LIBERTY
AND
SEXUALITY

Also by David J. Garrow

BEARING THE CROSS

THE FBI AND MARTIN LUTHER KING, JR.

PROTEST AT SELMA

THE MONTGOMERY BUS BOYCOTT AND THE WOMEN
WHO STARTED IT (editor)

THE EYES ON THE PRIZE CIVIL RIGHTS READER
(co-editor)

LIBERTY AND SEXUALITY

The Right to Privacy
and the Making of *Roe* v. *Wade*

David J. Garrow

Updated with a
New Epilogue

UNIVERSITY OF CALIFORNIA PRESS
Berkeley · Los Angeles · London

University of California Press
Berkeley and Los Angeles, California

University of California Press, Ltd.
London, England

© 1994 by David J. Garrow
Preface and Epilogue © 1998 by David J. Garrow

First Paperback Printing 1998

Library of Congress Cataloging-in-Publication Data

Garrow, David J., 1953–
    Liberty and sexuality : the right to privacy and the making of *Roe* v. *Wade* / David J.
Garrow ; updated with a new epilogue.
        p.   cm.
    Originally published: New York : Macmillan Pub. Co. ; Toronto : Maxwell Macmillan
Canada ; New York : Maxwell Macmillan International, c1994.
    Includes bibliographical references and index.
    ISBN 0-520-21302-5 (pbk. : acid-free paper)
    1. Abortion—Law and legislation—United States—History. 2. Birth control—Law
and legislation—United States—History. 3. Sex and law—United States—History.
4. Privacy, Right of—United States—History. I. Title.
KF3771.G37   1998
342.73′0858—dc21   97-52173
                                                                                          CIP

Printed in the United States of America

9 8 7 6 5 4 3 2 1

The paper used in this publication is both acid-free and totally chlorine-free (TCF).
It meets the minimum requirements of American Standard for Information Sciences—
Permanence of Paper for Printed Library Materials, ANSI Z39.48-1984. ♾

CONTENTS

Preface   ix

1. The Waterbury Origins of *Roe* v. *Wade*   1

2. No Further Service: Connecticut's Struggle for the
   Legalization of Birth Control, 1940–1953   79

3. One Vote Shy: Estelle Griswold, Fowler Harper, and the
   U.S. Supreme Court, 1954–1961   131

4. Creating the Right to Privacy: Estelle Griswold and the
   U.S. Supreme Court, 1961–1965   196

5. Lonely Voices: Abortion Reformers and the Origins
   of Change, 1933–1967   270

6. From Reform to Repeal: The *Right* to Abortion, 1967–1969   335

7. Into the Courts: *Roe*, *Doe*, and the Right to Abortion,
   1969–1971   389

8. The Right to Abortion and the U.S. Supreme Court,
   1971–1973   473

9. Liberty and Sexuality Since *Roe* v. *Wade*   600

   Epilogue   705

   Afterword   741

   Acknowledgments   743

   Acknowledgments (1998)   749

   Notes   751

   Bibliography   978

   Index   1009

LIBERTY
AND
SEXUALITY

PREFACE TO
THE 1998 EDITION

This big book tells three sequential stories. First, it relates how the forty-year struggle to overturn Connecticut's criminalization of even married couples' *use* of contraceptives finally triumphed in the landmark 1965 Supreme Court right-to-privacy ruling in *Griswold* v. *Connecticut*.

Second, *Liberty and Sexuality* details how that recognition of a fundamental right to privacy in *Griswold* opened the constitutional door to a previously unimagined argument: that women with unwanted pregnancies ought to have access to legal abortion as a fundamental right. The earliest abortion law reformers had sought liberalization of the strictures that had outlawed—but not actually prevented—almost all abortions since the middle of the nineteenth century, but between 1966 and 1969 that goal of reform was quickly supplanted by repeal: state antiabortion laws could be challenged in federal court as infringements of women's newly recognized constitutional right to privacy. Out of that litigation campaign—a quest that got under way late in 1969 and triumphed in January 1973—came both *Roe* v. *Wade* and its lesser-known but equally important companion case, *Doe* v. *Bolton*. The second part of *Liberty and Sexuality*—chapters five through eight—tells the story of the early activists and young lawyers who created those cases and the Supreme Court justices who in 1972–1973 accepted their constitutional claims.

Third, *Liberty and Sexuality* describes the twenty-five years of abortion litigation and congressional debates that have transpired since *Roe* and *Doe*. The first portion of that aftermath culminated in part in the huge setback that sexual liberty claims suffered in 1986 with the explicitly antigay Supreme Court decision in *Bowers* v. *Hardwick*. Far more encouragingly, repeated threats to *Roe*'s protection of abortion rights, threats that in 1989–1991 looked likely to prove fatal, surprisingly climaxed instead in the landmark 1992 Supreme Court ruling in *Planned Parenthood of Southeastern Pennsylvania* v. *Casey* which powerfully reaffirmed *Roe*'s constitutional core.

The second portion of the post-*Roe* story, the many developments that have occurred since 1993, is newly added to this edition of *Liberty and Sexuality*. The year 1994 witnessed two double homicides of abortion workers by right-to-life terrorists, but it also witnessed passage of a comprehensive federal statute, the Freedom of Access to Clinic Entrances Act (FACE), which quickly put an end to the violently obstructive mass protests that had besieged so many abortion clinics during the late 1980s and early 1990s.

Antiabortion protests were well past their peak by the time of *Roe* and *Doe*'s twenty-fifth anniversaries in January 1998. However, in one of the two most important developments of the post-*Casey* years, abortion opponents garnered significant political success by making "partial birth" abortions the subject of debate in legislatures all across the country. Courts constrained antiabortion legislation less comprehensively than they limited antiabortion protests, but the Supreme Court, in a crucial post-*Casey* milestone, gave gay Americans their greatest legal victory ever in a 1996 ruling, *Romer* v. *Evans*, that left *Bowers* in symbolic shreds.

Roe v. *Wade*'s creation and *Roe* v. *Wade*'s legacy represent one of the two greatest stories—the other is *Brown* v. *Board of Education*—in twentieth-century American legal history. *Liberty and Sexuality* seeks to tell that story as comprehensively as possible, for it—like *Brown*—has altered and improved the lives of millions of Americans.

CHAPTER ONE

The Waterbury Origins
of *Roe v. Wade*

Katharine Houghton Hepburn had never doubted that Sallie Pease was an ideal president for the Connecticut Birth Control League (CBCL). Hepburn's next-door neighbor in Hartford since 1927, a Smith College graduate, and the mother of three school-age boys, Pease was only thirty-seven—nineteen years Hepburn's junior—when she became league president in 1934. For eleven years, since 1923, when nationally noted birth control crusader Margaret Sanger had first visited Hartford, Kit Hepburn had played a central role in holding the league together. Little headway had been made toward the league's goal of winning legislative repeal of Connecticut's unique 1879 criminal statute that made the use and/or prescription of any form of birth control a crime for both woman and doctor alike, but in the summer of 1935 Sallie Pease had taken the lead in the league's dramatic but initially unpublicized decision to go ahead and simply *open* a public birth control clinic in Hartford. Just as the league had hoped, no one moved to enforce the law or to close the clinic, and in its first year of operation the clinic's women doctors provided birth control counseling and devices to over four hundred married women, many of them first- or second-generation ethnic immigrants from Hartford's poorer neighborhoods.[1] Quietly ecstatic at their success in extending to poor women the same medical advice that privately was available to those who could afford family physicians, by the summer of 1936 the Connecticut League also had clinics functioning in Greenwich, New Haven, and Stamford. The following two years witnessed similar growth and expansion, as clinic services opened in Norwalk, Danbury, New Britain, New London, and Bridgeport.[2] The Bridgeport city prosecutor expressly told inquiring reporters that the 1879 statute represented no bar to the services that the Bridgeport clinic was providing,[3] and six months later, in October of 1938, the league achieved its hope of having clinic services available in all of Connecticut's large cities when a one-morning-a-week clinic quietly opened in downtown Waterbury, Connecticut's most ethnically diverse—and most heavily Roman Catholic—city.

Sallie Pease and Kit Hepburn were rightfully proud of the tremendous progress that had been attained by simply going ahead and opening clinics, rather than by unsuccessfully continuing to petition each biennial session of the Connecticut legislature for a statutory change, as the league had from 1923 through 1935. Neither public officials nor religious groups seemed actively interested in mounting any effort to enforce a now seemingly dead-letter law, and the Connecticut League would be able to continue moving forward with its real purpose of providing actual services to more and more needy women who wanted to limit the number of their children.

So when the Connecticut League convened for its annual luncheon meeting at the Farmington Country Club on Thursday, June 8, 1939, Sallie Pease had no hesitancy in speaking plainly about their new successes. The general director of the national Birth Control Federation of America (BCFA)—the newly renamed organization that was the direct descendant of Margaret Sanger's initial work two decades earlier—Dr. Woodbridge E. Morris, had himself come up to central Connecticut for the luncheon, and while Hartford reporters took notes on Morris's remarks about the regrettable level of maternal mortality in America, they also listened to Sallie Pease's presidential report, in which she highlighted the opening of the Waterbury clinic as the league's most prominent achievement in the preceding year. What was especially notable, she stressed, was that the Waterbury clinic, unlike any of its other Connecticut predecessors, was operating "in a public institution," in the Chase Dispensary outpatient building of the Waterbury Hospital. So far, Pease said, it has "received no publicity, but it is there in working order and will grow."[4]

Sallie Pease was a brash and flashy person, quite different in style and persona from the Greenwich and Fairfield County women who comprised much of the Connecticut League, and she hadn't given any thought to the possible press coverage of her luncheon remarks.[5] Friday morning's *Hartford Courant* ran a modest story on page twenty-four, noting in passing the newly announced Waterbury clinic in the Chase Dispensary, but the Associated Press put the *Courant* story on the state news wire, and Friday morning's *Waterbury Republican* printed it on page fifteen, under a headline reading "U.S. Maternal Mortality Rate Reported Poor." Several paragraphs down, however, it stated how

Pease had reported "that during the year the first clinic in a public institution in Connecticut was opened at the Chase Dispensary in Waterbury."[6]

The *Waterbury Republican*, and its sister paper, the afternoon *Waterbury American*, were not the city's only newspapers, however. There was also the afternoon *Waterbury Democrat*, which in many ways—as its name indicated—was the antithesis of the *Republican*. *Republican-American* publisher William J. Pape had been an outspoken and crusading opponent of the city's mostly corrupt Democratic political establishment, and it was in large part because of the *Republican*'s efforts that Waterbury Mayor—and Connecticut Lieutenant Governor—T. Frank Hayes and over twenty fellow defendants were currently on trial for looting the city treasury. The *Democrat* had spoken up for the Hayes regime, and if the Pape papers were a voice for the Anglo-Saxon Yankee population that found its political home in the Republican party, the *Democrat* was viewed as the voice for Waterbury's Irish, Italian, French-Canadian, and Lithuanian immigrant populations. Some 72,000 of Waterbury's 99,000 citizens were either first- or second-generation immigrants to America, and while the ethnic parishes where most of them attended church might differ greatly in custom and in language, they were almost all Roman Catholic.[7]

Friday afternoon's *Waterbury Democrat* featured a front-page headline, "Birth Control Clinic Is Operating In City," and quoted Chase Dispensary supervisor Jeannie Heppel as confirming Sallie Pease's unintentional announcement. "Pastors of Catholic churches had no comment to make today," the *Democrat* went on, but the paper hardly had to tell its readers that Connecticut's Catholic hierarchy, the Diocese of Hartford, was a staunch and unyielding opponent of birth control. Church representatives had turned out at every legislative session from 1923 to 1935 to oppose the CBCL's petitions for statutory change, and just four weeks earlier the Reverend John S. Kennedy, associate editor of the diocese's weekly newspaper, the *Catholic Transcript*, had been prominently quoted in the *Democrat* as telling three hundred Waterbury Catholics at a special Mother's Day Communion breakfast that he was puzzled as to why some Connecticut prosecutors were "so anxious" to go after bingo game operators "while birth control clinics were allowed to flourish." One Hartford woman who had received a birth control circular, Kennedy said, had contacted the *Transcript* to complain. Kennedy's remarks, the *Democrat* volunteered, had been "most inspirational."[8]

Different readers reacted to the *Democrat*'s story in different ways.

Waterbury Hospital superintendent Dr. B. Henry Mason and gynecology clinic chief Dr. Charles L. Larkin both told reporters that no "birth control clinic" was operating at the Chase Dispensary, and Saturday's *Republican* prominently headlined their claim—"Doctors Deny Birth Control Clinic in City"—despite Heppel's statements to the contrary. The problem, Dr. Mason explained, was simply a matter of terminology. A gynecological clinic, the *Republican* said, "includes in the normal course of its work the giving of some information on birth control." But such advice, Mason said, "is provided purely on a health basis. A woman whose health would be seriously endangered by child bearing might get medical advice at the clinic on birth control, but not robust, healthy women." Dr. Larkin agreed: "That's a long way from the popular conception of a birth control clinic where any woman may go who doesn't want to have children."[9]

By Saturday morning the hospital staffers finally had their stories straight, as that afternoon's *American* emphasized: "Miss Heppel Agrees With Dr. Mason: Waterbury Has No Birth Control Clinic." But Heppel's actual statement, much like Mason's and Larkin's, did not exactly square with the headline: "Nobody can come here for information unless they are referred by doctors for reasons of their health," supervisor Heppel explained. "People can't just come in as they please and get information." Clinic sessions were held each Tuesday, the *American* added, had begun last October, and were actually conducted by two young doctors, William A. Goodrich and Roger B. Nelson, who reported to Larkin.[10]

But the hospital officials were not the most significant readers of the Waterbury press. Friday's *Democrat* had observed that the city's Catholic clergy "might" refer the matter to Hartford Bishop Maurice F. McAuliffe, but Father Eugene P. Cryne, president of the Catholic Clergy Association of Waterbury, already had called a special meeting of the association for Saturday morning in the rectory of Immaculate Conception parish, Waterbury's oldest Roman Catholic church. Cryne was not the most prominent or the most senior of Waterbury's Catholic clergy, but Immaculate's own pastor had been formally installed only one year earlier, and Monsignor Joseph Valdambrini, pastor of Our Lady of Lourdes parish and the son of a Vatican banker with a royal title, was out of town on a four-month visit to Italy. A fifty-six-year-old Connecticut native, Cryne, like many Connecticut priests, had received his religious training at St. Thomas Seminary. He had become pastor of St. Patrick's Church, one of Waterbury's more modest parishes, but with seventeen hundred members, mostly of Irish background, in 1933, after having previously served in a junior role at Immaculate and then in parishes just outside of Waterbury.[11]

Eugene Cryne was, however, in the eyes of his fellow priests, "a very forceful individual" who had a very definite sense of right and wrong. "When rules and regulations were made, they had to be abided by," a younger priest who served under Cryne explained. Although a "very kind" man, Eugene Cryne was "a very determined person." And the resolution that was drawn up at that special Saturday morning meeting of Waterbury's Catholic clergy at the Immaculate rectory was a very determined and very forceful resolution:

> Whereas, it is the teaching of the Catholic church that birth control is contrary to the natural law and therefore immoral, and
>
> Whereas, it is forbidden by statute law to disseminate birth control information for any reason whatsoever or in any circumstance, and
>
> Whereas, it has been brought to our attention that a so-called birth control clinic, sometimes called a maternal health center, is existing in Waterbury as admitted by the superintendent of Chase Dispensary, according to the papers, therefore, be it
>
> Resolved, that this association go on record as being unalterably opposed to the existence of such a clinic in our city and we hereby urge our Catholic people to avoid contact with it and we hereby publicly call the attention of the public prosecutors to its existence and demand that they investigate and if necessary prosecute to the full extent of the law.[12]

William B. Fitzgerald, the State's Attorney in Waterbury, had like Father Cryne seen the stories in the Friday and Saturday Waterbury newspapers. And while news of the Catholic Clergy resolution did not appear in the Sunday *Republican*, Bill Fitzgerald certainly heard of it Sunday morning at the latest, for he faithfully attended St. Margaret's Roman Catholic Church, and that morning—as Bill Fitzgerald remembered even decades later—the text of the clergy's resolution was read from the pulpit of each and every Catholic church in Waterbury and in surrounding towns.[13]

Bill Fitzgerald had been State's Attorney for only one year. Thirty-seven years old, a Waterbury native, and an alumnus of Holy Cross College, Fitzgerald had opened a Waterbury law office immediately after graduating from Harvard Law School and passing the bar in 1926. Two years later he became a prosecutor in the city's misdemeanor court, and in 1931 he became assistant state's attorney, both part-time positions that supplemented an attorney's private law practice. In May 1938, however, the special grand jury that had been impaneled to investigate Mayor Hayes and the city's financial scandals issued a detailed, seventy-four-page report to accompany its charges, and included in it was a brief but harsh condemnation of Fitzgerald's boss, State's Attorney Lawrence L. Lewis, for failing until very recently to take any action against the presence of gambling devices in Waterbury social clubs. "The fact that these violations of the law were known but not prosecuted by State's Attorney Lewis," and others, "is a matter of distinct concern to this Grand Jury. The law enforcement authorities of the city and of the district are, therefore, deserving of the severest censure for having permitted this widespread and flagrant violation of law to continue."[14]

Larry Lewis felt he had no choice but to resign and return to full-time private practice in his firm of Bronson, Lewis & Bronson, but Bill Fitzgerald rebuffed Lewis's notion that Fitzgerald too had to step down, indicating instead that he'd like to be Lewis's successor. That choice lay with Waterbury's local judges, particularly resident Superior Court Judge Frank P. McEvoy, the first Roman Catholic member of Connecticut's premier trial court bench, and on June 6, 1938, Bill Fitzgerald received their official blessing and became the first Roman Catholic State's Attorney at Waterbury. Fitzgerald voiced high praise of Larry Lewis at his swearing in, but moved swiftly to eliminate gambling from the city, with widespread raids receiving coverage even in the *New York Times*.[15]

Bill Fitzgerald "had a first class mind," one lifelong attorney friend and courtroom adversary later remembered, but he was "a very, very strict Catholic." Another attorney friend, also once a communicant at St. Margaret's, agreed that Fitzgerald was "very bright," but was nonetheless "a very parochial, insular guy," someone "very strongly receptive to and influenced by the clergy." Bill Fitzgerald was active in a number of civic and church groups, and, like Judge McEvoy, served on the advisory board of Waterbury's Diocesan Bureau of Social Service, which was directed by Father Eugene Cryne. But most people who knew Bill Fitzgerald felt that the pressure to act came largely from within, rather than from without, that even in the absence of a phone call, Bill Fitzgerald believed there was only one thing to do. After all, just one year earlier his predecessor had had to resign because of public complaints that he had failed to enforce the often-ignored but nonetheless still-valid gambling laws aggressively, and the old 1879 prohibition against birth control was certainly still on the statute books. Yes, Bill Fitzgerald was a "devout" Catholic, but "I don't think Fitzgerald was any crusader at all," his one-time fellow member of St.

Margaret's emphasized. As almost everyone saw it, the state's attorney simply felt he had to do his duty. Eight days later Fitzgerald would indicate that he had been "acting upon complaints" in the wake of the newspaper stories, but probably as early as Saturday morning Bill Fitzgerald had decided that an active investigation of the Chase Dispensary clinic would have to be mounted.[16]

Monday morning's *Republican* headlined the Catholic Clergy Association's resolution, but devoted more attention to the continuing claims that the clinic was not what its critics said it was. Like Doctors Mason and Larkin, Dr. William A. Goodrich was portrayed as minimizing the clinic's work: "Out of 250 women who come to the clinic yearly, he said, an average of perhaps 15 come for birth control advice. They get the same advice, he said, that women who can afford personal physicians get from their own physicians." More pointedly, the *Republican* also highlighted a conversation the newspaper had had with a Hartford attorney who had represented the original CBCL clinic there. He asserted "that there is apparently no state statute under which a birth control clinic can be prosecuted as long as the clinic is operated on a health basis," the *Republican* said. "The lawyer pointed out that prohibiting the giving of birth control information to women for health reasons would run counter to the public health laws of the state. The Hartford authorities were asked to prosecute, he said, by the Hartford Catholic clergy, and decided at the time that there was no basis for prosecution."[17]

But the *Republican*'s effort was in vain. Early Monday morning William Fitzgerald took a search warrant application to the chambers of Judge McEvoy. Fitzgerald's request stated "That he is informed and that he suspects and has reason to suspect that books, records, registers, instruments, apparatus and appliances used and kept for the purpose of violating the criminal laws," specifically Sections 6246 and 6562, "are kept, deposited, stored and used in" the Chase Dispensary at 43 Field Street.[18]

Birth control was not a new subject to Frank P. McEvoy. A sixty-year-old Waterbury native, an active member of Blessed Sacrament Roman Catholic Church, and, like Bill Fitzgerald, a member of the advisory board of Father Cryne's Diocesan Bureau of Social Service, Frank McEvoy had attended a small Roman Catholic college in New York, graduated from Yale Law School in 1907, and practiced law in Waterbury until being named a superior court judge in 1930. Friends thought of him as "soft spoken" and knew he was an "ardent horseman," but Waterbury attorneys considered him "narrow and reluctant to accept change." A much younger fellow Catholic attorney remembered McEvoy as "wildly Irish Catholic" and "very parochial." Perhaps most notably, seven years earlier his wife had played the leading role in blocking any endorsement of birth control by the state convention of the Connecticut League of Women Voters. As the *Republican* had described it, Mrs. McEvoy "opposed it violently and threatened that she and all Catholic women would resign if it were adopted. Largely because of this, the proposal . . . was voted down," and Mrs. McEvoy had received nationwide praise from some Catholic spokesmen for her activism on the issue.[19]

Frank McEvoy immediately granted the warrant application that Bill Fitzgerald put in front of him: "I find probable cause exists for said complaint." Minutes later, a little before 10 a.m., Deputy Sheriff Al Francis and County Detective Koland G. Alling took the warrant and went the three short blocks that separated the Chase Dispensary from the state's attorney's office in the courthouse. Dispensary supervisor Jeannie Heppel had left on Saturday on vacation, but her assistant, Berta Verba, showed the two lawmen to the second floor rooms at the northwest corner of the building that the birth control clinic used. As the clinic operated only on Tuesday mornings, no one else was present, but as the *Waterbury Democrat* described it, the two officers "confiscated several bags and boxes of articles and returned with them to the courthouse."

Bill Fitzgerald declined comment to inquiring reporters and sat down with his assistant, Walter Smyth, and Detective Alling to review the seized materials. They prepared a show-cause order, signed later that day by Judge McEvoy, directing Waterbury Hospital superintendent B. Henry Mason to appear in court the following Monday to explain why the diaphragms and other contraceptive articles that had been seized should not be condemned and destroyed. But much more importantly, Bill Fitzgerald noted two other things as he examined what Alling and Francis had seized. First, all of the patient records, the clinical cards that would identify who had been seen and for what reasons, were not at the dispensary, but were in the possession of a young Junior League volunteer, Virginia Goss, who maintained the clinic's records and was married to a prominent young executive at Waterbury's most famous manufacturing firm, Scovill Brass. And then, second, Bill Fitzgerald also learned that the founder and moving force behind the Waterbury Maternal Health Center was not one or another of the doctors from Waterbury Hospital, but instead was his next-door neighbor and family friend, Clara Lee McTernan.[20]

★   ★   ★

Kit Hepburn and her children would always remember the phone call that had interrupted her daughter Marion Hepburn Grant's wedding that Monday in the garden of the Hepburn family home at 201 Bloomfield Avenue in Hartford. But then it was utterly natural for Clara McTernan to call Kit Hepburn, for not only had Hepburn come to Waterbury to spur creation of the clinic, she had been making political waves across Connecticut years before Margaret Sanger had ever thought up the phrase "birth control."[21]

Katharine Houghton Hepburn was a twenty-six-year-old newlywed when she and her husband, Dr. Thomas N. Hepburn, first moved to Hartford in 1904. Orphaned as a teenager when her father committed suicide and her mother died of cancer, Katharine Houghton graduated from Bryn Mawr in 1899, earned a master's degree there the following year, and met Tom Hepburn, a medical student at Johns Hopkins, through her sister Edith, who was also in medical school. Thomas Hepburn's internship and residency took place at Hartford Hospital, and in 1905 their first son was born, followed two years later by their first daughter, Katharine's namesake, who later would win a 1934 Academy Award and Hollywood fame.

The following year Kit Hepburn, perhaps at the urging of her sister Edith, attended a speech at Hartford's Parsons Theatre by English suffragist Emmeline Pankhurst and adopted women's right to vote as her cause too. The Connecticut Women's Suffrage Association (CWSA) had been founded back in 1869, but now was slightly moribund. Kit Hepburn's urge to activism was initially hindered by a tremendous fear of attempting to speak in public, but she soon overcame it, and along with her friend and neighbor Josephine Day Bennett she helped create the Hartford Equal Franchise League. In 1910 Hepburn and Jo Bennett expanded their efforts into the CWSA itself, with Kit Hepburn becoming president for 1910–1911 and again in 1913. Kit Hepburn was also busy having additional children—two more boys in 1911 and 1913, and two more girls in 1916 and 1918—and Dr. Tom Hepburn was channeling much of his energy into antivenereal disease work. He played a significant role in the 1913 founding of the American Social Hygiene Association, and a very central role in its affiliate, the Connecticut Social Hygiene Association. One of Kit's older colleagues in CWSA work, Annie Webb Porritt, an immigrant from England, was also very active in the antivenereal disease efforts, as was Jo Bennett's father, George H. Day. Jo's mother, Katharine Beach Day, was a major source of funds for her daughter and Kit Hepburn's female suffrage endeavors.[22]

By 1917 Kit Hepburn was testifying before the Connecticut legislature's Judiciary Committee on behalf of the CWSA and appearing with Montana Congresswoman and suffragist Jeanette Rankin at a Parsons Theatre rally. But in the fall of that year, in the wake of Alice Paul and other national activists' departure from Carrie Chapman Catt's National American Woman Suffrage Association (NAWSA) to form the National Woman's Party (NWP), Kit Hepburn resigned the presidency of the 35,000 member CWSA and along with Jo Bennett and her other colleagues began directing most of her energies into the NWP. Both groups championed congressional approval of a federal constitutional amendment that would give American women the right to vote, but Hepburn and others felt that the NWP was the more active force. In January 1919, the House of Representatives approved a woman's suffrage amendment, and in June the Senate followed suit. Fourteen months later, in August 1920, Tennessee became the crucial thirty-sixth state to ratify the Nineteenth Amendment, and female suffrage had been won. Several weeks later the Connecticut legislature added its assent.[23]

The suffrage victory allowed the Connecticut activists to direct their energies toward other issues. Annie Porritt, already an elected member of the Hartford Board of Education, helped set up the League of Women Voters as a direct successor to NAWSA, continued her work with Dr. Hepburn in the Social Hygiene Association, and became active in the Joint Committee on Delinquent Women.[24] But another issue that both Mrs. Porritt and Katharine Beach Day began to take an interest in by the fall of 1921 was birth control.

Margaret Sanger's first enthusiastic follower in the state of Connecticut was a male attorney from Hazardville, a small village in the north-central part of the state, Henry F. Fletcher. Single-handedly, Fletcher four years earlier, in January 1917, had prevailed upon his local representative in Connecticut's lower house to introduce, "by request," a bill repealing the 1879 antibirth control statute. How Fletcher's interest first occurred is unknown, but by the fall of 1916 most readers of the American press knew full well who Margaret Sanger was. Then thirty-seven years old, Sanger had first begun championing a woman's right to control her own fertility in the summer of 1914 in her self-published monthly magazine *The Woman Rebel*. Heavily influenced by her own and her husband William's political roots in socialist politics, and particularly by the perspective of Emma Goldman, Margaret quite purposefully hoped that her in-print advocacy of birth control would launch a direct challenge against the enforcement of the 1873 federal antiobscenity and anticontraception statutes that most everyone spoke of as the "Comstock Laws," after their still very active principal proponent, New York moralist Anthony Comstock.[25]

Sanger's hope of generating a federal case in which to take on those prohibitions against the interstate shipment or importation of any goods, articles or literature dealing with sexuality or reproduction quickly came to pass: in August 1914 the U.S. Attorney's office in New York charged her with four counts of violating the Comstock statutes. Rather than prepare a defense, Sanger sat down and wrote a sixteen-page statement of her views, arranged for the printing of a hundred thousand copies of it under the title *Family Limitation*, obtained false identity documents, and fled to England rather than stand trial. The ensuing twelve months in Europe constituted perhaps the most intellectually important period in Sanger's long life, but her flight from prosecution did relatively little if any harm to America's growing popular support for women's right to control their fertility.[26]

While Sanger was away, however, her husband Bill was entrapped into giving a copy of the *Family Limitation* pamphlet to a government agent, and in September 1915, he was tried, convicted, and sentenced to a thirty-day jail sentence. One later historian calculated that Bill Sanger's arrest "proved a powerful magnet which drew many hundreds into active participation in the birth control movement," and that "Sanger's trial generated considerable support for birth control as a free-speech issue." That blossoming support also helped convince Margaret that the time was right to return to the United States, and in October 1915 she did. While she had been away the country's first birth control advocacy group, the National Birth Control League, had been formed by Mary Ware Dennett and a number of other upper-class, northeastern women. In January 1916—with Margaret rejecting lawyers' advice that she agree to a negotiated guilty plea in order to dispose of the 1914 federal charges still pending against her—the new league held a heavily publicized New York dinner honoring Sanger the evening before her scheduled trial. Indecisive prosecutors postponed the case once, and then again, as press interest heightened, before finally simply dropping the charges on February 18, 1916.[27]

The government's surrender elevated Margaret Sanger to celebrity status. Several weeks later she began a three-and-a-half-month coast-to-coast speaking tour, and birth control became more heavily publicized in America's newspapers than ever before. In Portland, Oregon, local authorities arrested her for handing out copies of *Family*

Limitation, but a supportive judge immediately released her. In Boston, however, when a young man named Van Kleeck Allison decided to distribute birth control pamphlets to passersby who soon included an undercover detective, a speedy trial resulted in a quick conviction and a three-year sentence, which later was reduced to sixty days. Allison's experience did have the effect of stimulating creation of an Allison Birth Control Defense League that then changed its name to the Birth Control League of Massachusetts, and local birth control groups also emerged in other cities across the country as a result of Sanger's triumphant tour.[28]

Upon returning to New York, however, much of Sanger's energy went into a deepening competition with Mary Ware Dennett for leadership of this burgeoning national movement. Sanger intensely resented that someone other than she had founded the first national birth control group, and while the NBCL was of very modest size, Dennett in early 1917 succeeded in getting a birth control legalization bill introduced into the New York State legislature. Just as with Henry Fletcher's contemporaneous legislative effort in Connecticut, however, Dennett's bill attracted almost no support and never emerged from committee. But Sanger's primary interest was not legislative lobbying, and on October 16, 1916, along with her sister and fellow nurse Ethel Byrne, and several other women supporters, Margaret Sanger opened America's first public birth control clinic at 46 Amboy Street in the Brownsville section of Brooklyn.[29]

Sanger had been unable to recruit a licensed physician to operate the clinic, but even on its first morning of operation a waiting line of forty-five women had formed on the sidewalk. Sanger and her colleagues fully expected to be raided and closed down by the police within days or even hours of opening, but nine days passed before a transparently obvious female undercover police officer arrived and insisted upon paying two dollars for one of Margaret's ten-cent pamphlets. The next day she returned with three fellow officers. The clinic's supplies were seized, and Sanger and an aide were carted off to jail. Ethel Byrne was promptly arrested as well. Released on bail after one night in custody, Sanger soon reopened the clinic but was quickly raided and rearrested.

Sanger and Byrne's lawyer, Jonah J. Goldstein, was determined to use the arrests to challenge the constitutionality of New York's Comstockian anticontraception statutes, and at one preliminary hearing he told the presiding judge that the law denied a woman "her absolute right of enjoyment of intercourse unless the act be so conducted that pregnancy be the result of the exercise. This clearly is an infringement upon her free exercise of conscience and pursuit of happiness." The judge, however, expressed astonishment at Goldstein's argument: "A right of copulation without conception is asserted upon behalf of women in general; defendant claims this is a personal right that cannot be invaded by the Legislature." Any such contention was hogwash, he held: "That men and women and boys and girls lacking in moral stamina are deterred from fornication by the fear of detection through the pregnancy of the female cannot be doubted."[30]

Goldstein nonetheless mounted a variety of legal challenges on behalf of his defendants, but in early January 1917, Ethel Byrne went to trial and was convicted. Margaret's sex education pamphlet which Ethel had given the undercover officer was titled "What Every Girl Should Know," but the trial court commented that "This contains matters which not only should not be known by every girl, but which perhaps should not be known by any." On January 22 Byrne was sentenced to thirty days' confinement and was soon jailed despite Goldstein's protests that she be freed pending appeal. Byrne announced she would go on a hunger strike until she was released, and amidst heavy publicity and flourishing support from the upper-class women of the NBCL, Margaret's own trial then got underway on January 29. Goldstein attempted to persuade both Sanger and the court to accept a guilty plea accompanied by only a suspended sentence so that his constitutional arguments could be appealed to higher courts without Margaret having to accept punishment in the interim, but no agreement could be arranged. On February 2, one day after Ethel had been released from jail on account of her rapidly failing health, Margaret was convicted and chose thirty days' imprisonment in lieu of a five-thousand-dollar fine.[31]

Margaret's own jail time passed quietly, and four months later an intermediate appellate court affirmed her conviction. Goldstein then took his arguments to New York's highest court, and in January 1918, that bench reaffirmed her conviction but also stated, in an indirect but nonetheless tremendously important victory, that New York's anticontraception statute could not prevent a physician from prescribing birth control to a married woman for whom it would help prevent "disease," a word which the court then defined in a most broad and inclusive manner. Goldstein resolved to appeal the case yet further, to the U.S. Supreme Court (which eventually dismissed the appeal), but the birth controllers had already registered a crucial if underpublicized triumph.[32]

The New York court's emphasis upon doctors' rights and obligations to protect patients against threats to their health significantly encouraged Margaret Sanger's ongoing evolution toward a more professionalized—and less politically radical—championing of birth control. Mary Ware Dennett was committed to advocating the complete *repeal* of all state and federal anticontraceptive statutes, and early in 1919 created the Voluntary Parenthood League, largely a successor to her earlier NBCL, to help recruit a congressional sponsor for a federal repeal bill. Sanger, however, was increasingly persuaded that milder reform measures, legalizing only the "medically supervised" prescription of birth control, stood far, far better chances of winning support and approval. Writing in mid-1919, Sanger now argued that "when instruction in the use of contraceptives is given, it should be given by the kind of persons best suited by training and experience to give it scientifically and accurately. If everyone is permitted to impart information, those who receive it have no guaranty that it is correct or suitable to the individual's physical requirements. Incorrect, unscientific information may bring good results in some cases, but it is more likely to cause a vast amount of disappointment and anxiety in others."[33]

In November 1921 Sanger and her supporters convened the First American Birth Control Conference at New York's Plaza Hotel. Intended in part to refocus the birth control spotlight on Sanger rather than Dennett, it also brought out-of-town birth control supporters to New York, including Katharine Beach Day, Annie Porritt, Jo Bennett, and Henry Fletcher and his wife from Connecticut. The conference's concluding event was a large public meeting on November 13, but it was interrupted almost before it could begin by a band of New York City policemen who said they were acting at the behest of Roman Catholic Archbishop Patrick Hayes. They removed a prominent English guest speaker from the stage, and then carted Sanger off to jail when she objected. The police action set off a firestorm of press criticism and coverage, and generated a major municipal investigation of how it had been instigated. The church's blunder transformed the conference into a national news story, and as *The New Republic* observed two weeks later, thanks to the church "the outlook for the birth control movement is brighter than it ever was."[34]

One of Sanger's primary aims for the conference was to create a new national organization of her own, which was christened the American Birth Control League (ABCL). Katharine Beach Day played a principal financial role in helping launch the new group, and by the spring of 1922 Annie Porritt was taking a major role in the editing and publication of its monthly magazine, the *Birth Control Review*, which Sanger had initiated several years earlier. Before the year was out both Day and Porritt were formal members of the ABCL's board of directors, and in October 1922, some weeks after returning from a London birth control conference that both she, Sanger, and Porritt had attended, Mrs. Day told Hartford reporters that Mrs. Sanger would be coming to town to speak in January. In mid-November both Day and Porritt attended the annual convention of the Connecticut League of Women Voters, distributed birth control literature, and spoke about mounting an effort in the upcoming 1923 Connecticut legislature to amend the state's 1879 anticontraception statute. By early January ABCL organization secretary Clara Louise Rowe was in Hartford planning for Sanger's visit, and Henry Fletcher had recruited Enfield state representative Samuel Sisisky to introduce a birth control bill when the legislature convened.[35]

Creation of state birth control leagues as affiliates of her national organization was a central part of Sanger's plan for the ABCL, as was her firm conviction that medically supervised birth control was the goal to advocate. Just a few weeks earlier, after finally recruiting a willing female doctor, Sanger had quietly opened a New York birth control clinic, right across the hall from her ABCL office, under the rubric of a "clinical research bureau." In Washington, Mary Ware Dennett had finally, after several years effort, found a member of Congress who was willing to sponsor a Comstock repeal measure, but in Connecticut Representative Sisisky's House Bill 504, formally introduced on January 25, provided only that the "giving of information or advice or medicine or articles for prevention of conception by a doctor or nurse shall not be a violation" of Connecticut's 1879 statute.[36]

Neither Sisisky, nor Henry Fletcher, nor the other 1923 Connecticut reformers had a clear understanding of how or why the 1879 law had come into being in the form that it had, largely because neither the surviving legislative records nor the contemporaneous newspapers provided any explanatory comments or details about the statute's consideration or passage. It had been introduced by New Haven state senator Carlos Smith just two days after a similar bill had been put before the Massachusetts legislature as a result of the efforts of the New England Society for the Suppression of Vice, a Comstock organization that boasted the presidents of Amherst, Brown, Dartmouth, and Yale among its members. The New England Society had been created as an antiobscenity lobby following a May 1878, visit to Boston by Comstock himself, and in Massachusetts its bill quickly passed the legislature without any apparent dissent or debate. The Connecticut bill was referred to the legislature's Joint Committee on

Temperance, favorably reported less than a week later, and passed by the senate, but then returned to the committee by the house. The committee, chaired by sixty-nine-year-old Bridgeport Representative and temperance advocate Phineas T. Barnum, of circus fame, then prepared a substitute bill, including for the first time the unique language that forbid not only trafficking in "obscene" literature and materials concerning sex or reproduction, but also the *"use"* of "any drug, medicine, article, or instrument" for the "purpose of preventing conception." The revised measure was adopted by the senate, explained to the house by Barnum, approved by the house in slightly amended form, and then again concurred in by the senate. On March 28, 1879, it became law.[37]

The kickoff event for the 1923 reform campaign was a Sunday afternoon rally and speech by Margaret Sanger at Hartford's Parsons Theatre, just two days before the legislative joint committee hearing on Sisisky's bill at which Sanger herself would also testify. The Sunday event drew an impressive crowd of eight hundred to twelve hundred people, approximately two thirds of whom were women, and received extensive coverage in the Connecticut press. The *Hartford Courant* characterized Sanger as "speaking with a sincerity which her listeners seemed quick to appreciate," and explained that "at the close of her talk many in the audience wrote questions which were brought up to the stage for Mrs. Sanger to answer." In her speech she had emphasized that "We want to free women from incessant child bearing; we want to free her from undesired pregnancy"; during the question and answer period she "bitterly attacked" the Connecticut statute while also emphasizing that birth control "must be handled in clinics," "places with doctors and nurses in charge where a man or woman may come for individual instruction in the use of contraceptives."[38]

During her Hartford visit Sanger stayed at the home of Mrs. Day, and either that evening or the next Mrs. Day and her daughter Jo Bennett had Katharine Hepburn join them for dinner with Sanger. Day and Porritt had already been laying the groundwork for formally starting a Connecticut branch of the ABCL, and that night at dinner the plan was ratified, with Mrs. Day becoming the group's president. Tuesday afternoon February 13, when the legislature's joint House/Senate Judiciary Committee convened for a ninety-minute hearing on Sisisky's bill, "the old Senate chamber was packed, people standing in the back of the room and on both sides," and with the galleries full as well. Henry Fletcher and then Annie Porritt spoke first for the birth control proponents, with Mrs. Porritt declaring that "We ask this knowledge for the poor; it is now obtainable by the rich." Hartford attorney and city corporation counsel Robert P. Butler, an active Democrat, added his endorsement, and then Margaret Sanger stepped forward. She "was loudly applauded when she took the floor," the *Courant* reported the next morning. "She wore a dark dress and a string of large amber beads. She talked directly to the committee in a low voice, but so clearly that it carried to the gallery." Sanger spoke "not on the bill specifically, but on the general subject of birth control," one paper said, and she "emphasized strongly that the advocates of birth control are not in favor of abortion, but desire only to prevent the beginning of life."

Then opponents of the bill, beginning with Hartford Alderman and Catholic Council of Men representative Francis E. Jones, had their turn. He was followed by Roman Catholic Auxiliary Bishop John G. Murray of Hartford, who "talked directly at Mrs. Sanger and the advocates of the bill" in a manner that one reporter characterized as "intense." "This method is a violation of a natural law," Murray declared. "The Creator gave the sex function for just one purpose and to exercise it for any other purpose is a perversion of that function." The Bishop went on to say, the *Courant* reported, that many families already were having too few children: "The races from northern Europe which he called the finest type of people, are doomed to extinction, unless each family produces at least four children." After two female opponents also spoke, the hearing concluded with Sanger being given a few moments for a brief and very effective rebuttal. "The gentlemen say it is against the laws of nature to prevent conception," Sanger declared, "yet they themselves are celibates." As the crowd applauded, Sanger closed by joking that by her opponents' standards, men shaving their beards also violated the law of nature and ought similarly to be prohibited.[39]

By any public standard the hearing and its press coverage, like the Sunday rally, had been a great success and an auspicious debut for the Connecticut birth controllers. But their rhetorical success with the crowds stood them in little stead with the legislature, for several weeks later, without debate, both the house and then the senate accepted and approved the judiciary committee's rejection of the Sisisky bill.[40] In Washington Mary Ware Dennett's efforts with the U.S. Congress fared no better, as two days of hearings in early 1924 were similarly followed by judiciary committee rejection of the repeal proposal. Sanger's ABCL—which now, with Katharine Hepburn's addition, had three Connecticut women on its board—was quite open in all but opposing

Dennett's congressional efforts. The March issue of the ABCL's *Birth Control Review* stressed the league's opposition to the "indiscriminate dissemination" of birth control information and declared that any "campaign for the repeal of these Federal laws was of secondary importance until some educational work had been done." Indeed, the league warned, "removal of the Federal restrictions would almost certainly be followed by a flood of widespread advertising, of hastily written and probably misleading books and pamphlets." Instead the ABCL was drafting a bill which "would free the hands of the medical profession and enable the clinical data to be passed from one group of doctors to another." The essence of Sanger's political strategy was conveyed most starkly in a frosty letter that Annie Porritt sent to Dennett, removing her name from Dennett's list of sponsors. After careful study, Porritt declared, "I am emphatically of the opinion that Birth Control is primarily, in its practical aspects, a medical question, and I am also convinced that promiscuous distribution of advice without medical examinations and care, would tend to degrade the whole question, and to prevent that hearty cooperation on the part of the medical profession which is the chief hope of success."[41]

The 1923 Connecticut legislative hearing had featured only one rather tardy appearance and endorsement of birth control by a medical doctor, but the reformers carefully arranged to have Boston M.D. James F. Cooper, whom Sanger had recently hired as the ABCL's medical director and primary ambassador to physicians, in attendance along with Sanger herself when the 1925 hearing convened on March 12. The 1925 reform bill, in clear contrast to the 1923 one, authorized medically supervised birth control by amending the old 1879 statute so as to provide for a "fifty dollars fine where drugs which may prevent conception are sold without physician's prescription." The 1925 hearing drew a smaller crowd than the 1923 one—about one hundred proponents and some fifteen opponents, the *New Haven Journal-Courier* estimated, but "the idea seemed to have gained in popularity since it was brought up two years ago." Dr. Cooper was the principal speaker for the reformers, supplemented by Sanger, Katharine Hepburn, and an Episcopalian minister from New York. The judiciary committee "was plainly on the defensive throughout the hearing," the *Hartford Times* commented, but the "questions asked by the committee indicated much skepticism." One senator asked Sanger if birth control information ought to be available to unmarried women, and Sanger said no: "Married women are entitled to the information, because they have moral obligations, which unmarried women haven't." The clergyman,

Reverend Thomas H. Garth, contended that "no woman can be free
. . . until she has the right of her person and can say how many children she shall bear and when," but he was quickly contradicted by the
day's only opposition speaker, Mrs. Louise H. Fisher, representing the
Connecticut Council of Catholic Women. "Legislation of this kind will
increase the trend toward evading of responsibilities on the part of
married people," Fisher warned. "Persons shouldn't enter into the
married life unless they are willing to accept the obligation of children." Noting that she herself was a mother of five, Mrs. Fisher closed
by declaring that "There is already too much love of luxury and ease
and this bill would encourage that very thing."

Once again, as in 1923, the Connecticut reformers were generally
pleased with the hearing, but just like two years earlier the judiciary
committee quickly recommended rejection of the bill, a recommendation that was accepted without debate by both the senate and house.[42]
Katharine Beach Day turned some of her attention toward assisting
Sanger in new political explorations that the ABCL was making in
Washington with an eye toward finding a congressional sponsor for a
reform bill. Henry Fletcher provided Day and ABCL executive secretary
Anne Kennedy with a letter of introduction to Connecticut Senator
George P. McLean, whom the women found "most sympathetic," but
neither McLean nor any of a number of other senators with whom Day
and Kennedy visited early in 1926, including Nebraska's George W.
Norris, stepped forward to sponsor a bill. Mary Ware Dennett had
already given up her Washington efforts and retired from the scene, and
by the end of 1926, the ABCL had pulled back as well.[43]

Birth control activism was ebbing significantly, with the ABCL registering only 2,800 new members in 1926, as opposed to over 13,000 in
1923 and over 10,000 in 1924, and in mid-1926 Connecticut showed
only forty-seven subscribers to the ABCL's *Birth Control Review*. Sanger
spent much of late 1926 and most of 1927 in Europe, on leave from the
ABCL, and when Connecticut's 1927 legislative hearing occurred in
early March, Dr. Hannah M. Stone, the director of Sanger's Birth
Control Clinical Research Bureau in New York, came in her boss's
stead. In 1927 the Connecticut women had resolved to champion a
repeal bill, and Annie Porritt told the ABCL that while "it will be a
miracle if it passes," the Connecticut women "would not consider anything else." Porritt explained in another letter that "You can buy condoms and pessaries at the drug stores" if you knew to ask for articles
that were not on open display, and that the real and continuing harm
done by the 1879 statute stemmed from how it "undoubtedly has

deterred the doctors from recommending something which it would be illegal for his [sic] patients to put into practice." The hearing itself featured Hannah Stone, accompanied by Day, Porritt, Fletcher, and Hepburn, telling the judiciary committee that "contraception is distinctly a medical problem" and that "it should be the duty and the privilege of the physician to advise his patients in regard to it." The only opposing speaker, Mrs. Richard F. Jones of West Hartford, who claimed "that there are more women in hospitals as a result of the use of preventives than on account of natural births," was apparently not questioned on her unintended acknowledgment that tens of thousands of Connecticut women indeed did want to limit and control their fertility. Although both the Connecticut senate and house once again without debate ratified a judiciary committee recommendation that the repeal bill be rejected, one small press report stated that the negative vote in committee had been by a margin of only seven to six.[44]

By early 1928 Margaret Sanger was back in the United States, but Eleanor Dwight Jones, who had been the acting ABCL president during Sanger's absence, was successfully resisting Sanger's efforts to reassume her previous level of organizational control. With the ABCL board, including board secretary Annie Porritt, resolutely backing Jones, Sanger in June 1928 resigned as ABCL president. Political struggles persisted throughout the year as Sanger and Jones fought for control of both the Birth Control Clinical Research Bureau and the *Birth Control Review*, with Sanger winning on the former and losing on the latter. Porritt tried to be something of a mediator, warning Jones that "Mrs. Sanger is scarcely sane on the point of her antagonism to you," but adding that she fully agreed with Sanger that the Clinical Research Bureau was a separate enterprise. Otherwise the Connecticut women were largely untouched by the New York battling, and focused their efforts on building some visible local support for birth control legalization in advance of the 1929 legislative session. ABCL staff organizer Constance Heck was detailed to the Fairfield County towns of Greenwich, Norwalk, and Darien to stimulate the creation of local birth control committees, and contacts were made with Protestant ministers in Hartford, Bridgeport, Stamford, and Waterbury. Up in Massachusetts the arrest and quick acquittal of one female doctor, Dr. Antoinette F. Konikow, for giving a lecture on birth control had had the effect of reviving a state league that had been moribund for almost a decade, but the great New England success of 1928 came in November when the general conference of Congregational Churches in Connecticut endorsed the upcoming repeal bill at the behest of ministers who had been recruited by the Connecticut women.[45]

The success with the Congregational clergy, and the creation of a total of fourteen local town or city birth control committees, gave the birth control advocates a major boost going into the 1929 legislative session. Margaret Sanger said no to Katharine Hepburn's request that she come up for the February 28 hearing, but an overflow crowd of almost a thousand people turned out, and the Associated Press reported that "The support was stronger this session than ever before." Hepburn, Porritt, Jo Bennett, and Henry Fletcher were joined as affirmative speakers by Leon F. Whitney of New Haven, executive secretary of the American Eugenics Society, Bridgeport's Reverend T. F. Rutledge Beale, the prime mover behind the Congregational Church endorsement, and prominent Hartford physician James Raglan Miller, an old acquaintance of Porritt and the Hepburns from the Social Hygiene Association.

The afternoon was without a doubt the most lively legislative hearing the Connecticut effort had yet experienced. At the outset, Katharine Houghton Hepburn stole the show. "Three quarters of the men and women in this room are common criminals and ought to be in jail," she declared, drawing "indignant whispers" and "scattered hisses" from some as the crowd understood her allusion to the anticontraception law. Instead, she went on, "The crime is in having too many children where parents are too poor, too unintelligent to raise many children, in raising children that can never be adjusted to society." Also, Hepburn said, even "Roman Catholic women are coming to realize that this is their concern and not that of their priests; that they, and not the priests, have to bear the children." When she finished, the *New Haven Journal-Courier* reported, "Tremendous applause went through the room."

At least half-a-dozen members of the legislature, including three women, stood to register their support for the bill, and then it was the opponents' turn. "The leader of the opposition," B. L. Garrity of Shelton, announced that he had been told to oppose the bill by his wife, the mother of their nine children. "More humorous than serious," the *Journal-Courier* added, "the opposition leader advised that, instead of birth control being allowed among the 'upper stratum' a law be passed that all couples married ten years should be forced to have five children, or be sent to jail for the rest of their lives." "If they want the sex relationship," he declared, "let them take what goes with it." Garrity went on to compare birth control clinics to houses "which people don't speak about in polite society," but when a female committee member sought to ask Garrity whether having so many children had threatened his wife's health, "a fight nearly developed" and the committee chairman ruled the question out of order as too personal. Louise Fisher's opposition testimony produced no such outbursts, but another Hartford woman asserted that the bill "savors of barbarism and paganism." Katharine Hepburn was allotted several minutes for a closing rebuttal, and tried to reiterate her earlier point that immigrant women "don't believe it's any business of the priests, since they, the women are the real sufferers," but she was angrily interrupted by an opposing legislator from Bridgeport who shouted that people simply needed to "control their lust." "Let them practice self-control, not birth control!" The hearing concluded with the committee asking the audience for a show of hands, pro and con, which one reporter estimated looked essentially even, "about 400 to 400."[46]

Only five days later, however, the judiciary committee issued a negative report on the bill, and even its supposed sponsor, Senator Ernest W. Christ, told reporters that he was not in disagreement with the committee's action. The Connecticut women were sorely disappointed, but soon learned, as Katharine Beach Day later reported, that "The Republican leaders had decreed the defeat of the bill." The women's organizing efforts had in part been for naught because they had insufficiently appreciated the extent to which legislative policy decisions in Connecticut were made in a "top-down" manner. In the largely one-party Republican world of the Connecticut legislature, where Republicans that year dominated the house by 194 to 68, and the senate by the much narrower margin of 21 to 14, most members followed the recommendations issued by their leaders.

One member who did not, however, was sixty-nine-year-old Bristol lawyer and legal scholar Epaphroditus Peck. While the senate accepted the judiciary committee's negative recommendation without debate, Peck forced a floor debate and vote in the house—the first time a birth control bill had gotten that far. Like the earlier hearing, however, the floor debate turned into a raucous affair. With Katharine Hepburn in "a front row seat in the well-filled gallery," Representative Peck spoke about how the anticontraception statute was essentially religious legislation and how there had never been a prosecution under it. He noted how at the hearing opposition to its repeal had come "exclusively from Roman Catholic sources," and emphasized how the entire topic involved "matters purely personal."

The primary opposition speaker was Representative Caroline T. Platt of Milford, who admitted that some liberalization might be desirable for women with health problems but contended that even most Protestants did not favor total repeal. "Trembling, seemingly with deep emotion," Mrs. Platt argued that if birth control was legalized, population growth would come only from immigrants, and "she pleaded for 'keeping up the proper element.'" This bill, she went on, "opens the way for every girl to become a prostitute," and "seventy-five per cent of them will." That statement generated "such a chorus of protesting hisses that Mrs. Platt was silenced, standing erect, her trembling hand holding a sheet of paper with her notes." Platt then concluded by calling for "a conference of 'conscientious doctors and wise lawyers'" to draft an amendment. Her speech, the *Hartford Courant* declared, had been "the first time in the history of the State" that "occupants of the galleries hissed a member of the House for arguments advanced on the floor."

Six other representatives, four of them women, also spoke before the vote was tallied. The *Courant*, terming the debate "bitter," explained that "applause for speakers both for and against the bill from onlookers and legislators went unchecked throughout the long discussion." Representatives Helen Lewis of Stratford, Georgina Davids of Greenwich, and Marjory Cheney of Manchester all spoke in favor. In opposition, Mrs. Marion Roberts of Hartford declared that "birth control is an unnatural process and leads to degeneracy," and a male representative from Clinton advanced an economic argument: "The workers come from the lower classes and it is here that births would be limited by such a bill. Workers are needed, and the upper classes should not put into effect legislation that will tend to reduce their number." Then the tally was taken, and the repeal bill was rejected by the overwhelming margin of 226 to 18. Eight of the affirmative votes were from women.[47]

The house debate had been the most dramatic event in the Connecticut struggle to date, and the women praised Peck's effort while welcoming the extensive favorable press coverage. Several weeks later, however, the birth control movement received its biggest national publicity boost since the New York police action in 1921 canceling Sanger's mass rally when another New York City police raiding party descended upon the Birth Control Clinical Research Bureau on April 15. The eight officers had arrest warrants for Dr. Hannah Stone, another physician, and three clinic nurses, and carted them off in patrol wagons while also seizing all of the clinic's medical and patient records. The raid had clearly been in preparation for some time, for undercover policewoman Ann K. McNamara had made several visits to the clinic under the guise of being a patient, and two examinations had found McNamara experiencing "several pelvic disorders." Sanger was outraged, noting that the clinic had been "minding its own business and hoping that its powerful ecclesiastical neighbors would mind theirs," but her new attorney, Morris L. Ernst, and many supporters found the raid nothing short of astounding, for the 1918 New York court decision in Sanger's own case had explicitly ratified doctors' provision of birth control advice and devices in any and all situations where they were medically appropriate for a woman's health.

Authorities returned the patient records four days after the raid, but New York doctors were infuriated at such a police invasion of doctor-patient confidentiality, and within a week the New York County Medical Society officially adopted a resolution condemning the raid. An initial hearing on the charges against the staff members was adjourned after only Officer McNamara's testimony, but Ernst explained his defense strategy to the press: "If the doctor is acting in good faith with the thought that the birth control information will prevent disease, that is all we have to prove. It is the burden of the prosecution to prove the bad faith of the doctor." Five days later, when the defense got its turn in court, several very prominent doctors, including a former city health commissioner, took the stand on behalf of the clinic workers. The presiding magistrate reserved decision, but the city police commissioner issued what the *New York Times* termed "a virtual apology" to the clinic and the medical community, saying he agreed "absolutely" that "the relationship between patient and physician should forever remain inviolate." Several days later the police commander responsible for the raid was demoted, and three days after that the court dismissed the charges, agreeing with Ernst that "good faith" on the part of the doctor was indeed "the test of guilt or innocence."[48]

The police and/or church blunder of raiding the New York clinic, just like the 1921 intrusion, redounded greatly to the birth control movement's advantage. The *Birth Control Review* declared that the controversy had "furthered the cause of birth control beyond the most optimistic hopes of its supporters," especially because of how "the medical profession aligned itself more definitely than ever before on the side of birth control." Just days before the raid Sanger had resolved to take new congressional soundings on the prospects for a federal reform bill by creating what she called the National Commitee on Federal Legislation for Birth Control, and while Catholic spokesmen continued to decry birth control as "intrinsically evil," Sanger responded that it will "enable a woman to act as a free, self-directed, autonomous personality."[49]

By the fall of 1929 Sanger was attempting to recruit a hesitant

Katharine Hepburn as legislative chairman for her National Committee, and the Connecticut women were looking ahead to the 1930 elections, hoping to boost the number of birth control supporters who would sit in the 1931 legislature. Nationwide there was now a grand total of fifty-five birth control clinics in twenty-three cities in twelve states, but while Katharine Beach Day reported to the ABCL that "it is very evident that there is a steady growth of sentiment throughout the state in favor of birth control," she also stated that "it is impossible to attempt to establish a clinic until the doctors shall be free from their present dilemma" under the 1879 statute. Sanger's National Committee sporadically sent staff organizers into Connecticut to raise money and recruit new supporters, and these efforts generated some funds, plus modest numbers of new endorsers—including, on one small Waterbury list, Miss Jeannie Heppel. However, a preliminary contact by one staffer in the summer of 1930 with a small group of Greenwich women who had had some initial discussions about possibly sponsoring a clinic just across the state line in New York came to naught.[50]

While the newly titled Connecticut Birth Control League had no discernable impact on the state's November elections, the results nonetheless were extremely notable: for the first time in twenty years a Democrat—grandfatherly Yale English professor Wilbur L. Cross—won the governorship. Liberals were ecstatic, believing that Cross's triumph over the one-party conservative Republican dominance of the state represented a "stinging rebuke" to the reticent millionaire power company president, J. Henry Roraback, who had served as Republican state chairman since 1912 and was widely believed to choose Republican gubernatorial candidates—and legislative leaders—quite single-handedly. Reformers had long accused passive state Democratic leaders of having an insidious but informal working relationship with Roraback, and while the Republicans still controlled both houses of the legislature, many thought that a new political era might be dawning in Connecticut.[51]

Not long after that election the CBCL women decided that their 1931 initiative would have to be a "doctors' bill" rather than a repeal one. There was "a pretty general feeling," they told the ABCL, "especially on the part of the women members of the legislature, that there would be less opposition to the 'doctors' bill' than to a straight repeal bill," which some supporters had "criticized as too 'radical' a step." In New York, however, the national birth control strategy debate had taken a new and very important turn when one young supportive woman lawyer, Dorothy Kenyon, had advanced the novel contention that rather than continuing to focus on winning legislative repeal of federal and state anticontraception laws, it would be preferable "to get away from the law by the simple expedient of forgetting about it." Terming this option "nullification," Kenyon argued that it would be better to bypass legislative bodies "and concentrate upon public opinion, in the hope that some day the sentiment of the community may be strong enough to impress our enforcement officers" into nonenforcement. Kenyon's article stimulated considerable discussion. Birth control historian Norman Himes agreed that the key would be "the failure of prosecutors to bring cases before the courts," and attorney Alexander Lindey concurred: "nullification promises the only speedy relief." Morris Ernst saw it somewhat differently: "Nullification will take place by the constant whittling away of the law by judicial decisions." Birth control statutes "will not be repealed until they have already been nullified," Ernst predicted, but the essence of change would be judicial incrementalism: "Courts which are too cowardly to declare laws in conflict with our basic Constitution wheedle out of dilemmas by casting new interpretations on old statutes, eventually destroying the word of the law givers." One of the very few dissents came from semiretired Mary Ware Dennett: not only was legislative repeal "far easier to accomplish than has been assumed," but "under the nullification process, one can never know where or when the lightning of occasional prosecution may strike."[52]

Ernst appeared quite prescient when, hardly two weeks later, the U.S. Court of Appeals for the Second Circuit ruled in a trademark infringement lawsuit involving the manufacturer of Trojans brand condoms that there was nothing improper about such items since, under the New York court decision in Sanger's case twelve years earlier, physicians could supply or prescribe contraceptive articles for health purposes, and condoms of course could prevent the spread of disease. Legal commentators heralded this *Youngs Rubber* ruling as a major step toward nullifying the federal 1873 Comstock provisions, but Margaret Sanger remained focused upon pursuing congressional approval of a doctors amendment. She had finally succeeded in recruiting a sponsor—ageing lameduck Massachusetts Senator Frederick H. Gillett—and in mid-February 1931 a judiciary subcommittee held two days of hearings on his bill, even though it had no prospects for passage, or even committee approval. Katharine Hepburn preceded Sanger as the proponents' first speaker, telling the subcommittee that human beings should not be denied "the right to regulate intelligently the birth rate."

A prominent doctor, a well-known Protestant clergyman, and a woman representing the New York City Junior League also spoke in favor. For the opponents, an attorney representing the National Patriotic League alleged that birth controllers were puppets of "communistic agents" and a spokesman for the National Catholic Welfare Conference warned against "perverting youth through the spread of contraceptive propaganda." An American Federation of Labor official, a female member of Congress from New Jersey, and Massachusetts Representative John W. McCormack—a future speaker of the House—completed the opponents' roster, with McCormack declaring that "I can conceive of no more dangerous piece of legislation to the future of America" than Sanger's modest reform bill.[53]

Hardly a week after the Washington session, a legislative hearing was held in Boston on a doctors-exception bill that was the first significant initiative to come from Massachusetts birth control advocates in over a decade. The Birth Control League's female officers had carefully recruited physician support, even to the extent of sponsoring a supportive article in the *New England Journal of Medicine*, but the bill went nowhere and some Massachusetts activists argued that efforts should be directed toward simply opening a clinic rather than appealing to the legislature.[54]

In Connecticut the 1931 birth control campaign followed much the same path as in Washington and Boston. Annie Porritt was now the acting chairman of the league, as an ageing Katharine Beach Day spent more and more time in Florida, and Porritt had taken the lead in being sure that an advance text of a doctors-exception bill had been circulated among Connecticut M.D.s for their endorsement. When prominent Hartford gynecologist James Raglan Miller appeared as the leadoff speaker at the judiciary committee's birth control hearing on February 24, he was able to present the members with a list of more than four hundred Connecticut doctors who were backing reform. The CBCL women had been deeply pleased by the extent of medical support, and while the proponents' presentation was heavily directed toward portraying the issue as a medical question, the same standing-room-only crowd of female supporters was once again present. Three other doctors joined Miller and Katharine Hepburn among the affirmative witnesses, but primary opposition speaker Francis E. Jones, representing the Bishop of Hartford, was joined by an opposing M.D. as well as by one Mrs. T. M. Sullivan of Hartford, who warned that if the bill passed, "twenty-five years from today the State of Connecticut will be a mass of crumbling ruins." The largely female audience laughed loudly when Mr. Jones was

forced to concede that "child-bearing has its difficulties," but the oppos-
ing doctor, Daniel E. Shea, firmly told the committee that if
Connecticut doctors really backed reform, the Connecticut State
Medical Society itself would be appearing before them.

The judiciary committee's reactions were noncommittal, but some
three weeks after the hearing the committee *favorably* reported an
amended and more modest bill, allowing for doctors to prescribe birth
control, but only for specific individual health needs. While it was the
first time that any birth control bill had received a committee endorsement, birth control advocates voiced mixed reactions, with Katharine
Hepburn terming it "much too conservative." Although the *Hartford
Courant* termed the favorable report "one of the surprises of the session," the day before house floor action the *Courant* also reported that
"opponents of the bill have been energetic in bringing pressure to bear
upon their representatives ever since the bill received a favorable
report." The paper added that "A considerable number of legislators are
loath to vote contrary to the wishes of constituents and equally unwilling to vote against the bill. A good many of the members of both houses are exceedingly anxious to avoid a record vote on the bill."

When the committee's bill was brought up for house floor debate on
April 1, Bristol's Epaphroditus Peck, as in 1929, led the fight for the
proponents, joined by Marjory Cheney of Manchester and a new
young Republican from Stratford, Raymond E. Baldwin. One of the
three M.D.s in the house, Clinton's David A. Fox, spoke against the
bill, saying that passage would result in young people having "a bottle
of gin in one hand and a birth control certificate in the other."
Legislative leaders attempted to avoid a recorded vote, but fifty-two
members, all Democrats—and just two more than the required minimum—forced a formal tally. When the numbers were totaled, the bill
was rejected by 172 to 76—a wide margin, but considerably closer than
1929's 226 to 18. Nine women representatives voted in favor and ten
against. The following day the judiciary committee's favorable report
was taken up in the senate. One of only two senate proponents told his
colleagues that "The state has no business telling me or you or anybody
else how we shall conduct our marital affairs." His compatriot added
that "some day we will laugh at our fear of passing such a bill," but
when a voice vote rejecting the bill was taken, reporters judged that
only three or four of the thirty-three senators present voted aye.[55]

That legislative struggle and defeat mobilized a number of new
medical supporters of birth control, and in very short order led to a significant alteration in the leadership—and the agenda—of the

Connecticut League. Taking the lead in these changes was fifty-four year-old Yale public health professor Charles-Edward A. Winslow, who had founded the public health program at Yale and who had long known Porritt, the Hepburns, and Mrs. Day through their mutual earlier involvement in the Social Hygiene Association. Along with two gynecologist friends, A. Nowell Creadick and Yale faculty member Herbert Thoms, Winslow resolved that medical men ought to "take some rather active steps to lay a foundation" for a successful 1933 legislative effort. The first step, Winslow and his colleagues told other doctors, was "to reorganize the Connecticut Birth Control League so that it can be made a really vigorous and effective organization. What we expect to do is to concentrate our efforts entirely on the amendment that was proposed" in the 1931 legislature—i.e., authorizing doctors to provide birth control advice and supplies *only* to women whose health needs justified it—"and to build up an organization throughout the counties and towns of the state so that we can really exert some influence."

The New Haven trio, along with two New Haven female supporters, Betty Whittemore and Elizabeth Reed, laid plans for a June 1 annual meeting of the CBCL and agreed that Creadick would become the league's new president, "as it seems very important to have a medical man in that position and he seems by far the best fitted." In advance of that session, however, Doctors Thoms and Creadick successfully brought the issue of birth control before the May 21 annual meeting of the Connecticut State Medical Society. Thoms had prepared a statement saying that the CSMS supported "legalizing the dissemination of contraceptive advice for medical purposes by licensed practitioners" as per the judiciary committee's bill, and Creadick delivered a stem-winding speech on its behalf, explicitly denouncing the doctors in the state house who had failed to back that bill. "Dr. Creadick's discussion evoked applause" from the delegates, the Society's minutes recorded, and it was "voted (unanimously) . . . that the sentiments expressed in the above statement be approved by the Society." Ten days later, at a luncheon at the New Haven Lawn Club, the CBCL elected Creadick as its new president and unanimously resolved to pursue a 1933 edition of the judiciary committee bill in the next legislature. Annie Porritt and Katharine Beach Day remained on the board, with Porritt's daughter-in-law, Alison Hastings Porritt, becoming the new CBCL treasurer, and Mrs. Hepburn's friend Sallie Pease being named Hartford County chairman.[56]

On the national scene the American Birth Control League continued to endorse practical nullification arguments while stressing that the actual opening of clinics, rather than Sanger's emphasis upon appealing to the Congress, was the direction in which birth control activists should move. New England's first public birth control clinic was opened in Providence in July 1931 by the newly formed Rhode Island Birth Control League, and encountered no legal difficulties, but Sanger, in an autobiographical book published in September, continued to call for winning "the ultimate victory through congressional legislation." The Connecticut activists, now headquartered at Creadick's office at 79 Trumbull Street in New Haven, took note of the Rhode Island step, but resolved that an educational campaign aimed particularly at rural legislators was their only option: "The Board felt that no step towards the establishment of clinics could be taken so long as the law makes penal the use of contraceptives, and thus puts any clinic in the position of being a school of crime."[57]

In February 1932 Creadick, in conjunction with New Haven's Leon Whitney, executive secretary of the American Eugenics Society, invited Margaret Sanger to town for a major speech, with Creadick informing Sanger that "the ladies of my Board are eager to meet you and entertain you." New Haven Police Chief Philip T. Smith did not share those sentiments, and announced he would have Sanger arrested "if she says one word over the bounds" during her March 8 talk at the Fox College theater. Sanger drew a capacity crowd of fifteen hundred, including numerous police officers, but she was not interrupted, and Smith told reporters that "I don't propose to make a martyr of any group." Sanger thanked Creadick for the Connecticut League's steadfast defense of her right to speak, writing that "I had to rub my eyes to remember that this was the year of 1932 and not back in the days of 1914." Sanger added that she had come to the "definite conclusion . . . that no man or woman with Catholic affiliations has any moral right to hold a position of authority for the State. They cannot help but give their first allegiance to the Church and become subject to the demands of any high official of the Church."[58]

Sanger's leading preoccupation remained her focus on pursuing a congressional reform bill, and in May 1932 both a Senate judiciary subcommittee and the House Ways and Means Committee held hearings on similar bills introduced by two openly noncommittal legislators, West Virginia Senator—and doctor—Henry D. Hatfield and North Carolina Representative Frank Hancock. Katharine Hepburn accompanied Sanger to both hearings, telling the House committee that birth control advocates were not opposed to large families. "I personally believe in large families. I have one." Sanger herself stressed to the committee that birth control "does not mean the interruption of life after conception occurs." The Senate committee, however, never even voted on the bill, and when the House one did, it was defeated by a margin of 19 to 4.[59]

In New England, however, birth control discussion was increasingly turning to clinics, not legislatures. Nowell Creadick acknowledged in a spring report to his CBCL colleagues that their emphasis upon winning modest future legislative reform "has brought us opposition and criticism from friends," including some within the league, but Creadick and his fellow doctors remained opposed to what he termed "the flagrant violation method" of opening a clinic. There had been some talk of filing a court case to seek a judicial declaration that doctors were not breaking any law when they sought to protect their patients' health, but Creadick and his colleagues noted that a suit "takes time and the outcome is uncertain. It will lead us nowhere except to permit any doctor to prescribe in his office to one of his patients." Again at their instigation, however, the 1932 annual meeting of the Connecticut State Medical Society approved a resolution backing legislation which would legalize birth control in cases where "pregnancy would be detrimental to the health of the patient."[60]

Other members of the league, however, and particularly the group of Greenwich women, focused more and more on the question of simply opening a clinic. In May 1932 several of them, particularly Nancy Carnegie Rockefeller and Florence Borden Darrach, launched the Greenwich Committee for Maternal Health with a well-attended mass meeting at Greenwich High School that was addressed by Mrs. Darrach's husband, a prominent doctor who had just stepped down as dean of Columbia University's medical school. Nancy Rockefeller in particular had been in contact with New York birth control advocates for almost two years, and several weeks after the rally they took further encouragement when they learned that the Birth Control League of Massachusetts had just opened that state's first clinic, the Brookline Mothers Health Office. By early August Rockefeller and her colleagues were committed to opening a clinic in Port Chester, New York, just across the state border, with the hope of subsequently moving it into Connecticut proper. Rockefeller asked Hannah Stone, still the director of Sanger's New York Birth Control Clinical Research Bureau, to recommend a willing physician to them, and in early September 1932, Dr. Cheri Appel, a thirty-one year-old graduate of New York University Medical School, began seeing Connecticut patients at the Port Chester facility. At long last Connecticut—almost—had a clinic.[61]

Most of the Connecticut League's work, however, continued to point toward lining up backers of a modest reform bill in advance of the 1933 legislature. In late August the league lost one of its three formative figures when Annie Porritt was killed in a Hartford auto accident. A decidedly formal woman—much unlike both Katharine Day and Katharine Hepburn—who had no interest in small talk and whom even her closest friends always called "Mrs. Porritt," she had been as central as anyone during the league's first decade, even if her role had receded some when the medical men had moved to the fore. In December Margaret Sanger delivered speeches in Hartford and at Wesleyan University in Middletown, but the more important event was the league's recruitment of the incoming house majority leader, Raymond E. Baldwin of Stratford, as sponsor of its 1933 bill. The general election had returned Wilbur Cross to the governorship, and the Roosevelt tide had carried a narrow Democratic majority into the state senate, creating divided control of the legislature for the first time in twenty years. Baldwin was young, a relative liberal, and visibly independent of the J. Henry Roraback tradition of Connecticut Republicanism. While the Democrats might be the more liberal party on most issues, the heavy concentration of most Catholic officeholders in Democratic rather than Republican ranks increasingly made the latter party the vehicle of choice for the birth control advocates, and Baldwin was an ideal Republican champion.[62]

Baldwin's House Bill 519 provided that the 1879 ban "shall not apply to [a] licensed physician when in his opinion pregnancy would be detrimental to the health of the patient." The judiciary committee's hearing on it took place on March 1, and the CBCL doctors recruited Dr. Charles W. Comfort, a top officer of the Connecticut State Medical Society, as the proponents' principal speaker. Comfort described the bill as "a purely medical measure for the purpose of preserving the health of our women." Then Hartford's Dr. James Raglan Miller detailed how during the final six months of 1932 fifty-seven Connecticut women had died in pregnancy, at least nine from illegal abortions and at least five from heart or kidney problems that would not have proven fatal in the absence of pregnancy. Dr. Creadick presented the committee with some five thousand petition signatures endorsing the bill, including more than a thousand from Connecticut doctors—considerably more than half of the state's practicing physicians. Opponents, however, countered by presenting four doctors of their own to supplement Louise Fisher of the Connecticut Council of Catholic Women, who had represented opponents eight years earlier in 1925. One of the opposing doctors warned that passage of the bill would result in "moral degeneracy," while Mrs. Fisher declared that "the laws of nature and of God are violated by the use of devices preventing conception." The only morally acceptable answer, she explained, was simple: "for the problems, both ethical and physical, there is but one solution, marital continence."[63]

Eight weeks passed before the judiciary committee voted on Baldwin's bill, and when it did, the result was an 8 to 8 tie. Five days later that unfavorable report went to the house floor, and floor leader Baldwin offered an amendment expressly limiting application of the bill's medical exception to *married* women. Representative Peck of Bristol, a veteran from previous years, sought to emphasize that this year's bill was being championed by doctors, not the league, but Republican Montgomery C. Tiers of Colebrook asserted that passage would "open wide the gates of prostitution," and William J. Lyons of Norwalk insisted that the bill "gives physicians the right to kill." Peck responded that "the real question is whether you have the right to impose your judgment on me and send me to jail if my judgment is not the same as yours," and when the tally was taken, Baldwin's amended bill passed by the impressive margin of 169 to 80. Republican representatives backed the measure by 151 to 35, while Democrats totaled 18 in favor and 45 opposed. Fifteen of eighteen women members voted in favor, and the *Hartford Courant* noted that while proponents had not previously been optimistic about their chances in the senate, the dramatic house margin now left them "greatly encouraged."

Two days later, however, the senate without debate first rejected, by 18 to 12, the limiting amendment that Baldwin had added in the house, and then the bill itself, with twenty votes in the negative. Dr. Creadick responded by telling reporters that "We have come a long way in the past ten years" and vowing "two years of careful campaigning" to change the result come 1935, but the *New Haven Journal-Courier* decried the outcome as one that "inhibits medical freedom" and regretted how the opposition was "purely religious."[64]

Raymond Baldwin, however, was not ready to give up, and on May 9, at his initiative, the house "voted to insist" on its previous endorsement of his bill and appointed two members, Peck of Bristol and Helen Kitchell of Greenwich, to serve as a conference committee to discuss the bill further with the senate. A single opponent, Raymond J. Devlin, represented the senate, and on May 18 Peck and Kitchell presented the house with a further revised and weakened version of the original Baldwin bill. This newest version would authorize a doctor to provide birth control information and supplies to a married woman if her health in the doctor's judgment called for such, so long as that doctor's judgment was "concurred in by another licensed physician" who would be designated by the state health commissioner after a request was filed by the initial doctor. This new amendment, the *Courant* reported, "was drafted on information that it would be acceptable to a sufficient number of senators to insure adoption of the bill in that body."

On May 23 the house adopted the new amendment on a vote of 149 to 45, with Representative Peck explaining quite explicitly that it had been prepared by a senator who previously had voted against the bill. The house then approved the bill itself, by an increased margin of 171 to 72, but the following day the senate simply tabled the entire matter, leaving the issue in abeyance. Among the bill's ostensible proponents, however, vocal dissent from the further compromise represented by the final house bill was growing, and on May 26 Margaret Sanger sent identical telegrams to Nowell Creadick and to Katharine Hepburn: "Have read with amazement House bill suggesting consultation [with] two physicians for women [to] receive information. Sincerely hope you will protest such shortsighted legislation. I beg you not to accept such compromise with principle and fairness. Better to leave legislation as it is." Hepburn cabled back that "[I] Entirely agree with you," but further internal debate over that fundamental strategic choice was precluded when the senate, on June 6, on a motion by Hartford senator Joseph P. Cooney and without apparent opposition, tabled the bill indefinitely.[65]

In the wake of the 1933 battle, however, Nowell Creadick stepped down as president of the league and was briefly replaced by Hartford minister William T. Hooper, who himself resigned on grounds of ill health in May 1934. The Greenwich women continued to operate successfully their clinic facility in Port Chester, New York, with Dr. Appel seeing 395 women in the first twelve months of operation and then an additional 523 new patients in the clinic's second year of existence. In November 1933, the league won a significant victory when the Connecticut League of Women Voters reversed their 1931 stance and voted by a narrow margin of 56 to 51 to endorse birth control, and most league activists looked forward to the 1935 legislature with considerable optimism.[66] Katharine Hepburn joined Margaret Sanger for two more sets of Washington congressional hearings on birth control bills that Sanger's National Committee was backing, and on the senate side a "doctors' bill" actually made it to the floor before finally being killed. One commentator observed that "There is little doubt that the bill would have passed had a fair roll-call vote been taken," but a more wide-spread view was that increasing numbers of people viewed the legislative effort as largely a symbolic enterprise, since the availability of some con-traceptives, particularly condoms, had increased very noticeably in the wake of the federal appellate court decisions in *Youngs Rubber* and anoth-er subsequent case. Some journalists warned that manufacturers who suggestively advertised "feminine hygiene" products as supposed contra-ceptives were taking advantage of this new atmosphere to misleadingly market many products that were far less dependable than physician-fit-ted diaphragms, and *The New Republic* contended that "the contraceptive business has outgrown the birth control movement." Even Sanger admitted that "all progress has been through judicial decisions or inter-pretations" and conceded that her congressional bill would merely "incorporate in the federal laws the exemptions that have already been judicially recognized," but she continued her legislative efforts in the new Congress that began early in 1935.[67]

In October 1934 the Connecticut League named Hepburn's friend and neighbor Sallie Pease as its president and carefully scrutinized the upcoming legislative elections. The November results for the state sen-ate were mixed, and both Pease and Dr. Creadick, now the league's leg-islative chairman, attempted to count possible votes in what ostensibly looked like close to a prospective tie. In late January the 1935 birth control bill, a doctors' measure, was introduced by Willington Representative Dr. Frank C. Converse, but prospects for a favorable report from the joint judiciary committee looked bleak, and hence house proponents attempted unsuccessfully to have the measure referred to the Public Health and Safety Committee instead. A judicia-ry committee hearing on the bill was not scheduled until April 5, but the weekly newspaper of the Hartford diocese significantly enlivened the biennial battle by publishing a harsh editorial attack on Katharine Hepburn and Margaret Sanger. "If the communistic theories imported from Russia are widely propagated in our American colleges, it seems quite probable that Mrs. Hepburn and Mrs. Sanger shall come forth from their protracted campaign crowned with the laurels of victory." The *Transcript* additionally alleged that during Katharine Hepburn's own childbirths, her entire family had been invited in to watch the event, and that suggestion was enough to propel Hepburn into sending the diocese what press reports termed "a sizzling telegram." In the next issue, in an editorial prominently headlined "We Apologize," the *Transcript* retracted its odd accusation.[68]

The April 5 judiciary committee hearing took place in front of

another overflow crowd, with the proponents' prominent physicians—
James Raglan Miller, Charles Comfort from the Medical Society, and
Representative Converse—supplemented this year with New Haven
attorney James Wayne Cooper and Episcopalian clergyman William T.
Hooper, the former league president. Dr. Comfort declared that if the
law was not changed, "it is high time there were some prosecutions
under it," and recommended that "if evidence of violation is to be
secured, a law officer should be stationed in each bedroom, bathroom,
and doctor's office." Cooper argued that without a medical exception,
the law was probably unconstitutional under both the Connecticut
Constitution and the Fourteenth Amendment to the U.S.
Constitution, as an unreasonable infringement of guarantees protecting
individual life and liberty. Reverend Hooper added that "It is the sacred
right of each and every individual person to determine the size of his
family." For the opponents, four state senators were joined by four
M.D.s, as well as by Louise Fisher, this year officially representing the
Bishop of Hartford, Maurice F. McAuliffe, plus a spokesman for the
Knights of Columbus. The Knights representative called for passage of
a bill prohibiting lectures about birth control, and one James W.
Fitzpatrick of Waterbury denounced the bill as "the last gesture of an
outworn, discredited, degenerate capitalistic system." In rebuttal,
Katharine Hepburn—whom one paper described as having "a striking
resemblance" to her now-famous daughter—emphasized that "the
greatest bulwark against immorality is happy marriage, and this bill will
promote early and happy marriages."

Prospects for any affirmative committee action, however, looked
very poor. Sallie Pease reported that "we thought that we had a fighting
chance but the Senate has had an almost complete reversal. The reason
is simply that they have had a FLOOD OF MAIL FROM THEIR
CATHOLIC CONSTITUENTS," and proponents would have to
answer in kind. Hartford supporter Dr. Hilda Crosby Standish
responded with a letter to the editor, asking rhetorically, "what kind of
birth control shall we have in this state? Shall we have the boot-legged
variety, which for the most part is dangerous to health, plus abortion
for the foreign born who cannot read English?" Birth control proponents, she explained, were "mostly women interested in saving the
health and lives of other women," and what they proposed was "a safe
and harmless method to be taught only by licensed physicians and only
to married women who are ill." Writing to state senators, Standish concluded, might help "save some woman's life." By early May, however,
hopes had dimmed even further, with reports indicating that a tie vote

existed within the judiciary committee and that the bill would not emerge, and in early June senate chairman Kenneth J. Bradley confirmed that the bill was indeed dead.[69]

On Tuesday, June 4, the Connecticut League held its annual luncheon meeting in Hartford. As Sallie Pease later remembered it, the mood was "most discouraging." "We had failed dismally in the Legislature and it seemed as though nothing but gloom had descended over the Connecticut Birth Control movement." Before lunch the board heard an up-to-the minute report on the legislative impasse, and at the luncheon itself that news was shared with a larger group. Afterward Pease was approached by a Hartford woman, Lillian Leiterman Joseloff, whose husband operated a successful grocery store chain. There had been talk for several years, particularly in New Haven, about expanding upon the Greenwich program and opening a clinic actually *in* Connecticut, but nothing had come of the talk. Lillian Joseloff, however, was more direct: "I would like to finance a clinic in Hartford."

Sallie Pease was more than eager to accept and agree. As she later put it, "we were determined not to become discouraged" and simply "wait until the next Assembly to again undertake the same campaign which had gotten us nowhere for the last twelve years." Joseloff's offer to support the first year of a clinic's operation was more than enough to propel Sallie Pease into immediate action, and by the very next day she was writing to friends and potential advisors, soliciting their help. In less than three weeks' time Pease put together an organizational structure and a board of sponsors for what would be called the Hartford Maternal Health Center, recruited two principal physicians, Hilda Crosby Standish and Eleanor Taylor Calverly, to see patients and fit diaphragms, and endorsed Dr. Standish's plan to rent four rooms on the ground floor of an apartment building at 100 Retreat Avenue in Hartford, directly across from Hartford Hospital, for the clinic's physical space. Standish had visited Sanger's Clinical Research Bureau several times while she had been attending medical school in New York, and Pease herself made several quick visits to gain pointers from clinics operating in nearby states. On June 26, twenty-one members of the new board of sponsors attended a founding meeting at which Pease and Standish detailed their plans for the clinic, which would be open six hours every day to make appointments for the two afternoons each week—Tuesday and Friday—when the physicians would see patients. Standish aimed to hold the first actual clinic session on Tuesday afternoon, July 9—and, thirteen days later, she did.[70]

Pease had recruited an impressive board of sponsors, but she, Standish, and their colleagues had two principal initial fears: publicity and legal vulnerability. One of her most important board recruits, prominent young attorney Lucius F. Robinson, Jr., gave her reassurance on the second score, and the Hartford press itself, Pease later explained, helped on the first: "when we were gathering people together in order to sponsor our clinic it reached the newspapers. We went to the newspapers, asked them to withhold the story for a while, told them our aims, our backers, and gave them full information." They went along, and throughout the first three months of the Hartford clinic's successful operation not a word of its existence appeared in either of Hartford's two newspapers.

Since "the only advertising was by person to person," the clinic's initial numbers were modest, with a total of fifty-three patients seen by its doctors in the first eleven weeks of operation. Additionally, Pease and Standish mandated purposely strict rules as to which women could be seen by clinic doctors: "Married, living with husband, at least one child unless physically unfit for pregnancy, physically or economically unable to have another pregnancy at present and unable to pay for private care." Fiscally the clinic—which cost a modest two hundred and fifty dollars per month to operate—was separate from the Connecticut League, with its own distinct—but very heavily overlapping—board, but physically the two organizations were hardly distinguishable, as the league moved its own office into the clinic's rooms at 100 Retreat Avenue in early September.[71]

The Hartford clinic's publicity-free inception came to a sudden and unplanned end when Katharine Hepburn mentioned the new facility during a talk at Connecticut State College in Storrs on the evening of October 23 and the Associated Press put a story on the wire, thus forcing the hands of the Hartford newspapers. Lucius F. Robinson, Jr., moved quickly to head off any problems: "The birth control clinic confines itself strictly to advising married patients whose health, in the opinion of competent medical experts, requires the giving of such service," he told the press. "I do not believe that the" 1879 anticontraception statute "was intended by its framers to preclude such action. If it is to be construed otherwise, then I believe that grave doubts exist as to its constitutionality."

Hilda Standish was surprised by the talk that there might be an actual threat of prosecution, but the Hartford papers said that "a complaint" had been filed with city prosecutor Nicholas F. Rago on October 24 and that "the possibility of legal action" was being studied. "No warrants for

arrests had been issued by mid-afternoon," the *Hartford Times* ominously reported, and the next morning's *Courant* featured an unnamed clinic
official—probably Sallie Pease—saying she was "awfully upset that the
whole thing has come out so publicly. We have felt that our best work
could be done privately, in cooperation with doctors and social workers"
who referred appropriate needy patients. "We realize that the subject is
controversial and we have no desire for antagonism."

Pease and Standish were nonetheless confident "that it was such a
stupid law [that] it would never stand up in court," and the
Connecticut press wasted no time in coming to the clinic's defense.
The *Hartford Times* supportively declared that the clinic operators "have
not set out to defy the law but to carry out a medical and sociological
service," and the *New Haven Journal-Courier* emphasized that there had
never been a known prosecution under the 1879 law. "Its enforcement
would require a police surveillance over the intimacies of family life
[that is] apparently impractical." But, the paper added, "whether such
[birth control] advice can be forbidden under the state and federal constitutions is a question requiring settlement."

On October 29, with prosecutors having made no move, the
Maternal Health Center's board met to review the situation. Lucius
Robinson reported that Rago "does not wish to prosecute unless pressure is brought" upon him, and while there was some possibility that
either Pease or Standish might be arrested, Robinson full well expected
that nothing further would come of the matter. Dr. Standish asked the
board "if some patients could be taken for economic reasons only," but
the issue was parried and it was reiterated "that there should be a strict
rule that no patient should be taken unless she were referred directly
by a recognized social worker or physician and that her social history
should be checked up." Robinson additionally recommended that each
patient should sign her case history, and that "there must be a medical
reason and only those whose health requires information should be
accepted at present."[72]

The brief but successful Hartford crisis convinced the Greenwich
women that they now could safely move their Port Chester clinic operation into Connecticut, and on November 15 the Greenwich Maternal
Health Center saw its first patient in its new quarters at 191 Lake
Avenue in Greenwich. Florence Borden Darrach, the chairman of the
Greenwich group, had solicited an extensive review of their possible
legal vulnerability from a prominent lawyer who lived in Greenwich,
Luke B. Lockwood, and it at least partially reassured the women who
reviewed it. Under the 1879 statute, now Section 6246 of the

Connecticut Code, and a companion "accessory" statute, Section 6562, which provided for punishment of anyone who "aided or abetted" the commission of a substantive offense under 6246, it would first be necessary, Lockwood pointed out, for a prosecutor to prove that a female patient "had actually used the articles in question for the purpose of preventing conception, and second that the person charged with accessoryship did actually lend assistance to the principal. As you can imagine," he went on, "the practical difficulties in the way of proving guilt under Section 6246 are very great and I doubt whether evidence could ever legally be obtained which would result in a conviction." However, Lockwood added, "the question of whether or not a conviction could be obtained is entirely different from the question of whether or not the activities in question are legal or illegal," and "it must be obvious . . . that the activities are illegal but that the chance of a conviction is fairly remote." Of much greater practical concern, Lockwood warned, was a different provision also dating from the 1879 statute, Section 6244, which prohibited the possession of "any article or instrument of indecent or immoral use or purpose," which Lockwood feared might be applied to diaphragms and other birth control supplies. In light of "the very real danger of prosecution" under that provision, anyone working for the Greenwich clinic "should be advised of the danger involved." "I cannot help but feel," he concluded, "that any such activity would be very unwise."[73]

Lockwood's comprehensive but cautious counsel did not cause the Greenwich women to hesitate, and as clinic operations moved forward both there and in Hartford, Sallie Pease became convinced that the extensive newspaper publicity had been all to the good, as the number of patient referrals increased steadily. New Haven and Stamford women were discussing opening clinics in their cities, and New Britain and Winsted supporters were planning to drive women from those towns to the Hartford clinic. Patient acceptance rules were being gradually liberalized, and a favorable early 1936 federal district court decision in a New York case involving birth control supplies that had been shipped from Japan to Dr. Hannah Stone was read by the Connecticut women as another sign that any possible legal problems could be overcome. When both Katharine Hepburn and Dr. Standish spoke at a January 13 meeting of Hartford birth control supporters, the *Courant* gave the event prominent coverage, and noted Standish's report that the Hartford clinic had now had over two hundred patients, of whom, she added, "more than 50 per cent were Catholics."

The printing of that statistic, however, was enough to energize one

Hartford priest, Reverend Andrew J. Kelly of St. Anthony's Roman Catholic Church, who the following Sunday alleged that the Hartford Public Welfare Department and doctors at Hartford Hospital were instructing women clients to go the Maternal Health Center under the threat of losing aid if they did not. "Busybody humanitarians from West Hartford," a wealthy suburb, should not "foist their kind of morality" on city residents, Kelly declared. Katharine Hepburn immediately denounced the allegation of coercion, but welfare department officials and hospital doctors offered only vague comments on the issue of referrals, with one physician telling the *Courant* that "It is too bad the subject has to be brought up." Sallie Pease bluntly responded that "It's a lucky thing that there are humanitarians in West Hartford who believe that it is merciful to save the life of a mother of eight children," and the story quickly subsided. Several weeks later Pease in a Boston talk jokingly thanked Father Kelly for his help, saying "We have since been getting his parishioners," and advising fellow birth control supporters that "I cannot make too strong an appeal [for you] to secure publicity every way you can."[74]

Throughout the spring and summer of 1936 the Connecticut clinic facilities continued to expand. A New Haven clinic began operating on May 11, and a Stamford one opened several weeks later. The Greenwich women began providing "visiting" clinic services in Danbury, Westport, and then Norwalk, and the Hartford clinic expanded its patient hours to three afternoons a week. Doctors Standish and Calverly, and Mrs. Hepburn, all kept up a heavy schedule of speaking engagements before church and women's groups, and word of the league's clinic services spread more and more widely. When the league's annual meeting took place in Hartford in mid-June, Sallie Pease stressed that "The opening of more and more clinics all over the State is the work cut out for the League." There had been ongoing talk as to whether any statutory reform effort should be mounted in the upcoming 1937 legislature, or whether it would be better to "continue as we are now" and "'let a sleeping dog lie.'" At the meeting "it was decided to leave it entirely in the hands of the doctors and for the League to take no part unless it was requested to do so." Worries about actual legal vulnerability under the existing statute had almost entirely ceased, as prosecutors to date had done nothing, and in early September Lucius Robinson confidently predicted that "I doubt very much if they ever do."[75]

On December 7, 1936, the U.S. Court of Appeals for the Second Circuit gave birth control proponents their most significant legal achievement ever when it affirmed the earlier district court ruling against the government's efforts to seize birth control devices that had been shipped to Dr. Hannah Stone from Japan. Stone and Margaret Sanger's lawyer, Morris Ernst, immediately heralded the ruling, *United States* v. *One Package*, as "the end of birth control laws," and later called the decision "the successful termination of a 60 year struggle." By holding that the federal 1873 Comstock statute could not be applied in ways that obstructed public health, the appellate decision—much like the New York ruling in Sanger's case almost two decades earlier— effectively meant that birth control could be prescribed and distributed in all instances where doctors believed that the avoidance of pregnancy would be beneficial to a woman's health. Some commentators read the decision more modestly than Ernst, but most observers agreed that it was likely the final word, as the chances of review by the U.S. Supreme Court seemed slim at best. Sanger and her colleagues, including Katharine Hepburn, held two days of discussions in New York about the decision, and Hepburn emphasized that neither in Congress nor in Connecticut was there any practical value to further legislative efforts: with both clinics and the necessary supplies now fully available, Ernst was right: "I think we should say we have won." Even Sanger was now persuaded, and she heralded the ruling as a long-sought triumph, "an emancipation proclamation to the motherhood of America." Through the judiciary, she said, "an informed and potent public opinion finally found expression," and legal scholars both then and in later years wholeheartedly agreed. The May 1937 issue of the *Columbia Law Review* observed that "it is difficult to escape the conclusion that the Comstock Act . . . has been almost emasculated by judicial nullification," and one respected commentator later termed the *Youngs Rubber* to *One Package* set of holdings "a striking illustration of the court[s] adjusting a statute to changing public information and sentiment."[76]

Public opinion polling—just beginning to become dependable in the late 1930s—appeared to support Sanger's interpretation: a clear consensus now existed among the American people that birth control information and supplies should be fully available to those married women and couples who desired them. A May 1936 American Institute for Public Opinion query asked respondents, "Should the distribution of information on birth control be made legal?," and 70 percent of those who expressed an opinion said yes. A *Fortune* magazine survey several weeks later asked "Do you believe in the teaching and practice of birth control?," a decidedly more intimate question, and received 63 percent yes. In July 1937 the American Institute asked "Do you favor the birth control movement?," and found a 71 percent yes among those who offered an opinion. When the *Ladies Home Journal* asked women respondents "Are you in favor of birth control?," 79 percent answered yes, including 51 percent of Catholic women. In 1937 North Carolina became the first of several states to offer birth control information through its public health program, and when in October 1938 the American Institute, picking up on this development, asked "Would you like to see a government agency furnish birth control information to married people who want it?," 62 percent said yes and only 24 percent said no. By late 1939 those proportions had shifted to 71 percent yes and 18 percent no.[77]

One group that had been lagging significantly behind American public opinion, however, was organized medicine. While the Connecticut State Medical Society had endorsed the legalization of birth control back in 1931, the premier national doctors' group, the American Medical Association (AMA), had avoided any affirmative statement despite intensive efforts by birth control proponents, particularly Dr. Robert L. Dickinson, to get the Association on record. Dickinson and Morris Ernst saw the *One Package* decision as a significant aid in prodding the AMA forward, and when U.S. Attorney General Homer Cummings announced in late January 1937 that the government would not even appeal the Second Circuit's ruling to the Supreme Court, Ernst and Sanger's National Committee heralded the legal development as "the liberation of the medical profession." Some doctors, however, and particularly the Director of the AMA's Bureau of Legal Medicine and Legislation, Dr. W. C. Woodward, took a decidedly different stance toward *One Package*. In early April the AMA *Journal* editorialized that the decision "has no reference to the right of physicians to advise the practice of contraception . . . or to prescribe or supply articles for the prevention of conception," and explicitly criticized the National Committee's statements: "This propaganda is essentially misleading." When Ernst and several prominent colleagues submitted a letter of rebuttal, Dr. Woodward simply hardened the *Journal*'s stance: "the committee's propaganda seemed likely to bring physicians unwittingly into conflict with federal and state laws."

But Robert Dickinson and other birth control supporters on the AMA's Committee on Contraceptive Practices, particularly Massachusetts's Dr. John Rock, now had a clear majority of votes, and on June 8, the AMA's House of Delegates formally adopted a committee report endorsing the dissemination and teaching of the best methods of birth control. The *New York Times* called the action a "landmark in the annals of American medicine," and printed extensive excerpts from the committee's report in a front-page story. The AMA report read as if it could have been drafted by Sanger or Ernst, and it went out of its way to say that *One Package* also ought to control the remaining laws in places like Connecticut and Massachusetts: "Although the statutes in force in the several states that forbid the dissemination of information concerning methods for the prevention of conception do not in express terms exempt physicians from their operation, it seems fair nevertheless to assume that the state courts, if called on to construe them, will adopt lines of reasoning similar to those followed in the case cited and in other cases decided by the United States courts, leaving physicians free to give information concerning contraception when required to meet the medical needs of patients." Sanger was so pleased that she termed the AMA action "really a greater victory" than *One Package* itself, and with seemingly all obstacles to the establishment of clinics all across the United States now removed, she and her colleagues dissolved the National Committee and declared victory.[78]

The Connecticut Birth Control League was happily busy operating its four clinic facilities, all of which continued to chalk up steadily increasing numbers of new patients. The league and Connecticut's doctors had passed up any 1937 legislative campaign, but the issue nonetheless had received helpful publicity when one of the legislature's most bombastic members, Representative John G. Fitzgerald of Ansonia, had introduced an antibirth control bill specifying that "All members of the legislature who advocate birth control must be sterilized within 30 days after adjournment, by surgeons appointed by the government."[79] One young member of the Connecticut League, however, Catherine Jackson Tilson, a recent graduate of Yale Law School and a former patient of Hannah Stone's, thought that the rosy legal predictions being offered by Ernst and Sanger were highly misleading, and shared her opinion both with her Connecticut colleagues and with Sanger. Tilson feared that optimistic observations "may do us considerable harm," particularly in Connecticut, because they raised the danger of "antagonizing now latent opposition." She personally believed that any Connecticut court case would come out favorably, but "an adverse decision is not without the realms of possibility." Morris Ernst, however, remained fully optimistic, and he told a Hartford audience of birth control supporters that any legal risks were minimal: "I am of the opinion that no locality will successfully attack any practice approved by the federal courts."[80]

On June 3, 1937, however—just five days before the AMA's formal ratification of its landmark birth control resolution—Lieutenant Charles Duffee of the Salem Police Department and three colleagues, armed with a search warrant signed by John J. McGrath of the Salem Board of Health, arrived at the North Shore Mothers Health Center in Salem, one of seven birth control clinics now being operated by the Birth Control League of Massachusetts. As they knew—for undercover policewoman Beatrice V. Clark and a female colleague had just left the clinic—Dr. Lucille Lord-Heinstein was in the midst of seeing patients, and the patients were detained and questioned while the officers packed up the clinic's medical records and supplies. While the staff "displayed marked calmness and at times amusement at" the police methods, Dr. Lord-Heinstein, nurse Flora Rand, and social worker Carolyn T. Gardner were taken to Salem police headquarters for questioning, and all three women were charged with violating the Massachusetts birth control statute by distributing contraceptive devices.

The Salem clinic had been operating for seven months, and the BCLM had heralded its opening by announcing that it had "the backing of a large committee from Salem and nearby towns, comprised of leading physicians, ministers, public spirited citizens and representatives from the boards of welfare agencies." The BCLM had also noted that in the opinion of its lawyers, the prominent Boston firm of Palmer, Dodge, "advice given for medical reasons does not come under prohibitions of our statutes," and in April 1937, when the chief of police in Fitchburg and local Catholic clergy had raised questions about a new clinic that the league had opened there, the league's attorneys had successfully impressed the chief by stressing that six other clinics were already operating across the state.

But when the three Salem defendants appeared in court on June 22, Judge George B. Sears refused to return the patient records that had been seized and set trial for July 13. The prosecution's first witness that day was Policewoman Clark, who testified that she had first visited the Salem clinic in late May under a false name, and then had returned on June 3 along with a civilian woman, Rose Barlotta, whom she had paid for her assistance. Mrs. Barlotta had been examined, was found to have severe hypertension, and was fitted for a diaphragm, which she had then turned over to the officers as evidence. Defense attorney Robert G. Dodge put all three defendants, plus three well-known Massachusetts doctors and prominent clinic chairwoman Dorothy Bradford on the stand, and Judge Sears said he would reserve his decision. Dodge filed a posttrial brief that Sears commended as "very able,"

but one week later, on July 20, Sears entered a verdict citing the 191
Massachusetts Supreme Judicial Court affirmation of Van Kleec
Allison's conviction and concluding that "I must find the defendant
guilty" even though they did not believe "they were acting contrary t
law." He imposed a fine of one hundred dollars upon each of th
defendants, and the league filed notices of appeal.[81]

Two weeks later, on the evening of August 2, vice squad officer
interrupted a clinic session at the Brookline Mothers Health Office
the Massachusetts League's oldest facility. They seized all of the clinic'
supplies, one medical file, and identified and questioned the eigh
patients who were present. "The raid was conducted in a very courte
ous manner," Dr. Ilia Galleani reported, "except when one of the lieu
tenants asked one of the new patients if she were a single woman. T
this she replied indignantly that she had seven children and had ha
eight." Criminal charges were soon filed against Dr. Galleani, and th
very next morning Boston police arrived at the South End Mother
Health Office. Lacking a warrant, the clinic staff refused them entr
and promptly removed all records and supplies from the office befor
the officers returned that afternoon. At that same time other officer
visited the headquarters of the Massachusetts League and questione
president Linda M. Hawkridge and staff member Caroline Carte
Davis, both of whom were charged and then arraigned the followin
day. Shell-shocked by the rapid-fire succession of raids and arrests, th
league board, with only one member dissenting, quickly voted to clos
all clinics in the state "temporarily."

Linda Hawkridge sought to take a somewhat more confident stanc
in public than the doctors and league members exhibited in private
"We gladly welcome this investigation, which we hope will clarify th
Massachusetts law," she told reporters. "We have no intention of break
ing the law, and we have nothing to hide. We have never denied that w
gave contraceptive advice, for we consider that a doctor has the right t
do what he can to preserve the life of his patients."[82]

Ilia Galleani's September 15 trial was the next legal step for th
Massachusetts League. Two Brookline police officers testified that the
had gathered their evidence against Dr. Galleani by secretly sitting
under a clinic window one evening a week before the raid and listening
to her conversations with patients. Galleani herself took the stand, anc
defense attorney John M. Raymond attempted to emphasize the *On
Package* precedent to Judge Philip S. Parker, but Parker, like Sears in th
Salem case, was unpersuaded. "There is a great difference, in my mind
between advice given privately by a physician in a particular case t

preserve life and an office that is openly conducted like this with free administration and advice to anybody who might apply." "To open a clinic," he added, "does not come within the purview of the statute or of the decisions, and to open a clinic may lead to abuse. . . . Of course," Parker went on, "contraception may be a good thing. Many people believe in it—I do—although a large number of persons in our community do not believe in it. But there you get into the legislative field, and it would be absolutely improper for a court to say that birth control ought to be practiced. That is a legislative proceeding entirely. While I might be in favor of it, it is not my province to pass on that question." Dr. Galleani, he said, was guilty, and would be fined four hundred dollars.[83]

Within the following week the cases against the three Salem defendants, plus a fourth colleague, clinic volunteer Pamelia Ferris, were set for a hearing in Superior Court, and initial proceedings took place in the cases against Hawkridge and Davis. On October 6 they were found guilty and fined two hundred dollars each, and on October 15 Essex County Superior Court Judge Wilford D. Gray upheld Sears's verdicts against Lord-Heinstein, Gardner, and Rand, and also levied a hundred-dollar fine against Ferris. BCLM leaders were most pessimistic about the cases against Hawkridge and Davis, who were being prosecuted for the general distribution of birth control literature, rather than for medical instruction of individual patients, as in the Salem and Brookline cases, but everyone involved was shaken. Ilia Galleani told league vice-president Loraine Campbell, "How sad that all that we worked for has been suddenly smashed. I sincerely hope that it will be temporary for the sake of all those poor women who needed the advice so badly. . . . But let us hope that the higher courts will judge in our favor. It seems difficult to believe that they will not."

League activists were upset that most of the trial proceedings had been marked by an "absolute failure to show what our work really consisted of," but the lawyers managed to postpone any further proceedings in either the Brookline or Boston cases while appeals of the Salem convictions went forward to the Massachusetts Supreme Judicial Court. In New York, preeminent birth control lawyer Morris Ernst made light of the Massachusetts worries. "It will take an aroused medical profession to influence the judiciary in Massachusetts," he told one medical audience, but "I am not much worried." "If the cases in Boston are fought, as I am sure they will be, in a forthright manner, and if you doctors and lawyers and people with the same point of view will pass your resolutions along to the birth control people in Boston and will give them support, there is no question of the outcome. I say that for this reason: I do not believe there is any such thing as law in the abstract. . . . The law is nothing more or less than the pressure of public opinion at any particular time on particular judges."[84]

Fifteen Massachusetts doctors, including John Rock, wrote to the membership of the Massachusetts Medical Society to ask that each doctor join in a statement of protest. "Two fundamental rights of physicians have been violated," they declared. "First, in the seizure and holding of confidential medical records by the police; second, by police interference with the right of physicians to practice medicine in accordance with accepted methods." Both *One Package* and the June AMA resolution had backed "the rights of physicians to give contraceptive advice," they emphasized, and within several weeks more than seventeen hundred Massachusetts doctors, more than one third of those in the state, joined their petition of protest.

Ernst might hope that such statements would be determinative, but the Massachusetts women already were seeking their lawyers' reassurance that the Salem case could be appealed to the U.S. Supreme Court in the event that the Massachusetts court, which would hear the appeal in early February 1938, affirmed rather than reversed the convictions. One person, however, who was vocally unhappy with the way that Massachusetts matters were being handled was Katharine Houghton Hepburn, and as usual she minced no words in stating her opinion. Telling Massachusetts League president Linda Hawkridge that "I am sorry to have said anything that annoyed you," Hepburn nonetheless insisted that the Massachusetts women were erring seriously: "I can't help feeling that going to jail is better tactics than paying fines. Have no fines been paid anywhere in Massachusetts? I spoke in Springfield and they had just closed up the clinic without the police even asking them to. It just seemed to me foolish." Perhaps the Massachusetts League needed more aggressive lawyers, Hepburn volunteered, such as New York's Morris Ernst.[85]

Aside from Hepburn, the Connecticut women had paid the Massachusetts crisis relatively little heed. Busy with expanding and extending clinic operations across the state, Sallie Pease and her colleagues pressed ahead with plans to start additional clinics. The Hartford Maternal Health Center, helped by twelve volunteer interns from Hartford Hospital, had seen almost seven hundred new patients in calendar 1937. A New London doctor, Dorothea H. Scoville, was fitting diaphragms for every needy woman whom league supporters in that area referred to her, and a new clinic had just opened in New

Britain. Essential to Pease's expansion plans was the hiring of a skilled, part-time field worker, someone who could approach and draw together interested potential clinic sponsors in the two major Connecticut cities, Bridgeport and Waterbury, that still lacked clinics. Seeking to reach beyond the very modest fifteen-hundred-dollar annual budget of the Connecticut League, Pease mentioned her hope to Clarence J. Gamble, a wealthy and idiosyncratic nonpracticing Pennsylvania doctor who was affiliated with neither Sanger nor the American Birth Control League but who was actively subsidizing the establishment of new clinics. Gamble told Pease he would be happy to pay half of the salary for such a field worker, and recommended that the league hire forty-five-year-old Leah Tapper Cadbury, a Haverford native and Bryn Mawr graduate with an "attractive personality" who had done birth control work in Philadelphia for Gamble after previously serving as a volunteer nurse during World War I and as executive secretary of the Women's Educational and Industrial Union of Boston. Cadbury, Gamble said, "would be very effective as an organizer," and Pease, overjoyed by the recommendation, immediately agreed and sent Cadbury a telegram inviting her to Hartford two days later. On November 15, 1937, Leah Cadbury—with one half her salary paid by Gamble, and the other half by Hartford's Lillian Joseloff—began work in Bridgeport for the Connecticut League.[86]

Cadbury's work in Bridgeport went exceedingly well, and on January 25, 1938, she spoke with her initial Waterbury contact, Anne Chase Hart, a daughter of one of Waterbury's most prominent families, the founders of the Chase Brass Company, and visited with two local physicians, Joseph L. Hetzel and Waterbury Medical Association president J. Harold Root, both of whom reacted enthusiastically to the idea of a Waterbury clinic. Anne Hart gave Cadbury the names of other Waterbury women, including her sisters Edith Chase and Mildred Chase Ely, and her sister-in-law, Florence Chase, who might be supportive, and on January 29 Cadbury returned to Waterbury intent on organizing an initial meeting of potential clinic sponsors. Some Waterbury residents were preoccupied by the burgeoning news reports of the financial scandals within the city government, but Cadbury was able to schedule a meeting for Monday afternoon, February 7, at the downtown home of Ruth Northrop, and also visited with Waterbury Hospital superintendent Dr. B. Henry Mason and with several Protestant clergymen. She tried firmly but unsuccessfully to persuade Mason to attend the meeting, telling him it would be "quite inadequate without you." "The public medical service in Waterbury is so completely your province that we can make little progress without your direction and criticism." One of the clergymen did agree to attend, and another recommended, perhaps surprisingly, that she call on two Roman Catholic clergymen, Eugene P. Cryne and Joseph Valdambrini, and she did. As Cadbury reported back, "I have seen both Father Cryne and Father Valdambrini. Each explained that he could not possibly come to the meeting, but we had, to me, an interesting and delightful interview. Thank you for your suggestion that I see them."

The two-hour February 7 meeting at Mrs. Northrop's drew thirty-two women and the sole clergyman. Cadbury had carefully arranged for Lillian Joseloff, Dr. Eleanor Calverly, and administrator Mabel Robbins from the Hartford clinic to arrive during a break halfway through the session, but first she spoke about the prospects for a Waterbury clinic and invited those present to offer their comments. "Some people thought that no immediate action could be taken at this meeting because they didn't want to rush into something while they are all upset by the scandals in their city government," Cadbury reported, but then "Miss Edith Chase suggested, and others agreed, that they all ought to go home and think over the possibility of starting a clinic, and then get together about a month hence, when they could decide if they would like to try to open a clinic with help from the League." Then Dr. Calverly described to the group how a clinic operates, and the meeting adjourned. "I am much encouraged," Cadbury wrote to Sallie Pease, "first by the number and the quality of the women there; and second by their suggesting themselves a plan for future activity instead of leaving this to me."[87]

Cadbury quickly followed up on her initial success. Writing to Edith Chase to thank her for her "very wise" suggestion of a second meeting, Cadbury said she wanted to send out a letter describing the first session to people who were not present but might be interested, and hoped she could include a date and place for the second meeting. Chase responded by suggesting Monday afternoon February 28 at her sister Mildred Ely's home, but emphasized to Cadbury that the Waterbury women had a particular concern: "Many are interested in the legal side of the matter—and it would be worthwhile, I think, to have some sheets of printed matter showing exactly the Connecticut laws on the subject." Cadbury then sent out more than ninety copies of a letter describing the first meeting, inviting people to the second, and enclosing several sheets that discussed Connecticut clinics and the law. "A few doctors in the city are already giving contraceptive advice to poorer residents at little or no charge," she informed her recipients. "It was the feeling of

the group" at the first meeting, "however, that a local, properly organized, birth control service is much needed; and that, even if some
obstacles now stand in the way, means may be found to remove or
avoid them." Cadbury stated the potential obstacles frankly: "Will some
groups in the city be actively hostile?" "Is it dangerous to attempt anything in Waterbury just now which may be illegal?" She closed by
encouraging everyone to visit the Hartford clinic whenever might be
convenient, and wrote to Sallie Pease that her expectations for
Waterbury were very bright: after the second meeting, she estimated, "I
doubt if there will be any need for me, even in organizing a committee
for a center. All of the women interested are experienced in such
work—they know how to form good committees, and how to raise
money."

Cadbury's upbeat portrayal of the first meeting, however, drew gentle
dissents from some recipients of her letter. Mildred Ely emphasized that
while she was happy to host the second session to discuss a clinic, "I am
not yet interested enough in it to sponsor it here in Waterbury and am
very decidedly against starting a clinic here at the present time," since
other existing local charities were already finding it difficult to secure
funds and "it would be almost impossible to raise enough money to get
it started." Ely's sister Anne Hart, Cadbury's initial contact, sounded a
similar but different note while apologizing that she would be out of the
state and unable to attend: "I do feel that there is much feeling of opposition right now in town and think a later time might be better." Edith
Chase and others, however, told Cadbury that the number one reason
for hesitation was fear of legal trouble. "I have the greatest sympathy
with the dread which many of you feel about any possible difficulties
with the law," Cadbury wrote one concerned woman, but "it appears
incredible, however, that any group as astute as the Catholics could
attempt a prosecution under the Connecticut law."[88]

Only twenty-two people attended the February 28 meeting, in part
because of bad weather, but two doctors, two ministers, a hospital
social worker, a female employment supervisor at Scovill Brass, and an
experienced former nurse were among those who did. The two doctors
spoke condescendingly about how inept poorer patients had proven to
be with diaphragm usage, and Miss Ruth A. Davis, the social worker,
indicated that she sometimes provided contraceptive advice to hospital
clinic patients. "The two ministers," Leah Cadbury later reported,
"were surprised to hear that reputable doctors gave contraceptive
advice. They had often wanted it for their parishioners, but had not
dared to ask for it, thinking that the doctors would be offended."

But then the most significant comment in the meeting, indeed the most significant event in Leah Cadbury's time in Waterbury, suddenly took place. Clara Lee McTernan, a thirty-nine-year-old former nurse who had not been present at the first meeting, "offered to try to start a transportation service," taking Waterbury women to the Hartford clinic. Until that moment, Leah Cadbury's initially optimistic hopes for Waterbury had looked increasingly uncertain. The Chase sisters had appeared to be backing away from any possible sponsorship of a clinic, legal concerns appeared widespread, the disappointing turnout for the second meeting was ten people fewer than had attended the first, and Cadbury's own time in Connecticut was soon coming to an end. But Clara McTernan meant what she said, and Millicent Pond, the Scovill supervisor, quickly volunteered that she would be willing to drive. For Leah Cadbury, the remainder of the discussion was of lesser significance, and afterward she spoke with both McTernan and Pond. The very next day Clara McTernan drove to Hartford to meet the clinic staff there, and Mabel Robbins "showed her all the workings of the Hartford Center."[89]

Writing to Sallie Pease, Leah Cadbury could scarcely contain her delight at the emergence of Clara McTernan. "I believe that she will accomplish something," Cadbury predicted. McTernan had lived in Waterbury for six years, since her 1932 marriage to widower Charles C. McTernan, seventeen years her senior and founder and headmaster of the McTernan School for boys. Clara, a nursing graduate of St. Barnabas Hospital in Newark, had initially worked as a nurse in the Newark public schools and at a summer camp that Charles McTernan and his first wife operated on the Connecticut shore in Old Saybrook. Two years after the 1930 death of the first Mrs. McTernan, Clara had married Charles, who had two college-age sons, and had moved to Waterbury and begun working at the family school that adjoined their home on Columbia Boulevard. "She has been much concerned," Leah Cadbury told Pease, "at the lack of facilities for giving the poorer women contraceptive advice." As a school nurse in Newark "she made constant use of the maternal health center there, and is entirely familiar with clinic service." And, given the social prominence of the McTernan School, "she is in touch with many people in Waterbury."

Mabel Robbins had given McTernan the names of all Waterbury-area women who had visited or written the Hartford clinic. "Her immediate plan," Cadbury explained, "is to go to some ministers and directors of welfare agencies and offer to arrange transportation of women whom they may want to send to Hartford, provided they will take care of the clinic fee of three dollars for each patient. She hopes to make arrangements for four women by the end of the month." Additionally, Cadbury would pass on to McTernan the "card file of more than 100 names of the people with whom I have had some contact, or of whose real interest I have learned, so that she will not have to break ground anew for herself, but she has a hard job ahead of her." The Chase sisters, Cadbury conceded, "do not want to take any active part in the work," although they might be persuaded to make modest financial contributions. Any idea of trying to establish an independent clinic, Cadbury went on, was almost certainly unwise, particularly because fund-raising obstacles might be heightened further if emergency tax assessments were imposed on residents to make up the large municipal deficit that was one product of the city's newly revealed financial scandals. But also, Cadbury mentioned for the first time, trying to finance an independent Waterbury clinic might simply prove unnecessary as "there seems to be a good chance of introducing birth control into the maternal health service of the Chase Dispensary, in the not impossibly distant future."[90]

Little more than two weeks after her initial visit to the Hartford clinic, Clara McTernan took her first two patients there for a fitting. Leah Cadbury, back home in Pennsylvania, told McTernan she was overjoyed at the news: "Eighteen days to get going! You compete with radishes for speed! . . . I have been thinking with much appreciation of your courage and determination to start some kind of birth control work in Waterbury," and explained how "one of the advantages of birth control work over other social reforms is that *individuals* can really accomplish something! You could slave yourself to death for peace and not make a dent in the armed frontiers of the world, but already you've g[iven] two whole families a tremendously important boost toward a fundamentally sound home life. They can never be completely hopeless and without some control over circumstances again. It's the effectiveness of individual effort in this work that I find so perfectly thrilling."

Cadbury also reminded McTernan of the additional plans they had both discussed for Waterbury, and recommended she talk with Edward H. Davis, an enthusiastic supporter and a colleague of Millicent Pond's at Scovill, about "mapping out your final approach to the Hospital Board about using the Dispensary. I wish you could wangle it somehow so that you don't have to ask them to approve or disapprove of birth control, but take advantage of Dr. Mason's statement: 'It's none of our business what the doctor and the patient talk about. We hire him

to do a good job, and what he prescribes is up to him and the patient.'"
Hence, Cadbury suggested, "Perhaps without going to the Board officially, you can make the arrangements with the doctors themselves. But
connecting with the Dispensary is work for the future. I think that you
are starting in just the right way to build up interest and a demand for
local service."[91]

Less than a month after Clara McTernan took her first patients to
Hartford, the other portion of Leah Cadbury's Connecticut work came
to fruition as a committee of Bridgeport area women publicly
announced that a clinic would open there on May 1. The following day
city prosecutor John P. Flanagan said that unnamed opponents of the
clinic had asked him to examine the matter, but within twenty-four
hours Flanagan told reporters that "there are no statutes prohibiting
such a clinic and that, therefore, he cannot act in the matter." Flanagan
added that "instructions will be given to . . . the police department that
plans for the clinic will not be stopped and that there must be no move
toward prosecution, as had been demanded by several of the complainants."[92]

If prospects for the future seemed bright in Connecticut, such was
not the case in Massachusetts, where the Birth Control League's appeal
of the Salem convictions had been argued before the state Supreme
Court by attorney Robert G. Dodge on February 7 and 8. Dodge had
filed an impressive seventy-page brief with the Massachusetts court,
giving particular emphasis to the *One Package* precedent, and a supporting amicus brief had been submitted on behalf of twenty-one doctors,
including John Rock and a former state medical society president,
Channing Frothingham. Essex County assistant district attorney John
J. Ryan, Jr., answered with an exceedingly modest seven-page submission that argued a simple but basic theme: "If the Legislature had
intended to make any exceptions in favor of doctors, nurses, social
reformers, or any other class of individuals, it would have been a simple matter to expressly state the exception in the statute" prohibiting
the distribution of birth control devices, Ryan stressed. "If these defendants are dissatisfied with the existing laws of this Commonwealth,
they should address their complaint to the Legislature."

Even Dodge himself felt that the Massachusetts' judges questions at
oral argument had been "not very encouraging," but he told league president Linda Hawkridge that if they lost there they should "certainly"
appeal to the U.S. Supreme Court. "I do not like to predict the decision
of that court on any constitutional point, but I should say that the
chances would be sufficiently good to make it distinctly advisable to take

the case to Washington." But some interested observers were still convinced that the Massachusetts League was mishandling the situation,
and Katharine Hepburn remained among the most vocal complainants.
"I am awfully sorry to have bothered you by things that I have said," she
once again apologized to the Massachusetts leaders, "but closing the
clinics, even in towns where they were not raided and appealing cases
instead of just refusing to pay the fines is to me—well, I'd better not say
what I think. I just wish that you'd had Morris Ernst for your lawyer
instead of what you've got. I don't know him—not even his name—so
there's nothing personal about it—but I hope that I don't meet him on a
dark night—I might shoot him. Seriously, I wish you the best of luck
and will try to keep my mouth shut—but it's hard."[93]

But Hepburn's best wishes did not do the trick, for on May 26 the
Massachusetts court unanimously affirmed the Salem convictions,
fully accepting Ryan's contention that the federal and New York precedents notwithstanding, it was not the province of the judiciary to create
exceptions to inclusive statutory language. "The relief here urged," the
court said, "must be sought from the law-making department and not
from the judicial department." The Massachusetts League announced
that it was "undaunted" and would appeal to the U.S. Supreme Court.
It criticized the Massachusetts ruling as "a decision so out of touch
with the realities of the world," and attorney Dodge told Linda
Hawkridge that their appeal to the Supreme Court would focus on the
issue of "whether a state legislature may interfere with the practice of
medicine under the guise of the police power" regulation of morality
and health.

But now even Hawkridge was wondering whether the
Massachusetts League should stick with stodgy and proper Robert
Dodge, and on June 14 she called on prominent Harvard Law School
professor Felix Frankfurter, widely noted as a potential nominee for
both past and future Supreme Court vacancies, to seek his advice on
whether the league should replace Dodge with New York's Morris
Ernst. Frankfurter's recommendation was clear and blunt: "Mr. Ernst
is a friend of mine and is a fine person for this Jersey City type of thing
[a reference to an ongoing case in which Ernst was representing labor
union organizers against tough Jersey City Mayor Frank Hague and his
political machine], but he is not the person for the United States
Supreme Court. Mr. Dodge is." Frankfurter cautioned Hawkridge,
however, that the league's chances might not be good no matter who
argued their case, for "everything that is foolish and socially wrong is
by no means unconstitutional." Dodge's best strategy, Frankfurter hint-

ed, would be to employ the social and health policy emphases of a "Brandeis brief," but he added that "More I ought not to say."

The Massachusetts outcome also finally raised serious worries in national birth control circles, with Margaret Sanger terming the decision "the most serious setback the movement has ever had." But while Ernst agreed with Dodge that a Supreme Court appeal was essential, and while Ernst's junior associate Harriet Pilpel told birth control leaders that *Gardner* would be "one of the most important cases ever to go before the court," another prominent birth control lawyer, Charles E. Scribner, contended that any such appeal "would be utterly futile" since the Massachusetts court was clearly correct that statutory changes must be made by the legislature. To settle this strategic disagreement, both Sanger and the leaders of the American Birth Control League, along with Dodge and Hawkridge, convened a lengthy late June meeting in New York. Everyone present agreed that there was much to gain and little to lose by pursuing an appeal, and one ABCL legal advisor reported that he had even half persuaded Scribner, who was absent, that an appeal was the best course. Without any dissent the meeting formally voted to endorse an appeal, but also to do everything possible to keep publicity about the case to an absolute minimum. Six weeks later Dodge filed his petition for Supreme Court consideration, and the Massachusetts Attorney General's office informed the Court that they would file no opposing papers until the justices ruled in early October on whether they would hear the appeal. Many New England birth control workers, however, were far more pessimistic than the lawyers. Dr. Mabel H. Pearson, who supervised the Connecticut League's Danbury clinic, wrote to a friend who worked for the Massachusetts League that "to press this legal fight in Massachusetts" was "a great pity. " "The law is on the statute books, the courts are bound to confirm it, and it is most unlikely to be considered unconstitutional. The legal battle causes a great deal of most unfortunate publicity, and its failure gives tremendous impetus to the antagonists of birth control, especially the Catholic faction. They are now only waiting for the final adverse decision to demand a show-down in Connecticut and this may easily result in our clinics being closed also. It would seem to be a much better plan (and this is the considered opinion of many in this state) to abandon the losing legal fight which only clinches the unfortunate result, and to concentrate your money and resources and influence in trying to change the law" in the legislature. Any Supreme Court victory "is most unlikely . . . and I fear very much that the birth control movement will suffer a bad set-back from this attempt to force their hand."[94]

In Connecticut, however, all tangible developments continued to be favorable, and league leaders certainly did not share Pearson's bleak forebodings. Sallie Pease told the CBCL's annual meeting in early June that "the wind is blowing our way and our ultimate objective—the recognition of birth control as an established social service to the community—is coming slowly but surely." New state board members elected at that meeting included Clara McTernan, and by late that summer McTernan's efforts to begin providing birth control services at the Waterbury Hospital's Chase Dispensary in downtown Waterbury were well on their way to fruition. Undoubtedly Clara McTernan's most important new Waterbury recruit was a young man whom she had known for years, ever since he had served as a counselor at Charles McTernan's summer camp while an undergraduate at Yale—William A. Goodrich. A Waterbury native whose father had practiced medicine there until his death in 1929, Bill Goodrich had graduated from the Loomis School, then Yale, and had entered Columbia Medical School in 1931. When he graduated four years later, he went on to a two-year internship at Hartford Hospital, and he had been one of the dozen young interns who had worked with Hilda Standish and Eleanor Calverly at the Hartford Maternal Health Center. In the summer of 1937 he had married and opened his own obstetrics and gynecology practice in Waterbury, and in the summer of 1938 he readily accepted Clara McTernan's request that he become the lead doctor for what would be called the Waterbury Maternal Health Center.

Bill Goodrich in turn recruited as a second doctor for the clinic his new friend Roger B. Nelson, an obstetrician who had moved to Waterbury hardly two months earlier after graduating from Cornell Medical School in 1934 and then taking internships and residencies in Rochester and New York City. Nelson had been drawn to Waterbury by one of the city's senior obstetrician/gynecologists, Dr. Charles L. Larkin, who served as the chief of gynecology at the Waterbury Hospital's Chase Dispensary and whose son had just graduated from the McTernan School. McTernan discussed with Goodrich her hope of offering birth control services at the Chase Dispensary, either under the auspices of the weekly gynecology clinic or under the auspices of a new and distinct birth control clinic, and Goodrich spoke to a number of the other doctors on her behalf. By mid-September McTernan had recruited another woman with nursing training, Kathryn Jennings, to help her in assisting the two doctors at clinic sessions, another interested supporter, Harriet Griggs, to serve as clinic treasurer, and one of the young Junior League members who often assisted at dispensary clinics, Virginia Goss, to keep the clinic's records. She wrote to hospital superintendent Dr. Mason to ask formal permission for once-a-week use of two rooms at the dispensary, and with most of her preparations complete, she drafted a proper statement of purpose for the nascent Waterbury clinic:

> Believing that there is a definite need for a clinic where the poor of Waterbury may go for scientific advice about birth control, it is our aim to establish such a clinic in Waterbury. We shall ask the Board of Directors of the Waterbury Hospital to let us use rooms in the Chase Dispensary for this clinic, but it is to be a separate organization and is not to be connected with the Hospital or Dispensary in any way. Funds for its maintenance are to be raised by volunteer subscriptions.
>
> The clinic will be known as the Waterbury Maternal Health Center and will be affiliated with the Connecticut Birth Control League and the Birth Control Clinical Research Bureau of New York City. Records will be kept according to standards set up by these organizations. It will have a Board of Sponsors of about fifty representative Waterbury citizens.

Three doctors—Charles L. Larkin, Charles Brown, who had attended one of Leah Cadbury's meetings, and John G. Foster, another local birth control supporter—"will be the advisory physicians in charge," McTernan wrote. "Dr. William Goodrich and Dr. [Roger] Nelson will be the acting physicians. At each clinic session there will be a graduate nurse and a secretarial worker in attendance. The services of these workers as well as the services of the doctors will be given without charge." Information and supplies, she added, "will be given only to married women living with their husbands," and "the object of this organization is to serve women of limited means." By early October, without personally having spoken with either Mason or any of the three physicians who ostensibly would be "in charge," Clara McTernan nonetheless was just about ready to begin conducting weekly Tuesday morning birth control sessions with her young recruits in second-floor rooms at the hospital's Chase Dispensary.[95]

On Monday morning October 10, 1938, the United States Supreme Court, in a ruling that stunned and dismayed the birth control lawyers, dismissed the Massachusetts League's appeal of the Salem convictions. At nine a.m. the very next morning, Tuesday, October 11, Clara McTernan arrived at the Chase Dispensary to begin the first of the Waterbury clinic's weekly sessions.

If the *Gardner* ruling had no immediate effect on Clara McTernan, however, it shocked and disheartened the Massachusetts and New York activists. Robert Dodge told Linda Hawkridge that "I did not expect that the result would be what it is, namely a decision on the merits to the effect that our attack upon the constitutionality of the statute is without any substantial basis." On Friday the four Salem defendants appeared in court and each paid their hundred-dollar fines, and several days later Hawkridge and Caroline Carter Davis, the defendants in the separate Boston case, withdrew their appeals and each paid their fines of two hundred dollars.

In New York Morris Ernst and his colleagues now thought that the Massachusetts League had made a huge error in allowing the Salem case to go to the Supreme Court without a detailed account of the clinic's actual birth control work being included in the record of the appeal. "Interpretation of the statute," Ernst later wrote, "was asked of the Court in the most abstract and lifeless terms. . . . No specific evidence was introduced. No particularized human problem was presented," and in the absence of such, "a naked statement as to clinic procedure was insufficient to stir the Court to a liberalized interpretation of the prohibitory statute." Instead, Ernst's junior colleague Harriet Pilpel suggested, what was needed was "a case in which a person's life and health would be seriously jeopardized if birth control information were denied her." If that was demonstrated at a trial, "It is not unreasonable to suppose," Pilpel hypothesized, that "a different result might follow."

On October 19 Ernst visited Boston and told the Massachusetts League that while the *Gardner* outcome was "a tremendous blow" to birth control nationally, they had no choice but to fight. Ideally, he suggested, they might generate a new court case, perhaps one in which some prosecutor could be persuaded to contest the sale of a *book* concerning contraception to a willing doctor or to fight an action brought by a doctor and a patient. With Robert Dodge unwilling to serve as Ernst's junior partner in any such endeavor, the Massachusetts women recruited Boston's Samuel Hoar as new local counsel, but Katharine Hepburn, watching from Hartford, continued to insist that the best tactics of resistance were being ignored. Caroline Carter Davis replied that Hepburn was wrong: "the question of refusing to pay fines has been discussed again and again and the practically unanimous verdict is 'Very harmful to the cause—an insane idea.'" Instead, Davis said, "we plan to stage other cases which will be of such a definite, appealing nature that it will be impossible for the courts to befog the issue. Our chance of winning them is very slight," she conceded, "but we feel that they will furnish the best possible publicity for education should we have to resort to legislation."

But recruiting a willing doctor, even from among the league's leading supporters, proved seemingly impossible because of how a case that
would imaginably risk any sort of conviction might thereby place the
physician's license to practice medicine in danger. Finally, in May 1939,
just after deciding to change its name from the Birth Control League of
Massachusetts to the "Massachusetts Mothers' Health Council," the
Bay State group resolved to proceed with a "book" case, but by that
time attorney Hoar's schedule for the balance of the year was seemingly full and the women were left in much the same position they had
been in eight months earlier when *Gardner* had been dismissed by the
Supreme Court.[96]

In January 1939 birth control forces had won a significant but little-
publicized victory when a federal judge in Puerto Rico had dismissed
criminal charges of distributing contraceptive articles that had been
brought against two San Juan doctors and four assistants under the old
federal Comstock statutes. Relying directly on the *One Package* precedent, District Judge Robert A. Cooper expressly held in *United States* v.
Belaval that "prescribing or furnishing contraceptive materials by a
physician is an exception to the statute. " "It is inconceivable," he went
on, "that Congress could by legislation prevent a physician from prescribing properly to save life or guard health." Since even antiabortion
statutes contained exceptions for life-threatening circumstances,
Cooper added, "It can hardly be successfully contended . . . that a
physician is prohibited from giving contraceptive advice and materials
in a case where in good faith . . . he believes it is necessary for the
preservation of life or health." "It is not only the right but the duty of a
physician, when in his judgment such is necessary for the protection of
life or health," Cooper concluded, "to prescribe contraceptives."[97]

More prominent public attention, however, was given to a January
meeting marking the formal ending of the eleven-year-old rift between
Sanger and her Birth Control Clinical Research Bureau on the one
hand and the American Birth Control League, which Sanger had left in
1928, on the other. Now, with Sanger herself increasingly living in
semiretirement in Arizona, the two long-competing groups would
merge into one, which would be called the Birth Control Federation of
America (BCFA). ABCL president Dr. Richard N. Pierson would
become president of the new group, and a younger doctor, Woodbridge
E. "Woody" Morris, would soon come on board as general director.

In Connecticut, the months between Clara McTernan's successful
opening of the Waterbury clinic on October 11 and Sallie Pease's fate-
ful remarks at the Connecticut League's June 8 annual meeting passed

quietly and productively. The once-a-week Waterbury sessions drew very modest numbers of patients, a significant proportion of whom had already received diaphragm fittings at the Hartford or New Haven clinics. Only about one new patient per week had an initial consultation with either Bill Goodrich or Roger Nelson, at which they received a fitting and were instructed to return a week later for contraceptive jelly once they had successfully mastered the diaphragm's insertion. While in part the small initial numbers testified to the success Clara McTernan already had had in arranging transportation to the Hartford clinic for needy women, McTernan and her colleagues nonetheless felt satisfaction at being able to assist new patients who, as in one case, had had one child each year for four years in a row, or, in another, four children within a five-year period. In both Hartford and New Haven the new patient totals outstripped Waterbury's by hundreds and hundreds, in part because of patients who were also referring their friends, and also because both clinics had now quietly dispensed with the prior requirement that specific health grounds exist before a married woman could receive a diaphragm fitting and jelly. Like Hartford, New Haven too was discovering that "Catholics predominate more than ever, numbering 214 as against 163 Protestants and 20 Jews", among new patients, and New Haven's chairman gave an upbeat report to the same luncheon audience that heard Sallie Pease's proud remarks about their notable achievement in Waterbury: "we feel that the clinic has made a place for itself in the community and that the future holds in store a period of expanding usefulness."[98]

Bill Fitzgerald's top priority late Monday morning June 12 was to locate and obtain the clinic's patient record cards that were in the possession of Virginia Goss. By that time Ginny Goss already had heard about what had transpired that morning at the Chase Dispensary, and when her good friend Dorothy Chase Carmody, whose attorney husband Ed was one of Bill Fitzgerald's closest friends, called to tell her that the state's attorney wanted the clinic's records, Ginny Goss had no doubt what she should do. With hardly a moment's hesitation, Ginny Goss took the four dozen or so large yellow record cards and the clinic's other paperwork and "got out of Waterbury," heading for a summer home on Fisher's Island, New York, off the Connecticut shore.

But Bill Fitzgerald would not be so easily stymied. A young attorney in Ed Carmody's firm of Carmody and Thoms, M. Heminway Merriman, Jr.—hence "Junie" to all who knew him—had previously been recruited as Waterbury's representative on the Connecticut

League's Legal Advisory Board. Clara McTernan had never had a substantive conversation with him about the clinic, but now Merriman was pressed into service by Ed Carmody. Merriman called Ginny Goss at Fisher's Island and instructed her to return to Waterbury posthaste, and to bring the clinic records with her. She complied, gave the records to Merriman, and by midday Tuesday Carmody and Thoms had handed over the clinic records—patient cards and all—to Bill Fitzgerald.

Sallie Pease and Katharine Hepburn were absolutely livid when they learned that Merriman and Carmody had voluntarily surrendered the patients' medical records to the state's attorney, and the two women wasted hardly a moment before heading to Waterbury in person. There, in a scene that Pease would later recall as "brief, concise, and thunderous," she and Hepburn told the Carmody and Thoms lawyers exactly what they thought of them and announced that the Connecticut League would having nothing further to do with them. In consultation with Clara McTernan and several of the clinic's local supporters, they began casting about for Waterbury counsel that would energetically defend the clinic's and the league's interest, and by late Wednesday, June 14, Pease and Hepburn had found just the right person: J. Warren Upson, a thirty-five-year-old Yale Law School graduate who was a junior partner to former State's Attorney Larry Lewis in one of Waterbury's most distinguished law firms, Bronson, Lewis & Bronson.[99]

Warren Upson knew Bill Fitzgerald well, in part because of Fitzgerald's seven years of service as Larry Lewis's deputy. But Warren Upson was already one of Waterbury's most significant political figures: as attorney for publisher William J. Pape and for the *Republican-American* newspapers, he had played a leading role in the fight against T. Frank Hayes's political machine for several years before Hayes and his cronies had finally been indicted on the fiscal corruption charges for which they were now standing trial. Part of Hayes's operation had been to control the local Republican party, in addition to his own Democratic one, through voter-registration fraud which had allowed dual Republican registration for several thousand loyal Democrats, a scheme that Upson and Pape had successfully challenged in state courts. Afterward, Upson had been the unsuccessful 1936 Republican candidate against local U.S. Congressman J. Joseph Smith, and in 1939 he was in his third year as Republican town chairman, a post that kept him almost constantly in the local news. Waterbury reporters thought of him as "frank and honest," "brilliant of mind and bed-rock in character."[100]

The legal situation that Warren Upson inherited on Thursday morning June 15 was unsettled but threatening. Bill Fitzgerald had been telling the newspapers little more than "no comment" for three days: "I haven't anything to say about the investigation and will make no announcement until the investigation is thoroughly completed." Other figures were similarly evasive, with hospital superintendent Dr. B. Henry Mason insisting "I am too busy to hear anything or think anything about dispensaries or clinics today." Gynecology chief Dr. Charles Larkin also "said he was too busy to think about the investigation," but did volunteer that he "hoped he would not be brought into the matter." Dispensary deputy Berta Verba, whose boss Jeannie Heppel was still away on vacation, declared "I have nothing to say and I don't know anything about the details."

BCFA general director Dr. Woody Morris in New York was fully abreast of the situation, and late Wednesday he managed to get Dr. Mason on the phone. The superintendent indicated "that he was anxious to clear his skirts of the birth control clinic. I inferred from him that the hospital would prefer to be considered as an accommodating landlord," and nothing more. Morris asked Dr. A. Nowell Creadick in New Haven to be sure that the Waterbury doctors did not lack either resolve or medical support within the state, and Margaret Sanger wrote Creadick to express the same sentiments, warning somewhat prematurely that "the case will never get anywhere unless they do allow themselves to be arrested and take the case to the highest courts."

Wednesday's and Thursday's *Waterbury Democrat* accorded front-page coverage to statements endorsing the Catholic Clergy Association resolution and Fitzgerald's investigation that had been issued by the Notre Dame Alumnae Association and the Irish-American Social Club, but behind the scenes Warren Upson knew that the real danger lay in the ongoing interviews that Fitzgerald's office was now conducting with former women patients of the clinic whose identities and addresses had been on Ginny Goss's yellow record cards. Late Thursday afternoon Fitzgerald's deputy Walter Smyth told Upson that the state's attorney wanted Clara McTernan to come in Monday morning for formal questioning, and when Larry Lewis visited with Bill Fitzgerald on Friday, Fitzgerald told him that and more.

The state's attorney would proceed with a prosecution before the end of the month, but "He is undecided as to whom to prosecute—a number or all connected with the local office. If one he probably will select Mrs. McT[ernan]." While Fitzgerald indicated that there was some prospect that he would charge league officials in addition to

Waterbury clinic personnel, he also indicated that he would be willing to proceed by a detailed stipulation of the facts, rather than by going to trial and "calling witnesses who might be somewhat embarrassed by the nature of the testimony." He might even agree, Fitzgerald told Lewis, "that in each case there was a health motive behind the instructions and contracepti[ve]s given, but he would refuse to agree that in each case the health of the user was directly or vitally concerned." That would leave Lewis and Upson to decide "whether it is advisable to take the dignified course of having the question disposed of upon a stipulated statement of facts submitted eventually to the Supreme Court, or whether it is advisable to proceed to the rough and tumble" of a trial. Fitzgerald's immediate priority, however, he told Lewis, was to establish precisely *who* was the legal owner of the diaphragms and other supplies that had been seized in the raid: the hospital, the Connecticut League, the clinic group, or some number of individuals. The hospital would certainly refuse to appear at Monday's scheduled show-cause hearing to assert any claim to the seized materials, and while Lewis and Upson were relatively certain that they themselves would either appear or request a continuance, they were uncertain as to precisely who the claimant ideally ought to be.

But Warren Upson was far more worried about their substantive prospects than about the Monday hearing. While the BCFA office in New York already had had Harriet Pilpel send him a detailed file on *One Package*, Upson and Lewis also had discovered and read the Massachusetts court decision in *Gardner*, and they immediately appreciated its significance: "Mass. case probably is decisive & will be followed by Conn. Court," Lewis jotted to Upson.[101]

Saturday morning Sallie Pease issued a bold public statement declaring that the Connecticut League was "delighted that the question of the legality of the birth control clinics throughout the state has been brought up." "Laws and the interpretation of laws must change with changing times. The growth of birth control clinics all over the United States has been in response to tremendous public demand," and no "medieval law" such as the 1879 Connecticut statute "can halt the march of progress and health." Saturday afternoon she, Upson, Kit Hepburn, and Clara McTernan met with Margaret Sanger, BCFA lawyer William J. "Mac" McWilliams, and Harriet Pilpel at Pilpel's country home in Newtown, not far from Waterbury, along with Bridgeport attorney Johnson Stoddard and New Haven lawyer Morris Tyler, both of whom had supported and advised the league clinics in their cities. The New Yorkers were highly impressed with Upson as he described the Waterbury situation, and the group agreed that Upson and Lewis should appear at Monday's hearing on behalf of both the Connecticut League and the Waterbury Maternal Health Center. They would seek a continuance of the hearing on the seized materials, and after Fitzgerald filed criminal charges against one or more individual defendants, they would seek to proceed by stipulation rather than conduct a full-blown trial.

Monday morning Upson and Larry Lewis, as well as Bill Fitzgerald, appeared before Superior Court Judge Frank McEvoy. Deputy Sheriff Al Francis and Detective K. G. Alling brought four bags and two boxes containing all the seized contraceptive supplies into the courtroom, and Fitzgerald informed McEvoy that the materials had been "kept to violate the criminal laws of the state" and that the Waterbury Hospital had disclaimed any interest in the articles. Upson explained that both the league and the Waterbury clinic wanted to contest Fitzgerald's motion to have the supplies destroyed, and while McEvoy "examined several of the objects" he pressed Upson to identify exactly who the officers of the Waterbury clinic were. With obvious reluctance Upson named Clara McTernan, Virginia Goss, and Harriet Griggs, whose names thus appeared in the local press for the first time that afternoon, and McEvoy then agreed to continue the hearing on the fate of the seized materials until July 3.

Soon after the proceeding before McEvoy concluded, Warren Upson and Clara McTernan appeared as scheduled at the courthouse office of Bill Fitzgerald. With Walter Smyth, Detective Alling, and a stenographer looking on, the state's attorney undertook a polite but firm interrogation of his next-door neighbor. Holding the yellow patient record cards, Fitzgerald asked McTernan to confirm that the Waterbury clinic had begun operation in October 1938, and that even earlier she had been referring women patients to Hartford. Fitzgerald asked whether she had ever personally spoken with any members of the executive committee of the Waterbury Hospital's board of directors, or with Dr. Mason, and McTernan said no. She had sent Mason one letter, "asking if we could have use of the dispensary," but "I never received an answer." Fitzgerald then asked her if she had had any personal contact with Doctors Larkin, Brown, and Foster, the clinic's ostensible advisory committee. "I never spoke to any of these men . . . I understood from Dr. Goodrich that these men had consented to be on the committee."

Fitzgerald moved on to the question of the clinic's financing, and McTernan noted that "the majority of patients did not pay anything."

Indeed, as some of the seized records showed, the clinic's entire income since the day it had started had totaled only ninety-seven dollars, and of that only ten dollars had come from patients. And those patients, she emphasized, "they just couldn't come there—they were sent either by a doctor or came through the gyn[ecology] clinic." Fitzgerald had also obtained a twelve-name list of people identified as the "Waterbury Committee," and while Clara McTernan readily conceded that these people were the clinic's official sponsors, she stressed that for many of them it involved only pro forma lending of their names. Only Edith Chase, her friend Lucy Burrall, Burrall's sister Mary, Edward and Edith Davis, and Deborah Elton had contributed any money, and while one or two others, including Ruth Northrop, had attended the group's only meeting, some on the list—including Jeannie Heppel—had not done even that.

Bill Fitzgerald was also very curious about whether Ginny Goss and Kathryn Jennings, like McTernan herself and the two doctors, had been at all involved in giving contraceptive instructions to patients, but McTernan repeatedly stressed that they had not. He asked whether Sallie Pease had attended a clinic meeting, and McTernan said no, but she answered in the affirmative when he inquired about Katharine Hepburn. Finally, Fitzgerald asked, "in anticipation of opening the clinic or Health Center, did you receive any legal advice or seek any legal advice of, or take into consideration any opinion rendered by any attorney?" "No, I did not," McTernan responded. "Did it occur to you that it may have been illegal?" "No. Not when a doctor gave advice to a patient for health reasons."

That afternoon Ginny Goss underwent similar questioning, and by late in the day Fitzgerald made it clear to Upson and Lewis that criminal charges would be filed by the end of the week, apparently against only McTernan, Goodrich, and Nelson. Fitzgerald agreed that he would furnish them with a draft stipulation at that same time, and Upson formally notified all three prospective defendants that the Connecticut League had engaged him to handle their defense at no cost to themselves. Sallie Pease readily sent Upson an initial retainer of a thousand dollars, which had been contributed by a friend or relative of Kit Hepburn's, but Pease registered her dissent from the strategy that the Saturday meeting had been agreed upon: "Please have a jury trial and not a stipulation. They are no good." And when Upson notified her that "I don't believe that there is any possibility of any person connected with the state organization" being charged by Fitzgerald, Pease was downright distressed: "I am terribly disappointed that he won't arrest me—the big sissy."[102]

Monday night Kit Hepburn called Upson to report on her efforts to mobilize the Connecticut State Medical Society, but the group's new executive secretary, Dr. Creighton Barker, was saying that he could do nothing more than reiterate the general endorsements of birth control that the society had rendered back in 1931 and 1932. Upson was preparing to have Goodrich and Nelson—whom he told Harriet Pilpel "are cooperative to the fullest extent"—and several senior doctors such as A. Nowell Creadick review Fitzgerald's draft stipulation as soon as it was made available, and with criminal charges on the immediate horizon the Connecticut League appointed a special five-person executive committee—Pease, Hepburn, Upson, Creadick, and Johnson Stoddard—and instructed its other clinics "to proceed with their work as usual."

Late Thursday Upson informed Pease that he believed Fitzgerald would be ready to proceed against the three defendants by sometime Friday, and early Friday afternoon Lewis and Upson, at Fitzgerald's request, brought Clara McTernan, Bill Goodrich, and Roger Nelson before Superior Court Judge Kenneth Wynne. As all the parties stood before the bench, Wynne formally issued the arrest warrants that Fitzgerald had prepared, and all three defendants immediately pled not guilty. Fitzgerald requested bail of five hundred dollars per person, and Larry Lewis objected, saying such a requirement was unnecessary. Judge Wynne—a savvy veteran of state politics who had served as executive secretary to Governor Simeon Baldwin in 1914–15 and to Wilbur Cross from 1931 to 1935—immediately agreed: "no one can gainsay the fact that they are acting in accordance with what they think they have a right to do," and released the defendants to Lewis's custody. Newspapers all across Connecticut greeted the charges with prominent front-page headlines, and accorded significant attention to supporters' statements. Woody Morris termed the arrests "an outrage to every physician," and Nowell Creadick insisted that "We welcome the opportunity now offered for a final adjudication." The old 1879 statute, Kit Hepburn declared, "was designed to prevent immorality and indecency, and not to interfere with competent physicians in protecting the health and well-being of their patients."[103]

The precise charges against the three defendants alleged that Goodrich and McTernan had both violated the Connecticut law by furnishing birth control devices to three specific women: a twenty-two-year-old mother of two who had visited the dispensary no fewer than forty-four times for a variety of illnesses in less than four years, a twenty-two-year-old mother who had borne three children within three years, and a twenty-three-year-old mother who had borne four children within four years—and all of whom had made "repeated" use of the devices, the charges said. Roger Nelson similarly was charged with having furnished birth control devices to three other women, one of whom had had four children within five years.

Upson and Harriet Pilpel met again on Saturday to review Fitzgerald's straightforward and largely unobjectionable draft stipulation of facts and to discuss what arguments against the Connecticut law Upson should stress in filing his demurrer—as the document was termed in Connecticut courts—challenging the constitutionality of the charges against McTernan and the doctors. There was some question as to whether Fitzgerald's declaration in the charges that the women patients had indeed "used" the furnished devices was wholly sufficient to prove the "use" that would be required to convict the three defendants under the accompanying "accessory" section of the law, but Upson and Pilpel were more interested in whether particular "health" grounds for contraception could be shown for most if not all of the Waterbury clinic's patients. Upson sought unsuccessfully to persuade Fitzgerald to return the patient record cards, both for that purpose and on the grounds that they were really the physicians' property, but the league did assign a nurse from the Hartford clinic, Mrs. A. L. Wasserman, the difficult task of contacting and interviewing all of the patients beyond those cited in the charges to see if health grounds could be shown. Both Goodrich and Nelson, as well as Woody Morris, reviewed the stipulation, giving particular attention to Fitzgerald's descriptions of the six particular women patients who were cited, but Upson was disappointed, although not surprised, that Mrs. Wasserman's inquiries were "not accomplishing much as far as finding more health reasons."[104]

On Thursday, June 29, both Upson and Fitzgerald again appeared before Judge Wynne. Fitzgerald filed slightly amended charges which acknowledged that Goodrich and Nelson were "duly licensed physicians" and McTernan a "duly qualified nurse," and Upson filed a three-page demurrer which straightforwardly challenged the anticontraception statute as "an unconstitutional interference with the individual liberty of the citizens" of Connecticut under both the state constitution and the Fourteenth Amendment to the U.S. Constitution, particularly when there was no exception for a physician "where the life or health of a patient is at stake." Upson also stressed to the court that Goodrich and Nelson had *not* received remuneration for their clinic work, and Judge Wynne set July 25 as the deadline for Upson's full brief challenging the charges and the statute and August 15 for

Fitzgerald's reply. In the interim the question of an actual trial would remain on hold until Wynne ruled on Upson's basic constitutional challenge. Four days later Judge McEvoy, after hearing a concise exchange in which Fitzgerald cited *Gardner* to prove that the statute "must be enforced unless it is repealed," and Upson responded by quoting *One Package* and *Belaval*, agreed to an identical briefing schedule for the seizure case.[105]

In early July all of the Connecticut League's supportive attorneys met and agreed that henceforth all of the state's clinics should specify in writing a particular health reason for each married woman to whom they provided birth control services. A sensationalist weekly newspaper that circulated widely in the state, the *Bridgeport Herald*, printed a baseless front-page, banner-headlined story alleging that Fitzgerald's Waterbury probe "may reveal before long, startling facts concerning alleged abortion practices of two or more Brass City medicos." The suggestion was wholly fictional, but even more than fifty years later, Roger Nelson and his wife Rosalie remembered the implicit accusation in the *Herald* as their clearest and most painful memory of the Waterbury case.

On July 25 Warren Upson filed a powerful and impressive fifty-four-page brief in the case before Judge Wynne and a similarly detailed argument in the seizure proceeding. "The decisions of the federal courts are uniformly to the effect that statutes with respect to contraceptive[s] are not to be construed as interfering with the bona fide practice of medicine," he emphasized. Additionally, Upson argued, the clear intent of Connecticut's 1879 legislature "was to prohibit the production and dissemination of obscene information and literature," and "any use of a contraceptive device upon the advice of a physician is not an offense against morality." What the statute intended to prohibit was the immoral and hence unlawful use of contraceptives, not *all* use of contraceptives, Upson contended: "it is admitted that, for instance, the indiscriminate dissemination of contraceptive information to high school girls could be prohibited. This would be a justified exercise of the police power, because if contraceptive information was widely available to high school students, the restraint upon immoral practices inherent in the fear of pregnancy would be removed."

Upson presented lengthy renditions of the *Belaval* and *One Package* decisions, and then shifted to a higher philosophical plane, asserting that the 1879 statute "does violence to the inherent rights of man." The state, he went on, "has no right to govern or attempt to govern the conduct of a citizen of a State if his conduct does not in any degree

impinge upon a similar freedom of conduct of other citizens of the
State." Relying upon an obscure 1888 decision by the Wisconsin
Supreme Court, Upson added that "any citizen of Connecticut may
deal with his own body in any way he wants to, and it is his natural
right to do, if, in so doing, he does not impair any similar right on the
part of another citizen."

Then Upson moved to the specifics at hand: "The power to commence a pregnancy is one of the inalienable rights of the citizens of
Connecticut." Having already called contraception the "antithesis" of
abortion, he returned to that contrast: "the State has the right to control abortions, but in the attempt to control conception, the State interferes with a natural right which inheres in its citizens. . . . the decision
as to whether or not a married couple shall have children is a decision
peculiarly their own. . . . If the people of Connecticut have any natural
rights whatsoever, one of them certainly is the right to decide whether
or not they shall have children, and to this natural right, the right to
use contraceptive devices is a natural concomitant."[106]

Four days later, and well ahead of schedule, Bill Fitzgerald filed considerably shorter and more modest briefs with both Wynne and
McEvoy. Relying almost wholly on the Massachusetts Supreme
Judicial Court opinion in *Gardner*, Fitzgerald insisted that "Every
claimed constitutional defect asserted by the defendants" here also
"was present in the Massachusetts statute involved in the Gardner
case." Within forty-eight hours Frank McEvoy notified Upson and
Fitzgerald that the seizure matter would proceed to a full ruling on the
merits, and Upson pondered whether to introduce additional evidence—by having McTernan, Dr. Creadick, and perhaps Sallie Pease
take the stand at a formal hearing—or simply let the matter proceed to
a decision based upon the written contentions that already had been
filed. He knew it would be "undesirable to have Dr. Nelson and Dr.
Goodrich testify" because that would "enable the State to examine
them exhaustively as to the medical indications of all of the patients
treated at the Waterbury clinic," and after discussing the issue with
both Connecticut and New York colleagues, Upson on August 4 notified McEvoy that the claimants would add nothing further.[107]

Shortly before noon on Monday, August 7, Judge Kenneth Wynne
filed a brief opinion upholding Warren Upson's demurrer to the
charges against Clara McTernan and the two doctors. Expressly rejecting Fitzgerald's claim that *Gardner* was determinative, Wynne brusquely noted that the Massachusetts statute prohibited *distribution* of
contraceptive articles, while the Connecticut one prohibited *use*. "The

court has no right to read exceptions into the statute" for qualified medical personnel, Wynne acknowledged, "but is convinced that without these proper exceptions the statute is defective on the broad constitutional grounds" articulated by Upson.

Bill Fitzgerald was away on vacation, and while Warren Upson had little doubt that the state's attorney would appeal Wynne's decision to the Connecticut Supreme Court, Upson told reporters that he would move for the formal dismissal of the criminal charges when the local Superior Court resumed its normal term in September. Connecticut papers quoted Kit Hepburn as calling the ruling "a wise and humane decision," and Sallie Pease termed it "a great triumph of common sense over a ridiculous" law. Woody Morris hailed the outcome as a "milestone," but in private Warren Upson warned both Pease and BCFA staffers that McEvoy quite likely would rule against them in the seizure case, and that they should keep their expectations in check: "we have been successful so far, but this does not mean ultimate success necessarily."[108]

Clara McTernan was away from Waterbury in mid-August but was overjoyed by the news of Wynne's decision. "You must be the world's best lawyer to have accomplished what you did," she wrote Warren Upson. "I would like to open the clinic again in September, or whenever you think it advisable." She and others also heartily congratulated Upson for his stand against Mayor Hayes, who had been convicted on August 16 after a seven-month trial and would soon resign his office. But not everyone was pleased with Wynne's ruling, and the pastor of Bill Fitzgerald's St. Margaret's Roman Catholic Church used his August 13 sermon to declare that Wynne's decision had no weight and that regardless of state law, the Catholic church "will continue to follow the law of nature and of God which is opposed to birth control."

At two p.m. on August 23 Frank McEvoy filed a lengthy opinion surveying Connecticut's birth control struggles reaching all the way back to 1917 and vociferously upholding the 1879 statute and its application to the Waterbury clinic's supplies. Relying literally word-for-word on Fitzgerald's July 29 brief, McEvoy stated that the Connecticut use statute was similar to the Massachusetts distribution one and that "Every claimed constitutional defect asserted by the defendants to exist in section 6246 . . . was present in the Massachusetts statute involved in the Gardner case." Furthermore, the Connecticut League and its clinics were organized "for the express purpose of violating the plain provisions of section 6246," and the supplies should indeed be condemned and destroyed. Upson quickly announced that he would appeal

McEvoy's decision to the state Supreme Court, and Sallie Pease told reporters that "I fail to see how he can rule upon the intention of the Connecticut Birth Control League or on physicians with whom it cooperates when they have not appeared before him in court."[109]

Upson advised a chagrined Clara McTernan that she should not start making plans to reopen the clinic, but he did approve her request to quietly accept contributions so that the Hartford clinic could provide new supplies of contraceptive jelly to the Waterbury clinic's indigent former patients. McEvoy's rhetorical emphasis upon how the Waterbury Hospital had disclaimed any interest in the clinic sufficiently irritated Sallie Pease that she made new efforts to see if any supportive statement could be extracted from the hospital's board of directors, principally through Ruth Northrup, who had hosted Leah Cadbury's first meeting and whose husband was the board's treasurer, but the effort did not come to fruition.[110]

On Thursday afternoon September 21 Warren Upson brought McTernan, Goodrich, and Nelson before Judge John A. Cornell to seek formal dismissal of the charges pursuant to Kenneth Wynne's August ruling. But Cornell, who was sitting in Waterbury pursuant to the rotational system of assignments employed for Connecticut's Superior Court judges, indicated, much to Upson's astonishment and consternation, that he was not fully persuaded that Wynne's opinion included an explicit finding that these individual defendants *had* indeed been working in a professional medical capacity when they provided birth control services at the Waterbury clinic. Upson understandably thought that this was at best a highly picayune and trivial distinction, but even after he and Lewis, plus Fitzgerald, spent over an hour discussing the matter with Cornell the following day, the judge remained unpersuaded. Four days later Cornell again postponed any decision for another week, and both Upson and Fitzgerald, who could not actually appeal Wynne's decision until Cornell granted the pro forma dismissals, became even more exasperated with the persnickety judge. In a move that was just as unusual as Cornell's behavior, the two adversaries jointly went to Hartford to call upon the Chief Justice of Connecticut, William M. Maltbie, to explain their quandary and seek his advice. Maltbie, who himself had served eight years as a Superior Court judge before joining the Supreme Court in 1925 and ascending to the chief justiceship in 1930, was known to his colleagues for his "easy friendliness" and "warm and gentle humility," and he willingly considered his visitors' novel predicament. He agreed to review the copies of each side's papers that Fitzgerald and Upson left with him, and within a day of their visit he sent each of them, and Judge Cornell, a friendly but firm letter intimating that perhaps a further joint stipulation would resolve Cornell's difficulty and pointedly observing that "The primary purpose is to secure a decision as to the proper interpretation of the statute and its validity rather than to penalize the defendant[s]."[111]

Oddly but unfortunately, even Maltbie's missive did not convince Cornell to resolve the matter. Upson met with him once again, and several days later Cornell informed both Upson and Fitzgerald that he had decided to write to Maltbie and would continue to hold the judgment in abeyance. Upson and Pease consulted with one of Morris Ernst's junior partners, Alexander Lindey, and Upson concluded that he could either try to persuade Bill Fitzgerald to drop or nolle the charges against Goodrich and Nelson—"so that whatever happens . . . their right to practice medicine and earn a livelihood will not be affected" by a conviction that would place their medical licenses in jeopardy—and proceed to an eventual ruling on the merits based simply on Clara McTernan's case, or apply to the Connecticut Supreme Court for a writ of mandamus ordering Cornell to enter a judgment.

Early in October Cornell reassured Upson and Fitzgerald he would act once he had a response from the chief justice, but two more weeks passed without news, and finally in late October Bill Fitzgerald wrote to Maltbie, politely observing that the McEvoy case was now on the Supreme Court's docket and that it made sense for both cases to be heard jointly. Finally, on October 31 Maltbie broke the six-week-old logjam by giving Fitzgerald a letter formally assigning Kenneth Wynne to return to Waterbury for one day to enter the necessary judgments. On Friday afternoon November 3 the three defendants appeared before Wynne, and in a brief, five-minute hearing the judge entered judgments of "not guilty." State's Attorney Fitzgerald announced he would appeal, but Warren Upson now felt confident that irrespective of whether the Connecticut Supreme Court affirmed or reversed Judge Wynne on the merits regarding the 1879 statute, "it is almost certain that none of the accused will be convicted or go to jail for violation of the Connecticut law." Five days later the case was officially forwarded to the Connecticut Supreme Court, with oral argument expected sometime before Christmas. Upson himself remained circumspect about estimating their chances for success with the high court, but his New Haven friend and colleague Morris Tyler confidently told BCFA director Woody Morris that "My own feeling is that our chances are 90 to 10 of a favorable decision."[112]

While Upson had been busy attempting to extract their apparent legal victory from the procedural morass created by Judge Cornell, the Connecticut League, in part at the urging of the national Birth Control Federation, had been seeking to use the legal crisis as an opportunity to highlight public and medical support for birth control. BCFA representative Edna Rankin McKinnon, the youngest sister of well-known pacifist Jeanette Rankin, pressed the Connecticut League "to emphasize the medical side" and sponsor a Committee for the Defense of Medical Rights which would distribute tens of thousands of flyers stressing the threat to doctors. "This intrigued all except the president," Sallie Pease, who "was not enthusiastic" about such a strategy, McKinnon told her BCFA superiors, and in short order the BCFA staff began to view Pease as an obstacle to the professional public-relations effort they believed the Connecticut situation required. Upson and his fellow lawyers, however, vetoed any mass mailings while the cases remained in the courts, but the attorneys welcomed the suggestion that a major amicus brief on behalf of doctors be prepared for the Connecticut Supreme Court. Nowell Creadick and the other members of the league's Medical Advisory Committee issued a strong warning to fellow M.D.s that "the liberty of the doctor to practice as he sees fit" was in danger of "intolerable restraint" if the courts upheld Fitzgerald, and even the Waterbury Women's Club unanimously passed a resolution calling for quick judicial action so that "physicians may fulfill, without legal handicap, their medical obligations."[113]

On November 20 Bill Fitzgerald, confined to bed with "a bad attack of grippe," requested that the Connecticut Supreme Court hearing be postponed from December until early January. Upson and the Connecticut attorneys, along with BCFA's advisors in New York, engaged in repeated discussions of how a doctors' amicus brief should be handled, with some fearing that such an effort would only serve to stimulate submission of an opposing amicus brief on behalf of Roman Catholic M.D.s. In early December the question was finally resolved when Laurence A. Janney, a New York lawyer and Connecticut resident whose wife was active in the state league, took the initiative and volunteered to write one without charge. Focusing on questions of statutory interpretation and presumed legislative intent, rather than on the broader constitutional issues that Upson had emphasized before Judge Wynne, Janney's skillful brief was submitted to the court on behalf of seventy-six Connecticut doctors.[114]

Upson's own briefs in both the seizure case and in Fitzgerald's appeal of Wynne's dismissal of the three criminal charges closely tracked what he had submitted to Wynne and McEvoy, repeating word-for-word the natural rights and individual liberty arguments he had made five months earlier. He devoted somewhat more attention than previously to arguing that *Gardner* was an inapposite precedent, in that it did not involve a statute criminalizing the *use* of contraceptives, but just as before, both of Bill Fitzgerald's briefs emphasized *Gardner* very extensively. "To say that the Gardner case differs from the cases at bar because Connecticut General Statute 6246 penalizes the *use* of contraceptives and the Massachusetts statute does not in terms do so is to split hairs," Fitzgerald declared. What was central here, the state's attorney stressed, was "the constitutionally permissible purpose of preventing immorality, discouraging promiscuous sexual intercourse . . . promoting the public morals . . . protecting purity, preserving chastity, encouraging continence and self-restraint, defending the sanctity of the home," and "lessening the incidence of the commission of the crime of abortion by those persons married or single who would otherwise be encouraged by the dubious and unproven but supposed power of artificial contraceptives to defeat the process of nature." Fitzgerald then devoted six full pages, some twenty percent of his brief, to quotations describing how "natural" family planning, or the "rhythm method," was a perfectly legal alternative to the use of contraceptives for those Connecticut couples who wanted to limit the number of their children.[115]

On Thursday, January 4, both Upson and Fitzgerald argued their cases before the five-member Connecticut Supreme Court of Errors—a particularly appropriate name, unsuccessful litigants often joked—and the tenor of the exchanges left both Upson and Sallie Pease extremely worried as to what the decision would be some weeks hence. The justices "did not seem to be particularly favorable to our point of view," Upson told Woody Morris, as they were not much interested in the federal precedents and "seemed to have a feeling that the law in question was one for the determination of the legislature" rather than the courts. "I am rather pessimistic about the outcome," Upson warned Mac McWilliams, and he alerted Alexander Lindey that they ought to give some advance thought to preparing for an appeal to the U.S. Supreme Court. Sallie Pease articulated her concern about the Connecticut justices more poignantly, later recalling that "We left with a sinking feeling in our hearts, for they seemed so old, so remote from the urgencies of life, so entangled in the musty depths of the law."[116]

Just as Pease thought, the composition of the Connecticut Supreme Court offered few reasons for optimism. Four of the five justices had attended Yale Law School, and the fifth, Harvard, and four were

Congregationalists and the fifth a Baptist, but it was not an aggressive or creative court. The two youngest members were each fifty-seven years of age, all five justices were Republicans, and all five had previously served as Superior Court trial judges, in line with a long-established Connecticut tradition. Three of the five had themselves served as members of the legislature, and a fourth, George E. Hinman, had served as an important legislative staff member in half-a-dozen terms. Chief Justice Maltbie was known to be a believer in judicial restraint, and when he retired a decade later, a cumulative tally showed that in his twenty-five years on the court he had written only thirty-three dissents while taking part in over 3,600 decisions. The court's other most notable member, Newell Jennings, was the only nonlegislative veteran, and while he was known for brief, pithy opinions, he was not viewed as terribly more liberal than Maltbie. Hinman, just weeks away from mandatory retirement at age seventy, was small and visibly frail, and Allyn Brown, the youngest justice, later wrote of their fifth colleague, Christopher L. Avery, a description that in many observers' eyes could have applied to all five members: "conservative in his views and inclined to be laconic in speech . . . he could be described as 'a typical Yankee.'"[117]

As Upson, Pease and their colleagues awaited an early or mid-March decision from the Connecticut court, all of the league's other clinics continued to operate normally. In late January one central Connecticut man thoughtfully wrote to the Hartford clinic to say that his wife, a patient of the clinic for over a decade, had recently left him: "I understand that she is running around a great deal. The authorities tell me that she must be an oversexed person as well as mental." Dr. Eleanor Calverly immediately wrote on the woman's chart "Separated from husband—Give her no more supplies. Discontinued," and Dr. Hilda Standish acknowledged the husband's letter: "We are very glad to have the information you sent us about your wife as it is not our policy to furnish any supplies to married women who are not living with their husbands."

The Connecticut clinics continued to receive supportive press attention, and magazine stories chronicled a new total of at least 553 birth control clinics nationwide, but Warren Upson had realized that he and the league might be in an insoluble strategic bind should the Connecticut Supreme Court reverse Wynne, much as he now feared. If that did happen, he explained to Woody Morris, "I expect that thereupon all these cases would be nolled by Mr. Fitzgerald and the accused would be discharged," leaving them without punishment but also leaving the league without any means by which to appeal to the U.S. Supreme Court a Connecticut decision affirming the validity of the 1879 statute. "It does not seem to me," Upson went on, "that we can ask these accused to refuse to accept a nolle," and hence stand trial on the original criminal charge, "if it is offered by the State. Certainly the two doctors, who want to preserve their status as citizens, so that they can practice medicine, should not jeopardize their future by refusing a nolle." However, "Mrs. McTernan, if she saw fit to do so, could, I suppose, stand trial in order to have this question clearly presented to the United States Supreme Court," so long as Fitzgerald nonetheless agreed to grant the two other nolles, and in New York in particular there was a clear appreciation that "it would be better for the future status of the movement if one case could go through the courts to its conclusion."[118]

On Wednesday, March 20, the Connecticut Supreme Court handed down its decision in *State of Connecticut* v. *Roger B. Nelson et al.*: a 3 to 2 ruling, written by elderly Justice George E. Hinman, that the 1879 statute should not be read as having any implicit exception for doctors and that it *could* constitutionally be used to prosecute the three Waterbury defendants. Hinman's opinion—joined by Chief Justice Maltbie and by Justice Allyn Brown—emphasized all the occasions from 1923 through 1935 when the state legislature had declined to repeal the ban on contraception or amend it to exempt qualified medical personnel from its coverage. "Rejection by the Legislature of a specific provision is most persuasive," Hinman wrote, "that the act should not be construed to include it." On Upson's constitutional argument, Hinman went on, there was not only the Massachusetts court's rejection of it in *Gardner*, but more importantly, there was also the U.S. Supreme Court's dismissal of the *Gardner* appeal: "We infer that this action may not be interpreted otherwise than as confirming the constitutionality of the Massachusetts statute in the respects in which it was attacked in the *Gardner* case," and the Waterbury trio's claims here were "essentially analogous."

Finally, the Hinman majority offered some more general views:

> Whatever may be our own opinion regarding the general subject, it is not for us to say that the Legislature might not reasonably hold that the artificial limitation of even legitimate child-bearing would be inimical to the public welfare and, as well, that the use of contraceptives, and assistance therein or tending thereto, would be injurious to public morals; indeed, it is not precluded from considering that not all married people are immune from temptation or inclination to extra-marital indulgence,

as to which risk of illegitimate pregnancy is a recognized deterrent deemed desirable in the interests of morality.

Hinman concluded with a common refrain for judicial restraint in the face of suspect statutes: "If all that can be said is that it is unwise or unreasonably comprehensive, appeal must be to the Legislature, not to the judiciary." Justices Newell Jennings and Christopher Avery dissented without filing an opinion. Almost as little more than a footnote, the Connecticut court unanimously reversed Frank McEvoy in the seizure case, holding that the statute under which McEvoy had granted Fitzgerald's initial search warrant properly applied only to searches for gambling devices: "the judgment is set aside and the case remanded with direction to dismiss the proceeding and order return of the seized property to the defendants." In the context of the other decision, this was, to say the very least, an utterly hollow victory.[119]

Within several hours of the announcement of the Court's decision, Warren Upson, Sallie Pease, and several other league activists met hurriedly in New Haven. Hilda Standish was already being quoted by the press as calling "this stupid, outmoded law" and the decision affirming it "a disgrace to our state," but Sallie Pease had presumed for weeks that if indeed the case was lost, the Connecticut League would have no choice but to close down all of its clinics. Hence, by early afternoon telegrams in her name went out to all of the eight other centers, saying simply "I suggest that it is advisable to close." Without dissent the local committees agreed; Florence Darrach in Greenwich told reporters that "since this organization is responsible and law abiding, there will be no further service." And for more than twenty-five years—from March 20, 1940, until the middle of 1965—with only one brief and dramatic exception, there would indeed be no further service until P. T. Barnum's 1879 handiwork was finally voided by the United States Supreme Court.[120]

CHAPTER TWO

No Further Service:
Connecticut's Struggle
for the Legalization
of Birth Control, 1940–1953

Many national newspapers viewed the Connecticut Supreme Court decision upholding the 1879 statute as an inexplicable oddity. The *News and Observer* of Raleigh, North Carolina, commented on Connecticut's "strange backwardness," and the *Des Moines Tribune* forthrightly declared that "the law is an ass." But the *Waterbury Democrat*, which had championed the clinic raid from the first, enthusiastically called the outcome "encouraging." Connecticut, it said, "has taken the very defensible position that legally and morally birth control cannot be countenanced through the instrumentality of the medical profession as a clearing house for the dissemination of such information and aid as would defeat the very purpose of matrimony. It is no easy thing to overthrow a natural law and to sustain arguments therefor."

Warren Upson's first reading of the *Nelson* decision convinced him that birth control proponents had only one alternative: to mount a major campaign to change the statute in the 1941 legislature. Bill Fitzgerald initially declined any comment on the ruling, but both he and Upson faced the question of what to do next when Superior Court in Waterbury reconvened two weeks hence on April 2. Upson, Pease, Florence Darrach, and Catherine Tilson met in New York on March 21 with Woody Morris, Harriet Pilpel, and Morris Ernst, and Upson described his hope of possibly persuading Fitzgerald to nolle the charges against the two doctors while proceeding with Mrs. McTernan alone as a test case. He realized the chances were substantial that Fitzgerald would not be willing to invest the time and energy such an exercise would require, but within the BCFA national staff in New

York several significant figures thought that the real lesson that should be drawn from *Nelson*, as from *Gardner* before it, was that the national organization needed to exert much more dominant control over its local affiliates than previously had been the case.[1]

Sallie Pease called a major meeting of the Connecticut League for two p.m. Monday afternoon, March 25, at the Hartford Golf Club, and more than two hundred people attended. The meeting heard Johnson Stoddard and other advisors voice their reactions to the *Nelson* decision, but aside from general talk about the inevitability of a 1941 legislative push, no particular strategic decisions were made. One set of recommendations presented at the meeting, however, came from BCFA public relations director Charles Magill Smith on behalf of the BCFA staff. The CBCL, he declared, needed to make "changes in organization," including "formation of a new committee with full authority" whose members would be chosen "primarily for their qualifications" rather than for previous involvement and who would include BCFA as well as Connecticut individuals. Such a committee could then create the Committee for the Defense of Medical Rights that the BCFA staff had been envisioning for six months as the preferable Connecticut publicity vehicle, and it could also take the place of the CBCL's previous legal advisory committee, which "should disband," since legal strategy decisions needed to be made primarily within a national rather than a state context. "It will probably seem wise to permit the state leagues and existing committees to become temporarily inactive," Smith said, and "the hope of victory in this fight depends largely on complete recognition that we are fighting the Catholic Church."

Smith's flat-footed effort was referred to the CBCL's Future Policies Committee for consideration, but so blatant an attempt by the BCFA staff to take control of the Connecticut scene in the wake of the *Nelson* defeat infuriated both Sallie Pease and Kit Hepburn. The very next day the two women went to New York and demanded an opportunity to join a scheduled meeting of the BCFA board's executive committee. They presented an angry memo protesting Smith's effort and how his suggestions represented "an insult to the intelligence" of the Connecticut lawyers and advisors, but the committee, withdrawing into executive session, dodged the challenge by explaining that it lacked a quorum and hence could not reach any decisions. Pease and Hepburn headed back to Hartford no less angry than they had come, but the tumultuous scene brought to a head the antipathy that the BCFA staff had been developing toward the independent-minded

Pease—and her outspoken mentor—for more than six months. Florence Rose, the BCFA staffer who was Margaret Sanger's primary confidante and aide in the New York office, claimed to her boss that "Mrs. Pease has long been a headache to lots of the Connecticut people" but stressed that "the sad part is that she and Mrs. Hepburn are evidently 'buddies' . . . which we did *not* realize." Pease and Hepburn had "misrepresented grossly the facts" about Smith's recommendations, Rose claimed, and Hepburn had apparently told BCFA executive committee chairman Gilbert Colgate precisely where he could go: "She is apparently losing her sense of fitness and propriety," Rose asserted. The best hope, Rose added, would be for Sanger to contact her old friend Hepburn directly: "she can be such a valuable asset if her loyalty to you is greater than to Mrs. Pease."[2]

While the BCFA staff was busily plotting the takeover of the Connecticut League, Warren Upson was hard at work on the next and final steps in the Waterbury cases. On March 27 Frank McEvoy entered a formal order resolving the seizure case, and two days later the clinic's now-ageing supplies were returned and then sent to the Clinical Research Bureau in New York, where they could be used legally. Upson had continued to ponder the possibility of attempting to go forward with simply the charges against Clara McTernan, but in a phone conversation with Morris Ernst on the afternoon of March 27 they reluctantly agreed that it "would be undesirable" because no particular health reasons for birth control had existed with the three patients whom McTernan was accused of aiding and abetting. Hence, Upson concluded, "Under the circumstances, if the State offers a nolle, we must accept one," and on Friday, March 29, he and Sallie Pease met Clara McTernan, Bill Goodrich, and Roger Nelson for lunch at the Waterbury Country Club to review what likely would happen in the formal court session on April 2.[3]

The tenor of the lunch conversation quickly erased Warren Upson's remaining ambivalence about accepting three nolles. "It is apparent," he wrote Morris Ernst several hours later, "that the doctors and Mrs. McTernan want to get out of these cases as quickly as possible. They certainly show no indication of wanting to have any further contest made, and in the light of their point of view, regardless of what the Birth Control League desires, there is only one thing for me to do, and that is to procure a nolle for them, if possible." After lunch he had spoken again with Bill Fitzgerald, whose position was firm but reasonable: "His view is that the Waterbury doctors are guilty of violation of the law, but that to punish them would be unjust, in view of the fact that there are so many culprits in the State who will go without punishment for this crime. His disposition, therefore, is to nolle the cases," because "he does not feel that it would be fair to secure a conviction under the circumstances," even though "he is being subjected to pressure from different sources."

At three p.m. on Tuesday, April 2, Clara McTernan, Bill Goodrich, and Roger Nelson filed into the Waterbury courtroom, and some minutes later the clerk called their cases and Bill Fitzgerald rose to read a five page prepared statement. He traced the early course of his investigation, and described how he understood the clinic had come into being: "through the superintendent of the Waterbury Hospital the informal permission of the hospital's board of directors for the use of space at the Chase Dispensary was obtained. It was the understanding of the superintendent of the hospital and of the defendants Goodrich and Nelson, that three senior members of the hospital gynecological staff had been constituted, and had agreed to function, as an advisory board for this contraceptive clinic, although these physicians, who were supposed to constitute the advisory board, profess complete ignorance of the matter."

Fitzgerald acknowledged that the defendants had "cooperated fully in establishing all of the material facts" of the case, and then he began his conclusion: "I am satisfied that these defendants believed that they had a right to do the acts referred to in the informations in these cases. They donated their time and services to what they regarded as a charitable work. I do not believe that they intended to violate the criminal laws of this state. When this Waterbury clinic was opened there were in open operation elsewhere in the state at least eight other contraceptive clinics which had been in existence for a long period of time and no question as to their right to operate had been raised in any court. These facts were known to and relied upon by these defendants."

In "the absence of any actual criminal intent," the charges would be nolled, for "it seems to me unjust to destroy the professional careers of these physicians by a conviction." However, Fitzgerald emphasized in closing, "Henceforth any person, whether a physician or layman, who violates the provisions of these statutes, must expect to be prosecuted and punished in accordance with the literal provisions of the law." With that, Judge Carl Foster dismissed the three defendants.[4]

Bill Goodrich was only thirty, and Roger Nelson thirty-one, and within three years each would be gone from Waterbury, called into military service. After the war Bill Goodrich switched from gynecology to radiology, helped his wife Elizabeth raise two children, and established a successful practice in Hartford before dying at the very young age of forty-nine. Roger Nelson returned from the war and eventually switched from obstetrics to a career as a hospital administrator, spending most of his life quietly in Ann Arbor, Michigan, and outliving his friend Bill Goodrich by well over thirty years.

The Fitzgeralds and the McTernans would continue to live just across the driveway from each other until 1948, when Charles McTernan retired as headmaster of the family school and he and Clara moved full time to their summer home on the Connecticut shore in Old Saybrook—where the Fitzgeralds would sometimes visit them. The McTernans "never had any ill feeling" toward Bill Fitzgerald, Clara's stepson John later explained, because "he really didn't have a choice." Clara "wasn't upset by it," and "took it in stride," especially since Bill Fitzgerald had conveyed to them that "he hated to do what he was doing." Once Bill Fitzgerald privately took the opportunity "to apologize for what he was doing," and Bill's son Tony, born four years after the case was concluded, also grew up witnessing both the family's friendship with the McTernans and his father's distaste for what had happened: it was as if he had been "kind of holding his nose" during those events of 1939 and 1940.[5]

Sallie Pease and her colleagues at the Hartford clinic resolved to keep the office open even if birth control supplies could not be distributed, and a plaintive "Dear Patient" letter was sent to the hundreds of women who had been helped there. "Some day," Pease told them, "if we all work together, we will have the clinics open again." But all working together was not the spirit that was emanating from the BCFA office in New York, and within a day of the final resolution of the Waterbury charges, Sallie Pease received a personal letter from Margaret Sanger that was as unfair and unpleasant as anything Pease and Hepburn had ever suffered at the hands of birth control opponents.

Sanger began by volunteering that the Charles Smith recommendations which Pease and Hepburn had found so offensive seemed like "excellent advice," and went on to blame Pease for the 3 to 2 loss in the Connecticut Supreme Court: "something certainly went wrong somewhere in the Connecticut League, to have lost that case and to have had so adverse and medieval an opinion." Then Sanger moved toward her real goal: "it is the duty of some one to seek out the cause of this and to eliminate persons or even groups if future progress is to be attained. Weak leadership guided by professional limitations, either legal or medical, usually ends in defeat." Sanger knew next to nothing about

the Connecticut people who had played the major roles over the past
ten months, but that did not stop her from offering a clear prescription: "resignations of dead wood or professional bias should be in
order," for "when leadership fails in achieving its goal it resigns its
position and lets a new group take hold. . . . As President of the
Connecticut League I hope you and Kate will analyze your material
and face the future with a clean slate for that is what is needed."

If some would have thought the letter harsh, Sanger told Woody
Morris she feared she had been too gentle: "I should have liked to have
been a little more explicit and said definitely that Mrs. Pease should
resign the presidency but as I do not know how good a president she
has made I only surmise that she has been a weakling."[6]

Sanger's woeful ignorance was only one aspect of a rapidly developing situation, however. When the BCFA board met two days after the
nolles were formally entered, outside counsel Morris Ernst announced
a dramatic suggestion, one he repeated in a letter to Pease the following
day: all Connecticut clinics should be reopened at once, and several
additional clinics should be opened in *churches*. Ernst's reasoning was
that the *Nelson* opinion, upon careful study, offered them some small
but significant room for maneuver, as the Connecticut court had not
explicitly spoken to whether the 1879 statute would be valid in a case
where the need to avoid pregnancy—and utilize contraceptives—
involved a threat to a woman's very *life*. Hence, he advised, "a statement should be prepared indicating that the Supreme Court had not
held that birth control is illegal; it merely held that the statute could be
enforced if the test of use was one of general health," and further indicating that the reopened clinics would prescribe birth control in those
cases where pregnancy might involve "jeopardy to life." In practice
such a phrase could be "a generous term," Ernst told Pease, for "jeopardy to life does not mean jeopardy of death," and the league should
have its friendly doctors draw up an exhaustive and inclusive list of all
ailments whereby pregnancy might exacerbate a threat to life, a list that
clinic doctors then could make specific reference to in examining each
and every woman seeking birth control. "The statement of publicity in
regard to the opening should be most dignified," Ernst advised, should
"in no way attack the court and in no way indicate that you are looking
for a test case or trouble." The stakes were high, but decisive action was
required: "if you do not take such a step the movement will be dissi-
pated in Connecticut," which in turn "will encourage further attacks in
other jurisdictions."[7]

The following day, Saturday, April 6, the Connecticut League's lawyers, doctors, and officers all met in New Haven to hear Sallie Pease present and endorse Ernst's bold plan of action. She explained that Ernst of course presumed that implementing his plan *would* generate a test case, but several of the Connecticut attorneys, including Morris Tyler and Warren Upson, firmly believed that such a course would *not* generate any Connecticut Supreme Court opinion that birth control proponents would welcome. Additionally, any such venture would require the doctors staffing the reopened clinics to put their medical licenses and futures on the line, and, in light of Fitzgerald's firm statements about enforcement when the Waterbury charges were nolled, it was very likely that such doctors *would* pay a stiff price if the Connecticut court once again affirmed the 1879 statute. Upson then formally recommended that the Connecticut League focus upon legislative rather than litigative remedies, and his proposal was adopted. Tyler and Johnson Stoddard further proposed that the league advise its clinics *not* to reopen until the statute was amended, and both that *and* a vaguely worded addendum saying that clinics *could* reopen on "life only" grounds if they so chose were approved, subject to revision by a small subcommittee.

Pease and Hepburn were about the only Connecticut activists who felt that Ernst's strategy of reopening the clinics was the wisest. Hilda Standish, the doctor who had opened the initial Hartford clinic in 1935 and helped operate it for almost five years, understood their sentiments but believed that the potential risk to M.D.s' medical licenses was simply too great a danger to face. Ernst himself was disappointed that the BCFA staff had little interest in his idea, especially as Justice Hinman's retirement raised the possibility that his successor, Arthur F. Ells, might vote differently. Ernst told friends that he thought the birth control movement was losing the fighting spirit that had carried it through the 1910s and 1920s, but Edna McKinnon of the BCFA explained to others that the national staff was more interested in ousting Pease than in listening to Ernst. Margaret Sanger remained more than a little confused about the Connecticut scene, erroneously continuing to believe that Pease and Hepburn, rather than BCFA, were the primary obstacles to aggressive action. "If there was only a good crowd of women up there who will open the clinics and keep them open until everyone of them were put into jail, they would have a better opportunity to get that law changed," she blustered to Clarence Gamble. "God only knows how weak and timid and full of fears respectability has made the birth control movement. If we had just half of the fighting spirit that the Roman Catholics have we would lay them low and mow them down."[8]

But in Connecticut matters were finally beginning to move forward. One of Sallie Pease's biggest burdens was the problem of paying the remaining bills from the Waterbury cases, and when Warren Upson, who so far had received only a very modest fifteen hundred dollars for all his time and efforts, submitted a final statement requesting an additional twenty-six hundred dollars, Pease reluctantly sent her old friend and Bridgeport attorney Johnson Stoddard to ask if he would settle for only a further thousand dollars. Upson raised the question with his partners, and senior partner Richardson "Dick" Bronson endorsed the modification: "I fear we are stuck. When it happens that men of the quality and association of Johnson Stoddard interest themselves to get down on their metaphorical knees and ask that we accept less than that which they admit is our due, we cannot afford to be mussy about it. . . . We have got to swallow it." In return Upson received only a thank-you letter from Kit Hepburn for his "very generous" contribution to the league, but the firm's resolution of an otherwise small matter reflected once again the dedication and distinction with which Upson had handled the Waterbury cases since the first day Pease and Hepburn had come to him.[9]

More significantly, other Connecticut activists, particularly Florence Darrach from Greenwich, were now fully convinced that a professionally managed 1941 legislative campaign had to be the league's next focus, and BCFA staffers from New York were all too happy to encourage this cohort as replacements for the tough-talking, independent-minded duo of Pease and Hepburn. The league's Future Policies Committee, at Darrach's initiative, unanimously endorsed the idea of a Committee for the Defense of Medical Rights that had been pending since the previous fall, and even Sallie Pease reluctantly told Morris Ernst that virtually everyone now agreed that a "life-threat" test case would not be an adequate solution: "even if the case were successful . . . it would not be worthwhile" to limit clinic services to only such patients. "This is really their basic reason for not wanting to go to the courts."

While both Pease and Kit Hepburn believed that the increased Roman Catholic presence in the state legislature, particularly in the state senate, meant that a legislative effort was almost certainly fore-doomed to be little more than a waste of money, a special plenary meeting of the Connecticut board was called for April 24 to hear a formal proposal from Darrach and the BCFA's principal public relations firm, the John Price Jones Corporation (JPJ), a twenty-year-old organization with a staff of fifty. One of JPJ's principal officers, D. Kenneth

Rose, had played a primary role in the merger that had created BCFA two years earlier, and both Rose and a deputy, Paul Franklin, attended the Hartford meeting. They described JPJ's past experience with BCFA and the consulting assistance they also had provided in recent years to both the Massachusetts and New York state groups. Rose contended that what the Connecticut struggle needed was "a publicity theme that will capture public interest," and, alluding to the desirability of launching some newly named group, asserted that "what you decide on as the final name and type of organization is going to determine whether you will win or lose." Franklin conceded that JPJ's services were expensive but explained that "the chief benefit you get from our type of organization lies in group judgment." Their specific proposal had two parts: first an intensive ten-week survey of the Connecticut scene and prospects by a JPJ executive at a fee of more than twelve thousand dollars, out of which would come a more detailed—and far more expensive—game plan that the CBCL could either adopt or dismiss. Rose volunteered that "We hope you will hire us to go right through," for "We won't take a job unless we think we shall succeed." A motion approving the initial ten-week study was easily approved, with Darrach promising that Greenwich supporters would meet much if not all of the cost, and a new steering committee to work with JPJ—including Pease and Hepburn—was also ratified. As almost everyone realized, for worse or for better the Connecticut League had taken a step very different from any prior one in its two-decade history.[10]

In early May the new CBCL steering committee ratified the hiring of JPJ and within less than a week JPJ Vice President Paul Franklin began functioning as executive director of the Connecticut League. He undertook long conversations with Nowell Creadick and Warren Upson to help familiarize himself with the Connecticut scene, and both men agreed that now "the Catholic opposition was much more effectively organized than it had ever been before." Creadick advised Franklin that doctors were the most effective representatives for birth control before the legislature, while the women could lobby candidates on the issue prior to elections. Upson, like Pease and Hepburn, cautioned Franklin that Democratic—and Roman Catholic—success in the fall elections for the 1941 legislature would leave them with very dim prospects indeed. Birth control supporters suffered a modest setback when the annual meeting of the Connecticut State Medical Society sidestepped the question of reaffirming the society's 1931 and 1932 endorsements, but Florence Darrach told her colleagues that the Greenwich women had raised more than sixteen thousand dollars within hardly three weeks to finance the JPJ study. Franklin devoted most of his time to one-on-one conversations with attorneys, judges, and political observers from across the state, and the growing presence of Roman Catholic members in the legislature—particularly among Democrats in the state senate—was cited again and again as a serious if not insuperable obstacle. Several savvy politicians noted that ideally one could lobby for the selection of *non-Roman Catholic* nominees for state senate seats; otherwise, a former house speaker warned, "a legislator's obligation to the church will outweigh his desire for votes." Some of the attorneys also pointed out that the Connecticut Supreme Court would be highly unlikely to reverse itself in any test case that attempted to capitalize on Ells's replacement of Hinman, and that Ells might simply follow Chief Justice Maltbie.[11]

On June 10 Pease, Darrach, Upson, and Franklin met in New York with Sanger, Harriet Pilpel, Loraine Campbell of the Massachusetts group, and D. Kenneth Rose, who had just moved over from JPJ to become national director of the Birth Control Federation. The experience of both *Nelson* and *Gardner* had convinced Sanger that her congressional focus back in the 1920s and early 1930s had indeed been right: "Court victories . . . are temporary in their effect; legislation is a final answer, for it is an expression of the will of the people." The others mostly agreed, but with the exceptions of Pease—who voted against any legislative campaign—and Darrach, who voted against any further consideration of a test case, the participants did not clearly identify a specific strategy for the Connecticut effort to follow.

On both June 18, at the annual meeting of the Hartford clinic, and on June 26, at the annual meeting of the Connecticut League, Sallie Pease delivered her valedictory speeches as president of the Connecticut struggle. Poignant, powerful, and moving, she spoke of the emotional peaks and valleys of the preceding year, of the many intense moments since her speech a year earlier that had kicked off the Waterbury confrontation. But the bottom line, she reminded everyone, was both clear and simple: "The Women of Connecticut must have the right to decide for themselves when their children shall be born."

The league's annual meeting affirmed two important JPJ and Florence Darrach initiatives: formal creation some weeks hence of a publicity vehicle that would be called the Connecticut Committee to Make Birth Control Legal, and installation of the very handsome and proper president of the Hartford Seminary, Robbins W. Barstow, as figurehead president of the Connecticut League. Paul Franklin stressed to reporters that the league had reached no decision on pursuing either a

1941 legislative effort or a court case, and several weeks later, when JPJ's initial ten-week contract with the league was about to expire, the relationship was extended—with only Sallie Pease voting no—even though everyone acknowledged that no funds were being raised anywhere except in Greenwich.[12]

Florence Darrach appreciated that the league's best political chance lay in obtaining firm support from the Republican party, but she realized too that not all Connecticut Catholics were Democrats. She told her Massachusetts counterpart Loraine Campbell that it was too bad that Connecticut, unlike Massachusetts, did not have the option of proposing a popular referendum on the issue, but in mid-July she and Franklin went to have a long private chat with Connecticut's first-term Republican governor, Raymond E. Baldwin, who seven years earlier had been the primary legislative sponsor of the league's reform bill. A narrow upset winner over Wilbur Cross in 1938, Ray Baldwin represented a state Republican party that had transformed itself from the era of J. Henry Roraback into the progressive garb of the party's 1940 presidential candidate, Wendell Willkie. Baldwin told Franklin and Darrach that personally he was "in sympathy with the birth control movement," but that he did not want the issue interjected into the upcoming fall elections. "He asked Mrs. Darrach if she wanted to see him Governor again and if so said the quickest way to kill his chances and the chances of the Republican party would be for the League or Committee to introduce the birth control issue into the campaign." The governor advised that "it would be infinitely better for all concerned for the Committee to do nothing in a political way until after the November elections. He said that the birth control issue was not as important as people believe because in the last election when he ran for Governor none of his opponents brought up the fact that he was known to be [a] supporter of birth control." Darrach and Franklin restrained themselves from pointing out that if indeed this was so, it could in no way harm Baldwin's reelection prospects for the issue to be raised, but they did directly ask the governor "if he would use his influence in bringing about a change in the law if the Committee agreed to do nothing in political circles until after the election." "Of course," Franklin noted, "he refused to answer this query."[13]

The Connecticut activists continued to flummox around without settling on any firm strategy. Laurence Janney volunteered to draft a bill for the 1941 legislature, and Paul Franklin, after undertaking an amateurish poll of citizens' opinions on birth control, sent out a low-visibility press release asserting that 93 percent of Connecticut residents backed a doctor's right to prescribe it. Judge Kenneth Wynne told Franklin in an off-the-record conversation that a court case stood no chance of success, and while some league members did make queries about local legislative candidates, an early September newsletter correctly confessed that "the real work of the organization has yet to begin."

By mid-September Sallie Pease and her Hartford colleagues were in open revolt against the way things were going, formally notifying the statewide steering committee that they would decline to contribute toward paying any further fees for JPJ and bluntly suggesting that need for "a workable, clear and practical plan which can be carried out mainly by volunteers" rather than "the present costly arrangement." The Hartford group warned that "the continued employment of a high priced publicity firm from New York" might well be seized upon by birth control opponents come the 1941 legislature, and even a good Hartford friend of Darrach's warned her that it "is not difficult to stir up an illogical opposition to measures proposed and advocated by those of you who reside so near the New York border" in wealthy Fairfield County.[14]

In late October Warren Upson pointed out to his Connecticut colleagues a mid-September ruling by the Massachusetts Supreme Court that potentially could be viewed as a retreat from *Gardner*. A Boston pharmacist, Lewis Corbett, had been arrested and convicted under the Massachusetts statute prohibiting the distribution of contraceptives for the crime of selling condoms to an undercover policeman. The court had reversed his conviction on the grounds that condoms could be used for protection against disease as well as for contraception, and in the absence of evidence that the seller knew which use a customer had in mind, no intent to violate the statute could be shown. It was a limited ruling, covering only condoms—as Harriet Pilpel later wrote, "the result of the holding is that practically speaking only the best type of contraceptives," diaphragms, "are effectively barred from use in Massachusetts." However, the tenor of the decision, as the *Yale Law Journal* noted, "is antithetical to that expressed two years earlier by the same court" in *Gardner* and then relied upon so centrally by the Connecticut Supreme Court in *Nelson*. Massachusetts lawyers did not pursue the matter, but to Upson and others in Connecticut *Corbett* at least offered plausible grounds for asking the Connecticut court to revisit the subject of *Nelson*.[15]

Rather than a court case, the Massachusetts activists had set their eyes on getting a popular referendum vote on medically sanctioned

birth control onto the 1942 Massachusetts ballot. In May 1940, with
that possibility in mind, they had commissioned a statewide poll. The
results showed that 64 percent of respondents—and 45 percent of
Roman Catholics—said yes when asked "Do you think people should
be allowed to obtain birth control information from public clinics here
in Massachusetts?" Even more notably, 82 percent of people—and 72
percent of Catholics—said yes when asked "Do you approve or disapprove of allowing Massachusetts doctors to provide birth control information to married women for health reasons?" Those answers
indicated that birth control liberalization stood a far better chance with
Massachusetts voters than with state legislators, and the first step
toward obtaining a 1942 referendum vote was to file a minimum of
twenty thousand petition signatures by late 1940. To aid in that campaign, Margaret Sanger herself scheduled a series of appearances across
the state, and all went smoothly until Roman Catholic pastors in the
industrial city of Holyoke called for the cancellation of her upcoming
talk there. Sanger was scheduled to speak at Holyoke's First
Congregational Church, which initially held firm in its commitment
until several church board members who were businessmen received
personal calls from a prominent Catholic priest who expressed concern
about future patronage of their businesses unless the Sanger talk was
canceled. Only twenty-four hours before Sanger was to speak the
church board reversed itself, and after at least one other unsuccessful
attempt to secure an attractive venue, Sanger ended up delivering her
remarks in a union hall. The potential lessons of this experience for a
1942 statewide referendum campaign on birth control should have
been hard to ignore.[16]

For the Connecticut activists, the November 1940 election results
were even worse than they had anticipated: Republican Governor
Baldwin was turned out of office by Democrat Robert A. Hurley, and
estimates were that as many as nineteen members of the thirty-five seat
state senate would be Roman Catholics. No more than thirteen likely
supporters of any birth control bill could be identified, but while the
Connecticut proponents realized that their chances for success were
"remote" at best, they nonetheless concluded that they had no real
choice except to put forward at least a modest version of a doctors-ori-
ented reform bill. A legislative campaign, even if wholly unsuccessful,
would keep the issue in the public eye; it also would make a subsequent court case seem more justified. Realizing that under the circumstances a modest legislative effort would be adequate, the relationship
with JPJ was terminated as of early December and a full-time local

executive director, Bice Clemow—a journalist and close friend of one of Mrs. Hepburn's sons-in-law—was hired instead. Many New York voices, including Ernst, Pilpel, and BCFA officials, as well as Pease and Hepburn, objected to the idea of a knowingly hopeless legislative campaign on behalf of any far from ideal bill, and Ernst attempted to sell the Connecticut lawyers on the same idea of a test case involving some birth control publication that he had unsuccessfully advocated in Massachusetts. The Connecticut attorneys were more interested in a test case involving an affirmative or declaratory civil suit brought on behalf of a physician who wanted to prescribe birth control for women patients, as distinct from a clinic opening and a defense against ensuing criminal charges, but one of their advisors, United States District Judge Carroll Hincks, warned that "the difficulty is to have an actual controversy" clearly shown in any such declaratory action. Consideration turned toward recruiting both a doctor/plaintiff and a senior lawyer of the "highest reputation in the bar" to bring the case, with Eleanor Calverly, who had worked for five years at the Hartford clinic, reluctantly bowing out because of family considerations.[17]

By mid-January 1941 a consensus had evolved that both a declaratory test case and some legislative effort should be mounted. The first two high-status attorneys who were approached each declined, but the third, former state bar association president Frederick H. "Fritz" Wiggin of the prominent New Haven firm of Wiggin and Dana, readily agreed. Some advisors were surprised by Wiggin's acceptance, for while he had with some hesitance helped Laurence Janney with the doctors' amicus brief in *Nelson*, he had also told Paul Franklin some months earlier that any test case "was doomed to failure" and that legislative reform was the league's only recourse. Wiggin told Florence Darrach that the case would have to involve a situation where "a married woman would be very likely to lose her life" in pregnancy if refused birth control, and opined that in the Connecticut courts "this question might be decided either way, which is the equivalent of saying that I think there is a fair chance of a favorable decision." Wiggin was unenthusiastic about but not flatly opposed to a legislative effort, and with his acquiescence Upson, Pease, Clemow, Creadick, and former house speaker William Hanna spent a long evening closeted with State Senator Alfred M. Bingham at Hartford's Bond Hotel drafting what would be the league's 1941 birth control bill.[18]

So as purposely *not* to overlap with the upcoming court suit, the Bingham bill—and a similar one introduced in the state house by Westport representative Anne Arnold—spoke of authorizing "hospitals or other health institutions" with five or more M.D.s—but *not* individual private doctors—to "prescribe contraceptive devices to meet health problems of married women." Some doctors complained privately about that approach, but with the legislative hearing some eight weeks away, the bills attracted hardly any public attention. Instead, birth control news focused upon an angry interreligious debate between the league's figurehead president, Robbins Barstow, and Hartford's Father Andrew J. Kelly, who five years earlier had denounced the "busybody humanitarians" who had opened the Hartford clinic. The Barstow-Kelly brawl had been preceded by an exchange of opposing letters in the *Waterbury American* between Father Francis J. Barrett and Clara McTernan, but within short order the Kelly-Barstow exchanges were front-page news all across Connecticut.

Some weeks earlier Barstow had made the simple observation that birth control was an issue of "public welfare and not morality," to which Kelly had responded by saying that the Hartford Diocese would withdraw from an annual interfaith service on account of such sacrilege. Barstow sought to assuage Kelly's concern, explaining that he of course thought birth control "was distinctly a moral and spiritual matter," and for several weeks the dispute seemed to fade. Then, just after the Bingham bill was introduced, Barstow declared in another speech that "it is contrary to our American principles of civil liberty to permit a situation where one particular religious viewpoint controls legislation governing the private lives of those who do not hold that doctrinal allegiance." Kelly responded by accusing Barstow of "aligning himself with pagan forces" and "identifying God-fearing parents with stud farm animals." The seminary executive ought to "choose between his position as president of a Christian foundation and president of a subversive league," Kelly added, for "if he is Christian, I am not." Barstow replied to this outburst with polite understatement, but Kelly persevered, labeling Barstow an "agnostic" who was championing a philosophy that was "essentially, admittedly and soundly pagan." The league subtly responded with a *Hartford Courant* story noting that the majority of clinic patients between 1935 and 1940 had been Roman Catholic, and for ten days the uproar subsided.[19]

Then, in a February 27 speech at Wesleyan University in Middletown, Kit Hepburn criticized the *Nelson* decision and made an innocuous passing reference to Father Kelly that was picked up by the *Hartford Courant*. Kelly responded that Hepburn, as a devotee of the philosophy of "naked paganism," obviously had "little understanding of human nature" or "the content of morality." Wesleyan President

James L. McConaughy then told the *Courant* that while he was "very sorry" about Connecticut's anticontraception law, he was also "just a little sorry" that Hepburn had criticized the Connecticut Supreme Court during her talk, for "I can hardly see how they could have decided otherwise than they did." He then released a letter to Hepburn asserting that "I ardently wish that we might have birth control clinics," and Hepburn responded that she was sorry if she had embarrassed him by her criticism of the court's "anti-social" ruling. Another Catholic cleric, Reverend Francis J. Sugrue of South Norwalk, eagerly joined the exchange by condemning birth control's "lecherous leaders" for advocating "reckless irresponsibility." Kelly added that Margaret Sanger had once advocated requiring advance licensing before mothers could have children, and when Sanger called the *Courant* to deny it, Kelly cited a 1934 Sanger article. As matters quieted once again, Connecticut League executive director Bice Clemow told the BCFA staff in New York that "Catholic opposition is rising in the state like a tidal wave."[20]

While the public and many activists had been preoccupied with these exchanges, Fritz Wiggin had sought and found a willing plaintiff. Dr. Margaret Tyler, who for four years had worked in the New Haven clinic, had abashedly refused, but in early February Wiggin, helped by longtime league activist Betty Whittemore, successfully recruited sixty-five-year-old Yale Medical School professor and private practitioner Wilder Tileston. A quiet and private man who was well-known throughout the New Haven medical community, Tileston—with active help from Margaret Tyler—set about identifying and documenting the cases of three local women for whom a pregnancy, and the absence of birth control, could be a tangible threat to their lives. On March 13 he examined "Jane Doe," a forty-one-year-old mother of five who was referred to him by New Haven Hospital through the efforts of Dr. Tyler. Jane Doe had had her last child just two months earlier and was suffering from extremely high blood pressure; when told she must avoid another pregnancy, she had asked how. Four days later New Haven Hospital referred "Mary Roe," a twenty-two-year-old newlywed who was suffering from ongoing lung problems as a result of having contracted tuberculosis five years earlier, for which she had spent four years in a sanitorium. Lastly, on March 20, Tileston saw "Sarah Hoe," a twenty-five-year-old poverty-stricken mother of three children, the youngest of whom was six months old.

That same day, March 20, Wiggin filed his formal complaint in Superior Court, naming New Haven County State's Attorney Abraham S. Ullman—who had been in the post for less than four months—as the defendant. It described the three women's medical problems; Tileston stated that a pregnancy would be "exceedingly perilous" to Jane Doe's life, and that "the best and safest medical treatment" for her was contraception as a "necessary preventative measure." For Mary Roe, a pregnancy "would have a strong tendency" to reactivate her tuberculosis, which in turn "would undoubtedly disable her for a long time to come, and might cause her death." If, through contraception, Mary Roe could avoid pregnancy for two to three years, she then should be able to have children without undue risks to her health. Sarah Hoe was presently "in good health," the suit conceded, but another pregnancy so soon after her recent childbirth "would probably have a serious effect on her general health and might result in her permanent disability." Additionally, a fourth child "would aggravate an economic condition already difficult, and hazardous to the health of the mother and her children."

Having described the three cases, where "conception would probably cause (a) her death; (b) serious permanent injury to her health; (c) injury to her general health," Wiggin asserted that the 1879 statute prohibiting Tileston from prescribing birth control for these women violated two provisions of the Connecticut Constitution and three amendments to the U.S. Constitution. Most significantly, he and Tileston contended that the law offended the Fourteenth Amendment's guarantee against "depriving any person of life without due process of law" and also, in the context of the Amendment's similar due process protection against deprivation of property, infringed upon Tileston's "privilege of practicing his profession" as a doctor.[21]

Only five days after the case's filing was news of it released to the press, and it received very limited publicity. Tileston told the Associated Press that "Connecticut doctors have been faced with the alternatives of turning away mothers to whom another pregnancy may mean permanent injury to health or even death itself, or of subjecting themselves to criminal prosecution," and that the law's intrusion had to be remedied. On April 1 there was a very brief initial hearing in New Haven which received absolutely no news coverage, and nine days later attention turned to the long-delayed legislative hearing on Senator Bingham's reform bill.

While Robbins Barstow was the leadoff witness for the bill's supporters, emphasizing how it would insure "the individual liberties of married citizens," the proponents had purposely weighted their presentation to women who could speak firsthand about the importance of clinic services: Dr. Hilda Standish, Daisy M. Dennison, who had worked in the Norwalk clinic, and six former clinic patients. As two onlookers from BCFA noted, "The members of the committee listened more attentively to these women than to any of the speakers." Twenty legislators also appeared to register their support, and then the other side took the floor, with Mrs. Francis E. Jones—whose husband had represented the opponents back in 1923 and 1931—saying that the Bishop of Hartford had asked her to register his opposition, along with that of some 131 affiliated groups for whom she also spoke. Among half a dozen opposing speakers the most notable was seventy-year-old State Labor Commissioner Cornelius J. Danaher, whom the BCFA visitors described as "a big, bull-necked, loud mouthed individual" who "pulled out all the stops" and characterized Margaret Sanger as "the crown princess of race suicide." Then, as the hearing was breaking up, the dramatic highlight of the day occurred as forty-eight-year-old Republican Representative Bernard Matthies of Seymour, a birth control supporter, told the much larger Danaher that his had been "the damnedest speech I ever heard" and that "I have a good mind to punch you in the nose." Danaher replied that "I'll punch you in the nose if you don't get out of here," and as other legislators stepped between the two men, Matthies ended the confrontation by asking "How much did the priests pay you?"[22]

Proponents and press observers agreed that the bill had no prospects in the senate, and hence might not even be brought up for passage in the house, but opposition forces continued their push, with the diocesan newspaper, the *Catholic Transcript*, lambasting birth control as both "a flight from decency" and also "a flight to calamity." Feeling obligated to address the hearing testimony of the former clinic patients, the *Transcript* declared that "the real problem is the rotten, inequitable economic system of which these people are the victims and of which many of the socially prominent birth prevention advocates are the vigilant guardians and fat beneficiaries."

Pondering their hopeless legislative chances, Florence Darrach and other Connecticut activists realized they had seriously erred nine months earlier when they had accepted then-Governor Baldwin's advice that birth control not be raised as an issue in the 1940 elections. In 1942, Darrach told one reporter, that mistake of deferring to the Republican leadership would not be repeated: "We didn't start out to be politicians, but we're sick of any party solidarity which soft-pedals our effort to legalize birth control clinics." Mitigating that irritation was the widespread belief that the *Tileston* suit might well resolve the problem. Harriet Pilpel volunteered that "the complaint is an excellent job," and Darrach told one friend that "*many* lawyers think that we are going to win the test case. . . . I am hopeful that by autumn we may be opening a few clinics" even if the legislative effort went nowhere.[23]

On May 13, at the prodding of birth control supporters and against the wishes of the Republican leadership, the house Public Health and Safety Committee voted twelve to three to send an amended version of the Bingham bill, one that would allow *all* doctors to prescribe birth control, to the house floor. One week later, after a brief and perfunctory debate and rejection by 169 to 71 of a motion to table, the house passed the bill on a vote of 164 to 64. The senate members of the Public Health and Safety Committee voted two to one against the measure, but on May 27, largely through the efforts of Senator Bingham himself, the bill nonetheless reached the senate floor, where Bingham and leading opposition Senator Joseph P. Cooney of Hartford engaged in what one paper called a "stirring" debate in front of "the largest audience of the session," most of whom were women. Bingham declared that the central issue was "whether freedom is to be given to human beings," but when the senate roll was called, only nine members voted in favor of the bill, and twenty-three against. Of those opponents, twenty-one were Democrats, and twenty were Roman Catholics. The Connecticut League announced that the "battle of 1943" was now beginning, and said it would single out for special attention "any politician who himself practices medically sound birth control but denies it to ill and under-privileged families."[24]

Eight days after the Connecticut senate vote both houses of the Massachusetts legislature took the next step toward assuring a statewide 1942 referendum when they declined to pass the birth control proposal. Proponents had successfully overcome an attempt by opponents to derail the referendum plan on the grounds that the Massachusetts Constitution barred popular votes on religious issues, with the Massachusetts Supreme Judicial Court stating that the birth control amendment was not a religious matter. Following those legislative votes the proponents would have to submit a modest number of additional petition signatures that summer, but the referendum plan appeared to be on track for a 1942 vote.[25]

With the conclusion of the 1941 legislative session, the Connecticut activists vowed to take an aggressive interest in the 1942 selection of state senate candidates, particularly in politically competitive districts. Clemow and others were disappointed at the relative slowness with which the *Tileston* case was progressing, and because of crowded court dockets the entire summer passed without any significant developments. By mid-September Wiggin and State's Attorney Ullman had agreed to proceed by stipulation rather than conduct an actual trial, and the Connecticut League spent the fall impatiently waiting for the case to move forward. The league's active membership dwindled significantly in the absence of a conspicuous program, and a well-publicized mid-October dinner in Hartford featuring Kit Hepburn and chaired by Sallie Pease drew only seventy-five people. Hepburn used the occasion to reflect upon her thirty years of political activism, explaining that birth control had attracted her because "I felt that women would always be hopelessly handicapped if they did not have control of how many children they produced." "It's perfectly all right," she added, "for Catholics to follow the dictates of their church, but to force their idea on other people is Nazi procedure." Outspoken Father Kelly quickly responded by asserting that "We shall enjoy civil liberties only so long as religion is entangled with our laws," but no rejoinder ensued. By late November Clemow warned the league's officers that "Every week we suffer from dwindling interest and flagging courage."[26]

Finally, on December 2—just five days before the Pearl Harbor attack transformed the entire American scene—Wiggin and Ullman filed the *Tileston* stipulation in New Haven County Superior Court. Dr. Tileston's medical evaluations of Doe, Roe, and Hoe had been reviewed and endorsed by four prominent fellow doctors, including James Raglan Miller, and a New Haven M.D. who examined all three of the women on behalf of Ullman, Dr. Samuel J. Goldberg, likewise concurred. In Jane Doe's and Mary Roe's cases, Goldberg agreed, pregnancies would pose a serious threat to the woman's life and "should be prevented by any means available." Pursuant to both sides' agreement, Superior Court Judge Earnest C. Simpson signed a brief order referring the questions of law posed by the suit to the Connecticut Supreme Court, and oral argument before the high bench was scheduled for early February of 1942.

The full-scale outbreak of World War II significantly hampered the Connecticut League's ability to attract volunteers and funds, and led the officers to focus their hopes even more heavily upon eventual success in the *Tileston* case. In late January Fritz Wiggin and his junior colleague, John Q. Tilson, Jr., filed their brief with the Connecticut Supreme Court, arguing that the 1879 statute had been intended solely as an antiobscenity measure and should not be construed as applying to medically approved contraception in cases where serious health threats existed. The *Nelson* ruling, they contended, "is not inconsistent with" such a position, for it "clearly reserved for future decision the question of whether a physician may lawfully prescribe contraceptive devices where medical prescription is necessary to the life of the patient." If the 1879 statute *was* read as prohibiting the prescription of birth control in such serious cases, they added, "it would be an unreasonable interference with the life and liberty of the physician and of his patients" as protected by the Fourteenth Amendment and hence would be unconstitutional.

Wiggin and Tilson maintained that *Gardner* was "much weakened as authority" by *Corbett*, which signaled "a distinct change in the opinion of the Massachusetts court." The unspoken inference was that if the Massachusetts court could so quickly and nimbly change direction, so too could the Connecticut one. They echoed Upson's emphasis from two years earlier that citizens possess an inherent right to protect their lives and health, and that "any attempt by the Legislature to outlaw medical contraception would be arbitrary and invalid since it would be taking from the citizen his inalienable right to liberty and health." They concluded by trying to magnify the differences between *Tileston* and *Nelson*, for "the facts in this case are far different" and *Nelson* "has no application to a situation where serious injury to health or danger to life is involved."

"Ab" Ullman was viewed as a friendly professional adversary by Wiggin and Tilson, and Ullman's brief in opposition was calm and straightforward. It noted, as the proponents had unspokenly conceded, that Sarah Hoe's case, unlike Doe's and Roe's, was indistinguishable from *Nelson*, and cited both the Connecticut precedent and *Gardner* as holding that "The language of these statutes forbids an exception for physicians under any circumstances." Additionally, in light of Connecticut's recent history, "The repeated rejection of proposed changes demonstrates the legislative intent to include all persons and all cases" under the statute. "We may doubt the wisdom of the statute or question its propriety," Ullman conceded, "but the manifest intention of the Legislature of this State for all-out prohibition cannot be denied," and for the court to hold otherwise "would in effect constitute legislation by judicial interpretation."[27]

Fritz Wiggin firmly instructed the league that he did *not* want a large turnout of members for the February 4 oral argument, for "This would be unusual, and . . . might irritate the Judges," but Wiggin received a slightly frosty reception, particularly from Chief Justice Maltbie, even in the absence of any visible crowd. One league officer congratulated Wiggin on his "calm and dignified answers" to Maltbie's many questions, and league office secretary Mabel Robbins said that she had been similarly impressed: "I do not see how we can fail to get a favorable ruling after listening to your argument. The Chief Justice showed a decided prejudice at the beginning but it seemed to me you had no difficulty later in overcoming it." Robbins added that her certainty that they would prevail had been further strengthened by Ullman's argument, for it seemed as if "the prosecuting attorney was more for than against us."

Wiggin himself, however, was a good deal less optimistic. "The Chief Justice said very frankly during the argument," he told one activist, "that what bothered him the most was the repeated refusals of recent sessions of the General Assembly to amend the law in any way even to permit contraception under the advice and direction of physicians. He said it was asking a good deal in the face of this to request the court to read an exception into a statute which on its face has no exceptions. I gave him the best answers I could to that but I feel that if certain members of the court are favorably disposed to us, which I hope is so, they will have a hard time bringing the Chief Justice around."[28]

For the next four months the Connecticut League did little more than sit and wait for the court to issue its decision. Kenneth Rose had succeeded in changing the name of the national group from the Birth Control Federation to the Planned Parenthood Federation of America (PPFA), and in May the Connecticut League followed suit, becoming the Planned Parenthood League of Connecticut (PPLC). Then, on June 2, came the decision from the Connecticut Supreme Court: a 3 to 2 affirmance of both the statute and *Nelson*. As before, Justices Newell Jennings and Christopher Avery dissented, but the majority opinion, supported both by Chief Justice Maltbie and Justice Brown, was authored by the Court's sole new member since *Nelson*, and the hypothetical swing vote, Justice Arthur F. Ells. The legislature, both in 1879 and from 1917 to the present, had clearly intended that *all* contraception be forbidden: "The manifest intention of the legislature of this state, to date, for all-out prohibition cannot very well be denied." Additionally, the legislature was constitutionally entitled to believe, and mandate, that abstinence from sexual relations, rather than the use of contraceptives, should be practiced by married women for whom a possible pregnancy could prove life-threatening. Avery and Jennings voiced agreement with the plaintiff's contention that *Nelson* had been largely based upon *Gardner*, which *had* been fundamentally undercut by *Corbett*, but they were the minority.[29]

The Connecticut League was disappointed but not stunned by the outcome, and immediately vowed to appeal to the U.S. Supreme

Court. National PPFA quickly suggested that PPLC engage Morris Ernst to handle the appeal, and, in part because it initially was indicated that Ernst would do it for free, and in part because Wiggin did not at first seem especially interested, the Connecticut leadership readily agreed. Everyone appreciated that it was not certain that the Supreme Court would choose to hear the appeal, but PPLC officials felt they had little choice but to hope for the best, because, as Mabel Robbins told one colleague, "it would be tragic to have to go to the Legislature again."

In late August Ernst and Pilpel filed the initial appeal papers with the Supreme Court. A month later Ab Ullman filed a brief opposing statement, emphasizing that "the real parties in interest" in the case were Doe, Roe, and Hoe, rather than Dr. Tileston, and that in their absence as actual plaintiffs, no decision of the case on its merits could properly take place. Two amicus briefs, one by Warren Upson on behalf of Connecticut doctors, and one by Charles E. Scribner of New York on behalf of other M.D.s, were also being prepared, and a "Dear Doctor" letter soliciting signatures for the Connecticut amicus brief was mailed to some fifteen hundred physicians. Over five hundred affirmative replies quickly came in, but the letter's tough language, indicating that physicians' rights were "under attack" by Ullman in "a barefaced assault on the entire medical profession" understandably angered the exceedingly cooperative state's attorney. Upson took upon himself the task of remedying the frayed relationships, and after two weeks of time-consuming exchanges among all the parties a "Dear Doctor" letter was sent out in Upson's name telling recipients that Ullman was simply "a conscientious public servant who is doing his duty." Finally, in late October, both Ernst's principal brief and the two amicus briefs were filed, with a total of over seven hundred doctors listed as endorsers, a tally that drew great considerable attention in the Connecticut press.[30]

On November 3, however, birth control supporters suffered a huge and embarrassing setback when the voters of Massachusetts overwhelmingly *rejected* the referendum proposal that would have legalized the medical prescription of contraception for married women for whom a pregnancy would threaten their health. In the eyes of the Massachusetts proponents, the margin of defeat—58 to 42 percent—was wholly the result of what they viewed as an intensive Roman Catholic advertising campaign against the measure, a campaign whose featured slogan had been "Birth Control Is Against God's Law—Vote NO." Six months before the vote the proponents had overcome yet another legal maneuver aimed at derailing the plebiscite, but the fall campaign had been an intense and emotional affair, and the Massachusetts activists were not wholly surprised at the outcome.[31]

The PPLC viewed the Massachusetts result as extremely disheartening, but was overjoyed at Connecticut's own election results: Republican Raymond E. Baldwin was returned to office as governor, and, more importantly, for the first time in twelve years there was a Republican majority in the state senate as well as in the house. This offered "a fighting chance for success" in the 1943 legislature, Florence Darrach told league members, but PPLC's hopes remained focused on the *Tileston* case, and when the U.S. Supreme Court announced on November 9 that it would hear the appeal, those hopes were raised even further.

Inside the Supreme Court, however, *Tileston* v. *Ullman* looked like an unremarkable and probably fatally flawed appeal. Two serious problems were readily apparent. First, as law clerk Vern Countryman related to Justice William O. Douglas: "no 'case or controversy,'" as required by the U.S. Constitution, "is presented on this appeal." Ullman's and Wiggin's initial stipulation a year earlier stated only that prosecutors "claim or may claim" that medical prescription of birth control violated the 1879 statute, and, as Countryman pointed out, "This does not evidence a present controversy—it shows no more than that there may be a controversy now, or there may be a controversy arising in the future, or that no controversy will ever arise" with actual criminal charges being filed against an offending physician. Second, and even more notably, Countryman told Douglas, "I don't believe that [the] Appellant," Dr. Tileston, "has the standing to raise the constitutional questions here asserted. All of the constitutional rights which [the] Appellant contends are violated belong not to him, but to his patients"—just as Ullman had emphasized in pointing out that the three women were the real—but missing—plaintiffs in the case. "Were it not for these jurisdictional defects," Countryman volunteered, "I believe that the case on the merits under due process is a substantial one," and that the Court's affirmance of *Gardner* four years earlier was not determinative: "this case is not similar. In the *Gardner* case there was no showing of the circumstances of the patients for whom the physician prescribed the contraceptives." But Fritz Wiggin, however, had failed to include the women themselves as plaintiffs.[32]

Morris Ernst and Harriet Pilpel had some sense of the serious procedural obstacles that they faced, and in late November they moved to recruit the country's top expert in declaratory judgment suits—and a personal friend of Dr. Tileston's—Yale law professor Edwin Borchard, to their side. The proponents also agreed that both Upson and Scribner would submit supplementary amicus briefs, but despite almost daily correspondence amongst all the attorneys throughout the month of December, neither Borchard nor Ernst devoted much thought to the possibility that the Justices would consider the omission of the three women patients as plaintiffs to be a fatal flaw.[33]

The oral argument of *Tileston* v. *Ullman* before the Supreme Court began late in the afternoon of Wednesday, January 13, 1943, and Morris Ernst was no more than two minutes into his initial remarks when Chief Justice Harlan Fiske Stone interrupted him to ask whether the Fourteenth Amendment issue in the case, in light of Wiggin's initial complaint, was limited simply to the question of whether the Connecticut statute deprived someone of "life" without due process of law. Ernst answered that in the initial appeal papers to the U.S. Supreme Court he had cited the full Fourteenth Amendment panoply of "life, liberty, or property," but Stone replied that the issue here was of course limited to whatever the Connecticut Supreme Court itself had passed upon. Ernst responded that the life of the patient was indeed involved, but Stone rightfully countered that the life claim had to involve the life of the plaintiff who was invoking the Fourteenth Amendment, namely Dr. Tileston. Justices William O. Douglas and Robert H. Jackson followed up with other questions, but then Chief Justice Stone jumped back in to ask whether there really was any actual controversy here, since the original complaint had not alleged any real threat of prosecution. Ernst answered that *Nelson* was powerful evidence of just such a threat, and Stone replied that the complaint might have satisfied that problem had it cited *Nelson*, but it had not. Fortunately for Ernst, who later called the experience "most uncomfortable," the Court adjourned each day at precisely four-thirty p.m. Warren Upson believed that Ernst had done "a splendid job" at coping with Stone's onslaught, but there was no way of curing the original shortcomings that had been inherited from Fritz Wiggin.

Upson, Ernst, and Charles Scribner spent a good part of the evening looking up references that might help to extricate Ernst from his predicament when the argument resumed on Thursday morning, but Ernst made no more headway against the Chief Justice then than he had on Wednesday. Finally, in open acknowledgment of how dire the situation was, Ernst volunteered that if the Court concluded that Stone was indeed correct, he would request a continuance and seek a formal clarification from the Connecticut Supreme Court that "liberty" and "property" had indeed been at issue. Then Ernst introduced his colleague Edwin Borchard, who also tangled with the Chief Justice over the question of whether the 1879 statute's very existence represented a threat of prosecution sufficient to create an actual controversy.

New Haven attorney William L. Beers, whom Ullman had hired six weeks earlier to help with *Tileston*, opened the opposition argument. Beers focused upon the procedural problems, contending that Dr. Tileston "had shown no substantial right of his own" to be at issue. Then Ab Ullman addressed the merits, saying that "a state has the right to control the marital relations of its citizens" and that birth control involved "moral and sociological problems that are appropriate for the legislature but not for the courts." Ernst had reserved a few minutes of his time for rebuttal, and finally for the first time was able to speak to the merits without being interrupted by questions about the technical flaws.[34]

Afterward both Ernst and Upson were appropriately downcast about the likely outcome. Upson wrote Ab Ullman that "I thought that you and Bill Beers did altogether too well in arguing your side," and to Nowell Creadick he explained that the real problem was not their opponents, but the combination of Fritz Wiggin and the Chief Justice. "I think that there are some members of the Court who would like to decide in our favor," but "I think that the technical difficulties may prevent a decision on the merits." If that indeed was the case, "I think we can safely assume that the majority of the Court was not with us." Ernst told one friend that he fully expected the Court to reject the appeal, and when he and Upson met with the leaders of the Connecticut League to advise them about introducing a bill into the 1943 legislature, both men strongly recommended that a legislative campaign be mounted, for the chance of success in the Supreme Court now looked very modest indeed.

Ernst and Borchard were sufficiently perturbed at how the oral argument had gone that they agreed to take a decidedly unusual step: a postargument letter addressed to Chief Justice Stone that reiterated once again their assertion that the simple presence of *Nelson* as a precedent served as a more than adequate threat of criminal prosecution for a doctor such as Wilder Tileston should he prescribe contraception for a Jane Doe or Mary Roe. "During the oral argument several observations were made by members of the Court as to which there was no opportunity for comment," Ernst cheekily asserted. "If this letter may properly be circulated and if in your judgment it would be of aid to the Court, I respectfully urge its distribution."[35]

Harlan Fiske Stone neither circulated nor acknowledged Ernst's impudent letter. He had no need to, for the outcome of *Tileston* v. *Ullman* had been decided two days after oral argument and two days before Ernst had mailed his missive. Just as the barrage of questions at the argument had suggested, there was no doubt or disagreement within the Court that *Tileston* was indeed a fatally flawed case. As Justice William O. Douglas jotted to himself during the Justices' private conference, Wiggin's citation of "'life' only" under the Fourteenth Amendment was not correctable. Tileston—or Wiggin—"need not have [limited] his const[itutional] claim but he did." Stone or some other Justice noted the apparent "close collaboration between pl[aintiff] and def[endant]" that was reflected in the case's record, and in the absence of clearer evidence of a true controversy, "we have no case here . . . we take cases only where there is [a] case or controversy as defined in [the] Constitution." Chief Justice Stone said that he would prepare a brief, unsigned per curiam opinion on behalf of his unanimous colleagues explaining the case's defects and dismissing the appeal.

On Monday, February 1, the *Tileston* decision was announced. It noted that Wiggin's original complaint "contained no allegations asserting any claim under the Fourteenth Amendment of infringement of appellant's liberty or his property rights." Additionally, the complaint's reference to "life" clearly meant that of Dr. Tileston's patients, not the doctor himself, and for that constitutional argument to be made, the patients themselves, and not merely their doctor, would have to be plaintiffs in the case.[36]

The Connecticut League's lawyers were disappointed but not surprised by the Court's quick and decisive action. Dr. Tileston called the result "not unexpected" and pointed out that the issue would now go before the 1943 legislature. Warren Upson told Morris Ernst that "everybody feels that you did a superb job under difficult handicaps," but conceded that any "further action through the courts will be difficult. The only possibility" would be "a criminal suit in which a patient is actually prosecuted," and such a case "obviously" would be difficult to generate.

Ernst himself was both angered and embarrassed. He tried to persuade Wiggin and John Tilson to consider petitioning the Connecticut Supreme Court to reopen *Tileston* so that the initial defects could be corrected and the case resubmitted to the U.S. Supreme Court, but Wiggin wanted nothing more to do with the matter. Ernst broached the same idea to Upson, and Upson discussed the question with William Beer, who in turn raised it both with Ab Ullman and, very privately, with Chief Justice Maltbie and Justice Arthur Ells. Ullman already had greeted news of the decision with an odd statement for the supposed victor, stressing that the ruling "did not involve the merits of birth control" and that the statute could soon be reviewed by the legislature. Ullman was unenthusiastic about any reopening of *Tileston*, however, and Beer further told Upson that "both Maltbie and Ells are hostile to any clarification in the Connecticut Supreme Court."[37]

Morris Ernst wanted both PPLC and PPFA to commit themselves immediately to mounting another case, this time on behalf of a patient as well as a doctor, but in Connecticut, league officials were now focusing upon the legislative session that lay immediately ahead. The *Hartford Courant* had responded to *Tileston* by stating that now the birth control debate would occur "in a considerably different climate from the one that prevailed a few years ago," and that "a different outcome" might result because of the new Republican majority in the state senate. Upson and Yale's Dr. C.-E. A. Winslow had helped an enthusiastic Republican house member, C. William Janson of Westport, draft the league's reform bill, a purposely novel measure stating that only registered pharmacists could sell contraceptives. By mid-March, however, even the resolute Upson thought its chances in the senate were no better than "doubtful," and in private league activists began to talk of searching for a willing plaintiff or two as soon as the legislative session concluded.[38]

The 1943 legislative hearing took place on March 31, with Warren Upson taking advantage of the unconventional bill to stress that at present the *sale* of contraceptives—as distinct from both "use" and the attendant "aiding and abetting" statute—was neither prohibited nor regulated by state law. Louise Fisher, once again leading the opposition on behalf of the Bishop of Hartford, forthrightly insisted that the measure "basically attacks the Catholic principles of family life and is an infringement on the moral rights of the individual in that it attempts to alter the natural law and encourages the abuse of a normal human faculty." Labor Commissioner Cornelius J. Danaher repeated his bravura performance from the 1941 hearing, this time invoking the costs of World War II as an additional reason for opposing a bill that represented "a direct assault on our strength as a nation." It was "a matter of national survival," Danaher insisted, that "America must propagate the family and perpetuate the species. . . . There should be no rationing of babies." Shifting to more natural ground, the commissioner added that "contraception is an offense against the moral law" before returning to his patriotic theme that "We need more men and women who think more of their country and less of their own comfort, convenience or pleasure."

Danaher's rhetorical dominance of the hearing was bad enough in itself, but the Hartford papers stressed the more serious news that quiet vote counting within the thirty-six-member state senate showed at least twenty firm votes against the Janson bill. On April 14, after reject-ing several opposition amendments, including one to pay women two hundred fifty dollars per childbirth, the house passed the measure on a vote of 155 to 84. One week later, however, when the bill was debated in the senate, the final roll-call vote was even worse than expected, a 24 to 11 defeat. Upson and others turned a new ear toward Ernst's and Pilpel's renewed suggestions that a new court case be developed, and one senator advised Upson that he should discard any hope of ever get-ting any birth control bill through the state senate, for "in a highly Catholicized state" that "is almost next to the impossible."[39]

PPFA staffers recommended that the Connecticut and Massachusetts leagues consider joining forces behind some case, but Upson warned PPFA director Ken Rose that too much emphasis on creating another case could be detrimental to PPLC: "I think it would be harmful to the organization to have the members get the impression that all they have to do is raise the money and leave it to the lawyers to win the battles." New PPLC president Harriet Crawford Janney, an experienced social worker whose husband had authored the amicus brief in *Nelson*, agreed with Upson's warning, but after one meeting of both Connecticut and Massachusetts activists to discuss a joint educational program, little occurred in either state until the beginning of the fall.[40]

Throughout September PPFA staffer Edna McKinnon explored test case possibilities in both Massachusetts and Connecticut. Some thought was given to the idea of simply opening a clinic, probably in Greenwich, if a willing doctor could be found, but several months passed without any significant progress. Late in the year the Connecticut attorneys realized that league sponsorship of a clinic could leave all league officers and board members open to criminal charges under the state's all-purpose conspiracy statute, and enthusiasm under-standably cooled. National public opinion polls indicated that popular acceptance of birth control was continuing to grow, with 85 percent of women—and 69 percent of Catholic women—endorsing the availabili-ty of contraceptive information. But birth control opponents remained vocal, with Father Edgar Schmiedler, Director of the Family Life Bureau of the National Catholic Welfare Conference, writing in *Reader's Digest* that birth control was "a cause that threatens the whole

Western world" and in particular was "a decided menace to the future leadership of the white race." Offering a decidedly unique view in the midst of World War II, Schmiedler explained that "Japanese birth-control devices in the homes of America can be more destructive than Japanese bombers over Pearl Harbor. Bombs destroy. Birth control not only destroys but poisons." But Schmiedler sounded pessimistic about the American future irrespective of Japanese imports, decrying "the putrid cess-pool that so much of American family life has become." And the spread of birth control was the cause: "Loosen one thread in the moral fabric and the whole garment speedily disintegrates."[41]

By early 1944 both the Connecticut and the Massachusetts activists were still trying to identify a possible test case plaintiff. Finally, in mid-March, Harriet Janney discovered an interested doctor, Josephine Evarts, in Litchfield County in northwestern Connecticut, and on March 20 both Janney and Edna McKinnon visited her. Born forty-three years earlier in Vermont, Jo Evarts had graduated from Vassar and then from Columbia University's College of Physicians and Surgeons. She had practiced in Kent, Connecticut, since 1929, and she told Janney and McKinnon that she was intrigued by the idea of a test case in part because her father had been an attorney. She of course dispensed contraceptives to her own patients, and there were two women, one with high blood pressure, and one with kidney disease, either or both of whom might make ideal coplaintiffs. Evarts struck them as "completely fearless" yet "cautious," and ten days later Evarts had lunch in New York with PPFA director Ken Rose and two of the organization's legal advisors, Charles Scribner and Morris Hadley. Evarts told them that one of the patients was leaving the area, and that while she herself remained willing if a case could proceed without publicity, that she also hoped "that a doctor could be found in some other county." The lawyers nonetheless began making discreet inquiries with attorneys and local judges in Litchfield County, and Pilpel and Ernst moved assertively to ensure that if a case indeed developed, this time they would not be left trying to repair errors that others had made at the outset.[42]

By the time of PPLC's annual meeting in mid-May the prior idea of doing a public education campaign in conjunction with the Massachusetts league had been discarded, but in considering it an effort had been made to identify a possible director for the program, and a recently widowed PPLC board member, Mary Van Zile Cunningham, had become the leading candidate. "Molly" Cunningham's late husband Gerald, the longtime rector of Stamford's

St. John's Episcopal Church, had been an officer of the Connecticut League as early as 1928, and Molly herself had been active in the Stamford clinic in the late 1930s. Now, with the Massachusetts venture shelved and the 1945 legislative session on the horizon, the league decided that the time had come to return to having a full-time executive director of the sort that Bice Clemow had been in 1941, and Molly Cunningham was the choice.

Hiring Molly Cunningham was the best move the Connecticut League had made since Sallie Pease and Kit Hepburn had been effectively deposed four years earlier. Born in 1888 in New York City, where her father was a reporter for the *New York World* and her mother a Republican district leader on the East Side, Molly Cunningham grew up in a political family; a much-discussed uncle on her mother's side was one-time Connecticut Governor Morgan G. "Crow Bar" Bulkeley, so named because of the implement he had used to gain access to the state house chamber during one particularly contentious legislative session in the 1890s. After marriage, living on the Lower East Side of Manhattan, Molly Cunningham had worked as a poll watcher at East 12th Street and Avenue C; even forty years later she would recall her happiest experience in life as having been the historic rally at the Cooper Union celebrating the ratification of the Nineteenth Amendment and the winning of female suffrage.

In seeking to legalize women's access to birth control, "We are fighting for the same fundamental principle as the suffrage," Molly Cunningham told that PPLC annual meeting. But no concrete progress was being made on the possible test case involving Dr. Evarts, and, despite Morris Ernst's energetic prodding, no case was developing in Massachusetts, either. Cunningham and Connecticut president Janney began to discuss commissioning a professional public opinion poll of state voters' views on the birth control issue as a useful weapon in the 1945 legislative session, and sometime in the summer Cunningham went to see Dr. Evarts, who indicated she was so busy that "she has not a minute for anything but her profession." By early in the fall the Connecticut activists were focusing on the 1944 elections and the 1945 legislature, and a dispirited Morris Ernst was telling Margaret Sanger that in spite of all the meetings, letters and phone calls, "somehow nothing seems to develop" in either Massachusetts or Connecticut.[43]

The November 1944 elections once again returned Ray Baldwin to the Connecticut governorship, but otherwise the results were a Democratic sweep, resulting in perhaps the most unfavorable state senate the Connecticut League had ever faced. Molly Cunningham acknowledged that any 1945 birth control bill would face "sure defeat," but an effort nonetheless had to be made. In a situation where there was little if anything to lose, Cunningham immediately undertook a most creative stratagem, politely writing to the Bishop of Hartford, Maurice F. McAuliffe, to ask "if you think any useful purpose would be served" by her and Harriet Janney meeting with him to discuss what sort of bill the league might pursue in the 1945 legislature. Not surprisingly, Bishop McAuliffe wrote back without delay to say that any meeting "would be useless" and "unprofitable," for "the opposition of the Catholic Church to artificial birth prevention is a matter of fundamental natural moral principle upon which there can be no compromise."[44]

Cunningham and Janney also lost no time in approaching Ernst and Pilpel to see if a test case could indeed be mounted as an alternative to their hopeless legislative prospects. Ernst immediately sent out a polite but pointed letter of inquiry to Dr. Evarts, asking to meet with her soon: "I am quite persuaded that a properly conducted case could be won in the United States Supreme Court without any hazard to the doctors or patients involved. The great difficulty resides in the lack of courage on the part of the medical profession." Morris Ernst would never be accused of excess subtlety, nor of lacking in hopefulness; a prominent profile of him earlier that year in *Life* magazine had highlighted his "quick-smiling charm" and "constitutional optimism"; it had also noted his "constant mouthing of well-known names," his "overpowering preoccupation with sex," and his "mild and middle-aged tendency toward bottom pinching." The Connecticut women were already well acquainted with both aspects of Ernst's personality, but for them the primary question was finding a willing plaintiff, and Ernst's upbeat insistence that victory could indeed be won was deeply heartening. Ernst similarly continued to press the Massachusetts League, but by early 1945 no case was developing there, and he likewise had received no response from Dr. Evarts to either his first letter or to a second.[45]

In late January Representative Philip Curtis of Norfolk introduced a bill authorizing physicians to prescribe birth control "when necessary to save life or prevent serious injury to health," and four weeks later PPLC released the results of a statewide survey that pollster Elmo Roper had conducted in December. Seventy percent of respondents answered yes when asked if doctors should be able to supply birth control to all married couples who requested it; 85 percent said yes if the married woman "would probably become an invalid" as a result of another pregnancy. The poll news received disappointingly modest coverage in Connecticut newspapers, and no one suggested that the clear evidence of overwhelming popular support for the Curtis bill would have any effect on the state legislature.

On February 23—eleven months after Harriet Janney had first contacted her—Dr. Jo Evarts finally met with the eager Morris Ernst. She suggested he contact a Lakeville attorney whom she knew, G. Campbell Becket, and four days later Becket saw Ernst in New York. Becket in turn visited with the state's attorney for Litchfield County, J. Howard Roberts of Thomaston, and broached the idea of an adversarial but friendly test case. Roberts said he was not at all eager to defend the Connecticut birth control statute, but nonetheless told Becket that "he would cooperate in every possible way" and that any patients' names could of course be kept private. Evarts "still seems enthusiastic and ready to go," Becket reassured Ernst and Pilpel, and Ernst began trying to schedule a personal meeting with Howard Roberts.[46]

On May 1 the public hearing on the Curtis bill took place before the joint legislative Committee on Public Health and Safety. The PPLC women played only supporting roles, and the principal affirmative speaker was a Roman Catholic union member and blue-collar worker from Stamford, John J. Hinman, who appeared on behalf of no organized group. He was followed by several ministers who were members of PPLC's new Clergy Advisory Committee; Reverend C. Lawson Willard of New Haven's Trinity Episcopal Church told the committee that "If this bill does not pass it will mean that one group in this state which is not the majority of the people," will be able to "force the rest of us who are not members of that church and who do not accept their practice to conform with a practice in which we do not believe."

The redoubtable Louise Fisher once again appeared as the leadoff opposition speaker on behalf of the Diocese of Hartford. "Contraception and contraceptive devices are against the law of nature and the law of God," she reiterated, and twenty years of PPLC publicity "has helped to tear down the moral fiber of our young people," leading to a new wave of "free love and trial marriages." She was joined by a new opposition representative, Lebanon attorney Thomas J. Dodd, but their remarks were almost unnecessary. Three weeks later the Public Health and Safety Committee killed the Curtis bill without even a recorded vote, and a downcast Molly Cunningham offered a bleak forecast: "It requires more imagination than the average person possesses to become excited about the attainment of a goal as remote as changing the birth control law in Connecticut seems to be at this point." [47]

Harriet Janney unsurprisingly told those who attended PPLC's annual meeting that "court action is indicated as the way to accomplish our objectives," and on June 14 Ernst and Pilpel finally met with State's Attorney J. Howard Roberts. Prosecutor Roberts was polite but noncommittal as Ernst, Pilpel, and "Cam" Becket discussed a possible case, and promised to think it over and get back to them. Becket subsequently told Ernst "obviously" Roberts "doesn't relish the extra work" that such a thankless venture would entail, and four months passed without Roberts saying anything more than that he was too busy to offer a conclusive answer.

By early fall it looked as if a helpful Bridgeport attorney, Irwin E. Friedman, whom Ernst had happened to meet in a Nantucket restaurant during the summer, might have secured a cooperative prosecutor in the Fairfield County town of Westport, but that possibility then required the recruitment of a willing Westport area doctor in place of Jo Evarts, and Molly Cunningham had no such success. In November Ernst spent several days back in Litchfield County meeting with Becket and Jo Evarts, with Dr. Evarts telling him that she now had found two ideal patients, but in the absence of any firm commitment of cooperation from Howard Roberts the matter remained stationary. Ernst pondered sending Roberts a formal letter, either from himself or Evarts, detailing the patients' cases and notifying him that the law was being broken, but 1945 turned into 1946 without any further developments.[48]

Molly Cunningham warned her colleagues against "a certain defeatism" that was openly emerging within the Connecticut League, but four months later, with nothing new having transpired, even she was confessing to the board that "the line between realism and defeatism is a rather fine one." The widespread apathy, she said at PPLC's annual meeting, no doubt was "due in part to the fact that many doctors continue to give and private patients receive contraceptive service" and the resulting "general impression that everyone has access to birth control information"; hence many people believed that the old 1879 statute had no actual effect on anyone. At that May 1946 annual meeting Harriet Janney stepped down after three years as league president and was succeeded by Barbara Davenport, but less than three months later Davenport resigned because her husband's business activities required her to be in New York City full time. Two months went by before a successor, Julie Howson, a longtime activist who fifteen years earlier had been a staff member at the American Birth Control League office, was selected and confirmed, and most of 1946 passed without the Connecticut League wrestling with anything more significant than these dual successions of officers.[49]

In mid-October of 1946 PPLC finalized plans to introduce another doctors' bill in the upcoming 1947 legislature, and arranged for the measure to be formally sponsored by a committee of one hundred leading Connecticut physicians. When the November elections resulted in a huge Republican sweep, Molly Cunningham rapidly spread the word that "the legislative outlook is the best in a great many years," as twenty-seven Republicans—and only nine Democrats—would be in the 1947 state senate. Hence the bill would have "more than a good chance of success," and Cunningham notified Ernst and Pilpel that the still-uncertain test case prospects should be put on hold until after the spring legislative outcome was known.[50]

On Friday, February 7, Avon Republican Representative John deK. Alsop introduced House Bill 953, authorizing physicians to prescribe contraceptives if a doctor believed that a pregnancy "would endanger the life or injure the health of a married woman." Alsop, a thirty-two-year-old Yale graduate who had won a Bronze Star and France's Croix de Guerre for a high-risk operation behind Nazi lines while serving as a captain in the OSS, was a prominent young star in state politics and was widely viewed as a likely future governor. His sponsorship was a major coup for PPLC, but the bill's prospects were nowhere near as rosy as Molly Cunningham initially had predicted. The composition of the Public Health and Safety Committee was less than ideal, and, much more importantly, ten of the senate's twenty-seven Republicans were Roman Catholic, as were seven of the nine Democrats. Alsop warned Cunningham that Republican Party leaders were saying privately that the bill's chances were "quite doubtful," and he recommended that the proponents keep a low public profile until the bill had been reported out of committee. The savvy Cunningham took Alsop's warning to heart, and called on Harry B. Strong, chief of staff to newly elected Republican Governor James L. McConaughy, who had been caught in the crossfire of the Kit Hepburn–Father Kelly birth control exchanges six years earlier when he was president of Wesleyan. Back then McConaughy had said publicly that "I ardently wish that we might have birth control clinics," but now, Strong told Cunningham, "the Governor will take no sides in the matter. . . . He will neither interfere nor make any expression on the bill." Just as Alsop had indicated, evidence was mounting that the Republican leadership, now facing a new political scene in which a good portion of the party's own supporters and elected officials were Roman Catholics, wanted no part of championing the legalization of birth control, especially if it might prevail and Republicans receive the potentially harmful credit.[51]

The tenor of the 1947 legislative battle underwent a sudden and angry shift in early March when the Diocese of Hartford threatened to cancel the Catholic hospital staff privileges of five physicians whose names had appeared in state newspapers as members of the Committee of 100 doctors backing the Alsop bill. Two Bridgeport M.D.s, Elwood K. Jones and Allen F. Delevett, were notified that "it is utterly incompatible for a doctor on St. Vincent's Hospital Staff . . . to *publicly* endorse and *engage* in the Planned Parenthood Program" and that "either you withdraw your name from the Committee" within one week "or you must resign from the Courtesy Staff. . . . We feel strongly that right is right and there can be no other alternative." Similar notices were sent to three Waterbury doctors regarding their staff privileges at St. Mary's Hospital.

The March 11 legislative hearing on the Alsop bill took place just several days after those letters were circulated, and two of the Waterbury doctors, Joseph L. Hetzel and Arthur H. Jackson, were among more than a dozen Connecticut physicians who joined other sponsors to speak in support of the measure. Alsop himself tried to sound optimistic about his bill's chances, and sought to rebut newspaper reports that it had little likelihood of passage, but even the optimistic Molly Cunningham showed a private tally of sixteen firm no's, only thirteen yes's, and seven uncommitteds. Opponents from previous years such as Louise Fisher and Thomas Dodd were joined by a new representative of the Hartford Diocese, former state Senator Joseph P. Cooney, but the extensive press coverage of the hearing focused almost exclusively on news of the imminent dismissals facing Hetzel, Jackson, and their equally unrepentant colleagues.[52]

The Alsop bill remained quietly in committee for the balance of the month, but the diocesan threats against the doctors helped mobilize new support for the legalization of birth control. The *Hartford Courant* editorialized that the only real issue was "the right of physicians to put science at the service of their patients," but that endorsement provoked Hartford's vociferous Father Andrew J. Kelly to insist that "human legislators have no jurisdiction to change divine laws." The "suicidal individualists" who were the "proponents of birth prevention are not out to change a particular statute," Kelly warned. "They would change, and by change I mean liquidate, the eternal moral code which makes man, in all his human acts, responsible to his Divine Creator."

In late March the five targeted doctors wrote to Hartford Bishop Henry J. O'Brien firmly requesting reinstatement of their staff privileges at St. Vincent's and St. Mary's, but on April 2 Father Lawrence E. Skelly, the diocesan director of hospitals, notified them that the church would not reconsider: "The action taken by the Hospital has nothing to do with your right to your opinion or belief in any matter professional or otherwise." If the diocese did not terminate their privileges, Skelly said, "your public action might give the impression that the Hospital endorses your views on this question. . . . The Hospital had no choice save to take action which would as directly, as distinctly and as publicly disassociate itself from your stand." The doctors responded with a public letter sent to each member of the Connecticut legislature, emphasizing how the diocesan retaliation for their taking a public stand on an issue pending before the General Assembly represented "a serious threat against the right of physicians to free speech on medical subjects."[53]

Several town and county medical societies released formal statements condemning the dismissals, and a veteran Republican legislator from Bridgeport called for terminating state grants to the offending hospitals until the doctors were reinstated. A representative of the Waterbury Ministerial Association met privately and unsuccessfully with the diocesan chancellor to urge reconsideration, and the American Civil Liberties Union contacted the doctors seeking a full report on what had transpired. Then, on April 24, the Public Health and Safety Committee approved the Alsop bill by a vote of thirteen to six, and public attention shifted back to the legislative scene. Reporters were saying that confirmed senate opponents numbered at least twenty-two, while sympathetic legislators indicated it was only nineteen, and PPLC activists focused upon a series of evanescent rumors that one or another declared opponent was privately having second thoughts.

Late in April the Connecticut State Medical Society's House of Delegates voted overwhelmingly to endorse the Alsop bill, and on May 7 the house passed the measure by a wide margin in a standing rather than recorded vote. But the outlook for the senate vote, scheduled on May 14, remained either bleak or hopeless. The *Courant* weighed in with another powerful editorial, declaring that "this is a vote on the legal rights of responsible physicians, and nothing else," but when senate Republicans caucused privately on the Alsop bill later that same day, the internal tally showed twelve no's, eleven yes's, and four uncommitted or absent. The two most committed senate backers of the bill, Herbert S. MacDonald and Charles S. House, had planned to push for a roll-call vote on the floor if the private Republican tally looked more promising, knowing that several wavering members would more likely vote in the affirmative if their position was to be formally recorded, but the caucus result precluded that effort. The following day, May 14, when the bill was called up on the senate floor, the outcome was preordained, and the roll was not called. Reporters watching the voice vote on which the bill was defeated guessed that the margin was 23 to 12, with all nine Democrats being joined by fourteen Republicans, but Senator MacDonald later remembered hearing "19 audible 'Nos' . . . 14 vociferous 'Yeas', and three carefully disguised mumbles."[54]

The legislative defeat was yet another dispiriting experience for PPLC. The *Courant* noted that the absence of a recorded senate vote "reflects little credit" on the legislature, and rued that P. T. Barnum's "hypocritical anachronism" would continue to remain a valid state law. "One of these days Connecticut will yet emerge into the twentieth century." The more conservative *Hartford Times*, however, rebuked its morning rival by editorializing that "it is idle for proponents of the legislation to insist that only a medical or health question is involved and not a religious or moral one, as long as a great religious organization holds to the contrary and its members"—or at least those holding legislative office—"are loyal to it." Dr. Hetzel of Waterbury hoped the ACLU would consider possible legal action against the Catholic hospitals for dismissing the doctors in retaliation for exercising their right of free speech, and when four doctors in Massachusetts—where birth control proponents were just beginning to work toward another referendum vote in 1948—were similarly terminated in late May, Hetzel suggested joint action and pointed out that the retaliatory actions had widened the birth control effort into a wider civil liberties struggle. Molly Cunningham made much the same point at PPLC's annual meeting, reminding her colleagues that "our particular fight is merely part of a larger and broader battle," but in Waterbury Dr. Charles L. Larkin, the senior medical staff member at St. Mary's—and the same man who had played such a shy and curious role in the 1939 Chase Dispensary situation—publicly rebuked Hetzel for pursuing the matter. There was no doubt, Larkin said, that Hetzel and his colleagues had been "working against one of the basic beliefs of the Catholic Church." There was likewise no doubt that the diocesan authorities had "a right to make such a ruling," and "There is no reason why we cannot go along just as we have in the past."[55]

The ACLU offered the doctors its formal support, but by mid-June most of Hetzel's colleagues had decided not to initiate a law suit. Both Hetzel and one other physician, Oliver L. Stringfield, pondered the question for several more months before likewise deciding no, and PPLC as well again turned its attention toward possible court case challenges to the Connecticut law. Nothing new emerged there, however, and the league began to consider involving itself in the 1948 state legislative elections on a specific senate district by senate district basis. By mid-October seven senate districts whose incumbents had not supported the Alsop bill, and which were susceptible to an electoral switch, had been identified, and PPLC started targeting those specific seats for intensive efforts in advance of the 1948 elections. By early 1948 actual organizing work was underway in four of those seven districts, and in April a half-time field worker, Nancy Doggett Williams, was hired to concentrate upon those areas. "Armed with a Vassar Alumnae address book and her own ingenuous personality," PPLC president Julie Howson told league officers, "she is able to find committee chairmen in the most hopeless districts." Also that spring, Boston Archbishop Richard J. Cushing delivered a major antibirth control speech in Hartford, declaring that "contraception is anti-social and anti-patriotic as well as absolutely immoral," but otherwise the first six months of 1948 were relatively quiet. John Alsop advised Molly Cunningham that a PPLC defeat of even a single opposing senator could very well trigger enough reaction to insure 1949 passage of a birth control bill so long as Republicans did relatively well in the 1948 elections, and hopes for actually winning such a long-awaited triumph gradually increased.[56]

By July 1948 PPLC was concentrating its efforts upon two districts whose Republican incumbents had opposed the Alsop bill: Stanley Stroffolino in South Norwalk and Darien, and Alice V. Rowland in Ridgefield and Danbury. An attempt to block Stroffolino's renomination as a Republican had failed, and a similar effort against Rowland was torpedoed when the families of the two principal PPLC volunteers were explicitly threatened with economic retaliation or worse if they did not desist. The leading volunteer had brushed off a visit by three unknown men who had "told her that she would be wise to stop her political efforts and hinted that there were many ways" in which she or her family might be penalized, but one week later the woman, "obviously on the verge of tears," phoned Molly Cunningham: "My husband and I thought that we were unreachable, but we find we are not. We have just had a letter from a lawyer that is upsetting to us both. I am not at liberty to tell you any more about" it, the woman said, other than that it involved a local Danbury police court. PPLC then turned its efforts toward supporting Rowland's Democratic—and probirth control—opponent, Minna Geddes, but on the Sunday before the November election a statement was read from the pulpits of each and every Catholic church in the district, informing parishioners that the

Republican candidate, rather than Geddes, had to be backed: "support of any candidate advocating birth control measures is a violation of the natural law of God which the Catholic church and Catholics are duty bound to uphold, and for any person to support such a program is a violation of the Sixth Commandment of Almighty God." As Father John J. Kennedy of Danbury's St. Peter's Roman Catholic Church told reporters, "this is not a political issue, but one of a question of natural moral law," and "no Catholic person in conscience can support any candidate favoring such legislation."[57]

Alice Rowland and Stanley Stroffolino both won reelection, and elsewhere other results were even worse: Democratic victories across much of Connecticut insured a total of at least twenty-one birth control opponents in the state senate, and in Massachusetts the referendum vote to legalize medically necessary birth control went down to defeat by a large margin—57 to 43 percent—that was almost as wide as the 1942 loss. Boston Archbishop Richard J. Cushing and the Boston Archdiocese had mounted a major campaign against the measure, utilizing weekly pulpit announcements and extensive radio ads that employed an updated slogan hearkening back to 1942: "Birth control is *still* against God's law." The church effort had been much more intense and outspoken than six years before; several months prior to the vote Boston College Law School Dean William J. Kenealy had told a legislative audience that use of birth control transformed marital sex into "mutual masturbation" and "a gross abuse of a God-given faculty" that hence amounted to nothing more than "pleasure by means of an unnatural act." Any form of contraception, Kenealy had insisted, was "intrinsically evil and is therefore never justified"; the "only moral remedy is either periodic or total abstinence."[58]

In the aftermath of both the Massachusetts and Connecticut setbacks, Molly Cunningham and her PPLC colleagues resolved to go through the motions of supporting a 1949 version of the Alsop bill even though there admittedly was no chance of success. Casting about for other options, PPLC thought again of initiating some kind of test case; as Cunningham told Harriet Pilpel, "I am becoming obsessed slowly but surely with a desire to somehow get off the dead center in which we find ourselves." Cunningham's deputy Nancy Williams wrote to her old friend Dorothy Bowles, whose husband Chester had won the Connecticut governorship in the Democratic sweep, but Mrs. Bowles responded brusquely that "I am afraid I cannot discuss with you the subject most on your mind. The Planned Parenthood Program is unquestionably a religious issue and for that reason I really cannot discuss your problem." Just as with previous, supposedly progressive governors such as Republican Ray Baldwin and Democrat James McConaughy, so too with liberal Democrat Chester Bowles would the legalization of birth control remain an untouchable issue.[59]

In early February a 1949 edition of the doctors' bill was introduced in the legislature by Bozrah Republican Representative Lawrence M. Gilman. New PPLC president Katharine B. McKinney attempted to recruit Margaret Sanger to come to the state and speak at PPLC's annual meeting, confessing that "We are at a low ebb in our efforts to get the law changed here and we badly need the inspiration." The effort went awry, however, when McKinney was told that "Mrs. Sanger was willing to speak . . . provided that [PPLC] was willing to adopt a militant policy against the Roman Catholic Church. It was decided," the board concluded, "that the League could not adopt such a policy at this time and therefore would withdraw the invitation to Mrs. Sanger to speak."

The legislative hearing on the Gilman bill took place on April 12 and was largely a rerun of previous years' proceedings. Gilman himself announced that he would willingly amend the measure so as to authorize the medical prescription of birth control only in life-threatening situations, but less apologetic proponents included a representative from the Connecticut Conference of Congregational Churches and the president of the Connecticut State Medical Society. Other doctors who spoke for the bill included Hilda Standish and Josephine Evarts; the opponents also featured several physicians plus diocesan representatives Louise Fisher and Joseph P. Cooney, as well as a Meriden state senator who had introduced a bill prohibiting legislative consideration of any birth control proposals for the next four years. A representative from Ansonia tellingly declared that "A bill of this nature is an insult to the Catholic people in our great state," and Ridgefield Senator Alice Rowland inquired as to why the proponents did not favor a statewide referendum vote, as in Massachusetts, even though Connecticut law did not provide for such an option.[60]

Three weeks after the hearing the Public Health and Safety Committee approved the Gilman bill on a secret ballot vote of twelve to five, but with observers reporting a minimum of twenty-six senators in firm opposition, the measure was not brought to the floor of either the house or the senate. Molly Cunningham immediately told her colleagues that "It is not at all too soon to be thinking about the nominations and elections" of 1950, but nothing of any political significance occurred during the balance of 1949. PPLC president Katharine

McKinney passed away unexpectedly in September after a sudden illness, and was replaced by her predecessor, Julie Howson, at much the same time that the leaders of the Massachusetts League were told by their lawyers that any test case should be brought not there but in Connecticut. Molly Cunningham continued to look for just such an opportunity throughout the fall and then into the early months of 1950, but nothing whatsoever materialized. In mid-February the sixty-two-year-old Cunningham informed the board that she wanted to step down as executive director as of the end of May, and the board easily and immediately agreed that Nancy Doggett Williams should step up to be Cunningham's successor.[61]

On May 18 Molly Cunningham delivered her sixth and final annual report as PPLC's executive director. She emphasized that "one of my greatest disappointments is that no suitable court case has been found," and reminded the board that "the fundamental issue of our fight to change the Connecticut birth control law is that of civil liberties." She had to concede that the outlook was not bright; doctors' enthusiasm for actively supporting reform seemed to be waning, and two Yale Law School students who had undertaken an exhaustive survey of the league's strategic options had come up with little to recommend. A new president, Mary Parker Milmine, would be succeeding Julie Howson, and Cunningham herself was not exactly retiring; that fall she would win election to the state house as a Republican representative from New Canaan.

Other than Cunningham's victory, PPLC activists found relatively little to celebrate in the November 1950 election results. Chester Bowles was turned out of office by Republican John Davis Lodge, but the Democrats retained a nineteen to seventeen majority in the state senate. Back in 1948 a few Republicans privately had mused as to whether the birth control issue was partially to blame for Bowles' victory, in that the Catholic church's electoral activism in selected legislative races might well have increased turnout among top-of-the-ticket Democratic voters, and now the same theory was bandied about once again to explain the narrow loss of Republican U.S. Senate nominee Prescott Bush to Democrat William Benton—even though Lodge at the same time had topped Bowles by some seventeen thousand votes.[62]

Given the dim legislative outlook, new PPLC president Molly Milmine, a Bryn Mawr graduate whose husband was assistant headmaster of an exclusive prep school, pressed for continued consideration of test case ideas as well as preparations for a 1951 doctors' bill. The initial legislative plan was to have four identical bills introduced—one each by Republican and Democratic members of both the house and the senate, but only three materialized, as not a single senate Democrat was willing to publicly support the legalization of contraception. In part the problem was that party leadership control of the legislature, and particularly the senate, had grown tighter and tighter in the five years since Hartford political boss John M. Bailey had become Democratic state chairman, with real authority being exercised by Bailey rather than by the elected legislators; in part the problem more specifically was the result of Bailey's extremely close, life-long friendship with former Hartford state Senator Joseph P. Cooney, who had been hired as principal legislative counsel and lobbyist by the Hartford Diocese several months after Bailey had become head of the state Democratic party.

Bailey was forty-seven, a graduate of Catholic University and Harvard Law School; Cooney was forty-four, a graduate of Georgetown University and Georgetown Law School, and in 1929 the two had begun a law practice together. In early 1933, during the second of four terms in the state senate, Joe Cooney had successfully sponsored Bailey for Bailey's first public post, a two-year appointment to a Hartford Police Court judgeship. The two had remained close ever since, and once Bailey became Democratic party chairman in 1946, the centralization of political power in Connecticut quickly returned to a level that had not been seen since the heyday of Republican J. Henry Roraback two decades earlier. By the time that the 1951 legislature convened, Bailey's power reached even well beyond the unusual authority of selecting Democratic floor leaders and committee chairmen; in the senate he employed the private caucus of the Democratic majority as a vehicle for all but totally eliminating public roll call votes from the senate's procedures. During the entire 1951 session only *eight* roll-call votes took place in the senate, and on *none* of them did even a single Democratic senator vote against the Bailey leadership's position.[63]

PPLC's three identical doctors' bills were introduced in the house and senate on January 30, but league officials had no serious hopes of success. Prior to the April 11 hearing the issue received almost no public attention, but officials of the Hartford Diocese convened two private meetings, one in New Haven and one in Hartford on the day of the hearing, to be certain that opponents would be appropriately represented and otherwise well-prepared. Diocesan chancellor Monsignor John J. Hayes chaired both sessions and was responsible for overall strategy, Joseph Cooney later indicated, while Cooney himself was in charge of organizing the appropriate speakers for the hearing. "The purely political aspects of the matter," Cooney explained, "were taken care of by Monsignor Hayes," who "directly approached the senators." Hayes also "arranged to have letters sent to Senators and Representatives by constituents," and also "arranged for women to sit in the galleries at the hearing and to voice their opposition."

The official diocesan representatives, including Cooney and Louise Fisher, played a smaller role at the actual hearing than did a number of outspoken legislative opponents of birth control. Bridgeport Representative Wilton Reinhardt insisted that "I think these bills can well be a step toward legalizing abortion," but overall, as the *Hartford Times* observed, "much of the bitterness evidenced at previous hearings was lacking" at the 1951 one. The two principal affirmative speakers were New Haven's Reverend C. Lawson Willard and West Hartford urologist Dr. Robert H. Hepburn, whose mother—and PPLC's landmark activist—had passed away less than a month earlier. Willard afterward thanked the committee and formally reminded them that the bills were designed "entirely to protect the health and lives of mothers," rather than to facilitate "the limitation of the number of children," but the proponents full well realized that no birth control bill, under whatever rationale, would ever be passed by John Bailey's state senate.[64]

The prominence of the Bailey-Cooney alliance influenced a number of onlookers, including PPLC president Molly Milmine and executive director Nancy Williams, to adopt a harsher, Sanger-like attitude toward the Catholic hierarchy than previously had characterized the Connecticut reformers. One New Haven protestant minister, new to the state, told Milmine after watching the opponents' performance at the hearing that "When you witness the bigotry and the blindness of the Totalitarianism of the Roman Catholic Church in this country, you can see that we have a real problem on our hands here." Milmine replied that he was quite right: "I entirely agree with you that we are fighting here something which is potentially as dangerous as Totalitarianism, and am tempted sometimes to rush the League into this more important and imminent fight." By mid-May, with the birth control bills still in committee, Nancy Williams underscored "the growing problem of Catholic domination in government" to PPLC's board. "The undeniable control by the Roman Catholic church of the Democratic party" had forged "the chains which bind the state Senate"; it also raised, in Milmine's words, the larger issue of "the danger the church is to the freedom of the individual." And, as Williams trenchantly explained, it was all on account of "a law which the Catholics themselves do not respect and which stays on the books for one reason only. It is a symbol of Catholic power."[65]

By the third week of May the Public Health and Safety Committee had voted eleven to four in favor of a birth control bill, but only after herculean efforts by Cornwall Representative Frank E. Calhoun did the measure actually make it to the house floor. On May 28 it passed on a vote of 121 to 62, with only three Democrats in favor, and ninety-two members not voting. Senate Public Health and Safety chairman Frank J. Monchun refused to bring the measure to the senate floor, however, despite a PPLC letter-writing campaign and distribution of leaflets in his Windsor district. The flyers attacked the 1879 law as "an infringement of personal liberty" and explained how PPLC's doctors' bill would protect "this 'freedom of choice' which is our birthright." Molly Milmine attempted to arrange a face-to-face meeting with John M. Bailey, "but each and every attempt to approach him proved futile." As close observer and former state Senator Herbert S. MacDonald commented on the unbreakable 1951 senate logjam, "All too obvious was the force of the State Democratic Chairman whose allegiance to the Catholic Church was all that was needed!"[66]

In the wake of yet one more legislative defeat, the PPLC leadership once again turned its focus toward potential court cases. At least one board member suggested they consider opening clinics in several cities "to test the actual enforcement of the present law," but Milmine continued to ponder some of the complicated declaratory judgment possibilities that had been suggested by the two Yale Law School students a year earlier. More experienced legal advisors judged those options too difficult to succeed, and spoke more positively of an actual clinic venture, but when Nancy Williams solicited Wiggin and Dana's opinion, Fritz Wiggin offered a distinctly chilly evaluation. There was no reason to believe that the Connecticut Supreme Court would decide differently on the basic question than it had back in *Tileston*, Wiggin declared. While there was "a reasonable possibility" that the United States Supreme Court might void the statute on Fourteenth Amendment due process liberty grounds if a criminal conviction under it was placed before them, any Connecticut prosecutor faced with a clinic opening might well proceed simply under the state's all-purpose conspiracy statute rather than get tied up in trying to win convictions under the use and aiding-and-abetting provisions. Faced with Wiggin's pessimistic perspective, Milmine, at the urging of Hartford insurance lawyer Buist Anderson, turned instead to a new and much younger possible lawyer, Hartford tax specialist John H. Riege, and in October PPLC formally asked Riege to survey test case prospects and report back by mid-December.[67]

In early November Riege met privately with retired Connecticut

Chief Justice William M. Maltbie "and had a very interesting and help-ful discussion with him for an hour or so concerning some of our problems," Riege told Milmine. Then in December Riege briefed the PPLC board on their potential legal options, explaining that the best possibility appeared to be a suit by a doctor and several patients requesting a declaratory judgment and an injunction against the 1879 statute from a *federal* district court. "The probability of obtaining a favorable decision in the [federal] District Court is greater than in the Connecticut Supreme Court," Riege explained. Additionally, any case involving an actual criminal prosecution of a doctor and/or patient would run the risk of significant punishment if the Connecticut courts, as expected, continued to follow *Nelson* and *Tileston*, and if the U.S. Supreme Court—as was "perhaps even probable," Riege warned—declined review pursuant to *Gardner*. Accepting Riege's projection that the chances of success were "reasonably good" in a federal declaratory action, the PPLC board authorized him and Milmine to proceed with further work toward creating such a case.[68]

During the early months of 1952 PPLC attempted to settle on a more experienced federal appellate litigator who could handle a case in conjunction with Riege. Some members objected to selecting Morris Ernst, and the Connecticut lawyers turned toward two other New York possibilities, Whitney North Seymour, of Simpson, Thacher and Bartlett, and John M. Harlan, a partner of the husband of one of PPLC's board members, Laura Bushby. Talk of PPLC's plans spread, and Riege scheduled a mid-March meeting with Seymour. Then, early in March, Milmine, Nancy Williams, and Laura Bushby all received telephone calls from the campaign manager for 1952 Republican Senate contender Prescott Bush. The manager "asked that the Planned Parenthood court case be postponed for the sake of Mr. Bush's cam-paign," but Molly Milmine "had replied that in her opinion postpone-ment would be impossible." When this news was shared with the board's executive committee, former president Julie Howson "suggest-ed that information about the nature of the case might reassure Mr. Bush, and it was agreed that this information [would] be given through Mr. Wilkie Bushby," the board member's husband. Riege's meeting with Whitney Seymour and his son Whitney, Jr., as well as PPFA attorney Fifield Workum, another Simpson, Thacher partner, took place as scheduled on March 20, and by early May preparatory work was underway, with a clear understanding that nothing would be ready for actual filing in advance of the November 1952 elections.[69]

PPLC's annual meeting agreed to shift the state office from

Hartford to New Haven. Office manager Mabel Robbins, who had been with the league for over sixteen years, going back to the early days of the original Hartford clinic, would be retiring at the end of June, and by late May PPLC had arranged to rent space at 38 Trumbull Street, in a largely residential block of lovely nineteenth-century town houses, just down the street from where Nowell Creadick had housed the league's office in the 1930s at 79 Trumbull. In late August, with nothing further having occurred concerning the possible court case, Seymour, Jr., alerted Riege that he and his father were coming to think that the procedural hurdles involved in any federal suit were considerable, and that even if those were overcome, the likelihood of success on the merits was "no better than fifty-fifty." He recommended that PPLC focus instead on legislative reform possibilities, but Riege reminded him in reply that "there is practically no chance of obtaining relief from the Connecticut Legislature" and that odds of fifty-fifty in a court case were much better prospects than anything else available. To Milmine, Riege put their choice somewhat more bluntly: "we do not see how the political situation could deteriorate much further."[70]

In mid-October Milmine and Riege went to New York for a major meeting with both Seymours. Seymour, Sr., now estimated their chances at 45 percent and recommended that PPLC wait until the conclusion of the spring 1953 legislative session; he also suggested that they probably should file an action in state rather than federal court. Three weeks later PPLC's strategic options shifted dramatically when the fall election results showed a Republican sweep and an apparent count of seventeen or perhaps eighteen firm supporters of birth control legalization in the thirty-six member state senate. In mid-November the board agreed to concentrate upon a legislative campaign, and Milmine advised Riege to focus on who ideally could litigate a state court test case come mid-1953 should that indeed prove necessary. By mid-January Riege had recommended and Milmine had interviewed a young partner at the Hartford law firm of Robinson, Robinson, and Cole, Bruce W. Manternach, and a legal fallback seemed ready should the legislative route fail once again.[71]

On February 3 the 1953 version of PPLC's doctors' bill was introduced by Fairfield Representative Norman K. Parsells. Within several weeks, however, indications of its likely prospects turned starkly negative with word that Republican Party leaders were fearful of future electoral fallout should the bill indeed pass and then be signed into law by Republican Governor John Davis Lodge. Moving swiftly to try to sidestep any Republican leadership decision to simply keep the bill in committee, PPLC leaders requested a personal meeting with Governor Lodge.[72]

On Thursday, March 12, Nancy Williams and PPLC legislative committee chairman Jane Daniells met with Lodge and his chief of staff, former state Senator Charles S. House. Apparently the session was an unmitigated disaster, with the prickly Lodge believing that the PPLC duo had obtained the appointment under "false pretenses." Within several days, as PPLC supporters from around the state wrote to Lodge urging him to back the Parsells bill, the governor apparently concluded that Williams and Daniells erroneously had passed the word that Lodge was opposed to passage. "I did not express an opinion on [the] legislation & I did not say I wanted to kill it," an angry Lodge jotted to himself. Lodge evidently had intimated to his visitors that perhaps the legislature might pass a bill providing for a popular referendum on birth control legalization, with the unspoken suggestion being that he and the Republican leadership would approve only this, as no referendum outcome could be blamed on the governor or his party. Republican National Committee member Meade Alcorn then sent Lodge a brief memo John Riege had prepared at Alcorn's suggestion, arguing that if a bill was not passed in 1953, the issue would only loom larger in future elections, and another PPLC supporter, Fairfield County attorney Leonard D. Adkins, began peppering the governor with feisty letters challenging him to start enforcing the 1879 statute if he did not believe it should be altered. The often-indecisive Lodge replied only that "I have expressed no opinion" on the Parsells bill.[73]

The 1953 hearing on the birth control measure was held on April 1, and it was a relatively brief and understated affair. Joe Cooney once again led the way for the diocesan opposition, and he quickly took the opportunity to throw down the political gauntlet of a popular vote resolution of the issue in the face of the bill's proponents: "It is our contention that the opponents of this bill are not a minority, and that any time the legislature wants to place the matter on a referendum, it will prove conclusively that our viewpoint is upheld by the majority of Connecticut citizens." Four days later Cooney repeated his suggestion, recommending that a birth control referendum be held in conjunction with any regularly scheduled state election, and Connecticut's newspapers gave wide voice to his challenge.[74]

PPLC lost little time in objecting to the referendum idea, arguing that it would be unconstitutional, very costly, and likely would incite religious strife. The Public Health and Safety Committee on April 7 voted 12 to 9 against a referendum proposal, in spite of reports that Governor Lodge and Republican leaders strongly backed the idea. Committee reconsideration was scheduled for April 15, and a number of advisors and supportive legislators advised PPLC to accept a referendum measure, whether or not it would prove constitutional. Senate committee chairman Benton H. Grant of Stamford privately advised Molly Milmine that "a bill with referendum may be able to pass the Senate," where as one without such a requirement stood "no chance whatsoever," but on April 14 the PPLC board voted unanimously to oppose any referendum proposal and to seek legal action to block it should it emerge from the legislature.[75]

On April 15 the Public Health and Safety Committee adopted a referendum amendment by 10 to 8 and then approved the amended bill by 11 to 8. The following day, amid rumors that the Roman Catholic hierarchy, despite Cooney's public pose, actually *opposed* any birth control referendum, diocesan Chancellor Hayes met privately with Governor Lodge in Stamford. Hayes reminded the governor how strongly the church supported the 1879 statute, evidently stressing how "the use of the sex function solely for pleasure . . . is an unnatural practice." Of course, Hayes noted, "we are not trying to impose our religious views on others," but "we feel that the moral principles which are the foundation of this law are unchangeable." Much more pointedly, the chancellor also told Lodge that "passage of the bill would be indelibly associated with your party administration and your leadership," and warned that any referendum would only stimulate interfaith bitterness. "We would, of course, win overwhelmingly as they realize, but at the risk of much unpleasantness."[76]

Senate chairman Grant, who had emerged as a reluctant champion of the referendum measure, tried to persuade Molly Milmine that PPLC should change its mind and accept a popular vote, but on April 23, to Milmine's tremendous relief, Legislative Commissioner Elmer S. Ryan formally ruled that any referendum bill would be unconstitutional. That resolved PPLC's most immediate worry, but it also all but guaranteed that no other version of a birth control bill would emerge from the 1953 Connecticut legislature. Senator Grant explained to one constituent that given the number of districts that encompassed urban, Catholic voters, the religious composition of the state senate, irrespective of party, was unlikely to change anytime soon. Hence the prospects for any legislative legalization of birth control were unlikely to get any better even in future legislatures: "I do not expect the existing statute to be altered in any way within a generation."

Molly Milmine and other onlookers reluctantly acknowledged that Senator Grant was undeniably correct. Milmine already had put Bruce Manternach in touch with a Sharon physician, Dr. Robert L. Fisher, who had suggested he might act as a test case plaintiff along with a patient or two, and now Warren Upson added his voice, telling Milmine he was "enthusiastically in favor" of court action. "I believe that the existing law is unconstitutional" and would be so declared if and when the question came before the United States Supreme Court on the merits.[77]

PPLC nonetheless did not want to give up the 1953 legislative fight without at least some further struggle, but on May 5 the Public Health and Safety Committee tabled the birth control bill by a vote of 11 to 8. The birth control story remained in the news, however, when Yale Law School professor Vern Countryman—Justice Douglas's clerk on *Tileston*—took United Press International correspondent David Robinson on a Saturday afternoon visit to a Liggett Drug Store in Hamden, where for three dollars Countryman easily purchased a box of Ramses condoms. "From the drug store," Countryman later recounted, "Robinson and I went to the Hamden Police Station where I approached the lieutenant on duty at the desk, showed him my purchase, and said I wished to file criminal charges against the drug store. The lieutenant's response was that the articles I had purchased were legal." Countryman unsuccessfully tried to persuade first the lieutenant, and then a Hamden police detective, otherwise, but was told to see the local prosecutor, who was away from home. Early Monday morning Countryman and Robinson called on the prosecutor, who "was not enthusiastic" and, per *Corbett*, noted the difference between prophylactic and contraceptive uses. Countryman reiterated his desire to file charges, but then the prosecutor mentioned that the Liggett's was a locally owned franchise, not a corporate property. For Countryman, who purposely had chosen a chain store, that was a fatal flaw, for he had not wanted to target some unfortunate individual druggist. Countryman dropped his request, and his venture immediately faded from Connecticut's front pages.[78]

The day after Countryman's saga concluded, Cornwall Representative Frank Calhoun, the 1951 birth control sponsor, and New Canaan Representative Molly Cunningham, PPLC's former executive director, began circulating a discharge petition to bring the 1953 bill to the house floor with or without a Public Health and Safety Committee report. Within four days they had more than the 140 necessary signatures, and the bill was placed on the house calendar.

Leonard Adkins and several other PPLC supporters in the Norwalk area attempted a different version of the Countryman ploy by mailing condoms to the Fairfield County state's attorney and to Governor Lodge, but they attracted only news coverage, not indictments. The prosecutor contented himself with saying that yes, mailing the rubbers *was* a violation of the law; the governor continued to decline comment, but even four decades later many small foil packages of desiccated, 1953-vintage condoms could still be found safely stapled to the incoming letters in Lodge's official papers in the Connecticut State Archives.[79]

On May 27, following a ninety-minute debate, the house passed PPLC's doctors' bill on a vote of 147 to 75, with only four Democrats among the yeas. Almost a dozen opponents warned against "the subjugation of man to passion and artificial sensuousness" or the danger of "race suicide"; one Wallingford representative recommended that "if our women would only get out their knitting bags and knit a few booties for the future generations, I think they would be well satisfied and happy, instead of self-centered." The following day a somewhat different bill was brought to the senate floor, but only after a private Republican caucus had agreed that the measure would be killed on an unrecorded voice vote. Only two senators spoke publicly on behalf of it; afterward one of them, Public Health and Safety Committee chairman Ben Grant, bluntly told his constituents that the bill had failed on account of one single organization: "I do not know of one non-Catholic opposed to the bill." The thirty-year battle over birth control, he said, showed Connecticut's democratic institutions to be feeble and dishonorable: "The issue hangs like a ghost over the Legislature. It causes more double talk, insincerity, cringing and juggling than all other issues put together. . . . Representative government is revealed at its frightened worst."[80]

Molly Milmine reacted to the legislative denouement by trying to pump renewed effort into PPLC's search for a test case and willing plaintiffs. Only in the state's more rural counties were court dockets free from serious backlogs that would delay action on a case for many months after it was filed, and by early August Milmine believed she had found an appropriate and eager female patient, someone to combine with Dr. Fisher, through a recommendation from Jo Evarts. Bruce Manternach, however, the Hartford attorney who earlier had been retained to handle a case, now had a full fall schedule, and by early October he was telling Milmine that it would be December or January before he would have any time for PPLC's potential endeavor.[81]

PPLC since 1946 had been providing a very modest subsidy for a

Yale infertility clinic that was directed by Dr. Herbert Thoms, the chairman of the medical school's obstetrics and gynecology department, and by late in the summer of 1953 PPLC had agreed to lend similar financial assistance to a marriage consultation service, based in the department of psychiatry, so that a part-time psychiatric social worker, Miriam Cohen Harper, could be added to the staff. Then, late in August 1953, Nancy Doggett Williams told Molly Milmine that she would be tendering her resignation as executive director, effective September 30, in order to take another job that was closer to her home. On top of that, PPLC fund-raising was running twelve thousand dollars behind the projected annual budget, and Williams's one assistant, Jennie Heiser, who was primarily responsible for fund solicitations, had indicated that she would be leaving sometime within the next four to eight months.

No real efforts to locate or identify a replacement for Williams took place during September or October, and budget worries were somewhat alleviated by the absence of having to pay a director's salary. Milmine continued to try to stimulate development of a test case, and a board subcommittee discussed future legislative options, but as of early November some board members wondered whether hiring a new director should be further postponed so that expenses could be minimized. One officer recommended that Milmine contact Helen Buxton, the wife of the newly named Yale ob/gyn department chairman and infertility clinic director, who was succeeding the retiring Dr. Thoms, as one of a number of potential new donors, and by the end of November the sense of imminent financial crisis had passed, even if the director's job remained vacant.[82]

Then one day Jennie Heiser was saying hello to the woman whose home was next door to the office, at 40 Trumbull, a woman in her fifties whom both Heiser and Molly Milmine knew as the executive secretary of the New Haven Human Relations Council. The neighbor understood that Nancy Williams had not yet been replaced, and Heiser, referring to their delayed search for a successor, half-seriously asked, "How would you like to be director of Planned Parenthood?" The neighbor answered "Phooey," but Heiser mentioned the idea, and the conversation, to Molly Milmine, who agreed that it was worth following up. So the subsequent day or soon thereafter, Molly Milmine went next door to talk with Estelle Trebert Griswold about the possibility of becoming the new executive director of Connecticut Planned Parenthood.[83]

CHAPTER THREE

One Vote Shy:
Estelle Griswold, Fowler Harper,
and the U.S. Supreme Court,
1954–1961

Estelle Trebert Griswold had mixed feelings about Molly Milmine's suggestion that she consider becoming executive director of Connecticut Planned Parenthood. On one hand, as she later explained, "I needed a job very desperately," for while being executive secretary of the New Haven Human Relations Council might seem professionally significant to Milmine and others, it was no longer a paying position; there simply was no money. On the other—well, Estelle Griswold did not feel she should explain that to Molly Milmine either.

Birth control was something Stelle Griswold of course had heard about; she and her husband, Dick, both Connecticut natives, had moved back to the state three years earlier. But birth control was not something Stelle Griswold knew very much about; in fact, as she explained it later, at the time of her first conversation with Molly Milmine, Stelle Griswold had never seen a diaphragm, did not know what one was, and was not sure what the word really meant.

Having been born Roman Catholic, in Hartford, in June 1900, was not the reason. Although her father, Frank, a toolmaker, was not especially religious, her mother, Jennie Church Trebert, was Catholic, and even decades later Stelle would acknowledge that "I'm still considered a Catholic on the rolls." Stelle had thought her parents had "a very strange marriage," for her father was "a very volatile person" while her mother was "very placid." There had been two older sons, only one of whom, Raymond, was still living when Stelle was born, and church-going never played a significant role in Stelle's youth. She attended the Hartford public schools, skipping both the fourth and seventh grades, and then

Hartford High School, where she later said she was "kind of a tom boy" who had been suspended more than once for playing hookey and recruiting boys to do the same. Many of Stelle's acquaintances, like her friend Hilda Crosby, who also graduated in 1920, came from somewhat better-off families, and most of them, unlike Stelle, went on to college. "I was very upset," she recalled years later, "when they all went to college and there was no money nor interest on the part of my parents."

Stelle wanted to be a singer. "She had a beautiful contralto voice," Hilda Crosby Standish later remembered, and for three years Stelle attended Hartford's Hartt School of Music, rooming there and working in a bank to support herself. More than once, she later said, she went for medical checkups to Dr. Thomas N. Hepburn, who lived near Stelle's grandmother and whose wife was the well-known suffragist. Then, in 1922, without ever previously having left greater Hartford, she defied her family's wishes and simply moved to Paris. Stelle got an office job as a bookkeeper, started singing at the American Cathedral, and quickly learned colloquial French. "I can swear in French with the best taxi driver there is," she later boasted. She caught tuberculosis, spent some time in Nice, became engaged to a playwright, and ended up back in another office job in Paris.

Then word reached Stelle that her mother was extremely ill, and reluctantly she returned to Hartford. She took a job in a bank, and first her father, and then her mother, passed away. Stelle went to New York to audition for singing jobs, was sent to Chicago for a position there, traveled from city to city singing with a show group for six months, and then ended up back in Hartford, working as a secretary to a gentleman who was the Belgian consul for New England. In Hartford she remet Richard Whitmore Griswold, two years her senior, whom she had known at Hartford High School before he had gone off to Yale and to brief service in World War I. Dick Griswold had had a series of advertising jobs in New York and New England, and had unsuccessfully tried to start an agency of his own in Hartford. By the fall of 1927 Stelle and Dick had decided to marry, and Dick took a salaried job with the Guardian Life Insurance Company in New York. They were married on October 20 at the Cathedral of St. John the Divine, with Hilda Crosby and other Hartford friends in attendance, and Stelle lined up various radio singing jobs while Dick commuted into the city from their home in Mount Vernon. She and her singing tutor took a long trip to France, but an illness of Dick's forced Stelle to return home prematurely.

Early in 1935 Guardian Life transferred Dick Griswold from New

York to Washington. Stelle's singing tutor died, and Stelle gave up her idea of a career in music. After an illness of her own, Stelle ended up working as an office volunteer for her own doctor, and started taking courses at George Washington University toward a certificate as a medical technologist. That developed into a full-time job at GWU, and when Dick was called to active duty in Washington in Naval Intelligence in the fall of 1941, Stelle continued to work as a lab instructor at George Washington.

Immediately upon the fall of Berlin in 1945, Dick Griswold was dispatched there to take charge of "investigative teams" under the rubric of the U.S. State Department's Office of Political Affairs. Stelle went first to London, and then in late 1945 obtained a refugee resettlement job in Holland with the United Nations Relief and Rehabilitation Agency. Some months later Stelle was shifted to Frankfurt, then to Munich, and then Bremen, while Dick eventually was moved to Bremerhaven. By 1947 Stelle's resettlement work was under the aegis of the American Christian Committee for Refugees, which in early 1948 was absorbed by Church World Service (CWS), a part of the World Council of Churches. Much of Stelle's work involved helping people from eastern Europe relocate to South America, and Stelle herself endured a memorable but unpleasant month-long crossing of the Atlantic to Argentina on an overcrowded ship.

In December 1950 Estelle returned to the United States, working for CWS in New York and commuting on weekends up to Connecticut, where Dick already had bought a house near New London. In mid-1951, tired of both the CWS bureaucracy and the long weekly commute, Estelle took the job with the New Haven Human Relations Council, Dick shifted his advertising work to New Haven, and they purchased the attractive town house at 40 Trumbull Street. Two years later, at Thanksgiving 1953, with the Human Relations Council out of money, Dick and Stelle were still there, and were eager to remain.[1]

Molly Milmine was extremely impressed by her first long conversation with Estelle Griswold. "Her qualifications are perfect," Milmine told Molly Cunningham, and other PPLC officers agreed "that there is no point to look further." Stelle had led Milmine to believe that she "had two other offers which may get her away from us," but Milmine hoped to convene the PPLC board by early the next week so that a formal job offer could be authorized.

As Estelle Griswold pondered whether to accept the forthcoming offer, she thought of one old friend, someone she had not seen in some years, who certainly could offer some knowledgeable advice—Hilda Crosby Standish. Stelle knew that Hilda once had been very active in the Connecticut League; indeed, perhaps the last time Stelle actually had seen Hilda was sometime in the late 1930s, when Hilda had told Stelle about how much she enjoyed being medical director of the Hartford clinic. "I met her on a train one day," Stelle recalled, "and she told me what she was doing. I wasn't interested. It just left me cold. I wanted children and hadn't been able to have them."

Stelle in 1953 was not going to raise that with Hilda, or with Milmine, but she did want to hear Hilda's views on PPLC, and so after an initial phone call, Stelle drove up to Hartford to visit her old high school classmate. Hilda Standish had been busy raising her own family, and she thought Connecticut Planned Parenthood in 1953 was but a dim shadow of what the league had been fifteen years earlier in the era of Kit Hepburn and Sallie Pease. "It's practically dead," she told Stelle after retracing some of the earlier history. "If you really want to work your head off and get it above ground and going again, there's no better place to work," but the odds on making it a success were very long indeed. But Estelle, Hilda Standish later remembered in describing that conversation, was someone "for whom that was a real challenge." "She was that type of person; that was just the thing that set her off." "I thought if anybody could do it, Stelle could," because "she always had her own ideas," and "she got things done . . . like Mrs. Hepburn."

Within two or three days of her visit to Hilda Standish, Estelle Griswold received Molly Milmine's letter formally stating that the PPLC board on December 8 had voted unanimously to offer her the position of executive director, starting January 1, at an annual salary of five thousand forty dollars. The board, Milmine said, had been extremely impressed by her "phenomenally interesting experience." Stelle, particularly affected by what was undeniably "a very good salary" offer, paused only two days before accepting. "I didn't know a thing about it," she later remembered, but it was too good, too convenient, and too challenging to imagine turning down. She was "honored and pleased" and "happy to accept," Estelle wrote Milmine. "Under your leadership and guidance I hope to make a real contribution."[2]

Being such a close and immediate neighbor offered Estelle Griswold an easy excuse for beginning to familiarize herself with PPLC's office and programs even before she officially went on the payroll. A mid-January board meeting at which Estelle would formally be introduced was snowed out, but Molly Milmine brought her quickly up to speed

about the present status of the long-delayed possibility that Bruce
Manternach would file a court suit on behalf of the northwestern
Connecticut woman who had been recommended by Jo Evarts. The
patient remained ready and willing, but wanted assurance, simply in
light of her husband's employment at a prep school with a potentially
troublesome headmaster, that a case could be filed and taken forward
without her actual name having to appear in any of the public papers.
Milmine was hopeful, but Manternach immediately replied that that
would not be possible: "she will have to be a plaintiff and her name
will have to be used in the title of the action." When Milmine passed
along that unhappy news, the result was just what she had expected.
"Our Kent witness has folded up," Milmine told Manternach—"fear
for her husband's position and the reaction of his chief." "I find it discouraging to have to wait so long to find someone, but I can easily
sympathize with them for not longing for the inevitable publicity."[3]

By early February Estelle Griswold was getting fully acclimated. On
February 4 she and Jennie Heiser attended a Yale School of Public
Health seminar on planned parenthood that featured a Yale gynecologist, Dr. Luther Musselman, and an outspoken professor from the Yale
Law School, Fowler V. Harper, whose wife Miriam held the social
work position at Yale's marriage consultation service that was subsidized by PPLC. Finances were a serious concern, Estelle told the board
members when she finally met them on February 9, for in January the
organization had spent nineteen hundred dollars while taking in only
three hundred dollars. She already was attending meetings of local
PPLC supporters in Norwalk, New Canaan, Darien, and Hartford,
and in early March Estelle told the board that those visits, along with a
thorough review of PPLC's files and an introductory visit to PPFA in
New York, had convinced her that much more outreach was needed.
PPLC's program, she stressed, "must stem from locals, not be super-
imposed" from above. The organization "must reach and represent not
only a small intellectual group"—namely the upper-middle class people who were so well-represented on PPLC's board—"but become a
mass movement."[4]

Molly Milmine continued to hope that they could find a willing and
appropriate plaintiff for a test case, but the spring months passed without progress. The new director of the Yale infertility clinic that PPLC
had long subsidized, Dr. C. Lee Buxton, introduced himself and
inquired about increased funding, but a commitment already had been
made to try to channel additional dollars into the marriage consultation
service. PPLC's annual meeting, on May 18, agreed that a 1955 legisla-

tive effort no doubt would be mounted, and Estelle Griswold, in her most extensive remarks so far, reminded everyone that the planned parenthood movement, both in Connecticut and nationally, would have to enlarge and expand if it was to succeed. "For thirty-seven years the upper upper and upper middle classes have been our support, but it is only the mass of people that can swing the vote." Additionally, PPLC's need for ethnic and economic diversity was also clear. The departing Jennie Heiser's financial job would be filled part time by a young black woman, Frances McCoy, whom Estelle had just recruited, but more was needed, as everyone who had seen that morning's head-lines—on the momentous U.S. Supreme Court school desegregation decision in *Brown* v. *Board of Education*—ought to realize. "We must show active interest in better housing, employment, good schools, and minority rights as related to our problem," Estelle insisted. Molly Milmine, in her own remarks, went more than slightly out of her way to underline what an energizing and transformative effect Estelle Griswold already was having on Connecticut Planned Parenthood:

> She has brought us new interests, new connections, and a new eye to our problems. She, in the five months she has been with us, has already brought us new ideas, new thinking, and new friends and affiliations. She admits to no experience with legislative or political activities, but at the rate she has caught up with us already, I see no reason why she can-not do almost anything. We are very fortunate to have been able to gain her interest and her wide experience.[5]

The summer of 1954 witnessed a minor stir over a new requirement adopted by Connecticut's Commissioner of Food and Drugs, who had regulatory authority over pharmacists, that druggists should dispense diaphragms to women only upon presentation of a written prescription from an M.D. Some private doctors were reluctant to put their names on such written documents, and some druggists were perturbed that certain private physicians were simply purchasing and then supplying diaphragms themselves, thus leaving pharmacists out of the business. After much private uncertainty, the matter was resolved in September when the commissioner privately circulated a letter stating that "there is no reason why vaginal diaphragms may not be prescribed or ordered by a physician and such order filled by a pharmacist. . . . Such order may be given orally or in writing."[6]

Even by mid-1954 Estelle Griswold believed that it would be some time before PPLC would be organizationally strong enough to win the legalization battle that still lay ahead. "We have a long way to go," she lectured the board in one report, "before we make a real impact on the public." "It is somewhat discouraging at times," she allowed to one PPFA staffer, "but I am convinced that with a little patience, hard work," and "good counsel," that matters would soon improve. "If we keep in mind the work," she told one discouraged PPLC supporter, "that gave us our Constitution, the Emancipation Proclamation, the U.N., votes for women and many other privileges that we accept for granted today, we should continue to work for our cause. We may not have 'success in our time,' but we may help to achieve it for future generations."[7]

By the fall of 1954, with the 1955 legislative session on the horizon, PPLC's financial picture had modestly improved. Fran McCoy moved from part-time to full-time work, and when Dr. Buxton met with the board to ask for an additional three or four thousand dollars for the infertility clinic in 1955, the request was eventually approved. Two new part-time employees, secretary Anita Beloff and publicity director Ellen Switzer, also joined the staff, and an increased number of public meetings—including one in New Haven featuring Reverend C. Lawson Willard and law professor Fowler V. Harper—began to be held across the state. The November election results were unsatisfying, with a Democratic majority of twenty state senators in the offing, but Molly Milmine continued to hope that they might yet discover some qualified female patient who would be a willing test case plaintiff.[8]

In late January both a doctors' bill and a repeal measure were introduced in the 1955 Connecticut legislature at PPLC's behest. Press observers forecast "certain defeat" for both proposals even well in advance of the April 20 hearing, at which Reverend Willard and Dr. Hilda Crosby Standish led the proponents, with another M.D. reading a statement on behalf of a busy Dr. C. Lee Buxton. The opponents were managed once again by diocesan spokesman Joseph P. Cooney, who included a personal attack on Hilda Standish in his remarks, alleging that she was "well known" as an advisory board member of the Euthanasia Society. Several opposing legislators offered defenses of "the laws of God," and one opposing doctor warned that PPLC "is a small, local part of a large, well-financed international movement" that was not further identified, but by previous years' standards, the 1955 hearing was relatively tame.[9]

On May 3 the Public Health and Safety Committee on voice votes overwhelmingly approved both the repeal measure and the doctors' bill. Two weeks later both bills came to the house floor, with opponents monopolizing much of the debate. One Bridgeport representative alleged that the repeal measure could "be interpreted as legalizing abortion," and a Plainfield member complained that the trouble with the bill's proponents is that "they want to play, but they don't want to pay," but both the doctors' bill, by a margin of 150 to 91, and the repeal measure, by a vote of 132 to 91, passed easily. On May 23, however, the senate rejected both bills on voice votes with hardly any debate, and the 1955 legislative effort to legalize birth control came to a quick and quiet end.[10]

After the 1955 session, PPLC realized more clearly than ever before that there simply would never be a way to get any birth control bill through the state senate in the absence of a decisive Republican majority. Democratic Party chairman John Bailey, PPLC's officers told the PPLC annual meeting, "has become so powerful that the Bishop no longer needs to watch over the Senate on this bill." The party chairman, although of course not a member of the senate, attended each day's private caucus of Democratic senators, and as one freshman Democrat later explained, Bailey's "ability to help or restrain the ambition of the aspiring politician plays no insignificant role" in ensuring that not a single Democratic senator would step out of line on any bill about which Bailey had a decided preference.

Estelle Griswold appreciated the partisan dynamics, and was trying to channel more and more PPLC effort into building groups of local supporters all across the state, especially in the eastern half of Connecticut, where PPLC never had had any significant presence. Estelle herself had attended and spoken at approximately seventy local PPLC meetings of one sort of another in just her first five months on the job, and now, with Molly Milmine stepping down as president after six years, Estelle hoped to begin drawing a new wave of volunteers into the organization. The new president, Claudia McGinley of New Canaan, fully agreed, and later explained that it was largely because of Estelle Griswold's vitality and dynamism that she had agreed to accept the presidency. One of McGinley's first new moves was to persuade Dr. Lee Buxton to become chairman of a revived medical advisory committee, and Buxton did so only after endorsing Estelle Griswold's view that wider political organizing, rather than professional lobbying, would be the only way to prevail: "if the people of the State through their Legislature, do not want to pass the legislation which the League advocates, the medical profession as such is not the organization to try to put it across."[11]

By early June Estelle for the first time was turning her own attention toward test case possibilities, and a review of all the prior years' unpro-

ductive correspondence convinced her that the league's remaining relationship with both John Riege and Bruce Manternach, if any, needed
immediate review. Estelle went to New York for an introductory chat
with Harriet Pilpel and a similar discussion with Patrick Malin, the
executive director of the American Civil Liberties Union (ACLU).
Estelle concluded that a functioning legal advisory committee had to be
revived, and by early September both she and Claudia McGinley began
meeting with Yale Law School professors Fowler Harper and Ralph S.
Brown. A fund-raising shortfall led to the termination of PPLC's support for Miriam Harper's marriage counseling position, but Estelle and
McGinley started thinking about a brand-new initiative, namely open
and publicly advertised PPLC referrals for poorer women desiring
diaphragm fittings to the birth control clinic that Planned Parenthood
of Eastern Westchester operated in Port Chester, New York, just across
the Connecticut state line from Greenwich. The Port Chester clinic
already quietly offered reduced-rate services to Connecticut residents,
and in early November Griswold and McGinley held their first meeting with the Port Chester directors to discuss an open and official
referral program.[12]

On December 1 PPLC sponsored a public forum at Yale Medical
School that featured both Fowler Harper and Lee Buxton, and by
Christmastime Griswold and McGinley's referral plan had received
official approval from PPFA in New York. In mid-January Estelle distributed a proposal recommending formal adoption of a public referral
service, and noting that if any Connecticut authorities sought to challenge the policy, PPLC in conjunction with its Yale advisors and the
ACLU would be able to defend the program on First Amendment
freedom of speech grounds. An office would be opened in Norwalk to
coordinate appointments and transportation to the Port Chester clinic;
an additional benefit of such a public outreach effort might be the
identification of an ideal patient for a test case. "Our first aim," Estelle
wrote, "is to help women, for health or economic reasons, to regulate
the size of their families." PPFA, highly impressed with the "high pow-
ered, efficient dynamo" now directing the Connecticut League, agreed
to contribute three thousand dollars, or about half the first year cost of
the program; PPLC would raise the rest.

On January 24 the PPLC board, with two Port Chester representatives in attendance, formally approved the referral operation. By mid-
February PPFA had secured initial funds from an "anonymous"
donor—actually St. Louis vaginal foam manufacturer Joseph Sunnen—
and PPLC was beginning to train volunteers for handling the actual

referrals. Many of the lawyers were somewhat dubious that a First Amendment claim would be a decisive defense if the referral service did draw prosecutorial attention under the 1879 statute and the auxiliary aiding and abetting provision, but all agreed that any such interference was relatively unlikely.[13]

In mid-March the upcoming opening of the referral service was announced to the Connecticut press, with significant stories running in seemingly every newspaper in the state. Most quoted Claudia McGinley as emphasizing that "we feel that it is our right under the First Amendment to the U.S. Constitution to give information about such centers in other states to husbands and wives who seek it." The standard dispatch also added that "Planned Parenthood believes that all married couples have a democratic right to this knowledge," and on April 10 the first formal referrals from the Norwalk office were transported to the Port Chester clinic.[14]

Estelle Griswold and her colleagues were deeply pleased with the success of the referral project. No legal complaints or challenges were voiced, and for the first time since Estelle's arrival more than two years earlier, PPLC finally had a tangible program. More importantly, as the minutes of May's annual meeting noted, the referral program also represented "the first actual service rendered by PPLC for fifteen years." Estelle explained her desire to eventually expand the referrals to other Planned Parenthood clinics in Mt. Kisco, New York, and Providence, Rhode Island, but PPLC as yet had neither the personnel nor the funds for that scale of activity. Everyone also hoped that a test case patient might somehow appear, but no wide-ranging search for one was underway. "We are fortunate in having as a director a person of imagination, experience, and organizational ability," Beatrice Hessel, who headed one board committee, told the meeting, but "we have a small, much too small, nucleus of *working* volunteers."[15]

The financial burden of the referral project led PPLC to notify Lee Buxton that its support for the infertility clinic would have to end at the close of the year, and throughout the summer and into the fall Estelle continued to hope for a test case. PPFA and its "anonymous" donor, Joseph Sunnen, were somewhat unhappy that the referral project, although quite successful, was not generating any national publicity or press attention, and both Griswold and McGinley had to invest unnecessary time in persuading PPFA to actually hand over the promised funds. As the fall elections approached, Molly Milmine in particular kept a close eye on the nominations and contests for different state senate seats, but when the November results and Dwight D.

Eisenhower's coattails registered an unprecedented Republican sweep—thirty-one Republicans and only five Democrats in the state senate—PPLC's legislative hopes immediately soared higher than ever before.[16]

PPLC quickly decided to go with a doctors' bill rather than a repeal measure in the 1957 legislature, and by early December it was well appreciated that the thirty-one senate Republicans might not be quite as promising a group as some first thought, for some thirteen of them—along with the five Democrats—were Roman Catholics, a potentially lethal opposing bloc. As of late January, when Kent Representative Francis C. Cady formally introduced House Bill 572, Molly Milmine believed PPLC had sixteen firm senate supporters and a good shot at winning either support or convenient absences from up to five more. "This session is our big chance for success," she told Griswold and the board, and "the hearing will be as medical as we can make it."[17]

Lee Buxton willingly acceded to Milmine's request that he prepare to play a leading role in the mid-March hearing. Reviewing the transcript of the 1955 one, he told Milmine, left him both "amused" and "disturbed" at the misleading nature of the opposing physicians' claims. "I do think that the simple presentation of two or three cases which have had tragic sequelae here" at Yale's ob/gyn ward at the Grace–New Haven Hospital within recent weeks "might make a fairly dramatic impression" on legislators: a twenty-eight-year-old woman, "Irene W.," who had died three days earlier from severe rheumatic heart disease that had been exacerbated by her six-month pregnancy; a twenty-three-year-old woman with very high blood pressure and in her fourth month of pregnancy, "Ruth O.," whom Buxton feared might very well die because of a severe cerebral hemorrhage. Milmine encouraged him in his preparations, and by late February she had also arranged for Sharon's Dr. Robert Fisher—PPLC's willing prospective plaintiff of several years earlier—to likewise be a featured witness. A week later Milmine gave the board's executive committee her most optimistic report yet, saying "we now have eighteen senators who are with us," although "some more firmly than others," in addition to two others who "will not vote at all." Other observers estimated the dependable total at only fifteen, but Milmine mused about whether Democratic Governor Abraham Ribicoff—who had voted against birth control legalization as a house member—would sign this bill should it reach his desk. Experienced advisors stressed that PPLC's low profile was all to the good, especially in light of a major sectarian battle that was brewing over Archbishop Henry J. O'Brien—and Joseph Cooney's—decision that Catholic forces would go all-out to win legislative approval for a bill that would authorize publicly funded school bus transportation for nonpublic—i.e., parochial—school students.[18]

At the March 21 hearing, Buxton, in countering some of the opponents' 1955 remarks, emphasized that birth control and abortion—"killing another individual by therapeutic abortion"—were highly dissimilar. The latter involved "the killing of an unborn child" whereas birth control "is as different from abortion as day is from night." Buxton, Fisher and a third colleague were followed by Joseph Cooney and several opposing physicians. One of them sought to persuade the committee that any use of birth control was harmful both to a woman and to any children she might have. "Sexuality . . . must be fully satisfied in order to maintain emotional health and equilibrium," Dr. Salvatore Carraba of Hartford asserted. "Many women using contraceptive devices are frigid, and present a variety of ailments which are really a manifestation of their lack of sexual gratification." Carraba was not asked what experiences his opinions were based upon, nor was he questioned about his second major claim: "Psychiatrists have noted that the problem child's behavior can be traced to the emotionally unstable and sexually frustrated mother using birth control measures."[19]

A dismayed Lee Buxton criticized such "irresponsible medical comments" privately to Estelle Griswold, and in early April the Public Health and Safety Committee approved the bill on a vote of 15 to 6. Press observers reported, in distinct contrast to Molly Milmine's earlier optimism, that there were some twenty-two firm no votes in the senate, but on April 17 the house passed the bill by the impressive margin of 170 to 58. One week later, however, a private senate caucus in advance of the public floor vote resulted in a tally of fourteen yeas, twenty nays, and two abstentions. Hence the principal proponent, Wethersfield Republican Elmer S. Watson, agreed to simply a voice vote on the floor, and the bill was quickly defeated in what the *Hartford Courant* estimated was "about ten seconds."[20]

Estelle and her colleagues were disappointed but not surprised at the legislative denouement. The referral service was an ongoing success, and Stelle told PPLC's annual meeting in late May that "Our program is growing but our organization and fund-raising are still weak." PPLC's number one priority, she said, was to "Raise more money!"; privately her hopes of generating one or two test cases, right there in New Haven, were distinctly higher than ever before. Claudia McGinley privately praised her as "a dynamo of energy," and sometime in early June, after more than one attempt, Estelle finally succeeded in arranging a private conversation with New Haven County State's Attorney Ab Ullman, still in office more than fourteen years after his victory in *Tileston*. Ullman conceded that PPLC had no chance of modifying the anticontraception statute in the legislature, but he apparently was noncommittal as to whether he would at all welcome another situation that would place him in the position of having to defend a statute that he personally disliked.[21]

The summer and fall of 1957 were seemingly quiet for PPLC. In late June the office moved five doors up Trumbull Street, to number 48, where they could enjoy substantially more space than had been available at number 38. Stelle's salary was increased to six thousand dollars, and in October she attended an International Planned Parenthood conference in Berlin, where for the first time she met the ageing Margaret Sanger. But much more importantly, by sometime early in January 1958 her hope of actually filing a test case was beginning to approach fruition as Lee Buxton resolved that he and—presumably—several of his patients would go to court in the case that everyone had discussed—but no one had ever filed—in the fourteen years since the Supreme Court's rejection of *Tileston v. Ullman*.[22]

Charles Lee Buxton had been chairman of Yale's ob/gyn department, and responsible for its services at Grace–New Haven Hospital, for almost four years at the time that he agreed to be the lead plaintiff whom PPLC had been seeking for so many years. Fifty-three years old, he had grown up in St. Paul, Minnesota, where his father operated a lumber business. While attending a New Jersey prep school he had suffered a football injury that required multiple operations on his spine, and eighteen months recuperation, but he had gone on to graduate from Princeton and then earned his M.D. degree at Columbia in 1932. After internships and residencies, he joined Columbia's medical faculty in 1938, specializing in research into cures for female infertility. World War II drew Buxton into the Navy for three years, but afterward he returned to Columbia and by 1951 he was a full professor with a lucrative private practice. But his uppermost professional goal was to have a departmental chairmanship, and when Yale, in 1953, offered him just that, he eagerly accepted, even at the cost—a very substantial cost—of giving up his private practice in return for extensive and unremunerative administrative duties. His four children—ages six to eleven—were all in school, and his wife Helen, a native of Massachusetts, was more than a little ambivalent about the move from cosmopolitan New York to modest New Haven, and about the challenges that their dramatically reduced income would pose for family finances. But for Lee Buxton the chairmanship was more than worth it, and he had plunged eagerly into all its duties—"he was really married to the job," Helen recalled almost forty years later. The PPLC-supported infertility clinic was one of those responsibilities, and when the request had come to testify at the March 1957 legislative hearing, Lee Buxton had willingly accepted.[23]

The death of Irene W., and the serious illness of Ruth O.—the two serious pregnancy-related cases from early 1957—had each influenced Buxton's legislative testimony about how the 1879 statute hindered women's health care, but after the hearing, as he later recalled, "I sort of gave up the idea for a while." But the problems did not go away. There was apparently another pregnancy-related fatality, and Ruth "Oldendorf"'s[24] pregnancy and extremely high blood pressure, while not fatal, nonetheless had had tragic results: she had suffered a serious stroke, and in June 1957 had miscarried a stillborn, seven-month fetus. The aftermath of the stroke had left her with impaired speech, only partial use of her right leg, little if any use of her right arm, and only modest hopes for future improvement. It had been a devastating experience for both Ruth and her husband, and another pregnancy would undeniably prove fatal. Additionally, just a few weeks after his legislative testimony, another patient, Anne K., who because of a blood disorder already had endured three unsuccessful pregnancies, suffered yet another full-term miscarriage. Both she and her husband, Hector, had felt traumatized by the repeated experience, and increasingly despaired about their hope of having children.

Lee Buxton saw a good deal of both Ruth and Bob Oldendorf, and Anne and Hector Kinloch, during those months, and their difficulties were much on his mind. Then early in the fall another case presented itself. Elizabeth "Odegard"[25] had arrived at Grace–New Haven Hospital just a few weeks earlier, with an incurably ill infant. Her two previous babies had already died in very early infancy—at nine and six days, respectively—within the previous three years, also because of unidentified congenital effects, and on October 17, at age ten weeks, this little boy too passed away. For the Odegards, as for the Oldendorfs and the Kinlochs, these tragic results of unsuccessful pregnancies threatened to be truly overwhelming.

The simultaneous presence of these cases, where three women all faced serious pregnancy-related threats to their physical and emotional health, raised the question of the anticontraception statute in Lee

Buxton's mind once again. "So one day at a party," he later remembered, "I talked with Fowler Harper," whom he knew from their previous mutual panel appearances. Buxton told Harper about his patients and their medical needs for birth control, "and he thought maybe we could make a case for the law's being unconstitutional—infringing on my rights as a doctor and the patient's right to be treated—if I got together the evidence." Buxton agreed to do so, and he did not delay.[26]

Buxton apparently approached Anne and Hector Kinloch first. Hector, a graduate of Cambridge University in England and a U.S. Army veteran, was working on his Ph.D. in Yale's history department and serving as director of the university's International House, where they lived. Anne, a native of Rhode Island, was working as secretary to Yale's Episcopal chaplain. They had been married two years, and had experienced an unsuccessful pregnancy in 1956 as well as the late miscarriage in the spring of 1957. Anne had had two earlier unsuccessful pregnancies in a previous marriage, and Lee Buxton had held out some hope that they might be able to circumvent the RH-negative incompatibility that underlay the repeated miscarriages. "It was a very difficult, indeed tragic" situation, Hector recalled thirty-five years later, a "searing" experience. They had both seen Lee Buxton "many times" in the course of 1957, and had been his patients for quite a while before he first broached the question of being anonymous fellow plaintiffs in a test case against the Connecticut statute. They readily agreed.[27]

Buxton knew Ruth and Bob "Oldendorf" best. Bob and Ruth were both New Haven natives, and had married shortly before Bob went off to military service in Korea in 1954. Upon his return he took a job with a dairy company, and then in the spring of 1957 came Ruth's pregnancy and stroke. They too, like Anne and Hector, had seen Buxton many times in the course of the year, and Buxton raised the topic of an anonymous court case with them somewhat tentatively at first, explaining that while he already had other participants, Ruth's situation would make her a highly appropriate plaintiff—"he said he needed somebody to be 'Jane Doe,'" Bob Oldendorf recalled years later. Buxton explained the statute to them, and how most Connecticut residents, and doctors, circumvented it in a quiet or "underhanded" manner. Beyond authorizing pseudonymous use of their names, Buxton said, "'You won't have to do anything,'" and "'you'll probably never get involved in it.'" Ruth was not in good health, and Bob was preoccupied with her prospects for recovery. But Lee Buxton had gone out of his way to do all that he could for Ruth, and while Bob at the time "didn't really fully understand" what Buxton's request entailed, he also did not doubt that they should accede to this very modest request from someone who had been so kind and helpful. "That's why I went along with it," Bob remembered.[28]

Lee Buxton had seen much, much less of Elizabeth and David "Odegard." Both natives of the west, David's employer had transferred him from Indiana to New Haven in early September of 1957, when their third child was just five weeks old. Their first two babies had died in January 1954 and April 1955, and the prospects for this boy were highly uncertain. Their Indiana doctor had instructed them to go to Grace–New Haven Hospital immediately upon arrival in Connecticut, and had sent their medical records on ahead of them. It was a time of "a lot of stress for us," Elizabeth later said with considerable under-statement, and on October 17, just five weeks after their arrival in New Haven, this third child too passed away. Some weeks later, Buxton—who had not been their principal physician—raised the test case subject with them. After being assured of complete confidentiality, they put aside their initial hesitation and agreed. Thus by sometime in early January 1958, Lee Buxton had three compelling medical cases—and human stories—tentatively ready to take to court.[29]

Medical tragedies were of course not the only events taking place at Yale during the fall of 1957. Jean Cressey and Marvin Durning were two students who met each other there that September. Jean was a Massachusetts native and Oberlin graduate who had spent a year in the Philippines and was just beginning Yale's master of arts in teaching program. Marvin had graduated from Dartmouth in 1949 and had taken one year of classes at Yale Law School before winning a Rhodes Scholarship to England. That had been followed by four years in the Navy, and only in September 1957 was he returning to finish his final two years of law school. By Christmastime Jean and Marvin had decid-ed to marry, and sometime just after New Year's Jean made an appoint-ment at Yale's student health service to request birth control advice and a diaphragm. Although she remembered the battle over the 1948 Massachusetts birth control referendum, she was nonetheless taken aback when the female physician at the Yale health service informed her that such devices could not be fitted or provided in Connecticut, and that the closest Planned Parenthood clinic was across the state line in Westchester County, New York. Jean had a full course load, a stu-dent-teaching assignment, and several big exams fast approaching. Having to take most of a day to drive all the way to Port Chester and back for such a simple matter was inconvenient and irritating. "I was really annoyed," she later remembered, "at the idea that I would have to find my way to New York, to the closest Planned Parenthood, to get birth control advice." Within a few days she made the trip down to Westchester. "I drove into town. I had the address, but I couldn't quite find it right away, and I found a policeman, and I stopped and asked him. I didn't ask by the full number of the address, I just asked where is 'Fowler' Street or whatever it was, and he said something like 'Go up to the second traffic light, turn left, it's in the first block on the right.' A young woman in Connecticut license plates asking for the street was enough for him to know where I was going."

Jean's trip was successful, but Marvin too was more than a little irritated at the inconvenience that the old Connecticut statute had caused Jean. "I was quite upset," he recalled, and complained about it the next day at lunch in the law school to several friends. Afterward he went upstairs and mentioned his annoyance to his civil liberties professor, Tom Emerson. A quiet and understated man whom conservatives nonetheless viewed as a dangerous radical, Tom Emerson had a quick and specific reaction when Marv related Jean's experience: "Go talk to Fowler Harper. Fowler is thinking about a case."

Durning knew Harper from having taken his torts course back in 1949–1950, and Harper welcomed Emerson's recommendation that Marvin see him. Perhaps several weeks had passed since his conversation with Lee Buxton at that party, and Marvin's description of Jean having to drive all the way to Port Chester and back stimulated Harper's indignation in an even more pointed way than had Buxton's three case descriptions. "Fowler was outraged," Tom Emerson later said in remembering Harper's reaction to Durning's visit, at the "governmental intrusion" into marital privacy that the old statute represented. "I don't think that there had been a final decision to do something at the time of my first conversation with him," Marvin Durning recalled, but within days of that visit, Fowler Harper, like Lee Buxton, made a firm decision that the 1879 statute should indeed be challenged in court as an unconstitutional exercise of government power.[30]

Fowler Harper had been at Yale Law School for nine years when he had those two successive conversations with Lee Buxton and Marv Durning, but he had had a significant and colorful career long before moving to New Haven. Born in Germantown, Ohio, in 1897, Harper began taking law classes at Ohio Northern University in 1918 and passed the Ohio bar even before his 1921 graduation. He took a job as football coach at a small Ohio college, survived a nearly fatal stabbing by an unidentified assailant in Kalamazoo, Michigan, and married an Iowa woman, Grace Gill. They had a daughter in 1925, and Harper completed a master's degree in English at the University of Iowa before earning a graduate law degree at the University of Michigan. He began publishing extensively in law journals, and after teaching law for several years at the University of North Dakota, in 1929 he moved to the Indiana University Law School. By the late 1930s Harper was a protegé of Indiana Governor—and former Indiana law dean—Paul V. McNutt, and in August 1939 McNutt, now in Washington, named him General Counsel of the Federal Security Agency, a New Deal bureaucratic construct that included the National Youth Administration, the Civilian Conservation Corps, the Public Health Service, the Office of Education, and the Social Security Board. Harper stayed in the position for only a year before returning to I.U., but in May 1942 McNutt appointed Harper deputy chairman of the War Manpower Commission, a high-profile position that Harper held for twelve months before resigning with a public blast that the commission's work was too heavily influenced by private corporate interests. He moved for a few months to the Office on Economic Warfare, and then in September 1943 was named Solicitor of the Interior Department by Secretary Harold Ickes. After two years in that job, Harper returned to the I.U. Law School in the fall of 1945.[31]

While in Washington Harper had been a delegate to both the 1940 and 1944 Democratic National Conventions; he also had been a leading member of the National Lawyers Guild, an association of liberal and progressive attorneys which he first had joined in early 1937, and through the NLG Harper had become good friends with many fellow New Deal progressives, including Thomas I. Emerson. Back in Indiana, Harper in the summer of 1946 was one of the first signatories of a petition to put the Communist Party on the state ballot, and within a few months local American Legion chapters were charging that Harper was a leading figure in Indiana communism. State and Chicago newspapers heralded the allegation, and in early December 1946, seventeen years after first arriving in Bloomington, Harper submitted his resignation to I.U.'s Board of Trustees. "I am not a political sympathizer with the Communist party nor have I ever been in sympathy with its political philosophy, practices or objectives," Harper declared, explaining that he had signed the petition at the request of a regional CIO official. Harper quickly filed suit against the *Chicago Herald American* over one outlandish story, later received a fifteen-thousand-dollar settlement, and by September 1947 had joined his friend Tom Emerson on the Yale Law School faculty.

A thorough FBI probe into Harper's politics and affiliations in

Indiana uncovered only acquaintances who characterized him as an "enthusiastic dice player" and a self-described best friend who reported that "Harper has the idea he can drink anyone 'under the table.'" Some colleagues attributed Harper's heavy drinking to his time in Washington, while others saw its roots in his wife's nervous condition, a circumstance which led to their 1950 divorce and to Harper's subsequent very painful estrangement from his daughter. But the Indiana controversy and the move to Yale did not lessen Fowler's active interest in politics and world affairs; within months of his arrival in New Haven he and another progressive colleague, Fred Rodell, persuaded twenty-two of the law school's twenty-seven professors to sign a public letter calling for the abolition of the House Un-American Activities Committee, a declaration that resulted in heavy public criticism. Fowler also served as vice-chairman of the American League for a Free Palestine, and in September 1948, along with a U.S. Representative from New York, he narrowly escaped being killed by an Egyptian mortar shell during a trip through southern Palestine. In 1949, along with a small number of other progressives or leftists, he testified against the nomination of Attorney General Tom C. Clark to a seat on the U.S. Supreme Court, and two months later, at the instigation of a Yale undergraduate named William F. Buckley, Jr., Harper debated internal security policy with top-ranking FBI executive Louis B. Nichols. Throughout the early 1950s Harper published a raft of essays in such magazines as *The Nation* and *The Atlantic Monthly*, attacking Truman administration internal security policies and lambasting the Supreme Court for anticommunist holdings such as *Dennis* v. *United States*, which Harper termed "the worst blow to democracy since the Dred Scott decision" upholding slavery in 1856.[32]

In December 1950 Fowler married Miriam Cohen, a progressive social worker at New York's Jewish Board of Guardians, and Miriam moved up to New Haven. Fowler's outspoken opinions and occasionally flamboyant style drew criticism from some Yale trustees and law school alumni, especially since the faculty also boasted two other well-known progressives, Emerson and Rodell—or "Tommy the Commy" and "Fred the Red" among right-wingers. One gentleman who met Fowler at a New Haven card game went so far as to write to Yale's Provost to register a formal complaint about Harper's poor manners at poker: "when he fails to win, which is very often, [he] tears the cards up and scatters the pieces around the room." Considerably more serious were the ongoing complaints that Harper was some sort of subversive, and in March 1953, perhaps as a direct result of defending Dr.

John P. Peters of Yale's Medical School against allegations that he was a communist, Harper apparently was asked to prepare an informal but written response to the charges. "I do not belong to any organization which I regard as a communist front," he stated in a letter addressed to law school colleague Eugene V. Rostow. He recently *had* resigned "because of communist domination" from the National Committee for the Arts, Sciences and Professions, and he vowed that he would resign his membership in the National Lawyers Guild "immediately" if "I ever conclude that the Guild is communist dominated." Two months later, however, when he told a Washington audience of the General Federation of Women's Clubs during a debate that communists should be allowed to teach at American colleges, he was booed and hissed in a scene that drew front-page coverage in Washington newspapers. To add injury to insult, three days later the *Washington Times Herald* attacked Harper editorially and noted that he was the same person who had resigned from the Indiana faculty in 1947 amidst allegations of communist affiliation.[33]

Not all of Harper's life in the early 1950s was consumed by controversy, however. In 1952 he published *Problems of the Family*, a book that addressed policy issues by combining social science with the law, and it was reviewed positively in a wide range of professional journals. Three decades later one legal historian singled out the volume as "a radical departure from traditional casebooks on domestic relations in its organization and in the help it sought from other disciplines." Harper's other scholarship also ranged widely, from a review of Alfred Kinsey's *Sexual Behavior in the Human Female* to his primary specialty of torts. In 1956, after several years of work, Fowler and his colleague Fleming James published *The Law of Torts*, a major treatise that would make their names familiar to several generations of American law students and lawyers.[34]

Harper was one of the most popular members of the law school faculty, both with students, who found him highly accessible as well as personable, and with his colleagues, even those who disagreed sharply with his political views. Fleming James later remembered him as "the most truly altruistic and compassionate man I have ever known," and Gene Rostow, not one of Harper's particular friends, acknowledged that "he was without malice" and "everyone recognized his generosity of spirit and the purity of his motives." Tom Emerson noted that Fowler's "unorthodox nature did not take kindly to organizational routine or compromise" and that often "he did not care whose toes he stepped upon." Rostow called him "a crusader by temperament" who was "acutely sensitive to injustice" and had a low boiling point. He took great pleasure in all the many battles, Emerson and Rostow both agreed, and "the more violent the controversy the greater was his delight," Emerson thought. Harper's colleague and future federal judge Lou Pollak found both Fowler and Miriam to be "terribly gregarious people," and Fowler and Miriam's closest New Haven friend, psychologist Elizabeth Phillips, who earlier had worked with Miriam in New York, heartily agreed, adding—as someone who named her daughter for her friends—that he was particularly "wonderful with children."[35]

But Fowler never shied from a controversy. In April 1954 he and his colleague Vern Countryman—the erstwhile Hamden condom purchaser and former Douglas clerk—faced off against Bill Buckley and L. Brent Bozell in a widely publicized debate about McCarthyism, and that same year—at the height of the Red Scare—Fowler sent a public greeting to a dinner marking the thirtieth anniversary of the Communist Party's newspaper, *The Daily Worker*: "If the government can destroy your newspaper, with which I disagree, I am most fearful that it can and sometime will suppress publications with which I agree." Harper and Emerson that same year fought and lost a major battle within the law school to win tenure for Countryman, who had joined Harper in Dr. Peters' case and would subsequently join him in filing a Supreme Court amicus brief in another major Communist Party case, *Yates* v. *United States*.

The following year Dr. Peters finally prevailed in the Supreme Court, with Thurman Arnold and Paul Porter handling the final argument instead of Harper, while Fowler himself triumphed in the Connecticut Supreme Court in a long-running and legally complicated damage suit he had brought against a dishonest real estate agent who had finagled Harper out of sixty-three acres of additional land in the course of selling him a seventeen-acre farm in Haddam, Connecticut in 1948–1949. Harper had recruited Catherine Roraback, a 1948 Yale Law School graduate whom both he and Tom Emerson previously had known in progressive circles in Washington, and who now was a colleague of theirs in the New Haven Civil Liberties Council, to try *Harper* v. *Jere Adametz et al.* They had lost in the trial court, but in March 1955, in a 4 to 1 decision written by Justice—and former governor—Raymond E. Baldwin that cited some of Harper's own work on torts, the Connecticut Supreme Court held that Adametz had committed fraud and that the sixty-three acres would be conveyed to Fowler at a price of one thousand dollars. It was a classic Harper contest and victory, and it carried the promise of at least a modest future windfall. The following year, in August 1956, Fowler and Miriam set off to spend a year at Lucknow University in India on a Fulbright fellowship. Once a month Fowler also delivered lectures in Delhi, and at the end of the academic year the Harpers toured the countries of the Mediterranean and drove from Italy to Copenhagen before embarking on a cruise home. Then, within six months of Fowler's return to New Haven, Lee Buxton had come up to him at that party and raised the subject of birth control.[36]

Within a day or two of Marvin Durning's stimulating visit, Fowler Harper called Lee Buxton to tell him the interesting news and was himself told of Buxton's encouraging conversations with the Kinlochs, the "Oldendorfs," and the "Odegards." Fowler quickly began envisioning the related set of multiple cases that could be brought on behalf of Buxton, his patients, and—as of February 1, 1958—newlyweds Jean and Marvin Durning. Lee Buxton called Estelle Griswold to let her know of the hopeful developments, and Estelle immediately set to work to push things forward. She asked both Lee and Fowler to prepare their thoughts and be ready to share them with PPLC's top officers, and she notified both PPLC president Claudia McGinley and first vice-president Bea Hessel that a real test case was now very much at hand. Sometime late in January she scheduled a luncheon meeting at the New Haven Lawn Club, and as Fowler looked ahead toward it, he explained to Estelle that since he had no experience in Connecticut trial courts, and was not even a formal member of the Connecticut bar, that they would have to bring in someone else to argue the cases prior to any appeal to the U.S. Supreme Court, where Fowler would handle things. Estelle readily assented, and Harper picked up the phone and called Katie Roraback.

Fowler had known Katie for fifteen years, respected her political views, and had been pleased with their success in the Adametz litigation. A 1941 graduate of Mount Holyoke College, Katie had grown up principally in Brooklyn, New York, where her father was a Congregationalist minister. Her family's roots, however, lay in northwestern Connecticut, where her grandfather had practiced law before serving on the Connecticut Supreme Court and where her uncle, J. Henry Roraback, had quietly built his fortune while creating his quarter century dominance of the Republican party and Connecticut state government.

But Katie Roraback was about as politically different from J. Henry as someone could get. An economics major at Mount Holyoke, her most important undergraduate experience had been her interaction with female factory workers in a nearby city through the Student Industrial Club. After graduation Katie had worked in Washington, first at the Agriculture Department and then for the National War Labor Board, and had met both Fowler and Tom Emerson. In 1945 she had entered Yale Law School, and after graduation she had begun practicing in New Haven, focusing principally on commercial and labor law.

Fowler in that initial phone call described the patients' cases and asked Katie if she would like to participate. Roraback jokingly asked him, "In what capacity are you calling me, as an attorney or as a woman?" But she readily said yes, and Fowler asked her to join him at Estelle's upcoming Lawn Club luncheon. It was there that she first met both Lee Buxton and Estelle, and it was there that Claudia McGinley and Bea Hessel, on behalf of PPLC, formally pledged the organization's financial backing for the set of cases that Fowler, Lee, and Katie would now begin to prepare. Fowler explained to everyone that their goal would be to reach the United States Supreme Court and to win there, on constitutional grounds; no one should have any realistic expectation that the 1879 statute would be reinterpreted or struck down by the Connecticut courts. He explained as well that they would pose a series of challenges: Lee's professional claim that a doctor should not criminally be barred from giving his patients appropriate medical advice and treatment, the patients' own three claims that the wives' health and, in at least one case, her very life would be at very serious risk in the absence of birth control, and, finally and most importantly, Jean and Marvin Durning's more basic assertion, in what Fowler called the "civil rights" case, that any married couple should be able to obtain and use contraceptives without obstruction or intrusion by the state.

Katie at that luncheon voiced only one request as a condition for her participation: "that I refused to have anything to do with Morris Ernst," PPFA's counsel and an aggressive anticommunist as well as a ham-handed sexist. Griswold, McGinley, and Hessel readily agreed that Ernst would have absolutely no role as the cases went forward, and Katie and Fowler left the Lawn Club fully committed to getting to work on the formal papers that would be necessary for filing suit in New Haven County Superior Court.[37]

Sometime in April Fowler notified Estelle that they were about ready to go, and either late that month or early in May both Fowler and Katie went to Jean and Marvin Durning's apartment at 6 Trumbull Street to have them sign a copy of the formal complaint that would soon be filed on behalf of "Ralph and Rena Roe." Katie had already met Ruth "Oldendorf," who would indeed become "Jane Doe," and was tremendously touched by both her struggle and Bob's supportiveness. Everyone had assumed without question from the outset that pseudonyms would be employed all around, except with regard to Lee Buxton, and everyone additionally understood that it was highly unlikely that any of the non-M.D. plaintiffs would ever have to appear in court. Hector and Anne Kinloch would file suit as "Harold and Hanna Hoe," and David and Elizabeth "Odegard" would be spoken of as "Paul and Pauline Poe." On May 12 Fowler told Claudia McGinley that they were within a week to ten days of actually filing the cases, and on May 22 the five sets of papers were formally served on State's Attorney Ab Ullman and officially docketed in Superior Court. Six days later Katie filed brief motions in four of the five actions seeking formal "permission to use fictitious names."[38]

The initial complaints in *Buxton* v. *Ullman* and the four companion cases were relatively brief and simple, in part because both Roraback and Harper were all but certain that Superior Court would simply refer the basic constitutional questions to the Connecticut Supreme Court. Buxton's suit alleged that the 1879 statute infringed upon his "property and liberty" in contravention of the Fourteenth Amendment to the U.S. Constitution; *Poe* v. *Ullman* understandably cited both "life and liberty" in making a Fourteenth Amendment challenge, and *Roe* v. *Ullman* most basically cited simply "liberty." Roraback told Estelle Griswold that if they were fortunate the cases would reach the Connecticut Supreme Court before the end of the year, and PPLC's late May annual meeting included a serious discussion of the expanded fund-raising that the organization would have to undertake. The cost of Katie Roraback's time, plus simple expenses, was estimated as likely to come to between five and six thousand dollars, and while Fowler Harper came for free, PPLC informed Port Chester and the Mt. Kisco and Providence clinics that it would have to suspend payment of the contributions that previously had been offered to help subsidize their services to Connecticut residents.[39]

Roraback had hoped to keep publicity about the cases to an absolute minimum until they reached Connecticut's highest court, but on June 6, two weeks after their filing, the *New Haven Register* and the Associated Press made the suits front-page news all across the state. The newspapers provided only the bare-bones descriptions of the plaintiffs that had been offered in the official complaints, and no follow-up coverage ensued. The American Civil Liberties Union immediately began discussing whether they should lend some sort of legal hand, but Estelle felt highly confident that these suits would bring eventual success irrespective of additional aid, telling one supporter that "we are already thinking and planning for the day we will open up a center in New Haven."[40]

Neither Ab Ullman nor the state Attorney General's office moved quickly to respond to Roraback's filings, and the summer and early fall passed without any substantive developments. In New York City a major controversy over an unspoken but long-standing policy that prohibited doctors in the city's public hospitals from providing birth control services remained in the news for months before culminating in a rule change that represented a significant Planned Parenthood victory, and a number of commentators, including several Roman Catholics, cited the New York events, and the Connecticut statute, as stellar examples of why public policies should not be guided or determined by church doctrine. Jesuit scholar John Courtney Murray expressly attacked the church's defense of Connecticut's contraceptive ban, contending that "Since it makes a public crime out of a private sin, and confuses morality with legality, and is unenforceable without police invasion of the bedroom, the statute is indefensible as a law." The New York Archdiocese insisted that "No indication or need can change an action that is intrinsically immoral into an action that is moral and lawful," but the Catholic magazine *Commonweal* firmly retorted that it was in Catholics' own interest to keep moral questions separate from legal issues. In particular reference to Massachusetts and Connecticut, another *Commonweal* essay bluntly noted that the decades-long battles over laws that "are merely decorative" served "no real purpose other than" to allow for an ongoing "Catholic-Protestant power struggle."[41]

In mid-September Morris Ernst, Harriet Pilpel and a third associate went up to New Haven to see Fowler Harper about the Connecticut cases, and Katie Roraback gritted her teeth and attended, largely so as to be sure that warm-hearted Fowler would not allow the New Yorkers to insinuate themselves. Harper and Roraback's successful brush-off of the PPFA lawyers quietly raised some hackles in New York, however, and PPFA president Loraine Campbell, a Cambridge resident and a twenty-five-year veteran of the Massachusetts birth control wars, decided she had better check out Fowler Harper with several of her friends on the Harvard Law School faculty. Benjamin Kaplan praised Harper as a "tremendous fighter" of "enormous courage" who, like his Yale colleagues, was nonetheless a "soggy thinker," but Lon L. Fuller, a figure of considerable repute, angrily denounced Harper as "a sleazy

character" whom Fuller would "not have anything to do with." He told
of Harper's departure from Indiana, called *Problems of the Family* "rather
unsound," and termed Fowler a "left winger" and "exaggerated liberal
who delights in shocking people." A concerned Campbell drafted a letter to Claudia McGinley offering PPFA funding if PPLC would like to
hire other attorneys, but finally contented herself simply with writing
to Harper to offer praise of Lee Buxton and to request an update.[42]

In early October Joseph Sunnen, the St. Louis vaginal foam manufacturer, donated a thousand dollars to PPLC to help with the cases,
but the ongoing delay disappointed everyone. PPLC began making
plans to sponsor a bill in the upcoming 1959 legislature, and Loraine
Campbell and Harriet Pilpel repeatedly compared notes about how the
Connecticut litigation might be improved. Pilpel and Ernst had
encouraged Harper and Roraback to think about adding some additional cases in which ministers would complain that the 1879 statute
interfered with religious liberty by prohibiting them from advising
parishioners about the advisability of birth control, but Pilpel and Ernst
were also eager to detect shortcomings in Harper and Roraback's original complaints, with Ernst griping that the *Doe* case was a poor selection since her condition was so serious that only sterilization would
really be appropriate. Campbell was concerned that the anonymity of
the patients might eventually become a problem, but Pilpel assured her
that Harper had said that at least two of the pseudonymous plaintiffs—
namely Jean and Marvin Durning—would be willing to step forward if
it became necessary. Pilpel also sought to leaven Campbell's ongoing
worries about Harper, jokingly telling her that the only serious problem was that Harper "drinks too much in the evening, but we can meet
at day time!"[43]

Late in October a frustrated Roraback, who already had tried several
times without success to prod the defendants into action, filed a formal
motion requesting a default judgment on account of her opponents'
failure to plead. On November 7 the state Attorney General's office, in
a clear signal that it was taking over defense of the actions from
Ullman, filed similar two-page demurrers in all five cases, contending
that the issues had been "conclusively determined" in *Nelson* and
Tileston and that "there is no uncertainty" in any of the cases. "The passage of time and a change in Court personnel," Assistant Attorney
General Raymond J. Cannon said, "cannot be grounds for seeking a
review." An additional problem in four of the five suits, Cannon added,
is that the plaintiffs "are fictitious persons and as such cannot invoke
the powers of the Court to solve purely academic questions."[44]

Harper and Roraback were more concerned about the growing signs of intramural unhappiness within the New York world of Planned Parenthood than about Cannon's response, for as Harper attempted to reassure Loraine Campbell, "We assume that we will lose in the state and our hopes are pinned upon an appeal to the Supreme Court." They also lined up C. Lawson Willard and two other willing ministers as additional potential plaintiffs as Pilpel and Ernst had suggested, and in mid-November Harper went down to New York for a long conference with Ernst, Pilpel, Campbell, and PPFA director William Vogt in order to try to lay their concerns to rest. Ernst and Pilpel, perhaps still sensitive fifteen years later because of the damage caused by Fritz Wiggin's initial error in the *Tileston* complaint, grilled Harper in some detail about language disparities in different paragraphs of the *Doe* complaint, and suggested that amended complaints might be advisable. Additionally, right after the meeting Campbell called Lee Buxton to be sure that he would suggest to Harper the advisability of an amicus brief that could be signed by prominent doctors.[45]

On December 5, more than six months after the suits had been filed, Katie Roraback finally squared off against Ray Cannon of the state Attorney General's office in an initial hearing before Superior Court Judge Frank T. Healey—a Waterbury native who twenty years earlier had been a fellow advisory board member along with Bill Fitzgerald for Father Eugene Cryne's Diocesan Bureau of Social Service. Cannon, like the judge, was a Roman Catholic graduate of Holy Cross College and Yale Law School, and now he reiterated the two points he had stressed in his preliminary papers. First, all of the legal issues "presented in the present complaints have been so authoritatively determined by the *Nelson* and *Tileston* cases that there is not now any justiciable issue" remaining. Both decisions explicitly held that the judiciary "is without power to create any exceptions in the subject statutes," and by asking for such the plaintiffs "are in effect seeking to have the Court act in a legislative capacity." Second, he repeated his earlier assertion that the anonymity of plaintiffs in four of the five actions raised a serious and perhaps fatal procedural problem. Katie Roraback responded by telling Healey that another Superior Court judge, James Shannon, had verbally assured her that the Doe-Poe-Hoe-Roe usages were acceptable, and she rebutted Cannon's substantive reliance on *Nelson* and *Tileston* by emphasizing the plaintiffs' core contention: "These people have the right to be allowed to continue normal marital relations without being inhibited by the state." Irrespective of the precedents, the 1879 law was so intrusive as to be inherently unconstitutional: "A statute which by its very terms may inhibit the most personal relationships of marriage is itself unreasonable" and hence void. Judge Healey said only that he would take their arguments under advisement, and issue a decision sometime in the future.[46]

Soon after that hearing the internecine tensions involving national Planned Parenthood took an odd but ultimately very important turn. For almost thirty years, since the 1929 raid on the Clinical Research Bureau, Morris Ernst had been Sanger's—and then PPFA's—principal lawyer. For much of that time he had prided himself on taking a less hostile attitude toward Roman Catholicism than was true of Sanger or some others within Planned Parenthood. Now, however, just after having reached his seventieth birthday, Ernst underwent something of a shift, insisting repeatedly to PPFA president Loraine Campbell that the organization needed to adopt a more hard-nosed stance. In mid-November Ernst had erupted at Campbell in front of several strangers, criticizing her "in the most vituperative way" for PPFA's restraint, and Campbell had complained to many of her colleagues about this "utterly indefensible behavior on the part of the official counsel." Harriet Pilpel, for twenty years Ernst's principal deputy but now a forty-seven-year-old partner in her own right, advised Campbell to have a quiet lunch with her now-ageing mentor. A date was made for early December, and that very same morning a furious Claudia McGinley called Campbell to rebuke her for Ernst's office having sent a junior associate to monitor the New Haven hearing and further lobby Fowler Harper on behalf of the New Yorkers' tactical recommendations. Campbell angrily told McGinley that the young observer had been dispatched at *her* request because of the unresponsiveness of the Connecticut lawyers, but at lunch Ernst had little interest in discussing the Connecticut scene and instead returned to his "extremely rude" assault on Campbell's and PPFA's political cowardice. Ernst twice threatened to resign as PPFA's counsel if his advice was not better heeded, and as Campbell later wrote, "I did everything I could to placate him because he really was in a dangerous and irrational mood and I was afraid that he might go out and shout from the housetops about what a lot of damn fools we are." Campbell wondered if Ernst in part might be distraught over the fact that the Connecticut problem was finally on its way back to the Supreme Court, but without he himself playing a significant role, but in the aftermath of the angry lunch Harriet Pilpel attempted to reassure Campbell that both she and Ernst felt comfortable with Fowler Harper. Campbell wondered too if Ernst was upset that PPFA had largely ignored his advice during the New York City hospitals controversy several months earlier, but it was Campbell's explicit instructions to PPFA's staff that later made the lunch so significant: in the future "all legal matters should be routed through Mrs. Pilpel herself and not through Morris." After more than thirty years on the front lines, Morris Ernst would spend his remaining years talking mostly to himself.[47]

On January 5, 1959, Frank Healey issued a sloppy and careless two-page decision upholding Cannon's substantive objections to the five test case complaints. Failing to note even the U.S. Supreme Court ruling in *Tileston*, Healey erroneously stated that *Nelson* had involved a patient and then offered little more than a brief reprise of the Connecticut Supreme Court's majority opinion in *Tileston*. Two weeks later Ray Cannon moved for a formal entry of judgment, and once that was done Katie Roraback in early February filed notices of appeal to the Connecticut Supreme Court. Fowler Harper was hopeful that oral argument there would take place sometime late in the spring, but within days of Healey's decision Jean and Marv Durning informed him that they would be moving to Seattle once Marvin completed his final semester of law school courses that spring. Fowler, knowing that *Roe* v. *Ullman*, the most important of the five cases, would have to then be withdrawn once they left the state, immediately began looking for another young married couple who could take the Durnings' place.[48]

PPLC's thinking about a 1959 legislative effort had been influenced both by the lawyers' discussions about the advisability of filing several religious freedom cases on behalf of ministers and by the results of the November 1958 elections, in which the greatest Democratic sweep in decades had resulted in a twenty-nine to seven margin of Democratic control in the state senate and the first Democratic majority in the state house (141 to 138) since 1876. Estelle and others, recognizing that the legislative effort would of course be truly hopeless, decided to frame it in such a way as to give a publicity boost to the ensuing litigation: the 1959 bill would be a religious freedom as well as a maternal health measure, and would call for a statutory exception to the 1879 law when contraception was practiced "pursuant to spiritual or medical advice." Harper himself drafted the measure, and Estelle recruited official support for it from the Connecticut Council of Churches and several other ministerial groups. Representative Dorothy Miller of Bolton formally introduced it in late January, and PPLC's board agreed that the ministerial law suits that Harper had prepared would be held in abeyance until the legislative demise of the bill was sufficiently obvious so as to supply an appropriate occasion for the public filing of the cases.[49]

Not until late April did the 1959 legislative hearing take place, with attorney Frank P. Lockard from the Council of Churches serving as coordinator for the bill's proponents. New Haven ministers George Teague of the First Methodist Church and C. Lawson Willard of Trinity Episcopal Church were the primary affirmative witnesses, with Willard testifying that the 1879 law represented "a curtailment and an infringement of my religious liberty" by prohibiting him from recommending birth control to parishioners. Joseph Cooney was once again the leading representative for the bill's opponents, and when Bethany Representative Jack Turner began energetically questioning a Hartford physician who had spoken against the measure, Cooney jumped in and interrupted. Public Health and Safety Committee chairman Senator Norman Hewitt admonished him bluntly: "Mr. Cooney, I am sure you won't allow that to happen again. . . . Mr. Turner has the right to ask any question that he desires and that right will be respected." Turner himself told Cooney that "I don't think your outburst was called for," but when Turner resumed questioning the doctor, the diocesan lobbyist again interrupted in an effort to end the interrogation. An angry Hewitt rebuked him again: "Mr. Cooney, I am the chairman of the hearing and we will terminate it when we are ready."

Cooney's insolent performance offended the legislators, but it could not save the bill from its inevitable fate, and six days after the hearing the committee voted by secret ballot to reject it.[50] PPLC wasted no time in moving along with the next step in its plans, and four days after the committee vote ministers C. Lawson Willard, George Teague, and Luther Livingston each filed suit in New Haven County Superior Court, alleging that the 1879 statute was an unconstitutional infringement of their religious liberty and pastoral counseling rights as protected by the free exercise clause of the First Amendment. Harper had recruited another young New Haven attorney, Louise Evans Farr, whom he—and Willard—knew from the New Haven Civil Liberties Council, to handle the ministerial suits, and he had some hope that they might catch up to the others either at the Connecticut Supreme Court or at the U.S. Supreme Court.

Harper also hoped, more fervently, that one other case might catch up to the initial ones. Sometime in March, just prior to the formal withdrawal of *Roe* v. *Ullman*, Marv Durning approached one of the few other married students at Yale Law School, David Trubek, who was in the first-year class. David, like his wife Louise, who was in the second-year class, was a New York native and a graduate of the University of

Wisconsin. They had been married the previous summer, just before David had started law school, and while neither of them had ever given the birth control issue much thought, they were both willing to sit down with Fowler Harper and discuss becoming the new plaintiffs making the crucial argument that *any* married couple, irrespective of health issues, had an inherent Fourteenth Amendment liberty right to use contraceptives. David and Louise Trubek not only agreed to be Marv and Jean Durning's successors, they agreed to do so under their own actual names, and on May 20, following a pro forma consultation between the Trubeks and Lee Buxton, Katie Roraback filed *Trubek* v. *Ullman* in New Haven Superior Court.[51]

Katie Roraback had filed her briefs on behalf of Lee Buxton and his patients with the Connecticut Supreme Court in mid-April, but Ray Cannon requested and received several extensions of the deadline for filing the state's responses, insuring that oral argument would be put off until sometime in the fall. Roraback's filings were substantive and professional, highlighting the physical and emotional traumas that the Does, Poes and Hoes each had faced, and noting, in contrast to *Gardner, Nelson,* and *Tileston* that "Never before have individual citizens"—i.e., patients rather than doctors and clinic personnel—"raised these questions, nor have their rights been adjudicated, either in this court or in the Supreme Court of the United States." She also frontally addressed the notion that the criminal prohibition of the use of contraceptives could not be unreasonable and unconstitutional *if* abstinence was indeed a reasonable alternative for married couples facing serious pregnancy-related health threats, as the Connecticut court had concluded back in *Tileston.* "If their rights to life and liberty have meaning," Roraback wrote, "they must . . . include the right to marriage and the enjoyment of the fullest bounties which that relationship can give. . . . Sexual intercourse is not a mere adjunct of marriage, which may or may not be engaged in depending on the health and bent of the husband and wife. It is a part of the basic fabric of the whole marital relation." Lastly, Roraback also directly confronted Cannon's contention that *Nelson* and *Tileston* were thoroughly controlling: "we do not believe that the questions here presented have been authoritatively settled. Even if this were not so, our courts are not so limited that they cannot re-examine vital questions of constitutional interpretation and individual rights when called upon to do so in the light of new events and experience."[52]

If Roraback, Harper, and Griswold were pleased with the briefs, however, their ostensible allies in New York were not. Harriet Pilpel gently informed Harper that the Connecticut lawyers should plan to file additional reply briefs once Cannon had submitted his arguments, and hinted that if they chose not to do so, PPFA could file an amicus brief. Harper, after consulting with Roraback, firmly told Pilpel that that would be inadvisable, and Pilpel then informed PPFA that "some rather vigorous action" was called for to convince the Connecticut activists of the New Yorkers' superior wisdom. Loraine Campbell responded that the national organization "might as well let them go to Hell their own way," but Pilpel continued to lobby Harper and Roraback toward submitting a reply brief. They tolerated the prodding politely, but Bea Hessel, who was just succeeding Claudia McGinley as PPLC president, called Loraine Campbell to complain about the "unethical" conduct and to point out how Roraback and PPLC had expressly stipulated at the outset that there would be no involvement by Ernst and Pilpel's law firm. Campbell understandably told Hessel that she too was no fan of Ernst's, but several days later Claudia McGinley phoned to repeat PPLC's complaint. In early June Pilpel went up to Yale to repeat the New York insistence on some additional filing to Harper in person, and while Harper was cordial and courteous, the following day Hessel again called Campbell to say that the ongoing New York pressure was infuriating Roraback. Campbell bluntly told Hessel "that we are frankly not happy [at] the way the cases are being developed," that "it all seemed rather amateurish," and that PPLC did not understand its subordinate relationship to PPFA.[53]

In mid-June Fowler Harper, after consulting with both Roraback and Griswold, wrote Pilpel to present what he hoped would be an implicit compromise that would halt the internecine warfare. He reiterated that "any intervention on behalf of the national organization in the Connecticut proceedings is undesirable" since Roraback "insists, as I thought she would, that she cannot effectively collaborate with anyone else in the writing of a reply brief"—the first acknowledgment that there now indeed would be one. Suggestions would be welcome, but any PPFA amicus brief for the Connecticut court would not be. However, once the cases were appealed to the U.S. Supreme Court, a PPFA amicus brief there would indeed be appreciated: "since presumably I will be the only attorney directly concerned, you may count on my cooperation."

Loraine Campbell continued to fret about the competence of the Connecticut litigation. She tried unsuccessfully to get one friend's spouse to have Whitney North Seymour review and critique Roraback's work, and Campbell's predecessor as PPFA president,

Frances Hand Ferguson, declined to ask her father, famed federal appellate judge Learned Hand, to prepare any such appraisal. Bea Hessel again told Campbell that the Connecticut League wanted "no further interference" while the cases remained in the state courts, but in early July Pilpel sent Harper a lengthy and detailed written critique of Roraback's briefs. None of the points was either central or serious, but Harper continued to tolerate the incessant hectoring far more dispassionately than Roraback or Hessel.[54]

In late July Ray Cannon finally filed his defense briefs, and again he sought to challenge the legitimacy of the anonymous patient plaintiffs. Since "Harold and Hanna Hoe," for example, were "fictitious" names, "the real parties in interest have not disclosed their identity." Thus, Cannon illogically continued, "If the plaintiffs are fictitious persons, it must also follow that the questions which they seek to have adjudicated are academic in nature and do not apply to specific individuals." This in fact did *not* follow, but Cannon went on at some length to warn the court that the pseudonyms were "an extremely dangerous precedent" that potentially could open the door to fraudulent litigation.

Cannon offered almost no substantive defense of the Connecticut statute, and Katie Roraback, who had indeed accepted the advisability of submitting reply briefs, told Pilpel that Cannon's efforts "are hardly enlightening exercises in the arts of the law." Roraback stressed that her reply briefs would incorporate "many of the suggestions which you so kindly made," and when she filed them in late August their argumentation was distinctly more vigorous than Roraback's earlier submissions. She countered Cannon by noting that the original complaints described the plaintiffs in "elaborate" detail and stated that Dr. Buxton maintained that "he is entitled to prescribe the use of contraceptives under any (not limited) circumstances, when in his professional opinion their use will protect the life and health and promote the welfare of his patients." Since actual patient cases had never before been adjudicated, the Connecticut court ought to willingly reconsider *Nelson* and *Tileston*, "especially where the facts so urgently called for the reassessment of prior pronouncements."[55]

Neither Roraback nor Estelle Griswold held out any serious hope of prevailing in the Connecticut Supreme Court. They both knew that now-Chief Justice Raymond E. Baldwin had backed birth control liberalization twenty-five years earlier as a state legislator, although not when he was governor, and while Stelle and Bea Hessel were already thinking of being able to open a New Haven clinic sometime in 1961, they presumed that would occur only in the wake of a U.S. Supreme

Court ruling. A mid-September hearing sent the *Trubek* case forward for Connecticut Supreme Court consideration, and on October 7— sixteen months after their filing—the Connecticut high court finally heard oral argument by Roraback and Cannon on *Poe-Hoe-Doe* and *Buxton*. Loraine Campbell and Harriet Pilpel went up to Hartford to observe, and Chief Justice Baldwin and Justice John H. King dominated the hearing with a wide range of challenging questions. Katie Roraback thought the argument went "quite well on the basic questions," but was concerned that "a good deal of questioning and doubt was raised as to the propriety of the use of fictitious names." She and Harper estimated that a decision ought to come by Christmastime, and although the ministerial cases were being delayed by the state, everyone in PPLC sat back to wait for the anticipated defeat that would then allow them to take their challenge onward and upward to the U.S. Supreme Court.[56]

In late November birth control became a front-page national issue when a number of Roman Catholic bishops, acting through the National Catholic Welfare Conference, issued a public statement denouncing any use of public funds, either domestically or in foreign-aid programs, to disseminate birth control services. Prominent Protestant leaders strongly criticized the statement, but President Dwight D. Eisenhower seemed to endorse it, saying that birth control was "not a proper political or governmental activity or function or responsibility." Other press coverage noted that the American Civil Liberties Union had recently voted to endorse PPLC's challenge to the Connecticut anticontraception statute on both First and Fourteenth Amendment grounds, but the sectarian controversy more importantly offered an opportunity for journalists to highlight how widely accepted contraceptive practices now were in almost all portions of American society. Survey data indicated that some 81 percent of married white women of childbearing age now used or had used contraceptive devices, a significant increase from even five years earlier, and that approximately 38 percent of Roman Catholic women in that group also used devices and methods that their church hierarchy condemned. Just as Hilda Standish and her colleagues at the Hartford clinic had recognized twenty years earlier, there was a very large—and now growing—gap between the practices of Catholic lay people and the proclamations of church officials.[57]

On December 22, 1959, the Connecticut Supreme Court unanimously upheld the 1879 law criminalizing the use or counseling of birth control. The opinion, written by Chief Justice—and one-time birth control proponent—Raymond E. Baldwin, offered a lengthy recital of all the unsuccessful legislative efforts to alter the statute before insisting that "Courts cannot, by the process of construction, abrogate a clear expression of legislative intent, especially when, as here, unambiguous language is fortified by the refusal of the legislature, in the light of judicial interpretation, to change it." Baldwin conceded that "By reason of the facts in the instant cases, the claims of infringement of constitutional rights are presented more dramatically than they have ever been before," but that *Nelson* and *Tileston* nevertheless were controlling because the basic issues raised here were "essentially the same." The chief justice also admitted that "It may well be that the use of contraceptives is indicated as the best and safest preventive measure which medical science can offer these plaintiffs," but if the Connecticut legislature nonetheless chose to prohibit that measure and insist on abstinence instead, there was nothing that either Lee Buxton or the Connecticut judiciary could do about it.

Baldwin's opinion completely avoided ever dealing with the individual rights and constitutional liberty claims that Roraback had advanced on behalf of her plaintiffs. Some months later, however, when a curious and amazed woman from Houston wrote to Hartford to ask if it actually was true that the practice of birth control was a criminal offense in Connecticut, Baldwin himself wrote her a long and detailed personal letter describing why the Connecticut Supreme Court had felt it had no other choice. The plaintiffs' requests, he explained, "could not be granted without overruling two prior decisions and the presumed will of the state legislature." The legislative branch, Baldwin stressed, has "always had the authority to pass statutes to promote the public health, safety and morals. Courts do not often interfere with such legislative determinations of how these objectives can best be served unless they are manifestly unreasonable," and in *Buxton* the Connecticut court "refused to find that the legislation was so unreasonable that the collective judgment of the legislature should be overturned."[58]

Few if any observers were surprised by news of the Connecticut ruling, however. Several national newspapers editorialized against the holding, with the *New York Herald Tribune* declaring that birth control is "quintessentially a matter of private, not public morality, and one to be resolved as a matter of individual conscience." Estelle Griswold admitted privately to one friend that she had been surprised by the unanimity of the Connecticut defeat, but Fowler Harper moved immediately to appeal the decision to the U.S. Supreme Court. He had arranged for

his friend Eugene Gressman, a Washington attorney who was perhaps
the nation's leading expert on Supreme Court procedure, to handle
much of the technical minutiae, and early in January Gressman advised
Fowler that the clerk's office at the court had recommended that they
file two separate appeals, one of behalf of Dr. Buxton and the other on
behalf of the patients. Just a few days later Harper learned that Anne
and Hector Kinloch would be leaving New Haven in June to move to
Australia, where Hector had accepted a history faculty appointment,
and their departure would necessitate dropping "Harold and Hanna
Hoe" from the set of cases. *Trubek* had not yet caught up, and hence
only *Doe* and *Poe* would go forward, even though—unbeknownst to
Harper—David and Elizabeth "Odegard," or "Paul and Pauline Poe,"
had no longer been Connecticut residents even when *Poe* was initially
filed.[59]

Both the ACLU and its small Connecticut affiliate, the CCLU, were
already aiming toward filing an amicus brief on behalf of Buxton and
his patients, and by early February Harper had contacted Whitney
North Seymour, Sr., about coordinating the preparation of an amicus
brief that could be filed on behalf of nationally prominent doctors.
Katie Roraback continued to press forward with *Trubek*, even though
the ministerial cases seemed inextricably stalled, and by mid-March it
had been agreed that Harriet Pilpel would prepare a Supreme Court
amicus brief on behalf of PPFA. Harper himself was hard at work on
drafting the initial substantive submission for the high court, the jurisdictional statement that would set out Buxton and the patients' arguments for why the Supreme Court should hear their appeal. Gressman
reviewed a first draft and recommended more attention to the constitutional rights claims and less to the medical acceptance of birth control, and on March 23 the two documents—one for *Buxton*, one for *Poe*
and *Doe*—were formally filed.[60]

Harper's *Poe* submission was the longer and more important document. He described "Jane Doe" and "Pauline Poe's" medical problems
in greater detail than Roraback had employed in the original complaints, and then presented the crux of his constitutional argument.
The Connecticut statutes, he noted, "purport to regulate the behavior
of married persons in the privacy of their homes in an arbitrary manner
which restricts their liberty and seriously jeopardizes the lives and
health of spouses." Four decades earlier, in 1923, the Supreme Court in
Meyer v. *Nebraska* had spoken of "the right of the individual . . . to
marry, establish a home and bring up children," and Harper, citing that
precedent, forthrightly insisted that "The right to marry and establish a

home . . . necessarily implies the right to engage in normal marital relations. And the right to engage in such relations embodies a personal
freedom or privilege to procreate or not procreate as the individuals
may desire or as medical factors may dictate. This right must therefore
be considered as one of the bundle of rights which are 'fundamental to
the very existence and survival of the race,'" a category the Court had
spoken of eighteen years earlier in *Skinner* v. *Oklahoma.* "Legislation
which leaves total abstention as the only alternative to death or
impaired health is on its face arbitrary and unreasonable," Harper contended, and represents "an unreasonable and arbitrary intrusion in the
private affairs of the citizens of Connecticut."

Harper went on to point out that birth control had widespread public acceptance, citing a recent Gallup Poll result showing that 72 percent of respondents believed that contraceptive advice should be
available to anyone who wanted it. Then he returned to the essence of
his argument, seeking to persuade the nine justices of the clear unreasonableness of the Connecticut statute:

> When the long arm of the law reaches into the bedroom and regu-
> lates the most sacred relations between a man and his wife, it is going
> too far. There must be a limit to the extent to which the moral scruples
> of a minority, or for that matter a majority, can be enacted into laws
> which regulate the sex life of all married people.
>
> Appellants are not contending that their rights of privacy, as such, are
> directly protected by the Fourteenth Amendment. They do submit,
> however, that their privacy is mercilessly being invaded by these laws
> and that, this being so, it is a highly important factor for this Court to
> consider in weighing the hardship upon individuals against the theoreti-
> cal, if not entirely fictitious, advantages of the laws as promoting public
> morality.

Harper reiterated the privacy point several times. "The normal and
voluntary relations of spouses in the privacy of their homes is regarded
as beyond the prying eyes of peeping Toms, be they police officers or
legislators." He drew a contrast between the Connecticut case and a
1952 Court decision, *Public Utilities Commission* v. *Pollak,* where a challenge to the broadcasting of radio programs on public busses was
rejected on the grounds that the unwilling listeners were, after all, out
in public rather than at home. The patient plaintiffs here, Harper said,
"complain that it is precisely their privacy in their homes and, indeed,
in the most private part thereof that is invaded. They want to be let
alone in the bedroom"—an implicit reference to a famous phrase, "the

right to be let alone," that had been coined by the legal scholar Thomas M. Cooley in 1888. "They insist that marital intercourse may not be rationed, censored or regulated by priest, legislator or bureaucrat. Certainly, they contend, the 'liberty' guaranteed by the due process clause includes this, among the most sacred experiences of life."

Harper closed his *Poe* statement with one final chorus: "These married persons contend that they have a constitutional right to marital intercourse in the privacy of their homes under medically approved conditions and under circumstances mutually satisfactory to them. What right, it may be asked, is more fundamental or more sacred?" In his much shorter, companion submission in *Buxton*, Harper understandably focused upon the statutes' infringement upon doctors' professional obligation to safeguard their patients' lives and health, decrying them as "laws which fly in the face of science."[61]

Within the Supreme Court, some six weeks passed before *Poe* v. *Ullman* and Harper's jurisdictional statements came under active consideration within the chambers of the Court's nine justices. In order for such an appeal to be accepted for review, at least four justices would have to vote in favor of such consideration. The State of Connecticut had made no submission, and when Harper's documents were reviewed in the different justices' chambers, the brand-new law school graduates who were the justices' law clerks had a wide variety of reactions. Justice William O. Douglas's clerk, Steven Duke, offered little reaction other than that the patients' claims were obviously stronger than Dr. Buxton's, while Justice Tom C. Clark's clerk, Cecil Wray— obviously not aware of Fowler Harper's testimony against the justice's nomination eleven years earlier—commended the Yale professor for writing "a very persuasive brief" and picking out "very strong cases" with which to challenge the statute. The Connecticut Supreme Court's opinion "isn't very strong," and overall the plaintiffs appeared to have "a good case."

Chief Justice Earl Warren's clerk, Murray Bring, was similarly impressed both by Harper's "very persuasive" work and by the specific and "very well stated" facts of the patients' cases. "If there is anything left of the doctrine of substantive due process"—the use of the Fourteenth Amendment's "liberty" language to void a statute simply because it was an excessive and unreasonable infringement on individual freedom, a usage that the Court had largely abandoned after 1937 following enormous criticism of its extensive utilization to invalidate government regulation of business—"then it would be difficult to find a more appropriate case for an application" of it. Of course the subject of birth control, with its sexual and religious overtones, might be "difficult and ticklish" for some—such as perhaps the rather prudish Chief Justice himself—but "I think it will be some time before a case will come along in which the facts are as appealing or the counsel is as competent."

Howard Lesnick, Justice John Marshall Harlan's clerk, took a decidedly less sanguine view. The merits of the case, he asserted, "are clouded by the poor quality of Professor Harper's brief," for Harper has "largely forgotten the particular claims of his clients" in favor of "a broadside attack on the statute." Lesnick too thought that the patients' claims were more significant than Buxton's, and remarked that the patients' real interest was in being able to have intercourse. "If the interest is thought sufficient to entitle it to constitutional protection, the question is one of substantive due process." Regarding the subject matter, he noted that "This issue, ticklish as it is, is not so bad as *Naim* v. *Naim*"—a case challenging Virginia's criminalization of interracial marriage that the Court twice had dodged four years earlier. But, Lesnick added, the Connecticut statutes "have not been enforced against any of the appellants, and the Court could duck the whole question by finding a lack of sufficiently ripe controversy."[62]

On Friday, May 20, the nine justices, meeting in the absolute privacy of their conference room, voted to hear *Poe et al.* and *Buxton v. Ullman*. Five members of the Court—Chief Justice Warren, and Justices Douglas, Harlan, William J. Brennan, and Potter Stewart—one more than necessary, voted in favor, while three justices—Hugo L. Black, Clark, and Charles E. Whittaker—voted to dismiss the appeal and thereby affirm the Connecticut court. For reasons he did not disclose, Justice Felix Frankfurter—PPLM's informal advisor back in the late 1930s—declined to vote on whether to accept *Poe*.[63]

Three days later the Court announced its acceptance of *Poe* and *Buxton*, with the twofold nature of the case meaning that three full hours—ninety minutes for each side—would be scheduled for oral argument sometime in the fall of 1960. PPLC held its annual meeting the day after the announcement, and while everyone was pleased, there was considerable mystification as to why Frankfurter had recused himself. Loraine Campbell told the Connecticut activists that neither Frankfurter nor his wife had ever contributed to PPLM, and Fowler Harper, as well as Harriet Pilpel, turned their attention toward coordinating the content of the different but complementary briefs that would be due in Washington by late August. Pilpel's amicus brief for PPFA would be responsible for showing why sexual abstinence was not a reasonable alternative to the use of contraception, while Whitney North Seymour's on behalf of prominent doctors would emphasize physicians' professional responsibilities to their patients. Connecticut's Raymond Cannon, in a very unusual move, refused to grant the state's pro forma consent to the filing of the PPFA and doctors' briefs, hence requiring those amici to obtain the Court's formal approval for their submissions.[64]

The Supreme Court's acceptance of *Poe* drew some press attention. The *New York Herald Tribune* editorially welcomed the action and said it looked forward to the high court voiding a statute that "is a clear infringement of both professional and personal liberty" and that makes "the particular doctrine of the Catholic Church binding, on penalty of imprisonment, on persons of all faiths." A Catholic priest writing in a relatively obscure religious journal stated that "a Catholic can justifiably favor repeal of the Connecticut and Massachusetts anti-contraceptive laws," and *Newsweek* magazine ran a story reporting his remarks. Several weeks later, when a Catholic journalist's monograph critiquing the statutes was issued by a small think-tank, *Newsweek* ran yet another story and an Associated Press dispatch highlighting his work appeared in almost all Connecticut newspapers.[65]

In early July the U.S. State Department offered Fowler Harper a four-month visit to Africa as a visiting legal consultant to several different countries, and with some reluctance Harper wrote to the Supreme Court Clerk's Office to request that the oral argument in *Poe* be postponed until sometime after he returned from the trip in late January of 1961. Harper's friend Gene Gressman warned that he had "heard some discouraging comments about the ultimate outcome from someone who spoke to one of the outgoing clerks," since a new group of fresh young law school graduates arrived at the Court each summer, but work on all the various briefs proceeded apace. ACLU Assistant Legal Director Melvin Wulf had undertaken some initial research for the ACLU/CCLU amicus brief, but Yale's Tom Emerson had volunteered that his wife Ruth Calvin Emerson, a 1950 Yale Law School graduate, was interested in helping, and by late August both Ruth Emerson and Wulf had completed revised drafts of parts of the brief.[66]

By mid-September all of the Supreme Court briefs had been completed and Fowler and Miriam Harper were off to Africa. Katie Roraback and Ray Cannon faced off before the Connecticut Supreme Court for the oral argument of *Trubek* v. *Ullman* on October 6, and within the following two weeks the U.S. Supreme Court—with Felix Frankfurter continuing to recuse himself—formally approved Harper's request for *Poe*'s postponement and also officially accepted all of the amicus briefs for which Cannon had refused to give Connecticut's consent. Cannon had told the Connecticut court that David and Louise Trubek's problem was not the 1879 statute but the fact that they sought to "avoid some of the responsibilities of the marital status," but the national climate regarding issues such as birth control continued to liberalize, with Catholic Democratic presidential nominee John F. Kennedy telling an audience of Protestant ministers in Texas that he desired an America "where no religious body seeks to impose its will directly or indirectly upon the general populace or the public acts of its officials." A major medical magazine, in a story picked up by national newspapers, quoted Connecticut doctors as explaining how the state law actually affected only those citizens too poor to pay private physicians for diaphragm fittings, but a prominent Catholic periodical, reacting both to *Poe* and to Kennedy's comments, acerbicly complained that "Unfortunately a growing number of Americans look upon contraception as their inalienable right."[67]

Fowler Harper's Supreme Court brief expanded upon but closely paralleled the arguments he had emphasized in his initial jurisdictional statement six months earlier. He spoke of how the Connecticut statutes "invade the privacy of the citizen," "the privacy of the home" and "regulate the private sex life of all married people"—a slight emendation of his earlier language, where the adjective "private" had not appeared. He repeated his insistence that "These spouses want to be let alone in the bedroom," noted the antecedents of that phrase, and reiterated in slightly altered wording his contention that married couples have "a constitutionally protected right to marital intercourse in the privacy of their homes." Harper concluded by charging that the Connecticut provisions "interfere mercilessly with the most intimate and sacred experiences in life."

Neither the Seymour amicus brief, presented on behalf of sixty-six physicians, nor the PPFA brief, submitted in the names of Ernst and Pilpel, offered any especially notable arguments. Ruth Emerson and Mel Wulf's ACLU/CCLU brief, however, expanded significantly upon the privacy emphasis articulated by Harper, and offered an explicit Fourteenth Amendment due process liberty basis for their contentions: "the Fourteenth Amendment protects persons from invasions of their privacy by the states. The Connecticut statutes in issue, on their face, seek to regulate an aspect of marital conduct that is inherently private and beyond the reach of government." They cited a 1949 Fourth Amendment search and seizure decision, *Wolf* v. *Colorado*, written by

Frankfurter, as their primary privacy precedent. *Wolf* had held that "security of one's privacy against arbitrary intrusion" is "'implicit in the concept of ordered liberty,'" a landmark constitutional phrase and standard signifying a right of such especially significant importance that the Supreme Court would protect it under the Fourteenth Amendment's "liberty" from any infringement by a state. Emerson and Wulf also quoted former Justice Louis D. Brandeis's 1928 adoption of Thomas Cooley's "right to be let alone" expression, and then presented the core of their argument:

> The invasion of privacy here is two-fold. First, the statute on its face restrains married couples from employing the most effective means of contraception when engaged in sexual intercourse. Secondly, as applied, the statute confronts appellants with the choice of engaging in sexual intercourse without contraceptive devices, thereby immediately threatening the life and health of the female spouses, or of abstaining entirely from sexual intercourse.

"Marriage and the family are the foundations of our culture, and the focal points about which individual lives revolve," they went on. "No other rights are entitled to greater privacy than that normally bestowed upon the acts of intercourse and procreation."

Thirty years later, in his midsixties, Mel Wulf archly insisted that writing the *Poe* brief had been particularly compelling. "I was then a single man, living in the Village, and sexually active if not promiscuous . . . I had a personal commitment to birth control, and also abortion." The brief, however, understandably stressed marital and family values to the utmost. Emerson and Wulf maintained that the Connecticut statute should evoke "the same quality of outrage to civilized sensibilities" that Frankfurter had enunciated in an earlier case that had denounced compulsory pumping of a drug suspect's stomach in order to secure evidence. They also noted that there were at least four additional Supreme Court precedents, reaching well beyond the search and seizure context, where the Court at least implicitly had acknowledged "a private right to conjugal or domestic matters," including two—*Meyer* v. *Nebraska* and *Pierce* v. *Society of Sisters*—which expressly recognized "marriage and the family as the ultimate repository of personal freedom."[68]

With Harper in Africa and the case on hold, the final months of 1960 passed relatively quietly. Loraine Campbell continued to gripe about PPLC, but Pilpel wrote Estelle Griswold a commendatory letter to say that "You have done such a wonderful thing in making these cases possible." Estelle declined the honor, insisting that "my part has been a secondary one. Had it not been for the professional courage of Dr. Buxton and Fowler Harper there might not have been a lawsuit for years to come. All I have done is to coordinate and help raise the funds," which now totaled some fifteen thousand dollars in legal expenses. "In fact, at all times, our League has tried to avoid publicity in connection with the cases to give credit for independent action on the part of the litigants."

Estelle was "reasonably sure of success" once the Supreme Court did hear *Poe*, and she kept up a regular correspondence with Harper in Africa, seeking his instructions as to whether an immediate appeal of *Trubek* to the U.S. Supreme Court would be worth the additional costs once the Connecticut Supreme Court issued its anticipated decision. Harper immediately replied that he could compose the necessary documents himself, even in Africa, and he also arranged to review Ray Cannon's brief in defense of the Connecticut statutes once it was filed with the Court in mid-October. Cannon's modest seventeen-page effort emphasized the many occasions on which the state legislature had declined to alter the law before attempting to justify the statute's continued validity. "There is no obligation that the most modern or scientific remedy be chosen" by the legislators as a lawful practice, he insisted, for "it seems obvious that the Connecticut Legislature, speaking for the people of Connecticut, believes that the indiscriminate use of contraceptives will have an eroding effect upon the moral standards of its people." He disparaged Harper's brief by contending that "for the most part appellants' argument is sociological and physiological rather than legal," and ended by objecting to a passing reference Harper had made indicating that "artificial devices to prevent conception are available in Connecticut to unmarried persons."[69]

Fowler informed Estelle that Pilpel's notion that they ought to file a reply brief in answer to Cannon's contentions was utterly unnecessary, and when the Connecticut Supreme Court, as expected, unanimously rejected *Trubek* on November 15, Fowler was still hoping that it might yet be combined with *Poe* in time for U.S. Supreme Court oral argument. PPLC had agreed that a repeal bill, written by Katie Roraback and ostensibly sponsored by the CCLU, would be introduced in the 1961 Connecticut legislature, and in late January two female representatives, Katherine Evarts of Kent and Evelyn Fisher of Oxford, put one forward. Various news stories and articles, including a critical essay on Harper's and the ACLU's briefs in the *Yale Law Journal*, all highlighted the upcoming high court consideration of *Poe*, and early in the new year the National Council of Churches explicitly condemned anticontraception statutes as violations of "the religious and civil liberties of all citizens." Fowler Harper returned from Africa in mid-January, and just a few days later he received official notification that the Supreme Court oral argument of *Poe* had been scheduled for February 27.[70]

In preparation for the *Poe* hearing, several of the nine justices, as was their common practice, had one or another of their young law clerks prepare lengthy private memos analyzing the issues and the briefs that had been submitted in the case. Charles Fried, a 1960 Columbia Law School graduate who was one of Justice John Marshall Harlan's two clerks, prepared a *Poe* memo that expanded upon the critical comments Howard Lesnick had offered Harlan ten months earlier. "Neither one of the parties gives us any help in deciding this case," Fried began. "Fowler Harper's jurisdictional statement is execrable and so is his brief on the merits—it misses the whole point that can be made for his position. The state, perhaps wisely, says as little as possible, on a sit-tight theory." Nonetheless, Fried enthusiastically agreed with Harper's basic position: "the right to privacy is one which enjoys specific consti-tutional sanction," particularly with regard to "the right to privacy of the home being the purpose behind" the Fourth Amendment. Hence "a married couple, enjoying that status in the eyes of the state, in their intimate and specifically marital relations may follow their inclinations and consciences without interference" by the state. It was undeniable that "the substantive right" at issue here "is one of privacy," particularly with regard to the home, and that "individual married couples have a right to engage in marital relations in the privacy of their own con-sciences and free of the intrusion of the criminal law." Connecticut "cannot say," Fried went on, "that a law intruding the criminal law into the privacy of the marital bedroom is *just like* a law forbidding adultery, fornication or homosexuality." Indeed, as was well known, Connecticut's "use" statute was utterly unique, and "If reasonableness is to be the test where the state admittedly encroaches on substantive rights, it is difficult indeed to conceive of more conclusive evidence of unreasonableness."

Nonetheless, the case was not without visible problems. First off, one could argue that as yet "there has been no showing that there is a danger of enforcement" of the Connecticut statute. Similarly, "One cannot escape the feeling that at least as to the complaint of the couple here that this is a totally unnecessary piece of litigation," and as to Dr. Buxton "clearly there is no such right" as a physician's privilege "to practice his profession as he sees best" without any state regulation. Any focus on the specific facts of *Poe*, Fried felt, would lead to a conclusion that "The only possible argument that can be made is that married couples have a right to engage in marital relations without the fear—in some cases—of death or serious illness." However, "the trouble with this argument is that it assumes what is to be proven: that married couples have some kind of innate right to marital relations, and that if the choice must be between contraception on one hand and abstinence or serious danger on the other that the couple has the right to resort to contraception. To my mind," Fried concluded, "this is a much more debatable proposition" than the other, decidedly broader answer that the Court could announce, and that Fried himself expressly recommended: that "married couples have a right to privacy in their intimacy."[71]

Justice William J. Brennan's clerk for *Poe*, however, offered a radically different—and far more skeptical—evaluation of the case than had Charles Fried. Richard S. Arnold, a 1960 Harvard Law School graduate, had, like all Brennan clerks at that time, been selected for the post by Harvard professor Paul Freund without ever having met or spoken with the justice himself. Prior to Harvard, Arnold had been an undergraduate at Yale and an active member of its Episcopal parish; years later he would happen to volunteer that perhaps his favorite Yale instructor had been a history graduate student whose wife he also knew through her job at the church: Hector and Anne Kinloch.

But if Richard Arnold had of course never heard of "Harold and Hanna Hoe," his two long memos to Justice Brennan were decidedly unfavorable to "Paul and Pauline" *Poe*. While Arnold believed there was no question that the appeals were rightfully within the Court's jurisdiction, he nevertheless seriously doubted whether *Poe* and *Buxton* were, in an important but elaborate judicial term of art, "justiciable" and hence worthy of a decision on the merits. The problem was the sketchiness of the cases' earlier development: "There was no trial, no witnesses were heard . . . no findings of fact were made." Yet "on this record the Court is asked to declare that the Connecticut legislature has exceeded its power," and the record was simply "not all one might wish on which to base a decision of a difficult constitutional issue," particularly in the absence of "the refining and sharpening influence of an adversary trial." It was unclear "just how much of an interference with individual liberty does this law entail," and the record was also silent on the question of whether the "rhythm" method of trying to avoid pregnancies was distinctly less dependable than diaphragms or other prohibited devices. "If they exceed in reliability the next best method by only a small margin, then the choice which Connecticut has made may be more reasonable than plaintiffs would have us believe."

Arnold had a further objection, however, one that literally had not dawned on Harper, Roraback, Cannon, or anyone else who so far had been involved with *Poe*. If the Connecticut courts had erred in sustaining Cannon's objections to the suits, Arnold told Brennan, then apparently, under Connecticut's procedural rules, should the U.S. Supreme Court reverse the decision below, such a holding would then require Harper and Roraback *to go to trial* to prove their original contentions, rather than immediately and directly void the 1879 law. Hence the Supreme Court appeal "is somewhat premature. Since there is going to be a trial anyway, if appellants are to succeed, why not have the trial before this Court decides the constitutional issue, instead of after." In short, Arnold said, the high court should "put off a decision" and delay "the evil day when this Court must tell Connecticut whether its law is valid." "This is no hardship for the appellants," he added, "since if we reversed at their request they would have to go to trial on remand anyway."

Several days later Arnold gave Brennan a second long memorandum focusing on the constitutional questions in *Poe* and arguing that if the Court did reach those merits, "the skimpiness of the record will probably compel it to uphold the statute." But Arnold readily conceded that "on a properly constructed record a holding of unconstitutionality would be required," for while Connecticut could cite a valid interest "in prohibiting extramarital intercourse" as underlying the statute, "the appellants have on their side of the balance not only the general interest in marital privacy and autonomy, but also their particular interests in health and life." In the final analysis, "when physical harm and possible death is thrown into the balance, I think the statute becomes unconstitutional as applied."[72]

Fowler Harper had agreed to share a portion of his oral argument time with Harriet Pilpel, and on Monday morning the two attorneys, accompanied by Katie Roraback, Pilpel's associate Nancy Wechsler, Bea Hessel, Estelle Griswold, Miriam Harper, and the Harpers' close friend Betty Phillips all arrived as scheduled at the Supreme Court. Lee Buxton was absent since he was spending the spring in Geneva, but immediately upon everyone's arrival at the Court, Harper received surprising and troubling news: the oral argument was being postponed for two days because Justice Frankfurter was absent due to laryngitis. But Frankfurter had explicitly *not* taken part in *any* of the preliminary decisions regarding the case, so did this now mean both that he had changed his mind regarding recusal, *and* that he was *especially* eager to take part? Harper was both perturbed at the delay, and worried about what Frankfurter's conduct might mean. Hoping to get a better under-standing of what was going on, in the absence of any explanation from the clerk's office, Harper did a *very* highly unusual thing for counsel in a Supreme Court case: remembering that one of Justice Potter Stewart's clerks, Jerry Israel, was a former Yale Law School student whom he had known in passing, Harper went to Stewart's chambers, asked for Israel, and queried the highly surprised clerk as to whether he had any idea what was going on. Not surprisingly, Israel didn't.

In fact, at about eight p.m. on Sunday evening the 26th, Frankfurter had called Chief Justice Warren at home to request the postponement on account of his laryngitis, and the Chief had agreed. The involuntary two-day delay did offer Pilpel and the Connecticut group, especially Griswold, Roraback, and Hessel, a much better opportunity to get to know each other in a friendly, nonadversarial setting, and Pilpel's deputy, Nancy Wechsler, later mused that perhaps the unplanned and enforced camaraderie occasioned by the Supreme Court delay went a good way toward erasing most of the tensions that previously had so heavily colored the PPLC-Pilpel interactions.[73]

By Wednesday, March 1, Felix Frankfurter had his voice back, and at two forty-five p.m. that afternoon *Poe et al.* and *Buxton* v. *Ullman* were called for oral argument before the full bench of nine justices. Fowler Harper, in an impressively strong and clear voice, began his presenta-tion by offering understated but extremely powerful descriptions of "Jane Doe's" and "Pauline Poe's" medical situations. Justice Potter Stewart interrupted with the first question, asking if he was correct in thinking that no Connecticut statute aside from the accessory one pro-hibited the sale or prescription of contraceptive articles, and after Harper answered yes, Stewart followed up by asking whether Harper was challenging Connecticut's use statute only in the context of women facing serious health threats. Harper, slightly off stride for the first time in the hearing, replied that the plaintiffs were challenging the statutes both "on their face" and as applied, and then Felix Frankfurter jumped in to querulously ask Harper why no First Amendment free speech argument was being made on behalf of Dr. Buxton. Harper par-ried, conceding that that was true, but Frankfurter pursued him: "And why is that? I don't understand it." Harper paused for a considerable time, explained that there were other cases, the clergy ones, still pend-ing below, and then gently conceded that perhaps a speech contention should have been included in the pleadings, but that since it was not, he could not argue it now. Another justice quietly interjected that the

Fourteenth Amendment also prohibited state interference with constitutionally protected speech, but Frankfurter again broke in, telling
Harper "It's not for me to decide how you should argue." Laughter
rippled through the courtroom, and Harper moved on to emphasize.
"the liberty of the marital relation" and how "these laws mercilessly
invade the privacy of a married couple." Potter Stewart interrupted to
ask whether freedom to practice one's religion was involved, and
Harper answered yes while noting that these plaintiffs had not made
that contention.

Harper's argument proceeded without interruption for some ten
minutes before Justice Harlan asked him how many prosecutions a
year there were under the Connecticut statutes. Harper responded that
he did not know, and Stewart then asked, "Is the law really enforced?"
Harper responded somewhat lamely than "I'm ignorant of the extent to
which the law is enforced . . . so far as I know it has never been
enforced against a person who used a contraceptive. . . . Police do not
peek into people's bedrooms to see whether they're using contraceptives . . . I know of no prosecution of an individual for use." Then he
recovered and pointed out how, since the *Nelson* decision, "no public or
private clinic for the purpose of advising on contraception" had operated in the state. "The people in Connecticut who need contraceptive
advice from doctors most—the people in the lower income brackets
and lower educational brackets—the people who need it most, do not
get it, because there are no clinics available." Justice Brennan asked
Harper whether there were any similar statutes elsewhere, and after
describing the Massachusetts one, Harper concluded his initial forty-
five minutes and yielded to Harriet Pilpel.

Pilpel, relying heavily on her notes, spoke almost exclusively to
medical considerations. Some eight minutes passed without a single
question from any justice until Stewart queried her about what the
medical view of contraception might have been in 1879, and Pilpel
returned to her disquisition for another long stretch before Frankfurter
inquired about Connecticut's sterilization law and opined that perhaps
Buxton should have sterilized "Jane Doe" and "Pauline Poe." Pilpel
pointed out that sterilization was irreversible, and then Frankfurter,
joined by Justice Whittaker, began peppering her with questions as to
whether doctors were more knowledgeable than legislators. Pilpel
acknowledged that "we recognize that we have the heavy burden in
this case," and then further conceded that "my argument is restricted to
these cases" of Poe and Doe's specific medical conditions alone.

Just before four p.m. Raymond Cannon began his argument in

defense of the Connecticut statutes. A far less effective speaker than Harper, or even Pilpel, Cannon floundered from point to point before Chief Justice Warren interrupted him with a pointed question as to whether Connecticut rightfully could deny life-saving treatment to someone in "Jane Doe's" situation. "It is our view," Cannon replied, "that it is the problem primarily for the legislature to determine what is the greater good and how to accomplish the greater good." That answer provoked both Warren and Potter Stewart, who sarcastically told Cannon that that was like telling a patient that they had appendicitis and would die unless it was removed, but that appendix removals were not allowed. Then Warren followed up, expressing amazement that the law, in a situation such as Jane Doe's, could prohibit her from receiving appropriate medical treatment. Cannon responded that "There are proper ways to prevent conception through the natural means which they call rhythm. . . . The legislature has adopted one system. The legislature is free to adopt whichever system it sees fit, provided it's reasonable for the purpose for which the law is intended." Felix Frankfurter drew Cannon into a colloquy about popular government and legislators, observing that "in a democracy they have a right to elect even ignorant people" to office. Frankfurter wondered whether there might be some "outside authoritarian power" that was coercing the Connecticut legislature to adopt a minority preference, and Cannon forthrightly declared that "I don't believe there's any outside power in Connecticut influencing the legislature." Justice Brennan asked whether Cannon regarded the sale of certain articles for the prevention of disease to be legal in Connecticut, and Cannon said no, for any use of such articles was a violation of the 1879 law. Cannon added that he knew of at least two unreported cases some years earlier where store owners had been arrested for having contraceptive vending machines on their premises. Justice Hugo Black got Cannon to readily acknowledge that the law indeed prohibited Dr. Buxton from saying some things to patients that he professionally might want to, and then, at four thirty p.m., the Court adjourned for the day.

Shortly after noontime on Wednesday, March 2, the oral argument resumed with Felix Frankfurter all but monopolizing Ray Cannon's remaining time. He asked Cannon whether contraceptives were widely available in the state, and when the assistant attorney general replied that "I have no personal knowledge of this," the justice quipped that "I wasn't attempting to explore your personal knowledge." Frankfurter pursued the theme that actual convictions under the use statute were necessarily nonexistent, musing that "we're talking about a theoretical

thing here, aren't we?" Cannon gently demurred, saying "It may be
academic, but it has some effect," and a surprised Frankfurter responded with a sharp "What?" Cannon replied that the statute had a deterrent effect in protecting the "moral qualities" of Connecticut citizens.
Frankfurter offered Cannon several opportunities to articulate additional purposes for the statute, and when Cannon failed to volunteer
what Frankfurter was anticipating, the justice explained to the harried
attorney that encouraging population growth was obviously a major
premise for the law. John Harlan asked Cannon whether "Connecticut
can pass a statute that impinges on the privacy of the marriage relationship," and Cannon responded that since marriage of course effected
the morals of a society, that the state necessarily could regulate the relationship.

Shortly after one p.m. Fowler Harper resumed his argument for the
final twenty-five minutes of the hearing. He emphasized that contraceptive articles, including diaphragms, were quietly available for purchase in Connecticut pharmacies, and Justice Stewart, seemingly in
agreement, interjected that "this may all be an abstract attack on the
law" and that "the law has no impact." Harper tried to back pedal
rapidly, declaring that "The law certainly has an impact on Poe and
Doe, and under it no clinics can function." Justice Brennan immediately broke in, asking "Isn't the operation of clinics what's at stake here
really?" Harper indicated yes, and just as the final time expired
Brennan observed, as much to himself as to Harper, that "I take it that
the Poes and Does can get what they need almost anyplace in
Connecticut."[74]

The PPLC and PPFA contingent were unanimously impressed with
what a superb job Fowler Harper had done, especially in handling
Justice Frankfurter's many challenges, but they acknowledged to each
other that the outcome was far from certain. Savvy press observers,
including a UPI reporter and a *Time* magazine correspondent, however, frankly predicted, as the latter writer put it, that the peppery justice
"had laid the basis for an opinion that the case was hypothetical" and
hence nonjusticiable. And when the nine justices convened on Friday
morning, March 3, to discuss and vote on *Poe v. Ullman* and the other
cases that had been argued earlier that week, the journalists' prognostication proved all too prophetic.[75]

Chief Justice Earl Warren presided at each of the Court's private
conferences and spoke first. PPLC's Bea Hessel had thought during
the oral argument that the white-haired Chief Justice had "the mien of
a loving father," and his warm manner and kind-hearted nature made

him a popular figure among most of his brethren and among law clerks and court employees. Many of his clerks across the years appreciated that the Chief Justice was very much a family man and a traditionalist, someone who was discomforted not only by the pornographic materials which the court often had to review in obscenity cases but also by any discussion concerning sex. Some of the clerks would acknowledge as well the Chief's relative disinterest in doctrinal technicalities, but clerks who watched carefully also noted Warren's long private visits to Justice Brennan's chambers the day before each of the Court's weekly conferences.

Warren began the discussion of *Poe* v. *Ullman* by observing that he could not call the Connecticut statute unconstitutional on its face, for to do so would represent a return to the largely abandoned doctrine of substantive due process. Just as importantly, the plaintiffs had made the justices "guinea pigs for an abstract principle," and Warren did not want the Court to decide "contrived litigation" when contraceptives could be purchased in any Connecticut drugstore and where there was no indication that the 1879 statute had ever or would ever be enforced. In short, *Poe* might well fail to meet the constitutional requirement that the Court decide only real "cases or controversies." Additionally, there were undeniable problems with the record: could a doctor be convicted under the accessory statute without proof of a patient's use of a contraceptive, and was or was not the sale of such articles in Connecticut actually legal. Harper and PPFA's medical evidence was in no way dispositive, and, all in all, whether or not the 1879 statute was unconstitutional as applied could be determined only after a trial had generated extensive evidence and findings. In short, the Chief would vote to dismiss the appeal and return *Poe* to the Connecticut courts.

The most senior associate justice, Hugo L. Black, spoke next. An Alabama native and former U.S. Senator, Black was an enthusiastic tennis player who deeply enjoyed serving on the court. Blessed with an encyclopedic memory and deeply committed to a literalist judicial philosophy that lent both a consistency and a predictability to his votes, Black relied less upon his two law clerks for help in drafting opinions than perhaps any other member of the court. An outgoing man who was not shy about trying to persuade his colleagues to support his own intense views, Black nonetheless believed that philosophical differences should not interfere with friendly relations. His years of disagreements with Frankfurter had created some "real distance" between the two men, but when a clerk once referred to the other justice as "Felix," Black firmly reprimanded him for such implicit disrespect.

Black was generally viewed as a liberal, but his closest friend on the court was the patrician John Harlan, whom many observers pigeon-holed as a colorless conservative. Black like Warren was something of a prude on sexual matters, and while some clerks had ambivalent if not critical feelings about the justices for whom they worked, Black's almost always felt that their justice was a wonderful man with an almost fatherly interest in furthering their appreciation of the law.

On *Poe* v. *Ullman*, Black began by noting that ten months earlier he had voted to affirm the Connecticut court without hearing the appeal. He still felt that way with regard to the Poes and Jane Doe, Black explained, because it was not appropriate for the judiciary to review the reasonableness of Connecticut's policy against any use of contraceptives. Personally, Black volunteered, it made no difference to him whether people used such devices, but the Court should not use the Fourteenth Amendment's due process clause as a vehicle for second-guessing legislative choices on a topic where the Constitution set forth no explicit barrier. Regarding Dr. Buxton, however, Black felt very differently, for a doctor was entitled under the First Amendment to *talk* to his patients about everything or anything without any statutory interference or punishment. Black's absolutist view of the First Amendment's protection of speech was well known and well understood by his brethren, and his explanation that no doctor could be prosecuted as an "aider and abettor" did not surprise any of his colleagues. With regard to "the ladies," however, Black would affirm.

The third justice to speak was the redoubtable Felix Frankfurter. An intense proponent of his views, especially with regard to the indispensable need for judicial restraint, Frankfurter's stubborn persistence had visibly alienated both Warren and Brennan. Never close to Black, some clerks also believed that Frankfurter was barely on speaking terms with William O. Douglas. Frankfurter's own clerks, with only a rare exception, were—like Brennan's—selected for him by Harvard law professor Paul Freund, but Frankfurter regarded every clerk in the court as a potential recruit and never hesitated to discuss substantive issues with other justices' clerks. Some clerks viewed Frankfurter as a troublesome "busybody" or "perverse character" who was sometimes openly "patronizing" toward one or another of his less-gifted brethren, but more than two decades of service on the Court had done nothing to dilute Frankfurter's intellectual intensity or personal aggressiveness.

On *Poe*, Frankfurter's remarks in conference followed naturally from his persistent queries during the oral argument. The Chief Justice was correct that the appeal should be dismissed, Frankfurter began, for to reach the merits in this sort of a declaratory judgment action with such a minimal record would run the risk of issuing an improper, advisory opinion. He could not imagine, Frankfurter went on, any doctor not giving contraceptive advice for fear of going to jail; what the plaintiffs clearly wanted was authorization to open clinics. Instead they should take the risk of going to jail and then bring the case to the Supreme Court if they were actually prosecuted. Additionally, Frankfurter said, how could this Court simply rule that "rhythm" was no good?

The next most senior justice, William O. Douglas, went after Frankfurter with alacrity. Indeed, he had been battling angrily with Frankfurter, among others, for all of his more than twenty years on the high court. Acknowledged as truly brilliant even by those who personally detested him, Douglas nonetheless was viewed as an intellectually lazy underachiever even by those who considered themselves his relative friends. Far and away the most reclusive and aloof of the justices, Douglas would never lobby any of his colleagues for support in a case and often would not even say hello to clerks whom he passed in the hallways. Only Douglas had one rather than two clerks, and almost without exception Douglas would scrawl out the first—and sometimes the only—draft of an opinion on a legal pad without any preparatory work by the clerk. Some years Douglas would hector the young man, others he would all but ignore him; among clerks from other chambers the almost unanimous impression was that William O. Douglas was "not a very nice human being."

Frankfurter, Douglas bluntly declared, was wrong on all counts. *Poe* was a legitimate declaratory judgment action, and undeniably involved a valid case and controversy. Moreover, the 1879 Connecticut statute was clearly unconstitutional on its face. The appeal should not be dismissed, and the Connecticut court's decision should be reversed.

Tom C. Clark, the fifth justice to speak, was a Texan who had been Harry Truman's Attorney General before being nominated and confirmed as a justice despite Fowler Harper's 1949 testimony against him. Personally popular among his colleagues and among the clerks, Clark was viewed by many of the clerks as "a wonderful politician" who was miscast as a Supreme Court justice. Some clerks judged him to be "by far the weakest intellect on the Court," but he nonetheless was often a crucial swing vote, and he was on especially good terms with the similarly personable Warren. On *Poe*, Clark's comments were simple and highly succinct: the suit did not meet the constitutional case or controversy requirement, and the appeal should be dismissed.

Next came John Marshall Harlan, the conservative and understated New Yorker who nine years earlier, while still in private practice, had been recommended to PPLC as a possible attorney for a declaratory judgment action. A justice for six years now, he was both a careful craftsman and a consistent yet thoughtful conservative—"a Frankfurter without the mustard," one clerk from another chambers quipped. Among the clerks, Harlan was perhaps the most respected justice of all, and he was personally close to both Frankfurter and the court's most junior member, Potter Stewart.

"We have no business dismissing these cases," Harlan began. The suits were not fictitious or feigned, they met the case or controversy standard, and there was no uncertainty as to how the Connecticut court had construed the 1879 law: it prohibited the contraceptive practices that the women plaintiffs had been told by their doctor were imperative. On the merits, Harlan said, it was not a close call: the statute was unconstitutional on its face, and indeed was "the most egregiously unconstitutional act I have seen since being on the Court." For someone of John Harlan's quiet and sober style, such a forceful and passionate statement was extremely unusual. The oral argument, Harlan went on, had submerged the real constitutional questions. He could not, like Black, vote to strike the Connecticut law on First Amendment grounds, but for him the Fourteenth Amendment's due process clause, protecting "life, liberty, or property," against state action, had substantive content apart from the specific provisions of the first eight amendments that the Court sometimes had "incorporated" to apply to the states through the language of the Fourteenth. And due process liberty, Harlan continued, protected "the right to be let alone." Despite states' broad powers to legislate in the area of health, the due process clause imposed limits, and a state could not use any and all means to regulate marital relations. The Connecticut law, he reminded his colleagues, was a "use" statute and as such was uniquely different from laws regulating the sale or prescription of such articles. Nothing could be more offensive to the concept of a "right to be let alone" than interjecting the criminal law into the privacy of the marital relationship. Police officers should not be able to get a search warrant to see if contraceptives could be found, and all other searches would pale in comparison to those that could follow from the Connecticut law. No matter what kind of record this case might have, the statute was unconstitutional on its face.

Justice William J. Brennan, the Court's only Roman Catholic member, had already told his two clerks, Richard Arnold and Dan Rezneck, after the oral argument that he was definitely inclined to agree with what appeared to be the majority of his colleagues—and Arnold's earlier recommendation—that *Poe* v. *Ullman* should be dismissed for failure to state an adequate controversy or to present a full and detailed record. They and other clerks were well aware of Brennan's special closeness to the Chief Justice, and Brennan's warm and approachable demeanor made him, like Tom Clark and Warren, one of the Court's most personable and popular justices. Generally a quiet figure at oral arguments, Brennan's remarks about *Poe* at the Friday conference were brief and succinct: it simply failed to meet the case or controversy standard.

Charles E. Whittaker similarly had little to say. A justice for four years, Whittaker had been a Kansas City corporate attorney before being named to the federal bench, and then elevated to the Supreme Court, largely because of his close friendship with the president's brother, Arthur Eisenhower. His own clerks viewed Whittaker as a quiet and "extremely conscientious man" who unfortunately was quite uncomfortable with and hence very indecisive about many constitutional questions. As a result, he had become a particular target of Felix Frankfurter's incessant lobbying, and a wide range of clerks who had witnessed Frankfurter's behavior toward the insecure Kansan felt that the situation was unpleasant and offensive. Whittaker's chambers were next to those of Hugo Black, and while Black too would energetically woo him, Whittaker's clerks thought that Black came as close to being Whittaker's friend as anyone on the court. Black's clerks watched with particular chagrin as Frankfurter "hounded and hounded" the neighboring justice, and when an unnerved Whittaker finally gave up and resigned from the Court a year later, more than one clerk readily concluded that Frankfurter unintentionally had "chased poor Whittaker off the Court." But for *Poe* v. *Ullman*, Whittaker said, Frankfurter was indeed correct: *Poe* did not satisfy the case or controversy requirement.

The Court's ninth and most junior member was Potter Stewart, a forty-six-year-old Ohio Republican who was in only his third year as a justice. Already close to John Harlan, whose chambers were right next door, Stewart too was a moderate conservative with a clear attraction to issues of jurisdiction and procedure. Although he never failed to win the respect of his own clerks, in other chambers during Stewart's early years on the high court many of the young assistants viewed him as something of a cipher.

On *Poe*, Stewart's comments echoed those of Harlan. It would be "cynical," he remarked, "to dismiss a case on the grounds that a law will not be enforced. A law is a law, and it is not a dead letter," especially when "as a practical matter there's no clinic in Connecticut." On the constitutional merits, Stewart said, he also fully agreed with John Harlan.

The discussion concluded, the tally was relatively clear: there were at least five clear votes—Warren, Frankfurter, Clark, Brennan, and Whittaker—for dismissing the appeals, and only three justices— Douglas, Harlan, and Stewart—who would reverse the Connecticut court and void the statute. Hugo Black apparently could be counted as a sixth vote for the majority in *Poe*, but certainly not in *Buxton*. Early Monday morning, three days later, when the Chief Justice's assignment sheet was circulated to all chambers, the opinion for the Court in *Poe* v. *Ullman* was assigned to the justice who had almost recused himself: Felix Frankfurter.[76]

Before the day was out, Frankfurter had jotted down a short but internally complex outline of how he wanted his clerks to go about drafting a *Poe* v. *Ullman* opinion, emphasizing that there should be a comprehensive canvassing of prior decisions in which the Court had similarly declined to reach the merits of a case that had been appealed. Frankfurter perchance had three clerks, rather than the usual two, for the 1960–1961 term, and that relative luxury offered him an opportunity that he chose to take full advantage of with *Poe*: he gave his brief memo to both Dan Mayers, a Harvard Law School graduate who had been chosen for him by Paul Freund, and to Anthony "Tony" Amsterdam, a University of Pennsylvania Law School graduate and the special third clerk whom Frankfurter had taken on because of truly exceptional reports that Amsterdam was as brilliant a law student as anyone anywhere had seen in some time. Frankfurter's instructions to Mayer and Amsterdam were unusual but not wholly out of character: *both* of them should work on preparing *separate* drafts of a *Poe* opinion in line with his framework, and, until the first of them had finished, they should *not* share or discuss their work with each other or with their third colleague, John French.[77]

At much the same time that Felix Frankfurter was outlining *Poe*'s demise, Fowler Harper was pondering how the Court's obvious doubts about whether there actually was any realistic threat that the Connecticut statute would be enforced against anyone, doubts that had been so manifest in the repeated questions voiced during the oral argument, might be refuted and disproved. Remembering that the last reported effort to enforce the 1879 law was of course *State* v. *Nelson*, and knowing that the very same William B. Fitzgerald who had prosecuted *Nelson* was still, twenty-one years later, the State's Attorney at

Waterbury, Fowler Harper had an idea. He picked up the phone and called J. Warren Upson, who also, like his longtime friend Bill Fitzgerald, was still a leading figure on the Waterbury legal scene. Now fifty-seven years old, Warren Upson had been out of touch with the PPLC for over a decade, but he was immediately willing to try to help with Fowler Harper's request: would Bill Fitzgerald be willing to execute a formal affidavit affirming that now, in 1961, he would pursue enforcement of the 1879 statute against any birth control clinic just as he had back in 1939–1940?

Wednesday, March 8, Warren Upson had "a long conference" with Bill Fitzgerald about their long-ago settlement of State v. Nelson two decades earlier, and while Fitzgerald affirmed that his position remained unchanged from what he had said in his formal statement in court on the day that the criminal charges against Clara McTernan and the two young doctors had been nolled, Fitzgerald nonetheless was unwilling to execute an affidavit for Fowler Harper to send along to the United States Supreme Court. Mulling the alternatives, Warren Upson selected the next best option: he unearthed a three-page copy of the court reporter's transcript of Fitzgerald's remarks back on April 2, 1940, and executed his own affidavit. He identified himself as counsel for the Nelson defendants and affirmed that the 1939 charges "were instituted in no sense with the prior knowledge of the accused and there was no pre-trial acquiescence by the accused that said actions would be instituted to test the constitutionality of the statutes in question." He immediately sent both documents off to Harper, who in turn sent them at once to the Supreme Court for formal consideration. Chief Justice Warren alerted Frankfurter to the submission, and they both agreed that it should not be made an official part of the record or circulated to all nine chambers. But Frankfurter read both Upson's affidavit and Fitzgerald's 1940 declaration that "any person" who violated the 1879 statute "must expect to be prosecuted and punished in accordance with the literal provisions of the law," and contemplated what if anything he should do about the apparent contradiction between this evidence of prosecutorial intent and the Court's forthcoming decision that Poe should be dismissed because of the absence of any credible evidence that the patients or Dr. Buxton faced any tangible threat that the old law would be enforced against them. Even Frankfurter's most supportive clerks realized that their justice was "such a rash character" that at times his actions could surprise anyone, but when Bill Fitzgerald picked up the phone and an unfamiliar voice introduced himself as Felix Frankfurter, the state's attorney for a moment wondered if someone was pulling his leg. But Frankfurter was Frankfurter, and as a "quite stunned" Fitzgerald subsequently related to his family, the justice wanted to talk about *State v. Nelson*. Precisely what was said in the "pretty extraordinary" conversation was not recorded by either party, but whatever transpired did not alter Felix Frankfurter's conviction that the legacy of *State v. Nelson* represented no barrier to the U.S. Supreme Court dismissing *Poe v. Ullman* on the grounds that no immediate threat of prosecution faced the *Poe* plaintiffs.[78]

Fortunately or unfortunately, however, neither Felix Frankfurter nor Fowler Harper kept up with the *Wallingford Post* or ever happened to hear of Thomas Coccomo. Forty years old and a resident of Deep River, Connecticut, Mr. Coccomo's 1961 endeavors included a modest, wholesale effort to furnish contraceptive articles—condoms—to gas station operators interested in offering such items to retail customers. On March 3, 1961—the very same day that the nine justices of the U.S. Supreme Court were privately voting to dismiss *Poe v. Ullman* on the grounds that there was no evidence that the 1879 Connecticut anticontraception was ever enforced against anyone—Mr. Coccomo's vocation took him to several service stations in North Haven, Connecticut. Someone apparently complained about his toils, for at one station his sales pitch was interrupted by Lieutenant Walter Berniere and Sergeant Thomas Nerreau of the North Haven police. They ascertained that Mr. Coccomo had approximately a hundred dollars' worth of contraceptive articles in his car, and they promptly seized his merchandise and arrested him for violating the aiding and abetting portion of the 1879 statute.

Mr. Coccomo retained legal counsel, and four weeks after his arrest appeared in Wallingford Circuit Court before Judge John Daly. The prosecutor indicated that an agreement had been reached: Mr. Coccomo would plead guilty, and only a modest fine would be recommended as punishment in light of the fact that the constitutionality of the statute was under review by the U.S. Supreme Court. Coccomo's attorney stated that he believed the maximum possible fine was fifty dollars, but Judge Daly disregarded his comment and imposed a penalty of seventy-five dollars. The North Haven Police Department would be instructed to burn all of the seized condoms. For better or for worse, Mr. Coccomo's criminal conviction—and the *Wallingford Post*'s front-page coverage of it—never entered into the Supreme Court's consideration of whether *Poe v. Ullman* was anything more than an academic challenge to an unenforced statute.[79]

While Felix Frankfurter's clerks set to work on a majority opinion for *Poe* v. *Ullman*, Fowler Harper and PPLC waited patiently for a decision that they expected would be announced sometime in late May or early to mid-June. Harper submitted a jurisdictional statement for *Trubek* v. *Ullman* to the high court that largely copied his earlier arguments in *Poe*, and PPLC made modest preparations for an April 12 legislative hearing on its 1961 repeal bill. Joseph Cooney chose to submit simply a written statement of opposition on behalf of the Connecticut Catholic hierarchy, and in the absence of any actual opponents, the 1961 hearing was a relatively brief and low-key affair. The principal affirmative witness, David Leventhal of the CCLU, devoted most of his remarks to emphasizing that the right to privacy was "perhaps *the* primary right guaranteed to the people of this state under the Constitution," but committee chairman William F. Hickey told the hearing that his panel would "hold off action as long as possible" on the bill in anticipation that the U.S. Supreme Court might very well resolve the problem once and for all. Two weeks later the Public Health and Safety Committee approved the repeal bill, but proponents, knowing that the measure had no chance of passage in the state senate, simply left it on the calendar for the remainder of the legislative session rather than bring it up for a floor vote even in the house.[80]

Estelle Griswold, like Fowler Harper, was not at all sure what the Supreme Court's decision would be, but by mid-May she was certain of something else: that if the Court were to rule against PPLC and dismiss *Poe* v. *Ullman*, the Connecticut League would move as quickly as possible to ignore and defy the old statute by openly offering some form of birth control services. PPLC had some sixty thousand dollars on hand to finance the opening of a clinic, especially should the law indeed be struck down, and Estelle discussed the possibilities with both outgoing president Bea Hessel and her incoming successor, Lucia Parks of Southport, whose PPLC involvement went back to the Hepburn era when she had worked as a volunteer at the Bridgeport clinic in 1938. At PPLC's annual meeting on May 24, with everyone crossing their fingers in anticipation of a Supreme Court ruling that might well come any day, Fowler Harper spoke optimistically about their prospects and read from a hilarious forthcoming student essay that parodied the Connecticut law by analyzing how pet owners might be arrested if they utilized a new oral contraceptive that recently had been developed for animals. More seriously, Harper told the PPLCers that if the Supreme Court did rule against them, their principal challenge might then become finding a way to get Estelle Griswold jailed.[81]

It was not until June 3, three full months after the conference discussion that had decided *Poe* v. *Ullman*, that Felix Frankfurter finally circulated to his colleagues a printed draft of an opinion for the Court. Both Dan Mayers and Tony Amsterdam had each prepared several successive drafts of a modest-sized opinion, and in the end Frankfurter chose to work from Amsterdam's version, revising and modifying Amsterdam's draft to a significant but not overwhelming extent. As soon as the Frankfurter opinion was distributed, John Harlan immediately sent a note to all his fellow justices notifying them that he would circulate a dissenting opinion "very shortly." Harlan had been away from the Court for several weeks since the conference discussion of *Poe*, undergoing surgery for a stomach ulcer, and he had turned over responsibility for preparing the opinion to one of his two clerks, Charles Fried. Harlan had orally instructed Fried to draft a dissent that stated that *Poe* was indeed justiciable, and while he said relatively little to his clerk about how, or at what length, to address the constitutional merits, both Fried and his coclerk, Philip Heymann, had heard the justice voice his outrage at the invasion of marital privacy that the Connecticut statute represented, and Fried knew full well that Harlan more than agreed with the enthusiastic advocacy of constitutional protection for marital privacy in the home that Fried had offered two months earlier in his initial memo on *Poe*. Hence in Harlan's absence Fried prepared a sixty-page typescript draft of an opinion that spoke both to the appeal's justiciability and, at some length, to the plaintiffs' constitutionally protected marital privacy. When Harlan returned from his hospitalization Fried waited curiously to see whether the justice would feel that he had gone too far. Little was said about it—"we didn't have a lot of discussion," Fried remembered thirty years later—but Harlan clearly liked the draft, and gave it only a modest pencil editing before sending it to the Court's print shop and then, on June 14, to all of his eight colleagues.[82]

Fried's fellow clerks in other chambers were in many cases both impressed and more than a little amazed by the dissent that Justice Harlan circulated. Generally not privy, except in some chambers at second hand, to the comments that justices uttered in the court's private conferences, Fried's colleagues had heard neither Harlan's passionate conference comments on *Poe* nor the similarly vociferous remarks that the justice had made to his own clerks. Some of them hence viewed Harlan's strong denunciation of the Connecticut law as a constitutionally offensive violation of marital privacy and liberty as distinctly out of character for such a conservative and solemn justice. A few, such as Brennan clerk Richard Arnold, who would often give Fried a ride to work in the mornings, already knew secondhand how strongly Harlan felt, but for many others the tone and content of the Harlan dissent came as quite a surprise. Virtually all of the clerks ate lunch together almost every day, and after ten months of close companionship the group had reached a clear consensus as to who were the undeniable intellectual stars—Amsterdam, Arnold, and Fried—and also knew their friends' predilections and styles. Hence when the Harlan dissent was circulated and read, "Everyone knew it was Charles," one colleague explained years later.[83]

The same day that Harlan's dissent circulated, a similar but considerably shorter one by William O. Douglas was also distributed to all chambers. Douglas usually prepared his dissents very soon after the initial conference, and this one had been ready for internal dissemination since late March. Douglas was also well-known for being extremely eager that the Court adjourn as early in May or June as was possible so that he could leave Washington, D.C., for his summer home in rural Washington state. On two recent mornings in succession the usually standoffish Douglas had sat down in the Court cafeteria beside a clerk from another chambers to whom he had never before spoken and asked the slightly startled young man, "When do you think we'll get out of here?" The clerk had twice mumbled noncommittal responses, wondering the second day whether Douglas even realized he was reenacting the previous morning's conversation. Then Douglas each time had launched into a soliloquy on how splendid the schedule had been in the late 1930s, when Douglas first came on the Court, and Charles Evans Hughes saw to it that they were done by Memorial Day. "Now there was a Chief Justice!"

Douglas's dissent in *Poe* was more thorough and carefully crafted than many Douglas opinions, and on the evening of June 13 Douglas had told fellow justice William J. Brennan that he would circulate it the following day. Two months earlier Brennan had sounded like a firm member of what appeared to be a five-vote Frankfurter majority, but now he was uncertain, and on the thirteenth and fourteenth he made that clear both to Douglas and to his own clerks. He indicated to Douglas that he might well choose to join Douglas's own dissent, but Douglas, rather than welcoming and encouraging Brennan's new inclination, instead warned him that such a shift would cause a serious problem: so far only two members of Frankfurter's ostensible majority, Clark and Whittaker, had formally joined the opinion, and if either Brennan and/or Chief Justice Warren failed to go with Frankfurter, the absence of a fifth vote—in the context of Justice Black's unique

stance—would leave the Court without any clear majority for deciding
Poe. Most importantly, Douglas noted, if they got tied up in any extensive reconsideration of *Poe*, the hope of concluding the term next
Monday, June 19, could very well be endangered. Hence it would be
better, Douglas told Brennan, for him to 'stick with Felix so we can get
this case decided and get out of here.'[84]

Other cases too—particularly a 5 to 4 Fourth Amendment search
and seizure decision that was being written by Justice Clark, *Mapp* v.
Ohio, were also scheduled for final ratification at a Friday conference
and announcement on Monday the 19th, but throughout Wednesday
the 14th and Thursday the 15th, Brennan remained undecided about
Poe, pondering whether he might prepare a small separate concurrence
of his own rather than join either Frankfurter or Douglas. Hence the
question of whether there would be a majority disposition of *Poe*
remained highly uncertain, and on Thursday Frankfurter circulated a
very slightly revised version of his previous draft. He pointed out to his
colleagues in a cover letter that at two places in the opinion he had
added sentences strengthening the decision's reliance on the fact that
no prosecutions under the statute had ever been pursued and that
there were no indications that the law presently was being enforced
against anyone.

The other uncertain member of the tentative Frankfurter majority
was Earl Warren. The Chief Justice had not been fully persuaded by
the initial version of Frankfurter's opinion, and even the Thursday
emendations had not completely eliminated his discomfort. He told
his clerks that "I just hate to strike down any law that's passed in the
name of the public interest," and while it seemed unlikely that he
could imaginably join either Harlan or Douglas, heading into the
Court's final conference of the term neither Earl Warren nor Bill
Brennan had firmly decided what they would do with *Poe* v. *Ullman*.

Friday morning in advance of that final conference Brennan
instructed his clerk Richard Arnold to draft a brief separate concurrence, endorsing the dismissal of *Poe* on the grounds that the real
Connecticut dispute concerned clinics, for Brennan to review right
after the meeting. Then, once the conference was underway, Brennan
just before eleven thirty a.m. sent out a note informing Arnold that the
term was indeed going to conclude on Monday, that he *was* going to
join in the dismissal of *Poe* by means of a separate concurrence, which
he had promised his colleagues would be circulated before the end of
the day, and that Arnold immediately should prepare a draft. Arnold sat
down and did just that, and within a half hour sent in to Brennan for

his approval a five-sentence statement of Brennan's views. Five minutes later Brennan sent out another note informing Arnold that his
draft was fine and that it should be typed up and then distributed to all
chambers.

After the conference concluded, Arnold and other clerks learned the
final score: the Chief Justice by the end of the day would join either
the Frankfurter opinion or the Brennan concurrence, thus guaranteeing five clear votes for a dismissal of *Poe*. Justice Black would be
recorded as dissenting without opinion. By the end of the afternoon
Justice Stewart, the other dissenter, circulated a three-sentence statement that hinted, but did not expressly state, that he shared the views
of both Harlan and Douglas. Also late in the afternoon Earl Warren, at
the urging of at least one of his clerks, sent Felix Frankfurter a two-
word note—"I agree"—indicating that he would join Frankfurter
rather than Brennan. The conference had similarly decided that the
appeal in *Trubek* v. *Ullman* would also be dismissed, with Justices
Douglas, Harlan, and Stewart in disagreement. Privately but perhaps
most notably of all, Justice Brennan in recounting the conference to his
clerks firmly revealed that were he actually to reach the merits in *Poe*,
he definitely could not vote to affirm the decision below and would
instead vote to void the statute as applied. Thus by only the tiniest of
margins had *Poe* v. *Ullman*—and PPLC—come up one vote shy of convincing the United States Supreme Court that P. T. Barnum's long-
lived 1879 criminalization of birth control should finally be held
constitutionally void.[85]

On Monday morning, June 19, the Supreme Court formally handed
down its 5 to 4 dismissal of *Poe* v. *Ullman*. The final version of the
Frankfurter opinion that commanded only four votes came to just
eleven small pages in print. It emphasized the "lack of immediacy" of
any threat of prosecution, called the *Poe* challenge "abstract," and
brushed aside *Nelson* as a "test case." "Neither counsel nor our own
researches have discovered any other attempt to enforce" the 1879 law,
and this "undeviating policy of nullification" of the old statute highlighted the "unreality" of the *Poe*, *Doe*, and *Buxton* lawsuits. "Federal
judicial power," Frankfurter emphasized, "is to be exercised to strike
down legislation . . . only at the instance of one who is himself immediately harmed, or immediately threatened with harm, by the challenged" law. Where there was no "realistic fear of prosecution,"
Frankfurter concluded, "[t]his Court cannot be umpire to debates concerning harmless, empty shadows."[86]

William Brennan's brief concurrence was simple and straightforward. The *Poe* appeal, he said, failed to present "a real and substantial controversy" and was based upon a "skimpy record." He was unconvinced that the individual plaintiffs actually faced any real dilemma; the "true controversy" in Connecticut was instead "over the opening of birth-control clinics on a large scale." Unless by some chance the state of Connecticut actually did make "a definite and concrete threat to enforce these laws against individual married couples," the Court could "decide the constitutional questions urged upon us when, if ever, that real controversy" over the opening of clinics "flares up again."[87]

Beyond the very brief indications of dissent filed by Justices Black and Stewart,[88] both William O. Douglas and John M. Harlan filed significant dissenting opinions. Douglas rebutted Frankfurter's characterization of *Nelson* as simply a "test case," invoked the First Amendment on behalf of Buxton, and concluded that the Fourteenth Amendment liberty rights of the "Poes" were undeniably violated by the 1879 statute. Privacy was among the components of liberty, and "'Liberty' is a conception that sometimes gains content from the emanations of other specific guarantees" in the Constitution "or from experience with the requirements of a free society." Douglas noted how the Connecticut law "reaches into the intimacies of the marriage relationship," and how, if enforced, it could "reach the point where search warrants issued and officers appeared in bedrooms to find out what went on." *Any* possible enforcement against married couples, Douglas declared, would be "an invasion of the privacy that is implicit in a free society," a privacy that "emanates from the totality of the constitutional scheme under which we live."[89]

John Marshall Harlan's dissent was more than twice the length of Douglas's and three times the size of the Frankfurter opinion. He explained at some length why *Poe* was indeed justiciable and gave a detailed critique of Frankfurter's characterization of *Nelson*. Harlan quoted from both the April 1940 Fitzgerald statement and from Warren Upson's affidavit that Harper had submitted, and also included a long footnote taking issue with the comments that Brennan had offered in his brief concurrence. On the constitutional issues, Harlan minced few words: "a statute making it a criminal offense for *married couples* to use contraceptives is an intolerable and unjustifiable invasion of privacy in the conduct of the most intimate concerns of an individual's private life" and hence violated the due process clause of the Fourteenth Amendment. The Constitution's language clearly indicated that the clause's protection of "liberty" could not be reduced to any simple definition or formula, Harlan emphasized, but what it shielded was "a freedom from all substantial arbitrary impositions and purposeless restraints." The Connecticut law intruded upon "the most intimate details of the marital relation" and "allows the State to enquire into, prove and punish married people for the private use of their marital intimacy." The "privacy of the home in its most basic sense" *must be* "a most fundamental aspect of 'liberty,'" and not only within the contours of the Fourth Amendment's protection against unreasonable searches and seizures. Harlan quoted a long segment from Justice Brandeis's well-known 1928 espousal of "the right to be let alone," and asserted that "the Constitution protects the privacy of the home against all unreasonable intrusion of whatever character." Fourteenth Amendment liberty protected that privacy of the home not as a matter of property rights, but because it was the locus of what a prior decision had once termed "the private realm of family life which the state cannot enter." "[I]t is difficult to imagine," Harlan observed, "what is more private or more intimate than a husband and wife's marital relations."

The right of privacy, Harlan acknowledged, "is not an absolute. Thus, I would not suggest that adultery, homosexuality, fornication and incest are immune from criminal enquiry, however privately practiced." But "the intimacy of husband and wife is necessarily an essential and accepted feature of the institution of marriage, an institution which the State not only must allow, but which always and in every age it has fostered and protected. It is one thing when the State exerts its power either to forbid extramarital sexuality altogether, or to say who may marry, but it is quite another when, having acknowledged a marriage and the intimacies inherent in it, it undertakes to regulate by means of the criminal law the details of that intimacy."

All in all, Harlan concluded, "the appellants have presented a very pressing claim for constitutional protection" against the "utter novelty" of Connecticut's "obnoxiously intrusive" statute. And although Lee Buxton, Estelle Griswold, and Fowler Harper had come up one vote shy in *Poe v. Ullman*, what John Harlan had said in dissent would prepare the way not only for their eventual victory four years later over the legacy of P. T. Barnum, but would open the door as well for a further expansion of the struggle that neither Harlan nor Harper nor even Estelle Griswold had yet envisioned.[90]

Creating the Right to Privacy: Estelle Griswold and the U.S. Supreme Court, 1961–1965

Neither Lee Buxton nor Estelle Griswold was terribly surprised when news of the Supreme Court's 5 to 4 dismissal of *Poe* v. *Ullman* reached them that Monday, June 19. Estelle had known for some weeks what course of action she would push for should *Poe* be turned aside, and early Tuesday morning June 20, she, Fowler Harper, and PPLC president Lucia Parks headed to New York to talk with PPFA officials before PPLC made any public announcement of its resolve to now go ahead and open at least one birth control clinic in the state as soon as it could.

After conferring with PPFA public relations director Fred Jaffe and others, a joint press release immediately was issued in the names of Lucia Parks and PPFA president Cass Canfield. Rather than deplore the Supreme Court's action, the statement declared that "we welcome the recognition by the Court that the law has in fact become a nullity" and promised that PPLC would move "as rapidly as possible" to publicly offer contraceptive services. Estelle told reporters that September would be PPLC's target date for opening an initial clinic in New Haven, and stated that since the Supreme Court had declared the law to be "a dead duck," PPLC had "an open road" for eventually opening multiple clinics. "We merely desire freedom in this most intimate of all our practices," Estelle emphasized. "We don't wish to impose birth control on anyone." She added, however, that if authorities did choose to move against the first clinic that "We would of course welcome prosecution by the state" so that the "absurd and antiquated" 1879 law could be removed from the books.[1]

Editorial responses to the "puzzling" and "regrettable" decision in

Poe generally praised Harlan's "powerful and persuasive" dissent while decrying the Court's failure to void Connecticut's "extreme and repressive" statute. An exasperated Lee Buxton told one reporter that "It all adds up to the rich getting contraceptives and the poor getting children," and in some interviews Estelle emphasized a similar theme, explaining that "It is the woman of the lower socio-economic group who does not know she can space her children, who cannot afford to go to a private doctor, who is being discriminated against by the Connecticut law."

Fowler Harper, with particular encouragement from Harriet Pilpel, quickly set to work preparing a petition for rehearing to the Supreme Court. Normally an almost certain waste of time, such petitions were granted only in the rarest of circumstances, but the Clerk's Office of the Court on Tuesday the 20th had indicated to Pilpel that in *Poe* such an effort might not be wholly futile. More realistically, Harper also immediately began researching the potential legal vulnerabilities that might be faced by clinic personnel. Estelle herself was already scouting the surrounding neighborhood for an available building that could offer sufficient space for both clinic facilities and PPLC's offices, and on June 22, with Buxton's approval, she and Lucia Parks sent a letter to several dozen New Haven–area physicians inviting them to a June 28 luncheon meeting to form a medical advisory committee that would advise and oversee the opening a New Haven clinic.[2]

Lee Buxton prepared carefully for the June 28 meeting. He had already sent memos to both the dean of Yale's Medical School and to the administrator of Grace–New Haven Hospital privately notifying them that as of July 1 the ob/gyn staff would begin giving birth control advice unless they forbid it, and when he phoned the hospital administrator on the morning of the 28th to inquire as to whether there would be any written acknowledgment, Buxton was told not to expect a reply. Both PPFA medical director Mary Calderone and new PPFA national director Alan F. Guttmacher, an exceptionally prominent physician who had long been an outspoken liberal on reproductive issues, came up to New Haven for the June 28 session, and heartily endorsed Buxton and Griswold's resolve to move ahead posthaste with a clinic. Later that day PPLC announced the formation of the medical advisory board to the New Haven papers and declared its hope of opening a clinic on or about September 1.[3]

Some observers thought Buxton was being truly courageous to lead the charge toward open defiance of the old statute, but when the ageing Morris Ernst sent him a midsummer fan letter, Buxton responded with self-effacing humility. "Quite frankly I do not feel particularly heroic about this effort . . . It seemed a necessary thing for a person in my position to do—being Chairman of the Department of Obstetrics and Gynecology in the only medical school in Connecticut. Possibly the economic security of a full-time position in a medical school made it possible for me to take this stand without fear of financial damage, although I think that the attitude of most of the professional people in Connecticut, even Catholics, is overwhelming in favor of nullification or repeal of these laws." Perhaps surprisingly, the weekly *Catholic Transcript* had offered no comment whatsoever in the wake of the *Poe* decision, and extensive attention had been drawn to a well-publicized article by Catholic physician John Rock in a popular national magazine recommending that "All restrictions, written or unwritten, should be lifted" from the public provision of birth control. Perhaps it was possible that PPLC's long-standing opponents, just as they had at the 1961 legislative hearing, might be deciding to withdraw from any further active battle rather than continue to fight.[4]

On July 7 Fowler Harper formally filed his petition for a rehearing of *Poe* with the U.S. Supreme Court. He contended that *Nelson* represented "a definite policy of enforcement" on the part of the state and expressly challenged Justice Brennan's attempted distinction between the practices of private M.D.s and the opening of clinics by pointing out that "If a clinic is opened in Connecticut, this Court will not have the 'clinic' before it, praying for a decision, but Dr. Buxton." Harper asserted that the June decision should be reconsidered because it "encourages violation of the law and dignifies the doctrine of nullification as a policy of government" and also because it represented nothing more than "an open invitation to appellants to violate the criminal law of the state because it is *unlikely* that they will be caught." He emphasized that Dr. Buxton "*has not given contraceptive advice to appellants Poe and Doe* in the hospital or any place else," and concluded that the June decision "appears to tell these appellants that they must be arrested and prosecuted before they can have their constitutional rights adjudicated." Harper had his colleague Tom Emerson carefully review the petition before it was filed, and he told his Washington friend Gene Gressman that although the odds against any such petition were indeed very high, he nonetheless had some hope of persuading either the Chief Justice or Justice Brennan.[5]

Unbeknownst to Harper, *Poe* indeed was very much on the mind of William J. Brennan. In a July 10 talk to a group of English barristers in London, Brennan brought up *Poe* almost immediately. "We must indeed find difficulty in imagining a more indefensible invasion of privacy than an invasion of the marriage chamber by government," he told his audience, but the Court, he explained, had not addressed the constitutional issue "since apparently the plaintiffs were not truly caught in an inescapable dilemma and actually were seeking invalidation of the Connecticut statute in the interest of the opening of birth control clinics." Brennan told the Londoners, just as he had said in his *Poe* concurrence, that the Court could decide the constitutional question "when and if the Connecticut statute is applied to a birth control clinic."

A week and a half later Harper received an unusual letter forwarded to him by PPFA president Cass Canfield. A well-known ethicist, Joseph Fletcher, who had several acquaintances at PPFA, had written Canfield to ask whether "you and/or Fowler Harper" could "give me any idea of some other *constitutional* ground upon which" *Poe* "might have been argued" before the Supreme Court. Fletcher offered a circumlocutious but clear enough explanation for his inquiry:

> Discretion forbids me to say more than that I had dinner the other evening with one of those who decided the fate of the case—one of the brothers Above, as they say—and he is very troubled about the whole thing.
>
> The point is: if I got from you any sort of helpful lead I would be glad to pass it on to him. Any more attempts will have to lie before him.

It was an amazingly audacious notion, particularly from an ethics specialist no less, and Harper politely but coolly told Fletcher no thank you: "I do not believe that there are any substantial constitutional arguments that could have been used . . . other than those which were actually used, or with which the Justices were already familiar. In any event, I should not think it proper for me to suggest anything further, with a view to your passing it on to one of the Justices." A partially chastened Professor Fletcher thanked Fred Jaffe at PPFA for a copy of Harper's petition for rehearing and other materials, volunteering that "Some of it I may pass on to my unnamed justice. But I gather that Fowler Harper is afraid, properly, to do or say anything sub judice or what ever it's called."[6]

In a distinctly different realm, and fully on the up-and-up, in late July Estelle signed a lease for nine rooms in a building just one block up Trumbull Street from PPLC's existing office. Although she did not know it, her selection of space on the second floor at 79 Trumbull—a striking nineteenth-century home that once might have deserved the word "mansion"—represented an ironic return home for PPLC, for it was in that same building that Nowell Creadick had housed the Connecticut League's offices back in the mid-1930s. On July 31 PPLC shifted its offices up the street to the new rooms, and Estelle told the New Haven newspapers that she now hoped to open a clinic by approximately October 1. Lee Buxton was working to obtain a quiet donation of surplus examining-room equipment from Grace–New Haven Hospital, and inquiring reporters, reacting to Estelle's announcement, were unable to evoke any evidence of interest from legal authorities. The state attorney general's office commented that the subject was "entirely within the discretion of the local prosecuting attorneys," and the New Haven state's attorney's office said that it had received no complaints. Estelle told one friend that "if we are not closed up in New Haven," additional clinics would be opened in Hartford and then Norwalk as soon as funds were available, and in early September she told a New York reporter that even in advance of opening "We have been getting about ten to fifteen calls a week" from women seeking appointments.[7]

By mid-September PPLC had pushed its projected opening date back to November 1. Refurbishing the clinic rooms at 79 Trumbull was taking more time than had been anticipated, and Fowler Harper was privately recommending that they wait until the Supreme Court ruled on the rehearing petition. Birth control nonetheless remained in the news in virtually every Connecticut paper when the Associated Press reported that both Middlesex County State's Attorney Thomas W. Flood and Hartford County State's Attorney John D. LaBelle were investigating complaints that a paperback book, *The Complete Book of Birth Control*, by PPFA's Dr. Alan Guttmacher, was widely available for purchase. A Durham bookstore owner and retired journalist who was a member of both PPLC and the ACLU immediately issued a public invitation to Mr. Flood to drop by and pick up a copy, and Flood's admission that the book was not actionable under the 1879 statute was almost lost in a slew of humorous but nonetheless pointed press coverage. "If the state permits its sale," bookstore owner Keith Henderson rhetorically asked, "how can it logically move to close up a birth control clinic?"[8]

On Monday, October 9, the Supreme Court without comment routinely denied Harper's petition that it reconsider *Poe*. Three days later Estelle told Fowler that she hoped to announce an opening date within ten days or so, with three two-hour clinic sessions to be offered each week. New Haven PPLC members would supply much of the staffing, and Lee Buxton had recruited four additional doctors who would each

volunteer several hours of their time. In line with national PPFA practice, "No unmarried woman will knowingly be accepted as a patient,"
except for premarital fittings where the woman was referred by a
member of the clergy. "It is our hope," Estelle told one acquaintance,
"that someone will complain and that the State Attorney in New
Haven will act to close the center. We shall then carry our case to the
U.S. Supreme Court and this time we feel they shall have to make a
decision." Finally, on the evening of October 26, PPLC notified the
press that a news conference would be held at 79 Trumbull on
Thursday, November 2.[9]

Estelle, Lee, and Fowler planned their opening event carefully, and
with dozens of eager potential patients calling the office, Estelle set the
first ten appointments for Wednesday evening November 1—the night
before the news conference. Those examinations and consultations went
without incident, and on Thursday morning Estelle and Fowler faced
only one problem—the reluctance of the self-effacing Lee Buxton to
show up at the press session. Fowler successfully badgered him by
warning that "You won't be able to stop them from taking your picture
when you get taken into court," and a hesitant Buxton joined Harper
and Griswold in meeting the more than forty media representatives
who showed up at 79 Trumbull. Estelle and Lucia Parks announced the
Wednesday evening kickoff and described how many inquiries and
supportive calls PPLC had been receiving. Clinic sessions would be
held each Wednesday evening, Friday afternoon, and Tuesday morning,
Estelle explained. Lee Buxton spoke briefly about the two 1957
patients, "Irene W.," who had died, and Ruth "Oldendorf," or "Jane
Doe," whose cases had had such a deep personal impact upon him, and
then Fowler bluntly blurted out their most pressing hope: "I think it
would be a state and community service if a criminal action were
brought. I think citizens and doctors alike are entitled to know if they
are violating the law."

Reporters seeking to find out whether Harper's wish would indeed
come true received mixed signals. Under a recent reorganization of
Connecticut's local court structure, a violation of the birth control
statute, since it was a misdemeanor, not a felony, presumptively would
fall within the jurisdiction of circuit court prosecutor Julius Maretz,
who declined comment. New State's Attorney Arthur T. Gorman, who
had succeeded his longtime boss Ab Ullman only five months earlier,
was slightly more forthcoming: "If other people don't enforce the law, I
will have to take some steps. But it is up to the police and Circuit
Court at this stage."[10]

Although Fowler Harper would not know about it until the following afternoon, by early Thursday night his hope was indeed well on its way to fruition. One local reader of the evening newspaper was deeply outraged at the news of the clinic's opening and the noncommittal remarks of the prosecutors, and resolved that if they were not pursuing such a scandalous violation of the law, he certainly would. James G. Morris, a forty-two-year-old West Haven Roman Catholic father of five, was the night manager of Avis Rent-a-Car's Downtown Garage at 280 Crown Street, and his first reaction was to call the Connecticut State Police. They told him it was a matter for the New Haven Police Department, and sometime Thursday evening Morris called there, only to be told that his complaint could not be accepted and that he would have to talk to the chief. Friday morning Morris resumed his crusade and, taking that suggestion one step further, instead called the office of New Haven Mayor Richard Lee. There too he was told he was in the wrong place, and that he should phone the assistant chief of police. Finally Morris did succeed in reaching Assistant Chief Simon P. Reising, who said he would discuss the matter with circuit court prosecutor Maretz. Morris paused for perhaps an hour, griping to reporters that "the clinic is being given special privileges by the New Haven Police Department." Then Morris himself called Maretz, who told him he had received no complaint by way of Reising and was not aware that any law was being broken. Morris bluntly told him he did not agree, and within the half hour showed up at Maretz's office in person. Yielding reluctantly, the circuit prosecutor brushed aside Morris's request that he accept a written complaint but acquiesced and said that he would request a police investigation.[11]

Julius Maretz knew almost everyone in New Haven law enforcement. Born in Russia sixty-nine years earlier, he had come to New Haven as a child, graduated from Yale Law School in 1912, and served as part-time prosecutor in the city police court since 1945. Jewish and a registered Republican, he had been named chief prosecutor in the new circuit court when Connecticut's judicial system had been restructured a year earlier. At about one p.m. on Friday, just moments after he had shooed Mr. Morris from his office, Maretz walked over to the detective division of the city police department. He told Captain William Holohan that he had received a complaint about the birth control clinic and was thus requesting an investigation. A few minutes later Holohan called in Detectives John A. Blazi and Harold Berg, and at about two ten p.m. the two officers arrived at 79 Trumbull Street and climbed the stairs to PPLC's second floor reception room.

Blazi and Berg's arrival happened to coincide with PPLC's second clinic session. Some half-dozen women were in an adjacent waiting room, and in another room Dr. Virginia Stuermer was speaking with several other patients. Several of the women, realizing who the visitors were, worried that perhaps their appointments would now be canceled, but Stuermer went right ahead with her counseling and fittings. A volunteer at the front desk quickly summoned Estelle, who was ecstatic at the news of the officers' arrival. She went out, introduced herself, and enthusiastically invited the two detectives into her private office, saying she would be more than happy to give them whatever information they might want about the clinic. Berg, a ten-year veteran of the New Haven department, had not previously met Griswold, but John Blazi, also a department veteran, had had in earlier years a good deal of contact with the Human Relations Council. Well-known in New Haven for his "keen and innate sense of humor" and for emceeing various functions, Blazi had taken Spanish classes at Yale and had become a fluent speaker of the language. He handled most of the department's cases involving Puerto Rican citizens, and in 1958 the council had presented him with an award.

Blazi and Berg quickly realized that Estelle Griswold was quite overjoyed to see them. Once in her office, she offered them multiple copies of all the clinic's literature and pamphlets, and waited hardly a moment before telling them that she very much hoped that the anticontraception law would indeed be enforced against her and the clinic so that the statute's constitutionality could again be challenged before the U.S. Supreme Court. Then, as Blazi struggled to take notes, Estelle Griswold launched into what was clearly the speech of her life, a speech for which she had been preparing for almost eight years. She told the two detectives far more than they needed or wanted to know about the procedures the clinic used in determining fees (a maximum of fifteen dollars), taking patients' histories, and in fitting and instructing women in the use of a diaphragm and contraceptive jelly. "Upon giving us this step of the procedure," Blazi wrote in his formal report on the investigation, "Mrs. Griswold informed us that she realized that this particular step was a violation of the law." Estelle herself later boasted that she had tried to use "all the medical terminology that I knew" in delivering her extensive rendition, and the interview went on for more than ninety minutes. Shortly after four p.m., with Dr. Stuermer having been called away in order to deliver a baby, Lee Buxton arrived and immediately stuck his head into Estelle's office. Blazi summarized for Buxton the notes he had taken on Estelle's descriptive comments, and Buxton willingly volunteered that they were all accurate. Buxton also took the opportunity to emphasize that while there were other doctors, nurses, and social workers volunteering their time at the clinic, that "actually only Mrs. Estelle T. Griswold and himself were directly responsible as directors for the operation of the Center." Then, just as Blazi and Berg were preparing to leave, Estelle delivered the final portion of her soliloquy: "Mrs. Griswold stated," as Blazi recorded it, "that although she welcomed arrest and a chance to settle the question of the Connecticut State Statute's legality, she would refuse to be pictured and finger-printed, feeling that she had not committed any crime, would not accept bail, and would physically resist and repel any effort on the part of the police to seize as evidence the personal clientele files of the Center, as she felt that, as doctor's medical records, the information contained therein should be kept confidential." With that Berg and Blazi each shook hands with both Estelle and Buxton and departed.[12]

Curious reporters mused that both Griswold and Buxton would soon face charges, but Estelle simply said "We don't know what the next step will be" and Maretz declined comment other than to confirm that the detectives had indeed visited the clinic at his direction. Mr. Morris continued to sound off, telling the media that "every moment the clinic stays open another child is not born," but both the third clinic session, on Tuesday morning, November 7, and the fourth, on Wednesday evening the eighth, took place without event or interruption.

Early Thursday morning November 9, Julius Maretz, having reviewed Blazi's report on the interview with Griswold and Buxton, instructed the two detectives to go back to the clinic and ask Griswold for the names of at least two women who had received birth control instructions and supplies there. If such voluntary witnesses could be found, it would obviate any struggle or dispute over patient records. Blazi and Berg immediately returned to 79 Trumbull and put the prosecutor's request to Griswold. Estelle said she was sure she could arrange for two such patients to provide statements to the officers, and that she would try to have them call at the detective division before the end of the day. Not wanting to miss a further educational opportunity, Estelle also insisted that both detectives dip their fingers into some of Joseph Sunnen's Emko Vaginal Foam before they went on their way.

Estelle's first thought with regard to the detectives' request concerned a woman she had spoken with just the previous evening as the Wednesday night clinic session was concluding. Joan Bates Forsberg, a thirty-three-year-old Yale Divinity School graduate and mother of three, previously had been making the same trek to the Planned

Parenthood clinic in Port Chester, New York, that had so infuriated Jean and Marvin Durning four years earlier. With her husband pastoring the Inner City Parish in a poor area of New Haven, Forsberg had never wanted to spend money on a private physician, and when she read about the new PPLC clinic in a local newspaper, she quickly called for an appointment. Forsberg and several other women first listened as Estelle described the different methods of birth control that were available, and each made a choice before having an individual examination with a doctor and a nurse. Forsberg chose the new oral contraceptive pill, of which the doctor gave her a supply, but just as she paid her two-dollar fee and turned to leave, Griswold reappeared and Forsberg paused to thank her for what she and PPLC were doing. "I know you're running a risk, and if there's anything I can do to help, let me know."

And so that very next morning, once the detectives had gone, Estelle called Joan Forsberg to take her up on her offer. "You said you would be glad to do anything you could to help," Griswold began. "Yes," Forsberg said. "We'd like you to make a statement to the police that in fact you went to the clinic, to turn state's evidence so we can get this into court." Forsberg was at first unsure exactly what Griswold meant, and Estelle slowed down and described the situation in greater detail. Once Forsberg understood it, and once Griswold reassured her that the detectives would not pursue Forsberg herself and that no public testimony was likely to be required, she readily agreed to arrange to go down and give Blazi a statement sometime that afternoon.

Estelle could not immediately think of a second patient whom she might similarly call or impose upon. Perhaps more seriously, Joan Forsberg had been examined not by Lee Buxton but by another doctor, and, with some worry, Estelle phoned Fowler. Always resourceful, Fowler said he would find her another willing patient and solve the problem without delay. One of Harper's favorite younger colleagues on the law school faculty, Robert Stevens, had been married for less than a year to a young woman who was now a graduate student in Yale's Public Health School. Both from England, they had impressed Harper at dinner parties as a young couple of sufficient moxie to probably be willing to follow in the footsteps of the Durnings and the Trubeks. Harper went to Robert Stevens's office and put the question directly: would he and his wife, Rosemary, be willing to enlist in the birth control struggle by arranging an immediate appointment for Rosemary with Lee Buxton, and then furnishing an appropriate statement about it to the New Haven police? Stevens was willing, but with one caveat: both he and Rosemary were English citizens with American "green cards," and would not want to be deported if they had to testify that they had violated the Connecticut birth control statute. Harper laughingly volunteered that he would happily take that case to the U.S. Supreme Court as well, and then explained that they had to move quickly. Rosemary was located and readily agreed, and it was arranged that she would rendezvous with Buxton at the PPLC office at two thirty that very afternoon. From there she would go directly to the police department.

At two p.m. Joan Forsberg arrived at the detective division and sat down with Blazi, Berg, and Lieutenant Mae Gilhuly. Under friendly interrogation by Blazi, who typed out the questions and answers as they proceeded, Forsberg described how she had come to visit the PPLC clinic and what services and supplies had been provided to her there. She had been furnished a two-month supply of birth control pills, but had not yet had occasion to begin using them. Offered the opportunity by Blazi, Forsberg concluded her statement by observing that "I shall be very happy to see the time when information about birth control is legally made available to all married women in this state."

At three forty-five, straight from her visit to 79 Trumbull Street, Rosemary Stevens similarly appeared at the detective division and sat down with Blazi, Berg, and Gilhuly. Her answers to Blazi's questions acknowledged that she had visited the clinic at two thirty that afternoon, in order to be sure that the diaphragm with which she had been fitted in England eleven months earlier was still effective; she said she had learned of the clinic "from friends." She explained that she had been examined by Dr. Buxton, and that Estelle Griswold had furnished her with a new tube of contraceptive jelly, at a charge of fifteen dollars. Blazi did not inquire as to whether she had yet had occasion to use it, but, as with Forsberg, Blazi concluded by asking Stevens about her interest in the issue. She explained that she wanted to delay any pregnancy until she had completed her graduate education, and added more generally that "This opportunity should be made available to all women in this state." Blazi interrupted his typing to ask, "Don't you mean *married* women, Mrs. Stevens?" With considerable hesitance, and only because Blazi had been so friendly and helpful, Rosemary Stevens reluctantly agreed to Blazi's adding "married" to her statement before she signed it. "I still feel badly about that," she explained over thirty years later.[13]

Friday morning, November 10, Julius Maretz gave Blazi and Berg arrest warrants for Estelle Griswold and Lee Buxton that had been signed by Judge J. Robert Lacey. He then called Katie Roraback, with whom he also had spoken concerning the matter of patient records, to inform her that Griswold and Buxton should surrender at the detective division's office at three that afternoon. Roraback called both of them, and Fowler instructed Estelle that since they had now reached this stage, clinic services would have to be discontinued.

Right on schedule, Estelle and Lee, accompanied by Roraback and by Estelle's deputy, Fran McCoy, appeared at police headquarters. Buxton wore a conservative suit and tie; Estelle looked as if she were headed for an Easter Sunday service, not an arrest proceeding. Estelle only half jokingly reprimanded Roraback for having allowed her to miss out on her one chance for a ride in a patrol wagon, but the formal charges in the warrants for both Griswold and Buxton were not intended to be humorous. They alleged that both defendants "did assist, abet, counsel, cause and command certain married women to use a drug, medicinal article and instrument, for the purpose of preventing conception," and further stated—in line with the companion statute—that the women "did in fact use said drugs, medicinal articles, and instruments for the purpose of preventing conception." Both Estelle and Lee declined to make any statement to the police, and neither mug shots nor fingerprinting was included in the booking process. Each defendant was released on a hundred-dollar bond, with an initial court appearance set for November 24. Buxton told waiting reporters that he was sorry that clinic services had had to be discontinued, for "It's very disappointing not to be able to treat patients who need medical advice so badly. It's like not being able to use penicillin for anyone who needs it." Estelle told the journalists that scores of upcoming clinic appointments had been canceled, and explained that each woman would receive a letter from PPLC listing seven contraceptive products that were widely available for commercial purchase in Connecticut as well as giving the addresses and phone numbers of the neighboring Planned Parenthood clinics in New York and Rhode Island. Reporters who asked Julius Maretz whether the charges meant that he disagreed with the Supreme Court's statements in *Poe* were told only that "There has been a crime committed in my opinion and we issued the warrant on that basis."[14]

The week's developments delighted birth control supporters all across the country. Harriet Pilpel wrote Harper that "I am sure I don't have to tell you what a magnificent job we feel that all of you in Connecticut are doing. We don't want to be in the position of back seat drivers," she asserted, but she hoped Harper and Roraback were aiming on an actual trial rather than proceeding by stipulation. Also, as she and Harper had discussed at a weekend dinner, neither Forsberg nor Stevens had as of Thursday actually used the materials that Griswold and Buxton had been arrested for furnishing them, and that would have to be corrected in order to avoid a fatal procedural problem later on.

Episcopal Bishop James A. Pike, erroneously assuming who had initiated the Connecticut charges, told PPFA's Cass Canfield that the New Haven prosecution "either represents very fine planning on the part of the Planned Parenthood Federation, or real stupidity on the part of the Roman Catholic Church." Maverick Catholic physician John Rock wrote to Buxton to say that "I am very grateful to you for doing what I might have considered doing here in Massachusetts if it were not for the religious scandal it would have generated," and Buxton replied that "unfortunately for my ego," he did not "feel very much like a martyr." In an odd coincidence, apparently stimulated by a letter Fowler Harper had signed calling for a change in American policy toward Cuba, rather than by the events with PPLC's clinic, the New Haven office of the Federal Bureau of Investigation early that same week, in response to a previous prodding from FBI headquarters, also took the notable step of adding the sixty-four-year-old law professor to Section A of the Reserve Index, bureau-speak for one of several secret lists of people who were to be picked up and interned in the event of a national emergency. The New Haven office cited Harper's ongoing membership in the National Lawyers Guild, his 1946 Indiana ballot petition signature, and his professorship at Yale—"In this position Harper is in a position to influence others against the national interest"—but not his representation of PPLC, as grounds for formally certifying him as a threat to national security.[15]

On Tuesday, November 14, Julius Maretz sent detective Berg back to PPLC to see whether clinic operations were continuing and to ask Griswold if she could send them an additional willing patient or two. Berg discovered that the only other nonstaffers present were two reporters from *Look* magazine, and Griswold promised that she would try to send them an additional patient. The following afternoon Marie Wilson Tindall, a thirty-seven-year-old black woman who had visited the clinic on November 7 along with her husband, a New Haven social worker, gave Berg a statement and also handed over to him the diaphragm, contraceptive jelly, and other articles that she had been furnished for seven dollars and fifty cents during her visit to the clinic. The following day Rosemary Stevens again visited the detectives to dictate a brief supplementary statement. She specified that beginning on the evening of November 9, there had now been four occasions on which she had used the contraceptive jelly that Estelle Griswold had furnished her, and Detective Berg took possession of one "partially used tube of vaginal jelly." The next morning Joan Forsberg also came to headquarters to supply a supplementary statement attesting to the fact that she had now begun using the birth control pills that PPLC had provided. She handed over the remaining pills to the detectives, and then immediately went home and called Griswold to ask for replacements. "I said I really don't mind going to jail for this cause, but getting pregnant is another story."[16]

One interested observer who was *not* happy with the ongoing developments was the high-strung Mr. James G. Morris. Some might have thought that Morris would be overjoyed at news of the charges against Griswold and Buxton, but instead he was highly dissatisfied that only two defendants had been arrested and that they had then been released on bail rather than incarcerated. Morris told the reporters from *Look* that initially "I thought somebody else would act, some organization like the Knights of Columbus," but when they did not, he did. He explained that "I think that a Planned Parenthood Center is like a house of prostitution. It is against the natural law, which says marital relations are for procreation and not entertainment." Morris was willing to concede that "Birth control is a private thing, and people do have a right to believe in birth control. But the doctors who prescribe contraceptives in Connecticut are breaking the law," and in Morris's judgment that 1879 statute "is a good law, and it should be enforced." Even in the PPLC clinic's very brief existence, Morris emphasized, it "did an awful lot of damage."

Morris complained to Maretz about the insufficiently zealous enforcement and demanded an opportunity to file a more inclusive complaint, but the prosecutor told him in no uncertain terms that the only help he wanted was from the police. Morris then refocused his attention on the department's two top officers, and after securing a meeting with the chief, finally was afforded an opportunity to dictate a written complaint to Detective Berg. What initially had angered him, Morris told Berg, was that PPLC could hand out "what I consider immoral literature to anyone that would walk into their place." Concerning his own public involvement, Morris explained that

I did this to protect my five children because I did not want any of this to fall into their hands and to stop the bad publicity that was in the papers, that they had to listen to on the television, radio and that they read in newspapers. I also did it because it is against the law to practice birth control and to give any information on it in this state. The same doctor that worked this immoral house also has the right to practice medicine in our hospitals; if he breaks the law this way what guaranty do the hospitals give me that he won't break these laws of impurity where I must send my children. If this woman who claims to be the head of this so-called clinic breaks this law th[en] she would not break the law by running a house of prostitution.

Morris added that "I also do not understand why they are a nonprofit organization when they are breaking the law. I filed this complaint to protect my children and all children and people against juvenile and adult delinquency." He said that registered letters he had sent to the governor and other elected officials protesting PPLC's activities had not been answered; PPLC's efforts, he explained, "cause many innocent people to break the law of this state." Before finally getting rid of Morris, Berg asked him what he would think if the 1879 statute no longer existed. Morris replied, "I would say that they had a right then to operate."[17]

On November 24, at a hearing that lasted no more than five minutes, both Estelle Griswold and Lee Buxton pled not guilty to the charge of violating the 1879 law. Katie Roraback filed a short demurrer contending that the statutes deprived the defendants of both their Fourteenth Amendment liberty and their First Amendment freedom of speech, and Judge J. Robert Lacey postponed a further hearing until December 8 so that both sides could prepare briefs. Harriet Pilpel continued to worry that the Connecticut activists were not taking every precaution or making every argument imaginable, but Lee Buxton told one journalist that he was thinking of having a partially paralyzed patient—i.e., "Jane Doe," Ruth "Oldendorf"—testify in his behalf at trial.[18]

Katie Roraback prepared a twenty-two-page brief for Lacey's perusal and submitted it just prior to the December 8 hearing. Much of its constitutional argument drew upon Harper's filings and the Harlan dissent in *Poe*—the statutes invaded "the most sacred area of family life" and represented an "extreme invasion of the privacy of the marital relation" as protected by "the right to liberty"—but Roraback also made the First Amendment argument which Pilpel had been encouraging. Maretz and one of his part-time assistants, Joseph B. Clark, on the other hand, filed only a three-page brief which did little more than cite the previous Connecticut Supreme Court rulings in *Nelson*, *Tileston*, and *Poe-Buxton*. At the actual half-hour hearing Roraback stressed that "courts are not bound to follow the dead letter of the law where that law is no longer applicable to current circumstances and situations." She also firmly articulated the basic constitutional claim: "The married person in his own privacy of his own home has a right to engage in marital relations and to do so in such manner as he sees fit— he and she, forgive me, see fit. To hold otherwise would invade the very innermost sanctums of privacy in violation of the rights of individuals to privacy which are embodied in the term 'liberty' in the Fourteenth Amendment."

Julius Maretz most revealingly began his oral presentation to Lacey by reading the Connecticut statute that directed prosecutors to pursue *all* statutory violations of which they became aware. "We felt it was our duty" to pursue the matter, and "it became incumbent upon our office" to file these charges, Maretz apologetically emphasized. He also noted that unlike the 3 to 2 rulings in *Nelson* and *Tileston*, the 1959 Connecticut Supreme Court affirmation of the 1879 statute had been unanimous. Judge Lacey made it clear to both attorneys that that precedent gave him no leeway in considering Roraback's Fourteenth Amendment liberty argument, but he questioned both counsel as to whether First Amendment grounds had been considered in any of the prior rulings before seeming to indicate that he thought that possibility might well be foreclosed by the modest opinion that the Connecticut high court had issued in *Trubek*. "I have got to approach this problem with extreme caution," Lacey stated, indicating that while he initially had thought about issuing a ruling later in the day as to whether the charges would go forward to trial, he now had concluded that he should take everything under advisement and file a written decision sometime later.[19]

While Lacey pondered a ruling, good old James Morris continued to wonder why a more vigorous and extensive prosecution of PPLC was not being undertaken. He had attempted without success to lobby the governor's office on the matter, and a week after the New Haven hearing he sent a long handwritten letter by registered mail/special delivery to Connecticut Chief Justice Raymond E. Baldwin asking him to investigate the supposed shortcomings in Maretz's probe. The fact that Maretz was not pushing harder, Morris alleged, indicated that "something in the case hasn't got a nice order [sic]. As a father of five children who want protection from these law breakers," Morris warned that "If they do it in a clinic, next it will be the hospitals." He ungrammatically declared that "C[onnecticu]t courts have always kept us pure from immorality but are these to be new rules for special people or must they obey the laws too. The Governor said it's your job, not his." Baldwin simply acknowledged Morris's missive without further comment.[20]

On December 22 Judge Lacey filed a brief decision citing *Nelson, Tileston, Poe-Buxton*, and *Trubek* and concluding that no birth control counseling that led to a violation of the use statute could claim protection under the First Amendment. He set a trial date of January 2, 1962, and pro forma subpoenas were issued summoning PPLC's three volunteer patients to appear as prosecution witnesses on behalf of the state. Estelle told a friend that "without doubt" she and Buxton would be found guilty, and that she had no expectation of any success until their appeals eventually reached the U.S. Supreme Court.[21]

The nonjury trial of *State of Connecticut* v. *Estelle T. Griswold and C. Lee Buxton* got underway shortly before eleven a.m. on Tuesday, January 2, before an audience of about one hundred people. Julius Maretz called Detective John Blazi to the stand as his first witness, and Blazi described his and Berg's initial conversation with Estelle. The birth control pamphlets she had given them were entered into evidence, and Katie Roraback conducted a short and uneventful cross-examination. Harold Berg testified briefly in support of Blazi's account, and then Joan Forsberg was called to the stand. She recounted her visit to the clinic, and her unused birth control pills were entered as evidence. Marie Tindall followed Forsberg, and after a break for lunch, Rosemary Stevens succeeded her. Journalists were somewhat disappointed at how "surprisingly routine" the trial seemed, and the cordial and relaxed atmosphere was illustrated when Maretz during his questioning of Stevens mistakenly referred to "Dr. Griswold." "I am trying to promote you," he apologized, and friendly laughter filled the courtroom as Estelle replied, "You are very gracious."

Once the prosecution rested, Estelle Griswold took the stand as the first defense witness. Despite objections from Maretz, Katie Roraback led her through a long account of the clinic's work, and Estelle, alluding to *Poe*, volunteered that "If the Supreme Court had declared this law a nullity, a dead word and a harmless empty shadow, I do not see how I could commit an offense against such a law." She was followed to the stand by Lee Buxton, and Roraback led him through a disquisition on the widespread acceptance of birth control. "It is the overwhelming opinion of expert medical testimony in this country that this type of advice is an aspect of medical care which is the responsibility of every doctor who is caring for patients to give when in his opinion the patient should have it."

The only unusual event of the trial came toward the end of Buxton's testimony when the ubiquitous James G. Morris stood up from his seat in the spectator's section, waved his arms, and started speaking. Judge Lacey instructed the bailiff to remove the interloper from the courtroom, and Morris desisted. "All right, I won't say any more." "You will conduct yourself properly," Lacey stated, "or remove yourself from the courtroom." "You want me to go?" Morris asked. "Is that a choice, your honor?" the bailiff inquired. "No," Lacey responded, "remove him from the courtroom."

Roraback attempted to call two physicians who had not been affiliated with the clinic to buttress Buxton's testimony about the medical necessity of birth control, but a somewhat peeved Maretz successfully objected to virtually every question Roraback asked them. After a brief recess just before five p.m., Lacey offered Maretz and Roraback a choice of whether to hold off on closing arguments until the morning or stay late and finish, and Roraback answered firmly that she would like to proceed. Neither she nor Maretz offered lengthy final remarks, with the prosecutor again emphasizing that so long as the legislature did not alter the statute, he had no choice other than to bring these charges. Once they concluded, Judge Lacey immediately and without ceremony announced that he was finding both defendants guilty and fining each of them one hundred dollars. Notices of appeal would be due within fourteen days.[22]

Estelle resolutely told reporters that she would continue to provide birth control *information* to anyone who requested it, and the trial outcome was noted both in national newspapers and in weekly news magazines. A major, well-reported article on the New Haven events in *Look* magazine drew special coverage in Connecticut papers and reaction pieces in other journals; when one periodical suggested that PPLC would do better with the state legislature than in the courts, Estelle sent off a corrective letter explaining that so long as Roman Catholic state senators were not able to vote in favor of reform or repeal, "the only way that this issue will ever be settled is in the courts."

By mid-January Katie Roraback had filed the necessary appeal papers, and several weeks later, in line with Connecticut procedure, she submitted to Lacey a sixteen-page draft of the findings that he had to enter into the record before the appeal of Griswold and Buxton's convictions could be considered by an intermediate three-judge court of appeals. In New York Harriet Pilpel continued to worry about whether the Connecticut matters were being adequately handled, but all the attorneys agreed that early 1963 was the soonest the case would be decided by the Connecticut Supreme Court, hence making U.S.

Supreme Court review late that same year the best that could be hoped for.[23]

All the attention drawn by the trial generated resolutions of support for PPLC from various ministerial and student groups, and by April of 1962 a local PPLC chapter like the one that had helped launch the short-lived New Haven clinic had also been established in Hartford. Press items about PPLC's forty-five-thousand-dollar 1962 fund drive, however, reactivated the briefly quiescent James G. Morris, who sent a handwritten missive to State's Attorney Arthur Gorman asking why PPLC should be allowed to raise money in the wake of Griswold and Buxton's convictions. Morris further suggested that anyone who contributed to PPLC ought to be charged under the aiding and abetting accessory statute, and explained that if the police were not eager to act, "It is up to your office to see that a raid is held."

Morris received further attention when a production crew from the television show "CBS Reports" visited New Haven in mid-February to film interviews with all the principals. Eventually broadcast nationally in early May, the show divided its attention between the Connecticut controversy and a recent Chicago battle over whether birth control services would be provided at Cook County Hospital. The Connecticut half of the show began with Morris explaining that he was "a hundred percent against birth control, because it's immoral; it's the same as prostitution, or abortion, or in any other in those immoral things." Morris was allowed to detail his extensive efforts to generate a raid or arrests; Julius Maretz repeated his standard explanation that "we are duty-bound as officials, prosecutors, to follow the decisions of our Supreme Court, and we did so in this case." Lee Buxton explained how the practical effect of the Connecticut statute's prohibition of clinics was to discriminate against poor women who could not afford to patronize private doctors, and Fowler Harper gave a powerful rendition of Griswold and Buxton's constitutional argument concerning "their right to advise people with respect to matters of their privacy." "One of the most intimate and sacred relations of life is the relation of a man and his wife in the privacy of their home. And when the long arm of the law reaches into the bedroom and prohibits a man and his wife doing what they want to do, and what medical advice suggests that they do, it seems to me that this is a merciless invasion of the freedom and liberty of the citizens of this country."[24]

Connecticut papers gave considerable attention to the CBS broadcast. The *New Haven Register* was puzzled as to why CBS narrator Eric Sevareid had spoken of the birth control case as "the Yale project," since "This was the first those close to the subject here had heard of this reference," and many state newspapers noted an attack on the show by Father John C. Knott, the new director of the National Catholic Welfare Conference's Family Life Bureau. Father Knott, who for over a decade had been an official of the Hartford Archdiocese, complained that CBS's treatment of the birth control battles had been lacking in "objectivity and impartiality." And several weeks after the CBS special, James G. Morris, always on guard against threats to Connecticut's morality, filed a complaint with the New Haven police alleging that an article on birth control in a current issue of the *Saturday Evening Post* magazine violated the 1879 statute. Police department officials told New Haven reporters that they had referred Morris's complaint to the city corporation counsel.[25]

By mid-June Roraback and PPLC were becoming increasingly frustrated over Judge Lacey's ongoing failure to file the "findings" that Roraback had requested in January and which were necessary for moving ahead with Griswold and Buxton's appeal. Joseph Clark, acting for Maretz, had filed an unremarkable response to Roraback in February, but Lacey's delay was well beyond the bounds of propriety. Private inquiries were made elsewhere in the Connecticut judiciary, and finally, on July 25—but with an ostensible face date of June 12—Lacey filed the necessary but unremarkable finding. Katie Roraback was thus able to move forward with the necessary paperwork for placing the appeal before the appellate division of the state circuit court, and by late September oral argument in the case had been scheduled for October 19.[26]

Although Harriet Pilpel still wondered whether Roraback was doing an ideal job, Roraback's forty-two-page brief for the appellate panel was another solid rendition of Harper's and Harlan's constitutional views, emphasizing "the realm of familial privacy" and privacy as an aspect of liberty. The oral argument itself, between Roraback and Joseph Clark, took place in New Haven before a three-judge panel that included Bernard Kosicki, who seven years earlier had been Roraback's opposing counsel in Fowler Harper's successful land-fraud suit. The argument itself was uneventful, and the PPLC activists once again settled back to wait for a decision. Come mid-December a disappointed Lee Buxton complained to one reporter that "If the medical profession were as desultory as lawyers, most of our cases would be dead by this time." Estelle told one correspondent that they knew they would lose there too, as well as in Connecticut's highest court, but that they remained confident that the U.S. Supreme Court would strike down the statute once the case got there.[27]

Other than the slow progress of *State of Connecticut* v. *Estelle T. Griswold and C. Lee Buxton*, PPLC's situation and the birth control scene were relatively uneventful. Connecticut's Consumer Protection Commissioner launched an effort to coerce pharmacies to remove contraceptive foam from their shelves after a Torrington teenager was discovered to have purchased some, but widely reported results from a new Gallup national survey showed that some 72 percent of respondents—and 56 percent of Roman Catholics—now favored open availability of birth control information. PPLC, finding itself too cramped for space on the second floor of 79 Trumbull Street, purchased for thirty-five thousand dollars a wooden frame house at 406 Orange Street, right around the corner from Estelle's home at 40 Trumbull. Although the building came with a carriage house, the main structure required more extensive, and expensive, renovations—about twenty thousand dollars—than had been planned, and only in late November did PPLC shift its offices to the new location. Six weeks later PPLC also opened an information office in Hartford, staffed by local volunteers, which Estelle and others hoped would be the beginning basis for opening a Hartford clinic once the anticontraception statute was indeed voided.[28]

Both Fowler Harper and the ACLU's Mel Wulf experienced considerable intellectual excitement when they learned of a new law review article expanding on Justice Harlan's powerful advocacy of Fourteenth Amendment "liberty" in his *Poe* dissent by New York University law professor Norman Redlich. "To assert that the people have certain rights other than those specifically mentioned in the Constitution would not dilute the Bill of Rights but would add to it," Redlich contended. "There are two possible paths to travel" in advancing such an interpretation, he explained. One—like Harlan—"is to revert to a frankly flexible due process concept even on matters that do not involve specific constitutional prohibitions. The other is to attempt to evolve a new constitutional framework." The principal building block in such a new framework, Redlich advocated, ought to be a new appreciation of the meaning of the otherwise extremely obscure Ninth Amendment to the U.S. Constitution—"The enumeration in the Constitution, of certain rights, shall not be construed to deny or disparage others retained by the people." Especially when read in conjunction with the neighboring Tenth Amendment, Redlich said, the message was clear that the framers of those amendments thought that "words were considered inadequate to define all of the rights which man should possess in a free society." Hence there were express constitutional grounds for identifying and protecting "rights adjacent to, or analogous to, the pattern of rights which we find in the Constitution." Simply because "there exists no purely objective set of criteria" for determining what those unenumerated rights were, "does not mean that they do not exist." Marital privacy in the context of contraception, Harper and Wulf both realized, was a seemingly ideal example of the sort of constitutionally unspecified but clearly protected right that Redlich was discussing.[29]

On January 17, 1963, the three-judge Appellate Division panel, in a unanimous opinion authored by Kosicki, unsurprisingly affirmed the convictions of Estelle Griswold and Lee Buxton. They held that the prior Connecticut Supreme Court rulings reaching back to *Nelson* were controlling, and suggested that the underlying legislative purpose of the 1879 statute must be to encourage population growth: "each civilized society has a primordial right to its continued existence and to the discouragement of practices that tend to negate its survival." The panel formally certified Roraback's constitutional claims to Connecticut's high court, a move that some thought would speed consideration of the appeal. Lee Buxton termed the opinion "absolutely incredible," and by the end of January Katie Roraback had filed the appropriate papers with the Connecticut Supreme Court. On February 19 the justices granted the petition, with oral argument likely to occur either in June or early in the fall.[30]

PPLC was preparing to go through the motions of sponsoring a repeal bill in the 1963 Connecticut legislature, but the surprising birth control news of the spring came when Boston Archbishop Richard Cardinal Cushing told a local radio audience that the Roman Catholic church no longer advocated anticontraception statutes such as those in Massachusetts and Connecticut. "Even in that field," the Cardinal stated, "I have no right to impose my thinking, which is rooted in religious thought, on those who do not think as I do." If another legislative reform effort or referendum drive were to occur in Massachusetts, he added, the church's reaction "would be just to explain our position, but not to go out campaigning." Somewhat similarly, when the brief and uneventful legislative hearing on the 1963 Connecticut repeal bill took place on April 11, "the room—filled mostly with women—gasped and then broke into applause when a call for opponents brought no one to his feet." Joseph P. Cooney was indeed present, but he told curious reporters that he had simply filed a written statement with the Public Health and Safety Committee recommending that no action be taken until the state supreme court had ruled on the New Haven appeals. Public impressions of an ongoing Catholic shift were reinforced once again two weeks later when Massachusetts physician John Rock—himself a good friend of Richard Cardinal Cushing—published a small but heavily publicized book entitled *The Time Has Come: A Catholic Doctor's Proposals to End the Battle Over Birth Control*. Stories on Rock's volume appeared in most Connecticut newspapers and in several national magazines, further strengthening the perception that the decades-long birth control controversy might be about at an end.[31]

Unfortunately for Estelle Griswold, however, the spring months of 1963 were very full of controversy even without any efforts by birth control opponents. Instead PPLC was deeply wracked by internal controversy stemming from the 1962 purchase and renovation of its new offices at 406 Orange Street. Several members of the New Haven Planned Parenthood chapter had convinced themselves that the state league had taken on far too great a financial burden, but they also were upset at the nascent suggestion that the carriage house at the rear of the property would be purchased by Estelle and Dick Griswold as a new and probably permanent residence. Estelle's interest in the possibility stemmed almost wholly from the fact that Dick, a lifelong heavy smoker, was suffering more and more from emphysema and had an increasingly difficult time coping with the many flights of stairs in their house at 40 Trumbull.

In a relatively short time the internal dispute took on an extremely nasty tone, with the New Haveners increasingly indicating that their objections were less to the carriage house proposal than simply to Estelle Griswold personally. Even Estelle's closest friends would readily acknowledge that she was "super-aggressive," stubborn, "sometimes a bit maddening," and "something of a snob." "There was never a dull moment with Estelle," one PPLC board member laughingly remembered, but the New Haven women alleged that they felt both stifled and patronized. Estelle responded to their initial complaints by strongly defending the financial advisability of the Orange Street purchase, but the internal attacks took a very significant emotional toll. Believing to at least some degree that the state league officers had not mounted as energetic a defense of her as they might, Estelle sent PPLC President Lucia Parks a formal letter of resignation on April 17. Expressing "sincere regret," Estelle asked that it take effect on May 27. "After nine and one half years with Planned Parenthood and with the best relations with officers and board, working in mutual confidence, you may be assured that I have not made this decision without serious thought. However, the divisive element that has recently developed, and apparent lack of confidence on the part of certain members of the Board makes it impossible for me to continue." She added in closing that "I have also consulted with our attorney, Miss Roraback, and find that my resignation will in no way jeopardize the lawsuits."[32]

Word of Estelle's threat created considerable consternation throughout PPLC as the news spread. Former president Julie Howson, whose involvement went back to the 1920s and who was now very aged and infirm, wrote to Parks—and Griswold—to protest such a "dreadful" and "appalling" development. "How can we get along without Mrs. Griswold? Her really remarkable ability as a speaker, her first rate hold on the many problems that we have to meet, her personal charm and the fact that she can outargue anyone all seem to me the elements necessary to an executive" director. Even more outraged was another senior veteran, Hilda Crosby Standish. "It must not be!," Standish began a note to Estelle. "This organization to which you have given your life blood needs your vision, wisdom, and enthusiasm as much now, perhaps more, than when first you manned the helm and dragged it up from the depths." Knowing something of what had been brewing, Standish acknowledged that "Your feeling of utter frustration is indeed understandable. I am sure I would react in the same way, for life is too short to work under a constant emotional strain, yet because you have given so much and brought the Connecticut League so far you deserve to see the job finished. We would stand to lose much of what has been gained without your continuing magnificent leadership. If the local group does not see the absolute necessity of cooperation, and the Board beg you to reconsider, I will lose my faith in the women of Connecticut."

To the PPLC board, Hilda Standish spoke even more strongly. The danger of Estelle's resignation "saddens and alarms me. I beg each of you to try to realize what this might mean if accepted." Estelle had performed "an absolutely unique job" and it would be "*impossible* to replace her." Standish retraced PPLC's history from the *Nelson* defeat to the time of Estelle's hiring, comparing that era to the years since 1953:

> In this job Estelle has given her all, with results that are almost unbelievable. It has been her vision that has inspired us, her courage that has made us proud, her sacrifice in time and energy that has made the Connecticut League one of which we may all be proud. Almost single handed she has brought it up from the depths, but if she is to continue at the helm it *must* be with the cooperation and respect of everyone of us. To do the job *we* must have a strong leader, and in being strong *she* must be allowed to take forward steps with our full support. The con-

stant emotional strain of dissension in our ranks is more than she can be expected to endure.

Lucia Parks and the other top PPLC officers were in full agreement with Hilda Standish's insistence that the board act in such a way that Estelle would choose to withdraw her resignation. Several members drafted resolutions supportive of Estelle in preparation for a penultimate May 2 meeting of the board's executive committee, and when that session convened, Parks began it by reading Estelle's letter of April 17 in full. Former president Bea Hessel immediately moved that the resignation not be accepted, and that motion carried unanimously. With Estelle present, Hessel then made a second motion, which was also promptly passed, requesting that the board endeavor to determine what would make Estelle reconsider her resignation. "Mrs. Griswold," the minutes recounted, "expressed the feeling that it was impossible for her to work effectively without proper support from the Board, and that the policy and relationship between the Executive Director, the State Board, and the local leagues must be clarified. She stated that it is not proper for members of local leagues to act independently without consulting either the Executive Director or the Board. This kind of action causes confusion, puts the Director in an impossible position, and in the end hurts the cause for which we are all working."

Lucia Parks then noted the many letters similar to Howson's and Standish's that she and other officers had received commending Estelle and asking that her resignation be withdrawn. A prepared resolution expressing appreciation for Estelle's leadership and pledging full cooperation in the future was read and adopted, as was a second motion in which the Board expressed regret that Estelle might mistakenly have thought that it had anything other than full confidence in her. Bea Hessel read a letter of praise for Estelle that Fowler Harper, who was teaching in Miami that spring, had sent to the board, and then Estelle spoke up and announced that she indeed would withdraw her letter of resignation. Lucia Parks thanked her on behalf of the board for that decision, and former president Claudia McGinley moved that copies of all the resolutions and commendatory letters be sent to all members of the entire board.[33]

That three-hour meeting largely but not completely resolved PPLC's internal battling. Estelle ended any further discussion of the carriage house project, and the board, seemingly in return, authorized her to use PPLC's office car, a small Fiat, for other than workaday obligations. PPLC's annual meeting reelected Lucia Parks for a third and final year as president, and elevated a relative newcomer to the board, Cornelia Jahncke of Greenwich, to the number two post of first vice-president. The 1963 Connecticut legislative session developed in much the same way as previous ones, with committee approval of a repeal bill being followed by easy passage in the house—149 to 66— and no floor action at all in the senate. By the summer of 1963, PPLC once again was in a position of having to wait for the very slow processes of appellate litigation to gradually move forward.[34]

Katie Roraback spent a good deal of the summer preparing a sixty-two-page *Griswold-Buxton* brief for the Connecticut Supreme Court, and throughout it all she once again had to devote considerable time to fending off intrusive suggestions from PPLC's ostensible New York allies. ACLU Executive Director John "Jack" Pemberton wanted the ACLU to file an amicus brief in the Connecticut court as well as eventually with the U.S. Supreme Court, and he also suggested that perhaps a parallel amicus brief in support of PPLC could be submitted to one or both such courts on behalf of a small, professorially oriented Roman Catholic group, the Catholic Council on Civil Liberties. Roraback enthusiastically welcomed both proposals vis-à-vis the U.S. Supreme Court, but again insisted that the relative rarity of amicus briefs in the Connecticut court would make any such filing—especially by an out-of-state group—either unhelpful or perhaps potentially harmful. Harriet Pilpel, worried about Roraback's own plans, complained privately to PPFA executives that "My general impression is that Catherine has no intention of doing more than filing the same kind of skimpy legalistic document she filed on previous occasions," and one PPFA board member and attorney very unsubtly wrote Roraback and asked to see a draft of her proposed brief. Roraback politely reminded him that the chances of the Connecticut court reversing Griswold and Buxton's convictions were "almost negligible," but in mid-August she did send an advance copy of her brief to Pilpel, who replied forthrightly that it was "a very good job." The lengthy filing was a significantly more substantive document than anything the PPLCers had generated since Harper's Supreme Court brief in *Poe*, and it made explicit use of both the Harlan and Douglas dissents there as well as Norman Redlich's law review article and other scholarly sources. It made repeated references to judicial recognition of the "right to be let alone," and emphasized the "constitutional protections inherent in this concept of privacy." After reviewing it, Pilpel told Roraback that "It is difficult to imagine a more fundamental civil liberty than the right to decide whether and when to have children."[35]

The "profound ferment" within Roman Catholic circles concerning birth control continued apace in the wake of John Rock's book. Journals like *Commonweal* continued to publish essays noting that measures such as the Connecticut statute were "bad" even "strictly in Catholic terms," but some reactionaries did strike back. Father Knott of the National Catholic Welfare Conference's Family Life Bureau proclaimed that "the Catholic Church has always, does now and will continue to consider contraception as a serious moral evil," and Knott even attacked Rock personally, declaring that he was "not a Catholic, but a propagandist for Planned Parenthood." More significantly, however, a liberal Notre Dame theologian, writing in a popular Protestant journal, advocated that "no one group may impose its distinctive creedal or moral viewpoint through the clenched fist of legislative fiat." When one did, "it is an utterly unwarranted infringement of the constitutional rights of others and is doomed to failure. Its only result is the generation of bad blood, bitterness, hatred and strife." Connecticut and Massachusetts's political experiences since the 1920s could easily be cited to support that conclusion.[36]

On October 1, six weeks in advance of oral argument before the Connecticut Supreme Court, assistant circuit prosecutor Joseph Clark, who largely had taken over responsibility for the Griswold-Buxton case from Julius Maretz, filed a modest twenty-one-page brief with the high court. Much of his material was utterly familiar, but Clark did provide a new twist to some themes, such as in rebutting Buxton's medical rationale. "The State is of the opinion," Clark wrote, "that the practice of medicine was directed to the treatment, cure, and prevention of disease. Certainly pregnancy for a healthy married woman cannot be a disease."

The November 12 oral argument was largely dominated by John H. King, who had ascended to the chief justice's chair with the retirement of Raymond E. Baldwin three months earlier. Katie Roraback told the five member court that the right to privacy was receiving "increasing recognition" in the United States, and sought to emphasize the importance of marriage. "Since the marital relationship is a private one, can the state invade and regulate it?," she asked. "Persons have the right to the pursuit of happiness and this must include a happy marriage and the right to plan for children." King told Roraback that her "most telling argument" was this contention concerning the statute's very broad sweep, and Roraback also followed up on King's suggestion that the statute's failure to differentiate between married and unmarried individuals might similarly raise a question.

Chief Justice King gave Joe Clark a distinctly harder time than he afforded Katie Roraback. Why could it be thought that a "reasonable General Assembly could have felt that this was a proper way to curtail illicit relationships between unmarried persons," King asked him. "What we're trying to determine is the reasonableness of this sweep which covers everybody." Clark parried, saying that the state had a proper interest both in protecting morality and in guarding the size of its population. But King persisted. "Does this law really protect morality?" he quizzically asked. The statute's "prohibition of use, instead of sale, presents policing problems," he noted. "How are you going to know if someone uses contraceptives unless they tell you?" Clark dodged again, but King repeated his query. "How do you know about the use unless the user tells you? I assume you are not going to raid bedrooms?" Clark assented, but King returned to his basic point about reasonableness and overbreadth: "Would it be a reasonable approach to abolish all liquor to prevent drunken driving?" Clark replied that married couples had the alternative of abstinence, and Julius Maretz jumped in to assert that if that law was voided, there would be an increase in the incidence of illicit intercourse in Connecticut. The oral argument went on for almost two and a half hours before it concluded, and Estelle Griswold, one of about a dozen PPLC onlookers, told her colleagues that she thought it had gone well.[37]

PPLC once more sat back to wait for a decision, and in early December the New Haven women publicized the opening of a birth control information center in the PPLC offices at 406 Orange. The announcement had the unintended effect of reactivating one prior participant in PPLC's work, James G. Morris, who on the morning of December 9 appeared outside of 406 Orange with a picket sign saying "The Law is The Law, or is it? Morality is in danger." Morris continued his one-man demonstration long enough for newspaper photographers to arrive, and the next day wire-service pictures of Morris's protest appeared in most Connecticut papers accompanied by descriptive captions. The Associated Press, describing the photo, noted that "Morris holds rosary in right hand."

One animated PPLC board member wrote Estelle to express regret that they had to put up with Mr. Morris's ongoing antics, but Estelle quickly wrote back to correct her understanding of what was taking place. "Actually Mr. Morris is doing so much for us and if we do not heap coals on his head and give some Roman Catholics reason to come to his defense, we gain their support just through their shame for him."

Morris's contributions notwithstanding, the winter and spring months of early 1964 were privately difficult for Estelle. She and Dick were now, because of his health, living in a downtown high-rise apartment building rather than around the corner on Trumbull, but Dick's emphysema was worsening significantly and in March he had major surgery. Most people who knew Estelle through PPLC saw very little of Dick; at least one president, as well as Lee Buxton's wife Helen, never actually met him. But Hilda Standish and other special, longtime friends could tell that Dick and Estelle were an especially close couple, even if his deteriorating condition was something she almost never mentioned at the office. Similarly, Fowler Harper, who was again teaching for the spring at the University of Miami Law School, was also undergoing treatment for prostate cancer, and Fowler's stiff drinking and heavy smoking, just like Dick Griswold's, were certainly not therapeutic.[38]

In late April 1964 Cornelia Jahncke succeeded Lucia Parks as PPLC president, and then, two weeks later, the Connecticut Supreme Court issued its decision affirming Estelle and Lee Buxton's convictions. The unanimous and very brief opinion, written by junior Justice John M. Comley, offered a familiar recitation of how *Nelson*, *Tileston*, *Poe*, and *Trubek* were controlling precedents. This appeal too, just like those prior rulings, was governed, Comley declared, by "the principle that courts may not interfere with the exercise by a state of the police power to conserve the public safety and welfare, including health and morals, if the law has a real and substantial relation to the accomplishment of those objects." Estelle told reporters that she was "very disappointed," and Lee Buxton termed the Connecticut court's perspective "unrealistic," but Katie Roraback announced that she and Fowler Harper were already at work on Griswold and Buxton's next appeal, to the Supreme Court of the United States.[39]

Virtually no one was actually surprised by the state court's ruling, and local editorialists looked forward to the U.S. high court doing Connecticut a favor by finally voiding the law that state legislators still could not bring themselves to strike. One New Haven paper noted that while all four *Poe* dissenters remained on the Supreme Court, two members of the five-vote majority—Felix Frankfurter and Charles E. Whittaker—had departed, and that one or both of their replacements—Byron R. White and Arthur J. Goldberg—could well make for a different majority this time. Fowler Harper, in Miami and about to undertake a six-week teaching stint in Puerto Rico, told Estelle he was looking forward to preparing the jurisdictional statement for the high court, and part-time assistant prosecutor Joe Clark, appreciating how much work now lay before him, unsuccessfully sought assistance from the state attorney general's office. Harriet Pilpel and Harper agreed that once again there would be both a PPFA amicus brief and an ostensibly independent one on behalf of prominent physicians, and ACLU staffers—with vexatious encouragement from the ageing but still active Morris Ernst—revived the idea of a supportive amicus brief from the Catholic Council on Civil Liberties (CCCL). In early August Buffalo law professor Robert B. Fleming, who would write the CCCL brief, met with Pilpel and Ernst, and by that same time Harper had a draft of the jurisdictional statement ready for colleagues' review.[40]

Harper formally filed the *Griswold* appeal and the jurisdictional statement with the U.S. Supreme Court in early September. He argued that the two convictions raised three principal constitutional questions: whether the 1879 statute deprived Griswold, Buxton, and their patients of liberty in violation of the Fourteenth Amendment's due process clause, whether the statute violated their First Amendment right to free speech, and whether the statute both on its face and "as applied to married patients of these appellants and other married couples" represented "an unreasonable and unjustifiable invasion of their privacy contrary to the Fourth, Ninth and Fourteenth Amendments." The document had more than its share of errors—such as calling Justice Brennan's concurrence in *Poe* a dissent, and referring to another opinion written by Justice "Stuart"—but it laid heavy emphasis on the liberty and privacy themes that Justices Harlan and Douglas had articulated in their *Poe* dissents. Harper devoted some attention to social policy benefits of birth control, observing with regard to the new federal "war on poverty" that "to fight poverty without birth control is to fight with one hand tied behind the back," but the privacy concept received his most extended attention. The Ninth Amendment, he stressed, either "as directly applicable to the States or as made so by the Fourteenth, should be interpreted to protect aspects of what has been called the rights of privacy as a protection additional to that afforded by other Amendments." The "so-called 'right of privacy,'" Harper went on, "is a broad general term which in fact includes a number of 'rights' or 'interests.'" The privacy claim that Buxton and Griswold's female clinic patients had a fundamental right to use birth control is "certainly closely akin to other aspects of privacy specifically recognized in the Constitution." Indeed, "freedom from coerced marital conformity in the bedroom" was "in many respects" a "far more important" privacy rights claim than some—e.g., the Third Amendment's prohibition against the quartering of troops in private homes during peacetime— that were expressly stated in the Constitution. Noting again the Ninth

Amendment's recognition of other rights "retained by the people," Harper argued that "the invasion of the interest of married spouses in the sanctity and privacy of their marital relations . . . is a violation of precisely the kind of 'right' which the Ninth Amendment was intended to secure."[41]

Thanks in part to the influence of Norman Redlich's 1962 article, Harper's initial filing in *Griswold* was constitutionally a good deal more robust and profound than the analyses that had been submitted in *Poe*. PPLC's board, in part because of their six-year indebtedness to Harper, and in part because of his clearly weakening health, resolved soon after that filing to bestow a several-thousand-dollar "gift" upon their ailing counsel. Estelle informed Miriam Harper of the news first, and Fowler then wrote her to say that the gesture had "utterly overwhelmed" him. "I would be less than frank if I didn't say that I am delighted," Harper told her, "although my first reaction was that I should not accept such a fee. However, it didn't take me long to change my mind."

Estelle was beginning to worry that even though PPLC was in stronger financial shape than ever before, the organization nonetheless was not financially ready to begin providing the clinic services that would be obligatory should *Griswold and Buxton* v. *State of Connecticut* prove successful in the U.S. Supreme Court. Estelle's insistence that new fund-raising would have to be undertaken, particularly by the PPLC local leagues that would be expected to sponsor future clinics, however, renewed the deep antipathy toward her that had continued to fester among some of the New Haven members. New Haven president Dorothy Giles informed PPLC president Cornelia Jahncke that "there is no possibility of effecting any mutual understanding" between the New Haven group and Griswold, and complained about "the complete dominance of the board by the Executive Director." In late September PPFA sent a senior staff member up to New Haven to try to mediate, since Giles and her cohorts were insisting that the principal issue was the question of how much autonomy local groups should have vis-à-vis the state league, but instead the New Haveners treated the visitor to a nonstop personal lambasting of Estelle Griswold. "The Executive Director is a rigid, unyielding person who never sees but one side of a question and who does not allow anyone or anything to stand in her way," the New Haven president perhaps shrewdly asserted. "It is impossible to work constructively with her," in part because of Griswold's supposed "inability to accept new ideas." It was further alleged that Griswold "does not let us forget that we thwarted her desire to have a home in the barn" or carriage house, and the New

Haveners also pointedly asserted that it would be "an impossibility" to "work with the Executive Director on a clinic project."

Estelle herself dismissed the criticisms as "bargain basement bickering and brainwashing" and told PPFA's Fred Jaffe that she did not "know of any legitimate basis for these complaints." Cornelia Jahncke firmly reprimanded the New Haveners for failing to submit pro forma reports to PPLC and also for wanting to discuss what should be done should the Supreme Court appeal be lost rather than won, and by late October the New Haven group was discussing whether to petition PPFA for direct affiliation with the national federation, wholly separate and apart from PPLC. PPFA reluctantly convened a New York meeting of all the warring parties, and Estelle complained that seemingly every new New Haven league member was being "given an orientation session in non-cooperation and personal animosity toward me and other members of our staff." Estelle also volunteered that in the fourteen years she had lived in New Haven, she had never encountered any of PPLC's complainants as active members of any other local civic group.

The New York session settled nothing, but as word of the renewed tensions spread, Estelle's supporters once again spoke up. An angry Lee Buxton, believing that PPFA was being insufficiently supportive of Estelle, sent PPFA president Alan Guttmacher a letter resigning from his largely pro forma role as chairman of PPLC's Medical Advisory Committee. PPFA's Jaffe reassured him that "We do recognize Estelle's great contributions and have told her so in person and in other ways repeatedly." A board member from Newtown wrote the New Haveners to rebut their attacks on Estelle and to assert that her "astute and judicious leadership" had given "a new impetus" to PPLC. "With Mrs. Griswold's broad range of public activities and contacts in every walk of life," she had made it possible for PPLC to take part in many social welfare projects where Planned Parenthood participation had previously not been welcome. In particular, this board member declared, "I have known Mrs. Griswold too long to believe that 'social standing' is of undue importance to her. . . . I find this particular criticism not only untrue but bordering on the ridiculous."[42]

Nonetheless, at a PPLC Executive Committee meeting on November 6, Estelle once again tendered a formal letter of resignation, this time to take effect December 1. An executive session discussion decided that the New Haveners ought to be put in their place and that both Buxton and Griswold should be asked to withdraw their resignation letters. However when the full board met eleven days later, New Haven president Dorothy Giles twice declared that her group could not and would not work with Estelle Griswold. A week later the executive committee resolved that eventual opening of a clinic at the 406 Orange Street building would be undertaken by PPLC itself, and not in any way by the local New Haven group, who would be told that whatever their plans might be, they should find space elsewhere. That declaration seemed to establish at least a temporary internal truce, and Griswold and Buxton both withdrew their resignations.[43]

While PPLC had been preoccupied with its internecine disputes, assistant prosecutor Joe Clark had filed his own Supreme Court motion asking that the *Griswold* appeal be dismissed for lack of a substantial federal question and because the two convictions were virtually identical to the ones that the high court had refused to review or reverse in *Gardner* twenty-six years earlier. Harper filed a short and succinct rebuttal, and Harriet Pilpel informed him that she had been told by liberal Catholic academician Robert F. Drinan that work was indeed progressing on a CCCL amicus brief. But at the same time that Pilpel was sending friendly and reassuring missives to the increasingly ill Harper, she was simultaneously warning PPFA's Alan Guttmacher and Fred Jaffe about potentially "serious defects" and "deficiencies" in the *Griswold* record and appeal, particularly with regard to Harper's jurisdictional statement, due to the fact that "our advice in most substantial respects has not been followed" by Harper and Katie Roraback. That contention was factually incorrect in the extreme, but Pilpel nonetheless expressed "astonishment and dismay" to the PPFA executives that Harper had had his three-page reply to Clark's motion printed and filed without seeking her prior approval. Perhaps Pilpel was simply seeking to avoid future criticism should something go wrong with *Griswold* in the Supreme Court. Or perhaps being in New York simply did make one superior and smarter, even relative to someone with Harper's professional record, a phenomenon that the PPLCers had of course had many prior opportunities to ponder.[44]

In mid-October the national wire services and all the Connecticut papers gave considerable play to a further declaration that Boston Archbishop Richard Cardinal Cushing favored terminating Roman Catholic opposition to repeal of anticontraception statutes. The occasion for the renewed attention to even the Catholic hierarchy's apparent liberalization was an article in the *New England Journal of Medicine* by a young Catholic doctor, Joseph L. Dorsey, whose close relationship to the Boston archdiocese was well-known; perhaps uniquely, the article carried a one-paragraph introduction and endorsement by the monsignor who was editor of the archdiocesan weekly newspaper. The physician author noted in the context of the Massachusetts statute that "After talking with many well informed priests about this law, I have failed to find one . . . who favors retention" of it. Cushing himself had recently acknowledged that "although natural law does not change, our here-and-now interpretation and awareness of it does," but Dr. Dorsey concluded that the "change in attitude" had come about "primarily through the development of a different attitude toward laws in general in a pluralistic society." A forthcoming survey, however, found that 78 percent of Catholic respondents—as compared with 82 percent of Protestants, and only 53 percent of Catholics just two years earlier—now agreed that "birth control information should be available to anyone who wants it." And, quite similarly, demographic studies disclosed that more than half of married Catholic women were now using methods of birth control that the church hierarchy continued to condemn. Perhaps for once the clergy—although grudgingly if not almost furtively   were following the laity rather than vice-versa.[45]

Within the U.S. Supreme Court, initial consideration of whether to hear the *Griswold* appeal was scheduled for the justices' private conference of December 3, and in advance of that discussion summary memos were prepared by the young clerks in at least four of the chambers. For three of them there was no doubt, Joe Clark's contentions notwithstanding, that *Griswold*—or *Poe* "round two" as John Harlan's clerk, Michael Maney, labeled it—was an important appeal warranting full consideration. However, John Hart Ely, one of Chief Justice Earl Warren's three clerks, introduced it to the Chief Justice in a manner that almost seemed reminiscent of a horror movie sequel—"Dr. Buxton is back"—and depending on one's constitutional tastes, maybe it was. "For me, this is not an easy case on the merits," Ely informed Warren, but nonetheless it was "clear that the issues are significant." Warren and all eight of the other justices agreed on at least that latter point, for when the *Griswold* appeal was considered at the December 3 conference, all nine members of the Court voted unanimously that the case should be heard.[46]

On Monday, December 7, the Court announced publicly its acceptance of the *Griswold* appeal. Estelle told reporters she was "very gratified" by the action. "We're quite confident that when the court hears the case, this will be the final episode." Lee Buxton sounded similarly optimistic, commenting that "in the past five years the thinking on this issue has changed considerably," both in Connecticut and elsewhere. Estelle agreed, explaining that PPLC would move to reopen a clinic as soon as the old 1879 statute was finally voided. "I think the time has come. Times have changed, and there is a dialogue going on all over."[47]

But Estelle and Lee's happiness that the decisive round of PPLC's forty-two-year struggle to make birth control legal was finally beginning was largely vitiated by an advancing tragedy whose terribly ironic timing made it all the more painful. By the time of the court's actual decision to take *Griswold* and face the inescapable constitutional challenge that it had so clumsily ducked in *Poe*, Fowler Harper entered Grace–New Haven Hospital for what he knew would be the final time.

Fowler had borne up under the increasing pain of his terminal cancer with the same combative determination he had long brought to all his many endeavors. Unbeknownst to him, the New Haven office of the FBI had just renewed his membership in the Bureau's top-secret list of dangerous subversives to be rounded up in the event of some national emergency. In addition to its decades-old evidence of such dastardly deeds as that 1946 ballot petition signature and membership in the National Lawyers Guild, this year the New Haven office was able to cite much fresher evidence, a vintage Fowlerism that Harper had uttered to a tabloid news reporter who had asked him why it seemed that his political positions often followed the communist line. The error, Harper told the reporter, was in looking at the matter backward, so to speak. It wasn't that Harper followed the communist line, just that "sometimes it appears that the communists follow my line. They're always welcome to agree with me, but I don't see how I can be blamed when they do."

Only a few months before the onset of his final illness Fowler had finally completed a longtime labor of love, a biography of one-time Supreme Court Justice Wiley B. Rutledge, a Harper friend whose relatively brief service on the Court had been cut short by his sudden death in 1949. Fowler also had been energetically and successfully pursuing a libel suit against his old Yale bête noire from a quarter-century earlier, William F. Buckley, Jr. Buckley's *National Review* magazine had editorially alleged that Harper and other initiators of a 1962 petition opposing American military involvement in Vietnam had been communist-inspired, and Fowler's litigious nature would not let that aspersion pass unanswered. Just before Christmas of 1964 a New York trial court judge ruled in Harper's favor, and some months later Mr. Buckley settled the suit by making a payment of more than thirteen thousand dollars.[48]

Tuesday morning, December 8, someone in the clerk's office at the Supreme Court attempted to reach Fowler, only to be told by Miriam that he was in the hospital and that she would have someone else get in touch with them. Miriam spoke with Estelle, and later that day Estelle went to Grace–New Haven to ask Fowler what they should do. Fowler already had privately raised the issue with his longtime friend and colleague Tom Emerson, and now he told Estelle that the time indeed was at hand for formal responsibility for *Griswold* to be passed to Tom. Estelle sent Emerson a friendly official letter welcoming his willingness to assume PPLC's cause, and tried to reassure Fowler, or herself, that of course his condition would improve.

From a distance many people thought of Tom Emerson and Fowler Harper as political if not personal twins. Up close, however, they were stylistic opposites. Tom like Fowler was a New Deal veteran who had been an active leader of the National Lawyers Guild; shortly after joining the Yale faculty in 1946 he had briefly been the Connecticut gubernatorial candidate of Henry Wallace's Progressive Party. Fifty-seven years old when he inherited *Griswold* from Fowler, Tom had graduated from both Yale College and Yale Law School before going to Washington; since joining the Yale faculty his most notable achievement had been coauthoring an innovative and highly praised casebook, *Political and Civil Rights in the United States*. After his first wife passed away in 1958 he remarried, and Ruth Calvin Emerson had helped prepare the ACLU amicus brief in *Poe*. A deeply committed civil libertarian, Tom maintained an active interest in a wide range of political and legal issues. But highly unlike the outgoing and extravagant Fowler Harper, Tom Emerson was a very reserved and undramatic man, a "very unemotional" teacher even when he dealt with subjects about which he felt strongly. People who expected a fire-breathing leftist were again and again surprised that Tom Emerson in person—as several students and colleagues all described him—was simply "very, very staid."[49]

Within two days of Estelle's visit to Fowler and her formal note to Tom, Emerson was hard at work trying to get up to speed on *Griswold* as quickly as possible. Now that the Supreme Court had agreed to hear the appeal, the appellants' brief was due in Washington in approximately eight weeks. Emerson read through Fowler's files in preparation for one meeting with Buxton, Roraback, Estelle, and Cornelia Jahncke and another one with Harriet Pilpel. On December 16 Tom notified the Supreme Court that he would be assuming Fowler's role, and although Fowler was in Lee Buxton's words "gradually losing his strength," Tom was able to have several conversations with him about the case before the end of the year. When PPLC's executive committee met for the first time in 1965 on January 7, Estelle and Cornelia Jahncke obtained approval to make an additional gift of twenty-five hundred dollars to Fowler immediately. The gesture came just barely in time, for early the following morning Fowler Harper died at Grace–New Haven Hospital.

Estelle and Lee both felt a very deep sense of loss. Several weeks later at a memorial service at the law school Gene Rostow spoke of the "serenity" with which Fowler had faced his "long and painful" illness, and Wiley Rutledge's son Neal spoke of the "trace of loneliness, and the courage to be alone, that added a quality of mystery" to Fowler's character. Federal judge William H. Hastie spoke of his friendship with Fowler going back to the late 1930s in Washington, and Tom Emerson lovingly spoke of how Fowler had been "one of the country's best and most belligerent watch-dogs. . . . At times I thought he was quixotic; he thought I was a compromiser." Tom spoke of how much energy and commitment Fowler had put into first *Poe* and then *Griswold*; left unspoken was the probability that Fowler's most important legacy, one that he had not lived to see, still lay ahead of him, perhaps five months in the future.[50]

In mid-January Tom Emerson had his first conversation with his opposite number, assistant prosecutor Joe Clark. Clark too was hard at work on his brief, and fairly frustrated that neither his new superior, circuit prosecutor Philip Mancini, nor state officials in Hartford had provided him much in the way of support or assistance. A friend and colleague, Irwin P. Harrison, was giving him some help on procedural matters, but a formal request for more extensive aid resulted only in the pro forma appointment of the recently retired former circuit prosecutor, Julius Maretz, as a supposed special assistant. Clark himself was nonetheless repeating Raymond Cannon's odd precedent from *Poe* of refusing to give customary consent to the routine filing of amicus briefs that would support Griswold and Buxton. Requests from Pilpel's office, on behalf of PPFA, from the ACLU, from Whitney North Seymour for many of the same prominent physicians who had supported *Poe*, and from Robert Fleming for the Catholic Council on Civil Liberties were all turned aside with the assertion that Clark "fail[ed] to see" how any one of the briefs "would serve any useful purpose."[51]

By late January final drafts of Emerson's and several of the amicus briefs were being privately circulated. Pilpel and her deputy, Nancy Wechsler, pronounced Emerson's expedited work "simply superb," and PPFA's Fred Jaffe was enlisted to supply Tom with up-to-date demographic and medical citations. Lee Buxton was similarly impressed with Emerson's feat but reprimanded Whitney Seymour, who once again was responsible for the PPFA-sponsored doctors' brief, for a PPFA letter that spoke of *Griswold* as "our" case. Otherwise, aside from some modest financial haggling, the Connecticut–New York tensions remained largely in repose. Within PPLC, however, efforts to enforce the earlier board of directors mandate upon the rebellious New Haven members continued to generate sparks, and only after being threatened with formal disaffiliation by the board did the New Haveners agree to surrender their presence at 406 Orange so that preparations toward opening a PPLC clinic after a Supreme Court victory could get underway.[52]

On February 11 Tom Emerson filed a ninety-six-page brief on behalf of Estelle Griswold and Lee Buxton with the Supreme Court. It was an impressive if not exhaustive piece of work, especially in light of the suddenness with which it had had to be prepared, and it offered two main arguments: first, that the 1879 law contravened the liberty protected by the Fourteenth Amendment, and, second, that its application to Griswold and Buxton also violated their First Amendment freedom of speech. Emerson subsumed the privacy argument into the liberty one. "The Connecticut statutes violate due process in that they constitute an unwarranted invasion of privacy. Whether one derives the right of privacy from a composite of the Third, Fourth and Fifth Amendments, from the Ninth Amendment, or from the 'liberty' clause of the Fourteenth Amendment, such a constitutional right has been specifically recognized by this Court. Although the boundaries of this constitutional right of privacy have not yet been spelled out, plainly the right extends to unwarranted government invasion of (1) the sanctity of the home, and (2) the intimacies of the sexual relationship in marriage. These core elements of the right to privacy are combined in this case."

Emerson critically surveyed the possible legislative purposes which may have underlain the 1879 enactments, noted how widespread the acceptance of birth control now was within American society, and then returned to his argument that the First, Third, Fourth, and Fifth Amendments taken in tandem "embody a general principle which protects the private sector of life." Additionally, "the interest of married spouses in the sanctity and privacy of their marital relations involves precisely the kind of right which the Ninth Amendment was intended to secure." All told, Emerson concluded, "the demands of modern life require that the composite of these specific protections be accorded the status of a recognized constitutional right," and reiterated again that "the sanctity of the home and the wholly personal nature of marital relations" together form "the inner core of the right of privacy."[53]

The four supportive amicus briefs were filed soon after Emerson's, and were generally unremarkable. Pilpel and Wechsler, on behalf of PPFA, emphasized the extensive popular approval now accorded birth control, and Seymour's brief for the doctors repeated well-known themes. Robert Fleming for the Catholic Council on Civil Liberties emphasized that the right of privacy was "within the liberty protected by the Fourteenth Amendment," and the ACLU's submission highlighted exactly the same point. Earlier Court decisions such as *Meyer* and *Pierce* recognized "marriage and the family as the ultimate repository of personal freedom," and reaching beyond those previous holdings stood "the wife's right to order her childbearing according to her financial and emotional needs, her abilities, and her achievements."[54]

The amicus briefs, especially the Catholic one, drew a significant amount of press attention, and the attorneys on each side had a fairly good sense of where they stood. Joe Clark replied to one law student's inquiry by remarking that "I have the good fortune, or lack thereof, to be" arguing *Griswold* for the state, while Tom Emerson expressed considerable optimism in response to the persnickety Morris Ernst. Harriet Pilpel notified Emerson that she was asking the Court for thirty minutes of oral argument time for herself in addition to the one hour each that both Emerson and Clark would have, although she acknowledged that the chances of the Court granting her request were "virtually nil."[55]

On March 11 Joe Clark submitted his brief in defense of the 1879 statute, a thirty-four-page effort that attempted to find a variety of procedural flaws in the case while also asserting that "There has been no invasion of anyone's privacy in this case." Although it was not apposite, Clark also volunteered that any suggestion "that single people should be allowed to use a contraceptive device is so contra to American experience, thought, and family law that it does not merit further discussion." Five days after Clark's filing, the clerk's office informed all parties that the oral argument of *Griswold* v. *Connecticut* would commence on March 29 and that Pilpel's request to participate had been denied.[56]

At the same time that *Griswold* was moving forward toward argument before the Supreme Court, new efforts to change the old anti-contraception statutes were underway in both Massachusetts and Connecticut. The Bay State attempt had started with a reform bill introduced by state Representative Michael S. Dukakis, but what drew sudden and extensive nationwide attention was a statement read on behalf of the hospitalized Richard Cardinal Cushing at a March 2 legislative hearing on the measure. "It does not seem reasonable to me to forbid in civil law a practice that can be considered a matter of private morality," Cushing declared. He went on to say that "Catholics do not need the support of civil law to be faithful to their own religious convictions and they do not seek to impose by law their moral values on other members of society." His "admirable" testimony drew prominent national editorial praise as "sensible, tolerant and thoroughly commendable," and with Cushing's encouragement the Dukakis bill was referred to a study commission for further action.[57]

In Connecticut, where reapportionment litigation had led to the cancellation of 1964 legislative elections and a second, 1965 session for the same legislators who had served in 1963, Katherine Evarts again introduced a repeal bill. Several days before the March 23 hearing, Joseph P. Cooney announced on behalf of the Hartford Archdiocese that no opponents would appear at the session in light of *Griswold*'s presence before the U.S. Supreme Court, and the most notable event at the very brief public session was the affirmative remarks that were volunteered by a female Roman Catholic Republican legislator from Stonington. Evarts's bill was expected to win a favorable report from the Public Health and Safety Committee, but no one was anticipating that the state senate would move to vote on the measure just weeks before the U.S. Supreme Court might well erase the problem once and for all.[58]

In the judgment of many of the young clerks, and perhaps several of the justices, the 1964–1965 Supreme Court term had seemed relatively uneventful. To at least several clerks, the major case of the year was *Estes* v. *Texas*, in which the Court finally decided that the presence of television cameras in a courtroom infringed upon a criminal defendant's right to a fair trial, although others attached greater significance to *Dombrowski* v. *Pfister*, where the Court approved federal judicial intervention in an ongoing state criminal proceeding. Early in the term a significant number of clerks had been taken away from regular duties to proofread the final draft of Warren Commission Report on the assassination of President John F. Kennedy, and another, with his justice's permission, had been recruited into full-time work for President Lyndon B. Johnson's reelection campaign. John Harlan thought the Warren Commission involvement was an undeniable violation of the separation of powers, but one clerk who took part in the work explained that the most extensive attention was directed largely toward the girlie photos from Jack Ruby's nightclub.

Many clerks were puzzled by the highly critical attitude that William O. Douglas was displaying toward the Court's newest member, Justice

Arthur Goldberg. Several also looked up to the other Kennedy appointee, Byron R. White, because of his status as the first former clerk to become a justice, but some were highly aggravated by White's behavior as an exceptionally dirty basketball player during pickup games in the Court gym.

Among the clerks themselves, Warren's John Hart Ely was the subject of more intramural talk than most, in part because of the perception that Ely in one otherwise unremarkable case, *Hanna* v. *Plumer*, had successfully persuaded the Chief to adopt a viewpoint that Ely himself had focused upon while still a student at Yale Law School. But *Griswold* v. *Connecticut* was undeniably of special interest to Ely, and several weeks in advance of oral argument he gave Warren a thirty page memorandum on the case. The six briefs, Ely explained, were on the whole somewhat disappointing. Emerson's failed to offer any extensive argument as to whether the Connecticut statute might be vulnerable under the Fourteenth Amendment's equal protection clause, "which to me seems very important," and the amicus ones "really raise no arguments different from those" made by Emerson. More regrettably, Joe Clark's brief "unfortunately does not put forth as good a defense of the law as can be made." Although one of Clark's procedural contentions might have some validity, "One would hope that the case for the State would be argued by someone other than the man responsible for the brief, but it appears that you will not be so lucky."

On balance, Ely recommended, "I think the conviction should be reversed, but that the Court should carefully choose its ground of decision, for some of those urged by appellants have dangerous implications." First and foremost among those was the notion that there is a constitutional right to privacy. "I do not think," Ely opined, that "the Court should enforce clauses which are not there. No matter how strong a dislike for a piece of legislation may be, it is dangerous precedent to read into the Constitution guarantees which are not there." No matter how many writers, or justices, might pontificate about a "right to be let alone," "the Constitution says nothing about such a right." Regarding Emerson's contention that four or five different amendments all speak to such a right, Ely argued that "it by no means follows that because several parts of the Constitution protect aspects of what might be called privacy, the Constitution therefore contains a general right of privacy, with a content over and above the content of the various specific provisions. To say that the 9th Amendment protects privacy, without any demonstration of such a right predating the adoption of the Amendment, or any intention to cover privacy, is of course to beg the question."

Ely went on to draw a special bead on one of Emerson's principal linchpins. "Harlan's opinion in *Poe* boils down to a statement that he does not like the Conn[ecticut] law. This vague, 'outrage' approach to the 14th Amendment comprises, in my opinion, the most dangerous sort of 'activism.'" Instead, Ely suggested, the Chief Justice should look at *Griswold*, and how the Connecticut statute prevented the operation of birth control clinics for the poor, but not the provision of similar services to better-off patients of private physicians, in the light of an eighty-year-old equal protection decision, *Yick Wo* v. *Hopkins*. There, in 1886, the Supreme Court had declared that "Though the law itself be fair on its face and impartial in appearance, yet, if it is applied and administered by public authority with an evil eye and an unequal hand, so as practically to make unjust and illegal discriminations between persons in similar circumstances, material to their rights, the denial of equal justice is still within the prohibition of the Constitution." In conclusion, Ely thus recommended that "an opinion along these lines would be far more satisfactory than one based on the right to privacy."[59]

Estelle, Lee Buxton, Cornelia Jahncke, and Lucia and Charles Parks were among more than a dozen PPLCers who flew to Washington for the March 29 oral argument. Miriam Harper and Ruth Emerson also attended, as did Katie Roraback, who joined Tom Emerson at the counsel's table in the front of the courtroom. Reporters noted that the capacity crowd also included Ethel Kennedy, the wife of the former attorney general and newly elected senator from New York, as well as Treasury Secretary Henry Fowler. Consideration of *Griswold* began at about one thirty in the afternoon, and Tom was no more than a minute into his opening remarks when he was interrupted by the first of many questions from the bench. Tom explained that their challenge to the 1879 statute "goes only to the application to married women," and Justice Hugo Black broke in: "Well, why wouldn't it be a denial of equal protection of the laws to draw such a distinction, if women need that?" "Well, it might be," Emerson conceded. Then, responding to another query, he repeated the error Fowler Harper had made four years earlier by telling the court that under the statute "there have been no prosecutions for sale." Justice Brennan, picking up on Black's question, asked Emerson why he was not making an equal protection argument, "which on the face of it, it seems to me, might have considerable merit." Tom parried by saying that that claim was subsumed under their due process clause challenge, and after Black again jumped in, Tom reiterated his point: "We pitch it on due process in the basic sense" that the statute "is arbitrary and unreasonable, and in the special sense that it constitutes a deprivation of right against invasion of privacy. The privacy argument is a substantially narrower one than the general argument." Emerson said he also was making a First Amendment claim, and added that "We argued the Ninth Amendment as part of the privacy . . . we refer to that as a basis for the right of privacy."

Hugo Black, in little doubt of where Emerson's argument would take the Court, came back once again, asking Tom whether he expected the justices to find the statute "sufficiently shocking" as to be void under the due process clause—a symbolic standard against which Black had railed for many years. Tom immediately denied that he was asking the Court to return to substantive due process as it had been employed in the early twentieth century: "we are not asking this Court to revive *Lochner*," the most infamous such holding. But Black fought back. "It sounds to me like you're asking us to follow the constitutional philosophy of that case." Tom again denied it. "No, your honor, we are not. We are asking you to follow the philosophy of *Meyer* against *Nebraska* and *Pierce* against the *Society of Sisters*." Black suggested that Emerson was thus making an argument that the Connecticut statute was overbroad, and Tom agreed: "The reason that it is overbroad is because it denies rights to married couples that should not be denied." Black then asked what in addition to the due process clause was Tom resting his constitutional claim upon. "We rely on the Third, Fourth and Fifth Amendments, insofar as they embody a concept of a right of privacy" and were incorporated to apply against the states by the Fourteenth. Justice Goldberg inquired as to whether Emerson was saying that privacy, with regard to the Ninth Amendment, was "a right retained by the people," and after first responding "It could very well be," Tom caught himself and sounded a much stronger note. "If there's any right that you would think would be reserved to the people and which the government should not interfere with, it would be this right." Potter Stewart somewhat oddly inquired as to whether Emerson had any data "as to the breadth of the use of these devices" back in 1791 when the Ninth Amendment was adopted, and Tom simply said no.

John Harlan spoke up to ask whether Emerson would be coming back to amplify his First Amendment argument. Tom self-effacingly responded, "Well, I'm not getting far on any of my arguments," and the courtroom rang with laughter. Then Tom explained how "It's a religious principle that's being enacted into law, that it is immoral to use contraceptives even within the marriage relation." Otherwise, "there is no objective basis for the statutes." Then, in order to preserve the final ten minutes of his time for rebuttal the following day, Tom concluded by again emphasizing "the right to decide whether to have children voluntarily."[60]

Connecticut journalists had anticipated that the Washington face-off would be a less than even match. One New Haven paper, predicting that Griswold and Buxton "will win overwhelmingly," had emphasized that Joe Clark was "a young man in his early thirties with no experience before the Supreme Court." A graduate of Notre Dame University and the University of Connecticut Law School, Clark had been in private practice in New Haven for four years before being named to the part-time assistant prosecutor post in 1961. A New Haven native whose father had been extremely active in state and local Democratic party politics, Clark was active in the Knights of Columbus and the St. Joseph Holy Name Society and would eventually have six children.

Clark had no illusions about his chances with the Supreme Court. Acknowledging that the 1879 statute was "a very difficult thing to defend," he had concluded that "the handwriting was clearly on the wall" back in December when the Court had taken the appeal and thereby rejected his motion to dismiss. Personally he though that the Connecticut law was "foolish" but not unconstitutional; "legislatures have the right to enact stupid laws." Julius Maretz, Irwin Harrison, and several other attorney friends had accompanied Clark to Washington, and his portion of the *Griswold* argument began just a few minutes before the Court's scheduled adjournment for the day at two thirty p.m. He started by trying to use the Supreme Court's own history with birth control cases to his advantage: "Actually, the issue that this Court is being asked to decide is not a new issue here. It is: Should the case of *State* versus *Sanger* from New York, and should the case of *State* versus *Gardner* from Massachusetts, decisions of this Court, be overturned? In both those cases, this Court was involved with a situation where clinics were being run. . . . And in both cases, this Court held that this was not a federal question." Clark also had time to volunteer that there had indeed been convictions for selling contraceptive articles before the two-thirty adjournment was upon him.

When the oral argument resumed on Tuesday morning shortly after ten a.m., Potter Stewart immediately asked Clark what the purpose was of the 1879 statute. "I think it's to reduce the chances of immorality," Clark responded, "to act as a deterrent to sexual intercourse outside of the marital relationship." Stewart, joined by Arthur Goldberg, pressed him further, noting that all the women involved in *Griswold* were married. Clark replied that "there are other methods available to married people" besides contraception, and volunteered that legislatively "this is a question of pure power," supported by a desire "to preserve morality." He went on to say that privacy had nothing to do with the facts of this case. The two defendants, he emphasized, "were running a clinic. They were holding themselves out to the world."

Clark bore up extremely well under very persistent questioning. "This case is purely a case of legislative power reduced to its narrowest sense. Does the legislature have the power to enact laws in this area," or does it not. "Married couples do not have the freedom to do what they want," and the Supreme Court's refusals to review *Sanger* and *Gardner* decades earlier demonstrated "that it was within the power of the states to control these contraceptive clinics."

When Clark's time expired, Tom Emerson rose for approximately ten minutes' worth of rebuttal, beginning with the First Amendment speech argument he had not been able to get to on Monday. Hugo Black broke in with a different question: "Would your argument concerning these things you've been talking about relating to privacy, invalidate all laws that punish people for bringing about abortions?" Tom responded, "No, I think it would not cover the abortion laws or the sterilization laws, your honor. Those—that conduct does not occur in the privacy of the home." Tom paused, and then reiterated the point. "The conduct that is being prohibited in the abortion cases takes place outside of the home, normally. There is no violation of the sanctity of the home." Then Byron White interjected, "Well, apart from that, Mr. Emerson, I take it abortion involves killing a life in being, doesn't it? Isn't that a rather different problem from contraception?" Tom immediately agreed: "Oh yes, of course." Black jumped back in: "Are you saying that all abortions involve killing or murder?" Tom hesitated. "Well, I don't know whether you need characterize it that way. But it involves taking what has begun to be a life." With that the argument concluded, and *Griswold* was submitted for decision.[61]

The private conference discussion of *Griswold* by the nine justices took place three days later, on Friday, April 2. Some of the justices, such as Harlan and Douglas, knew without a moment's doubt how they felt about the case. But Earl Warren was highly uncertain, and in advance of the conference he looked over the long memo that John Ely had given him four weeks earlier, and sketched out his own reactions. First, "I would give the Legis[lature] a chance to dispose of it by waiting, if possible, to adjournment," to see whether the 1965 Connecticut General Assembly might amend or repeal it. Second, Warren was certain of several things he could not do. "I cannot say that it affects the 1st Amend[ment] rights of doctors." Additionally, "I cannot say the state has no legitimate interest—that would lead me to trouble on abortions." Also, "I cannot balance the interest of the state against that of the individual," and "I cannot use the substantive due process approach." Likewise, "I do not believe the equal protection argument is sound," and "I do not accept the privacy argument." The Chief Justice realized that did not leave him with many other options, and Ely's recommendation might be the best course: Warren could support voiding the law either "on a *Yick Wo* theory or on the basis that the statute is not tightly drawn."

When the April 2 discussion of *Griswold* commenced, the Chief articulated to his colleagues most of the thoughts he had jotted down to himself. He was "bothered with the case," and certainly held out some hope that the Connecticut legislature "may repeal the law." He "can't say it affects the First Amendment rights of doctors," and "can't say the state has no interest in the field," for such a holding "could apply to abortion laws." Warren further recited that he could not employ substantive due process or equal protection, and could not accept a privacy argument. Then he explained that he might rely upon *Yick Wo* since there was no effective prohibition on contraceptive sales in Connecticut and since prosecutors did not "go after doctors as such but only clinics." He would favor an opinion saying that any statute regulating the practice of contraception had to be clearly, carefully, and narrowly drawn, since basic rights were involved—"we are dealing with a confidential association, the most intimate in our life."

Hugo Black spoke next, and from the tenor of his questions to Emerson, none of his colleagues doubted where Black would come out, his apparent dissent in *Poe* notwithstanding. He could not vote to reverse on any ground, Black said, not on a First Amendment speech basis or on any freedom of association claim. The First Amendment right of association, Black explained, "is for me the right of assembly, and the right of husband and wife to assemble in bed is a new right of assembly to me." He could not see why the statute was not within the state's power to enact, and while he was open to being shown that the law might somehow be unconstitutionally vague, he was firmly opposed to any due process balancing analysis of the case.

William O. Douglas immediately challenged Black's comments. The right of association is more than a right of assembly, Douglas explained; it is a right to join with and associate with others. A right to send a child to a nonpublic school, as in *Pierce*, was on the periphery of the First Amendment right to association, just as the Court had held that the right to travel also lay within the periphery of First Amendment protection. So too was this present right of association, for there was nothing more personal than this relationship, and even on the periphery it was within First Amendment protection.

Four years earlier Tom Clark, like Earl Warren, had joined the

Frankfurter opinion in *Poe*, but now he firmly and succinctly agreed with Douglas. Alluding to *Meyer* and to *Pierce*, he said that there was a right to marry, to maintain a home, and to have children. This indeed was an area where people have the "right to be let alone." Hugo Black interrupted him to assert that "a state can abolish marriage," but Clark let the remark pass and reiterated his position—this was an area where people have the right to be let alone, and he preferred that principle as the grounds for reversing the Connecticut convictions.

The ageing John Harlan restated his position from *Poe v. Ullman*. He would reverse on the basis of Fourteenth Amendment due process liberty, but he noted that he would feel differently if the Connecticut law were not a 'use' statute and did not apply to married couples.

Next, Bill Brennan, who had been the decisive swing vote in *Poe*, briefly said that he agreed with the Chief, Clark, and Douglas, and favored reversal because of how the statute infringed upon the realm of privacy.

But Potter Stewart, who had clearly intimated in *Poe* that he shared Bill Douglas's and John Harlan's objections to the Connecticut statute, now said that he could not find anything in the Bill of Rights that touched upon this. Nothing in Amendments One, Three, Four, Five, Nine or in any others prohibited such a statute, and hence he would have to vote to affirm. The place to get relief from the 1879 statute, Stewart said, was in the Connecticut legislature.

The eighth justice to speak was Byron R. White. Nominated to the Court in 1962 to take the seat of the retiring Charles E. Whittaker, White was best known as a former college football star from the late 1930s rather than for his role in Kennedy's presidential campaign and his one year as Deputy Attorney General. After service in World War II and graduation from Yale Law School, White had clerked for Chief Justice Fred M. Vinson and had then practiced law in Denver until being drawn into Kennedy's Justice Department. He had been on the Court for less than three years at the time *Griswold* was argued, compiling an unremarkable and sometimes unpredictable voting record. On *Griswold* he told his colleagues simply that he too would vote to reverse.

The ninth and most junior justice was Arthur J. Goldberg, Kennedy's Secretary of Labor until he was named to succeed the retiring Felix Frankfurter five months after White had replaced Whittaker. A 1929 graduate of Northwestern University Law School, Goldberg had had a highly distinguished career as a labor lawyer before taking the post in Kennedy's cabinet. While White in his two years plus had

become best known within the Court for his rough approach to basketball, Goldberg had quickly emerged as an intellectually active and
effervescent justice who had developed especially good relationships
with Brennan, Warren, and Harlan.

On *Griswold*, Goldberg said that he too favored reversal, relying on
Meyer and *Pierce*. Connecticut had no compelling interest that justified
the 1879 statute, and the law clearly infringed upon associational rights
as protected by the First Amendment. Two fairly recent cases involving
penalties imposed upon former or present Communist Party members,
Schware v. *Board of Bar Examiners* and *Aptheker* v. *Secretary of State*, had
involved parallel concerns, Goldberg said, and if one had the right to
join a political organization then one "can join his wife and live with
her as he likes."

At the end of that discussion, the tally on *Griswold* was clear and
straightforward: seven votes for reversing the convictions and two
principled votes—Black and Stewart—against any reversal. The following Monday morning Earl Warren circulated the assignment list for
new opinions, and to the dismay of at least one or two chambers,
Griswold v. *Connecticut* was assigned to William O. Douglas.[62]

The assignment to Douglas was most distressing to John Harlan.
Now largely blind, he had perhaps less of a relationship to Earl Warren
than he did with any of his other colleagues. Increasingly viewed as the
Court's most prominent conservative voice following the retirement of
Felix Frankfurter, Harlan nonetheless still felt strongly about his *Poe*
dissent and rightfully appreciated the stature the opinion had won for
itself. But from Earl Warren's vantage point, assigning *Griswold* to John
Harlan would only have created doctrinal trouble, for Harlan's
Fourteenth Amendment due process "liberty" orientation was, at least
in form if not in substance, wholly unacceptable to at least two members of the prospective seven-vote majority: Warren himself as well as
Bill Douglas. Warren knew full well that the often-cavalier Douglas
was nowhere near the careful judicial craftsman that John Harlan still
was, and Douglas's behavior as the court's quintessential loner meant
that he would make no special efforts to prepare an opinion that would
generate consensus among all seven prospective majority votes, but
Douglas's remarks at conference had been far closer to the nascent
doctrinal center of that majority than had John Harlan's.

The *Griswold* assignment opened Douglas to some risqué kidding
from one colleague who shared his taste for off-color humor, Byron
White. Appreciating that the challenge in preparing an opinion would
be to persuasively articulate how one or another accepted constitution-

al doctrine applied to the Connecticut statute, White sent Douglas a teasing note recommending four possibilities and suggesting that "any one of the following dispositions would be wholly justified." Number one, White scrawled, would be a Fourth Amendment search and seizure holding, "because the Conn[ecticut] law would authorize a search for the intra-uterine coil." Number two, there was *Escobedo* [v. *Illinois*] and the right to counsel—from a Dr." Or, thirdly, one could apply *Robinson* v. *California*, a 1962 decision which had held that someone could not be criminally punished for the status of being a drug addict, to the Connecticut situation "since there is an obvious addiction to sex involved & it is cruel & unusual punishment to deprive one of it or to permit it only at the cost of having children. A grizzly choice." Lastly, there was a possibility that Tom Clark already had jokingly suggested to Douglas, building on the landmark 1964 reapportionment case of *Reynolds* v. *Sims*, in which the Court had adopted the memorable slogan of "one man, one vote." Now it could simply be altered and expanded a bit, Clark and White said: "one man, one child." Douglas laughingly indicated that he preferred the last of the four possibilities, sending a note back to Clark that "I think your 'one man one child' formula is a flash of genius." Clark responded that it ought to be patentable pursuant to another recent decision.[63]

While the Court was snickering over *Griswold*'s implications, the parties took stock of their prospects in the wake of the difficult oral argument. Joe Clark remained less than sanguine about his chances despite having been quite pleased with the hearing, while Tom Emerson was both very hopeful and perceptively astute about the likely implications of different justices' questions. "I am fairly optimistic that the Court will go with us on the case," he wrote to one old friend the same day that the justices were holding their private conference. "Black was very strongly opposed; he just will not go for substantive due process of any kind, and he thinks that a right of privacy argument is nothing but natural law and the work of the devil. Warren also seemed a little uncertain. But I think we have the other seven with us, or at least five of them. They never let me give my argument, but kept up a running barrage of questions throughout the whole time. The result was that I felt rather frustrated, though not unhappy."

Tom took a distinctly more confident stance with his two clients. He told Lee Buxton that "I would be quite amazed if the Court went against us," and he said to Estelle that he remained "very optimistic." In fact, "I would be much surprised if we didn't win by seven to two," although he cautioned her that it was unlikely that the Court would issue a decision until mid-June.[64]

William O. Douglas, however, was a fast if not thoughtful writer, and within ten days of being assigned *Griswold* he had scrawled out the first draft of an opinion in blue ink on a yellow legal pad. Typed up double-space it came to only six pages, but this was not atypical for a Douglas opinion, for as one former Douglas clerk wrote years later, with little if any overstatement, "Many were drafted in twenty minutes. Some were written on the bench during oral argument" of other cases, since Douglas rarely asked questions. Douglas's sole clerk during the 1964–1965 year, Stanford Law School graduate James Campbell, had already learned that Douglas had no interest in having a clerk help him in any significant way with his majority opinions. While Douglas was more than happy to have a clerk prepare drafts of dissenting opinions, when it came to a case such as *Griswold*, "he wouldn't let me near this."

Douglas's initial draft in *Griswold* may have taken more than twenty minutes, but not much. After giving a brief rendition of the basic facts, he immediately disclaimed any reliance on Fourteenth Amendment due process clause liberty: "Overtones of some arguments suggest that *Lochner* . . . should be our guide. But we decline that invitation. . . . We do not sit as a super-legislature to determine the wisdom, need, and propriety of laws that touch economic problems, business affairs, or social conditions. Were this law one that dealt with the sale or market- ing of contraceptives we would think no substantial federal question would be presented by this appeal. This case, however, has no com- mercial aspect or any marketing aspect. It deals with an intimate rela- tion of husband and wife."

"The association of husband and wife is not mentioned in the Constitution nor in the Bill of Rights," Douglas acknowledged. But decisions such as *Meyer* and *Pierce* had construed the First Amendment to include certain "peripheral rights," particularly in the realm of politi- cal associations, as highlighted in several cases protecting members of the National Association for the Advancement of Colored People (NAACP) from state harassment. "Marriage does not fit precisely any of the categories of First Amendment rights. But it is a form of associa- tion as vital in the life of a man or woman as any other, and perhaps more so. We would, indeed, have difficulty protecting the intimacies of one's relations to the NAACP and not the intimacies of one's marriage relation. Marriage is the essence of one form of the expression of love, admiration, and loyalty."

Then Douglas reached for a rhetorical climax. "We deal with a right of association as old as the Bill of Rights, older than our political par- ties, older than our school system. It is a coming together for better or for worse, hopefully enduring, and intimate to the degree of being sacred. This association promotes a way of life, not causes; a harmony in living, not political faiths; a bilateral loyalty, not commercial or social projects."

Douglas concluded the little opinion by sounding a different note: "The prospects of police with warrants searching the sacred precincts of marital bedrooms for telltale signs of the use of contraceptives is repulsive to the idea of privacy and of association that make up a goodly part of the penumbra of the Constitution and Bill of Rights."[65]

Douglas's clerk Jim Campbell suggested two modest additions to the draft opinion, one concerning privacy and both drawn in part from Douglas's far lengthier dissent in *Poe*, before it went to the Court's print shop for typesetting. Once that was done, Douglas privately sent a copy of it only to Bill Brennan, and in the Brennan chambers the reaction to Douglas's handiwork was not enthusiastic. Brennan himself was beginning to believe, as he explained publicly years later, that Bill Douglas was fast losing interest in the work of the Court. Undeniably as bright or brighter than anyone else on the Court, Douglas's disinterest and carelessness stemmed not from lack of ability but from lack of commitment. Even those who saw the most of Douglas during the 1964–1965 term wondered on occasion whether he was "mentally absent," and the *Griswold* draft that Brennan and Brennan's clerk Paul Posner reviewed certainly seemed like evidence of such.

Posner, a hard-driving Harvard Law School graduate, sat down and drafted a long letter for Brennan to send Douglas suggesting extensive revisions in the initial draft. Deferential yet insistent in tone, it began by saying that "while I agree with a great deal" of Douglas's draft, "I should like to suggest a substantial change in emphasis." Douglas was "absolutely right" to reject *Lochner*-style substantive due process, and also correct in identifying the absence of any explicit protection for marriage in the Bill of Rights as "the obstacle we must hurdle." "But I hesitate," it went on,

> to bring the husband-wife relationship within the right to association we have constructed in the First Amendment context. Any language to the effect that the family unit is a sacred unit, that it is unreachable by the State . . . may come back to haunt us just as *Lochner* did. If a suitable formulation can be worked out, I would prefer a theory based on privacy, which, as you point out, is the real interest vindicated here. In the First Amendment context, in situations like *NAACP* v. *Alabama*, privacy is necessary to protect the capacity of an association for fruitful advocacy. In the present context, it seems to me that we are really interested in the privacy of married couples quite apart from any interest in advoca-

cy. . . . we have to strain hard to find a First Amendment interest in advocacy or expression in the marital relationship, where that is not really the primary interest.

Then Posner's draft of the Brennan letter to Douglas articulated the affirmative case for a different approach:

> Instead of expanding the First Amendment right of association to include marriage, why not say that what has been done for the First Amendment can also be done for some of the other fundamental guarantees of the Bill of Rights? In other words, where fundamentals are concerned, the Bill of Rights guarantees are but expressions or examples of those rights, and do not preclude applications or extensions of those rights to situations unanticipated by the Framers. Whether, in doing for other guarantees what has been done for speech and assembly in the First Amendment, we proceed by an expansive interpretation of those guarantees or by application of the Ninth Amendment admonition that the enumeration of rights is not exhaustive, the result is the same. The guarantees of the Bill of Rights do not necessarily resist expansion to fill in the edges where the same fundamental interests are at stake.

Thus the Connecticut statutes violated the right to privacy "created out of the Fourth Amendment and the Fifth, together with the Third, in much the same way as the right to association has been created out of the First. Taken together, those amendments indicate a fundamental concern with the sanctity of the home and the right of the individual to be let alone. We need not say how far it would extend, nor intimate even remotely whether it would encompass 'privacy' in the common law sense" of "invasion of privacy" as an issue in tort law. "All that is necessary for the decision of this case is the recognition that, whatever the contours of a constitutional right to privacy, it would preclude application of the statute before us to married couples. For it is plain that, in our civilization, the marital relationship above all else is endowed with privacy."

Justice Brennan reviewed Posner's draft of the letter with pencil in hand and made just a handful of modest alterations, adding a few further touches of deference and inserting a specific mention of "the self-incrimination clause of the" Fifth Amendment where Posner had referred to that amendment. He changed and expanded the concluding sentence so that it highlighted one additional advantage of his newly suggested approach: "I think there is a better chance that it will command a court." With that, a properly retyped copy of the letter was signed and sent on to Justice Douglas.[66]

Douglas took Brennan's suggestions very much to heart, and when he privately sent a significantly revised version of the draft to both Brennan and Earl Warren three days later on April 27, Brennan and Posner at least were deeply pleased at the extent to which they had helped provoke a notable improvement. "This is a signal victory," Posner wrote in a cover note to Brennan. "The approach is, I think substantially in accord with your note of April 24," particularly with regard to how a principal emphasis on privacy had replaced the previous focus on a right of association. There were additional specific suggestions that could be made, particularly with regard to seeking greater specificity in Douglas's mention of how there were "penumbras" and "emanations" in the Bill of Rights, and with "beefing up" Douglas's reference to the Ninth Amendment. "As a tactical matter, he might want to specify the Ninth Amendment as an alternative, without saying whether he specifically relies upon it." Perhaps Brennan might want to have a conversation with Douglas about these points, in the context of "getting a Court," before the draft opinion was circulated to all chambers within the next day or so, but the major battle appeared to have been won.[67]

One reader of that revised April 27 circulation who was not pleased, however, was John Hart Ely in the Chief Justice's chambers, and he immediately gave Warren a five-page cover memo advising that "I do not think you should join this opinion." Ely said that "I agree with you that the Constitution says nothing about privacy," and that nothing in the Connecticut statute intruded upon any privacy concept unless Douglas's hypothesized police searches of bedrooms did come to pass. "When one seizes upon a right which does not appear in the Constitution, that right can be given whatever shape and scope the person discussing it wishes it to have." Even more strongly than at the outset, Ely again warned that "this opinion incorporates an approach to the Constitution so dangerous that you should not join it." Either Warren could "wait and see what is written" by other justices, for "perhaps someone will circulate an opinion you can join." However, "If no acceptable concurrence appears, I do not think it would be much trouble for us to write a brief concurrence" saying that the "Connecticut law is void under *Yick Wo*" because "it is only against the clinics that the law is enforced," if Warren wanted to do so.[68]

On April 28 a largely unchanged text of the Douglas opinion was circulated for the first time to the other six chambers. Tom Clark told Douglas almost immediately that he liked it, particularly the rhetorical peroration, and later in the day sent a follow-up note: "Yes, I like all of it—it emancipates femininity and protects masculinity." The following day Arthur Goldberg sent Douglas an almost equally enthusiastic note, saying "I am very glad to join your fine opinion" and offering just two minor suggestions for improvements in wording. John Harlan also sent Douglas an acknowledgment, asking him to indicate in a separate line at the bottom of the opinion that Harlan concurred in the judgment of reversal on the grounds of his *Poe* dissent. "As I told you on the Bench, I may decide to write something in addition, but I have not yet made up my mind." Lastly, Potter Stewart sent a note to all of his colleagues saying that "In due course I expect to circulate a dissenting opinion."

Those initial responses seemed to give Douglas four votes—his own, Brennan's, Clark's, and Goldberg's—but *only* four votes, for what was supposed to be a majority opinion. Neither Warren nor White had signaled a response, and while Harlan was a fifth vote for the outcome, he had made it clear that he was not considering formally joining the Douglas opinion. Much of the justices' and clerks' attention necessarily shifted to other cases as the Court's workload built toward the final six weeks of the term, but within the world of the clerks, Douglas's Jim Campbell got more than a small amount of teasing about the revised draft that had been circulated to everyone on April 28. The *Griswold* opinion was "very badly received," Campbell recalled years later, and "attracted considerable scorn in other chambers," such as the Chief Justice's, where another of the clerks was a Campbell classmate from Stanford. "We felt bad for Jim," one clerk explained, because it was common knowledge within the Court that Douglas rarely allowed any clerk to have significant input into his principal opinions. One clerk in Goldberg's chambers had been "shocked" by what a "very weak opinion" the Douglas circulation was, and in breakfast and lunchroom chatter it was clear that many other clerks had had a similar reaction. "No one who read it liked it," Campbell remembered, and in particular Douglas's references to "emanations" and "penumbras" "attracted the giggles" of other clerks.[69]

As something of an implicit consensus emerged that the Douglas opinion "was not adequate to the task," the two focal points of attention became the Warren and Goldberg chambers. Potter Stewart, as promised, circulated in early May a draft of a small dissent reiterating his conference comments that no provision of the Constitution barred the Connecticut law, but the real question of whether there would be a fifth vote for the Douglas opinion, or any majority opinion, focused upon Earl Warren and his reluctance, with or without John Ely's urgings, to join the Douglas opinion.

At some point in very early May Warren discussed his doubts with

Arthur Goldberg, who privately had been toying with the possibility of saying something more about the Ninth Amendment angle that had been raised in Harper's jurisdictional statement, that Goldberg himself had brought up to Tom Emerson at oral argument, and that Douglas had made a passing reference to in his draft opinion. Warren's expressions of disquiet were enough, at least as Goldberg later remembered the sequence, to propel him into action, and right after that conversation Goldberg walked into the room shared by his two clerks, Stephen Breyer and Stephen Goldstein, and told them that they had a new assignment: "I have a good idea. We're going to do something on the Ninth Amendment." Breyer was designated to undertake the appropriate research and preliminary drafting, and on May 14 an initial version of a Goldberg concurrence that was twice as long as Douglas's ostensible majority opinion was circulated to all chambers. In a cover note to Douglas, Goldberg said simply that "I have added some of my views about the 9th Amendment, which, as I recall the Conference discussion, you are not free to do as reflecting the views of all in the majority."[70]

Goldberg did not view his circulation as a competing alternative to the Douglas opinion, which he already had joined, and Goldberg, who could be quite an intra-Court lobbyist when he chose to, did not actively try to recruit additional supporters for his concurrence. Three days after it was distributed, Bill Brennan formally joined it, and even the critically minded John Hart Ely told Chief Justice Warren that "I think this is a good opinion." Its articulation and advocacy of the Ninth Amendment's declaration that the enumeration of "certain rights" in the Constitution "shall not be construed to deny or disparage others retained by the people" was an especially welcome rebuttal to Stewart's contention "that the enumeration of certain rights *should* be construed to disparage others." But, Ely warned Warren, Goldberg just like Douglas "is disturbingly unclear as to the dimensions of the right which is being recognized. All we are told is that it has something to do with marital privacy." He again intimated that the Chief might want to consider a concurrence of his own, but Warren did not move either to join Goldberg or to give Ely a go-ahead of his own.

Five days after Goldberg's circulation, Byron White, the so far silent seventh member of the *Griswold* majority, distributed a six-page concurrence of his own. Jim Campbell told Justice Douglas that "I am not sure he is saying anything other than what you have said," and wondered if White might be open to joining Douglas if a modest change or two were made. John Ely, however, was quite impressed by how White, unlike either Douglas or Goldberg, avoided any express recognition of

a privacy right in nonetheless finding that the Connecticut statute violated due process, and told Earl Warren that "I think this is the best
opinion which has yet been circulated in this case." White almost certainly would be willing to add the sort of *Yick Wo* discussion and citation that Ely and Warren had both focused on, and the very next day
the Chief Justice formally joined the White concurrence.[71]

While the Supreme Court was privately wrestling with *Griswold*,
PPLC was slowly proceeding with plans to open a clinic once a decision against the 1879 statute was indeed handed down. Estelle and others hoped such an opening could take place within a week or two of
such a ruling, but the ongoing low-grade warfare between the PPLC
board and the New Haven group had slowed such preparations. In
early May the 1965 legislative repeal bill had been sent to the house
floor with a favorable committee report, and on May 18 it had been
passed by an impressive margin of 130 to 47. One last-ditch opponent
warned his colleagues that since he was one of seventeen children, "If
Connecticut had had birth control, I might not have been here," but
his admonition failed to generate any alarm. In the state senate, however, no action was taken on the measure, as legislative leaders preferred
simply to wait another three or four weeks for the Supreme Court to
end the dispute once and for all.[72]

Within the Court, the apparent muddle as to whether there would
or would not be an actual majority *opinion* to accompany the majority
vote against Griswold and Buxton's convictions and the 1879 statute
remained a subject of relatively low-key concern. On May 21 Hugo
Black circulated a relatively brief dissent that he himself had first written out in pencil a week earlier, and the next day Potter Stewart formally joined it, followed in turn by Black then formally joining Stewart's
similar, previously circulated dissent. That same week the Court handed down a decision in *Lamont* v. *Postmaster General*, a First Amendment
case that afforded constitutional protection to the right to *receive* publications, and a Brennan concurrence, joined only by Goldberg, contained one assertion quite parallel to the sort of language that they and
Douglas had been preparing for *Griswold*: "the protection of the Bill of
Rights goes beyond the specific guarantees to protect from congressional abridgment those equally fundamental personal rights necessary
to make the express guarantees fully meaningful."

By Friday, May 28, William O. Douglas had resigned himself to the
fact that his opinion in *Griswold* was unlikely to garner a majority of the
Court. The seven votes for voiding the two convictions remained firm,
but only four of those stood behind Douglas's opinion. Byron White's

concurrence had his vote plus Earl Warren's, and John Harlan's separate statement simply concurred in the judgment. Jim Campbell asked Douglas whether he wanted to strengthen his privacy language by adding a discussion of Justice Louis Brandeis's well-known articulation of the "right to be let alone" in a 1928 dissent in a wiretapping case, *Olmstead* v. *United States*, but Douglas let the suggestion pass unheeded. Campbell also recognized that there of course remained some chance that the Chief Justice would either switch from the White concurrence to Douglas's opinion, or join the latter as well, thus reelevating the Douglas statement to majority stature, but *Griswold* was only one of a good number of cases on the Court's plate as the term headed into its final two weeks.

On Wednesday, June 2, John Harlan distributed a brief page-and-a-half concurrence in place of his previous pro forma statement that he would concur in the judgment. Then, as a result of an unrecorded conference discussion or individual conversation on Friday, June 4, Earl Warren did just what Campbell had been hoping for, but in a way that Campbell's scenario had not envisioned: Warren did indeed remove his name from Byron White's separate concurrence, but rather than directly join the Douglas opinion, he instead joined Brennan and Goldberg on the latter's concurrence. Since the Goldberg opinion expressly indicated that the justices for whom it spoke also joined Douglas, Warren's action created a five-vote majority for the Douglas opinion—and the clear impression that Warren indeed supported it—without the Chief Justice having to join Douglas's handiwork directly. From the outside it was a distinction without a difference, but given how long and hard the Chief had wrestled with the constitutional implications of *Griswold* ever since John Ely's first lengthy memo on the case more than six months earlier, it was a distinction that doubtless made Earl Warren feel somewhat more comfortable about signing on to so potentially open-ended a decision. By the end of that Friday the Court's juggling of *Griswold* was complete, and final revisions of the six different opinions in the case were sent to the print shop.[73]

Monday morning, June 7, the Supreme Court publicly handed down its 7 to 2 decision reversing Estelle Griswold and Lee Buxton's convictions and holding Connecticut's 1879 anticontraception statute unconstitutional. The final version of William O. Douglas's opinion for the Court covered less than seven pages. It repeated his original language declining any invitation that *Lochner* should be the Court's guide, and denying that the Court would function as any sort of "super-legislature" determining the wisdom of legislative enactments.

It moved on to his original discussion of a right of association, relying upon *Meyer*, *Pierce*, and *NAACP* v. *Alabama*, the latter of which had expressly protected the privacy of one's political association memberships. "In other words," Douglas said, "the First Amendment has a penumbra where privacy is protected from governmental intrusion." He cited several other cases, including *Schware*, the bar admissions case that Goldberg had mentioned in the conference discussion, and then enlarged upon his First Amendment point: "The foregoing cases suggest that specific guarantees in the Bill of Rights have penumbras, formed by emanations from those guarantees that help give them life and substance," citing his own dissent in *Poe* as support. "Various guarantees create zones of privacy. The right of association contained in the penumbra of the First Amendment" was one, and the Third, Fourth, and Fifth Amendments similarly each protected another "facet" or "zone" of privacy.

Douglas then simply quoted the Ninth Amendment, without any explanatory comment, before returning to additional citations of Fourth and Fifth Amendment precedents and two law review articles. His two closing paragraphs emphasized how *Griswold* "concerns a relationship lying within the zone of privacy created by several fundamental constitutional guarantees" and involved a statute which, in its "use" provision, "seeks to achieve its goals by means having a maximum destructive impact upon that relationship." He then employed in revised form the language from his original draft rhetorically asking would not police searches of "the sacred precincts of marital bedrooms" be "repulsive to the notions of privacy surrounding the marriage relationship." Douglas's final paragraph was the paean to the importance of marriage that had appeared in his initial version, except that the original assertion that "We deal with a right of association as old as the Bill of Rights" had been revised to say that "We deal with a right of privacy older than the Bill of Rights."

The Goldberg concurrence, endorsed by both Warren and Brennan, was twice the length of the Douglas opinion. With regard to Fourteenth Amendment due process, it acknowledged that "the concept of liberty protects those personal rights that are fundamental, and is not confined to the specific terms of the Bill of Rights." The liberty concept "embraces the right of marital privacy" even though the latter was not explicitly mentioned in the Constitution, a conclusion that was supported both by judicial precedents and by the language of the Ninth Amendment. He highlighted his desire "to emphasize the relevance" of the Ninth Amendment to that holding, and stressed that "the Framers of the Constitution believed that there are additional fundamental rights, protected from governmental infringement, which exist alongside those fundamental rights specifically mentioned" in the Bill of Rights.

Goldberg then devoted several pages to surveying the comments of the Ninth Amendment's principal author, James Madison, and an authoritative nineteenth century commentator, Supreme Court Justice Joseph Story, before reiterating his basic contention, one that directly contradicted the arguments put forward by dissenting Justices Black and Stewart: "To hold that a right so basic and fundamental and so deep-rooted in our society as the right to privacy in marriage may be infringed because that right is not guaranteed in so many words by the first eight amendments to the Constitution is to ignore the Ninth Amendment and to give it no effect whatsoever."

The significance of the Ninth Amendment for constitutional interpretation, Goldberg asserted, lay in its "strong support" of the view that due process "liberty" was an inclusive and open-ended phrase. He quoted from both Douglas's and Harlan's dissents in *Poe*, and at some length from Brandeis's poetic articulation of the right to be let alone in *Olmstead*. "The entire fabric of the Constitution," Goldberg declared, demonstrated that "the rights to marital privacy and to marry and raise a family" were just as fundamental as any that were explicitly enumerated in the document. The Court's reaching this conclusion, he noted in closing, "in no way interferes with a State's proper regulation of sexual promiscuity or misconduct." He quoted Harlan's language in *Poe* disavowing any shielding of adultery or homosexuality, and concluded that "the right of privacy in the marital relation is fundamental and basic—a personal right 'retained by the people' within the meaning of the Ninth Amendment."[74]

John Harlan's three-page concurrence was a restatement of his long-held belief, articulated so powerfully and persuasively in *Poe*, that the Fourteenth Amendment's due process clause protection of "liberty" represented a substantial limitation on state action wholly independent of the specific constitutional guarantees spelled out in Amendments One through Eight. He took issue with Hugo Black's judicial literalism, and emphasized that "the teachings of history" and appreciation of "the basic values that underlie our society" were the best guides for defining and applying the Constitution's guarantee of personal liberty.

Byron White's individual concurrence also stressed the independent definition and application of Fourteenth Amendment due process clause liberty. He devoted several pages to attempting to plumb the legislative purpose underlying the Connecticut law, made the *Yick Wo* point that Ely and Warren had urged about the apparent history of enforcement only against clinics, and concluded with a discussion of how the statute's impact on married couples vastly exceeded any possible deterrent effect the law might have with regard to illicit sex.

Hugo Black's twenty-page dissent, by far the longest of the six opinions in the case, began with a forthright admission that "the law is every bit as offensive to me as it is to my Brethren of the majority." He criticized "privacy" as a "broad, abstract and ambiguous concept which can easily be shrunken in meaning" as well as expanded, and then volunteered in a memorable line that "I like my privacy as well as the next one, but I am nevertheless compelled to admit that government has a right to invade it unless prohibited by some specific constitutional provision." Whether one employed the due process liberty approach of Harlan and White, or the Ninth Amendment argument articulated in Goldberg's concurrence, "on analysis they turn out to be the same thing—merely using different words to claim for this Court and the federal judiciary power to invalidate any legislative act which the judges find irrational, unreasonable, or offensive." Such an inherently standardless approach, Black explained, offered far less dependable protection for core constitutional rights than the firm literalism that he for many years had championed.

Potter Stewart's much briefer dissent conceded that the Connecticut statute was "an uncommonly silly law." He volunteered that "I believe the use of contraceptives in the relationship of marriage should be left to personal and private choice," and that "professional counsel about methods of birth control should be available to all." But, like Black, whose dissent he joined just as Black joined his, he could find no specific constitutional guarantee which the Connecticut law infringed upon, and hence he too had no alternative but to vote to affirm.[75]

Tom Emerson and Katie Roraback had told Estelle Griswold and Lee Buxton that the Supreme Court decision was quite likely to be announced on Monday morning, June 7, and so there was little sense of surprise—at either the timing or the outcome—when the word reached New Haven shortly before noon. "We were pretty sure the ruling would be favorable," Estelle confessed to one reporter, and she directed many of her remarks toward praising Lee Buxton, who was attending a daughter's prep school graduation in Massachusetts before leaving that evening to fly to France for a professional conference in Paris. Buxton himself told journalists that "It's a great advance for married couples in our state to be able to live a normal life without breaking the law." And Estelle, privately very disappointed that PPLC's preparations were not much further along, also emphasized to the press that "As soon as we have the funds and the professional staff, we will reopen our clinic here in New Haven for married women."

The Roman Catholic hierarchy's reaction was relatively subdued. Hartford Archbishop Henry J. O'Brien told the Associated Press that "Catholics, in common with our fellow citizens, recognize this decision as a valid interpretation of constitutional law. However," he went on, "I must emphasize that this is a judicial opinion, and it in no way involves the morality of the question," for "artificial contraception remains immoral by the law of God." Father John Knott of the National Catholic Welfare Conference's Family Life Bureau noted that the Connecticut law "was a bad one because it was unenforceable," and, echoing Cardinal Cushing's statement a year earlier, added that "the church does not seek to use the power of the state to compel compliance with its moral views."[76]

Editorial reaction to the Court's decision was largely but not unanimously positive. The *New York Times*, noting how "once again ... the failure of the states to protect individual liberties has impelled the Court to move onto untrod ground," nonetheless welcomed *Griswold* as "a milestone in the judiciary's march toward enlarged guardianship of the nation's freedoms." Somewhat more enthusiastically, the *Washington Post* declared that the "protection of privacy is the central purpose of the Constitution, or at least of its Bill of Rights," and added that indeed "the idea of privacy is implicit in the idea of a government of limited powers." Black's and Stewart's dissenting rationale, the *Post* observed, "strikes us as judicial restraint carried to the point of abdication."

The conservative *Richmond Times-Dispatch* sided with Hugo Black, and the *Boston Herald* called the Douglas opinion "rather a fuzzy one." Several other Massachusetts papers each called the decision "wise," but the *Worcester Telegram* observed that the justices would not get "high marks for judicial precision" even though "by common consensus" there was of course a "zone of privacy" surrounding marriage. *Life* magazine, in a substantial piece that otherwise was more sympathetic to Black than to Douglas, nonetheless conceded that in circumstances where legislatures failed to act, "it is surely better that the Court should fill the gap than that nobody should."

Roman Catholic editorial reaction was somewhat muffled but generally positive. The Jesuit magazine *America* noted the irony of some of the justices essentially having to rely on "higher law" or "natural law" derivations in order to strike down a law that the church for so many decades had defended on quite different but similarly labeled "natural law" grounds, and the progressive journal *Commonweal* welcomed *Griswold* as "long overdue" even though legally "muddy." Both in Connecticut and Massachusetts, *Commonweal* added, the Catholic hierarchy should have dropped its opposition to legislative change long before *Griswold* or even *Poe* started on its way to the Supreme Court: "The entire round of court struggles was unnecessary, a dubious tribute to the power of a determined minority to impose their moral values on others."[77]

In the eyes of many PPLC members and veterans, the credit for *Griswold* and for winning the struggle that Kit Hepburn had first undertaken forty-two years earlier largely if not wholly went to the woman whose name had ended up on the decisive case—and who had quietly celebrated her sixty-fifth birthday on June 8, the day after the decision was announced. Mabel Robbins, hired as the league's first full-time staff member in the Hartford clinic thirty years earlier and now long-retired, wrote Estelle to say that "I felt three-fourths of the victory was due to your leadership and judgment, above everyone else." Hilda Standish, one of the other very few surviving veterans from the Hepburn era, felt likewise. Given PPLC's very limited prospects for success as of 1954, when Estelle first arrived, she had accomplished a task "that not many people could have done," Standish believed.

Years later former PPLC president Claudia McGinley would claim that "Estelle had all the ideas; we all helped implement them." Virtually all of Estelle's colleagues would use one and the same adjective as their first word or in their first phrase when asked to describe her: *dynamic*. "She was an inspiration of energy and determination and dedication to getting the job done," McGinley recalled. "She loved doing it and we loved her for doing it." Lee Buxton's then-wife Helen thought Estelle was "an incredible woman." "If it hadn't been for her energy, I sometimes wonder what might have happened." Two decades later, Lucia Parks, PPLC president from 1961 to 1964, thought she knew the answer: "Without her we might *still* have that birth control law." Estelle, she said, "carried Planned Parenthood along as no one else could have . . . I am practically able to believe that, help or no help, and given time, Estelle Griswold could have gotten the Connecticut birth control law thrown out all by herself."[78]

But Estelle herself thought they were all wrong. Years later, in the only extended interview reflecting back on the events that had propelled her name into virtually every book concerning American civil liberties and constitutional law, her attitude was much the same as it had been that Monday when the decision came down. "I have always been a little uncomfortable about the case being called *Griswold* versus *Connecticut* because actually the case in my mind should be *Buxton*." And indeed, ten years later, when an entirely different generation of PPLC members sought to bring her back to New Haven for an anniversary dinner, Estelle Griswold declined. "I would feel pretentious sitting at the head table now that Dr. Buxton and Fowler Harper are gone."[79]

Estelle's greatest regret about the victory they had won was that *Griswold*'s principal architect had not lived to see the civil liberties triumph to which he had devoted much of his final seven years of life. And to no one, not even Estelle, did *Griswold* mean more than it meant to one person whom no reporter thought to call for comment that Monday afternoon. But the very next morning Miriam Harper sat down and wrote to William O. Douglas, whom Fowler had known years earlier, to thank him for the very personal monument that the Supreme Court had constructed:

> Having lived with Fowler through almost every facet of the Birth Control case for the past many years, I cannot refrain from writing to tell you how pleased Fowler would have been with your opinion this week. It is one of the great sadnesses of life that he could not see his work come to fruition. As you know, I'm sure, Fowler's cause was always for the civil rights of people, and in this case to keep the sanctity of the home and the marital relationship. I feel the outcome of this case is a fitting memorial to Fowler and will have widespread effects.[80]

Lee Buxton flew to Paris from Boston's Logan Airport that same evening that *Griswold* was announced, but first he took the time, as Tom Emerson would recall it in later years, to call Emerson and congratulate him on the win. "In spite of the long years of effort, it really may have been worthwhile," Lee told Tom in a follow-up note. Lee like Estelle insisted that no special accolades were due him personally, and he told PPFA's Fred Jaffe that "full credit for all of this should go to the extraordinary amount of legal persistence and patience that was put in by Fowler Harper, Kate Roraback and Tom Emerson." But on the phone that afternoon, at least as Tom later remembered, Lee had more than half seriously said to him that they were not yet done, that they ought to consider tackling laws prohibiting most if not all therapeutic abortions. Tom had laughed and said something like "Well, that's going to take twenty-five years," but the very next day Helen Buxton, writing Tom a thank-you note of her own in Lee's absence, made much the same point. Picking up on a *New York Times* profile that morning that had termed Lee a "gentle crusader," Helen expressed displeasure at the paper's choice of adjectives and noted that now "maybe he will take on another cause such as the abortion laws." Years later Helen, remembering some of those 1965 comments, would reaffirm that Lee had indeed been thinking in that direction, "very much so. It was the next step. If he hadn't gotten sick, I'm sure he would have taken it on."

But Lee Buxton was sick, and it was a sickness that would preclude any second crusade with either Tom or Estelle. At times it seemed as if Estelle silently wondered whether some unspoken pressures from being involved in the case had taken a deep and debilitating toll on Lee, inflicting damage that otherwise would not have occurred, but Lee's rapid decline in the wake of the Court victory was just as painful for Estelle and others as the tragic and untimely death of Fowler Harper.

Helen Buxton always thought that the illness and decline were not a price that Lee paid for *Griswold*, but were instead the result of "a family characteristic, a physical thing that was catching up with him." One friend characterized it succinctly as "a genetic predisposition to clinical depression," and alcohol abuse coupled with the use of barbiturates played a central role as it accelerated. By late in the fall of 1965 Lee's situation had deteriorated to the point where he was forced to go on leave from Yale, and by the end of the year he had been admitted first to the psychiatric ward at Columbia-Presbyterian Hospital in New York and then to an institution in Fairfield County, Connecticut. Antidepressant drugs for a time alleviated matters somewhat, but by the fall of 1966 Lee's condition had worsened significantly and he returned to Columbia-Presbyterian. In the spring of 1967 he had improved to the point where he was able to return to Yale and to some involvement in other professional activities, but by that stage his family had broken apart. Lee married the widow of a former colleague, and took a long trip through the Far East, but within two years he was dead. One year later his eldest son, only twenty-eight years old, was dead as well. Lee had "faced his personal problems with an extraordinary amount of courage and humor," one close colleague remembered in a memorial address. "It is unfortunate that calamity should strike such a man at the peak of his success."[81]

Tom Emerson never bragged to a soul about how his prediction of a 7 to 2 Supreme Court victory had proven to be precisely correct. Just like Estelle and Lee, he too declined to take any special credit for what had been won. When Cornelia Jahncke wrote him formal thanks on behalf of PPLC, Tom replied self-effacingly that "the basic work on the case had already been done by Fowler Harper and Catherine Roraback," though "I was happy to have a hand in it at the end." Several months later, reflecting upon what PPLC and the Supreme Court had wrought, Tom observed that the new status accorded a right to privacy was "a bold innovation" on the part of the Court but also noted that the more basic doctrine of how the liberty language in "the due process clause protects certain fundamental rights not expressly mentioned in the Bill of Rights or elsewhere in the Constitution is well established" already. In the future, he said, it was quite possible that the novel usage that *Griswold* made of the Ninth Amendment "might be utilized to expand the concept of privacy, or, perhaps, to guarantee other basic rights. It would hardly be surprising, however, if this development were some decades away." Noting how all of the affirmative opinions had placed significant rhetorical emphasis upon the importance of *marital* privacy, Tom pointed out that "It is conceivable that in future cases the Court will limit the doctrine to the marriage relationship." However, he emphasized, "such an outcome seems unlikely, since constitutional doctrines have a way of expanding beyond the boundaries of the original case." "It is conceivable," he remarked, "that sometime in the future, as mores change . . . all sexual activities of two consenting adults will be brought within the right of privacy." Additionally, if *Griswold*'s privacy doctrine did develop expansively, it was also possible, Tom said, perhaps hearkening back to Lee and Helen Buxton's earlier comments, that "the way would be open for an attack upon significant aspects of the abortion laws."[82]

The constitutional right to privacy created by the Supreme Court in *Griswold*, as Tom Emerson's doctrinal comments clearly reflected, was not without suggestive precursors. Thomas Cooley's 1888 coining of the "right to be let alone" was among the best known, but even "the right to privacy" itself, although in a very different legal application than that of *Griswold*, had already been quietly present on the American legal scene for three quarters of a century. Less than two years after Cooley's treatise appeared, a well-known journalist writing in *Scribner's Magazine*, E. L. Godkin, first spoke of "the right to privacy" in the context of criticizing personally salacious and intrusive newspaper reporting. Five months later two young Boston lawyers, Samuel D. Warren and Louis D. Brandeis, used that simple phrase as the title for a *Harvard Law Review* essay that discussed how "political, social, and economic changes entail the recognition of new rights" and called for affirmation of "a general right to privacy for thoughts, emotions, and sensations." Like Godkin, it was "the unwarranted invasion of individual privacy" by the press that troubled Warren and Brandeis, and in calling for shielding of "the private life, habits, acts, and relations of an individual" they emphasized that "the general object is to protect the privacy of private life." Their advocacy of new statutory protection against the excesses of the "yellow" press drew widespread approbation, but neither popular magazines such as *The Nation* nor professional journals such as the *Northwestern Law Review* saw much chance for actual legislative action that would open the way for tort law civil damage suits against irresponsible publications.[83]

Warren and Brandeis's article generated considerable ongoing attention in legal circles, and several years later Augustus N. Hand—who in 1936 would author the landmark federal circuit court opinion in *United States* v. *One Package*—enthusiastically endorsed their argument, saying that privacy was "an extension if not a part" of what he termed "the right of personal liberty." In 1902, however, New York's top court in a 4 to 3 ruling in *Abigail Roberson* v. *Rochester Folding Box Co.* refused to apply the Warren and Brandeis concept on behalf of a young woman whose permission had not been sought or attained before her photograph was employed as an illustration in a baking products advertisement which characterized either her and/or the product as the "flour of the family." That decision met with "a storm of professional, as well as popular, disapproval," and three years later the Supreme Court of Georgia, in the first ever victory for a tort law right of privacy, ruled in favor of an Atlanta man, Paolo Pavesich, who had filed suit after a life insurance company had used his picture in an advertisement without permission. "Each person has a liberty of privacy," the Georgia court declared, "derived from natural law" and protected by the constitutional language of due process. "The right of privacy has its foundation in the instincts of nature. It is recognized intuitively, consciousness being the witness that can be called to establish its existence."[84]

Pavesich v. *New England Life Insurance Co.* was welcomed and praised throughout the legal profession, and by the time Louis D. Brandeis joined the U.S. Supreme Court in 1916 the privacy concept he had helped introduce a quarter century earlier was slowly gaining official favor. Even before his arrival the high court had given some form of passing recognition to personal privacy on at least three occasions, and even in advance of his well-known statement in the 1928 wiretapping case of *Olmstead* v. *United States*, Brandeis had occasion to speak of "the privacy and freedom of the home" in a 1920 dissent. His *Olmstead* statement was only of persuasive, not precedental value, for no other justice joined him in it, and it was made wholly within the bounds of the Fourth Amendment's prohibition against "unreasonable searches and seizures," but it nonetheless became a much-celebrated declaration of individual civil liberties. The framers of the Constitution, Brandeis said, "conferred, as against the Government, the right to be let alone— the most comprehensive of rights and the right most valued by civilized men. To protect that right, every unjustifiable intrusion by the Government upon the privacy of the individual, whatever the means employed, must be deemed a violation of the Fourth Amendment."[85]

Meyer (1923), *Pierce* (1925), and *Prince* (1944) all contained at least symbolic bows toward what Justice Rutledge in the latter of them termed "the private realm of family life which the state cannot enter," but while Brandeis's vision of a "right to privacy" continued to have a modestly accepted presence within some states' civil law of torts, the only significant Supreme Court notations of the concept between *Olmstead* and the 1961 dissents in *Poe* came from *Griswold*'s own author, William O. Douglas. In 1942, in a well-known equal protection decision voiding a state statute that allowed for punitive sterilization of some selective categories of recidivist criminals, Douglas had not mentioned privacy but had spoken of marriage and procreation as "one of the basic civil rights of man." Chief Justice Stone had concurred on due process liberty grounds, but in *Griswold* Douglas failed to cite either of those opinions. Nor did he refer to his opinion for the Court in a 1948 Fourth Amendment case, *McDonald* v. *United States*, where he spoke of "the constitutional barrier that protects the privacy of the individual" as well as the constitutionally protected "privacy of the home." Four years later, dissenting in a District of Columbia case, *Public Utilities Commission* v. *Pollak*, Douglas wrote movingly about "the constitutional right to be let alone" and declared that "Liberty in the constitutional sense must mean more than freedom from unlawful government restraint; it must include privacy as well, if it is to be a repository of freedom. The right to be let alone is indeed the beginning of all freedom." Douglas likewise made no reference to those 1952 remarks in his *Griswold* opinion, and neither did he footnote his extensive but off-the-bench comments regarding privacy in a 1958 book where he also, in the context of discussing the right to travel, spoke of it as lying "in the vague penumbra of the law." Privacy or the "right to be let alone is a guarantee that draws substance from several provisions of the Constitution, including the First, the Fourth, and the Fifth Amendments," and "the right to be let alone" was itself a "congeries" of rights that "concern the right of privacy—sometimes explicit and sometimes implicit in the Constitution. This right of privacy protects freedom of religion and freedom of conscience. It protects the privacy of the home and the dignity of the individual."[86]

Douglas's 1961 dissent in *Poe*, even more so than his 1958 remarks in the book, did a significantly better job of articulating a strong basis for constitutional protection of procreative marital privacy than did his opinion for the Court in *Griswold*, as a number of legal commentators were quick to point out. More than three dozen critiques of *Griswold* appeared within the following two years, and while a good number expressed disquiet over the "nebulous language" Douglas had employed, virtually all of them endorsed the outcome of the case, if for no other reason than that it was "probably the only reasonable one in view of the facts involved."[87] A few observers praised the decision, with one well-known professor asserting that "*Griswold* marks an important advance in the protection of individual and group liberties in this country." "It is that quality, rather than the specific holding, which gives significance to the decision," he conceded, and he went on to explain that Douglas's approach no doubt resulted from a desire to avoid both the substantive due process heritage associated with John Harlan's approach to Fourteenth Amendment liberty and the literalistic limitations championed by Hugo Black.

One perceptive commentator, Robert G. Dixon, took issue with some of the simple rhetorical labels that might be applied to *Griswold*, pointing out that "The privacy issue" is not "simply a right to be let alone; rather, it takes on an aspect of an affirmative right of access to information concerning a very private sphere of life," for "information relevant to marital privacies is what *Griswold* . . . comes down to." Dixon explained that "By invoking the married couples' fictional fear of prosecution for *use* of contraceptives to give the clinic defendants standing to defend themselves from actual prosecution for giving *advice*, the Court tied marital privacy and access to information together into a single bundle of rights." He emphasized that "unless some kind of information-access theory is recognized as implicit in *Griswold*, then it stands as a decision without a satisfying rationale."[88]

But a significant proportion of law school critics were troubled by Douglas's "curious, puzzling mixture of reasoning" and by its "ambiguous and uncertain" reach. One splenetic commentator attacked *Griswold* as "a malformation of constitutional law which thrives because of the conceptual vacuum surrounding the legal notion of privacy," but more common complaints were that the opinion was "far from satisfying," "shot through with serious weaknesses," or "rather opaque." "Only the rhapsody on marriage," one subsequent writer opined, "saves an opinion whose concepts fall suddenly in a heap."[89]

Some *Griswold* critics focused upon Douglas's and especially Arthur Goldberg's utilization of the Ninth Amendment,[90] while others drew a particular bead on Douglas's use of the term "penumbra." Originally coined by astronomer Johannes Kepler in 1604 to describe the area of partial or shaded illumination occasioned by an eclipse, many commentators found Douglas's use of the spatial metaphor "obfuscating rather than clarifying,"[91] even though—as many critics failed to realize—the term already had been employed more than twenty times in previous Supreme Court opinions. Oliver Wendell Holmes had used it in an 1873 law review article—"the penumbra between darkness and light"—then employed it three times at the turn of the century while on the Massachusetts Supreme Judicial Court, and subsequently utilized it in four Supreme Court opinions, including a dissent of his own in *Olmstead* v. *United States*, where he spoke of "the penumbra of the Fourth and Fifth Amendments." Learned Hand, Benjamin Cardozo, and Douglas himself had all employed "penumbra" on multiple earlier occasions, and even Felix Frankfurter had used it once. One of the most perceptive students of *Griswold* later noted that "Douglas could have replaced penumbra with periphery or fringe with no loss of meaning or force," but his usage of so unusual a word in such a central role in the opinion became an easy target for those whose objections to either Douglas's formulation or the decision itself were otherwise more diffuse.[92]

Within a half-dozen years of the decision, however, a one-time Yale Law School colleague of both Fowler Harper and Tom Emerson emerged as *Griswold*'s most prominent and outspoken critic. Originally Robert H. Bork had started out as a rather pronounced fan of the ruling. Writing in 1968 he had conceded that Douglas's opinion was "shallow, murky," "rhetorical" and of "poor quality," but nonetheless Douglas and the Court's basic "idea of deriving new rights from old is valid and valuable. The construction of new rights can start from existing constitutional guarantees, particularly the first eight amendments, which may properly be taken as specific examples of the general set of natural rights contemplated" by the Framers and specifically by the Ninth Amendment. Out of that base, Bork explained, "the judge can construct principles that explain existing constitutional rights and extrapolate from them to define new natural rights," just as the Court in part had done in *Griswold*.

But within three years Professor Bork's tune had changed complete-ly. Writing in a 1971 article that became famous within the legal profession long before its author became a public figure, Bork expressly retracted his 1968 remarks and now insisted that a judge "must stick close to the text and the history, and their fair implications, and not construct new rights." *Griswold*'s right to privacy, he now explained, "fails every test of neutrality. The derivation of the principle was utterly specious, and so was its definition. In fact, we are left with no idea of what the principle really forbids." That meant that *Griswold* "is an unprincipled decision, both in the way in which it derives a new constitutional right and in the way it defines that right, or rather fails to define it," since it provided "no idea of the sweep of the right of privacy and hence no notion of the cases to which it may or may not be applied in the future." *Any* application of due process liberty "is and always has been an improper doctrine," and "Courts must accept any value choice the legislature makes unless it clearly runs contrary to a choice made in the framing of the Constitution."[93]

In subsequent years Bork further intensified his attack on *Griswold*, telling one audience in 1982 that "The result in *Griswold* could not have been reached by proper interpretation of the Constitution" and a 1985 interviewer that "I don't think there is a supportable method of constitutional reasoning underlying the *Griswold* decision." Two years later Bork had occasion to expand on his feelings, explaining that *Griswold* was "not a case of Connecticut going out and doing anything" to enforce the 1879 statute, but had been cooked up by his Yale Law School colleagues "because they like this kind of litigation." "The only reason" the "utterly antique" Connecticut law had "stayed on the statute book was that it was not enforced," Bork explained. "If anybody had tried to enforce that against a married couple, he would have been out of office instantly and the law would have been repealed." However, "some professors found that law in the books and tried to frame a case to challenge it on constitutional grounds," but "they had trouble getting anybody arrested." Then, after *Poe*, they had "engaged in enormous efforts to get somebody prosecuted," and "they had a terrible time, the Yale professors did, getting these doctors arrested." The "only person who could get arrested was a doctor who advertised that he was giving birth control information," Bork went on, "and the thing was really a test case on an abstract principle." "I think both sides regarded it as an interesting test case. The whole case was practically an academic exercise."

Bork willingly conceded that "the Connecticut law was an outrage and it would have been more of an outrage if they ever enforced it against an individual." If faced with such a law as a legislator, "I would vote against that statute instantly," for with regard to *Griswold*'s result, "I agreed with it politically." Bork also concurred that "No civilized person wants to live in a society without a lot of privacy in it," and acknowledged that the framers of the Constitution "protected privacy in a variety of ways" in a number of provisions in the Bill of Rights. "There is a lot of privacy in the Constitution," and "as to the marital right of privacy, I think it is essential to a civilized society." Indeed, "I think marital privacy is a right older than the Bill of Rights."

But "the mere fact that a law is outrageous is not enough to make it unconstitutional," Bork explained. Moreover, Justice Douglas's specter of police searches of marital bedrooms in *Griswold* was "wholly bizarre and imaginary," for "privacy was not the issue in that case. It was the use of contraceptives." There was a much more basic problem with *Griswold*, however, for "the right of privacy, as defined or undefined by Justice Douglas, was a free-floating right that was not derived in a principled fashion from constitutional materials." Douglas's right to privacy "does not having any rooting in the Constitution" and instead "comes out of nowhere." Bork sought to explain that "it is not a right of privacy I am opposed to. It is a generalized, undefined right of privacy that is not drawn from any constitutional provision." "I certainly would not accept emanations and penumbras analysis, which is I think less an analysis than a metaphor," and in *Griswold* he would have joined Justices Black and Stewart in dissent.[94]

Offered an opportunity to review and reconsider his *Griswold* remarks, Bork continued to maintain that "*Griswold*, even in 1965, was for all practical purposes nothing more than a test case." He dismissed *Nelson*, noted Frankfurter's opinion in *Poe*, and, not having considered the experiences of Ruth and Bob "Oldendorf," or even of Jean and Marvin Durning, concluded that "it cannot realistically be said that failure to invalidate the Connecticut law would have had any material effect on the ability of married couples to use contraceptives in the privacy of their homes."

Two years later, and with much more time available to insure the accuracy of his comments, Bork asserted that "the spurious right of privacy that *Griswold* created" had arisen from a case involving "two doctors" where "the lawyers had a difficult time getting the state even to fine two doctors as accessories." "Anyone who reads *Griswold* can see that it was not an adjustment of an old principle to a new reality but the creation of a new principle by *tour de force* or, less politely, by sleight of hand." Contending that "the reasoning of *Griswold* was not meant to be taken seriously by judges, only by the general public," Bork also went out of his way to expressly reject John Harlan's landmark dissent in *Poe* as well as the opinions in *Griswold*: "Harlan's arguments were entirely legislative. The stark fact is that the Constitution has nothing whatever to do with issues of sexual morality," and "*Poe* v. *Ullman* led directly to the intellectual catastrophe of *Griswold*."[95]

Bork's critique of *Griswold* certainly did not prevail, but it did smooth the way for other legal commentators who similarly advocated scholarly and judicial rejection of the decision. One law journal writer, explaining that "the Court and the American polity have been ill-served by the creation of a general constitutional right of privacy," insisted that "it is time to cast *Griswold* aside" and contended that "no reason exists for not leaving the resolution of privacy-related issues to the political branches." An undistinguished but often-quoted one-time Justice Department official and op-ed contributor called *Griswold* "one of the worst decisions the court ever handed down" and later seemed to suggest that Griswold and Buxton's convictions indeed should have been affirmed rather than voided on "utterly incomprehensible" grounds. A serious legal historian, while conceding that the Connecticut statute was "utterly unreasonable," nevertheless termed *Griswold* the single "most egregious example" of excessive Warren Court activism. And the Solicitor General of the United States in the early 1980s called *Griswold* "pernicious" and explained that "the Court was basically wrong to infer a general right of privacy from shadows allegedly cast by the Bill of Rights . . . We have to accept that there's a difference between laws that embody bad policy and laws that a state legislature lacks the power to enact. A law can be bad—like the Connecticut law in *Griswold*—without being unconstitutional."[96]

But the vast majority of experts who sought to pronounce judgment upon *Griswold* not only—like Robert Bork—knew nothing of the real-life experiences of Ruth and Bob "Oldendorf" and Jean and Marvin Durning, they also had not the slightest idea who "Griswold" was. A 1970s book on the right to privacy sponsored by the American Civil Liberties Union told readers about a case that had involved "Mary Griswold" and "Dr. George Buxton,"[97] and several years later a prominent political scientist asserted that "the ACLU had been, in large part, responsible for the successful litigation of *Griswold*."[98] Another political scientist presented Estelle as the "wife of a Yale University professor"[99]—that dangerous band whom Robert Bork blamed for the case—and a Princeton thesis writer presented a much fuller biographical identification: "Mrs. Whitney Griswold, a very prim and proper elderly lady from New Haven and widow of the former president of Yale University."[100] An extremely prominent Yale Law School professor *twice* wrote about "The fact that Estelle Griswold was suing Connecticut," apparently as a plaintiff, rather than noting that she was a defendant appealing a criminal conviction.[101] Another well-known law professor highlighted his criticism of *Griswold* by stressing that "it is significant that the Connecticut legislature was on the point of repealing the statute ... when the Court obligingly preempted the question,"[102] and a curmudgeonly political scientist claimed that since one house of the Connecticut legislature had voted for repeal, "a Brandeisian court would have withheld decision for a reasonable period to give the legislature an opportunity to complete its work." Historical accuracy notwithstanding, such restraint would have ostensibly allowed the case to become moot and thus "Mr. Griswold's conviction would have died by abatement."[103]

A long list of *Griswold* commentators joined that critic in presuming that "Griswold" of course was male,[104] like themselves, and a good number of others joined Robert Bork in presuming that "Griswold," even if not expressly masculine, was certainly "Dr. Griswold."[105] One supportive but sometimes addled United States Senator took matters one creative step further, either misunderstanding the nature of the prosecution, or presuming a different sort of partnership between Estelle and Lee Buxton, when he discoursed on "the married couple in the *Griswold* case."[106]

Whether or not latter-day legal experts knew a single thing about the story that underlay PPLC's final victory after forty-two years of struggle, Estelle Griswold had two primary intentions in the weeks that immediately followed the June 7, 1965, Supreme Court decision. Her top priority was to make up for lost time and move as quickly as possible to open an initial New Haven clinic. Her second decision, one she privately had been mulling even in advance of the ruling, was to tell Cornelia Jahncke and PPLC's other officers that she would step down as executive director and go into at least partial retirement after the clinic was opened and some time before the end of 1965.

The ongoing tensions between Estelle and the New Haven women continued to hinder and distract from efforts to speed the opening of the clinic, and not until mid-August was it finally resolved that Dr. Virginia Stuermer—one of the volunteer clinic physicians from November 1961—would serve as medical director once the facility opened sometime in September. In New York at midsummer the state legislature repealed the partially nullified nineteenth-century anticontraception statute under which Margaret Sanger had been convicted almost fifty years earlier. Similarly, despite an August rebuff in one house of the Massachusetts legislature, that state too altered its long-standing Comstock law several months later, replacing its 1879 language with a provision that followed *Griswold*'s apparent lead by legalizing the provision of birth control services to married—but *only* married—individuals.[107]

On Monday evening, September 20, 1965, on the first floor of PPLC's headquarters house at 406 Orange Street in New Haven, the first session of new clinic services took place with nine patients in attendance. Almost four years had passed since the November events of 1961; twenty-five years and six months—to the very day—had passed since Sallie Pease had closed the league's clinics on March 20, 1940, in the immediate wake of *State v. Nelson*. Clinic sessions would be held three times a week; six months later a second PPLC clinic would open in Stamford, soon followed by a third in Hartford.[108]

Estelle Griswold had completed her mission. She asked that her resignation take effect as of November 1, but PPLC's internal tensions so hampered a search for a successor that she extended her tenure first to the end of November and then until the end of the year. The board presented her with a formal resolution commending her "great skill, integrity and courage," and expressing their "abiding esteem and affection." PPFA honored her and Lee Buxton with the Federation's major prize, but with Fowler gone and Lee so clearly ailing any sense of joy was more than tempered by the personal tragedies that had accompanied the legal triumph.

The legacy of Estelle Griswold, like the legacy of Kit Hepburn before her, would very much live onward. Biologically, Estelle was undeniably childless, but legally and politically *Griswold* would have many children—some of whom were already attending law school. As Estelle herself said, "I knew that there was another job to be done."[109]

CHAPTER FIVE

Lonely Voices:
Abortion Reformers
and the Origins of Change,
1933-1967

Alan F. Guttmacher was no radical, but he was as respectable a rebel as any doctor could be. The son of a rabbi, both he and an identical twin brother, Manfred, had been born in Baltimore in 1898. Alan graduated from Johns Hopkins University in 1919 and then four years later from Hopkins's Medical School. He did a three-year residency at Johns Hopkins Hospital, and in 1929 joined its staff, but in later years he would sometimes suggest that he had learned less at Hopkins than from "a decade of Monday-night beer drinking with H. L. Mencken and a small group of his intimates in the back room of a mid-town Baltimore Gasthaus."

But during his Hopkins residency Alan Guttmacher had three experiences that always stayed with him. The first was the death of a mother of four children. The second was the death of a fifteen-year-old girl, and the third was the death of a woman in middle age. All were victims of illegal abortions at the hands of untrained nonprofessionals. And soon after, when Guttmacher sought to perform an abortion for a twelve-year-old girl who had been impregnated by her father, his distinguished mentor, J. Whitridge Williams, had said no. Only if the local district attorney would provide a written letter, excepting them from any culpability under Maryland's criminal statute prohibiting all abortions except those necessary to save a woman's life, would a Hopkins doctor be allowed to proceed. Lacking such legal permission, seven months later Guttmacher delivered the twelve-year-old's baby.[1]

By the early 1940s Baltimore featured two quite competent and privately well-known doctors who performed abortions. Guttmacher knew them both, and on appropriate occasions would make referrals to the one he knew best—G. Lotrell Timanus, "Dr. Tim." In 1942 Alan Guttmacher became chief of obstetrics at Baltimore's Sinai Hospital, and that same year, speaking in New York at the annual meeting of the Birth Control (soon to be Planned Parenthood) Federation of America, he gave voice to his strong feelings and expressly called for extensive liberalization of antiabortion laws so as to allow for legal "therapeutic" abortions whenever a woman's health might be at risk. The *New York Times* thought such a declaration by a reputable, university-affiliated doctor to be newsworthy, and gave prominent attention to Guttmacher's assertion that "the patent hypocrisy and holier-than-thou attitude of the medical profession in regard to this problem is revolting."[2]

Alan Guttmacher was not the first person to call for significant liberalization of America's nineteenth-century antiabortion laws, but the number of predecessors was very modest indeed. The first such statute had been enacted in 1821 in—where else—Connecticut, and was strengthened in 1830, but even then followed the traditional seventeenth-century English standard of criminalizing abortions only if they took place after the "quickening"—or detectable movement—of the fetus. In 1828, however, New York became the first American state to follow a more recent English judicial precedent by enacting a statute that made abortion at any stage of pregnancy a felony, thereby erasing the importance otherwise assigned to "quickening." Still, enforcement of the new standard was erratic at best, and by 1850, by one expert's later estimate, "American women were aborting at least one of every five pregnancies."

But starting in the mid-1840s a new wave of pressure for tougher antiabortion statutes, and more serious enforcement efforts began to build, with medical doctors often taking the political lead. By the end of the 1850s, the physicians' antiabortion efforts were making significant headway, and in 1860 Connecticut, again leading the way, passed a comprehensive new law eliminating the quickening distinction, prohibiting any abortion-related advertising, and mandating criminal punishment for a woman who obtained an abortion as well as for whoever performed it. "This 1860 Connecticut law," a principal historical expert later explained, "set the tone for the kind of legislation enacted elsewhere in the United States during the succeeding twenty years." By the final two decades of the nineteenth century an "official consensus against abortion" had solidified in the law of each and every state of the union, with almost all of the prevailing statutes prohibiting all abortions, irrespective of the stage of pregnancy, except in cases where a woman's life was directly at risk. Those years after 1880 witnessed both a very steep decline in the number of abortions taking place across the United States and a very pronounced increase in police and court enforcement of substantial criminal penalties against those who provided abortions.[3]

By 1930, when Alan Guttmacher began to take an active interest in the problem, the best-available demographic estimates were that at least eight hundred thousand illegal abortions a year were taking place in America, at a human cost of perhaps somewhere between eight thousand and seventeen thousand women's deaths each year. The principal abortion statistics expert of that time, Frederick J. Taussig, inescapably had to work with numbers that often were little better than well-informed guesses, but most observers, both then and later, estimated that over the course of the Depression decade of the 1930s, the overall proportion and number of American pregnancies that ended in illegal abortions was increasing significantly.[4]

The apparently expanding scale of the problem generated the first smattering of calls for legal reform. The first outspoken call for change, however, came not from an American but from a highly individualistic Canadian-born female leftist in England, F. W. Stella Browne, who styled herself as a sexual radical and supported herself by working as a librarian and translator. Browne had been calling for the legalization of abortion in England since as early as 1915, but her remarks never attracted any significant attention, even in professional circles, in the United States. Browne championed *repeal* of abortion laws, not simply liberalization for some "therapeutic" reasons, and in a 1929 paper at a London Sexual Reform Congress, Browne had forthrightly advocated "absolute freedom of choice on the woman's part in the early months of pregnancy," or "up to the fourth month." Perhaps quite appropriately, given her venue, Browne's advocacy of "the full right of free motherhood" was couched less in terms of family planning than in a context of sexual freedom. It was important, she explained, for women to be able "to enjoy and benefit by normal intercourse without enforced motherhood," and it was "essential" to "separate the fulfillment of the sexual impulse from the procreation of children." "Not abortion, but forced motherhood, is the crime," she told her audience.

Six years later, in another conference paper, Browne reiterated her firm position: "The woman's right to abortion is an absolute right, as I see it, up to the viability of her child. . . . It should be available for any woman, without insolent inquisitions, nor ruinous financial charges, nor tangles of red tape. For our bodies are our own." Stella Browne, however, remained almost completely unknown in the United States, and the first American publication of any of her remarks, in a little-known educational journal, did not occur until 1952, just three years before her death.[5]

In 1933, however, two American doctors each published small books advocating legal change. William J. Robinson had been a well-known proponent of birth control, and the author of several dozen diminutive books and pamphlets concerning reproduction and sexuality, since just after the turn of the century. In *The Law Against Abortion*, issued by the Eugenics Publishing Company, Robinson spoke of "the right of the woman to her own body" and advocated an ideal goal of "the complete and total abrogation of any law against abortion." If that proved impossible, he would heartily welcome "at least a very radical modification," and since "there are cases in which the induction of an abortion is inevitable, necessary, [and] imperative, it is important that both the attitude of the public and the law be changed." Robinson willingly conceded that "Abortion is an evil, but in some cases it is so decidedly the lesser of two or three evils that there can be no question of the *proper* choice."

What Robinson actually had in mind with regard to statutory change, however, fell well short of total repeal. Instead, "a clause could be inserted permitting abortion only until the end of the third month, and only a certain number of times in the case of any given woman." He explained that "As a general rule, abortion should be permitted up to the end of the third month only. Only in exceptional cases and for valid reasons should abortion be permitted in the fourth, fifth or sixth month. Of course therapeutic abortion should be permitted in any month according to the physician's judgment."[6]

If Dr. Robinson seemed to write without fully organizing his thoughts, gynecologist Abraham J. Rongy expressly favored a statutory liberalization which would give sanction "to the performance of abortions under circumstances justified by the health of the patient, her economic condition, the danger of a social stigma, or any one of a number of valid reasons." Rongy believed that "the tide of public opinion is swelling in favor of greater freedom in the matter of childbearing," but he acknowledged that "the national timidity on the subject has proved to be an effective bar against a rational examination of what the problem is." What was first necessary, he stressed, was the attainment of "a temperate legislative attitude toward all sex problems and primarily toward birth control, and the dissemination of contraceptive information." Of that he was quite hopeful, and "When that has been fully achieved the time will be ripe for a valid code on abortion."[7]

Neither Rongy's nor Robinson's book was widely distributed, but, unlike Browne, their statements were at least cited by other writers considering the subject. One or two law journal notes included passing remarks supporting "unconditional repeal," and an occasional article in the popular press intimated clear support for legal change. With few exceptions, however, open discussion of whether abortion should to some greater degree be legalized simply did not take place. Even the American Birth Control League's *Birth Control Review* referred in passing to abortion as "the murder of the unborn child," and as late as 1939 Morris Ernst and Harriet Pilpel, also writing in the *Birth Control Review*, explicitly termed abortion "the antithesis of contraception." When a Denver doctor who was also a Colorado state Senator, George A. Glenn, wrote that same year to Margaret Sanger to inform her of his intent "to introduce a bill that would legalize the option of any woman in procuring an interruption of her pregnancy," Sanger and Birth Control Federation officials almost panicked. The Coloradan's bill referred to abortion as an "act of birth control," and the New Yorkers, fearing that such a measure would further confuse some people as to the distinction between contraception and abortion, begged him to change plans. Glenn explained how his interest had resulted from the fact that "Recently various magazine articles have expressed the desired freedom of women under man-made laws," and correctly noted that "I have never known of this type of legislation being offered before." Fortunately, at least in the judgment of Sanger and the BCFAers, Glenn's bill attracted no attention whatsoever and was not emulated elsewhere.[8]

The dangers of illegal abortion were considerable, especially for the lives and health of the women who ended up with nonprofessional practitioners rather than with doctors operating at the margin of their profession. Police enforcement of antiabortion statutes understandably tended to net the most unskilled practitioners rather than the most successful, but even the rare magazine article that hinted at "possible legislation" so that existing laws could be "adjusted" nonetheless laid more emphasis on the dangers that the procedure entailed. The National Committee on Maternal Health sponsored a 1942 conference on "The Abortion Problem," but it was only the very rare doctor who explicitly called for legal change. "The whole underground movement of abortion with its butchering quacks, midwives and incompetent doctors is the result of these statutes now in force," one dissenting physician wrote in 1942 in a southern medical journal. "There must be room for a doctor's honest discretion—flexibility is needed. Only completely legalized abortion can untangle the unhappy mess that 75 years of blind and inhuman legislation has created."[9]

As of even the early 1950s, however, the level of open discussion of the subject, even in limited-circulation professional journals, was truly minuscule.[10] In 1955 newly hired PPFA medical director Mary S. Calderone organized a conference on "Abortion in the United States," principally to highlight "the need for contraception in order to avoid the need for illegal abortion." The one scheduled legal speaker, Yale professor Fowler Harper, was at the last moment unable to attend, but other participants included Alan Guttmacher and his low-visibility, now-retired Baltimore friend, G. Lotrell Timanus. A Yale law student whom Harper sent in his stead, Edwin M. Schur, authored a contemporaneous magazine article that drew attention to what he called "abortion's skyrocketing death rate"—an annual American loss of somewhere between three thousand and eight thousand women's lives. Schur recommended that "Completely legalized abortion would probably be the best solution," but acknowledged that "the real impediment to progress is public indifference."[11]

But abortion made news only when gruesome deaths or notable criminal convictions supplied an occasion. In early 1956 *Time* magazine ran an extensive story on the four-month jail sentence meted out to a seventy-two-year-old Akron, Ohio, doctor who estimated that he had performed two to three hundred abortions every year since 1934, at a cost of two hundred dollars each. He had never experienced a fatality, and had never previously been arrested, but *Time* emphasized how his conduct had resulted in "5,500 babies deprived of life."[12]

Modest reform suggestions occasionally appeared from within the legal community. One prominent scholar, Glanville Williams, gave several 1956 lectures at Columbia University that advocated therapeutic liberalization, and the following year his remarks appeared in book form, explicitly calling for the legalization of prequickening or previability abortions in cases where a woman faced a serious health threat. A modest law review essay similarly suggested that "an exception to preserve health, whether achieved by statutory reform or judicial interpretation, is clearly desirable," but realistically concluded that "the status quo will remain undisturbed until either public opinion becomes aroused sufficiently to enforce abortion laws, or existing mores change enough to make legalized abortion a legislative feasibility."[13]

In mid-1958 Calderone's edited proceedings of the 1955 PPFA abortion conference were published, and the explicit contribution of Dr. Timanus, who surveyed his detailed and fatality-free records of the more than five thousand abortions he had performed over the years, drew news attention in *Time* magazine. *Time* stressed that the actual number of abortions in the United States was now "astronomical," but the Calderone volume itself represented no clarion call for reform. Indeed, with the exception of Alan Guttmacher, the medical contributors to the book were a seemingly timid group, and the conclusory statement signed by the conference participants represented only the most modest and limited endorsement of liberalization.[14]

Despite its own timidity, the Calderone volume nonetheless occasioned book reviews that gave voice to nascent liberalization sentiments. A prominent commentary in *Scientific American* termed existing abortion laws "fanatically narrow and backward" and observed that "a frank admission of the dimensions of the problem might force remedial action which would provoke intense religious and social opposition." Both Fowler Harper and Lee Buxton were among the volume's other reviewers, and while Buxton did indeed volunteer that "an abortion of any kind is the taking of a life," he nonetheless also offered a clear and optimistic endorsement of statutory reform: "The probability is that . . . legal modifications will occur in abortion laws throughout the country, very probably liberalizing genetic, socio-economic, and psychiatric indications, but this will never be done without the constant prodding of thoughtful and concerned individuals."[15]

Soon after the Calderone book's publication, one member of a standing committee of the American Civil Liberties Union's board of directors brought up the subject of abortion law reform for the second time in two years. In December 1956 the committee had turned aside any consideration of endorsing liberalization efforts on the grounds that since no such efforts were known to be under way, nothing needed to be said. Now, in October 1958, ACLU board member and New York lawyer Dorothy Kenyon, who almost thirty years earlier had first suggested "nullification" as the means for eliminating anticontraception laws, raised the subject again. Kenyon told her ACLU colleagues that "there was an important individual right that should be given weight. A woman should have the right to determine whether or not she should bear a child." Her fellow committee members were not persuaded, however, and with only Kenyon dissenting agreed that the issue "was not one to which the ACLU should properly devote its time."[16]

Only a few weeks after Kenyon's effort, Alan Guttmacher was back in the New York newspapers with a call for therapeutic abortion liberalization at a scholarly conference. Six years earlier Guttmacher had moved from Baltimore to become director of obstetrics and gynecology at Mount Sinai Hospital in New York, and the shift to New York had magnified his medical influence. As he had in Baltimore, he created a five-doctor committee whose unanimous approval was necessary before any therapeutic abortion could be performed there. The numbers involved were very modest—only 207 abortions took place at Mount Sinai between 1953 and 1960—but Guttmacher's reputation as a distinctive liberal nonetheless raised hackles. "Many members of the staff," a younger colleague wrote twenty years later, "felt that Dr. Guttmacher had breached normal medical-moral discipline by allowing abortions to be performed at the hospital."[17]

Early in 1959 Guttmacher's twin brother, Manfred, took him along to a meeting of the seemingly obscure but extremely influential American Law Institute (ALI), an organization of professionals from a number of fields whose major focus was the drafting and promulgation of a comprehensive set of statutes, including a Model Penal Code, for American states to consider for enactment. Guttmacher went along because that May 21 session at New York City's Harvard Club would consider Columbia Law School professor Herbert Wechsler's draft recommendation that the group endorse therapeutic abortion liberalization, so as to allow for an abortion if two doctors agreed that there was a "substantial risk that continuance of the pregnancy would gravely impair the physical or mental health of the mother," if the fetus itself had a "grave physical or mental defect," or if the pregnancy was the result of rape or incest. The proposal was approved by an "overwhelming" voice vote of the thirty or so men present, but Guttmacher was taken slightly aback when the elderly and famous federal appellate judge, Learned Hand, seated near him, muttered that the reform proposal was "a rotten law; it's too damned conservative." The *New York Times* ran an immediate news story heralding the ALI action, and in later years both Guttmacher and prominent antiabortion activists such as future federal appellate judge John T. Noonan, Jr., would agree that the ALI endorsement had been the first major stimulus toward significant liberalization.[18]

Another almost equally pivotal event that month was the seemingly unremarkable publication in the *Stanford Law Review* of a detailed survey of how more than two dozen California hospitals were actually interpreting and applying the state's antiabortion statute that authorized exceptions only if a woman's life was in danger. Perhaps unsurprisingly the two researchers found that in practice "the standards of the law are not being strictly complied with," and that while the total numbers of therapeutic abortions being performed were modest indeed, there nonetheless was "a significant disparity between what the law commands" and what doctors really were doing. This explicit finding that some practitioners and institutions were already employing ALI-like therapeutic standards in the cases of some women patients thus raised the more-than-hypothetical possibility that doctors and hospitals could well be criminally vulnerable under the California statute for following what had already become accepted medical practices. While the two authors, Herbert Packer and Ralph Gampell, observed that "the deviation from the legal norm is not unwitting," they also noted that legislatively "the means exist to take this problem entirely out of the realm of the criminal sanction and entrust its resolution to arrangements imposed by the responsible judgment of the medical profession." Their most explicit recommendation, however, was that "the law ought to be brought into greater conformity with the practices of reputable members of the medical profession." By putting at least some mainstream doctors on notice that they too, and not just dingy abortionists, could potentially be at risk under existing statutes, Packer and Gampell significantly expanded the potential universe of influential and self-interested liberalization supporters.[19]

In midsummer 1959 Alan Guttmacher published a book-length statement of his views that was excerpted in popular magazines such as *Redbook* and *Reader's Digest* and that the *New York Times* again treated as a newsworthy event. Guttmacher's *Redbook* article, which the *Times* highlighted, endorsed liberalization reforms "for general health, including the socio-economic environment, too many children," and so forth, but sought to protect his backside by fervently asserting that "Lest it appear that I am advocating unrestricted legal abortion, let me hasten to say that I would vigorously oppose any such proposal." The *Times* also picked up on Guttmacher's Packer and Gampell-like admission that more than 90 percent of the therapeutic abortions that were performed at Mount Sinai technically "were illegal," and supportively quoted San Francisco physician Dr. Glenn Craig, head of the leading professional specialty association, the American College of Obstetricians and Gynecologists (ACOG), as saying that such ALI-standard therapeutic abortions were "morally and medically correct" even though they were illegal. "It is impossible to change the law," Craig added. "It must be left up to the enforcement officers. Our responsibility is for the health and welfare of our patients."

In the book itself, titled *Babies By Choice or By Chance*, Guttmacher briefly lambasted the Connecticut anticontraception statute for making "the citizens of that state the largest mass criminal population in America" before moving on to a more extended argument in favor of abortion law reform, which he conceded "is not going to happen soon." What the United States ideally needed, Guttmacher explained, was "a uniform abortion law" covering all states. Such a law would have to be "clear-cut" and "permissive but at the same time restrictive," authorizing abortions where a pregnancy involved a "high likelihood of injury to the health of the mother," a "strong probability" of a fetal defect, a pregnancy that was the result of rape, or "feeble-mindedness" in the mother or parental unfitness due to drink or drugs. Progress toward such liberalization could be made only "through an aroused citizenry," and Guttmacher quoted a letter he previously had written to a convicted abortionist, explaining that if doctors and prosecutors actually abided by the true strictures of existing laws, legal change would come *sooner* than if therapeutic liberalization occurred privately and quietly: "the more precisely one sticks to these laws the more likely it is that the body politic will rise up against them and cause their modification." Guttmacher again stressed, however, that "I am strongly opposed to modifying the law to permit abortion on demand. There must be important medical or sociological necessity" for each abortion. But Guttmacher seemed to hint that changes reaching well beyond his own recommendations could of course be envisioned. "How long will it take the reactionary state legislatures to adopt such conservative modifications of the archaic abortion statutes? By the time they do, the proposed modifications have a fair chance of being judged archaic."[20]

Guttmacher's writings, the Packer and Gampell study, and the ALI recommendation all had effects. A young and inexperienced Maryland state legislator, Joseph D. Tydings, wrote Guttmacher to say that he had seen one of his articles and wanted to learn more about therapeutic reform. "I plan to study it very seriously with the thought of introducing legislation into the Maryland House of Delegates." Guttmacher replied that Tydings should review the Packer and Gampell article and volunteered that he would be happy to testify in favor if Tydings went ahead. "I admire your courage in attempting to modify the Abortion Law in Catholic Maryland," Guttmacher added, and Tydings indeed did not introduce any such bill.[21]

Another new, young participant in the slowly burgeoning discussion was a twenty-nine-year-old Los Angeles County assistant district attorney, Zad Leavy, who had graduated from law school only the year before. During his early months in the DA's office Leavy was assigned to handle a number of abortion prosecutions generated by a special six-member police detective squad that investigated *only* abortion cases. Leavy quickly learned "how much suffering was going on" within the world of illegal abortion and also soon realized, in dealing with uncooperative witnesses, that "women were very grateful to good abortionists." That fall Leavy authored an article in the *Los Angeles Bar Journal* calling for therapeutic liberalization and reiterating the Packer and Gampell argument that "it is common knowledge among medical men as well as legal authorities that only a small percentage of therapeutic abortions performed today are legal."

One supportive reader of Leavy's essay, Santa Monica psychiatrist Jerome Kummer, who was working on an article advising doctors that the legal risks of performing therapeutic abortions were declining rapidly, called Leavy to ask whether he would be interested in coauthoring—one doctor, one lawyer—a paper for the upcoming annual meeting of the American Medical Association. Leavy agreed, and in June 1960 Kummer's presentation of their joint work at the AMA session garnered newspaper headlines—"Law on Abortions Called Too Strict"—all across the country. Subsequently published in *California Medicine*, Kummer and Leavy's essay called for the same liberalization measures advocated by the ALI, observed that without doubt "the primary goal" of existing antiabortion laws was "to prevent death or injury to the mother," and asserted that "there is a rather direct derivation of attitudes concerning abortion from the prevailing attitudes toward sex in general." They contended that the notion that some women suffered psychologically from grief or other ill effects in the wake of therapeutic abortions was "grossly exaggerated," and estimated that "the weight of public opinion most probably favors a cautious relaxation of the present abortion laws." "If the medical profession fails to assume the leadership in this campaign," they concluded, "it will be only a matter of time before an informed citizenry will cry out and demand the necessary changes in law."[22]

PPFA medical director Mary Calderone was also gradually expressing more interest in abortion, but in a major late 1959 paper she explicitly eschewed any call for legal change or liberalization and volunteered that "abortion is the taking of a life." She also avoided any overstatement of the extent of the problem, pointing out that probably some "90 percent of all illegal abortions are presently being done by physicians" and noting that "in 1957 there were only 260 deaths in the whole country attributed to abortions of any kind." Several months later PPFA counsel Morris Ernst prodded Calderone on abortion, telling her that "I have a hunch that it is about time we a got a well-reasoned opinion on the subject from some upper court," but only at the end of 1960 did Calderone make a move, suggesting to Alan Guttmacher that they along with other prominent doctors should consider whether "the time may have come" for "the establishment of an Abortion Service." Women with therapeutically persuasive situations could have their cases reviewed and approved before the procedure was performed at a clinic that might best be located in Maryland, where the unique language of the state law allowed somewhat more room for abortions on "health" grounds than anywhere else.[23]

Nothing came of Calderone's suggestion, but liberalization exhortations continued to attract attention. A Ralph Gampell speech at a meeting of the American College of Surgeons drew widespread news coverage, and *Newsweek* magazine ran a three-page proreform story stating that the national death toll from illegal abortions was some five thousand women a year. It asserted that "most doctors strongly advocate reforms in the laws," and termed Alan Guttmacher "one of the most outspoken crusaders." *Newsweek* also noted Leavy and Kummer's involvement, and indicated that in light of Packer and Gampell's findings, "most doctors feel they should stretch the abortions laws still further."[24]

A number of law reviews also published articles endorsing the ALI therapeutic reform proposal, but the *Georgetown Law Journal* published a two-part, 220-page attack on the burgeoning liberalization drive. Author Eugene Quay, in surveying the nineteenth-century history, emphasized how "none of the modern legislation in the United States and England can be traced to any political influence of the Catholic Church," and alleged that "the present pressure is for freedom to have abortions for the convenience of the mother." Hence, Quay said, "there is obvious need for a guardian or attorney to defend the interest—the right to life—of the child." Reform proposals that would allow for abortions on the basis of a woman's health, or a pregnancy resulting from rape, were especially undesirable, Quay suggested. "A mother who would sacrifice the life of her unborn child for her own health is lacking in something." Instead, "it would . . . be in the interests of society to sacrifice such a mother rather than the child who might otherwise prove to be normal and decent and an asset." Other disposable or despicable women facing an unwanted pregnancy, Quay argued, would turn to another option, for "many an errant female if caught will call herself a rape victim," as "many false charges of rape are made." In Quay's version of reality, there was no need for a therapeutic rape provision whatsoever, for "there seems to be little likelihood of any pregnancy resulting from a rape by force or from any intercourse in which the woman's consent was *wholly* refused throughout."[25]

Nevertheless, additional voices for liberalization emerged early in 1961. *The Christian Century*, a prominent voice of liberal Protestantism, published a strongly worded editorial calling existing abortion laws "barbaric and cruel" and repeating *Newsweek*'s figure of some five thousand deaths per year. But the magazine stressed that its support was for reform, not repeal; "few doctors and few responsible people outside the medical profession would argue that all restraints should be lifted or that pregnancies should be interrupted because of some married mother's whim or some unmarried mother's shame or fear." Six weeks later the board of the National Council of Churches, in a resolution endorsing birth control, also indicated support for abortion liberalization, but in language that conveyed the real message only if a reader appreciated the significance of the word "health": "Protestant Christians are agreed in condemning abortion or any method which destroys human life except when the health or life of the mother is at stake."[26]

The following month, at the initiative of the New Hampshire Medical Society, a bill legalizing the performance of a therapeutic abortion during the first twenty weeks of pregnancy if the mother's *life* was endangered passed the New Hampshire house of representatives by a margin of 209 to 156 and then the New Hampshire state senate on a vote of 15 to 8. New Hampshire's nineteenth-century antiabortion law, perhaps as a result of a printer's error, contained no such exception, and state doctors who had encountered one particularly serious case pushed to bring the law into compliance with accepted medical practice. The Roman Catholic Bishop of Manchester had denounced the bill, but with the added support of the New Hampshire Council of Churches and the Manchester Ministerial Association, the medical society prevailed in both houses. Then, however, conservative Republican Governor Wesley Powell made good on a promise to veto the measure, and proponents' efforts to get the two-thirds support necessary to override the governor's action fell far short. This first legislative struggle over abortion anywhere in America in many years indicated apparent support for at least tepid liberalization, but the effort received almost no national news attention, although the Catholic weekly *America* did note the developments for the purpose of implicitly rebuking the New Hampshire Protestants: "If the churches do not guard morality in a democratic state, the determination of morality tends to go by default to the majority vote and the popular will"— apparently an ominous risk.[27]

On April 12, 1961, a newly elected member of the California Assembly, John T. Knox of Contra Costa County, introduced an ALI-style therapeutic reform bill in the state legislature. Knox had never forgotten a story he had seen several years earlier about a Colorado woman who had been unable to get an abortion for a pregnancy that was the result of a rape, and an attorney friend in state government who had seen the Packer and Gampell study had reinforced Knox's interest in the issue. The rape story had "made a very deep impression on me," Knox recalled twenty years later, and although no immediate action was taken on his measure, his initiative was nonetheless notable and unique.[28]

Soon after Knox's move the *Saturday Evening Post* published a major, three-part series of articles on abortion by well-known journalist John Bartlow Martin. Two of the three pieces focused upon the medical horror stories of women who suffered death or serious injury as a result of illegal abortions, and repeated the estimate of perhaps five thousand fatalities nationwide each year. The final one, noting that "present abortion laws are neither obeyed nor enforced," sounded a restrained call for reform and highlighted the involvement of Kummer, Leavy, and Guttmacher. "No one," Martin added, "has proposed to repeal the abortion laws outright, though feminist movements assert the right of a woman to decide whether to continue a pregnancy."[29]

One interested reader of Martin's series, New York state senator and Public Health Committee chairman George R. Metcalf of Auburn, noticed Alan Guttmacher's call for legal reforms and wrote Guttmacher to say that he would like to hear his specific recommendations. Guttmacher told Metcalf that the existing New York antiabortion law was "an utterly unworkable legal anachronism" and that he would be happy to meet and discuss the subject further. Eventually, Guttmacher put together a group of some nineteen interested professionals—including two or three Roman Catholic priests—who attended a working lunch with Metcalf at the New York Academy of Medicine on December 1. The proposal on the table was whether a liberalization bill that would simply add "and health" to New York's sole existing exception allowing for abortions "to preserve the life" of the mother ought to be introduced in the legislature. The monsignors, however, forcefully indicated that the Roman Catholic hierarchy would oppose any such measure with all of their energies, and Guttmacher—and Metcalf—gave up their hopes for any legislative reform drive in New York. "The only thing that could be done," Guttmacher wrote to his old friend, retired abortionist Tim Timanus, "would to be organize a society for the reform of the abortion laws," but "I think it would be awfully tough to get any meaningful group together in our own country." Abortion law change would be attained only sometime in the distant future. "It is a tough assignment and one which our children will have to fight."[30]

By coincidence, however, the same day on which Guttmacher wrote Timanus, a thirty-three-year-old California woman, Pat Maginnis, wrote to Guttmacher to tell him about her newly formed Citizens' Committee for Humane Abortion Laws. Brought up as one of seven children in a devoutly Roman Catholic and conflict-ridden family, Maginnis had had her first illegal abortion in Tijuana, Mexico, in the mid-1950s, and then had managed to abort each of two subsequent unwanted pregnancies by herself. She had read about Assemblyman Knox's bill in the local San Jose newspaper, had made a stab at circulating a petition in favor of it, and in January 1962, along with a half-dozen friends, created CCHAL. Maginnis appreciated Guttmacher's championing of reform, but clearly indicated that her hope was for repeal, not for individual therapeutic approval from some committee of doctors. She and other women, Maginnis told Guttmacher, did not like the idea of having "to appeal their case to a battery of people."[31]

Abortion continued to draw increased public attention. Two convicted physician-abortionists—one styling himself as "Dr. X"— each published inherently reformist paperback memoirs, and a CBS television series, "The Defenders," drew Roman Catholic ire by airing a segment on an abortionist entitled "The Benefactor." The *New York Times* stated that the show "amounted to an appeal for revision of the law," and reported that the network "overrode assorted objections and reservations of sponsors, affiliated stations and others" to broadcast it. A major New York City radio station soon followed with a repeated editorial announcement calling existing laws "out of date" and advocating reform, and both *Time* and *Newsweek* magazines published prominent and implicitly proreform stories. *Time* cited an increasing number of American women who were traveling to Japan for abortions to highlight what it called "a striking case of conflict between the mores of a people and their legal code." It reiterated that "nearly 5,000 women die each year" from illegal abortions, and emphasized the reform proposals that had now been formally ratified by the ALI. *Newsweek* profiled a sixty-six-year-old Oklahoma family doctor and longtime abortion provider who had pled guilty to manslaughter and received a four-year prison sentence following a 1961 procedure that resulted in a woman's death. W. J. Bryan Henrie, *Newsweek* emphasized, was a former city council member, founder of his small town's public library, and 1960 PTA Father of the Year. His neighbors held a townwide thank-you and farewell party for Henrie before he left to begin his imprisonment.[32]

Crusty old Morris Ernst, now seventy-four years old, had significant time on his hands once primary responsibility for PPFA legal work shifted to his partner Harriet Pilpel following his battle with Loraine Campbell, and Ernst increasingly turned his remaining energies toward abortion, or at least toward crotchety letters insisting that nothing was holding up extensive liberalization except medical and legal cowardice. Ernst had contributed an introduction to "Dr. X's" memoir, and in it he had insisted—just as he had previously in birth control cases—that "no statute may be constitutional if it calls for the impairment of the health of the people." Not only was it true that "abortions are necessary for the health of the women of our land," but also, Ernst insisted, "abortions are legal and we must await a tiny speck of social decency on the part of organized medicine and the legal profession" to enable everyone to appreciate it. What he really had in mind, he again told PPFA's Mary Calderone, was "a liberalization of abortion law by judicial opinions," so long as courageous doctors and lawyers were willing to undertake the necessary cases—and abortions. Ernst made the same point to Alan Guttmacher, telling him that *One Package* and other birth control precedents "will expedite the change on abortion whenever a few people feel strongly about the matter and are ready to stop Talmudic discussions."

In July 1962 Ernst published an occasionally cranky statement of his views in a moderately obscure medical magazine. He characterized long-dead Anthony Comstock as a "proven psychopath" and attacked what he called the "defeatist concept of therapeutic abortion." He reiterated his call to arms, telling physicians that "The health of our nation in this area of abortion awaits no more than some simple dignified and thoughtful leadership. Only men in the health discipline are fit to so lead our people." One friend of Alan Guttmacher's wrote him to be sure that Guttmacher, who had just retired from Mount Sinai to accept the challenge of becoming president and chief executive of PPFA, had seen the Ernst piece. On July 17 Guttmacher replied that he had, and that the issue of abortion reform "is certainly coming to a boil. I am quite certain that doctors all over the country will be made cognizant of the problem through all media in the next twelve months." But Alan Guttmacher did not know just how prescient he was, or that the time frame would be more like twelve days, rather than twelve months.[33]

Sherri Chessen Finkbine was a twenty-nine-year-old pregnant mother of four when she first read a story about the link between thalidomide and fetal defects in her local newspaper, Phoenix's *Arizona Republic*. A local television hostess on a "Romper Room" children's show, Sherri over the past few months had used a considerable number of headache tablets that her husband Bob, a high school history teacher, had happened to bring back from a trip to England the previous summer. Thalidomide had never been approved for use in America, but it had been employed in Europe, and it soon was identified as a cause of fetal defects. The newspaper story made Finkbine wonder about those English capsules she had taken, and after seeing a second piece on thalidomide, she called her doctor and asked him to check on the pills she had used, Distaval. The following day, Friday, July 20, he called her back to say that they did indeed contain thalidomide and that as a result there was a very considerable chance that her pregnancy would result in a highly deformed child. The following day, Sherri's thirtieth birthday, she and Bob visited her doctor, who strongly recommended that she undergo a therapeutic abortion. He showed the Finkbines pictures of thalidomide babies that had appeared in a recent medical journal, and for Sherri the photos removed whatever doubts she had had. The physician explained that he already had checked with the three-doctor committee at Good Samaritan Hospital, and that their approval of the procedure was assured. The Finkbines then and there wrote out a letter of request, and their physician projected that once the paperwork was complete, the procedure itself would be scheduled for Wednesday or Thursday.

On Sunday Sherri had the bright idea of calling the *Republic*'s managing editor, J. Edward Murray, a friend of the Finkbines, to thank him for how the *Republic*'s stories had alerted her and enabled the Finkbines to avert a potential personal tragedy. She reached Mrs. Murray instead, and during the conversation Sherri suggested that perhaps the *Republic* would want to do a more prominent story to alert other women who might be in her same situation. Later that same day *Republic* medical editor Julian DeVries called the Finkbines, and Monday morning the *Republic*'s front page featured a story headlined "Pill Causing Deformed Infants May Cost Woman Her Baby Here." The piece described the Finkbines' situation without identifying them, but the story drew considerable attention, and Tuesday afternoon Good Samaritan Hospital administrator Steven Morris canceled the scheduled abortion on the grounds that Maricopa County Attorney Charles N. Ronan had refused to voice his consent without approval from a court.

Late Wednesday, July 25, attorney Walter Cheifetz filed a brief declaratory judgment petition in Maricopa County Superior Court on behalf of the hospital, its administrator, and the Finkbines. The court suit, which named Arizona Attorney General Robert Pickrell and prosecutor Ronan as defendants, put the Finkbines' names into the public record, and Thursday morning stories on their predicament ran in most newspapers in America. That afternoon the Finkbines reluctantly held a press conference, and Bob Finkbine explained their rationale for seeking a legal abortion. "There is a fifty-fifty chance our baby would be a basket case if it were allowed to be born. We feel very strongly about this and believe we are doing the right thing." A clearly shaken Sherri added that "My wish is that God would step in and do this naturally. I honestly believe I would be giving birth to a living death."[34]

While the doctors, who had been intending to support the abortion on mental health grounds, checked the high-strung Sherri into Good Samaritan under an assumed name to shield her from the mushrooming news coverage, attorney Cheifetz, deputy county attorney Felix Gordon, and a representative from the attorney general's office appeared at a one-hour Friday hearing before Superior Court Judge Yale McFate. Gordon contended that the Finkbines' argument was with the hospital, not county or state authorities, and despite Cheifetz's claim to the contrary, Gordon assured McFate that Ronan's office had not threatened Good Samaritan or its doctors with criminal prosecution if they went ahead with Finkbine's scheduled procedure. McFate took the matter under advisement over the weekend, but on Monday he issued a simple four-page order dismissing the case on the grounds that the Finkbines and the hospital had failed to demonstrate any real controversy with county or state authorities.

The Finkbines, the hospital, and attorney Cheifetz briefly considered proceeding nonetheless, but the following day Bob Finkbine released a statement saying that "we have concluded to seek help in a more favorable legal climate." The statement, concurred in by the hospital, added that "There have been repeated published suggestions of prosecution" and declared that "we and our physicians do not wish to undertake a solution that might be considered outside the framework of the law." That same day the Finkbines privately applied for passports and that evening they both flew to Los Angeles, where on Wednesday Bob went to see the local Japanese consul to request visas for Japan. The consul told him that it would take from four to seven days to receive approval from Tokyo, and with Sherri desperately wanting to proceed as quickly as possible, they changed plans and booked a flight to Stockholm without having had any contact with any Swedes aside from the New York correspondent of the *Expressen* newspaper. That gentleman kindly arranged for the paper's medical editor to meet them at the Stockholm airport, and a newspaper vice president provided them lodging in his home.

American reporters energetically followed the Finkbines' travels, with stories appearing almost daily in all major U.S. newspapers. Sherri twice tried to disguise herself by donning sunglasses and a blond wig over her dark hair, and in one interview before they departed Los Angeles she told an American journalist that one of the most painful aspects of the experience was the scores of hostile letters that were already pouring in. "We don't believe in abortions, really," Sherri disclosed, "But the main thing is to do what is right for the baby." "I don't feel it morally right to bring a deformed child into the world."[35]

On August 5 the Finkbines arrived in Stockholm to the warm welcome arranged by *Expressen* and also to news of a direct personal attack on Sherri by Vatican Radio, which had declared that each and every fetus is a full human person from the moment of conception and that, with regard to each and every abortion, "Homicide is never an act of goodness." Sherri had her first appointment with a Swedish psychiatrist on August 7, and another a few days later, but since the Royal Medical Board, which had to authorize each abortion, met only once a week on Fridays, the Finkbines had to sit and wait until the board considered Sherri's case on August 17. News reports indicated that 40 percent of requests were rejected, but when that Friday finally came, the three-man committee approved Sherri and she immediately checked in to Karolinska Hospital. The next day, in her thirteenth week of pregnancy and under a general anesthesia, the abortion was finally performed, and the hospital told reporters that the fetus had indeed been highly deformed. The doctors told Sherri it was "not a baby" but an "abnormal growth," and while Sherri remained hospitalized for almost a week of recuperation, Bob told journalists that "we both feel extremely relieved." Their long and traumatic journey had cost them some four thousand dollars, Bob estimated, and as they prepared to head home, Vatican Radio again denounced them and called Sherri's decision "a crime." "Crime is the only possible definition," the Vatican pronounced, because "the victim was a human being."[36]

Sherri Finkbine's very public ordeal, and the extensive news coverage it received, altered the national consciousness concerning abortion far more profoundly than anything Alan Guttmacher or Morris Ernst could say or do. Finkbine's medically tragic case, and her heavily publicized Arizona tribulations, represented "a perfect vehicle for challenging the status quo in the most narrow (and hence most persuasive) possible way," an insightful scholar later wrote. An avowedly antichoice historian subsequently acknowledged that Finkbine was "the perfect suburban housewife and mother," and that her story marked a fundamental shift from the prior journalistic consensus that abortion was a subject that newspapers covered largely within the context of crime news and police raids against death-dealing nonprofessionals.[37]

The Finkbines' experience had effects both large and small. Karolinska Hospital in Stockholm found itself deluged for months to come with abortion requests from American women wealthy enough to envision a possible trip to Sweden, and a number of U.S. doctors queried their state medical associations to ask whether the threat of thalidomide-induced fetal defects was acceptable grounds for proceeding with an abortion under one or another state's law. Legal counsel for the Texas Medical Association reminded doctors there that "saving the life of the mother" was the only proper basis for an abortion in Texas and that the statute's "stringent and simple" command was "rigidly limited." A Dallas newspaper noted that a Veteran's Administration physician had told a laymen's group at Dallas's First Unitarian Church that the Texas law should be extensively liberalized, but some members of the Roman Catholic church's American hierarchy echoed Vatican Radio by insisting that the Finkbines had grievously erred. Father John C. Knott, director of the National Catholic Welfare Conference's Family Life Bureau, reiterated that "to deliberately abort is to deliberately kill" and minimized the danger that the Finkbines had faced by declaring that "most people you meet have some physical or psychological deformity or defect." Knott added, in an odd sort of sarcasm, that "Since it seems relatively easy to secure physicians to act as a volunteer board for the elimination of embryonic life, it should not be too hard to secure a few more doctors (and qualified laymen, of course) to act as a committee for the elimination of deformed and defective adults."[38]

In mid-September the Gallup Poll told respondents that "As you may have heard or read, an American woman recently had a legal abortion in Sweden after having taken the drug thalidomide, which has been linked to birth defects. Do you think this woman did the right thing or the wrong thing in having this abortion operation?" Fifty-two percent of all respondents answered that Finkbine had done the right thing, and 32 percent said the wrong thing. Sixteen percent had no opinion. Among Protestants the responses ran 56, 27, and 17, while among Roman Catholics the breakdown was 33, 49, and 18. Fifty-four percent of men said Finkbine had done the right thing, 30 percent the wrong thing; among women the two percentages were 50 and 33.[39]

The Dallas Unitarians were not the only small-scale evidence of the Gallup Poll's notable majority. A woman from Lynbrook, New York, wrote to Morris Ernst from "out of the blue" to say that she and her husband along with three other couples, two Jewish and one Roman Catholic, had privately begun discussing "the need for liberalization" of the New York antiabortion statute but had had no success in persuading any local doctor to join them in some public effort, even though the physicians had indicated that privately they agreed. The group's hope was "to promote new legislation," but "we are at a loss as to the next step to take," and asked for Ernst's advice. Ernst simply passed her inquiry along to a doctor friend, and seemingly did not answer at all when the woman wrote again to repeat their request. "It is our hope that all of the people who feel the way we do can join forces and get some legislation as soon as possible." Six weeks later Ernst himself gave a talk advocating abortion law nullification to a group of Westchester County doctors, but all he earned for his effort was an editorial attack in a local newspaper calling his argument "indefensible."[40]

On December 17 and 18, 1962, a California Assembly committee held hearings in San Diego on Assemblyman Knox's therapeutic reform bill. Zad Leavy, Jerry Kummer, and prominent physician Keith P. Russell were among the first day's affirmative witnesses, and all three men emphasized that the bill would simply codify existing medical practices as had been documented by the Packer and Gampell study. One witness, George McLain, the president of the National League of Senior Citizens, volunteered his belief that Knox's bill did not go far enough, and that "Regardless of the circumstances, I believe the woman should have the right to determine whether or not she wishes to be a mother." Father Timothy E. O'Brien, appearing on behalf of the California Conference of Catholic Hospitals, opposed the measure on the grounds that "the unborn child is a human being and has the basic rights attributable to any other human being," and San Jose's Pat Maginnis submitted some 350 petition signatures backing liberalization that had been gathered by her small Citizens' Committee for Humane Abortion Laws. "Women do challenge the existing law and always have," Maginnis told the committee. "Not as an organized body of people, but rather as a chaotic scattering of individuals." Maginnis later estimated that the hearing had drawn an audience of only about six people, and the sessions provided no apparent stimulus for reform proponents. Early in 1963 Maginnis's small group recruited a willing Alan Guttmacher as an endorser, and when Assemblyman Knox, troubled by friends' opposition to his measure, declined to reintroduce it in the new legislative session, the bill was put forward instead by thirty-year-old Beverly Hills freshman representative Anthony C. Beilenson.[41]

National attention continued to be drawn to abortion by a number of prominent magazine and wire service stories. Sherri Finkbine recounted her ordeal for *Redbook* and volunteered that "I hope it has advanced the day when our nation ... will take a fresh, unprejudiced look at its abortion procedures." United Press International quoted well-known anthropologist Margaret Mead as saying that abortion laws "should be changed" and indeed eliminated. "We should not prescribe the conditions under which abortion is permissible." The *Yale Daily News* endorsed liberalization in an editorial that Guttmacher praised as "courageous," and hardly a week later the *Columbia Spectator*, picking up on an article in the university alumni magazine, did the same. The magazine piece, by thirty-eight-year-old Columbia Presbyterian gynecologist Robert E. Hall, cited the Finkbine case and noted that no present U.S. statutes allowed for abortions on fetal deformity grounds. Hall observed that doctors "in general ... are a timorous group" and suggestively added that "doctors should not be asked to determine which women qualify for abortions."

Hall's modest article deeply agitated the excitable Morris Ernst, who badgered Alan Guttmacher into arranging a luncheon where Ernst could berate Hall with his hobbyhorse notion that increased courage on the part of physicians was the only thing standing in the way of widespread liberalization. Hall politely insisted that reformers needed to focus on broadening state laws, and in private Ernst was having no better success in arguing with Harriet Pilpel over what sort of advice their law firm should give PPFA with regard to its stance toward abortion. Ernst unavailingly lobbied Pilpel toward a more forceful stance, insisting that "I want to see an immediate revolution in thinking by doctors and others." Some longtime PPFAers, such as former president Loraine Campbell, worried that Alan Guttmacher already was too outspoken on the subject for the organization's own good, but Guttmacher continued to have very modest expectations of potential progress, advising one doctor who queried him on behalf of the American Humanist Association that legislative change in any state having a significant Roman Catholic population "is a virtual impossibility at least for the next several decades." Just as he had told Tim Timanus a year earlier, Guttmacher again confessed that "I am afraid the fight will have to be won by our children."[42]

In mid-May of 1963 the Unitarian Universalist Association endorsed liberalization in a resolution that at least implicitly bridged much of the distance between reform and repeal. Acceptable grounds for an abortion, the Unitarians said, included a risk of "grave impairment" to a woman's physical or mental health, a serious fetal defect, a pregnancy that had resulted from rape or incest, or "some compelling reason, physical, psychological, mental, spiritual or economic." The following week a low-visibility legislative hearing took place in Sacramento on Beilenson's ALI-style reform bill, and while previous indications had been that the committee might well be prepared to report the measure favorably, a heavy flood of Roman Catholic opposition mail significantly altered the situation. One opposition witness, former Boston College Law School dean William J. Kenealy, who fifteen years earlier in Massachusetts had denounced birth control as "intrinsically evil," emphasized his opposition to *all* abortions, even when a woman's life was at stake: "reason supplies no justification for killing the child to save its mother." One leading affirmative witness, Dr. Edmund W. "Ned" Overstreet, privately stressed to Beilenson that his modest bill "would have if anything an infinitesimal effect" on the number of illegal abortions taking place in California, but even its prospects for passage were clearly negligible. Pat Maginnis rued the low level of activity on behalf of liberalization, particularly by women, and told Morris Ernst that "the men have given us the greatest support."[43]

Alan Guttmacher continued to hope that there might be some means of action on the East Coast, and on at least two occasions in the summer and early fall of 1963 he spoke with Harriet Pilpel about an ageing doctor whom a friend of Pilpel's had recommended to her as a willing and interested abortion test case participant. Guttmacher suggested in a state medical journal essay that there was "growing sentiment" in the country for altering the "anachronistic and puritanically punitive" existing laws, and candidly asked, "Would it not be helpful if a broadly based committee were appointed to investigate the problem and to render a report which will include recommendations?" Nothing developed on either of these two fronts, and Guttmacher noted in another essay that while full repeal was a good goal, he did not now advocate it because such a position would offend too many people. "Social progress should be made by evolution, not revolution," he averred.[44]

Various law journal commentators continued to voice support for reform, and other occasional figures, such as a Unitarian minister in Seattle, Peter S. Raible, publicly indicated a preference for full repeal over ALI-style therapeutic reform. But when the California activists arranged a major roundtable discussion, longtime reformer Jerry Kummer brushed aside a suggestion that there might be a woman's right to abortion as outside their purview. Kummer willingly conceded that a reform bill such as Beilenson's would legalize only 5 percent of the existing demand for abortions, but there was clear agreement that such a measure was a necessary first step, with one lawyer cavalierly declaring "Let us worry about the 95 percent later."[45]

But a radically different analysis was being suggested by another Californian, Garrett Hardin, a forty-eight-year-old University of California at Santa Barbara biologist. Hardin had opposed abortion until he read and pondered that 1959 *Scientific American* review of the Calderone book, but by the spring of 1963 he had become convinced that complete repeal, not therapeutic reform, was the proper course. Even more importantly, he argued in an October lecture to a large audience at UCSB, reform could very well significantly *postpone*, rather than hasten, complete repeal, for "a trifling improvement of this sort might well delay for generations the much larger step." And Hardin articulated the basis for pursuing that larger step in a way that no one, even the obscure Stella Browne, had ever yet done: "any woman, at any time, should be able to procure a legal abortion for herself *without even giving a reason*. The fact that she *wants* it should be reason enough." No committee approval or institutional permission should ever be necessary. "The right to abortion should be hers, and hers alone."

Hardin's feminist declaration was, in Alan Guttmacher's typology, a call for revolution, not evolution. And Hardin had an equally succinct and prescient analysis of what the chances were that that goal would be attained: "Whether our anti-abortion laws will be repealed depends, I think, on one thing: whether women will band together to repeal them. Don't expect men to do much; men don't get pregnant.... It is women who must lead the fight. When the majority of women come out against the anti-abortion laws, the legal structure will topple like a house of cards."[46]

Hardin's speech created no news, but in its own quiet way it represented just as significant a milestone of fundamental change as had Sherri Finkbine's heavily publicized ordeal fourteen months earlier. Some weeks later Hardin sent a copy of his text to Alan Guttmacher, and Guttmacher warmly thanked him for such a "unique and fascinating" argument. "I too feel that in the ultimate the woman has the right to make the decision whether she should or should not remain pregnant," Guttmacher disclosed, but he repeated his belief that legal progress would be evolutionary, not revolutionary. "I think we can change the abortion statutes inch by inch and foot by foot, but not a mile at a time. Therefore, I believe in liberalizing the law—not amputating it." Guttmacher added that he agreed with Hardin's biological belief that "the fertilized egg is no more sacred" than an unfertilized egg, "but again I feel we would be voted down by the body politic."

Hardin answered Guttmacher's reactions by explaining that "I am of two opinions on the feasibility of a radical change in the laws." On the one hand, he realistically believed that Guttmacher's argument for gradualism would prove correct, but on the other, it nonetheless was the case that "what we say influences the truth." Specifically with regard to abortion, "a radical shift in opinion on this matter may be in the offing," and "the 100 years I believe you have spoken of, may in fact turn out to be 10." Hardin acknowledged that Guttmacher's role as president of PPFA might limit what Guttmacher could say, but Hardin had the advantage of being simply "a completely independent maverick." "I want to continue assuming an extreme position, using my words as an irritant and probe," and an abortion speech already scheduled for April in Berkeley would be his next opportunity.[47]

The early months of 1964 offered several reflections of ongoing change. Harriet Pilpel and Guttmacher joined two antiabortion speakers at a March symposium on abortion at Columbia Presbyterian Medical Center, and Pilpel's remarks reflected her increasing acceptance of Morris Ernst's perspective. "It is because the doctors have not until now taken a forthright position," Pilpel contended, "that so little progress has been made in this field. . . . As soon as you as a group are ready to say 'we believe . . . that this woman should have an abortion,'" that her well-being "'is threatened by this pregnancy,' then many of us lawyers believe you have a legal right to perform an abortion." Doctors simply had to "give the courts and the judges . . . the facts of medical life," Pilpel told the physicians. "If you do this courageously, and as a group and with determination, what you say those laws mean has got to become what they do mean." "Gentlemen, it is up to you," Pilpel concluded. "There is no one else who is competent to do that job."

Guttmacher straightforwardly told Pilpel that she—and Ernst—were wrong. "I think it is the extreme cases which are going to change the law," and "I think it will be swifter even to get the legislators to change the law than to have us doctors do it." Guttmacher subsequently expressed regret to one friend that as yet there was "no organization of any stature that seeks to soften the abortion laws," but four weeks later that too began to change in the wake of a White Plains abortion symposium sponsored by the Westchester Ethical Society at which both Pilpel and Robert E. Hall spoke. Pilpel repeated her Ernst-like position, insisting that "abortion statutes will be interpreted to mean what the doctors say they mean" and declaring that she found it "hard to believe" that any court would ever rule against a doctor who said he had done an abortion for reasons of maternal health. Bob Hall on the contrary voiced a Guttmacher-like argument for legislative liberalization by means of an ALI-style therapeutic reform bill, and several audience members, including Sylvia Bloom and her husband Daniel, a dentist, began to talk about the desirability of actually setting up an organization to advocate abortion law reform.[48]

In late April Garrett Hardin gave a revised version of his 1963 Santa Barbara lecture, now titled "Abortion and Human Dignity," to a sizable audience at the University of California in Berkeley. He reiterated that "any woman, at any time, should be able to procure a legal abortion without even giving a reason," and that such a practice—what he memorably called "a policy of abortion on demand"—was "the *only* morally defensible arrangement." The "underlying justification for all birth control practices," Hardin emphasized, was simple and undeniable: "to free women from a now needless form of slavery, to make a woman the master of her own body. The emancipation of women is not complete until women are free to avoid the pregnancies they do not want."[49]

Once again Hardin had articulated the core of the issue more powerfully than anyone before him, but also once again no outside attention immediately focused on his remarks. Alan Guttmacher, speaking in his old stomping grounds of Baltimore, Maryland, confessed to an academic audience that he recently had had to refer a pregnant rape victim to an illegal abortionist after New York's Mount Sinai Hospital had refused her and she lacked the money to fly to the Japanese doctor to whom Guttmacher referred most women who asked him for help. Guttmacher added that he had repeatedly been surprised to discover how many of his own prominent doctor friends very quietly performed abortions, but when one audience member asked if Guttmacher's remarks meant that PPFA might soon endorse abortion liberalization, Guttmacher seemed startled. He confessed with more than a little embarrassment that "I have not had the fortitude to even present this to them" and admitted that "I think I would have a tough time in getting them to take a stand." Any open support for legal change, he said, "is going to take a long time."[50]

In private Guttmacher mused to forty-five-year-old journalist Larry Lader, who a decade earlier had authored a Sanger biography and was now starting an abortion book, that the fundamental question was not whether he or any other single doctor was willing to undertake the sort of legal test that Ernst and Pilpel had in mind, but whether he or any other doctor could find a *hospital* that would allow them to carry out such an abortion using *its* facilities. A law professor friend told Ernst that he was "a complete pessimist" concerning Ernst's notion and that there appeared to be "little prospect that anything can be done," but

Lader was just as impressed when he read Garrett Hardin's argument as Guttmacher had been earlier. Seattle minister Peter Raible, who had delivered the prorepeal sermon six months earlier, told Lader that there were no reform efforts underway in Washington, and said he shared "Dr. Guttmacher's pessimistic view as to the possibility of getting new statutes" rather than simply having to hope for some liberalizing interpretations of existing laws.[51]

As Lader began to survey the small national band of liberalization advocates, he told Pilpel that he agreed with her and Ernst's view that "the whole situation needs only a few strong test cases" and some willing doctors. Pilpel herself, at a summer ACLU meeting, posed in rhetorical form a question similar to what Dorothy Kenyon had asked the civil liberties group six years earlier: "Does it not unconstitutionally deny a woman life, liberty and the pursuit of happiness, for example, if despite her wishes and the opinions of concurring doctors she is forced to bear a child she doesn't want?" That formulation fell short of what Garrett Hardin was articulating, but posing it in constitutional terms reached significantly beyond ALI-type therapeutic reform proposals. Anthony Beilenson's California reform bill, which Beilenson acknowledged would legalize only some 2 to 5 percent of illegal abortions, was debated at a mid-July legislative hearing, and at another in September, but no committee endorsement of it was forthcoming.

Connecticut's Lee Buxton told Lader that the issue "is a terribly complex subject for which I doubt if there is really any solution." Existing laws created "an incredible amount of hypocrisy," but "if there weren't any checks of abortion practices . . . it might be even worse." An extensive survey of abortion in Texas by the *Houston Chronicle* estimated a statewide total of perhaps eighteen thousand abortions a year—and at least twenty-three deaths in 1963—and found an increasing number of doctors backing liberalization. The authors of a competent and newly published study of illegal abortion repeated the annual national death figure of approximately five thousand and offered a distinctly pessimistic portrait of any prospects for change. "One could hardly imagine a New York State senator of any faith (or no faith) actually introducing a bill on the subject at the present time," they prophesied, but by mid-September the Westchester group that had invited Bob Hall and Harriet Pilpel to discuss abortion reform back in the spring were well on their way to creating an organization to encourage just that.[52]

Calling themselves the Committee for a Humane Abortion Law, Sylvia and Dan Bloom, along with their fellow Westchester Ethical

Culture friend Fred Dusenbury, believed that there was a "great" need for such an organization "and that some degree of success is possible." They asked Alan Guttmacher and other notables to serve on their advisory board, and explained that they believed "There should be no undue restriction against physicians to recommend and implement an abortion if, in their judgment, it is indicated for the health and well-being of the woman" or if there was a "serious risk" of a fetal defect. Guttmacher, Bob Hall and others responded favorably, and on October 27 the group had its first formal meeting and named Dr. Hall as its presiding officer on the grounds that "the future of the organization can best be served by a physician in the role of chairman."[53]

The new group made its public debut in late November when both Bob Hall and Harriet Pilpel testified about abortion and birth control respectively before the New York State Commission on Revision of the Penal Law. Pilpel, offering an optimistic reference to the briefs that she, Fowler Harper, and the ACLU were about to file with the Supreme Court in *Griswold*, told the group that "recognition in the law of the fundamental right of privacy is developing in the direction of acknowledgment that there is a basic constitutional right for a married couple to decide . . . how many children are appropriate." Two weeks after that hearing the Committee on Public Health of the New York Academy of Medicine revised earlier endorsements of therapeutic abortion reform and issued a resolution backing the ALI-style recommendations with regard to physical and mental maternal health and fetal defects. Both the *New York Times* and at least one national news magazine publicized the action, but none of the leading New York reformers had any expectation that legislative progress would follow. The Westchester group had resolved to change its name to the more succinct Association for Humane Abortion (AHA), and by early 1965, thanks to one moderately wealthy New York City member, Ruth Proskauer Smith, who had found a midtown office and agreed to serve as executive secretary, America's first notably active abortion reform organization was about to get officially underway.[54]

In part through his new role as president of AHA, and in part because of his own independent research work, Bob Hall increasingly began to join, and sometimes replace, the much-older PPFA president Alan Guttmacher as a primary public advocate of abortion liberalization. In late January, just as AHA prepared for its first public function, the New York papers devoted extensive attention to the results of a survey of New York state obstetricians that Hall had carried out in response to a question at the Penal Commission hearing as to what evidence was there that reform advocates had the backing of New York doctors. Hall's poll of twelve hundred obstetricians showed that some 87 percent supported ALI-style therapeutic liberalization, and Hall announced the results to reporters while at the same time stressing that "We are not trying to legalize abortion. We just want to get a change so that we can protect the health, as well as the life, of the mother and the developing fetus."[55]

Hall and AHA clearly were articulating a far more modest agenda for change than what Garrett Hardin had envisioned, but his survey announcement generated a proreform editorial in the *New York Times*, perhaps the first significant newspaper endorsement of abortion liberalization in the entire twentieth century. "The present barbarous law ought to be revised" on both health and fetal defect grounds, the *Times* said, but the editorial drew a quick rebuttal from a Fordham Law School professor, Robert M. Byrn, who asserted that the existing antiabortion law had a symbolic as well as practical importance. "The law deters more by virtue of the moral climate which it absorbs and preserves than by the punishment which it enacts and imposes." And with particular regard to deformities, "if the law were to devalue fetal life for one purpose, a significant segment of public moral opinion would devalue it for many other purposes."

AHA's official launching was marked by a public meeting that both Alan Guttmacher and Harriet Pilpel addressed, with Pilpel directly raising the possibility of a court case: "The Fourteenth Amendment . . . should be made to apply in connection with seeking an abortion . . . if test cases were brought, we would win." Journalist Lader, ethicist Joseph Fletcher, and additional high-status doctors such as Louis M. Hellman and Carl Goldmark, Jr., joined Hall, Guttmacher, and Pilpel on AHA's board, and Lader told California's Pat Maginnis that it was his hope that AHA's founding would lead to the creation of "one national group" advocating liberalization. Lader realized that Maginnis, like Garrett Hardin, envisioned change reaching well beyond therapeutic exceptions, but when even a publication like *The Nation* was featuring a prominent article calling for case-by-case *court* authorization of each and every abortion, reformers' hopes indeed remained modest. A newly elected black member of the New York State Assembly, Percy E. Sutton, along with Manhattan state senator Manfred Ohrenstein, had enlisted Alan Guttmacher's help in fashioning a liberalization bill that fell well short of even ALI standards, and the measure, with no prospects for even committee consideration, drew almost no public attention. In California Anthony Beilenson reintroduced his reform measure in the new session of the legislature, but his chief aide, Alan Charles, told Lader that the explicit opposition of the hierarchy of the Roman Catholic Church tempered any hopes for success. "We are optimistic about its eventual acceptance, but are realistic enough to know it will be a slow and tedious process of educating the public and the Legislature." Charles said that the California reformers, like Pilpel, had considered the possibility of test cases, and while the state courts seemed "sympathetic," they nonetheless did "not seem willing ... to go much beyond ad hoc reversals of convictions" of reputable M.D.s who had been arrested for performing abortions and reach the "more fundamental constitutional issues." "Unless a very positive constitutional case can be made out," Charles explained, "I doubt that test cases will ever be of any lasting good."[56]

A low-visibility statutory reform effort was also being made in New Mexico, where a retired public relations executive who believed that "every woman has the right to defend herself against abnormal mental and physical anguish" had persuaded a state representative to introduce a therapeutic liberalization bill that twice was killed in committee. Another journalistic inquiry into abortion availability in the neighboring state of Texas concluded that "It's easy to find an abortionist in Dallas" and quoted a retired practitioner as estimating there were about twelve non-M.D. abortionists in town, none of whose services she would recommend. The city had recorded only one abortion death in 1964, and the word was that several competent doctors also quietly performed a few abortions.

A much more important journalistic examination of the subject was a CBS television documentary, "Abortion and the Law," that was broadcast nationally on April 5, 1965. The show included an interview with the retired Tim Timanus and also referred to another "relatively well-known" physician-provider who was still active in Pennsylvania. A New York psychiatrist, Dr. Robert Laidlaw, voiced support for repeal rather than reform, saying that "it should be a part of the Bill of Rights that a woman can decide for herself whether she will or will not continue an existing pregnancy." Alan Guttmacher concurred to some extent, agreeing that "Ideally, a woman should choose to have a baby. If she does not want one, I think that her pregnancy should be terminated safely. This is what the ideal is, but it is not very practical for America today. We have to move forward in stages, liberalizing our laws a little each generation." Roman Catholic legal scholars Robert F. Drinan and Walter Trinkhaus spoke against abortion on behalf of fetuses, and Tony Beilenson forthrightly acknowledged that his "deliberately restrictive and conservative" reform bill would have "absolutely no effect on the great majority of abortions" now being performed illegally. The show indicated that there was "little hope" for legislative liberalization any time in the near future, but the program represented at least an implicit recommendation of reform, and two days later the *New York Times* cited the broadcast in again editorializing about how existing antiabortion statutes represented "an example of man's inhumanity to man—or, more directly, to woman." "Civilized compassion," the *Times* said, "demands a liberalization of abortion law."[57]

In late April, just as AHA was changing its name to "ASA"—the Association for the Study of Abortion—journalist Larry Lader had a prominent article on "The Scandal of Abortion Laws" in the *New York Times Magazine*. "Until a few years ago," Lader observed, "prospects for changing the abortion laws seemed hopeless," but now, he optimistically asserted, there was "a national chorus calling for reforms." Legislative change, however, "will be extremely difficult to achieve," and thus, Lader indicated, quoting Harriet Pilpel, prospects in the courts would undeniably be brighter. In private Pilpel and a junior associate had already suggested to the New York Civil Liberties Union that the existing antiabortion law "deprives women of the liberty to plan their families in violation of the Due Process clause of the Fourteenth Amendment" and that a bill that would leave the decision to a woman and her doctor up through the first twenty-six weeks of pregnancy should be considered. A lawyer friend of Lader's since college, Cyril C. Means, Jr., had also begun to take an active interest in the constitutional questions, and once Means concluded that "there is not the chance of a snowball in Hell" that any reform bill would win passage in the New York legislature, he quickly agreed with Lader that "a court test is really the only hope."[58]

By May 1965 an important new factor had begun to enter the abortion picture, a factor just as influential as Sherri Finkbine's experience three years earlier. The new element was rubella, or German measles, and while most Americans who had contracted the disease during a recent epidemic had suffered no serious ill effects, any woman who caught it during the early stages of a pregnancy ran about a 50 percent risk that she would deliver a seriously damaged fetus. In mid-May the *Los Angeles Times* had publicized the fact that several local hospitals were readily performing abortions for such women in clear violation of California law, but the district attorney's office indicated that no action would be taken. *Life* magazine devoted a very prominent story to the problem in early June, and it quickly became clear that the tragedy of rubella pregnancies was further widening the already-explicit gap between actual medical practice and literal statutory rules. Many of the rubella abortions took place under the rubric of a life-threatening "mental health" crisis brought on by a woman's great psychological fear of giving birth to a severely deformed infant, and that formulation in turn placed significant pressure on psychiatrists to certify the existence of suicidal tendencies in women whose only desire was a powerful wish to be rid of a potentially disastrous pregnancy. Two California doctors were already tracing the "marked lack of consistency and uniformity" exhibited by psychiatrists who were asked to gauge the impact of an unwanted pregnancy, with a range running "from those who essentially never recommend therapeutic abortion to those who seem always to do so." In both rubella and nonrubella cases, they concluded, "psychiatrists seem to be forced into the position of making decisions which are basically nonscientific."[59]

In the closing days of the 1965 California legislative session Anthony Beilenson had agreed to a significant watering down of his reform bill in an unsuccessful effort to bring it to a floor vote, and in the wake of that perceived setback the California reformers were forced to turn their thoughts to trying again in 1967. Pat Maginnis had been away from California for significant parts of 1963 and 1964, but upon her return she reactivated a small Society for Humane Abortion (SHA) and began distributing copies of Garrett Hardin's talks to a modest but nonetheless significant network of readers. Hardin's analysis had had a major impact upon Maginnis and her two principal collaborators, Robert N. Bick and Rowena Gurner, and Bick recounted their shift to one reporter: "We started out much less radically, looking for a change in [the] laws. . . . We say now that a woman's body is her own and she has a right to it."[60]

Widespread newspaper and news magazine coverage of the abortion choices posed by rubella resulted in a growing public awareness of the issue, and within one three-month period in the late summer and early fall of 1965, *The Atlantic*, *Time*, *Redbook*, and *Look* all published prominent stories on abortion. Fordham's Professor Byrn was only one of a number of Roman Catholic writers who responded that all pregnancies, even those involving rubella or resulting from rape, represent "innocent human life." The fundamental issue, he declared, "is to bring the public to a realization of the fact that pre-natal life is innocent human life." Robert F. Drinan agreed, and warned that since June of 1965 repeal proponents had gained a powerful new weapon: "advocates of the abolition of anti-abortion laws will no doubt urge, as one of the principal arguments, the right to marital privacy as that right is explained in the *Griswold* decision."[61]

In late 1965 New York County—Manhattan—Medical Society president Dr. Carl Goldmark, Jr., an ASA board member, drew press attention when he explicitly declared that abortion law *repeal* would be preferable to therapeutic liberalization, but he stressed that legal approval for rubella abortions was doctors' most pressing priority. New York City's Women's Medical Association quickly followed with a call for legal change, but when the American Medical Association's Committee on Human Reproduction—including Lee Buxton and Mary Calderone—recommended at a December meeting that the AMA's House of Delegates endorse ALI-style therapeutic reform, the recommendation was placed on hold rather than approved. Several leading newspapers responded editorially to the AMA action, with the *New York Times* again voicing support for ALI-like legislation and asserting that "the consensus is that nearly 10,000 women die each year." Proreform articles continued to appear in prominent medical and legal journals, and in more and more states the beginnings of proreform legislative efforts started to emerge. In Texas the president of the state Association of Obstetricians and Gynecologists, Dr. Hugh W. Savage of Fort Worth, began to lobby officers of the Texas Medical Association on behalf of a reform resolution that would highlight how the existing Texas antiabortion statute "is in conflict with present medical practice in many reputable hospitals," and one Oregon legislator started to ponder a similar move there.[62]

Public opinion polling also reflected the growing trend. The Gallup organization, in the first abortion question employed since the immediate aftermath of the Finkbine story, asked respondents in January 1966, "Do you think abortion operations should or should not be legal in the following cases?" and offered three prototypes: "where the health of the mother is in danger," 77 percent said legal and only 16 percent not legal; "where the child may be born deformed," the tally showed 54 percent legal and 32 percent not legal; and "where the family does not have enough money to support another child," only 18 percent endorsed abortion and 72 percent opposed it.

The Association for the Study of Abortion (ASA), which was struggling to raise enough money to meet basic operating expenses, nonetheless funded a study by sociologist Alice S. Rossi of results from a December 1965 National Opinion Research Center poll that included a six-item question similar to Gallup's. "Please tell me whether or not you think it should be possible for a pregnant woman to obtain a legal abortion if," respondents were asked, (1) "the woman's own health is seriously endangered by the pregnancy"—71 percent yes, 26 percent no—(2) "she became pregnant as a result of rape"—56 percent yes, 38 percent no—(3) "there is a strong chance of serious defect in the baby"—55 percent yes, 41 percent no.

For those three grounds, clear majorities of the American people supported therapeutic reform. But for the three other reasons that the NORC question presented, the results were, as with Gallup's question about financial stringency, dramatically different: if "the family has a very low income and cannot afford any more children," only 21 percent yes and 77 percent no; if "she is not married and does not want to marry the man," 18 percent yes and 80 percent no; if "she is married and does not want any more children," only 15 percent yes and 83 percent no.

To reporters, Rossi and ASA emphasized the 71 percent health figure as showing what a heavy majority backed legal reform. Even 64 percent of Roman Catholic men and 58 percent of Roman Catholic women, they added, supported the availability of legal abortion when a woman's health was in danger. But the wide gap between those numbers and the ones responding to the latter items powerfully highlighted how greatly different were the political prospects for ALI-type reform as opposed to more far-reaching repeal. The Catholic weekly *America*, in an unhappy editorial entitled "Growing Consensus on Abortion," ruefully observed that "if three-quarters of the American people seriously want broader grounds for abortion written into the law, their wishes will eventually prevail."[63]

Increasing concern within the national Roman Catholic hierarchy over the spread of proreform sentiments led the National Catholic Welfare Conference to issue a well-written sixty-page pamphlet critiquing the idea of liberalization and arguing that even existing statutes allowing for abortions in life-threatening cases represented "substantial concessions and compromises" that should not be expanded. Conservative columnist William F. Buckley, Jr., warned readers of his *National Review* that "there is great pressure to ease the abortion laws," and a worried Catholic lawyer in Los Angeles warned that "almost overnight abortion has become the subject of national interest and concern." But press attention that was at least implicitly supportive of liberalization continued to grow, with both the *Wall Street Journal* and the *Atlanta Constitution* devoting front-page stories to the rubella issue and the solidly Republican *Chicago Tribune* reporting that "the number of fatalities is increasing" and "the national debate over abortion laws is getting louder."

Pat Maginnis's SHA held a day-long public conference on abortion laws in San Francisco early in 1966, and one of Maginnis's principal colleagues, Lana Clarke Phelan, termed existing statutes "sexual discrimination laws" that impose "slavery in its cruelest sense" upon women. She termed modest reform measures like Beilenson's "a lie and a cruel farce" and with implicit reference to *Griswold* decried the "political interference in the realm of marital privacy and denial of constitutional rights" that any restrictive statute represented. Another conference participant, however, Northern California Civil Liberties Union attorney Marshall Krause, firmly told Phelan that she and those who agreed with her were looking in the wrong direction. "Those people who attempt to say that there is a constitutional right to have an abortion are stretching the Constitution beyond bounds which it has ever gone and ever will go for a long time." *Griswold*'s voiding of the Connecticut anticontraception statute, he contended, would not extend to abortion because "you have a greater legislative interest in protecting whatever it is that is protected by anti-abortion statutes . . . You would have a difficult time saying that a court should come in and protect this as a right of privacy. So, as far as a prediction, and I would hope to be wrong, I don't think that the problem of harsh abortion laws is going to be solved by the United States Supreme Court's ruling them unconstitutional. This is an area which the courts will leave to the legislatures, so the primary pressure and effort should be on legislative changes."

Maginnis quickly emphasized that she disagreed with Krause on "the possibility of creating a constitutional case," but Krause insisted that "the energy, the devotion of people interested in this cause must be toward education of the public." SHA's ensuing newsletter nonetheless asserted that *Griswold* "has done much to stimulate questions about abortion as a human and civil liberty" and reiterated what it termed "each woman's right to govern her own body in matters of reproduction." It added that "the Society is seeking lawyers willing to donate time to examine the constitutionality of the California Penal Code statutes on abortion, and, possibly, prepare a test case and carry it through, if necessary, to the highest court."[64]

Most public activism on abortion, however, remained firmly within a legislative context and reflected largely a reform orientation. In early March 1966 the New York State Assembly Public Health Committee held its first hearing on the ALI-style bill that Percy Sutton had introduced a year earlier, but several of the ostensibly supportive witnesses, particularly Harriet Pilpel, devoted their testimony to detailing why reform measures were an inadequate and undesirable response to the abortion issue. Speaking on behalf of the New York Civil Liberties Union, Pilpel led off the hearing by saying that the CLU did not believe the bill "will accomplish the result intended" and that if enacted it instead "would further aggravate an already intolerable situation." Ideally it should be left to a physician "to decide what the health of his patient requires" and if "in this field any additional protection is necessary, surely a corroborative opinion from one or two other physicians would suffice." Under questioning Pilpel forthrightly volunteered that "I believe it is a right of a woman to decide whether she should have children," and a Unitarian minister from Albany and a representative of New York's Liberal Party also voiced personal preferences for repeal. Journalist Larry Lader tactfully asked that "the broadest possible reform bill be passed," but Dr. Hall and Assemblyman Sutton recommended ALI-style liberalization. The *New York Times* coverage of the hearing stressed that Sutton's bill had "little chance of enactment," but editorially the *Times* once again commended the measure as a "compassionate" replacement for the "cruel and unrealistic" existing statute.[65]

ASA remained a relatively unfocused and low-visibility enterprise, though it did sponsor a mail opinion survey of American psychiatrists that showed more than 90 percent favoring statutory reform but less than 25 percent backing repeal. In private, Alan Guttmacher continued to insist that "the task of this generation is to broaden our laws significantly, but not repeal them." "I do not advocate abortion on demand," he told one woman, "because (1) I think America isn't ready for it and (2) It makes people disregard the use of effective contraception and (3) It develops in both the medical profession and the laity a lack of reverence for life." A South Dakota representative introduced a liberal reform bill in that state's legislature, and in Texas Dr. Hugh Savage's effort to get that state's doctors on record as backing reform began to bear fruit as the Texas Medical Association appointed a six-doctor study committee to draft a recommendation to the state legislature endorsing therapeutic liberalization. "All we're asking," TMA president Dr. James D. Murphy told reporters, "would be to give legal status to procedures now being done."[66]

But the most significant political developments of early 1966 regarding abortion took place in California, where wealthy St. Louis contraceptive foam manufacturer—and one-time PPLC contributor—Joseph Sunnen had decided to finance a new proreform organization, the California Committee for Therapeutic Abortion (CCTA). The new organization would have two principal aims: first to generate widespread support for an ALI-style Beilenson bill in advance of the 1967 session of the state legislature, and second, and far more importantly, to pave the way toward full repeal by either legislative or judicial action. In late March Sunnen and his top deputy, Al Severson, approached two suitable Californians, UCLA public health professor Ruth Roemer and Episcopal clergyman Lester Kinsolving, who had written about abortion in Protestant periodicals and was a top protégé of California Bishop James A. Pike, with their proposal. Kinsolving quickly assured Sunnen that the Episcopal Diocese would he happy to receive and pass on his contributions to CCTA, and Severson immediately sent Kinsolving a check for twenty-five thousand dollars, saying that "The money is to support the pioneer work in California to bring light and hope to the thousands of people who suffer . . . the miseries and heartbreak of back-street abortions." Roemer, assigned to find an appropriately high-status chairman for CCTA, first approached University of Southern California Medical School dean Roger O. Egeberg, who declined but strongly recommended his friend and colleague, prominent obstetrician Keith P. Russell. Before the end of March Russell had accepted the chairmanship and a paid executive director, Dorothy Stolz, was formally on staff.

Sunnen's creation of CCTA represented more money than had ever before been invested toward abortion law change anywhere in America, and he explicitly envisioned making a total investment of somewhere between two hundred and five hundred thousand dollars to achieve abortion law repeal in California. Sunnen and Severson explained to Kinsolving and Roemer that one top priority ought to be a possible test case, perhaps using a very young and respectable woman who would seek court approval to abort a pregnancy that had resulted from rape. Kinsolving noted that such a case could rely in part upon *Griswold*, and in search of other test case possibilities he also surveyed the records of all twenty-two people presently incarcerated in California for abortion offenses. He was very disappointed to find that only one of the twenty-two was an M.D., and that his record also featured six narcotics and two murder convictions—not a plausible test case plaintiff.[67]

In March 1966 the California Medical Association formally endorsed therapeutic reform, and a close attorney friend of Roemer's, Norma Goldstein Zarky, encouraged a UCLA law student to explicate some of the test case thoughts that were being bandied about. Some eight weeks later, however, a potential test case was handed to the CCTA leadership when the state Board of Medical Examiners, at the behest of one outspoken member, Roman Catholic Los Angeles obstetrician James V. McNulty, brought unprofessional conduct charges—as distinct from criminal complaints—against two San Francisco M.D.s, J. Paul Shively and Seymour P. Smith, with regard to some ten rubella and fetal defect abortions that they had performed in licensed hospitals with colleagues' approval. One CCTA board member and physician, Edmund "Ned" Overstreet, pressed for creation of a CCTA-backed defense fund for Smith, Shively, and another half-dozen San Francisco doctors whom the Medical Examiners Board soon added to its target list on similar grounds, but at an early June meeting of CCTA's board Joseph Sunnen himself downplayed the significance of the Shively case on the grounds that no matter how it developed it was unlikely to pose a direct, frontal challenge to the constitutionality of California's existing antiabortion law. The doctors moved to challenge the Medical Examiners' charges in state court, and Ned Overstreet hoped that Sunnen would shoulder their legal fees in addition to a constitutionally oriented amicus brief that CCTA would sponsor on behalf of other doctors and that Zad Leavy would prepare.

Pat Maginnis's SHA contributed to the increasing California activity by doing some well-publicized leafletting in downtown San Francisco with pamphlets featuring first the names and addresses of dependable Mexican abortionists and then directions for how to perform self-administered abortions. In late July Maginnis was arrested but the charge was soon dismissed, and despite police monitoring of at least one "do-it-yourself" instruction session taught by Maginnis, no further controversy ensued. A statewide Field Poll in July showed that 65 percent of Californians backed therapeutic liberalization, but the hopes of the professionals in CCTA turned increasingly toward the courts. They realized far better than casual observers how very modest an achievement the Beilenson bill would be even if passed into law, and while they applauded the September endorsement of it by the California State Bar Association, they welcomed the judicial prospects of the Shively challenge even more enthusiastically. Zad Leavy told one legal colleague that Griswold "gave us the beginning of an answer if the legislature cannot find it," and in late September the Southern California ACLU announced its conclusion that a woman's decision regarding abortion represented a "fundamental right" and not a legislative policy choice. "Under the right of privacy guarantees of the First, Third, Fourth, Fifth, Ninth, and Fourteenth Amendments to the U.S. Constitution, it is for each individual to determine when and whether to produce offspring," the ACLU branch said, "without interference by the state." "The present laws prohibiting abortion in California infringe upon this fundamental right."[68]

The increasing sense of change was not simply a professional phe-

nomenon, however. CCTA executive director Dorothy Stolz, informing the board in midfall about ongoing public education efforts, indicated that "Our speakers are reporting a change in response of
audiences. Women's groups in particular seem to accept the [ALI]
Model Penal Code indications for abortion without question and are
interested in considering social and economic indications." New locally based reform groups were being created in Minnesota, Wisconsin,
Ohio, and Illinois, and in Texas Dr. Hugh Savage's efforts to move the
Texas Medical Association toward backing a reform bill in the 1967 legislature were proceeding apace. The New York activists, with author
Larry Lader in the lead, similarly resolved to make a new legislative
push in 1967, and by late October Lader and Bob Hall had recruited
Assembly Public Health Committee chairman Albert H. Blumenthal
as principal legislative sponsor for a bill that Lader hoped would reach
well beyond ALI-style reform. Lader was also discussing a possible
abortion test case with a longtime doctor friend, William B. Ober, who
was on the staff of Manhattan's Knickerbocker Hospital and who had
just authored a highly visible article in the *Saturday Evening Post* entitled
"We Should Legalize Abortion." Ober's sentiments were little different
from those that Garrett Hardin and Dorothy Kenyon had articulated
previously, but Ober's received a circulation that was many thousand
times greater. "Every woman should be able to have an unwanted pregnancy aborted at her own request, subject only to the consent of her
husband and the advice of her physician," Ober declared. "To me, it is
unthinkable that a civilized society should require a woman to carry in
her womb something she does not want, whatever the reasons."[69]

Ober's essay was noted in other periodicals, and *Newsweek* magazine, picking up on a talk by Bob Hall, ran a one-page article entitled
"The Abortion Epidemic." Other coverage noted the endorsement of
at least therapeutic reforms by groups including the American
Lutheran Church. The *New York Times* published a story on Pat
Maginnis's California self-instruction efforts, the first national attention Maginnis or SHA had ever received, but the piece managed to call
the thirty-eight-year-old Maginnis both "a zealot" *and* "a spinster." The
New York-based ASA was momentarily preoccupied with the contentious firing of executive director Ruth Smith and the hiring of her
replacement, Jimmye Kimmey, a young female academic. In Illinois,
however, several energetic Chicagoans who five years earlier had established a pro-birth control group now announced formation of what
would be America's first organization that explicitly backed repeal
rather than reform, the somewhat ungainly and misleadingly titled
Illinois Citizens for the Medical Control of Abortion (ICMCA).[70]

ICMCA's guiding spirit was a forty-four-year-old female anesthesiologist and mother of five, Caroline Rulon "Lonny" Myers, a Hartford native and Vassar graduate who in late 1961 had taken the lead in founding Citizens for the Extension of Birth Control Services to advocate the availability of birth control advice to public aid recipients at Chicago-area public hospitals. It had taken several years before that issue had finally and favorably been resolved, and in the immediate wake of that victory, Myers had told her two principal colleagues in the birth control group, attorney Ralph E. Brown and Episcopalian clergyman Don C. Shaw, who actually worked as education director of Chicago Planned Parenthood, that abortion repeal should be their next goal. First Unitarian Church in Hyde Park, where Myers was a member, offered ICMCA office space, and by early in 1967 ICMCA was up and running as a tangible organization. "The ultimate decision regarding an abortion," Myers declared in an initial letter announcing ICMCA's formation, "should rest only with the pregnant woman and her physician."[71]

Unlike Myers and Shaw, California's CCTA had a far less pronounced preference for repeal over reform, but CCTA's most important accomplishment in late 1966 was its sponsorship of Zad Leavy's amicus brief in J. Paul Shively's initial judicial challenge to the disciplinary hearing that the Board of Medical Examiners was seeking to hold concerning his and his colleague's past performance of hospital-approved rubella abortions. In late November Leavy and Herma Hill Kay, a young University of California at Berkeley law professor, filed the thirty-nine-page amicus brief with the California Supreme Court on behalf of several hundred nationally prominent doctors, including Alan Guttmacher, Bob Hall, and Lee Buxton. Far more significant a document than the procedurally oriented brief submitted by Shively's own principal counsel, Robert Lamb, the Leavy brief represented the first judicial filing to expressly argue that the privacy holding of *Griswold* could and should be applied to abortion.

"The primary purpose of the anti-abortion laws" dating from the nineteenth century, Leavy and Kay asserted, "is to protect the woman from unskilled abortionists and others operating outside the scope of sound medical practice." In their right to privacy analysis, they reached back and offered a two-page recapitulation of the 1936 decision in *One Package* before proceeding to an inclusive statement of the meaning of *Griswold*: "It is a palpable invasion of the right of privacy guaranteed by the due process clause of the Fourteenth Amendment for the state to inject itself into the sanctity of the marital relationship and dictate that the advice of the physician may not be followed, when that advice lies within the ambit of sound and accepted medical practice." Relying in part directly on an analysis that Leavy and his friend Jerry Kummer had just published in a law review article, the brief went on to assert that "The striking similarity of the anti-abortion laws and the Connecticut anti-contraceptive statute is too patent to be overlooked." "Both statutes invade the intimate realm of marital privacy," Leavy said, twice citing Tom Emerson's 1965 article and its reference as to how *Griswold*'s right to privacy might also apply against abortion laws. "The enforcement of these statutes strikes a sharp blow at the right of privacy of married persons by preventing them from making a personal, intimate and crucial decision which may affect their own health and well-being as well as that of their family for the rest of their lives." "It is constitutionally repugnant," he went on, "for the government, through regulation of physicians, to invade the privacy of a husband and wife to dictate a decision which is intimate and personal to the marital relationship, and which deeply affects the health and well-being of the wife and the family. It seems no less an invasion of personal privacy for the state, through regulation of its physicians, to dictate to any person a decision deeply affecting her health and well-being."[72]

Within four weeks of that filing, however, the California high court would issue an order favorable to Shively but of only procedural, not constitutional import in countering the board's upcoming administrative hearings. Nationwide the abortion agenda would turn to a legislative focus—but on a scale dramatically larger than anyone had envisioned possible in 1965 or even in the summer of 1966. Therapeutic reform bills would be considered by the legislatures of at least *twenty-five* states during the first eight months of 1967, and while surprising successes would be registered in several, in none of them would the press coverage, or the religious controversy, exceed that of New York. Before six months were out, developments in three other states—Colorado, North Carolina, and California—would outstrip in tangible, short-term importance the earlier New York legislative battle over reform, but in several prominent ways the New York contest would set the stage not only for 1967 events elsewhere but for New York's and other states' struggles in future years as well.

Even before the end of 1966 the New York State Council of Churches, the Episcopal Diocese, and Governor Nelson Rockefeller all called for the passage of reform legislation in the upcoming legislature. The *New York Times* resumed its editorials in favor of modification of the "cruel and out of date" existing law, but the journalistic consensus was that passage of any reform measure was "unlikely" in the face of opposition by both Democratic assembly speaker Anthony J. Travia and Republican senate majority leader Earl W. Brydges. On January 17, along with more than three dozen cosponsors, Manhattan Assemblyman Albert H. Blumenthal introduced an ALI-style reform bill that was promptly attacked by the New York Catholic Welfare Committee as authorizing the "slaughter of the innocents." The Roman Catholic Bishop of Albany, Edward J. Maginn, said he was "saddened and shocked" that Protestant churches would support a bill that was "neither Christian nor reasonable," and at an initial February 3 hearing on the Blumenthal measure affirmative witnesses including Harriet Pilpel were opposed by leading Catholic spokesmen. Pilpel once again articulated a firm preference for repeal over reform, explaining that "The right to free choice in the area of procreation is as fundamental a civil liberty and constitutional freedom as the right to life and liberty itself," but a second day of hearings on February 8 was marked by especially intense Catholic attacks on even the notion of therapeutic reform.

Journalists predicted that such opposition meant the bill had little chance of success, and one black Roman Catholic legislator who supported it, Manhattan Assemblyman Basil A. Paterson, emphasized that "We're not telling Catholics they have to get abortions. We're only asking them not to dictate to the rest of the population what they can and cannot do." On February 12, however, the state's eight Roman Catholic bishops issued a joint letter—the first such document ever—and had it read from every Roman Catholic pulpit in New York. Reporters disclosed that Speaker Travia had removed Blumenthal from an important Democratic Party policy position without giving a reason, and the following day two Roman Catholic assemblymen from Brooklyn delivered floor speeches bitterly attacking Blumenthal for sponsoring the bill. Democrat Lawrence P. Murphy cited the hierarchy's missive and told his colleagues that "I have to believe my eight Catholic Bishops who tell me how to believe."

The New York Times renewed its endorsement of reform in an editorial that asserted that there were "2,000 abortion deaths every year" in the state, and New York's junior U.S. Senator, Robert F. Kennedy, himself a Roman Catholic, publicly announced that "there are obvious changes that have to be made" in the existing statute. His Senate colleague, Republican Jacob Javits, quickly agreed, saying that "intelligent reform is long overdue." The Times repeated both senators' remarks in another editorial endorsement of reform, and underlined the modesty of that position by publishing an op-ed article that termed Blumenthal's bill "only one small step toward a truly enlightened solution" and asked "what business has the state in dictating to a woman what she is to do with her own body?" Pessimistic legislative predictions continued amidst Roman Catholic clergy attacks on Senator Kennedy over his statement, and national stories testified to a burgeoning wave of reform efforts. One medical weekly announced that "the push for reform is gaining momentum from coast to coast," and the AMA's *Journal of the American Medical Association* (*JAMA*), published a proreform editorial highlighting how more and more doctors were becoming acutely aware of the disparities between accepted medical practice and century-old statutes. Nationally some ten thousand "legal" therapeutic abortions a year were now being performed, usually on mental health grounds and in large part because of the rubella epidemic, under statutes that authorized abortions only to save a woman's life. "American medicine," *JAMA* thus noted, "is therefore confronted with a situation where many of its conscientious practitioners are daily acting contrary to existing laws," as California's Shively case so bitterly highlighted. All of this was evidence, *JAMA* said, of "a profound restiveness for reappraisal and updating of our statutes to keep pace with 20th-century medical practice."[73]

Americans for Democratic Action (ADA), a mainstream liberal group, endorsed repeal and declared that "a woman has the absolute right to decide whether or not she should have an abortion," but they were quickly attacked by the ostensibly liberal Protestant weekly *The Christian Century*, which complained that "new laws based on ground as unsure as absolute rights can be as inhumane as the ones they seek to replace." One New York City minister, Howard Moody, a forty-five-year-old Dallas native and Marine combat veteran, wrote in another Protestant journal that present-day supporters of the old laws were motivated by "a desire to inflict retribution and punishment upon women" and that *Griswold* showed the path toward judicial repeal. "The control of a fetal appendage in the body of a woman ... by civil law can only be viewed as an infamous invasion of individual privacy and denial of the freedom of choice. I believe the Supreme Court will eventually find our abortion laws unconstitutional."

Time magazine ran an article highlighting the growing religious tensions, and the usually liberal Catholic weekly *Commonweal*, which had been among the first Catholic voices to speak out against the anticontraception statutes, printed a hard-line editorial attacking the New York reform bill. A human fetus at any stage of development, it said, was either a full human person or, dichotomously, "nothing but another chunk of matter." "We doubt there can be a middle ground," *Commonweal* insisted. Catholic law professors such as Fordham's Robert Byrn weighed in with similar articles in professional journals, and in a subsequent short essay in *Commonweal* itself Byrn reiterated the view that "there is no qualitative difference between life at conception and life at birth." Well-known Catholic scholar Robert F. Drinan warned in the Jesuit weekly *America* that "The advocates of abortion clearly have the initiative at this time," but Drinan implicitly suggested that a compromise on reform might help stave off the much more far-reaching change of repeal. "One can wonder . . . whether the indiscriminate availability of contraceptives today would have come about if Catholics, instead of seeking to retain an absolute ban on all contraceptives, had negotiated for a law restricting their sales to married persons by a physician's prescription."

Moderate reformer and ASA president Bob Hall went so far in one symposium as to say that "the decision to destroy a pregnancy more rightfully belongs to the pregnant woman than to her physician," and the American Civil Liberties Union, after previously turning aside Dorothy Kenyon's repeated entreaties on the subject, now began to wrestle with the prorepeal positions that had been adopted by its New York and Southern California chapters. Perhaps surprisingly, however, Kenyon's position attracted little more support than it had in prior years, with the appropriate board committee reporting to the full ACLU board that "There was almost unanimous agreement that restrictive laws were not unconstitutional on their face. The Committee felt that restrictive abortion laws . . . while unduly restrictive, are not so unreasonable as to be unconstitutional. The Committee felt that society could decide . . . to place such value on the life of the unborn child as to render abortion possible only in a narrow range of circumstances." As a matter of legislative policy, as distinct from a question of rights, the board committee "felt that a woman ought to have an unfettered right to decide to have an abortion up to the first 20 weeks."

When the full ACLU board considered the subject in mid-February, Kenyon had no better success there than in committee in convincing her colleagues that the choice involved a question of individual rights rather than legislative preference. One board member unsuccessfully complained "that we cannot neglect the father's right to have a child," and Harriet Pilpel moved to address one question the committee had not mentioned by advocating that therapeutic ALI standards be used to decide any post-twenty weeks abortion requests. Kenyon spoke up vociferously, saying—in the words of the Board's minutes—"that she does not concede that the state has any legitimate interest in protecting the life of an unborn child, even after 20 weeks" and that she was "unwilling to impose any time limits on the mother's unfettered discretion to abort herself." The board, however, first weakened the committee recommendation by moving even the preferred legislative dividing line forward from twenty weeks to the first three months of pregnancy, and then sent back to committee the entire subject of what exemptions if any should be endorsed for the six latter months.

An angry Dorothy Kenyon circulated a letter calling the board discussion "a shambles of irrelevance and illogic" and reminding her colleagues that "For lo! these many years I have been a Cassandra crying out in the A.C.L.U. wilderness against the crime of abortion laws and man's inhumanity to women." She reiterated her contention that "the abortion law is a violation of civil liberties because it imposes upon woman a kind of bodily slavery," but one ACLU officer quickly circulated a letter of rebuttal, emphasizing that "everyone present" at the meeting except Kenyon "thought it entirely impractical to support any such extreme position." One female colleague from Philadelphia wrote Kenyon to voice her agreement, saying "There should be *no* restrictions upon the basic human right of a woman not to bear a child that she does not want." Frustrated within the ACLU, Kenyon nonetheless continued to champion her long-held position in other venues, including television talk shows. In an article in an ADA publication she termed therapeutic reform bills "woefully inadequate" and called for abolition of the "cruel and unconstitutional abortion laws" that infringed upon "the right to control our own bodies."[74]

Another combative rebel within the growing ranks of repeal advocates was a thirty-three-year-old former medical student from Long Island with a highly developed taste for publicity, William R. Baird. Two years earlier, in May of 1965, Baird had been let go from a marketing job with Joseph Sunnen's Emko Pharmaceuticals when his crusading urge to challenge New York's remaining statutory ban against the distribution of contraceptives by nonprofessionals became more than the company wanted to bear. A week after first going public, Baird had succeeded in getting arrested in the town of Hempstead for dispensing birth control materials, but six months later, in November of 1965, the charges had been dropped. In August of 1966 Baird had drawn press attention by picketing St. Patrick's Cathedral in midtown Manhattan along with his wife and two of his four children to protest the Catholic church's opposition to birth control, and a month later Baird managed to get himself arrested in Freehold, New Jersey, for displaying contraceptives in violation of an antiquated state statute. Baird's initial conviction and hundred-dollar fine were subsequently reversed by the New Jersey Supreme Court on the grounds that the old law was unconstitutionally vague, but within weeks of the New Jersey arrest Baird and about fifty young followers turned out to picket the PPFA annual awards dinner at New York's Waldorf Astoria. Baird told puzzled reporters that they were protesting both the excessive fees he said Planned Parenthood clinics charged poor women for birth control pills, and PPFA's bestowal of its top prize, the Margaret Sanger Award, which the previous year had gone to Estelle Griswold and Lee Buxton, to President Lyndon B. Johnson. Baird's demonstration certainly did not endear him to his ostensible allies within Planned Parenthood, and in mid-February 1967, with New York press interest in abortion at a new peak because of the battling over the Blumenthal bill, Baird and a previously publicity-shy ally, Nathan G. Rappaport, made a joint public appearance in Hempstead.

Nathan Rappaport was in his own obscure way, like Tim Timanus, quite well-known. Sixty-six years old at the time of his appearance with Baird, the swarthy-looking Rappaport had spent nine of the last sixteen years in jail and estimated that he had performed some twenty-five thousand abortions since he had first begun practicing medicine in the Jackson Heights section of Queens in the 1920s. Rappaport had achieved a certain sort of word-of-mouth status from his anonymous 1962 memoir in which he had styled himself as "Dr. X," and Baird for some time had been quietly referring abortion seekers to him. Others in the New York activist community, however, understood that whatever Rappaport's medical skills might have been in earlier years, his specific technical competence was no longer sufficiently error-free as to merit adequate confidence.

In their Hempstead appearance, however, Rappaport was a secondary figure in Baird's hope that a public display of abortion instruments, accompanied by descriptive remarks, would be sufficient to win arrest by the Hempstead police, Nassau County detectives, and Nassau County assistant district attorney who made up a good proportion of the modest audience, but the lawmen refused to play their assigned role. "It's your duty to arrest me," Baird insisted. "I have clearly violated the law." An unhappy Baird had to go home rather than to jail, but his entry onto the abortion scene introduced a dramatic and confrontational player into the flourishing national drama.[75]

New York of course was far from the only state where abortion had become a public and legislative issue during January and February of 1967, and while in some reform measures died quickly, in others they generated considerable attention and heat. In Connecticut a female state senator introduced an extremely modest reform bill that called simply for adding an exception for pregnancies resulting from rapes to the state's nineteenth-century statute allowing only abortions necessary to save a woman's life. Literally no proponents showed up to testify in favor of the measure, but longtime PPLC adversary Joseph P. Cooney did appear, on behalf of Connecticut's three Roman Catholic bishops, to attack the bill on moral grounds and warn that it undoubtedly would become too permissive. Not surprisingly, neither that bill nor a subsequently introduced ALI-style bill even emerged from committee.[76]

In Arizona the state Medical Association, which had endorsed therapeutic reform in April 1966, had its legislative counsel aid four Democratic state senators in introducing a bill whose language directly mirrored the association's position. The Senate Public Health Committee held hearings on the measure in January of 1967 and approved it by a 5 to 3 vote, but then the state's Roman Catholic bishop sent a vociferous letter of opposition to every member of the legislature and also instructed pastors to read it from the pulpit at Sunday services. Legislators were immediately deluged with a considerable quantity of opposition mail, and the Medical Association backed away from the issue as a second round of hearings took place before the Senate Judiciary Committee. Ten days after the bishop's letter had been distributed, the committee formally killed the reform bill. A subsequent survey of Arizona's Catholic clergy found that 79 percent of them identified abortion as a "very important"—as distinct from just an "important"—issue, and 55 percent of them indicated that they had *personally* contacted one or more legislators after receiving the bishop's letter. While reform proponents had melted away or failed to take the field, reform opponents had mustered their forces most impressively.[77]

In Georgia, state representative Richard L. Starnes, Jr., of Rome prepared an ALI bill in conjunction with staff members of the Medical Association of Georgia, the state doctors' group, and after relatively pro forma hearings and judiciary committee consideration the state house passed it on March 1 by the overwhelming margin of 129 to 3. At that point, however, potential opponents began to mobilize, and an editorial attacking the bill immediately appeared in the weekly newspaper of the Atlanta Archdiocese. Several Roman Catholic clergymen contacted Senate Judiciary Committee chairman Robert H. Smalley, Jr., of Griffin, and when Starnes appeared before that committee on behalf of his bill several days later, it quickly became clear, he later explained, that "most of them felt I had thrown them a hot potato which they had just as soon I had left alone." On March 14 the Senate Judiciary Committee voted four to two to defer action on the bill, and proponents indicated that they would try again at the outset of the 1968 legislative session.[78]

While the 1967 Arizona and Georgia reform measures were being turned aside, the New York reformers and their many journalistic supporters were still trying to advance the Blumenthal bill there. The *New York Times*'s editorials now emphasized that therapeutic reform "would not legalize abortion indiscriminately," and ASA's Bob Hall, in conjunction with John V. P. Lassoe, Jr., of New York's Episcopal Diocese, and wealthy liberal philanthropist Stewart R. Mott, created an Ad Hoc Committee for Abortion Law Reform to convey the impression that a popularly based lobby group backed the bill. *Life* magazine weighed in with an editorial declaration that "present laws are badly out of step with life" and noted that 71 percent of Americans, including 61 percent of Roman Catholics, endorsed abortion when a woman's health was at risk. "Each year 5,000 of the desperate die," *Life* emphasized, and "present laws refuse to recognize that these women face a real problem. Laws that lead hundreds of thousands to risk their lives to break them need restudy and reform."

New York legislative leaders deferred committee action on the Blumenthal bill for more than a week, and a small group of Roman Catholic laity issued a statement backing the measure and saying that the law ought to allow "individual citizens the free exercise of their conscience." But on March 7 the Assembly's Codes Committee voted 15 to 3 to kill the reform measure, and sponsor Blumenthal said he was "disappointed" while Republican Governor Nelson Rockefeller termed the defeat "unfortunate." The following day Blumenthal publicly requested that Rockefeller appoint a special commission to study and report on the issue of abortion law change, and the following evening, at a private dinner party in Manhattan, the governor told a fellow guest, Alan Guttmacher, that he was indeed inclined to accept Blumenthal's suggestion. Guttmacher several days later sent Rockefeller a long list of possible members for such a commission, but most other abortion activists were not about to wait quietly until some such commission report a year hence could be used to resuscitate legislative prospects for reform.

Three days later Bill Baird led 150 marchers in a protest outside St. Patrick's Cathedral that "attracted little attention" in the judgment of the *New York Times*, and Larry Lader and John Lassoe held a press conference to announce that a network of ministers would soon begin publicly offering abortion provider referrals to pregnant women. Lader had found himself privately deluged with such requests ever since his book, simply titled *Abortion*, had been published ten months earlier, and he had first raised the possibility of organizing such a referral system with Howard Moody, the Manhattan pastor who shared Lader's prorepeal sentiments, back in September 1966. Lader himself had initially referred women either to Robert D. Spencer, a now ageing doctor in Ashland, Pennsylvania, who had just recently retired from a longtime career as a family practitioner and abortion provider, or to a distinguished Arkansas physician who had contacted Lader soon after his book had appeared. By now most of Lader's private referrals were going to a brusque and iconoclastic Serbian-born physician in Washington, D.C., Milan Vuitch, who had successfully weathered two attempted criminal prosecutions in Maryland and Virginia, but the idea of a public referral operation struck some longtime reform backers as distasteful, and Bob Hall publicly disassociated himself and ASA from Lader and Lassoe's announcement.

Defeat of the Blumenthal bill also stimulated Lader to revive his and William Ober's previous discussions about creating an abortion test case. Ober had raised the subject several times with a forty-seven-year-old gynecology colleague at Knickerbocker Hospital, Dr. Wayne Decker, and now Lader told Ober, Decker, and lawyers Harriet Pilpel and Cyril Means that "it seems important to proceed with our plans . . . in the next few months." Lader and Ober had talked about either a teenager or an older, married woman who did not want another child as an ideal test-case patient, and while Lader aspired to "the broadest possible judicial interpretation," he nonetheless worried that "if we cannot guarantee that the woman's identity can be kept out of court and out of the press, it may be extremely difficult to find a case." In early April Lader met to discuss legal possibilities with Pilpel and Means, but the somewhat pompous Means insisted that any notion that they should argue that existing antiabortion statutes were unconstitutional in light of the Fourteenth Amendment's due process clause liberty language was "so perspicuously absurd" that he would not join such a case.

In a follow-up letter, Means instructed Lader and Pilpel that "I can discern a respectable and cogent constitutional argument in two, but only in two, cases: (1) pregnancy caused by rape; (2) pregnancy that will predictably result . . . in birth of a deformed child." All other pregnancies, Means explained, fell well within the "fundamental notion of law and morals that one can be held responsible for the natural consequences of one's acts." Hence, except for pregnancies involving rape or deformities, "I perceive none in which there is the faintest chance that any court would sustain a contention of unconstitutionality." Means said that "I believe in abortion on demand" as a legislative policy preference, but that if Lader and Pilpel went ahead with any test case, "there will be a resounding defeat." Worst of all, he claimed, the resulting judicial opinion "will be quoted triumphantly by the enemies of abortion law reform in the legislative forum for years to come. If someone had asked me to suggest some step which abortion law advocates of reform could take which would be as counterproductive as possible, I doubt if I could have hit upon anything so admirably adapted to that purpose as this test case."

Means's dismissive broadside irritated both Lader and Pilpel. Lader believed strongly that a rubella–fetal defects case was far too narrow a claim to be worth litigating, and Pilpel told Means that she "could not disagree more" with his constitutional perspective, especially in light of an unpublished essay she had just received by a young scholar that argued that such constitutional attacks on abortion statutes "have an excellent chance of prevailing." Pilpel's rebuttal humbled Means and "delighted" Lader, who was also happy that Ober had obtained the support of Knickerbocker Hospital's executive director, Alvin Conway. Other activists such as John Lassoe were already focusing on 1968 New York legislative prospects, but Lader hoped that if a willing patient could be found, the abortion struggle could make headway in the courts even before the next session convened.[79]

New York, Arizona and Georgia were not the only states where reform advocates had suffered early 1967 legislative defeats. In Indiana an ALI-style bill that had the backing of the state medical association and the Indiana Council of Churches had passed the state House but had been "gutted" in the state senate so that only pregnancies resulting from rape or incest would be added as statutory exceptions. The senate had passed this watered-down measure, but Indiana's governor then vetoed it. In North Dakota a reform bill introduced by a first-term female legislator had been defeated by a five-vote margin, and in Hawaii, where both a reform bill and a repeal measure had been introduced, the reform proposal won approval in one committee before being tabled in another. Reform bills had also been rejected in New Mexico and Nebraska, and in New Jersey a 4 to 3 decision by the state Supreme Court drew extensive attention to the abortion issue there.

The court dismissed a "wrongful birth" claim brought by a couple who contended that their doctor improperly had failed to alert them to the danger that a deformed infant would result from the mother's bout with rubella, and that the doctor should have recommended an abortion. The court's narrow majority declared that any such recommendation would have been improper, and, focusing upon the deformed fetus, rather than the traumatized parents, asserted that "the sanctity of the single human life is the decisive factor" in deciding the case. "The right of their child to live is greater than and precludes their right not to endure emotional and financial injury," the court asserted. Some observers, including New Jersey prosecutors, called for a statutory review in light of this apparent declaration that each and every rubella abortion would violate the existing state statute, but Governor Richard J. Hughes and state legislative leaders brushed the matter aside.[80]

Even before Bill Baird's demonstration outside St. Patrick's Cathedral in the wake of the New York legislative defeat, Baird had been recruited for another protest venture by the student newspaper at Boston University, the *B.U. News*, and its editor, Raymond Mungo. *B.U. News* announced to its readers in early March that it had invited Baird to visit the campus four weeks hence to "distribute free lists of abortionists and birth control devices to interested coeds" and to give a lecture. The *News* also ran an article by Baird in which he explained how his interest in providing birth control and abortion services for poor women had grown out of an experience he had had while representing Emko in which he had witnessed the emergency-room death of a woman who he was told was a twenty-nine-year-old mother of eight, following a bungled illegal abortion. Baird claimed in his piece that the 1966 national death toll from illegal abortions had been more than ten thousand, and he noted that Massachusetts, even after the 1966 post-*Griswold* revision of its birth control statute, still had a law, similar to those under which he had been arrested in New York and New Jersey, prohibiting the display and/or distribution of contraceptive materials other than to married people by a physician. "I am now ready to test this law in Massachusetts as well," Baird proclaimed, and he emphasized that "no group, no law, no individual can dictate to a woman what goes on in her own body. That decision must remain her own."[81]

Soon after that article appeared, Baird received a petition signed by some seven hundred B.U. students seconding the *News*'s invitation, and on Thursday, April 6, Baird appeared on the stage of B.U.'s Hayden Auditorium before an overflow crowd of some fifteen hundred to two thousand people, and 65 percent female. Editor Mungo introduced Baird and told the audience that "We are here to test the legal aspects of the birth control and abortion laws in the state of Massachusetts." That was not difficult to tell, as seven Boston Police Department officers and detectives were present, in part because advance publicity concerning Baird's appearance and intent had led state senate Public Health Committee chairman William X. Wall to call for Baird's arrest if he followed through on his declared intent. Three vice squad officers stood right behind the stage curtain as Baird began his sixty-minute talk and listened as he told the students that they were being "enchained by men who have no right to dictate to you the privacy of your bodies." Toward the end of his lecture Baird explained that he was about to distribute both a mimeographed list of abortion providers outside the United States and packages of Emko vaginal foam. He called upon the watchful officers "to do their duty" and told the audience that "the only way we can change the law is to get the case into a court of law." He then invited those in the audience who wanted packages of foam to come up to the stage, and about twenty women immediately came forward. Baird himself handed packages to approximately six of the women, and others took packages from a carton on the podium. The officers on the stage then finally moved toward Baird, and one of them, Lieutenant—and later Boston Police Commissioner—Joseph M. Jordan, placed his hand on Baird's shoulder and Baird asked the crowd if ACLU attorney James Hamilton was in the audience. He had to repeat the question a second time before Hamilton headed toward the stage amidst a standing ovation from the crowd, and Jordan and officer Edward McHale informed Baird that he was under arrest. None of the young women to whom Baird had handed packages of foam were identified or detained, though one told a reporter that "None of us were planted." Baird was placed in a car and taken to police headquarters, where he was released on one hundred dollars bail for an initial court appearance the next day. "I feel I have achieved my purpose of bringing the law into the courts," Baird told reporters, and at his Friday arraignment he pled not guilty and a court date four weeks later was set.

In the ensuing two weeks Baird gave well-attended talks at Harvard, Tufts, and other Boston-area colleges without repeating his distribution of contraceptive foam, but at least one of the speeches, at Simmons College, was monitored without incident by Boston police. Baird's B.U. sponsors began a defense fund to meet his court costs, but the Massachusetts Civil Liberties Union, uncertain as to whether prosecutors would proceed against Baird for anything he had *said* or only on the issue of having distributed the foam, let him know that they were uncertain as to whether they would continue to represent him. Baird was put in touch with another Boston attorney, Joseph J. Balliro, who agreed to defend him without fee, and Baird thus dispensed with any further assistance from the lukewarm ACLU. Balliro represented Baird at his next court appearance in early May, where the case was formally passed along to Superior Court for indictment and trial. Sixteen student pickets turned out to protest Baird's prosecution, but the Planned Parenthood League of Massachusetts (PPLM), in its May newsletter to supporters, went out of its way to disassociate itself from both Baird and his court challenge to the existing Massachusetts statute. Baird "is in no way connected with Planned Parenthood," the newsletter declared, and the current laws forbidding the distribution of contraceptive articles to unmarried individuals "do not . . . deny anyone his constitutional rights to *use* contraceptives or to talk about them—therefore there is nothing to be gained by court action of this kind. The only way to remove the limitations remaining in the law is through the legislative process."

Baird told two sympathetic journalists who nonetheless characterized him as "a little too intense, a little too filled with the vision of himself as a martyr" that "Planned Parenthood is a middle class monopoly." He asserted to a more impressionable reporter from *B. U. News* that "I never dreamed another birth control group would attempt to destroy me personally," even though they were "protecting a vested business interest," but no Boston publication noted the prior history of Baird picketing PPFA's annual dinner. PPLM received about a dozen letters, apparently from Baird's young supporters, asking for its view of Baird, and executive director Hazel Sagoff replied that PPLM was "not too disturbed" that the present Massachusetts law "directs women to physicians" and said that "We are told by our lawyers . . . that there is no violation of constitutional rights in the present law," which distinguished between unmarried and married individuals in authorizing the dissemination of contraceptives only to the latter. "They tell us, and we agree, that the only way to liberalize the current law is through the process of filing a bill in the legislature and working for its passage." Sagoff added that PPLM "has no official position on abortion" and noted that Baird "is openly critical of the predominant faith in Massachusetts." Some years later former PPFA president Loraine Campbell, whose active involvement in the Massachusetts league stretched back a full thirty years to the days of *Gardner*, acerbicly called Baird "a thorn in our flesh for years." "He was always talking about abortion under the aegis of birth control, when we were trying to avoid the issue of abortion at that point." On balance, Campbell said, "Baird did more good than harm," but then, as she memorably declared, "every social change and every forward step in history requires its nuts."[82]

On the very same day that Bill Baird was busy being arrested in Boston, the 1967 nationwide abortion reform effort registered its most surprising and most significant victory when the Colorado state senate passed an ALI-style bill by a vote of 20 to 13. The April 6 tally was surprising both because Colorado had no organized group of proponents on the order of California's CCTA, and because the bill had been introduced in the legislature only six weeks earlier by a newly elected and otherwise largely unknown thirty-one-year-old Denver representative, Richard D. Lamm, who had lived in the state for only five years since moving from California. Indeed, Dick Lamm's reform bill came from what seemed to be purely happenstance origins, for the first draft of the bill had started out in December of 1966 as a course work assignment prepared by a third-year University of Denver Law School student, Susan Graham Barnes. Her friend Cindy Kahn showed a copy of Barnes's work to her husband Ed Kahn, who in turn mentioned it to Lamm, but initially Lamm had no particular thought of introducing any such measure. He told a Unitarian church audience on January 15 that an abortion reform bill "wouldn't have a chance" in the Colorado legislature, and at a first ad hoc meeting of potential reform proponents the prevailing opinion, Lamm later recalled, "was one of pessimism, because it was our feeling that an attempt to change the law at that point in time" would certainly fail and "would probably hurt more than help toward the eventual passage of a liberalizing law."

That meeting left some reformers thinking more about educational work than a legislative effort, but as several members of an unofficial steering committee for the group approached other legislators beyond Lamm, "a cautious optimism began to grow" that a reform bill was indeed passable. A good number of legislators cited how the initially hesitant 1965 approval of a measure authorizing the provision of birth control information to public aid recipients had nonetheless proven successful, and "the support in public acceptance" of that initiative "had gone far to pave the way for abortion reform in the minds of legislators," Lamm later explained. Worries there that political controversy or electoral troubles might ensue had proven wholly chimerical, and the small group of reformers began to appreciate that over "the last few years an immense change" had taken place in public attitudes concerning reproductive issues. Denver Republican Representative Carl H.

Gustafson, a Lutheran who had been significantly influenced by his denomination's recent endorsement of therapeutic reform, agreed to join Lamm in cosponsoring a revised draft of Barnes's ALI bill, and after setting a minimum target of recruiting at least twenty other advance supporters, they began canvassing other members. "To our great surprise," Lamm remembered, "virtually every legislator we approached not only agreed to put his name on the bill but manifested great enthusiasm." It quickly became apparent that there was a much higher chance of actual success than the ad hoc steering committee initially had imagined, and Lamm and Gustafson, along with former Colorado Planned Parenthood president Ruth Steel of Englewood, who had served as the primary lobbyist for the 1965 birth control bill, reached out for wider support. They recruited additional supporters in the medical community, sought the endorsement of the Colorado Council of Churches, and accompanied by at least one minister and one doctor, made courtesy calls upon all of the major media outlets in Denver, particularly the *Denver Post*, to request editorial support.[83]

By the time Lamm formally introduced the reform bill on February 23, less than a month after he had made his own firm commitment on the subject, the measure had forty-six recorded sponsors, almost half the membership of the entire Colorado legislature. The thirty-five representatives backing the bill represented a majority of the sixty-five member state house, and the eleven senators, out of a body of thirty-five, included two influential Republicans, John Bermingham and Ruth Stockton. Within a week's time the number of senate sponsors had jumped to sixteen, and on March 9 a three-hour House Health Committee hearing on the bill took place before an audience of more than one hundred. In preparation, Lamm later explained, the bill's supporters had agreed to emphasize "that it was strictly a health matter" and "to use as proponents of the legislation the most conservative and responsible people we had at our disposal," namely "ministers, doctors, and lawyers who had not previously been involved in controversial legislation of any kind." Over a dozen opposition witnesses squared off against some twenty supportive speakers, but within two weeks of the hearing the committee approved the bill by eleven to four after Lamm had agreed to several amendments requiring parental consent for a teenager under eighteen, spousal consent in the cases of married woman living with their husbands, and unanimous rather than simply majority approval of every procedure by each hospital's three-doctor abortion committee.[84]

On March 29, by a vote of 40 to 21, the Colorado house approved the therapeutic reform bill. Five days later the Senate Health and

Welfare Committee held its hearing on the measure, and a crowd of angry Roman Catholics turned out to register their opposition. Several foes brought bottled human fetuses to display to the committee, and one opponent's irate jeers at the committee so embarrassed the two members of the Catholic Lawyers Guild who had sought to coordinate the opposition that they left the session and later formally apologized to the committee for the crowd's behavior. The following day the senate committee approved the bill by a vote of eight to two, and the day after that it moved to the senate floor. About fifty female opponents of reform staged a brief protest outside the state capitol, but on April 6— just a few hours before Bill Baird's arrest in Boston—the Colorado senate passed the reform bill by a margin of 20 to 13. The state house then ratified that final version of the measure by a Saturday vote of 40 to 20, and the bill then went to the desk of conservative Governor John Love, who told reporters that "I have not yet made up my mind what I will do with it." Love previously had hinted that he would indeed sign the measure, and after some four days of apparent indecision, Love on April 25 signed the bill into law. That same day, however, he privately summoned the president of the Colorado State Medical Society to his office and very firmly recommended that doctors and hospitals implement the new measure in a conservative and responsible fashion. Reform proponents' jubilation over their amazingly quick and obstacle-free victory was somewhat tempered by the realization that only a modest percentage of women seeking abortions would qualify for legal ones under the provisions of the new Colorado statute. That limitation, however, did nothing to stop the wave of national press attention that descended upon the Colorado reformers and their first-in-the-nation achievement. Dick Lamm with some humility told New York's Larry Lader that he was merely someone who had been "in the right place at the right time," and other Colorado reform backers emphasized to reporters that the new law would be no panacea, especially if the Colorado medical community followed Governor Love's guidance in implementing it. "The intent of" the new measure, Adams County District Attorney Floyd Marks stressed to one journalist, "is to promote the well-being of the mother, to avoid impairment of her health. If the doctors can't face up to their responsibilities," and implement the statute with that purpose in mind, "this new law will be a farce." Indeed, Marks noted, Colorado's modest step forward might simply serve to highlight the inadequacy of the entire therapeutic reform approach. "In time, I think we will all accept the proposition that no woman should be forced to bear a child against her will."[85]

In Colorado, the reformers' success was achieved without any significant participation by the organized medical community. In almost all other states that witnessed 1967 reform efforts, however, the backing for legislative initiatives came principally from state doctors' groups, and when one medical magazine surveyed over forty thousand American physicians on the question of therapeutic liberalization in March, it found—as the *New York Times* and other newspapers prominently highlighted—that some 87 percent backed ALI-style changes. That overall statistic included 49 percent support for reform from among Roman Catholic M.D.s, but only 14 percent of all respondents said they supported abortion law repeal. In Texas, where Fort Worth's Dr. Hugh Savage had been working within the Texas Medical Association for well over a year to be sure that a 1967 reform bill would be placed before the state legislature, his efforts resulted in the successful recruitment of a surprisingly unlikely legislative sponsor. In mid-January Savage and several TMA colleagues, including Dallas's Dr. James T. Downs III, as well as Page Keeton, dean of the University of Texas Law School, dined with sixty-seven-year-old Dallas state senator George Parkhouse, a sixteen-year veteran of the senate whom one state newspaper characterized as an "outspoken and often cantankerous" "hard rock conservative." The state's weekly Roman Catholic newspaper had already published an editorial attacking what it knew would be the TMA's upcoming reform bill, but Parkhouse was undeterred by such flak and willingly accepted the TMA's request. On February 21 he introduced an ALI-style bill requiring written endorsement of each prospective abortion by two doctors and majority approval by a five-doctor hospital committee.

Several days later Drs. Savage and Downs, along with Mrs. Harry L. Logan, Jr., a former president of the Fort Worth Junior League, announced the creation of the Texas Committee for the Modernization of Therapeutic Abortion Laws and released a membership list that featured leading Texas doctors and socially prominent women, such as Mrs. Perry R. Bass and Mrs. Robert S. Strauss. Hugh Savage emphasized how many medically appropriate abortions, such as those involving rubella, were technically illegal under existing state law, and in mid-March, when the Senate Public Health Committee held a three-hour hearing on the Parkhouse bill, both Dr. Savage and Mrs. Logan were among eight affirmative witnesses. Two Roman Catholic doctors and the director of the Texas Catholic Conference were among eight opposing witnesses, but after a motion to table the measure was defeated on a vote of seven to six, the committee concluded the hearing by voting to send the bill to the senate floor, where journalists predicted stiff opposition.

Then, on the evening of May 5, with the reform bill awaiting a senate debate and vote, Savage and his allies experienced an unexpected and embarrassing defeat when the TMA House of Delegates, at its regular annual meeting, voted in a narrow and initially disputed tally to approve a committee recommendation that "mental health has no place in consideration of a therapeutic abortion" and that the TMA bill should therefore be substantially revised. An unhappy Senator Parkhouse told reporters that that sealed the measure's fate. He added that passage had already seemed "beyond any hope" because of the absence of any affirmative "propaganda," and especially in light of the well-organized opposition. "There has been a lot of pressure from the Catholic press and from members of the church clergy." Colorado's success had occurred so quickly that church officials might have been taken by surprise, but in states where they were ready and prepared, such as Texas and Arizona, legislative proponents quickly discovered that state medical associations alone did not have the political weight to recruit majority support for seemingly controversial legislation.[86]

But Colorado was not the only surprising and unexpected success for reform proponents in the spring of 1967. While the Colorado bill had been sponsored by thirty-one-year-old Dick Lamm, in North Carolina a freshman legislator more than twice Lamm's age, sixty-five-year-old Arthur H. Jones of Charlotte, a retired North Carolina National Bank vice president, similarly put forward an ALI-style measure. Much of the initiative for Art Jones's bill came from his good friend and Mecklenburg County Public Welfare Director, Wallace Kuralt, who had long had an interest in reproductive policy issues. Jones himself had met and interviewed Margaret Sanger during the 1920s when he had been an undergraduate at Oberlin College, and both he and his wife, who worked as a counselor in Mecklenburg County family court, had taken an active interest in related issues during the years before his entry into electoral politics. But the original idea for a 1967 initiative was Wally Kuralt's, and even though Kuralt had never seen the ALI's Model Penal Code abortion provision, soon after the 1966 election Kuralt discussed his idea with several Charlotte ob/gyns, who reinforced his inclination that the liberalization focus ought to be on the "health of the mother." Then he and a welfare department attorney, Myles Hanes, wrote out a first draft of a reform bill, and Kuralt took their handiwork to Charlotte state Senator Herman Moore to ask his help in finding a sponsor. Moore then mentioned the idea to Jones, whom Kuralt had not approached on the assumption that a big-city freshman might not be the ideal proponent, and Jones immediately leapt to the task and eagerly volunteered for the role. Jones then went over the language of Kuralt's draft with several other doctors, and settled on "preserve the life or health of the mother or the child" as the operative phrase. Jones recruited a veteran Guilford County house member, Charles Phillips, as a cosponsor, while Senator Moore enlisted a fellow Democrat, Cleveland County's Jack White, to sponsor the measure in that chamber, and by early March the Kuralt-Jones reform bill was ready to be introduced into the North Carolina legislature.

Even before the Jones bill was submitted, word that it was coming reached North Carolina Medical Society (NCMS) president Dr. Edgar T. Beddingfield, Jr., who was dismayed that a reform effort was going to be mounted on behalf of something other than the widely accepted ALI language. Beddingfield had two mutual friends ask Jones to meet with himself and the NCMS executive director and legal counsel before proceeding, and after sitting down with those three men on March 9, Jones readily agreed to go ahead with an ALI bill rather than the one that he and Kuralt had put together. On March 15 Jones, Phillips, and the only female member of the North Carolina house, Nancy Chase, formally introduced it there, and Jack White did likewise in the senate.

Now a second-term state senator, White had thought about possibly introducing an abortion reform bill in 1965 after seeing one or more news magazine stories on abortion, but had decided that it was too late in the session. The 1967 proponents agreed to hold off house action and allow White's senate committee to move first, and in late March a small, seven-witness hearing took place. Three of the four supportive speakers were doctors who had been recruited by NCMS executive director James T. Barnes, and the fourth was the pastor of Raleigh's largest Methodist church. The three opposing witnesses, a science professor and two lawyers, had all been contacted by the Roman Catholic diocesan representatives, but neither set of speakers greatly impressed the committee members. Two days later the committee heard briefly from a fourth Roman Catholic opponent, and then sent the bill to the senate floor after agreeing to some tightening of the bill's medical terms, defeating one major opposition amendment by a 4 to 3 margin, and adding a four-month residency requirement. Several additional modest amendments were agreed to on the senate floor on April 4, and the following day it was formally approved with only two senators voting no.

The reform bill's successful transit through the state senate had drawn no significant press attention and no public comment by the

Diocese of Raleigh, whose bishop, Vincent Waters, presided over a state that was only 1 percent Roman Catholic, the lowest figure in the entire United States. Art Jones was more than happy to proceed with the senate-amended version of his bill, and after asking house leaders to delay action for two weeks to give him time to lobby among his colleagues for support, Jones spoke face-to-face with some seventy-five members of the 120-seat house and came away with a tally of sixty-eight firm commitments. A committee hearing took place on April 20, with NCMS president Beddingfield appearing as one of three affirmative witnesses, and then continued on April 25, with opponents turning out in greater numbers than they had for the senate hearing but nonetheless not offering particularly effective testimony. Two days later the health committee unanimously sent the bill to the house floor, and on May 4 it was called up for action. Art Jones gave a speech on its behalf that some legislative observers judged as one of the most persuasive addresses of the entire session, and a final vote was scheduled for the next day. A number of serious weakening amendments offered by opposition legislators were defeated, and the house then passed the reform bill on a voice vote that onlookers estimated at better than two thirds in support. Three days later the senate ratified that final version by a vote of 46 to 7 and the measure thereby became law.

The North Carolina success drew somewhat less national attention than had Colorado's cutting-edge achievement. To some observers North Carolina's law seemed somewhat narrower, in that it included a residency requirement and did not expressly authorize abortions on *mental* health grounds, yet it also provided for a somewhat more fluid medical process by mandating simply the approval of three doctors, rather than unanimous consent by a standing, three-doctor hospital committee. But politically the North Carolina victory, like the one in Colorado, owed its success to two difficult-to-replicate factors. First, proponents in both states had benefitted tremendously from very adept and perceptive principal sponsors, Dick Lamm and Art Jones, both of whom had happened into their roles without any grand planning on the part of reform advocates. Second, and far more importantly, the legislative reform drives in both states had emerged from seemingly nowhere with remarkable suddenness and had each been able to prepare and introduce a bill before any public attention or threat of controversy was drawn to their efforts. Perhaps particularly in North Carolina Roman Catholic opponents would not have been able to mount a successful opposition campaign no matter how much notice and opportunity to prepare they had been afforded, but it was undeniable that in both of abortion reform's first two legislative triumphs, swiftness and a large element of surprise had been major and probably decisive advantages.[87]

The one state where abortion reformers at the beginning of 1967 anticipated relatively good chances of success, but certainly with no element of surprise, was California, where the ongoing efforts of the CCTA had continued to pave the way toward a plausible reform drive. Tony Beilenson had improved his position in the legislature by winning election to the state senate, and the general reapportionment that the state had undergone had produced both a distinctly more liberal state senate and a much-higher than normal freshman presence in the state assembly. Beilenson and his administrative assistant, Alan Charles, refined the 1965 reform bill, enlisted well-respected Riverside Republican Craig Biddle as principal sponsor in the assembly, and recruited a conservative Glendale Republican, John L. Harmer, a long-time Democratic veteran, Alan Short of Stockton, and a liberal Republican freshman, Lewis Sherman of Alameda, as senate cosponsors. In late February the bill was formally introduced, and Beilenson purposefully delayed a Senate Judiciary Committee hearing on the measure until late April so as to be able to privately lobby fellow members of the closely divided committee ahead of time. Going into the April 27 hearing it appeared that chairman Donald Grunsky, a Watsonville Republican, would be the deciding vote on the thirteen-member committee, and Roman Catholic opponents of the bill turned out in force for the evening hearing. Keith Russell, Ned Overstreet, Zad Leavy, Herma Hill Kay, and California Medical Association president Malcolm Todd all joined Beilenson in speaking on behalf of the measure, and it was eleven p.m. before opposing witnesses got their turn. Roman Catholic bishop Alden Bell was joined by two Protestant clergymen appearing on behalf of the Northern California Right to Life League as well as by several Roman Catholic lawyers, including John T. Noonan, Jr., and Richard P. Byrne. The general tone of many of the opposing speakers was highly emotional and their predominant theme was that each and every abortion was an act of murder since a fetus was a human person from the moment of conception onward. When the testimony finally concluded sometime after two a.m. on the morning of April 28, chairman Grunsky voted with the proponents and the Beilenson bill was sent to the senate floor by a razor-thin vote of 7 to 6.

The bill's opponents were clearly surprised by the committee's approval, and the following day the senior Roman Catholic prelate in

California, James Cardinal McIntyre of Los Angeles, attacked the measure as a "trend away from divine authority." Initial floor action two days later indicated that the bill possibly although not certainly had the twenty-one votes needed for senate passage, and the careful Beilenson again chose to wait and proceed slowly rather than risk an immediate floor vote. On May 9 the *San Francisco Chronicle* reported that a new California Poll showed 73 percent popular support for therapeutic reform, up from 65 percent a year earlier, and 67 percent support among Roman Catholics, a jump of sixteen points in one year. Four days later Republican Governor Ronald Reagan, whose support would be necessary to sign any bill into law, said publicly that he did not like the fetal defects provision that was included in the Beilenson measure, and for the first time the governor's staff spread the word among Republicans that they should not back the bill. Beilenson and Assemblyman Biddle met privately with Reagan, who was noncommittal, but at a May 23 gubernatorial news conference a supportive journalist pressed Reagan to articulate his specific objections to the reform measure. The governor said that removal of the fetal defects clause and reduction of the age at which any intercourse was by definition statutory rape to fifteen were his two requirements for being able to support the measure.

Beilenson briefly pondered his options, and then on May 27 presented his own amendments to bring the bill into line with Reagan's requirements. On June 6, confident that he had the necessary votes, plus another likely "no" who would switch to "yes" if absolutely necessary, Beilenson brought his amended bill up for a final senate vote and won passage by a margin of 21 to 17. Governor Reagan acknowledged that he would sign the senate-passed version, and the measure went to the assembly with full confidence that it could win comfortable approval there. An assembly committee hearing that was largely a rerun of the senate one quickly took place, and on June 13 the senate measure reached the assembly floor. Then Governor Reagan, whose 1966 campaign managers had just days before been hired as political consultants by the Catholic hierarchy, indicated that he was having second thoughts and that perhaps the bill should be further amended to add a residency requirement. Reagan's self-contradictory remarks and last-minute timing generated resentment rather than helping the opposition, and later that same day the assembly passed the senate version by a vote of 48 to 30 after beating back by almost equally comfortable margins several opposition attempts to weaken the bill significantly. Two days later Reagan signed it into law, with the new provisions scheduled to take effect some months later, in early November, after the close of the legislative session.[88]

Knowledgeable observers of the California success gave principal credit for the victory to Tony Beilenson, without whose personal skills the bill almost certainly would not have emerged from the state senate. Careful onlookers also noted that within the legislature "the bill was sold primarily as a means to alleviate the tragic results of rape and incest," and even Beilenson's aide and law partner, Alan Charles and Zad Leavy, readily acknowledged that "the Act's basic intent is to provide relief for women in situations of hardship." CCTA activists such as Ruth Roemer, as well as Beilenson himself, recognized full well that the California reform triumph, just like the similar new measures in Colorado and North Carolina, would provide legal abortions for less than 5 percent of all women who were seeking them, but in terms of where the national reform movement had stood in December 1966, the achievements of early 1967 in the three states that had registered reform victories were a pleasant and largely surprising success indeed.[89]

That was especially true when looked at in the context of the many other legislative defeats that had been suffered in addition to the early losses in New York, Arizona, Georgia, and Texas. Lonny Myers's Illinois group, ICMCA, had taken an essentially neutral stance toward an ALI-style reform bill sponsored by state representative Leland Rayson, but that measure failed to make it out of committee. They and other liberalization proponents had higher hopes for another bill, sponsored by Lake Forest Republican John Henry Kleine, that provided for the appointment of a special Illinois abortion study commission, but that measure was vetoed by Democratic Governor Otto Kerner after being passed by both houses of the state legislature.[90] Reform bills had also failed to get out of committee in Minnesota, Michigan, Iowa, Ohio, and Pennsylvania, while in both Missouri and Alabama bills that made it out of committee never progressed further.[91] In both Nevada and Maryland reform measures passed the lower house of the legislature but were voted down in the upper chambers, and in Oklahoma a reform bill passed the state house before being tabled in the senate after the governor announced that he would veto it. The Maine state senate passed an ALI measure by a vote of 20 to 12, only to have it voted down in the state house by a margin of 90 to 39, and the Florida state senate also approved a therapeutic bill only to have it expire in the state house.[92]

The nationwide spate of spring 1967 legislative activity both reflected and influenced ongoing abortion discussions within a wide range of organizations. In mid-May the American Baptist Convention endorsed ALI-style reform, and in mid-June, under continuing pressure from Dorothy Kenyon, the board of the ACLU distinctly strengthened its support for abortion liberalization. Most importantly of all, however, on June 21 the House of Delegates of the American Medical Association formally put *the* organization of America's doctors on record as formally endorsing ALI-style therapeutic reform. To date only seven state doctors groups had explicitly backed such liberalization, but in the subsequent three months ten more would move to follow the lead of the national body.[93]

Even more notable than the AMA's action, however, was a decidedly more unconventional announcement that the *New York Times* prominently displayed on its front page: twenty-one New York clergymen, stimulated by Larry Lader's initial suggestion to Howard Moody eight months earlier, declared that they would provide publicly advertised abortion counseling *and* abortion referral information to any pregnant woman who cared to contact them. Formally titled the Clergy Consultation Service on Abortion (CCS), the group was not so much an organization as a network, a network organized around a phone number and an answering machine located at Moody's Judson Memorial Baptist Church on the south side of Washington Square Park in Manhattan's Greenwich Village. Women who called in would initially be referred to one or another clergyman for a private, face-to-face conversation, and only in that context would a woman actually be given specific information on abortion providers. Many of CCS's referrals went to doctors in Puerto Rico, but some went to Milan Vuitch in Washington, with whom Lader had been in contact for some months. Others went to a doctor in Pennsylvania, and after some months an additional excellent provider was discovered in New Orleans. Referrals were made only to credible, licensed physicians practicing outside New York, and the CCS volunteers scrupulously avoided any comment on whether they believed their referral work was or was not legal. The initial announcement in the *Times* had taken place with considerable trepidation, but no prosecutorial initiatives ensued. Substantial numbers of pregnant women, however, did start calling Judson's special number, and it became clear within the first few weeks of CCS's operation that the essence of the program—providing referrals for actual, safe abortions—was clearly meeting a tremendous need that neither reform nor repeal advocates—apart from Lader and California's Pat Maginnis—had ever before directly begun to address. Perhaps just as significant as its tangible provision of a badly needed service, however, was CCS's open and aboveboard operating style, which conveyed to all who might take notice that abortion on request could hardly be presumed to be an immoral and despicable act if substantial numbers of upstanding clergymen were serving as volunteer middlemen between needy women and legitimate doctors.[94]

The immediate success of CCS, however, was not the only goal of Lader and his fellow New York activists. John Lassoe continued to coordinate discussions aimed at mounting a renewed New York state legislative effort in 1968, and Lader and Bill Ober continued their conversations about recruiting Wayne Decker or another willing doctor for an abortion test case. Harriet Pilpel sent Decker a full copy of the NYU law student's essay on the unconstitutionality of abortion statutes which had so impressed her back in April and which so thoroughly rebutted Cyril Means's notion that no liberty-based constitutional challenge to existing laws was even worth considering. Lader's hopes of pursuing a test case through the good offices of Knickerbocker Hospital fell through once it became clear that the hospital's director had had serious second thoughts about the institutional wisdom of joining in such a legally risky enterprise, but Ober introduced Lader to another sympathetic gynecologist, Bernie Nathanson, and Lader pondered whether a test case might be built around a fifteen-year-old New York teenager who was pregnant as a result of being raped by her stepfather.[95]

But such an extreme and fact-specific case would not speak to Lader and Pilpel's most basic hope that a constitutionally broad-gauged judicial challenge to existing antiabortion laws could indeed be enunciated, crafted, and filed. For that they would willingly, and at first eagerly, turn to the initial representative of a new and younger generation of liberalization advocates, a generation whose unquestioned inclinations ran toward repeal rather than reform, and—because they had indeed read *Griswold* while still in law school—toward the federal courts rather than toward state legislatures. The first representative of the new wave truly had still been at NYU Law School when *Griswold* was decided, but—as Pilpel had immediately recognized when she read his unpublished paper in mid-April—he was undeniably the first person to fully articulate on paper the vision of the future that would become *Griswold*'s true and remarkable legacy. Estelle Griswold never met Spurgeon LeRoy Lucas, Jr., but if indeed there were children of *Griswold*, Roy Lucas was certainly the first, and for the next five years he would, for better or worse, indisputably be the most important.

CHAPTER SIX

From Reform to Repeal:
The *Right* to Abortion,
1967–1969

Roy Lucas was only twenty-five years old when the initial draft of his law school essay arguing that a woman's right to choose abortion was a fundamental individual freedom protected by the U.S. Constitution's guarantee of personal liberty first had such a powerful and uplifting effect on Harriet Pilpel and Larry Lader. A native of Columbia, South Carolina, where his father sold insurance and served as a deacon in a Baptist church, Lucas had graduated from the University of South Carolina in 1963 with a degree in chemical engineering. He had applied for a prestigious Root-Tilden fellowship at New York University's law school, with the idea of perhaps pursuing a career in patent law, after seeing a bulletin board announcement of the program. A personal interview in Baltimore with an NYU selection committee which included U.S. Circuit Judge Simon E. Soboloff proved successful, and in September 1963, after attending the August 28 civil rights March on Washington, Lucas began his first year of classes at NYU.

Following an academically successful but otherwise unremarkable school year, Lucas spent the next summer working in the patent law department at Texas Instruments in Dallas, and then returned to New York to begin his second year of classes. The young, very southern-sounding student's top interest beyond his course work was the burgeoning civil rights revolution, and in early October Lucas and a classmate took an overnight train down to Washington in order to watch U.S. Solicitor General Archibald Cox argue the constitutionality of the newly passed Civil Rights Act of 1964 before the U.S. Supreme Court in two cases from Atlanta and Birmingham.

Decades later Lucas would remember that "the word 'abortion' did not enter my vocabulary or mind" until that second year of law school, and when it did, it did not come from a casebook. Shortly before Christmas Lucas's distraught girlfriend told him that she was pregnant, and Lucas frantically but discreetly started making inquiries about how they might solve this highly unwanted problem. Through one or another NYU faculty member Lucas was given telephone entree to a well-known figure whom he had never before heard of, Alan F. Guttmacher, and sometime in December 1964 Guttmacher explained to his young and unseen caller that he and his girlfriend needed to make plans for a brief holiday trip to San Juan, Puerto Rico, and should call in advance for an appointment with either a Dr. Otero or a Dr. Palmiero, both highly competent, American-trained specialists with whom Guttmacher was acquainted through old Baltimore connections. Lucas followed Guttmacher's instructions, made contact with the first of the recommended doctors, and flew to San Juan with his girlfriend. The clinic was in a "dingy, alien neighborhood," and while the procedure itself took place without complications, that did not change the fact that the entire ordeal was "degrading" and "not an uplifting experience" for them both. The "relationship ended because of this," and "[I] felt very bad about it," Lucas remembered years later.

That spring, with an eye towards gaining a good deal of public speaking experience, Lucas applied for and won a Rotary Foundation fellowship that would enable him to spend the 1965–1966 academic year at the University of Glasgow in Scotland while devoting much of his actual time to speaking appearances before scores of Rotary Clubs all around England and Scotland. He spent the initial summer working with a German patent lawyer in Stuttgart, where he met a young German woman, Uta Henkel, who soon became a close girlfriend, and in April 1966, just before returning to the United States, Roy and Uta were married in Germany. Lucas spent part of the ensuing summer back in Dallas at Texas Instruments, and part of it working for a New York law firm, Fish and Neave, and then began preparing for his third and final year of classes at NYU Law School.

Before heading to Glasgow, Lucas had already been elected to the staff of the *NYU Law Review*, but now, rather than return to the law review staff, Lucas decided that he would devote a significant proportion of his third year to another academic option, preparing a major essay as a senior-year project. His topic, one he had thought about while in the U.K., would be the constitutionality of American antiabortion statutes. His primary faculty mentor, Norman Dorsen, did not initially seem especially enthusiastic about Lucas's chosen topic, and so for formal sponsorship of his independent study Lucas turned to another experienced constitutional scholar who seemed somewhat more receptive, law school dean Robert B. McKay.

The subject was so novel, Lucas told a journalist three years later, that "People thought it was a weird idea. My professors kind of laughed at me, but I went ahead and spent six months at it." Looking back at his choice of topic some three decades later, Lucas acknowledged that his Puerto Rico experience was no doubt "one motivating factor" in his decision, as was the fact that during his year in the U.K. the British press had been full of reports concerning an ongoing abortion reform debate in the House of Lords. The English debate had resonated with his own feelings about his traumatic trip to Puerto Rico, but even before going to Britain, and especially upon his return, Lucas had been more than a little intrigued by the much-discussed June, 1965, Supreme Court decision in *Griswold*. During Lucas's year in Great Britain Robert McKay had been one of a number of legal scholars who had contributed to a special symposium issue of the *Michigan Law Review* on *Griswold*, but when Lucas looked at that December 1965 number, the essay that had far and away the greatest impact on him was the contribution by Tom Emerson.

"The first time I ever saw any mention in the literature of the possibility that there may be some constitutional limitations on abortion laws" was in Emerson's article, Lucas remembered several years later. Come the fall of 1966 Lucas was quite surprised that no one else had yet expanded upon Emerson's brief suggestion that *Griswold*'s privacy doctrine might well open the way "for an attack upon significant aspects of the abortion laws," and he began an intensive effort to read everything he could find, particularly in case law and legal literature, that in any way touched upon abortion. Lucas was much impressed with Larry Lader's newly published book on the subject, and he also paid full attention to the *New York Times*'s coverage of the early 1967 legislative debates on reform statutes in Albany and elsewhere. He took special note of how Harriet Pilpel stood out as a repeal supporter who seemed to appreciate the clear potential linkage between *Griswold* and abortion, and Lucas had even further opportunity to ponder *Griswold*'s significance in a civil rights seminar that he took with NAACP Legal Defense Fund attorney Robert Carter. Lucas's primary paper for Carter was a predecision study of a pending Supreme Court case, perhaps the best-named case in American legal history, *Loving* v. *Virginia*, where a state criminal statute outlawing interracial marriages was under constitutional challenge in an attack that relied significantly upon *Griswold*'s celebration of the importance of marriage and that would soon prove successful.[1]

Lucas made initial contact with Harriet Pilpel even before he completed work on his essay in the spring of 1967, and as Pilpel so pointedly told Cyril Means and Larry Lader in mid-April, she, like Lucas's NYU professors, was extremely impressed with the persuasive case his paper made that affirmative federal court challenges to the constitutionality of existing state antiabortion statutes might very well succeed. Robert McKay was so impressed with Lucas's paper that he gave it the highly unusual grade of A+, and Lucas, deeply encouraged by such enthusiastically supportive reactions to his work, resolved to revise and shorten the paper for publication in one or another law review following his June graduation. Fortunate enough to have already been offered assistant professorships in the law schools at both Florida State and the University of Alabama, Lucas decided to accept the latter position and early that summer he and Uta moved to Tuscaloosa, where Roy began teaching summer school and revising the paper.[2]

By the time he arrived in Tuscaloosa in the summer of 1967, Roy Lucas fully realized that his interest in a federal constitutional challenge to state antiabortion laws was not purely academic. A reform bill was under active but eventually unsuccessful consideration in the Alabama legislature that summer, but Lucas's first thought upon arriving in Alabama was to explore the possibilities for a declaratory judgment case against the state abortion statute. When Larry Lader wrote Lucas in early August seeking an update on the status of the Alabama reform bill, Lucas told him that he had already written to the three Alabama doctors whose names had appeared among the scores of supportive physicians from across the country who had endorsed Zad Leavy and Herma Hill Kay's amicus brief in the *Shively* case in California to see whether they might be interested in helping mount a challenge to the Alabama law. "The test case I am planning to prepare," Lucas told Lader, "would be a class action by a number of physicians and hospital abortion committee members for a declaratory judgment that the state has no power to interfere in physician-patient decisions concerning the termination of pregnancy." Revising his NYU paper had increased his confidence in both the substantive and the procedural aspects of such a case, Lucas explained, and he sent Lader both a short, two-page outline of the case strategy that he hoped to discuss with the Alabama doctors and a full copy of his lengthy revised essay.

Although a case would feature high-status physicians as the named plaintiffs, the substantive focus would be upon "the fundamental interests of a woman in marital privacy and personal autonomy in controlling her reproductive processes." *Griswold*, Lucas emphasized, "pointedly rested on the broad principle of marital privacy and the physician's right to advise on the use of contraceptives for the purpose of family planning. It follows, therefore, that state abortion laws may well be found unconstitutional when tested according to the same reasoning."

In the long revised paper, Lucas again emphasized that abortion ought to be acknowledged as "a fundamental right of marital privacy, human dignity, and personal autonomy reserved to the pregnant woman acting on the advice of a licensed physician," and that such a right was protected by the "values embodied in the express provisions of the Bill of Rights" and most specifically by an "altogether reasonable application" of *Griswold*. "The values implicit in the Bill of Rights suggest that the decision to bear or not bear a child is a fundamental individual right not subject to legislative abridgement—particularly in light of *Griswold*," Lucas explained. If this perspective was indeed constitutionally plausible, "a frontal attack on the very assumptions of abortion legislation can be made through judicial enforcement of the guarantees of human rights found in the" Bill of Rights. "The state interest in regulating abortion is a subjective judgment of value based upon a belief of a religious character," and if a constitutional challenge could be properly mounted, the odds were excellent that the U.S. Supreme Court would conclude that "abortion prohibitions violate substantive due process in contravention of values expressed in the Bill of Rights."[3]

An enthusiastic Lader immediately cited Lucas's conclusions in a final unsuccessful effort to convince the director of New York's small Knickerbocker Hospital to help sponsor a test case, and also invoked it in trying to convince John Lassoe of the Episcopal Diocese that such an effort ought to be welcomed at the church-affiliated St. Luke's Hospital. Bob Hall of ASA told an interviewer that "some day—probably after many of the state laws have been changed" by legislative reform—"there will be a test case in which the courts will declare all anti-abortion legislation unconstitutional," but that generating such a case would not be easy: "even when we get a woman willing to see herself on the front pages for months, we'll need to find a reputable doctor and reputable hospital willing to join her there." Lucas's strategy, unlike Hall and Lader's presumption, would require only willing doctors, and not an actual abortion or a cooperative hospital, but that important legal distinction was not readily appreciated. Hall was certain that "'abortion on demand' is just not going to happen in the foreseeable future," but that as increasing numbers of states gradually adopted reform bills, "eventually they will lead to complete legalization."

California's Garrett Hardin expressly disagreed with that final sentiment, insisting that "small reforms are the worst enemy of great reforms," but the major public abortion event of the fall was an implicitly *anti*reform symposium sponsored by the Joseph P. Kennedy, Jr., Foundation and the Harvard Divinity School over three days in mid-September in Washington, D.C.[4]

Rather grandiosely titled the International Conference on Abortion, the meeting's tacit purpose was clear enough from its advance agenda that Pat Maginnis and several California colleagues arrived on the first day to publicly picket the proceedings. Some repeal supporters, such as demographer Christopher Tietze, were included among the speakers, and Supreme Court Justice Potter Stewart was among at least one day's onlookers, but the heavy majority of participants were opposed to liberalization in any form. One Roman Catholic Florida doctor and legislator who had worked energetically on behalf of a reform bill in his state complained that the meeting "was a 'sell' job," and while many journalists recognized the same thing, *Newsweek* magazine published a two-page story on the symposium and told its readers that "the most surprising aspect of the entire conference was the wide-spread antipathy against abortion itself."[5] ASA's quarterly newsletter quietly noted how one Catholic publication had celebrated the conference as a "significant road-block . . . thrown in path of" ongoing reform efforts, but new liberalization groups were springing up in a variety of states such as Michigan and preexisting ones in states such as Illinois and Wisconsin were making new efforts to expand.[6]

In Georgia three Atlanta Unitarians, minister Edgar T. Van Buren, British-born attorney Alan Bonser, and Emory University psychologist Kenneth Anderson, met with state representative Richard Starnes, sponsor of the earlier reform bill, to map out a renewed reform effort in the 1968 legislature, and they soon announced creation of a new proreform group, Georgia Citizens for Hospital Abortions.[7] In Connecticut, Mystic attorney Richard M. Bowers, who had been interested in the subject for more than a year, took the lead in creating a new group that soon came to be called the Connecticut League for Abortion Law Reform. Hartford attorney Donald Cantor, who had spoken up on behalf of a nascent reform bill some months earlier after first encountering the subject at a local ACLU symposium, soon joined forces with Bowers, and among those attending the group's first meeting was Lee Buxton. Both Buxton and Estelle Griswold were soon elected to the new group's board of directors, but while Buxton now evinced a clear preference for repeal rather than reform, the group as a whole was slow to come to any decisive conclusion on the matter.[8]

If *Newsweek* unwittingly had thrown a major bouquet to liberalization opponents with its gullible coverage of the September conference, *Time* several weeks later featured the first prominent media story that reflected a distinct preference for repeal over reform. "Written by men, anti-abortion laws cannot quell the desperation of women for whom a particular pregnancy is a hateful foreign object," the story bluntly declared. It rebutted the notion that any significant proportion of women felt "deep guilt" after having abortions, and emphasized that "in fact, most women react with a feeling of great relief." The story noted the while a heavy majority of Americans endorsed abortions predicated upon a threat to a woman's health, an even greater proportion opposed abortion being available simply as matter of a woman's choice. As with other matters involving sex, *Time* commented, "the surveys suggest that Americans disapprove publicly what they practice privately."

The *Time* story went on to say that with regard to the Colorado, North Carolina, and California reform statutes, "the key question is whether limited legislation is any solution," since "the new laws merely codify what hospitals are already doing" and would provide legal abortions to only a very small percentage of women who wanted one. It noted how one well-known Roman Catholic legal scholar who had spoken at the September conference, Robert F. Drinan, had offered the novel analysis that from his *anti*abortion perspective, *repeal* of abortion statutes would be *preferable* to reform since it would remove the subject from governmental review rather than place the state in the position of expressly approving some abortions while disapproving others. The story then concluded with a final sentence that was explicitly instructive: "The way to deal with the problem forthrightly is on terms that permit the individual, guided by conscience and intelligence, to make a choice unhampered by archaic and hypocritical concepts and statutes."[9]

Time's remarkable piece touched only in passing on one aspect of the debate that more and more reformers and journalists were beginning to focus upon: how very few additional legal abortions actually were being performed pursuant to the new reform laws. California's revised statute would not take effect until November, but in both North Carolina and Colorado only about *twenty-five* legal abortions a month were taking place. "Hospitals are definitely leaning over backward to keep the number down," reform bill sponsor Richard Lamm told Larry Lader, and mental health ones were proving *more* difficult to obtain than before the new law had been passed. Few hospitals outside of Denver were performing any abortions, and even in the capital city most abortions were taking place at just a few facilities. Denver

General Hospital was accounting for more than one third of all abortions in the state, with two thirds of those taking place on psychiatric grounds, but even Denver General's three-doctor abortion committee was rejecting more than 20 percent of women who provided a psychiatric endorsement of their request. When Great Britain's new abortion statute was formally approved in late October, some American press accounts noted that it was distinctly more liberal than the Colorado law, but within medical circles the actual advent of the new reform measures, while eliminating much of the previous worry about potential legal vulnerability, also served to further highlight the inherently standardless charade involved in doctors deciding which women's "mental health" was sufficiently threatened by an unwanted pregnancy and which women's were not. "To get around the law is no substitute for bringing about a change in the law," one unhappy California psychiatrist wrote in his discipline's principal national journal, and gradually more and more signs began to appear that the passage of reform bills might actually serve to illuminate the inadequacy of therapeutic reform and the preferability of the seemingly far more radical step of repeal.[10]

Time's highlighting of Robert Drinan's unique and intriguing *anti*abortion argument *for* repeal rather than reform contributed significantly to a burst of reflective rethinking in some Roman Catholic intellectual circles. The Jesuit magazine *America*, in a prominent editorial introducing a special issue on abortion that included a piece by Drinan, asked "should the Catholic Church ... adopt a more flexible attitude and engage actively in abortion law reform?" and without pause answered yes, "We think it should." The journal explained its surprising position by emphasizing that "changes are going to come (and come quickly) whether we oppose them or not," and even a much more hard-line contributor, Fordham law professor Robert Byrn, pessimistically estimated that some twenty states would soon adopt reform statutes and that three years hence "1970 will see ... the abortion movement triumphant." Another antiabortion Catholic law professor extended *America*'s analysis and concluded that since abortions within the first thirteen weeks of pregnancy involved only "an organism which is striving to develop the form of a human being," rather than "an identifiable human organism" as was the case with more mature fetuses, such early procedures could indeed be tolerated. Drinan, offering a fuller explanation of his preference in another essay rather quixotically titled "The Right of the Fetus to Be Born," maintained that "repeal would not mean that the state approves of abortion but only that it declines to regulate it." The moral imperative, he explained, was "to keep the state out of the business of decreeing who is to be born." The number of abortion essays appearing in a wide range of religious, legal, and medical journals continued to increase, but nowhere was the evidence of the growing move toward liberalization more marked than in such Roman Catholic contributions.[11]

The intellectual ferment was of course not all-controlling, however, and in mid-October of 1967, when idiosyncratic abortion activist Bill Baird finally stood trial for his April arrest at Boston University, Massachusetts Superior Court Judge Donald B. Macaulay immediately pronounced Baird guilty of improperly distributing contraceptive materials after a proceeding that lasted less than two hours. Baird's student supporters had publicly denounced Planned Parenthood's lack of interest in his case and turned out more than two hundred strong for the hearing, where Baird, seeking a decision on the constitutionality of the Massachusetts statute, waived a jury trial and presented no defense witnesses to rebut anything that police lieutenant Joseph Jordan said in response to questions from assistant district attorney Joseph R. Nolan. Baird's volunteer lawyer, Joseph Balliro, cross-examined Jordan and sought to convince Macaulay that the Massachusetts statute was unconstitutional, but the judge was unpersuaded. He did agree to delay Baird's sentencing until Baird's appeal could be heard by the Massachusetts Supreme Judicial Court, and Baird unsurprisingly was unfazed by his conviction. "I know I will win on appeal," he told journalists, only some of whom publicized his declaration that he was actively referring pregnant women to cooperative American doctors for illegal abortions. "I know the law won't have a snowball's chance in hell of being declared constitutional."[12]

Another significant but much less publicized call for repeal of reproductive controls came at the second annual convention of the National Organization for Women (NOW) in mid-November of 1967. Founded just a year earlier, NOW was still a low-visibility group in the national press, and until well-known author Betty Friedan pressed the issue of endorsing abortion law repeal at the 1967 meeting, NOW had not previously addressed the issue. Friedan's effort succeeded, but only at the cost of profoundly alienating a significant number of members who, while not necessarily antiabortion, did not believe that the issue had to be addressed by a women's rights organization. Many of the women who left NOW over this disagreement several months later created a new group, the Women's Equity Action League (WEAL), but national NOW did not follow up on its endorsement of repeal by taking any active role in legislative efforts or potential test case discussions.[13]

More important than the national NOW repeal resolution was the involvement of some NOW members in local-level liberalization efforts, and nowhere was that more significantly the case than in New York, where Long Island housewife Ruth P. Cusack, who lived in the home district of state Assembly Republican Minority Leader Perry B. Duryea, quickly emerged as the most influential lobbyist on behalf of a 1968 legislative effort. Cusack had recently moved to New York from California, where her initial interest in liberalization had been stimulated by news of Garrett Hardin's unprecedented public lectures in favor of repeal. Hardin had introduced Cusack to Pat Maginnis and her colleagues in SHA, and even in 1965 Cusack had written to her assemblyman, former reform bill sponsor John T. Knox, to *oppose* Beilenson's therapeutic measure on the grounds that its passage "would benefit very few women" and might "lead to complacency, making it difficult to arrive at the only decent solution to the matter of abortion, which is the repeal of any laws whatsoever which prevent any woman who wants one from obtaining an abortion." She had told Knox that reform failed to acknowledge "the right of a woman to own her own body, the right to decide for herself if and when she is to bear a child," and she had pointed out how "it is degrading for a woman to have to petition a committee for the right to receive simple medical treatment to terminate an unwanted pregnancy, almost as degrading as forcing a woman to obtain this service illegally." The "only humane approach," Cusack had declared, "is for a woman to be able to receive an abortion from a physician at her own request, quickly, quietly, and inexpensively."

By late 1967 Cusack was voicing similar sentiments to both Duryea and 1967 reform bill sponsor Al Blumenthal as she tried to convince New York liberalization backers that repeal was infinitely preferable to reform. Cusack advised one friend that "abortion should be a civil right," and she privately explained that while she "was upset to find the ASA so conservative," the discovery had "strengthened my resolve to work for repeal." In one letter to fellow Unitarians, Cusack noted that "abortion on request . . . permits freedom of choice, a cherished American principle," and emphasized that Margaret Sanger's fifty-year-old "fight for a woman's right to birth control . . . will not be won until *every* method of birth control, including abortion, is available to every woman who wants it." Cusack wrote to every legislator in the state, describing abortion as "a private decision between physician and patient" and contending that "there is no legal justification for making abortion a crime any more than there would be legal justification for declaring it a crime to use birth control pills or condoms." She asked both Blumenthal and Duryea to champion repeal rather than reform in the 1968 legislature, and while Blumenthal was noncommittal, Duryea, who at first may not have fully understood the distinction, told Cusack that "I totally agree with your position." ASA commissioned a statewide public opinion survey, which found that 25 percent of New Yorkers said they knew at least one woman who had had an abortion and which registered a whopping 75 percent support for therapeutic reform. Even among Roman Catholics who said that religion was very important to them, 63 percent endorsed therapeutic liberalization, and only 17 percent of the entire sample opposed any changes in the law.[14]

The *New York Times*, extending its support of liberalization beyond the editorial page, opened 1968 with a prominent overview story informing readers that "many more states" would soon follow the abortion reform lead of Colorado, North Carolina, and California. Robert McCoy of Minnesota's liberalization group stated that "It's really remarkable how much the climate of public opinion has changed in just a few years," and he added that "I wouldn't be surprised if several states including Minnesota soon repealed their abortion laws." The story also highlighted the ongoing referral work being done by Howard Moody's group and Larry Lader, and cited Al Blumenthal, who had just reintroduced a reform bill, as estimating that the prospects for passage were "much improved." The very next day New York Governor Nelson Rockefeller announced his support for liberalization, and the *Times* gave his statement page-one coverage and also prominently cited the results of the ASA poll. A spokesman for the Roman Catholic Archdiocese of New York, Monsignor William F. McManus, requested time to reply to one television station's endorsement of liberalization and used his appearance to object to any type of therapeutic reform in the strongest possible terms. "If feticide is carried out for the prevention of defect, would not infanticide be a logical and medically preferable consequence? Errors in prenatal diagnosis, dangers to the mother, and sacrifice of normal fetuses would be avoided" if infant-killing were adopted in place of abortion.[15]

Sensing a need to generate additional legislative support in advance of any serious consideration of Blumenthal's measure, Governor Rockefeller quickly followed up on his endorsement of liberalization by appointing just the sort of special study commission that Blumenthal himself had recommended a year earlier. Of the eleven members, the four Roman Catholics, who included Monsignor

McManus and Fordham law professor Robert Byrn, were publicly presumed to be liberalization opponents, while at least another six, including Alan Guttmacher, Cyril Means, and demographer Christopher Tietze, were all believed to support at least therapeutic reform.

The appointment of what was formally called the Governor's Select Committee to Review the State's Abortion Law significantly fueled the already burgeoning private debate amongst liberalization backers over the relative merits of reform versus repeal. Chicago's Lonny Myers had just written to ASA president Bob Hall and ASA's board members, including Alan Guttmacher and Larry Lader, to demand that ASA's published literature at least acknowledge that repeal was a plausible option. Bob Hall responded organizationally by maintaining that "The contention that abortion is an individual right, though shared by most of us who work in this field, cannot be officially expressed by a tax-exempt education group" such as ASA. Larry Lader, whose board term was expiring, told Myers that Hall in a certain way was quite correct, since "ASA's tax-free status makes it generally ineffective." He added that "I think we will have to form an organization for complete legalization here when enough people can get the time." Two additional board members, Lader's doctor friend Bill Ober and prominent ethicist Joseph Fletcher, similarly told Myers that they essentially agreed with her. "Nobody should be compelled to bear a child against her will," Fletcher responded, but "most of the ASA people are much more conservative ethically, especially the medical members." Ober concurred that "abortion is a private matter between the woman and her doctor," but the far more influential Guttmacher replied to Myers's letter with much the same message he had been voicing for many years. In his role on Rockefeller's commission, Guttmacher explained, "I shall not attempt to repeal the statute," because "Such an attempt would be impractical and the people are not ready for it." He would "try for something broader than the ALI," however, by proposing that abortions also be allowed for all women with three or more children, for all women over the age of forty, for all unmarried girls under eighteen, and in all situations where the parents' circumstances "would create an adverse environment for a child." Guttmacher did not explain why he perceived such a significant distinction between simple repeal and such a potentially very liberal list of allowable exceptions, but he nonetheless remained a surprising holdout from the rapidly growing sentiment for repeal.[16]

In early February 1968 the Assembly Codes Committee voted 12 to 4 to send Blumenthal's reform bill to the floor, but amid journalistic prognostications that the measure's chances were "dubious, at best,"

Blumenthal announced that floor action would be delayed until after Rockefeller's special commission concluded its study and submitted its report. Privately Blumenthal told repeal advocate Ruth Cusack that "a majority is not now obtainable for the view you espouse" and that "the only feasible approach is an abortion law which would permit abortions for medical indications and for rape and incest." Liberalization proponents announced creation of a new umbrella-group coalition, Organizations for Abortion Law Reform, which included supporters of repeal as well as reform, and in late February Rockefeller's commission held a day long hearing in New York City at which a long list of witnesses, including Cusack and Harriet Pilpel, appeared to testify.[17]

Four weeks later, by the surprisingly large margin of 8 to 3, the commission submitted to the governor a fifty-page majority report calling for the enactment of a liberalized statute reaching somewhat beyond the standard ALI provisions. The one Roman Catholic woman on the panel had joined with the majority, and Rockefeller announced that he "concurred fully" with the recommendations, although he did decline to endorse one specific, Guttmacher-style provision allowing abortions for women who already had four or more children. The three committee dissenters submitted a separate statement far longer than the majority report, and a spokesman for the state's Roman Catholic bishops denounced the recommendations as "shocking and appalling." Howard Moody's Clergy Consultation Service expressed "deep disappointment" that the majority recommendations went no further than they did, but four days after the report was submitted a hopeful Blumenthal proceeded to a floor debate and roll call vote on his reform bill in the state assembly. Proponents had believed they had three or four votes more than necessary, but once the roll call itself got underway, several anticipated supporters unexpectedly voted no and Blumenthal interrupted the tally and moved to recommit. "We had four votes we needed and they backed out," Blumenthal candidly told Albany reporters. "It's dead for this year. We'll absolutely try again next year." His most consistent supporter, the *New York Times*, termed the defeat "more disappointing" than in 1967 but confidently predicted that "the climate for reform should continue to improve."[18]

While the New York measure had been awaiting that frustrating final outcome, reform proponents in Georgia had mounted a far more successful 1968 reprise of their previous year's campaign. Senate Judiciary Committee Chairman Robert H. Smalley, Jr., who had not supported Representative Richard L. Starnes's 1967 ALI-style bill, now took the lead in revising Starnes's measure in close collaboration with

Medical Association of Georgia staff members Jim Moffett and John L. Moore. They settled on a four-month residency requirement plus a provision mandating that abortions could take place only in certain better-equipped hospitals that were approved by the nationwide Joint Commission on Accreditation of Hospitals (JCAH), and in early January Smalley himself introduced the revised bill. A new opposition group which had been formed by two Catholic housewives, the "Concerned Committed Citizens," spoke out against the bill and told journalists they were unhappy with the "defeatist" attitude of Georgia's Roman Catholic hierarchy. No diocesan spokesman was among twenty-one opponents who testified against the bill at a January 16 hearing, and while a number of prominent doctors, including W. Newton Long and Robert Hatcher, spoke on behalf of the measure, the most conspicuous opponent was Atlanta attorney Ferdinand Buckley. Two days after the hearing Smalley's committee endorsed the bill on a vote of 5 to 2, and two weeks later in an initial floor vote the full senate approved the measure by a tally of 33 to 17. The Georgia house made some slight changes in the bill during February, and then on February 26 both the senate, by 39 to 11, and the house, by the overwhelming margin of 144 to 11, passed a final version. Georgia's notoriously segregationist governor, Lester Maddox, had indicated little interest in the issue, and while both Atlanta newspapers encouraged him to sign the bill, Maddox took no action whatsoever and hence on April 15 the Georgia reform statute became law without his signature.[19]

"Emotionalism was strikingly absent" from the 1968 Georgia debate, a thorough contemporaneous study accurately concluded, and neither the passage of Georgia's new law nor the subsequent approval of a similar ALI-style reform measure in Maryland received anywhere near the amount of national notice that had been accorded the 1967 reform successes in Colorado, North Carolina, and California. In Florida and Hawaii reform bills failed to get out of committee, but since many state's legislatures met only biennially, 1968 was a far quieter year legislatively than 1967. In Connecticut a legislative study commission announced that it would recommend reform to the 1969 legislature, and in New Jersey, where local liberalization groups had sprung up in both Princeton and Plainfield, the state medical society voiced its backing for therapeutic reform. In Texas Dr. Hugh Savage had continued his efforts to win firm Texas Medical Association (TMA) backing for a 1969 reform bill, and TMA's 1968 annual meeting decided to take a mail poll of the full membership in order to determine whether the organization would indeed endorse reform.[20]

In California, liberalization advocates held a statewide conference on abortion in Santa Barbara in February, a meeting that clearly reflected how passage of the Beilenson reform bill had dramatically *narrowed* the differences that previously had separated reformers from supporters of repeal. CCTA, the Sunnen-funded reform organization, had essentially gone into eclipse following passage of the 1967 bill, and the exceedingly modest impact of the new law was leading more and more reformers to conclude that repeal indeed should be pursued. The two leading California attorneys, Zad Leavy and Norma Zarky, had both thought about mounting a potential test case, but as Zarky indicated at the Santa Barbara conference, it was presumed that some sort of charges against a doctor, either by a local prosecutor or by the state Board of Medical Examiners, would be needed to set such a case in motion. The board was still administratively pursuing its 1966 charges against J. Paul Shively and his colleagues over their earlier rubella abortions, and Zarky bluntly told the Santa Barbara meeting that "a court case is a gamble and I do not think this movement should hinge on a gamble." Garrett Hardin and Pat Maginnis both suggested that sponsorship of a 1970 statewide popular vote on a repeal initiative should be considered, and CCTA lent its support to that idea while also midwifing the creation of a Los Angeles-based Clergy Consultation Service referral group modeled on Howard Moody's success in New York.[21]

Joseph Sunnen had decided to create a repeal advocacy group, called the Nevada Committee for the Rights of Women, in a neighboring state where legislative passage of a 1969 repeal bill was thought to be possible, and with funds from Sunnen channeled through CCTA, the Nevada group was in operation by late May. New external funding was also being sought by ASA, which was primarily being supported by two members of the Rockefeller family and by heiress Cordelia Scaife May, but ASA's lack of "an aggressive program" led several foundations to demur. One significant ASA contributor, idiosyncratic liberal millionaire Stewart Mott, argued angrily with Bob Hall over ASA's relative moderation and strenuously objected to the organization's heavy investment in an upcoming fall conference on abortion at a Virginia resort. Mott dropped his support entirely, but Hall maintained his commitment to ASA's restricted role, even while telling reporters that he personally favored repeal and hoped that "the Supreme Court will declare all these laws unconstitutional."[22]

In late March 1968 the American Civil Liberties Union further strengthened its endorsement of liberalization by additionally declaring that "a woman has a right to have an abortion . . . prior to the viability of the fetus," and six weeks later the American College of Obstetricians and Gynecologists endorsed extensive liberalization.[23] Much more importantly, however, in late May Lonny Myers's Chicago group, ICMCA, formally endorsed Myers's recommendation that initial steps be taken to create a new nationwide organization to bring together all backers of abortion law repeal. Myers envisioned holding a founding conference in Chicago sometime the following winter, and by mid-July, thanks to the munificence of two Chicago businessmen, the nascent and as yet unnamed national organization had two staff members planning the winter conference. Two weeks later Myers went to New York to meet several of the activists there and was pleased to have Larry Lader remind her that he had suggested the idea of creating just such a national repeal organization to her in a letter six months earlier. They enthusiastically agreed to join forces in assembling the Chicago conference, and quickly recruited California's Garrett Hardin to provide further geographical balance among the meeting's top sponsors.[24]

Lader suggested to Myers and Hardin that they call their new organization the National Association for Repeal of Abortion Laws (NARAL), but his overall outlook on their prospects was not optimistic. "Experience shows that getting a bill through a state legislature to repeal all laws is an agonizing and possibly fruitless procedure." Hence "the main attack" should "be through the courts," but while "a few of us have worked on this a long time," we "have still failed to get a prominent gynecologist in an established hospital to launch such a case." As he had learned from his and Bill Ober's experience with Knickerbocker Hospital, "The key question is whether it must be done in a hospital or whether a doctor in his office provides a reasonable framework." Lader doubted the latter option, and thus "I am still at a loss as to how to find the gynecologist and hospital to do this." Therefore "the only practical immediate program I see is an extension of the clergymen's committees and referral services," which required significant work, especially with regard to identifying willing *and* competent physicians. Lader's favorite doctor, Milan Vuitch, had been raided and arrested by Washington, D.C., detectives four months earlier, and although Vuitch could shift his practice between offices in Maryland and D.C., many of the New York clergy referrals began to be directed to a physician in New Orleans, while Lader sent others to a group of providers in the Riverdale section in the Bronx. The New York activists, like those in California, no longer had any doubts about the utter inadequacy of reform laws; as CCS coordinator Howard Moody and his chief administrative aide, Arlene Carmen, frankly put it, "our day-to-day work taught us how few women wanted abortions for the reasons most liberals conceded were justifiable."[25]

By mid-1968 even the mainstream press was beginning to question the value of therapeutic statutes like the one in Colorado, where the *New York Times* reported a grand total of only 289 legal abortions had been performed during its first year on the books. Reform bill sponsor Dick Lamm indicated that he was extremely unhappy at how conservative doctors and hospitals had been in implementing the new law, but Dr. Myron C. Waddell, a former president of the Colorado State Medical Society, told one reporter that "It's working beautifully." The institutional review procedure mandated by the law, he explained, has "given real stature to the hospital committees; the committee members have the final word, and they call the shots as they see them." Needless to say, this was exactly the medical attitude that repeal proponents wanted to free female abortion applicants from having to experience.[26]

Larry Lader's utter pessimism about the prospects for initiating a test case that could lead to a successful voiding of existing statutes was about to undergo a friendly and most welcome challenge, however. Roy Lucas had spent an interesting twelve months teaching law in Alabama, and while he had had no success in persuading any of the state's leading gynecologists to become voluntary test case plaintiffs, he had had his NYU Law School paper accepted for publication in the June 1968 issue of the *North Carolina Law Review* and had gotten some initial real-world legal experience. Quite curious about the newly emerging field of students' rights cases, Lucas had driven down to Montgomery to watch one particular case contesting the expulsion of a student newspaper editor from Alabama's Troy State University be tried before nationally known U.S. District Judge Frank M. Johnson. The volunteer attorney representing the student, Morris Dees, was one of the small number of Alabama lawyers working with the ACLU, and after Lucas introduced himself and expressed his interest, Dees later graciously offered to allow Lucas to handle the case when the university unsuccessfully appealed an unfavorable decision to the U.S. Court of Appeals. It was Lucas's first courtroom experience, and while Dees believed that the ACLU's litigation priorities needed some reordering, he mentioned Lucas's interest in students' rights issues to ACLU southern regional director Charles "Chuck" Morgan. Through Morgan's contacts Lucas ended up spending a good part of the spring of 1968 writing an amicus brief on behalf of the U.S. National Student Association for an important Supreme Court case, *Tinker* v. *Des Moines Independent Community School District*, which would be argued that coming fall.

By the end of the spring Lucas was hoping to find some foundation funding for a book-length study of student rights and academic freedom cases, but the widespread discussion that had sprung up around his abortion article even before its actual publication resulted in an unforseen grant offer: Bob Hall's ASA, which had already given Cyril Means financial support for a historical inquiry into the origins of American antiabortion laws, asked Lucas if he would devote the first half of his summer to preparing a model court brief for just the sort of declaratory judgment case challenging the constitutionality of abortion statutes that he had outlined in his article. Lucas eagerly accepted and set to work, and just several weeks later he was presented with yet another attractive opportunity: one of the New York foundations he had approached about his students' rights work, the Twentieth Century Fund, invited him to join its staff as a program officer. Lucas had presumed he would remain a law professor, perhaps somewhere other than Tuscaloosa, until some recent conversations with Dees had led him to ponder Dees's idea that another liberal litigation group should be created to handle issues such as economic indigency and educational rights that were not being fully addressed by the ACLU. Dees was about to have the financial wherewithal to make his idea a reality, for prior to turning back to the practice of law, he had created a phenomenally successful mail-order cookbook company that he now was in the process of selling to the Times-Mirror Corporation for some six million dollars. Once the sale was concluded, a new litigation institute could become a reality, and an interim New York base for Lucas at a well-established public policy foundation would supply a perfect lead-in for the eventual opening of a New York office for such an institute. Lucas immediately accepted the Twentieth Century Fund offer, and set to work finishing the model abortion brief for ASA before packing up to move from Tuscaloosa to New York.[27]

In early July Lucas sent copies of the final draft of a 106-page model brief to both ASA and to ACLU legal director Mel Wulf. Eleanor Holmes Norton, Wulf's deputy, had suggested that the ACLU look into the possibility of an abortion case even before she had read an advance copy of Lucas's article, but perusing it led her to renew her request that the ACLU approach Hugh Hefner's Playboy Foundation for financial backing. "Are there some bunnies we can get who have particular influence with management?" Norton jokingly asked. Wulf too was very excited about Lucas's "really first-class" constitutional analysis, and even before Lucas first arrived in New York in mid-July, Wulf explicitly asked him if he would be willing to take charge of organizing a number of cases against different states' abortion statutes. Lucas responded enthusi-astically, telling Wulf that the new brief could serve "as a working model for cases to make America free for abortionists."

In a cover memo to ASA, Lucas explained that declaratory judgment cases could raise the fundamental issue of the unconstitutionality of antiabortion statutes "without the risk of a physician's license, without embarrassment to patients, and without the emotion-charged clamor too often brought on by opposition to legislative reform." Since by fed-eral statute such constitutional challenges to state laws could be heard by special three-judge district courts, whose decisions were then directly reviewable by the U.S. Supreme Court, such cases also reduced the amount of time and money that normally would be required for an initial district court decision and then intermediate review by one of the federal circuit courts of appeal. Such a condensed timetable would allow for "a final decision in slightly more than two years after the suit is filed," Lucas explained.

Substantively, such a case would allege that certain crucial terms in abortion laws, such as "life" and "health," were so inherently imprecise as to make those statutes void and unconstitutional on grounds of vagueness. More significantly, the suit would also contend that the First Amendment's "freedom of association includes the physician-patient relationship, and that treatment of the patient is a constitution-ally protected feature of this relationship unless the state can show an overriding interest." Additionally, "a patient has a fundamental right to regulate the size of her family," a right that "is a corollary of the right to marital privacy" enshrined in *Griswold*.

In mid-July, just after arriving in New York from Alabama and just before flying to Europe to see his wife's family, Lucas met with Mel Wulf, Harriet Pilpel, and Bob Hall and Jimmye Kimmey of ASA to dis-cuss preparation of an actual declaratory test case. While all agreed that Lucas's model brief would be the basis for the suit, the group told Lucas "that the brief should emphasize more strongly the rights-of-the-physician argument." Everyone concurred that they needed the benefit of Cyril Means's ongoing work into the history of abortion statutes, but the major focus of discussion was on *where* an initial test case should be brought, and particularly on whether some reform statute should be challenged in addition to one or more cases against traditional antiabortion laws. After considerable exchange they decided that the first case would be brought against New York's fairly represen-tative statute, and that "Dr. Hall will get a prestigious group of M.D.'s ... to act as plaintiffs as well as women who have been denied abortions in hospitals. We have to decide what kind of affidavits we want from the plaintiffs." Getting these necessities squared away would certainly take at least several months, but by sometime late in 1968 or early in 1969, the small group agreed, a constitutional challenge that would probably implicate every antiabortion statute in America ought to be underway.[28]

In late July the hopes of many progressive American Roman Catholics for a clear signal of doctrinal moderation on matters of sexuality and reproduction were thoroughly dashed when the Vatican released a new papal encyclical staunchly reiterating the church's hardline opposition to any and all forms of "artificial" birth control. Demographic studies had continued to show that more and more Roman Catholic American women were forsaking traditional church teachings in their own private reproductive choices, with one survey indicating that the proportion of Catholic women using diaphragms, the pill, or some other "artificial" method was now well over 50 percent and indeed approaching two thirds.[29]

But litigation developments would remain unaffected by such doctrinal disappointments, and just several days later a California Superior Court judge fully vindicated Dr. J. Paul Shively's effort to dismiss the state Board of Medical Examiners' ongoing effort to administratively discipline him for the rubella abortions he had performed four years earlier. Shively, Judge Andrew J. Eyman concluded, had "acted in good faith in accordance with the practices and procedures recognized and approved by those reasonably skilled in his profession." The board declared that it would appeal its loss to the California Supreme Court and continue its similar proceedings against Shively's colleagues, but a potentially even more significant legal showdown was looming in California's high court over a criminal conviction of a well-known Beverly Hills gynecologist, Leon P. Belous, who had been found guilty of referring a distraught pregnant college student to a Mexican doctor who had moved his abortion practice into southern California even though he lacked an American medical license.

Leon Belous had been an active although far from central member of CCTA, the Sunnen-sponsored reform group, even before his August 1966 indictment, but none of his abortion reform colleagues knew of his unpublicized criminal predicament until Zad Leavy by chance happened to walk into his actual trial in mid-January of 1967. Belous had practiced medicine in California for more than thirty-five years, and while many female liberalization backers were extremely supportive when word of his trial—and conviction—first spread among abortion activists, most reform-minded physicians had far more ambivalent feelings. Many were not troubled by their belief that Belous himself had quietly been doing significant numbers of abortions for many years, but almost all believed that the particular circumstance in which he was arrested was one in which he was receiving kickbacks from the practitioner to whom he was making the referrals.

Leavy himself had handled the initial appeal of Belous's conviction to a three-judge panel of the Second District Court of Appeals, but the appellate panel rejected Leavy's attempt to invoke *Griswold* by saying simply that the pregnant student whom Belous referred had been unmarried. The panel clearly read the trial evidence as showing that Belous did indeed receive kickbacks for such referrals, and affirmed his conviction without further ado. Belous engaged two well-known California civil rights attorneys, A. L. Wirin and Fred Okrand, to quarterback his appeal to the California Supreme Court, and the southern California ACLU affiliate swiftly asked Norma Zarky to prepare an amicus brief on their behalf. Belous's conviction had taken place prior to the enactment of the Beilenson reform bill, but the limited provisions of the new law offered Belous no legal shelter and in no way altered the basic constitutional arguments that could again be made on his behalf in this next appeal. The California activists consequently concluded that *Belous*, rather than *Shively*, might now be the best vehicle for confronting California's high court with the essential issue of the underlying constitutionality of antiabortion statutes, and thus CCTA's leadership put aside its earlier ambivalence and agreed to lend a prestigious hand on Belous's behalf.

Los Angeles attorney Charles T. Munger, an important figure in California legal circles and an unobstrusive financial supporter of both CCTA and the Los Angeles clergy referral service, similarly recognized that *Belous* could well be a crucial case. Along with his extremely wealthy friends and investment partners, Warren and Susan Buffett of Omaha, Nebraska, Munger volunteered to finance and otherwise facilitate a major amicus effort by CCTA, prominent doctors, and well-known attorneys. Zad Leavy would prepare another brief along the lines of his landmark 1966 contribution at an earlier stage in *Shively*, and CCTA, through Munger's good offices, would also engage one of the most prestigious attorneys in the state, former California bar association president Burnham Enersen, to offer the state supreme court oral argument on behalf of the amici supporting Dr. Belous's constitutional claims. "We need the establishment," Munger straightforwardly told Leavy in explaining his carefully conceived strategy. In early

October the high court scheduled oral argument of Belous's appeal for early 1969, and the California attorneys began drafting briefs that had some chance of spawning abortion law liberalization that might reach far beyond the 1967 therapeutic reforms.[30]

With Roy Lucas off in Europe and then busy getting settled in at the Twentieth Century Fund, two months passed without any progress toward the planned test case. New York activist Ruth Cusack, now the chairperson of an abortion committee created by the New York chapter of NOW, was busy investigating the possibilities for a repeal rather than a reform bill in the 1969 session of the New York legislature, and in August of 1968 she succeeded in recruiting a Republican assembly-woman from Ithaca whom she had first met at a NOW meeting at the home of Betty Friedan, Constance E. Cook, as a willing sponsor of a 1969 repeal bill. A six-year veteran of the legislature and a graduate of Cornell Law School, the forty-nine-year-old Cook was well-respected in Albany, and when Cusack informed Republican assembly leader Perry Duryea of this new development, Duryea answered that "I feel confident that I could support a repealer introduced" by Cook and vol-unteered "to assist in any way possible." Cusack and her colleagues lined up Manhattan assemblyman Franz Leichter as a second sponsor of the repeal measure, and turned their efforts toward attempting to persuade Al Blumenthal *not* to reintroduce his reform bill in the upcoming session so as to leave the field clear for an all-out battle for repeal.[31]

In mid-October Lucas and his colleagues on what they had come to call the "Ad Hoc Test Case Committee" finally turned their attention to the litigation plans that had been left hanging since their decisive meet-ing in July. Hall and ASA had not yet firmly recruited any M.D. or patient plaintiffs, and while Lucas had considered the possibility that they might wait until a California decision was issued, after a little reflection he decided that they had best proceed very early in 1969 so that initial argument in the New York case could take place in advance of any potentially unfavorable outcome in *Belous*. He believed the like-lihood of "great success" in the declaratory case was "very high," but the most serious obstacle within the small New York group was Cyril Means's continuing insistence that no *Griswold*-style constitutional challenge to abortion statutes had any credible chance of success. Means's lengthy inquiry into the history of New York's antiabortion statute had convinced him that the *sole* legislative purpose for enacting the nineteenth-century abortion ban had been dire concern about the dangers that the procedure entailed for women's lives and health in that medically unsophisticated era. Means zealously believed that with the twentieth-century advent of medical knowledge that made abortion extremely safe when carried out by a knowledgeable practitioner in sterile surroundings, antiabortion statutes that *had* been legitimate in their original day and age had *become* unconstitutional as the factual predicate motivating their enactment had evaporated. "Judges are much more likely to accept a historical argument" than any privacy-oriented reasoning that a woman's individual choice was a fundamental liberty. Thus it was "impossible" for Means to concur in Lucas's brief, and he urged the test case committee to substitute his historical argument for "the to us obvious proposition that constitutional wisdom was born with Harriet Pilpel, Roy Lucas, et al."[32]

Lucas and his colleagues brushed aside Means's idiosyncratic contentions and pressed ahead with their plans. Thoughts of preparing an additional amicus brief for *Belous* were put aside after an initial draft of Norma Zarky's planned submission easily convinced both Lucas and Mel Wulf that the essential constitutional claims were already in good hands, and in early November, just after Richard M. Nixon's hard-fought presidential election victory over Hubert H. Humphrey, Lucas sketched out a full game plan for the New York case. An early 1969 filing would generate an initial three-judge panel decision by late summer or early fall. Review by the U.S. Supreme Court then would take place sometime in 1970, with a decision being issued no later than the spring of 1971. Nixon's victory gave Lucas serious concern, for "at present there is a delicate balance" on the high court which could easily change for the worse if Nixon was presented with the opportunity to name one or more new justices to seats vacated because of death or retirement. Lucas believed that they might very well have a majority receptive to their case on the present court, but Nixon's victory meant that time was of the essence. If the New York case did not reach the high court until 1971, Lucas warned his colleagues, their prospects might be endangered, for "Douglas and Harlan may not last that long. They are two of the principal figures upon whom we are depending, but they are also two of the oldest."[33]

In mid-November virtually all professional supporters of abortion law liberalization gathered for ASA's long-planned International Conference in Hot Springs, Virginia. Just the week before, both national Planned Parenthood (PPFA) and the American Public Health Association (APHA) publicly endorsed quasi-repeal resolutions, with the APHA statement speaking of a woman's choice as a "personal right." The *New York Times* noted these "advanced positions" while condemning New York's absence of therapeutic exceptions as "a tragedy and a disgrace," but a cautious-sounding Alan Guttmacher told *Time* magazine that anything more than reform was legislatively impossible because "the public does not want abortion on demand and is not prepared to accept it." Efforts to prepare for 1969 reform bills were going forward in states such as Michigan and Minnesota, and in Texas the state medical association poll of its members had found 4,435 in favor of liberalization and only 536 against, but more and more national coverage, like that *Time* story, was highlighting how the very modest increase in the number of legal abortions allowed under reform statutes was "too small even to make an appreciable dent in the number of illegal" ones. Lonny Myers and her colleagues were still pointing towards a national repeal conference in February in Chicago to launch their nascent idea of NARAL as an organization, and in the state of Washington the sixteen-member Citizens' Abortion Discussion Group, which had privately been discussing liberalization options since January 1967 without taking any public action, announced its existence and said it would champion a repeal bill in the 1969 state legislature. State Senator Joel Pritchard, one of several already-committed sponsors, told journalists that "our chances look good."[34]

The Hot Springs ASA conference followed an academic format, with different panels of speakers focusing upon different aspects of abortion. A major initial speech was delivered by one of ASA's principal financial patrons, John D. Rockefeller III, who said that repeal "will inevitably be the long-range answer" and that in the interim reform statutes had to offer "a broad interpretation of mental health" that would allow many if not all women to qualify under such a provision. California's Ned Overstreet, in a talk that was highlighted in the *New York Times*'s coverage of the conference, explained how his state's reform statute "really satisfies no one" and emphasized that "the voices raised in favor of abolishing all abortion statutes are growing in number and vigor with a speed that is simply astonishing." In particular, Overstreet observed, *Griswold* "is being quoted increasingly frequently as a manifesto which points to the right of the individual woman to decide against pregnancy even though abortion is involved."

Zad Leavy sounded a similar note in a lawyers' panel, commenting that "I believe we are going to see recognition in the courts before we see it in the legislatures." A law professor not involved in the litigation efforts, B. J. George, suggested that federal courts might well brush aside declaratory judgment cases challenging abortion statutes that actually had not been used to prosecute reputable physicians, but Roy

Lucas carefully explained to everyone present that those sorts of procedural hurdles, so serious even just seven years earlier with *Poe* v. *Ullman*, had been all but eliminated by more recent Supreme Court cases, particularly a decision just a few months earlier in which the high court had enthusiastically upheld a declaratory judgment challenge to an Arkansas statute that prohibited the teaching of evolution. Larry Lader spoke for almost all participants in the conference when he emphasized that "complete repeal is the only real solution," and the *New York Times*'s account of the conclave, like one in *Newsweek*, stressed that "The consensus at the end of the meeting . . . was nearly unanimous: Abolish all existing abortion laws." Many who had gone thinking that they were members of a growing minority favoring repeal learned that their assumption was wrong and that such views were now very much in the majority. As Lader captured the realization in a subsequent letter to the absent Lonny Myers, "It seemed to me that almost everyone at Hot Springs (including people who were moderate a year ago) are now for repeal."[35]

Bob Hall, highly pleased with the success of his long-planned conference, returned to New York and convened a mid-December dinner meeting with Roy Lucas for some prospective physician plaintiffs in the declaratory judgment test case. Lucas realized that their timetable was receding toward a possible actual case filing sometime in mid-spring, but Hall in particular seemed enthusiastic about proceeding, and even his long-standing moderation about the proper stance for ASA now no longer held him back from declaring in a magazine piece that "abortion must be the right of every woman." The New York legislative repeal advocates had reached agreement with assembly members Cook and Leichter on the text of an actual repeal bill for the 1969 legislature, but a mid-December press conference announcing their initiative received almost no news media attention. Alan Guttmacher told one acquaintance that while repeal "must obviously be our eventual goal," it would be "a long time before the state of New York was willing to legislate abortion on demand."[36]

Activists in a number of other states felt that same way, calculating that therapeutic exception bills were the most they could possibly attain from 1969 legislatures and deciding that something was better than nothing. "I am working for reform, but I believe in repeal," Connecticut activist Evelyn Warren told a friend about upcoming plans in that state. Reform bills were also being introduced in New Hampshire and in Texas, where thirty-two-year-old second-term state representative James H. Clark, Jr., of Dallas became the new legislative sponsor for Dr. Hugh Savage and the Texas Medical Association's long-sought liberalization provisions.[37]

But new reform proponents were often outnumbered by prior reform supporters who now advocated repeal. Colorado's Dick Lamm went public with his unhappiness about the exceedingly modest impact his 1967 measure had had, writing in the *Denver Post* that "the right to control her fertility is a right every woman should have" and contending that "compulsory pregnancy is a form of involuntary servitude." Atlanta's Alan Bonser, the primary activist in Georgia Citizens for Hospital Abortions, told Larry Lader that the new 1968 reform statute there "is terrible compared to what I personally think we should have." The *New York Times Magazine* ran a prominent story bluntly titled "How California's Abortion Law Isn't Working," and quoted Garrett Hardin as terming the 1967 reform statute "virtually worthless." A *Washington Post* reporter located Sherri Finkbine, who was now operating an Arizona dress shop, to see how her views had evolved over six years, and Finkbine forthrightly answered that "abortion should be the right of the woman . . . It should be a private, introspective decision."[38]

Bob Hall's ASA had spun off a sister organization, the Abortion Reform Association, or ARA, whose mission was to make modest grants to local-level liberalization groups, but when Lonny Myers's Chicago group, ICMCA, twice requested funds to support a 1969 campaign for a repeal bill in the Illinois legislature, Hall and John Lassoe, ARA's other principal figure, repeatedly turned them down. ICMCA was receiving some significant financial backing from Midas Muffler executive Gordon Sherman and from Hugh Hefner's Playboy Foundation, but hackles were raised when Hall and Lassoe frankly informed Myers and her colleague Don Shaw—like Lassoe an Episcopalian executive—that while they all agreed that repeal was preferable to reform, ARA would not abide ICMCA's *opposition* to reform. While Myers and Shaw, like others before them, had concluded that passage of a reform bill would more than likely *hinder* chances for legislative repeal, Lassoe strongly disagreed, arguing that a reform statute, "by demonstrating how few people it does help," can "provide the impetus for repeal," as the recent—and ongoing—history of reactions to the California and Colorado measures clearly indicated.[39]

Neither Hall nor ASA executive director Jimmye Kimmey attended Myers and Lader's mid-February Chicago conference that would give formal birth to their new national repeal organization, NARAL. Kimmey lamely told the Chicagoans that ASA's tax-exempt status prohibited her from coming, but she expressed the hope that as a result of the meeting "some too-timid reformers will be encouraged to seek more and that some too-adamant repealers will learn useful lessons in political reality." More than 350 people attended the three days of sessions at Chicago's posh Drake Hotel, and those participating ranged from wealthy financial contributor Joseph Sunnen to oft-imprisoned abortionist Nathan Rappaport. Author Betty Friedan and American Public Health Association president Lester Breslow both gave powerful speeches advocating repeal, and even Alan Guttmacher offered a slightly tentative endorsement of repeal. On the conference's final day a sometimes chaotic plenary session was devoted to choosing a steering committee which would be responsible for creating an actual organization to be called NARAL, although considerable unhappiness resulted when nine of the twelve members—including Larry Lader, Lader's doctor friend Bernie Nathanson, Ruth Cusack, politician Percy Sutton, philanthropist Stewart Mott, and Friedan—ended up being New Yorkers. NARAL's creation received prominent coverage in virtually every major American newspaper, and one New York ACLU activist reported to the national office that the most significant aspect of the repeal conference was in how it reflected "the rate at which this drive is accelerating." Within two weeks' time Lader and his steering committee colleagues had opened a New York office and hired a New Jersey woman, Lee Gidding, as executive director, and soon after that Lader himself was formally elected as chairman of NARAL's board.[40]

Several of the attendees at the Chicago conference, and not just Nathan Rappaport, embodied the increasing ties that were gradually developing between the repeal movement and the older, generally quite secretive world of actual abortion providers. Rappaport, because of his many arrests and significant jail sentences, was a considerably more public figure than any of his putative colleagues, but a more representative figure who attended the Chicago conference and began to take an active part in NARAL activities was Detroit's fifty-five-year-old Dr. Ed Keemer. A 1936 graduate of Tennessee's traditionally black Meharry Medical College, Keemer performed his first abortions in 1938 in Richmond, Indiana. He refused to serve in the armed forces after being rejected on explicitly racial grounds for an officer's commission that would have brought him into the service as a doctor rather than a grunt, and then pursued an interest in political change by becoming an active member of the Socialist Workers Party and writing a regular column for the party paper, *The Militant*, under the pen name "Charles Jackson." Keemer was far from alone in being an activist black M.D. who did a thriving business in abortions; Dr. T. R. M. Howard, a prominent figure in Mississippi's nascent civil rights movement in the 1950s until being forced to flee the state, soon thereafter established a highly remunerative practice in Chicago. In August 1956, however, Ed Keemer's luck ran out in Detroit when he and three other physicians were arrested in an abortion raid by city police. Convicted and sent to prison in 1959, Ed Keemer, like Tim Timanus in Maryland, struck up something of a correspondence with Alan Guttmacher after seeing an article in which Guttmacher endorsed reform. Keemer was released after serving fourteen months, and once his medical license was restored a year or two later, he carefully resumed his prior practice and then in late 1960s had his abortion trade suddenly snowball once he was discovered by the Clergy Consultation Service network.

Ed Keemer was a credible and significant representative of a world that up until early 1969 had received virtually no public attention other than occasional and never friendly police beat stories on arrests and convictions. Like Ed Keemer, Ruth Barnett Bush had performed her first abortion decades earlier, in Portland, Oregon, where she and several other regular providers practiced their profession rather openly and with only occasional legal interference. First raided in 1951, Bush was convicted and served four months in jail before resuming her work until a second arrest in 1956. That conviction resulted in a ten-month sentence in 1958, but then almost eight years passed until—at the age of seventy-two—Bush was arrested and convicted in the summer of 1966. After that conviction was affirmed on appeal, Bush entered prison in early 1968 and served five months before being paroled. In jail she had the time to draft her memoirs, and in early 1969, just as the NARAL conferees were assembling in Chicago, Bush's small autobiography was published to little if any public notice. "Abortion is a matter of personal decision," Bush wrote, and she had "long believed that every woman has the right of abortion if she believes it necessary."[41]

That same month the doctor who posthumously would become America's most celebrated abortionist died at the age of seventy-nine in his small home town of Ashland, Pennsylvania. Robert D. Spencer had received his medical degree from the University of Pennsylvania in 1916 and had opened his practice in Ashland three years later. Spencer had begun performing abortions in the mid-1920s, with most women initially being referred to him by other doctors whom Spencer knew or by mutual friends. Over the years, as word of Spencer's friendly manner, great competence, and exceptionally modest fees—never more than a hundred dollars, even in the 1960s—spread by word of mouth, a veritable network of Spencer alumnae gradually came into existence,

both in Pennsylvania and eventually in New York City. Spencer estimated that all told he had performed somewhere between thirty and
forty thousand abortions, and while he was arrested on three occasions,
the two cases that actually went to trial both ended in verdicts of
acquittal.

Spencer's fame first broke print in a 1966 *Village Voice* story that
spoke only of "Dr. S," but eight months later, following his retirement,
a *New York Times* piece identified him by his full name and called him
"the saint." *Time* magazine later named him as well, and although he
was far too ill to attend ASA's Hot Springs conference in person, Bob
Hall asked Spencer to submit a paper recapping his life's work, which
John Lassoe read in his absence. Written with considerable understatement but with unmistakable pride, Spencer described how in his later
years several of his patients were brought to him by their mothers,
whom he previously had helped in similar circumstances. "To me," he
wrote in his ASA remarks, "a good and sufficient reason" for abortion
"is the simple fact that the person has firmly decided she does not want
the baby."

When Spencer died in January 1969, the *New York Times* accorded
him a substantial obituary that erroneously credited him with having
performed over a hundred thousand abortions. Just a month earlier Dr.
Rappaport had taken New York writer Susan Brownmiller and a young
correspondent for *Medical World News* to meet Spencer, and after his
death Brownmiller published a front-page obituary in the *Village Voice*
and *Medical World News* ran a two-page profile. *Newsweek* magazine followed up with an obituary story of its own, and a month later the *Los
Angeles Times* offered its readers a lengthy, front-page profile of the
Pennsylvania physician, entitled "Defiant of Law, Full of Life, Doctor
Won Town's Esteem."[42]

But few abortion providers ever received even a fraction of the public recognition posthumously accorded Dr. Spencer. Indeed, neither
then nor in later years did the netherworld of illegal abortion get any
significant amount of attention from serious journalists or scholars.
One anthropologist prepared a nine-page ethnographic study of an
apparently quite competent clinic located just across the Mexican border from California, where the daily routine was most notably distinguished by the fact that "at no time is the word abortion used." A
Harvard sociology student devoted her doctoral dissertation to a top-
quality study of the acquaintance networks that women used when
searching for an abortion provider, and two Virginia researchers
painstakingly tried to come up with a reliable estimate of the total

number of illegal abortions that had been sought in their state during 1967, and settled on a figure of 21,000. A young sociologist at an Atlanta-area college prepared a brief but breathtaking paper for ASA's Hot Springs conference based upon interviews with five abortionists— and thirty of their surviving patients—who "practiced" in one city of about a quarter-million people. The "most successful" provider, a chiropractor with more than twenty years' experience in his sub-rosa field of endeavor, estimated that he performed hundreds of procedures each year but was unavailable for reinterview when he left town hurriedly following a patient's death. Another twenty-year veteran was a black midwife and nurse whose regular job was at a local hospital, and a third was an antique and drug dealer who had been expelled from medical school at least three decades earlier. The lowest price in town was apparently charged by "a young white automobile mechanic," who had in turn learned his technique from a friend who also had been expelled from medical school. He generally requested a fee of fifty dollars, although "he will accept less if they permit him to have sexual relations with them." Hence it was no small wonder that providers like Ed Keemer were much appreciated, or that within the network of Spencer alumnae the Pennsylvania physician was sometimes spoken of as "the saint of Ashland."[43]

By early 1969 the Clergy Consultation Service, with support from Stewart Mott, had expanded into a national network with a rapidly growing number of local affiliate groups, and its roster of providers had grown significantly, with even quite mainstream doctors such as Bernie Nathanson accepting a significant number of patients.[44] But while Lader and many other repeal activists were for the moment primarily concerned with getting NARAL off the ground and continuing to build the referral network, most abortion litigators were preoccupied with the preparatory work leading up to the potentially all-important March 4 oral argument of *Belous* before the California Supreme Court. A. L. Wirin and Fred Okrand's brief for Dr. Belous was supplemented by three supportive amicus briefs: by Norma Zarky on behalf of the ACLU's chapters, by Herma Hill Kay for eighteen prominent attorneys recruited by Charles Munger, and by Zad Leavy on behalf of a highly impressive nationwide roster of prominent physicians pulled together by CCTA and including Alan Guttmacher and Bob Hall from New York and Lee Buxton from Connecticut. Zarky told her CCTA colleagues that "I don't suppose any of you who are not lawyers can appreciate how deeply Mr. Munger reached into the establishment for signers of the lawyers' brief," and that submission, like Wirin and

Okrand's, laid heavy emphasis upon how abortion involved precisely the same sort of liberty and privacy concerns to which the Supreme Court had given constitutional protection in *Griswold*. "We think proper constitutional interpretation," the lawyers' brief said, "requires both contraception and early abortion by licensed physicians to remain private matters."

The California signers of Leavy's impressive brief included University of Southern California Medical School Dean Roger O. Egeberg as well as CCTA mainstays Keith Russell and Ned Overstreet. Much as in his earlier *Shively* brief, Leavy offered the court an extensive constitutional argument, contending that the Bill of Rights and particularly the right to privacy "reserves to the individual control of the procreative function free from unreasonable restriction by the state." The old California abortion statute "drastically interferes with a woman's right to control the use of her own body," and additionally "an even stronger claim to constitutional protection can be asserted by the married woman acting to preserve and protect her family, with the support of her husband under the guidance of her doctor." Repeatedly invoking *Griswold*, Leavy argued that "the mere fact of fertilization should not *ipso facto* and *eo instante* abolish or limit the constitutional right of the married couple to decide whether to have a child." "For all the reasons which led to the striking down of Connecticut's prohibitions against pre-fertilization birth control in *Griswold*, this Court should strike down California's statute prohibiting post-fertilization birth control."

Egeberg and his colleagues were highly pleased with Leavy's work, but Charles Munger alerted everyone that their opponents were investing almost as much effort in *Belous* as they were. In addition to the expected defense of the antiabortion statute, and Belous's conviction, submitted by California Attorney General Thomas C. Lynch and his deputy, Phillip G. Samovar, the diocesan counsel for James Cardinal McIntyre of Los Angeles, Joseph J. Brandlin, arranged for preparation of an antiabortion amicus brief. Its signers included former state Board of Medical Examiners member Dr. James V. McNulty, who had instigated the Shively charges, and the diocese also retained a Jewish attorney who was highly respected by some members of the California court, Herman F. Selvin, to present oral argument on behalf of those amici.

The March 4 Sacramento hearing before the seven-justice California Supreme Court was a major production that thus featured four different attorneys all offering oral argument: Wirin and former bar association president Burnham Enersen for Belous and the Belous

amici, and deputy attorney general Samovar and Selvin for the state
and its diocesan supporters. Roy Lucas flew all the way from New York
simply to watch the argument, but it was immediately clear that the
justices, particularly Justice Raymond E. Peters and Chief Justice
Roger Traynor, were much more interested in Wirin's contention that
California's pre-1967 statute was excessively and hence unconstitutionally vague than in Enersen's argument that the court should reach the
more fundamental constitutional issues. Lucas, Zad Leavy, and Norma
Zarky all left the Sacramento hearing feeling quite optimistic, based
upon the justices' questions, about the chances for a reversal of
Belous's conviction, but Leavy expressly told his CCTA colleagues that
he expected a ruling based upon the narrow grounds of vagueness and
Zarky added that she "felt sure they are not going to reach *Griswold*."[45]

Lucas discussed his plans for a New York declaratory suit with the
California attorneys, and Leavy and Wirin agreed that a similar case
might have to be considered in California should *Belous* turn out unfavorably. Lucas had also agreed to a request from a New Jersey attorney,
Jacob Balk, who had read Lucas's *North Carolina Law Review* article, to
take the lead in preparing a longshot petition asking the U. S. Supreme
Court to review a state court decision dismissing a case that Balk had
filed on behalf of a rubella-damaged baby and his parents against the
physicians who had failed to advise them of the risk of fetal defects or
to raise the option of seeking an abortion. The New Jersey Supreme
Court had itself declined to review the lower court dismissal of *Morin*
v. *Garra*, but Lucas gamely told the U.S. Supreme Court that "The
importance of this case far transcends its particular facts and the interests of individual litigants. It raises the conflict between the state laws
on abortion and the woman's interest in not being compelled to bear
offspring each time she conceives. This is a conflict which will increasingly appear in petitions to this court, and one which deserves serious
and immediate attention. Its ultimate resolution will determine
whether the women of these United States are to be treated as citizens
with control over their reproductive capacities, or instruments of the
State who must perpetuate the human race in the way specified by a
majority of their state legislators." The principles of *Griswold* undeniably ought to protect "the personal autonomy of a woman with respect
to her reproductive capacities," and "Certainly the right to control the
planning of one's own family is a corollary of the broad right of marital
privacy whether contraception or abortion after the failure of contraception is at issue." To no one's surprise the Supreme Court without
comment declined to review *Morin*, and similarly refused to hear an

abortion appeal by a Louisiana doctor with a heavily checkered record, Sidney C. Knight, whose medical license was being pursued by state regulatory officials.[46]

The major east coast abortion focus in early 1969 was not court litigation, however, but the renewed legislative liberalization drive in New York. Connie Cook and Franz Leichter had indeed introduced a repeal bill, and although Al Blumenthal's far more modest therapeutic reform measure also was up for consideration again, almost all liberalization energy was directed toward promoting the Cook bill, not Blumenthal's. Ruth Cusack's abortion committee of the New York NOW chapter had evolved into a quasi-separate group that called itself first Citizens for Abortion Law Repeal and then New Yorkers for Abortion Law Repeal, but the first major splash made on behalf of legislative repeal came not from these proponents of energetic lobbying but from a decidedly more theatrical presentation staged by about thirty members of a more radical feminist group, Redstockings, at a mid-February hearing on the Blumenthal and Cook bills held in Manhattan by the legislature's Joint Committee on Public Health.

Redstockings was not the first women's liberation group to appear on the New York political scene, but it was the first to devote particular attention to the issue of abortion law repeal. Previous groupings, starting with New York Radical Women, had appeared as early as December 1967, but as one of the first true activists in the movement, Jo—then Joreen—Freeman, later noted, "women's liberation did not begin in New York." Freeman herself in Chicago, along with three friends in several cities, initiated in March 1968 the first publication that marked the emergence of this new wave, *Voice of the Women's Liberation Movement*, and other early women's liberation groups appeared in such different cities as Gainesville, Florida, and Detroit, in addition to Chicago.

Redstockings decided to disrupt the February 1969 New York legislative hearing in part because the witness list on the subject of abortion featured fourteen men and one woman—a Roman Catholic nun. The disruption forced a brief adjournment before the hearing resumed in private quarters, and one repeal supporter, Democratic Senator Seymour Thaler of Queens, denounced the women for tactics that he believed hurt rather than helped their cause. At the end of the seven-hour hearing three Redstockings representatives were allowed to address the committee, and the events of the day received modest but not prominent media attention. "We are particularly interested in exposing the concept of expertise, as opposed to letting people make decisions about their lives," Ellen Willis, one of Redstockings' most prominent members, later told a journalist.

New York newspapers were full of a seemingly almost endless stream of small stories announcing that more and more mainstream groups—New York City's Presbyterian and Episcopal churches, the state Correctional Association, the Liberal Party, and both the city and state Councils of Churches—were explicitly endorsing abortion law repeal, but legislative observers gave Cook's bill no chance of coming even close to passage. Journalists believed that Blumenthal's ALI-style reform bill had much better prospects, in part because the new Republican Assembly Speaker, Perry B. Duryea, Jr., who already had been fully educated on abortion by Ruth Cusack, favored liberalization and also because, as the New York Times put it, the 1969 session reflected "an unmistakable change of climate" on the abortion question. Public Health Committee chairman Senator Norman Lent had said in mid-January that "It is not a question of whether a law will be passed; it is a question of what form it should take," and the serious legislative jockeying focused upon what particular therapeutic exceptions should be allowed, not on the possibility of full repeal.[47]

In late February PPFA president Alan Guttmacher, now seventy-one years old, distributed a public letter announcing his long-delayed but now more-than-full conversion from reform to repeal: "I personally strongly favor the Cook bill and removal of abortion from the criminal code." Guttmacher acknowledged that the Cook bill "has little chance to pass," and then he made a far more astounding declaration: now, like Garrett Hardin and Lonny Myers before him, he too was convinced that reform hindered rather than hastened the prospects for eventual repeal. "I fear only that the Blumenthal bill or something worse will become law," Guttmacher said. "I believe this would be a catastrophe for it would postpone real liberalization for another decade or two," and would lead to a situation—as in Colorado—where medical implementation of a reform statute might very well make it even more conservative in practice than its legislative sponsors had intended. Absent full legislative repeal, Guttmacher indicated, the best course for meaningful liberalization lay in the courts, where he understood "that there is a good chance for a favorable decision."

Two weeks after Guttmacher's memorable letter, the New York legislature's joint Public Health Committee endorsed an amended version of the Blumenthal reform bill by a margin of 8 to 3. Blumenthal believed that he had five or six votes more than he needed to pass the bill on the floor of the state assembly, but when it was called up for debate in mid-April, an "emotional" and "highly personal" attack on the measure, particularly its fetal defects provision, by Martin Ginsberg, a polio-crippled Nassau County Republican who had previously backed the bill, suddenly and unexpectedly turned the tide. Some fourteen anticipated supporters, all but one a Republican, shifted sides and voted no, and what Blumenthal had projected to be a comfortable victory turned into a highly embarrassing 78 to 69 defeat.[48]

The New York loss was not the only painful setback experienced by abortion reformers in the spring of 1969. In Texas the overwhelming 1968 endorsement of liberalization by the members of the state medical association led both Hugh Savage and the primary legislative sponsor of reform, Dallas Representative James H. "Jim" Clark, Jr., to attempt another big push, but officials of the Texas Catholic Conference strenuously opposed Clark's bill and San Antonio Archbishop Robert E. Lucey publicly declared that any legislator who would vote for it was "a murderer." Clark initially thought the bill had a good chance of being favorably reported by the Public Health Committee, but in the wake of the Catholic onslaught he frankly conceded that "I don't have enough votes to get it out of committee." The legislators themselves were not opposed to reform, Clark explained; "It's the political repercussions they fear from the Catholic opposition. Minorities, if they are militant enough, and determined enough, can stop things." By late March it was clear that Clark's bill was dead, and a frustrated Hugh Savage told reporters that "it's time the public got stirred up—doctors can't pass legislation." After all, he stressed, there was nothing radical about Clark's reform bill; "we're just trying to legitimize what already is being done."[49]

Reformers had distinctly better luck in neighboring New Mexico, where an ALI-style therapeutic reform bill passed the state house by a narrow margin of 36 to 34 and the state senate by 25 to 15. Roman Catholic Governor David F. Cargo had the power to veto it but chose not to, announcing in late March that "I do not feel that my own personal religious beliefs should interfere with the enactment of this statute." Hence the bill became law without Cargo's signature, and took effect three months later in June. In Arkansas a reform bill successfully made its way through the state legislature without attracting any significant national attention, and in Kansas the state senate, also without any national news coverage, passed a *repeal* bill by a vote of 25 to 12. Once it reached the house floor, however, extensive weakening amendments were adopted that transformed it into a reform measure. A conference committee resolved the differences in favor of the house version, and in late April the reform bill was signed into law. Several weeks later an extremely liberal reform bill that had been championed by the Oregon Committee for the Legal Termination of Pregnancy, a group originally created by the First Unitarian Church of Portland, was adopted by the Oregon legislature. It was soon signed into law by the governor, and in Delaware a reform bill that had squeaked through the legislature by a one-vote margin in the state senate also became law. All told, five new states had adopted reform bills, doubling to ten the pre-1969 total of five where therapeutic exceptions now gave at least a few pregnant women some chance of securing a legal abortion.[50]

With support from Bob Hall and John Lassoe's New York-based ARA, the Connecticut League for Abortion Law Reform (CLALR) was able to open a Hartford office and hire a staff member for the 1969 Connecticut legislative session, but neither CLALR president Don Cantor nor any of his colleagues had any serious hope of passing even a reform bill during that 1969 session. CLALR board member Estelle Griswold, now living in retirement in Essex, Connecticut, told a Hartford reporter that the issue of legal access to abortion was just like the question of legal access to birth control in the years before 1965. "It's the same old story. Women of influence and means can get therapeutic treatment denied to the poor," because the first group, unlike the latter, either "knew someone or could go out of state." At bottom, Estelle said, "This is basically a civil rights issue and rights that are denied to women." The Connecticut Civil Liberties Union spoke out in favor of repeal and in opposition to reform at a mid-April legislative hearing, but even before a reform proposal was defeated by 89 to 69 on the house floor, Cantor and others were already thinking more of court action than of legislative success. Cantor appealed to Yale's Tom Emerson for input and advice, telling him that both "Dr. Buxton and Mrs. Griswold, who are members of our Board of Directors, were quite certain that you would be interested in participating." Emerson agreed, but nothing tangible developed and Katie Roraback advised the national ACLU that "I do not think that the issue will be resolved for a long time."[51]

Reform bills failed to emerge from legislative committees in Iowa and in Minnesota, where the Minnesota Council for the Legal Termination of Pregnancy was furious when a group from the Radical Women's Caucus disrupted a House Health and Welfare Committee meeting much as had happened in New York. In Nevada, where Joseph Sunnen had once had high hopes for passage of a repeal measure, a reform bill was defeated in the state assembly by one vote. In

Hawaii a reform bill was approved by a comfortable margin of 39 to 12 in the state house but was not brought to the senate floor after the chairman of the relevant senate committee, Vincent Yano, a Roman Catholic father of ten, told supporters that he wanted to read more about the issue, and learn more about doctors' sentiments, before making up his mind.[52]

In Illinois a repeal bill lost by only two votes in the state senate, and abortion activists were disappointed both with their own lobbying efforts and with one of their principal legislative sponsors. Michigan activists also made a push for a repeal bill, but in the end even a reform bill fell four votes short of passage in the state senate. They began to consider the possibility of petitioning for a popular referendum vote on repeal, and similar consideration of a referendum or initiative option also came to the fore in Washington state, where an all-out effort by Catholic opponents had succeeded in keeping a repeal bill bottled up in a senate committee. Seattle's small Citizens' Abortion Discussion Group, led by psychologist Samuel Goldenberg, changed its name to Washington Citizens for Abortion Reform (WCAR) in preparation for a statewide 1970 vote, and began debating whether to commission a private poll before making a definite decision to go the popular-vote route.[53]

While the many 1969 spring legislative battles were being resolved, Roy Lucas was moving to implement the plans for a new litigation group that he and Morris Dees had mapped out nine months earlier. Having firmly decided to hold off on filing a New York case until sometime in the fall, by which time a potentially helpful *Belous* decision might be in hand, Lucas began recruiting trustees for the James Madison Constitutional Law Institute (JMCLI), which would begin operation in September 1969 thanks to Dees's largesse from his windfall deal with Times-Mirror. Norman Dorsen from NYU was the first to agree, soon followed by Tom Emerson, whom Lucas successfully wooed with a fan letter highlighting the importance of *Griswold* for upcoming abortion litigation. ACLU legal director Mel Wulf, his deputy Eleanor Holmes Norton, NYU's Robert McKay, former Fowler Harper student Edwin Schur, and ASA's Dr. Bob Hall all signed on, along with a host of prominent law professors—and oftentimes former Supreme Court clerks—from across the country: Anthony Amsterdam, Jesse Choper, Charles Black, and William Van Alstyne. By midsummer Lucas had prepared a snappy brochure, announcing that the nascent JMCLI would initially concentrate on issues of access to higher education and abortion and "will pioneer new constitutional frontiers. Only cases involving questions of constitutional law not presently settled or accepted will be pursued." Lucas would be "Director and General Counsel," Dees the president; a young lawyer with a special interest in students' rights cases, Douglas J. Kramer, would be the one other staff attorney in addition to Lucas. The JMCLI brochure flatly announced that "Morris has agreed to place one million dollars of his personal funds in trust for the Institute as its financial base," and by the end of the summer Lucas had formally left the Twentieth Century Fund and opened the JMCLI's first office on West Ninth Street in Manhattan with himself, Kramer, and a secretary as the new staff.[54]

Lucas and others were waiting expectantly for *Belous*, but even in advance of that Lucas stumbled upon a seemingly obscure law review article that looked like as influential an endorsement of his litigation strategy as anything possible: an explicit endorsement of a *Griswold*-based right to abortion by recently retired Supreme Court Justice Tom C. Clark, who had stepped down from the high court when his son Ramsey had been named U.S. Attorney General. Clark's eleven-page text was perhaps all the more unusual for appearing in the *Roman Catholic*-affiliated *Loyola University Law Review*, but in it the former justice laid out a firm critique of the inadequacy of therapeutic reform laws before proceeding to note both the inherent vagueness of such statutory language and then the constitutional meaning of *Griswold*'s right to privacy. Clark had joined Douglas's 1965 opinion, not John Harlan's concurrence, but Clark's articulation of how judges "must look to the collective conscience of our society in determining which rights are fundamental and therefore protected" under Fourteenth Amendment due process liberty echoed Harlan's dissent in *Poe* much more than Douglas in *Griswold*. But there was no doubt, Clark went on, that "abortion falls within that sensitive area of privacy—the marital relation. One of the basic values of this privacy is birth control," but it certainly was not the only. With abortion, Clark said, "the vital issue becomes one of balancing," and he articulated what that balance might be in a formulation that was prescient even if it did not explicitly speak of fetal viability: "until the time that life is present, the State could not interfere with the interruption of pregnancy through abortion performed in a hospital or under appropriate clinical conditions."[55]

If the Clark article was unexpected good news for incipient litigators like Lucas, some modestly surprising bad news was the Massachusetts Supreme Judicial Court's 4 to 3 *affirmance* of Bill Baird's 1967 conviction for handing a package of Emko vaginal foam to a presumably unmarried young woman after his Boston University lecture. Six months earlier at oral argument, assistant district attorney Joseph R. Nolan had told the justices that Baird's entire B.U. performance had been "an invitation to promiscuity and sexual license," but that warning notwithstanding, the Massachusetts court voided on First Amendment grounds the second count on which Baird had been convicted for merely *exhibiting* contraceptives. The old Massachusetts statute provided for up to *five years* imprisonment for anyone who "sells, lends, gives away, exhibits, or offers to sell, lend, or give away" any article "for the prevention of conception or for causing unlawful abortion," and in 1966, after *Griswold*, it had been amended only to the extent of creating express exceptions for doctors, nurses, and pharmacists to provide such articles to married persons. Baird's distribution of the foam, the four-vote court majority said, added nothing to the content of his constitutionally protected lecture, and the ongoing validity of the Massachusetts law as amended rested upon its regulation of *who* could distribute such items, not on the marital status of the recipient, the court stated. Baird was not a doctor, nurse, or pharmacist, and hence the majority affirmed his criminal conviction for handing out the Emko foam. This affirmance, they insisted, was fully compatible with *Griswold*: "we rest this decision wholly upon the Federal Constitution and largely upon its construction by the Supreme Court."

The Massachusetts court's three dissenters contended that Baird's handing out of the foam ought to be similarly protected, arguing that "the distribution should be considered part of constitutionally free speech and protest." The usually irrepressible Baird was stunned by the outcome, explaining later that he had expected the Massachusetts high court would "knock the whole thing out." Three weeks later he appeared before Suffolk County Superior Court Judge Donald M. Macaulay for his previously postponed sentencing, and prosecutor Nolan requested that a six-month jail sentence be imposed. When Macaulay meted out a term of three months' imprisonment, one reporter described Baird as "visibly upset by the jail sentence." The idea that someone in 1969 could actually go to prison for giving away a nonprescription product that was openly and legally on sale in thousands of American stores seemed almost too bizarre to consider, but it was now a very real possibility for Bill Baird. Despite Nolan's opposition, Macaulay stayed Baird's actual incarceration to allow Baird's volunteer attorney, Joseph Balliro, to petition the U.S. Supreme Court to review the 4 to 3 Massachusetts decision, and in late July Balliro filed the appropriate papers. Two members of NOW's New York chapter who were also very active members of New Yorkers for Abortion Law Repeal, Jim Clapp and Cindy Cisler, sought to persuade NOW to commission Roy Lucas to prepare an amicus brief, since whatever the Supreme Court did with *Baird* could well be "an important precedent" for Lucas's yet-to-be filed New York abortion case. Their effort was unsuccessful, and Massachusetts Attorney General Robert H. Quinn told the Supreme Court, in answer to Baird's petition, that Baird's argument that the Massachusetts anticontraception statute was infirm under *Griswold* "reads too much from too little. . . . nothing in *Griswold* indicates that a state cannot limit the distribution of drugs and medical aids to properly trained personnel."[56]

Baird's odd and unexpected setback was only one incongruous piece of a rapidly developing mosaic, however. Several weeks later many of the country's abortion activists gathered at a CCTA-sponsored conference in San Francisco, and national news coverage of the meeting once again highlighted the strong distaste that almost all the activists now felt toward reform-style statutes. The *Los Angeles Times* quoted Colorado's Dick Lamm as lamenting that "we have replaced one cruel, outmoded law with another one," and California's Ned Overstreet confessed to his colleagues that "I can scarcely believe the change in my own thinking that has taken place in the last decade" as he like others had shifted from reform to repeal. ASA's Jimmye Kimmey tried to temper the zeal for repeal by suggesting that some activists were "unable to see that . . . the perfect can be the enemy of the good," and by emphasizing that "it is not enough to be self-righteously right—it is necessary to be politically effective." "In some states," she contended, "the no-compromisers may have been detrimental to other reform efforts. One branch of the no-compromisers—the radical feminists— may have been instrumental on occasion in defeating the move to reform the law short of their ideal."

Kimmey shifted to a less critical theme, however, by stressing that "it may be that disagreements over the content of legislation are not only debilitating to the movement but irrelevant to the goal." Her point was that "the vital constituency" for real liberalization "is the medical community," and that in actual practice "reform or repeal of the law" might not be the most crucial question, since "the objective is not merely to reform the law but to change medical practice."[57]

Kimmey's modest rhetorical overstatement did not significantly undercut her more basic truth that day-to-day physician behavior was actually of far greater practical importance than the dry black and white wording of statutes. That was precisely the lesson that more and more activists and observers were drawing from the postreform experience in Colorado and in other early reform states, where statistics increasingly suggested that the real impact of reform was very modest indeed. Dick Lamm told one medical journal that his 1967 reform measure had been "a bill that would help about 5 percent" of pregnant women seeking abortions but that "the doctors and hospitals have turned it into a 3 percent bill." A Colorado hospital director volunteered that "it's probably more difficult now to get a hospital abortion than it was before the law passed because of all the publicity and official scrutiny." North Carolina reform law sponsor Art Jones complained that "the net result of the new law was merely to make legal what doctors actually had been doing previously," and little if anything more, and a Georgia accounting showed that a grand total of only seventy-three abortions had taken place pursuant to that state's reform law during the balance of 1968, with no increase occurring in 1969. A comprehensive survey by the magazine *Modern Hospital* concluded that "most hospitals in states where a reform abortion law is in effect are, to varying degrees, restricting themselves beyond the requirements of the law," and a Maryland study revealed that every hospital in the state was limiting therapeutic abortion services to Maryland residents even though the reform statute imposed no such requirement.[58]

Particularly in California there was significant medical tension and disagreement over the manner in which the reform statute's mental health exception was being implemented, with one very sympathetic study in a leading journal concluding that "There is general knowledge that psychiatrists are prone to identify as suicidal patients who are not. This creates skepticism and resistance by other physicians." A prominent essay in the *New England Journal of Medicine* similarly highlighted "the humanitarian need that frequently masquerades under the hypocrisy of a pseudo-psychiatric label such as 'suicide risk,'" and longtime CCTA activist and psychiatrist Jerry Kummer publicly acknowledged "a marked tendency for psychiatrists to indicate suicidal risks when indeed none exist." A California survey undertaken by CCTA president Keith Russell and a colleague revealed that while 88 percent of California's roughly five thousand hospital abortions in 1968 had taken place under a mental health rubric, standards varied tremendously from one part of the state to another: greater San Francisco accounted for 23 percent of California's births and 64 percent of abortions, while greater Los Angeles hospitals had 44 percent of births and only 19 percent of abortions. Just as Kimmey suggested, the medical practices that determined how a law would be implemented counted for a good deal more than the language of the statute itself.[59]

Not long after the CCTA conference Kimmey's boss, ASA president Bob Hall, went so far as to dismiss reform bills by asking "What will the passage of such laws do to the practice of abortion? Not much." Abortions during the first twenty weeks of pregnancy should, and ultimately would, be legal, Hall said, with "the ultimate solution" coming from the courts, and perhaps fairly soon. Even *Reader's Digest* published a prominent article highlighting the shift from reform to repeal, and *Time* magazine featured Harris poll results showing that 64 percent of Americans now "believe that abortion should not be a matter of the law but should be left to the prospective parents and their doctor; even a 60% majority of Roman Catholics agree." A more scholarly study of those rapidly evolving attitudes noted how "in only a few years abortion has been transformed from a taboo topic to daily newspaper copy," but stressed that while very heavy majorities indeed did back legal abortions in specific therapeutic cases, only a small minority—*Time*'s presentation notwithstanding—actually endorsed repeal.[60]

The nationwide Clergy Consultation Service referral network continued to expand apace, but in May and June 1969 two events caused significant scares among the growing ranks of participants. On May 24 New York City police raided an abortion facility quietly housed in an apartment building in the Riverdale section of the Bronx and arrested its four principal staff members, including a doctor licensed to practice in the Dominican Republic, although not in the United States. Bronx District Attorney Burton Roberts coupled his announcement of the arrests with a somewhat surprising declaration that "the law needs modification and liberalization so we can face the problem realistically," but Larry Lader and other New York activists who had been using the Riverdale group as one of their primary referral facilities were terrified that they too—just like Bill Baird—might soon be on their way to jail. Roberts subpoenaed more than fifty people—including Lader, several ministers, and Bernie Nathanson, who cited the Fifth Amendment and declined to testify—to appear in front of a grand jury pondering criminal charges, but in the end only the actual staff was indicted. Several eventually settled the charges simply by paying modest five-hundred-dollar fines, and none actually ever stood trial, but the raid greatly disrupted the functioning of the east coast referral network.

Two weeks after the Riverdale raid, a Massachusetts grand jury, pursuing charges against a Massachusetts doctor who eight years earlier had been prosecuted on another abortion charge, Pierre V. Brunelle, also indicted a thirty-five-year-old Cleveland minister, Reverend Robert W. Hare, who had never visited Massachusetts or spoken with Brunelle but who had given Brunelle's name to a young Cleveland woman as part of the Clergy Consultation Service operation in Ohio. Many observers thought it highly unlikely that Massachusetts's prosecution of Reverend Hare would succeed, but the first indictment of a ministerial participant in the clergy referral network dramatically highlighted the possible risks being run by those who openly conducted the clergy service.[61]

On Friday, September 5, 1969, the California Supreme Court issued its much-awaited decision in *People* v. *Leon P. Belous*. Although the vote was a razor-thin 4 to 3, Justice Raymond A. Peters's majority opinion voided Belous's conviction on the grounds that California's pre-1967 antiabortion statute was unconstitutionally vague. The one exception in the old statute allowed an abortion if it was "necessary to preserve" the pregnant woman's life, and the four-vote majority held that both "necessary" and "preserve" were excessively vague. "A showing of immediacy or certainty of death is not essential for a lawful abortion" under the old language, and once that was conceded, the majority indicated, the statute offered a doctor no clear guidance as to which health-related abortions *were* "necessary to preserve" a woman's life and which—in the eyes of a prosecutor or jury—might not be.

But the California majority did not limit itself simply to that issue of statutory interpretation. Without expressly indicating whether its additional comments were or were not an essential part of its holding, the Peters majority much more significantly asserted that "The fundamental right of the woman to choose whether to bear children follows from the Supreme Court's and this court's repeated acknowledgment of a 'right to privacy' or 'liberty' in matters related to marriage, family, and sex." Citing *Griswold*, *Loving* v. *Virginia*, and several other precedents reaching back to *Meyer* v. *Nebraska* and *Pierce* v. *Society of Sisters* in the 1920s, the California court also stated that the fact "That such a right is not enumerated in either the United States or California Constitutions is no impediment to the existence of the right."

The *Belous* majority extensively and explicitly relied upon Zad Leavy's amicus brief on behalf of the 178 medical school professors and deans, and argued at some length that if an antiabortion statute like California's *was* interpreted to require a "certainty of death" before an abortion could be allowed, such a reading would create a "great and direct infringement of constitutional rights," particularly where "abortion is sought during the first trimester" of pregnancy. Justice Peters also analyzed how the vague but worrisome threat of criminal prosecution that the abortion statute placed over any doctor evaluating a woman's abortion request inescapably created a situation where a physician, rather than relying solely upon best medical judgment, might very well give more weight to minimizing any chance of prosecution than to provide the best possible care for the patient and thus refuse to perform an abortion that even under the statute *should* take place. The state, "in delegating" to a doctor "the power to decide whether an abortion is necessary, has skewed the penalties in one direction: *no* criminal penalties are imposed where the doctor refuses to perform a necessary operation, even if the woman should in fact die because the operation was not performed. The pressures on a physician to decide not to perform an absolutely necessary abortion are," the Court said, "enormous."[62]

Although the Peters opinion was not always a model of clarity, what it lacked in precision it more than made up for with its outspoken, *Griswold*-oriented constitutional suggestiveness and with its explicit hint that the stage of pregnancy during which an abortion might take place could well be of particular significance. The next morning's *Los Angeles Times* immediately labeled the decision a "Landmark Ruling," and both medical publications and the popular press gave it extensive attention, with *Time* magazine remarking upon the "awesome list of supporters" who had endorsed one or another of the Munger-initiated amicus briefs. Keith Russell, Roy Lucas, *American Medical News*, and counsel for the California Medical Association all adopted the "landmark" characterization, and an ecstatic Zad Leavy termed the decision "the most significant opinion in an abortion case in Anglo-American jurisprudence since the inception" of antiabortion statutes in the early nineteenth century. "The real thrust of the decision," Leavy asserted, "was the enumeration for the first time of certain basic rights of women over their own bodies," and Keith Russell, in a deeply moving letter to the many signers of Leavy's amicus brief, acknowledged *Belous*'s "landmark" importance while describing the victory as "but a single episode in a long endeavor to obtain appropriate freedom for women and licensed physicians."[63]

California Attorney General Thomas Lynch moved to have the state court reconsider its decision, contending that the purpose of the old statute was to "protect the unborn child," but the California court quickly denied his motion. Lynch announced he would seek review by the U.S. Supreme Court, but the CCTA network of lawyers estimated that the chances of *Belous* being disturbed were very low indeed. Norma Zarky stressed that what the California court had said with regard to vagueness, as well as with its acknowledgment of "the fundamental right of the woman to choose," made every abortion statute in America highly vulnerable to constitutional attack, and Roy Lucas in particular welcomed *Belous* as exactly the sort of high-status endorsement of his *Griswold*-based litigation strategy that he had been hoping for in advance of filing a federal court declaratory judgment challenge to the New York antiabortion statute. The Peters opinion had cited his 1968 *North Carolina Law Review* article, and without delay Lucas began making the final preparations in New York. *Belous* also energized Morris Dees to begin exploring whether there might now be an Alabama doctor willing to help reactivate Lucas's earlier idea of filing a challenge to that state's antiabortion law, and in New York Lucas settled on a three-pronged strategy of attack. A lead suit would be filed on behalf of physicians, and two companion cases would be brought in the names of clergy referral activists and poor women who might desire abortions. Tactically Lucas would move to secure a special three-judge panel, and sought to time the actual filing of the lead action, the doctors' case, so that the motion requesting the panel would be heard by a reputedly sympathetic federal district judge.[64]

The doctors' case would be cosponsored by Lucas's Madison Institute, the ACLU, and ASA, but in Lucas's eyes nothing about this first affirmative case ever to contend that abortion entailed a fundamental individual liberty would be more important than the reputations and professional stature of the physician plaintiffs. And nothing said more about how dramatically expert sentiment on abortion had shifted from lobbying for reform to litigating for repeal than the identities of the four prominent doctors whose names would appear at the top of formal complaint that Lucas filed in Manhattan's federal district court on Tuesday, September 30: Robert E. Hall, Alan F. Guttmacher, Seymour L. Romney, and Louis M. Hellman. Romney and Hellman, who had long been an active member of ASA's board, were both well-known professors of gynecology at New York medical schools; Hall and especially Guttmacher—as the public record of the previous decade amply revealed—had been the most outspoken medical champions of reform before finally endorsing repeal. The presence of their two names on Lucas's suit signified more strikingly than anything else how the long and usually friendly wrestling match between reform and repeal had indeed been concluded by the reformers themselves becoming repealers.

Norman Dorsen, Harriet Pilpel, and the ACLU's Mel Wulf also signed the complaint in what would be styled *Hall* versus Louis

Lefkowitz, the New York State Attorney General. The filing of the suit received widespread press coverage in out-of-town papers like the *Washington Post* as well as in the *New York Times*, but the ACLU's desire to claim press release credit for a case "it has filed"—as well as for *Belous*—set off a brief but intense private battle over whether one organization was unfairly trying to hog publicity for legal work that very largely had been carried out by others. ACLU executives tried to brush aside Lucas's angry complaints about their self-serving behavior, and Lucas drafted but did not send a tart letter naively telling the ACLU that "that kind of jockeying for position has little place in a movement."[65]

California's Charles Munger, understandably quite pleased at how successful his and Warren Buffett's quiet investment of more than fifty thousand dollars to sponsor the *Belous* amicus briefs had turned out to be, commended Lucas on the filing of *Hall* and recommended on pragmatic grounds the same tactics the Californians had employed in *Belous*: "using separate amicus briefs signed by substantial groups of 'establishment' lawyers and doctors. This can't hurt, and may help with one or more key judges of a cautious or conservative type." Munger and Buffett were continuing to finance the Los Angeles clergy referral service, even to the point of helping the principal clergyman, J. Hugh Anwyl, start a new church after being dismissed from his previous pulpit, but Munger stressed to Lucas that in his judgment the practical impact of *Belous* within California would be so substantial in dramatically liberalizing the availability of abortion that no actual litigation challenge to the newer, 1967 reform statute would really be necessary. Munger immediately began channeling some of his financial largesse into the actual provision of abortion services, and his forecast as to how significantly the medical situation in California would change in the powerful wake of *Belous* would soon prove extremely prescient.[66]

Lucas's two planned companion cases to *Hall* v. *Lefkowitz*, one on behalf of clergymen and one filed by several legal services attorneys on behalf of poor women, were soon joined by a third. *Abramowicz et al.* v. *Lefkowitz* made much the same complaint against the New York abortion statute as the *Hall* trio—that the law invaded "plaintiffs' right of privacy or liberty in matters relating to marriage, family and sex" and infringed upon "the fundamental right of a woman to choose whether to bear children"—both phrases that were drawn directly from the Peters opinion in *Belous*. The all-female group of *Abramowicz* plaintiffs initially numbered more than 125, and while formally they were represented by an all-woman team of lawyers, press coverage of their early October filing stated that much of the legal work had been done by

New York attorney Gerald Lefcourt. Their suit was combined with the three other cases, and in late October U.S. District Judge Edward Weinfeld—precisely the jurist whom Lucas had been aiming for—heard argument on Lucas's motion to convene a special three-judge court. Within a week Weinfeld issued a brief opinion granting the motion, and although the three judge panel unsurprisingly denied a request for an order blocking any further enforcement of the New York law in advance of the actual trial and decision of the four conjoined cases, the composition of the panel—Weinfeld, Circuit Judge Henry J. Friendly, and District Judge Harold R. Tyler, Jr.—left Lucas and his colleagues extremely optimistic. Once what in all likelihood would be *the* abortion case was indeed heard and decided by that panel sometime in the spring, the judgment, whether favorable or unfavorable, would then be directly reviewable by the U.S. Supreme Court. If the promise of *Belous* indeed proved true, all antiabortion laws across the entire United States might well be declared unconstitutional by perhaps June 1971.[67]

Lucas had long intended the New York case to be not the only federal court suit against a state abortion law, but simply the first of several, and it soon became clear that *Belous* would mobilize any number of lawyers and potential plaintiffs. Dees was having no success finding willing doctors in Alabama, but at a small, ARA-sponsored meeting in New York in mid-October a tall and strikingly handsome man—Hugh W. Savage—introduced himself to Lucas and said that he and a number of other Texas doctors were interested in bringing a *Hall*-type suit there. Savage also suggested that funds to support such a case could be generated in Texas, and Lucas responded with particular enthusiasm, in part because arcane complications in Morris Dees's remunerative deal with the Times-Mirror Corporation were likely to leave the Madison Institute with considerably less financing than had earlier been envisioned. A Texas case would require perhaps twenty-five thousand dollars over several years, Lucas told Savage, plus a Texas attorney knowledgeable about federal courts and constitutional litigation. Such a Texas case would be one of several companions for *Hall*, Lucas explained, because ideally "it would be desirable that five or six cases reach the U.S. Supreme Court simultaneously."

Lucas immediately had a research assistant prepare a memo summarizing every Texas case involving abortion or the fetus going back to the nineteenth century, and he put Texas right at the top of his short list of other states likely to generate good test cases with ideal, high-status physician plaintiffs. The aftermath of *Belous* had produced a widespread expectation among abortion activists that other, probably even more dramatic legal successes were not far off, and in late October ARA's John Lassoe told Illinois's ICMCA that because of *Belous* and *Hall*, ARA had decided "that we will not fund activity aimed at influencing legislation in those states whose legislatures will not be in session during 1970. Our feeling is that, by 1971, legislative action may be irrelevant."[68]

Then, on November 10, came a second and wholly unexpected legal breakthrough almost as momentous as *Belous*: U.S. District Judge Gerhard A. Gesell dismissed the pending criminal prosecution of Washington's Dr. Milan Vuitch on the grounds that the District of Columbia's antiabortion statute—unchanged since 1901—was unconstitutionally vague. The D.C. law—allowing abortions that were "necessary for the preservation of the mother's life or health"—was significantly broader than most antiabortion provisions, but the word "health," just like "necessary" and "preserve" in *Belous*, was unacceptably vague, Gesell ruled. "There is no clear standard" for a doctor to follow, and hence the D.C. law "fails to give that certainty which due process of law considers essential in a criminal statute." Gesell cited *Griswold* and *Loving* to document what he termed the "increasing indication in decisions of the Supreme Court . . . that as a secular matter a woman's liberty and right of privacy extends to family, marriage and sex matters and may well include the right to remove an unwanted child at least in early stages of pregnancy." Gesell went on to say, however, that "the asserted constitutional right of privacy, here the unqualified right to refuse to bear children, has limitations. Congress"—which had direct legislative authority for District of Columbia statutes—"can undoubtedly regulate abortion practice in many ways, perhaps even establishing different standards at various phases of pregnancy." A new D.C. abortion statute, Gesell indicated, would almost certainly have to be prepared.

Gesell's ruling was a significant victory for the beleaguered Dr. Vuitch, but much more importantly it was also a second highly publicized judicial endorsement of the litigation strategy embodied in *Hall*. Like *Belous*, *Vuitch* indicated that the judicial climate—like other expert opinion before it—was rapidly evolving. A prominent *New York Times* story emphasized that abortion attorneys such as Lucas were increasingly optimistic about an eventual victory in the Supreme Court, and *Times* court correspondent Fred Graham stressed that more and more activists "are coming to view abortion as a fundamental right." Vuitch himself—a fifty-four-year-old native of Serbia who had attended medical school in Hungary before marrying an American woman and immigrating to the United States in the mid-1950s—had started performing abortions in the D.C. area in 1962, soon after receiving his first American medical license. Abortions had become his full-time specialty in 1964, and in the ensuing five years Vuitch had been arrested more than a dozen times in Maryland, Virginia, and Washington. Aside from one conviction in Montgomery County, Maryland, four months earlier that was now on appeal, Vuitch otherwise had never been found guilty, even though he readily admitted to performing anywhere between ten and twenty abortions a day, five days a week. Until his D.C. arrest eighteen months earlier, Vuitch had been a mainstay of the east coast referral network, and now with Gesell's voiding of the D.C. statute, Vuitch was able to return to a high-volume operating schedule in an even more open manner than before.[69]

The *Vuitch* decision significantly hastened the litigation plans that had gotten started in a number of states in the nine weeks since *Belous*. New Jersey attorney and ACLU member Richard "Dick" Samuel had agreed right after *Belous* to help the state ACLU affiliate handle a federal appeal for an imprisoned doctor, Sherwin H. Raymond, whose 1967 abortion conviction had been affirmed on appeal and then not accorded review by the New Jersey Supreme Court. A number of attorneys from around the state who were interested in mounting a broader case were brought together with both Samuel and Roy Lucas by state ACLU executive director Stephen M. Nagler, and a group of Princeton women who had been actively interested in abortion repeal for more than a year were also drawn into the effort. In mid-December the ACLU publicly announced its intentions, and by the end of 1969 Samuel, Nagler, and Lucas had made significant headway in preparing an actual case for filing sometime early in 1970.[70]

In Iowa the state Civil Liberties Union cited *Belous* in announcing its intent to look for an attorney to file an abortion suit, and Illinois's ICMCA likewise referred to the California decision in saying that it was considering a constitutional case. An ACLU-affiliated lawyer in Charlotte notified the national office that he would soon initiate a case against North Carolina's 1967 reform law, and in Colorado Dick Lamm, who had discussed with Lucas at the mid-October ARA meeting in New York the possibility that at least one case should be brought against a reform statute, found that several physicians at the University of Colorado Medical School were quite willing to take part if Lamm would bring a federal challenge against his own 1967 reform law. The doctors, Lamm told Lucas, were "a particularly prestigious group" with "great influence in the entire Rocky Mountain area," and a case brought in their names, Lamm believed, would have a "vast influence on the entire area." Lamm's view was in full accord with Lucas's own firm belief that prominent physicians were the best possible plaintiffs to take before federal judges, and Lamm likewise now also believed, as he wrote in the nation's leading magazine for lawyers, that *Griswold*'s right to privacy "would seem to apply with equal force to laws that restrict the availability" of abortion. Even a therapeutic reform statute, Lamm said, "invades the sacred realm of marital privacy by denying married couples the right to plan the future of their family." Asked by a Denver journalist to explain his planned constitutional challenge to the very law he himself had sponsored less than three years earlier, Lamm said that "From the beginning, I have believed that abortion should be a strictly private, medical decision between a woman and her doctor." Just as with Bob Hall and Alan Guttmacher, the reformers had indeed become the repealers.[71]

In Seattle, where the obstetrics and gynecology department at the University of Washington Medical School had quietly initiated an abortion referral service, Sam Goldenberg, the leading activist in Washington Citizens for Abortion Reform (WCAR), had turned his thoughts toward a possible court case after attending the same mid-October ARA meeting in New York where Hugh Savage and Dick Lamm had both spoken with Roy Lucas. Goldenberg raised the possibility with Seattle attorney David Hood, who quickly agreed that *Belous* and now *Vuitch* indicated that a court case in all likelihood would succeed in Washington as well. Four days later the Seattle press announced that a physician in suburban Renton, Dr. A. Frans Koome, had notified the governor that he was performing abortions and intended to continue, and amidst the ensuing public hoopla it quickly became clear that neither law enforcement nor medical authorities were eager to tackle Dr. Koome. No witnesses willing to testify against him could be found, and the Renton police chief, who perchance was Koome's next-door neighbor, told one Seattle reporter that Koome was "a good medical man." Some observers interpreted the all-but-explicit tolerance of Koome as a clear sign that most officials believed that some sort of significant liberalization would indeed be approved by the 1970 legislature, but WCAR's principal legislative champion, State Senator Joel Pritchard, was "pessimistic" as to whether the legislature would approve a simple repeal bill. Attorney Hood, with Goldenberg's blessing, began recruiting willing doctors as potential plaintiffs, but in mid-December Goldenberg and his WCAR colleagues decided—in part because of cost worries—to hold off on immediate preparation of a suit until actual legislative prospects could be assayed with the opening of the 1970 session in January.[72]

The aggregate impact of *Belous* and *Vuitch* was also readily apparent outside the confines of litigation strategy. A host of additional medical groups and associations endorsed repeal during the fall months, and a mid-November Gallup poll found that 40 percent of respondents—including 31 percent of Roman Catholics—now endorsed a woman's access to legal abortion "anytime during the first three months" of pregnancy. A widely publicized survey of more than twenty-seven thousand American doctors revealed that more than a majority now backed repeal, and Alan Guttmacher, speaking to a mid-November meeting of the Minnesota Council for the Legal Termination of Pregnancy, told the group that with the prospects for the legal demise of old abortion laws now so bright, "you were probably lucky" that a reform bill failed to pass in the 1969 Minnesota legislature. New York assembly members Franz Leichter and Connie Cook announced that they would again introduce a repeal bill in the 1970 legislature, and press coverage noted that while ten months earlier they had been the only two members to publicly support repeal, their 1970 bill would be cosponsored by more than twenty additional colleagues, including assembly Democratic minority leader Stanley Steingut. An optimistic Leichter told reporters that "we have a good chance" of success, and noted that since *Hall* would be heard sometime that coming spring, perhaps "a race might develop on whether the court or the Legislature will act first."[73]

Roman Catholic opponents of liberalization openly acknowledged that *Belous* and *Vuitch* had placed them very much on the defensive. The Jesuit magazine *America* argued that fetuses ought to be given a major role in defending antiabortion statutes against court case challenges, a role reaching well beyond simply written arguments in amicus briefs: "What the unborn child needs is the additional right to present evidence and to cross-examine the opposing witnesses." Catholic legal scholar John T. Noonan, Jr., the most prolific opponent of abortion liberalization, acknowledged that "the shift in influential sentiment is palpable" but tried to insist that *Griswold* was of no constitutional relevance to the abortion issue since "the usual statute restricting abortions does not affect the sexual relations of husband and wife." Seeking to propagate a quite literal interpretation of *Griswold*, Noonan argued that "Prevention of abortion does not entail . . . state interference with the right of marital intercourse, nor does enforcement of the statute require invasions of the conjugal bedroom."[74]

In the aftermath of *Vuitch*, however, repeal proponents began to think about providing abortion services in a way that would represent a dramatic expansion of the referral network operation. A doctor friend of Bob Hall's, William Rashbaum, proposed to both Hall and Alan Guttmacher that a group of interested New York physicians set up a "private, non-profit medical facility" under the ostensible sponsorship of the Clergy Consultation Service. It would offer outpatient abortions for about one hundred fifty dollars to women whose pregnancies were no more than ten weeks along, and each abortion would be endorsed in writing by two or more doctors on pro forma psychological grounds. Hall's initial reaction was "enthusiastic," although he envisioned it would take some months to raise the necessary start-up funds and obtain and furnish appropriate facilities, and the clergy response was enthusiastic as well. Larry Lader and his NARAL colleagues were hoping to take advantage of the Gesell ruling by creating a similar facility in Washington that would expand upon the flourishing practice of Dr. Vuitch, but the knowledge that the government intended to appeal Gesell's decision to the Supreme Court inhibited any other D.C. physician from joining the NARAL plan. Alan Guttmacher, however, was even more interested than Bob Hall in the possibility of opening a nonlegal clinic in New York sometime in early 1970, and just before Christmas he sent out a letter to some thirty physicians saying that such an idea was in the "very early" planning stage and that he wanted to sample "the attitude of the leaders of the New York medical profession" concerning such a venture. "If enough of you approve," Guttmacher told his colleagues, "the next hurdle would be to find out the attitude of the" district attorney right after the first of the year. Assemblyman Leichter had perhaps seemed prescient when he had wondered out loud as to whether the *Hall* court or the state legislature would act first to void the existing New York statute, but now it appeared that there might be a third route to repeal—essentially Dorothy Kenyon and Morris Ernst's old idea of nullification—as well. Having moved from reform to repeal, now Alan Guttmacher was willing to champion an approach that went well beyond simply signing on as a named plaintiff in a federal court suit.[75]

But federal litigation was where almost all of the activists believed the real breakthroughs would come, and as Roy Lucas surveyed the national scene in December 1969, he was more inclined than ever to think that Texas, along with New Jersey, might be the best state from which to generate a Supreme Court companion case or two for *Hall*. The Gesell decision, and the naming of the New York panel, Lucas told Hugh Savage, "make me more optimistic about further cases. I hope that your interest has not waned, and that you will be able to participate in a test case yourself." On December 4 Lucas and Savage spoke by phone, and Lucas explained how Texas's location in the Fifth Circuit—whose judicial climate was generally regarded as one of the most liberal and innovative of all ten regional federal court circuits—could very well prove to be a major plus. Besides Savage himself, Lucas said, they would need "two or three other physicians from the Fort Worth–Dallas area who share your views about the need for substantial alteration or repeal of the present laws as to physicians." "Each of you must be willing to take the position that: (a) the present law is unclear to you in application; (b) because of the present law you have to refuse to advise and treat women who request interruption of pregnancy; [and] (c) a change in the law would substantially affect your advice and treatment." The cost of such a case, including fees for Lucas and a Texas attorney, would come to perhaps fourteen thousand dollars at the three-judge district court stage and then another nine thousand dollars when it reached the Supreme Court. "The suit should probably be filed no later than mid-March if it is to reach the Supreme Court for consideration in the fall of 1970," Lucas advised in a follow-up letter recapping their discussion. "It would also be possible, and preferable, to file the case late in January."

Two days after his long conversation with Savage, Lucas enthusiastically told NARAL executive director Lee Gidding that a Texas case was definitely in the works. If they were able to file it expeditiously enough, by late January or early February, a timely three-judge panel decision might be ready for Supreme Court review by the fall of 1970, when the high court might very well be considering both the government's appeal of *Vuitch* and an appeal of the initial decision in *Hall*. Lucas told her that the Texas case would be particularly valuable "because it concerns establishment people" and because filing it in the federal judicial district that included Dallas and Fort Worth almost certainly meant that one of the three panel members would be a woman jurist, Sarah T. Hughes, known to millions of Americans as the judge who had administered the oath of office to Lyndon B. Johnson on November 22, 1963. The other two members, Lucas explained, would be selected by the chief judge of the Fifth Circuit, John R. Brown, a former Houston lawyer and an acquaintance of Savage's who had sat on the appellate court for almost fifteen years and who was well-known, Lucas said, for having written "some of the best civil rights decisions in the South." For these reasons, Gidding noted, "Roy is convinced that this case will be won."

During the ensuing three weeks it also became clear that in addition to ideal plaintiffs and extremely promising judges, Texas could also offer good and eager local counsel for an abortion test case. Just three days after talking with Gidding, Lucas received from ASA's Jimmye Kimmey a copy of a letter from a Texas attorney handling a criminal appeal for a physician who had been convicted of abortion six months earlier, Dr. C. W. Thompson. The Thompson appeal, his lawyer said, contained "all the necessary elements to support constitutional arguments" should the abortion litigators be interested in coming in as amici and seeking to make it a test case.

Two weeks later Kimmey forwarded Lucas a second letter from another Texas attorney, Roy L. Merrill, Jr., who had written to ASA, NARAL, and the ACLU on behalf of a Dallas-area doctor, James Hubert Hallford, who had been indicted on two felony counts of having performed abortions in his small-town office in Carrollton, Texas. Merrill and his senior partner, well-known Dallas defense attorney Fred Bruner, knew about *Belous* and *Vuitch*, and hence, Merrill explained, "We are planning to challenge the constitutionality of the Texas laws concerning abortion" as part of Hallford's defense. Merrill asked the New Yorkers for whatever information and advice they could provide, and an enthusiastic Roy Lucas, replying on their behalf, eagerly volunteered his help. "I have undertaken already a great deal of research on the Texas law for a possible federal court declaratory judgment action there, in Dallas or Fort Worth." Moreover, Lucas explained, "Dallas was once a second home to me," during his two summers of student work at Texas Instruments. Proceeding with a Texas case made ideal sense strategically, given Dr. Savage, Judge Hughes, Judge Brown, and now attorney Merrill, and it might well be enjoyable as well as successful.

And indeed a constitutional challenge to the Texas abortion statute *would* be filed in Dallas in early 1970. But it would not emerge from the litigation strategies of Lucas or other experienced attorneys, nor would it be filed on behalf of Hugh Savage or other "establishment" physicians. For unbeknownst to Lucas, to Merrill, and to Savage, two other groups of Texans were simultaneously preparing to file a federal test case, and out of *their* combined energies would come the decisive attack upon the constitutionality of Texas's antiabortion statute and—eventually—almost all others as well.[76]

CHAPTER SEVEN

Into the Courts:
Roe, Doe, and the Right
to Abortion, 1969–1971

Judy Smith moved to Austin to enter the Ph.D. program in molecular biology at the University of Texas in the summer of 1968. An Oklahoma native who had grown up in Dallas and graduated from Brandeis University in Massachusetts in 1966, Judy had spent a year in the Peace Corps in West Africa and then some time in San Francisco before arriving in Austin.

The center of progressive student life at UT was *The Rag*, a two-year-old underground newspaper published by a free-floating group of former and present UT students, many of whom also belonged to the Austin chapter of SDS, Students for a Democratic Society. At *The Rag* Judy met Jim Wheelis, a twenty-six-year-old native of the Texas panhandle who had just started law school at UT; through her graduate work and SDS she met Victoria "Vic" Foe, another biology student, Barbara Hines, a graduate student in Latin American studies, and Beatrice Vogel, a Montana native with a Yale Ph.D. in biology and two preschool-age children.

In March 1969 SDS's National Council met in Austin, and the disagreeably sexist behavior of SDS's male national leaders, most of whom were housed with different members of the Austin chapter, was a defining experience for many of the Austin student activists. The outsiders' treatment of the Austin women was "quite unpleasant" and "pretty alienating," Judy Smith later explained, and Jim Wheelis described the national SDSers as "fairly offensive, sexist people." Bea Vogel, who was somewhat older than her colleagues, recalled that "we were quite astonished to find out how sexist it was" and remembered that the experience "kind of crystalized" the feelings of several of the

Austin women that sex and gender issues deserved more attention than they had yet received.

Not long after the SDS gathering some eight or ten of the Austin women—including Judy and her sister Linda Smith, Bea Vogel, Barbara Hines, Vic Foe, and Barbara Wuensch—met for the first of what became almost weekly conversations about gender and women's roles. Sometime late that spring or early in the summer someone passed around several copies of an early version of *Our Bodies, Our Selves*, a handbook generated by a similar women's group in Boston, and discussions about it soon led to extended conversations about issues of sex and reproduction. At least one member of the group had had the experience of performing a successful self-abortion seven years earlier so that she could continue her education, and in late April *The Rag* ran a brief story describing how Austin women seeking abortions could drive south and cross into Mexico. Doctors there offered abortions for under four hundred dollars, *The Rag* said, and the entire trip could be completed in less than a full day.[1]

In early July the UT administration, at the behest of several reactionary members of the university's Board of Regents, banned the sale or distribution of *The Rag* on the UT campus, and petitioned a state court for an order requiring *The Rag*'s staff to comply with that directive. Several *Rag* staff members persuaded a thirty-five-year-old labor lawyer who had just moved to Austin, David R. Richards, to help them oppose the university's effort, and on August 1 Richards filed suit in federal court to block UT's move on the grounds that any such ban on the sale of a newspaper was a gross violation of the First Amendment's constitutional protection of freedom of speech and of the press. Six weeks later a special three-judge federal court was named to hear *The Rag*'s case.[2]

Although that legal excitement was the major event of the summer for Austin's student activist community, the women's group centered around *The Rag* continued their discussions, and late in July Judy Smith published an initial essay in *The Rag* reflecting the group's thoughts. "We in Women's Liberation," she explained, "deny any inherent differences between men and women and regard everyone as human beings with the same potential." "All of us are trapped by the society that created our roles," and those confines had to be torn down. "We are questioning the ideals of marriage and motherhood," and in the process "the very society that has created these roles and values must also be questioned." Several weeks later the group published a second piece in *The Rag*, entitled "Why Women's Liberation?," and explained that part of the answer was

that "Women's problems are rooted deep in society, and women's liberation cannot be successful until much of what is wrong with society is
corrected. The task is almost too great to be contemplated. Yet there is
freedom in the striving."[3]

But the women did not believe that articles in *The Rag* should be the
only result of their discussions, and by the end of the summer there
was a clear consensus that the group ought to undertake some tangible
projects. "What do we *do*?" Judy Smith remembers them asking each
other. They had known since the spring that birth control counseling
and materials could prove difficult to obtain for unmarried female UT
students, as some but not all physicians at the student health service
rebuffed such requests and since the local Planned Parenthood refused
to serve UT students. By early September there was general agreement
that one tangible project they could undertake would be to establish a
birth control information center in their tiny cubicle next to *The Rag*'s
office, and they announced their plan both in the paper and at the
group's first general meeting of the fall semester on September 25.
"The treatment of women as inferiors is all pervasive in our society,"
Bea Vogel explained in *The Rag*, and through this project as well as others "the Women's Liberation movement is dedicated to freeing women
from the inferior role society has defined for her."

On Wednesday evening October 1 Vic Foe hosted a meeting to
begin setting up the birth control project, and within four weeks they
were advertising the opening of the Women's Liberation Birth Control
Information Center next to *The Rag* office in the university YMCA,
right across the street from the UT campus. Each weekday one or
more volunteers from the group would staff the office from three to
eight p.m. "Every woman has the right to control her own body, to
decide when and if she wants a child," their first announcement
emphasized. "Here in Austin it is very hard to obtain birth control
information if you are unmarried, especially if you are under 21," and
the counseling program hoped to meet this need.

The group did not initially intend for the birth control project to deal
with the question of abortion, even though their first announcement
stated that "By making abortions illegal, our society makes the abortion
operation a punishment for sin." However, it soon became clear, as each
day's volunteers fielded a half-dozen or more face-to-face inquiries from
UT women, that abortion availability was a question the counseling
project would have to confront. Several of the women were greatly concerned that any detectable involvement with abortion might bring them
to the unfriendly attention of local police and prosecutors, and everyone

appreciated that however surprisingly, abortions were not available in Austin, either from doctors or nondoctors. But the requests continued, and the issue of abortion was becoming more and more visible. Even Austin's principal newspaper, the *American-Statesman*, which ignored the student activists almost entirely, featured a story in which the chairman of UT's botany department, B. L. Turner, declared that "I believe in abortions. If the mother doesn't want the child, that's a good enough reason. The government ought to make it possible for the woman alone to make the decision." The women in the counseling project whole-heartedly agreed, and not long after they first advertised the availability of birth control advice, they quietly but actively began to seek out dependable information about the availability of safe abortions and about whether they could then provide that knowledge to women who contacted them without fear of being criminally prosecuted.[4]

Everyone knew about the option of driving to Mexico, but no one had very much information about the skills, safety, and dependability of the Mexican providers, the most convenient of whom were located in the town of Piedras Negras, just across the border from Eagle Pass, Texas. Among the first people whom the women approached with their quandary was Bob Breihan, a Methodist minister who had been affili-ated with the UT campus for more than two decades. Breihan had already heard Howard Moody speak about the Clergy Consultation Service network at a campus ministers conference in Michigan, and while he was quite willing to help with the women's search for dependable providers, he was dubious about their belief that he, as a minister, would be immune from prosecution in ways that they would not. Breihan raised their query with a friend who was a criminal defense attorney, Perry Jones, and Jones soon passed along the name of a Hispanic woman in San Antonio who supposedly had a good reputa-tion for a nondoctor. Some Austin referrals began to go there, others to a similar woman in Dallas, and then a few to an actual M.D. in a small town just north of Dallas, James Hubert Hallford, who had had at least a modest number of Austin patients even before the counseling project first came on the scene.

The Austin women's quiet inquiries and very careful referral efforts had not progressed too far when a Piedras Negras provider with a medical degree, Dr. Leopoldo Bruno, made contact with them. Judy Smith and Vic Foe discussed the unusual development with Bob Breihan, who was similarly intrigued, especially by the relatively rea-sonable fee that had been quoted—three hundred fifty dollars. Smith and Foe took the initiative and drove down to Piedras Negras to speak with Bruno and have a look at his clinic, and came away quite favorably impressed. Now the Austin women and Breihan had a dependable, moderately priced and reasonably convenient provider; the remaining question was how certain could they be that discreet distribution of that information to women who asked for abortion referral assistance would not land one or more group members in the Austin city jail.[5]

One Saturday morning at a garage sale Judy Smith and Bea Vogel raised that issue with a young female lawyer, Sarah Weddington, whose husband Ron was a close friend and law school classmate of Judy's friend Jim Wheelis: Would open and aboveboard provision of referral information leave the project volunteers vulnerable to arrest, as some of them feared. Weddington was not sure, but she agreed to look at the Texas antiabortion statutes and let them know. Judy had taken Sarah to one earlier meeting of the entire women's group, but Sarah was "much straighter than we were," one key participant later explained, and had not taken part in either the group's many discussions or in the world of student activism centered around *The Rag*. Sarah's husband Ron, a twenty-seven-year-old Texas native who had been drafted into the Army before returning to Austin to finish his undergraduate degree and then begin law school, was one of several additional plaintiffs who had lent his name to *The Rag*'s federal court suit against the UT Regents, but Sarah, who had graduated from the UT law school in August 1967, a year before the couple had married, had never become involved in campus political life. In part it was because she had had to hold down a variety of part-time jobs—as a secretary, insurance clerk, hospital librarian, and sorority house mother—in order to support herself while in law school, but far more so it was because Sarah's previous life and church-centered upbringing had made her fundamentally middle-class in both style and attitude. As she explained a few years later, "I had never even been to a party where liquor was served until after I graduated from college." Sarah's resolutely proper demeanor inescapably separated her from many aspects of Austin's student counterculture; as one close acquaintance at the time later put it, Sarah's manner and outlook made her seem "more like my parents than like a peer."[6]

But Sarah had had one experience—one she never shared with Judy or Bea or ever discussed with anyone else besides Ron for more than two decades—that made her much more responsive to their legal query than might otherwise have been the case. Two years earlier, in 1967, after she and Ron had become seriously involved during her final year of law school, Sarah had unexpectedly and distressingly discovered that she was pregnant. Neither she nor Ron had any desire to interrupt their schooling in order to become parents, and Sarah was mortified at the thought of having to tell her parents, a Methodist minister and a teacher, or her two younger siblings. While Sarah had never previously given much thought to abortion, she had no doubt about what they ought to do. Ron spoke with several acquaintances, made a call or two, and the following Friday morning they drove south toward Eagle Pass and the Mexican border. They checked in to an American motel and then walked across into Piedras Negras for a scheduled rendezvous with an unnamed man who led them to a small but clean clinic. The fee was four hundred dollars cash, but the staff was pleasant and the doctor friendly. Sarah was anesthetized during the abortion itself, and no difficulties or complications ensued. After a woozy evening in the Eagle Pass motel, she and Ron drove back to Austin the following day and resumed their normal schedules.

Sarah's secret trip to Piedras Negras was perhaps the one extraordinary event in an otherwise unremarkable and successful early life. Only twenty-two years old at the time of her brief visit to Mexico, Sarah Ragle Weddington had grown up in a variety of small west Texas towns where her father had been a pastor at a succession of churches. A good enough student to have skipped both sixth and twelfth grades, Sarah graduated from Abilene High School when she was only sixteen and then from Abilene's small McMurry College in December 1964. Having set her eyes on attending law school—in part because one college advisor told her that it would be far too difficult for a girl—Sarah moved to Austin in early 1965 and worked as a typist in the state legislature before beginning classes at the University of Texas Law School in June 1965. Only four other women were among the 120 law students who started that summer, and out of the law school's total enrollment of some sixteen hundred students, only some forty were female. Despite having to juggle both her course work and the succession of part-time jobs, Sarah did well academically and, by taking classes straight through during three successive summers, she completed the normal schedule of three years' work by the end of 1967.

With such an excellent academic record, Sarah found it deeply frustrating when not a single job offer resulted from her interviews with a variety of law firms. Female attorneys were still relatively rare in Texas in 1967, with sex discrimination open and explicit, but one of her favorite professors at the law school, John Sutton, who was also in charge of supervising preparation of a new Code of Professional Responsibility for the American Bar Association's Committee to Reevaluate Ethical Standards, solved Sarah's employment dilemma by offering her a multiyear position as his assistant.[7]

Sarah was well into her second year of work for Sutton when Judy and Bea posed their abortion law query to her at that Saturday morning garage sale in November 1969. The UT law library was in the same law school building where she worked for Sutton, but her review of the Texas statutes on abortion and on aiding and abetting gave Sarah no clear answer as to how criminally vulnerable the counseling project's volunteers might be as a result of the group's judicious abortion referral efforts. She reported her uncertain findings to Judy and several of the other women, and the project's quiet efforts continued on as before. Toward the end of the month, on November 26, the special three-judge federal district court that had been named to handle *The Rag*'s case against the UT Regents assembled in Austin to hear oral arguments on several procedural matters. *The Rag*'s success in winning such an impressive-looking federal court proceeding in its battle against the UT administration was a subject of considerable talk within the Austin student activist community, and one morning either just before or just after that Wednesday hearing, Judy Smith raised the subject with Jim Wheelis at breakfast. He and his fellow law students, Judy commented, talked a lot about the federal courts. Making any headway on abortion legalization in state legislatures in Texas and elsewhere looked like a pretty dim prospect. What would it take, she asked, to bring an abortion suit much like *The Rag*'s. "Do you think it would work in the federal courts? What would we need?" Jim's initial response specified the bare minimum: "About fifteen dollars and an attorney." Judy replied, "What about Sarah?" Jim agreed that it was a possibility, and later that day Jim stuck his head into Sarah's office at the law school: Judy and her colleagues had another abortion question for her. Several hours later Sarah met with Judy and Jim at the law school snack bar, and Judy quickly broached the idea she had first voiced to Jim at breakfast: a federal lawsuit ought to be filed challenging the constitutionality of the Texas antiabortion statute. Sarah did not dismiss the idea, but she was more than a little taken aback by Judy's suggestion that *she* consider filing it. "No, you need someone older and with more experience," Sarah told Judy. "You need somebody in a firm, with research and secretarial backup." But Judy asked her to give the idea some further thought, and Sarah agreed.

As Judy and women's group colleagues such as Barbara Hines talked about the possibilities, everyone agreed that Sarah was the only female attorney whom they knew who might be persuaded to file such a challenge, especially given how the Austin women's liberation group had virtually no money for fees or expenses. Judy, Jim, and one or two of the others discussed the case idea again with Sarah one evening over dinner at Jim and Judy's, and Sarah somewhat reluctantly agreed to look into pursuing it. Jim and Ron both suggested that she talk with one of their favorite and most approachable professors in the law school, Bernard "Bernie" Ward, about the federal court procedural hurdles that would have to be overcome, and then several days later, when Sarah was in Dallas, she realized that a former classmate from law school, Linda Coffee, who after graduation had gone on to a year-long clerkship with U.S. District Judge Sarah T. Hughes, might also be a good source of advice and, given her background, might indeed be willing to file such a case herself.[8]

Linda and Sarah had been two of the five women who had entered UT law school together in the summer of 1965, and while they had sometimes studied together, they had not been particular friends nor had they been much in touch since graduating almost two years earlier. Linda like Sarah had been a lifelong academic standout, first at Woodrow Wilson High School in Dallas and then at Rice University in Houston. At age seventeen she had spent more than six months in New Zealand on an exchange program, and while a German major at Rice she had spent a summer in West Germany. A few years later Linda explained that she had decided to attend law school because "it just seemed intriguing," but the small number of women at UT had made her experience somewhat discomforting; "I was always self-conscious," she subsequently remembered. Linda had spent several months during law school doing legal aid work in Austin, and when she took the Texas bar exam in March 1968, she tied for the second highest score in the state. That same spring Linda's mother had heard that Judge Hughes was looking for a new law clerk or two, and after Linda sent in a resumé, Hughes immediately called her up.[9]

Linda began her one-year clerkship with Hughes in June 1968, and found the experience both educational and enjoyable. The Dallas federal courthouse was a small community of its own, with three district judges and one circuit judge in residence plus a customary population of court staffers, prosecutors, local attorneys and a few regular reporters from Dallas's two main newspapers. Sarah Hughes was well-known in town from her twenty-six years as a state court judge prior to joining the federal bench in 1961; liberal U.S. Senator Ralph Yarborough had recommended Hughes for the appointment over her principal local competitor, Dallas County District Attorney Henry Wade. Barely five feet tall, Judge Hughes had won election to three terms in the Texas state legislature, starting in 1930, before joining the judiciary. Almost seventy-two years old when Linda Coffee became her law clerk, Hughes had graduated Phi Beta Kappa from Maryland's Goucher College before getting her law degree from George Washington University by taking classes at night while working as a D.C. policewoman during the day. She and her husband George, who had died in 1964, had moved to Dallas in 1924, and Sarah Tilghman Hughes had immediately plunged into a lifelong career in law and politics. "We didn't want any children," she explained years later. "I never wanted the care of young children. I was interested in a career," and no matter how rare women attorneys, let alone female legislators or elected state judges were in Texas in the 1930s and 1940s, Sarah Hughes persevered and generally prevailed. She lost one race for Congress and another for the state supreme court during her years on the state bench, but achieved minor national fame when her name was placed in nomination for the vice presidency at the 1952 Democratic National Convention. An outspoken proponent of women's rights throughout her years in Texas politics and on the state bench, her elevation to the federal judiciary had only slightly cramped her style. Known to most people from the famous scene in which she had administered the oath of office to Lyndon B. Johnson on Air Force One on the afternoon of November 22, 1963, Sarah Hughes much preferred to be known for her advocacy of women's rights and for the judicial outcomes she dispensed from the bench.[10]

Sarah Hughes was unquestionably a unique federal judge, and vastly more colorful than either of her district court colleagues in Dallas, William M. "Mac" Taylor and Chief Judge Joe Estes, but there was unanimous agreement around the Dallas federal courthouse that the building's most remarkable and impressive character was Fifth Circuit Court of Appeals Judge Irving L. Goldberg, an energetic and outspoken man with a voice that two law clerks later described as having "the resonance of a tuba spiked with the twang and pitch of a banjo." Born in 1906 in the east Texas town of Port Arthur, Irving Goldberg graduated from Harvard Law School in 1929 and then returned to his home state to practice law and take an active role in a wide range of Jewish organizations. Long-acquainted with Texas politicians such as Representative and later Senator Lyndon B. Johnson, Goldberg in 1950 had joined with several other longtime friends, including Robert Strauss, to found a law firm that was initially named Goldberg, Akin, Gump, Strauss and Hauer. Sixteen years later President Lyndon Johnson nominated Goldberg to a newly created seat on the Fifth Circuit, and within little more than two years, Irving Goldberg deservedly acquired a well-known reputation for being as vocal and dominating a courtroom presence as any member of the federal appellate bench.[11]

In May 1969, just as she was about to complete her clerkship with Sarah Hughes, Linda Coffee accepted a position with a small but attractive Dallas bankruptcy firm, Palmer and Palmer. That same month, one of her oldest friends, a young attorney whom she had known since childhood more than twenty years earlier when they had both attended Dallas's Gaston Avenue Baptist Church, sought Linda's advice and assistance with an unusual and—for 1969—truly novel declaratory judgment case he wanted to file in federal district court. Henry J. McCluskey, Jr., looked about as straight as a twenty-six-year-old Baptist graduate of Waco's Baylor University and Baylor Law School should, but Henry had one client, Alvin L. Buchanan, who was openly and actively gay and whose efforts to find similarly inclined sexual partners had led to one arrest in a bathroom at Dallas's Reverchon Park in February and another two months later in a department store restroom. Buchanan had been convicted in local trial courts for both offenses, and one jury had recommended five years' imprisonment as appropriate punishment for consensual oral sex. Henry was appealing Buchanan's convictions within the Texas courts, but he also wanted to file a federal case alleging that Texas's nineteenth-century sodomy statute was unconstitutionally overbroad. Since the statute criminalized all acts of oral or anal sex, whether heterosexual or homosexual, and provided no exception for married couples who might otherwise be arrested if they happened to be caught committing such a crime, the law in light of *Griswold* and *Griswold*'s reverential celebration of marital privacy appeared to be particularly vulnerable to just such a constitutional challenge.

Linda enthusiastically encouraged Henry in his effort, and offered him a number of pointers. In late May McCluskey filed his initial complaint in *Alvin L. Buchanan* v. *Charles Batchelor*, Dallas's chief of police, and by the end of the summer Fifth Circuit Chief Judge John R. Brown had named three of the Dallas-based jurists—Goldberg, Hughes, and Taylor—as the three-judge panel to hear McCluskey's challenge to the constitutionality of the Texas statute. Three additional plaintiffs—a married couple complaining of their vulnerability under the statute, and a gay man alleging that his private, as distinct from public, sexual acts were similarly outlawed—were added to the case before the panel heard oral argument late that fall. By the time that Sarah Weddington first called Linda Coffee on December 3 to ask that she consider filing a federal case against the Texas abortion statute,

Henry McCluskey's parallel challenge to the sodomy law was under submission and awaiting decision by the three-judge panel.[12]

Weddington explained to Coffee that the idea of filing a constitutional test case had originated with the women's group in Austin, and that their present assumption was that the case would be brought on behalf of the Austin group, if upon examination it looked reasonably certain that such a group—actively involved in encouraging and advising violators of the statute—would have sufficient legal standing to be acceptable plaintiffs for such a challenge. Coffee already knew about the California Supreme Court decision in *Belous,* and she responded eagerly to Weddington's request that she consider bringing a Texas abortion case, so long as her colleagues at Palmer and Palmer had no objections. Linda sought and obtained their approval later that same day, and the next morning Coffee wrote to Weddington in Austin to accept the offer:

> I am very enthusiastic about the possibility of your organization in Austin (I can't remember what name you told me yesterday) bringing an action to challenge the Texas Abortion Statute. There are a few procedural points that I will need to check into, but at the present time I am reasonably sure that the organization would have the requisite standing to challenge the statute. I would appreciate it very much if you would bring the matter up

with the Austin group for its formal approval "as soon as possible," Coffee suggested. "Would you consider being co-counsel in the event that a suit is actually filed?" she asked Weddington. "I have always found that it is a great deal more fun to work with someone on a law suit of this nature. If you are not at the present time admitted to practice before the Northern District of Texas," the formal name of the federal district court in Dallas, "it will be a simple matter to have you so admitted sometime before any actual hearings are scheduled." Palmer and Palmer had given her permission to proceed, Coffee said, and "I will be looking forward to hearing from you soon."[13]

Weddington soon called with a hearty assent, and Coffee began to think about how to put together an actual case. Two principal questions loomed large. One major strategic consideration, Coffee quickly realized, was that while Dallas was indeed in the Northern District of Texas, where Sarah Hughes would be a likely presence on any three-judge panel, Austin was in a different district, the Western. That alone strongly suggested that they ought to proceed with a Dallas-area plaintiff rather than the Austin women's group. Secondly, Coffee began seriously examining whether such a group would actually have adequate standing. She soon realized that there was no clear guarantee that it would, and Coffee and Weddington quickly agreed that they had better find one or more individual plaintiffs whose standing would be unchallengeable, such as a pregnant woman who wanted an abortion, in addition to any organizational plaintiff. Weddington explained the need to Judy Smith, and Judy and several other Austin volunteers broached the question with a few women who contacted the group seeking referral information, but it soon became clear that for virtually every woman who was seeking an abortion, their undesired pregnancy was "a part of their life they wanted over," rather than prolonged in the interest of a court case. Linda and Sarah believed that they needed a woman who not only had an unwanted pregnancy, but a woman whose pregnancy would continue at least until the case was actually filed. Otherwise, if the plaintiff went ahead and actually had an abortion, the case might then turn out to be moot.

"I didn't know how we would find" such a pregnant woman, Linda later explained. Perhaps if they went forward and simply filed on behalf of an organization, additional and better plaintiffs would come forward as a result of the initial publicity, just as had happened with Henry McCluskey's sodomy law case. She discussed the problem with Henry, and mentioned her search to a number of other friends and at several informal gatherings. Christmas and then New Year's passed without a clear solution presenting itself. Then in early January 1970 the Women's Alliance of Dallas's First Unitarian Church announced a January 13 meeting on abortion law change where two members of Dallas Planned Parenthood, Virginia Whitehill and Pat Cookston, would lead the discussion. The Women's Alliance had been planning such a meeting since late September, soon after the *Belous* decision had been publicized, and at the January 13 session both Ginny Whitehill and Pat Cookston explained to the other women present how the subsequent *Vuitch* decision in D.C. was further evidence that fundamental abortion law change would likely come from the courts rather than from legislatures. One interested observer at the meeting was *Dallas Times-Herald* reporter Barbara Richardson, and the next day her story on the discussion appeared under a headline that was in the form of a question: "Answers Lie With Courts?"[14]

In the wake of Richardson's story, two people who learned about the active interest of the Women's Alliance in abortion law change made contact with one or another group member, and then with each other: Linda Coffee and Marsha King. Linda was happy to discover a preexisting Dallas group that could offer support for a court case and potentially help in locating one or more plaintiffs; Marsha King was passionately interested in the issue because of an extremely traumatic abortion experience that she had gone through less than two months earlier.

Marsha Diane Cooper King was twenty-six years old when she first met Linda Coffee and Ginny Whitehill. A native of Atlanta, where her mother was a longtime teacher in the public schools, Marsha had graduated from Emory University as a physics major in 1964 and had then gone on to earn a master's degree in physics at Georgia Tech. An engineering job with General Dynamics had brought her to Fort Worth, Texas, just west of Dallas, where she had met and fallen in love with another General Dynamics employee, David Garth King, a native of Tyler, Texas, who had earned a marketing degree and then an MBA from Southern Methodist University in Dallas. Marsha and David were married in Fort Worth in July 1968, but in the summer of 1969, soon after Marsha had taken a new job, she began to experience vision problems, severe backaches, and erratic mood swings, including significant periods of depression. One of several doctors recommended that she switch from birth control pills to a diaphragm and spermicidal foam, and while her vision did normalize, in late October Marsha became pregnant. Confirmation of the pregnancy "was the worst possible news," she later explained. "My feeling about the pregnancy was that a horrible cancer was growing in my body that would ruin my life." Marsha was still taking a variety of medicines for both her back pain and her mood swings, and felt so sick that she could barely cope with her job. Neither she nor David believed they were ready to parent a child, and they immediately called a Mexico City abortion clinic they had heard about. Three days after her pregnancy was confirmed, Marsha flew to Mexico City and underwent a lengthy and painful procedure. When it finally was over she felt "filled with a feeling of joy and freedom," with "relief and happiness." Her back pain prevented her from getting much if any sleep, and on the plane back to Dallas she was so weak that the flight attendants gave her oxygen. The abortion had been successful but extremely stressful, and the intensity of her experience gave Marsha an acute interest in making safe abortions legally available right there in Texas.[15]

Soon after Linda Coffee first met Marsha King, Coffee's Dallas abortion case prospects received a tremendous boost when Judges Goldberg, Hughes, and Taylor unanimously sustained Henry McCluskey's constitutional privacy attack upon the Texas sodomy statute. Sarah Hughes's opinion on behalf of the panel cited *Griswold* in holding that the Texas law was indeed unconstitutionally overbroad in that it "operates directly on an intimate relation of husband and wife." Without speaking in any direct way to the issue of homosexual intimacies, the panel nonetheless ruled that traditional moral disapproval of sodomous sex acts "is not sufficient reason for the State to encroach upon the liberty of married persons in their private conduct." Hughes noted how a 1968 ruling by the Seventh Circuit Court of Appeals, *Cotner* v. *Henry*, freeing from prison a man who had already served three years for the crime of having anal intercourse with his wife, had by implication already extended *Griswold*'s constitutional protection to such marital acts. The Supreme Court had not disturbed the Seventh Circuit's ruling, and thus Hughes and her colleagues formally held that the similar Texas law was "void on its face for constitutional overbreadth insofar as it reaches the private, consensual acts of married couples."[16]

Buchanan was a signal victory for Henry McCluskey, but most of Henry's practice involved much more mundane matters such as arranging adoptions. Sometime in mid- or late January, either just before or just after *Buchanan* was decided, a young and somewhat marginal osteopath who was facing a federal insurance fraud indictment, Dr. Richard Allen Lane, sent McCluskey a pregnant young woman who had failed in her search for a safe and affordable abortion and was going to need adoption assistance with her unwanted pregnancy. Norma Nelson McCorvey was a tiny twenty-two-year-old when she first met Henry McCluskey. A high school dropout whose parents had divorced when she was thirteen, Norma Nelson was a sixteen-year-old carhop at a Dallas–Fort Worth drive-in when she met Elwood "Woody" McCorvey, a twenty-four-year-old twice-divorced sheet metal worker from Buffalo. Six weeks later they were married, and soon they were on the road to California, where Norma excitedly discovered she was pregnant. Her new husband, however, angrily denied responsibility and violently accused Norma of playing around. Bruised and frightened, Norma sold enough of her few possessions to get bus fare back to Dallas, where she got a job as a waitress in a lesbian bar. In May 1965 she gave birth to a daughter, Melissa.

Over the ensuing four years, Norma worked a succession of jobs in generally lesbian Dallas-area bars and found herself a female roommate. Norma's mother, upset with Norma's all but openly bisexual life-style, took charge of Melissa and moved to Louisiana, where she and her second husband gained formal custody. By the end of 1966 Norma was again pregnant—"every time I went to bed with a man I got pregnant," she later observed. She did not want to keep the child, but the father did, and after giving birth at Dallas Osteopathic Hospital, where Dr. Frank J. Bradley had also delivered Melissa, Norma happily surrendered custody of her second daughter.

In the summer of 1969 Norma had a brief affair with an older man named Bill, whom Norma rather liked and who said his money came from successful gambling. Early that fall, however, Norma took a job as a ticket-seller with a traveling carnival, and a few weeks later, with the carnival in Florida, Norma realized that she once again was pregnant. Upset and distraught, Norma headed back to Dallas and tried to find a place to live. She went to see Dr. Bradley for a pregnancy test, which was indeed positive, and she immediately told Bradley that she did not want to give birth to another child. Bradley was "absolutely appalled" when he realized she wanted an abortion, Norma recalled years later, and she understood she would have to look elsewhere. She ended up at Dr. Lane's office, where another woman in the waiting room, upon hearing Norma's story, told her that she ought to tell the doctor that she had been raped, for that news might well make the difference. She took the advice and concocted an elaborate tale of being assaulted one night while working for the carnival, but Lane, like Bradley, told her he could not be of help; if she had five hundred dollars and could get herself to California or New York, he said, maybe she could succeed there. But Norma, whose utter lack of funds had forced her to move in with her father, could not imagine raising anywhere near that figure. Now perhaps almost three months pregnant, it might be getting a little too late in any event, and Lane gave her the name of an adoption attorney. Norma went to see the man and loathed him almost immediately. He asked her several suggestive and demeaning questions, and she quickly left. She pondered her options, and went to look at one place she had been told abortions were available, only to find it deserted. Finally she returned to Lane's office, and he gave her the name of a second attorney to try: Henry McCluskey.

When Norma first saw McCluskey after an initial brief telephone conversation, she very quickly warmed to his awkward but friendly manner. He answered no when Norma asked if he knew of any possibilities for arranging an abortion, and their conversation turned to how he would handle the baby's adoption, placing it with a good family in return for their paying all of Norma's childbirth expenses. They agreed to be in touch, and either that day or perhaps the next Henry McCluskey phoned his old friend Linda Coffee to say that just like she had helped him with *Buchanan*, now it looked like he might be able to assist in her abortion case, for he had just met a young woman who was going to have to go forward with her unwanted pregnancy. Linda was delighted, and asked to meet her. Henry phoned Norma at her father's apartment and told her that he had a female attorney friend whom he would like her to meet, that his friend wanted to talk with her about her belief that legal abortion ought to be available. A day or two later Henry McCluskey introduced Norma McCorvey to Linda Coffee, and Linda was immediately struck by how small—and how visibly pregnant—her potential test-case plaintiff looked. Linda explained to her the court case idea that she and Sarah had been developing, and Norma, her educational background notwithstanding, responded very enthusiastically. Linda stressed that being a plaintiff would not take much time, would not entail any costs, and almost certainly would not require any courtroom testimony or public identification. Linda emphasized that a lot of the details were not yet certain, and that her colleague from Austin would also want to meet and talk with Norma, but Norma was quite willing to take part. Linda swiftly called Sarah in Austin with the good news, and Sarah arranged to come up to Dallas a few days later so that the two attorneys together could have a further conversation with Norma.

Linda told both Sarah and Norma to meet her at a Colombo's Pizza Parlor in the 5700 block of East Mockingbird Lane in northeast Dallas, just six blocks north of Linda's apartment on McCommas Boulevard. Norma was still holding out some slight hope of actually getting an abortion, but both Linda and Sarah, conscious of their belief that they needed a still-pregnant plaintiff with whom to go to court, gently indicated to Norma that that seemed quite unlikely, especially since it looked to them that Norma was now probably more than four months pregnant. Norma made a brief reference to her rape story, much as she had to both Linda and Henry previously, but it was of little moment to either of the attorneys, for they were intent upon filing a full-scale attack upon the Texas abortion statute, not a case seeking therapeutic exceptions for rape victims. Norma was quite willing to sign on as a prospective plaintiff, and the dinner conversation broke up with both Linda and Sarah convinced that they now had at least the beginnings of an actual federal court case.[17]

Both attorneys fully appreciated that Norma's highly unsettled life and high-strung, emotionally vulnerable personality meant that she might not prove to be the most stable or dependable of plaintiffs, and they agreed that Norma would have to be supplemented by one or more others. On January 27 both Linda and her new friend Marsha

King went to the morning meeting of the Women's Alliance at First Unitarian Church. One committee chair, Virginia Fielding, told the group that her members, who had been instrumental in sponsoring the abortion discussion two weeks earlier at which Ginny Whitehill and Pat Cookston had spoken, had scheduled a February 11 meeting aimed at launching a new and broader-gauge organization that would champion abortion law repeal. Then both Marsha and Linda addressed the group on the subject of the incipient federal court case, and each explicitly asked the Alliance to join the case as an organizational plaintiff and authorize Linda to represent them. A good deal of discussion ensued, and a consensus was reached that any formal decision should be put off until a subsequent meeting and perhaps a polling of the entire membership.

The February 11 meeting drew a varied group of about eighteen people, including Marsha and David King, Ginny Whitehill, and Barbara Richardson from the *Times-Herald*, but aside from agreeing to organize themselves as the Dallas Committee for the Study of Abortion (DCSA), those present had widely divergent opinions about what tangible actions the group should pursue aside from sponsoring some sort of public forum. As Linda Coffee and Sarah Weddington considered their plans, however, Linda's increasing doubts about whether any organization would actually be accorded standing to challenge the Texas abortion statute led them to drop their idea of using the First Unitarian Women's Alliance as a group plaintiff. Even before Linda's first contact with Norma McCorvey, Marsha King had volunteered to serve as an anonymous plaintiff, and while Linda, and then Sarah, had put the idea aside on the grounds that Marsha was not currently pregnant, by mid-February Linda and Sarah had agreed that using both Marsha and her husband David as plaintiffs made far more sense, both with regard to possible standing and with regard to having a married couple who could invoke *Griswold*'s celebration of marital privacy, than trying to recruit the Unitarian women's group.[18]

By late February Linda was beginning to sketch out the beginnings of a formal complaint both for Norma McCorvey, who would be called Jane Roe, and for David and Marsha King, who would be spoken of under the common legal sobriquet of John and Jane Doe. Linda was a bit uncertain about precisely what sort of motion to prepare to request appointment of a three-judge court, but on March 1 or 2 a courthouse reporter for the *Times-Herald* who had heard about Linda's plans called and suggested that she might run an item on the upcoming suit even before it was actually filed. That comment prodded Linda into immediate action, and by the morning of March 3, doing her own typing, she had readied a three-page complaint on behalf of Norma McCorvey and a five-page one on behalf of David and Marsha King. They both asked the court for a declaratory judgment holding the Texas abortion statute facially unconstitutional and for a permanent injunction barring any further enforcement of it. Each of the two complaints named Dallas County District Attorney Henry Wade as the defendant, and both of them alleged that the plaintiffs could not afford to travel to other jurisdictions where abortions might be available. The first one stated that the Texas law infringed upon "Jane Roe's" "right to safe and adequate medical advice pertaining to the decision of whether to carry a given pregnancy to term" and upon "the fundamental right of all women to choose whether to bear children." It also alleged that the statute infringed upon "Roe's" "right to privacy in the physician-patient relationship," and upon "Roe's" "right to life" as protected by the Fourteenth Amendment. The second complaint prepared on behalf of "John and Jane Doe" specified that the law encroached upon "plaintiffs' right to marital privacy" and that fear of an unintended pregnancy without access to a legal abortion was "having a detrimental effect upon Plaintiffs' marital happiness." The complaint also, by way of implicit reference to the Kings' involvement in the newly formed DCSA and to the work of the Austin volunteers, additionally alleged that the plaintiffs feared prosecution under the Texas law for any counseling or referral work they might take part in.

With Weddington in Austin and hence unavailable to review Coffee's two documents, Linda put only her own name on the two complaints and at midmorning on March 3 went to the clerk's office in the Dallas federal courthouse and paid thirty dollars from her own pocket—fifteen dollars apiece—to file both *Roe* v. *Wade* and *Doe* v. *Wade*. Both that evening's *Dallas Times-Herald* and the next day's *Dallas Morning News* ran front-page articles on the cases' filing. The *Times-Herald* followed up with one story surveying the views of local doctors, none of whom were identified, and another which estimated that perhaps three thousand illegal abortions a year took place in Dallas, with prices ranging from one hundred fifty to one thousand dollars. Two days later the *Times-Herald* devoted a long editorial to Coffee's challenge, and while the paper conceded that the existing law was "badly in need of an intelligent overhaul" and that therapeutic liberalization was "long overdue," it nonetheless concluded that abortions should be available only under "tightly controlled conditions." "We have no sympathy," the *Times-Herald* said, "with the attempt of a married couple and of a single woman to get the existing Texas abortion law declared unconstitutional by a Dallas federal court." Abortion "is too serious a matter to go unregulated and uncontrolled," and while it should be available on individual mental health grounds, "there are, most assuredly, circumstances in which abortion is not at all justified," such as "when it is undertaken for sheer caprice." Coffee's suit was also a mistake, the paper said, because the plaintiffs "are tossing an extremely sensitive and complex moral issue into the laps of a mere handful of individuals—the judges who are to decide the case." Legislators, not jurists, should resolve the abortion law issue, the *Times-Herald* concluded.

Several days later Barbara Richardson essentially responded to her own newspaper's editorial criticism of the law suits with a long story anonymously and sympathetically profiling Marsha and David King. Richardson characterized them as "a church-going, articulate young couple," and described Marsha's serious health problems and her Mexican abortion. Marsha was quoted as saying that "The biggest thing motivating us is . . . freedom of choice," and that "we do feel the abortion law is unconstitutional." David said that "We both felt a moral imperative to file the suit," because "our personal moral and ethical codes were outraged by the law." When legislative reform failed to occur, "we became convinced if redress could not be gotten there, we would turn to the courts." More basically, however, David explained that "I have had strong convictions about abortions ever since I've been old enough and wise enough to consider it. I realized a long time ago the abortion laws were anachronistic and unnatural. We filed the suit anonymously to dramatize the plight of every woman capable of conceiving. We don't really stand for two people who, because of our particular situation, found abortion necessary. We stand for everybody—for woman's right to freedom of choice."[19]

While *Roe* and *Doe* v. *Wade* had been on their several-month journey from Judy Smith's initial suggestion to Linda Coffee's actual filing, abortion repeal efforts in other states had been occurring at an even faster pace. Both Larry Lader's NARAL circle and Alan Guttmacher's group of doctors had pressed ahead with their efforts to set up large-scale, publicly visible abortion clinics in Washington and New York respectively. The D.C. situation remained highly unsettled, however, with the Justice Department appealing Judge Gesell's *Vuitch* decision to the Supreme Court, and in New York many activists had been preoccupied with strategic disagreements over precisely what form of an abortion bill should be championed in the 1970 state legislature. One small group of activists ostensibly affiliated with NARAL, New Yorkers for Abortion Law Repeal, led principally by Lucinda Cisler and James Clapp, announced before the first of the year that they would *oppose* Connie Cook and Franz Leichter's forthcoming repeal bill on the grounds that its requirement that legal abortions be performed by doctors was fundamentally unacceptable. Several New York NARAL members who vociferously disagreed with that rigidly absolutist stance responded by setting a new group, straightforwardly called the Committee for the Cook-Leichter Bill, to lobby in favor of the repeal measure. New York journalists estimated that there was "much stronger sentiment" than before in support of repeal, but one *New York Times* story noted that many legislators wanted to leave the entire issue to the courts, especially since the actual trial of *Hall* and its three companion cases was now scheduled for April 15. While Al Blumenthal had again introduced a reform bill, both he and Martin Ginsberg, who had spoken so effectively against reform a year earlier, were now among the three dozen official *sponsors* of the Cook-Leichter repeal bill.[20]

In mid- and late January there were several days of widely reported public depositions in the *Hall* and *Abramowicz* cases, with some witnesses, such as New York writer Susan Brownmiller, testifying about their own personal experiences with abortion. On January 25 the *New York Times Magazine* ran a major story by reporter Linda Greenhouse entitled "Constitutional Question: Is There a Right to Abortion?" and Greenhouse focused much of the piece on twenty-eight-year-old Roy Lucas, who she said "could properly be called the father of the new abortion" movement. Greenhouse noted how influential Lucas's *North Carolina Law Review* article had become, and explained how in light of *Griswold*, for Lucas "a right to abortion is only a logical extension of the right to contraception." She reported how Lucas's opposing counsel in *Hall*, Joel Lewittes, was attempting to contest the relevance of *Griswold* by arguing that with abortion "we are no longer in the sacred precincts of the marital bedroom," and she briefly mentioned the historical argument being put forth by Cyril Means, who somewhat oddly characterized himself as "a hopeless reactionary." Greenhouse concluded the story with Assemblyman Blumenthal explaining that legislative reform was no longer his preeminent desire: "Repeal is the correct route now, and if the courts could solve the problem it would be both preferable and faster."[21]

Greenhouse's important essay stimulated similar but less notable stories, also highlighting Lucas, in publications ranging from *Life* magazine to the *St. Louis Post-Dispatch*. Everything was on track for the mid-April trial of the potentially decisive *Hall* suit, but Hall himself was beginning to get extremely cold feet about Alan Guttmacher's abortion clinic plan. In early February he warned his colleagues that Guttmacher's idea was "unnecessarily reckless," but one week later Guttmacher, Harriet Pilpel, and New York County Medical Society president Carl Goldmark met privately at Goldmark's apartment with Manhattan District Attorney Frank Hogan to gauge how he would respond to such a clinic. Hogan said that while he would welcome such a test of the existing New York abortion law, once the facility received any publicity a grand jury investigation would begin and indictments of whomever was performing the abortions would be likely. As Pilpel recorded it, Guttmacher responded by asking "if he could not be the guinea pig instead of young doctors who would be doing the abortions, and Hogan indicated very clearly that he would not 'take Dr. Guttmacher on.'" Hogan said he personally had not found *Belous* at all persuasive in its statutory vagueness holding, and he expected that the U.S. Supreme Court would avoid any definitive ruling on abortion. He "indicated strong sympathy for what we [are] trying to do," Pilpel recounted, "and said he was hopeful that possibly the legislature would clear up the situation itself." Guttmacher and Goldmark had already scheduled another meeting of likely medical supporters, but Louis M. Hellman, one of New York's most prominent doctors and a fellow plaintiff in *Hall*, was so upset about the continued clinic planning that he angrily resigned as ASA's board chairman. Opening such a facility might harm their chances in court and would certainly "polarize opposition that now lies dormant." Such a step would also "certainly have an adverse effect upon the legislature," where liberalization proponents had received a very unexpected boost from conservative state senate majority leader Earl W. Brydges. Guttmacher pulled back in the face of his friends' opposition, and similar clinic aspirations on the part of Clergy Consultation Service coordinator Howard Moody likewise foundered when no physician other than Lader's friend Bernie Nathanson proved willing to contemplate possible arrest.[22]

Roy Lucas was putting the finishing touches on a 164-page brief for the three-judge court in *Hall* and had also been enlisted to write the response to the Justice Department's petition seeking Supreme Court review and reversal of Gesell's decision in *Vuitch*. Lucas and others assumed that it was indeed very likely that the high court would hear *Vuitch*, but the Court's action in two other notable and relevant cases had failed to send any clear message as to what might be in the offing.[23]

First, on January 12, to almost everyone's surprise, the high court with
only William O. Douglas dissenting, had refused to hear Bill Baird's
appeal of his Massachusetts conviction. Even Baird's prosecutor,
Joseph R. Nolan, told reporters that he had expected the Supreme
Court to hear the appeal and void Baird's sentence for having handed
out the packages of contraceptive foam following his lecture, but now
Baird was looking at the unexpected likelihood of actually serving his
three-month jail sentence. Illness prevented Baird's immediate incarceration, and his volunteer attorney, Joseph Balliro, filed a habeas corpus petition in federal district court seeking to block Baird's actual
jailing, but in the absence of action by U.S. District Judge Anthony J.
Julian, Baird on Friday, February 20, was forced to surrender himself to
Sheriff Thomas Eisenstadt at Boston's Charles Street jail. One week
later Julian finally heard oral argument on Balliro's petition, but three
more weeks passed before Julian formally denied it in an opinion that
explicitly endorsed the earlier 4 to 3 Massachusetts Supreme Judicial
Court affirmation of the state's narrowly amended anticontraception
statute. "Baird's crime," an angry *Boston Globe* editorialized, "was that
he preached aloud what millions practice in private," and "if he belongs
in jail, so does a large part of the Massachusetts population." Julian's
long-delayed decision, however, finally allowed Balliro to appeal the
denial to the First Circuit Court of Appeals, which acted almost immediately to grant the request and release Baird from jail pending a full
consideration of his appeal. Baird had served thirty-five days for his
supposed violation of the Massachusetts statute, but the circuit court
explicitly volunteered that "we find it difficult to think that the appeal
lacks merit."[24]

Far less puzzling than the Supreme Court's apparent disinterest in
Baird was its February 24 denial of California's petition that it review
the state Supreme Court's decision in *Belous*. The justices gave little if
any consideration to the state's defense of its now-obsolete, pre-1967
law, and in California itself, just like in New York, there were more and
more signs that support for reform had now evolved into a widespread
preference for repeal. In conservative Orange County a municipal
court judge called the 1967 reform statute unconstitutional while dismissing four abortion charges that had been filed against a local physician, and Norma Zarky and Zad Leavy continued to consider the
possibility of filing a *Hall*-like federal court suit against the 1967 law.
Some California repeal proponents were still entertaining the idea of
sponsoring an initiative that would result in a statewide popular vote
on abortion, but virtually everyone believed that one or another court

case would resolve the entire question more quickly and more surely. Less visibly but just as importantly, evidence was also mounting that the actual availability of "therapeutic" abortions on mental health grounds was becoming more and more liberal with each passing month. The efforts of Charles Munger and CCTA to convince doctors that *Belous* had opened the door to far-reaching, practical liberalization were clearly succeeding, and while one young doctor, John Shriver Gwynne, succeeded in a well-advertised effort to get himself arrested for publicly operating an abortion clinic, a highly permissive trend was rapidly emerging. Another municipal court judge reviewing an abortion charge against a northern California physician followed the lead of his Orange County colleague, and a San Diego physician, surveying the changing standards of hospital abortion-approval committees, frankly concluded that "the present climate is one in which 'abortion on request' is effectively being practiced."[25]

While the idea of a popular referendum was put aside by the California activists, in Washington state just such a proposal was approved by the state legislature with the support of liberalization proponents. Some national activists had been horrified when they learned of the Washington strategy, and both New York's Bob Hall and Colorado's Dick Lamm wrote to Marilyn Ward, the top lobbyist for the measure, to warn of the tremendous nationwide damage that liberalization efforts would suffer should such a popular vote result in defeat. Hall termed the plan "terribly dangerous," especially in light of some poll results that suggested a close outcome, and asked that Ward and chief legislative sponsor Joel Pritchard choose some other course. One or more test cases ought to reach the Supreme Court by the fall, and while a November referendum victory would of course be wonderful, a defeat "could seriously jeopardize the entire court action." Hall warned that such a vote might well mobilize strong Catholic opposition, and Lamm asked them to ponder the national consequences of a loss, for "There is the old saying that the Supreme Court follows the election returns." Within the Washington legislature, however, a referendum repeal measure was passable, whereas simple legislative repeal was not, and the Washington activists pushed ahead. On January 27 the state house approved such a measure on a vote of 60 to 36, and three days later the state senate, after adding a three-month residency requirement and a sixteen-weeks-of-pregnancy ceiling, passed the bill by a margin of 25 to 23. Liberalization proponents shelved their previous plans to institute a court case, and began charting a campaign strategy for the November 3 vote.[26]

Washington was far from the only state where liberalization proponents made a major legislative push during the early months of 1970. In South Carolina a therapeutic reform law was enacted without drawing any national attention, and in Vermont a reform bill passed the state house but was voted down in the state senate. The Massachusetts house defeated a liberalization measure by the overwhelming margin of 184 to 32, and an Iowa repeal bill failed to emerge from committee. The Arizona house approved a repeal measure that opponents then blocked from reaching the senate floor, and in Michigan an effort to pass either a repeal bill or a reform measure ran aground despite editorial backing for repeal from the *Detroit Free Press* and extensive public support.[27] Thus the first state to enact a repeal law more definitive than the Washington referendum measure became Hawaii, where state Senator Vincent Yano, the Roman Catholic father of ten who in 1969 had blocked the passage of a reform bill so as to give the subject further study, stunningly emerged as a new champion of legislative repeal.

The key person in helping Vincent Yano become a sponsor of abortion law repeal was Joan Eames Hayes, a Radcliffe graduate and mother of three who had moved to Honolulu with her family in 1968 and quickly become legislative chairman of the local chapter of the American Association of University Women (AAUW). Hayes had testified in favor of the reform bill in April of 1969, but as she read and thought more about the issue over the following few months, she quickly became an advocate of repeal. Senator Yano also did a good deal of reading in the course of the summer, and was particularly impressed by Robert Drinan's Roman Catholic argument that repeal was preferable to reform. Yano told Hayes that he would like to know what Hawaii's doctors actually thought, and with the backing of the Hawaii Medical Association, which had endorsed reform two years earlier, University of Hawaii public health school professor Roy G. Smith undertook a mail questionnaire of the state's eight hundred doctors. Hayes had also been told by Republican Senator Percy Mirikitani of Manoa Valley that legislators would have to see evidence of actual constituent support for such a change in order for it to be enacted, and in early September 1969 Hayes organized a major public forum on the subject of abortion law change. Much to almost everyone's surprise, Senator Yano used the occasion to announce that he would introduce a repeal bill in the legislature come January. Several weeks later Governor John A. Burns, also a Catholic, indicated that he too saw repeal as preferable to reform, and in late October the state's newspapers reported that Professor Smith's poll of Hawaii doctors had found

96 percent supported some form of liberalization. Both the Hawaii AFL-CIO and then the Hawaii Chamber of Commerce also publicly endorsed repeal, and while the state's Roman Catholic hierarchy began speaking out in opposition to any prospective change, Yano's explanation that he supported repeal while personally opposing the act of abortion severely undercut the church's efforts. The *Honolulu Star-Bulletin* energetically backed repeal, and a clear consensus soon emerged that repeal was an eminently reasonable position backed by a wide range of thoughtful and respectable individuals and organizations.

In early February of 1970 a two-day senate committee hearing on Yano's repeal bill drew sixty witnesses who spoke in favor, including one Catholic nun, and only eighteen opponents, all of whom were Roman Catholic. Many legislators were particularly impressed by the affirmative testimony of doctors, and also by Professor Smith's. The comments of one witness from the Hawaii Women's Liberation Front, however, prompted one prorepeal committee member to ask the young woman whether she was hoping to help the repeal cause or hurt it, and as two careful students of the Hawaii campaign later observed, "the incident demonstrated vividly the importance of the repeal campaign's conservative and dignified approach." The Roman Catholic Bishop of Hawaii, John Scanlan, requested a private meeting with legislators that took place two days after the hearing but with little effect, and on February 9 the committee sent the repeal bill to the senate floor with a report voicing Yano's Drinan-like explanation of what repeal actually represented: "Your Committee's position for repeal is *NOT* legalization but rather that we choose not to control or regulate this matter by law and further that we neither approve nor disapprove of abortion." The very next day the senate took up Yano's bill and after a restrained debate passed the measure on a vote of 17 to 7.

A Yano rival blocked immediate endorsement of the senate bill by the state house, and in subsequent conference committee negotiations Yano was forced to accept first a limitation that all abortions take place in hospitals, then a ninety-day residency requirement, and finally a restriction that abortions could be performed only prior to fetal viability, i.e., the point at which a "fetus can exist individually outside of the mother's womb." On February 20 the house approved that significantly amended version of Yano's bill by a vote of 31 to 20, and four days later the senate adopted it on a tally of 15 to 9.

Faced with actual legislative approval of a repeal bill, devoutly Catholic Governor Burns now hesitated over what to do. Burns had ten working days in which he could either sign or veto the measure; if he did neither, the bill would become law even without his signature. Halfway through that ten-day period Burns met with Hayes and other repeal supporters and told them how he still remembered having seen victims of ineptly performed illegal abortions years earlier when he was a young Honolulu policeman. On March 10, his final day of decision, Burns had his staff prepare both a veto message and a statement explaining why he had allowed the measure to become law; after a teary-eyed conversation with a similarly ambivalent reporter, Burns sat alone until midnight and the next day released a seven-page explanation of why he had let the repeal bill become law. His decision "reflects my best judgment as Governor," and "not the private and personal whim of John A. Burns." "My reputation has been unfairly and seriously attacked," Burns complained, "by a number of my fellow Roman Catholics who do not appear to understand precisely the separate roles of State authority and Church authority." Personally, Burns said, he believed that individual human lives did begin at biological conception. Hence, "I could not in good conscience condone what the ... bill permits by signing it into law. On the other hand, I do consider the abortion question as a matter involving individual conscience."[28]

Hawaii's first-in-the-nation enactment of a law allowing female state residents to choose to end an early or midterm unwanted pregnancy drew widespread attention. Both *Newsweek* and *Time* magazines ran stories on the action, and the *New York Times* heralded it as a reflection of "the revolutionary change in public attitudes toward abortion." But most proponents of repeal remained more oriented toward litigation than toward legislative change, and within days of the Hawaii action a three-judge federal court sitting in Milwaukee issued a unanimous opinion holding Wisconsin's traditional antiabortion statute unconstitutional, a decision that potentially could be the most significant abortion ruling to date.[29]

The Milwaukee opinion, by U.S. District Judges John W. Reynolds and Myron L. Gordon and Circuit Judge—and former Illinois Governor—Otto Kerner, stemmed from an effort by a local doctor, Sidney G. Babbitz, to block his upcoming state court trial on a criminal abortion charge being prosecuted by Milwaukee County District Attorney E. Michael McCann. Judge Reynolds three months earlier had rejected Dr. Babbitz's petition for a temporary restraining order to halt the prosecution, but had approved his request that a special three-judge court consider his substantive constitutional attack on the Wisconsin statute. Suburban Milwaukee housewife Edith Rein, the chairman and founder of the very small, three-year-old Wisconsin

Committee to Legalize Abortion, which had quietly provided referral advice for some time, had heard of Babbitz long before his 1969 arrest. A Minnesota native and mother of two, Rein had first gotten interested in abortion liberalization after seeing a subsequent showing of the 1965 CBS television documentary, "Abortion and the Law." She cheerfully acknowledged to local reporters that being a repeal advocate in heavily Catholic Milwaukee was a challenging task, but Rein emphasized that "I want my daughters to grow up in a world where women have the right to decide their own reproduction."[30]

After Babbitz initiated his federal court petition, Rein admitted privately to national activists that "we have unhappy reports on him, and most of us avoid sending people to him." Nonetheless, Rein explained, given Wisconsin's hopeless legislative prospects for even a reform bill, she was very happy to have the opportunity to mount a constitutional attack on the state's antiabortion statute that Babbitz's federal court move provided. Thanks to Milwaukee attorney Clifford K. Meldman, Rein's Wisconsin Committee submitted an impressive, *Griswold*-oriented amicus brief to the three-judge panel in advance of Babbitz's January 23 hearing. *Griswold*'s right of marital privacy included "the right of the woman to decide when, or whether, she shall bear children," Meldman contended, and "the denial of the right of an abortion is thus inconsistent with the undenied right to use contraceptives." Rein herself was "very optimistic" after observing the questions that the three jurists put to the opposing counsel at the January 23 hearing, and when the panel's decision was publicly released on March 5, just two days after *Roe* and *Doe* v. *Wade* had been filed in Dallas, the holding in *Babbitz* v. *McCann* undeniably offered an even clearer articulation of a constitutionally protected right to choose abortion than had been voiced in *Belous* or *Vuitch*.

Unlike California's Justice Peters or Washington's Judge Gesell, the Milwaukee federal court panel expressly declined to rely even in part on the notion that traditional antiabortion laws were so vaguely worded as to offer no constitutionally adequate statutory notice to doctors. Instead, the panel said, the Supreme Court's interpretation of the Ninth Amendment in *Griswold* "compels our conclusion that the state of Wisconsin may not . . . deprive a woman of her private decision whether to bear her unquickened child," a nineteenth-century concept that distinguished the point at which a woman first detected fetal movement and which had been incorporated in Wisconsin's initial 1858 antiabortion law that made only postquickening abortions a crime. "There is no topic more closely interwoven with the intimacy of the home and marriage than that which relates to the conception and bearing of progeny." The panel cited retired Supreme Court Justice Tom C. Clark's law review endorsement of applying *Griswold* to abortion, and said that while a state did have an identifiable interest in protecting unborn fetuses, "a balancing of the relevant interests" nonetheless compelled a decision that "a woman's right to refuse to carry an embryo during the early months of pregnancy may not be invaded by the state" without some compelling interest. "When measured against the claimed 'rights' of an embryo of four months or less, we hold that the mother's right transcends that of such an embryo," and a mother "has the right to determine whether to carry or reject an embryo that has not quickened."[31]

The very same day that *Babbitz* was issued in Milwaukee, Roy Lucas and his New Jersey colleague Dick Samuel filed a declaratory judgment suit in federal court in Newark that Lucas presumed would become the primary non-New York counterpart to *Hall*. Featuring seven doctors and two organizations among a grand total of some thirteen plaintiffs, *Young Women's Christian Association of Princeton* v. *George A. Kugler*, New Jersey's attorney general, was very much a cross-Hudson duplicate of *Hall*. New Jersey like Wisconsin was a state where even a therapeutic reform bill stood virtually no chance of legislative approval, and Lucas had long envisioned New Jersey as his secondary locus for a case that could go directly from a special three-judge panel decision right to a final ruling in the U.S. Supreme Court. *Griswold v. Connecticut*, he stressed to the panel in his 135-page brief on the merits, "is not an isolated decision confined to its facts, but is one in a continuing line of decisions involving various aspects of personal privacy and family autonomy."[32]

Similarly, *YWCA* like *Babbitz* was far from the only case joining *Hall* and the Texas duo as new federal court abortion suits. In Illinois a federal judge rejected a request for a temporary restraining order prohibiting enforcement of the state antiabortion statute against a doctor who had been requested to perform an abortion on a pregnant sixteen-year-old rape victim, but three days later the Seventh Circuit Court of Appeals rescinded that rejection. Another new case was quietly filed in Indiana, and in Michigan, where several attorneys had considered starting a federal action, a state trial court judge declared Michigan's antiabortion statute unconstitutional in dismissing a criminal abortion charge pending against a physician. Citing *Belous* and *Vuitch*, Judge Clarence A. Reid held that the commonly worded exception provided by Michigan's statute—allowing only those abortions "necessary to preserve the life" of the woman—was unconstitutionally vague. He also concluded that the law "infringes on the right of privacy in the physician-patient relationship" and that "the woman has a right to privacy in matters relating to marriage, family, and sex." One week later a South Dakota trial court judge, Clarence P. Cooper, issued an extremely similar decision holding that state's antiabortion law unconstitutional and dismissing a criminal charge against Rapid City physician H. Benjamin Munson. Invoking *Babbitz* as well as *Belous* and *Vuitch*, Cooper declared that the South Dakota statute "interferes with private conduct without serving any vital interests of society."[33]

Potentially far more important than those public trial court rulings was the wholly private consideration the U.S. Supreme Court was giving to the Justice Department's appeal of Judge Gesell's voiding of the D.C. abortion law in *Vuitch*. U.S. Solicitor General Erwin Griswold—no relation to Estelle—had told the high court in his initial petition in early February that Gesell had erred in holding that the crucial statutory exception language, allowing abortions "necessary for the preservation of the mother's life or health," was unconstitutionally vague. While the law might have to be construed so as to absolve any doctor who performed an abortion in a good faith belief that a health threat did exist, the law should also be read to require at least some case-by-case application of medical judgment, Griswold said. "The unconditional availability of abortions, unrelated to medical justification," would be contrary to Congress's intent in enacting a restrictive statute, and "without ambiguity" the law *could* be applied against doctors whom a judge or jury decided had not exercised *any* case-by-case "medical judgment at all."

Both Roy Lucas, whom Larry Lader had introduced to Vuitch, and Joseph L. Nellis, an experienced Washington litigator, had been brought in to supersede Vuitch's original attorney, Joseph Sitnick, in defending the Supreme Court appeal. Lucas prepared a lengthy submission invoking a wide range of arguments to support the contention that Gesell's decision was "so manifestly correct as not to warrant further argument before it is affirmed by this Court." Everyone realized full well that such a summary affirmance was extremely unlikely, and while Justice John M. Harlan's clerk observed in summarizing the appeal that Judge Gesell had "made a fairly strong case for his ruling," Harlan along with fellow justices William J. Brennan and particularly Potter Stewart were initially concerned with a far more abstruse question, namely whether Gesell's decision was eligible for direct appeal to the Supreme Court or whether the government first had to take its case to the U.S. Court of Appeals for the District of Columbia.

When the justices discussed *Vuitch* at their private conference on

Friday, March 27, they reached quick agreement that Harlan and Stewart's concern that the appeal might well belong in the circuit court merited serious attention and that both the government and Vuitch's attorneys should be asked to address the issue in supplementary filings. On March 31 the court's chief clerk sent just such a letter to the opposing parties, requesting additional submissions by April 14, and unsurprisingly both Griswold's office and Vuitch's lawyers reiterated their previous positions that the appeal was indeed within the Supreme Court's jurisdiction. At a subsequent private conference on April 23 the justices decided, with only Stewart and newly confirmed Chief Justice Warren E. Burger disagreeing, that further debate over the jurisdictional issue should be postponed until the Court actually heard the case sometime that coming fall or winter. On April 27 the Court formally announced that step, and with reporters interpreting the move as a clear sign that a decision in *Vuitch* thus probably would take place sometime in early 1971, major newspapers such as the *New York Times* and the *Washington Post* gave front-page coverage to the Court's seemingly mundane action. Eight weeks later, however, in a move that received no journalistic attention but was seen as extremely significant by interested attorneys, the Court at Harlan's behest expressly propounded three questions, all concerning the jurisdictional status of the appeal, for the opposing parties to address in their subsequent briefs.[34]

To thoughtful attorneys if not to journalists, the Supreme Court's series of steps, starting with the March 31 letter, strongly suggested that the Court might very well be intending to dispose of *Vuitch* on one or another jurisdictional issue rather than use the case to say anything substantive about the constitutional status of antiabortion laws. As of early April that seemed to further increase the already substantial likelihood that *Hall*, scheduled for trial on April 15, would indeed become *the* first case in which the high court would frontally address the constitutionality of abortion statutes. Then, however, with virtually no advance warning, all prior expectations concerning how repeal efforts would progress were suddenly and totally upended by the surprising outcome of the 1970 legislative effort in New York.

As of mid-March, repeal proponents in the New York legislature had been openly divided over the strange question of whether conservative, Roman Catholic senate majority leader Earl Brydges's support of a repeal bill was somehow sincere or was instead an elaborate strategy aimed at torpedoing any possible liberalization measure. Repeal sponsor Connie Cook, who had discussed repeal provisions at some length with Brydges's aide Don Zimmerman, was uncertain yet open-minded, but even after a senate committee approved Brydges's own repeal bill for floor action, many proponents continued to believe that Brydges was opposed to any liberalization and was bringing forward a repeal bill, instead of a reform one, only because he felt certain that repeal could *not* win on the floor. "It's a hoax, a conspiracy by the archenemy of reform," angry Queens Democrat Seymour Thaler told reporters. One week later, however, with well-respected Newburgh Republican D. Clinton Dominick leading the way, the New York state senate voted in favor of abortion law repeal by 31 to 26 after an emotional, five-hour debate. Majority leader Brydges did indeed vote against the measure, and some onlookers thought he was stunned by its surprise passage, but afterward Brydges again insisted that his goal was to see the best possible bill become law and that a twenty-fourth week of pregnancy ceiling ought to be added to the senate-passed measure for all abortions except those where a woman's life was at risk. With grudging support from repeal proponents, the state assembly committee that received the senate bill did exactly that, and on March 30 the amended bill went to the assembly floor.

Both supporters and opponents knew that the final tally, on which the bill had to receive 76 votes in order to pass, would go one way or the other by the narrowest of margins. An eight-hour debate stretched long into the night, with "some of the most dramatic anti-abortion speeches," Cook later recalled, being "made by men who told me privately that of course I was right, that they were very glad when they could get their daughter or their lover an abortion." Late in the evening, two supporters of the bill, in line with legislative tradition, left word of their votes with the clerk and departed. When the final roll was called, however, Assembly Speaker Perry Duryea, a longtime liberalization supporter who had promised Cook that he himself would if necessary provide the crucial seventy-sixth vote despite the standard custom that the speaker did not vote, ruled that the two absent members' votes would *not* be counted. That left the affirmative tally at seventy-three, three short of what was needed. Cook immediately made the necessary parliamentary move to preserve an opportunity for another vote on the bill one week later, and amidst a variety of recriminations the already intense lobbying of assembly members escalated still further.

"No issue in recent years has resulted in the degree of bitterness and emotion" within the legislature that the 1970 abortion repeal debates had produced, the *New York Times* reported. Several Catholic legislators from New York City who had voted for the bill on that initial roll call let their colleagues know that powerful church pressure meant that they would have to vote no on the second tally, but proponents also knew they would pick up the votes of a black Buffalo assemblyman who had missed the first vote on account of a "headache" and a female Roman Catholic member whose family had been the target of Catholic opponents. Cook and her supporters also had to contend with well-advertised and sometimes vituperative *opposition* to the repeal bill, and especially to the twenty-four-week ceiling, from Cindy Cisler of New Yorkers for Abortion Law Repeal. Cisler and her sidekick Jim Clapp were so convinced that the *Hall* case would result in a complete voiding of New York's existing abortion statute that they vociferously argued that such an upcoming triumph in the courts would be totally preferable to the middling step forward that they thought the pending repeal bill represented. Asked about Cisler years later, Cook explained that "for a while there I thought we were going to lose the bill because of her activities."

The *New York Times* predicted that the April 9 roll call would be "a toss-up," but the unflappable Connie Cook quietly yet firmly told reporters that "it will pass." What Cook knew that they did not was that one assemblyman, a Jewish Democrat from a traditionally Republican district adjacent to Cook's own, had privately told her that despite his no vote on the first tally, he—and his family—would not allow himself to be *the* vote that killed the bill. "He said," Cook later recalled, "'If it's one vote away, then you have my vote.'"

That knowledge made Cook considerably more optimistic than her supporters when the assembly roll began to be called after four hours of debate on April 9. Her upstate neighbor voted no when his turn came, and at the end of the roll call the number of yes votes stood at seventy-four—one vote shy, given Speaker Duryea's pledge to be the seventy-sixth if it would be determinative. As the realization of the repeal bill's defeat began to sweep the assembly floor and gallery, Cook's obscure friend, fifty-nine-year-old Auburn Assemblyman George M. Michaels, a Brooklyn Law School graduate and a World War II Marine Corps veteran, rose to his feet and struggled to get Duryea's attention. Gradually the chamber began to quiet as people understood what Michaels was about to do. "I realize, Mr. Speaker, that I am terminating my political career, but I cannot in good conscience sit here and allow my vote to be the one that defeats this bill. I ask that my vote be changed from 'no' to 'yes.'" As the tally of yeas thus rose to seventy-five, Perry Duryea cast his vote as the seventy-sixth, and abortion repeal dramatically—and tearfully—passed the New York state assembly.[35]

   The following day the New York state senate, after a relatively subdued debate that nonetheless featured majority leader Brydges reading the imaginary autobiography of a soon-to-be-aborted fetus, again approved the measure on a vote of 31 to 26. The bill then went to the desk of Republican Governor Nelson Rockefeller, who signed it into law on April 11. Scheduled to take effect on July 1, the New York measure, unlike the earlier one in Hawaii, included no state residency requirement and no provision specifying that abortions had to take place in hospitals. Repeal proponents such as Alan Guttmacher quickly began to warn that New York, and especially New York City, might be all but inundated by a nationwide flood of women seeking to terminate unwanted pregnancies once the magic date arrived, and hasty discussions got underway as to what sort of specialized clinic facilities could be established and what size caseloads existing hospitals would be willing to bear.[36]

   One very important casualty of the remarkable New York legislative victory was Roy Lucas's potential landmark court case of *Hall* v. *Lefkowitz,* which was effectively mooted by the legislative repeal of the statute whose constitutionality it had challenged. Lucas without regrets turned his attention toward the similar New Jersey action, and three days after Rockefeller's signing of the New York bill a declaratory judgment action challenging the constitutionality of Oregon's *reform* statute was filed in Portland by Betty Roberts, who as a state senator had sponsored a 1969 repeal bill, and her husband and fellow attorney, Keith Skelton.[37] Similar evidence of growing support for repeal was visible all across the country, and Robert F. Drinan, whose earlier writings had proven far more influential than many observers yet realized, published another widely visible essay arguing the moral preferability of repeal over reform measures. Drinan also asserted that the Catholic hierarchy should speak with restraint on the subject, and forcefully repeated his prior criticism of what he termed "inappropriate intrusions in a pluralistic society" by ecclesiastical officials who wrongly assume that they "can pronounce a moral and uniform position" for the church "on a legal-political question." The very defensive stance of liberalization opponents was explicitly reflected in an April 22 statement by the National Conference of Catholic Bishops that decried the passage of the New York law and lamely observed that "there has been a radical turn of events during this past year." One bishop, seemingly in accord with Drinan's advice, told a reporter that the Conference was "concerned only with a statement, not political action," and another, who had supervised preparation of the resolution, expressly volunteered that "We have no desire to effect a legislative program" and "would recognize existing legislation."[38]

The state of Virginia approved a modest reform bill on almost the same day that the New York repeal measure attained final passage, but the most heated southern legislative struggle of 1970 took place in Georgia, where many of the same activists who had played significant roles in the 1968 passage of that state's reform bill mounted an all-out attack on their own prior handiwork in the hope of winning legislative passage of a repeal measure. In the fall of 1969, Alan Bonser, the young, English-born attorney and financial services executive who had first created Georgia Citizens for Hospital Abortions (GCHA) back in 1967, brought the small group back together to begin organizing a 1970 repeal drive. Along with two Emory University Medical School doctors, James L. Waters and W. Newton Long, and Emory University Presbyterian chaplain J. Emmett Herndon, an active member of the clergy referral network, Bonser had been talking publicly of the need for repeal since midsummer.

One newcomer to Atlanta and the Emory community who saw an announcement of Bonser's first fall meeting and went was Judith Bourne, a Washington state native and trained nurse who had arrived in town just weeks earlier with her husband Peter, a physician whose father was a prominent member of the Emory faculty. Judith was aware of illegal abortion's human toll from when she previously had taught nursing in California during Peter's medical residency, and in the fall of 1969, having arrived in Atlanta too late to obtain an academic year teaching post, she was the one member of GCHA's small band of repealers who had both the willingness and the time to serve as the group's legislative chairman for the upcoming session.[39]

Early in December GCHA sponsored a public forum on abortion law change, with Judith, whom the *Atlanta Constitution* told its readers was "an attractive brunette," stressing that the group wanted complete repeal, not further reform. She and Bonser recruited two well-respected legislators, Killian Townsend and Grace Towns Hamilton, the first black woman ever to serve in the Georgia legislature, to sponsor the 1970 repeal bill, and Judith and a GCHA colleague, Annis Pratt, circulated a "Dear Friend" letter encouraging people to contact their own legislators and pointing out that "the women of Georgia are deprived of their constitutional rights as long as the state may dictate in any way what they do about the privacy and dignity of their own reproductive life." "Abortion is a private matter," Judith emphasized in an early January interview with the *Atlanta Journal*. "The government does not have the right to insist that a woman bear a child against her will," and passage of a repeal bill would "make abortion a private decision between a woman and her doctor." In addition, the complicated and time-consuming application and review procedure mandated by the 1968 reform statute for every woman seeking a legal, therapeutic abortion "involves so much red tape that it's really ineffective," Judith explained. Furthermore, virtually all hospitals that did perform therapeutic abortions pursuant to the 1968 law, such as Atlanta's large Grady Memorial Hospital, which was primarily staffed by Emory-affiliated doctors, imposed a firm but unspoken monthly quota on the maximum number of abortions—six in the case of Grady—that would be approved, regardless of applicants' individual situations.

On Monday, January 19, the Georgia repeal proponents suffered a stunning emotional loss when Alan Bonser went to the Regency Hyatt House and committed suicide by jumping from the twenty-first floor of the hotel's famous interior lobby. With the legislative hearing on GCHA's repeal bill only two weeks away, Judith Bourne was named the group's new chairman, and with editorial support from the *Atlanta Constitution*, the repealers mounted a major effort at the February 3 hearing. Much to their surprise, immediately after the hearing the committee in a secret ballot voted 6 to 2 to table the measure, and the sponsors quickly vowed that an attempt to revive it would take place the following week.[40]

Judith Bourne responded to the committee vote by publicly announcing that GCHA would seek donations to help Georgia women travel out of state to obtain medical abortions. An Associated Press photo of Judith, accompanied by an explanatory caption, ran in any number of national newspapers, including the *Dallas Morning News*, and the Bournes soon found their Atlanta home phone ringing off the hook with callers wanting referral information. Early the following week legislators reiterated to Atlanta reporters that the repeal bill almost certainly would be revived once a hospitalization requirement and a provision compelling married women to obtain their husband's consent were both added. However, on February 11 the repeal proponents received yet another unpleasant legislative surprise when the committee, again by secret ballot, killed the repeal bill on an 8 to 6 tally despite the fact that seven members claimed to have voted yes. Committee chairman Virgil Smith, who would have broken such a tie vote by supporting the measure, announced that the bill now would not be revived, and a "profoundly disappointed" Judith Bourne told Atlanta journalists that GCHA would now "strongly consider" filing a court case.[41]

Over the previous several months Judith had been reading a considerable range of materials concerning abortion, but even more than twenty years later she could immediately describe the two items that had had far and away the greatest impact on her thinking: Judge Gesell's November 1969 decision in *Vuitch* and Roy Lucas's landmark 1968 law review article on the constitutional infirmity of antiabortion statutes. As yet no one else had actually moved to file such a challenge against one of the 1967–1968 *reform* laws, but in the immediate wake of the February 11 legislative defeat, Judy Bourne wasted no time at all in starting to put together just such a federal case.

Through her husband Peter, Judy already knew Agnes "Ruste" Kitfield, the executive director of the American Civil Liberties Union of Georgia, and within a day or two of the legislative loss Judy called Kitfield to seek her advice and help in finding one or more interested attorneys. Ruste Kitfield was a central figure in the small world of liberal Atlanta activists, and she, like many others, already respected Judy Bourne as "a dynamo of energy and intelligence." Kitfield immediately thought of several women lawyers whom she believed would probably be willing and able to help mount such a case. Just a week or so earlier at one or another party she had chatted with one of Atlanta's more experienced female lawyers, thirty-six-year-old Margie Pitts Hames, a former partner in the firm of Fisher and Phillips. Hames had gone on leave from the firm just before the birth of her first child in December 1968, and had not returned. Now she was eight months pregnant with a second child, and Kitfield had gotten a clear impression that Hames might well have some available time.

Hence Margie Hames was the first person Ruste Kitfield called after getting Judy Bourne's request, and her initial question to Hames was direct but generic: "She asked me would I be interested in doing a women's rights case." Hames had replied that "'That would be fun,'" but reminded Kitfield that since she was almost nine months pregnant, "'I can't do anything for a while.'" Kitfield responded that all they needed to do at the moment was begin planning it, and Hames willingly agreed to participate. Kitfield said she would recruit several other women lawyers to also take part, and she made successive calls to several female attorneys who worked for one or the other of two analogous legal groups, the Atlanta Legal Aid Society, which provided representation for poor people in the city proper, and Georgia Legal Services, which performed a similar role for needy individuals in the rest of the state.

Sometime in late February an initial abortion case planning meeting took place at Ruste Kitfield's ACLU of Georgia office in downtown

Atlanta. Judy Bourne and Kitfield took the initial lead in explaining what they hoped to pursue; in addition to Margie Hames the all-female group also included Tobiane Schwartz, a supervisory attorney with Atlanta Legal Aid, and Elizabeth Roediger Rindskopf, who worked at the Emory Neighborhood Law Office, a legal services affiliate adjoining Atlanta's leading university. Kitfield's trio of women lawyers came from a variety of backgrounds. Hames, a Tennessee native, had graduated from Vanderbilt Law School in 1961 after spending her first five post-high school years working as a legal secretary in Murfreesboro. Women law students had been something of a rarity at conservative Vanderbilt in the late 1950s; years later Hames would credit the supportive friendship of a successful upperclassman, Fred Graham, as being crucial to her first-year survival. After practicing for a year in Tennessee, Margie's marriage to fellow attorney William Hames brought her to Atlanta and Fisher and Phillips in 1962.

Almost exactly the same age as Margie Hames, Tobi Schwartz was originally from West Virginia, where she had graduated from law school in 1959. She had spent seven of her first ten years of law practice in West Virginia as well, and had come to Atlanta to join Atlanta Legal Aid only a year earlier. Elizabeth Rindskopf, whom Kitfield knew through Elizabeth's husband Peter, who had been practicing civil rights law in Atlanta since 1965, had graduated from the University of Michigan Law School in 1968. She had joined the Emory legal services office that same year, and already had accumulated an unusual amount of federal court experience.

The lawyers met two or three times with Bourne and Kitfield during late February and early March, and on at least one occasion two additional female attorneys, Betty Kehrer from Georgia Legal Services, and private practitioner Orinda Evans, also joined in. Bourne and her GCHA colleagues were coping with a steady flood of callers seeking referral assistance, but as the lawyers' discussions built towards identifying what sorts of plaintiffs ought to be sought out, both Bourne and Hames took on significant additional tasks. Everyone involved in the planning agreed that a wide range of plaintiffs, including doctors, interested nurses, and clergy counselors such as Emmett Herndon should all be recruited, and Judy and Margie divided up the responsibility for making most of the calls. Judy's husband Peter, whose Emory responsibilities included overseeing a community mental health center, would of course be one, and Peter in turn helped enlist a variety of others. Judy first approached Emory's Dr. Robert A. Hatcher, a well-known expert on contraceptive technology, and counted him as a particularly important recruit; Emmett Herndon and outspoken medical proponents of repeal such as Jim Waters and Newton Long also happily signed on.[42]

Both Judith and Margie, however, fully agreed that their lead plaintiff ought to be—and, indeed, perhaps *had* to be—an unwillingly pregnant woman who had tried but failed to successfully negotiate the institutional approval maze created by the 1968 therapeutic reform law. Many of the counselors and nurses, and several of the doctors, who staffed the abortion service at Atlanta's Emory-affiliated Grady Memorial Hospital were GCHA members and personal friends of Judy and Peter Bourne, and by early March Judy had asked two of the women responsible for interviewing and evaluating abortion applicants, Sallie Craig Huber and Kit Young, to keep an eye out for an applicant who might run afoul of Grady's quota ceiling and thus be a potentially ideal plaintiff for a federal court challenge to the 1968 provisions.

On March 12, just one day after Margie Hames gave birth to her second child, Kit Young interviewed just such a woman. Twenty-two-year-old Sandra Bensing was several weeks into her fourth pregnancy. The daughter of an Atlanta sanitation worker and a mother who was sixteen when she was born, Sandra had dropped out of school in the ninth grade, in part due to a bout with Bell's palsy, and at age seventeen had married an Oklahoma drifter, Joel Lee Bensing. A son, Joel Lee, Jr., was born in May 1966, and a daughter, April, followed in November 1967. Joel worked only occasionally, and Sandra briefly had a job at a hamburger stand. The marriage was continuously conflict-ridden, and Joel was arrested several times for attempting to abuse different children. In June 1968, Sandra's mother, angry at the entire situation, attempted to have Sandra committed to the Central State Hospital at Milledgeville, but Sandra left after only a short stay and resumed living with Joel. In May 1969, with Sandra seven months pregnant, Joel left and headed to Oklahoma, and Sandra went to the Atlanta Legal Aid Society to begin divorce proceedings.

Joel "tries to molest girls small or big," Sandra stated in explaining her desire for the divorce. "He's been in jail several times for sex crimes." The following month, however, Sandra joined Joel in Texas to attempt another reconciliation, and briefly took a job in a plastics plant. In July 1969 she gave birth there in Texas to her third child, a girl who was given up almost immediately for adoption. That fall Sandra and Joel made their way back to Atlanta, and by early 1970 both of the older children had been removed from their custody and placed in a foster home.

Once in early January, and again in late February, Sandra went to Grady's emergency room with various ailments. Then in early March, just days after leaving Joel and moving in with her mother, Sandra realized that she was again pregnant. On March 12 she went to Grady for that initial conversation about obtaining an abortion, and four days later she returned to the hospital for a series of interviews with psychiatrist Dr. Charles W. Butler and two psychologists. She told them she had renewed her effort to divorce Joel, and that she would be unable to care for a new child if this present pregnancy went forward. On March 24 and then again on March 28 Sandra returned to Grady for additional psychiatric consultations, and on April 1 she went for an obstetrical exam. Although she did request that her application for a therapeutic abortion be considered by Grady's review committee, Sandra also told one or another of the staff members whom she saw on April 1 that she "doesn't want it done if she is more than 3 months, [for she] feels that it would be like killing a baby." The following week, on April 10, Dr. Butler told her orally that her application had been denied.

Sometime prior to receiving that April 10 news, but apparently well after her initial conversation with Kit Young, Sandra came to the attention of both Tobi Schwartz and Judy Bourne. Tobi first met Sandra when Sandra renewed her effort to have Atlanta Legal Aid help with her divorce; Judy learned of Sandra's unsuccessful application to Grady either from her friends there or from Tobi. By at least Monday, April 13, Tobi, Judy, and Margie Hames knew that they now had just the sort of unsuccessful abortion applicant whom they had been seeking as a lead plaintiff, and over the following several days Margie and Tobi put the finishing touches on their draft complaint.[43]

Thursday morning April 16, Sandy Bensing formally executed an affidavit reciting her fruitless effort to obtain a therapeutic abortion at Grady Hospital and authorizing the filing of a federal court challenge against the 1968 reform law on her behalf. Agreeing to be publicly designated as "Mary Doe" for the purpose of the case, Sandra's affidavit described how all three of her previous children were no longer in her custody and noted her prior stay at Milledgeville. It made no reference to her hope for a divorce, but it did assert that "she and her husband are financially unable to support and care for another child."

Later that same day Margie Hames and Tobi Schwartz filed both their thirteen-page complaint and Sandra's sealed affidavit in federal district court for the Northern District of Georgia. "Mary Doe" and Peter Bourne headed a list of twenty-four individual and two organizational plaintiffs. The other individual complainants—eight more physicians, seven nurses, five ministers, and two social workers—included Judy, Reverend Herndon, and Doctors Hatcher, Waters, and Long. GCHA was joined as an organizational plaintiff by Planned Parenthood of Atlanta, whom Judy had recruited only after agreeing to remove Grady Memorial Hospital, one of whose top doctors also chaired Planned Parenthood's medical committee, from its intended position as the case's lead defendant.

In Grady's place Margie and Tobi instead named Georgia's Attorney General, Arthur K. Bolton, followed by Fulton County District Attorney Lewis R. Slaton and Atlanta Chief of Police Herbert T. Jenkins. They asked for the appointment of a three-judge court to hear their request for both declaratory and injunctive relief against enforcement of the 1968 statute, and filed an additional motion, drawn up by Gale Siegel, a young legal aid colleague of Elizabeth Rindskopf's, seeking a temporary restraining order against any further application of the law even in advance of an initial hearing. The complaint described "Mary Doe" as "recently abandoned" by her husband and sought to suggest that her denial at Grady was especially puzzling in light of her prior status as "a mental patient" at Milledgeville. Constitutionally, Hames and Schwartz cited *Griswold*, *Belous*, *Vuitch*, and *Babbitz* in asserting that "Mary Doe's" "right of privacy or liberty in matters related to marriage, family and sex," as well as "the sacred right of every individual to the possession and control of her own person" and "the right to be let alone" were all infringed upon by the restrictions contained in the 1968 Georgia reform law.[44]

The April 16 filing of *Doe* v. *Bolton* was front-page news all across Georgia, but that very same day in Minneapolis, a similarly titled but potentially more dramatic challenge to Minnesota's traditional antiabortion law, *Doe* v. *Randall*, was filed on behalf of a twenty-three-year-old mother of three with a rubella-scarred nine-week pregnancy that her obstetrician, Dr. Jane E. Hodgson, had recommended she abort. Minnesota's "Jane and John Doe" were Nancy K. and Ronald R. Widmyer, a Lakeville couple who had been married six years; Dr. Hodgson, at fifty-five, had practiced for twenty-two years as St. Paul's only female obstetrician and gynecologist. She and her husband, Dr. Frank Quattlebaum, were the parents of two teenage girls, and since 1967 she had served, with a growing sense of frustration, on the Minnesota State Medical Association's Ad Hoc Abortion Committee.

Jane Hodgson had begun thinking about a possible abortion law test case well before she first met Nancy Widmyer in January or confirmed the rubella threat to Widmyer's pregnancy just two days before *Doe* v.

Randall was filed. In a mid-November, 1969 talk in which she expressed regret that the Medical Association had refused to endorse a repeal bill in the Minnesota legislature, Hodgson had referred to both the *Belous* and *Vuitch* decisions and observed that "it is possible that change for all of us will come quickly via the Supreme Court." A year later Hodgson remarked that "I think that perhaps for years, I was looking for a test case," but as she subsequently explained, she realized full well that any test case plaintiff had to be "very carefully chosen" and certainly had to be married. "I really had been looking for some-body," and when Nancy Widmyer's flawless and potentially tragic situation presented itself, Jane Hodgson quickly concluded "that it was a once-in-a-lifetime perfect case." Thinking back to the immediate context of mid-April, 1970, she also reflected that "I think what spurred me on was New York's passage of their law" just a few days before Nancy Widmyer's rubella exposure was confirmed.

Hodgson had long been acquainted with the small band of liberal-ization advocates who made up the three-and-a-half-year-old Minnesota Council for the Legal Termination of Pregnancy, and partic-ularly with Robert McCoy, a founding member of the group who, by 1969–1970, was openly running a sizable one-man referral operation. Bob McCoy had introduced her to attorney Stewart Perry, and the day before Nancy Widmyer's rubella exposure was verified, Perry agreed to represent Hodgson on a volunteer basis in filing a federal test case. *Doe* v. *William Randall*, the Ramsey County prosecuting attorney whose jurisdiction encompassed St. Paul, would seek injunctive protection for the therapeutic abortion, as well as a declaratory judgment that Minnesota's antiabortion law was unconstitutional, on behalf of the Widmyers, Hodgson, and three other supportive doctors.

Even in advance of the April 16 filing, Jane Hodgson had personally consulted with several physician colleagues to obtain formal endorse-ments that a therapeutic abortion was indeed appropriate for Nancy Widmyer. The most prominent of those colleagues was Dr. Joseph H. Pratt of the Mayo Clinic, who forthrightly wrote on a copy of Nancy Widmyer's medical record that "There is no question in my mind as to the proper course of treatment for the above patient. The chance of congenital mal-development with rubella contracted in the first month of pregnancy is very high. Therefore one should advise and discuss with such a patient the procedure for a therapeutic abortion. Since the patient is approximately 8 weeks pregnant the sooner such an operation could be done the less risk involved for the patient."

Stewart Perry offered precisely that argument when he and Jane

Hodgson appeared before U.S. District Judge Edward J. Devitt on April 20, with Hodgson submitting that given the progression of Nancy Widmyer's pregnancy, the abortion should take place before May 1. Faced, however, with substantive and procedural objections both from Randall and from two attorneys speaking on behalf of Minnesota Citizens Concerned for Life, an antiabortion group hoping to intervene in the case, Judge Devitt agreed to delay any decision in the matter for at least one week and made clear his impression that no federally justiciable controversy existed with regard to the injunctive question in advance of the abortion itself and subsequent possible state charges against Dr. Hodgson. Perry told reporters he was "extremely upset" by the judge's one-week delay, and while Devitt at the ensuing April 27 hearing agreed to convene a three-judge panel to consider the constitutional challenge, he again repeated his belief that no advance injunctive protection could be provided by the federal judiciary.

Two days later, on the morning of April 29, Jane Hodgson went ahead and performed Nancy Widmyer's therapeutic abortion. She and Perry announced the news to the press and formally notified Devitt; on May 1, officers from the St. Paul police department arrived to formally question Dr. Hodgson. She was not surprised. She had assumed from the outset that criminal arrest and prosecution might well ensue, and after the first of Devitt's hearings she had concluded that it was certainly "a good possibility." Joe Pratt wrote her on May 6 to say that "I agree with the stand you took," but five days later county attorney Randall confirmed to reporters that criminal charges were indeed likely. On May 19 Judge Devitt and two colleagues formally ruled that there was as yet no federally justiciable "case or controversy" in the matter; forty-eight hours later Jane E. Hodgson was officially indicted for the crime of abortion.

Jane Hodgson's May 26 arraignment before Judge Ronald E. Hachey marked *the* first time in American history that a licensed physician had been criminally charged for performing a medically approved hospital abortion. Perry sought unsuccessfully to convince the federal panel that this development inescapably cured any prior absence of a "case or controversy," but Devitt and his colleagues again refused to act. Perry also challenged the constitutionality of the Minnesota statute in state court, but with little delay Judge Hachey dismissed Perry's arguments in a brief opinion that Jane Hodgson correctly described as embodying "the theology of the Catholic church." A November trial date was soon set, and it immediately became apparent that depending on that trial's outcome, one of the declaratory judgment cases such as

Roe v. *Wade* or *Doe* v. *Bolton* might not be the first clear-cut constitutional challenge to an abortion statute to reach the U.S. Supreme Court.[45]

By late April 1970 it was also apparent, regardless of how Washington state's fall referendum might turn out, that Hawaii and New York would not be the only two states whose legislatures would enact repeal measures. One contender, seemingly just as improbable as Hawaii, was Alaska, where two decidedly different individuals played the principal roles in making a repeal bill a strong candidate for legislative passage. One was Helen Nienhueser, a thirty-three-year-old Brown University graduate and mother of two with a background in social work. First inspired to take an interest in the abortion issue by several January newspaper articles that highlighted how the Alaska Medical Association had endorsed liberalization but would not mount a major legislative push, Nienhueser along with several other Anchorage women started circulating a petition backing a change in the law and soon created a small organization that called itself the Alliance for Humane Abortions. Unitarians and members of conservation groups were among the most supportive Alaskans, and a Methodist clergyman from Juneau, Reverend John Shaffer, emerged as a particularly important religious representative.

Within the legislature itself, Anchorage state senator John L. Rader, a longtime Alaska resident whose family physician was chairman of the state medical association's legislative committee, took the lead in drafting a bill to legalize all abortions performed by a doctor during the first twenty weeks of pregnancy. Originally unable to recruit even a single cosponsor, Rader believed his measure had no prospects whatsoever for passage until the work of the grass-roots lobbyists suddenly began to have a clearly demonstrable effect. In early March Rader brought the bill up for an initial test on the senate floor, where it fell only one vote short of the eleven needed for passage. Then Rader learned of Hawaii's repeal victory, and, after revising his measure in line with Hawaii's, several weeks later he brought an amended bill back to the floor. One ill and previously absent senator had stepped aside and been replaced by his wife, and during the April 2 debate that new member, Roman Catholic Senator Kay Poland of Kodiak, declared her support for Rader's bill, which thus passed by the minimum margin of 11 to 9. Eight days later the state house approved it on a comfortable vote of 26 to 12, but one week after that repeal proponents received an unpleasant surprise when Alaska Governor Keith Miller unexpectedly vetoed the measure. To override Miller's veto would require a minimum of forty votes in a joint roll call of both houses, but Rader immediately indicated that he was relatively confident of success. That confidence proved justified on April 30, when the combined tally of the entire legislature resulted in a better than two-thirds affirmative majority of 41 to 17. Looking back on what had happened, Senator Rader explained that "It was an amazing display of public and political change which permitted the swing of legislative opinion from adverse to overriding the Governor's veto in approximately a three month period." Alaska's new provisions would become effective on July 29, four weeks after New York's repeal measure took effect.[46]

An initially similar chain of events also marked Maryland's consideration of legislative repeal. Following a February hearing, Delegate Allen B. Spector's repeal bill won passage in the lower house of the Maryland legislature by a two-vote margin in mid-March. Ten days later the state senate, in the face of clear indications that Governor Marvin Mandel might well veto the measure, nonetheless also approved it on a vote of 23 to 18. With the governor's signature affirmatively required in order for the bill to become law, Mandel was able to postpone any action for upwards of eight weeks while repeatedly letting journalists know that an eventual veto was all but certain. Finally, in late May, Mandel formally issued a veto message contending that the bill was unacceptable because it included no residency requirement, no explicit term of pregnancy ceiling, and no provision for spousal or parental consent or notice in the cases of married women or teenagers.[47]

Mandel's action, however, appeared as little more than a small blip on an otherwise rapidly cresting curve. In the course of just four days in mid-May 1970, declaratory judgment challenges to four different states' abortion statutes were filed in federal courts in North Carolina, Kentucky, Missouri, and California. *Corkey* v. *Edwards*, the North Carolina case, featured five plaintiffs: four prominent obstetrician-gynecologists and former Charlotte legislator Arthur H. Jones, the onetime sponsor of the 1967 reform law that the case was constitutionally attacking. Jones told reporters that going to court would now be "quicker" than attempting to pass a repeal bill through the legislature, and the lead attorney in the case, Charlotte's vibrant George S. Daly, Jr., who had sought out Roy Lucas's assistance in preparing the suit, responded to comments about the stature of his clients by explaining that "We didn't want a pregnant hippie as a plaintiff."[48]

While the case against the Kentucky statute ran into immediate difficulties and delays at the hands of a seemingly hostile U.S. district judge,[49] the Missouri suit, filed by attorneys Charlotte Thayer and Frank Susman, also utilized Lucas's cooperation and drew upon his litigation strategies; four physicians led the list of plaintiffs.[50] Lucas's counsel was also solicited by Moses Berman, the attorney for California's young Dr. John Shriver Gwynne, who since his willful abortion arrest in Los Angeles in March had accumulated a roster of six felony charges before shifting his operations to Santa Ana in Orange County on May 13. He was arrested there that very first day, and while Berman immediately filed suit in federal court against the Orange County District Attorney, neither the California activists, who had at best ambivalent views about both Gwynne and Berman, nor Lucas made any move to lend an active hand.[51]

But those four suits did not even begin to exhaust the rapidly widening drive for legislative and litigative repeal. In Connecticut, where several New Haven women were beginning to discuss a potential federal case, the principal liberalization group changed its name from the Connecticut League for Abortion Law Reform to the Connecticut League for Abortion Law Repeal. Attorneys in Ohio and university activists in New Hampshire both sought Lucas's advice on whether federal cases should be initiated in their states, and several ongoing cases involving physicians offered other possible avenues for legal gains. In South Dakota, where prosecutors were appealing the constitutionally based dismissal of criminal charges against Dr. Ben Munson to the state supreme court, Munson's local counsel, Homer Kandaras, brought in Lucas to supplement the defense. In Louisiana, where an effort by the state board of medical examiners to revoke the license of a physician on abortion-related grounds was being constitutionally contested in federal court, Benjamin E. Smith, the old-line civil rights lawyer representing Dr. Isadore I. Rosen, similarly enlisted Lucas's assistance. Additionally, several weeks later, in early June, yet another federal declaratory case got underway when Planned Parenthood of Phoenix and several affiliated doctors filed suit against Arizona's attorney general in a constitutional challenge to that state's abortion statute.[52]

The abortion case that was moving forward most swiftly, however, was in Texas. In the immediate aftermath of Linda Coffee's March 3 filing of *Roe* and *Doe* v. *Wade*, the most significant early development came when Roy Merrill, the young Dallas lawyer who already had been in touch with Lucas in preparation for contesting the constitutionality of Texas's abortion law as part of the criminal defense of indicted Carrollton physician James Hubert Hallford, heard about

Coffee's suit and immediately contacted her. Merrill explained that he and his senior partner, Fred Bruner, wanted to join the case by introducing Hallford as an additional party. Coffee was overjoyed both by the prospect of having a medical plaintiff added to the suit and by the additional legal help that Merrill and Bruner could provide, and readily welcomed their participation. On March 19 they filed an initial request to formally intervene, and four days later they submitted a full-scale complaint.

Merrill and Bruner's client, James Hubert Hallford, was facing an April 20 trial date in state district court on two charges of criminal abortion. A forty-three-year-old native of Wichita Falls, Hallford had grown up in Enid, Oklahoma, and had graduated from Oklahoma Baptist University. He received his medical degree in 1958 from the University of Texas's Southwestern Medical School in Dallas, and, following a two-year internship in Oklahoma City, he began practicing medicine in the small town of Carrollton, just north of Dallas, in 1960. Married and with several young children, Hallford nonetheless struggled for several years with an increasingly serious drug problem, and in December 1963 he was brought before the Texas Board of Medical Examiners on charges that he had been improperly writing prescriptions so as to furnish himself with Demerol. One year later, when those charges were renewed, the board revoked Hallford's medical license on the grounds "of writing narcotic prescriptions for himself, using the names of fictitious persons." In December 1965 Hallford's license was reinstated on a probationary basis, and he resumed his Carrollton practice.

An active member of Carrollton's First Baptist Church and the part-time health officer and city physician for municipal employees, Hallford was thought of by many as "a sound citizen" and was known among the regulars in Carrollton's small downtown as a man who could always be found with a Coca-Cola in his hand. Both Fred Bruner and Roy Merrill quickly realized in 1969 when they first met Hallford that a substantial number of abortions had been a significant part of Hallford's practice for at least several years, and in a town as small as Carrollton, the inevitable visibility of that enterprise eventually led to Hallford's undoing.

William R. "Bill" Fuller and Frank Johnson handled criminal investigations for Carrollton's sixteen-member police department. With an "odd traffic" of up to seven or eight out-of-town women arriving each day for extended stays at Hallford's office just off Carrollton's main square, "it wasn't too difficult" for Fuller and Johnson to realize what was going on. Most of the female patients looked like young college students, and early in 1969 Fuller and Johnson began a discreet visual surveillance of Hallford's office. Some days the number of unfamiliar women visitors reached more than a dozen, and the investigators wondered whether the scale of Hallford's profitable practice might be explained by a need to generate enough money to support an ongoing drug addiction. The officers were all but convinced that Hallford had to be aware of their interest, and they speculated that perhaps Hallford believed they would not be savvy or persuasive enough to be able to make a case against him.

As they observed the stream of young female visitors, Fuller and Johnson took down license plate numbers and concluded that many of Hallford's patients were students from the University of Texas at Austin. With names and addresses obtained from the vehicle registrations, Fuller and Johnson paid a quiet visit to Austin. They located and confronted one of Hallford's recent patients, Jane "Wilhite," and under questioning she acknowledged that Hallford had indeed performed an abortion at her request. That was all Fuller and Johnson needed, and shortly after returning to Carrollton they both testified before a Dallas County grand jury that Jane "Wilhite" had confirmed that on January 4, 1969, Dr. Hallford had violated the Texas antiabortion law. On May 5 the grand jury formally indicted Hallford, and Fuller and Johnson went to Hallford's office to tell him he was under arrest. Hallford reacted with complete calm, but several months later a second woman willingly contacted the police, and in October 1969 a second abortion indictment was added to the first.

Hallford's retention of fifty-three-year-old Fred Bruner as his principal attorney was unsurprising, for Bruner was widely regarded as one of Dallas's better criminal defense lawyers. A former number-two prosecutor in the Dallas County district attorney's office, Bruner had won at least one well-remembered abortion conviction of a physician back in the 1950s. Bruner considered Hallford "a competent general practitioner" with at least one chronic problem, and Roy Merrill, Bruner's younger associate, viewed their client as something of an introvert yet certainly "a good person" despite his troubles. Bruner's estimate of Hallford's abortion practice was that the doctor "wasn't an idealistic person," but Merrill, after once asking Hallford about his personal views, came away with a somewhat more nuanced impression. "'It's not an issue for me,'" Hallford had answered. While finishing his medical training, Hallford explained, he had seen any number of women admitted to Dallas's Parkland Memorial Hospital who had been injured by unskilled abortionists. Hence, "'it's real, real easy for me,'" Hallford said, "'because when a woman comes to me, by the time I ever see her, she's already made up her mind: she's going to have an abortion. . . . It's just a question of who's going to do it.'"[53]

Bruner and Merrill's move to hitch Hallford's constitutional claims to the federal court opening provided by *Roe* and *Doe* v. *Wade* was not the only significant development that quickly followed Coffee's well-publicized initial filing. In line with the court's standard sequential practice, the two cases were respectively assigned to District Judges Sarah Hughes and William "Mac" Taylor, and hence it came as no surprise to Coffee or anyone else when Dallas papers reported, on the very same day that Hallford's first petition was noted, that Hughes, Taylor and Dallas's resident Circuit Judge, Irving Goldberg—the very same panel that had ruled favorably for Henry McCluskey in *Buchanan*—had been named by the chief judge of the Fifth Circuit, John R. Brown, as the three-judge court that would hear both *Roe* and *Doe*. Coffee and Merrill both appreciated that Hughes and Goldberg's appointments were indeed promising, and Hughes quickly granted Merrill and Bruner's request that Hallford be added as an intervening plaintiff.

Beyond Merrill and Bruner, the other party who quickly responded to Coffee's filing of *Roe* and *Doe* was the one named defendant in the cases, Dallas County District Attorney Henry Wade. First elected to the local prosecutor's post in 1950, the fifty-six-year-old D.A. had long ago deservedly earned a reputation for fairminded toughness; years later observers would single out Wade's successful prosecution and jailing of one of his own brothers for drunken driving as a signature story from Wade's years in office. Hallford aside, almost all abortion prosecutions undertaken by Wade's office were of nonmedical practitioners who had badly or fatally injured one or more women; proactive antiabortion raids were not a principal feature of either Wade's office or the Dallas police department. Wade himself, responsible for supervising a staff of more than one hundred attorneys and with no particular interest in the subject matter, made no effort to have any direct input into his office's response to the two abortion cases in which he had been named the sole initial defendant. *Roe* and *Doe*'s initial paperwork was channeled to assistant district attorney Wilson Johnston, whose first reaction was to notify the state attorney general's office in Austin about the cases and to "earnestly invite you to participate in the defense."

The chief of Wade's appellate section, John B. Tolle, was a thirty-six-year-old graduate of Notre Dame and Southern Methodist

University's law school. As the attorney responsible for all of Wade's office's participation in federal cases, Tolle on one hand viewed *Roe* as "just a routine assignment," similar in some respects to Henry McCluskey's successful sodomy law challenge, which Tolle had also handled, just several months earlier. But Tolle on the other hand also recognized *Roe* as "a serious case" because Linda Coffee was the attorney who had filed it. Tolle had had a good deal of interaction with Coffee during her 1968–1969 clerkship with Sarah Hughes, and had developed "a lot of respect" for her. "I didn't think Linda Coffee would involve herself in an oddball thing."

On March 23, Tolle filed a two-page initial response to *Roe*, arguing that "Jane Roe" lacked judicial standing to bring the case, since "the statutes complained of operate only against persons who perform an abortion, not against pregnant women upon whom abortions are performed." The following day two one-page submissions signed by Johnston lodged a similar objection against Marsha and David King's contentions in *Doe*: the plaintiffs lacked standing and the suit amounted to little more than a request for an improper advisory opinion. The state attorney general's top deputy, Alfred Walker, had directed Robert Flowers and Jay Floyd, the chief and assistant chief of that office's appropriate division, to respond to Johnston's letter and to definitely participate in the case, and in response to that initial acknowledgment, Johnston with some embarrassment sent Floyd copies of the *Doe* filings with an apology for how "hurriedly and horribly" the papers had been drafted: "I even failed to point out that Mary Doe is not now pregnant and may never be."[54]

While the Dallas and Austin officials were struggling to coordinate credible responses to the two cases, Sarah Hughes moved swiftly to get *Roe*, her assigned case, on a fast track to a quick hearing. On March 26 she wrote Coffee, Bruner, Tolle, and the attorney general's office to summon them to a pretrial conference in her chambers on Friday afternoon, April 3, and at that officially unrecorded session, almost all of the procedural underbrush of both *Roe* and *Doe* was decisively cleared away. Hughes told the five attorneys—Coffee, Bruner, Merrill, Tolle, and Jay Floyd—that *Roe* and *Doe* would be consolidated, that the state of Texas would be permitted to intervene, that Coffee and Weddington would be allowed to file an amended complaint, designating *Roe* as a "class action" on behalf of all women similar to "Jane Roe," and that a formal hearing of the case before the full three-judge panel would be scheduled for two p.m. on Friday, May 22. Tolle had filed a request to question "Jane Roe" as soon as possible, and Linda Coffee parried by explaining that "Roe" would be continuing her pregnancy right up until childbirth. Hughes set a schedule for the filing of everyone's additional briefs leading up to the hearing, and Jay Floyd left the session with decidedly pessimistic expectations, telling Alfred Walker that "From all indications we do not appear to be in very good shape in these cases."[55]

While Coffee, Hughes, and Hallford's lawyers had been moving forward with *Roe*, both the Dallas and Austin women's groups had continued their abortion work. The Austin women, who were actively continuing their referral service, were also approached by a commercial referral operator from California, Wray Morehouse, who was hoping to expand his network for providing Mexico City abortions from an initial Texas base in Houston to both Austin and Dallas. The Austin activists concluded that the medical reputation of his service was less than desirable, and announced their stance in *The Rag*.[56] In Dallas, the far more visible Dallas Committee for the Study of Abortion (DCSA) repeatedly publicized its support for repeal, and in early May its sister group, the Unitarian Women's Alliance, sponsored a talk by Linda Coffee and discussed whether they could sponsor an amicus brief in federal court. In mid-May DCSA held a well-attended public forum at which both Ginny Whitehill and Representative Jim Clark spoke, but much of the news coverage focused on a third speaker, Southern Methodist University chaplain J. Claude Evans, who had made front-page news in Dallas several weeks earlier when he had delivered a sermon championing abortion liberalization after attending a campus clergy conference in New Orleans that had featured Dallas native Howard Moody. Just as with Judy Bourne in Atlanta, Evans's sudden notoriety led to a deluge of phone calls from women seeking referral information, and within days Evans and his associate chaplain, Robert O. Cooper, found themselves operating a nascent Clergy Consultation Service of their own.[57]

On the litigation front, state court judge Jerome Chamberlain indefinitely postponed Dr. Hallford's criminal trial in deference to the federal court's consideration of his constitutional claims in *Roe*, and in mid-April Fred Bruner and Roy Merrill filed an extremely impressive fifty-four-page brief on Hallford's behalf with the Dallas three-judge court. Weddington and Coffee soon followed with an amended complaint and a far more modest fourteen-page brief of their own. A profusion of typographical errors testified to Linda's rusty skills as a typist, and the brief repeatedly cited Merrill and Bruner's submission in support of various points while attaching a photocopy of the constitutional portions of Lucas's brief in *Hall* as a supplemental reference. At the end of April Jay Floyd submitted an unremarkable memorandum on behalf of the state contending that none of the plaintiffs had adequate standing to pursue the case, and just days before the May 22 hearing John Tolle of Wade's office filed a three-page brief bluntly asserting with regard to "Roe" that "the right of the unborn child to life is greater than the Plaintiff's right to privacy." Most basically, Tolle said, "the preservation of the life of the unborn 'human organism' is a matter of compelling interest sufficient to give the State of Texas constitutional authority to enact laws for that purpose." At that same time, the only amicus brief in the case, a five-page effort from the Dallas Legal Services Project on behalf of poor women, was also filed, quickly followed a nine-page supplemental statement from Merrill and Bruner.[58]

The day before the May 22 hearing Coffee and Weddington completed the trial court record by filing two affidavits. One was from Dr. Paul C. Trickett, since 1968 the director of the student health service at the University of Texas in Austin, who had been introduced to Weddington some time earlier by campus minister Bob Breihan. Trickett had taken more than his share of criticism in *The Rag* for the health service staff's inconsistent responses to women students' requests for contraceptive assistance, but the number of women coming in for postabortion checkups after visits to Mexico, Carrollton, or wherever had made a significant impression on him, and he briefly voiced his views in a four-page statement.

Coffee and Weddington's second affidavit was an anonymous three-page statement from Norma McCorvey, submitted in lieu of the questioning that John Tolle had sought. Drafted in large part by Coffee, McCorvey's declaration offered a lengthy justification for her anonymity, asserting a fear that "the notoriety occasioned by the lawsuit would make it impossible for me to secure any employment in the near future and would severely limit my advancement in any employment which I might secure at some later date." It went on to say that "I consider the decision of whether to bear a child a highly personal one and feel that the notoriety occasioned by the lawsuit would result in a gross invasion of personal privacy." Although the affidavit did not expressly note that McCorvey was now almost eight months pregnant, it did explain that she had "wanted to terminate my pregnancy because of the economic hardship which my pregnancy entailed and because of the social stigma attached to the bearing of illegitimate children in our society." While Weddington and Coffee, given their concern that an abortion could possibly have mooted the case, were privately thankful

that McCorvey was carrying the pregnancy to term, McCorvey's affidavit concluded by describing how she was too poor to travel outside
Texas for an abortion or to pay for a medically competent illegal one; "I
fear that my very life would be endangered if I submitted to an abortion which I could afford."[59]

Only one member of the three-judge panel, Sarah Tilghman
Hughes, had given much thought to *Roe* v. *Wade* in advance of the May
22 hearing. One of her two clerks, Randy Shreve, had been assigned to
pull together relevant materials in addition to the spotty briefs that
made up the case's formal record, and Shreve had gone to the extent of
calling Roy Lucas in New York to ask for information. Lucas sent off a
package of what he termed "numerous articles and briefs to which you
may or may not already have had access," but whether or not Shreve
was cognizant of it, Sarah Hughes already knew full well what she
thought of the substantive issue posed by *Roe* v. *Wade*. Asked later
whether she had had a personal opinion on the question prior to hearing the case, Hughes answered frankly that "Oh, well, I was in favor of
permitting abortion."

Neither of the other two panel members, Irving Goldberg and
William M. "Mac" Taylor, Jr., had ever given the subject any particular
consideration. Goldberg, asked about it two decades later, explained
that he had "had no contact" with abortion and had "never thought
about it" prior to *Roe*. Taylor, who passed away in 1985, had been
named to the district court bench by Lyndon Johnson at the very same
time that Goldberg had been nominated for the circuit court in June
1966. Sixty-one years old when he heard *Roe*, Mac Taylor had graduated from Southern Methodist's law school in 1932 and had spent several years as a junior prosecutor before moving into private practice.
After serving four years as a state court trial judge in the early 1950s,
Taylor had returned to private practice up until the time of his federal
nomination. A "soft-spoken, even tempered" man who never raised his
voice, Taylor was a popular if unremarkable figure in Dallas's federal
courthouse, and no one who knew him expected him to play a dramatic role on a three-judge panel that included the resolutely liberal
Hughes and the energetically outspoken Goldberg.[60]

When Goldberg called the hearing to order at two p.m. on May 22
in Sarah Hughes's courtroom in the federal courthouse and post office
in downtown Dallas, a largely female crowd—including Marsha and
David King, but not Norma McCorvey—had filled almost every seat
in the room. John Tolle explained to the panel that there were no disputed facts in the case and that neither side thus had any testimony

they desired to present. Goldberg hence said that each side would be given thirty minutes to speak to the competing motions for summary judgment and for dismissal, and both Fred Bruner and Tolle indicated that each side's attorneys had already agreed on how to divide their time amongst themselves. Bruner and Merrill had spoken by phone with Linda Coffee about how they planned to handle Hallford's claims; Coffee and Weddington had worked out a division of labor between themselves, and Tolle and Jay Floyd from the attorney general's office had arranged to split the defense's allotment.

Linda Coffee led off for the plaintiffs, explaining that she would address the procedural issues and Weddington the substantive ones. Coffee argued that the federal panel should declare the Texas abortion law unconstitutional since there was no acceptable or "saving" construction that state courts could give to the provisions, but as soon as she mentioned that the case also involved First Amendment issues, Sarah Hughes quickly asked what they were, and Coffee answered, "Well, the right of privacy," citing a 1969 Supreme Court First Amendment decision, *Stanley* v. *Georgia*, that had condemned "unwanted governmental intrusions into one's privacy" while voiding the obscenity conviction of a man who had been found to have three pornographic films in his home. Irving Goldberg immediately inquired as to whether Coffee drew any distinction between the First and the Ninth Amendments, and Coffee tried to parry the issue. Then both Goldberg and Hughes proceeded to bombard her with a series of questions and observations on a variety of points, and for the entire balance of her time Coffee was unable to utter more than two consecutive sentences without being interrupted.

Then Weddington rose to address the constitutional issues, and she was only halfway through her initial effort to list the prior decisions that had recognized a privacy right in the context of abortion when Goldberg interrupted to say that "I don't read *Vuitch* that way." Weddington responded by immediately beginning to read Gesell's own language, and the peppery Goldberg for once was satisfied. Weddington referred to the law review exposition of a privacy-based abortion right that had been offered by retired Supreme Court Justice Tom Clark, a Texas native and onetime Dallas County prosecutor, but Goldberg broke in to ask her whether the state had *any* compelling interest in regulating the performance of abortions. Weddington answered that the only valid such interest lay in requiring that they be performed by doctors, and Goldberg immediately interjected "Or the state of pregnancy or anything?" Weddington conceded that "the state of pregnancy gives me some pause," and noted how the *Babbitz* panel had spoken of the fourth month, but quickly went on to say that "a more persuasive argument is that you could recognize life when the fetus is able to live outside the body of the mother," somewhere between twenty-two and twenty-six weeks of pregnancy. Picking up on Goldberg's earlier intimation, Weddington contended that "under the Ninth Amendment . . . those women have a right to abortion," but Goldberg again and again pushed Weddington to speak to the issue of whether there were any additional compelling state interests in the area. Weddington finally indicated, without using the word viability, that some ceiling point limitation would indeed be constitutionally proper. Then Goldberg concluded their colloquy by asking whether "you think this statute is more vulnerable on Ninth Amendment grounds or on vagueness," and Weddington forthrightly answered that "I believe it is more vulnerable on the Ninth Amendment basis."

As part of the prior arrangement worked out with Coffee, Fred Bruner devoted most of his ten minutes to arguing, in line with both *Belous* and *Vuitch*, that Texas's single statutory exception, allowing abortions necessary for "saving the life of the mother," was indeed unconstitutionally vague. Then Jay Floyd began the defense argument by contending that none of the plaintiffs had adequate legal standing to bring the case, but both Goldberg and Hughes firmly indicated that they found the assertion unpersuasive. Hearkening back to Coffee's initial constitutional reference, Floyd declared that "I cannot perceive, your Honors, how it would fall under religion, speech or press of the First Amendment," and while Hughes quickly interjected that "We agree with you on that," Irving Goldberg pressed him to "go to the Ninth Amendment and what about vagueness." Floyd responded by noting that he failed to see how the references in the plaintiffs' briefs to the constitutional guarantee of equal protection had any relevance, and Goldberg, indicating agreement, brusquely told him to "Skip it." Both Goldberg and Hughes's questions seemed to reflect the influence of *Belous* and *Vuitch*, but toward the end of Floyd's presentation, yet another reference to privacy caused Goldberg to voice something of an objection. "Well," he volunteered, "I think it's a bad word in this area, but apparently everybody wants to use it. I think it's something different from privacy, but I haven't come up with a phrase myself yet, but I just know 'privacy' won't do."

John Tolle concluded the attorneys' presentations by reechoing the position Wade's office had articulated in its earlier filings. "The state has got a right to protect life that is in being at whatever stage it may be in being," and policy-making toward that end "is a matter for legislative determination." Under the existing Texas statute, once a pregnancy had occurred "the right of that child to life is superior to that woman's right to privacy." Tolle experienced far fewer interruptions that any of the other counsel had suffered, but just as the hearing was coming to a close, Irving Goldberg directed a pointed hypothetical question to Sarah Weddington: if the panel perchance did enjoin Henry Wade's office from any further enforcement of the Texas abortion statute, where would that leave all the dozens of other district attorneys in Texas. Weddington answered that she thought the state attorney general was now a party-defendant, but both Goldberg and Hughes instantly told her that he was *not* a party. "Do you have any response to the question?" Goldberg asked. Weddington hesitated. "We goofed," she exclaimed, and laughter rippled through the crowd as the hearing ended.[61]

As the three judges retired to the small library situated right behind Hughes's courtroom, the respective attorneys and some of their supporters began to mull over the possible results of the hearing. Linda Coffee, whose performance some of the supportive onlookers had found less reassuring than Sarah Weddington's, was nonetheless "very confident" that the plaintiffs would prevail at least on vagueness grounds and "fairly optimistic" that they would win a decision on the more far-reaching constitutional merits as well. Both Roy Merrill and Fred Bruner, however, came away with a sense that Goldberg and perhaps Hughes were more likely to hand down a Ninth Amendment decision rather than one based on vagueness or any of the potential procedural problems. On the other side, both Jay Floyd and John Tolle came out of the hearing in fairly upbeat spirits. "I felt that they were not going to declare the statute unconstitutional," Floyd remembered. "I was confident." Tolle recalled that he "thought we did a pretty good job" and had made "a good presentation," but he had no particular expectation as to what sort of a decision the panel was likely to render.

Among the onlookers, Ginny Whitehill, who had never before met Weddington, left the room "more optimistic" than she had been at the outset, largely because of how well Sarah had coped with Goldberg's sustained questioning. Weddington herself, however, felt "let down" and "less optimistic," in spite of how promising Goldberg's strong interest in the Ninth Amendment might well be. The hearing had been Weddington's first courtroom appearance ever as a practicing attorney, and hence "I was petrified" during that part of the proceeding, she later explained. The most reassuring moment, she said, came when

Sarah Hughes looked down, made eye contact and "gave me a reassuring smile" and then "winked at me as if to say, 'It's going to be all right.'" Indeed, Weddington's performance, particularly in the face of Goldberg's onslaught, had actually gone far better than she thought. The least experienced participant in the hearing had arguably turned in the best showing of the day, but all of the attorneys realized full well that their impressions and evaluations would probably count for very little once the panel itself sat down to make a decision and got to work on an actual opinion.[62]

The hearing in *Roe* came three weeks before the similar proceeding in Georgia's *Doe* v. *Bolton*. Once Margie Hames and Tobi Schwartz had filed suit in mid-April, the next substantive development in the case took place late that month when Fifth Circuit Chief Judge John Brown named three Atlanta jurists—District Judges Sidney O. Smith, Jr., and Albert J. Henderson, Jr., and Circuit Judge Lewis R. Morgan—as *Doe*'s special three-judge court. At that same time, a Roman Catholic Atlanta attorney, Ferdinand Buckley, petitioned Judge Smith for appointment as the "guardian ad litem" for "Mary Doe's" fetus, with the corresponding opportunity to thus become a full-fledged participant in the case. Smith initially granted the petition, and then eight days later revoked it as "improvidently" granted after Margie Hames protested that Buckley's status would obstruct the ongoing effort to arrange a legal abortion for Sandra Bensing at some hospital other than Grady.

Late in April both Dr. Peter Bourne and Dr. Donald L. Block, an obstetrician/gynecologist at Georgia Baptist Hospital on the east side of Atlanta, met with "Mary Doe" and began the process of obtaining approval for Sandra's abortion. On May 5 both Sandra and her husband Joel Bensing executed supportive affidavits, with Sandra stating that "I am very nervous and upset at the thought of raising another baby. . . . I cannot love another baby and I am depressed all the time thinking about my pregnancy." Joel straightforwardly declared that "I don't want her to have this baby" and "I do not want this baby either." Later that same day Georgia Baptist's abortion committee approved Sandra's request, and Margie, Tobi Schwartz, and the Bournes started piecing together the several hundred dollars that would be required to pay Sandra's hospital costs for the procedure.

In mid-May the *Bolton* defendants filed a pro forma motion to dismiss, but several days later Judge Smith set the formal three-judge hearing for ten a.m. on Monday, June 15, and notified all the attorneys that briefs would be due by June 8. Hames and her colleagues set to work on their principal arguments, and Judy Bourne's small GCHA group, which already had helped more than 150 women with referral assistance, continued its work and confidently predicted a judicial victory to the Atlanta newspapers. Then, however, sometime in the third week of May, the Bournes and the attorneys received startling news: Sandra had failed to show up for her scheduled abortion at Georgia Baptist, and indeed was nowhere to be found. Quiet but frantic inquiries produced reports that Joel, once again on the lam from the law, this time for relatively minor theft, had fled to Oklahoma and had taken Sandra with him. More than a week's worth of very nervous days passed as the attorneys began trying to identify some other unsuccessful abortion applicant whom they could substitute for Sandra or simply add to the case. They had already started to consider such an option while worrying about the mootness issue that might arise if Sandra did indeed obtain an abortion, and by early June they had identified two possible new plaintiffs: Linda "Smith," a twenty-four-year-old mother of two who had been turned down at Grady and then fired from her job once her twenty-week pregnancy had become visible, and Martha "French," a forty-one-year-old mother of seven whose husband was a severe alcoholic.

Then, no more than week before the scheduled hearing, Sandra called Margie Hames from Oklahoma. Joel had taken off and left her there with essentially no money; equally if not more important, Sandra also said she had felt fetal movement in her now four- to five-month pregnancy and that experience had convinced her that she no longer wanted an abortion. Hames told her that no one wanted to force her to go ahead, that continuing the pregnancy was actually better in terms of the court case, but that the lawyers did very much want her to come back to Atlanta so that she could be present at the June 15 hearing. Sandra agreed, and after confronting and overcoming a variety of logistical problems, Tobi Schwartz arranged to use the money they had put together to underwrite Sandra's abortion to instead finance a prepaid airplane ticket that would bring Sandra back to Atlanta from Oklahoma. On Sunday, June 14, Tobi met Sandra at the airport and took her to Margie's, where they acquired some proper clothes for the hearing and also worked out written answers to a set of basic, factual questions that the defendants had propounded for "Mary Doe" just four days earlier. Tobi then had Sandra spend the night at Tobi's own home and arranged for a Legal Aid staff member to accompany her to the ten a.m. Monday hearing.[63]

The six briefs filed with the three-judge court in *Doe* represented a considerably more extensive set of arguments than had been provided to the Texas panel in *Roe*. Hames, Schwartz, and Rindskopf had relied very extensively and very directly on the most recently updated materials that Roy Lucas had filed in late April in the New Jersey declaratory judgment case, and hence their fifty-eight-page submission cited both Tom Emerson's 1965 remark about how *Griswold* might well prove applicable to abortion and retired Justice Tom Clark's law review article as well as *Belous, Vuitch*, and *Babbitz*. They precisely repeated Lucas's contention that "*Griswold* is not an isolated decision confined to its facts, but one in a continuing line of decisions involving various aspects of personal privacy and family autonomy," and went on to assert that since "the State has no compelling interest to justify interfering with a woman's basic right to privacy in matters related to sex, family and marriage," therefore even the 1968 Georgia reform statute "is an unconstitutional invasion of the right to privacy."

Alan Charles, a young California protégé of Zad Leavy and Tony Beilenson's, filed a solid amicus brief in support of the *Doe* plaintiffs, and Ferdinand Buckley, the erstwhile fetal rights intervenor, submitted a fifty-two-page statement on behalf of "Mary Doe's unborn child" and other "unborn children." Tony Hight, an assistant district attorney representing Fulton County district attorney Lewis Slaton, and Atlanta city attorneys Henry Bowden and Ralph Witt, representing Atlanta Police Chief Herbert T. Jenkins, each filed modest, six-page statements; of the three named defendants, the lead role in speaking up on behalf of Georgia's 1968 law thus fell to Dorothy T. Beasley, the one female assistant attorney general on Arthur Bolton's staff of some twenty-six such deputies.[64]

A New Jersey native who had earned her law degree at Washington's American University in 1964, Dorothy Toth Beasley had moved to Atlanta with her husband in December 1967. At a Christmas party she had remarked to one new acquaintance, Owen Forrester, that she was looking for a job, and Forrester had recommended that she call one of his fellow partners at Fisher and Phillips, Margie Hames. An interview with Hames was arranged, and by the end of January Dorothy Beasley had joined the firm. She practiced there until shortly before joining the criminal division of Bolton's staff in October 1969, just six months prior to when Bolton and criminal division chief Marion O. Gordon had assigned her *Doe*. Bolton had a high opinion of Beasley, and privately thought she was perhaps the best lawyer on his staff. "She didn't get it simply because she was female," the outspoken attorney general emphasized years later in explaining that the statute deserved as good a defense as his office could provide. "I really left it up to her."[65]

None of the three members of the special panel before whom Beasley and her former colleague Margie Hames appeared on Monday morning June 15 had the sorts of reputations that had allowed Linda Coffee to feel so optimistic about the Dallas court that had featured Sarah Hughes and Irving Goldberg. The one circuit judge on the Atlanta panel, Lewis R. Morgan, had been promoted to the Fifth Circuit in 1968 after having served as a district judge in north Georgia since John F. Kennedy had nominated him in 1961. A LaGrange native whose father had been a doctor, Morgan had earned his law degree at the University of Georgia, where he had been a close friend of future Georgia Senator Herman Talmadge, and had served in the state legislature in the late 1930s. Fifty-seven years old in 1970 and widely regarded as a judicial moderate, Morgan was popular with his colleagues and rarely authored dissenting opinions.

The second member of the *Doe* panel, silver-haired Albert J. Henderson, had been named to the district court bench at the same time that Morgan had been elevated to the Fifth Circuit. A forty-nine-year-old native of Marietta, Henderson had earned his undergraduate and law degrees from Mercer University in Macon and had served seven years as a juvenile court judge and then seven years as a state superior court judge before joining the federal bench. An exceedingly quiet man, Henderson was viewed as undoubtedly the most conservative member of the panel by the *Doe* attorneys.

The youngest and most intriguing member of the *Doe* panel was the judge who had taken preliminary responsibility for the case right from the start, Sidney O. Smith, Jr. A Gainesville native and World War II Army veteran who had graduated from Harvard before earning his law degree at the University of Georgia, Smith had been elected a state superior court judge in 1962 and had been named to a federal district court judgeship by Lyndon Johnson in 1965. A friendly man with an easy sense of humor, he teasingly told Elizabeth Rindskopf, who was herself pregnant, that they could stipulate that Rindskopf was not "Mary Doe." Like Rindskopf, Margie Hames viewed Smith as far and away the *Doe* plaintiffs' most likely supporter on this particular panel.[66]

When Lewis Morgan called the June 15 hearing to order before a "standing-room only crowd" that included a significant number of pregnant women, and not just Sandra Bensing, both Margie Hames and Tobi Schwartz were prepared to present a number of well-prepared witnesses, including Doctors Donald Block and W. Newton Long, who were ready to testify about the significant obstacles and delays that the Georgia reform statute placed in the path of women seeking approval for a legal, therapeutic abortion. The three-judge panel, however, had caucused privately in advance of the hearing to discuss their concerns, and Morgan began the proceeding by asking Hames to address the most basic issue of whether the court had jurisdiction to hear the case. When Hames sought to parry, Sidney Smith immediately jumped in and seconded Morgan's point, exclaiming that "The question that concerns us is what do the federal courts have to do with the case. What is the federal constitutional right that requires a federal district court to pass on the matter?" Hames responded by citing "the First and Ninth Amendment right of privacy and right to control her own body," and Smith immediately replied by saying that "I understand that you are basing this primarily on the *Griswold* case. Now, I do not see in the Constitution in reading it a federal constitutional right to the right of privacy, and this is the underlying question." As Hames tried to respond, she and her colleagues silently wondered whether this was an indication that their chances of success were exceedingly slim, and Smith reiterated his concern, saying that "I am having difficulty making a federal constitutional right out of the underlying question." Lewis Morgan broke in to seemingly give Hames a hand, and Hames made reference both to *Babbitz* and to Henry McCluskey's victory in *Buchanan*. She offered to file a brief detailing them both, and when Morgan quickly asked if she could do so within ten days, Hames readily agreed.

When the panel members turned their attention for a moment to Ferdinand Buckley, Judge Smith twice referred to the issue of "the unborn child." He then further volunteered that since *Doe* was a facial challenge to the 1968 Georgia law, "I don't see what we need any evidence for to reach that question," and Morgan agreed, saying that "I was under the impression there wouldn't be any evidence." Hames politely but repeatedly tried to say that the plaintiffs very much did want to present testimony, but Smith and his colleagues remained firm: "I see no need for any evidence," particularly the sort of detailed descriptions of hospital abortion committee functioning that Hames, Schwartz, and their witnesses had been prepared to offer. Morgan called a brief recess so that the panel could consult privately, and when they came back in, Morgan announced that they were in agreement that there were two issues here, jurisdiction and the merits. Tobi Schwartz took over from Margie and recited almost verbatim the entire Lucas sentence about how "*Griswold* was not an isolated decision confined to the facts . . ." that they had employed in their brief. All three of the panel members tried to press her as to whether a fetus's father should have any rights or standing, and then Morgan asked whether the panel should simply wait until the Supreme Court decided *Vuitch*. Schwartz said no, since *Vuitch* had turned on vagueness, and the panel called upon the defense attorneys to offer their arguments.

Fulton County assistant district attorney Tony Hight led off for the trio of defendants, focusing upon how the record did not indicate *why* Grady had rejected "Mary Doe's" abortion request and further contending that an application for a hospital abortion did not involve "the private marital state that is referred to in *Griswold*." Then Dorothy Beasley took over, firmly asserting that if "Mary Doe" wanted to avoid having children, she had the options of sterilization, birth control, or abstinence from sexual relations. "She has voluntarily put herself in the position to have this child and once that life is kindled in her, the state takes the position that it has the right to be born because it is regarded as a life." Judge Morgan responded by pointing out, as he had to Hight, that the Georgia reform law nonetheless already allowed for the abortion of some fetuses, and Beasley replied that while a balance would always have to be struck between the rights of the woman and those of the fetus, "a good argument could be made for it to be a federal constitutional right for the unborn child to have a right to live. . . . I think the child has a right to life from the moment of its conception."

Both Ralph Witt, on behalf of Chief Jenkins, and Tony Hight advised the judges that they supported Ferdinand Buckley's desire for a full roll in the case, and the panel allowed Buckley to speak for some time about fetal interests. Then Margie Hames was given several minutes to recapitulate the plaintiffs' contentions. She returned immediately to *Griswold*, asserting that "the basic holding of that case . . . established the basic right to determine the size of one's family." For Mary Doe and others struggling with unwanted pregnancies, "abortion should be available to these women as a backup method to make the *Griswold* holding effective." She purposely announced that "Mary Doe is present in court," and went on to conclude by noting that "'Abortion on demand' is not our terminology and this is not what we are talking about. We are talking about abortion as a medical procedure and a decision between the woman and her physician." Sidney Smith broke in to declare that "You either have a basic constitutional right for this that is not subject to control by the state, or the statute is good," and then further volunteered that no equal protection attack was going to succeed. Hames interjected apologetically that "lawyers are inclined to use the shotgun approach," and Smith replied with a smile that "We got blasted in this one." The clock showed almost 12:45 p.m., and Lewis Morgan brought the hearing to a close. "If the court determines to decide this case, if evidence should be considered, we will reconvene it; otherwise, we will pass on the argument."[67]

Margie Hames, Tobi Schwartz, Elizabeth Rindskopf and Judy Bourne took Sandy Bensing to lunch at a nearby French restaurant and discussed their reactions. Margie felt fairly confident, especially in light of Smith's final remarks, that the panel would indeed reach the constitutional merits of the case, but she, like Tobi and Elizabeth, was greatly disappointed and somewhat worried at the panel's disinterest in hearing any of their factual witnesses. Margie in particular been somewhat surprised by how fetally oriented an approach her former colleague Dorothy Beasley had taken, but before the lunch ended they all agreed that Elizabeth would take charge of preparing the supplemental brief on the constitutional issues that Judge Morgan had so explicitly requested. Filed nine days later, Rindskopf's submission again reiterated the *Griswold* emphasis that they had stressed in their initial brief and that both Margie and Tobi had voiced at the hearing. If, with regard to birth control, "the right to make such a family decision is constitutionally protected from state interference before conception, one should ask how does it lose its status as a constitutional right after conception," Rindskopf tellingly asked.

That supplemental question, however, would not be the final suggestion that the *Doe* panel would consider, for all four of the opposing parties also submitted supplemental briefs, with Ferdinand Buckley's and particularly Dorothy Beasley's being the most significant. Beasley's statement reiterated, in dramatically stronger language, the fetal emphasis she had articulated at the hearing. She asserted that "the *real* liberty" sought by the plaintiffs was "the right to destroy a living child without 'State interference,'" and she alleged that the actual goal of abortion applicants such as "Mary Doe" was "to have someone kill the life developing within her." Beasley went on to explain that "The child within the woman is not a 'part' of her and/or her body; from its earliest stage it is already a boy or a girl, with its own organs, nervous system, digestion, etc." She contended that "*Griswold* offers no authority for the proposition that restrictions on abortion are an impermissible limitation of the right of privacy," and she harshly attacked the plaintiffs' interpretation of constitutional privacy, alleging that in their view "the right embraces an unlimited freedom to so invade another's right to privacy that he may be exterminated." With the conclusion of Beasley's fervently worded supplemental brief, the trial court record in *Doe* v. *Bolton* was complete.[68]

★   ★   ★

Less than forty-eight hours after the conclusion of the Atlanta argument in *Doe* v. *Bolton*, the Dallas panel of Hughes, Goldberg, and Taylor filed their unanimous decision and opinion in *Roe* v. *Wade*. Immediately after the close of the May 22 hearing in Sarah Hughes's courtroom, the three panel members had retired to her small adjacent library to discuss the case. It was not a room Sarah Hughes had much use for. "I don't like to go in that library," she later explained while criticizing the Supreme Court for issuing opinions that "are too long." "There are some judges that like to write opinions and like to study. I don't. I have never written an opinion that I didn't have to write."

The panel's private discussion lasted less than five minutes. The three judges had all known each other for years, and they quickly established that they were in almost complete agreement concerning *Roe*. "It was actually an easy case for us," Irving Goldberg recalled years later. "The statute we had before us was clearly bad. It made criminal almost any type of abortion by anyone," including those with strong therapeutic justification. "You cannot tell me," Goldberg explained, "that a woman who gets pregnant due to rape cannot have the burden removed from her body." Two decades later, Goldberg described the decision as "almost inevitable," as one that "just flowed from the statement of the facts." The attractiveness of a Ninth Amendment basis, particularly in an era when "new concepts were born every day," stemmed in large part from the undeniably basic recognition that "you just couldn't deny the woman the right." "Talk about life, liberty, or anything you want to; you can't even begin to talk about the constitutional rights if this is prohibited," Goldberg recounted.

For Sarah Hughes, the issue was even more cut and dried. Asked some years later whether she had been impressed by the plaintiffs' presentation at the hearing, Hughes forthrightly said "No, I don't remember what it was. It was just unconstitutional, that's all. It was a privilege for a woman to decide what she wanted to do, and it was an invasion of that privilege." Stating her position on abortion a few years after the decision, Hughes explained that "I see no reason for any law. It is between a woman and her doctor, and I wish people would stop talking about it."

There were no long talks at that brief post-hearing conference. Mac Taylor expressed his concurrence with his more opinionated colleagues, and the trio quickly agreed that since *Roe* was formally on Hughes's docket, it would be her responsibility to prepare an opinion stating their views. Hughes indicated that she would prefer to issue an injunction prohibiting any further enforcement of the Texas abortion statutes as well as to hand down the declaratory judgment sought by the plaintiffs, but the more savvy Goldberg said no. To do that would dramatically increase the chances that their decision would be reviewed and reversed, for there were increasing signs that the Supreme Court firmly believed that federal injunctions against the enforcement of state statutes should be issued only in unusual circumstances where officials were engaging in clearcut misbehavior. It would be strategically preferable, Goldberg believed, for the panel simply to hold the Texas provisions unconstitutional and then see how Wade's office and state officials responded. Mac Taylor agreed, and Sarah Hughes reluctantly consented.

Within little more than a week of that May 22 conference, Hughes sent copies of an initial typescript draft of her opinion to both Taylor and Goldberg's chambers. As Hughes's minimalist attitude toward the preparation and significance of written opinions clearly augured, the draft that she circulated to her colleagues was neither lengthy nor elaborate. Irving Goldberg was of course in no way surprised, but Goldberg's clerk, Clarice Davis, who was accustomed to seeing the work of such renowned Fifth Circuit judges as Louisiana's John Minor Wisdom, was "appalled" at Hughes's draft. It did indeed rely upon the Ninth Amendment in much the way that Goldberg had suggested, but it provided little of the additional discussion or analysis that was customary in appellate opinions. Goldberg and Davis drew up a fairly extensive list of changes and amplifications they wanted to see made in the initial draft, and discussed how they might best persuade Hughes to adopt some if not all of their suggestions. Goldberg, after deciding that it might well be disrespectful to his longtime friend if he himself visited her to ask for so many changes, sent Davis off to see Hughes in the hope that she would accept at least some of their prospective revisions.

Sarah Hughes grudgingly accepted several of the improvements that were at the top of Irving Goldberg's list, but once the scope of Clarice Davis's mission became clear, Hughes coolly but politely indicated that she had absolutely no interest in pursuing the sort of line-by-line rewrite of her draft that Goldberg and Davis had been hoping for. "When she saw the amount of writing on the paper," Davis recalled years later, "she said, 'That's too much. I won't talk about that much.' And so then I said, 'Let's start with this,'" but Hughes's patience expired inside of five minutes. "It just wasn't the sort of thing she was interested in," Davis explained. "Judge Hughes was a very impatient lady, very impatient with the niceties of grammatical structure and legal reasoning and scholarship . . . She was a bottom-line person," and "She wouldn't go over the opinion again because she didn't give a rip."

Goldberg had told Davis to expect much the sort of reception that she received, and he was bemused rather than angered when his momentarily inconsolable clerk returned to report the seeming failure of her nonetheless partially successful mission. Davis herself wondered whether Goldberg might be willing to prepare a separate concurring opinion of his own to supplement Hughes's, but Goldberg's sense of personal and judicial manners again constrained him. "He just didn't get to say what he wanted to say," and "he didn't see anything he could do about it," Davis later explained. Goldberg himself in subsequent conversations about *Roe* itself would not go beyond the polite observation that "maybe we should have written more," but he never shied from expounding a decisive and forthright view of opinion-writing. "If the subject matter permits it, then I think an opinion should be a crusading force," Goldberg emphasized. "An opinion should have not only a beginning and an end, but a future."[69]

What the *Roe* panel handed down on Wednesday, June 17, came to less than nine pages in the law books, and would hardly merit description as a "crusading force," but it nonetheless represented a good part of what Linda Coffee and Sarah Weddington had been hoping for. Issued per curiam instead of in the name of any one particular panel member, the panel found that both "Jane Roe" and Dr. Hallford, but not "John and Mary Doe," had sufficient standing to litigate the case. Both the Ninth Amendment issue and Hallford's vagueness challenge, the panel stated, posed significant constitutional questions that had to be faced. With regard to the plaintiffs' most basic complaint that the Texas provisions "deprive single women and married couples of their right, secured by the Ninth Amendment, to choose whether to have children," the panel simply and directly said "We agree. The essence of the interest sought to be protected here is the right of choice over events which, by their character and consequences, bear in a fundamental manner on the privacy of individuals." They quoted from Arthur Goldberg's concurrence in *Griswold*, and then avowed that "freedom to choose in the matter of abortions has been accorded the status of a 'fundamental' right in every case coming to the attention of this Court where the question has been raised": *Belous*, *Vuitch*, *Babbitz*, and the South Dakota trial court dismissal in *Munson*. They quoted from the first two and from former Justice Clark's law review analysis, and then went on to acknowledge that indeed there were "several compelling justifications for state presence in the area of abortions. These include the legitimate interests of the state in seeing to it that abortions are performed by competent persons and in adequate surroundings. Concern over abortion of the 'quickened' fetus may well rank as another such interest. The difficulty with the Texas Abortion Laws is that, even if they promote these interests, they far outstrip these justifications" by prohibiting virtually all abortions. The "Ninth Amendment right to choose to have an abortion is not unqualified or unfettered," the panel reiterated, but "We need not here delineate the factors which could qualify the right of a mother to have an abortion." The opinion concluded by formally holding that the Texas provisions were both unconstitutionally overbroad and unconstitutionally vague, and by briefly discussing an earlier Supreme Court decision in explaining why no formal injunction against further enforcement of the Texas laws would actually be issued.[70]

The *Roe* ruling was front-page news all across Texas. Linda Coffee told reporters "We consider it quite a victory" and that "Jane Roe" was "very satisfied" with the decision, even though it would not affect her own situation, since she was now just a few weeks away from giving birth. David and Marsha King, as "John and Mary Doe," told Barbara Richardson of the *Dallas Times-Herald* that they considered the outcome a victory even though they themselves had been denied standing, and while no comment was forthcoming from Dr. Hallford, Fred Bruner stressed that he himself was "no crusader. I'm just representing my client." Dr. Hugh Savage called the decision "a step in the right direction" toward full-fledged repeal, but the Austin Women's Liberation group, commenting in *The Rag*, warned that the ruling actually meant "very little." What it did signify, they emphasized, was how everyone's focus now ought to shift to what sort of new law the 1971 state legislature might enact as a replacement statute, especially since it appeared likely that the legislature would choose reform rather than repeal. The *Dallas Times-Herald*, for example, termed the court decision "unfortunate" yet called a reform law "long overdue" while nonetheless opposing repeal. Similarly, Fort Worth state senator Don Kennard told the *Dallas Morning News* that "the feeling and attitude" within the legislature had "shifted a great deal in the last two years," but observers agreed that while a reform bill would now have a good shot at passage, a repeal one would not.

Perhaps the most surprising reaction to the judicial ruling was offered by Mrs. Peter J. Collora, president of Catholic Women of the Dallas Diocese, who told the *Times-Herald* that "I have great faith and trust in our courts" and that "this decision is the only one the court could have made. You couldn't prosecute under those terms. They really were too vague and too broad. Why have a law you can't enforce?" More predictable but also somewhat confusing were the comments voiced by District Attorney Henry Wade and Texas Attorney General Crawford Martin. On the day after the panel's decision, Wade said he would appeal the ruling and was confident that the statute would eventually be upheld. He forthrightly added, however, that "I am of the opinion if the law has been declared unconstitutional you can't try people for it. But we won't dismiss any pending abortion charges against anyone until the Supreme Court rules." One day later, however, after he had had more time to focus upon the panel's decision not to issue an injunction, Wade seemed to step back from his earlier statement by declaring that "Apparently we're free to try them, so we'll still do that." Attorney General Martin seconded Wade's comment that the ruling would indeed be appealed and emphasized that "I do not agree with the court decision that the Texas statutes are overbroad and vague."[71]

Texas doctors initially were not sure what to make of the situation. In Dallas, Parkland Memorial Hospital administrator C. J. "Jack" Price spoke with Wilson Johnston of Wade's office and was told that no change in the public hospital's abortion policy should follow from the decision, and several months later the doctor who headed obstetrics and gynecology at Parkland and at Dallas's University of Texas Southwestern Medical School declared that "the only marked impact of the *Roe* v. *Wade* decision was to increase the frustration felt by many of the faculty members of my department regarding the matter of abortion." Very similar experiences were registered at medical schools and public hospitals in other major Texas cities, and it soon became clear that as a practical matter the Austin women's evaluation of *Roe*'s impact—"very little"—might prove far more accurate than many interested observers had initially realized.[72]

Far more widely publicized than the intensified frustration of the Texas physicians was the remarkable news that the principal governing body of the American Medical Association, which had backed therapeutic reform only three years earlier, had voted by a margin of 103 to 73 to endorse what amounted to a prorepeal position. Also drawing a highly unusual level of national attention was a lengthy new book on the legality of abortion by Daniel Callahan, a thoughtful scholar who emphasized that he had evolved into a repeal supporter in the course of completing his project. *Newsweek* magazine gave Callahan a rave reception, and the *New York Times*, which had just run a front-page story declaring that reform statutes had made "barely a dent in the criminal abortion rate," similarly accorded him significant notice. Abortion laws, Callahan concluded, "should be free enough to place the final decision in the hands of the pregnant woman," for "abortion on request as a *legal* position . . . represents good public and legal policy," wholly apart from whatever moral preferences different people might have. "The Roman Catholic position does not genuinely allow . . . consideration of the woman's welfare or that of her family to have an integral place in the making of abortion decisions," and such decisions "should be private decisions," Callahan emphasized. "The goal of a permissive law," he explained, "should be that of removing the necessity that a woman convince others, who in effect thus sit in judgment upon her, that she ought to be allowed to have an abortion."[73]

Much more prominent in the news than either Callahan, the AMA, or the *Roe* decision in Texas, however, was the watershed July 1 date when New York's landmark repeal law would take effect. The six weeks leading up to July 1 featured intense debates over precisely how the new statute ought to be implemented, with the New York City Health Department, joined by the New York Academy of Medicine and ASA president Dr. Bob Hall, suggesting that on safety grounds abortions should take place only in hospitals, and not in unaffiliated or "free standing" clinics. Some observers, including Hall, also worried that in the absence of any statutory residence requirement, New York City in particular would be swamped with thousands of abortion-seeking women from across the country. Their pessimistic scenario foresaw significant delays, the hasty emergence of for-profit clinics with slipshod medical standards, and so much potential for chaos and serious injuries to women that the New York state legislature might end up reconsidering the entire statute. "I'm even naive enough," Hall pointedly added, "to believe that Supreme Court justices read the papers, and that they will wonder why they should legalize abortion."

Many press accounts pictured Hall as a conservative and abortion clinic supporters such as Alan Guttmacher and Bernie Nathanson as liberals, but Hall's position was more sophisticated than many appreciated. "I want to see the hospitals forced to perform abortions," he explained. "If we let them off the hook by setting up clinics, they'll never accept their responsibilities." In fact, once July 1 actually arrived, the first few weeks went very smoothly, with no crush in New York City, no plethora of injuries, and an approximate statewide total of about three thousand abortions a week.[74] Bob Hall himself, however, was forced to file suit against his own hospital, Columbia Presbyterian, when hospital administrators refused to allow him to abort an unmarried eighteen-year-old woman without approval from her parents. Some hospital executives had not forgiven Hall for his leadership role in the earlier New York court case, but when the new case bogged down in court, the young lady's procedure was simply performed at another hospital.[75]

Implementation of the new repeal statutes in Hawaii and Alaska, both of which included residency requirements, received far less attention and involved far more modest numbers than the new system in New York. In California, where a repeal bill sponsored by Anthony Beilenson was going nowhere in the legislature, more and more hospitals nonetheless were clearly but quietly evolving toward what in practice amounted to abortion on request.[76] Several other states with reform laws, such as New Mexico, Maryland, and North Carolina, were also witnessing modest yet significant medical liberalization trends,[77] and several additional court actions, including a challenge to the Colorado reform law filed by its onetime sponsor, Richard D. Lamm, were also getting underway. One Pennsylvania trial court judge, R. Paul Campbell, citing *Griswold* and *Belous,* even went so far as to hold that state's antiabortion law unconstitutional in a decision vacating the abortion conviction of an already jailed motorcycle mechanic.[78]

Somewhat more significantly, on July 6 the federal First Circuit Court of Appeals, following up on its March action in releasing peripatetic activist Bill Baird from Boston's Charles Street jail, reversed his 1967 conviction for distributing vaginal foam, and held Massachusetts's restrictive birth control statute unconstitutional. Despite the state's argument that the law was intended to protect people from potentially harmful goods, "it is impossible to think of the statute as intended as a health measure" because of its express exception for married people, the appellate panel observed. The state's additional contention that prohibiting the distribution of contraceptives to unmarried individuals was aimed at deterring the crime of fornication was equally unpersuasive, the court said, since the maximum penalty for the misdemeanor crime of fornication was three months yet for the felony of distributing contraceptives a criminal could receive up to five years. The panel thus concluded that the law's real purpose was simply to declare that "it is contraceptives per se that are considered immoral," and that the statute lacked any other rational basis. Massachusetts responded by promptly announcing that it would appeal the ruling to the U.S. Supreme Court.[79]

On the final day of July, the Atlanta panel of Judges Smith,

Henderson, and Morgan handed down a unanimous decision in *Doe* v. *Bolton*. Notwithstanding the several potential obstacles that the jurists had identified at the mid-June hearing, the Atlanta trio, just like their Dallas colleagues, had no difficulty whatsoever in quickly agreeing that the 1968 Georgia reform law was indeed unconstitutional. They likewise readily concurred that while the state could not limit the grounds on which a woman could obtain an abortion, a statutory requirement that hospitals oversee each individual physician's decisions with some sort of committee approval system, as Georgia did, was certainly constitutional. They too, just like the Dallas court, also agreed that while a declaratory judgment should issue, no formal injunctive relief prohibiting state enforcement should be granted. The panel delegated the drafting of its opinion to Sidney Smith, who had had primary responsibility for *Doe* since its filing, and along with his law clerk, Jeffrey Nickerson, Smith set to work preparing the decision. Neither Lewis Morgan nor Albert Henderson had any significant changes to suggest when Smith first circulated his draft in late July, and six weeks after the hearing, *Doe* v. *Bolton* became the first judicial decision to hold that even a reform statute unconstitutionally infringed upon women's rights.

"While the Court agrees that the breadth of the right to privacy encompasses the decision to terminate an unwanted pregnancy," the panel said, "we are unwilling to declare that such a right reposes unbounded in any one individual." They stated that "although the state may not unduly limit the reasons for which a woman seeks an abortion, it may legitimately require that the decision to terminate her pregnancy be one reached only upon consideration of more factors than the desires of the woman and her ability to find a willing physician." They indicated some sympathy to Dorothy Beasley's arguments, saying that "once the embryo has formed, the decision to abort its development cannot be considered a purely private one affecting only husband and wife." For example, "the legislature might require any number of conditions, such as consultation with a licensed minister or secular guidance counselor as well as the concurrence of two licensed physicians or any system of approval related to the quality and soundness of the decision in all its aspects. It certainly has a clear right to circumscribe a decision made by a woman alone or by a woman and a single physician," but only "so long as they do not restrict the reasons for the initial decisions." "The reasons for an abortion may not be proscribed," Smith's opinion reiterated in conclusion, but "the quality of the decision as well as the manner of its execution are properly within the realm of state control."[80]

Margie Hames reacted to news of the ruling by calling it "great" and "a real victory" while nonetheless expressing regret that the panel had upheld the hospital committee process that in real life was much "too cumbersome." Judith Bourne said she was "very, very pleased" and considered it "a victory for everyone in the state." Bourne added that it apparently meant that "no further legislative action will be necessary," and Dr. Robert A. Hatcher, one of *Doe*'s medical plaintiffs, joined Hames in noting that with each female applicant still required to undertake "an obstacle race which exposes her to one indignity after another," their judicial victory, while quite important, was by no means complete. Emory's Reverend Emmett Herndon struck a similar note, commenting that "At least we won—whether the victory means anything or not."

Georgia Attorney General Arthur Bolton told reporters after receiving initial word of the decision that "I think we'll probably appeal it," but that "I haven't discussed the matter with our lawyers who handled the case." Several weeks later Dorothy Beasley indicated that Georgia would indeed appeal, and Judge Smith denied her request that the panel formally stay its decision pending such a move by the state. Awareness of the decision seemed to stimulate a slow increase in the number of therapeutic abortions being approved in Georgia, and a September survey by the state medical association found a clear plurality of doctors—48.9 percent—expressly endorsing abortion "on request," while only 35 percent opposed it. The association's lawyer termed that outcome "a surprisingly liberal response" and called the transformation of medical opinion since 1967–1968 "astounding." Indeed, "seldom has one seen so rapid a change in the opinion of the country on any subject."[81]

Just one week after the *Doe* decision, however, abortion rights litigators suffered their first significant federal court defeat when a special New Orleans panel voted 2 to 1 to reject the constitutional arguments that Roy Lucas and Benjamin E. Smith had put forward on behalf of Dr. Isadore I. Rosen in his effort to stave off disciplinary proceedings by the Louisiana State Board of Medical Examiners. The majority opinion, written by Judge Robert A. Ainsworth, the first Roman Catholic member of the Fifth Circuit Court of Appeals, explicitly rejected the conclusions that had been reached in *Belous, Vuitch, Babbitz,* and *Roe.* "Exercise of the right to abortion on request is not essential to an effective exercise of the right not to bear a child, if a child for whatever reason is not wanted. Abstinence, rhythm, contraception, and sterilization are alternative means to this end." Ainsworth noted that "the root problem in the controversy over abortion is the one of assigning value to embryonic and fetal life," and asserted that "*Babbitz* and *Roe* were decided upon theories of life and being which a large part of this country does not entertain." Ainsworth concluded that "we are not persuaded that the Louisiana abortion laws infringe on any fundamental principle as understood by the traditions of our people," and "we do not recognize the asserted right of a woman to choose to destroy the embryo or fetus she carries as being so rooted in the traditions and collective conscience of our people that it must rank as 'fundamental.'"

Ainsworth's view was directly rebutted by the interpretation of *Griswold* offered by *Rosen*'s sole dissenter, District Judge Fred J. Cassibry, who emphasized that *Griswold* "rested upon the broadest and most sweeping principles of substantive constitutional law." *Griswold*, he argued, "contains a broad command. It says, to this and other courts: You must protect the privacy and intimacy of family life, for such relationships lie at the very core of a free society." He added that "in some ways the right to have an abortion is even more compelling than the rights involved in *Griswold*," and noted that indeed there were *two* fundamental rights involved in a woman's abortion decision: "the mother's autonomy over her own body, and her right to choose whether to bring a child into the world."[82]

Lucas and Smith moved to appeal their New Orleans defeat, and several weeks later the federal three-judge panel considering the similar declaratory challenge to Missouri's abortion statute dismissed that suit on the grounds that "the complaint merely seeks an opinion on the construction of the statutes." As the Missouri plaintiffs prepared to appeal that loss to the U.S. Supreme Court, new declaratory cases against additional state abortion statutes were filed in federal courts in Utah, Pennsylvania, and Ohio. Some consideration was also being given to instituting a declaratory action in Massachusetts, but in the minds of Roy Lucas and most other interested lawyers, the appellate prospects for both *Roe* and *Doe* were far and away the two most pressing concerns.[83]

In the immediate aftermath of the *Roe* panel decision and the comments by Wade and Texas Attorney General Martin that the defendants would appeal, the plaintiffs similarly considered whether *they* should appeal the panel's refusal to enjoin any further enforcement of the Texas statute. In light of several almost contemporaneous Supreme Court procedural rulings, *Roe*'s technical status was such that while Wade and Martin would have to appeal their declaratory loss to the Fifth Circuit Court of Appeals, the Dallas panel's denial of injunctive relief allowed the plaintiffs to appeal directly to the Supreme Court. Linda Coffee and

Sarah Weddington had initially been fearful of the time and expense that a full-fledged review of *Roe* by the Fifth Circuit in New Orleans would entail, and hence they were relieved as well as grateful when Roy Lucas made contact and explained that an immediate appeal could be lodged with the Supreme Court. John Tolle of Wade's office had filed a formal notice of appeal to the Fifth Circuit in mid-July, followed shortly there-after by both Fred Bruner for Dr. Hallford and Linda for "Jane Roe" and the "Does," but in mid-August, just as the attorney general's office was signaling Tolle that they would take primary charge of the appeal, Coffee and Bruner moved to have *Roe* considered by the U.S. Supreme Court. Lucas had also volunteered to take the lead in preparing the initial juris-dictional statement that would be due at the high court by early October, and with Coffee and Weddington happy to accept his offer of assistance, primary responsibility for *Roe*'s appeal quietly shifted from Dallas to New York.[84]

In late August, Lucas wrote Fort Worth's Dr. Hugh Savage to request financial support for the *Roe* appeal and to explain to him that Coffee and Weddington had "turned it over" to Lucas's Madison Institute. Savage was on the verge of winning Texas Medical Association (TMA) endorsement of a repeal bill for the upcoming 1971 legislature, and a statewide poll showed better than two-to-one popular support for at least a reform measure. The head of the Texas Catholic Conference, Callan Graham, told reporters that "no law would be an improvement over either the existing law or the liberalization approach," and the Dallas women's group, which had just changed its name to the Abortion Education Committee of Dallas, continued to attract significant prorepeal news coverage. Norma McCorvey, having given birth to the "*Roe*" baby, resumed her peripatetic life-style, and Marsha King, faced with another unintended and traumatic pregnancy, found herself having to make a return trip to the same Mexico City clinic she had visited in late 1969.[85]

On October 6, Lucas filed a thirty-three-page jurisdictional state-ment formally asking the U.S. Supreme Court to hear the plaintiffs' appeal of *Roe v. Wade*. He pointed out to the justices that "*Griswold* has been applied in the abortion context by numerous state and federal courts," and asserted that *Roe*'s substantive questions "are novel issues of profound national import, affecting the lives of many thousands of American citizens each year." Lucas devoted seven pages to contending that the Dallas panel should have granted injunctive relief, and three pages to attempting to resuscitate the "Does'" standing, but he stressed several times that at the core of his constitutional argument lay "the reasoning of *Griswold*." Alluding deftly to how *Griswold* did not expressly speak to the rights of unmarried individuals, Lucas emphasized nonetheless that "Under *Griswold*, it is clear that a husband and wife are constitutionally privileged to control the size and spacing of their family by contraception." Several weeks later Jay Floyd of the Texas Attorney General's office filed a modest seven-page response to Lucas's submission, but Floyd's reply was silent on the constitutional questions and instead argued that "Roe's" claim was moot, that there should be no federal court interference in the state's prosecution of Hallford, and that the entire case should first be considered by the Fifth Circuit Court of Appeals.[86]

In Texas, a victorious Hugh Savage appeared before a legislative committee on behalf of the TMA to announce that "We favor a complete repeal of the present law," and Claude Evans's Dallas clergy counseling service drew expanded public attention and assisted in an increasing number of referrals, with many of the women being directed to a credible Unitarian physician practicing in a small town ninety minutes southeast of Dallas. In mid-November the Abortion Education Committee hosted a Dallas meeting of abortion activists from across the state, and the participants voted to launch a new confederation, the Texas Abortion Coalition, in order to press for repeal and *oppose* any reform bill. "The greatest disaster for our cause would be the substitution of the ALI model law or some variation thereof," the Dallas women warned. "The small reform is truly the enemy of the big one. We are unalterably opposed to the therapeutic abortion law." Any such legislative move would be "a step backwards," particularly since it appeared, as Sarah Weddington indicated at the Dallas symposium, that the passage of *any* new Texas abortion statute would inescapably moot *Roe*'s challenge to the present one. Only by insisting upon repeal, or nothing, would the Texas activists help advance what Dallas's Ginny Whitehill termed "freedom of choice for the individual."[87]

While Roy Lucas had been eminently successful in his effort to take command of the Supreme Court appeal of *Roe* v. *Wade*, he fared much more poorly when he attempted to do the exact same thing with *Doe* v. *Bolton*. Just as in *Roe*, the *Doe* attorneys, once they had reflected upon their highly incomplete victory, decided, after some internal disagreement, that the three-judge court's upholding of the hospital abortion committee review process ought to be appealed. As with *Roe*, the Atlanta panel's refusal to order injunctive relief gave the plaintiffs an opportunity for direct appeal to the Supreme Court, and on August 28 Lucas phoned Margie Hames to volunteer to also prepare *Doe*'s jurisdictional statement. Hames and her colleagues had already agreed that Margie, with advice from regional ACLU attorney Reber Boult, would take charge of preparing the *Doe* appeal, and Hames politely but firmly told Lucas that she and Boult were more than capable of doing the work without additional outside participation. Lucas immediately responded with a three-page letter admonishing Hames for failing to appreciate that the *Doe* appeal was so crucial as to deserve the best possible preparation. She and Boult had neither the depth of experience with the issue, nor the necessary amount of time, that *Doe* would receive if Lucas himself took charge, he asserted. Whatever the Supreme Court might do with *Doe* would affect not just Georgia but all other states with reform statutes, and thus "you have personal responsibility to all of the individuals in the twelve ALI states to put aside any consideration other than the need for the utmost in preparation, writing, and comprehension of the issues in the case," especially "when someone else with three years' background in the area is willing to do the work." Additionally, Lucas claimed, what would happen if *Doe* was set for oral argument in the Supreme Court and Hames had to respond to far-reaching questions from the justices: "will you be able to give a state-by-state account of the existing legislation, and litigation in both state and federal courts?" If Hames would accede, she and her colleagues could of course still have their names on the brief, Lucas offered in closing. "The content of the brief, however, is too important to be lightly put aside, unless you are willing to put aside with it the interests of several thousand poor women who cannot afford what should rightfully be theirs."[88]

Lucas's presumption was motivated in some part by the Madison Institute's weakened financial condition as well as by substantive concerns and a very large dose of simple ego. As Morris Dees and Lucas had slowly grown further and further apart, Dees's involvement with the Institute had slackened and by mid-1970 his donations had dropped to three thousand dollars per month. The Institute had also received some support from Planned Parenthood and from the United Methodist Church's Board of Christian Social Concerns, but by the fall of 1970 Lucas was highly uncertain as to where funds for 1971 would come from, especially if other litigators were handling the case or cases that potential donors thought most likely would present the U.S. Supreme Court with the crucial constitutional questions. By late in the fall Emko vaginal foam manufacturer Joseph Sunnen had promised fifty thousand dollars for 1971, and John D. Rockefeller III the modest sum of fifteen thousand dollars, but matters were considerably shakier than Lucas had envisioned one year earlier. Lucas personally was far from poor, in part because of the private income he was receiving for his role in assisting with Dr. Vuitch's Supreme Court appeal, but Lucas was increasingly bitter at how small a part Planned Parenthood and Harriet Pilpel were playing in support of cutting-edge cases and at how little interest Larry Lader's NARAL had in actual litigation. Relations between Lucas and Lader had been strained since the spring, when Lader and others had first learned that Lucas privately was representing one of the more conspicuous for-profit New York–based commercial referral services, and by fall the tensions had grown significantly. Finally, in late October, Lucas resigned from his somewhat pro forma position as chairman of NARAL's legal committee, citing his need to do more toward fund-raising for the Institute.[89]

Hames's rebuff of his brazen request left Lucas highly irritated, and the very next day he wrote California's Alan Charles to complain that *Doe*'s lawyers "leave something to be desired" and that "too much is at stake" for Hames to handle the appeal. He griped about what he viewed as Hames's relative ignorance of both constitutional and abortion issues, and a week later, in the course of soliciting the Rockefeller Foundation for Institute funding, Lucas again groused about how oftentimes "local counsel have insufficient training to handle a major federal case with any degree of professional competence." The Georgia lawyers, Lucas claimed, "won a little victory, in spite of their performance, but the Supreme Court is a big league arena," and it would be regrettable if the most knowledgeable litigators were relegated to filing amicus briefs with "the kind of arguments which should have been thoroughly made in the first place."[90]

Hames was unaware of the intensity of Lucas's resentment, and with Boult's counsel she forged ahead both with *Doe*'s Supreme Court appeal and with two astute but unsuccessful efforts to build *Doe*'s evidentiary record and perhaps persuade the Atlanta panel to reconsider its refusal to void the hospital committee system. In mid-September Hames moved to add a new plaintiff to *Doe*, an unmarried young woman whose abortion request had just been rejected by Atlanta's Georgia Baptist Hospital. She also tried to launch an additional action against Grady Memorial Hospital on behalf of another young woman who had been turned down there, explaining to Judge Smith that with regard to the committee requirement, "we feel that Mary Doe and members of her class did not have their 'day in court' on these issues." That contention notwithstanding, in mid-October the three-judge panel issued a brief supplemental opinion affirming their earlier endorsement of the hospital review process. Three weeks later, just as her husband Joel was once again embarking on a string of child-molestation assaults, Sandra Bensing gave birth to her *"Doe"* baby, which was put up for adoption. Shortly thereafter, on November 14, Hames and her colleagues filed *Doe*'s jurisdictional statement in the Supreme Court, and several weeks later Dorothy Beasley, on behalf of Attorney General Bolton, responded with a motion contending that the appeal should be dismissed.[91]

The third federal three-judge court abortion decision potentially headed to the Supreme Court was Wisconsin's *Babbitz* v. *McCann*. Following the Milwaukee panel's March declaratory judgment holding the state's antiabortion statute unconstitutional, Dr. Babbitz had again renewed his previously unsuccessful request that the federal court also enjoin Milwaukee County District Attorney E. Michael McCann from continuing to prosecute him in state court. Just as in *Roe* and *Doe*, U.S. District Judge Myron L. Gordon had reiterated the panel's refusal to intervene directly in the prosecution, but Babbitz's Milwaukee attorneys failed to appeal from the denial of the injunction, thus negating the possibility of obtaining direct review by the Supreme Court. District Attorney McCann *had* appealed the panel's declaratory decree to the high court, but just as Lucas and other knowledgeable observers anticipated, in mid-October the justices dismissed the appeal on the grounds that in the absence of any injunction McCann's appeal of the declaratory ruling rightfully belonged in the Seventh Circuit Court of Appeals in Chicago. McCann responded by scheduling Babbitz's criminal trial for late November, and Washington attorney Joseph L. Nellis, Dr. Vuitch's lead lawyer, was brought in to try to redeem Dr. Babbitz's federal court prospects. Nellis presented a new petition for injunctive relief to the three-judge panel at an October 28 hearing that Roy Lucas also attended on behalf of Edie Rein's Wisconsin Committee to Legalize Abortion. The panel members, particularly Circuit Judge Otto Kerner, gave McCann's representative an extremely frosty reception, stating that they believed the popularly elected district attorney was proceeding with Babbitz's prosecution in the face of their earlier opinion out of political motivation. Three weeks later the federal panel took the rare step of formally prohibiting McCann from proceeding with Babbitz's trial, and when the district attorney protested that order to the Seventh Circuit, the appeals court swiftly affirmed their lower court colleagues. McCann reluctantly obeyed while appealing the entire matter to the Supreme Court.[92]

While the *Babbitz* litigation was proceeding, another abortion battle that also had begun in the spring was similarly coming to a climax. Washington state's popular referendum vote on abortion repeal would take place on election day in early November, and starting back in April Seattle Archbishop Thomas A. Connolly had begun a major effort to quietly mobilize as much opposition as possible. Four diocesan planning meetings, he explained in a letter sent to every priest in the state, had decided that "the campaign must operate on two levels." One would be "the broadly inclusive citizen organization, without denominational or sub-group identity"; the second would be efforts openly sponsored by the Roman Catholic church itself. Each priest was directed to attend a full-day educational session on the campaign, and by midsummer the ostensible "citizen organization," named Voice for the Unborn, was readying a serious advertising drive. Its first large-scale venture was billboard displays picturing a four-month fetus with the caption "Kill Referendum 20, Not Me." Archbishop Connolly told his priests that it represented an "excellent campaign" and that Voice for the Unborn was "desperately in need of funds" to expand it, but public outcry was so great that the repeal opponents shifted to a different slogan. Their new motto, "Let Him Live," unsurprisingly drew additional criticism for its glaring gender premise, and one commentator on the referendum campaign later noted that "Voice for the Unborn was constantly on the defensive responding to charges of tasteless tactics." When the November 3 election returns were tallied, the abortion repeal measure, which incorporated a ninety-day residency requirement and a sixteen-week ceiling, attracted more than 56 percent popular support and passed by a margin of more than 130,000 votes. The earlier fears of national activists that such a referendum might prove disastrous had been resoundingly disproven, and repeal forces had won perhaps their most politically important victory so far.[93]

Not long after the Washington state triumph, the *New York Times* reported that "A dramatic liberalization of public attitudes and practices regarding abortions appears to be sweeping the country" and cited the Washington tally as notable evidence. It quoted one Catholic priest as saying "I'm certain there has been a great swing among Catholics toward favoring abortion reform," and concluded that Catholics' "traditional hard-line opposition to abortion appears to be declining."[94] One place where that did not seem to be happening, however, was Minnesota, where Dr. Jane Hodgson's criminal indictment back in May for having terminated Nancy Widmyer's rubella-scarred pregnancy had survived multiple courtroom challenges and was now proceeding to trial. Both the Minnesota Supreme Court and the local U.S. District Court had refused to block Ramsey County District Attorney William Randall's prosecution of Hodgson, and by late in the summer Dr. Hodgson had herself gone to New York to recruit Roy Lucas to join Minnesota attorney Stewart Perry in handling her defense. Lucas had signed on more than willingly, for not only was Hodgson a bright, charming, and courageous client, but her case "could not be better," as it posed abortion's basic constitutional issues in the most compelling context. In late September Lucas and Perry appealed both the federal court's and the state supreme court's refusals to intervene to the U.S. Supreme Court, and in early October Lucas asked the high court, first in one appeal and then in the other, to issue an order postponing Hodgson's mid-November trial. "The central question presented is the application of *Griswold*," he told the justices, but on October 19 the first request was denied with only Justice William O. Douglas dissenting and on November 6 the second one was rejected without comment.

Once it was certain that the constitutional challenge posed by Jane Hodgson's high stakes test case would be frontally addressed by the Supreme Court only *after* her trial, if at all, she forthrightly took the position that the trial hence ought to result in her *conviction* so that the case *could* be appealed and thus might still serve as a vehicle for obtaining Supreme Court review of the basic constitutional issues. If by some chance such a conviction was subsequently upheld rather than reversed, the price would likely include the loss of her license to practice medicine, but Hodgson valiantly insisted that she would take that risk, even though Stewart Perry was highly uncomfortable at helping defend a client who was frankly hoping to be convicted. Hodgson expressly waived a trial by jury so as to avoid the possibility that sympathetic citizens would derail the case by acquitting her, and when the trial commenced on November 12 before Judge J. Jerome Plunkett, the only witnesses whom the prosecution found it necessary to call were Nancy Widmyer herself and the pathologist who had routinely examined the rubella-deformed fetus. Widmyer was similarly the lead defense witness, followed by Dr. Joseph H. Pratt of the Mayo Clinic and two other physicians who also testified in support of Hodgson's decision that it had undeniably been in her patient's interest for her to proceed with the abortion. Jane Hodgson herself was the final defense witness, and on Thursday, November 19, after hearing all of the testimony, Judge Plunkett announced just the verdict Jane Hodgson had been hoping for: guilty. The following day Plunkett commended Hodgson's courage while pronouncing a suspended sentence of thirty days in jail, and Lucas made plans to appeal the conviction to the

Minnesota Supreme Court in the hope that it would then be on its way to the U.S. Supreme Court as quickly as possible.[95]

The first abortion case which *was* scheduled for a full hearing by the U.S. Supreme Court, tentatively in mid-December, was the government's appeal of Judge Gesell's voiding of the D.C. abortion statute in *United States* v. *Milan Vuitch*. Just as Roy Lucas had succeeded in taking charge of Jane Hodgson and *Roe*'s appellate prospects, and had tried so forcefully to do the same with *Doe*, by midfall he had also parlayed his initial role in preparing *Vuitch*'s Supreme Court brief into an increasingly dominant role in representing Washington's premier abortion provider. Lucas had already submitted an amicus brief on behalf of ASA to the Maryland appellate court which was considering an appeal of Dr. Vuitch's one actual conviction, and Vuitch was now facing additional criminal charges in D.C., subsequent even to the Gesell ruling, largely because of a May abortion which had resulted in the death of a seventeen-year-old girl.[96]

In late September Lucas, along with Nellis and Vuitch's original attorney, Joseph Sitnick, submitted to the U.S. Supreme Court their principal brief contending that the high court did have jurisdiction of the appeal and that Gesell's ruling should be affirmed. It repeated Lucas's now-standard line that "*Griswold* is not an isolated decision confined to its facts, but is one in a continuing line of cases involving various aspects of personal privacy and family autonomy," and went on to cite retired Justice Tom Clark's law review article and prior Supreme Court decisions reaching from *Meyer* and *Pierce* in the 1920s to *Skinner* v. *Oklahoma*, the 1942 antisterilization ruling, and the 1969 First Amendment holding in *Stanley* v. *Georgia*. It contended that the D.C. antiabortion statute gave "little consideration to a woman's feelings, pains, thoughts, and emotions. It impinges severely upon her dignity, her life plan, and her marital relationship if she has one. It is a first order invasion of her privacy with irreparable consequences," and in light of prior Court rulings such as *Skinner*, if "the right to have offspring enjoys a constitutional presumption of protection, should not a right *not* to have offspring be of equal stature under the Constitution?" In short, Lucas asserted, "there are certain sacred rights associated with individual privacy and the marital relation," just as the additional lower court holdings in *Belous*, *Roe*, and *Doe* had also acknowledged.[97]

Lucas had his hands full with a multiplicity of legal tasks, ranging from the *Babbitz* appearance in Milwaukee to a three-judge court hearing in Toledo on the declaratory case against Ohio's abortion law just the day before Jane Hodgson's trial commenced, but Vuitch and his wife Florence, who actively managed all of the business aspects of her husband's medical practice, had decided by sometime in October that they wanted Lucas rather than Joe Nellis to present the oral argument in *Vuitch* in the U.S. Supreme Court. In part their decision stemmed from tensions with Nellis over legal fees, just as they had likewise previously quarreled with Joseph Sitnick, but more fundamentally their desire stemmed from Lucas's undeniable expertise and from his pronounced eagerness to take on the lead role in their case too. Dr. Vuitch mentioned his preference to Nellis in late October, and on November 3 Vuitch filed a formal motion with the Supreme Court asking that Lucas rather than Nellis be allowed to appear on his behalf. Copies of the motion were sent to the government attorneys in the case, but not to Nellis or Sitnick, Vuitch's own supposed attorneys of record. The motion explained to the Court that Lucas is "the author" of Vuitch's brief and that in determining who should speak for him, Vuitch believed that it was of "particular importance" that Lucas was also "principal counsel in three other appeals to the Court this term involving very similar issues"—*Roe* and the two *Hodgson* cases. The request was looked upon favorably in the chambers of at least one justice, but in mid-November Joe Nellis, even without knowing about Vuitch's motion, sent Lucas an exceptionally tough and threatening letter demanding his "immediate withdrawal" from all legal matters pertaining to Dr. Vuitch. Nellis already had been extremely angered by Lucas's turning up in Milwaukee for the *Babbitz* hearing, and now he charged Lucas with "unprofessional and unethical" actions in both the *Vuitch* and *Babbitz* contexts. Nellis alleged that Lucas had told the Vuitches that Nellis's Milwaukee performance on behalf of Dr. Babbitz had left something to be desired, and Nellis asserted that such comments would be "among the most unethical actions" any lawyer could commit. Nellis charged that Lucas's behavior was motivated by the potential fees involved—rather than by the credit which would stem from a Supreme Court success—and closed the letter by warning that if Lucas failed to respond, he and Sitnick would "take whatever measures seem to us to be necessary and desirable" with bar association disciplinary committees and with the courts.

Four days after sending that missive to Lucas, Sitnick in the course of a phone conversation with Supreme Court chief deputy clerk E. P. Cullinan learned for the first time about Vuitch's November 3 motion to replace Nellis with Lucas at oral argument. Nellis and Sitnick fired off an immediate letter of protest to the Court, followed several days later by a formal response to the Vuitch request in which they labeled

Lucas "inexperienced" and said they would pursue a professional griev-
ance. By the time that response arrived, however, the clerk's office
determined that this brawl had gone far enough, and phone calls went
out to at least two of the participants telling them that the dispute
should be halted immediately. Before the day was out both Dr. Vuitch
and Joseph Nellis submitted letters formally withdrawing their earlier
filings for and against Lucas's participation at oral argument, and both
men expressed agreement, as Nellis put it in his own letter to the
clerk's office, that "the case will be orally argued by myself and a third
party to be selected by Dr. Vuitch, not Mr. Roy Lucas."[98]

As the smoke began to clear, the clerk's office postponed the *Vuitch*
argument from mid-December to the second week of January, and
Lucas, with Vuitch's permission, recruited his friend and former mentor, New York University Law School professor Norman Dorsen, to
enter the case as the second attorney who would share the Supreme
Court argument with Nellis. Lucas licked his wounds quietly, but took
deep pleasure when the Maryland appellate court reviewing Vuitch's
criminal conviction issued an opinion the very same day the Supreme
Court fracas came to a head that expressly criticized Joseph Nellis.
Vuitch's attorney, the Maryland panel said in affirming the conviction,
had erroneously failed to raise the basic constitutional questions that
were "readily apparent prior to trial" until the proceeding's latter stages,
"and then only by an inappropriate motion . . . submitted without
comment, or illuminating argument."[99]

Lucas understandably took far less pleasure, however, when a 2 to 1
negative decision in the Ohio declaratory judgment case was handed
down several weeks later. The majority opinion, by District Judge Don
J. Young, focused upon the importance of the fetus and was sarcastically dismissive of the plaintiffs' constitutional privacy arguments. "Once
human life has commenced, the constitutional protections found in
the Fifth and Fourteenth Amendments impose upon the state the duty
of safeguarding it," Young held. "It may seem cruel to a hedonist society that 'those who dance must pay the piper,' but it is hardly unusual,"
Young said in a tone not generally found in federal court decisions. "If
it is known generally that an act has possible consequences that the
actor does not desire to incur, he has always the choice between
refraining from the act, or taking his chance of incurring the undesirable consequences," Young added. "This is peculiarly true with respect
to the bearing of children. If one gambles and loses, it is neither statute
nor constitution that determines the price, or how it shall be paid. The
result is not punishment, but merely the quid pro quo." District Judge

Ben C. Green argued in dissent that *Griswold* stands for "the proposition that the interests of the embryo or fetus must be balanced against the interests of the pregnant woman," and cited Tom Clark's article before observing that "I do not consider the protection of an embryo in its early stages of existence as a compelling state interest." Green concluded that "a woman has the private right to control her own person, which necessarily encompasses the fundamental right to choose whether to bear children."[100]

The same week that the Ohio decision came down, the long-delayed oral argument in Lucas's New Jersey declaratory judgment suit and a companion case that also had filed nine months earlier finally took place. Attorney Nancy Stearns told the federal three-judge panel that "any woman who feels she needs an abortion has a constitutional right to one," but the New Jersey litigation was now so far behind *Roe* and *Doe* that it was almost guaranteed to not be *the* case that would generate a constitutionally definitive Supreme Court abortion ruling. Lucas, having been denied a starring role in *Vuitch*'s Supreme Court argument, was now significantly more convinced than ever before that the high court would *not* use *Vuitch* to provide a decisive decision. Now it seemed "most unlikely" that *Vuitch* would "have any impact" beyond the District of Columbia or be resolved on any basis broader than the vagueness holding made by Judge Gesell, Lucas told Texas's Hugh Savage while reiterating the potentially paramount importance of *Roe* and his need for funds. Although only Jane Hodgson's case was absolutely certain to force a clear decision on the central constitutional issues, if her conviction was indeed sustained by Minnesota's highest court, her possible appeal would reach the Supreme Court only well after it had decided or disposed of *Roe* and *Doe* in some fashion. "In my judgment," Lucas told Savage, "the Texas case will be the turning point. A broad decision in this case can have impact across the United States."[101]

In retrospect, 1970 would undeniably appear as the definitive year in America's abortion revolution. But just before the U.S. Supreme Court would hear its first abortion case ever, a once-prominent but now largely forgotten relic from another era would quietly be discarded. On January 8, 1971, four days in advance of *Vuitch*'s presentation in the high court, President Richard M. Nixon signed into law a measure legislatively repealing the ninety-eight-year-old federal anticontraception statutes. Sponsored in the House of Representatives by a Texas congressman who ostensibly supported another kind of repeal as well—whether to give birth to a child "should always remain a matter of individual choice," George Bush had written one constituent two months earlier—the new enactment rescinded the statutory legacy of Anthony Comstock. Still ahead, however, lay the far more momentous step that would finally eviscerate the ghost of P. T. Barnum and truly fulfill the legacy of Kit Hepburn.[102]

CHAPTER EIGHT

The Right to Abortion
and the U.S. Supreme Court,
1971–1973

Harry A. Blackmun was one of the three new justices of the U.S.
Supreme Court to hear oral argument in *United States* v. *Milan Vuitch* on
January 12, 1971, who had not been members of the Court when
Griswold v. *Connecticut* was decided in June 1965. Justice Thurgood
Marshall, a former federal appellate judge far better known as the
NAACP chief counsel who had successfully argued *Brown* v. *Board of
Education*, had been promoted to the high court from his post as U.S.
Solicitor General when Justice Tom Clark stepped down in 1967. The
second newcomer, Chief Justice Warren E. Burger, a Minnesota native
and a longtime federal circuit judge in the District of Columbia, had
joined the Court in the summer of 1969 following the retirement of
Earl Warren. An Eisenhower-era Justice Department official and an
active participant in Republican politics before ascending the bench,
Burger had been nominated for the post by newly elected Republican
President Richard M. Nixon after Lyndon Johnson's 1968 attempt to
promote Justice Abe Fortas, a close friend whom Johnson had named
to replace Arthur Goldberg three years earlier, to Warren's seat had
failed in the Senate. Fortas's nomination to be chief justice had
foundered amidst senatorial apprehension that his personal finances
and his cronylike relationship with Johnson had each led to repeated
violations of judicial ethics, and Nixon thus inherited the opportunity
to name Warren's successor. Just a few weeks before Burger's confirmation, however, Nixon was presented with a second vacancy when
new and more serious revelations of Fortas's financial indiscretions
forced him to resign from the Court in disgrace.

Nixon's first two nominees for the Fortas seat, Fourth Circuit Chief
Judge Clement F. Haynsworth, Jr., and undistinguished Fifth Circuit

Judge G. Harrold Carswell, were both rejected by the Senate after difficult and bitter confirmation fights, and only in May 1970 had Nixon's third candidate, Harry Blackmun, an eleven-year veteran of the Eighth Circuit Court of Appeals, finally won unanimous Senate confirmation to fill the long-vacant seat. A childhood friend of Warren Burger, the sixty-one-year-old Blackmun grew up in St. Paul, Minnesota, and graduated from both Harvard College and Harvard Law School before returning home to practice law. In 1950 Blackmun became resident counsel at Minnesota's famous Mayo Clinic, and nine years later he was named to the federal appellate bench. He had seemed an unremarkable as well as an uncontroversial choice for the high court after Nixon's two setbacks in attempting to name conservative southerners, and when Blackmun formally joined the Court in June 1970 he like Burger was believed to be a conventionally conservative Republican. Indeed, the two men's shared roots and presumably similar ideologies led some journalists to call them the "Minnesota Twins."

None of the three new justices had yet made a distinctive impact upon the Court. Thurgood Marshall was appreciated by his colleagues and by his own clerks as a talented storyteller whose liberal instincts would usually place him on the same side of controversial cases as William J. Brennan and William O. Douglas. Warren Burger certainly *looked* like a chief justice, and during his first year in the job many members of the small Court community had begun to think that the new "Chief" took more pleasure in the ceremonial aspects of his post than in the intellectual ones. Blackmun's first few months at the Court had occasionally reflected such uncertainty that some clerks in other chambers wondered when if ever the new justice would finally begin to grow into the job and establish himself apart from Warren Burger. A few abortion litigators had heard talk that Blackmun was a good friend of Mayo's Dr. Joseph H. Pratt, Jane Hodgson's most prominent Minnesota medical supporter, and even that Pratt had been Mrs. Blackmun's doctor, but no one was inclined to count either Blackmun or Burger as likely supporters of *Griswold*-style constitutional protection for a woman's right to choose abortion.[1]

Roy Lucas and other abortion lawyers understandably attached far greater importance to *United States* v. *Vuitch* than did any of the justices of the Supreme Court, and the night before the January 12 oral argument Lucas and Norman Dorsen spent several hours in a Capitol Hill hotel going over the constitutional points and potential questions with which Dorsen might have to cope. Only the next morning, just before the argument itself, did Dorsen and Joseph Nellis, who would be pri-

marily responsible for addressing the jurisdictional issues on behalf of
Vuitch, meet for the first time in the Court's lounge to discuss how
they would manage the unusual one full hour of argument time that
the Court had allocated to each side.[2]

When the actual argument got underway shortly after ten a.m., however, the first speaker was the government's representative, Samuel
Huntington of the Solicitor General's office, whose task was to persuade the nine justices that Judge Gesell had erred in holding that the
District of Columbia antiabortion statute—and particularly its crucial
word, "health"—was unconstitutionally vague. Responding to the
questions posed by the Court six months earlier, Huntington maintained that the high court did have proper jurisdiction of the government's direct appeal from Gesell's ruling and that the D.C. criminal
statute should apply to cases "where a doctor has made no attempt to
determine whether or not health reasons exist which would justify an
abortion." He added that "the constitutional rights asserted here are
novel and for the most part unexplored," and Justice Potter Stewart
broke in to ask if it should not automatically be assumed that any abortion performed by an accredited doctor was in the interest of a
woman's health. Huntington replied that "the term health means he
has to make an examination of the woman and determine that because
of some condition"—at which point Stewart interrupted to say that the
condition was pregnancy, drawing audience laughter—"beyond the
mere fact that she is pregnant." Stewart persisted, suggesting that
"whenever a doctor in good standing performs an abortion, that's the
end of it, it's not a criminal act," and Huntington said no, that a doctor
must "make a good faith judgment that there were special conditions"
that merited an abortion.

Huntington further asserted that the Court should restrict itself to
the vagueness issue in reviewing the merits of Gesell's ruling, and *not*
consider other points such as privacy, for "the very fundamental question" of abortion itself was "peculiarly within the province of the legislature." Additionally, Huntington said, the government's position was
that "the statute reflects a desire to protect fetal life," but Justice Hugo
Black asked "Why do we have to get into the fetal life problem when
the statute is limited to preserving the health or life of the mother?"
Huntington answered that "where the mother's health doesn't require
an abortion, the fetus should be protected," and when Justice
Blackmun asked if he was correct in thinking that under the D.C.
statute a woman would not be able to obtain a legal abortion because of
a rubella-scarred pregnancy, Huntington replied in the affirmative.

Huntington concluded his remarks after forty-five minutes by recommending to the Court the writings of several antiabortion legal scholars, and Chief Justice Burger, with an eye toward saving time, announced that while Huntington would be given five minutes for subsequent rebuttal, each side's time was being reduced from sixty to fifty minutes.

Joseph Nellis began Vuitch's presentation with an articulate explanation of why the Court did have jurisdiction of the appeal. He asserted that the subject was "a matter of landmark and historic importance in the area of constitutional law" and reminded the justices that "there are myriads of cases brewing in the lower courts." Potter Stewart invited Nellis to address the vagueness issue, but Hugo Black broke in to ask whether a woman had a right "to kill it." Nellis answered, "Well, your honor, I don't accept the notion that the abortion of an embryo before the twentieth week, before the common law quickening, is an act of killing at all." Black replied, "Well, suppose it's after that?" Nellis responded that postquickening there would have to be serious health grounds for an abortion, and Black interjected, "you mean to dispose of the child." Nellis tried to counter Black's usage, and the justice replied that "I'm not saying it's wrong; I just don't care to be cluttered up in a maze of words that mean something else." Nellis reacted tactfully. "Mr. Justice Black, I am not trying to obfuscate my answer. I cannot accept, if you don't mind my saying so, the word 'child' as related to a fetus."

Black allowed Nellis to move on, but when Nellis reiterated that the abortion issue was of "enormous national significance," Chief Justice Burger observed that the court might benefit from a case record offering more extensive medical evidence. Justice Blackmun noted that federal three-judge court decisions on abortion statutes included rulings both for and against, and when Nellis in expressing agreement made reference to the initial Minnesota refusal in Jane Hodgson's case, Blackmun replied that "I had this in mind." Nellis volunteered that "the multiplicity of suits which will be reaching—are reaching this Court now—could be very deftly and intelligently approached by a decision here," and when Blackmun interjected that some of these other cases, unlike *Vuitch*, would feature full trial records, Nellis gently demurred, replying that "there is nothing in the way of a factual record that would either enhance or detract from the ability of this Court to determine that right of privacy."

Justice Byron White gruffly asked Nellis how the statute's supposed vagueness could be challenged by a physician who simply provided abortions on request, and when Nellis answered that only nondoctors ought to be covered by a criminal abortion statute, White asked him what about cases where a woman seeking an abortion was in perfect health. Nellis responded that "health" as a word was inherently vague, and as White kept after him, Nellis finally declared that "I don't feel cornered." "No, you shouldn't," White replied, and as laughter spread through the courtroom, Nellis added that "socio-economic reasons in modern-day society approach health reasons." White refused to let go, and only several questions from Chief Justice Burger curtailed the White-Nellis exchange before it came time for Norman Dorsen to begin the second half of Vuitch's presentation.

Dorsen started with the vagueness issue, citing the California Supreme Court decision in *Belous* and noting each of the operative and arguably imprecise words in the D.C. statute: "necessary," "preserve," "life," and "health." Dorsen asserted that doctors' own standards were the only dependable criterion, and Justice Blackmun broke in, saying that "I shouldn't go on my own experience, but I have seen physician after physician say the same thing about malpractice that you have just said." Chief Justice Burger pursued the point, and Dorsen handled his queries superbly, emphasizing that only in the context of abortion was there a *criminal* threat hanging over a physician that instructed the doctor to act counter to the interests of the patient. "Underlying this case, in our judgment," Dorsen continued, "is a basic constitutional right, recognized by Judge Gesell—and he did not rule on the point specifically—and by courts in many other jurisdictions, that it is a right of a woman to make her own decision, unaffected by the criminal law of the state, whether or not to bear a child." Byron White broke in: "At any stage?" Dorsen parried. "We are not making the claim of any stage in this case. Certainly we would say up to the point where the embryo is viable." White responded, "Why does it become a different problem in terms of that fundamental right of the woman not to bear a child?" Dorsen ducked: "Now, this is a question I would not have an answer to in this particular case." "It is a difficult question, isn't it?," White asked. "Yes, it is," Dorsen agreed. "To draw a distinction," White added. "Yes, it is," Dorsen repeated, "and we are making the claim, as spelled out at some length in our brief, that certainly up to the traditional lines of twenty, twenty-two, twenty-four weeks there is a right of a woman to have an abortion."

Potter Stewart joined in: "You mean a constitutional right?" "That's correct, sir," Dorsen replied. "Under which provision or provisions of the Constitution?," Stewart asked. "Well, I would rely on the liberty of the woman" as protected by the language of due process, Dorsen answered. "The right comes from the liberty of the individual," he continued, citing *Skinner*, *Meyer*, and *Griswold*. "The position, in other words, is a position based upon both the right of privacy and the liberty of—." Stewart cut him off: "What does this really have to do with the right of privacy?" "I would suggest that if a woman wishes to use her body in a way which would mean disposing of the embryo, that that is a choice that she can make" and that a doctor should be able to implement without criminal sanction, Dorsen responded. "It's the use of the woman's body, which she has dominion over."

Warren Burger asked what about the rights of the father. Dorsen explained that his answer was that "It's the woman's right and not the father's right; that it is her body and that she should have the right to make the awesome decision of whether or not to bear the child." Justice Blackmun asked whether this ultimately would entail a right to commit suicide. "I'm not sure," Dorsen twice replied. "I'd be inclined to think it would, but I am not sure." Another justice pursued the suicide comparison, and Dorsen answered that with regard to abortion, "We're not dealing here with a human being in the same sense as a suicide case suggests." Several justices suggested that if Dorsen was correct about suicide, then a person could instruct a doctor to amputate their right arm, and when Dorsen indicated he had trouble with the hypothetical question of the arm, one questioner replied that "If you have trouble with the arm, I think you would have trouble with the abortion," especially if "the unborn child has some rights." Dorsen had only enough time remaining to cite retired Justice Tom Clark's law review article, and the morning's argument concluded with Samuel Huntington briefly reiterating his earlier insistence that a doctor must identify specific health grounds for any abortion. Huntington amended his earlier answer to Blackmun's rubella question, allowing that such a circumstance might well raise questions of psychological health, but both Justice Black and Justice Marshall reacted with skepticism to Huntington's basic contention.[3]

Interested observers found the court's reactions inconclusive. Cyril Means thought Black's repeated invocation of the word "child" was extremely unpromising, and while Larry Lader thought Dorsen had done a good job, Dorsen himself was wracked with worry that he had not done well enough. Dorsen had another case to argue before the high court just two days later, and while he enjoyed a pleasant dinner with Dr. and Mrs. Vuitch, he dropped a subsequent note to Roy Lucas expressing frustration about how difficult it was to tell how the Court was leaning.[4]

Although the jurisdictional questions which the Court had formally posed to the *Vuitch* parties six months earlier had drawn surprisingly little attention at oral argument, even before the nîne justices convened three days later for their private conference discussion of the case, John Harlan circulated a memo to his colleagues informing them that he had tentatively concluded that the Court *did* lack jurisdiction over the government's direct appeal. At the conference itself, however, Chief Justice Burger began the discussion of *Vuitch* by stating that he disagreed with Harlan about jurisdiction and believed they should reverse Judge Gesell on the merits. The language of the D.C. statute was not vague and the charges against Vuitch should not have been dismissed. Burger indicated that while he had not been impressed with either side's arguments, he definitely rejected Dorsen's contention that a woman has an "absolute right to decide what happens to her own body." Burger also noted that Jane Hodgson's Minnesota case was "on its way to the Minnesota Supreme Court" and then "will soon be here," and hence would offer a subsequent opportunity to address the constitutional merits of abortion law challenges.

Hugo Black agreed with the Chief Justice. The Court did have jurisdiction, and the D.C. law was not vague. There was "no right to an abortion" and Gesell "has no right as a judge to create that right." Additionally, Black said he too "can't go with [a] woman's claim of [a] const[itutional] right to use her body as she pleases."

William O. Douglas differed, saying they should affirm Gesell's ruling and that they did have jurisdiction. Laws could regulate the performance of abortions and still be constitutional, but the D.C. language *was* vague. "The definition of what is meant by health must be very broad today," Douglas professed. "Does this statute sufficiently notify [a] doctor [as to] what that means?" Douglas believed the answer was no.

John Harlan indicated that he still did not think the direct appeal was properly within the Court's jurisdiction, but if his colleagues were going to rule on the merits of Gesell's decision, Harlan believed that the statute was not vague and that the ruling below should be reversed. William J. Brennan stated that while he fully agreed with Harlan's memo that the Court did not have jurisdiction of the appeal, on the merits he agreed with Bill Douglas that Gesell had been correct in finding the D.C. law unconstitutionally vague.

Potter Stewart, the sixth justice to speak, maintained that they did have jurisdiction. Stewart went on to explain that while he like Douglas believed that "health" had to be given a very broad definition, that to him meant that Gesell's ruling should be *reversed*, since an appropriately liberal "saving" construction could be provided for the D.C. law. Stewart added, however, that the specific charge against Vuitch should indeed be dismissed, for he believed, as he had indicated at oral argument, that no licensed physician could be prosecuted under any such statute.

Byron White stated that the Court had jurisdiction and that the D.C law, in the absence of any trial record, was not facially vague. Thurgood Marshall said that he was not sure with regard to jurisdiction but would reverse Gesell on the merits, for "every doctor knows the meaning" of the statute and ought to "take his chances with a jury." The Court's junior justice, Harry Blackmun, said that he was troubled on the question of jurisdiction and had found Harlan's argument appealing. He was unpersuaded by Gesell's contention of vagueness, and hence on the merits would vote to reverse.

The outcome of the Court's discussion of *Vuitch* was clear but somewhat complicated. A clear majority of at least five—Burger, Black, Douglas, Stewart, and White—believed that the Court did have jurisdiction to decide the appeal, and a decidedly larger majority of seven—Burger, Black, Harlan, Stewart, White, Marshall, and Blackmun—clearly believed that Gesell's vagueness ruling was erroneous and should be reversed. Warren Burger waited almost two weeks before finally assigning the task of preparing a majority opinion in the case to the ageing Hugo Black, but by the second week of February one of Black's three law clerks, Robert W. Spearman, was finishing work on a eighteen-page typescript draft of an opinion that would affirmatively answer the question of jurisdiction and firmly reverse Gesell's decision on the merits.[5]

The Court's consideration of *Vuitch* had led the justices to postpone any discussion of the other abortion-related appeals and petitions which had been arriving since early in the fall. Even before Christmas the Court had put off any dispositive action on either of Jane Hodgson's pretrial petitions until decisions were ready in several non-abortion cases also involving requests for federal court action against state criminal prosecutions, and one week before the *Vuitch* conference the justices had deferred any consideration of either *Roe* v. *Wade* or *Doe* v. *Bolton* until after work on *Vuitch* was completed.[6]

In late January, however, one more abortion case began to head for the high court when a federal three-judge panel in Chicago held Illinois's antiabortion law unconstitutional by a two to one margin. Seventh Circuit Court of Appeals Chief Judge Luther M. Swygert, joined by Chief District Judge Edwin A. Robson, held that the exception language of the Illinois statute, allowing those abortions "necessary for the preservation of the woman's life," was unconstitutionally vague. Observing how some judicial panels had endorsed vagueness attacks upon such statutes while others had rejected them, Swygert emphasized that "If courts cannot agree on what is the essential meaning of 'necessary for the preservation of the woman's life' and like words, we fail to see how those who may be subject to the statute's proscriptions can know what it prohibits." Both "necessary" and "preservation" were "gravely amorphous" words, Swygert concluded. Then he went on to say, with several citations to retired Justice Tom Clark's law review article, that the entire constitutional question of abortion was indistinguishable from that of *Griswold*. "A woman's interest in privacy and in control over her body is just as seriously interfered with by a law which prohibits abortions as it is by a law which prohibits the use of contraceptives." Swygert noted the earlier decisions in *Belous*, *Vuitch*, *Babbitz*, and *Roe*, and explained that "the critical issue is whether the state has a compelling interest in preventing abortions." He answered that question by asserting that "a statute which forces the birth of every fetus, no matter how defective or how intensely unwanted by its future parents, displays no legitimately compelling state interest in fetal life." At least during the first trimester of pregnancy, he and Robson held, state laws could regulate the performance of abortions only to the extent of requiring that they be performed by doctors and in licensed facilities. In line with that declaratory judgment, and unlike the earlier panels in *Roe* and *Doe*, Swygert and Robson issued a permanent injunction barring any future enforcement of the Illinois antiabortion statute.

Senior District Judge William Campbell's dissent rejected Swygert's comparison of abortion and contraception and cited *Steinberg* v. *Brown*, the earlier federal court decision upholding Ohio's abortion statute, in arguing for the importance of fetal life. One of the two principal defendants, Cook County State's Attorney Edward V. Hanrahan, announced that he would immediately appeal both the decision and the issuance of the injunction to the Supreme Court, and on February 10 Justice Marshall granted a motion staying Swygert and Robson's injunction until such time that the full Court chose to act on the defendants' appeal.[7]

Three days after the issuance of the Chicago decision the three-judge panel considering the declaratory judgment suit against North Carolina's reform statute rejected the plaintiffs' basic challenge while nonetheless finding that the law's residency requirement was a violation of the right to travel. "Whether or not to bear a child is ordinarily and up to a point within the zone of privacy of a woman," Circuit Judge Braxton Craven wrote for the panel, and "she has the right to be let alone in making that determination. In short, it is none of the state's business whether a woman chooses to become pregnant." However, he added, "We do not find that an equation of the generalized right of the woman to determine whether she shall bear children with the asserted right to abort an embryo or fetus is compelled by fact or logic." The opinion then proceeded directly but without any attribution to exactly repeat several sentences that had appeared six months earlier in Circuit Judge Robert Ainsworth's opinion in *Rosen* upholding Louisiana's abortion statute: "Exercise of the right to an abortion on request is not essential to an effective exercise of the right not to bear a child, if a child for whatever reason is not wanted. Abstinence, rhythm, contraception and sterilization are alternative means to this end. . . ." Contrary decisions such as *Babbitz* and *Roe* involved "a value judgment not committed to the discretion of judges," the Charlotte panel concluded.[8]

That setback in *Corkey* v. *Edwards* brought to five the number of cases against state abortion statutes that had been *rejected* by federal three-judge panels: Minnesota, Louisiana, Missouri, and Ohio in addition to North Carolina. Only *Babbitz*, *Roe*, *Doe*, and the Illinois ruling could be counted in the victory column, but most activists agreed with Colorado's Richard Lamm, who expressed an attitude of "hopeful anticipation" toward the Supreme Court and told an early 1971 abortion symposium that "the major wave of future change lies with the courts," not state legislatures. Oregon Senator Robert Packwood, who already had emerged as the most outspoken congressional champion of a right to abortion, expressed a similarly optimistic perspective at that conference and explained to participants that "most of the legislators in the nation I have met and many members of Congress would prefer the Supreme Court to legalize abortion, thereby taking them off the hook and relieving them of the responsibility for decision-making."[9]

Lamm emphasized at that gathering, as he had previously to Texas's Ginny Whitehill, that legislative activists had to "go for repeal only— reform is not only no compromise but is counterproductive" to the real goal of achieving repeal. "If an ALI bill," like the one he had successfully sponsored just four years earlier, "is introduced by compromise-minded politicians," Lamm added forcefully, "it should be fought." In virtually every state where a repeal bill had been introduced in the legislature, however, prospects for passage appeared to range between bleak and nonexistent. One had been voted down in the

Montana house by a margin of 95 to 5, and in New Mexico one had been rejected in the state senate on a tally of 34 to 9. In Iowa the state house voted 55 to 45 against such a measure, and other repeal bills went down to defeat in Minnesota, Maryland, Colorado, and Massachusetts.[10]

Georgia repeal proponents succeeded in winning house committee approval for a repeal bill with a relatively narrow sixteen-week limit and a modest ten-day residency requirement, but several days later principal legislative sponsor Killian Townsend announced that he was withdrawing the measure because prorepeal doctors at Atlanta's Grady Hospital "told us they thought it would be worse if it passed at sixteen weeks than if it didn't pass at all." Judy Bourne explained to reporters that most Georgia women were traveling to New York City for abortions, but New York activists were becoming increasingly worried that conservative opponents in the legislature might try to reverse the one-vote victory that the repeal forces had eked out a year earlier. New York Governor Nelson Rockefeller had publicly indicated his willingness to accept a reduction in New York's statutory ceiling from twenty-four weeks to twenty, and repeal supporters feared that legislative consideration of a possible dilution of the 1970 law would open the door to a complete rollback. Many activists were livid when ASA president Bob Hall asserted in an op-ed piece in the *New York Times* that a residency requirement should be implemented and that all abortions should be performed in hospitals, and by early April repeal partisans were warning their supporters that the 1970 statute "is now in severe danger in the legislature." Governor Rockefeller sought to allay such concerns by emphasizing that he would veto any flat-out repeal of the 1970 measure, but he also indicated that the state was about to halt Medicaid funding for poor women's abortions. No up or down vote on the 1970 law would come until May or June, but the New York situation was not helped when President Richard M. Nixon publicly declared that abortion was "an unacceptable form of population control" and emphasized his "personal belief in the sanctity of human life—including the life of the yet unborn."[11]

NARAL executive director Lee Gidding, who had more direct contact with local level activists across the country than any other person, had felt for some months that the efforts of abortion opponents had been on the upswing ever since the New York measure had been approved a year earlier. In New York itself, as in the fall referendum campaign in Washington state, much of the opposition appeared to be emerging from the Roman Catholic hierarchy and from the newly visible National Right to Life Committee (NRLC), which had initially been created at the behest of Father James McHugh of the U.S. Catholic Conference's Family Life Division. NRLC lawyers in particular enthusiastically welcomed several late-February Supreme Court decisions in nonabortion cases that appeared to prohibit *any* federal court injunctive relief against state statutes such as that which the Chicago panel had granted with regard to Illinois's abortion law, and one of the opinions also indicated that even declaratory judgments against such statutes might now be infirm if the federal case had been brought on behalf of someone who already was facing related state charges—a ruling that likely would cover Doctors Rosen and Hallford and perhaps the first of Jane Hodgson's two appeals.[12]

Antiabortion forces, however, were not limited to the hierarchy around the NRLC, and even in Georgia opponents of repeal had outnumbered proponents by more than four to one at the 1971 legislative hearing. In late March *Time* magazine observed that there were more and more signs that antiabortion forces were "gaining momentum," and NARAL's Lee Gidding told one friend it increasingly looked as if "this is not our year." Perhaps the one legislative bright spot, relatively speaking, was Michigan, where the state senate had passed a quasi-repeal bill allowing a woman to choose abortion during her first three months of pregnancy, but proponents estimated that the measure had a less than fifty-fifty chance of winning approval in the state house.[13]

One of the most energetic 1971 legislative repeal campaigns was mounted in Texas, where the new confederation of Dallas, Austin, and Houston activists, the Texas Abortion Coalition (TAC), recruited two prominent legislative sponsors—state Senators Tom Creighton and Don Kennard—for a well-crafted repeal bill. Overcoming a variety of personal and stylistic tensions that led the Dallas women to create a separate group, Texas Citizens for Abortion Education, TAC organized a major public event in Austin to launch the repeal campaign, at which both Jane Hodgson and Roy Lucas appeared as featured speakers. Austin activist Vic Foe had solicited additional endorsements from various notables such as Alan Guttmacher, and Texas reporters noted that among the supportive telegrams read at the symposium was one from U.S. District Judge Sarah T. Hughes, who told the group that "I wish you well in your educational program on this important topic."[14]

Hodgson and Lucas were also honored guests at a well-publicized reception in Dallas, and while considerable press attention was devoted to Dr. Hodgson and her courageous test case stand, the Fort Worth paper also noted how Lucas "will be the lead counsel pleading the

Texas abortion case before the Supreme Court." While everyone waited to see what the Supreme Court might do with the *Roe* appeal, the Dallas three-judge panel quietly denied a request for an injunctive order under *Roe*'s rubric that had been filed some weeks earlier by Dallas Legal Services on behalf of a very young teenager who was seeking an abortion after having been raped by her father. The panel seemed to indicate that such a request was simply too far distant in time from their previous decision in the case, and public coverage of the Texas abortion scene focused on the upcoming legislative struggle as repeal proponents emphasized that *no* bill would be preferable to enactment of a reform measure that might very well have the effect of mooting *Roe*.[15]

Prospects for the Creighton-Kennard repeal bill did not look bright. Some legislators cited the *Roe* appeal as a reason why no action was necessary, and one of the state's major papers, the *Dallas Times-Herald*, called repeal "morally repugnant" while recommending the swift defeat of "a bill that would confer official sanction on a latter-day slaughter of the innocents" simply on account of "the whim of a momentarily inconvenienced mother." On March 29 several dozen witnesses, including Colorado's Dick Lamm and Dallas's Claude Evans, testified at a senate hearing on the Creighton-Kennard bill before an overflow audience of more than seven hundred people, but the Austin women, who had not signed up in advance to be among the speakers, were deeply disappointed when "nowhere in the presentation supporting the bill was the chief issue raised: the right of a woman to control her own body." Thanking Lamm for his visit, Dallas's Ginny Whitehill conceded that the prospects for success did not "look too promising," and while the committee approved the bill two weeks later, Senator Kennard readily acknowledged that he did not yet have the votes necessary to obtain passage on the senate floor.[16]

The same day that the senate hearing took place in Austin, the U.S. Supreme Court, citing its late-February rulings limiting federal court action against state statutes which plaintiffs otherwise could challenge in state court proceedings, vacated and remanded the declaratory decision voiding the Texas sodomy law that Henry McCluskey had won fourteen months earlier from the Dallas panel of Goldberg, Hughes, and Taylor. Texas newspapers speculated as to whether that dismissal might promise similar Supreme Court action in *Roe*, and the Texas activists feared that they might face setbacks on both the legislative and judicial fronts. The Texas Catholic Conference was taking a decidedly low-key stance in opposing liberalization, but a mid-April hearing on the house side of the state capitol brought forward a slew of non-Catholic repeal opponents as well as a prominent newspaper editorial opposing "abortion on impulse."[17]

The Austin Women's Liberation group had continued its undramatic but valuable abortion referral work on an all but daily basis, and by the spring of 1971, as word of the service spread far beyond the university community, the Austin group found themselves assisting an average of more than thirty-five women a week. The Austin women were not the only avowedly feminist network which was augmenting the more heavily advertised ministerial referral work being carried out by Howard Moody's Clergy Consultation Service and by such local volunteers as Atlanta's Emmett Herndon, Dallas's Claude Evans, and Austin's Bob Breihan, but in Chicago another feminist group, operating even more discreetly than the Austin women, had almost by accident taken the work of abortion referral a crucial step further.[18]

The Chicago Women's Liberation Union had begun an abortion counseling service in late 1969, with several housewives from the city's Hyde Park neighborhood and a number of graduate students from the University of Chicago among the early activists. At first the group had channeled its referrals to several men who they believed were doctors and who, after some lobbying, had agreed to a reduced fee of two hundred seventy-five dollars per abortion. Several of the group members assisted with the medical procedures, and in time one of the men taught one of the women the relatively simple task of how to perform the actual abortions. Shortly thereafter, early in 1971, the women happened to discover that the "doctors" were *not* physicians at all. From that initially surprising realization soon flowed a conclusion that was as powerful as it was natural—that "if *he* can do abortions, *we* can do abortions." Dispensing with the men, and reducing the onerous two-hundred-seventy-five-dollar fee to a maximum of one hundred dollars, the women carefully began to perform the procedures themselves and to teach the basic skills to additional members of the group. Using each others' apartments both as staging areas and as the locations for the actual abortions, the women expanded what had begun as a counseling service into an actual service-delivery organization that was performing approximately twenty-five abortions a day, three days a week—a total of approximately three hundred abortions each month. From the pseudonymous name they initially had employed when taking or returning women's phone calls—"This is Jane from Women's Liberation"—the service itself came to be called "Jane," a quasi-code name reflecting both the discretion and the communal identity involved in its work.

Troubled with police attention only once, "Jane" never experienced a fatality and performed thirty-five hundred abortions a year for Chicago-area women who otherwise might have paid far more to a potentially far less skillful provider or been left to carry an unwanted pregnancy to term.[19]

Early in March of 1971, just as the Supreme Court was announcing that it would hear Massachusetts's appeal of the First Circuit decision that had struck down the state's anticontraception law in Bill Baird's case,[20] the group of young feminist women in New Haven who had been discussing a possible legal challenge against Connecticut's abortion statute for more than a year finally filed suit in federal court. Katie Roraback had been recruited as one of several female attorneys to handle the case, and while a repeal bill covering the first twenty weeks of pregnancy had been introduced in the state legislature with the support of the Connecticut State Medical Society, repeal proponents gave the court case a far better chance of success than the legislative measure, which soon went down to a resounding 132 to 28 defeat just a few weeks after the suit was initiated.[21]

Shortly after the Connecticut case began, the Vermont chapter of a rapidly expanding two-year-old group with an active interest in abortion law repeal, Zero Population Growth (ZPG), sponsored a state court case against the existing Vermont statute brought by Burlington attorney Willis E. Higgins on behalf of six women and eleven doctors.[22] Three days later, on April 19, however, just as had happened with Henry McCluskey's *Buchanan* suit, the U.S. Supreme Court, with only Justice William O. Douglas dissenting, vacated the three-judge decision that had held Wisconsin's abortion statute invalid in *Babbitz* v. *McCann* and remanded the case to the lower court for reconsideration in light of the late-February rulings limiting federal court intervention against state statutes. Milwaukee's Dr. Babbitz had recently retired to Florida, but in far more liberal Madison, the home of the University of Wisconsin, Dr. Alfred Lee Kennan, a forty-five-year-old former full professor at the university's medical school, had privately opened a full-scale abortion clinic, the Midwest Medical Center, ten weeks earlier. Dane County District Attorney Gerald C. Nichol had met with Kennan and Kennan's attorney, David Pappas, the day after the clinic opened, to assert that the *Babbitz* ruling did not bar him from enforcing Wisconsin's abortion statute. Nothing further transpired, however, until Friday, April 16, when a seventeen-year-old young woman from Minnesota and a girlfriend were accosted as they were leaving Kennan's clinic by Madison police, who had been contacted by the young woman's furious mother. The parental and police endeavor was a bit too late, however, for the young woman displayed a receipt for payment of two hundred dollars, but the day's events convinced Nichol that now he should act. On Monday morning, just as the Supreme Court was remanding *Babbitz*, police officers acting at Nichol's behest and armed with a search warrant swooped down on Kennan's clinic, seizing all of his medical instruments and all of his patient records. The following day Kennan and Pappas filed suit against Nichol in federal court, seeking a declaratory judgment against the abortion statute as well as an immediate order blocking any further action and requiring Nichol to return the seized materials. U.S. District Judge James E. Doyle immediately issued a show-cause order directing Nichol to appear in court on April 26, but the very next day, April 21, Nichol filed criminal abortion charges against Kennan and several assistants and simultaneously moved for a state court injunction barring Kennan from performing any further abortions.

The day after the April 26 federal court hearing, Judge Doyle issued a temporary restraining order prohibiting Nichol from proceeding against Kennan and instructing the district attorney to return the instruments and records he had seized. At the same time, however, the state board of medical examiners announced an investigation of Kennan, thereby effectively inhibiting him from resuming abortion services. Nichol without success tried to get first the Seventh Circuit and then Supreme Court Justices Marshall and Harlan to stay Doyle's restraining order, and on May 5 Doyle issued a second order, directed against state Attorney General Robert Warren and the medical examiners, blocking any further efforts to pursue additional actions against Kennan. Three days later Doyle extended his order to include a state court judge before whom the prosecutors' request for an antiabortion injunction was pending, and finally, on Monday, May 17, four weeks after Nichol's raid, Kennan reopened his clinic and resumed performing abortions while the district attorney appealed Doyle's orders to the same three-judge panel handling the remand of *Babbitz*.[23]

The very same week that the battle of Madison commenced, the U.S. Supreme Court publicly announced its decision in *United States* v. *Milan Vuitch*. Justice Black had circulated an initial draft of a majority opinion to his colleagues on February 17, and within twenty-four hours John Harlan politely served notice that he soon would circulate an opinion contending that the Court lacked jurisdiction of the government's direct appeal of Judge Gesell's decision. William O. Douglas, who differed with Harlan on jurisdiction and with Black on the merits, circulated a dissent contending that Gesell should be affirmed, and while Warren Burger quickly endorsed Black's draft, several weeks passed without further developments as other justices such as Harry Blackmun waited to read Harlan's dissent on the jurisdictional question before committing themselves one way or the other on the Black opinion.

Only in late March did matters finally jell. Justices Blackmun, Brennan, and Marshall all endorsed Harlan's analysis that the Court lacked jurisdiction of the appeal. Of the other five justices who *did* believe the Court had jurisdiction, however—Black, Burger, White, Douglas, and Stewart—only the first three were willing to join Black's analysis of why Gesell should be reversed on the question of vagueness. Faced with such a splintered situation, first Blackmun and then Harlan, both of whom agreed with Black that Gesell had erred on the merits, moved to give Black a five-vote majority for the second portion of his opinion by formally agreeing that the D.C. abortion statute was *not* unconstitutionally vague while nonetheless dissenting from the other majority holding that the Court *did* have jurisdiction. With Douglas and Stewart joining Black with regard to jurisdiction, although not on the merits, Black's two-part opinion was able to garner two different five-vote majorities. On April 21 the Court's complicated resolution of *United States* v. *Vuitch* was publicly announced.[24]

Hugo Black's ten-page opinion of the Court dispensed with the jurisdictional issue routinely and declared that Gesell had made a mistake in finding that "health," the crucial word in the D.C. statute, was unconstitutionally vague. So long as "health" was correctly understood as including "psychological as well as physical well-being," Black said, the D.C. law was quite amenable to forthright application by Washington physicians. At John Harlan's request, Black had deleted three sentences from one footnote which Harlan thought might "intimate a view on the merits of the so-called *Griswold* issue," and hence with regard to the merits of the D.C. abortion statute the Black opinion expressly emphasized that "Since that question of vagueness was the only issue passed upon by the District Court it is the only issue we reach here." William O. Douglas's dissent from the vagueness reversal, however, quite explicitly indicated his view of the broader question as well. "Abortion touches intimate affairs of the family, of marriage, of sex, which in *Griswold* . . . we held to involve rights associated with several express constitutional rights and which are summed up in 'the right of privacy.'" With abortion as with contraception, Douglas added, "There is a compelling personal interest in marital privacy and in the limitation of family size."

The one other substantive opinion in the case, Potter Stewart's partial dissent on the merits, closely followed his earlier comments at the *Vuitch* conference. "I share at least some of the constitutional doubts about the abortion statute expressed by the District Court," Stewart volunteered, but he nonetheless agreed that Black was correct in delineating how the D.C. language could be acceptably construed by means of a broadly inclusive definition of "health." From that it should also follow, Stewart explained, "that when a physician has exercised his judgment in favor of performing an abortion, he has, by hypothesis, not violated the statute." He added that hence "I think the question of whether the performance of an abortion is 'necessary for the preservation of the mother's life or health' is entrusted under the statute exclusively to those licensed to practice medicine" and could not be second-guessed by a judge or jury. Hence any physician would be "wholly immune from being charged with the commission of a criminal offense under this law."[25]

The Court's decision was front-page news in major U.S. newspapers. Many reporters highlighted the subtle importance of Black's broad definition of "health," and most accounts portrayed the outcome as a 5 to 2 vote, with Justices Brennan and Marshall—who had joined Harlan's dissent with regard to jurisdiction but did not indicate any views on even the vagueness question—being omitted from a simplified tally. Dr. Vuitch told reporters that he had performed eight procedures that very day of the decision, and Washington observers quickly concluded that given Black's interpretation of "health," the Court's formal reversal of Gesell nonetheless would not allow for any new prosecutions of physicians in the District of Columbia. Indeed, it quite rapidly became clear that the decision would significantly increase rather than decrease abortion availability in the nation's capital. While Norman Dorsen had at first been deeply disappointed over reports of the outcome, he was extremely surprised and then greatly pleased when Harriet Pilpel called to congratulate him on his role in helping generate the Court's exceedingly helpful definition of "health." Pilpel in a subsequent memo also emphasized that "the persuasiveness of the constitutional arguments based on *Griswold* is in no way diminished by the *Vuitch*" outcome and opinions.[26]

While Pilpel and most other knowledgeable attorneys counted *Vuitch* as an implicit victory rather than an ostensible defeat, in Texas word of the ruling was greeted with dismay by abortion repeal proponents. "As a practical matter, the Supreme Court decision has hurt our chances," legislative sponsor Senator Tom Creighton told reporters. "People will just read that the Supreme Court has upheld an abortion law." Repeal backers needed twenty-one votes to bring their bill up for Senate floor action and had only sixteen. Cosponsor Senator Don Kennard explained that "the overwhelming feeling in the Senate is for the bill philosophically, but politically it's a different matter." House sponsor Representative Sam Coats sounded a similar note: "Some members of the Legislature would love to have the Supreme Court decide this for us."[27]

Given the backlog of additional abortion appeals and petitions that had accumulated at the Supreme Court over the previous eight months, the release of the *Vuitch* decision actually represented the onset of expanded Supreme Court action on the subject rather than any sort of conclusion. The justices had privately decided in late March that both of Jane Hodgson's pretrial challenges to her Minnesota prosecution should be dismissed, but only several weeks after *Vuitch* was announced did they ratify their earlier conclusion and publicly issue the appropriate orders.[28] Appeal papers in the Louisiana, Missouri, and Illinois cases had drawn relatively little attention or discussion within the Court,[29] but after the justices' January determination to postpone any consideration of either *Roe* v. *Wade* or *Doe* v. *Bolton* until *Vuitch* was decided, on April 22, the day after that decision, the Court by narrow but identical margins privately agreed to hear both of the cases. Five justices—Douglas, Harlan, Brennan, White, and Marshall—one more than the necessary minimum of four—voted to consider both *Roe* and *Doe*. The four other justices—Black, Stewart, Burger, and Blackmun—voted to affirm the lower courts' denials of the plaintiffs' requests for injunctive relief against the Texas and Georgia statutes and thus not review either those questions or the merits of the two declaratory judgments holding the abortion laws unconstitutional. Almost two weeks passed before those decisions were made public, but on May 3 the Court formally announced that sometime in the fall it would hear argument in both *Roe* v. *Wade* and *Doe* v. *Bolton*.[30]

News of the Court's action stimulated an immediate burst of activity on the part of abortion litigators. Roy Lucas immediately circulated two memos encouraging the preparation of significant amicus briefs in support of the plaintiffs, and he formally asked Margie Hames for permission to prepare a medically oriented amicus brief in *Doe* which hopefully both the American Medical Association and the American College of Obstetricians and Gynecologists might decide to endorse. Lucas went to some pains to underscore how unimpressive the amicus participation in *Vuitch* had been, and while Harriet Pilpel told colleagues she believed there was "an excellent chance" the Supreme Court would void the Texas law on either vagueness and/or privacy grounds, Lucas emphasized that "the vote will be close" and that a defeat would set back the abortion movement by "at least a decade." Privately, Pilpel worried that the Georgia reform statute at issue in *Doe* might be upheld even if the Texas law was not, and in Austin, where the repeal bill was now clearly not going to win legislative approval, the young Texas activists were far less sanguine than Pilpel. "I am *not* optimistic about the Supreme Court," Victoria Foe wrote Dallas's Ginny Whitehill. "I believe that this court will somehow continue to hand down a 'no decision' and to not rule on the substantive issue of privacy."[31]

Both Lucas and Margie Hames successfully asked the Court for routine extensions of the deadlines on which their initial briefs would be due until August 1, and Lucas renewed a suggestion he had first broached to Sarah Weddington more than a month earlier: since both Weddington and her husband Ron, who had spent the last eight months living and working in Fort Worth, where Sarah had become an assistant city attorney, ardently wanted to move back to Austin and open a private practice, Sarah could as a halftime responsibility open a "southwestern office" of Lucas's Madison Institute and do some of the work on *Roe* in Austin under that rubric. Linda Coffee, due to her law firm's commitments, had far greater constraints on her available time than did Sarah, and Linda was already referring legal inquiries about *Roe* to Lucas, the "lead counsel." By late May, when Lucas consulted with Weddington during a quick trip to Texas for a speaking appearance in Galveston, the "southwestern office" arrangement was set, and Lucas was beginning to worry about how to raise the necessary funds for *Roe*'s upcoming printing bills. Lucas wanted a significant portion of the money to come from Texas, and he hoped to persuade Dr. Hallford, who had already given a hundred dollars to help Ginny Whitehill's spring legislative efforts, that his ongoing participation in *Roe* merited a serious contribution toward the appellate expenses.[32]

Within two weeks of the Court's announcement that it would hear *Roe* and *Doe*, Harriet Pilpel invited many of the country's principal abortion case activists to a New York dinner meeting on the first weekend in June—when many of them would be in town for another abortion-related conference—to discuss the Texas and Georgia cases and particularly the amicus briefs that ought to be prepared. Many of the attendees—Pilpel and her colleagues Nancy Wechsler and Jane Zuckerman, Lucas, Norman Dorsen, Cyril Means, ASA's Jimmye Kimmey, and the ACLU's Mel Wulf—were from New York to begin with, but Margie Hames and Judy Bourne both came from Atlanta and Norma Zarky was in town from California. Dorsen stressed that the cases' prospects were "uncertain" because while *Griswold* "*can* be extended" to cover abortion, it "*need not* be," and Lucas, no doubt with his earlier rebuff by Margie Hames still clearly in mind, emphasized how regrettable it was that *Doe*'s crucial but as yet unsuccessful challenge to the Georgia statute's hospitalization requirement was going forward without any extensive trial court evidentiary record having been developed. Data on New York's now almost one-year-old experience with nonhospital procedures might be a potentially persuasive substitute if it was featured prominently enough in the *Doe* briefs, Lucas advised.

Some of the most important aspects of the New York meeting, however, took place not in the group discussion but in more private conversations, and one particularly significant interchange occurred when Cyril Means went out of his way to tell Margie Hames that any involvement by Roy Lucas in *Doe* v. *Bolton* would represent a great danger to her prospects for success in the Supreme Court. The origins of Means's intense although often-concealed animus toward Lucas dated back to the much-younger lawyer's initial 1968 appearance on the New York abortion scene, when Pilpel and others had been so taken with Lucas's *Griswold*-style privacy analysis of how abortion laws could be constitutionally challenged. In part Means's enmity was fueled by his zealous preference for a historically oriented argument that once-valid nineteenth-century antiabortion statutes intended to protect women from a then-dangerous procedure had become obsolete and thus invalid as medical progress had made early-term abortion safer than actual childbirth. In 1968 Means had futilely attempted to dismiss the entire utility of any rights-based litigation strategy, an approach which many participants and observers understandably believed Lucas personified, especially after Linda Greenhouse's prominent 1970 *New York Times Magazine* profile of the abortion rights struggle. Means's hostility had been fortified when Larry Lader had broken with Lucas over the latter's remunerative but admittedly controversial representation of for-profit commercial referral agencies, and it had been even further reinforced by the advent of Joe Nellis's fervent antipathy toward Lucas in the wake of their battle over who would argue *United States* v. *Vuitch*.

Lucas's audacious style—as Hames herself had personally experienced nine months earlier—sometimes helped create receptive listeners for Means's talebearing complaints. To Hames, Means explained that Lucas's previous attempt to move in on *Doe* v. *Bolton* was by no means unique, and he recounted the entire ugly contretemps between Nellis and Lucas over *Vuitch*. Means fortified his account with a dramatic but at best fourthhand story of how the *Vuitch* flurry of then withdrawn motions had left one or more justices "hopping mad" at Lucas's impertinence. Means and others had assiduously monitored how Lucas had not yet applied for formal admission to the Supreme Court bar, and Means told Hames how he and Nellis imagined that the Court might very well *reject* what otherwise would be a customarily routine application because of Lucas's conduct in *Vuitch*.

Hames was learning more than she wanted to know about New York's petty rivalries, but Means's assertion that the *justices* would look askance at any case in which Lucas was involved was a claim she could not afford to dismiss, even if she otherwise had been inclined to. The current plan, which Lucas had initiated four weeks earlier and which the dinner discussion had ratified, was that Lucas would prepare the most important, medically oriented amicus brief in *Doe* as well as the primary brief in *Roe*. Unlike Means, Hames knew from Lucas's earlier comments that Sarah Weddington was now a Madison Institute employee and that Lucas's involvement in the Texas case of course only postdated the panel decision, but the seriousness of Means's claim about the justices' feelings led her to raise the subject of *Vuitch* with Lucas later that same day. "He played dumb at first," Hames recounted in a memo she dictated for her own records a day later, but then Lucas fessed up and related his side of the entire story. "He characterized Nellis as a Mafia type lawyer and stated he had had trouble with him on the Wisconsin case also.... He claimed that Nellis had 'extorted' about $100,000 from Dr. Vuitch last year and the Doctor was getting tired of it." Lucas additionally explained that he had indeed just applied for formal admission to the Supreme Court bar, with New York University's Robert McKay and Oregon Senator Robert Packwood as his official sponsors, and that the clerk's office had assured him that there would be no problem. Hames declined to identify Means when Lucas asked about the source for her concerns, and the discussion ended. ASA's Jimmye Kimmey took charge of following up on the participants' informal agreements as to who would be responsible for which amicus briefs, and while some initial commitments—such as one by Means to prepare a "Catholic brief" that could be signed by other lawyers—soon fell by the wayside, others did move forward. The AMA had already declined to support any medical amicus brief, but Lucas would indeed prepare one for *Doe* and New York attorney Carol Ryan would oversee a much more modest one to accompany Lucas's primary brief in *Roe*. Norman Dorsen had explained that given the ACLU's formal sponsorship of *Doe*, the organization should not file an amicus statement in *Roe*, but Pilpel and her colleagues would prepare major submissions on behalf of Planned Parenthood and Norma Zarky would take charge of a brief to be filed on behalf of such women's groups as the American Association of University Women, the Young Women's Christian Association, and the National Organization for Women. Zarky and Hames agreed to closely coordinate their drafting, for as Hames explained to Zarky after citing some of the justices' comments at the *Vuitch* hearing, "I do not believe that this Supreme Court will recognize the right to control one's own body."[33]

Few promising legislative developments were occurring anywhere in the country. The antiabortion effort to revoke New York's 1970 repeal law had finally ground to a halt, but Governor Rockefeller had curtailed most state Medicaid payments for poor women's abortions. New York City authorities, fearful of the financial impact on municipal hospitals, had filed suit against the new policy in state court, and in mid-May a trial judge voided the new policy. Holding that *Griswold* encompassed "the right to determine when and whether to have children," and additionally citing *Belous* and *Babbitz*, Justice Samuel A. Spiegel ruled that "Since the right to decide not to have a child has been held to be a fundamental one protected under the Ninth Amendment, the State has an obligation to provide the indigent with adequate means to exercise that right." Six weeks later an appellate court affirmed that ruling on the first anniversary of the New York repeal statute. That very same day, July 1, a newly passed state law prohibiting all for-profit abortion referral services also took effect. Enthusiastically supported by most abortion rights proponents, the measure was a direct response to what many observers felt was widespread and unconscionable profiteering. Roy Lucas, who was continuing to take significant flak over his representation of such operators, unsuccessfully sought a federal court order against the new law on First Amendment grounds, and some weeks later a three-judge panel expressly affirmed the statute's validity.[34]

Antiabortion forces continued to maintain a high-visibility profile, especially in New York, and early in July Boston Archbishop Humberto S. Medeiros told a Sunday audience at New York's St. Patrick's Cathedral that the widespread availability of abortion in that city should be met with what he termed "vengeance." New York City's most intrepid Baptist minister, Clergy Consultation Service founder Howard Moody, told his nationwide network of abortion rights activists that a state-by-state survey of legislative prospects made it very clear "that the courts are the only real hope for change." Additional repeal bills had gone down to defeat in Illinois, Maine, Ohio, and North Dakota, and prospects now looked bleak even in Michigan, which repeal proponents had once counted as perhaps their best prospect for a 1971 victory. Both there and in North Dakota, local activists were beginning to organize for 1972 statewide popular-vote referenda of just the same sort that had proved so successful in Washington state in 1970, but for most repeal supporters, Howard Moody's conclusion was indeed the clear lesson of the first six months of 1971.[35]

Even in the courts, however, newer cases were experiencing at best a spotty reception. The Connecticut women's suit had been dismissed by an openly hostile Federal District Judge, T. Emmet Clarie, and Katie Roraback and her colleagues had appealed the action to the Second Circuit Court of Appeals. The earlier similar dismissal of the Kentucky case had been reversed by a Sixth Circuit appellate panel, but the Arizona suit was rejected by a three-judge panel that placed particular emphasis on the U.S. Supreme Court's opinions earlier in the year cutting back on federal court authority to entertain challenges to state criminal statutes. The New Jersey, Colorado, and Oklahoma cases were undergoing prolonged if not interminable judicial consideration, and the appeals of the Ohio and South Dakota ones also appeared to be going nowhere fast.[36]

There were several new judicial bright spots, however. In Missouri, where a federal case had initially proved unsuccessful, a state court trial judge sustained a constitutional complaint against Missouri's abortion law, but the decision was immediately appealed. In Florida, where a new federal suit was also about to run afoul of the early 1971 Supreme Court rulings, the highest state court, in a decision reversing a criminal abortion conviction, explicitly declared that the state's abortion law was unconstitutionally vague no matter how painstakingly a prosecutor might try to apply it against an accredited doctor. In California, where one court had already ruled that a female minor did not need her parents' consent in order to obtain an abortion, one intermediate appellate panel upheld the constitutionality of the state's 1967 reform statute while affirming a criminal abortion conviction of a licensed physician, but another appellate court voided significant portions of the 1967 law while reviewing a second such conviction. "We are impelled to conclude," the second panel observed after citing *Belous*, *Babbitz*, and the Texas opinion in *Roe*, "that a woman has a constitutional right to terminate her pregnancy, subject only to reasonably imposed state restrictions designed to safeguard the health of the woman, and to protect the advanced fetus." Both of the two divergent decisions, however, were appealed for more decisive review by the California Supreme Court.[37]

The most important legal undertakings of the 1971 summer, however, would be the preparation of the Supreme Court briefs for *Roe* and *Doe*. Margie Hames in Atlanta had principal responsibility for the primary brief in *Doe*, and while she had the benefit of additional input from ACLU southern office staff attorney Reber Boult, both Boult and in time Hames herself ended up spending a significant portion of the summer trying to help resolve racial disturbances that were wracking the west Georgia city of Columbus. A young ACLU intern from the University of Arkansas Law School, Pam Walker, had been assigned to assist Hames in preparing the brief, and while most of the other original *Doe* attorneys were now involved in name only, Tobi Schwartz from Atlanta Legal Aid had inherited the chief responsibility of coping with *Doe*'s lead plaintiff, Sandra Bensing. More than six months earlier, just weeks after Sandra had given birth to her *"Doe"* baby, Sandra's husband Joel had outstripped all of his previous criminal conduct toward young children by kidnapping a six-year-old black girl and taking the child all the way from Atlanta to Oklahoma. The visual incongruity of the duo soon led to Joel's apprehension and arrest, and in late January of 1971 Joel pled guilty and immediately began serving a twenty-year prison sentence. With Tobi's assistance, Sandra renewed her 1969 petition for divorce, and in mid-May the divorce was finalized. Temporarily reduced to living with her mother and stepfather, Sandra yearned to regain custody of her first two children, and by the end of the summer Sandra had remarried in the hope that she now could attain a new stability in life.[38]

While Schwartz and Hames were contending with those difficulties attendant to *Doe*, challenges also existed for the principal participants in *Roe*. Roy Lucas had met Marsha and David King, although not Norma McCorvey, during his early summer trip to Texas, and shortly thereafter Marsha King sent Lucas a lengthy letter thanking him for his work on the case and detailing all of the medical and contraceptive misfortunes that had been encountered by "Mary and John Doe." "We very much appreciate what you are doing," and "We would like to help in any way that we can. I have written down all of the things that I could think of with regard to my problems with pregnancy," and Marsha explained how in the wake of her second visit to Mexico City nine months earlier, she had "decided to take my chances with the pill" rather than practice abstinence. Marsha also described how she and Linda Coffee had been trying unsuccessfully for some time to locate

Norma McCorvey. "I guess that we will have to comb the bars, and I can't say that I am looking forward to that," Marsha explained. She and David—as well as Marsha's mother and grandmother—were planning to attend the Supreme Court argument in the fall, she said, and Marsha was also helping establish a Texas chapter of WEAL, the Women's Equity Action League, a group committed to attacking economic and employment discrimination. The Austin women, who remained more focused upon their ongoing referral work than on the courtroom status of *Roe*, found themselves having to devote increasing attention to containing the sectarian activism of several Socialist Workers Party (SWP) members whose interest in abortion more and more seemed to follow a centrally rather than locally defined agenda. Early in the summer the SWP's national leadership created a group called the Women's National Abortion Coalition (and later the Women's National Abortion *Action* Coalition, or WONAAC), and a mid-July conference in New York ratified plans for a Washington demonstration targeted at the Supreme Court just before the *Roe* and *Doe* oral arguments. Neither in Texas nor elsewhere, however, did the SWP initiatives interrupt the continuing work of earlier and more deeply committed activists.[39]

By late June it was becoming painfully clear that Roy Lucas's Madison Institute had undertaken a significantly larger summer workload than it might be able to complete. Deadlines for the briefs in *Roe* and in Jane Hodgson's criminal appeal to the Minnesota Supreme Court, as well as for the principal amicus brief in *Doe* and other items such as the jurisdictional statement for the Supreme Court appeal of the North Carolina case, *Corkey* v. *Edwards*, were all fast approaching. Most importantly, Lucas himself was actually the only full-fledged attorney at the Institute. Nick Danforth, a former colleague at the Twentieth Century Fund who was in charge of the Institute's increasingly strained financial affairs, and a young college graduate who was about to enter Yale Law School, Brian Sullivan, were the only other full-time, nonclerical employees. Danforth had recruited a friend with two years at Yale law, David Tundermann, as a summer intern, and a first-year law student from the University of Cincinnati, Dan Schneider, had been similarly directed to Lucas by a professor who had worked at the Institute a year earlier. That trio of students found themselves doing much of the Institute's substantive work, as Lucas was so overextended that he had to apologize to the Institute's trustees—who had not met since 1969—for not having sent them any update on the Institute's work in over a year.

One of the first people to realize how serious the summer overload might be was the Madison Institute's newest employee, Sarah Weddington, who had already begun to turn her attention to the *Roe* appeal after she and Ron had returned to Austin from Fort Worth. By mid-June, however, Sarah was beginning to worry that Lucas and his New York aides were not making any significant headway on the *Roe* brief. Hoping that no more than a three or four week stay would be involved, Sarah decided with considerable reluctance that she herself had better spend part of the summer in New York.

Thanks to Lucas's incidental affiliation with one of several abortion referral services, Sarah like Tundermann and Schneider had free yet extremely modest housing in a simple, clinic-connected building in the Gramercy Park area of Manhattan, only a fifteen-minute walk from the Institute's significantly fancier quarters in a Greenwich Village town house where Lucas and his wife Uta lived upstairs and which had once been the home of the poet e.e. cummings. Lucas in early July sent the Supreme Court formal notification that he would be arguing *Roe*, but as Weddington learned upon her arrival in New York, the Institute's most immediately pressing tasks were not the *Roe* or *Doe* briefs but the North Carolina and *Hodgson* submissions, both of which had even more urgent deadlines.

By mid-July, with Weddington pitching in and most staff members working twelve-hour days, the jurisdictional statement in *Corkey* had been submitted to the Supreme Court and work on the *Hodgson* brief was almost complete. Both documents quietly sought to emphasize that each of those cases presented questions which might well not be resolved by *Roe* or *Doe*. David Tundermann was overseeing most of the *Doe* amicus work, and the Institute staff was keeping Margie Hames regularly informed of their progress. On July 20 Lucas wrote to the clerk's office at the Court to request an extension of the deadline date for the *Roe* brief from August 1 to August 17, and several days later Hames, who was coping with a serious back injury as well as the Columbus disorders, requested an identical extension. Both applications were soon granted, but even when Lucas's letter was first dispatched, little more than the preparatory work of compiling *Roe*'s lower court record had actually been completed. Weddington contacted John Tolle of Henry Wade's office to secure written confirmation that the Dallas District Attorney would, in the absence of any injunction, continue to enforce the Texas abortion law despite the three-judge court's declaratory holding, and she also secured impressive affidavits from three prominent Texas medical school leaders attesting to the vagueness of the Texas statute and to how the *Roe* decision had in no way made legal abortions available in Texas. An elderly Boston friend of Danforth's family, Thomas Cabot, contributed fifteen thousand dollars toward the summer's rapidly mounting printing bills, and a wealthy San Antonio woman, Ruth McLean Bowers, whom Ginny Whitehill and Weddington had first met during the spring repeal effort in the Texas state legislature, sent the Institute a similar check for ten thousand dollars.[40]

The extension of the *Roe* and *Doe* deadlines until August 17 gave Weddington and the others some amount of breathing room, but when Ron Weddington arrived in New York in mid-July for a previously planned visit, Sarah quickly conscripted him as an additional contributor to the *Roe* brief. Like Sarah, Ron too had no other obligations until they actually could open an Austin law office, and Ron assumed responsibility for those portions of the *Roe* brief that would try to resuscitate the "Does'" standing and justify the involvement of Dr. Hallford, which appeared almost certainly foredoomed as a result of the earlier Supreme Court rulings.

Ron joined Sarah and the others at their no-rent lodgings as well as at the upscale offices, and while the youngest members of the Institute's very young team—Ron at twenty-nine and Lucas at thirty were the two relative oldsters—found the summer enjoyable as well as memorable, by late July everyone was working extremely long hours. Sarah and Ron had asked a number of Austin friends, including Bea Vogel, Barbara Hines, and Glen Wilkerson, a former colleague of Sarah's on the ABA ethics committee staff, for research assistance on specific state law items, and some of their efforts influenced small portions of the *Roe* brief. Lucas also had David Tundermann prepare a harshly critical review of Cyril Means's work on the original nineteenth-century legislative motives for the enactment of antiabortion laws, and Tundermann's devastatingly negative evaluation of Means's research reinforced Lucas's already strong predisposition to include hardly a single citation to Means's historical analysis in either his *Roe* or *Doe* briefs.

Despite Margie Hames's pronounced ambivalence, Lucas had decided that one way to repair *Doe*'s lack of any evidentiary record with regard to the Georgia reform statute's hospital requirement, which the Atlanta panel had upheld, was to append to the *Doe* amicus brief a supplementary appendix of more than four dozen prior court rulings and medical journal papers that all-told came to an imposing 477 pages, far larger than the brief itself. Lucas included former Justice Tom Clark's law review essay as well as medical studies by supportive doctors such as Bob Hall and Christopher Tietze, but Cyril Means's 1968 historical article was one of the few arguably relevant items which was *not* included in the otherwise comprehensive collection.[41]

Lucas's many obligations had often kept him out of town or otherwise away from the Institute's offices for much of the summer, but by early August, he was working until the early hours of each morning drafting, polishing and assembling different portions of the *Doe* and *Roe* briefs. Early Tuesday morning, August 10, one week before their deadline, Lucas left a daybreak memo for Sarah, a message that was as revealing as it was instructive, for it was a note to an employee, not a colleague: "It is 6 o'clock and the sun is coming up, but the *Doe* brief is complete. Today I expect you to take over to ensure that it is proofed and printed to perfection." A variety of additional directives—"Make certain . . . be certain . . . Correct Table I-2"—followed, and the memo ended with a curt and brusque admonition: "Do not make any proofreading or administrative mistakes."[42]

Four days later the *Doe* amicus brief was filed in Washington, followed within a week by the *Roe* brief, Margie Hames's brief in *Doe*, and a half-dozen other supportive amicus submissions. Lucas's *Doe* brief was notable less for its content than for its impressive list of signers, which even drew news attention in the *New York Times*. The three leading organizational endorsers—the American College of Obstetricians and Gynecologists (ACOG), the American Medical Women's Association, and the American Psychiatric Association—were joined by some 178 individually prominent medical leaders, including Alan Guttmacher and Hugh Savage plus Keith Russell, Ned Overstreet, and Jerry Kummer from California. Twenty-two individual signatories hailed from New York, but Minnesota—in a less-than-subtle effort to appeal to Justices Blackmun and Burger—topped all other states with a total of twenty-four, including Jane Hodgson and the Mayo Clinic's Dr. Joseph H. Pratt.

The first two thirds of Lucas's 145-page *Roe* brief—which also listed Sarah and Ron Weddington, Linda Coffee, Fred Bruner, Roy Merrill and Norman Dorsen as additional attorneys—was largely devoted to procedural matters and to emphasizing the breadth of medical support for legalized abortion. The constitutional privacy argument began only on page ninety-one, with a long quotation from retired Justice Clark's law review essay. Lucas cited the Court's 1923 decision in *Meyer* as well as *Griswold* in contending that the absence of any explicit constitutional enumeration of a privacy right "is no impediment to the existence of the right," and he cited language from a well-known 1905 ruling,

Jacobson v. *Massachusetts*, in arguing that "The right to seek and receive medical care for the protection of health and well-being is a fundamental personal liberty." He reached beyond the constitutional frame of reference to remind the justices that "Certainly the members of this Court know from personal experience the emotional and financial expenditures parenthood demands," and a relatively brief final section quickly dismissed the likely arguments that Texas might make in defense of its statute. Only a brief footnote on page 123, originally prepared by Ron Weddington, directly rebutted a common argument made by abortion opponents: "Section 1 of the Fourteenth Amendment . . . refers to 'All persons born or naturalized in the United States. . . .' There are no cases which hold that fetuses are protected by the Fourteenth Amendment."

Of the seven other favorable amicus briefs submitted in August, the two most significant were those prepared by Harriet Pilpel and her colleagues on behalf of PPFA and one by Nancy Stearns, who had helped file both the 1969 *Abramowicz* case in New York and one of the ensuing companion suits in New Jersey, on behalf of several small women's groups plus WONAAC. Pilpel and her two coworkers, Nancy Wechsler and Jane Zuckerman, sounded much the same note as Lucas, stressing that "the right to abortion must be viewed as a corollary of the right to control fertility which was recognized in *Griswold*" and stating that there is a "fundamental constitutional right under the Ninth and Fourteenth Amendments to choose whether or not to bear a child." Like Lucas, the PPFA brief also quoted from former Justice Clark's article to support the contention that "the right of a woman to choose whether or not to bear a child is an aspect of her right to privacy and liberty." Pilpel emphasized the linkage to *Griswold* again and again, however, asserting that from "the right to practice contraception and thus control fertility" flowed "the right to control conception. . . . The right to contraception implicitly includes the right to choose whether or not to become a parent."

Nancy Stearns's impressive submission focused more upon the realities of pregnancy than the PPFA brief's invocation of precedent. "Carrying, giving birth to, and raising an unwanted child can be one of the most painful and long-lasting punishments that a person can endure," Stearns explained, and "statutes which condemn women to share their bodies with another organism against their will" should be declared unconstitutional. A somewhat similar point was made in the far more modest amicus brief filed only in *Roe* by Carol Ryan on behalf of the exact same impressive list of signers whose names appeared on

Lucas's medical brief in *Doe*: "The freedom to be the master of her own body, and thus her own fate, is as fundamental a right as a woman can possess."[43]

Roy Lucas sent Cyril Means copies of the *Roe* and *Doe* briefs, in which Means's work received only a single, unindexed citation, as soon as they arrived from the printer, accompanied by a seemingly incongruous cover letter saying that "I was able to utilize your work a great deal, and . . . I regard the contribution of your article highly." Lucas also derisively told Means that "As you can see, I copied everything from the writings of Joseph Nellis and Harriet Pilpel (I mean, Miss Zuckerman), who have unwittingly allowed their drafts to slip into my hands." Roy and his wife Uta, whose relationship had recently become increasingly strained, left New York for an almost month-long trip to Germany, Italy, and Greece almost as soon as the briefs were filed, and Cyril Means invited both Margie Hames and Sarah and Ron Weddington to his summer home in Gloucester, Massachusetts, for an end-of-the-summer vacation. Hames had to decline, but told Means of her disagreements with Lucas over the *Doe* amicus brief and Lucas's huge supplementary appendix, and Means replied in a letter which again starkly reflected his spiteful attitude toward his perceived rival. "I was sorry to learn of all your tribulations this summer," and "I could not help chuckling at the thought of Spurgeon LeRoy Lucas, Jr., affecting to remain 'above it all,'" Means said. "Your hair would stand on end if you knew the telephone calls that have been made to me here by highly placed men he has been harassing in his now desperate quest for funds."

Just a few days later Sarah and Ron Weddington took the train from New York up to Massachusetts for a three-day visit with Means before they returned to Austin. Sarah had had only passing contacts with Means in New York, but had found "he was a pleasant person" and had been particularly impressed that "he took time to talk to me" and treated her as a colleague, not an employee. She had been delighted at Means's invitation that she and Ron visit him in Gloucester, and while little of the visit was ostensibly devoted to abortion litigation issues, it did provide Sarah and Ron with their first extensive exposure to someone within the New York abortion world who had a thoroughgoingly critical attitude toward Lucas both personally and professionally.[44]

The week after the Weddingtons' visit to Gloucester, Sarah on behalf of herself and the vacationing Lucas sent a formal letter to the clerk's office at the Supreme Court requesting additional oral argument time in *Roe* beyond the thirty minutes normally allotted each side. Their request, Weddington explained, came "primarily because of the two unusually important and complex issues involved" in *Roe*: first the generic question of "the propriety of injunctive relief against the enforcement of state criminal statutes" to which the Court had devoted so much attention in its spring decisions, and second the constitutional claim which "squarely presents the question of the application of the right of privacy to the abortion issue," a subject which was of "vital importance to countless women and their families." Those "issues are particularly important and complex," and she reminded the Court that a full hour initially had been allocated to each side in *Vuitch*. The letter closed by implicitly making a second request as well: "In view of the complexities of the case and the necessity that each aspect of the case be consummately presented, Mr. Lucas and I desire to share the responsibilities of oral argument. We respectfully request the Court to grant additional time for the oral argument."

Upon his return from Europe, Lucas indicated in a letter to the imprisoned Nathan Rappaport, better known as the authorial "Dr. X" of *The Abortionist*, that "I will be arguing *Roe* with a colleague," presuming that the Court assented. Lucas's most immediate concern, however, just as Cyril Means had indicated to Margie Hames, was how to generate sufficient funds to keep the Madison Institute going in the absence of any ongoing support from either Morris Dees or Joseph Sunnen. Lucas was receiving a significant personal income from his ongoing representation of Milan Vuitch in all three Washington-area jurisdictions, and in mid-September he also collected the first half of a twenty-thousand-dollar fee for filing suit against the Kansas reform statute, which restricted therapeutic abortions to large, specially accredited hospitals, on behalf of a Kansas City doctor, Dr. Lynn Weller, who was doing a booming business in a small, black-owned facility.[45]

Lucas was gradually becoming convinced, however, that many of the Madison Institute's fund-raising difficulties were due to the continuing dissemination of Joe Nellis's and Cyril Means's comments about him and his actions in *Vuitch*. In mid-September, just after his return from Europe, Lucas heard talk of a new strand of complaints, and in response he sent Margie Hames a firm but polite letter complaining as to how he recently had been apprised that "Someone involved in the *Doe* case apparently told several foundations that the ACOG brief was not wanted by the *Doe* counsel(s), and that it would be superfluous to file such a brief. This unkind commentary made it quite difficult to raise funds to cover the cost of the brief, and I find it difficult to believe that anyone could have made such a statement." Hames waited a week before responding, but when she did, her four-page letter of reply laid out all of her accumulated anger reaching back to Lucas's first attempt to move in on *Doe* thirteen months earlier. She began by recalling that in the earliest stages of *Doe*, ACLU legal director Mel Wulf had recommended that she and her colleagues contact Lucas for assistance. When they did so,

> We received a packet of reprints of medical articles and your law review article and a *bill* for $25.00. This did not get us off to a very good start and needless to say did not endear volunteer counsel to you. The next thing we heard from you was after the decision in our case; you called and offered to take over the appeal to the Supreme Court. I advised you that [the] ACLU would pursue the case. You then wrote me a very lengthy dissertation on your expertise and our lack of it. We were very foolish, according to you, to reject your help. We did not turn down your help; we did say you could not take over the case and argue it.

Hames went on to complain about how Lucas had begun to advertise his preparation of the *Doe* amicus brief even before the New York attorneys' meeting had approved that assignment with Hames ambivalently acquiescing. She had felt "that you should stick to the Texas case, which you had 'taken over' by then, and stay out of our case," but "there was no real alternative" to Lucas doing the medical brief. She had worried that Lucas was taking on more work than he could complete, and she detailed how Nellis's accusation that Lucas had tried to "take over" *Vuitch* seemed to parallel the way in which he had come after *Doe*. Those concerns, she asserted, had been reinforced by phone calls and queries from other abortion activists, and "the questions themselves were indicative that many people mistrusted you."

With regard to Lucas's specific complaint, "I never told anyone we did not want the ACOG brief," Hames stated, but when a foundation lawyer had called to ask her about Nellis's allegations and Lucas's earlier insulting letter to her, Hames had refused to provide any copies but had conceded her unhappiness about Lucas's handling of the amicus brief. Lucas's basic problem, she declared, was that "you are immature, somewhat irresponsible, and a super ego. I also feel you are very devoted to this movement and have accomplished many good things. Why don't you grow up?" Hames's most serious worry was the "forbidding" size of Lucas's supplementary appendix. "It is so overdone the entire thing may turn the Court off and they may choose to ignore it. Thus in this way your brief has jeopardized our case." Hames finally concluded her lambasting by telling Lucas that with regard to his fund-raising difficulties, "I refuse to accept responsibility for your problems. You should quit trying to blame someone else."[46]

The increasingly mean-spirited relations among the abortion lawyers fortunately remained an entirely private problem, but a potentially more public difficulty was brewing for Lucas within the organizational world of NARAL. Three weeks before the group's early October annual meeting, NARAL's nominating committee circulated a statement to the entire membership explaining that Lucas's name was being withdrawn from the list of nominees for NARAL's board of directors because of his courtroom representation of the for-profit abortion referral services. Lucas prepared a statement defending the propriety of his legal work for the commercial agencies, and various recipients of the NARAL circular began to inquire as to what was going on. John Cowles, the publisher of the *Minneapolis Star* and *Tribune* newspapers and a financial contributor to Jane Hodgson's legal defense fund as well as to NARAL, wondered whether the controversy would "adversely affect the effectiveness" of Lucas's upcoming representation of Hodgson before the Minnesota Supreme Court. Hodgson's supporters had already paid Lucas over thirty-two thousand dollars for his work, and local attorneys vouched for the "excellent" quality of the brief Lucas had submitted to the Minnesota court on her behalf while Minnesota activists knowledgeable about internal NARAL politics reassured Cowles and others that the dispute had more to do with personalities than anything else. "It was evident from the discussion," the minutes of one fifteen-person Minneapolis-St. Paul meeting recorded, "that several people present felt that Mr. Larry Lader," the NARAL chairman, "was prejudiced against Mr. Lucas."

Roy Lucas, who knew that Lader was a close friend of Cyril Means, felt exactly the same, and without using Lader's name nonetheless said just as much in a memorandum asserting that he would be too busy to contest the action in person at the annual meeting. NARAL, he brashly but accurately asserted, "has contributed almost nothing to the court cases" and its leadership—i.e., Lader—has "seemed only interested in holding press conferences to announce or pretend involvement in court cases wherein NARAL was not in fact at all involved, or to announce positions which carried no force." During a year "of impasse in both courts and legislatures" and during which "the anti-abortion forces have greatly increased in strength," NARAL had contributed relatively little, Lucas asserted in his dismissive rebuttal.[47]

In private, many activists agreed with some if not all of Lucas's analysis. NARAL executive director Lee Gidding had remarked to

Colorado's Dick Lamm several weeks earlier that 1971 so far had witnessed only "an impressive series of losses throughout the country" and she added that "those of us on the inside know what a beating the opposition dealt us this year" in state after state. A *New York Times* story reviewing the results of state legislative sessions highlighted how not a single new abortion statute had been approved in 1971, and what a particularly stark contrast that was from the dramatic events of 1970. NARAL activists such as Gidding and Kansas's Biddy Hurlbut, an outspoken supporter of Lucas's, also traded fears that perhaps both Lucas and Sarah Weddington were privately much more pessimistic about the chances that the Supreme Court would actually address the basic constitutional issues of abortion in *Roe* and *Doe* than they wanted openly to admit.

Then, within one six-day period in mid-September, just two weeks before the beginning of the Supreme Court's 1971 term, first Hugo Black and then John Harlan suddenly resigned from the Court because of rapidly deteriorating health. Black died just one week after stepping down, and the two departures transformed a nine-justice court into a seven-member bench to which conservative Republican President— and professed abortion opponent—Richard M. Nixon would now have the opportunity to nominate two new potential apostles. Abortion lawyers who had seen or heard of Black's questioning of Joe Nellis at *Vuitch* had never counted the elderly Alabamian—and *Griswold* dissenter—as a potential supporter, but John Harlan had seemed a winnable vote. The possibility that Richard Nixon would nominate even one justice who might be willing to extend *Griswold* to abortion seemed close to nonexistent.

NARAL's annual meeting, however, which convened in Washington the day before the Supreme Court began its 1971 term, featured far more discussion of Roy Lucas than of the forthcoming changes at the high court. Former ASA executive director Ruth Smith led an effort to revive Lucas's consideration for the NARAL board, and overcame opposition from both Cyril Means and Larry Lader to win agreement that a mail ballot on Lucas's status would be distributed to the entire national membership. Lucas portrayed that outcome as a signal victory, and told his Minnesota supporters that the battle was really "an effort by a handful" of New Yorkers "to harass me because they feel left out of the national litigation program. Quite frankly, I have ignored this clique" and what Lucas viewed as their false efforts to claim undue credit and public attention. In response, "the New York clique, having nothing else to do, and obsessed with malicious fantasies, has set out to malign my reputation and interfere with my work," especially with regard to the Madison Institute's fund-raising efforts. "My job is to be an advocate in court, not a businessman nor a politician," Lucas professed. "In matters of business and politics I have little competence."

Larry Lader's public focus at the NARAL meeting was on how abortion availability, now relatively good on both coasts thanks to the California situation as well as New York and D.C., had to be expanded in the Midwest, where only Dr. Kennan's clinic in Madison and Dr. Weller's operation in Kansas City offered readily available service. Lader announced that NARAL's top priority for 1972 would be to achieve repeal in Michigan, and in furtherance of that end longtime Detroit provider Dr. Ed Keemer was introduced to the press as a physician who now would openly perform "mental health" abortions for a significant number of women. Several weeks later, in preparation for the referendum on Lucas, both Lucas and his opponents mailed statements to the entire NARAL membership, with Lucas decrying "pointless and destructive infighting" and defending his representation of the for-profit referral services. "The existence of commercial agencies is obvious proof that they are needed and that they often provide cheaper abortions than non-profit groups," Lucas claimed. His adversaries' rebuttal noted how the federal courts had upheld New York state's ban on such agencies and sought to claim the moral high ground: "If we are to stand behind *free* abortion referrals, we cannot have any board member making high personal fees from a defense of commercial referrals." Privately, however, many participants acknowledged that the vote was as much a referendum on Roy Lucas as on commercial referral services. North Carolina's Art Jones, the 1967 reform law sponsor who had become first a repealer and then a 1970 plaintiff in the *Corkey* case against his own statute, confidentially notified Lee Gidding that he would resign from NARAL's board should the vote go against Lucas. "I feel it would be hard to find a person who has done more for repeal in this country than Roy."[48]

Sarah Weddington traveled from Austin to Washington to attend the NARAL meeting and took the opportunity to attend the opening day of the Supreme Court's term and get an eyewitness look at the way in which oral arguments were conducted. She too, like Lucas a few months earlier, had now been formally admitted to the Court's bar, and during her visit she had a chance to chat with one of the ranking officials in the clerk's office, who told her that *Roe* and *Doe* might well be postponed until the Court was back up to full strength and that her and Lucas's motion for additional oral argument time was unlikely to be approved. Sarah and Ron's effort to launch their Austin law practice was getting off to an extremely slow and unremunerative start, and while the Madison Institute was now so bereft of funds that Sarah's ostensible halftime job was a monetary fiction, the resulting state of affairs had left her with time for a mid-September visit to Dallas to see Marsha King and meet Norma McCorvey. Marsha had just been prominently featured in the Dallas press—"a diminutive brunette," the *Dallas Morning News* called her—when the WEAL chapter of which she was president had filed sex discrimination complaints with the U.S. Treasury Department charging that a significant number of Texas banks—including two of Dallas's largest, Republic National Bank and First National Bank—had absolutely no female directors or officers. Sarah shared with Marsha, as with Ruth Bowers in San Antonio and Ginny Whitehill, her growing doubts about Roy Lucas and the Madison Institute. No one was at all certain about *Roe*'s prospects in the Supreme Court, and the upcoming nomination and likely Senate confirmation of two more Nixon-selected jurists was even further discouraging.[49]

In late September the Utah declaratory judgment case was tossed out by a federal three-judge panel,[50] and then, on October 12, with only Justices Brennan and Douglas dissenting, the Supreme Court refused to hear Lucas's appeal of Dr. Vuitch's 1969 abortion conviction in Maryland, which the state's highest court had affirmed eleven months earlier. Lucas immediately filed a habeas corpus petition on Vuitch's behalf in federal district court in Maryland, thus blocking any effort by the state to move toward actual imposition of Vuitch's earlier one-year jail sentence and five-thousand-dollar fine. Vuitch himself told reporters that abortion was "a private matter between the physician and the patient," and confidently declared that "I may have lost the battle, but I'm going to win the war."[51]

The same day that the high court dismissed Vuitch's appeal, the justices denied Weddington and Lucas's request for additional argument time in *Roe*.[52] A few days later, both Dorothy Beasley on behalf of Georgia and Jay Floyd on behalf on Texas, finally filed their Supreme Court briefs after having obtained deadline extensions just as Lucas and Hames had done during the summer. Beasley, who had argued—and lost—her first Supreme Court case, involving a Georgia motor vehicle statute, seven months earlier against Elizabeth Rindskopf, one of the initial *Doe* attorneys, had hoped for an even longer extension, for up until Justices Black and Harlan's retirements, she had been scheduled to argue *two* major death penalty cases, *Furman* v. *Georgia* and

Jackson v. *Georgia*, on October 12. The capital punishment cases were, along with *Roe* and *Doe*, the major public issue on the Court's docket, but the diminution of the Court to seven members had quickly led to an order postponing that argument until such time as the court returned to full strength. That action had underlain the prognostication Sarah Weddington had been given that the abortion cases too would be held until Nixon's nominees were chosen and confirmed, but it more importantly had allowed Dorothy Beasley somewhat more time to polish her seventy-nine-page *Doe* brief before submitting it on October 15.[53]

Dorothy Beasley's solid but unremarkable submission was produced wholly in Atlanta, but the fifty-eight-page brief filed on behalf of Henry Wade and the state of Texas on October 19 had been composed in a somewhat more unusual way. Jay Floyd, the assistant attorney general who had had responsibility for *Roe*—as well as some fifty to sixty other cases—since the initial Dallas hearing, had started out with no particular feelings about abortion one way or the other, but by the time that the Dallas panel had rendered its decision, Floyd had become firmly convinced of the fetus's right to life and resolutely antiabortion. As early as June of 1970 one of Floyd's superiors in the attorney general's office had made initial contact with a Washington-based lawyer for the National Right to Life Committee, Martin F. McKernan, Jr., and a year later, in July of 1971, as Floyd was about to get to work on Texas's brief for the Supreme Court, McKernan traveled to Austin to meet with him and to recommend that Floyd include a significant amount of medical information concerning fetal development during pregnancy.

By early September, however, Floyd had not yet been able to get started on the *Roe* brief, but through McKernan's good offices he had been introduced to two partners in a Chicago law firm, Dennis J. Horan and Jerome A. Frazel, Jr., who were planning to submit an amicus brief in defense of the Texas antiabortion statute of behalf of some 222 physicians and who had authored a similar submission in *Vuitch*. They graciously offered to assist Floyd in preparing the state's brief, and on September 9 Frazel wrote Floyd to tell him that

> We are just about ready to send you the two sections of your brief, which we discussed on the telephone. The doctor from Mayo Clinic, who we've been working with, has done a very comprehensive job on rebutting the claim that induced abortions are not a health hazard any longer to the mother, and we have sharpened up our scientific information concerning the nature of the unborn child. Hopefully we will have these things in such a form that if you have the room you could just insert them without any further work.

"Our plan," Frazel went on, "still is to perhaps reproduce the sections as a separate amicus brief" on behalf of the physicians. "The material will be read in your brief, whereas it will just be part of the record in our amicus brief." Six other antiabortion amicus briefs were also being prepared, and Frazel noted that the likelihood was that "this avalanche of *amici* briefs will probably go for naught since they will not be able to read them all."

One week after that letter, Frazel's senior partner, Dennis Horan, followed through on his colleague's promise and sent Floyd an initial package:

> I am enclosing the first part of the medical [sic] for inclusion in the Texas brief. The medical [sic] has been brought up-to-date and revised from what you have previously seen in our amicus brief in *U.S.* v. *Vuitch*.
>
> We have written this medical [sic] referring directly to the Texas case so that it can be, if you desire, given directly to your printer without revision. However, you may want to draft your own beginning and conclusion.

"The second part of the medical [sic]," Horan explained, "concerning medical complications of abortion is in its final revision and will be forwarded to you shortly." If Floyd had any questions about what they were sending him, Horan added, "please call me collect." Five days later, Horan mailed Floyd "the second part of the medical [sic]" as well. "Once again," he said, "it has been tailored to fit the Texas situation, but feel free to make whatever changes you feel are necessary," and do "call me collect" if any problems appeared. Horan additionally sent Floyd eight pages from a lengthy antiabortion book that he felt "substantially repudiated" Cyril Means's historical work, and advised Floyd that in light of Justices Black and Harlan's resignations, "the presently sitting Justices would probably divide 4 to 3 against the Texas statute." Hence, "We are wondering if perhaps you ought to consider getting another extension of time in order to give President Nixon time to fill those two appointments in the hope that these two successors would support the Texas statute."[54]

Given the amount of material sent from Chicago to Austin, it was perhaps as unsurprising as it was notable that more than forty percent of Texas's brief in *Roe* v. *Wade*—approximately twenty-five of its fifty-eight pages—directly duplicated material that was also submitted to the *Roe* Court in the amicus brief filed by attorneys Horan and Frazel. While the overlap was most visible with regard to how the two briefs both used ten identical photographs of fetal development which the

Chicagoans had sent to Floyd, the lengthier seventy-nine-page amicus brief went on to offer even more detail about fetal growth than Floyd's heavily illustrated submission. For better or worse, however, the first half of Texas's brief was an original composition, and it straightforwardly argued that "the fetus is a human being" and "the right to life of the unborn child is superior to the right of privacy of the mother." Texas's presentation was marred by a number of glaring typographical errors—well-known Supreme Court decisions such as *Flast* v. *Cohen* and *Barrows* v. *Jackson* repeatedly became *"Flask"* and *"Burrows"*—but Floyd took on the *Griswold* analogy with forthrightness if not with perfect grammar: "Prevention of abortion does not entail . . . state interference with the right of marital intercourse, nor does enforcement of the statute requiring [sic] invasions of the conjugal bedroom." The most impressive of the six amicus filings, by Alfred L. Scanlan of Washington's Shea and Gardner on behalf of the National Right to Life Committee, made the same point more succinctly: "The Texas and Georgia abortion statutes do not affect the sexual relationships of husband and wife."[55]

On October 21, President Nixon went on nationwide television to announce his two nominees for the Black and Harlan vacancies on the Supreme Court: sixty-four-year-old Lewis F. Powell, Jr., a politically moderate Virginian who had once served as president of the American Bar Association, and forty-seven-year-old William H. Rehnquist, an extremely conservative assistant attorney general who had served as a law clerk for Justice Robert H. Jackson two decades earlier. Nixon had publicly broached several far less qualified candidates prior to actually naming Powell and Rehnquist, and Powell's selection was greeted with considerable praise, both because of his establishment credentials as a private practitioner and because his opposition to segregation while serving as chairman of the Richmond Public School Board and his involvement with the National Legal Aid and Defender Society made clear that he was no one's predictable conservative. Self-effacing and oftentimes almost shy, Powell drew almost no opposition, whereas Rehnquist, who had assisted in framing many of the Nixon administration's most controversial "law and order" policy proposals, was undeniably well to the right of any sitting justice. Joe Nellis sent Cyril Means a deeply pessimistic letter, advising that with regard to Powell and Rehnquist "I know of nothing in their backgrounds that would give any supporter of abortion law repeal or reform any comfort or hope for a favorable judicial solution." Justices Douglas and Stewart, Nellis said, were probably the only supportive members of the high court, and "I have the feeling that favorable court rulings turned the corner in 1970 and that the going will be heavy and downhill from here on in most jurisdictions, and particularly in the Supreme Court."[56]

While both sides in the abortion cases seemed fearful of judicial setbacks, in late October the *New York Times* gave front-page coverage to how the results of the first major national public opinion poll in several years to ask Americans about their views on abortion had revealed "a dramatic change in public attitudes," with a full *50 percent* now saying that during the early stages of pregnancy, the choice should be left to a woman in consultation with her doctor.[57] That news did little to lift the spirits of abortion litigators who were wondering whether the as yet unscheduled arguments in *Roe* and *Doe* would indeed be postponed until Senate confirmation of the Powell and Rehnquist nominations had returned the Court to full strength. Roy Lucas wrote Sarah Weddington to express new concern that the Court "may be interested in these cases primarily for purposes of defining federal jurisdiction," and then on November 2 the attorneys received additional bad news when the constitutionality of the Texas antiabortion law was expressly upheld in a decision affirming a Houston doctor's 1969 conviction by the Texas Court of Criminal Appeals, the highest state forum for such cases. The Texas court ignored the Dallas federal panel's 1970 ruling against the statute and instead cited Judge Campbell's dissent in the Illinois federal case, *Doe* v. *Scott*, as support for its conclusion that the state had a compelling interest in protecting fetal life. Ginny Whitehill criticized the decision in the Dallas press, calling it "a step backward in the struggle for human dignity" and the "right to choose," but antiabortion lawyers such as Al Scanlan notified Jay Floyd that the Texas court's reaffirmation of the statute was powerful grounds for asserting that the now arguably immaterial Dallas decision in *Roe* failed to present a "substantial federal question" and hence should not even be reviewed by the Supreme Court.[58]

A concerned Sarah Weddington sent a copy of the Texas court's opinion to Cyril Means along with a note describing how she had happened to meet a young new University of Texas law professor, Scott Powe, who had been one of Hugo Black's 1970–1971 law clerks. "He felt it would be inappropriate for him to discuss the cases," Weddington related, but he "did say 'good luck' in a way that silently added, 'because you are going to need it.'" She was also worried, Weddington explained, about Austin rumors that a prominent Texas law professor with substantial Supreme Court experience, Charles Alan Wright, might argue *Roe* on behalf of the state rather than Jay

Floyd. Privately, Weddington was more preoccupied with the issue of whether she and Lucas could split their side of the argument even though the motion for additional time had been rejected. "There is a Supreme Court Rule," Weddington explained to Ginny Whitehill, "that allows two people to argue a case by special permission of the Court where several parties are involved, so I'm contemplating that, much as Roy isn't going to like the idea." In late October Weddington called Lucas to broach that possibility. "I just told Roy I was going to draft a request for special permission to submit—he didn't say any-thing," Weddington subsequently told Whitehill.

One week later, however, Lucas sent Sarah a long letter articulating why he and not she should of course argue *Roe*. He began by rebutting what he knew were Cyril Means's various aspersions upon his court-room track record. Means, Lucas said, has been "consorting too much with people like Joe Nellis and Larry Lader who, like him, would have much more of the limelight they so desperately need if I were not alive. It is pitiful that they cannot put aside their animosity against a 'young upstart' to work for the common goal." He had also heard, Lucas said, "that Cyril has been trying to get you to persuade me to give up half of my time for the *Roe* argument. He should realize, however, how ama-teurish it looks to have a parade of different counsel getting up and down for argument." In *Roe*, Lucas went on,

> I have been working for a long time to prepare argument by keeping up with the developments in jurisdiction and on the merits, not to men-tion the fast-moving medical aspects of the question. There is no reason for multiple counsel, as I am certain you realize. It is enough of a burden for me to have to worry about the views of the nine different justices, the questions each might ask, the way to weave the argument into responses to questions, etc., without having to worry about what anoth-er counsel will say or how another counsel might respond to a difficult question.

Lucas's conclusion pulled out almost all the stops:

> It has taken me virtually years to read and absorb everything which might be relevant to the case, and it would be wasteful to not make full use of this experience. As I indicated before, you should be relatively well-prepared on all of the issues in the case in the event that I go down in an airplane accident, but every maxim of appellate advocacy demands that the case be presented by one attorney, and that the attorney be the most thoroughly prepared. This is particularly necessary when we know full well that the *Doe* case is in less than fully capable hands. While I like

Margie Hames as a person, her inexperience in this area of litigation frightens me. It seems almost irresponsible for her to risk such an important issue by preparing so little.

If Cyril has been "working on you" as I have been told, I trust you will put the best interests of the cause over any personal desires in the matter and will straighten him out. It would be a serious mistake to divide the argument, and it is completely out of the question.[59]

On November 15, the clerk's office at the Supreme Court notified the attorneys in both *Roe* and *Doe* that oral arguments in the cases had been scheduled for Monday, December 13, and asked for written confirmation of which lawyer would argue for each side. Roy Lucas promptly replied that in *Roe* "oral argument for appellants will be presented by Roy Lucas," but two days later, just before word of the scheduling reached Texas, Marsha King visited Austin to attend a meeting and while there discussed the subject with Sarah Weddington. "Marsha told me she wanted me to do the oral argument, but I was still inclined to let Roy do it," Weddington explained in a letter to Ginny Whitehill three days later. "Then everybody found out about the date having been set, and before I talked to her Marsha sent Roy a telegram saying they wanted me to do the oral argument."

Marsha's November 22 telegram was as unpleasant a shock as Roy Lucas had ever received. "David King had written a letter to me on behalf of Marsha and himself only a few weeks earlier, stating that he and Marsha were looking forward to hearing me argue and thanking me for the work I had done," Lucas recalled eight months later. "Yet, when I called him in response to their telegram, I was accused of being a sexist for asking to talk to him, and Marsha denied that there had been any understanding other than that" Sarah would present the case. "That was less than the complete truth," Lucas asserted in his subsequent rendition, for "I had the contrary in writing from them."

Lucas's November 23 phone conversation with Marsha had quickly turned unpleasant. Many of Marsha's comments about why Sarah rather than Roy should present the argument echoed Cyril Means's assertions about Lucas's shortcomings to an amazing extent. Roy tried to convince Marsha that she should speak with any number of people who were familiar at firsthand with Lucas's courtroom skills, such as Jane Hodgson, before firmly making up her mind, and later that day Sarah sent Ginny Whitehill an update explaining that the outcome was still unclear. "I have very conflicting emotions about it," Sarah confessed. "I would really like to do the oral argument and I am tremendously pleased that Marsha wants me to do it so much—but I really dislike the hassle. We'll just have to see what works out. It appears I may do it. My stomach is already in knots."

The following day, the Wednesday before Thanksgiving, Marsha and David King met with Linda Coffee in Dallas to discuss their choice. Like Marsha, Linda had by now heard the fourth or fifthhand story, just like Cyril Means had told Margie Hames six months earlier, that the justices themselves actively disliked Lucas because of his *Vuitch* behavior and that any case for which he spoke might thereby suffer. Marsha had touched base with Norma McCorvey as well, and Linda concurred with Marsha's insistence that it would be better for all concerned if Sarah rather than Lucas argued their case. Linda suggested that the best way to implement their decision would be for her to send a formal letter of notification to the Supreme Court, and later that day she addressed just such a missive to Court clerk E. Robert Seaver. "I am the general counsel for Norma McCorvey, Marsha King, and David King, who are Appellants Jane Roe, Mary Doe, and John Doe respectively," Linda explained. "In such capacity I wish to inform the Court that each of my clients requests that Sarah Weddington present the oral argument." She indicated that she was sending copies of the letter to Lucas as well as to Fred Bruner and Roy Merrill, and concluded by stating that "It is my understanding that all counsel of record have been informed of the above and consent."

The Monday after Thanksgiving, Sarah Weddington called Robert Seaver at the Court and described the situation. "I told her to call Lucas + work it out—that I said it seemed she had the prior right," Seaver jotted down in a note. Following their conversation, Sarah tried unsuccessfully to reach Roy by phone, and then typed out a letter to Seaver confirming that she and not Lucas would present the oral argument. She reiterated that "I was one of the two women lawyers who originally filed" *Roe* and that "Mr. Lucas has been involved in the case only since the district court decision." She "had hoped to speak with Mr. Lucas before taking any action to change the designation of counsel," but as she had not succeeded in reaching him by phone, "I do not feel that I can wait longer." She dispatched copies of the message to Seaver to both Roy Merrill and to Lucas, with the latter accompanied by a brusque letter claiming that Lucas had repeatedly misled her about the Madison Institute. She asserted that "both my husband and I quit our jobs in Fort Worth in reliance on your promise of support," and she declared that she wanted to terminate her affiliation with the Institute in early 1972. The following day, prior to either of Weddington's letters being received, Robert Seaver wrote to her, with copies to both Coffee and Lucas, saying that as far as the Court was concerned, the matter was now settled: "In light of the letter I received from Linda N. Coffee dated November 23 and your call yesterday, your name is being listed as counsel who will argue for appellants" on December 13. That ratification of Marsha King's decision left a deeply despondent Roy Lucas feeling that his expertise would now go to waste, but the apparently victorious Sarah Weddington was anything but relieved. A day or two after her correspondence with Seaver, she phoned Roy Merrill to give him an update, and Merrill never forgot the call. "'I'm going to argue the case,'" Sarah told him, "and then she just broke down crying. I mean, just wept."[60]

Before either Sarah Weddington or the Supreme Court would have to confront the *Roe* and *Doe* arguments on December 13, however, a related matter of much lower visibility would receive the seven justices' full-scale consideration on November 17: Massachusetts's appeal from the First Circuit's decision in Bill Baird's case more than a year earlier voiding the state's anticontraception statute that exempted married couples but prohibited the distribution of contraceptives to single people. The high court had accepted the appeal almost nine months earlier, and the principal briefs as well as three amicus briefs in support of Baird had been submitted by the middle of the summer. Early in the fall, however, two senior figures who had long been active in population affairs, former Alaska Senator Ernest Gruening and retired General William Draper, had prevailed upon Baird to replace the Boston attorney who had represented him without charge in the B.U. case for more than four years, Joseph J. Balliro, with recently defeated Maryland Senator Joseph D. Tydings, a well-recognized, high-status figure on the Washington political scene. Baird felt badly about deserting Balliro, and Balliro himself initially tried to block the substitution, but by the end of October Tydings and his law firm had assumed full command of Baird's representation.

Harriet Pilpel and colleagues who had prepared an amicus brief on behalf of PPFA organized a moot court session for Tydings in advance of the real oral argument, but the most notable of the briefs filed in the case was the fourth and final amicus submission, written by John A. Robertson on behalf of the American Civil Liberties Union. ACLU legal director Mel Wulf had advised Robertson to "stick entirely to the privacy point," and Robertson, hoping to encourage a broadly worded as well as affirmative opinion, wrote a brief that inclusively championed "the fundamental nature of the right to privacy in the context of intimate sexual relationships." Robertson emphasized that the existing decisions in several abortion cases, including *Roe* and *Doe*, expansively read *Griswold* "as establishing a right of sexual privacy which extends to both married and single men and women" alike. If such a "right of sexual privacy" did indeed protect the contraceptive practices of single individuals as well as married couples, Baird's 1967 distribution of contraceptive foam to a young woman who was presumably unmarried might well invoke just as "fundamental" a right as the marital one so explicitly acknowledged in *Griswold*. Under the existing Massachusetts statute which the First Circuit had voided, Robertson coyly noted, "Newlyweds face the peculiar dilemma of having to see a doctor after their wedding and before their wedding night."[61]

When the Supreme Court argument of *Eisenstadt* v. *Baird* got underway on the afternoon of November 17, Massachusetts prosecutor Joseph R. Nolan tried to insist that Baird's status as a nonphysician was the key fact in the case. Justice Brennan peppered Nolan with questions to such an extent that the Massachusetts attorney all but completely lost his focus. Nolan sought to regain the initiative by contending that "there are some very dangerous sidelights and side effects to the use of many contraceptives" and that Baird's public distribution of the foam meant that "There is no right of privacy involved here with him. This is not a *Griswold* situation." Nolan's failure to make any headway under sustained questioning, however, led Brennan to lament that "I'm sorry, I just don't follow you, that's all." Nolan responded by admonishing the seven justices that "You certainly do not sit as a super legislature" to determine the wisdom of the Massachusetts law, nor was the Court "being asked to determine whether or not contraception is, per se, evil or in violation of the natural law," even though he and others *did* believe that it was "against the natural law." Chief Justice Burger sought to help him by observing that Nolan's strongest possible argument was that the purpose of the Massachusetts law was "to protect people from harmful substances at the hands of nonphysicians," but by that point most of Nolan's time had expired.

Former Senator Tydings began his argument by highlighting federal efforts to encourage contraceptive practices, and asserted that the state statute was "inherently unconstitutional because there is no compelling state reason for it." At three p.m. the argument adjourned until the following morning, at which time Justice Stewart rather openly agreed with Tydings about the seeming illogic of the Massachusetts law. Tydings concluded his remarks well before his time had expired by observing that "what the *Griswold* case really held was what Justice

Harlan said in his dissent back in *Poe*," but prosecutor Nolan, in his brief rebuttal comments, again sought to sever any linkage to *Griswold*. Baird's offense had not involved a married couple, the actual use of contraceptives, or a physician. "If there's any case that's distinguishable with ease, it's the *Griswold* case," he blithely asserted.[62]

The *Eisenstadt* arguments had been less than dazzling, and, aside from a reference by Tydings to the "unborn child," they had illuminated no apparent linkages between this possible offspring of *Griswold* and the upcoming abortion cases. When the justices convened on Friday for their private conference, Chief Justice Burger began the discussion of *Eisenstadt* by saying that he would vote to *sustain* the Massachusetts statute and reverse the First Circuit's decision, primarily because Baird was not a doctor and the state ought to be able to regulate the distribution of contraceptives. This was in the "medicinal field + [the] state can select the person to dispense the matter," Justice Douglas recorded Burger as explaining. Douglas himself succinctly asserted that he would affirm on First Amendment grounds the reversal of Baird's conviction, but Justice Brennan, while agreeing with Douglas about the result, said that he "can't go on that ground" because "the man did more than talk—he handed out a device," an action that under the Court's own precedents clearly fell outside the protection of the First Amendment. Instead, Brennan said, he would hold that Baird's conduct was within "the penumbra of *Griswold*."

Potter Stewart bluntly volunteered that the Massachusetts law reflected "complete irrationality" as there was no health basis for distinguishing between married and unmarried individuals' access to contraceptives nor had Massachusetts shown why items such as vaginal foam should only be prescribed by doctors. Like Brennan, Stewart said, he would rest on *Griswold*. Byron White, however, indicated that he would vote to reverse the decision below, for under a 1963 Court decision disavowing any judicial review of the wisdom of state regulation of commercial matters, a state could decide "that bread can be sold only by license" if it so chose. "That's all there is to this case," White declared, although he conceded that there "might be something" to Tydings's argument that federal policy strongly supported contraceptive availability.

Thurgood Marshall quickly stated that he would vote to affirm the First Circuit, and Harry Blackmun, seeming to indicate at least some ambivalence, said that it would be "better to affirm" since the Massachusetts law was "not a public health statute." Blackmun went on to say that he was "bothered by [the] fact that" under the law "a device may be prescribed only by doctors," and Byron White jumped in to reiterate that a state *could* "have it sold only through doctors" or require a license. White did admit that a state "cannot distinguish between married and unmarried," but Warren Burger asserted that "this is like cigarettes—a vendor's license is needed." Bill Douglas said that a while a state could control a commercial operation, what Baird had done "was only free speech." In frustration Burger said that he would pass rather than vote either to reverse or affirm, since he "can't discover what the issue is."[63]

The justices moved on to other cases without explicitly deciding what to do with *Eisenstadt*, although it was apparent that there was a clear majority of at least five votes—Douglas, Brennan, Stewart, Marshall, and Blackmun—for affirming the First Circuit's ruling in one way or another. William O. Douglas prepared a brief written statement of his views within four or five days of the conference discussion, but only on November 23, after Bill Brennan had discussed the situation with both Douglas and Burger, did everyone agree that Douglas—as the senior member of the apparent majority—would assign the case to Brennan for the preparation of a relatively brief per curiam opinion simply acknowledging that several different rationales underlay the formal affirmance. Burger now indicated that "My vote is a questionable reverse with a note 'could affirm—depends on how written,'" and Douglas acknowledged that the per curiam solution was the best method for "accommodating all different points of view," with the likelihood being that several separate concurring opinions would also be filed. Within three weeks Brennan's chambers had prepared a first-draft opinion of the court, but when it was circulated to his six sitting colleagues on December 13—the very same day that *Roe* and *Doe* were argued—only Thurgood Marshall and then Potter Stewart formally joined Brennan's statement. Some days later Chief Justice Burger distributed a note saying that he would eventually file a dissent or join one from Byron White, and by the final days of 1971 it was clear that *Eisenstadt* v. *Baird*, not a high-priority case to begin with, would not actually be decided or announced until sometime in the early spring of 1972.[64]

One person who had gone out of her way to attend the Supreme Court oral argument in *Eisenstadt* was Margie Hames, who—in distinct contradiction of Roy Lucas's private aspersions—had taken her responsibilities in preparing for the presentation of *Doe* v. *Bolton* with the utmost seriousness. At the recommendation of her longtime law school friend Fred Graham, who was now the Supreme Court correspondent of the *New York Times*, Hames also had gone up to

Washington one month earlier to observe the oral argument of an even lower-visibility gender discrimination appeal, *Reed v. Reed*, which the Court disposed of with a speed and brevity that failed to indicate the case's subsequent importance. Hames had carefully reviewed a transcript of the oral argument in *Vuitch*, and after attending the *Eisenstadt* presentation she went so far as to write the Florida attorney who was counsel in an obscenity case which was scheduled for argument the same day as *Doe* and *Roe*—and which the Court also had accepted at the very same time—to explore the potential jurisdictional similarities that might well in the Court's view link the otherwise disparate cases.[65]

Hames like Sarah Weddington had no excess optimism about what the Court might do with *Doe* and *Roe*, but on November 30, with the Powell and Rehnquist nominations still awaiting final confirmation votes on the Senate floor, Texas's Jay Floyd filed a formal motion with the Court expressly requesting that the *Roe* argument be postponed for several weeks until the two new justices were officially seated and the Court had returned to full strength. The "extreme importance" and "far-reaching effect" of any decision on the constitutionality of antiabortion statutes, Floyd said, suggested that a decision should come from an unabridged rather than an incomplete Supreme Court. Just such a motion had of course been recommended to Floyd nine weeks earlier by Dennis Horan, the Chicago attorney who had helped prepare so much of Texas's brief, but it was an issue all of the lawyers, and a good many journalists, had also pondered. Weddington began rooting against Floyd's request from the moment she learned of it, for she, like many other participants and observers, accepted the likely accuracy of prognostications that foresaw a favorable 4 to 3 majority on a seven-justice bench—Douglas, Brennan, Stewart, and Marshall versus White, Burger, and Blackmun—but an unfavorable 5 to 4 margin once Powell's and Rehnquist's votes were added to what otherwise would be a trio of dissenters. One medical weekly, without naming its observer, quoted a "Washington attorney" who candidly expressed Joseph Nellis's pessimistic outlook: "The successful constitutional challenges may have reached their peak. It looks to me like it's downhill for a while."

A few of the justices' own clerks wondered whether Floyd's motion might indeed be granted, but no justice chose to champion it, and on December 7—one day after the Senate had confirmed Lewis Powell's nomination by a vote of 89 to 1—the Court denied the request without dissent. That action was viewed as surprising by at least some journalistic observers, and it strongly reinforced the view that the Court might well be preparing to dispose of *Roe* and *Doe* on jurisdictional grounds rather than use the two appeals to reach the constitutional merits of abortion laws. Three days after the denial the Senate likewise confirmed William Rehnquist's considerably more controversial nomination by a margin of 68 to 26, but neither Rehnquist nor Powell would actually take their seats on the high court until after the first of the year, thus leaving *Roe* and *Doe* to be heard—and decided—by the seven-member bench.[66]

In the ten days preceding the Supreme Court hearing, considerable public attention was also directed toward a bevy of other abortion law developments. The *New York Times* published a prominent story on a twenty-three-year-old Florida woman, Shirley Wheeler, who had been criminally convicted and sentenced to two years' probation for having undergone an abortion and refusing to divulge who had performed the procedure. Nancy Stearns and Cyril Means were assisting with a further state court appeal, and the SWP's WONAAC group was attempting to capitalize on Wheeler's utterly unique legal victimization to draw attention to its own organizational existence. More ominously, Fordham University law professor Robert M. Byrn, a prolific Roman Catholic critic of any form of abortion law liberalization, filed suit against the New York law on December 3 in a court whose judge willingly appointed Byrn as the official legal "guardian" of all fetuses between four and twenty-four weeks of development which were scheduled for upcoming abortions in all of New York City's municipal hospitals. The New York press devoted considerable attention to Byrn, a forty-year-old bachelor who still lived with his mother, but Roy Lucas warned the city's principal attorney that "the *Byrn* case is not the aberration of one nut, but may be the beginning of an aggressive litigation program by a power group of zealots." Lucas himself was displaying no public bruises from his painful and privately humiliating denouement with Sarah Weddington and Marsha King, perhaps in part because he had two important state Supreme Court presentations of his own just days in advance of *Roe* and *Doe*. On December 7 he argued against the constitutionality of the South Dakota abortion statute in Pierre on behalf on Dr. Ben Munson, and two days later he appeared before the Minnesota Supreme Court in St. Paul on behalf of Jane Hodgson's effort to win a constitutionally based reversal of her criminal abortion conviction from one year earlier. That same week, the California Supreme Court heard argument on both of the two contrasting lower court rulings in *People* v. *Pettegrew* and *People* v. *Barksdale*, the former of which had affirmed the constitutionality of the state's

1967 reform statute and the latter of which had voided it. An overflow crowd turned out for the hearing, and repeal proponents left the courtroom feeling decidedly optimistic, looking forward to a favorable constitutional ruling sometime in the first half of 1972.[67]

During the week leading up to the *Roe* and *Doe* arguments in Washington, Margie Hames in Atlanta and Sarah Weddington in Austin both made their final preparations. Sarah spent one long evening at the law school with six of her former professors throwing questions at her in an intensive moot court practice session, and she held several similar but far more informal dry runs with various other Austin friends. Sarah and Ron went up to Washington several days in advance of the actual hearing, and Cyril Means and Harriet Pilpel organized yet another moot court panel there for both Sarah and Margie. Sarah was very fearful that one or another justice would ask her a question for which she would not have an answer, and to Joe Nellis Sarah seemed "absolutely frightened" the day before the high court argument. That evening Sarah and Ron had dinner with Margie Hames and her husband so that the two attorneys would have a final opportunity to compare notes and agree upon which points one or the other would try to make in their successive arguments, and the next morning Sarah, along with Linda Coffee, arrived at the Supreme Court building more than an hour before the ten a.m. starting time for *Roe*'s oral argument.[68]

In a way the scene in the Supreme Court's impressive but intimate courtroom on Monday morning, December 13, included a significant number of the people who had helped bring the movement for abortion law repeal to the brink of victory. Sandra Bensing, Norma McCorvey, and Dr. Hallford were all unsurprisingly absent, but Ruste Kitfield and Judy and Peter Bourne, along with a slew of Margie Hames's legal colleagues—Tobi Schwartz, Reber Boult, Gale Siegel, and Pam Walker—were all on hand to represent *Doe*, and Marsha and David King, along with Ginny Whitehill, Ruth Bowers, Roy Merrill, and Fred Bruner had all made the trip up from Texas. Bob Hall, Jimmye Kimmey, Cyril Means, and Harriet Pilpel were among the group from New York, and Jane Hodgson was in town from Minnesota. A subdued Roy Lucas would join Sarah and Linda as the third attorney sitting at the counsel's table at the front of the courtroom, and most of the young men who had comprised the Madison Institute's summer staff—Nick Danforth, Brian Sullivan, and Dan Schneider—were in the audience as well. Only Dorothy Beasley and one assistant were on hand for Georgia, and Jay Floyd was almost alone on behalf of Texas, as neither Henry Wade nor John Tolle had seen any point in making the trip. Dennis Horan, however, had come from Chicago, and both Father James McHugh of the U.S. Catholic Conference and Alfred Scanlan, who had prepared the amicus brief of the National Right to Life Committee, were also in attendance.[69]

At a few moments after ten, Chief Justice Burger announced that the seven-member bench would hear argument in *Roe* v. *Wade* and called upon Sarah Weddington. Sarah began her thirty-minute presentation in a firm and confident voice, and the first question directed to her came from Burger himself, who asked whether *Vuitch* disposed of some of *Roe*'s issues. Sarah said no, since the D.C. statute, unlike Texas's more restrictive one, included that crucial word "health," and she took the opportunity Burger had provided to also note that the recent affirmation of the Texas law by the state Court of Criminal Appeals in *Thompson* had expressly rejected a vagueness challenge. Sarah then moved on to a point she had specially prepared for, and told the justices that "a pregnancy to a woman is perhaps one of the most determinative aspects of her life. It disrupts her body, it disrupts her education, it disrupts her employment, and it often disrupts her entire family life." "Because of the impact on the woman," she continued, "this certainly, in as far as there are any rights which are fundamental, is a matter which is of such fundamental and basic concern to the woman involved that she should be allowed to make the choice as to whether to continue or to terminate her pregnancy."

Sarah had stated the personal essence of her argument clearly and succinctly, but Potter Stewart brought her up short with a polite but pointed comment. "Mrs. Weddington, so far, on the merits, you've told us about the important impact of this law, and you've made a very eloquent policy argument against it. I trust you are going to get to what provisions of the Constitution you rely on." Sarah replied by referring to the Ninth Amendment and citing a brand-new historical article by Cyril Means which contended that as of 1791, when the Ninth Amendment was ratified, no common law prohibition against abortion existed in America. She moved on to mention *Griswold*, and acknowledged that since "it appears that the members of the Court in that case were obviously divided as to the specific constitutional framework of the right which they held to exist," hence "I'm a little reluctant to aspire to a wisdom that the Court did not, was not in agreement on. I do feel," she continued, "that the Ninth Amendment is an appropriate place for the freedom to rest. I think the Fourteenth Amendment is equally an appropriate place, under the right of persons to life, liberty, and the pursuit of happiness," a phrase that actually appeared in the

Declaration of Independence, and not in the Fourteenth Amendment. "I think," Sarah went on, that "in as far as liberty is meaningful, that liberty to these women would mean liberty from being forced to continue the unwanted pregnancy."

Stewart asked her if she was relying "simply on the due process clause of the Fourteenth Amendment." Sarah answered that "We had originally brought the suit alleging both the due process clause, equal protection clause, the Ninth Amendment, and a variety of others." "And anything else that might obtain," Stewart interjected, drawing laughter from the audience and a laughing "Yes" from Weddington herself. Sarah repeatedly cited both the Ninth and Fourteenth Amendments, and stated that "I think in as far as the Court has said that there is a penumbra that exists to encompass the entire purpose of the Constitution, that I think one of the purposes of the Constitution was to guarantee to the individual the right to determine the course of their own lives."

Sarah made a second reference to Means's article when one justice asked whether there was any legislative history as to what the state interest was in enacting the law in the nineteenth century, and when both Justices Stewart and White inquired as to whether the state had a proper interest in protecting the fetus during at least some stages of pregnancy, Weddington sought to elude the issue of stages by pointing out that the Texas statute made no such distinction in prohibiting *all* abortions except those necessary to save a pregnant woman's life. Pressed several times more on the matter, Sarah finally conceded that "Obviously I have a much more difficult time saying that the state has no interest in late pregnancy." Why is that, White asked her. "I think it's more the emotional response to a late pregnancy, rather than it is any constitutional" consideration, Sarah answered. She made another reference to how Means's article showed that the Constitution "attaches protection to the person at the time of birth" and not any earlier, and then she proceeded to articulate how a federal court injunction against the state statute was the only legal remedy open to Texas women, for Texas law included no declaratory judgment process and women themselves could not be charged as criminal defendants under the state abortion law. She had time to mention again the recent state court affirmance in *Thompson*, and then her thirty minutes were over.

Jay Floyd began his presentation with an ostensibly deferential comment that many listeners thought was inappropriate. "It's an old joke, but when a man argues against two beautiful ladies like this, they are going to have the last word." Margie Hames found the remark "very chauvinistic," and later recounted that "I thought Burger was going to come right off the bench at him. He glared him down. He got the point right away that this was not appropriate in that court." Floyd moved on to assert that "Mary and John Doe" lacked any standing to challenge the Texas law and that "Jane Roe's" claim was moot once she was no longer pregnant. Potter Stewart, however, immediately challenged Floyd's suggestion of mootness by noting that *Roe* was a class action and that the Court could of course "take judicial notice of the fact that there are at any given time unmarried pregnant females in the state of Texas." Floyd nonetheless tried to pursue his mootness point, and Stewart asked "what procedure would you suggest for any pregnant female in the state of Texas ever to get any judicial consideration of this constitutional claim?" Floyd responded that "I do not believe it can be done," and then added that "I think she makes her choice prior to the time she becomes pregnant." Stewart immediately shot back that "Maybe she makes her choice when she decides to live in Texas," and laughter filled the courtroom. Floyd somewhat testily—"May I proceed?"—tried to regain the floor, but Stewart jabbed him again, observing that "There's no restriction on moving, you know."

Floyd finally was able to continue, but in contrast to Sarah Weddington's smooth and articulate presentation, Floyd spoke slowly and at times haltingly, despite having prepared a detailed outline of what he hoped to cover. He readily volunteered that he had "no idea" as to whether the protection of the fetus was the original, nineteenth-century intent of the Texas statute, and as both Justices Stewart and Marshall pressed him to identify what state interests presently underlay the law, Floyd's exposition became more and more hesitant. Pushed to identify precisely when fetal "life" commenced, he conceded that "there are unanswerable questions in this field," which drew audience laughter, and when Justice Marshall answered that "I appreciate it," Floyd tried to back pedal, saying "This is an artless statement on my part." Marshall replied "I withdraw the question," which generated further laughter. Floyd stumbled again in erroneously suggesting that the lower court decision in the North Carolina case, *Corkey* v. *Edwards*, had somehow been affirmed by the Supreme Court, and then Stewart pointedly noted how Texas's abortion ban included no exception for women who had been raped. "Such a woman wouldn't have had a choice, would she?" he pointedly asked Floyd, and by the time that Floyd attempted to articulate a response, his thirty minutes had expired.

With only a moment's pause as the attorneys changed places, the

Court proceeded immediately to the oral argument of *Doe* v. *Bolton*. Tobi Schwartz and Reber Boult joined Margie Hames at the front table, and while Margie like Sarah later acknowledged that at first she "was very frightened," Margie's description of "Mary Doe's" situation and *Doe*'s lower court record proceeded smoothly. She emphasized that "our appeal here is directed primarily at the procedural requirements left standing by the District Court," especially the Georgia law's requirement that each doctor-sanctioned abortion also receive the endorsement of two other physicians and the approval of a three-member hospital committee. Hames explained that any claim of a "compelling state interest" in protecting the fetus was clearly untenable in a situation where a reform statute explicitly sanctioned the "therapeutic" abortions of many fetuses, but she directed most of her fire at the shortcomings of three-judge panel's ruling, and not at the state's contravening arguments. "It is our contention that the procedural requirements left standing by the court below have virtually manipulated out of existence the right to terminate an unwanted pregnancy," she told the justices. "These procedures are so cumbersome, costly, and time-consuming as to" deny "Mary Doe" and other women like her the Fourteenth Amendment due process liberty right that the *Doe* panel ostensibly had recognized in its basic holding against the Georgia reform law.

Dorothy Beasley began her argument just before the Court's noontime lunch break. Beasley in her first sentence emphasized that *the* issue in *Doe* was "the value which is to be placed on fetal life," and Beasley's remarkably vibrant and high-pitched voice gave her presentation an energetic and articulate air that outshone the three speakers who had preceded her. She devoted considerable attention to the fetus, and she tackled the *Griswold* issue quite directly: "A person has a right to be let alone, certainly," Beasley acknowledged, "but not when another person is involved, or another human entity is involved." After the luncheon recess Justice Douglas questioned her assertion that *Doe* no longer presented an actual controversy, and when Beasley sat down Margie Hames used her one remaining minute to recommend Cyril Means's new article to the justices and to remind them that "the right of privacy, as enunciated in *Griswold*, of course, is our basic reliance."[70]

The *Roe* and *Doe* attorneys were generally pleased with their presentations and understandably relieved to have gotten through them without any significant difficulties. Several supportive onlookers thought that the undeniable weakness of Floyd's exposition had given the *Roe* and *Doe* plaintiffs the better of the arguments, but other supporters conceded privately that Dorothy Beasley probably had been the most impressive speaker of the four. Weddington herself was inclined to count only Douglas and Stewart as all-but-certain yes votes, and a number of courtroom observers were far from sure that there was any majority, even on the seven-justice court, in favor of striking down either the Texas and/or Georgia abortion laws. Roy Lucas told two acquaintances that "It appeared to me unlikely from the tenor of oral arguments . . . that any earthshaking landmarks on the merits would be forthcoming soon," and while Lucas's pessimistic reaction was perhaps otherwise explainable, he nonetheless observed that "a decision to remand both cases to the Fifth Circuit appears more likely" than a ruling on the merits. Few other principals were quite that gloomy, and later in the day the Hameses held a reception for both the *Roe* and *Doe* supporters in their suite at the Hays-Adams Hotel. That evening Ruth Bowers gave a dinner at an Arlington steak house for all of the Texans, including Marsha and David King, as well as several of the Madison Institute's summer alumni, but Lucas understandably was not among the guests.[71]

Far more important than the reactions of the *Roe* and *Doe* supporters to the oral arguments were the reactions of the seven members of the Supreme Court, and on Thursday morning December 16, one day ahead of their normal Friday schedule, the justices convened for their private conference on the cases in which they had heard argument that week. Warren Burger began the discussion of *Roe* by summarizing the statuses of the different plaintiffs—"Jane Roe," the "Does," and Dr. Hallford—and the decision of the Dallas panel. Burger then offered his own views, saying that the most notable of their procedural decisions earlier in the year, *Younger* v. *Harris*, barred any federal court relief for Dr. Hallford and that the three-judge court had been correct in concluding that the "Does" did not have standing to sue. "Jane Roe," however, certainly had standing, for, just as Sarah Weddington had stressed at oral argument, "she can't be prosecuted and [the] state gave her no remedy. She didn't lose standing through mootness," and, apropos of Potter Stewart's comment during the argument, the class of women whom Jane Roe represented undeniably contained some who presently had unwanted pregnancies. Nonetheless, Burger said, for the Dallas panel to have issued a "declaratory judgment without [an] injunction is tantamount to [a] mere advisory opinion." "Jane Roe," he went on, was entitled to an injunction if the Texas abortion statute was indeed unconstitutional. The "balance here," Burger explained, "is between [the] state's interest in protecting fetal life and [a] woman's interest in not having children." However, he asked, did an unmarried woman like "Jane Roe" "also represent married women" and, if so, "what of the husband's interest" in a situation "where he won't consent?" After all that, Burger nonetheless concluded by saying that he could *not* find the Texas statute either vague or otherwise unconstitutional although it was "certainly archaic and obsolete."

William O. Douglas immediately disagreed. The statute *was* unconstitutional, and abortion was "basically a medical, psychiatric problem." Pursuant to Stewart's argument in *Vuitch*, the Texas statute was unacceptably vague "unless it gives a licensed physician an immunity for good faith abortions." In Douglas's judgment, all of the *Roe* parties had standing, and *Younger* represented no obstacle to a decision in *Roe*. William J. Brennan essentially agreed. "Jane Roe" and the other plaintiffs all had standing, and the Texas law was clearly infirm, for it would not allow for an abortion even for a twelve-year-old or a woman who had been raped. Brennan said that he was willing to hold that the statute was unacceptably vague, but that he would vote to affirm the Dallas panel's decision except with regard to the "Does'" standing.

Potter Stewart was inclined to agree that both the "Does" and Dr. Hallford also had standing, but those issues should not confuse the discussion, he said, "if we agree [that the] unmarried girl has standing to get a judgment on the merits. She clearly has standing," and the Dallas panel had been correct in issuing a declaratory judgment but not an injunction. On the merits, Stewart remarked, he agreed with Bill Douglas, although of course a state could legislate at least to the extent of requiring that abortions be performed by doctors and that after a "certain period of pregnancy" a woman could not have an abortion.

Byron White agreed with Potter Stewart on all the preliminary matters, but took the other view on the merits. The plaintiffs "want us to say that women have [a] choice under [the] Ninth Amendment privacy argument" to "get rid of [the] child" wholly "apart from health reasons." Thus the real question, White said, was "does [the] state have [the] police power to protect [a] fetus that has life in it as opposed to [the] desire of the mother." White concluded by indicating that he was "not at rest on [the] merits," and that prompted Stewart to reiterate that a "state can legislate in this field—they can require that only doctors can do this," Justice Douglas recorded him as saying.

Thurgood Marshall agreed with Bill Douglas and Bill Brennan even though the "time problem concerns me." While he did "not see what interest [the] state has in abortion in [the] week after conception," he nonetheless wondered why a state could not prohibit abortion after a "certain stage," for "if [the] fetus comes out breathing," to "kill it is murder." Constitutionally, Marshall said, he would base their decision on Fourteenth Amendment liberty, for "'liberty' covers about any right to have things done to your body."

Harry Blackmun stated that he too agreed that since "Jane Roe" had standing, the Court did not have to concern itself with the married couple or the doctor. On the merits, Blackmun said, the central question was "can a state properly outlaw all abortions?" If one accepted the thesis that there *was* fetal "life" from conception onward, a "strong argument" could be made "that it can." But, he went on, "there are opposing interests—[the] right of [the] mother to life and to mental and physical health, [the] right of [the] parents in [a] case of rape, [the right of the] state in [a] case of incest." Disagreeing with Thurgood Marshall, Blackmun said that "there is no absolute right to do with one's body what you like." "Jane Roe," he explained, did have Fourteenth Amendment rights here, and on top of that the Texas law did "not go far enough to protect doctors." The statute also impinged on "Roe's" Ninth Amendment rights and he not only would affirm the Dallas panel's declaratory judgment but "could go so far as to grant an injunction" against the Texas statute. In closing, Blackmun observed that the Texas and Georgia statutes represented a stark contrast, for until the Georgia law had been "ruined" by the Atlanta panel's ruling, Georgia had had "a fine statute."

Warren Burger then moved immediately into the discussion of *Doe* v. *Bolton*. The Chief Justice said that while he believed that "Mary Doe" certainly had standing, he nonetheless did not agree with how the three-judge court had "carved up" the Georgia reform statute. The state, Burger went on, had "a duty to protect fetal life at some stage" and the Atlanta panel had given no clear reasons for truncating the 1968 law. In short, Burger said, he would hold that the Georgia measure was constitutional.

William O. Douglas readily conceded that "This is [a] much better statute than Texas," but he sought to emphasize that in light of *Doe*'s highly abbreviated record, we "don't know how this statute operates. Is it weighted on [the] side of only those who can afford this? What about the poor?" All in all, Douglas said, his preference would be to remand *Doe* to the three-judge court for a full evidentiary hearing on whether the Georgia law in practice was discriminatory.

Thurgood Marshall jumped in to say that while a measure like Georgia's might work in an urban center, in rural areas where "there are no negro doctors" Douglas's fear would be correct. Then Bill

Brennan, speaking in turn, stated that he would vote to affirm the Atlanta decision and that he also would take the further step of voiding Georgia's hospital committee approval requirement as too restrictive. Brennan added, however, that he would not reach the issue as to whether the woman's Ninth Amendment right was absolute.

Potter Stewart simply and succinctly stated that he agreed fully with Brennan, and Byron White began his remarks by observing that *Doe* was "a hard case." Nonetheless, a "state has [the] power to protect [the] unborn child," and the Georgia statute was clearly not burdensome to the woman, for "Mary Doe" had had no difficulty in getting her abortion request reviewed by the Atlanta doctors. White said he believed that Georgia had "struck the right balance here" in view of the fact that a state does have "the power to declare abortions illegal," and hence he would vote to reverse the three-judge court.

Justice Marshall briefly said that he would affirm, since his view was somewhere between Bill Douglas's and Bill Brennan's. Harry Blackmun, the final justice to speak, stated that "medically this statute is perfectly workable." He believed the doctor plaintiffs like "Mary Doe" also had standing to challenge the law, and that neither Georgia's residency requirement nor the hospital approval process really troubled him. Some cases, Blackmun told his colleagues, are "borderline" and doctors preferred "the security" that such a review board provided. What he would like to see, Blackmun went on, was an "opinion that recognizes [the] opposing interests in fetal life and [the] mother's interest in health and happiness." The Georgia law "strikes a balance that is fair," though he too would like to see factual findings on the points that Justice Douglas had noted. Blackmun explained that he was "sympathetic to [the] psychiatric people" and that the Court "should try to provide standards" for how a measure like Georgia's ought to operate. He would be "perfectly willing," Blackmun concluded, "to paint some standards and remand for lower court findings as to how it operates," particularly with regard to whether the Georgia measure did "deny equal protection by discriminating against the poor." Byron White chimed in that while equal protection was certainly a real issue with regard to the provision of some medical services, and while he was willing to remand for such a hearing, he was not sure that equal protection was really present as an issue here.[72]

The outcome of the conference discussion of *Roe* and *Doe* was much clearer with regard to the former than with regard to the latter. Bill Brennan tallied the votes in *Roe* as 6 to 1 to affirm, though his own notes, just like Bill Douglas's, undeniably showed that the actual division was 5 to 2, with both Byron White and a somewhat ambivalent Warren Burger favoring reversal of the Dallas panel's declaratory judgment. In *Doe*, however, where Brennan had simply scribbled a question mark, the bottom-line result was hard to categorize, for while there were three clear votes for affirming the declaratory judgment— Brennan, Stewart, and Marshall—and two for reversal—Burger and White—both Bill Douglas and Harry Blackmun had seemed to favor remanding the case so that a richer and more detailed record could be generated.

For William O. Douglas, the 1971 Term was witnessing the most congenial relations he had had with any one year's law clerks in almost a decade. Even more widely regarded as an aloof and unfriendly loner in 1971 than he had been six or ten years earlier at the time of *Griswold* and *Poe*, Douglas in the first few months of the 1971 Term had nonetheless already developed the habit of sitting down with his three clerks—Dick Jacobson, Bill Alsup, and Ken Reed—over an open bottle of vodka immediately upon returning from each of the justices' private conferences. This Thursday afternoon Douglas was in an especially good mood, for he had been very pleasantly surprised by Harry Blackmun's comments about both *Roe* and *Doe*. Many of the clerks— and at least some of the justices—still adhered to the largely dismissive "Minnesota Twin" view of Blackmun as a predictable conservative which had emerged eighteen months earlier when he had been nominated and confirmed to the high court, and hence for Blackmun to disagree with Warren Burger in an important case was a highly significant development. The clerks had found Blackmun to be a friendly and considerate man who even would invite them to join him at breakfast, but among some clerks there was increasing talk about whether Blackmun's painstakingly slow pace of work meant that the new justice was in over his head. Blackmun's unwillingness to delegate even his most mundane opinion-writing tasks to his clerks was causing him to devote much of his own time to highly detailed work on obscure or complicated cases such as *Port of Portland* v. *United States*, and clerks in other chambers felt considerable sympathy for their friends who worked for Blackmun.

One of Douglas's clerks, speaking with one of Blackmun's clerks prior to Douglas's late afternoon return from the conference, had come away from the conversation with an explicit impression that Blackmun, at least in his clerk's view, was very much hoping to write the Court's opinions in both *Roe* and *Doe*. Thus when Douglas sat down with his clerks to recount the conference discussion of the abortion cases and particularly Harry Blackmun's pleasantly surprising stance, the clerk passed along the report that Blackmun was eager to have the abortion opinions assigned to him. Since Warren Burger was clearly a member of the 5 to 2 minority in *Roe*, Douglas as the senior member of the majority would be responsible for assigning the opinion, and he had already mentioned to Potter Stewart—who in turn told his own clerks—that he was inclined to assign *Roe* to Blackmun as an acknowledgment of the significance of Blackmun's divergence from Burger. His clerk's report seemed to further reinforce Douglas's inclination, but the next day Douglas received an extremely rude surprise when Warren Burger's assignment list for the week's cases showed that the Chief Justice—despite his own remarks in conference—had taken it upon himself to assign *Roe* as well as *Doe* to Harry Blackmun.

Douglas was offended by Burger's erroneous presumption that both *Roe* and *Doe* were his and not Douglas's responsibility to assign, but while the assignment of *Roe* to Blackmun was exactly what Douglas himself had intended to do, Burger's further effrontery in assigning *Doe* to Blackmun was a far more serious problem, for—at least in Douglas's mind—Blackmun in *Doe* was in the minority rather than in what Douglas believed was the majority. Rethinking the conference discussion of *Doe* without any careful review of his own notes, Douglas convinced himself that the conference had yielded a clear 4 to 3 split in which Burger, White, and Blackmun had been the minority. "In summary," Douglas scrawled to himself, "WOD, WJB, PS & TM agreed that a state abortion law could require all abortions to be performed by a licensed physician, that a woman's psychological problems as well as her health problems must be considered"—which was actually a point that *Blackmun* had touched on during the *Doe* discussion—"and that some period must be prescribed protecting fetal life."

The next day, a Saturday, Douglas dictated a polite but pointed note to Burger about the Friday listing of *Doe* v. *Bolton*. "Dear Chief," he began. "As respects your assignment in this case, my notes show"—at least in Douglas's memory—"there were four votes to hold parts of the Georgia Act unconstitutional and to remand for further findings, e.g. on equal protection"—another point where Blackmun actually had agreed with Douglas. "Those four were Bill Brennan, Potter Stewart, Thurgood Marshall and me," Douglas stated. "There were three to sustain the law as written—you, Byron White, and Harry Blackmun," he asserted. "I would think, therefore, that to save further time and trouble, one of the four, rather than one of the three, should write the opinion."

In standard Court practice, Douglas sent copies of his note to all the other justices, and on Monday Warren Burger did the same with his letter of reply. "At the close of discussion" in *Doe*, he told Douglas, "I remarked to the Conference that there were, literally, not enough columns to mark up an accurate reflection of the voting in either the Georgia or the Texas cases. I therefore marked down no votes and said this was a case that would have to stand or fall on the writing, when it was done. That is still my view of how to handle these two . . . sensitive cases, which, I might add, are quite probable candidates for reargument" once newly confirmed Justices Powell and Rehnquist formally joined the Court shortly after New Year's. "However," Burger concluded, "I have no desire to restrain anyone's writing even though I do not have the same impression of views" as Douglas had maintained.[73]

Warren Burger's response ended the exchange about the desirability of *Doe* as well as *Roe* being assigned to Harry Blackmun, and at least in later years Blackmun himself would profess that at the time he "was not very pleased to have the assignment come to me" and that he had accepted it and set to work on the two opinions "without enthusiasm." None of his colleagues expected Blackmun to circulate any drafts for at least several months, but by Wednesday, December 22, just two days after Warren Burger's note, William O. Douglas, in his usual speedy fashion, already had a rough draft of a *Doe* opinion that he was ready to share privately with Bill Brennan. "Let me have any of your suggestions, criticisms, ideas, etc. and I will incorporate them, and then we can talk later as to strategy," Douglas volunteered in his cover letter. Douglas's hastily prepared draft featured a long quotation from his *Griswold* opinion invoking the right to privacy and far briefer citations to additional Supreme Court precedents in *Pierce*, *Skinner*, and *Loving*. Douglas directly quoted and endorsed the Atlanta panel's conclusion that *Griswold*-style privacy also applied to abortion, but he added that "the state has interests to protect" and that abortion "is a rightful concern of society. The woman's health is part of that concern; and the life of the fetus after quickening is another concern. These concerns justify the state in treating the problem as a medical one." With the Georgia law, however, "the difficulty is that the statute as construed and applied does not give full sweep to the 'psychological as well as physical well-being' which saved the concept 'health' from being void for vagueness" in *Vuitch*. Returning to the larger constitutional issue, Douglas wrote that "The right of privacy described in *Griswold* is a species of 'liberty' of the person as that word is used in the Fourteenth Amendment. It is a concept that acquires substance, not from the predilections of judges, but from the emanations of the various provisions of the Bill of Rights, including the Ninth Amendment. There is no 'liberty,' in the absolute sense, to do with one's body as one likes," Douglas went on, and with regard to abortion, "the 'liberty' of the mother, though rooted as it is in the Constitution, may be qualified by the state." However, "where fundamental personal rights and liberties are involved, the corrective legislation must be 'narrowly drawn,'" and Georgia could not require the sort of elaborate, hospital committee approval mechanism mandated by the 1968 statute. Where a "good-faith decision of the patient's chosen physician is overridden and the final decision passed on to others in whose selection that patient has no part," there would be "a total destruction of the freedom of association between physician and patient and the privacy which that entails," Douglas asserted. In conclusion, he added that the case should be remanded so that the Atlanta panel could further determine whether the Georgia procedure in practice also violated equal protection.

One week later Bill Brennan phoned Douglas to say that while he would be sending Douglas a long, written reaction to his initial draft the following day, it would be best not to distribute any revision until Blackmun circulated at least a first draft in *Roe*, even though that might be several months away. Douglas agreed, and Brennan's ensuing letter laid out a comprehensive and analytically impressive survey of all the questions raised by both *Roe* and *Doe*. None of the preliminary issues barred reaching the constitutional merits, and with regard to the Georgia provisions at issue in *Doe*, "I would strike all of those procedures down except for the requirement that the abortion be performed by a licensed physician." Constitutionally, Brennan said, they should rely upon privacy rather than the First Amendment, and should emphasize that "the statute infringes the right of privacy . . . because it limits abortions to enumerated cases," and the Atlanta panel had been correct in holding that Georgia could "not limit the number of reasons for which an abortion may be sought." With regard to privacy, Brennan went on,

> I agree with you that the right is a species of "liberty" (although, as I mentioned yesterday, I think the Ninth Amendment . . . should be brought into this problem at greater length), but I would identify three groups of fundamental freedoms that "liberty" encompasses: *first*, freedom from bodily restraint or inspection, freedom to do with one's body as one likes, and freedom to care for one's health and person; *second*, freedom of choice in the basic decisions of life, such as marriage,

divorce, procreation, contraception, and the education and upbringing of children; and, *third*, autonomous control over the development and expression of one's intellect and personality.

Brennan cited a number of precedents, particularly *Jacobson* v. *Massachusetts*, the 1905 vaccination case, which offered language that would support his first category, and he added that he would "peg the right to care for one's health and person to the right of privacy rather than directly to the First Amendment partly because (1) it would seem to be broader than the right to consult with, and act on the advice of, the physician of one's choice and include, for example, access to non-prescriptive drugs and (2) it identifies the right squarely as that of the individual, not that of the individual together with his doctor." They ought to avoid any such associational formulation, in favor of a privacy-based holding "that there is a fundamental interest in the individual's safeguarding his health."

With regard to his second major category, Brennan explained that they should rely upon *Loving*, *Griswold*, and other older precedents in addition to his own recently circulated opinion in *Eisenstadt* that so far only Marshall and Stewart—and not Douglas—had formally joined. Brennan gently emphasized that his *Eisenstadt* draft, "in its discussion of *Griswold*[,] is helpful in addressing the abortion question," and he politely noted that if Douglas "could find it possible to join" his opinion in addition to filing a concurrence, *Eisenstadt* would be assured of a majority among the seven-justice court since the likelihood of Harry Blackmun's joining the opinion remained uncertain.

For his third category, Brennan said simply that he would cite the 1969 decision in *Stanley* v. *Georgia* and its explicit invocation of the privacy language that Louis Brandeis had used in his *Olmstead* dissent four decades earlier. All in all, Brennan observed, "The decision whether to abort a pregnancy obviously fits directly within each of the categories of fundamental freedoms I've identified and, therefore, should be held to involve a basic individual right." As had Douglas in his draft,

> I would next emphasize that that conclusion is only the beginning of the problem—that the crucial question is whether the State has a compelling interest in regulating abortion that is achieved without necessarily intruding upon the individual's right. But here I would deal at length not only with the health concern for the well-being of the mother, but with the material interest in the life of the fetus and the moral interest in sanctifying life in general. This would perhaps be the most difficult part of the opinion. I would come out about where Justice Clark does in his

Loyola University Law Review article—that "moral predilections must not be allowed to influence our minds in setting legal distinctions" (quoting Holmes) and that "the law deals in reality, not obscurity—the known rather than the unknown. When sperm meets egg life may form, but quite often it does not. [Indeed, the brief for the appellants in the Texas abortion case quotes an estimate of the rate of 'spontaneous wastage' of 50%]. The law does not deal in speculation. The phenomenon of life takes time to develop, and [only after] it is actually present, it cannot be destroyed." The inconsistent position taken by Georgia in allowing destruction of the fetus in some but not all cases might also be mentioned. Thus, although I would, of course, find a compelling State interest in requiring abortions to be performed by doctors, I would deny any such interest in the life of the fetus in the early stages of pregnancy. On the other hand, I would leave open the question when life "is actually present"—whether there is some point in the term before birth at which the interest in the life of the fetus does become subordinating.

"The right of privacy in the matter of abortions," Brennan concluded, "means that the decision is that of the woman and her alone." The Atlanta panel "was wrong in holding that the State has a legitimate interest in regulating the quality of the decision," and while he would affirm the panel's "conclusion that the reasons for an abortion may not be prescribed," he also "would further hold that the only restraint a State may constitutionally impose upon the woman's individual decision is that the abortion must be performed by a licensed physician." Since the Court could assume that Georgia, and Texas, would obey final declaratory judgments, the high court thus could also affirm the lower courts' refusals to issue federal injunctions against the state statutes.[74]

Bill Brennan's eleven-page, single-spaced letter to Bill Douglas was obviously much more than a commentary on Douglas's far less carefully considered draft statement in *Doe*, and both men—along with several of their clerks—recognized that it could prove to be a richly detailed outline for a full-scale opinion should Harry Blackmun's efforts prove unsatisfactory. Blackmun himself was openly uncertain as to whether he would or indeed should produce *Roe* and *Doe* opinions that would decide the two cases sometime in the early months of 1972, for when Warren Burger, ten days after Justices Powell and Rehnquist formally joined the Court, circulated a letter asking his colleagues to note which cases presently under consideration should be reexamined by all nine justices, Blackmun quickly replied that "I nominate for reargument the two abortion cases." "It seems to me," he explained in a letter that went to all eight of his colleagues, "that the importance of the issue is such that the cases merit full bench treatment" rather than resolution simply by the seven justices who had heard argument on December 13. Any formal decision was postponed, however, until Blackmun would be ready with his own first drafts, and while Bill Douglas continued to make private emendations in his *Doe* statement, the Court turned aside requests for action in other abortion cases. Only in Wisconsin's ongoing effort to prosecute Madison's Dr. Lee Kennan did the Court take any substantive action whatsoever, and even there, in simply affirming without opinion the earlier lower court injunction barring any prosecution, they acted expressly on procedural grounds.[75]

While the Supreme Court privately contemplated how and when to decide *Roe* and *Doe*, other litigation continued to percolate in lesser venues. The Second Circuit Court of Appeals reinstated the New Haven women's suit against Connecticut's abortion law that had been dismissed seven months earlier by a hostile jurist and set the case for full consideration by a three-judge panel. In New York an intermediate appellate court blocked Professor Byrn's ongoing effort to halt all abortions in the city's municipal hospitals, but the state's highest court, by a 4 to 3 margin, upheld the 1971 state policy denying Medicaid funding for nontherapeutic abortions, and a federal court challenge to the policy was initiated on Long Island.[76] In mid-January the Vermont Supreme Court struck down Vermont's antiabortion statute on state law grounds that were not appealable to the U.S. Supreme Court, and one month later the Florida Supreme Court bluntly reiterated in a second decision its previous ruling nine months earlier that that state's antiabortion law was unconstitutionally vague. The Florida court explicitly asked the state legislature to fill the ensuing void with "appropriate remedial legislation," and just seven weeks later Florida enacted a therapeutic reform statute, the first liberalization measure to win approval *anywhere* in the country since the Washington state repeal referendum had passed in November, 1970, a full eighteen months earlier.[77]

Similar referendum efforts aimed at the upcoming 1972 fall elections were underway both in North Dakota and in Michigan, where a federal case was also just getting started,[78] but in other states such as Oklahoma and Georgia, repeal bills died even in advance of legislative floor votes.[79] In Texas Sarah Weddington had announced her candidacy for an Austin seat in the state House, and increasing numbers of women seeking abortions were taking advantage of the remarkably liberal situation in California rather than travel to Mexico. Local activists like Ginny Whitehill told reporters that they remained hopeful of a Supreme Court victory but were also making tentative plans for the 1973 Texas legislature, and Whitehill told NARAL's Lee Gidding that the Texas activists hoped to recruit "more establishment type people" rather than the SWP members who had been so visible during the 1971 legislative campaign.[80]

In early February the generally conservative American Bar Association adopted a repeal stance with regard to the first twenty weeks of pregnancy, and five weeks later a twenty-four member presidentially appointed commission on population growth similarly endorsed "abortion on request" with only the four Roman Catholic members of the panel dissenting. In addition, January results from a nationwide Gallup poll showed that some 57 percent of Americans—including 54 percent of Catholics—believed that the abortion decision should be left to a woman and her doctor, but in the eyes of most repeal proponents, these promising signs were more than outweighed by the continuing evidence of widespread legislative resistance to abortion law liberalization. Activists as different in background and style as Bob Hall and Larry Lader both warned that the repeal movement had now been stalled for well over a year, and while both the lawyers and nonlawyers sought to remain optimistic with regard to the U.S. Supreme Court, some judicial developments—such as the Massachusetts Supreme Judicial Court's reinstatement of the criminal charges that had first been filed against Clergy Consultation Service member Reverend Robert Hare almost three years earlier—were certainly not promising.[81]

Roy Lucas had suffered a two to one defeat—108 to 54—in the NARAL referendum on his board candidacy, and by early in 1972 both the long and short-term financial prospects for the Madison Institute were looking exceedingly bleak. Lucas was beginning to ponder both a move from New York to San Francisco and a reincarnation of his litigation interests under a new rubric of a Population Law Center, but he continued to hear secondhand reports of the *Vuitch* allegations that he ascribed to Joe Nellis, Larry Lader, and Cyril Means. Nellis had launched an unsuccessful court suit *against* Dr. Vuitch in an effort to collect disputed legal fees, and while Lucas fully understood Nellis's animus, he professed puzzlement to a variety of colleagues as to why Lader and especially Means continued to engage in "adolescent games" against him. He acknowledged to one friend that "Cyril desperately needs recognition," but in a long letter to Harriet Pilpel, Lucas wrathfully con-

ceded that the "misleading" and "fraudulent" claims undeniably underlay his ouster from NARAL. However, he sarcastically told Pilpel, "with
Lader and Means at the NARAL helm, the whole matter is akin to being
asked to leave Nedicks." Lucas remained far more defensive about the
more principled dispute over his unsuccessful representation of the
commercial referral services, and while he told Pilpel that "population
and women's rights are the issue, not my professional fees nor yours,"
by March of 1972 the Madison Institute was on its deathbed and members of its pro forma board of trustees were resigning almost weekly.[82]

By early 1972 the New Jersey case that Lucas had once thought
would be the first abortion suit likely to reach the U.S. Supreme Court
had been under ostensible consideration for more than thirteen
months by the three-judge panel that had heard argument in
December 1970. Late in January 1972, attorney Nancy Stearns took the
unusual but appropriate step of writing to the court to ask when the
case might be decided, and in late February, several weeks after U.S.
Circuit Judge Philip Forman had apologized for what he acknowledged
was an "extraordinary" delay, the panel by a vote of two to one voided
the New Jersey law on grounds of both vagueness and the right to privacy. Judge Forman's majority opinion highlighted "the critical significance" of *Griswold*'s invocation of the Ninth Amendment and went on
to explain that "the absence of specific language in the Constitution
does not dilute or diminish the contention that there is a right of privacy which includes the right to seek an abortion in the early stages of
pregnancy." Forman and District Judge George H. Barlow concluded
that "a woman has a constitutional right of privacy cognizable under
the Ninth and Fourteenth Amendments to determine for herself
whether to bear a child or to terminate a pregnancy in its early stages,"
and in a separate opinion the third member of the panel, District Judge
Leonard Garth, endorsed Forman's reliance on *Griswold* but asserted
that *Griswold*'s marital privacy emphasis meant that the panel's extension of *Griswold* to abortion should thus be limited only to protecting
such a choice for *married* women.[83]

The New Jersey decision attracted considerable press attention, with
one Englewood Cliffs practitioner announcing that he immediately
would begin performing abortions and NARAL's Larry Lader excitedly
wondering whether the ruling might represent a "breakthrough point"
that would allow repeal proponents to regain the initiative.[84] Two weeks
later, in a far less publicized but substantively even more important
decision, a three-judge federal panel in Kansas City endorsed Roy
Lucas's challenge against the hospitalization and multidoctor approval

requirements set forth in Kansas's 1969 reform law. The Kansas provisions were almost identical to the Georgia ones which had been upheld by the Atlanta panel in *Doe* v. *Bolton*, and the Kansas City decision represented the first time that any court had voided the highly exclusive hospital criteria that significantly limited the number of facilities providing abortions in most "reform" states. The Kansas panel cited retired Justice Tom Clark's law review essay in holding that the "fundamental right to individual and marital privacy" authenticated in *Griswold* "includes within its scope the right to procure an abortion."[85]

Far more notable than either the New Jersey or Kansas holdings, however, was the March 22 release of the U.S. Supreme Court's 6 to 1 decision in *Eisenstadt* v. *Baird*. Justice Brennan had indeed finally received William O. Douglas's endorsement of the opinion which Brennan had first circulated the same day that *Roe* and *Doe* were argued, and Douglas's support—along with that of Thurgood Marshall and Potter Stewart—gave Brennan the four votes necessary to represent a majority of the seven-member Court that had heard *Eisenstadt*. Byron White in early February had circulated a brief opinion concurring in rather than dissenting from Brennan's affirmance of the First Circuit decision voiding the Massachusetts anticontraception law, and three weeks later Harry Blackmun joined White's concurrence rather than Brennan's opinion for the Court. Chief Justice Burger finally circulated a typescript draft of a dissent during the second week of March, but further delays on Burger's part postponed *Eisenstadt*'s actual announcement until March 22.

Much like the First Circuit ruling two years earlier, Brennan's opinion concluded that Massachusetts's criminal ban on the distribution of contraceptive articles to unmarried individuals only could not be defended as either a health measure or as a rational means for discouraging nonmarital sex. Since "it would be plainly unreasonable to assume that Massachusetts has prescribed pregnancy and the birth of an unwanted child as punishment for" the simple misdemeanor offense of "fornication," Brennan sardonically observed, the felony statute under which Bill Baird had been convicted violated "the rights of single persons under the Equal Protection Clause" of the Fourteenth Amendment by failing to demonstrate any "rational basis" for drawing a criminal distinction between married and unmarried individuals. Brennan insisted in a footnote that that fatal flaw meant that the Court did not have to expressly hold that the Massachusetts law "impinges upon fundamental freedoms under *Griswold*," but he went on to emphasize that whatever the right of the individual to access to contraceptives may be, the rights must be the same for the unmarried and the married alike.

If under *Griswold* the distribution of contraceptives to married persons cannot be prohibited, a ban on distribution to unmarried persons would be equally impermissible. It is true that in *Griswold* the right of privacy in question inhered in the marital relationship. Yet the marital couple is not an independent entity with a mind and heart of its own, but an association of two individuals each with a separate intellectual and emotional makeup. If the right of privacy means anything, it is the right of the *individual*, married or single, to be free from unwarranted governmental intrusion into matters so fundamentally affecting a person as the decision whether to bear or beget a child.

That crucial sentence had appeared in the Brennan opinion beginning with the very first draft that had been distributed the day of the *Roe* and *Doe* arguments, and while it had occasioned no correspondence from other justices, among the clerks there was full awareness that the sentence could and would be read as speaking to much more than simply Massachusetts's anticontraception statute. "Was that recognized at the time? Was it clear to me that that sentence would have some impact on the abortion question?" the clerk who worked most closely with Brennan on the *Eisenstadt* opinion asked twenty years later in rephrasing an obvious question. "Yes, I certainly knew that and I believe Justice Brennan did too." So, of course, did the clerks of other justices who joined the Brennan opinion. "We all saw that sentence, and we all smiled about it," for it seemed to have a "transparent purpose," one subsequently explained. "Everyone understood what that sentence in *Eisenstadt* was doing, but no one believed it would tie anyone's hands in the abortion context or bind anyone in the future."

William O. Douglas's additional concurrence simply reiterated his conference assertion that "This to me is a simple First Amendment case" where Baird's distribution of the vaginal foam was inseparable from his preceding lecture. Byron White's separate concurrence, in which Harry Blackmun joined, emphasized that the formal record of Baird's arrest, trial and conviction never actually indicated whether the young woman to whom he had handed the foam was married or unmarried. Hence, the fact that Baird under the Massachusetts law "could not be convicted for distributing Emko to a married person disposes of this case." White added that while it would be different had Baird handed out a contraceptive, such as birth control pills, that actually merited prescriptive regulation, *Eisenstadt* in fact presented "no reason for reaching the novel constitutional question [of] whether a State may restrict or forbid the distribution of contraceptives to the unmarried."

Warren Burger's lone dissent insisted that the issue in the case was not the marital status of Baird's recipient, as even the Massachusetts law itself clearly seemed to indicate, but was instead Baird's status as a layman rather than a medical professional. "I do not challenge *Griswold*," Burger opined, "despite its tenuous moorings to the text of the Constitution, but I cannot view it as controlling authority for this case." "I simply cannot believe," he went on, "that the limitation on the class of lawful distributors has significantly impaired the right to use contraceptives in Massachusetts. By relying on *Griswold* in the present context, the Court has passed beyond the penumbras of the specific guarantees into the uncircumscribed area of personal predilections."[86]

Both journalists and attorneys immediately identified Brennan's memorable paean to *"individual"* privacy and the fundamental choice of "whether to bear or beget a child" as *the* key statement in *Eisenstadt*. Every leading news report highlighted that crucial sentence, and both the *Washington Post* and the *New York Times* noted how that "broadly phrased" declaration might well "influence pending abortion cases," especially since the four signers of the Brennan opinion also constituted a majority of the seven-justice Court that had heard *Roe* and *Doe*. The following day Roy Lucas told a Minnesota colleague that while "the effect of the case is to extend privacy rights to the unmarried," Brennan's "bear or beget" language meant that "the opinion goes much further." Margie Hames reacted similarly, telling a Georgia journalist that *Eisenstadt* made her more optimistic about *Doe* and *Roe*, since "the argument for that case was the same as ours—the constitutional right of privacy."

Since almost all contemporary attention understandably focused upon Brennan's most quotable and suggestive statement, Brennan's footnoted assertion that the Court actually was *not* extending *Griswold* to establish an *individual* constitutional right of access to contraceptives was almost completely ignored until law professors in later years began to point out that compositional flaws in the Brennan opinion made it neither as coherent nor as consistent as its author might have wished. Some opponents of abortion—and perhaps of contraception as well— were quick to allege that the Brennan opinion in *Eisenstadt* was unprincipled both in its extension of *Griswold* and as an unmistakably calculating effort to pave the way for a constitutional right to choose abortion. One future federal appellate judge asserted that *Eisenstadt* "unmasks *Griswold* as based on the idea of sexual liberty rather than privacy," while a like-minded nonjurist alleged that *Eisenstadt* revealed how the Supreme Court's "family rationale of 1965 was simply an expedient fabrication." Another future circuit judge stated that *Eisenstadt*'s "revolutionary rationale was probably invented" with *Roe* and *Doe* in mind, and a prominent female law professor decried how *Eisenstadt* had "abruptly severed the privacy right from its attachment to marriage and the family." Far more insightfully, one of the country's most perspicacious conservative scholars later identified the basic problem with the *Eisenstadt* opinion bluntly and succinctly: Brennan had "begged the crucial question" of whether there was or was not a constitutionally protected right to fornicate.[87]

The Supreme Court's decision in *Eisenstadt* v. *Baird*—or, more precisely, Justice Brennan's singularly promising sentence—measurably raised the spirits of repeal proponents as they awaited the late June conclusion of the Court's 1971–1972 Term. Additionally, just four weeks after *Eisenstadt*, the three-judge court that had been convened to hear the New Haven women's challenge to Connecticut's antiabortion law voided the statute on both Ninth and Fourteenth Amendment grounds and then formally enjoined any further enforcement of it. The panel's 2 to 1 majority opinion prominently quoted *Eisenstadt*'s "bear or beget" language, and while U.S. District Judge T. Emmet Clarie, who had initially dismissed the suit before being reversed by the Second Circuit Court of Appeals, filed an angry dissent, fellow District Judge Jon O. Newman, in a scholarly concurring opinion that relied heavily upon the work of Cyril Means, emphasized that in light of *Griswold* there was "no doubt" that a "constitutionally protected zone of privacy" secured a woman's right to choose abortion. Connecticut officials unsuccessfully sought a stay of the panel's injunctive order from Supreme Court Justice Thurgood Marshall, and within hours of Marshall's denial, Governor Thomas J. Meskill—an antiabortion Roman Catholic Republican—called an emergency special session of the state legislature so that a new antiabortion measure could be enacted immediately. Within a week a bill allowing abortions only if a woman's life was in danger, and providing a five-year jail term for violators, was reported out of committee and passed by a vote of 120 to 49 on the house floor. One idiosyncratic senator who backed repeal mockingly introduced a substitute measure mandating the death penalty rather than five years' imprisonment, but when the senate by 22 to 13 adopted a provision allowing for abortions in cases of rape or incest and then passed the amended bill by a margin of 21 to 14, Governor Meskill announced that he would veto the bill as too liberal unless the senate reversed itself and adopted the more restrictive version. Adding the senate amendment, Meskill asserted, "amounts to abortion on demand. A woman can merely claim she was raped or it was an incestuous relationship. Everyone who wants an abortion will be reporting rape." Meskill's insistence was supported by energetic lobbying on behalf of the Roman Catholic church, and the very next day, with six senators switching their votes, the senate by a narrow margin of 18 to 16 approved the original bill. Meskill immediately signed it into law, and house majority leader Representative Carl Ajello, Jr., explained to reporters that "the impetus for the bill as it was drafted came directly from the Hartford Archdiocese. They didn't want any loopholes." The attorneys handling the New Haven women's suit quickly asked the federal three-judge court to extend its prior injunctive order to cover the new law as well, since it too was clearly unconstitutional under the panel's earlier decision, but not until midsummer did the court hold a formal hearing and take the matter under full consideration.[88]

Some legal observers, such as Cyril Means, interpreted Thurgood Marshall's refusal to issue a stay of the Connecticut court's initial injunction—especially in the wake of *Eisenstadt*, and especially when Marshall *had* issued just such a stay fifteen months earlier in the Illinois case—as a clear sign that the Supreme Court was just about to affirm *Roe*'s voiding of Texas's highly similar antiabortion law with "a fairly broad ruling in favor of a woman's fundamental right to terminate an unwanted pregnancy." Means warned Harriet Pilpel, however, that even if the final weeks of the Court's term did indeed produce such a constitutional victory, the growing political presence of antiabortion forces nonetheless meant that "we are in for a long, tough fight" that no doubt would "go on for years and years." In New York, the increasingly vigorous efforts of abortion opponents such as the Roman Catholic Knights of Columbus, who drew more than ten thousand demonstrators to a "Right to Life Sunday" rally, appeared to be making significant headway in the state legislature, where an antiabortion bill that would revoke the 1970 repeal statute and return the law to a traditional "life-only" exception was approaching a floor vote. NARAL's Larry Lader warned his colleagues that the legislative situation was now "more critical than ever before," and New York Governor Nelson Rockefeller, in a compromise gesture that pleased neither side, advocated reducing the 1970 abortion law ceiling from twenty-four to sixteen weeks of pregnancy. Rockefeller stressed that he would veto any all-out reversal of the 1970 statute, and senate majority leader Earl Brydges tried to convince antiabortion legislators that Rockefeller's pledge meant they instead should back the compromise measure, which Rockefeller had just shifted from sixteen to eighteen weeks.[89]

Then, however, on May 6, just one day after President Richard M. Nixon publicly rejected the abortion recommendation that had been made two months earlier by his commission on population growth, the Archdiocese of New York released to the press a private letter Nixon had sent to Terence Cardinal Cooke. "The unrestricted abortion policies now recommended by some Americans, and the liberalized abortion policies in effect in some sections of this country," such as New York, "seem to me impossible to reconcile with either our religious traditions or our Western heritage," Nixon stated. The letter went on to commend Roman Catholic antiabortion efforts on behalf of "unborn children" as "truly a noble endeavor," but the public release of Nixon's missive set off a firestorm of controversy. The *New York Times* decried what it described as "a President openly working through a particular church to influence the action of a state government" and denounced Nixon for "a blatant misuse of his high position." Fellow Republican Nelson Rockefeller unsurprisingly was reported to be furious at Nixon's action, and within forty-eight hours top presidential aide John D. Ehrlichman publicly apologized for the public release of the letter, which he said had been composed by White House speech writer Patrick J. Buchanan.

By that time, however, the bill to revoke the 1970 repeal measure had been passed by the state Assembly on a vote of 79 to 68 after a six-hour debate highlighted by one opponent's display of a fetus in a jar. Five members who had backed repeal two years earlier now voted to rescind it, and the following day the state Senate, by a margin of 30 to 27, also endorsed revocation. Three days later Governor Rockefeller made good on his promise and vetoed the bill, saying that "the extremes of personal vilification and political coercion brought to bear on members of the Legislature raise serious doubts that the votes to repeal the reforms represented the will of a majority of the people of New York State." Abortion supporters breathed a huge sigh of relief, and castigated themselves for having demonstrated what Larry Lader termed "overwhelming apathy" and only a "marginally effective" political presence in the face of such a "superbly coordinated" opposition onslaught. "Despite the fact that women's movement participants were aware of the magnitude of the threat," one National Organization for Women volunteer later recounted, "abortion activists had difficulty getting other feminists to write letters, make phone calls, [or] go to Albany." New York public opinion polls showed better than 60 percent popular support for the 1970 law, but the intensity and commitment of abortion opponents had more than offset that majority sentiment. Another major right to life effort to revoke the repeal law would almost certainly be launched in 1973, and many abortion partisans worried that if for any reason Nelson Rockefeller was no longer governor, next time the 1970 measure might not survive at all.[90]

New York was not the only state where antiabortionists appeared to be gaining strength despite the countervailing public opinion polls. In Pennsylvania, where several trial court rulings against the old abortion statute were pending before the state Supreme Court, the state house approved a new measure with only a maternal life exception by an overwhelming vote of 157 to 34, and in Massachusetts the state house by a similar landslide margin of 178 to 46 passed a measure that would bestow the full legal rights of children upon all fetuses beginning at the moment of conception. Even on the judicial front there was bad news, with a federal three-judge court in Kentucky upholding the constitutionality of that state's antiabortion law, and while some activists looked forward optimistically to the upcoming November popular referendum on a twenty-week repeal measure in Michigan, most interested observers continued to anticipate that the U.S. Supreme Court might very well resolve the entire matter sometime before the end of June.[91]

Inside the Court itself, the first tangible development in *Roe* or *Doe* since the inconclusive mid-January discussion of whether the cases should be reargued before the full nine-member Court came on May 18 when Harry Blackmun distributed a seventeen-page initial draft of a *Roe* opinion to his colleagues. "Herewith is a first and tentative draft for this case," Blackmun's cover note explained.

> Due to the presence of multiple parties and the existence of issues of standing and of appellate routes, it may be somewhat difficult to obtain a consensus on all aspects. My notes indicate, however, that we were generally in agreement to affirm on the merits. That is where I come out on the theory that the Texas statute, despite its narrowness, is unconstitutionally vague.
>
> I think that this would be all that is necessary for disposition of the case, and that we need not get into the more complex Ninth Amendment issue. This may or may not appeal to you.
>
> In any event, I am still flexible as to results, and I shall do my best to arrive at something which would command a court. Would it be advis-

able, rather than having numerous concurring and dissenting opinions immediately written, to have each of you express his general views in order to see if we can come together on something?

The Georgia case, yet to come, is more complex. I am still tentatively of the view, as I have been all along, that the Georgia case merits reargument before a full bench. I shall try to produce something, however, so that we may look at it before any decision as to that is made.

Blackmun's *Roe* draft was an almost wholly unremarkable document. Ten of its seventeen pages were devoted, as Blackmun's cover note indicated, to questions of standing and jurisdiction. Only on page eleven did he reach the merits, and just as he said, it discussed the Texas antiabortion law only within the context of whether the statute's language was inadequately clear. Blackmun concluded that it was indeed "insufficiently informative to the physician to whom it purports to afford a measure of professional protection" and hence was unconstitutionally vague. Thus there was no need, he stated, to consider either the Ninth Amendment argument on which the Dallas panel had based its decision or "the opposing rights of the embryo or fetus during the respective prenatal trimesters."

Blackmun's opinions in the abortion cases had been eagerly awaited in the chambers of those justices who comprised the apparent majority, but when his *Roe* draft arrived on Thursday the 18th, some clerks who read it were utterly amazed at what an "awful" and inadequate statement it really was. George Frampton, the Blackmun clerk whom the other clerks knew was working most closely with the justice on the abortion cases, was a popular and well-respected figure among his colleagues, and for several months he had been reassuring his friends in other chambers that Blackmun's vote to strike the Texas statute was indeed firm. Frampton's assurances had convinced his friends, and several of them in turn had conveyed their impressions to their own justices. William O. Douglas had remained wary, however, that Warren Burger might persuade his old friend to adopt a more deferential attitude toward antiabortion laws, and Douglas had also continued to worry that Burger might seek to have the cases held over so that Justices Powell and Rehnquist's votes could potentially shift the result. Blackmun's cover note significantly heightened the second of those fears, and the disappointing quality of Blackmun's draft immediately generated a good deal of additional woe in Douglas's chambers as well as in those of Justices Marshall, Brennan, and Stewart. Several of Frampton's friends lost little time in "giving George a fair amount of shit," as one clerk later put it, about his boss's unsatisfactory draft, and before the day was out a clear consensus had emerged that both Blackmun's opinion in *Roe* and his resolve about deciding *Doe* would have to be strengthened as quickly as possible.

Unsurprisingly, Bill Brennan was the first justice to respond to Harry Blackmun's request for comments. In a firm but polite note that very same day, Brennan explained that the *Roe* opinion would have be recast so as to address the basic constitutional question and that no basis existed for holding off on a decision in *Doe*. "My recollection of the voting on this and the Georgia case," Brennan began,

> was that a majority of us felt that the Constitution required the invalidation of the abortion statutes save to the extent they required that an abortion be performed by a licensed physician within some limited time after conception. I think essentially this was the view shared by Bill, Potter, Thurgood and me. My notes also indicate that you might support this view at least in this Texas case. In the circumstances, I would prefer a disposition of the core constitutional question. Your circulation, however, invalidates the Texas statute only on the vagueness ground. I see no reason for a reargument in the Georgia case. I think we should dispose of both cases on the ground supported by the majority.
>
> This does not mean, however, that I disagree with your conclusion as to the vagueness of the Texas statute. I only feel that there is no point in delaying longer our confrontation with the core issue on which there appears to be a majority and which would make reaching the vagueness issue unnecessary.

The next morning Bill Douglas sent Blackmun a letter that curtly seconded Brennan's observations:

> My notes confirm what Bill Brennan wrote yesterday in his memo to you—that abortion statutes were invalid save as they required that an abortion be performed by a licensed physician within a limited time after conception.
>
> That was the clear view of a majority of the seven who heard the argument. My notes also indicate that the Chief had the opposed view, which made it puzzling as to why he made the assignment at all except that he indicated he might affirm on vagueness. My notes indicate that Byron was not firmly settled and that you might join the majority of four.
>
> So I think we should meet what Bill Brennan calls the "core issue."
>
> I believe I gave you, some time back, my draft opinion in the Georgia case. I see no reason for reargument on that case.
>
> It always seemed to me to be an easier case than Texas.

The following Monday Blackmun acknowledged Douglas's letter with a brief note that simply expressed appreciation for how "very helpful" Douglas's *Doe* draft had indeed been, and indicating that Blackmun was about ready to circulate a *Doe* opinion of his own. "You may or may not agree with what I have come up with, but I suspect we are really not very far apart."[92]

Three days later Blackmun formally distributed a twenty-five-page first draft of *Doe* to his colleagues. In his cover memo, he explained that his opinion would void almost all of the remaining provisions of the Georgia reform statute—namely those requiring prior approval by other doctors and by a hospital committee and those restricting abortions to Georgia residents and to certain larger hospitals—that had not been struck down by the Atlanta panel. "What essentially remains is that an abortion may be performed only if the attending physician deems it necessary 'based upon his best clinical judgment,' if his judgment is reduced to writing, and if the abortion is performed in a hospital licensed by the State." In particular, Blackmun said, striking down the hospital committee requirement "was not the easiest conclusion for me to reach," since in Minnesota

> I have worked closely with supervisory hospital committees set up by the medical profession itself, and I have seen them operate over extensive periods. I can state with complete conviction that they serve a high purpose in maintaining standards and in keeping the overzealous surgeon's knife sheathed. There is a lot of unnecessary surgery done in this country, and intraprofessional restraints of this kind have accomplished much that is unnoticed and certainly is unappreciated by people generally.
>
> I have also seen abortion mills in operation and the general misery they have caused despite their being run by otherwise "competent" technicians.
>
> I should observe that, according to the information contained in some of the briefs, knocking out the Texas statute in *Roe* v. *Wade* will invalidate the abortion laws in a *majority* of our States. Most States focus only on the preservation of the life of the mother. *Vuitch*, of course, is on the books, and I had assumed that the Conference, at this point, has no intention to overrule it. It is because of *Vuitch*'s vagueness emphasis and a hope, perhaps forlorn, that we might get a unanimous court in the Texas case, that I took the vagueness route.

Blackmun's actual *Doe* draft cited *Eisenstadt, Stanley, Griswold, Skinner,* and other cases reaching back to *Meyer* and *Pierce* in the 1920s, as well as retired Justice Clark's law review article, to support the hold-

ing that "a woman's interest in making the fundamental personal decision whether or not to bear an unwanted child is within the scope of
personal rights protected by the Ninth and Fourteenth Amendments."
That interest, however, was not absolute, and because of the fetus,
abortion was "inherently different from marital intimacy, or bedroom
possession of obscene material, or marriage, or the right to procreate,
or private education," the subjects involved in those earlier cases.
Blackmun stated that "somewhere" during pregnancy, "either forth-
with at conception, or at 'quickening,' or at birth, or at some other
point in between, another being becomes involved and the privacy the
woman possessed has become dual rather than sole." Hence "the state's
interest grows stronger as the woman approaches term," even though
the Georgia statute's requirement that a hospital committee had to
approve all abortions, irrespective of the stage of pregnancy, "is unduly
restrictive of the patient's rights and needs."

Blackmun's *Doe* draft was a considerably more sophisticated and far-
reaching piece of work than his *Roe* circulation, but nonetheless Bill
Brennan's first instinct was to ask Blackmun for some significant
strengthening. However, quick conversations with Bill Douglas, Potter
Stewart, and Thurgood Marshall produced a speedy consensus that the
nascent *Doe* majority would be better advised to join Blackmun's opinion and *then* request changes rather than run the risk that extensive preliminary suggestions might incline Blackmun to move for reargument
of *Doe* and even *Roe* rather than press ahead toward actual decisions.
Thus before that very day was out, Justices Douglas, Brennan, and
Marshall all sent Blackmun written notes formally joining his *Doe*
opinion. Both Brennan and Marshall told Blackmun that they would
send along some suggestions for improvement, and Douglas's clerk,
Bill Alsup, went over several others with George Frampton, but the
three immediate and unqualified endorsements created an explicit
four-vote majority for deciding *Doe*. Taking note of that fact, Douglas
sent Blackmun an additional message, officially joining the *Roe* circulation which he had all but dismissed only six days earlier. "I had once
thought that this case should be remanded in light of the Georgia
case," Douglas asserted, "But I now think it best to hand it down as
you have written it."[93]

The next day, Friday, Blackmun sent his colleagues a memo recommending that his *Doe* draft be augmented to include a clear statement
of what would remain the law in Georgia following the Court's decision: "an abortion is a crime," his suggestion read, "except an abortion
performed in a licensed hospital by a licensed physician 'based upon

his best clinical judgment that an abortion is necessary.'" Additionally, the doctor would have to file a confidential statement to that effect with both the hospital and the state health department. On Monday, Potter Stewart phoned Blackmun to express "basic agreement" with the *Doe* draft and to request several changes that Blackmun willingly agreed to make. Stewart's support brought the number of *Doe* supporters to five of the seven justices who had heard the case, but later that same day, Byron White distributed an incisive and influential three-page dissent from Blackmun's earlier circulation in *Roe*. Blackmun's prospective opinion holding Texas's antiabortion statute to be unconstitutionally vague, White noted, "necessarily overrules" *Vuitch*, for "If a standard which refers to the 'health' of the mother . . . is not impermissibly vague, a statutory standard which focuses only on 'saving the life' of the mother would appear to be *a fortiori* acceptable."[94]

White's trenchant observation was a decisive if nonetheless eventually ironic contribution to the Court's consideration of *Roe* and *Doe*. Less than forty-eight hours later, Harry Blackmun circulated another memo to all of his colleagues:

> Nearly all of you, other than Lewis Powell and Bill Rehnquist, have been in touch with me about these cases. A number of helpful and valid suggestions have been made.
>
> You will recall that when we were canvassing the list for possible candidates for reargument when the bench would be full, I suggested that, although the Texas case perhaps might come down, the Georgia case should go over. This suggestion was not enthusiastically received. It was the consensus, as I recall, that I produce some drafts and we would see what reactions ensued. I have done this and, frankly, I prepared the Texas memorandum the way I did in the hope that we might come near to agreement there irrespective of the disposition of the Georgia case.
>
> Although it would prove costly to me personally, in the light of energy and hours expended, I have now concluded, somewhat reluctantly, that reargument in *both* cases at an early date in the next term, would perhaps be advisable. I feel this way because:
>
> 1. I believe, on an issue so sensitive and so emotional as this one, the country deserves the conclusion of a nine-man, not a seven-man court, whatever the ultimate decision may be.
>
> 2. Although I have worked on these cases with some concentration, I am not yet certain about all the details. Should we make the Georgia case the primary opinion and recast Texas in its light? Should we refrain from emasculation of the Georgia statute and, instead, hold it unconstitutional in its entirety and let the state legislature reconstruct from the

beginning? Should we spell out—although it would then necessarily be largely dictum—just what aspects are controllable by the State and to what extent? For example, it has been suggested that upholding Georgia's provision as to a licensed hospital should be held unconstitutional, and the Court should approve performance of an abortion in a "licensed medical facility." These are some of the suggestions that have been made and that prompt me to think about a summer's delay.

I therefore conclude, and move, that both cases go over the Term.

Hardly an hour passed before Blackmun's colleagues began to respond. Unsurprisingly, William O. Douglas told Blackmun that he felt "quite strongly" that *Roe* and *Doe* "should not be reargued."

> In the first place, these cases which were argued last October [sic] have been as thoroughly worked over and considered as any cases ever before the Court in my time.
>
> I know you have done yeoman service and have written two difficult cases, and you have opinions now for a majority, which is 5.
>
> There are always minor differences in style, one writing differently than another. But those two opinions of yours in *Texas* and *Georgia* are creditable jobs of craftsmanship and will, I think, stand the test of time.
>
> While we could sit around and make pages of suggestions, I really don't think that is important. The important thing is to get them down.
>
> In the second place, I have a feeling that where the Court is split 4–4 or 4–2–1 or even in an important constitutional case 4–3, reargument may be desirable. But you have a firm 5 and the firm 5 will be behind you in these two opinions until they come down. It is a difficult field and a difficult subject. But where there is that solid agreement of the majority I think it is important to announce the cases, and let the result be known so that the legislatures can go to work and draft their new laws.
>
> Again, congratulations on a fine job. I hope the 5 can agree to get the cases down this Term, so that we can spend our energies next Term on other matters.

Bill Brennan called Blackmun to convey a similar message, and then dispatched a follow-up note, emphasizing that "I see no reason to put these cases over for reargument. I say that since, as I understand it, there are five of us (Bill Douglas, Potter, Thurgood, you and I) in substantial agreement with both opinions and in that circumstance I question that reargument would change things." Thurgood Marshall likewise sent along a note saying that "I, too, am opposed to reargument," but late in the day Warren Burger dispatched a decidedly different message to his eight colleagues:

I have had a great many problems with these cases from the outset. They are not as simple for me as they appear to be for others. The States have, I should think, as much concern in this area as in any within their province; federal power has only that which can be traced to a specific provision of the Constitution.

Perhaps my problem arises from the mediocre to poor help from counsel. On reargument, I would propose we appoint amici for both sides, but that can wait. This is as sensitive and difficult an issue as any in this Court in my time and I want to hear more and think more when I am not trying to sort out several dozen other difficult cases.

Hence, I vote to reargue early in the next Term.[95]

Burger's memo set off alarm bells in at least four chambers. The angriest reaction came from William O. Douglas, who assumed that Burger would not try to postpone *Roe* and *Doe*, no matter how optimistic Burger might feel about adding the votes of Justices Powell and Rehnquist to his own and Byron White's, unless Burger believed that there was a potential fifth vote—i.e., Harry Blackmun—that could transform June's two-justice minority into an October majority. Douglas immediately resolved to dissent publicly if Burger and Blackmun did draw majority support to hold the cases over, and the next morning Douglas sent a short but pointed note to Burger, with copies to all other justices: "If the vote of the Conference is to reargue, then I will file a statement telling what is happening to us and the tragedy it entails."

Douglas's threat, however, failed to have the effect he desired, for later that day both Lewis Powell and then Bill Rehnquist distributed memos agreeing that the cases should be held over. Powell noted how he and Rehnquist after being seated had not taken part in the January discussion of what cases might merit reargument, but

The present question arises in a different context. I have been on the Court for more than half a term. It may be that I now have a duty to participate in this decision, although from a purely personal viewpoint I would be more than happy to leave this one to others. I have not read the briefs; nor have I read either of Harry's opinions. I am too concerned about circulating my own remaining opinions to be studying cases in which I did not participate. I certainly do not know how I would vote if the cases are reargued.

In any event, I have concluded that it is appropriate for me to participate in the pending question. I have read the memoranda circulated, and am persuaded to favor reargument primarily by the fact that Harry

Blackmun, the author of the opinions, thinks the cases should be carried over and reargued next fall. His position, based on months of study, suggests enough doubt on an issue of large national importance to justify the few months delay.[96]

Bill Rehnquist said simply that he agreed with Powell, and as it became apparent that there likely would be a five-vote majority in favor of reargument—even though Byron White had yet to be formally heard from—the anger of those who had briefly comprised Blackmun's now-evanescent majority openly exploded. Bill Douglas, in line with his earlier threat, drafted a furious memo—clearly designed for public rather than private consumption—denouncing what he thought Warren Burger was up to. It highlighted how the relatively complicated decision in *Vuitch* had been handed down almost within three months of oral argument, whereas close to six months had now passed since the arguments in *Roe* and *Doe*. It asserted that in the initial conference discussion Burger had "represented the minority view" and had "forcefully argued his viewpoint on the issues," yet nonetheless had assigned the majority opinions, "an action no Chief Justice in my time would ever have taken." Burger's behavior, Douglas went on, revealed that "there is a destructive force at work in the Court. When a Chief Justice tries to bend the Court to his will by manipulating assignments, the integrity of the institution is imperiled." In *Doe* and *Roe*, opinions had been circulated, "and each commands the votes of five members of the Court. Those votes are firm," and "The cases should therefore be announced. The plea that the cases be reargued is merely strategy by a minority somehow to suppress the majority view with the hope that exigencies of time will change the result. That might be achieved of course by death or conceivably retirement. But that kind of strategy dilutes the integrity of the Court and makes the decisions here depend on the manipulative skill of a Chief Justice."

Just as angry as Douglas, however, though less inclined to express it on paper, was Potter Stewart, who had become more and more upset about what he regarded as Burger's disingenuous conduct as the Court's year had progressed. Other justices such as Thurgood Marshall and Bill Brennan also believed that Burger's behavior with regard to opinion assignment had repeatedly verged on the improper, but Stewart's anger was especially acute, and Stewart's own clerks, as well as others, were quite aware of Stewart's "very intense" hostility toward Burger. The move to hold over the abortion cases further strengthened Stewart's feelings, and within a day or two of Burger's May 31 memo, he let Bill Brennan know exactly what he was thinking, as Brennan then described in a brief, handwritten note to Bill Douglas:

> I will be God-damned! At lunch today, Potter expressed his outrage at the high handed way things are going, particularly the assumption that a single Justice if CJ can order things his own way, + that he can hold up for nine months anything he chooses, even if the rest of us are ready to bring down 4–3s for example. He also told me he will not vote to overrule *Wade*, *Miranda* etc. + resents CJ's confidence that he has Powell + Rehnquist in his pocket. Potter wants to make an issue of these things—maybe fur will fly this afternoon.

Whether or not Stewart personally confronted Burger at conference—and if so, no notes were taken—Bill Brennan, while wholly sympathetic to both Douglas's and Stewart's anger, fully appreciated that if the battle became too intense, or if Douglas went public, both the Court itself, as well as the prospective decisions in *Doe*, *Roe*, and other cases in which Blackmun, Powell, or Rehnquist might prove decisive, could well end up among the gravely wounded. When Douglas on June 2 gave Brennan a printed copy of his prospective public dissent from any formal order for reargument, Brennan took his pencil and edited the statement extensively, taking special care to remove all of the personal references to Burger. Brennan was literally the only justice who had anything even approaching a personal friendship with the standoffish Douglas, and he returned the draft dissent with a "Dear Bill" note gently observing that "If anything is to be made public (& I have serious reservations on that score), I hope the pencilled out portions can be omitted." Two days later Byron White circulated his own formal statement affirming the view that *Roe* and *Doe* should indeed be reargued in the fall, and although Douglas in mid-June sent two copies of a revised version of his dissent to each of his colleagues' chambers, by the time Douglas left for his summer home in Goose Prairie, Washington, several days before the end of the Court's term, Bill Brennan's gentle but persistent entreaties had convinced him that his angry statement should indeed not be published. When the Court on June 26 publicly announced that *Roe* and *Doe* would be carried over and set for reargument sometime in the fall, the only appendage when the brief and unrevealing order was formally published was a simple indication that Justice Douglas dissented from the decision.[97]

News of the Court's action heightened the stress that the attorneys on both sides of the two cases already had been experiencing in anticipation of a late June decision. Roy Lucas, who by now had closed the

Madison Institute and moved to San Francisco, told a friend that "the suspense is getting to me." Both Linda Coffee and Sarah Weddington, who three weeks earlier had won a runoff primary for the Democratic nomination for a Texas House seat in heavily Democratic Austin, understandably felt that the news might well mean trouble. Margie Hames was similarly worried, while Jay Floyd, who had wanted Powell and Rehnquist to participate in the case seven months earlier, felt a slight burst of optimism. Dorothy Beasley, who had delivered three *additional* Supreme Court arguments since *Doe*—two extremely visible death penalty cases that would be handed down three days later plus a jury composition suit that had been decided the week before—experienced both a "terrible sinking feeling" at not having prevailed plus a sense of "tremendous relief" that she would have a second shot. Most journalists and commentators initially attached no particular meaning to the Court's action, but eight days later, on July 4, a front-page story in the *Washington Post* changed almost everything.[98]

Headlined "Move by Burger May Shift Court's Stand on Abortion," the unbylined story stated that the Chief Justice had "helped to prevent the Supreme Court from deciding two abortion cases this term and may have caused an ultimate shift in the court's position on abortion." Citing only "informed" and "reliable" sources, the *Post* said that "a majority of the seven-man court in tentative voting at the conference favored proponents of legalized abortion in both cases. Though the exact vote on each case is not known, Burger and Justice Byron R. White dissented in both." The story went on to refer to a William O. Douglas to Burger memorandum that had objected to Burger's assigning the cases to Harry Blackmun, and that Blackmun during the spring had prepared draft opinions holding both antiabortion laws unconstitutional on a variety of grounds, including the right to privacy. The story also reported that Blackmun had asked to have the cases held over, and that a majority of the Court, including Burger, had agreed, over Douglas's strenuous objection. The following day the *New York Times*, without ever mentioning the *Post*'s story, reported that while "Justices who could be reached refused to comment," "sources close to the Court" had confirmed the news.

One justice who could not be reached was William O. Douglas, whose summer home in Washington state did not have a phone, but the very day that the *Post* account appeared, Douglas had happened to call his wife Cathy back in Washington from the nearest accessible phone, and she immediately apprised him of the *Post*'s report. Douglas was truly mortified, and without delay he sent Warren Burger a handwritten letter of regret. Although Douglas's salutation of "Dear Chief Justice" was notably impersonal, he explained how Cathy had told him about the *Post*'s

> nasty story about the Abortion Cases, my memo to the Conference, etc. etc.
>
> I am upset and appalled. I have never breathed a word concerning these cases, or my memo, to anyone outside the Court. I have no idea where the writer got the story.
>
> We have our differences; but so far as I am concerned they are wholly internal; and if revealed, they are mirrored in opinions filed, never in "leaks" to the press.
>
> I am taking the liberty of sending a copy of this letter to you to the other Brethren.

Somewhat curiously, Douglas closed his letter "With affectionate regards," but while Douglas understandably expected that Burger and others would assume that he was the source of the *Post*'s unprecedented story, the more complicated truth was that the story had emerged in large part because of an indiscretion that had landed in the lap of Jack Fuller, a Yale Law School student who was working as a *Post* summer intern. In addition, the larger story of internal Court unhappiness with Burger was a favorite subject of the justice who loathed Warren Burger the most intensely of all, Potter Stewart. Several years later it would be no secret at the Court that Stewart, apropos of one young *Post* reporter—who in July 1972 was busy helping investigate a "third rate burglary" on the other side of town—"saw Bob Woodward as different from the press," as a well-informed observer put it. Likewise, numerous other participants in the internal life of the Court, even without being asked, would in later years bring up the subject of Stewart's acquaintance with another subsequently well-known journalist, simply to insist that it was of course "a friendship, not a relationship." Far less attention was ever paid to Stewart's friendship with an older *Post* reporter who covered the Court, and hence it was no accident that the intern's good luck resulted in so important a story appearing on the *Post*'s front page without any byline at all.

Most justices had left Washington for the summer by the time the *Post*'s story appeared, and it created no immediate crisis or flurry of memos. Harry Blackmun had returned to Minnesota to spend two quiet weeks in the medical library at the Mayo Clinic, where he looked into the history of state abortion statutes, the prior record of various medical and professional groups' attitudes toward abortion, and the traditional status accorded the antiabortion reference that appeared in doctors' Hippocratic Oath. George Frampton remained in Washington to help Blackmun incorporate his new research into the existing *Doe* and *Roe* drafts, for only in August would the new clerks for the Court's 1972–1973 term arrive to start work. Even in midsummer, however, Blackmun privately made it clear that there was no chance whatsoever that his position in the abortion cases would shift as a result of any lobbying by the Chief Justice. As one Blackmun intimate later recounted, "there was no question that Blackmun was tired of being referred to as a 'Minnesota Twin' and tired of being leaned on by such an overbearing son-of-a-bitch as Warren Burger."

Most of July passed without any follow-up developments to the *Post* story whatsoever, but late in the month Warren Burger wrote Bill Douglas a four-page, single-spaced "PERSONAL" and "CONFIDENTIAL" letter reviewing all of the earlier events, and mailed copies to the other seven justices as well. Burger asserted that he was "impelled" to compose the letter in light of Douglas's internally distributed but never published dissent, for it had contained "a number of factual errors . . . that should not be allowed to stand uncorrected." Additionally, since Douglas's "circulation of at least 18 copies" of the document had created the "obvious risk that the subject would, as it did, get outside the security of the Court, albeit in garbled form,"

something akin to "due process" suggests that the facts be clarified of record.

1. It is not accurate, as you state, that "The Chief Justice represented the minority view in the Conference" on the abortion cases, unless you add that there was no majority for any firm position. On the Texas case there was a consensus, if not unanimity, that the Texas statute had to fall. There were varying views as to the basis. No one's notes are controlling nor likely to be comprehensive, or even precisely accurate. Mine are "final disposition to wait on writing and grounds" as to both cases.

My notes show, and my recollection is the same, that on the Georgia case there was no "majority" in the sense of identifying the assigning authority. It is not in accord with my records of the Conference or my recollection that "out of the seven there were four who initially took a majority view," as you state. There simply was no majority for any clearcut disposition on all the issues or even the basic issues, and that is not at all unusual in a case of this kind. Some of us saw one aspect of infirmity in the Georgia statute; others saw different weaknesses. The discussion was extended and positions altered in the course of it—which is also not unusual.

In an odd sort of overkill, Burger went on at some length to empha-size that neither Douglas, Brennan, Stewart, White nor Marshall—the five justices besides himself and Blackmun who heard *Doe* —had *ever* expressly indicated that *they* rather than Burger should have assigned *Doe*. "The correct evaluation of the Conference discussion, as I see it, was made by at least three Justices during the Conference, when they said their final position, in the Georgia case particularly, would 'depend on how it is written.'" Douglas's "unprecedented" draft, Burger sug-gested, "seems to imply bad faith if positions are not firm, fixed and final when a Conference adjourns." Lastly, Burger insisted that "I have never taken to assign from a minority position," and that when Douglas eight months earlier had complained about Burger's making the assignment in *Doe*, no other justice had concurred. Thus, "there is not the slightest basis" for Douglas recapitulating that claim again and again.

Burger closed his long letter with incongruously warm greetings to Douglas and his wife from both himself and his spouse, and with little delay Douglas responded with a warm note that seemed to put the controversy to rest:

> Dear Chief:
> I have your memo relative to my earlier memo on the Abortion Cases. That chapter in the Abortion Cases is for me gone and forgotten.
> I wrote the memo for internal consumption only. I showed it to no one not on our staff. I did not "leak" it to the press.
> I believe in full candor on our internal procedures, for, as I said before, we are a group with fiercely opposed ideas but we have always been a friendly, harmonious group. That's the only way I want it.
> I did not write the memo for posterity. It would be the least interest-ing of anything to those who follow.
> My Conference notes obviously differ from yours. I think, quite respectfully, that mine are more complete. The reason Bill Brennan, not I, represented the consensus at the first Conference on the Abortion Cases was that I thought at the time that the cases—at least Georgia's—could be disposed of on Equal Protection grounds—a theory that did not hold up on further study. It was, however, clear that there were five who probably would reverse [*sic*: affirm]; and on assignments we all deal only with probabilities, not with certainties.

Douglas concluded by mentioning that in a few days' time Justice and Mrs. Rehnquist would be visiting him and Cathy at their summer home, and inviting Burger and his wife to soon do the same.[99]

The *Washington Post* story generated relatively little discussion or analysis among the relevant litigators, who neither dismissed nor fully accepted its rendition of events inside the Court. Both Sarah and Ron Weddington and Margie Hames attended the American Bar Association's summer meeting in San Francisco, where Sarah was told that "Blackmun's clerk stayed late this summer to finish writing the opinion" and where Justice Powell delivered what Weddington felt was a discouraging speech decrying America's growing sexual permissiveness. "I also had a few minutes to talk with Justice Douglas during the ABA meeting," Sarah told NARAL's Lee Gidding, "but he was extremely guarded about any comment regarding the case." Antiabortion activists, who met in Philadelphia for the third annual assembly of the National Right to Life Committee, were similarly uncertain about the Court and laid plans to push for a federal constitutional amendment reestablishing "the rights of the unborn" should the decisions invalidate antiabortion laws. More and more journalistic accounts were crediting the "right to life" forces with rapidly expanding political influence, and nowhere were those perceptions more readily apparent than in the refusal of the Democratic party and its newly chosen presidential nominee, South Dakota Senator George McGovern, to take any position whatsoever on the issue of abortion. Prominent feminist writers and political activists such as Betty Friedan and Gloria Steinem denounced McGovern for his repeated equivocations, but most commentators portrayed the Democrats' stance as a politically astute move in the face of President Nixon's efforts to capitalize upon his well-publicized opposition to abortion as part of his reelection strategy.[100]

On the legal front, Roy Lucas achieved another lower court triumph similar to his Kansas City victory when a federal district judge in Baltimore, citing *Griswold* and *Eisenstadt*, threw out Dr. Vuitch's 1969 Maryland abortion conviction and voided the hospitalization requirement that Maryland's reform statute, like the Georgia one under challenge in *Doe*, imposed upon all doctors.[101] Two weeks later New York's highest court affirmed the earlier dismissal of Professor Byrn's effort to challenge the constitutionality of that state's 1970 repeal statute on behalf of unwanted fetuses, holding by a 5 to 2 margin that "unborn children have never been recognized as persons in the law in the whole sense." Byrn announced that he would appeal again, this time to the U.S. Supreme Court, but several weeks later New York right-to-life forces suffered another setback when a three-judge federal panel acting on equal protection grounds overturned New York state's refusal to provide Medicaid funding for poor women's abortions, a policy that had previously survived challenge in state courts.[102] Across the Hudson River in New Jersey, however, antiabortion prosecutors who deeply resented the earlier federal court invalidation of their state's abortion statute, defiantly arrested the Englewood Cliffs physician who had greeted the decision by publicly announcing his willingness to perform the procedure. In Indiana, the state Supreme Court upheld the abortion law on the grounds that the measure reflected a compelling state interest in protecting fetal life, but in Michigan a state appellate court declared that "the question of whether any given woman should be given a therapeutic abortion during the first trimester is a question which is properly [left] to the discretion of the physician."[103]

Of far greater political significance than those court decisions, however, was the late August release of public opinion figures from a Gallup poll of almost sixteen hundred Americans two months earlier which showed that 64 percent of respondents—including a remarkable 56 percent majority of *Roman Catholics*—agreed that "the decision to have an abortion should be made solely by a woman and her physician." That 64 percent figure represented a 7 percent increase since a previous poll in January, and even a majority of the 31 percent of respondents who expressed disagreement with that statement nonetheless indicated that abortions should be allowed when a woman's physical or mental health was at issue. Only 7 percent of respondents expressed opposition to each and every one of the "therapeutic" exceptions that ranged beyond "life," and all of those results appeared to seriously contradict the widespread impression that antiabortion forces were rapidly gaining ground. Father James T. McHugh of the U.S. Catholic Conference's Family Life Bureau immediately attacked the wording of the Gallup question, pointing out that if Americans were asked whether they favored "abortion on demand," far less than a majority would assent. Two Catholic sociologists, however, reported in the Jesuit magazine *America* that a comparison of 1965 and 1972 polling data showed a striking change in Roman Catholics' abortion attitudes, and they emphasized that such a trend would likely continue, since the increasing support for liberalization was disproportionately concentrated among younger Catholics.[104]

As summer turned to fall, abortion activists' attention swung increasingly toward the upcoming November referendum in Michigan, where passage of the statewide ballot measure would permit a woman and her doctor to choose abortion at any time during the first twenty weeks of pregnancy. NARAL's national leaders cited the earlier lesson of New

York in warning that "we can be defeated by our own apathy, by our willingness to sit it out and wait for a Supreme Court decision," and Dr. Jack Stack of Alma, one of the most energetic Michigan activists, admonished his colleagues on the Michigan Abortion Referendum Committee that until midsummer "Many supporters withheld their energies and help in the belief that the Supreme Court would resolve the issue imminently." Now, with the virtual certainty that the Michigan tally would be recorded at least a month or more before any Supreme Court decision would be handed down, it had become all the more undeniable that "Victory in Michigan is essential to the movement nationwide." A mid-September poll by the *Detroit News* was extremely encouraging, for it showed that 57 percent of respondents planned to vote for the proposal, and only 37 percent against, with 6 percent undecided. Three weeks later, in early October, with the election only a month away, the *News* repeated its survey, and the indications continued to be most heartening: support had increased two points to 59 percent and opposition had slipped by one to 36 percent.[105]

Only on September 5 did the Supreme Court notify the opposing counsel in both *Roe* and *Doe* that the oral reargument of the cases would take place on Wednesday, October 11, but even several weeks in advance of that announcement, Roy Lucas sent Sarah Weddington a five-page letter recapitulating all of their earlier frictions and closing with a plaintive request that he be allowed to present the reargument in *Roe*. Alternately indignant and forlorn, Lucas's letter sought both sympathy and renewal. Being taken off the first argument, especially when the reasons "were either irrelevant or shallow," Lucas said, "was like being told: Thank you for getting jurisdiction, and for four years of your life, and for going into debt up to and beyond your ears, but no thanks. It seemed incomprehensible." He recounted his painfully penultimate 1971 phone conversation with Marsha King, and described how unmistakably clear it was that she had heard a detailed account of Cyril Means and Joe Nellis's slurs against him. "In every social movement," Lucas bitterly observed, "the young upstarts are defamed by others, and the abortion movement was no exception."

Lucas went on to offer a decidedly creative account of his initial involvement in *Roe*, asserting that "It was no small undertaking to agree to handle the appeal. I spent months and months of hard work . . . rather than to let the case die." Professing that he had presumed that Weddington and Coffee had turned the case over to him for good, Lucas claimed that "I thought you were all honorable people and would not attempt to take unfair advantage of me." Lucas did concede, with regard to the Madison Institute, that "you probably think I let you and Ron down too, since you both quit your jobs," but he quickly returned to *Roe*, acknowledging that their mutual friend and former colleague Nick Danforth "has probably told you how I thought your argument could have been improved" in the initial presentation. "It takes a lot of experience and dedication to be able to anticipate and respond to the Court's questions in a way which strengthens your case. When Justice Stewart suggested that you get off the policy arguments and talk about law (he put it nicely, though) it was a sign that you were talking to the general public and the audience. The Justices are interested in law," and Sarah had erred both in her handling of *Vuitch* and in failing to mention former Justice Clark's article, for "the Court is more likely to read that than any brief from mortals." Lucas did admit that "much of your argument was well done, but much could have been far better, and that is crucial with a sharply and closely divided Court." Given the circumstances, the reargument would be all the more critical. "Not only do a few Justices appear to be wavering, with Justice Burger leading the opposition lobbyists, but also the questioning will be much more difficult and intense."

After insinuating that Weddington herself had once confessed to Danforth that Lucas could have done a better job than she had, Roy emphasized that "my primary interest has been and remains to see that the abortion repeal movement, and the people affected thereby, receives the most thorough representation and advocacy available ... I only regret not having labored more, and especially not having maintained better personal relations with colleagues whose efforts I respect such as you and Ron and many others." However heartfelt the regret, Lucas closed by highlighting how "the fact of my being taken off the argument in *Roe* destroyed my fund-raising capabilities," but that Sarah now had an opportunity to make amends. "The boost of a well-done and successful argument in the fall would change all of that, and would even out our mutual obligations. Think about it. It is up to you."[106]

Sarah needed no time at all in order to make up her mind about Lucas's request, and whether or not Lucas had imagined that he might receive a reply, he should not have been surprised when he did not. Sarah was much more focused on her all-but-certain upcoming election to the Texas house than on sitting down to write a supplemental Supreme Court brief for *Roe*, but by the second week of September she had prepared a succinctly written seventeen-page statement that noted the relevance of *Eisenstadt* as well as of the favorable lower court abortion decisions that had been handed down in Vermont, New Jersey,

Kansas, Connecticut, and Maryland since *Roe*'s first argument. Weddington also directly confronted Texas's prior claim that the purpose of its 1854 statute was to protect fetal life, observing that "since self-abortion is not a crime in Texas, it is not logical to assume that the purpose of the legislature in passing the so-called 'abortion' law was to protect the fetus. It is logical that the legislative purpose was to protect the woman and her health."

Sarah's brief was somewhat more extensive than the nine-page supplemental submission that Margie Hames filed in *Doe*, which also stressed *Eisenstadt*, but whereas Sarah was able to note that abortion availability in Texas remained just as legally restricted as it had been when *Roe* was first filed, in Georgia, or at least in Atlanta, actual hospital practices had liberalized considerably over the past nine months. The one other supplemental brief, filed on behalf of PPFA by Harriet Pilpel and her colleagues, devoted much of its space to describing how current medical evidence from both reform and repeal states demonstrated that early legal abortions were now even safer for a woman than actual childbirth. Pilpel also sought to remind the Court that "Except possibly for military service, imprisonment and capital punishment . . . it is difficult to imagine a more drastic restriction on privacy or on the fundamental freedom to control one's body and one's life" than compulsory childbearing, a point that was also made in the one new amicus submission supporting the plaintiffs, filed on behalf of several small California organizations. Neither Dorothy Beasley nor Jay Floyd submitted supplemental briefs, but the general counsel of the National Right to Life Committee, Martin F. McKernan, Jr., prepared a short statement urging the Court to reverse the declaratory judgments against the Texas and Georgia laws on the grounds that federal courts should abstain from such holdings. McKernan himself recruited the attorneys general of Utah and Kentucky as signers, and at McKernan's request Jay Floyd willingly wrote to six other prospects whom McKernan suggested, seeking their endorsement of the impending amicus brief. In the end three other states—Connecticut, Arizona, and Nebraska—signed on to the Right to Life Committee's project, but when the actual ten-page document was filed with the Court in late September, it featured only the names of the five attorneys general, and no indication whatsoever that it had been initiated or written by the Right to Life Committee.[107]

The same day that the Attorneys General's ostensible brief was submitted, the three-judge federal court in Connecticut that had been considering the New Haven women's complaint against the state's newly reenacted antiabortion statute struck down the four-month-old law on much the same constitutional grounds that had led them to void its predecessor back in April. U.S. District Judge Jon O. Newman, writing for himself and Circuit Judge J. Edward Lumbard, explicitly acknowledged that annulling the new statute—which declared that Connecticut's policy was "to protect and preserve human life from the moment of conception," and allowed only those abortions "necessary to preserve the physical life" of a pregnant woman—was a much tougher decision than the one in the spring. Nevertheless, "the constitutionally protected right of a woman to privacy and personal choice in matters of sex and family life" was undeniable in the light of *Griswold* and *Eisenstadt*, and indeed, Newman said, quoting Justice Brennan's "bear or beget" sentence, the *Eisenstadt* opinion "may have anticipated the outcome of cases such as this." Reflecting at some length upon the meaning of *Griswold*, Newman observed that "The opinion of Justice Douglas appears to posit the right of marital privacy as an absolute right, totally immune from state abridgement. The opinions of Justices Harlan, White and Goldberg, however, all concede that the right may be abridged if the state can demonstrate that its regulation is founded upon a sufficiently compelling state interest." Thus, "It may well be that the right of a woman to decide whether or not to carry to term the fetus within her is a right immune from total governmental abridgement," especially since "the right to an abortion is of even greater concern to the woman than the right to use a contraceptive protected in *Griswold*." Like other jurists before him, Newman also concluded that "a fetus is not a person within the meaning of the Fourteenth Amendment" and "its capacity to become such a person does not mean that during gestation it is such a person." Indeed, Newman noted, "it is difficult to imagine how a statute permitting abortion could be constitutional if the fetus had Fourteenth Amendment rights." Hence he and Lumbard, over another angry dissent from Judge Clarie, granted the plaintiffs both declaratory and injunctive relief against the new statute, and Connecticut's effort to obtain a stay of their order while the state appealed was refused by Justice Marshall.[108]

Two far less favorable decisions soon followed, as the Supreme Courts of first South Dakota and then Missouri each reversed lower court rulings and upheld their states' antiabortion laws, but repeal activists remained preoccupied with the upcoming Michigan vote and the certainty of another large right to life effort in the 1973 New York legislature.[109] NARAL purposely held its early October annual meeting in Detroit, and while a *New York Times* story on the gathering stated that "Pro-abortion forces believe they are on the verge of major victories that will soon make abortion on request available throughout much of the country," New York City council member and outgoing NARAL president Carol Greitzer bluntly told her colleagues that repeal proponents, particularly in her home state, would have a difficult time even just preserving the achievements they had won to date. "The ultimate court decision we have been counting on has been delayed once again, and owing to the changing makeup of the court, the prognosis is less optimistic," Greitzer cautioned. Politically, "we have done little to broaden our base," and especially in New York "it is regrettable that more mature women who would make more of an impression on legislators have not been involved." There would have to be "a real effort to recruit activists and bodies from other established organizations," as well as "an end to divisiveness" and narrow-mindedness within the movement. "I deeply regret the chauvinism of some women's groups," Greitzer pointedly declared.

With reporters, Larry Lader and the Michigan activists struck a decidedly different tone, with Lader proclaiming that "This is the breakthrough year for abortion" and Jack Stack predicting that the Michigan referendum would pass with 61 percent support. NARAL executive director Lee Gidding emphasized that the Michigan vote would be "the most visible expression of public opinion in the nation," and stressed that a victory would be "terribly significant." Michigan repeal proponents had almost fifty thousand dollars, most of which had been contributed by the United Methodist Church, available for media advertising during the campaign's final four weeks, and so far the opposing forces had seemed all but invisible. Political observers believed that the North Dakota repeal referendum stood little chance of passage, but Michigan would be vastly more important, and former state senator Lorraine Beebe, who had sponsored one of the earliest abortion bills, told one reporter that "It would set the movement back ten years if we lose."[110]

In preparation for the October 11 rearguments of *Roe* and *Doe* in the Supreme Court, Sarah Weddington asked Harriet Pilpel to set up another moot court practice session the preceding afternoon for herself and Margie Hames, and Pilpel recruited Cyril Means, Joe Nellis, and St. Louis's Frank Susman to take part. Weddington herself had not been looking forward to the reargument, in large part because of the degree of mystery that the summer news reports and rumors had created concerning the Court's outlook, and several weeks earlier Sarah told one Texas audience that "I don't think anybody can say what the outcome of the case will be." The morning of the argument itself, Sarah and Ron Weddington had breakfast with Linda Coffee and Margie Hames, and when the time for the ten a.m. presentation came, Roy Lucas seated himself in the area reserved for members of the bar while Ron joined Linda and Sarah at the counsel's table.[111]

In contrast to ten months earlier, Sarah this time was able to deliver almost half of her presentation without encountering any substantive or sustained questioning from the nine-member bench. She summarized the prior history of the case, noted the abortion safety statistics presented in Harriet Pilpel's brief, reiterated the importance of *Griswold*, and directed the Court's attention to the recent decision by the three-judge federal court in Connecticut. When she paused for a moment to recall the name of the Connecticut opinion's author, it quickly became clear that some justices were already quite familiar with the ruling, for Potter Stewart politely interjected "Newman" to resolve Sarah's dilemma. She noted the New York court's *Byrn* decision when first Stewart and then Byron White asked her about the legal status of the fetus, and White pursued the question of whether a fetus should be regarded as a person with some persistence. Warren Burger broke in to ask whether Weddington would draw any distinction between the first and ninth month of gestation, and Sarah twice parried by indicating that Texas's statute did not.

Harry Blackmun asked Sarah whether she placed more reliance upon a vagueness challenge or upon a Ninth Amendment claim, and when Sarah refused to elevate either one above the other, Blackmun shifted subjects and asked whether she had any comment on the Hippocratic oath, which Blackmun said had not been mentioned in any of "the voluminous briefs that we're overwhelmed with here." Sarah floundered briefly, observing that the Hippocratic oath did not speak to the question of constitutional rights, but Blackmun persevered, noting that the oath was "the only definitive statement of ethics of the medical profession." Sarah replied that she had not cited it because it did not seem "pertinent to the argument we were making," and Blackmun changed topics again, inquiring as to whether Sarah felt "there is any inconsistency" between the Court's June decisions striking down the death penalty "and your position in this case." Sarah responded that since the fetus had never been held to be a person, no inconsistency would occur, and Blackmun followed up by asking whether "your case depends primarily on the proposition that the fetus has no constitutional rights?" Sarah stumbled slightly, saying that even if the Court held that a fetus had some rights, "you would still get back into the weighing of one life against another," and Byron White pounced on her immediately: "That's what's involved in this case, weighing one life against another?" "No," Sarah quickly answered, adeptly explaining that that would be the situation only *if* the state could prove that a fetus was a constitutional "person."

Potter Stewart followed up less combatively, but with the same basic question: "if it were established that an unborn fetus is a person," "you would have almost an impossible case here, would you not?" Sarah replied frankly and directly that "I would have a very difficult case," and Stewart responded "I'm sure you would." Warren Burger inquired as to whether Weddington thought that Texas could constitutionally declare that fetuses were legal persons "after the third month of gestation," and Sarah forthrightly answered that "I do not believe that the state legislature can determine the meaning of the federal Constitution. It is up to this Court to make that determination." Sarah deflected a follow-up question from Burger with another reference to *Griswold*, and reserved the final four minutes of her time for subsequent rebuttal comments.

The argument on behalf of Texas this time was presented by Robert C. Flowers, Jay Floyd's immediate superior and since 1968 the chief of the Texas Attorney General's Enforcement Division. A graduate of Texas A&M University and the University of Texas Law School, Flowers would confess to interviewers years later that he had not thought it necessary to prepare any sort of outline in preparation for his appearance. Flowers began straightforwardly, declaring that "it is the position of the state of Texas that upon conception we have a human being, a person within the concept of the Constitution." Stewart immediately inquired as to how one could know that a fetus was indeed a person, and Flowers answered that it was a question for legislatures to resolve. Stewart countered by asking whether Flowers knew of any case which had held that a fetus was a person, and when Flowers conceded that he did not but nonetheless tried to hold his ground, Stewart pointed out how the Fourteenth Amendment explicitly spoke of persons as being "born or naturalized." Flowers in response tried to invoke the eighteenth-century English legal commentator William Blackstone, and Justice Blackmun immediately broke in to ask whether it was "not true that in Blackstone's time abortion was not a felony?" Flowers agreed and sought to shift the discussion to the framers of the U.S. Constitution, but Blackmun pressed him to also acknowledge "that the medical profession itself is not in agreement as to when life begins," and Flowers again acceded. Both Blackmun and White pursued him further, and only when Thurgood Marshall drew audience laughter by asking whether Texas could authorize the killing of a husband so as to benefit a wife's health was Flowers able to utter two complete sentences in succession.

Flowers finally was able to return to his basic point that Texas did view fetuses as constitutional "persons." Harry Blackmun immediately interjected that "Of course, if you're right about that, you can sit down, you've won your case," and Potter Stewart added "Except insofar as maybe the Texas abortion law presently goes too far in allowing abortions." Flowers responded affirmatively, and Byron White rejoined the colloquy to ask whether "You've lost your case, then, if the fetus or the embryo is not a person, is that it?" Flowers answered "Yes, sir, I would say so," and both Burger and Marshall joined White in pressing Flowers still further with regard to Texas's view of the fetus. Stewart again raised the Fourteenth Amendment's postbirth usage of "person," and Marshall queried Flowers as to whether there was "any medical testimony of any kind that says that a fetus is a person as the time of conception." Flowers cited a dissenting opinion from two years earlier in the Illinois abortion case, and after a question from Justice Rehnquist established that even that opinion had not spoken to "the moment of conception," Potter Stewart returned again to the point he had made earlier: "Well, if you're right that an unborn fetus is a person, then you can't leave it to the legislature to play fast and loose dealing with that person. In other words, if you're correct in your basic submission that an unborn fetus is a person, then abortion laws such as that which New York has is grossly unconstitutional, isn't it?" Flowers agreed—"That's right, yes"—and Stewart reiterated that fact twice more before Harry Blackmun, and then Rehnquist, confronted Flowers with several historical questions about the nineteenth-century origins of the Texas law. When Flowers told Blackmun that he did not know what motives had underlain the enactment of such statutes, the ostensibly helpful Stewart volunteered that wasn't it the case that "they were enacted to protect the health and lives of pregnant women because of the danger of operative procedures generally around that time?" Flowers once again readily agreed—"I'm sure that was a great factor, your honor"—and as his thirty minutes expired, Sarah Weddington returned to the podium for her final remarks.

When Sarah began her rebuttal argument by highlighting how even Flowers had acknowledged that no one could prove when "life" begins, Justice White doggedly inquired as to whether Sarah thus meant that a state could not protect a fetus even during the later stages of pregnancy.

Sarah persistently avoided giving a direct answer, and Chief Justice Burger asked her whether the Court could preserve the Texas statute by reconstruing it in light of *Vuitch*. Sarah noted that *Vuitch* had not dealt with the right to privacy, and then spoke to Blackmun's earlier question by pointing out that the Hippocratic oath "was adopted at a time when abortion was extremely dangerous to the health of the woman." Moving toward a summation, Sarah emphasized that "We are not here to advocate abortion. We do not ask this Court to rule that abortion is good or desirable in any particular situation. We are here to advocate that the decision as to whether or not a particular woman will continue to carry or will terminate a pregnancy is a decision that should be made by that individual" and that "she has a constitutional right to make that decision for herself." Byron White suggested that this meant "you are urging upon us abortion on demand," and Sarah gave an appropriately measured response, saying she was urging that Texas's statute was unconstitutional and citing Justice Brennan's crucial sentence from *Eisenstadt* as powerful support. Chief Justice Burger noted that her time had expired, and with the argument in *Roe* v. *Wade* now complete, Margie Hames and Dorothy Beasley immediately stepped forward to begin the reargument of *Doe* v. *Bolton*.

Margie Hames commenced her presentation by stressing that the *Doe* plaintiffs were "relying principally on this Court's decision in *Griswold*" more so than on any particular constitutional provision. She described once again *Doe*'s challenge to the various provisions of the Georgia reform statute, and particularly the hospitalization requirement that the Atlanta panel had upheld, and during the first half of her presentation she was confronted with almost no questions from the nine justices. Blackmun and Lewis Powell eventually asked several questions about the hospitalization issue and both Rehnquist and Burger posed additional queries about medical self-regulation. Byron White unsuccessfully sought a direct answer to the question of whether or not a state could impose a twenty-week limit, and Hames reserved three minutes of her time for rebuttal comments before Dorothy Beasley stood up to deliver the argument on behalf of Georgia Attorney General Arthur K. Bolton.

Beasley began by investing several minutes in a long and unproductive colloquy with William Rehnquist about jurisdiction, and then Warren Burger posed a series of questions concerning tonsillectomies. Thurgood Marshall took issue with Beasley's characterization of the fetus, saying "I have great problems with this 'living being' point," and when Beasley sought to turn the constitutional tables on the plaintiffs by insisting that the fetus ought to have a Ninth Amendment right to be "let alone," Marshall retorted that "You can't recognize the Ninth Amendment for the fetus and not recognize the Ninth Amendment for the mother, can you?" Harry Blackmun commented that he had asked Beasley ten months earlier at the first argument why the Georgia statute failed to include an incest exception, and while Beasley time and again returned to her basic emphasis on Georgia's primary interest in fetal life, her distinctively keen and high-pitched voice increasingly seemed to take on a touch of anger as the argument progressed.

Precisely at noontime the Court adjourned for lunch, and when the argument resumed at one p.m. for the final ten minutes of Beasley's presentation, one questioner inquired as to whether different legal standards could be imposed subsequent to the first trimester of pregnancy. When Beasley again reiterated that "If there's anything emanating from the Ninth Amendment, it's the fetus's right to be left alone," Chief Justice Burger seemed to disagree, and as Beasley's time expired, Margie Hames returned to the podium for a final few moments of remarks that were almost exclusively devoted to a colloquy with Justice Blackmun about the Hippocratic oath. At one fourteen the presentation of *Doe* v. *Bolton* officially concluded, and without delay the attorneys began to ponder just what the morning's proceedings portended for their chances.[112]

Sarah and Ron Weddington had lunch with Linda Coffee, Marsha King, and Texas supporter Ruth Bowers, and while Linda was more optimistic than she had been four hours before, Sarah was decidedly less happy than she had been after the initial argument ten months earlier. Once again Sarah had encountered no major problems while delivering a solid and occasionally eloquent performance, but the far less intense questioning from the justices had been unsettling rather than encouraging, and made her think that "most of them already had their minds made up." Harriet Pilpel had told Sarah as they were leaving the Court that she believed they had a good chance of winning, but as Sarah and her colleagues counted the possible votes, the likely outcome looked very close indeed. Neither Warren Burger nor certainly Byron White had sounded like prospective supporters, and neither William Rehnquist nor Lewis Powell had said anything that was either encouraging or particularly revealing. Sarah and Ron had a sympathetic friend, a 1970 University of Texas Law School graduate, who was clerking for Powell and working on *Roe* and *Doe*, but that alone was no reason to consider Powell as a likely backer. Unless at least one of those four did turn out to be supportive, all five of the other justices—

Blackmun, Stewart, Brennan, Marshall and Douglas—would be neces-
sary in order to prevail. "I may be wrong," Sarah wrote Ginny
Whitehill several days later, "but I think we are going to win this case.
Not sure what grounds or how good the opinion will be, but really
think we'll win. However, I'm worried about the Georgia case. The
Court may just uphold facility restrictions, etc."

In contrast to Sarah's mixed expectations, however, Margie Hames
left the hearing significantly encouraged, both because she had sensed a
distinctly favorable shift in the tone of Warren Burger's questions and
because in her judgment Lewis Powell had also come across as a probable supporter. "I came away very optimistic," Hames explained four
months later. "I really felt like we were going to pick up Powell, and I
felt like we were going to pick up Burger." A markedly less sanguine
assessment, however, came from Roy Lucas, who—knowing full well
Cyril Means's proclivity for sharing with others the stories and letters
that came his way—sent Means a decidedly disparaging evaluation of
the *Roe* and *Doe* presentations. The high court, Lucas said, "must think
the abortion movement (on both sides) hasn't a competent attorney in
its ranks. By any standard, the arguments were amateurish and unin-
formed, even worse than last December. Hopefully the Court will do
as it has done before and perceive the cases in a more sophisticated
light than they were presented. A number of professional federal appellate advocates were in the audience, and you should have heard their
remarks. The respect for the women's movement was set back ten
years. Any law student who had skimmed" one or another standard
treatise "would have done better," Lucas sarcastically concluded. And
just as Roy Lucas might have expected, Cyril Means wasted no time
whatsoever in sending a copy of Lucas's letter to Sarah Weddington.
"Thank goodness I've heard good things from others," Sarah told
Ginny Whitehill after reading Lucas's deprecations. "Considering the
source," she added, "this 'rolls like water off a duck's back.'"[113]

Once again, however, the reactions of the interested litigators—
whether canny or just catty—would count for very little compared to
the reactions of the nine men who actually would decide both *Roe* and
Doe. When the justices convened for their private conference on the
two cases, they considered the cases in tandem rather than sequentially,
and Chief Justice Burger began the discussion by frankly stating that
the Texas statute was "bad" and "too restrictive." Burger explained that
he was uncertain as to whether he could support voiding it on vagueness grounds, as Blackmun's earlier draft opinion had done, but Burger
was sure that a state could not by means of a criminal statute aimed at

doctors restrict abortions to only those which would save a woman's life. *Doe*, however, was "much more complex," Burger said, because "a state has a right to legislate" with regard to abortions, as the Court previously had indicated in *Vuitch*. Additionally, Burger stated, "fetal life is entitled to protection at some point."

William O. Douglas concisely said that he agreed with Burger about Texas and also agreed with the *Roe* and *Doe* drafts that Blackmun had circulated back in May. Bill Brennan stated that he too endorsed both of Blackmun's drafts, and Potter Stewart announced that his position also remained the same as before. Stewart added, however, that it was essential for the Court to deal with the claim that a "fetus is not a person within [the] 14th Amendment," since both the Connecticut decision and the *Byrn* case in New York had confronted the issue. "That doesn't mean [a] fetus has no rights or can't be given them by the State," Stewart declared, but he also could not say that the Texas law was void for vagueness. Stewart explained that he very much liked Jon Newman's reasoning in the Connecticut case, and that constitutionally the Court should not rest upon the Ninth Amendment. "It's a 14th Amendment right, as John Harlan said in *Griswold*."

Byron White agreed that a fetus was not a "person" under the Fourteenth Amendment, but emphasized that this did not end either case, for the Court had to weigh the woman's Fourteenth Amendment right against the state's interest in protecting the fetus. "I'm not going to second-guess state legislatures in striking the balance in favor of abortion laws." Unless states were to be barred from prohibiting *any* abortions, including those based simply on the "personal convenience" of the mother, the Georgia and Texas statutes should not be held facially void. "Why cannot a state, at least after a certain period of gestation, say 'no abortion' or require cesarean operations for women who rest solely on convenience? No women in these cases assert injury to life or health." He would vote to uphold the Georgia statute, White said, and would pass in the Texas case, for he could not agree that the Texas law was vague.

Thurgood Marshall noted that in Texas a "woman who aborts herself is in the clear" and that "no doctor would perform" an abortion when a pregnancy was well advanced. Marshall indicated that he agreed with Potter Stewart regarding the fetus, and would stand by the outcomes that Blackmun had reached five months earlier.

Harry Blackmun himself offered the lengthiest remarks at what was otherwise an extremely concise conference. "I am where I was last spring," Blackmun told his colleagues, and "I'd make Georgia the lead case." He had revised both the Texas and Georgia opinions from where they had stood in May, and he reviewed point by point all the preliminary issues of jurisdiction, standing, and mootness that would have to be dealt with in the final decisions. Blackmun said he wanted to include a discussion of the history of abortion in the opinions, and that constitutionally he would rest upon the Fourteenth Amendment, not the Ninth. During pregnancy, Blackmun went on, "there is a point where other interests are at stake [and] where [a] state can regulate." He added that he would hold invalid the Georgia hospitalization requirement, although the opinion would indicate that states could require abortions to be performed in licensed facilities, and the *Doe* opinion would also strike down Georgia's residency requirement and the provision mandating prior approval by multiple doctors and a hospital committee.

Unlike the Georgia law, Blackmun continued, the Texas act was void for vagueness, and *Vuitch* could indeed be reconciled with such a holding. He would make *Doe* rather than *Roe* "the leading opinion," but Blackmun emphasized to his colleagues that "if [the] Texas act falls, abortion laws in a majority of our states fall." Hence, "we might hold [the actual] mandate for awhile," Blackmun explained, since he "wants to avoid complete disorganization."

The eighth justice, Lewis Powell, had privately made up his mind about *Roe* and *Doe* back in September, several weeks before the oral arguments, after giving both cases considerable thought toward the end of the summer recess. Upon returning to Washington, Powell told Larry Hammond, the clerk who was helping him with the two cases, that he wanted to have lunch at The Monocle, Capitol Hill's premier restaurant, to discuss *Roe* and *Doe*. Hammond pessimistically concluded that the fancy setting was intended as recompense for what Powell knew Hammond would regard as bad news, and hence it "hit me like a ton of bricks," Hammond later recalled, when the quiet and gentlemanly Powell began the lunch by saying, "Larry, I'm inclined to affirm" the Dallas and Atlanta panels' decisions. Neither Hammond nor Powell's other clerks had told their friends in other chambers about Powell's stance prior to the conference, and hence it came as news to almost all of his colleagues when Powell began his conference remarks by saying that he was "basically in accord with Harry's position" except for being concerned about allowing a doctor to rely on "economic considerations" or other such factors "unless they relate to health." Powell said that he thought *Roe* "should [be] the lead case" and that he would decide it not on vagueness grounds but on the more basic issue.

Powell's comment prompted Blackmun to volunteer that he would be "willing to bypass vagueness" and put the Texas and Georgia cases onto much the same grounds. That proposal met with no objections, and the conference discussion came to a quick end as Bill Rehnquist, the final justice to speak, said simply that he agreed with Byron White.

This time, in contrast to ten months earlier, the conference's outcome, especially in light of Blackmun's decisive willingness to accede to Lewis Powell's crucial suggestion and move beyond a vagueness holding in *Roe*, was quite susceptible to intelligible vote-counting: with Douglas, Brennan, Stewart, Marshall and Powell all expressing basic agreement with Blackmun, there were definite six-vote majorities for deciding both *Roe* and *Doe*, and in *Roe* it had sounded as if there was a seventh vote—Warren Burger—as well. Byron White and Bill Rehnquist had plainly indicated their determination to dissent from a decision voiding the Georgia statute, but their stance in *Roe* remained uncertain, as did Warren Burger's in *Doe*. Thus Harry Blackmun left the conference knowing that he would be revising his opinions on behalf of at least a seven-justice majority in one case and a six-justice one in the other. Equally important, because of both Blackmun's own resolute commitment and Lewis Powell's clear stance, the conference discussion also established that none of the fears that William O. Douglas and Potter Stewart had entertained five months earlier would actually come to pass.[114]

Looking back on those *Roe* and *Doe* discussions and his own momentous role six years later, Lewis Powell recalled that the decision had not been difficult. *Griswold*, he related, had protected "a personal and private relationship that should be free from state regulation," and *Roe* and *Doe* presented the same basic question. "The concept of liberty was the underlying principle of the abortion case—the liberty to make certain highly personal decisions that are terribly important to people," Powell explained. "It is difficult to think of a decision that's more personal or more important to a pregnant woman than whether or not she will bear a child."[115]

Following the conference discussion, five weeks passed before Harry Blackmun circulated revised opinions, and while external events did not alter the Court's course, for repeal activists those intervening developments raised the judicial stakes even higher. Most public attention with regard to abortion was focused on Michigan, where opponents of the November 7 repeal referendum first began broadcasting television ads against the measure only on October 13. Six days later another *Detroit News* statewide poll showed that 56 percent of respondents continued to support the proposal, but during the ensuing two weeks, as the thirty-second spots purchased by "Voice of the Unborn" continued to appear, public sentiment started to shift significantly, and when the *News* on November 3 publicized the results of a final poll that had been completed on October 31, the numbers revealed a startling turnaround: only 42 percent of respondents now backed the twenty-week repeal measure, and the proportion of opponents had shot up from 40 to 54. One month earlier, repeal activist Dr. Jack Stack had predicted a 61 percent victory when the ballots were counted, but when the votes were actually tallied late on the night of November 7, the statewide result was painfully ironic: only 39 percent of voters had supported repeal, and a whopping 61 percent majority had voted against it. In North Dakota the far less heralded repeal referendum went down to an even more overwhelming 77 percent to 23 percent defeat, but it was the Michigan result—and the considerable importance that repeal proponents all across the country had attached to it—that drew the most attention. Texas's Ginny Whitehill wrote to Stack mourning the "tragic outcome," and NARAL's Larry Lader privately confessed that it was "a terrible blow." Stack himself gallantly conceded that "Our opponents waged a fantastically sophisticated political campaign in the last three or four weeks" and he acknowledged how antiabortion forces had mustered "a tremendous grass-roots organization that we couldn't begin to match." ASA executive director Jimmye Kimmey, however, offered a far more specific analysis of why the early poll numbers had turned out to be so highly misleading. "The main thing going for the opposition," she explained, "was the 20-week limit," for evidence now suggested that that ceiling "was perceived as too late by a significant number of those who had, without at the moment thinking about the time limit, responded 'Yes' to the pollsters' question."[116]

The same day that the Michigan and North Dakota measures were going down to defeat, Sarah Weddington won election to the Texas house by a margin of almost fifty thousand votes. Both she and other Texas activists began making plans to champion a repeal bill in the 1973 legislature if the Supreme Court did not void the existing Texas law, and Ginny Whitehill pessimistically told one friend that the Texans were "still holding out a ray of hope for the Supreme Court to come through." The legislative prospects for a repeal bill, moreover, were already rather doubtful, and Whitehill ruefully confessed to one ally that "we know well that the opposition is gaining strength and momentum."[117]

Upcoming political struggles were even more of a concern for New York abortion activists, who had been increasingly apprehensive about their state's 1973 legislative session even before the stunning Michigan results were announced. Both PPFA and New York City Planned Parenthood leaders charted a major political outreach effort to defend the 1970 law, but officers of Planned Parenthood affiliates in such upstate cities as Albany and Schenectady vociferously objected to the organization taking a highly visible position on the subject. Albany's president warned that the affiliates' fund-raising prospects would be badly harmed if PPFA failed to "maintain a low profile on the abortion issue" and the Schenectady president reported that "Our Board has emphasized repeatedly that we should not jeopardize the rest of the services that we want to provide by having our community image locked in with the abortion hassle." Some New York activists feared that the greatest threat to the 1970 law would arise if President Nixon—whose willingness to work hand-in-glove with New York abortion opponents had already been proven—could entice Governor Rockefeller to resign in order to accept some irresistible appointment, thus placing antiabortion Lieutenant Governor Malcolm Wilson in a position to sign rather than veto a legislatively approved revocation bill. That worry was not openly broached when Rockefeller met privately with PPFA president Alan Guttmacher—still robust at age seventy-four—to discuss the upcoming battle, but Rockefeller did volunteer that he had "felt very lonely" when he vetoed the earlier revocation measure "because there was no public evidence of grass roots support for his stand."[118]

In late November abortion activists received yet another reminder of how perilous their political position now seemed when passage of an extremely restrictive new antiabortion law in Pennsylvania—allowing only those abortions judged necessary to save a woman's life by *three* doctors—was averted only by Democrat Milton Shapp's gubernatorial veto. Antiabortion forces had defeated an amendment that would have added a rape and incest exception to the bill, and only Pennsylvania's unusually stiff constitutional requirement of 75 percent support in both houses of the legislature prevented Shapp's veto from being over-ridden.

Just as worrisome to some activists as the New York, Michigan, and Pennsylvania evidence that antiabortion forces now had repeal advocates badly outgunned despite the countervailing national public opinion poll numbers was the increasingly prominent usage that right to life leaders were making of visually powerful pictures of aborted fetuses. NARAL's Larry Lader notified his colleagues that one television broadcast, a November 29 PBS show featuring black activist Jesse Jackson and three other abortion opponents, was "a disaster to the abortion movement," largely because one opponent, Marjory Mecklenburg of Minnesota, had been able to dominate the program both with fetal pictures and with what she said was a tape recording of a fetus's heartbeat. The broadcast amounted to "the most damaging national TV coverage in our history," Lader declared, in part because Mecklenburg represented "perhaps our most dangerous opponent, a good-looking woman." Two weeks later another PBS show, "The Advocates," permitted right-to-life representatives to show a series of fetal slides, and Lader admitted that "Their impact was overpowering." He advised that repeal proponents forego media appearances in which opponents would be able to use such pictures and tapes, and advocated that "We must refuse to give equal time in debate to a minority point of view whenever such a tactic is possible." Lader frankly conceded that "the abortion movement has been increasingly pushed to the defensive in recent months," and he acknowledged that "the opposition now employs superb strategy and organization." In short, he told his allies, "We are being steam-rollered." ASA's Jimmye Kimmey offered only a slightly less pessimistic outlook to the Associated Press. "Now that I have seen the fierceness of the opposition, I no longer feel if we got a favorable ruling" from the Court that the struggle "would be over." "Instead of it being the end," it would represent only "the beginning of a tough new era."[119]

One of the few pieces of good news for abortion activists during the final two months of 1972 was late November's 4 to 3 decision by the California Supreme Court striking down that state's pioneering 1967 reform statute on the grounds that one of the crucial phrases in the law's maternal health exception—would continuing a pregnancy "gravely impair" a woman's health—was unconstitutionally vague. The California majority expressly avoided any right to privacy ruling, and upheld the 1967 law's hospitalization requirement, but California activists nonetheless welcomed the decision as "a significant milestone" that officially made "therapeutic abortion at the request of the woman a reality in California." Washington state's best-known provider, Dr. A. Frans Koome, suddenly faced a criminal conviction for performing an abortion on a sixteen-year-old woman in violation of a court's order, but many other judicial matters remained essentially on hold, as lower courts waited for a definitive signal from the U.S. Supreme Court. Indeed, several weeks after the California ruling, the Minnesota

Supreme Court, faced with journalistic inquiries as to why it had not resolved the appeal of Jane Hodgson's conviction that had been presented more than a year earlier, actually issued a press release saying that it was reserving decision until the U.S. Supreme Court handed down opinions in *Roe* and *Doe*, which had originally had been argued just four days after *Hodgson*.[120]

On November 22, 1972, Harry Blackmun circulated to all eight of his colleagues a new draft opinion in *Roe* v. *Wade*. "This has proved for me to be both difficult and elusive," he explained in a cover memo.

> In its present form it contains dictum, but I suspect that in this area some dictum is indicated and not to be avoided.
>
> You will observe that I have concluded that the end of the first trimester is critical. This is arbitrary, but perhaps any other selected point, such as quickening or viability, is equally arbitrary.

Blackmun said that he had "attempted to preserve *Vuitch* in its entirety," even though that might create some complications, and he ended his memorandum on a decidedly self-conscious and subdued note, apologizing for what he termed both "the rambling character" of the draft "and for its undue length. It has been an interesting assignment. As I stated in conference, the decision, however made, will probably result in the Court's being severely criticized."

Blackmun's forty-eight-page *Roe* draft, and a considerably shorter revision of *Doe* that he circulated later that same day, definitely reflected the research Blackmun had performed over the preceding summer. The *Roe* opinion, after dealing with the case's jurisdictional and procedural issues, offered an extended survey of the history of abortion laws and practices reaching back to ancient times, including the Hippocratic oath, and then moved on to survey professional attitudes toward abortion law liberalization over the preceding fifteen years. Along with the draft, Blackmun sent an additional note to Bill Brennan, the Court's only Roman Catholic member, highlighting the fact that in the historical section of the opinion "I have referred to the development of the canon law and to the position of the Catholic Church. I personally would very much appreciate your paying particular attention to these passages. I believe they are accurate factually, but I do not want them to be offensive or capable of being regarded as unduly critical by any reader. Your judgment as to this will be most helpful."

Most importantly of all, as Blackmun had emphasized in his cover letter, the *Roe* draft, particularly in its two final pages, drew an extremely significant line at the end of the first trimester of pregnancy. During that first three months, Blackmun's opinion held, a state "must do no more than to leave the abortion decision to the best medical judgment of the pregnant woman's attending physician." However, "For the stage subsequent to the first trimester, the State may, if it chooses, determine a point beyond which it restricts legal abortions to stated reasonable therapeutic categories that are articulated with sufficient clarity so that a physician is able to predict what conditions fall within the stated classifications."[121]

Reactions to Blackmun's two circulations took several days in coming, but when they did, they were generally quite supportive. William O. Douglas endorsed both opinions and told Blackmun that he would file a revision of his earlier *Doe* statement as a concurrence. Douglas explained that he still believed the Court should uphold rather than dismiss Dr. Hallford's standing in *Roe*, but he stressed that "this is a mere fly speck in the total case. You have done an excellent job." Potter Stewart commended Blackmun for having done "an admirably thorough job" and expressed "basic agreement with the results," while adding that he too might file a concurring opinion. Byron White confessed that he had been "struggling with these cases," and would "probably end up concurring in part and dissenting in part." Three days later Bill Rehnquist wrote that "I am about where Byron said he was" and that he also would "probably concur in part and dissent in part." Lewis Powell informed Blackmun first in person and then in writing that he was "generally in accord with your fine opinions," and no doubt would formally join once he had the time to offer a few suggestions.

Along with Warren Burger, the only other members of the Court from whom Blackmun did not formally hear in the first two weeks following his November 22 circulations were Bill Brennan and Thurgood Marshall. Brennan and Marshall were two of Blackmun's most expressly declared supporters, and their formal silence was in large part a reflection of how close an interaction two of Blackmun's new clerks, Randy Bezanson and Jim Ziglar, had developed with their Marshall and Brennan counterparts concerning *Roe* and *Doe*. Within Brennan's chambers, the two cases were now the responsibility of Bill Maledon, a University of Notre Dame Law School graduate who had published a senior year paper in Notre Dame's law journal arguing that the "unborn child" had an inalienable right to life and insisting that "abortion has absolutely nothing to do with marital privacy." Even one of Blackmun's clerks had serious doubts about the constitutional status of *Roe* and *Doe*, doubts that led to lively intellectual exchanges within the Blackmun chambers, but Bill Maledon's deep discomfort with abortion was well-known by any number of fellow clerks, and one sympathetic colleague believed that Maledon was "under a considerable tension" in trying to assist Justice Brennan with Blackmun's *Roe* and *Doe* drafts.

In Thurgood Marshall's chambers, the new clerk assigned to the abortion cases, Mark Tushnet, had no hesitations about the Blackmun circulations, and told Marshall that the *Roe* opinion was "one the Court can be proud of." Tushnet recommended that Marshall join it "without reservation," but he also pointed out that the final two pages of Blackmun's draft could benefit from some tightening and clarification, particularly with regard to how it referred to a "compelling" state interest in regulating post-first trimester abortions.[122]

Marshall made no formal response to Blackmun's circulations, but sometime in the second week of December, after further conversations among the clerks from the three allied chambers, Bill Brennan personally raised with Blackmun a concern that he had also discussed with Marshall. In response, Blackmun on December 11 circulated to all of his colleagues a two-page memo that offered some far more extensive thoughts about the crucial bench mark he had employed in the opinions and which he had previously highlighted in his initial cover memo:

> One of the members of the Conference has asked whether my choice of the end of the first trimester, as the point beyond which a state may appropriately regulate abortion practices, is critical. He asks whether the point of viability might not be a better choice.
>
> The inquiry is a valid one and deserves serious consideration. I selected the earlier point because I felt that it would be more easily accepted (by us as well as others) and because most medical statistics and statistical studies appear to me to be centered there. Viability, however, has its own strong points. It has logical and biological justifications. There is a practical aspect, too, for I am sure that there are many pregnant women, particularly younger girls, who may refuse to face the fact of pregnancy and who, for one reason or another, do not get around to medical consultation until the end of the first trimester is upon them, or, indeed, has passed.
>
> I suspect that few could argue, or would argue, that a state's interest by the time of viability, when independent life is presumably possible, is not sufficiently developed to justify appropriate regulation. What we are talking about, therefore, is the interval from approximately 12 weeks to about 28 weeks.
>
> One argument for the *earlier* date is that the state may well be concerned about facilities and such things as the need of hospitalization

from and after the first trimester. If the point of viability is selected, a decision of this kind is necessarily left to the attending physician.

I would be willing to recast the opinions at the later date, but I do not wish to do so if it would alienate any Justice who has expressed to me, either by writing or orally, that he is in general agreement, on the merits, with the circulated memorandum.

I might add that some of the district courts that have been confronted with the abortion issue have spoken in general, but not specific, terms of viability. See, for example, Judge Newman's observation in the last *Abele* v. *Markle* decision.

May I have your reactions to this suggestion?

Even before the day was out, William O. Douglas replied simply that "I favor the first trimester, rather than viability," but the following day Thurgood Marshall signed and sent to Blackmun a crucially important letter that Mark Tushnet, after extensive conversations with Bill Maledon from Brennan's chambers, had drafted for the justice's approval. The clerks felt that Brennan's prior suggestions to Blackmun might make an initial letter from Marshall less obtrusive, and while Marshall made only one insignificant change in Tushnet's typescript, its content was as momentous as anything that had been written during *Roe*'s entire development. "Dear Harry," Marshall began,

I am inclined to agree that drawing the line at viability accommodates the interests at stake better than drawing it at the end of the first trimester. Given the difficulties which many women may have in believing that they are pregnant and in deciding to seek an abortion, I fear that the earlier date may not in practice serve the interests of those women, which your opinion does seek to serve.

At the same time, however, I share your concern for recognizing the State's interest in insuring that abortions be done under safe conditions. If the opinion stated explicitly that, between the end of the first trimester and viability, state regulations directed at health and safety alone were permissible, I believe that those concerns would be adequately met.

It is implicit in your opinion that at some point the State's interest in preserving the potential life of the unborn child overrides any individual interests of the women. I would be disturbed if that point were set before viability, and I am afraid that the opinion's present focus on the end of the first trimester would lead states to prohibit abortions completely at any later date.

In short, I believe that, as the opinion now stands, viability is a better accommodation of the interests involved, but that the end of the first trimester would be acceptable if additions along the lines I have suggested here were made.[123]

The next day Bill Brennan sent Harry Blackmun a similar but considerably longer letter following up on the verbal suggestions he had offered prior to Blackmun's latest memo. Brennan emphasized that he was "in basic agreement with" Blackmun's drafts, and thanked his junior colleague for "giving second thoughts to the choice of the end of the first trimester as the point beyond which a state may appropriately regulate abortion practices. But if the 'cut-off' point is to be moved forward somewhat, I am not sure that the point of 'viability' is the appropriate point, at least in a technical sense." Viability's appropriateness as the beginning point for state regulation was questionable, Brennan explained, because "if we identify the state's initial interests as the health of the woman and the maintenance of medical standards, the selection of 'viability' . . . as the point where a state may begin to regulate in consequence of these interests seems to me to be technically inconsistent" since viability focused upon the fetus rather than on the woman. "Thus considerations of 'viability,'" Brennan went on, "arise at a point in time after the state has asserted its interest in safeguarding the health of the woman and in maintaining medical standards."

"I have no objection," Brennan stated, "to moving the 'cut-off' point (the point where regulation first becomes permissible) from the end of the first trimester (12 weeks) as it now appears to a point more closely approximating the point of viability (20 to 28 weeks), but I think our designation of such a 'cut-off' point should be articulated in such a way as to coincide with the reasons for . . . creating such a 'cut-off' point." Brennan suggested that "rather than using a somewhat arbitrary point such as the end of the first trimester or a somewhat imprecise and technically inconsistent point such as 'viability,' could we not simply say that at that point in time where abortions become medically more complex, state regulation—reasonably calculated to protect the asserted state interests of safeguarding the health of the woman and of maintaining medical standards—becomes permissible." Then the opinion could explain, Brennan continued, "that this point usually occurs somewhere between 16 and 24 weeks (or whatever the case may be), but the *exact* 'cut-off' point and the specifics of the narrow regulation itself are determinations that must be made by a medically informed state legislature. Then we might go on to say that at some later stage of pregnancy (i.e., after the fetus becomes 'viable') the state may well have an interest in protecting the potential life of the child and therefore a different and possibly broader scheme of state regulation would become permissible." In other words, Brennan concluded, "our reasons for the choice of a 'cut-off' point (which I think we all agree must be found) should be consistent with the state interests which allow the states to select a 'cut-off' point."[124]

The same day that Blackmun received Brennan's long thought-piece, Warren Burger sent him a brief letter saying that he had "more 'ploughing' to do" on Blackmun's drafts and asking whether the opinions ought to "deal with whether husbands as such or parents of minors have 'rights' in this area." The following day, Potter Stewart wrote Blackmun to say that

> One of my concerns with your opinion as presently written is the specificity of its dictum—particularly in its fixing of the end of the first trimester as the critical point for valid state action. I appreciate the inevitability and indeed wisdom of dicta in the Court's opinion, but I wonder about the desirability of the dicta being quite so inflexibly "legislative."
>
> My present inclination would be to allow the States more latitude to make policy judgments between the alternatives mentioned in your memorandum, and perhaps others.

Stewart added that he had hoped to have a concurring opinion prepared by now, and would certainly circulate something by early January.

On December 15, Harry Blackmun sent yet another memo to all of his colleagues:

> I appreciate the helpful suggestions that have come to me in response to my memorandum of December 11. I now feel somewhat optimistic that the issues are in focus and that an agreement in some general areas may be in prospect.
>
> With your permission, I would like the opportunity to revise the proposed opinions in light of these suggestions. I have in mind associating the end of the first trimester with an emphasis on health, and associating viability with an emphasis on the State's interest in potential life. The period between the two points would be treated with flexibility. I shall try to do this revision next week and circulate another draft before the end of the year. It is my earnest hope, as you know, that on this sensitive issue we may avoid excessive fractionation of the Court, and that the cases may come down no later than the week of January 15 to tie in with the convening of most state legislatures.[125]

Six days later, on December 21, Blackmun circulated his revised and all-but-final drafts of both *Roe* and *Doe* along with a brief cover memo. Blackmun explained that "I have endeavored to accommodate the various views expressed to me orally or by letter," and highlighted how the principal change he had made occurred in the latter portion of the *Roe* opinion. "Here I have tried to recognize the dual state interests of protecting the mother's health and of protecting potential life. This, I believe, is a better approach than that contained in the initial memorandum. I have tried to follow the lines suggested by Bill Brennan and Thurgood." Blackmun noted that in response to Burger's query, "the rights of the father" were now mentioned in a footnote, but he acknowledged that "this will not be very satisfying" and concluded by observing that he was "somewhat reluctant to try to cover the point in cases where the father's rights, if any, are not at issue. I suspect there will be other aspects of abortion that will have to be dealt with at a future time."

Blackmun's colleagues appreciated that his revisions had fully—and sometimes quite precisely—responded to their suggestions. The very next day William O. Douglas formally joined both the *Roe* and *Doe* opinions, followed immediately after Christmas by Thurgood Marshall, Bill Brennan, and Potter Stewart. "I think your most recent circulations are even better than the original ones, and I was again greatly impressed with the thoroughness and care with which you have accomplished a difficult job," Stewart told Blackmun. Stewart added that he had now decided to dispense with a lengthy concurrence in place of a much briefer one, and before New Year's both Stewart and Douglas distributed their concurrences to their colleagues. Early in January Lewis Powell formally added his support, saying that he too was "happy with the revisions" and commending Blackmun for the "exceptional scholarship" of the opinions.[126]

On Thursday, January 11, 1973, both Byron White and Bill Rehnquist circulated initial copies of their brief individual dissents, but Blackmun's desire to announce the decisions sometime during the third week of January—Wednesday, January 17, had been tentatively scheduled—was foiled by Warren Burger's continuing inability to decide how he was going to come down in the two cases. Relations between Burger and some of his colleagues, particularly Potter Stewart, had remained decidedly strained throughout the early months of the Court's 1972–1973 term, and only toward the end of the second week in January did Burger finally indicate that he would join Blackmun's opinions in both *Roe* and *Doe* while filing an additional statement of his own. On January 16 Burger wrote Blackmun to say that he hoped to circulate a brief concurrence within a day or two and that *Roe* and *Doe* hence could be scheduled for announcement on Monday, January 22.

Soon after Burger's note arrived, Harry Blackmun distributed new prints of the *Roe* and *Doe* opinions to all of his colleagues along with a memorandum suggesting that public release of the two opinions be accompanied by an unprecedented eight-page explanatory statement. Blackmun explained that "I anticipate the headlines that will be produced over the country when the abortion cases are announced," and "Accordingly, I have typed out what I propose as the announcement from the bench in these two cases," an announcement that traditionally amounted to abbreviated summary excerpts from the opinions themselves and which never before had been issued or preserved in any written form. In *Roe* and *Doe*, however, Blackmun recommended, "I suggest that copies of this be given" to any reporters who wanted one, for "It will in effect be a transcript of what I shall say" and might help keep the press from "going all the way off the deep end" in reporting the news of the decisions.

Blackmun's proposed announcement noted the Court's realization that the abortion issue "is a most sensitive, emotional and controversial one," and acknowledged how "we are fully aware that, however the Court decides these cases, the controversy will continue." It underscored that "abortion is essentially a medical decision," and highlighted that "Fortunately, the decisions come down at a time when a majority of the legislatures of the states are in session." Speaking in the first person on the statement's final page, Blackmun said that "I fear what the headlines may be, but it should be stressed that the Court does not today hold that the Constitution compels abortion on demand." Neither was the Court saying, Blackmun added, "that a pregnant woman has an absolute right to an abortion." Instead, "for the first trimester of pregnancy," the opinions "cast the abortion decision and the responsibility for it upon the attending physician."

Lewis Powell told Blackmun that he thought the "excellent" statement "will help contribute to the understanding of the Court's decision," but the far more experienced Bill Brennan quickly convinced Blackmun that any such written announcement, no matter how well done, would likely create more problems than it would solve, for some people no doubt would treat the statement as a formal extension of the opinions themselves. Plans for such a release were abandoned, and when Warren Burger on Thursday the 18th finally distributed a three-paragraph concurrence, *Roe* v. *Wade* and *Doe* v. *Bolton* were set for announcement at ten a.m. on Monday morning, January 22, 1973.[127]

Outside of the Court, almost no one knew how imminent the decisions now were. In Texas, Sarah Weddington, who had just been sworn in as a member of the state house, formally introduced a repeal bill on January 19. Asked by one reporter what she thought the chances for success were in the Supreme Court, Sarah replied that she had "no idea what will happen." She added that "It could go either way," and Ginny Whitehill warned NARAL's Lee Gidding that "even if the Supreme Court comes through, I think we will have to be active to prevent fetal bills or whatever."

Perhaps the one person outside the Court's official family who *did* know what was about to happen was David Beckwith, a young *Time* magazine staff member who had learned the essence of the upcoming decisions after approaching any number of clerks for off-the-record comments. Beckwith had attended the University of Texas Law School at the same time as one of Powell's clerks, and the Powell clerk, knowing that *Roe* and *Doe* were listed for announcement on January 17 and hence would be covered in *Time*'s next issue, spoke "on background" with Beckwith about the upcoming decisions, unaware that Warren Burger's tardiness would cause the cases to be held over into the following week. When Burger's delay meant that Beckwith's superiors at *Time* had the makings for a scoop rather than some redundant background material, those editors went ahead and prepared a two-page story entitled "Abortion on Demand" for the Monday issue that appeared on news-stands just a few hours before *Roe* and *Doe* actually were announced. "Last week *Time* learned," the article boasted, "that the Supreme Court has decided to strike down nearly every antiabortion law" and to permit "only minimal curbs" upon abortion. *Griswold* would be "the basis" for the rulings, which "were also influenced by the 1972 opinion of U.S. District Judge Jon O. Newman" in the Connecticut case. "No decision in the court's history," *Time* predicted, "has evoked the intensity of emotion that will surely follow this ruling."[128]

Warren Burger was absolutely livid when he learned of *Time*'s story that Monday morning, but the magazine's scoop was short-lived. Just after ten a.m., with all nine justices on the bench, the Chief Justice turned to the author of the *Roe* and *Doe* opinions for the announcement of the Court's decisions, and Harry Blackmun began reading his eight-page statement while the Court's press office started to distribute copies of the two decisions to waiting reporters.

Blackmun's opinion for the seven-justice majority in *Roe* came to fifty-one pages in print. In the very second paragraph he directly addressed the concern that had led him to consider releasing his explanatory comments in some quotable form:

> We forthwith acknowledge our awareness of the sensitive and emo-
> tional nature of the abortion controversy, of the vigorous opposing views,

even among physicians, and of the deep and seemingly absolute convictions that the subject inspires. One's philosophy, one's experiences, one's exposure to the raw edges of human existence, one's religious training, one's attitudes toward life and family and their values, and the moral standards one establishes and seeks to observe, are all likely to influence and to color one's thinking and conclusions about abortion.

The Court's task, Blackmun emphasized, was "to resolve the issue by constitutional measurement free of emotion and of predilection. We seek earnestly to do this, and, because we do, we have inquired into, and in this opinion place some emphasis upon, medical and medical-legal history and what that history reveals about man's attitudes toward the abortive procedure over the centuries."

The first four sections of Blackmun's opinion succinctly dispensed with the issues of jurisdiction, standing, and mootness, and while the Court upheld "Jane Roe's" status in challenging the Texas abortion statute, it dismissed both Dr. Hallford and "John and Mary Doe." Then, following a brief introductory segment, Blackmun moved on to a nineteen-page historical section which owed much to his earlier summer research. He emphasized that "the restrictive criminal abortion laws in effect in a majority of States today are of relatively recent vintage," and then devoted considerable attention to reviewing the history of the Hippocratic Oath and to how abortion, both before and after the crucial stage of fetal "quickening," had been treated under English law across the centuries. His footnotes included multiple references to Larry Lader's 1966 book and to Cyril Means's two law review articles, and when his survey progressed to America's own legal heritage with regard to abortion, Blackmun noted that "at common law, at the time of the adoption of our Constitution, and throughout the major portion of the 19th century, abortion was viewed with less disfavor than under most American statutes currently in effect." Only at about the time of the Civil War, Blackmun observed, did most states decree that abortions before as well as after quickening were criminal offenses. In other words, until then, "a woman enjoyed a substantially broader right to terminate a pregnancy than she does in most States today. At least with respect to the early stages of pregnancy," Blackmun pointed out, "the opportunity to make this choice was present in this country well into the 19th century."

The *Roe* opinion attributed some responsibility for that nineteenth century shift to the antiabortion stance of the American Medical Association, and then proceeded to summarize the recently liberalized stances that the American Medical Association, the American Public Health Association, and the American Bar Association had all adopted.

Moving out of that lengthy historical section, Blackmun explicitly addressed the question of what legislative purpose underlay the enactment and continuation of antiabortion laws. In the nineteenth century, he noted, abortion had been highly dangerous for a pregnant woman, but present-day medical data indicated that "abortion in early pregnancy, that is, prior to the end of the first trimester . . . is now relatively safe." "Consequently, any interest of the State in protecting the woman from an inherently hazardous procedure," he concluded, "has largely disappeared," even though a state of course continued to have "a legitimate interest in seeing to it that abortion, like any other medical procedure, is performed under circumstances that insure maximum safety for the patient." Especially since "the risk to the woman increases as her pregnancy continues," hence "the State retains a definite interest in protecting the woman's own health and safety when an abortion is proposed at a late stage of pregnancy."

Quite distinct from any such health-based rationale for antiabortion laws, Blackmun acknowledged, was a state interest "in protecting prenatal life. . . . Logically, of course, a legitimate state interest in this area need not stand or fall on acceptance of the belief that life begins at conception or at some other point prior to live birth. In assessing the State's interest, recognition may be given to the less rigid claim that as long as at least *potential* life is involved, the State may assert interests beyond the protection of the pregnant woman alone."

Only well past the two-thirds mark in the opinion did Blackmun finally address the constitutional contentions advanced by "Roe" and other abortion case plaintiffs. "The Constitution," he began, "does not explicitly mention any right of privacy. In a line of decisions, however, going back perhaps as far as" *Botsford* in 1891, "the Court has recognized that a right of personal privacy, or a guarantee of certain areas or zones of privacy, does exist under the Constitution. In varying contexts the Court or individual Justices have indeed found at least the roots of that right in the First Amendment," citing *Stanley*, in the Fourth and Fifth Amendments, as reflected in a number of search-and-seizure cases, "in the penumbras of the Bill of Rights," as indicated by Justice Douglas in *Griswold*, "in the Ninth Amendment," as suggested by Justice Goldberg in *Griswold*, "or in the concept of liberty guaranteed by the first section of the Fourteenth Amendment" and recognized as early as *Meyer* in 1923. "These decisions," Blackmun went on, "make it clear that only personal rights that can be deemed 'fundamental' or 'implicit in the concept of ordered liberty,'. . . are included in this guarantee of personal privacy. They also make it clear that the right has some extension to activities relating to marriage," citing *Loving*, procreation, citing *Skinner*, contraception, citing *Eisenstadt*, "family relationships," citing *Prince* v. *Massachusetts*, "and child rearing and education," citing *Pierce* and *Meyer*.

"This right of privacy," Blackmun then continued, "whether it be founded in the Fourteenth Amendment's concept of personal liberty and restrictions upon state action, as we feel it is, or, as the District Court determined, in the Ninth Amendment's reservation of rights to the people, is broad enough to encompass a woman's decision whether or not to terminate her pregnancy." After listing some of the reasons for which a woman might choose to terminate a pregnancy, Blackmun cited the contention of some parties "that the woman's right is absolute and that she is entitled to terminate her pregnancy at whatever time, in whatever way, and for whatever reason she alone chooses. With this we do not agree." Any argument that Texas or another state "has no valid interest at all in regulating the abortion decision, or no interests strong enough to support any limitation upon the woman's sole determination, is unpersuasive." For instance, "a state may properly assert important interests in safeguarding health, in maintaining medical standards, and in protecting potential life. At some point in pregnancy, these respective interests become sufficiently compelling to sustain regulation of the factors that govern the abortion decision." Furthermore, Blackmun added, "it is not clear to us that the claim asserted by some *amici* that one has an unlimited right to do with one's body as one pleases bears a close relationship to the right of privacy previously articulated in the Court's decisions."

Thus, Blackmun said, "We therefore conclude that the right of personal privacy includes the abortion decision, but that this right is not unqualified and must be considered against important state interests in regulation." He devoted two long paragraphs to noting many of the recent lower court decisions on constitutional challenges to state abortion statutes, and observed that "most of these courts have agreed that the right of privacy, however based, is broad enough to cover the abortion decision; that the right, nonetheless, is not absolute and is subject to some limitations; and that at some point the state interests as to protection of health, medical standards, and prenatal life, become dominant. We agree with this approach."

Proceeding to a more direct evaluation of Texas's assertion that its antiabortion statute reflected a compelling state interest in protecting the fetal "person," Blackmun acknowledged how Texas's brief described "at length and in detail the well-known facts of fetal development. If this suggestion of personhood is established, the appellant's case, of course, collapses, for the fetus' right to life is then guaranteed specifically" by the Fourteenth Amendment. Blackmun also noted, however, Robert Flowers's admission at reargument that no case could be cited that had ever held a fetus to be a Fourteenth Amendment "person," and he further explained that while the Constitution "does not define 'person' in so many words," virtually every usage of the term in the document "is such that it has application only postnatally. None indicates, with any assurance, that it has any possible pre-natal application."

In a footnote, Blackmun additionally indicated that some considerable tension appeared to exist between Texas's fetal personhood contention and the maternal life exception in its antiabortion statute. "But if the fetus is a person who is not to be deprived of life without due process of law, and if the mother's condition is the sole determinant," Blackmun rhetorically asked, "does not the Texas exception appear to be out of line with the Amendment's command?" Also, if Texas truly viewed the fetus as a person, why did its laws not provide for any criminal abortion penalties for the woman herself? Similarly, the punishment for abortion was "significantly less" than the penalty for murder, and "If the fetus is a person, may the penalties be different?" Blackmun inquired.

In the text, Blackmun thus concluded that "All this, together with our observation . . . that throughout the major portion of the 19th century prevailing legal abortion practices were far freer than they are today, persuades us that the word 'person,' as used in the Fourteenth Amendment, does not include the unborn." Nonetheless, Blackmun recognized that on account of the embryo or fetus, "The pregnant woman cannot be isolated in her privacy," and that therefore the situation "is inherently different from marital intimacy, or bedroom possession of obscene material, or marriage, or procreation, or education, with which *Eisenstadt, Griswold, Stanley, Loving, Skinner, Pierce,* and *Meyer* were respectively concerned." Thus "it is reasonable and appropriate for a State to decide that at some point in time another interest, that of health of the mother or that of potential human life, becomes significantly involved. The woman's privacy is no longer sole and any right of privacy she possesses must be measured accordingly."

Blackmun explicitly stated that the Court "need not resolve the difficult question of when life begins. When those trained in the respective disciplines of medicine, philosophy, and theology are unable to arrive at any consensus, the judiciary, at this point in the development of man's knowledge, is not in a position to speculate as to the answer." He observed that "There has always been strong support for the view that life does not begin until live birth," but he also noted how the nineteenth-century focus on quickening as the most significant intermediate point in fetal development had over time been displaced by increased regard for "viability," the point at which a fetus is "potentially able to live outside the mother's womb, albeit with artificial aid." Viability, Blackmun said, was "usually placed at about seven months (28 weeks) but may occur earlier, even at 24 weeks."

Following a quick survey of other legal precedents concerning the status of the fetus, including two citations to Bill Maledon's Notre Dame law review piece, Blackmun frankly concluded that "In short, the unborn have never been recognized in the law as persons in the whole sense." Then, in an initial step towards a conclusion, Blackmun reiterated how a state had *both* "an important and legitimate interest in preserving and protecting the health of the pregnant woman" and "*another* important and legitimate interest in protecting the potentiality of human life. These interests are separate and distinct. Each grows in substantiality as the woman approaches term and, at a point during pregnancy, each becomes 'compelling.'"

Then Blackmun moved decisively toward the first crux of his holding:

> With respect to the State's important and legitimate interest in the health of the mother, the "compelling" point, in light of present medical knowledge, is at approximately the end of the first trimester. This is so because of the now-established medical fact, referred to above . . . that until the end of the first trimester mortality in abortion is less than mortality in normal childbirth. It follows that, from and after this point, a State may regulate the abortion procedure to the extent that the regulation reasonably relates to the preservation and protection of maternal health.

Equally important, Blackmun also explained that this meant that

> for the period of pregnancy prior to this "compelling" point, the attending physician, in consultation with his patient, is free to determine, without regulation by the State, that in his medical judgment the patient's pregnancy should be terminated. If that decision is reached, the judgment may be effectuated by an abortion free of interference by the State.

Blackmun immediately proceeded to the second principal aspect of the holding:

With respect to the State's important and legitimate interest in potential life, the "compelling" point is at viability. This is so because the fetus
then presumably has the capability of meaningful life outside the mother's womb. State regulation protective of fetal life after viability thus has
both logical and biological justifications. If the State is interested in protecting fetal life after viability, it may go so far as to proscribe abortion
during that period, except when it is necessary to preserve the life or
health of the mother.

In light of such standards, abortion laws like Texas's were "violative
of the Due Process Clause of the Fourteenth Amendment" and the
question of whether the sole exception for "saving the life of the mother" also made such statutes unacceptably vague did not have to be considered. The opinion then offered a brief summary of its earlier analysis:

(a) For the stage prior to approximately the end of the first trimester,
the abortion decision and its effectuation must be left to the medical
judgment of the pregnant woman's attending physician.

(b) For the stage subsequent to approximately the end of the first
trimester, the State, in promoting its interest in the health of the mother, may, if it chooses, regulate the abortion procedure in ways that are
reasonably related to maternal health.

(c) For the stage subsequent to viability the State, in promoting its
interest in the potentiality of human life, may, if it chooses, regulate, and
even proscribe, abortion except where it is necessary, in appropriate medical judgment, for the preservation of the life or health of the mother.

Blackmun noted that a state of course "may proscribe any abortion
by a person who is not a physician," and pointed out that while the
Roe and *Doe* opinions "are to be read together," that in neither case
was the Court addressing whether any "father's rights" existed with
regard to an abortion decision. Then Blackmun moved to his penultimate statement:

This holding, we feel, is consistent with the relative weights of the
respective interests involved, with the lessons and example of medical
and legal history, with the lenity of the common law, and with the
demands of the profound problems of the present day. The decision
leaves the State free to place increasing restrictions on abortion as the
period of pregnancy lengthens, so long as those restrictions are tailored
to the recognized state interests. The decision vindicates the right of the
physician to administer medical treatment according to his professional
judgment up to the points where important state interests provide compelling justifications for intervention. Up to those points the abortion

decision in all its aspects is inherently, and primarily, a medical decision, and basic responsibility for it must rest with the physician.

Thus, after a brief closing section stating the judgment and explaining that Texas's inevitable compliance with the ruling made it "unnecessary to decide whether the District Court erred in withholding injunctive relief," Blackmun's majority opinion in *Roe* v. *Wade* was complete.[129]

Blackmun's opinion in *Doe* v. *Bolton* was a somewhat shorter and more modest statement. It held that both "Mary Doe" and the physician plaintiffs had standing to challenge the Georgia reform law, and it affirmed those portions of the Atlanta ruling that had already invalidated as unacceptably narrow the therapeutic exceptions specified by the Georgia statute. Blackmun stated that while the law was not void for vagueness, all of its principal surviving provisions were themselves unconstitutional, and his opinion proceeded to nullify them one by one. In striking down Georgia's hospitalization requirement, Blackmun explained that "We feel compelled to agree with appellants that the State must show more than it has in order to prove that only the full resources of a licensed hospital, rather than those of some other appropriately licensed institution, satisfy these health interests" that the Court had acknowledged in *Roe*. Similarly, with regard to the hospital committee authorization mandated by the Georgia law, the *Doe* opinion concluded that "we see no constitutionally justifiable pertinence in the structure for the advance approval by the abortion committee." Lastly, the statute's edict that two other doctors endorse any given physician's recommendation of abortion was also unacceptable, for "Required acquiescence by co-practitioners has no rational connection with a patient's needs and unduly infringes on the physician's right to practice." Thus, just as *Roe* effectively voided the abortion laws of all thirty states whose statutes resembled the one in Texas, the *Doe* opinion invalidated not only the Georgia law but also the generally similar reform provisions that had been adopted by fourteen other states since 1967.[130]

Three members of the seven-justice *Roe* and *Doe* majorities filed individual concurrences in addition to joining the two Blackmun opinions. William O. Douglas's thirteen-page statement was the longest, and virtually all of it was devoted to an explication of the constitutional right to privacy. Like Blackmun, he acknowledged that "There is no mention of privacy in our Bill of Rights," but he too underscored how many earlier decisions had nonetheless "recognized it as one of the fundamental values those amendments were designed to protect." Douglas conceded that the Ninth Amendment "obviously does not create federally enforceable rights," but its reference to other unenumerated rights "retained by the people" included many that also came within the meaning of Fourteenth Amendment "liberty."

Douglas then outlined a three-part synopsis of what those privacy elements of "liberty" encompassed. "First is the autonomous control over the development and expression of one's intellect, interests, tastes, and personality." These "aspects of the right of privacy" were protected by the First Amendment as well as the Ninth, and in Douglas's view they were "absolute, permitting of no exceptions." Second, Douglas said, "is freedom of choice in the basic decisions of one's life respecting marriage, divorce, procreation, contraception, and the education and upbringing of children." *Loving*, *Skinner*, *Griswold*, *Eisenstadt*, and *Pierce* all involved such freedoms, and while these rights were subject to some control by the state, any such regulation had to be justified by a "compelling state interest." Douglas quoted Brennan's striking statement in *Eisenstadt*, noted Justice Brandeis's 1928 espousal of the "right to be let alone" in *Olmstead*, and denied in a footnote that *Griswold* and the other relevant decisions had invoked "substantive due process," insisting that that was "a bridge that neither I nor those who joined the Court opinion in *Griswold* crossed." Third and finally, Douglas declared, "is the freedom to care for one's health and person, freedom from bodily restraint or compulsion, freedom to walk, stroll, or loaf," as exemplified by cases that dated from 1891 to 1972.

All told, Douglas said, "the clear message of these cases" was that "a woman is free to make the basic decision whether to bear an unwanted child. Elaborate argument is hardly necessary to demonstrate that child birth may deprive a woman of her preferred life style and force upon her a radically different and undesired future." Like Blackmun, Douglas also recognized that a state had a proper interest both in protecting women's health and in "the life of the fetus after quickening," but he emphasized that "it is difficult to perceive any overriding public necessity which might attach precisely at the moment of conception," as both the Georgia and Texas statutes presupposed. Douglas presented a lengthy quotation from former Justice Tom Clark's law review essay in support of that position, and concluded that the Georgia law in particular was "overbroad because it equates the value of embryonic life immediately after conception with the worth of life immediately before birth."

Douglas observed in conclusion that "The right of privacy has no more conspicuous place than in the physician-patient relationship," and that the elaborate approval procedure mandated by Georgia and struck down in *Doe* represented "a total destruction of the right of privacy between physician and patient" and hence violated a "basic" Fourteenth Amendment liberty.[131]

A second but considerably briefer concurrence was filed by Potter Stewart, who sought to insist—in the face of Douglas's express denial—that with regard to the 1965 decision in *Griswold*, "it was clear to me then, and it is equally clear to me now, that the *Griswold* decision can be rationally understood only as a holding that the Connecticut statute substantively invaded the 'liberty' that is protected by the Due Process Clause of the Fourteenth Amendment." Implicitly referring to his own 1965 dissent, Stewart proclaimed that he now nonetheless accepted *Griswold* as a valid "substantive due process" holding, even though he continued to assert that "There is no constitutional right of privacy, as such."

Stewart also acknowledged that while "The Constitution nowhere mentions a specific right of personal choice in matters of marriage and family life," "the 'liberty' protected by the Due Process Clause of the Fourteenth Amendment covers more than those freedoms explicitly named in the Bill of Rights." He quoted at some length from John Harlan's dissent in *Poe* v. *Ullman*, from Brennan's crucial passage in *Eisenstadt*, and from Jon Newman's opinion in the Connecticut case. That *individual* right recognized in *Eisenstadt*, Stewart stated, "necessarily includes the right of a woman to decide whether or not to terminate her pregnancy," and indeed, he added, "it is difficult to imagine a more complete abridgment of a constitutional freedom than that worked by the inflexible criminal statute now in force in Texas."[132]

The third and shortest concurrence was Warren Burger's last-minute statement. Only three paragraphs long, it invoked *Vuitch* in emphasizing that both the Georgia and Texas statutes "impermissibly limit the performance of abortions necessary to protect the health of pregnant women." Burger announced, in explicit conflict with *Doe*'s actual holding, that he "would be inclined to allow a State to require the certification of two physicians to support an abortion," and he added that he did not read the two decisions as entailing "sweeping consequences." "Plainly," he somewhat gratuitously insisted in his closing line, "the Court today rejects any claim that the Constitution requires abortion on demand."[133]

Of the two dissenting opinions, Byron White's, which William Rehnquist also joined, was very brief, filling hardly two pages, but it was nonetheless quite tart. His majority colleagues, White said, were holding that prior to fetal viability, "the Constitution of the United States values the convenience, whim or caprice of the putative mother more than the life or potential life of the fetus." He added that "I find nothing in the language or history of the Constitution to support the Court's judgment. The Court simply fashions and announces a new constitutional right for pregnant mothers and, with scarcely any reason or authority for its action," wielded that right to void the existing abortion statutes of some forty-six states. "As an exercise of raw judicial power, the Court perhaps has authority to do what it does today; but in my view its judgment is an improvident and extravagant exercise of the power of judicial review." White argued that the Texas law was "not constitutionally infirm because it denies abortions to those who seek to serve only their convenience rather than to protect their life or health," and further contended that since "Jane Roe" had alleged no such therapeutic need, her case should not be allowed to cover such claims. In short, White said, the Court should not erect "a constitutional barrier to state efforts to protect human life" and give "mothers and doctors . . . the constitutionally protected right to exterminate it."[134]

William Rehnquist's dissent conceded that the *Roe* opinion "commands my respect" because of how Blackmun utilized "both extensive historical fact and a wealth of legal scholarship" in framing the decision, but he maintained that since the *Roe* record failed to indicate that "Jane Roe" was in her first trimester of pregnancy at the time the case was filed, her lawsuit could not properly be used to vindicate the constitutional rights of women with unwanted first trimester pregnancies. More substantively, Rehnquist also asserted that "I have difficulty in concluding . . . that the right of 'privacy' is involved in this case," for a medical procedure such as abortion "is not 'private' in the ordinary usage of that word." He expressed agreement with Stewart's observation that "liberty" was a better constitutional designation, but objected to the Court's applying the all but impossible "compelling state interest" standard of review to abortion statutes rather than the far more deferential "rational basis" standard. More pointedly, he also observed that the majority's effort "to break the term of pregnancy into three distinct terms and to outline the permissible restrictions the State may impose in each one" essentially amounted to "judicial legislation."[135]

When the nine members of the U.S. Supreme Court completed the public announcement of their decisions in *Roe* v. *Wade* and *Doe* v. *Bolton* on Monday morning, January 22, 1973, only Harry Blackmun had given extended consideration to what the consequences might be. He knew relatively little about Norma McCorvey and Sandra Bensing, not even their actual names, nor had he heard of Judy Smith or Judith

Bourne. Roy Lucas, Linda Coffee, Margie Hames, and Sarah Weddington, like Dorothy Beasley and Jay Floyd, were now familiar names, if not entirely familiar faces, even if neither Henry Wade nor Arthur Bolton—just like "Jane Roe" and "Mary Doe"—had personally attended either of the oral arguments. Similarly, Alan Guttmacher, Bob Hall, Larry Lader, and Cyril Means were now familiar bylines too. But Harry Blackmun was equally well acquainted, at least on the printed page, with the handiwork of Sidney Smith and Sarah Hughes and Irving Goldberg, just as he was also familiar with *Belous*, with Gerhard Gesell in *Vuitch*, with Jon Newman in Connecticut, with the other federal panel decisions reaching from New Jersey to Illinois and Wisconsin, and with the state court rulings that reached from New York back to California. Likewise, he appreciated the legacy of John Harlan's dissent in *Poe*, perhaps even more so than any of the opinions in *Griswold* or even Bill Brennan's contribution in *Eisenstadt*. Granted, he had never heard of Warren Upson, nor did he know Estelle Griswold or Lee Buxton, and if Fowler Harper was the coauthor of an oft-cited treatise on torts, well, Katharine Hepburn was that actress who had costarred with Spencer Tracy. Margaret Sanger was an acknowledged historical figure, even if no one at the Supreme Court had ever heard of Leah Cadbury, or Clara McTernan, or Eugene Cryne if not Bill Fitzgerald.

It had been a long time in coming—nearly two years, Harry Blackmun thought—but really it had been almost fifty years since Kit Hepburn had first welcomed Margaret Sanger to Hartford and more than thirty-three years since the priests of Waterbury had made it clear that Bill Fitzgerald had better enforce that statute, even if it literally did mean arresting the woman next door. But in the end, it had seemed far easier than Roy Lucas had envisioned in 1967, or Alan Guttmacher in 1963, or than Fowler and Estelle had found their challenge in 1958, or Kit Hepburn and Sallie Pease in that summer of 1939. Yes, there had been *Eisenstadt*, and, far more importantly, there had also been *Griswold*, but from New York University to Austin to Atlanta, as from Hartford to Waterbury to New Haven, there had of course been so much—and so many—more, even if neither Harry Blackmun nor any of his six supportive colleagues ever knew more than a few of their names. But in the end, Harry Blackmun grasped perhaps the simplest but eventually the most long-forgotten truth of all: "*Roe* against *Wade* was not such a revolutionary opinion at the time."[136]

CHAPTER NINE

Liberty and Sexuality
Since *Roe* v. *Wade*

Norma McCorvey had heard nothing at all about *Roe* v. *Wade* for many months when she suddenly saw the front-page newspaper article reporting the Supreme Court's decision. The unexpected death of former President Lyndon Johnson had taken priority as the day's top news story both in Texas and across the nation, but the coverage of the *Roe* and *Doe* rulings was almost equally substantial. "I was happy, sad and mad," Norma later explained, for "in a way I felt cheated because I didn't benefit" from the long-awaited victory. Since the fall of 1970, just a few months after Henry McCluskey had arranged for the adoption of her newborn "*Roe*" baby, Norma had been living with Connie Gonzales, whom she had first met as a coworker at a grocery store, but only now, for the first time, did Norma tell Connie that *she* was that "Jane Roe" in the newspaper story about the Supreme Court.

Within a day both Sarah Weddington and Linda Coffee telephoned Norma. Sarah was surprised at the breadth of the Court's decision, and slightly astonished that Warren Burger had joined the majority, but she told reporters that she was "very glad for the women of Texas." Linda was likewise startled by the 7 to 2 margin, and while she found the outcome "terribly satisfying" both "as a woman and as a lawyer," she explained in long interview with the Southern Baptist Convention's press service that "From my personal perspective as a Christian, it would tear me up to have to make a decision on abortion except in the very early stages, and I would have to have a compelling reason even then." Linda pointed out that "Legal personhood is separate entirely from a moral or religious view of personhood," but she emphasized that "the state should be neutral on abortion because it should never appear either to sanction an abortion or to interfere improperly with a doctor-patient relationship." In part through her mother, who worked at the Baptists' Christian Education Commission, Linda also intro-

duced Robert O'Brien, the Baptist Press correspondent, to her hereto-
fore anonymous client, and just four days after the Supreme Court
decision was announced, the Baptist news service distributed a story
identifying "Jane Roe" as twenty-five-year-old Norma McCorvey, a
"part-time delivery girl." O'Brien quoted Norma as saying that "It's
great to know that other women will not have to go through what I
did," and while the *Dallas Morning News* picked up O'Brien's scoop and
announced that "Abortion Reformer Sheds 'Jane Roe,'" the paper
nonetheless gave the story no greater prominence than placement on
page thirty. Three full days passed before Dallas's other daily paper
took note of the news, and aside from one or two southern dailies that
also picked up on the Baptist Press story, Norma McCorvey's identity
receded into full anonymity for most of the ensuing decade.[1]

Marsha and David King had moved away from Dallas even before
the Supreme Court reargument three months earlier. David had
changed jobs and Marsha, who was hoping to enter law school that
coming fall, was working temporarily in Washington until their plans
were certain. She knew about the decision even prior to a congratulato-
ry call from Sarah, but after Sarah sent her copies of the full opinions,
Marsha was truly exhilarated. While the ruling itself "was just too good
to believe," Blackmun's opinion was even better. "There was not a single sexist remark in the Texas decision—not even any patronization. It
was truly a feminist statement," Marsha told Dallas's Ginny Whitehill.
She was also happy that Norma had stepped forward, for "She
deserved some recognition" and Marsha remained sorry that they had
been unable to locate McCorvey so as to invite her to either of the
Supreme Court hearings. "She is such a lost, little soul," Marsha
lamented. "It makes me sad to think of her, but she will not be forced
to bear another unwanted child."

The other Texas repeal proponents were just as ecstatic about the
Court ruling as Marsha, and Ginny Whitehill told Dallas reporters on
the very first day that "This is more important for women than getting
the vote." SMU chaplain and clergy referral activist J. Claude Evans
termed the judgment "an ideal decision," and characterized
Blackmun's three-tier analysis of pregnancy as "a beautifully accurate
balancing of individual vs. social rights." The two long-pending criminal abortion charges against Dr. Hallford were soon dismissed, but,
unbeknownst to the other participants in *Roe*, six weeks before the
Supreme Court ruling Hallford's medical license had been quietly canceled by the Texas Board of Medical Examiners on account of another
recurrence of Hallford's prior problem with prescription drug abuse.

None of Hallford's subsequent efforts to win reinstatement of his license ever succeeded, but just five months after the *Roe* ruling a far more dreadful tragedy occurred when Linda's friend Henry McCluskey, without whom Norma McCorvey certainly would not have become "Jane Roe," was tied up and shot to death by a male acquaintance. Two weeks passed before Henry's body was found in a Dallas park, but exactly six years to the day after its decision in *Roe* v. *Wade*, the U.S. Supreme Court declined to review the death sentence that had been meted out to McCluskey's killer.[2]

Jay Floyd, who had handled most of Texas's defense of its antiabortion statute until the end of calendar 1972, when a new state attorney general, John Hill, had taken office, was both "disappointed" and "somewhat shocked" by the 7 to 2 Supreme Court loss. Dallas County District Attorney Henry Wade, who had never taken any personal interest in the case that bore his name, made no comments to the press and confessed years later that actually he had never read the decision. "I don't really have any views on it, either way," Wade would generally tell subsequent questioners, but when pressed, Wade would readily concede that "in some cases abortion is justified."[3]

In Atlanta, Wade's counterpart, Georgia Attorney General Arthur K. Bolton, likewise offered no immediate reaction to inquiring reporters, but two decades later Bolton willingly divulged that losing *Doe* v. *Bolton* had not personally bothered him a bit, for his own private view of abortion was that "it's strictly a woman's decision." Dorothy T. Beasley, in subsequent years a state appellate judge, would politely decline to characterize her own personal reaction to the *Doe* ruling, but when the Clerk's Office at the Supreme Court, following standard procedure, sent collect telegrams on January 22 to the *Roe* and *Doe* attorneys, formally apprising them of the decisions, Western Union notified the Clerk that "Dorothy T Beasley Asst Atty General of Georgia 132 State Judicial Bldg . . . declined to accept your message and charges."

If Dorothy Beasley was deeply upset at the Supreme Court's holdings in *Roe* and *Doe*, Margie Hames was "very pleased." She had felt from the very outset, she told Atlanta reporters, that "this is one of the most important women's rights cases," and on the very day of the decision she arranged for her old Vanderbilt Law School mentor, Fred Graham, to film a silhouetted interview with Sandra Bensing at Hames's law office for his new employer, CBS News. Over the ensuing six months both Margie and Tobi Schwartz would devote countless hours to helping Sandra acquire visitation rights so that she could again see her two oldest children, who each had been living with foster families for more than three years. A decade and a half later, however, Hames and Schwartz's efforts would be repaid in an odd and highly unpleasant way when Sandra, who had been introduced by her sister to an Atlanta-area pastor who was affiliated with the antiabortion group Operation Rescue, decided that she should attempt to reopen *Doe* v. *Bolton* and reverse the 1973 decision. Starting in December 1988 with an unlettered petition to Atlanta's U.S. District Court, Sandra explained that in 1970 "I was mentally unstable and not . . . totally aware of what was happening," and that she now believed that "I was used by my attorneys at that time." Once her effort and change of heart were publicized in the Atlanta press, two antiabortion attorneys volunteered to represent her, and Atlanta papers gave extensive coverage to Sandra's newfound conviction that signing on to be the lead plaintiff in *Doe* v. *Bolton* was "the biggest mistake I ever made." The federal court unsurprisingly turned aside Sandra and her new allies' effort to reopen a case that had been closed for over fifteen years, but the extensive publicity did allow eighteen-year-old Melissa Able, Sandra's *Doe* baby, to make contact with her mother for the first time. In subsequent years press reports would chronicle a host of ups and downs in Sandra and Melissa's new relationship, but twenty-three years after she had helped initiate *Doe* v. *Bolton*, Sandra Bensing Cano would forthrightly declare that "abortion is wrong for anyone." With one of the named parties from Georgia's landmark case a heartfelt convert and supporter of Operation Rescue, it was equally fitting, if not ironic, that the other, living quietly in retirement and contending with the ailments of old age, was so avowedly pro-choice.[4]

Among the New York abortion activists, reactions were just as jubilant as in Dallas and Atlanta. Cyril Means was in Albany when he first heard the news of the Court's action, and after taking an evening train back to New York City, he went directly to Harriet Pilpel's apartment on the assumption—which indeed proved correct—that Pilpel would have received copies of the opinions even though the decisions were hardly eight hours old. NARAL executive director Lee Gidding, observing how "the scope of the decision and the decisiveness of the vote mean total victory," wrote Ginny Whitehill to ask, with open amazement, "how many people do you know who have actually won, in total, the objective they set for themselves?" NARAL chairman Larry Lader, who had just completed a brief new history of the abortion struggle since the mid-1960s, remarked that *Roe* and *Doe* were "far broader in scope than anyone expected" and "even more conclusive than any of us dared to hope." Attorney Nancy Stearns expressed astonishment at how it had taken only "an amazingly short time in the courts to win recognition of the right to abortion once the ball started rolling," but she, like many others, emphasized that "one of the most dangerous things that could happen now is that women could sit back and think that they have won," irrespective of the antiabortion efforts that had proven so powerful during all of the previous year.[5]

In San Francisco, Roy Lucas first heard about the decisions when Dr. Vuitch's wife awakened him with an early morning phone call. Once copies of the opinions arrived later that day by plane, Lucas told a wire service reporter how different it all seemed now from when he had first begun work on his NYU Law School essay only a little more than six years earlier. "They laughed at it in 1966," he said with exaggerated reference to his former professors, but "Now it has a 7 to 2 majority behind it."

But even the remarkable approbation of the U.S. Supreme Court did not erase all of the resentments that Lucas had developed during the course of the previous two and a half years of internecine battling over *Roe* and *Doe*. Several weeks after the cases came down, Lucas phoned Margie Hames to offer congratulations on what a tremendous step forward *Doe*'s voiding of hospitalization requirements represented for both women and doctors all across the country, but he was somewhat taken aback when Hames, who had certainly not forgotten Lucas's earlier insolent letters, responded somewhat acerbicly. In rejoinder, Lucas replied with another letter that all but outdid any of his prior correspondence. His call, Lucas insisted, was simply a polite gesture. "You just did not understand what I was congratulating you about. Perhaps it was that you had finally figured out" what hospital accreditation meant "and understood that elimination of the mandatory hospitalization requirement was vitally necessary to the delivery of abortion services in the United States. Surely you cannot (with a straight face) assert that your argument and briefs made a lasting impression and deeply influenced the Court. The *Doe* opinion too frequently rejects assertions you made and too often relies upon arguments and evidence for which you were not responsible." Lucas went on to explain that eighteen months earlier he had decided that answering Hames's letter telling him to grow up "was a waste of time," in part because Hames's obvious "immaturity" was "enough to establish that your mind was closed." Likewise, Larry Lader's brand-new book, Lucas volunteered, was "incredible," but only because it created "new frontiers in abortion fiction." With *Doe*, however, Lucas reiterated how "I felt throughout that a realistic danger existed of your arguments being so weak" that the Supreme Court would uphold the hospitalization and committee approval requirements. He announced that "my view of your competence and ability to contribute to a sweeping decision was the inevitable consequence of considerable matured experience in litigating the issues I was afraid you would present inadequately." In closing, Lucas insisted that it was "nothing personal," for "As a person I think very highly of you," but he spitefully sent a copy of his letter directly to Cyril Means. In a postscript, however, Lucas nonetheless offered a stunningly insightful commentary that could just as well have been applied to many other intramural exchanges that had marked the private history of both *Doe* and *Roe*: "For two adult attorneys at law (I am 31 years old now), our correspondence is on a very low level."[6]

The first day's national news coverage of the *Roe* and *Doe* rulings emphasized not only the substance of the decisions but also how the Court's action would likely end most legislative battles over whether abortion law liberalization should be enacted or—in New York's case—revoked. The *New York Times* noted how Blackmun's opinions laid out "an unusually detailed timetable" for state regulation of a pregnant woman's choice, and New York Governor Nelson Rockefeller, deeply relieved that 1973 would not witness a replay of previous years' abortion battles, called the *Roe* decision "a wonderful thing." PPFA President Alan Guttmacher labeled the ruling "wise and courageous," but New York's Roman Catholic archbishop, Terence Cardinal Cooke, termed it "shocking" and "horrifying." *Newsweek* magazine asserted that the outcome was "an astonishing decision for the Nixon Court to reach," and added that "most astonishing of all was the broad scope and explicit detail of the decision." *Time* said the ruling was "bold and uncompromising," and, like several other publications, highlighted how new Gallup poll results showed that when Americans were asked whether an abortion decision during the first three months of pregnancy should simply be left to a woman and her doctor, 46 percent of respondents said "yes" and 45 percent "no." Some other national reporting, however, stressed that the decisions "surprised almost everyone" and that Blackmun's timetable "looked a good deal more like legislation than adjudication."[7]

Editorially, the nation's newspapers reacted to *Roe* and *Doe* with overwhelming praise. The *New York Times* welcomed the Blackmun opinions as "a major contribution to the preservation of individual liberties" and said that they offered "a sound foundation for final and reasonable resolution" of the abortion debate. "Nothing in the Court's approach," the *Times* added, "ought to give affront to persons who oppose all abortions for reasons of religion or individual conviction." The *Washington Post* termed the decisions "wise and sound," and the *Los Angeles Times* stated that they were "sensible" as well as both legally and historically "persuasive." The *Boston Globe* said it was "deeply gladdened" by the outcome, and the *Wall Street Journal*, while expressing "certain reservations," said that overall the Court had "struck a reasonable balance on an exceedingly difficult question." The *Philadelphia Inquirer* praised Blackmun's "admirably reasoned decision," and the *Pittsburgh Post-Gazette* said that the Court had acted with "compassion and intelligence." The *Atlanta Constitution* characterized the result as "realistic and appropriate," and the Raleigh *News and Observer* stated that the decisions should be "praised" for "upholding our traditional concept of personal freedom." The *Arkansas Democrat* asserted that the United States was "doubly blessed that this matter was settled by the court rather than by legislation," and the *St. Louis Post-Dispatch* said the Court's action was "remarkable for its common sense, its humaneness and most of all for its affirmation of an individual's right to privacy." Within Texas, the *Houston Chronicle* commended the judgment as "sound" and the *San Angelo Standard-Times* praised it as "a wise and humane decision," while the *San Antonio Light* concluded that "The ruling is not perfect, but it was as close to it as humanly possible."[8]

Jesuit theologian Robert F. Drinan stated that Blackmun's opinions were "balanced with extraordinary care," but conservative columnist William F. Buckley, hearkening back to an infamous nineteenth-century ruling in which the Court had upheld slavery, labeled the "outrageous" abortion ruling "the Dred Scott decision of the 20th century." The religious magazine *Christianity Today* asserted that "the majority of the Supreme Court has explicitly rejected Christian moral teaching" and has "clearly decided for paganism, and against Christianity." Protestant ethicist and abortion scholar Daniel Callahan concluded that "the Court should have left the matter in the hands of state legislatures," and black religious historian C. Eric Lincoln announced himself as a convert to the opposition cause, explaining that "unrestricted abortion . . . is but one more example of the retreat from responsibility which seems characteristic of the times." Antiabortion legal scholar John T. Noonan, Jr., decried *Roe* and *Doe* as perhaps "the most radical decisions ever issued by the Supreme Court," and in one of the more widely circulated attacks on the Court's rulings, *The New Republic* explicitly endorsed William Rehnquist's dissent and expressed astonishment that only two justices had refused to join a majority holding which "simply asserts the result it has reached." The entire issue of abortion, *The New Republic* claimed, "is not for the courts, but should have been left to the political process."[9]

Within medical circles, some physicians who had adopted a repeal stance, such as ASA president Bob Hall, felt that Blackmun had erred in placing fetal viability at twenty-four to twenty-eight weeks rather than at twenty or some other earlier point. Out of some 33,000 doctors who responded to a questionnaire distributed by *Modern Medicine* magazine, however, more than 64 percent voiced approval of the *Roe* and *Doe* decisions, even though in some states, such as Louisiana, majorities of up to 75 percent of physicians expressed opposition. Several weeks later, a nationwide Harris Poll found that 52 percent of respondents favored the Supreme Court decisions, with 41 percent registering disagreement and 7 percent saying they were unsure.[10]

One day after *Roe* v. *Wade* and *Doe* v. *Bolton* were publicly announced, Harry Blackmun distributed to his eight colleagues an eight-page memorandum with detailed recommendations for how they should affirm, dismiss, or otherwise vacate and remand the other abortion cases that had been sitting quietly on the Court's docket awaiting final disposition of *Roe* and *Doe*. The following day Blackmun and one of his clerks, Randy Bezanson, flew to Bezanson's home town of Cedar Rapids, Iowa, where Blackmun had long been scheduled to speak at Wednesday night's annual dinner of the Cedar Rapids–Marion Area Chamber of Commerce. More than four dozen antiabortion demonstrators turned out to greet Blackmun's appearance, and perhaps in response, Blackmun took the unusual step of devoting some of his remarks to the Monday decisions. The Supreme Court, he told his 560-person audience, "has not authorized abortion on demand," and he stressed that the justices "are aware of how sensitive an issue this is and how seemingly insoluble that problem is." He volunteered that he had very much favored holding the cases for reargument, since it was "too important a matter to study without two justices," and he went on to explain that "No matter how the Court ruled, it will be excoriated from one end of the country to the other." Most unusually and intriguingly of all, the *Cedar Rapids Gazette* also quoted Blackmun as saying with regard to abortion that "I really resent that it had to come before the Court because it is a medical and moral problem," more than a legal one.[11]

In both Austin and Atlanta, Texas and Georgia officials undertook the standard procedure of preparing formal petitions asking the Supreme Court to reconsider its two decisions. Connecticut Attorney General Robert K. Killian submitted a four-page statement in support of those requests at the same time that they were formally filed in mid-February, and Dennis Horan, the Chicago attorney who had been so helpful to Jay Floyd eighteen months earlier, likewise filed a petition objecting to the fact that *Roe* and *Doe* had been decided without "unborn children" being accorded formal representation during the Court's consideration of the cases. While the *Dallas Morning News* editorially welcomed these last-gasp efforts, the Supreme Court accorded the various submissions nothing more than pro forma consideration, and at a February 16 conference the justices privately ratified all of Harry Blackmun's recommendations as to how the other pending abortion cases should be resolved. On February 26 the high court publicly announced that the petitions for reconsideration of *Roe* and *Doe* had been denied, and that twelve additional cases—including those from Missouri, North Carolina, Utah, Kentucky, and South Dakota, plus three other criminal cases against doctors and two appeals each from both the Connecticut decisions and the Illinois case, had all been remanded to lower courts for resolution in light of *Roe* and *Doe* and that a thirteenth, Professor Byrn's appeal from New York, had simply been dismissed. Several weeks later the justices rejected rehearing petitions from both the State of Connecticut and Professor Byrn, and soon thereafter they also remanded the final abortion case on their docket, Dr. Rosen's suit against the Louisiana law.[12]

Within a few weeks of the Supreme Court's two landmark decisions, lower courts following *Roe* and *Doe*'s lead resolved a number of well-known and long-pending appeals. Minnesota's Supreme Court reversed Jane Hodgson's two-year-old conviction, and the Fourth Circuit Court of Appeals affirmed the earlier District Court judgment voiding Dr. Vuitch's 1969 Maryland conviction. Over the ensuing several months, other state courts applying *Roe* and *Doe*'s principles formally invalidated antiabortion laws in Oklahoma, Illinois, New Mexico, Colorado, Pennsylvania, Arizona, Michigan, South Carolina, and Wyoming. Additionally, at much the same time, federal panels struck down now-obsolete statutes in Tennessee, Rhode Island, Indiana, Montana, and Iowa.[13]

While judicial compliance with *Roe* and *Doe*'s mandate was unsurprisingly prompt, actual implementation of the rulings' tangible commands by American hospitals was generally slow and in many instances simply nonexistent. Both journalistic and professional surveys disclosed that many hospitals, both private and public, were manifesting no desire whatsoever to begin providing abortion services, but in some states, doctors who had already been performing abortions quickly moved to expand the scale of their clinic facilities.[14]

Far more visible than the hesitancy of medical institutions, and far more weighty than the editorial opposition of magazines like *Christianity Today* and *The New Republic*, however, was the overt political resistance to *Roe* and *Doe* that was quickly voiced both by members of Congress and by the national leadership of the Roman Catholic church. Only eight days after the two decisions were announced, Maryland Representative Lawrence J. Hogan introduced a constitutional amendment declaring that a fetus was a Fourteenth Amendment "person" beginning at the moment of conception, and one day later New York Senator James Buckley announced that he would submit a similar measure for Senate consideration. Soon thereafter, the National Conference of Catholic Bishops issued a harsh denunciation of the Supreme Court's decision, saying that "this majority opinion of the Court is wrong and is entirely contrary to the fundamental principles of morality." The Bishops asserted that "laws that conform to the opinion of the Court are immoral laws, in opposition to God's plan," and they insisted that "our American law and way of life comprise an obvious and certain recognition of the law of God . . . our legal system is both based in it, and must conform to it." Most pointedly of all, they declared in conclusion that "we reject the opinion of the U.S. Supreme Court as erroneous, unjust, and immoral."[15]

A significant number of Roman Catholic legal scholars, including the ubiquitous Professor Byrn, soon authored equally harsh or dismissive attacks on the *Roe* and *Doe* opinions, with one such writer decrying Blackmun's handiwork as a "shoddy performance, devoid of judicial craftsmanship,"[16] but amidst a veritable flood of law journal essays recapping and reviewing the two decisions,[17] the most telling attacks on the Court's rulings came from prominent legal academics who professed not to be personally opposed to abortion.

Far and away the most important critique of *Roe v. Wade* was written by a young professor who had been involved at firsthand in the Court's earlier consideration of *Griswold*, former Earl Warren clerk John Hart Ely. Some years later one commentator would call Ely's April 1973 *Yale Law Journal* essay, "The Wages of Crying Wolf," perhaps "the most famous and influential legal analysis of the past decade," and on the abortion decisions' tenth anniversary, one legal newspaper would term Ely's article the "classic diatribe against *Roe*." Ely's piece began with an almost apologetic reference to Byron White's and William Rehnquist's opinions, explaining that "Were the dissents adequate, this comment would be unnecessary. But each is so brief as to signal no particular conviction that *Roe* represents an important, or unusually dangerous, constitutional development." Ely offered up several almost flippant remarks—"Whether anti-abortion legislation cramps the life style of an unwilling mother more significantly than anti-homosexuality legislation cramps the life style of a homosexual is a close question"—and noted that Blackmun's focus on viability was insufficiently justified, but his fundamental goal was to point out what he saw as the wholesale inadequacy of the Court's constitutional analysis. On one central point, Ely noted how "the argument that fetuses lack constitutional rights is simply irrelevant," for "it has never been held or even asserted that the state interest needed to justify forcing a person to refrain from an activity, *whether or not that activity is constitutionally protected*, must implicate either the life or the constitutional rights of another person." Laws prohibited killing dogs, for example, even as some sort of political statement, without anyone having to contend that dogs, or birds, or what have you, themselves possessed any rights.

Ely did concede that "Abortion is too much like infanticide on the one hand, and too much like contraception on the other, to leave one comfortable with any answer," but in the constitutional context, the *Roe* opinion's "inability" to confidently state whether the right that was involved stemmed from the Ninth or from the Fourteenth Amendment should have raised the question of "whether the Constitution speaks to the matter at all." Ely stressed that he was not arguing for some sort of literalism, for "Surely the Court is entitled," and indeed "obligated, to seek out the sorts of evils the framers meant to combat and to move against their twentieth-century counterparts." Hence, "it seems to me entirely proper to infer a general right of privacy, *so long as some care is taken in defining the sort of right the inference will support.*" Ely went on to explain that "The problem with *Roe* is not so much that it bungles the question it sets itself, but rather that it sets itself a question the Constitution has not made the Court's business." Ely acknowledged that "*Roe* v. *Wade* seems like a durable decision," but more importantly, it was also "a very bad decision," he emphasized in closing. "It is bad because it is bad constitutional law, or rather because it is *not* constitutional law and gives almost no sense of an obligation to try to be."

Some months later, Ely spoke out even more strongly, declaring that "Nothing in the Constitution's text, nothing in the Constitution's history suggests any right to an abortion." He maintained that in the *Roe* and *Doe* opinions "the Court never adequately explains why a desire on the part of a State to permit a fetus to proceed to life is not a goal sufficiently important to support the legislative efforts in this area," and that in those opinions, the Court also "fails equally with respect to the other half of its inference," namely "the proposition that the right to an abortion is a constitutional right entitled to special constitutional protection." All in all, Ely volunteered, *Roe* and *Doe* "could be reversed ... without great danger of upsetting an entire body of doctrine."

Ten years later Ely would admit that his now-famous essay may have been a "little exuberant and oversimplified," and he would even allow that "In many ways, the country is better off because of" the *Roe* and *Doe* decisions. There was no denying, or erasing, however, the indisputably formative influence of his widely read 1973 essay, and Ely's severely dismissive attitude toward the Blackmun opinions directly stimulated and encouraged a swiftly growing torrent of legal criticism from what could have been supportive quarters.[18]

Only a month or so after Ely's landmark article first appeared, two other academic essayists, Philip B. Heymann and Douglas E. Barzelay—the first of whom had been Charles Fried's co-clerk with Justice John M. Harlan during the year that *Poe* v. *Ullman* was decided—published an understated defense of the new abortion rulings. Blackmun's *Roe* and *Doe* opinions "have already engendered much popular criticism," Heymann and his colleague acknowledged, and they further conceded that "the language of the Court's opinion in *Roe* too often obscures the full strength" of the argument underlying the decision. They also admitted that the Court "may well have gone too far in its seeming codification of detailed restrictions on health regulations and procedures," and that "the line" that Blackmun had drawn at viability "is presently vague, subject to troublesome modifications with the development of medical knowledge and technique, and, in any event, perhaps further along during pregnancy than the mother's interest requires." Heymann and Barzelay granted that "the question of constitutionality in the case of abortion statutes is a more difficult one than that involved in *Griswold* and *Eisenstadt*," but "only because the asserted state interest is more important, not because of any difference in the individual interests involved."

For the most basic constitutional question, however, Heymann and his coworker provided an authentically Harlan-like answer, explaining that "basic values related by principle and tradition to central, widely accepted, organizing concepts of our society" ought to be specified as the foundation for a decision such as *Roe*. "Sadly," they observed, "the Court failed to relate the body of long-emerging precedent it recognized as significant," reaching back even well before *Griswold*,

> to those articulable, widely shared principles that the precedents reflect and that are fundamental to many of our social and political arrangements. This failure leaves the impression that the abortion deci-

sions rest in part on unexplained precedents, in part on an extremely tenuous relation to provisions of the Bill of Rights, and in part on a raw exercise of judicial fiat. The holding in *Roe* is, nonetheless, far more solid than it at first appears, for it is fully consistent with, and reflects a groping toward, principles that are justified in both reason and precedent even if these principles were never adequately articulated by the opinion of the Court.[19]

Prominent antiabortion pedagogue John Noonan would later praise Heymann and Barzelay's concession-laden essay for being "far more articulate than the Court," but ensuing critical evaluations of *Roe* and *Doe* owed far more to John Ely's perspective than to Heymann and Barzelay's. Soon after those first articles appeared, two female legal scholars concluded that the Court's opinions "fail to yield a reasoned justification of the constitutional basis for protection of the woman's interest in terminating her pregnancy," since Blackmun "explains the weight of the mother's interest, rather than its source." Far more prominently, former Solicitor General and Watergate Special Prosecutor Archibald Cox, in a small book that repeatedly discussed the "Berger" Court and which misstated the *Roe* and *Doe* holdings so badly as to suggest that he actually had not read them, nonetheless asserted that "the Court failed to establish the legitimacy of the decision by not articulating a precept of sufficient abstractness to lift the ruling above the level of a political judgment based upon the evidence currently available from the medical, physical, and social sciences." The Court's "failure to confront the issue in principled terms," Cox claimed, "leaves the opinion to read like a set of hospital rules and regulations, whose validity is good enough this week but will be destroyed with new statistics . . ."[20]

Several years later, a judge on the Second Circuit Court of Appeals, Henry J. Friendly, who had served on the panel that would have decided *Hall* had not the New York repeal statute intervened, publicly decried the Supreme Court's "failure to articulate a defensible principle" in *Roe* and *Doe*, and one of the country's most prominent law professors, Gerald Gunther, stated that the decisions had entailed "infusing a value of questionable constitutional legitimacy into the basic document." He bluntly added that "I have not yet found a satisfying rationale to justify *Roe* . . . on the basis of modes of constitutional interpretation I consider legitimate." Another academic, boldly claiming that the pre-*Roe* "lower court decisions that struck down abortion statutes for impairing the right of privacy wholly neglected legal analysis," further asserted that "By taking an abortion case when it did, the Court forestalled the development of one of its traditional aids for deciding difficult questions—a thoughtful lower court case law." Declaring that "three years is hardly time enough for the judicial system to evolve sound analysis," he maintained that "the Court should not have decided an abortion case when it did," for by doing so the Court had "thrust itself into a political debate and stunted the development" of invaluable lower court litigation.[21]

One well-known legal analyst, William Van Alstyne, conceded that Blackmun's *Roe* opinion was "gratuitously sweeping" and that "its sheer sweep does leave it critically vulnerable," but he nonetheless emphasized that "Blackmun faced the collision of conflicting views with an admirable directness. Doubtless that extreme candor invited some of the criticism he (and his opinion) have since received. But it was also a degree of candor which commands respect." Six years later, however, Van Alstyne's attitude had become dramatically harsher, and he castigated *Roe* as "an aberration of judicial legislation" and insisted that *Griswold* "did not imply *Roe*, or anything even close." "There is no such thing," Van Alstyne declared, "as a personal, free-standing, fundamental right embedded in the Constitution of the United States to kill gestating life. *Roe* v. *Wade*, in suggesting otherwise, proceeded on an assumption not derived or derivable from *Griswold* v. *Connecticut*, from any previous case, or indeed, from any constitutional clause. It was rather judicial legislation."[22]

As the years passed, even Ruth Bader Ginsburg, a future Supreme Court justice who in 1973 had headed the American Civil Liberties Union's Women's Rights Project, joined the assault, alleging that in *Roe* "the Court ventured too far in the change it ordered and presented an incomplete justification for its action." Instead, she later explained, the Court should have simply invalidated the Texas statute "and said no more," rather than venture into "heavy-handed judicial intervention" in the way that it had. Ginsburg contended that *Roe* was impaired "by the opinion's concentration on a medically approved autonomy idea, to the exclusion of a constitutionally based sex equality perspective," and she further argued that "Academic criticism of *Roe* . . . might have been less pointed had the Court placed the woman alone, rather than the woman tied to her physician, at the center of its attention."[23]

Future Yale Law School dean Guido Calabresi was even more outspoken, terming the *Roe* decision "offensive" and labeling Blackmun's opinion "highly unfortunate" and "a disaster." Like Ginsburg, however, Calabresi also focused upon articulating a new perspective that had first been briefly suggested by New York University Law School professor Sylvia Law: that Fourteenth Amendment's equal protection clause, rather than a substantive, *Griswold*-style application of privacy or liberty analysis, ought to be the lens through which the constitutional status of abortion restrictions was appraised. Law had submitted that "The rhetoric of privacy, as opposed to equality, blunts our ability to focus on the fact that it is *women* who are oppressed when abortion is denied," and she had also maintained that the Court had erred in "falsely casting the abortion decision as primarily a medical question." Calabresi significantly expanded on Law's point, arguing that "without a right to abortion women are not equal to men in the law" and pointing out, in classic equal protection language, how antiabortion statutes in terms of gender were "laws enacted by a dominant group which disproportionately burden a disfavored group." The relevant Fourteenth Amendment command, he asserted, was "equality of access to sex— equality in *sexual freedom* among men and women," for "the right at stake is the right of women to participate equally in sex without bearing burdens not put on men."[24]

Any number of legal writers would go on to make the point that some alternative term or concept other than "privacy," such as either "autonomy" or simply "liberty," ought to be frankly acknowledged as the substantive core of what was at issue in *Roe*,[25] but Ginsburg and Law were far from alone in criticizing Blackmun's *Roe* and *Doe* opinions for being too solicitous of doctors and insufficiently supportive of women's individual liberty of choice above and beyond whatever medical advice they might be offered by one or another physician. Yale law professor Harry H. Wellington sarcastically observed soon after the decisions came down that Blackmun in *Doe* "treats the private physician with the reverence that one expects only from advertising agencies employed by the American Medical Association," and some years later another academic noted that "the Court's language in *Roe* . . . portrays the doctor and not the patient as the primary decision-maker in the abortion context."[26]

In subsequent years, sophisticated commentators such as John A. Robertson and Nancy K. Rhoden would highlight how the Court should have devoted more attention to acknowledging the gestational burdens a woman experiences during pregnancy and how too narrow a focus upon the concept of trimesters could distort *Roe* and *Doe*'s meaning. Rhoden pointed out that "the Court in *Roe* never spoke of a second or third trimester," but only of "a first trimester and then of stages demarcated by the time of viability," and she similarly noted how "the continuum of pregnancy contains no magic moment at which the maternal health interest becomes compelling." Rhoden also acknowledged that the Court's adoption of the potentially fluid frontier of viability meant that "control over the dimensions of a constitutional right has been wholly delegated to medical technology and the physicians who develop, utilize and assess this technology," but a wide variety of medical, philosophical, and legal commentators all agreed that while no absolutely precise lines of demarcation could be drawn at any stage during pregnancy, viability nonetheless was certainly "a proper cutoff point."[27]

Nonetheless, the resolutely critical perspective that had first appeared in John Ely's influential essay would increasingly prevail as the years passed. By the early 1990s even a leading federal appellate judge would feel no compunction, at least in off-the-bench writings, about ridiculing *Roe* as "a flop" and disparaging what he termed "the ineptitude of the opinion." Self-professed conservatives such as Charles Fried, far better known as Ronald Reagan's Solicitor General from 1985 to 1989 than for his role in helping prepare John Harlan's landmark dissent in *Poe v. Ullman*, could decry *Roe* as "a serious misuse of the Supreme Court's authority" that was "wrong in method and result" without fear of rejoinder, and even more heated denunciations—"The moral inadequacy of the *Roe* opinion is matched by its inadequacy as a piece of legal reasoning"—would raise nary an eyebrow.[28]

But in later years, just as in 1973, *Roe* and *Doe* would sustain far graver wounds from the friendly fire of professed supporters than from the explicit attacks of candid opponents. The nation's most quoted law professor of the 1980s, Harvard's Laurence H. Tribe, had initially greeted *Roe* with a law review article ruing how "the substantive judgment on which it rests is nowhere to be found" and asserting that there is "something deeply unsettling about the Court's conclusion that even after fetal viability, the state may not forbid any abortion that is 'necessary to preserve the life or health of the mother.'" Nevertheless, in 1981 Tribe accurately told a congressional committee that "*Roe v. Wade* was but a logical extension of *Griswold*," for the "limits on government power declared in *Griswold* left the Court no alternative other than to impose some limits on abortion regulation as well." *Roe*, he explained, "far from creating some novel and unprecedented liberty, simply recognized and extended some deeply felt and well-established principles about the limits of governmental power." Nine years later, however, Tribe's enthusiasm had once again slackened, as he emphasized that "the sensitivity of the abortion question counseled more restraint than the Court exhibited in *Roe*. A gradual enunciation and articulation of the line that separated permissible state laws from laws that violated the constitutional right to privacy" would have been a "more judicious" choice, and elsewhere, in his most influential book, Tribe reiterated that "nothing in the Supreme Court's opinion provided a satisfactory explanation of why the fetal interest should not be deemed overriding prior to viability."[29]

The worst casualties of the excessively negative but nonetheless pervasive consensus about *Roe*'s wrongheadedness, however, were astonishingly forgetful or ignorant journalists, not ambivalent law professors. Hardly four years after *Roe* and *Doe* were decided, *The New Republic* tried to tell its readers that "In the early 1970s, antiabortion laws were on the way out" and that *Roe* had "killed off the movement for abortion reform." Not long after that, *Newsweek* explained that abortion "was never fully debated in state legislatures" in advance of the 1973 rulings, and quoted an ACLU staffer as confirming that "The Supreme Court decision was too fast and too easy." Some years later, while opining that "the greatest weakness in *Roe*" was "its notorious 'trimester' analysis," *The New Republic*'s editors illuminated their historical perspective somewhat more fully by claiming that "Abortion was rapidly being legalized in 1973 and might well not even be controversial if politics had been allowed to take its course." Unfortunately, however, faulty historical memories were not exclusively limited to sophomoric magazine editors, for even one of Professor Tribe's colleagues at Harvard Law School, Mary Ann Glendon, would write that *Roe* had curtailed "the process of legislative reform that was already well on the way to producing . . . compromise statutes that gave very substantial protection to women's interests." Future Supreme Court justice Ruth Ginsburg similarly amplified her earlier criticisms by lamenting how *Roe* had been guilty of "stopping a political process that was moving in a reform direction," and progressive essayist Barbara Ehrenreich expressed regret as to how *Roe* had "cut off what might have been a grassroots pro-choice movement." "In the early 1970s," she explained, "There had been no national debate, no widespread feminist effort to reach out to, and convince, the undecided public of the justice of what we called abortion rights. In this sense," Ehrenreich concluded, "*Roe* v. *Wade* was tragically premature."[30]

From the immediate vantage point of 1973, however, with memories of both the devastating Michigan loss and the dire, narrowly averted threat that the right-to-life mobilization had posed to the New York repeal law so freshly in mind, no abortion activists, and no academic or journalistic supporters, expressed any regret that Harry Blackmun and six of his Supreme Court colleagues had ruled that a woman's choice with regard to abortion was a constitutionally protected right rather than a criminally punishable preference that could be left to the annual vagaries of state legislative votes or statewide popular referenda.

Opponents of the *Roe* and *Doe* decisions found relatively little support in Congress for any of the several "right to life" constitutional amendments that had been proposed in the immediate wake of the rulings, but as many state legislatures moved to update and revise their abortion-related statutes, abortion opponents in a few states, such as Rhode Island and Minnesota, adopted new laws that openly contradicted the Supreme Court's holdings. Lower federal courts swiftly voided such enactments, with one district judge dismissing Rhode Island's claims as "sheer sophistry," but in several cities abortion access proponents filed federal lawsuits of their own when municipally supported public hospitals refused to allow staff physicians to perform abortions. Federal judges ruled against the recalcitrant hospital authorities without exception or delay, and a three-judge Florida federal court, acting in a case that Roy Lucas had argued prior to the *Roe* and *Doe* decisions, struck down state statutes requiring spousal and/or parental consent before a married woman or a teenager could obtain an abortion.[31]

Abortion opponents showed increasing signs of popular support, however, and in the fall of 1973 the National Conference of Catholic Bishops publicly highlighted "the need for grassroots pro-life organization" on behalf of a "right to life" constitutional amendment and quickly followed up with a declaration that "there is a *moral imperative*" for "well-planned and coordinated political organization by citizens at the national, state and local levels." One Catholic intellectual pointed out that "a considerable gap exists between the official position of the Catholic Church and the thinking of many rank-and-file communicants" on the issue of abortion, and a Washington protest on the first anniversary of the *Roe* and *Doe* decisions drew only some seven thousand antiabortion demonstrators. In early March, however, when a Senate subcommittee finally and reluctantly opened hearings on the right to life constitutional amendments that had been introduced a year earlier, four Catholic cardinals—from Boston, Chicago, Los Angeles, and Philadelphia—all appeared as witnesses, the first time in American history that such high-ranking church officials had appeared before Congress.[32]

On April 12, 1974, in the most significant abortion law development since *Roe* and *Doe*, a Massachusetts grand jury charged Dr. Kenneth C.

Edelin, a thirty-five-year-old black staff physician at the Boston City Hospital, with criminal manslaughter for having aborted an approximately twenty-two or twenty-four-week fetus that at least one hospital colleague believed was definitely viable. Nine months passed before Edelin stood trial, but even though Judge James P. McGuire instructed the all-white jury that "a fetus is not a person and therefore not a subject for an indictment for manslaughter," the jurors deliberated for only seven hours before returning with a verdict of guilty. Stunned observers had believed almost unanimously that Edelin's acquittal was virtually guaranteed, and while some commentaries noted that ten of the twelve jurors were Catholic, *Time* magazine pointed out to its readers that "By finding him guilty of manslaughter, the jury decided, in effect, that a fetus approaching viability is a person and, as such, is entitled to the full protection of the law." Judge McGuire sentenced Edelin to simply one year's probation, and while almost two years later the Massachusetts Supreme Judicial Court would reverse the conviction on the grounds that the evidence against Edelin was so insufficient that the case should not even have gone to the jury, the Boston verdict nonetheless gave right to life advocates the most dramatic boost their cause had yet received.[33]

The 1974 congressional elections witnessed the defeat or retirement of many leading antiabortion champions, and while the paltry proportion of American hospitals that were performing *any* abortions—only 17 percent of public and 28 percent of private, one study showed—meant that actual availability was difficult for women in some states, right to life forces were making no significant headway in Congress. Part of the difficulty stemmed from proponents' inability to unite behind any single version of an antiabortion constitutional amendment, but some observers believed that the shrill tone exhibited in many right to life appeals was inherently self-defeating. One professor at a Catholic-affiliated law school, writing about *Roe* and *Doe* in a Catholic periodical, asserted that "the Court's decision in its basic concerns is more in accord with fundamental Christian principles, and certainly far more judicious in its projections, than the positions reflected in the rather strident criticisms it has received from certain Catholic sources." Indeed, Raymond G. Decker continued, "it is difficult to comprehend how the basic thrust of the decision in its concern to protect the right of conscience ('right to privacy' in legal terms) can be so severely criticized by those purporting to adhere to basic Christian beliefs."[34]

In April 1975 the U.S. Senate tabled by a margin of 54 to 36 an amendment that would have terminated federal Medicaid funding for abortions, and in mid-September of that year the Senate subcommittee that had been considering the various right to life constitutional amendments for upwards of two years rejected them all. The National Conference of Catholic Bishops responded forcefully to the Senate action, with a committee headed by New York archbishop Terence Cardinal Cooke announcing that the church had concluded that it was "absolutely necessary to encourage the development in each Congressional district of an identifiable, tightly knit and well-organized pro-life unit." This Pastoral Plan for Pro-Life Activities, Cooke said, was a response to how "We have been subjected to a brain-washing by people pushing abortion," but even the Jesuit magazine *America* expressed extreme discomfort at the Bishops' initiative, explaining that while their plan specified "in considerable detail the structure, objectives and modes of operation of these political action groups," the conference concurrently disavowed any formal affiliations, no doubt because of the tax-exemption repercussions that might ensue. "Simultaneous detailed exhortations and disclaimers of responsibility are not credible," *America* noted, while observing how it was "regrettable that there is no explicit recognition by the bishops that many Catholics have persistent doubts about the correctness and wisdom of the hierarchy's stand."

The bishops' explicitly political declaration, however, did nothing to unify the prolife cause around any one specific constitutional proposal, and early in 1976 one prominent antiabortion activist, Robert Lynch, wrote publicly about "the terrible and at times scandalous disunity that exists among the pro-life partisans." Some relative moderates, such as law professors John T. Noonan and David Louisell, favored an amendment that would simply return full authority for abortion law regulation to the states, thus permitting a wide range of results, while others supported *only* an amendment that would make every human embryo a Fourteenth Amendment person beginning at the "moment of conception" and expressed considerable irritation that other right to life advocates, including the bishops, remained open to less restrictive alternatives. Robert Lynch, who headed the National Committee for a Human Life Amendment, a close adjunct of the Bishops' Conference, acerbicly observed that "There are presently six national pro-life organizations, each with a different form of amendment, each with a different political plan, each refusing generally to communicate or work with the other." "It has been said," he added, "that jealousy and megalomania abound in the pro-life movement, and my experience confirms this charge to some degree." Lynch warned that "many Catholics are tired of the abortion issue or are apathetic about it," and cautioned that "the successes that state units enjoyed before the Supreme Court decision have generally been dulled by the events of the past three years." Both Cardinal Cooke and Archbishop Joseph L. Bernardin, president of the Bishops' Conference, appeared at a March 1976 House subcommittee hearing to speak in favor of some form of a right to life constitutional amendment, but when the full Senate, on April 28, voted 47 to 40 to table a fetal personhood proposal sponsored by North Carolina Republican Jesse Helms, the *New York Times* termed the defeat "a major setback" for the right to life cause.[35]

Nationwide public opinion polls showed no significant change in popular sentiment regarding abortion since *Roe* and *Doe*, and while one pair of researchers concluded that the decisions had given pro-choice sentiment something of a boost, numerous analysts viewed the rather surprising stability as a clear indication that most citizens—including many with ambivalent, ambiguous, and at times seemingly contradictory sentiments—had not changed their views since the 1973 rulings. Although considerable poll-to-poll variations could be identified depending on vital differences in the wording of questions, virtually all serious students of the numbers agreed that a very significant and largely stable proportion of respondents favored the availability of abortion for most reasons that a woman or doctor might identify as therapeutic while nonetheless refusing to endorse anything that appeared to represent "abortion on demand."[36]

At the same time that the national politics of abortion from 1973 through early 1976 played out largely in reaction to *Roe* and *Doe*, the Supreme Court's endorsement and extension of *Griswold*-style privacy analysis to the context of abortion also stimulated new legal curiosity as to whether *Eisenstadt* and *Roe*'s seeming abandonment of the "marital" emphasis that had been so explicit in *Griswold* meant that a fresh opportunity was now at hand for a renewed assault on sodomy statutes much like Henry McCluskey had first tried in 1969 with *Buchanan* v. *Batchelor*. As early as 1967 one journalist had prophesied that "If not next year or the next, then five years or ten years hence the United States Supreme Court will strike down existing state laws which make practicing homosexuals criminals," but both before and after its 1971 rejection of *Buchanan*, the Supreme Court on several occasions sidestepped any substantive consideration of cases contending that consenting adults ought to enjoy constitutional protection from criminal punishment for one or another private sex act, including one appeal by two Arkansas men who had each been sentenced to eight years in prison for engaging in oral sex in a parked car.[37] Even prior to *Roe* and *Doe*, Justice Marshall, dissenting in a case involving state regulation of topless bars, had volunteered that in light of *Griswold* "I have serious doubts whether the State may constitutionally assert an interest in regulating any sexual act between consenting adults," and several lower federal courts cited both *Griswold*'s and *Roe*'s protections of privacy in voiding disciplinary actions that nosy school boards in Nebraska and Alabama had attempted to take against unmarried female teachers.[38] In November 1973, however, the Supreme Court, in a brief per curiam opinion, unanimously reversed a Fifth Circuit Court of Appeals decision, written by Judge Irving Goldberg, which had found Florida's sodomy statute to be unconstitutionally vague. Exactly two years later, in a 6 to 3 per curiam holding from which Justices Brennan, Marshall, and Stewart dissented, the high court also reversed a Sixth Circuit decision which had held that Tennessee's sodomy law was unconstitutionally vague after it was challenged by a man who had been sentenced to five to seven years' imprisonment for the crime of cunnilingus. The Supreme Court majority called such oral gratification a "sexual aberration," and one otherwise sympathetic academic commentator termed the Court's embarrassingly strenuous effort to uphold the Tennessee law "truly extraordinary."[39]

In 1974, however, a homosexual man in Richmond, Virginia, with assistance from the National Gay Task Force and in-state lawyers affiliated with the American Civil Liberties Union, filed a federal declaratory judgment action much like *Buchanan* challenging the constitutionality of Virginia's sodomy statute. *John Doe v. Commonwealth's Attorney* was heard by a special three-judge district court, and while a two-member majority of the panel—seventy-six-year-old Albert V. Bryan and seventy-three-year-old Oren R. Lewis— did little more than cite the Supreme Court's recent endorsement of Florida's similar law in dismissing the challenge, District Judge Robert R. Merhige, Jr., penned a forceful dissent. "A mature individual's choice of an adult sexual partner, in the privacy of his or her own home, would appear to me to be a decision of the utmost private and intimate concern," Merhige wrote. "Private consensual sex acts between adults are matters . . . in which the state has no legitimate interest," as indicated both by Brennan's language in *Eisenstadt* and by the Court's earlier 1969 holding in *Stanley* v. *Georgia*.

One subsequent commentator labeled Judge Bryan's majority opinion "extraordinarily shoddy," and the *"Doe"* attorneys quickly appealed their loss to the Supreme Court, citing *Griswold*, *Stanley*, *Roe*, and especially *Eisenstadt* in support of their challenge. On March 29, 1976, however, with absolutely no warning, the high court by a 6 to 3 margin summarily *affirmed* the Bryan dismissal without even choosing to hear argument in the case. The Court's action generated front-page stories in the national press, with the *Los Angeles Times* terming it a "major defeat" of "far-reaching impact" for gay rights proponents and the *New York Times* emphasizing how the "ruling sharply departs from a 10-year trend in which the high court had increasingly expanded the concept of the constitutional right to privacy." Justices Brennan and Marshall, along with the Court's newest member, John Paul Stevens, a five-year veteran of the Seventh Circuit Court of Appeals whom President Gerald Ford had nominated to replace the incapacitated William O. Douglas and who had been unanimously confirmed by the U.S. Senate just four months earlier, were the three dissenters from the Court's summary disposition. *Time* magazine described civil libertarians as "thunderstruck" by the Court's action, and Bruce Voeller of the National Gay Task Force admitted that it was "an enormous disappointment."[40]

Academic reaction to the summary affirmance was vociferously critical, but some commentators acknowledged that it might well signal the end of any *Eisenstadt*-like extensions of *Griswold*, and a few even hinted that appealing the Virginia setback to the Supreme Court had been a tactical mistake. ACLU and gay rights attorneys nonetheless pulled out all the stops in petitioning the Court to reconsider its action and grant *Doe* full consideration on the merits, but on May 19 the Court unsurprisingly denied the petition for rehearing. Thanks to recent legislative revisions of old criminal codes, some eighteen states—a big jump from 1973's total of seven—had quietly decriminalized all sodomous sex acts, and seven others now boasted statutes that expressly excluded *married* couples from their penalties. Some gay strategists wondered whether *Doe* was a further and conclusive sign that ongoing decriminalization efforts should focus on legislatures rather than on courts, but national public opinion surveys nevertheless showed that some 72 percent of Americans thought that homosexual relations were "always wrong," and 59 percent believed that there should be laws "against sex acts between persons of the same sex," even though some 38 percent indicated that "what consenting adult homosexuals do in private is no one else's business."[41]

In spite of the *Doe* rebuff, ACLU attorneys hesitantly agreed that another Virginia case, in which a married couple who had recruited a

Jamaican immigrant for a "threesome" had been sentenced to several years in prison—and the Jamaican man deported—after the wife's two daughters from a previous marriage had shown photos of the encounter to school officials, should indeed be appealed to the Supreme Court. Aldo and Margaret Lovisi had initially met Earl Romeo Dunn, as he called himself, after he answered an ad they had placed in *Swingers Life* magazine, and on their third meeting, by means of a camera timer, the trio had taken photos of Margaret performing fellatio on both her husband and Mr. Dunn. Margaret's twelve and thirteen-year-old daughters, who did not care for their stepfather, took one or more such pictures to school, and after child welfare authorities were notified, local police obtained a search warrant and raided the Lovisis' home, seizing hundreds of sexual films, magazines, and photos, including those picturing the Lovisis with Earl Dunn. Aldo was charged with both cruelty to children as well as violating the Virginia sodomy statute—for allowing his wife to perform fellatio on him—and Margaret was arrested on two counts of sodomy, for performing oral sex both on her husband and on Mr. Dunn. At trial, the daughters testified unpersuasively that *they* had taken the photos of their mother, stepfather, and the Jamaican visitor, but the Lovisis were convicted on all counts. Appeals of the three sodomy convictions were routinely turned aside, and while the Virginia Supreme Court did void Aldo's initial child cruelty conviction on the grounds that the jury had received prejudicial instructions, the justices nonetheless volunteered that the photos depicting consensual oral sex in the privacy of the Lovisis' home "reveal unspeakably depraved conduct on the part of the three adults."

Aldo and Margaret were each given two years' imprisonment for their marital act of fellatio, while Margaret received an additional three years for having fellated Mr. Dunn. With the Lovisis both in jail and their normal appeals exhausted, Virginia ACLU attorney Richard E. Crouch filed a habeas corpus petition in federal court in Richmond, reiterating the privacy right claims that the convictions had scorned. District Judge Robert Merhige—who had not yet heard *"Doe"*—cited Blackmun's opinion in *Roe* and John Harlan's concurrence in *Griswold* in acknowledging that "the right to privacy inherent in the federal constitution may well extend to heterosexual relations involving oral-genital contact between consenting adults," and certainly "The right to privacy extends to sexual relations between husband and wife." In light of *Eisenstadt*, there was also "some doubt," Merhige went on, as to whether Virginia's sodomy statute "could constitutionally be applied to private sodomous acts between heterosexual consenting adults." The "rationale expressed in *Eisenstadt*," Merhige explained, "extends to protect the manner of sexual relations between unmarried persons. It is not marriage vows which make intimate and highly personal the sexual behavior of human beings. It is, instead, the nature of sexuality itself or something intensely private to the individual that calls forth constitutional protection."

Griswold and its progeny did protect "intimate sexual relations between consenting adults, carried out under secluded conditions," Merhige stated, and while the "existence of seclusion in a sexual act . . . is a necessary prerequirement to that act's being protected from state regulation by the Constitution," in this present case the sexual relations "were not private," because the Lovisis "relinquished the secluded aspect of their sexual relations" when the photographs were taken. Thereby, Merhige concluded, "the Lovisis did not meet the burden incumbent upon them to preserve the seclusion of their sexual acts. As such they relinquished their right to privacy in the performance of these acts, and they could lawfully be prosecuted."

Merhige's refusal to grant the habeas corpus petition was appealed to the Fourth Circuit Court of Appeals, but almost three years passed before the appellate court—some six weeks after the Supreme Court's summary affirmance of "*Doe*"—upheld Merhige's decision by a vote of 5 to 3. Chief Judge Clement F. Haynsworth—once an unsuccessful nominee for the Supreme Court seat that became Harry Blackmun's—wrote for the majority that "What the federal constitution protects is the right of privacy in circumstances in which it may reasonably be expected," and that the Lovisis' privacy had dissolved when Earl Dunn had joined them. The three dissenters contended that with regard to the Lovisis' twin convictions for engaging in fellatio with each other, "what would not be punishable sodomy in Dunn's absence is not rendered punishable sodomy by his presence," and the ACLU lawyers resolved to seek Supreme Court review. ACLU legal director Mel Wulf conceded that success was improbable, since likely "the Justices will just find the whole thing a little embarrassing," and five months later, without dissent, the high court did indeed decline to review the Lovisis' imprisonment and convictions.[42]

While both "*Doe*" and *Lovisi* got far more attention in the law reviews than they drew from the Supreme Court, by late 1975 several abortion cases were very much commanding the high court's attention. Missouri was as active as any state in post-*Roe* efforts to restrict the performance of abortions, and in mid-1974 a Planned Parenthood affiliate and two physicians had gone into federal court to challenge a new state law mandating parental and spousal consent as well as several potentially intimidating regulatory measures aimed at doctors. With Circuit Judge—and future FBI and CIA director—William H. Webster dissenting from his two colleagues' endorsement of the spousal and parental requirements, a special three-judge panel upheld most all of the provisions, the first time since *Roe* that such criteria had survived an initial court challenge. The plaintiffs appealed directly to the Supreme Court, and the high court stayed any enforcement of the Missouri law pending resolution of the appeal. Harry Blackmun quickly prepared a first draft of a per curiam summary disposition, hoping to reverse the Missouri panel before the June conclusion of the Court's 1974–1975 year, but when only Justices Brennan, Stewart, and Marshall readily signed on to Blackmun's initial circulation, the appeal—styled as *Planned Parenthood of Central Missouri v. John Danforth*, the Attorney General of Missouri, was held over for the 1975 Term and eventually scheduled for argument in March of 1976.

By the time that *Danforth* was finally argued, two other abortion cases were also before the Court. One, involving many of the same participants as *Danforth*, was a state appeal of an Eighth Circuit decision voiding a Missouri attempt to restrict Medicaid funding to only those abortions performed on therapeutic grounds. The second was an appeal by Massachusetts Attorney General Francis Bellotti from a three-judge court decree, requested by onetime *Eisenstadt* victor Bill Baird, that had voided a new 1974 state law making it a crime to perform an abortion on a woman under eighteen years of age without prior permission from *both* of her parents. The justices unanimously agreed that the Massachusetts case should be remanded so that the Massachusetts Supreme Judicial Court could have an opportunity to construe a brief provision allowing state court judges to grant exceptions in a sufficiently broad way that the statute might be saved, and while there was a heated but ultimately tangential disagreement in the Medicaid case about doctors' standing to mount such a challenge on behalf of their patients, the justices nonetheless agreed that the merits of the case should be returned to the appellate court for fuller consideration.[43]

In *Danforth*, Harry Blackmun circulated a new first draft of a majority opinion in late May, and while Justices Brennan and Marshall quickly signed on, a full month passed—and the end of the term approached—before first Potter Stewart and then Lewis Powell also agreed to join Blackmun's full opinion. John Paul Stevens had earlier indicated that he could support most sections of Blackmun's draft, but not the one striking down Missouri's parental consent provision, and while Warren Burger had not yet taken a clear position one way or the other, Stewart and Powell's agreement—in the context of Byron White and William Rehnquist's firm status as dissenters—gave Blackmun at least a five-vote majority across the board.[44]

On July 1, 1976, the Court handed down its first significant abortion decisions since *Roe* and *Doe*. *Bellotti* v. *Baird* and *Singleton* v. *Wulff*, the Missouri Medicaid case, understandably drew little attention, but Blackmun's *Danforth* opinion, striking down both the spousal and parental consent requirements and a number of other measures, was treated by the press as a major ruling. Early on, in a section of the opinion endorsed by all nine justices, Blackmun stressed how the Court had "recognized in *Roe* that viability was a matter of medical judgment, skill, and technical ability, and we preserved the flexibility of the term." The section voiding the spousal consent measure, however, was backed by just six justices, for only the day before Warren Burger had finally stated that he would join White and Rehnquist in dissent. Blackmun emphasized that the provision gave a husband "a veto power exercisable for any reason whatsoever or for no reason at all," and hence was constitutionally unacceptable, "inasmuch as it is the woman who physically bears the child and who is the more directly and immediately affected by the pregnancy." Similarly, with regard to the parental consent requirement, Blackmun concluded that the state "does not have the constitutional authority to give a third party an absolute, and possibly arbitrary, veto over the decision of the physician and his patient." A subsequent section also struck down a portion of the law that would have prohibited saline solution abortions after the twelfth week of gestation, and Justices Stewart and Powell added a short concurrence indicating that parental *consultation* mandates that also provided for judicially approved exceptions would indeed be permissible. Justice White's brief and unremarkable dissent was joined by both Rehnquist and Burger, and John Paul Stevens wrote separately to articulate his acceptance of parental approval.[45]

Aside from Warren Burger's shift, *Danforth* was an unmistakably clear reaffirmation of *Roe* and *Doe*, but the summer months of 1976 witnessed a new right to life congressional initiative to add an amendment prohibiting any Medicaid funding of abortions to the appropriations bill for the upcoming fiscal year. Illinois Republican Henry J. Hyde first successfully offered such a rider on the House floor in late June, but the Senate, by a wide margin, refused both then and again in late August to accept the House-passed ban. By mid-September the disagreement had been referred to a conference committee for a second time, and the deadlock was finally broken only when members from both houses agreed to endorse a slight weakening of the proviso so that abortions "where the life of the mother would be endangered" by an ongoing pregnancy would be excepted from the funding cutoff. Both the House and the Senate ratified that compromise, and passed the overall bill into law, overriding a presidential veto unrelated to the abortion tussle. The very day of that vote, abortion access proponents filed suit against the provision in federal court in New York, and on October 1, just as the Hyde Amendment was taking effect, District Judge John F. Dooling, Jr., enjoined any enforcement of the new prohibition until the challengers' case could be heard. Three weeks later Dooling issued a full decision upholding the merits of the plaintiffs' challenge, and the U.S. Supreme Court refused to issue an interim stay of Dooling's injunction while the government pursued a direct appeal.[46]

In November 1976, over an angry dissent by Byron White that both William Rehnquist and Warren Burger also joined, a six-justice majority summarily affirmed a lower federal court decision voiding an Indiana statute that would have required all first trimester abortions to be performed in hospital-quality facilities.[47] Early in 1977, however, the Supreme Court heard full-dress argument in three other abortion appeals, the most significant of which was *Maher* v. *Roe*, where a three-judge court had upheld a challenge to a Connecticut Welfare Department regulation which limited state Medicaid funding to only those abortions that were "medically necessary." The high court also had under consideration a New York appeal of a three-judge decision that had voided a state statute prohibiting the distribution of any contraceptive to anyone under age sixteen as well as distribution by someone other than a pharmacist even to an adult. Resolving the New York case first, Justice Brennan on behalf of a six justice majority reiterated that "the teaching of *Griswold* is that the Constitution protects individual decisions in matters of childbearing from unjustified intrusion by the State." Access to contraceptives "is essential to exercise of the constitutionally protected right of decision in matters of child-bearing that is the underlying foundation of the holdings in *Griswold*, *Eisenstadt* v. *Baird*, and *Roe* v. *Wade*," Brennan observed, and in a section speaking for only four justices he further held that "the right to privacy in connection with decisions affecting procreation extends to minors as well as to adults." Byron White, unlike John Stevens, acquiesced in that result, thus giving Brennan's holding in *Carey* v. *Population Services International* an official majority, and while William Rehnquist and Warren Burger dissented in toto, a somewhat reluctant concurrence from Lewis Powell made for an ostensible 7 to 2 outcome, although Powell complained that "the extraordinary protection the Court would give to all personal decisions in matters of sex is neither required by the Constitution nor supported by our prior decisions."[48]

Several weeks after the *Carey* ruling, the Court *reversed* both *Maher* and the two other abortion cases in 6 to 3 decisions written by Lewis Powell, with Justices Blackmun, Brennan, and Marshall in dissent. "*Roe* did not declare an unqualified 'constitutional right to an abortion,'" Powell explained. "Rather, the right protects the woman from unduly burdensome interference with her freedom to decide whether to terminate her pregnancy." Connecticut could indeed refuse to provide Medicaid funds for most abortions while nonetheless assisting poor women who carried their pregnancies to term, since *Roe* "implies no limitation on the authority of a State to make a value judgment favoring childbirth over abortion, and to implement that judgment by the allocation of public funds." Connecticut's policy, Powell said, "places no obstacles—absolute or otherwise—in the pregnant woman's path to an abortion. An indigent woman who desires an abortion suffers no disadvantage as a consequence of Connecticut's decision to fund childbirth." Powell acknowledged that Connecticut very well "may have made childbirth a more attractive alternative, thereby influencing the woman's decision, but it has imposed no restriction on access to abortions that was not already there. The indigency that may make it difficult—and in some cases, perhaps, impossible—for some women to have abortions is neither created nor in any way affected by the Connecticut regulation."

Powell emphasized, on behalf of the majority that decided both *Maher* and the two highly similar cases from Pennsylvania and St. Louis, *Beal* v. *Doe* and *Poelker* v. *Doe*, that "Our conclusion signals no retreat from *Roe*," but the three dissenters vociferously disagreed. "Today's decision seriously erodes the principles that *Roe* and *Doe* announced," William Brennan contended, and Harry Blackmun warned that states and cities could now "accomplish indirectly what the Court in *Roe* . . . said that they could not do directly." Under Medicaid, Brennan asserted, "the physician and patient should have complete freedom to choose those medical procedures for a given condition which are best suited to the needs of the patient."[49]

The Court's decisions in the *Maher* trio of cases sent an unmistakable signal that a *federal* funding limitation on Medicaid abortion payments, such as the 1976 Hyde Amendment, would now almost certainly pass judicial muster, and nine days later, as antiabortion lobbyists geared up to add another such rider to the appropriations bill for the upcoming year, the Court made that message even more explicit by vacating Judge Dooling's earlier decision against enforcement of the Hyde ban and pointedly instructing him to reconsider his nine-month-old injunction in light of the *Maher* opinions. That very same day the Senate, which a year earlier had initially stood fast against the Hyde initiative, added prohibitory language—albeit with a much broader therapeutic exception than the House was espousing—to the pending appropriations measure, and rejected by 56 to 42 an effort to delete any such proviso. In early August Judge Dooling did indeed dissolve his earlier order, while nonetheless commencing a lengthy trial on the merits of the 1976 challenge to the Hyde Amendment, and except in the one dozen states that continued Medicaid financing for nontherapeutic abortions out of nonfederal funds, the 1976 limitation went into effect, tangibly restricting the reproductive choices faced by poor pregnant women in the other thirty-eight states.[50]

Pro-choice activists immediately recognized that the *Maher* decisions represented "a substantial victory for antiabortion forces" and one that likely would pay significant political dividends for right to lifers both in Congress and in many states. New York's Howard Moody denounced the rulings as "discriminatory, unjust and dumb," and St. Louis attorney Frank Susman, who had argued *Poelker* as well as *Danforth*, labeled the three judgments "a full scale retreat from the case law spawned by" *Roe* and *Doe*. NYU professor Sylvia Law said that activists "should stop thinking in terms of going to court so often and begin to put more energy into pressuring state legislatures," but one major opinion poll showed that 55 percent of Americans opposed public funding for abortions. By midfall House and Senate conferees were well into their third month of unsuccessful efforts to agree upon restrictive Medicaid funding language for fiscal 1978, as the House hewed to a far harsher stance on a therapeutic exception than the Senate, and press accounts explained that the tenor of the Hyde debate, just like the *Maher* decisions, indicated how pro-choice forces were now very much on the defensive. "In nearly every state," the *New York Times* reported, "abortion rights advocates have failed to equal the opponents' network of dedicated activists," and throughout the autumn fallout from that pattern could regularly be seen in the House of Representatives as the funding language deadlock dragged into a fourth month and then a fifth. Only in early December, with the Christmas holidays fast approaching, did the House and the Senate finally agree upon just what therapeutic standard a pregnant, indigent woman would have to meet before she could qualify for a federally funded Medicaid abortion: "severe and long-lasting physical health damage" if her pregnancy was carried to term.[51]

Time magazine noted the passage of the second Hyde Amendment by asserting that "people who believe that abortion is every woman's right are in retreat," and many supporters privately agreed. A large group of prominent theologians and ethicists, including John C. Bennett, James H. Cone, L. Harold DeWolf, Beverly Harrison, George Kelsey, Rosemary Reuther, and Kenneth L. Smith, issued an unusual public statement declaring that "We support the Supreme Court decisions of 1973" and announcing that they also backed public funding. *Roe* and *Doe* had been decided "in accord with sound ethical judgment," and given the situations of many women's lives, "abortion may in some instances be the most loving act possible." More pointedly, the group also stated that "We are saddened by the heavy institutional involvement of the bishops of the Roman Catholic Church in a campaign to enact religiously based antiabortion commitments into law, and we view this as a serious threat to religious liberty and freedom of conscience." Most revealingly, the statement closed by saying that "We call upon the leaders of religious groups supporting abortion rights to speak out more clearly and publicly in response to the dangerously increasing influence of the absolutist position."[52]

One prominent Roman Catholic abortion opponent bitterly alleged that the Protestant theologians' "Call to Concern" was "infected" with "simple bigotry," but throughout the early months of 1978, most signs continued to indicate that antiabortion forces were making additional political headway. One survey showed that while more than 90 percent of abortions were now taking place during the first twelve weeks of pregnancy, only 30 percent were being performed in hospitals, with almost all of the others occurring in specialized clinics. The study emphasized, however, that half of those clinics were located in America's thirty largest metropolitan areas, meaning that women in many locales might face a considerable trek in order to actually have access to abortion services. In mid-February one Cleveland clinic was firebombed by abortion opponents, but more mainstream right to life activists, utilizing a previously untried constitutional provision, sought to persuade state legislatures to pass resolutions instructing Congress to convene a constitutional convention that could adopt one or another of the proposed amendments that were languishing in Congress. By the spring of 1978 only thirteen of the necessary thirty-four states had enacted such resolutions, but in early June, as abortion opponents launched yet another annual effort to add a Hyde Amendment to the federal appropriations bill for fiscal 1979, *Newsweek* magazine reported that abortion access was "under greater attack than at any time since" January 1973 and that right to lifers were making "considerable headway."[53]

Congress's five-month wrestling match over the 1978 Hyde Amendment occasioned less emotion and news coverage than 1977's, yet come mid-October generated the exact same result. However, the extremely protracted, still-ongoing New York trial of the two-year-old court challenge to the first Hyde Amendment before Judge Dooling began to engender increased bitterness and attention when abortion funding proponents used it to contend that antiabortion enactments like the successive Hyde bans violated the Constitution's First Amendment protection against any governmental establishment of religion because of how they were premised upon an inescapably theological belief concerning the human status of an embryo or fetus. Early in the fall the Supreme Court heard argument in one new abortion case, involving a long-pending challenge to a Pennsylvania antiabortion law, and several weeks later the Court agreed to hear another state appeal in Bill Baird's suit against Massachusetts's parental consent statute, which the Court had first considered and remanded more than two years earlier. Antiabortion activists registered further political gains in the ensuing November elections, especially in the U.S. Senate, and as 1979 dawned, right to life forces appeared to still have the upper hand.[54]

On January 9, 1979, the Supreme Court handed down its decision in the Pennsylvania case, *Colautti* v. *Franklin*, affirming a lower court ruling that had found a statute prescribing criminal penalties should a doctor fail to preserve an aborted fetus that "may be viable" void for vagueness. Written by Justice Blackmun, the high court's 6 to 3 majority opinion reiterated both *Roe*'s holding that "there is a right of privacy, implicit in the liberty secured by the Fourteenth Amendment" and *Danforth*'s explication of how the Court had purposefully left the point of viability "flexible for anticipated advancements in medical skill." *Roe* and especially *Doe*, Blackmun emphasized, had "underscored the importance of affording the physician adequate discretion in the exercise of his medical judgment." While viability was the point at which "there is a reasonable likelihood of the fetus' sustained survival outside the womb, with or without artificial support," that determination inescapably involved a case-by-case evaluation, above and beyond the length of the pregnancy and/or the size of the fetus. Pennsylvania's usage of so uncertain a phrase as "may be viable" as a criminal standard was constitutionally impermissible, for its law not only failed to "afford broad discretion to the physician," but also "conditions potential criminal liability on confusing and ambiguous criteria." Byron White's dissent, in which both William Rehnquist and Warren Burger joined, complained that "the Court has considerably narrowed the scope of the power to forbid and regulate abortion that the States could reasonably have expected to enjoy under *Roe* and *Danforth*."[55]

Six months later, just as a fourth consecutive annual round of congressional debate on yet another Hyde Amendment was getting under way, the Court also decided *Bellotti* v. *Baird*. Ruling against the constitutionality of Massachusetts's parental consent law by an 8 to 1 margin, with only Byron White in dissent, the Court's majority nonetheless was evenly split into two separate groups of justices, four of whom Lewis Powell spoke for in a controlling opinion and four of whom joined a brief statement by John Stevens simply concurring in the judgment. Both groups agreed that the statute's requirement that any pregnant teenager wanting an abortion must seek the consent of both her parents, and could petition a judge for special approval only *after* such dual consent had been refused, was unacceptable. "Every pregnant minor is entitled," Powell explained, "to go directly to the court for a judicial determination without prior parental notice, consultation, or consent," and if a jurist judged a young woman to be "mature," then the decision was indeed hers to make. Powell's quartet, which also included Potter Stewart, Warren Burger, and William Rehnquist, contained at least one highly ambivalent member, for Rehnquist volunteered in a separate concurrence that he nonetheless would be more than happy to reconsider and overturn *Danforth*, but the Court's basic holding was more than bolstered by the Stevens foursome. Stevens had privately told Powell that under *Danforth* the Massachusetts law was also constitutionally offensive because it "gives a judge an absolute veto over the abortion decision of every minor who does not receive the consent of both parents," and that the Court should simply strike down the statute without signaling what revised procedures *would* pass muster. His brief public statement, which Justices Blackmun, Brennan, and Marshall also joined, made that point explicitly and forcefully: "It is inherent in the right to make the abortion decision that the right may be exercised without public scrutiny and in defiance of the contrary opinion of the sovereign or other third parties," such as parents.[56]

In mid-October of 1979 Congress approved another Hyde Amendment, adopting even more narrowly restrictive language for fiscal year 1980 than had been applied in each of the two previous years. Six weeks later the Supreme Court announced that it would hear an Illinois appeal of a lower federal court decision that had struck down a state statute restricting Medicaid payments for poor women's abortions, and New York journalists suggested that Judge Dooling's long-pending decision in the case that had started out in 1976 as a challenge to the first Hyde ban ought to come down early in 1980. A *New York Times*/CBS News poll found that 69 percent of Protestants, and even 64 per cent of Roman Catholics, expressed agreement with the statement that "The right of a woman to have an abortion should be left entirely to the woman and her doctor," but more extensive academic surveys continued to show that a significant plurality of Americans had complex and often highly ambivalent feelings on the subject. Every major national survey also indicated that there had been almost no measurable shifts in popular sentiment in the seven years since *Roe* and *Doe*,[57] and researchers began focusing increased attention upon the small but highly motivated groups of activists, particularly on the right to life side, who were giving the abortion issue so much of its national visibility and intensity. A heavy majority of antiabortion activists, scholars determined, were married women of modest educational backgrounds who had children and were not employed outside the home. Rather than simply viewing these women's "crusade against abortion" as manifesting a primary concern for fetuses, their activism should instead be seen as a "symbolic defense of traditional conceptions of morality," one analyst reported, and also as reflecting a particular "hostility to freer sexual standards," other observers contended. Fundamental to "pro-life ideology is a conservative, traditional notion of the role of the family and of women in society," one thoughtful student explained. "There exist beneath the surface among pro-life groups a deeply rooted respect for and admiration of the traditional woman and the glories of motherhood. This is accompanied by a corresponding disrespect for and hatred of the modern woman as depicted by the feminist movement." For many right-to-lifers, this commentator recounted, the abortion crusade was essentially "a means to an end," for it was a highly visible way of "fighting the anti-family and anti-traditional image that abortion is seen to promote." A less sympathetic professor made the same point more bluntly: "the meanings resonating from abortion politics have more to do with compulsory heterosexuality, family structure, the relationship between men and women and parents and children, and women's employment, than they do with the fetus."[58]

Nothing gave greater promise to the social policy agenda of the New

Right, and especially to its focus on issues concerning the family and sexuality, than the flourishing Republican presidential candidacy of former California governor Ronald Reagan. His 1967 approval of the landmark Beilenson reform bill now long forgotten, Reagan by early 1980 had emerged as not only the leading Republican contender but also as a special favorite of right to life activists. In mid-January, antiabortionists were further provoked when New York's Judge Dooling, in a written opinion that came to 214 typeset pages, ruled that all of the successive Hyde Amendments violated both the constitutional guarantee of equal protection and the First Amendment's free exercise clause. Dooling stayed a reinstatement of his earlier 1976–1977 injunction against the Medicaid funding ban for thirty days so as to allow the government to appeal to the Supreme Court, but in mid-February, with Chief Justice Burger and Justices Rehnquist and Powell in dissent, the high court refused to further delay the impact of Dooling's order. At the same time, however, the Court also placed the government's appeal of the case, *Harris* v. *McRae*, on a highly accelerated schedule for full oral argument in late April, when the justices would also be hearing the similar Illinois case, *Williams* v. *Zbaraz*, which they had accepted three months earlier.[59]

The Court's consideration of *Harris* and *Zbaraz* took place against a backdrop of virtually unanimous recognition, even by clerks who were hoping for a ruling against the funding bans, that the Court's 1977 decisions in the *Maher* trio of cases were "nearly dispositive" of the questions posed by the two newest appeals. True, *Harris* and *Zbaraz* both involved challenges to statutes that prohibited Medicaid financing of even medically necessary abortions, whereas *Maher* had endorsed only a funding cutoff of nontherapeutic abortions for indigent women, but constitutionally the difference would be hard to distinguish. Hence there was no surprise at all within the private confines of the Court when the late April conference discussion that followed the oral arguments of *Harris* and *Zbaraz* registered a 5 to 4 majority in favor of affirming the prohibitions on government funding. Only in early June did Justice Stewart first circulate initial drafts of majority opinions in the two cases, and it was the final day of the month before the decisions were publicly announced.[60]

Stewart's opinion in *Harris*, which was joined by Chief Justice Burger and Justices White, Powell, and Rehnquist, announced that "although government may not place obstacles in the path of a woman's exercise of her freedom of choice, it need not remove those not of its own creation. Indigency falls in the latter category."

Following very much in the tradition of Powell's *Maher* holding, Stewart declared that "the Hyde Amendment leaves an indigent woman with at least the same range of choice in deciding whether to obtain a medically necessary abortion as she would have had if Congress had chosen to subsidize no health care costs at all." Citing both *Griswold* and the 1925 decision in *Pierce*, Stewart explained that "It cannot be said that because government may not prohibit the use of contraceptives . . . or prevent parents from sending their child to a private school," that government therefore "has an affirmative constitutional obligation to ensure that all persons have the financial resources to obtain contraceptives or send their children to private schools." Just as in *Maher*, government could indeed selectively choose to subsidize some but not all medical undertakings. The Hyde Amendment's approach "is rationally related to the legitimate governmental objective of protecting potential life," for abortion "is inherently different from other medical procedures, because no other procedure involves the purposeful termination of a potential life." Stewart's far briefer statement in *Zbaraz* made much the same point, but he closed the *Harris* opinion with a remark that spoke for himself and Lewis Powell, if not for the three other members of the narrow majority: "It is not the mission of this Court or any other to decide whether the balance of competing policy interests reflected in the Hyde Amendment is wise social policy. If that were our mission, not every Justice who has subscribed to the judgement of the Court today could have done so."

All four minority justices—Brennan, Marshall, Blackmun, and Stevens—filed dissenting opinions, with Brennan asserting that Congress's "deliberate effort to discourage the exercise of a constitutionally protected right" burdened and intruded upon a "pregnant woman's freedom to choose." John Stevens reminded his colleagues that with regard to any state desire to safeguard potential life, "*Roe v. Wade* squarely held that the States may not protect that interest when a conflict with the interest in a pregnant woman's health exists." Indeed, "Since *Roe v. Wade* squarely held that the individual interest in the freedom to elect an abortion and the state interest in protecting maternal life *both* outweigh the State's interest in protecting potential life prior to viability," the *Harris* majority was thereby doubly wrong.[61]

Medicaid payments for some medically necessary abortions continued for several weeks until the high court's judgment was formally transmitted to New York and Judge Dooling's earlier order was officially dissolved, but many commentators greeted the decisions with dismay. The *New York Times* pronounced the ruling "deeply troubling," and one usually thoughtful law professor proclaimed that *Harris* was "inconsistent with the narrowest possible coherent reading of *Roe*," namely that "government may not take action predicated on the view that abortion is *per se* morally objectionable." Another normally understated supporter of abortion rights asserted that "by permitting the state to place the welfare of the fetus ahead of the health and welfare of the pregnant woman," *Harris* "effectively overrules *Roe* v. *Wade*," and antiabortion attorney Dennis Horan, who had helped Jay Floyd with *Roe* itself, concluded that *Harris* "makes it unmistakably clear that the state may disfavor abortion and favor protection of fetal life." To Horan, *Harris* was an undeniable Court signal that legislatures in fact could "act upon a view of the human fetus so contrary to the underlying premises of its own decision in *Roe*." Indeed, Horan observed, "Under *Harris*, the Constitution would not be violated even if a woman is effectively surrounded, as an island by a sea, with public pressure and inducements to abandon her decision to abort."[62]

Despite such unpromising judicial developments, national polls continued to show significant majorities—62 percent in one *New York Times*/CBS survey in August—for a woman's right to choose abortion, and earlier in the summer voters in Toledo, Ohio, in America's first popular vote on abortion since 1972, had handed a resounding, two to one defeat to an antiabortion referendum proposal placed on the ballot by local right to lifers. Some public opinion polling also showed better than 60 percent opposition to any antiabortion constitutional amendment, but variations in question wording could generate remarkable differences, with 50 percent of respondents *in that same survey* answering "yes" when asked if they would support an amendment "protecting the life of the unborn child." Congress was beginning its approval process for yet another Medicaid funding rider that would allow states to choose whether or not to provide public funds to cover indigent women's abortions even in life-threatening circumstances, but the severe internal divisions that had long plagued the prolife cause were threatening to become more and more open, just as its beloved presidential candidate, Ronald Reagan, increasingly looked like a possible victor in the upcoming November election against unpopular Democratic incumbent Jimmy Carter. Monsignor George G. Higgins, a recently retired senior staff member of the National Conference of Catholic Bishops, publicly complained that some prolife groups, particularly those most insistent upon a no-exceptions constitutional amendment, "are being used as a vehicle to promote a much broader right-wing agenda." Higgins cautioned that "the association of right to life with the right wing will ultimately undermine and not broaden support for pro-life positions," and he most pointedly warned that "there is an increasingly grave danger that the right to life movement as a whole will be discredited as a right-wing sham."[63]

On November 4, Ronald Reagan swept to an easy presidential victory over Jimmy Carter, and antiabortion forces could celebrate their most important political triumph since the Michigan referendum victory exactly eight years earlier. Three days later, Thurgood Marshall privately circulated to his eight colleagues a first draft of a majority opinion in *H.L.* v. *Matheson*, an appeal challenging a Utah criminal statute requiring doctors to give prior notification to the parents of any teenager for whom they were scheduled to perform an abortion. The Court had accepted the case some months before, and had heard oral argument four weeks earlier, after which the conference discussion had generated a tentative 5 to 4 tally in favor of reversing the Utah Supreme Court's initial affirmance of the law. On the Monday after the election, however, Marshall's majority began to crumble when first one member—Potter Stewart—and then another—Lewis Powell—informed him that they would not be able to support his opinion. "My vote at Conference was to reverse," Powell explained, because the Utah statute, contrary to Powell's 1979 opinion in *Bellotti*, did not provide for an "independent decision-maker," such as a judge, for a pregnant teenager who did not want to notify her parents. Marshall's draft, however, similarly contravened Powell's *Bellotti* analysis by accepting the argument "that a pregnant minor, regardless of age or circumstances and without notice to parents, has a constitutional right to decide for herself, in consultation with a physician, whether to have an abortion."

Stewart and Powell's shift, Harry Blackmun privately commiserated to Marshall and Bill Brennan, "was not unanticipated," but now it was likely that one or both of those brethren would join with the four original dissenters, for whom Chief Justice Burger was writing, thereby creating a new majority. Hence Marshall's draft would be reduced to a minority statement on behalf of these three dissenters, and Blackmun asked Marshall to alter only a single phrase—changing "the pregnant woman's right to make the abortion decision through private, unfettered consultation with her physician" to "the pregnant woman's and her attending physician's right to make the abortion decision through private, unfettered consultation"—so as to avoid "the 'abortion on demand' criticism that so frequently, and wrongfully, appears in public comment."

More notably, however, Harry Blackmun also voiced some additional thoughts, which in part may well have been spurred by the election results one week earlier, and by their potential consequences for the Court. "I need not say how disappointed I have been in what I perceive to be the Court's noticeable withdrawal in recent cases from the more positive position taken in *Roe, Doe* and *Danforth*," he confessed to Marshall and Brennan. "I fear that the forces of emotion and professed morality are winning some battles. That 'real world' continues to exist 'out there' and I earnestly hope that the 'war,' despite these adverse 'battles,' will not be lost."[64]

Early in 1981, just before the Supreme Court announced its actual resolution of *H.L.* v. *Matheson*, both the Massachusetts Supreme Judicial Court and the California Supreme Court relied upon *state* constitutional grounds to issue abortion funding decisions that explicitly rejected the Supreme Court's decisions in *Harris* v. *McRae* and *Maher* v. *Roe*. The Massachusetts court, ruling in a case that had been filed nine days after *Harris*, found that that state's Declaration of Rights "affords a greater degree of protection" to a woman's right to choose abortion than did the U.S. Constitution as interpreted in *Harris*. California was one of ten states whose constitutions included language explicitly protecting "privacy," and California's high court voided legislative restrictions on state Medi-Cal funding of nontherapeutic abortions by bluntly declaring that "the asserted state's interest in protecting a nonviable fetus is subordinate to the woman's right of privacy." The "morality of abortion," the California majority noted, "is not a legal or constitutional issue; it is a matter of philosophy, of ethics, and of theology. . . . Once the state furnishes medical care to poor women in general, it cannot withdraw part of that care solely because a woman exercises her constitutional right to choose to have an abortion."[65]

On March 23, 1981, the U.S. Supreme Court handed down its decision in *H.L.* v. *Matheson*, with Lewis Powell's concurring opinion for himself and Potter Stewart expressing the case's actual holding more clearly and succinctly than Warren Burger's five-vote opinion for the full majority. Reiterating his *Bellotti* statement, Powell explained that "a State may not validly require notice to parents in all cases, without providing an independent decision-maker to whom a pregnant minor can have recourse if she believes that she is mature enough to make the abortion decision independently or that notification otherwise would not be in her best interests."[66]

That modest and unoriginal declaration attracted far less attention than was being focused on a new right to life push aimed at winning enactment of a congressional *statute* proclaiming that personhood begins at conception. Originally drafted by a young Harvard Law School graduate and then quickly adopted by Illinois Representative Hyde and North Carolina Senator Helms, the human life bill proposed to mandate in statutory form the same declaration that prolife forces previously had assumed a constitutional amendment would be required to accomplish. Most legal commentators, including many who opposed abortion, insisted that any such statutory enactment would be unconstitutional, but right-wing North Carolina Republican Senator John P. East nonetheless scheduled eight days of Senate subcommittee hearings on the measure, beginning in late April 1981. Conservative University of Texas law professor Charles Alan Wright, who had won notoriety helping represent Richard Nixon during Watergate, told the subcommittee that while he was "quite unpersuaded" by *Roe v. Wade*, as it failed to show "what abortion has to do with privacy," he also was troubled by the "intemperate criticism" the decision had attracted and was "skeptical about the ability of men to form judgments that concern an experience they can never have." Nonetheless, Wright emphasized that the human life bill was patently unconstitutional. Some weeks later, two former Solicitors General, Archibald Cox and Robert H. Bork, the latter of whom had once fired the former as Watergate special prosecutor, both appeared before the subcommittee to also oppose the bill. Neither man supported *Roe*, but Cox labeled the human life proposal "a radical and dangerously unprincipled attack upon the foundations of our constitutionalism." Bork told the senators that *Roe* was "an unconstitutional decision, a serious and wholly unjustifiable judicial usurpation of State legislative authority" and "perhaps the worst example of constitutional reasoning I have ever read," but he too denounced the human life bill as threatening "the destruction of the Court's entire constitutional role."[67]

In early July that subcommittee approved the measure on a partisan, 3 to 2 vote, but the bill languished in the full Senate Judiciary Committee as other Republicans such as Utah's Orrin Hatch focused instead on antiabortion constitutional amendments. In the fall of 1981 a subcommittee which Hatch chaired held nine days of hearings on the four different constitutional proposals that were pending, and in mid-December the subcommittee endorsed Hatch's own measure, a relatively moderate amendment that would upend *Roe* by authorizing each state to regulate or prohibit abortion to whatever extent it chose. Public opinion polls indicated that some 75 percent of American citizens *opposed* any amendment that would give Congress "the authority to prohibit abortions," and that 77 percent of respondents agreed that

"The decision to have an abortion should be left to the woman and her physician," but three months later the full judiciary committee approved Hatch's proposal on a vote of 10 to 7. In mid-September 1982, however, when a more extreme human life amendment sponsored by North Carolina's Jesse Helms became the first constitutional proposal to be brought up for a full vote on the Senate floor, it went down to a 47 to 46 defeat, well short of the two-thirds support that a constitutional amendment was required to attain.[68]

Not long before that Senate vote, the New Jersey Supreme Court took the same step that Massachusetts' and California's high courts had taken eighteen months earlier and invoked *state* constitutional grounds in voiding a legislative restriction that barred Medicaid funding for medically necessary abortions.[69] Several weeks later, on the final day of November 1982, the U.S. Supreme Court heard oral argument in three abortion appeals from Virginia, Ohio, and Missouri which it had accepted six months previously. Since the Court's decision in *H.L.* v. *Matheson* a year and a half earlier, one very significant change had taken place: in June 1981 Justice Potter Stewart had announced his retirement, and President Ronald Reagan had nominated a little-known Arizona state court judge, Sandra Day O'Connor, to be the first female justice in Supreme Court history. Some right to life groups had opposed O'Connor on the grounds that she had once voted against adding an antiabortion amendment to an unrelated bill while a member of the Arizona legislature, but O'Connor herself had made no substantive comment on *Roe* or its progeny. In late September 1981 O'Connor's nomination had been unanimously confirmed by the U.S. Senate, and by the time that the Supreme Court heard argument in *Simopoulos* v. *Virginia, City of Akron* v. *Akron Center for Reproductive Health* and *Planned Parenthood Association of Kansas City* v. *Ashcroft*, she had been a member of the high court for fourteen months.

Dr. Chris Simopoulos, represented by Roy Lucas, was appealing a criminal conviction for having initiated a saline abortion of a twenty-two-week pregnancy at his unlicensed clinic rather than at a hospital, as Virginia law required for all post-first trimester procedures. The seventeen-year-old patient had subsequently expelled the fetus in a motel room, where she left it in a wastebasket, and the motel had notified the police. The Akron case involved a comparable hospitalization requirement, which two lower courts had upheld, as well as ordinances mandating either parental or judicial approval for an abortion on any girl under the age of fifteen, and imposing a twenty-four-hour waiting period on all women who sought abortions, both of which had been voided by the Sixth Circuit Court of Appeals. *Ashcroft* likewise included constitutional challenges to both Missouri's second trimester hospitalization requirement, which the Eighth Circuit Court of Appeals had struck down, and a parental consent provision, which the appellate court had upheld.

One journalistic observer, sitting through the three hours of presentations—*Simopoulos* at ten a.m., *Akron* at eleven a.m., and *Ashcroft* after lunch at one p.m.—reported that "the long argument often seemed to lack focus," but the one exceptional highlight of the day—and perhaps the most dramatic moment in abortion litigation since *Roe* and *Doe* had themselves been decided—came when the Reagan administration's Solicitor General, Rex E. Lee, spoke for ten minutes as an *amicus* in *defense of* Akron's antiabortion regulations. Lee's office, in line with the administration's aggressive right to life stance, had already submitted a brief backing Akron's assertions, but when Lee personally stood up to make such claims on behalf of the United States government, Harry Blackmun challenged him forcefully.

"Mr. Solicitor General, are you asking that *Roe* v. *Wade* be overruled?"

"I am not, Mr. Justice Blackmun."

"Why not?"

"That is not one of the issues presented in this case," Lee responded, indicating it would not be proper for an amicus to introduce a question that the principal parties had not raised. Blackmun, however, repeated the point: "It seems to me that your brief in essence asks either that or the overruling of *Marbury* against *Madison*," the landmark 1803 decision that had established the Court's power of judicial review. "Neither, neither," Lee replied. Blackmun voiced another query, and Lee again stated that "we are not urging that *Roe* v. *Wade* be overruled. . . . That is an issue for another day." Lee's time was about up, but Blackmun's parting question was as pointed as could be. "Mr. Lee, did you write this brief personally?" "Very substantial parts of it, Justice Blackmun," the Solicitor answered, and no one in the courtroom could have doubted that the Reagan administration's advocacy of a rollback for women's constitutional right to choose had certainly produced some very strong feelings.[70]

When the Court, after an unusual delay, finally convened on December 16 to vote on the long list of questions presented by the three cases, the nine justices quickly agreed, with only John Stevens in dissent, that Dr. Simopoulos's conviction should indeed be affirmed. A solid five-justice majority—Brennan, Marshall, Blackmun, Powell, and

Stevens—favored voiding both Akron's and Missouri's hospitalization requirements as well as Akron's parental consent and waiting period provisions. Along with Byron White and Bill Rehnquist, Sandra O'Connor voted to uphold all of those limitations, and in *Ashcroft*, where Justice Powell believed that three other restrictions—one requiring the presence of a second physician for late-term abortions, another requiring pathology reports, and a third involving Missouri's provisions for parental or judicial consent—should survive judicial scrutiny, Warren Burger's eventual agreement with Powell would mean that a separate lineup would control the disposition of those discrete points. All three opinions were assigned to Lewis Powell, and three months later—in early March 1983—he circulated initial drafts that were accepted by his colleagues following only modest revisions. Three months later—on June 15, 1983—the trio of decisions was publicly announced.[71]

City of Akron v. *Akron Center for Reproductive Health* became the lead decision among the 1983 cases, and Powell's opinion for the six-member majority—including Warren Burger as well as Brennan, Marshall, Blackmun, and Stevens—stressed that "the doctrine of *stare decisis* . . . is a doctrine that demands respect in a society governed by the rule of law. We respect it today, and reaffirm *Roe* v. *Wade*." Indeed, Powell added, there were "especially compelling reasons" for adhering to the 1973 holding, for *Roe* "was considered with special care," including the two oral arguments and "extensive briefing." Powell quoted from John Harlan's famous dissent in *Poe* before emphasizing that "The decision in *Roe* was based on this long-recognized and essential element of personal liberty," and he firmly castigated Sandra O'Connor's dissenting opinion, in which both White and Rehnquist also joined, for articulating an approach which "is wholly incompatible with the existence of the fundamental right recognized in *Roe*." Powell noted how "the dissent would uphold virtually any abortion regulation," and he asserted that "the effect of the dissent's views would be to drive the performance of many abortions back underground free of effective regulation and often without the attendance of a physician."

Powell acknowledged that the safety of second-trimester abortions had increased dramatically in the ten years since 1973, thus undercutting much of the significance that *Roe* had attached to the end of the first trimester, but he declared that it was nonetheless prudent "to retain *Roe*'s identification of the beginning of the second trimester as the approximate time at which the State's interest in maternal health becomes sufficiently compelling to justify significant regulation of abortion." Thus *Roe*'s "trimester standard," Powell said, "continues to provide a reasonable legal framework for limiting a State's authority to regulate abortions. Where the State adopts a health regulation governing the performance of abortions during the second trimester, the determinative question should be whether there is a reasonable medical basis for the regulation." The Sixth Circuit, in upholding Akron's hospitalization provision, had "misinterpreted" the Supreme Court's view of second trimester regulation, for particularly because of the "primary burden" of increased cost, the hospitalization requirement clearly represented "a serious obstacle" to women seeking abortions of second trimester pregnancies. However in *Ashcroft*, "given the compelling interest that the State has in preserving life," Missouri's requirement that a second physician be present at each rare third trimester abortion was not unconstitutional, nor did the cost incurred by a mandatory pathology examination "significantly burden a pregnant woman's abortion decision."

Sandra O'Connor's dissent picked up on a phrase that the Court had first used seven years earlier in *Bellotti I* and then again in *Maher*—whether or not an abortion regulation was an "undue burden" for a pregnant woman—and asserted that "this 'unduly burdensome' standard should be applied to the challenged regulations throughout the entire pregnancy without reference to the particular 'stage' of pregnancy involved." Blackmun's trimester format, she alleged, "cannot be supported as a legitimate or useful framework," and was "completely unworkable." Most pointedly, O'Connor claimed that the distinctions which *Roe* had identified between different stages of pregnancy were diminishing at both ends of the spectrum, and that "It is certainly reasonable to believe that fetal viability in the first trimester of pregnancy may be possible in the not too distant future." Thus, O'Connor alleged, "The *Roe* framework, then, is clearly on a collision course with itself," and ought to be dispensed with. "Even assuming that there is a fundamental right to terminate pregnancy in some situations, there is no justification in law or logic for the trimester framework adopted in *Roe*."[72]

Many legal commentators disregarded O'Connor's attack on *Roe* and viewed the holdings as "a major victory for pro-choice advocates," with one writer confidently opining that "as a result of the Court's recent decisions, a woman's right to an abortion is now secured."[73] Less than two weeks after the rulings were announced, the U.S. Senate rejected Orrin Hatch's proposed constitutional amendment, aimed at returning legal control of abortion to the states, by a tally of 50 to 49, eighteen votes short of the two-thirds support necessary for approval.

That vote effectively signaled an end to meaningful congressional efforts to overturn *Roe* and its legacy, and the fall of 1983 was as quiet a period for abortion battles as anytime in over a decade.[74]

On October 3, however, in an otherwise obscure move, the U.S. Supreme Court agreed to hear a New York district attorney's appeal of a state high court ruling reaffirming and extending an earlier decision that had decriminalized all consensual adult sexual relations, heterosexual or homosexual, that took place in relative seclusion. Only four justices—White, Burger, Rehnquist, and O'Connor—the minimum number necessary, voted to hear the appeal, and while neither their number nor their names were publicly stated, within the Court no one thought that that constellation of justices had expressed interest in the case in order to affirm it. The New York decision, *People* v. *Uplinger*, had voided a statute against loitering in public for the purpose of soliciting "deviate sexual intercourse"; three years earlier, New York's highest court, in a far more significant case, *People* v. *Onofre*, which the U.S. Supreme Court had declined to review, had invalidated several convictions under the state's sodomy statute—which already included an express exception for married couples—that had involved consensual oral sex. An intermediate appellate court had already reversed Ronald Onofre's conviction for performing fellatio on another male at his own home on the grounds that "Personal sexual conduct is a fundamental right, protected by the right to privacy because of the transcendental importance of sex to the human condition, the intimacy of the conduct, and its relationship to a person's right to control his or her own body," and the New York Court of Appeals affirmed that decision. Constitutional privacy safeguarded "a right of independence in making certain kinds of important decisions," and in light of the Supreme Court's rulings in *Eisenstadt* and *Stanley*, which had protected "individual decisions as to indulgence in acts of sexual intimacy by unmarried persons and as to satisfaction of sexual desires by resort to material condemned as obscene by community standards when done in a cloistered setting, no rational basis appears for excluding from the same protection decisions—such as those made by defendants before us—to seek sexual gratification from what at least once was commonly regarded as 'deviant' conduct, so long as the decisions are voluntarily made by adults in a noncommercial, private setting."

That New York majority in *Onofre* was not alone. The New Jersey Supreme Court had already voided that state's fornication statute on similar constitutional grounds, holding that the right to privacy's protection of "independent choice" and "personal autonomy," especially pursuant to "the far more expansive concept of individual autonomy which the United States Supreme Court established in *Roe*," "necessarily encompassed" so "fundamental" a personal choice as a decision to fornicate. Citing the references to childbearing in *Carey*, the Supreme Court's 1977 contraceptives ruling, as well as *Roe*, the New Jersey court had observed that "It would be rather anomalous if such a decision could be constitutionally protected while the more fundamental decision as to whether to engage in the conduct which is a necessary prerequisite to childbearing could be constitutionally prohibited. Surely, such a choice involves considerations which are at least as intimate and personal as those which are involved in choosing whether to use contraceptives." Similarly, just seven months before the New York ruling, the Pennsylvania Supreme Court had struck down their state's criminal law against "deviate sexual intercourse" between unmarried individuals, saying that it served only "to regulate the private conduct of consenting adults." The Pennsylvania majority quoted at length from John Stuart Mill's 1859 essay *On Liberty* and explained that "This philosophy . . . properly circumscribes state power over the individual." The "marital status of voluntarily participating adults would bear no rational relationship to whether a sexual act should be legal or criminal," and "to suggest that deviate acts are heinous if performed by unmarried persons but acceptable when done by married persons lacks even a rational basis, for requiring less moral behavior of married persons than is expected of unmarried persons is without basis in logic." If the oral and anal sex acts were truly harmful, the Pennsylvania judges observed, "then they should be proscribed for all persons, not just the unmarried."

But *Onofre*, unlike *State* v. *Saunders* in New Jersey and *Commonwealth* v. *Bonadio* in Pennsylvania, had involved male homosexuals, not unmarried heterosexuals, and two members of New York's highest court had objected vociferously to their colleagues' analysis. "The right of sexual choice established today is really a wholly new legal concept bearing little resemblance to the familiar principles enunciated in *Griswold*," Judge Domenick Gabrielli complained on behalf of himself and Chief Judge Lawrence Cooke. "The decisions in *Griswold*, *Roe* and *Stanley* cannot fairly be interpreted as collectively establishing an undifferentiated right to unfettered sexual expression," and "western man has never been free to pursue his own choice of sexual gratification without fear of State interference." His colleagues' majority holding, Gabrielli protested, "represents a radical departure from cases such as *Griswold* and *Roe*."[75]

Rehnquist, Burger, White, and O'Connor's votes to accept *Uplinger* did not mean that other justices were not equally interested in the issue that the case presented. Justices Marshall, Brennan, and Stevens had all dissented from the Court's 1976 summary affirmance of *Doe* v. *Commonwealth's Attorney*, and in 1977 both Marshall and Brennan had voted against the Court's refusal to hear the appeal of a Washington state public school teacher who had been dismissed simply because he was known to be gay. One year later, when Marshall and Brennan were again alone in wanting the Court to hear an appeal by two Pennsylvania library employees who had been fired from their jobs because they had had a child and had begun living together, without benefit of marriage, while the man was still legally married to someone else, Marshall had filed an angry dissent. "Petitioners' rights to pursue an open rather than a clandestine personal relationship and to rear their child together in this environment closely resemble the other aspects of personal privacy to which we have extended constitutional protection," Marshall argued. "Individuals' choices concerning their private lives deserve more than token protection from this Court."

Early in 1980 both Brennan and John Stevens had voted to hear an appeal from a North Carolina man who had been convicted of committing a "crime against nature" after a trial judge had refused to instruct the jury that the alleged offense—heterosexual fellatio—would not be a crime if the jury found that it had been consensual, and just a few weeks after their four colleagues had voted to accept *Uplinger*, Marshall and Harry Blackmun had joined Brennan in dissenting from the Court's refusal to hear the appeal of a now-married couple who had both been fired from the Amarillo, Texas, police department after elaborate surveillance had shown that the two officers were guilty of off-duty cohabitation. "There is not the slightest hint in either the language or the prior interpretations of the city's rules that they forbid private, off-duty, lawful, and consensual sexual relations," Brennan complained. Moreover, he asserted with some emphasis, not only was the petitioners' conduct wholly legal, it also involved "fundamental rights."[76]

Many academic commentators and several federal judges had sought to project what the Supreme Court would do if and when it chose to decide a gay rights or otherwise novel sexual privacy case, and most law review writers heavily downplayed the significance of the 1976 summary affirmance in *Doe*. Federal District Judge Gerhard Gesell, who some years earlier had ruled in favor of Dr. Vuitch, addressed the question in a case brought by a gay Navy ensign who had been dismissed from the service after acknowledging his sexuality. In *Griswold*, *Eisenstadt* and *Roe*, Gesell noted, the Supreme Court had "explicitly recognized the right of privacy in sexual matters by repeatedly prohibiting interference by the state with relationships between men and women." The *Doe* affirmance, however, suggested that the sexual privacy right was limited to heterosexuals, and thus with evident reluctance Gesell explained that he was "constrained to conclude that an individual's right to privacy does not extend to homosexual conduct even where it occurs in private between consenting adults."

One gay rights strategist, noting how an unrelated 1975 Supreme Court ruling, *Hicks* v. *Miranda*, indeed meant that the *Doe* affirmance was substantively binding on lower federal courts, warned his colleagues that "we must be more selective in our test cases" than had been true with *Doe* and firmly recommended that they "place more emphasis on state courts and constitutions." A writer in the *Journal of Homosexuality*, however, asserted that "the degree of legal progress is truly remarkable" and blithely declared that "judicial attitudes and, consequently, judicial decisions will change as public attitudes change." A far more thoughtful legal scholar, however, Thomas C. Grey, noted that the Supreme Court's action in *Doe* had been followed by its refusals to hear both *Lovisi* and the Pennsylvania couple's appeal. "These cases strongly suggest," he contended, "that the Court meant what it said in *Griswold*: that the right of privacy protects only the historically sanctified institutions of marriage and the family, and has no implications for laws regulating sexual expression outside of traditional marriage." Too many commentators, he concluded, had overlooked the Court's "rigorous abstention from any support for sexual freedom in the privacy cases" and kept envisioning libertarian themes in those holdings despite "almost no encouragement by the Court."[77]

More substantively notable than any other gay rights ruling, pro or con, between *Doe* and the Supreme Court's acceptance of *Uplinger*, however, was the 1982 decision of Dallas federal District Judge Jerry Buchmeyer in *Donald F. Baker* v. *Henry Wade*. Don Baker was a religious, thirty-five-year-old Navy veteran and former schoolteacher. In late 1979, shortly before becoming president of the Dallas Gay Alliance, Baker had filed a declaratory judgment action—just like the late Henry McCluskey's *Buchanan* suit of a decade earlier—against Dallas County District Attorney Henry Wade, of *Roe* fame, seeking invalidation of Texas's sodomy statute, which in 1974 had been explicitly amended so as to cover *only* homosexual—and not heterosexual—acts. In advance of trial, Baker's attorney, James C. Barber, took a deposition from prosecutor Wade, and while Judge Buchmeyer noted in his subsequent opinion that Baker himself had been "a very sincere" and "very credible witness," Buchmeyer's opinion made especially trenchant use of Henry Wade's own comments about the Texas law he was supposed to enforce. Asked whether he could explain "how this statute furthers the state interest, if any, in procreation by permitting heterosexual sodomy, but prohibiting homosexual sodomy?" Wade frankly replied that "I didn't even know it permitted either one." Queried as to why the law "prohibits deviate sexual intercourse between persons of the same sex, but . . . does not prohibit private deviate sexual intercourse by members of a different sex," Wade answered that "I don't think procreation is involved in either one of them, is it?" Lastly, questioned with regard to the law's complete distinction between otherwise analogous heterosexual and homosexual acts, as to "What rational basis is there for that classification, if you know of any?" Wade candidly responded, "I don't know of any."

Judge Buchmeyer's analysis of the rationality of Texas's sex laws also led him to note that pursuant to the relevant statute, bestiality was a crime *only* if it occurred in public. "Thus, under the Texas Penal Code, one may engage in private sexual acts with 'an animal or fowl' . . . but may not engage in private oral or anal sex with a consenting adult of the same sex." More traditionally, Buchmeyer further pointed out that the Virginia statute at issue in *Doe* had criminalized *all* sodomous activity, rather than singling out only homosexuals, and he indicated that the precedental value of the *Doe* affirmance might well have been undercut by the Supreme Court's subsequent denial of the request that it review the New York Court of Appeals decision in *Onofre*. Texas's criminal distinction between otherwise identical gay and straight sexual activities violated the constitutional guarantee of equal protection, and Texas's law similarly contravened the constitutional guarantees contained in *Griswold* and subsequent progeny such as *Carey*. "The right of two individuals to choose what type of sexual conduct they will enjoy in private is just as personal, just as important, just as sensitive" as a couple's decision "to engage in sex using a contraceptive to prevent unwanted pregnancy." In short, "homosexual conduct in private between consenting adults is protected by a fundamental right of privacy."[78]

In mid-January of 1984 the U.S. Supreme Court heard oral argument in *New York* v. *Uplinger*, but it was already clear that a narrow majority—Brennan, Marshall, Blackmun, Powell, and Stevens, the five justices who had not favored taking the case—were in agreement that the Court's prior acceptance of the appeal should simply be dismissed without addressing the actual merits. New York Attorney General Robert Abrams was opposing the effort by Buffalo prosecutors to preserve the statute, and the three-paragraph decision that had been rendered by New York's highest court was so linked to *Onofre* as to create serious doubt as to whether *Uplinger* could be meaningfully reviewed without also reconsidering a case the Court had already declined to hear. William Brennan circulated an initial draft of a brief per curiam dismissal to his colleagues in early March, and at the end of May, after John Stevens had prepared a short concurrence, the Court handed down a little-noted 5 to 4 rejection of *New York* v. *Uplinger*. Justices White, Rehnquist, and O'Connor, plus Chief Justice Burger, insisted in dissent that the constitutional question should be decided, but the majority cited *Onofre* and stated that "a meaningful evaluation of the decision below would entail consideration of the questions decided in that case" as well. Thus *Uplinger* "provides an inappropriate vehicle for resolving the important constitutional issues raised by the parties."[79]

Less than three months later, however, a relatively new member of the federal Court of Appeals for the District of Columbia Circuit, former Solicitor General and Yale law professor Robert H. Bork, who had been nominated to the prestigious appellate bench by President Reagan and unanimously confirmed by the U.S. Senate early in 1982, authored an outspokenly antithetical opinion that received front page coverage in the *New York Times*. Joined by both a circuit court colleague, Antonin Scalia, and a third judge, Bork affirmed a lower court's dismissal of a suit brought by a Navy petty officer, James L. Dronenburg, who had been discharged from the service after acknowledging that he had had repeated homosexual encounters in a California barracks. "Whatever thread of principle may be discerned in the right-of-privacy cases," Bork wrote, "the Supreme Court has never defined the right so broadly as to encompass homosexual conduct." He noted John Harlan's remark in *Poe* that homosexuality was of course subject to criminal punishment, and described the 1976 *Doe* affirmance as a ruling on the constitutional merits. But Bork was just as interested in critiquing the Supreme Court's privacy jurisprudence as in rebuffing Dronenburg's appeal, and hence he went on to offer a comprehensive analysis of those precedents, beginning with *Griswold*. He discussed the imprecision of William O. Douglas's "penumbra," and stated that while *Griswold* had stressed the importance of marriage, "It did not indicate what other activities might be protected by the new right of privacy and did not provide any guidance for reasoning about future claims laid under that right." Bork quoted the signal passages from both *Eisenstadt* and *Roe*, but avowed that in *Roe* "the Court provided no explanatory principle that informs a lower court how to reason about what is and what is not encompassed by the right of privacy." He reiterated that none of the Supreme Court's precedents "covers a right to homosexual conduct," and volunteered that it was "impossible to conclude that a right to homosexual conduct is 'fundamental' or 'implicit in the concept of ordered liberty' unless any and all private sexual behavior falls within those categories, a conclusion we are unwilling to draw." Bork highlighted one assertion in Dronenburg's brief—"That the particular choice of partner may be repugnant to the majority argues for its vigilant protection, not its vulnerability to sanction"—and observed that "This theory that majority morality and majority choice is always made presumptively invalid by the Constitution attacks the very predicate of democratic government." Bork summed up his panel's rejection of Dronenburg's appeal by declaring that "If the revolution in sexual mores that appellant proclaims is in fact ever to arrive, we think it must arrive through the moral choices of the people and their elected representatives, not through the ukase of this court."[80]

Dronenburg appealed Bork's decision to the entire D.C. Circuit Court, but by a vote of seven to four the judges refused to grant the case a full en banc rehearing. The four dissenters, however, filed a remarkable opinion of their own, contending that "the panel's extravagant exegesis on the constitutional right of privacy was wholly unnecessary to decide the case" and that "the opinions of this court are not proper occasions to throw down gauntlets to the Supreme Court." They mockingly admonished Bork that "Judicial restraint begins at home," and labeled his opinion "an abdication of judicial responsibility," asserting that "Instead of conscientiously attempting to discern the principles underlying the Supreme Court's privacy decisions, the panel has in effect thrown up their hands and decided to confine those decisions to their facts." Bork and Scalia filed a defensive rebuttal, insisting that the *Doe* affirmance was indeed binding and reiterating that from *Griswold* onward, "no principle had been articulated that enabled us to determine whether appellant's case fell within or without that principle." Bork admitted that "It is difficult to know how to reach the conclusion that no principle is discernible in decisions without seeming to criticize those decisions," but he maintained that "our analysis of the privacy cases was both required and accurate."[81]

While the federal courts were increasingly having to face the possible sexual implications of *Griswold* and *Roe*, antiabortion activists intensified their attacks on women's right to choose. Anonymous terrorists bombed pro-choice facilities in Norfolk and Annapolis, and, just in advance of the Democratic National Convention, New York's Roman Catholic archbishop, John Cardinal O'Connor, announced that "I don't see how Catholics in good conscience can vote for a candidate who explicitly supports abortion." Once Democratic nominee Walter Mondale selected New York Representative Geraldine Ferraro, an abortion rights supporter and a Catholic, as his running mate, church sniping at pro-choice politicians intensified even further, and in early September eighteen Roman Catholic bishops from across the Northeast released a public statement announcing that abortion was "the critical issue" in the upcoming November balloting. Soon after the election, a new rash of abortion clinic bombings spread across the country, and pro-choice organizations reacted angrily when federal law enforcement officials insisted that there was no evidence that the terrorist attacks represented any sort of even loose-knit conspiracy. On December 30, federal agents charged a twenty-one-year-old man with carrying out four bombings of clinics in Pensacola, Florida, and early in 1985 they arrested three additional collaborators. After a man representing the "Army of God" claimed responsibility for an explosion at a Washington, D.C., clinic, even President Reagan publicly denounced the ongoing attacks, and several weeks later self-styled lay minister Michael Bray and two other men were charged with placing bombs at seven Washington-area clinics.[82]

More propitious attention was being drawn to the right to life cause by a new film, *The Silent Scream*, which purported to depict fetal pain but which drew most of its power from the narration of onetime NARAL activist Bernie Nathanson, now an antiabortion crusader. But terrorist violence against clinics remained the principal abortion story, and in early March a congressional subcommittee opened hearings on the subject, with one of the first witnesses being Joseph Scheidler, president of the Pro-Life Action League and author of a handbook entitled *Closed: 99 Ways to Stop Abortion*. Scheidler acknowledged that he was "aware of attacks against abortion facilities," and told the subcommittee that he very much understood "the moral outrage at the waste of human life that prompts this response. Some have condemned the destruction of abortion facilities. The Pro-Life Action League and others refuse to condemn it because we refuse to cast the abortionists in the role of victim when they are, in fact, victimizers." Scheidler admitted that "Nonviolent direct action to end abortion is preferable to bombing abortion chambers," but he warned that if such methods were unavailable, "the violence of abortion will inevitably be opposed by other means." Six weeks later the two principal Pensacola bombers were convicted and sentenced to ten years in prison, and in mid-May Michael Bray was found guilty of masterminding the Washington-area bombings and also received a ten-year sentence.[83]

Early in 1985, with Lewis Powell temporarily absent because of illness, the U.S. Supreme Court in a 4 to 4 tie affirmed without opinion a circuit court decision that the Oklahoma City school system could not fire teachers simply because they expressed public support for gay rights. Only Justices Brennan and Marshall, however, voted to hear an appeal by a high school guidance counselor who had been fired simply because she had told several colleagues that she was bisexual. Privately, the Court also deadlocked over whether to dismiss Pennsylvania's appeal of a Third Circuit ruling that had voided a host of state antiabortion regulations. For the first time since Sandra O'Connor's appointment, Warren Burger voted with Justices White, Rehnquist, and O'Connor in an abortion case, and in mid-April the Court simply announced that it would set the case, *Thornburgh* v. *American College of Obstetricians and Gynecologists* (ACOG), for full argument in the fall. Several weeks later the Court also accepted a similar appeal from Illinois, and in midsummer the Reagan Justice Department made front-page news with the announcement that this time its support of the appeals would include an explicit request that the high court overrule *Roe* v. *Wade*.[84]

Also in early 1985, in a clearly ominous action, the sixteen-member Fifth Circuit Court of Appeals agreed to grant an en banc rehearing to a challenge against Judge Buchmeyer's invalidation of Texas's sodomy statute in *Baker* v. *Wade*. Neither Henry Wade nor Texas Attorney General Jim Mattox had pursued an appeal of Buchmeyer's 1982 ruling, but a district attorney from Amarillo, along with a Dallas lawyer representing "Dallas Doctors Against AIDS," had unsuccessfully sought to persuade first Buchmeyer and then a three-judge circuit court panel to allow them to intervene in defense of the antigay law. Far more promising than the Fifth Circuit's portentous move, however, was an outspoken opinion by Richmond federal District Judge Robert Merhige, sustaining a declaratory judgment suit against the constitutionality of Virginia's fornication and cohabitation statutes. The "right to engage in heterosexual intercourse," Merhige explained, was "necessarily implicit" in the "right to bear or beget children." Hence, Merhige said, "the constitutional right of privacy extends to a single adult's decision whether to engage in sexual intercourse."[85]

Even more significant than Merhige's ruling, however, was a 2 to 1 late May decision by a three-judge panel of the Eleventh Circuit Court of Appeals holding that Georgia's criminal sodomy statute would have to satisfy the all-but-impossible "compelling state interest" test in order to be constitutional. Written by Judge Frank M. Johnson, Jr., and joined by former Chief Judge Elbert P. Tuttle, two of the most remarkable judicial champions of the southern civil rights era, the ruling vindicated an ACLU-sponsored test case that had begun after an extraordinary series of events befell a twenty-eight-year-old Atlanta man, Michael Hardwick, in 1982. Early on the morning of July 5, Hardwick left a gay bar carrying a beer. A twenty-three-year-old Atlanta patrolman, Keith Torrick, saw Hardwick and gave him a ticket for drinking in public. It listed twelve noon on Wednesday, July 13, for Hardwick's court appearance, but early on Tuesday afternoon, July 13—for July 13 *was* Tuesday—officer Torrick obtained a warrant for his arrest after Hardwick failed to appear in Atlanta Municipal Court. Hardwick was not home when Torrick showed up at about two p.m. at the house he shared with several other men, but Hardwick returned soon thereafter, learned of Torrick's visit, and immediately went to the courthouse and paid his fifty-dollar fine.

Three weeks later, on August 3, officer Torrick again showed up at Hardwick's residence. He asked a guest whether Hardwick was home, and the uncertain visitor pointed Torrick toward Hardwick's bedroom. There, with the door slightly ajar, Hardwick was engrossed in "mutual oral sex" with another man, a married schoolteacher from North Carolina. Some moments passed before either Hardwick or his friend realized they were being watched, but when they did, Hardwick asked the uniformed policeman the only conceivable question: "What are you doing in my bedroom?" Torrick answered that he had the warrant for Hardwick's nonappearance on the drinking ticket, but that both Hardwick and his friend were now under arrest for sodomy. Hardwick explained that the warrant had been canceled when he paid the ticket three weeks earlier, but Officer Torrick replied that he had been acting in good faith, and when he spied some marijuana in Hardwick's room, he added that offense too. Once Hardwick and his distraught companion put on some clothes, Torrick took them out to his squad car, handcuffed them, and took them first to a police substation and then to jail, where officers let everyone know that the duo had been arrested for "cocksucking." It took almost twelve hours for Hardwick to win release, and a little longer before his frightened friend was also set free.

The jailhouse experience "was a nightmare," Hardwick later said, and while his friend pled guilty to a lesser charge and paid a fine, so as to minimize the danger that word of his arrest would get back to North Carolina, Hardwick was quite receptive when a local ACLU activist who had heard of the incident contacted him several days later to ask whether he would be willing to help launch a constitutional test case challenging the sodomy statute. Hardwick's ordeal had been as classic as it was awful, for as one commentator later noted, what had transpired—"police intrusion into Hardwick's bedroom, followed by charges arising from his sexual conduct—was strikingly similar to the kind of police intrusion" that Justice Douglas's opinion in *Griswold* had envisaged as the ultimate violation of constitutional privacy. In late August Hardwick met with a group of Atlanta-area ACLU attorneys, and in mid-September two of them accompanied Hardwick to a municipal court appearance where he pled guilty to the marijuana charge and where the sodomy count was referred to Fulton County Superior Court.

Over the ensuing several months, however, it became clear that local prosecutors preferred not to pursue the sodomy charge, at least in part because Fulton County District Attorney Lewis Slaton believed it highly unlikely that any jury, given the circumstances of Hardwick's arrest, would return a conviction. Early in 1983 Slaton finally informed Hardwick's lawyers in writing that his office would not present the case to a grand jury for indictment unless "further evidence" developed. Thus frustrated from being able to pursue the issue as a criminal case, Hardwick's lawyers five weeks later filed a declaratory judgment suit in federal district court challenging the constitutionality of Georgia's sodomy statute. The complaint, filed on behalf of both Hardwick and a married couple, "John and Mary Doe," whom Hardwick knew, alleged that Hardwick "regularly engages in private homosexual acts" and that the Does "have been chilled and deterred from engaging in personal, private sexual activity by the existence of the Georgia sodomy statute and the recent arrest of Plaintiff Hardwick." The complaint asserted that there was "no rational relationship between any legitimate state purpose and the statute," which specified anywhere between one and twenty years' imprisonment for convicted offenders. Georgia Attorney General Michael Bowers was named as the lead defendant, and Hardwick's lawyers were expressly candid about the case's purpose: "Sexual conduct in private between consenting adults is protected by a fundamental right of privacy, guaranteed by the 1st, 3rd, 4th, 5th, 9th and 14th Amendments."[86]

Hardly two months after the suit was filed, however, District Judge Robert H. Hall dismissed it on the grounds that the Does lacked standing and that Hardwick's contentions were "foreclosed by the Supreme Court's affirmance" of *Doe* v. *Commonwealth's Attorney* seven years earlier. "All the constitutional arguments made by Hardwick here were rejected in *Doe*," Judge Hall maintained. Hardwick's attorneys appealed the dismissal to the Eleventh Circuit, but two full years—April 1983 to May 1985—passed before the appellate panel reversed Judge Hall. Frank Johnson's majority opinion agreed that the Does, unlike Hardwick, faced no reasonable likelihood of prosecution under the statute and hence lacked standing, but with regard to Hardwick he resolutely concluded that the *Doe* affirmance was in no way dispositive. Johnson held that Constitution protected "certain individual decisions critical to personal autonomy because those decisions are essentially private," and asserted that the "benefits of marriage can inure to individuals outside the traditional marital relationship. For some, the sexual activity in question here serves the same purpose as the intimacy of marriage." Johnson reiterated what he termed "the resemblance between Hardwick's conduct and the intimate association of marriage," and noted that "the constitutional protection of privacy reaches its height when the state attempts to regulate an activity in the home." For Hardwick, Johnson emphasized in conclusion, the "activity he hopes to engage in is quintessentially private and lies at the heart of an intimate association beyond the proper reach of state regulation."

Circuit Judge Phyllis A. Kravitch declined to join Johnson and Tuttle's ruling, believing that the *Doe* affirmance was substantively controlling, but gay rights activists welcomed the decision, and one national legal periodical labeled it "unprecedented." Attorney General Bowers wasted no time whatsoever in petitioning for Supreme Court review, and Hardwick's lead attorney, Kathleen Wilde, fearing a possible reversal, filed a statement in opposition, contending that "there is no basis for this Court's review" since the appellate decision was "well-grounded in established constitutional principles" and "does not involve the creation of any new rights." She stressed that Johnson's opinion did not "represent a departure from" the *Griswold* family of precedents and was indeed "the logical result of their application." Especially *Eisenstadt* and *Carey* "make it clear that the right of sexual privacy is the right of the individual to be free from unwarranted government intrusion into matters fundamentally affecting intimate personal decisions," and she understandably emphasized that Michael Hardwick had been "arrested for conduct which occurred in the privacy of his own bedroom."[87]

Michael Bowers's office filed a reply brief in early October 1985, prominently highlighting an intervening event that had taken place in late August: the Fifth Circuit Court of Appeals, by a en banc vote of 9 to 7, had reversed Judge Buchmeyer's decision in *Baker* v. *Wade* on the grounds that Robert Bork's opinion in *Dronenburg* had correctly held that the Supreme Court's seven-year-old summary affirmance in *Doe was* a substantively binding precedent that lower federal courts were obliged to follow. Irving Goldberg, one of the seven dissenters, declared with some exasperation that "If ever there was a constitutional right to privacy, Texas has violated it by blatantly intruding into the private sex lives of fully consenting adults," and when Donald Baker's attorney submitted a customary petition for rehearing, the circuit court majority issued an almost apologetic supplemental opinion. "We are sensitive and sympathetic to some of the complaints" Baker had voiced, but "it is not the role or authority of this federal court to decide the morality of sexual conduct for the people of the state of Texas." The nine judges sought to insist that Texas's same-sex sodomy statute "is directed at certain conduct, not at a class of people," and they stubbornly declared that "moral issues should be resolved by the people, and the laws pertaining thereto should be written or rescinded by the representatives of the people."[88]

When the nine justices of the U.S. Supreme Court first considered Michael Bowers's request that the Court hear *Bowers* v. *Hardwick*, only two of the four necessary votes—Byron White and William Rehnquist—favored granting Bowers's petition. In mid-October White circulated a short first draft of a dissent, contending that Johnson had erred and that the *Doe* summary affirmance "was a decision on the merits of the constitutional issues." Rehnquist immediately concurred, but *also* joining White's dissent was William Brennan, who of course held an antithetical substantive view but had long wanted the Court to confront the issue and understandably saw *Bowers* as an all-but-perfect case. The next day, Friday, October 18, the question of hearing *Bowers* was formally reconsidered at the justices' weekly conference, and when Thurgood Marshall, who often followed Brennan's lead, likewise changed his earlier stance and voted to grant, *Bowers* v. *Hardwick* had all four of the votes necessary for high court review.

One person who was extremely worried about the consequences of this highly unusual alliance was Harry Blackmun. Any Supreme Court majority that might vitiate Frank Johnson's privacy holding would pose a serious doctrinal danger to the underpinnings of *Roe* and the subsequent abortion decisions, and several days later Blackmun raised his concern directly with Brennan. One of Brennan's clerks remained enthusiastically convinced that *Bowers* was nothing short of ideal, but on October 23 Brennan sent a memo to his colleagues saying that he had given the case a "second look" and had "decided to change my vote. I vote to deny." That shift reduced *Bowers* to only three votes, but within twenty-four hours, Warren Burger circulated a follow-up to Brennan's note: "I, too, have taken a second look" and he now would grant, restoring the tally to four. Thurgood Marshall's law clerks, fully aware of Blackmun's anxiety, suggested that he like Brennan should seriously rethink his vote, but Marshall, who might have found it embarrassing to once again follow Brennan in quite so visible a fashion, was also very strongly committed to the home-privacy principle of his 1969 opinion in *Stanley*. His crucial vote did not change, and on November 4 the Court publicly announced that it was accepting the appeal of *Bowers* v. *Hardwick*.[89]

The very next morning, the justices heard oral argument in both *Thornburgh* v. *ACOG*, Pennsylvania's abortion case, and *Diamond* v. *Charles*, an appeal of a lower court invalidation of Illinois' antiabortion regulations that was being pursued by attorney Dennis Horan on behalf of a right to life physician but not by the state of Illinois itself. Clinic bombings and attacks in such cities as Toledo and Philadelphia had continued to attract far more public attention than did such appellate litigation, and that same day—the first Tuesday in November— voters in three New England towns, including Bristol, Connecticut, which was 70 percent Catholic—were going to the polls to reject anti-*Roe* referenda that abortion opponents had succeeded in placing on local ballots. At oral argument, the nine justices were frankly skeptical about the jurisdictional status of Horan's third-party plea, but *Thornburgh*, like *Akron* and *Ashcroft* three years earlier, was a serious and complex case. At the justices' private conference three days later there was virtual unanimity that *Diamond* should indeed be dismissed on procedural grounds, and when the tentative tally was taken on *Thornburgh*, it became more definite than ever before that with Warren Burger's unmistakable shift toward the stance taken by Justices White, Rehnquist, and O'Connor, *Roe* v. *Wade*'s actual margin of support in the U.S. Supreme Court had indeed slipped to only 5 to 4.[90]

The winter holiday season of 1985–1986 was marked by a significant upsurge in antiabortion violence, as letter bombs mailed to four Oregon clinics luckily malfunctioned and as actual explosions rocked facilities in New York City, Cincinnati, and Toledo. The Diocese of Providence officially excommunicated the Roman Catholic executive director of Rhode Island Planned Parenthood on the grounds that she was an "accomplice" to abortion, and while major public opinion polls

found virtually no movement in the complex mix of American attitudes on the topic, more than eighty thousand participants turned out
for an early March pro-choice demonstration in the nation's capital.
Later that month, however, antiabortion violence resurfaced in a particularly blatant form when former Ku Klux Klansman John Burt, the
commander of right to life forces in western Florida, led five followers
in a physical assault on a Pensacola clinic that left two staff members
injured and all six invaders under arrest.[91]

On the last day of March, the U.S. Supreme Court heard oral argument in *Bowers* v. *Hardwick*. The principal briefs, plus fourteen amicus
submissions, had all been filed several months earlier; in the interim,
the Fourth Circuit Court of Appeals, in an opinion written by Lewis
Powell's closest protégé, J. Harvie Wilkinson III, had vacated Judge
Merhige's ruling against Virginia's sex statutes on the grounds that the
heterosexual plaintiffs actually faced no plausible threat of prosecution.
Hardwick's brief, authored by his new lead counsel, Laurence Tribe,
and two associates, sought to highlight how the case involved "values
of intimate association, and of the sanctity of the home," and made virtually no references to homosexuality. The brief underscored how neither *Eisenstadt*, *Roe*, nor *Carey* had been confined by concepts of
marriage or family, and while it quoted several times from John
Harlan's dissent in *Poe*, it placed far more emphasis upon *Stanley*'s special concern for the home. The sexual relations involved in *Bowers*
ought to be viewed "solely as a facet of associational intimacy" that
already had received constitutional recognition, for "this Court's decisions upholding access to contraceptives involved not so much the
right to buy and use a particular pharmaceutical product, as the right to
engage in sexual intimacy as such."

Within the Court, most clerks agreed wholeheartedly with Tribe's
analysis. One of Marshall's young assistants, Dan Richman, recapitulated the arguments shortly in advance of the hearing: "To repeat the
point, which I'm sure many members of the Court will forget or
ignore: THIS IS NOT A CASE ABOUT ONLY HOMOSEXUALS.
ALL SORTS OF PEOPLE DO THIS KIND OF THING."
Hardwick's suit, he advised the seventy-seven-year-old Marshall,
involved sex acts which "are incredibly popular among a substantial
chunk of the population," and he pointed out that pursuant to *Griswold*
and *Roe*, "this Court (though it would never phrase it this way) has
essentially established a right to engage in recreational sex."

Among the clerks, however, expectations took a worrisome turn two
days before the oral argument when word spread that Lewis Powell,

apparently unaware that he himself had already employed numerous gay assistants during his fifteen years on the Court, told one astounded and discomforted clerk that he had never met a homosexual. On Monday morning, March 31, Georgia assistant attorney general Michael Hobbs faced off against Laurence Tribe, with Hobbs contending in his argument that no nonmarital sex of any sort, whether heterosexual or homosexual, merited any special constitutional protection. Once Tribe began his presentation, Lewis Powell immediately jumped in to ask what limiting principle Tribe would apply to the right to privacy argument. "It includes all physical, sexual intimacies of a kind that are not demonstrably physically harmful, that are consensual and noncommercial, in the privacy of the home," Tribe replied, stressing that the essence of his case was "autonomous personal control over intimacy."[92]

When the justices met privately on April 2 to decide *Bowers*, Warren Burger began the discussion by declaring that the only issue in the case was homosexuality, since the married plaintiffs lacked standing. Under the common law, Burger stressed, sodomy had been a crime for centuries, and privacy analysis could not be controlling, for without any limiting principle even incest would be protected. William Brennan, however, cited both *Griswold* and *Stanley* in contending that privacy was paramount and that noncommercial conduct in the home by consenting adults was constitutionally protected. *Bowers* was not just about homosexuals, Brennan told his colleagues, but Byron White said simply that he agreed with Burger, and Thurgood Marshall mentioned *Stanley* in announcing that he agreed with Brennan. Harry Blackmun commended Frank Johnson's "great" job and a "careful and craftsmanlike" opinion and emphasized how the case did not involve coercion, prostitution, or public activity outside the home. He warned that the Georgia law could spill over into marriage, and cited *Loving* v. *Virginia*. Lewis Powell said he had mixed emotions. He had "never met a homosexual," but Hardwick's conduct ought to be decriminalized, especially in the context of the home and particularly given the statute's history of nonenforcement. *Robinson* v. *California*, a 1962 decision in which the Court on Eighth Amendment "cruel and unusual punishment" grounds had thrown out a criminal conviction based simply upon a man's status as a drug addict might be relevant, Powell suggested, if sexual preference indeed was not simply a behavioral choice. Hardwick "gets his satisfaction in [the] home" and Georgia "can't imprison him for this affliction." William Rehnquist stated that he sided with Burger and White, and that *Stanley* was "unfortunate," since the "criminal law has moral underpinnings." John Stevens said that morality was not enough, and that while he disliked homosexuals—"I hate homos," one colleague quoted Stevens as saying—"we have to live with it," for it was a basic question of liberty. Sandra O'Connor noted that there was no absolute constitutional right to privacy, and that the state did have broad authority to enact morals legislation. Sodomy was clearly prohibited at the time the Constitution was adopted, even if Georgia had explicitly declined to prosecute Michael Hardwick.

The conference ended with five apparent votes for affirming Frank Johnson's ruling: Brennan, Marshall, Blackmun, Powell, and Stevens. At Harry Blackmun's request, Bill Brennan assigned the majority opinion to Blackmun, but over the ensuing several days a discomfited Lewis Powell continued to contemplate what the best aftermath would be. Hardwick's conduct should not be punishable, but at the same time Johnson's depiction of it as analogous to marriage went much too far. Powell knew what he thought; he simply was uncertain as to whether his stance meant that he should favor affirmance or reversal. Finally, on April 8, he circulated a memorandum to all eight of his colleagues:

> At Conference last week, I expressed the view that in some cases it would violate the Eighth Amendment to imprison a person for a private act of homosexual sodomy. I continue to think that in such cases imprisonment would constitute cruel and unusual punishment. I relied primarily on *Robinson* v. *California*.
>
> At Conference, given my view as to the Eighth Amendment, my vote was to affirm but on this ground rather than the view of four other Justices that there was a violation of a fundamental substantive constitutional right—as [the Eleventh Circuit] held. I did not agree that there is a substantive due process right to engage in conduct that for centuries has been recognized as deviant, and not in the best interest of preserving humanity. I may say generally, that I also hesitate to create another substantive due process right.
>
> I write this memorandum today because upon further study as to exactly what is before us, I conclude that my 'bottom line' should be to reverse rather than affirm. The only question presented by the parties is the substantive due process issue, and—as several of you noted at Conference—my Eighth Amendment view was not addressed by the court below or by the parties.
>
> In sum, my more carefully considered view is that I will vote to reverse but will write separately to explain my views of this case generally. I will not know, until I see the writing, whether I can join an opinion finding no substantive due process right or simply join the judgment.

Powell's memo was greeted with understandable dismay in the four chambers whose justices had suddenly been recast as *Bowers*'s dissenters. Before the afternoon was out, John Stevens dictated a brief "Dear Lewis" letter that when circulated to all eight justices early the next morning immediately became a top contender for the most droll missive in Supreme Court history:

> Your letter, which expresses some uncertainty as to whether your final vote would be one to reverse or to affirm brings to mind the disposition of the Court in *Coleman* v. *Miller*, 307 U.S. 433, 446–447, where the Court, with all nine justices participating, disposed of the question whether the Lieutenant Governor of Kansas was part of the state legislature, by stating that the Court was "equally divided" on the issue.
>
> Maybe we should follow a similar course in this case.
>
> Respectfully,

The gentlemanly Lewis Powell did not reply to Stevens's note in writing, but the very next morning, Warren Burger circulated a memo formally reassigning the majority opinion in *Bowers* v. *Hardwick* to Byron White. Within less than two weeks, after putting aside his clerk's draft in order to prepare an opinion that was very much his own, White circulated an initial print of a statement for the nascent *Bowers* majority. Only Bill Rehnquist immediately joined, and while Harry Blackmun advised that he would be writing a dissent, Powell told White after seeing the draft that "I will join the judgment but will probably write separately."[93]

Eight full weeks passed before any further developments occurred in *Bowers*. In the interim, the justices in late April dismissed Dennis Horan's appeal of *Diamond* v. *Charles* and then, on June 11, publicly handed down their five-to-four ruling against Pennsylvania's antiabortion regulations in *Thornburgh* v. *ACOG*. Blackmun's majority opinion resolutely declared that "again today, we reaffirm the general principles laid down in *Roe* and in *Akron*," and explained that Pennsylvania's restrictions "intrude upon the physician's exercise of proper professional judgment" in addition to infringing upon the rights of pregnant women. "The Constitution embodies a promise that a certain private sphere of individual liberty will be kept largely beyond the reach of government," Blackmun reiterated. "Few decisions are more personal and intimate, more properly private, or more basic to individual dignity and autonomy, than a woman's decision. . . . whether to end her pregnancy. A woman's right to make that choice freely is fundamental."

John Stevens contributed a sprightly concurrence, acknowledging that "the State's interest in the protection of an embryo . . . increases progressively and dramatically as the organism's capacity to feel pain, to experience pleasure, to survive, and to react to its surroundings increases day by day," but among *Thornburgh*'s dissenters, Warren Burger's opinion was perhaps the case's most remarkable statement. "Every member of the *Roe* Court," Burger asserted, "rejected the idea of abortion on demand. The Court's opinion today, however, plainly undermines that important principle." If both *Thornburgh* and the 1976 decision in *Danforth*, from which Burger had also dissented, "really mean what they seem to say, I agree that we should reexamine *Roe*." Byron White of course had believed for over thirteen years that *Roe* demanded more than just reconsideration, but his *Thornburgh* dissent, which William Rehnquist also joined, was as tough-spoken and fetally oriented as any prior statement on abortion by any justice. "I can certainly agree with the proposition—which I deem indisputable—that a woman's ability to choose an abortion is a species of 'liberty' that is subject to the general protections of the Due Process Clause," White seemingly conceded. "I cannot agree, however, that this liberty is so 'fundamental' that restrictions upon it call into play anything more than the most minimal judicial scrutiny." The presence of a fetus meant that the avowal of a right to abortion was "different in kind from the others that the Court has protected under the rubric of personal or family privacy and autonomy." The state's interest in protecting a fetus was just as "compelling" in advance of viability as afterwards, and only "the warped point of view of the majority" kept them from acknowledging that. Sandra O'Connor's dissent was far less harsh than White's, but she nonetheless contended that "no legal rule or doctrine is safe from ad hoc nullification by this Court when an occasion for its application arises in a case involving state regulation of abortion."[94]

Six days after the *Thornburgh* decision was handed down, Warren Burger made far more momentous news when he announced his retirement as Chief Justice at the upcoming completion of the Court's 1985–1986 term. President Ronald Reagan, whom Burger had notified in advance, simultaneously announced his nomination of William Rehnquist as the next Chief Justice and D.C. Circuit Court Judge Antonin Scalia—who had joined Robert Bork's privacy opinion in *Dronenburg*—to assume Rehnquist's seat. Considerable opposition to Rehnquist's promotion quickly arose, whereas Scalia's selection drew little critical comment, but inside the Court itself, as the justices moved into the final ten days of the term, one principal unsettled question remained the final disposition of *Bowers* v. *Hardwick*. Two days after Burger's announcement, Sandra O'Connor had joined Rehnquist in endorsing Byron White's draft opinion, while Lewis Powell had circulated a first print of his separate concurrence, but only on June 24, after both Harry Blackmun and John Stevens had distributed dissents, did Burger himself formally become the fourth vote in support of White. The following day, Powell for the first time appended to a third recirculation of his concurrence that "I join the opinion of the Court," thus giving White's statement official status as a majority opinion. Six days later, on June 30, the Supreme Court's 5 to 4 decision in *Bowers* v. *Hardwick* was publicly announced.[95]

White's opinion for the Court asserted that *Bowers* v. *Hardwick* involved "whether the Federal Constitution confers a fundamental right upon homosexuals to engage in sodomy." From *Pierce*, *Meyer*, *Prince*, and *Skinner* through *Griswold*, *Loving*, *Eisenstadt*, and *Roe*, White proclaimed, "none of the rights announced in those cases bears any resemblance to the claimed constitutional right of homosexuals to engage in sodomy . . . No connection between family, marriage, or procreation on the one hand and homosexual activity on the other has been demonstrated" and "any claim that these cases nevertheless stand for the proposition that any kind of private sexual conduct between consenting adults is constitutionally insulated from state proscription is unsupportable." Against the background of the Supreme Court's due process precedents protecting familial privacy, White maintained, "to claim that a right to engage in such conduct is 'deeply rooted in this Nation's history and tradition' or 'implicit in the concept of ordered liberty' is, at best, facetious." Warren Burger's concurrence reiterated that "there is no such thing as a fundamental right to commit homosexual sodomy" and observed that "To hold that the act of homosexual sodomy is somehow protected as a fundamental right would be to cast aside millennia of moral teaching."

Lewis Powell's supplemental concurrence agreed that Hardwick's case involved no substantive fundamental right, but Powell added that "This is not to suggest, however, that respondent may not be protected by the Eighth Amendment," especially since the Georgia law authorized imprisonment for as much as twenty years. "In my view, a prison sentence for such conduct—certainly a sentence of long duration— would create a serious Eighth Amendment issue." Powell noted that "In this case, however, respondent has not been tried, much less convicted and sentenced. Moreover, respondent has not raised the Eighth Amendment issue below. For these reasons this constitutional argument is not before us." In a footnote, Powell observed that even Professor Tribe had conceded that prior to Hardwick's experience "there had been no reported decision involving prosecution for private homosexual sodomy under this statute for several decades" and that especially in light of that fact, "for the reasons stated by the Court, I cannot say that conduct condemned for hundreds of years has now become a fundamental right."

Harry Blackmun's dissent, in which Justices Brennan, Marshall, and Stevens all joined, was a forceful rejoinder to Byron White. "This case is no more about 'a fundamental right to engage in homosexual sodomy' . . . than *Stanley* . . . was about a fundamental right to watch obscene movies, or *Katz*," a 1967 decision extending the Fourth Amendment's protection against unreasonable search and seizure to electronic surveillance, "was about a fundamental right to place interstate bets from a telephone booth. Rather, this case is about 'the most comprehensive of rights and the right most valued by civilized men,' namely 'the right to be let alone,'" as Justice Brandeis had said in *Olmstead* in 1928. Reiterating how "the majority has distorted the question this case presents," Blackmun emphasized that the Georgia sodomy statute covered heterosexuals as well as homosexuals and that Hardwick's claim that the law represented an "unconstitutional intrusion into his privacy and his right of intimate association does not depend in any way on his sexual orientation." Additionally, "Georgia's exclusive stress before this Court on its interest in prosecuting homosexual activity despite the gender-neutral terms of the statute may raise serious questions of discriminatory enforcement." Blackmun affirmed that "the right of an individual to conduct intimate relationships in the intimacy of his or her own home seems to me to be the heart of the Constitution's protection of privacy," and he decried the majority's "failure to comprehend the magnitude of the liberty interests at stake in this case." "Depriving individuals of the right to choose for themselves how to conduct their intimate relationships," Blackmun asserted, "poses a far greater threat to the values most deeply rooted in our Nation's history than tolerance of nonconformity could ever do."

John Stevens also filed a dissent, joined by both William Brennan and Thurgood Marshall, that cited the Court's 1967 voiding of Virginia's ban on interracial marriage in *Loving* as precedent for how "the fact that the governing majority in a State has traditionally viewed a particular practice as immoral is not a sufficient reason for upholding a law prohibiting the practice." The liberty right recognized in *Griswold*, *Eisenstadt*, and *Carey*, Stevens observed, "surely embraces the right to engage in nonreproductive, sexual conduct that others may consider offensive or immoral." Even Georgia had conceded that it could not constitutionally apply its sodomy statute against married couples, Stevens noted, and under *Eisenstadt's* equal protection extension of *Griswold* to single individuals, any sodomy prosecution of unmarried heterosexuals would be highly suspect. Hence the majority's declaration that Georgia could enforce the law against homosexuals, while the statute itself "presumably reflects the belief that *all sodomy* is immoral and unacceptable," inescapably posed a serious equal protection problem.[96]

The Court's announcement of *Bowers* v. *Hardwick* was greeted with widespread expressions of dismay and sharp attacks upon the tone and content of Byron White's opinion. Gay rights attorney Tom Stoddard termed the decision "a major disaster," and ACLU litigator Nan Hunter called it "as much of a setback as we can experience without an overturning of *Roe.*" The *New York Times* branded it "a gratuitous and petty ruling, an offense to American society's maturing standards of individual dignity," and constitutional scholar Paul Brest, writing in the *Los Angeles Times*, said that White's opinion was "so lacking in legal craft that it makes one wonder what was going on." Yale law professor Paul Gewirtz castigated White for a ruling that was "superficial, peremptory and insensitive," and warned that "the Court treats homosexuals' claims in such a dismissive way that it conveys a sense that similar treatment by legislatures would be appropriate." A Syracuse law professor opined that White "was simply mirroring and sanctioning societal attitudes about the unacceptability of homosexual conduct," and attorney Stoddard, in a subsequent commentary, contended that the Court's ruling "rests upon nothing more substantial than the collective distaste of the five justices in the majority for the conduct under scrutiny." Professor Brest, the *New York Times*, and even *The New Republic* all praised Blackmun's dissent as "eloquent," and Gallup Poll results showed that of the 73 percent of respondents who said they had heard of the decision, 47 percent of them expressed disapproval while only 41 percent said that they agreed.

Newsweek magazine featured those Gallup numbers in a story which declared that while the right to privacy was "Now regarded as one of our fundamental birthrights," the evolution of that right had come to "an abrupt halt" with *Bowers*. Several legal observers elucidated how *Bowers* and *Roe* were "inconsistent and irreconcilable," despite Lewis Powell's fifth-vote endorsement of both, and former White House counsel Charles Colson was only one of many abortion opponents who pointed out that "To apply the logic of the sodomy case to *Roe* v. *Wade* is to reverse *Roe* v. *Wade*." Indeed, as one gay rights litigator trenchantly noted, *Bowers* "is the decision that Justice White would like to write about abortion rights, but for which he does not have the fifth vote."[97]

A very few writers sided with White. One law professor who had filed his own amicus brief in *Bowers*, warning against the dangers of AIDS, complained that Blackmun's dissent "strikingly invoked the liturgies of autonomous hedonism," and an idiosyncratic former Blackmun clerk commended the "extraordinarily forceful reasoning" of White's opinion while celebrating how *Bowers* "rejects the philosophical underpinnings of *Roe*" and represented "a distinct philosophical break with the modern line of right to privacy decisions that began with *Griswold*." Many conservative constitutional scholars, however, were loathe to embrace the *Bowers* majority. *Roe* critic and Reagan administration Solicitor General Charles Fried subsequently disparaged "White's stunningly harsh and dismissive opinion" and characterized Hardwick's conduct as first and foremost "an act of private association and communication. The fact that sexuality is implicated seems an anatomical irrelevance." Legal pundit Bruce Fein, conservative even by Reagan administration standards, admitted that "the political case for judicial rescue of homosexuals from the legislative process was greater than that for the *Griswold* intervention on behalf of married couples," and warned that in light of the doctrinal contradictions between *Bowers* and previous holdings, the American public would "correctly" conclude that the Court's privacy decisions were based on simply "the varied personal policy predilections of the Justices" themselves.[98]

Within two weeks of the *Bowers* announcement, a front-page story in the *Washington Post* revealed how the end result had differed from the initial conference tally: "Powell Changed Vote in Sodomy Case." In the interim, the Supreme Court had quietly rejected an appeal of *Baker* v. *Wade*, and soon thereafter the Missouri Supreme Court invoked *Bowers* while reversing a lower court's invalidation of that state's sodomy statute. The Missouri high court also cited both Robert Bork's opinion in *Dronenburg* and "the general promiscuity characteristic of the homosexual life style" as additional support for its holding. Laurence Tribe prepared the customary petition requesting Supreme Court reconsideration of *Bowers* with tacit assistance from the light that the *Post*'s disclosure shed on Lewis Powell's concurrence, and Tribe's petition thus emphasized Eighth Amendment themes. Hardwick had indeed been jailed pursuant to his arrest, Tribe noted, but even more so, "it is the very criminalization of an involuntary condition, not the terms of any specific sentence imposed, that violates the Constitution." Tribe pointed out that the actual record "contains nothing as to the gender of Hardwick's partner," and he further stressed that "the effect of the decision in this case is to encourage the eventual overruling of decades of privacy decisions from *Meyer* . . . and *Pierce* . . . through *Griswold* . . . [and] *Roe*." The question before the Court, he reminded the justices, "is not what Respondent Michael Hardwick was doing in the privacy of his own bedroom, but what the State of Georgia was doing there."

In mid-September, however, the high court rejected the rehearing petition without comment. Four weeks later, in a separate action that many observers took as implicit confirmation of *Bowers*'s homophobic message, the justices declined to hear an appeal of an Oklahoma decision that had cited constitutional privacy grounds in voiding sodomy prosecutions of nonmarital but consensual heterosexual couplings. In Georgia, though, the fifteen months after *Bowers* witnessed two state supreme court decisions affirming sodomy convictions that involved very significant jail terms. In one, James A. Lambeth's sentence of five years for what a trial jury apparently had concluded was consensual, heterosexual anal sex was upheld, while in the other, James H. Gordon, Jr., received ten years for a half-dozen consensual encounters with an underage, sixteen-year-old male upon whom Gordon had performed fellatio and who in turn had anally sodomized Gordon. Three years later, Lewis Powell publicly acknowledged that while *Bowers* was a "close call" and "not very important," he nonetheless had concluded that "I think I probably made a mistake" in voting to uphold the law. *Bowers* "was not a major case, and one of the reasons I voted the way I did was the case was a frivolous case" which had been brought "just to see what the Court would do," Powell recalled. "When I had the opportunity to reread the opinions a few months later, I thought the dissent had the better of the arguments."[99]

Harry Blackmun of course agreed. Asked some months later whether he believed that his dissent would ultimately prevail, Blackmun agreed that "it will in the long run," for eventually *Bowers* "has to be overturned." But Blackmun's more pressing concern in the late summer and early fall of 1986 was the future of *Roe v. Wade*, for only one vote separated the *Thornburgh* majority from the *Thornburgh* dissenters. The Senate's unanimous mid-September confirmation of Antonin Scalia, following a more divisive vote that had elevated William Rehnquist to Chief Justice, had not altered the Court's numerical balance, for Scalia presumably would take Warren Burger's place among the *Thornburgh* minority, but the departure of any member of *Thornburgh*'s majority would jeopardize *Roe*'s entire thirteen year heritage. *Roe* was "a landmark decision" in the "emancipation of women," Blackmun acknowledged to one questioner, but "It may well be overruled," depending on shifts in the Court's membership. Most abortion news continued to focus on right to life violence against clinics—bombings in Kansas and New York, arson fires in Missouri and Michigan—but in the November elections antiabortion referendum proposals in Arkansas, Massachusetts, Oregon, and Rhode Island all went down to defeat. In midfall the Supreme Court announced that it would hear an Illinois appeal of a lower court decision that had voided several state antiabortion regulations, but in March 1987, just two days before the scheduled oral argument, the justices postponed the case until the fall and asked the parties for supplemental briefs.[100]

On Friday, June 26, the final day of the Court's 1986–1987 term, seventy-nine-year-old Lewis F. Powell announced his retirement. Five days later, after White House political advisors had carefully surveyed the votes necessary for Senate confirmation, President Reagan announced his nomination of D.C. Circuit Court Judge Robert H. Bork as Powell's successor. News accounts highlighted Bork's established track record as an outspoken critic of *Roe*, and pro-choice groups such as NARAL wasted no time in announcing that they would mount a full-scale campaign against the nomination. Senate Judiciary Committee hearings on Bork would not begin until mid-September, and while his opponents were leery about making *Roe* itself a focal point of their campaign, they also realized that Bork's academic attacks on *Griswold* would allow them to portray him as an enemy of the right to privacy. Early in August, an ad placed in the *Washington Post* by People for the American Way asserted that Bork "has argued many times that the Constitution does not specifically recognize the right to privacy. In one case, he said the state could prevent married couples from using contraceptives at home." Some readers may have thought that this referred to a decision Bork had rendered as a judge, but as the Senate hearings drew near, his opponents' invocation of privacy themes intensified. "According to Bork," a NARAL ad proclaimed, "A state can declare the use of birth control illegal and invade your privacy to enforce the law." An anti-Bork television commercial featuring the actor Gregory Peck told viewers that the nominee "doesn't believe the Constitution protects your right to privacy," and a *New York Times* ad placed by Planned Parenthood of New York City said that Bork had

termed *Griswold* "utterly specious" and warned that if he was confirmed, "you'll need more than a prescription to get birth control."

Democratic consultant Ann Lewis later underscored how anti-Bork
activists had recognized that the privacy emphasis was "the strongest
way to make the case" against the nominee. As liberal strategist Nikki
Heidepriem subsequently explained, in the effort to portray Bork as "a
rigid ideologue . . . with a stifling interpretation of a living document,"
the "key surrogate for that notion was privacy," for "privacy as an overarching concept gave us a chance to talk about control, as in choice,
and integrity of the home." Indeed, the very morning that the Senate
Judiciary Committee hearings on the nomination finally got underway,
a People for the American Way ad in the *New York Times* reminded
readers that "to this day" Bork still believed that "the Supreme Court
was wrong when it stopped one state from making the use of contraceptives by married couples a punishable crime."

While Bork's foes had undoubtedly capitalized on *Griswold* in seeking to arouse opposition to the nomination, Bork himself in his first
day of testimony bluntly restated his attacks on both *Griswold* and *Roe*.
"If *Griswold* v. *Connecticut* established or adopted a privacy right on reasoning which was utterly inadequate, and failed to define that right so
we know what it applies to," Bork told the Senators, then "*Roe* v. *Wade*
contains almost no legal reasoning. We are not told why it is a private
act, and if it is—there are lots of private acts that are not protected—
why this one is protected. We are simply not told that. We get a review
of the history of abortion and we get a review of the opinions of various groups like the American Medical Association, and then we get
rules. That's what I object to about the case. It does not have legal reasoning in it that roots the right to abortion in constitutional materials."
Committee chairman Joseph R. Biden, Jr., who had pointed out to his
own staffers that "if you don't have *Griswold*, you can't get to *Roe*"—
joined Massachusetts Democrat Edward M. Kennedy and Utah
Republican Orrin Hatch in extended colloquies with Bork about
Griswold's privacy holding, and the following day Senators Alan
Simpson, Arlen Specter, Dennis DeConcini, Charles Grassley, and
Howell Heflin all queried Bork about the case. Bork termed *Griswold*
"a radical departure" from the Court's previous jurisprudence while
trying to stress that he neither endorsed the old Connecticut statute
nor opposed the principle of marital privacy. Bork nonetheless insisted
that "It remains a live controversy" as to whether *Griswold* was correctly decided, and political participants as well as journalists increasingly
realized that Bork's deepening image as an unwavering opponent of

constitutional privacy was doing his nomination greater political harm than any other single factor. Once Bork's own testimony was complete, more and more signs appeared to indicate that his chances for confirmation were fast slipping away. On Monday, September 21, the sixth day of actual hearings, impetuous Wyoming Republican Alan Simpson spoke about both *Griswold* and the nomination in the past tense while complaining to no one in particular that "you cannot believe how much time we have spent on that nutty case and how much mileage the opponents of Bork got out of it. This was the key."

One week later, with judiciary committee testimony still continuing, a Louis Harris poll found that opponents of the Bork nomination now outnumbered supporters by 57 to 29 percent. The heaviest anti-Bork sentiment, Harris reported, centered on *Griswold*. One Harris query had used an invented quotation to ask respondents whether or not they were worried about Bork's opposition to a constitutional right to privacy: "Judge Bork has said, 'when a state passes a law prohibiting a married couple from using birth control devices in the privacy of their own home, there is nothing in the Constitution that says the Supreme Court should protect such married people's right to privacy.' That kind of statement worries me." An overwhelming 68 percent of respondents said that yes, they were worried, while only 27 percent were not, and two days later, when the Harris survey was officially entered into the judiciary committee's hearing record, Pennsylvania Republican Arlen Specter remarked that "*Griswold* is the most discussed case in America today."

The day after the hearings finally concluded, with Bork's prospects for Senate confirmation now viewed as next to hopeless, the nominee sent judiciary committee chairman Biden a fifteen-page letter, more than half of which was devoted to defending his criticisms of *Griswold*-style privacy reaching all the way back to 1971. Citing *Roe* and *Bowers*, Bork observed that "The difference between these two decisions illustrates my point that it is difficult, if not impossible, to apply the undefined right of privacy in a principled or consistent manner. It is difficult to understand why abortion is a constitutionally protected liberty and homosexual sodomy is not." Bork of course was not suggesting that *Bowers* had been wrongly decided, for while he would later say that he was "dubious about making homosexual conduct criminal," he nonetheless believed that Blackmun's dissent was "a constitutional debacle" as well as "the natural outcome of *Griswold*."[101]

Five days later the judiciary committee voted 9 to 5 against Bork's confirmation, and as additional Senators announced their opposition to the nomination, Bork himself resolved to push forward to a full floor vote despite the sure knowledge that he would lose. New York Democrat Daniel Patrick Moynihan, revealing his decision to vote against Bork, explained that "it is his restricted vision of privacy which troubles me most. I cannot vote for a jurist who simply cannot find in the Constitution a general right of privacy," for such a right "is a fundamental protection for the individual and the family against unwarranted state intrusion. Its importance is such that I cannot support anyone for a Supreme Court appointment who would not recognize it."

On October 23 the full Senate voted 58 to 42 to reject the nomination, and judiciary committee chief counsel Mark Gitenstein, looking back on the preceding weeks, would conclude that "if the Bork struggle was over any one case, it was *Griswold* v. *Connecticut*." Other constitutional commentators came to the same judgment, with one opining that the "Bork nomination hearings have made clear that 'privacy' . . . enjoys broad popular support as a constitutional value" and another deciding that "Bork was deprived of a seat on the Supreme Court largely because of his refusal to acknowledge the 'unenumerated' right to privacy as being part of the set of constitutional rights legitimately enjoyed by Americans." Bork's opponents, one analyst observed, had convinced most Senators that they "could use allegiance to *Griswold* as a useful litmus test for membership in the 'mainstream' of constitutional thought," and the same writer, quoting from a Supreme Court decision of four decades earlier, volunteered that "If the Bork hearings accomplished anything beyond the rejection of the Bork nomination itself, it was the enshrinement of *Griswold* v. *Connecticut* as 'a fixed star in our constitutional firmament.'" Bork's supporters unhappily concurred, with one warning that "any future nominee who has ever questioned the constitutional integrity or the political propriety of *Griswold* will suffer Bork's fate." *Griswold*, he indignantly agreed, had indeed "become the Senate's litmus test for federal judges."[102]

In subsequent years, after he resigned his circuit court judgeship, Robert Bork would further intensify his attacks upon both *Roe* and *Griswold*, decrying "the spurious right of privacy that *Griswold* created" and denouncing *Roe* as "the greatest example and symbol of the judicial usurpation of democratic prerogatives in this century." Regarding *Roe*, Bork would also allege that "in the entire opinion there is not one line of explanation, not one sentence that qualifies as legal argument," and eventually he would angrily insist that "it will probably never be too late to overrule the right of privacy cases, including *Roe*" and apparently even *Griswold*.[103]

In the immediate wake of Bork's overwhelming Senate defeat, the Reagan administration moved quickly to select another nominee for Lewis Powell's now-vacant seat. Its first choice was one of Bork's younger colleagues on the D.C. Circuit Court, Douglas Ginsburg, but just nine days after being nominated, Ginsburg was forced to withdraw from consideration when confronted with published reports that he repeatedly smoked marijuana while a professor at Harvard Law School in the late 1970s. Four days after Ginsburg's withdrawal, President Reagan nominated fifty-one-year-old Ninth Circuit Court of Appeals judge Anthony M. Kennedy, a moderately conservative Roman Catholic from Sacramento, as his third choice to succeed Lewis Powell. With no signs of controversy and little overt opposition, three short days of Senate Judiciary Committee hearings on Kennedy's nomination got underway in mid-December.

The very same morning that Judge Kennedy began his testimony before the Senate committee, the eight sitting members of the Supreme Court announced that they had deadlocked 4 to 4 over Illinois's abortion case appeal in which the high court had heard oral argument five weeks earlier. No longer was there any doubt that Lewis Powell's eventual successor would become the decisive vote on the legacy of *Roe* v. *Wade*, and at the Senate hearing, Anthony Kennedy implicitly but clearly emphasized that his view of constitutional rights was decidedly broader than Robert Bork's. "I think that the concept of liberty in the due process clause is quite expansive, quite sufficient, to protect the values of privacy that Americans legitimately think are part of their constitutional heritage," Kennedy told the judiciary committee. Chairman Biden followed up immediately: "Let me put it to you very bluntly. Do you think *Griswold* was reasoned properly?" Kennedy parried, saying that he would prefer not to address specific reasoning or results, but he did volunteer that "if you were going to propose a statute or a hypothetical that infringed upon the core values of privacy that the Constitution protects, you would be hard put to find a stronger case than *Griswold*." Kennedy unhesitatingly answered "yes" when Biden asked "Is there a marital right to privacy protected by the Constitution?," and the nominee added that "the value of privacy is a very important part" of the "substantive component" of the due process clause. "It is not clear to me that substituting the word 'privacy' is much of an advance over interpreting the word 'liberty,' which is already in the Constitution," he explained to the committee.[104]

In early February 1988, the U.S. Senate unanimously confirmed Anthony Kennedy as the ninth member of the Supreme Court, and with no abortion law cases scheduled for argument, Justice Kennedy's first six months of service passed without any opportunity for illumination of what his liberty views might mean for the future of *Roe*. Most abortion news focused on the disruptive efforts of Operation Rescue, a relatively new antiabortion group headed by former used-car salesman Randall Terry, to block women from entering abortion clinics, first in New York and then, in midsummer, during the Democratic National Convention in Atlanta. While some observers viewed Terry's emergence as evidence that pro-choice forces were on the defensive, other journalists interpreted right to lifers' adoption of such "direct action" tactics as indicative of how they so far had been largely unsuccessful in trying to combat abortion through normal legislative and judicial processes. In mid-September, just a few weeks before the high court began its 1988–1989 term, Justice Blackmun drew nationwide news coverage when he rhetorically asked a University of Arkansas audience "Will *Roe* v. *Wade* go down the drain?" and answered that "there's a very distinct possibility that it will, this term. You can count the votes." Clearly referring to Kennedy's possible stance towards *Roe*, Blackmun added that "One never knows what a new justice's attitude toward *stare decisis* is. It's now fifteen years old."[105]

In the November elections, antiabortion forces were heartened both by Republican presidential candidate George Bush's resounding victory over Democrat Michael Dukakis and by the defeat of referenda in Colorado and Michigan that would have restored state funding for indigent women's abortions. Then, just two days after the election, outgoing Solicitor General Charles Fried asked the Supreme Court to hear a Missouri appeal of a circuit court decision that had voided several state antiabortion restrictions. Fried's petition also noted how the case, *Webster* v. *Reproductive Health Services*, could provide an opportunity for the Court to reconsider *Roe* v. *Wade*, and at a private conference on January 6, 1989, at least four justices—White, Rehnquist, Stevens, and O'Connor—voted in favor of accepting the appeal. Three days later that action was publicly announced, and both attentive journalists and interested litigators began to lay odds on what the newly constituted Court—with Anthony Kennedy rather than Lewis Powell as the apparent swing vote—would do with—or to—the legacy of *Roe* v. *Wade*.[106]

In late February both Missouri Attorney General William L. Webster and Fried's interim successor as solicitor general filed briefs defending the state's regulations and taking aim at *Roe*. The Reagan administration's submission forthrightly contended that "*Roe* v. *Wade* unduly restricts the proper sphere of legislative authority in this area and should be overruled." It asserted that the abortion "controversy has, in substantial measure, been a product of the decision itself" and the "unworkable framework" *Roe* had created. Missouri's brief declared that "the trimester approach established in *Roe* v. *Wade* is inherently flawed because the point of viability is arbitrary and the State has a compelling interest in protecting life through all stages of pregnancy." Webster further maintained that "The textual, doctrinal, and historical basis for *Roe* v. *Wade* is flawed and is a source of such instability in the law that the Court should reconsider the decision, and on reconsideration abandon it and adopt the rational basis test for reviewing abortion regulations in accordance with *Bowers*," where White had applied that most deferential level of judicial scrutiny. "Criticism regarding the legitimacy of the right declared to be fundamental in *Roe* v. *Wade* continues unabated," Webster stressed, and the "Court's reasoning in *Bowers* constitutes a forceful basis for rejecting the philosophical underpinnings of *Roe*."

The brief for Reproductive Health Services, St. Louis's oldest and best-established abortion clinic, reminded the Court that "*Roe* was a logical and necessary outgrowth of the long line of cases preceding it which recognized a fundamental right to privacy in matters of childbearing and family life." Ten days after it was filed, a huge pro-choice march drew more than 300,000 participants to the nation's capital, and while public opinion polls continued to show that upwards of 60 percent of Americans favored leaving an abortion decision to a woman and her doctor, only a slim majority said they supported *Roe* and just a narrow plurality voiced opposition to laws that would make abortions harder to obtain. A veritable deluge of amicus briefs—seventy-eight in all, twenty more than the previous Supreme Court record of fifty-eight eleven years earlier in the *Bakke* affirmative action case—had been filed in *Webster*, including one heavily publicized defense of *Roe* submitted on behalf of almost three hundred historians. A distinct majority of the amicus filings, however, sided with Missouri, and just six days before oral arguments, Attorney General Webster tendered a final reply brief in which he again sought to underscore how "the fact that abortion involves the purposeful termination of a potential human life takes it altogether outside the bounds of the right to privacy."[107]

The highlight of the April 26 hearing was the ten-minute presentation of former Solicitor General Charles Fried on behalf of the Bush Administration. As in the government's brief, Fried immediately told the justices that the United States was asking that *Roe* be reconsidered and overruled because "abortion is different" from the intimate or familial decisions to which the Court had given constitutional protection in other privacy rulings. Justice Kennedy asked Fried if he thus believed that *Griswold* was correct, and Fried replied "exactly," because *Griswold* concerned "a right which was well established" and "quite intimate intrusions into the details of marital intimacy." Kennedy wondered whether *Griswold* hence stood for "a right to determine whether to procreate," but Fried demurred, answering that "*Griswold* surely does not stand for that proposition." Kennedy inquired as to what right *Griswold* did represent, and Fried stammeringly responded, "the right not to have the state intrude into, in a very violent way, into the details—inquire into the details of marital intimacy." Both Kennedy and O'Connor pressed Fried to address the question of women's liberty interests, and as Fried sought to maintain his "search and seizure" emphasis, he tacitly reached back into his own personal history, telling Kennedy that "That is how the Court analyzed the matter in *Griswold*. That is how Justice Harlan analyzed the matter in his dissent in *Poe* v. *Ullman*, which is, in some sense, the root of this area of law."

Justice Brennan forced Fried to acknowledge that *Griswold* was, of course, a Fourteenth Amendment case, not a Fourth Amendment holding, and when Frank Susman, the lead attorney for Reproductive Health Services, replaced Fried at the podium, he termed his predecessor's argument "somewhat disingenuous." "There no longer exists any bright line between the fundamental right that was established in *Griswold* and the fundamental right of abortion that was established in *Roe*," Susman explained. "These two rights, because of advances in medicine and science, now overlap. They coalesce and merge," and "we need to deal with one right, the right to procreate. We are no longer talking about two rights." Susman's presentation was far more articulate than most, and he invoked the classic 1937 due process language of *Palko* in telling the Court that "Procreational interests are indeed implicit in the concept of ordered liberty, and neither liberty nor justice would exist without them. It is truly a liberty whose exercise is deeply rooted in this nation's history and tradition."[108]

At the justices' private conference on April 28, William Rehnquist set the tone for the *Webster* discussion by saying that he "Disagrees with *Roe* v. *Wade*" and that on all particulars, the Missouri restrictions should be affirmed and the circuit court decision that had voided them reversed. Justices White, O'Connor, Scalia, and Kennedy largely agreed, and with even John Stevens saying that he believed the appellate ruling was partially in error, Thurgood Marshall tallied only himself, Bill Brennan, and Harry Blackmun as being in dissent. Three days later the Chief Justice formally assigned himself the majority opinion in *Webster*, and within less than four weeks Rehnquist circulated an initial twenty-three-page draft to his colleagues. After successive sections discussed each of the Missouri provisions, Rehnquist's final paragraph concluded that *Webster* "affords us no occasion to revisit the holding of *Roe*" and hence "we leave it undisturbed," even while acknowledging that "we modify and narrow *Roe* and succeeding cases" by upholding the Missouri regulations. Byron White and Anthony Kennedy each joined Rehnquist's opinion without delay, and John Stevens sent the Chief Justice a long letter of response, explaining that while some portions were "extremely persuasive," one section—sustaining a statutory mandate that physicians comprehensively test for fetal viability prior to any abortion where the pregnancy appeared to be "twenty or more weeks gestational age"—was "a different story." Here, Stevens told Rehnquist, "you make no attempt to explain or justify your new standard" of review—whether such a regulation "reasonably furthers the state interest in protecting potential human life"—a standard under which

> the woman's interest in making the abortion decision apparently is given no weight at all. A tax on abortions, a requirement that the pregnant woman must be able to stand on her head for fifteen minutes before she can have an abortion, or a criminal prohibition would each satisfy your test. Because the test really rejects *Roe* v. *Wade* in its entirety, I would think that it would be much better for the Court, as an institution, to do so forthrightly rather than indirectly.

Stevens pointed out that Rehnquist paradoxically was upholding the viability testing requirement while otherwise suggesting that the state interest in potential life was of equivalent weight throughout pregnancy, and hence the viability test actually was analogous to many other restrictions which likewise would pass Rehnquist's new test:

> They do further the state's interest in protecting potential human life because they place an additional burden on the abortion decision, but the same result could be accomplished by requiring tests of the woman's knowledge of Shakespeare or American history.
>
> As you know, I am not in favor of overruling *Roe* v. *Wade*, but if the deed is to be done I would rather see the Court give the case a decent burial instead of tossing it out the window of a fast-moving caboose.

Three full weeks after Stevens's piercing note, Harry Blackmun circulated a draft dissent. He highlighted how "the majority labors to obscure what is at stake in this monumental case and to cloak what it actually has decided." The fact was that "the two isolated dissenters in *Roe*, after all these years, now have prevailed," for Rehnquist's claim that *Roe* was "undisturbed" was "totally meaningless." "The simple truth," Blackmun asserted, "is that *Roe* no longer survives . . . I rue the violence that has been done to the liberty and equality of women. I rue the violence that has been done to our legal fabric and to the integrity of this Court." Given the evasiveness of Rehnquist's opinion, Blackmun declared, "the majority invites charges of cowardice and illegitimacy to our door. I cannot say that these are undeserved."

Both Brennan and Marshall immediately endorsed Blackmun's circulation, and the very next day Sandra O'Connor circulated a concurrence indicating she would join only three of the five principal parts of Rehnquist's prospective majority opinion. Four days later Nino Scalia distributed a concurrence of his own joining only the same portions of the Rehnquist opinion as O'Connor, and John Stevens circulated a separate statement endorsing but a single section of the Rehnquist draft. The following day Rehnquist distributed an updated reprint, now acknowledging that while three parts would indeed speak for a majority of the Court, the crucial portion which John Stevens had so disparaged four weeks earlier would carry the votes of only himself, Byron White, and Anthony Kennedy. Six days later, on July 3, the final day of the Court's 1988–1989 term, the somewhat fragmented and definitely less than decisive judgment in *Webster* v. *Reproductive Health Services* was publicly announced.[109]

The first two substantive sections of Rehnquist's opinion spoke for a five-justice majority—O'Connor and Scalia as well as White and Kennedy—in reversing the circuit court's invalidation of a legislative preamble declaring that "The life of each human being begins at conception" and likewise upholding a statutory ban on any public facility or public servant assisting in the performance of an abortion. As to the latter, Rehnquist explained that "Missouri's refusal to allow public employees to perform abortions in public hospitals leaves a pregnant woman with the same choices as if the State had chosen not to operate any public hospitals at all." Compared to the Court's earlier decisions in *Maher* and *Harris*, this prohibition was "considerably less burdensome" than the denial of public funding, but the bottom line was that "the State need not commit any resources to facilitating abortions." The entire Court agreed that a third segment of the Missouri regulations merited approval, and on the crucial provision mandating viability testing, both O'Connor and Scalia agreed with Rehnquist's core trio that the requirement should not be struck down, but they declined to endorse the analysis which Rehnquist proffered on its behalf.

The "rigid trimester analysis . . . enunciated in *Roe*," Rehnquist stated for himself, White, and Kennedy, "is hardly consistent with the notion of a Constitution cast in general terms," for the "key elements of the *Roe* framework—trimesters and viability—are not found in the text of the Constitution or in any place else one would expect to find a constitutional principle." He went on to say that "we do not see why the State's interest in protecting potential human life should come into existence only at the point of viability," and volunteered somewhat defensively that *Griswold*, "unlike *Roe*, did not purport to adopt a whole framework, complete with detailed rules and distinctions, to govern the cases in which the asserted liberty interest would apply. As such, it was far different from the opinion, if not the holding, of *Roe*." The concluding three-vote section of Rehnquist's opinion retained the characterization of *Roe* as "undisturbed" that Blackmun had earlier mocked, but the previous declaration that "we modify and narrow *Roe*" had been slightly changed to now promise only that "we would modify and narrow *Roe*."

In her concurring opinion, Sandra O'Connor stated that "Unlike the plurality, I do not understand these viability testing requirements to conflict with any of the Court's past decisions," and she pointedly emphasized that "When the constitutional invalidity of a State's abortion statute actually turns on the constitutional validity of *Roe v. Wade*, there will be time enough to reexamine *Roe*. And to do so carefully." Requiring the viability tests, she explained, "does not impose an undue burden on a woman's abortion decision," especially since "the State's compelling interest in potential life postviability renders its interest in determining the critical point of viability equally compelling."

Antonin Scalia's concurrence took a far different stance than O'Connor's. Like John Stevens and Harry Blackmun previously, Scalia too agreed that the viability section of Rehnquist's opinion that O'Connor had not joined "would overrule *Roe*." Scalia emphasized that "I think that should be done, but would do it more explicitly," and he expressed regret that "today we contrive to avoid doing it." Abortion, Scalia declared, was a field where the Supreme Court "has little proper business since the answers to most of the crucial questions posed are political and not juridical," and he volunteered that O'Connor's assertion that *Webster* did not require the Court to confront *Roe* "cannot be taken seriously." The judicial result, Scalia added, is "a chaos that is evident to anyone who can read and count," and he went on to ridicule O'Connor's adoption of the "undue burden" standard, saying with regard to Missouri's viability testing requirement that "I know of no basis for determining that this particular burden (or any other for that matter) is 'due.'" Finally, Scalia expressed exasperation at "the irrationality of what we do today" and dismissively labeled O'Connor's treatment of viability as "similarly irrational."

However annoyed Scalia and O'Connor might have been with each other as the fourth and fifth votes in such an outspokenly discordant majority, the dissenters were even less happy. John Stevens in the end disagreed with almost every portion of Rehnquist's holding, but the principal dissent, in which both William Brennan and Thurgood Marshall joined, was Harry Blackmun's. The lack of majority support for Rehnquist's viability section had allowed Blackmun to dilute some of the most dire comments that had appeared in his first draft, but he still warned how "at every level of its review" the Rehnquist opinion obscured its intentions except for "winks, and nods, and knowing glances ... The simple truth is that *Roe* would not survive the plurality's analysis." Almost poetically, Blackmun said "I fear for the future. I fear for the liberty and equality of the millions of women who have lived and come of age in the 16 years since *Roe* was decided. I fear for the integrity of, and public esteem for, this Court."

Blackmun highlighted how "in flat contradiction to *Roe*," the Rehnquist opinion "concludes that the State's interest in potential life is compelling before viability," and he avowed that the plurality's attack upon *Roe*'s trimester framework was merely "a mask for its hostility to the constitutional rights that *Roe* recognized." Blackmun noted that neither the plurality nor O'Connor now made any reference to O'Connor's unfounded 1983 claim in *Akron* that *Roe* was on a "collision course" with itself, and he characterized Rehnquist's assertion that *Webster* would leave *Roe* "undisturbed" as "unadulterated nonsense." Blackmun underscored how "In a Nation that cherishes liberty," a woman's ability to determine "whether or not to carry a fetus to term must fall within that limited space of individual autonomy that lies beyond the will or the power of any transient majority." In *Roe*, he reiterated, "we did no more than discharge our constitutional duty," and while "For today, at least, the law of abortion stands undisturbed," Blackmun warned in closing that the indications of reversal "are evident and very ominous, and a chill wind blows."[110]

Right to life groups welcomed the announcement of *Webster* as a landmark victory, while many pro-choice activists insisted that *Roe*'s funeral was indeed at hand. James Bopp, Jr., the general counsel of the

National Right to Life Committee, asserted that "*Roe* is dead" and that "*Roe* and its progeny are de facto overruled," but more prudent observers quickly stressed that in essence *Webster* "decided nothing at all" and that the decision "actually is notable as much for the Court's caution and indecision as anything else." Two commentators castigated the Rehnquist opinion for trying to use a "backdoor approach" to "eviscerate *Roe* without explicitly overruling" it, an attempt that they condemned as failing to meet even "the most minimal standards of sound judicial decision-making." Abortion rights litigators, however, took particular note of how the tone of Justice O'Connor's concurrence "was significantly less hostile to *Roe*" than her 1983 and 1986 abortion opinions. For arguments in future abortion cases, two prominent law professors noted, "the real audience is one woman," for Sandra O'Connor "is in the position single-handedly to decide the future of abortion rights."[111]

The very same day that the high court handed down *Webster*, it accepted three abortion appeals from Minnesota, Ohio, and Illinois for argument during its upcoming 1989–1990 term. The enormous public reaction to *Webster*, however, centered far less on the Court's potential next step than on the new opportunities for state restrictions on abortion that the decision had made possible, and while a swiftly completed Gallup Poll showed that 53 percent of Americans disagreed with *Webster*, right to life proponents in many states swung into immediate action. Florida Governor Bob Martinez called a legislative session to consider new antiabortion measures, and like-minded legislators in Louisiana announced an all-out effort to return that state's law to a pre-*Roe* status whereby only those abortions necessary for saving a woman's life would be allowed.

Webster's signal that states could now significantly restrict abortion access was an even greater stimulus to pro-choice supporters than for right to lifers, and by early fall it was clear that *Webster* had given abortion rights advocates a considerable political boost. In mid-October Governor Martinez's legislative attempt went down to an embarrassing, nationally publicized defeat just a few days after the Florida Supreme Court had all but unanimously decreed that the privacy language added to Florida's *state* constitution nine years earlier—"Every natural person has the right to be let alone and free from governmental intrusion into his private life"—guaranteed a woman's right to choose abortion independent of whatever the U.S. Supreme Court might do in the federal realm. A measurable increase in pro-choice sentiment was also visible in the U.S. Congress, but the two most important manifestations of the new, post-*Webster* politics of abortion came in Virginia and New Jersey, the only two states with 1989 gubernatorial elections. Two outspokenly pro-choice Democrats—L. Douglas Wilder and Jim Florio—were opposing two antiabortion Republicans, and even well in advance of the actual November tallies, all evidence pointed to how significant an advantage both Wilder and Florio enjoyed because of their pro-choice stances. When both men did indeed prevail in the November 7 balloting, political observers all across the nation concluded that in the wake of *Webster*, an antiabortion position could be a serious hindrance for a candidate even in relatively conservative states.[112]

One state where the antiabortion consensus was not shaken by *Webster*, however, was Pennsylvania, and less than two weeks after the Virginia and New Jersey elections, Pennsylvania Governor Robert P. Casey signed into law an "Abortion Control Act" that had passed both houses of the state legislature by overwhelming margins. Several days later, the pro-choice plaintiffs in the Illinois abortion case which was scheduled for Supreme Court oral argument the very next week obtained an advantageous settlement from state Attorney General Neil Hartigan. Hence when the high court convened on November 29 to hear the abortion appeals it had accepted five months earlier, only *Hodgson* v. *Minnesota* and *Ohio* v. *Akron Center for Reproductive Health* remained on its docket, and the questions they presented were limited to issues of parental notification and consent with regard to pregnant teenagers. *Hodgson*, with pioneering physician Jane Hodgson as the lead plaintiff, had successfully challenged a state statute requiring advance notice to *both* parents of any pregnant teenager's request for an abortion, but the Eighth Circuit Court of Appeals, in a 7 to 3 en banc vote, had partially reversed the district court decision. Hodgson's attorneys had petitioned for Supreme Court review, while in the Ohio case, where the state had sought review, the Sixth Circuit Court of Appeals had affirmed a lower court invalidation of a somewhat similar notification measure. After hearing the oral arguments, some of the nine justices were both frustrated and befuddled by the degree of statutory minutiae the two cases presented. Although the initial conference discussion indicated that a tentative majority favored invalidating the Ohio statute and approving the Minnesota one, Sandra O'Connor, after further consideration of both cases with John Stevens, changed each of her votes so as to favor reversal of the circuit court results in both *Akron Center* and in *Hodgson*, so that now the Ohio statute would be approved while the Minnesota one would be rejected. Chief Justice

Rehnquist assigned the majority opinion in *Akron Center* to Anthony Kennedy, while John Stevens took charge of writing on behalf of the five justices—himself, Brennan, Marshall, Blackmun, and O'Connor—who would reject Minnesota's parental notification statute.[113]

Early in 1990 a federal district court blocked the implementation of much of Pennsylvania's new abortion measure, and in the American territory of Guam, another federal district court judge enjoined enforcement of a far more comprehensive antiabortion statute that had been approved by both the legislature and the governor. Idaho Governor Cecil Andrus vetoed a model antiabortion law that right to life forces had propelled through the state legislature, and the National Conference of Catholic Bishops garnered front-page coverage—and widespread criticism—with the announcement that they had hired the public relations firm of Hill & Knowlton to produce a multimillion dollar antiabortion propaganda campaign. In late April right to life forces mounted a march of more than 200,000 people in Washington, D.C., but far more notable—and certainly more surprising—was the stunning news that Connecticut, thanks to explicit support from the state's Pro-Life Council and at least tacit approval from the Hartford Archdiocese, had enacted a new statute affirmatively *codifying* the provisions of *Roe* v. *Wade*. Simple and direct—"(a) The decision to terminate a pregnancy prior to the viability of the fetus shall be solely that of the pregnant woman in consultation with her physician. (b) No abortion may be performed upon a pregnant woman after the viability of the fetus except when necessary to preserve the life or health of the pregnant woman"—the Connecticut law was a landmark pro-choice achievement. Pro-Life Council executive director Regina Smith, a ranking officer of the National Right to Life Committee, defended her group's action on the grounds that the postviability prohibition was a worthy attainment, but a small band of abortion opponents opposed the measure until the end, charging that the prolife leadership had been "snookered." When the state senate sent the bill to Governor William O'Neill for his signature on a final vote of 32 to 3, the most vociferous of the three opponents was Waterbury Republican Thomas F. "Tim" Upson, whose views differed enormously from those of his now eighty-six-year-old father.[114]

Although the Connecticut accomplishment was indeed unique, prochoice forces gradually were beginning to appreciate that right to life political opposition was not the only significant hurdle they were facing. "The legal struggle over abortion rights in the United States," one sympathetic observer pointed out, "has consistently taken for granted that so long as abortion is legal, physicians will be trained and available to perform them." Increasingly, however, evidence indicated that "More Doctors Shun Abortion," as a front-page *New York Times* headline put it. With over 85 percent of all abortions now being performed in specialized clinics rather than in full-service hospitals, "doctors who perform abortions say they are being heavily stigmatized" and feel "largely isolated from medical colleagues." Only some 12 percent of obstetrics and gynecology residency programs for new physicians were providing abortion training, and professional lack of interest, rather than actual opposition or fear of Operation Rescue harassment, seemed to characterize the dwindling medical commitment. Many clinics reported difficulties in recruiting doctors, even though the scientific consensus regarding abortion appeared sturdier than ever before. "The question of when the fetus acquires humanness," two even-handed experts explained, "comes down to this: When do nerve cells in the brain form synapses?" That takes place between the twenty-fifth and thirty-second weeks of gestation, and while pregnancy is "a period in which it is hard to draw discrete boundaries," that combination of brain development with the onset of fetal viability at twenty-four to twenty-six weeks gestation meant that "humanness and the ability to survive outside the womb develop at the same time."[115]

Unlike *Webster*, viability was not an issue in *Hodgson* or *Akron Center*, but between January and June of 1990 the Supreme Court, especially Justices Stevens and O'Connor, continued to wrestle privately with the tentative decisions that had been reached concerning Minnesota and Ohio's parental notice provisions. In mid-January, John Stevens changed his mind and decided he could largely join Anthony Kennedy's majority position in *Akron Center*. Two months later, Sandra O'Connor similarly endorsed all but one section of Kennedy's opinion, and twelve weeks after that, O'Connor informed her colleagues that in *Hodgson* she would now support only one half of Stevens's tentative majority and would instead side with Kennedy, White, Rehnquist, and Scalia to hold that the other portion of the Minnesota law, mandating notification but also providing young women with a "judicial bypass" option, would indeed pass legal muster.[116]

On June 25, 1990, the two decisions in *Hodgson v. Minnesota* and *Ohio v. Akron Center for Reproductive Health* were publicly announced. While most news coverage focused upon how a five-justice majority had upheld the notification-with-bypass portion of the Minnesota law, the most important although widely overlooked aspect of the rulings was O'Connor's joining with Stevens, Brennan, Marshall, and Blackmun to hold that Minnesota's two-parent notice requirement "does not reasonably further any legitimate state interest." It was the first time in her entire nine years on the Court that Sandra O'Connor had voted to invalidate *any* abortion restriction, and a supplemental opinion by Thurgood Marshall, speaking for himself, Brennan and Blackmun, reiterated that "*Roe* remains the law of the land" and stressed how that part of *Hodgson* "reaffirms the vitality of *Roe*." The Kennedy opinions in both *Hodgson* and *Akron Center* were understated and moderate, but a separate concurrence by Antonin Scalia restated his fervent view that "the Constitution contains no right to abortion" and that "the Court should end its disruptive intrusion into this field as soon as possible."[117]

Most abortion news in the immediate wake of *Hodgson* and *Akron Center* concerned an ultimately unsuccessful effort by antiabortion legislators in Louisiana to enact a rigid ban despite successive vetoes by Governor Buddy Roemer, but a far more crucial event took place on July 20, when Justice William J. Brennan, a veteran of thirty-four years on the Supreme Court, announced his retirement at age eighty-four. Just three days later, President George Bush nominated a little-known, fifty-year-old federal circuit judge from New Hampshire, David H. Souter, as Brennan's successor. Widespread efforts to discover what views, if any, Judge Souter might have on abortion proved completely unavailing, and at his mid-September confirmation hearings before the Senate Judiciary Committee, Souter politely declined to address the status of *Roe* v. *Wade* while emphasizing that "the due process clause of the Fourteenth Amendment does recognize and does protect an unenumerated right of privacy." Acknowledging a preference for John Harlan's approach in *Griswold*, Souter impressed the committee as a thoughtful moderate, and on October 2 the full Senate by a vote of ninety to nine confirmed him as the newest and most junior member of the Supreme Court.[118]

The only abortion-related case on the Court's 1990–1991 docket, *Rust* v. *Sullivan*, was a challenge to the gag rule that the U.S. Department of Health and Human Services had imposed on all medical organizations that received federal funds under Title X of the Public Health Service Act, prohibiting their doctors from in any way counseling or referring patients with regard to abortion. A 2 to 1 panel of the Second Circuit Court of Appeals had upheld the new regulations not long before two other Circuit Courts, the First and the Tenth, had found them unconstitutional, and in May 1990 seven justices had agreed that the Supreme Court should review the Second Circuit's decision. At oral argument on October 30, brand-new Justice Souter seemed somewhat skeptical of Solicitor General Kenneth W. Starr's defense of the gag rule, but when the justices assembled for their private conference on Friday, November 2, a narrow majority of five— Rehnquist, White, Scalia, Kennedy, *and* Souter—readily agreed that the regulations were constitutionally acceptable. Rehnquist assigned the majority opinion to himself, and four weeks later he circulated an initial draft. Only Byron White responded with an immediate endorsement, and early in 1991, as Harry Blackmun prepared a draft dissent, both Scalia and Kennedy recommended changes that the Chief Justice willingly adopted. By late February both of them had formally joined Rehnquist's opinion, but more than two additional months passed before David Souter suggested some further modifications that Rehnquist amiably incorporated after making only minor alterations. A reference to "traditional zones of free expression" had to be eliminated, Rehnquist privately told Souter, because otherwise "I fear it will give rise to an entire new body of doctrine based on that phrase—and I don't think we need any new doctrines in the First Amendment area." Likewise, Rehnquist also expanded an assertion that the regulations "do not impinge upon the doctor-patient relationship" to "do not significantly impinge," explaining that "I do not feel that we can categorically say that it does not impinge at all" and warning that "if we say it doesn't impinge at all I am sure that Harry could find some examples, however obscure, indicating *contra* to incorporate in his dissent."[119]

Shortly thereafter, Souter too formally endorsed Rehnquist's opinion, and on May 23, 1991, the 5 to 4 decision in *Rust* v. *Sullivan* was publicly announced. Rehnquist asserted that the federal government "is exercising the authority it possesses under *Maher* and *Harris*," the earlier abortion funding cases, and that in this instance as in those, "the Government has not discriminated on the basis of viewpoint; it has merely chosen to fund one activity to the exclusion of the other." The "difficulty that a woman encounters when a Title X project does not provide abortion counseling or referral," he candidly admitted, "leaves her in no different position than she would have been if the government had not enacted Title X." Additionally, the majority also insisted, in the language that Souter and Rehnquist had both worked on, that the gag rule regulations "do not significantly impinge upon the doctor-patient relationship. Nothing in them requires a doctor to represent as his own any opinion that he does not in fact hold." A physician, they contended, "is always free to make clear that advice regarding abortion is simply beyond the scope of the program."

Sandra O'Connor and John Stevens each filed individual dissents as well as joining different portions of Blackmun's dissent, but in a part of his dissent that also spoke for Thurgood Marshall as well as Stevens, Blackmun reiterated that *Roe* v. *Wade* and its progeny "are not so much about a medical procedure as they are about a woman's fundamental right to self-determination . . . 'Liberty,' if it means anything, must entail freedom from governmental domination in making the most intimate and personal of decisions."[120]

At the very same November 2 conference where the justices had resolved *Rust*, they had also voted not to hear the most notable gay rights case since *Bowers*, *Watkins* v. *U.S. Army*. Sergeant Perry J. Watkins, who had told the Army about his homosexual orientation both when he was drafted into the service in 1967 and again following 1971 and 1974 reenlistments, had filed suit in federal court nine years earlier, in 1981, when the Army had moved to discharge him because he was gay. U.S. District Judge Barbara J. Rothstein, citing a 1975 review in which the Army had expressly decided *not* to discharge Watkins because of his sexual preference—and the fact that Watkins was a female impersonator whose performances had been covered by the *Army Times* newspaper as early as 1971—had blocked both the discharge and a subsequent Army effort to deny Watkins another reenlistment. A Ninth Circuit Court of Appeals panel had reversed the reenlistment ruling and sent the case back to Rothstein for further action, and after she dutifully upheld the Army's refusal, Watkins took another government job and sought further review by the Ninth Circuit. In February 1988 a three-judge appellate panel had ruled for Watkins on the grounds that the Army's regulations punished soldiers simply on the basis of sexual *orientation*, rather than for sexual *acts*, a distinction which the panel majority held was constitutionally unacceptable even in the wake of *Bowers* v. *Hardwick*. One member, however, Circuit Judge Stephen Reinhardt, reluctantly disagreed, saying that although he believed the Supreme Court had "egregiously misinterpreted the Constitution in *Hardwick*," his colleagues erroneously were refusing to acknowledge that *Hardwick* represented the Supreme Court's "willingness to condone anti-homosexual animus in the actions of the government," such as the Army's behavior toward Watkins. As appellate judges they were required to follow that mandate, no matter how mistaken it might be. Reinhardt predicted that in time "history will view *Hardwick* much as it views *Plessy*," the Supreme Court's infamous 1896 endorsement of racial segregation, and said that he was "confident that, in the long run, *Hardwick*, like *Plessy*, will be overruled by a wiser and more enlightened Court."

Fifteen months later, in May 1989, a reconsideration of the panel decision by an eleven-judge en banc sitting of the Ninth Circuit resulted in a 7 to 4 ruling in favor of Watkins and against the Army, but this time simply on contractual rather than constitutional grounds. After considerable delay, the Bush administration requested Supreme Court reversal of even this modest holding, perhaps because in early 1990 the high court had turned aside a petition from an openly lesbian Army sergeant, Miriam Ben-Shalom, whose initial federal district court success in contesting a highly similar discharge action had been reversed by a hostile Seventh Circuit panel in August 1989. Without dissent, however, the Supreme Court turned aside the Bush administration's petition that it review *Watkins* just as it had Ben-Shalom's request nine months earlier, and some weeks later the Army agreed to grant Sergeant Watkins full retirement benefits and one hundred thirty-five thousand dollars in back pay.[121]

While the Supreme Court thus avoided two contrasting if not contradictory opportunities to revisit the basic issue it had dealt with so disdainfully four years earlier in *Bowers*, other appellate rulings continued to take place in cases almost as unusual as Michael Hardwick's. The Rhode Island Supreme Court unanimously upheld a Family Court child custody order, requested by a divorced woman's ex-husband, prohibiting her from having overnight male visitors whenever her three children were at home, and the U.S. Supreme Court declined review. In Maryland, an intermediate appellate court, reasoning that *Bowers* had expressly limited *Griswold*'s privacy protection to marital sexuality, affirmed a five-year felony sentence that one Steven Schochet had received after being convicted under the state sodomy statute for consensual, heterosexual fellatio. Concluding that *Bowers* likewise had now limited *Eisenstadt* simply to the realm of contraception, the Maryland judges explained that "The argument . . . that the Supreme Court has created or recognized a constitutional right of privacy for consensual, adult, heterosexual fellatio simply cannot stand." Schochet's attorneys appealed, and just a few weeks before the Supreme Court refused to review *Watkins*, a higher Maryland court hesitantly reversed the conviction. The state's sodomy statute, it ruled, should not be applied to consensual, heterosexual, noncommercial fellatio carried out in a private home, but the judges nonetheless opined that in the wake of *Bowers* "the constitutional issue presented here is a very difficult one."[122]

More than a year later, on a decidedly more encouraging note, an intermediate court in Texas cited state rather than federal constitutional grounds for voiding Texas's same-sex only antisodomy law. Remarking that "the Texas Constitution accords individuals greater safeguards to their personal freedom than its federal counterpart does," the Texas judges stated that "we can think of nothing more fundamentally private and deserving of protection than sexual behavior between consenting adults in private." Under the Texas law, they emphasized, gay people could be criminally prosecuted for "engaging in the same conduct in which heterosexuals may legally engage. In short, the State cannot make the same conduct criminal when done by one, and innocent when done by the other."

A few months later, the Kentucky Supreme Court likewise emphasized how the Kentucky Constitution's liberty guarantees "offer greater protection of the right of privacy than provided by the Federal Constitution as interpreted by the United States Supreme Court" and struck down Kentucky's same-sex sodomy statute. "Sexual preference, and not the act committed, determines criminality," the Kentucky majority noted, but dissenting Justice Donald C. Wintersheimer disparaged the privacy precedents reaching all the way back to *Griswold*. "'Emanations and penumbras,'" he asserted, "are more suited to a seance or a psychic experience than to a judicial opinion at any level in any court," for "Only the people have the right to decide what are constitutional rights" and "what are not."[123]

Early in 1991, as abortion clinics across the country continued to be hit by firebombings as well as by Operation Rescue harassment of employees and patients, the Supreme Court granted an Operation Rescue request that it review a Fourth Circuit decision affirming a lower court order that had utilized an 1871 civil rights statute to prohibit abortion opponents from obstructing the entrances to Virginia clinics. Initially only three justices—Rehnquist, White and Scalia—voted to grant Operation Rescue's petition, but several days later the necessary fourth vote suddenly materialized when Anthony Kennedy changed his mind and concluded that the appellate decision merited reconsideration. Meanwhile in Louisiana, right to life forces pushed another hard-line antiabortion bill through the state legislature and this time succeeded in overriding a gubernatorial veto, but the new law was quickly blocked by a federal district court. Operation Rescue mounted an intensive, month-long assault on abortion clinics in Wichita, Kansas, that was eventually curtailed by an energetic federal District Judge, Patrick F. Kelly, under the same law that was at issue in the Virginia case, but the Bush administration, asserting statutory tenets rather than hostility to abortion, announced its opposition to any application of the 1871 law against clinic antagonists.[124]

On June 27, eighty-two-year-old Justice Thurgood Marshall announced his retirement from the high court, and four days later President Bush nominated District of Columbia appellate judge Clarence Thomas as his successor. Thomas had no track record on abortion aside from some lavish praise he had once bestowed on a rhetorically extreme right to life magazine essay, but his generally conservative views led abortion rights proponents to testify against his nomination, even though Thomas himself insisted to the Senate Judiciary Committee that he had never at any time expressed an opinion about *Roe v. Wade*. Thomas's jurisprudential leanings, however, were soon overshadowed by the intense controversy sparked by Anita Hill's allegation of sexual harassment, and when Thomas's nomination was finally approved by the Senate on October 15 by the narrow margin of 52 to 48, no one counted him as a likely vote to reaffirm *Roe v. Wade*.[125]

The day after Thomas's confirmation, the eight sitting members of the Supreme Court heard oral argument in Operation Rescue's harassment appeal, *Bray v. Alexandria Women's Health Clinic*. Harry Blackmun asked the Justice Department attorney who spoke on the side of Operation Rescue whether the government was "asking that *Roe v. Wade* be overruled," and when the lawyer responded that "the right to abortion is not implicated here," Blackmun replied that "It seems to me you've slipped a stitch somewhere." Five days later, in a decision that made front-page news across the country, the Third Circuit Court of Appeals almost totally reversed the district court ruling that had voided Pennsylvania's 1989 Abortion Control Act. The plaintiffs in the suit, *Planned Parenthood of Southeastern Pennsylvania v. Casey*, said that they would immediately appeal to the Supreme Court, and Pennsylvania Attorney General Ernest D. Preate, Jr., declared that the state too would seek high court review. Just a few months later, on January 21, 1992, the Supreme Court announced that it would hear the joint appeals sometime that spring.

Antiabortion harassment continued as one right to lifer armed with a sawed-off shotgun wounded two people at a clinic in Springfield, Missouri, before escaping, but in the state of Washington, a ballot initiative incorporating the provisions of *Roe v. Wade* into state law was narrowly approved by popular vote. In early March, the Supreme Court announced that oral arguments in *Planned Parenthood v. Casey* would take place on April 22, and several weeks later the justices granted a Bush administration motion requesting that the U.S. government be allowed to join Pennsylvania in arguing that *Roe* should be overturned. In early April abortion rights forces turned out more than 500,000 people for a pro-choice march in the nation's capital, and just six days before the Supreme Court hearing in *Casey*, a three-judge panel of the Ninth Circuit Court of Appeals declared that *Roe* v. *Wade* was indeed still the law of the land while affirming the earlier district court invalidation of Guam's new antiabortion law.[126]

The April 22 oral argument in *Planned Parenthood of Southeastern Pennsylvania* v. *Casey* was widely heralded as the most important event in abortion litigation since January 1973. Kathryn Kolbert, a widely experienced ACLU attorney, was the lead counsel for the petitioners, and her initial remarks to the Court firmly enunciated the plaintiffs' resolutely determined stance:

> Whether our Constitution endows government with the power to force a woman to continue or to end a pregnancy against her will is the central question in this case.
>
> Since this Court's decision in *Roe* v. *Wade*, a generation of American women have come of age secure in the knowledge that the Constitution provides the highest level of protection for their child-bearing decisions.
>
> This landmark decision, which necessarily and logically flows from a century of this Court's jurisprudence, not only protects rights of bodily integrity and autonomy, but has enabled millions of women to participate fully and equally in society.

Kolbert emphasized that *Casey*'s issues were virtually identical to those which the Court had considered six years earlier while reaffirming *Roe* in *Thornburgh* v. *ACOG*, and she forcefully noted that "Never before has this Court bestowed and taken back a fundamental right that has been part of the settled rights and expectations of literally millions of Americans for nearly two decades." No justice interrupted Kolbert's impressively articulate opening until Sandra O'Connor spoke up. "You're arguing the case as though all we have before us is whether to apply *stare decisis* and preserve *Roe* v. *Wade* in all its aspects," she observed, tersely asking Kolbert whether she planned to address the specific questions posed by Pennsylvania's abortion restrictions. Kolbert responded affirmatively, pointing out that in addition to Pennsylvania's spousal notification requirement, which the lower courts had annulled, regulations identical to two other Pennsylvania measures, mandating state-prescribed "counseling" and then a twenty-four-hour "waiting period" before an abortion could be performed, had been struck down in *Thornburgh* and before that in *Akron*.

Antonin Scalia engaged Kolbert in an extended colloquy after she commented that pursuant to *Brown*, *Griswold*, and *Loving*, the scope of American liberty could not be restricted only to rights that were expressly recognized when the Fourteenth Amendment was ratified in 1868. Anthony Kennedy, just like O'Connor, encouraged Kolbert to address the specifics of Pennsylvania's provisions, but Kolbert again responded by reiterating that the single most crucial question was whether the "strict scrutiny" standard which the Court had applied in all abortion cases from *Roe* through *Thornburgh*—but not in *Webster*—would or would not be the criterion employed here. Chief Justice Rehnquist interjected two brief questions, but Kolbert encountered few additional interruptions, and she reserved her three final minutes of time for rebuttal.

Pennsylvania Attorney General Ernest D. Preate, Jr., had barely uttered his second sentence before Harry Blackmun broke in to remind him that *Roe* "does not provide for abortion on demand" and to ask him "Have you read *Roe*?" Preate assured Blackmun that he had, but he was able to resume his presentation only briefly before Sandra O'Connor peppered him with more than half a dozen questions after he contended that the state's spousal notice requirement should pass muster under O'Connor's "undue burden" standard. Both John Stevens and Anthony Kennedy followed up on O'Connor's skeptical questions, and then Antonin Scalia—who had dismissively attacked O'Connor's standard in *Webster*—asked Preate how he should go about determining what was an undue burden. Both Stevens and O'Connor also joined in asking Preate to describe the standard, and O'Connor moved on to quiz Preate as to whether the notification provision, by compelling a woman to speak, might present a First Amendment issue. Preate in his final moments explicitly requested that the Court overturn both *Akron* and *Thornburgh* as being "unwarranted extensions of *Roe*," and his time expired as Justice David Souter confronted him with an additional question about spousal notification.

U.S. Solicitor General Kenneth W. Starr began his remarks by saying that the Court should apply in *Casey* the minimal standard of review that Chief Justice Rehnquist had articulated in the plurality opinion in *Webster*. John Stevens broke in to ask Starr what position the government took on the question of whether a fetus was a Fourteenth Amendment person, and Starr replied that the government did not have one. O'Connor and Scalia each followed up on Stevens's query, and when Stevens prodded Starr again, Scalia had to come to the solicitor general's rescue. David Souter observed that even a complete prohibition of abortions would meet *Webster*'s rational basis standard, and Starr replied that a statute which failed to provide a life-of-the-mother exception could face "very serious questions." Souter pressed Starr further, but the solicitor sought to demur, leading Souter to tell him that "you're asking the Court to adopt a standard and I think we ought to know where the standard would take us." John Stevens spoke up in agreement, reiterating Souter's point that rational basis review would allow for a total prohibition accompanied by criminal penalties. Starr replied that any law lacking a maternal life exception would not pass such a test, and with his time at an end, Kathryn Kolbert returned to the podium for her final three minutes. She politely highlighted Starr's seeming acknowledgment that any statute other than a complete prohibition would survive *Webster*-style scrutiny, and in closing she challenged the Court to reaffirm both that "the right to choose abortion is fundamental" as well as *Roe* itself.[127]

Kolbert had vastly outperformed her two fellow advocates, but in the wake of the *Casey* argument, few observers saw any prospects for *Roe* beyond a further *Webster*-style slide into feeble irrelevancy. Scalia and the Rehnquist-White-Kennedy trio from *Webster* all remained in place, and although newly seated Justice Clarence Thomas had not said a word during the *Casey* hearing, he—if not David Souter, who of course had joined the Rehnquist-Scalia quartet in *Rust* just twelve months earlier—would almost certainly provide the fifth anti-*Roe* vote that Sandra O'Connor had refused to furnish back in *Webster*. Harry Blackmun and John Stevens alone remained from the once-large ranks of *Roe* supporters, and even the ostensibly liberal *New Republic*, in an editorial denouncing the "brazen judicial activism" of 1973, called upon the Court to "Dump *Roe*." In early June, the Court announced without further comment that *Bray v. Alexandria Women's Health Clinic* would be passed over and set for reargument sometime in the fall, and most observers concluded that if the Court was deadlocked at 4 to 4 over Operation Rescue's appeal, newly arrived Justice Thomas would become the deciding vote.[128]

Hence on Monday morning, June 29, 1992, the final day of the Supreme Court's term, virtually no one in the press or spectator sections of the courtroom was at all prepared for what ensued after the Chief Justice announced that the decision in *Planned Parenthood of Southeastern Pennsylvania v. Casey* was ready for announcement. For more than twenty-three years, ever since the Little Rock school case of *Cooper v. Aaron*, when all nine justices had jointly signed their names to a ringing reaffirmation of *Brown v. Board of Education of Topeka*, every signed opinion of the Court had borne the name of a single principal author. But on this day, in what scholars would later acknowledge as the most important statement by the Court in more than twenty-eight years, the decisive opinion in *Planned Parenthood* v. *Casey* would jointly bear the names of three coauthors: Sandra Day O'Connor, Anthony M. Kennedy, and David H. Souter.

Only on unusual occasions would any justice recite a sizable portion of a decision from the bench, but on this morning all three of the coauthors would read successive sections of their joint opinion, sections that had also been joined by both Harry Blackmun and John Paul Stevens, thus making them a full-fledged majority holding. As the realization of what the trio had wrought spread through the courtroom, tears came to the eyes of even experienced journalists as the language of the joint opinion gradually made more and more clear that the constitutional legacy of *Roe* v. *Wade* was not dead but instead was very much alive.

"Liberty finds no refuge in a jurisprudence of doubt," the trio's opinion memorably began. They indicated that they disagreed with the starkly alternative options that Kathryn Kolbert had pressed upon the Court at oral argument, but they acknowledged that "our decisions after *Roe* cast doubt upon the meaning and reach of its holding." They declared that "the essential holding of *Roe* v. *Wade* should be retained and once again reaffirmed," and they explained that

> *Roe*'s essential holding, the holding we reaffirm, has three parts. First is a recognition of the right of the woman to choose to have an abortion before viability and to obtain it without undue interference from the State. Before viability, the State's interests are not strong enough to support a prohibition of abortion or the imposition of a substantial obstacle to the woman's effective right to elect the procedure. Second is a confirmation of the State's power to restrict abortions after fetal viability, if the law contains exceptions for pregnancies which endanger a woman's life or health. And third is the principle that the State has legitimate interests from the outset of the pregnancy in protecting the health of the woman and the life of the fetus that may become a child. These principles do not contradict one another; and we adhere to each.

The trio went on to detail how the Fourteenth Amendment's Due Process Clause had provided constitutional protection for individual liberty for over a century; they quoted from John Harlan's opinion in *Poe* both before and after observing that "there is a realm of personal liberty which the government may not enter." In a segment that Justice O'Connor read from the bench, the opinion spoke of how people could disagree about "the profound moral and spiritual implications of terminating a pregnancy, even in its earliest stage. Some of us as individuals find abortion offensive to our most basic principles of morality, but that cannot control our decision. Our obligation is to define the liberty of all, not to mandate our own moral code."

In the next portion, after references to *Carey*, *Eisenstadt*, and the 1944 decision in *Prince* v. *Massachusetts*, Anthony Kennedy read from the bench that "These matters, involving the most intimate and personal choices a person may make in a lifetime, choices central to personal dignity and autonomy, are central to the liberty protected by the Fourteenth Amendment. At the heart of liberty is the right to define one's own concept of existence, of meaning, of the universe, and of the mystery of human life." In abortion, he went on, "the liberty of the woman is at stake in a sense unique to the human condition and so unique to the law." In light of the burdens a woman confronted in carrying a pregnancy to term, "Her suffering is too intimate and personal for the State to insist, without more, upon its own vision of the woman's role, however dominant that vision has been in the course of our history and our culture. The destiny of the woman must be shaped to a large extent on her own conception of her spiritual imperatives and her place in society." Accepting that "in some critical respects the abortion decision is of the same character as the decision to use contraception," the opinion cited *Griswold*, *Eisenstadt*, and *Carey* and stated that "We have no doubt as to the correctness of those decisions. They support the reasoning in *Roe* relating to the woman's liberty." The trio added that "It was this dimension of personal liberty that *Roe* sought to protect, and its holding invoked the reasoning and the tradition" of those precedents in "granting protection to substantive liberties of the person. *Roe* was, of course, an extension of those cases," but they emphasized that "the reservations any of us may have in reaffirming the central holding of *Roe* are outweighed by the explication of individual liberty we have given combined with the force of *stare decisis*."

Undoubtedly the most powerful and eloquent section of the opinion was the ensuing discussion of *Roe* and *stare decisis* that had been crafted by David Souter. "For two decades of economic and social developments, people have organized intimate relationships and made choices that define their views of themselves and their places in society, in reliance on the availability of abortion in the event that contraception should fail. The ability of women to participate equally in the economic and social life of the Nation has been facilitated by their ability to control their reproductive lives." Souter reviewed "the succession of cases most prominently exemplified by *Griswold*" and described *Roe* as "an exemplar of *Griswold* liberty." He conceded that "time has overtaken some of *Roe*'s factual assumptions," but he underscored that

> the divergences from the factual premises of 1973 have no bearing on the validity of *Roe*'s central holding, that viability marks the earliest point at which the State's interest in fetal life is constitutionally adequate to justify a legislative ban on non-therapeutic abortions. The soundness or unsoundness of that constitutional judgment in no sense turns on whether viability occurs at approximately 28 weeks, as was usual at the time of *Roe*, at 23 to 24 weeks, as it sometimes does today, or at some moment even slightly earlier in pregnancy, as it may if fetal respiratory capacity can somehow be enhanced in the future. Whenever it may occur, the attainment of viability may continue to serve as the critical fact, just as it has done since *Roe* was decided.

Souter went on to stress how "An entire generation has come of age free to assume *Roe*'s concept of liberty in defining the capacity of women to act in society, and to make reproductive decisions; no erosion of principle going to liberty or personal autonomy has left *Roe*'s central holding as a doctrinal remnant," just as "no changes of fact have rendered viability more or less appropriate as the point at which the balance of interests tips."

Then Souter moved on to the core of his argument concerning *stare decisis*:

> Where, in the performance of its judicial duties, the Court decides a case in such a way as to resolve the sort of intensely divisive controversy reflected in *Roe* and those rare, comparable cases, its decision has a dimension that the resolution of the normal case does not carry. It is the dimension present whenever the Court's interpretation of the Constitution calls the contending sides of a national controversy to end their national division by accepting a common mandate rooted in the Constitution.
>
> The Court is not asked to do this very often, having thus addressed the Nation only twice in our lifetime, in the decisions of *Brown* and *Roe*. But when the Court does act in this way, its decision requires an equally rare precedential force to counter the inevitable efforts to overturn it and to thwart its implementation. Some of those efforts may be mere unprincipled emotional reactions; others may proceed from principles worthy of profound respect. But whatever the premises of opposition may be, only the most convincing justification under accepted standards of precedent could suffice to demonstrate that a later decision overruling

the first was anything but a surrender to political pressure, and an unjustified repudiation of the principle on which the Court staked its authority in the first instance. So to overrule under fire in the absence of the most compelling reason to reexamine a watershed decision would subvert the Court's legitimacy beyond any serious question.

Concluding that crucial section of the majority's holding, Souter recapitulated how "A decision to overrule *Roe*'s essential holding under the existing circumstances would address error, if error there was, at the cost of both profound and unnecessary damage to Court's legitimacy, and to the Nation's commitment to the rule of law. It is therefore imperative to adhere to the essence of *Roe*'s original decision, and we do so today."

In a long portion of their opinion which spoke only for themselves, and not for the full five-vote majority, O'Connor, Kennedy, and Souter addressed *Roe*'s crucial concept of viability. Prefacing their discussion with a reminder that "Liberty must not be extinguished for want of a line that is clear," the trio conceded that "Any judicial act of line-drawing may seem somewhat arbitrary, but *Roe* was a reasoned statement, elaborated with great care." However, the trio said, explaining a holding that would draw the separate support of *Casey*'s four dissenters, "we must overrule those parts of *Thornburgh* and *Akron I* which, in our view, are inconsistent with *Roe*'s statement that the State has a legitimate interest in promoting the life or potential life of the unborn." Nonetheless, viability, which they characterized as "the time at which there is a realistic possibility of maintaining and nourishing a life outside the womb," was an essential part of *Roe*'s holding, for "there is no line other than viability which is more workable." They bluntly added that "a woman who fails to act before viability has consented to the State's intervention on behalf of the developing child," but they reiterated that "the immediate question is not the soundness of *Roe*'s resolution of the issue, but the precedential force that must be accorded to its holding."

Roe, they reminded once again, "speaks with clarity in establishing not only the woman's liberty but also the State's 'important and legitimate interest in potential life.' That portion of the decision in *Roe* has been given too little acknowledgment by the Court in subsequent cases." Terming *Roe*'s "trimester format" an "elaborate but rigid construct," O'Connor, Kennedy, and Souter proceeded to outline *Casey*'s new standard:

> Though the woman has a right to choose to terminate or continue her pregnancy before viability, it does not at all follow that the State is

prohibited from taking steps to ensure that this choice is thoughtful and informed. Even in the earliest stages of pregnancy, the State may enact rules and regulations designed to encourage her to know that there are philosophic and social arguments of great weight that can be brought to bear in favor of continuing the pregnancy to full term and that there are procedures and institutions to allow adoption of unwanted children as well as a certain degree of state assistance if the mother chooses to raise the child herself.

They explained that "We reject the trimester framework, which we do not consider to be part of the essential holding of *Roe*," since "in practice it undervalues the State's interest in potential life." They commented that "not every law which makes a right more difficult to exercise is, ipso facto, an infringement of that right," and restated how the "rigid" trimester format "does not fulfill *Roe*'s own promise that the State has an interest in protecting fetal life or potential life. *Roe* began the contradiction by using the trimester framework to forbid any regulation of abortion designed to advance that interest before viability."

Citing Justice O'Connor's prior articulation of the undue burden standard, and tracing its usage all the way back to *Bellotti I* in 1976, the trio announced that "Not all burdens on the right to decide whether to terminate a pregnancy will be undue," and stated that "the undue burden standard is the appropriate means of reconciling the State's interest with the woman's constitutionally protected liberty." Admitting that not all prior invocations of the undue burden criterion had been consistent, O'Connor, Kennedy, and Souter underscored how "A finding of an undue burden is a shorthand for the conclusion that a state regulation has the purpose or effect of placing a substantial obstacle in the path of a woman seeking an abortion of a nonviable fetus." They stressed that "the means chosen by the State to further the interest in potential life must be calculated to inform the woman's free choice, not hinder it," but they proceeded to delineate why Pennsylvania's twenty-four-hour waiting period requirement was not an "undue burden" or a "substantial obstacle" to "the right to make family decisions and the right to physical autonomy" that *Roe* protected. The trio added that with regard to mandatory counseling, "a State is permitted to enact persuasive measures which favor childbirth over abortion, even if those measures do not further a health interest." Then, after a strongly worded section, joined by Blackmun and Stevens, affirming the Third Circuit's invalidation of the spousal notice provision, the trio—plus in one instance Stevens—proceeded to uphold two lesser-noted restrictions that had been sustained by the Third Circuit.[129]

The primary dissenting opinion was authored by William Rehnquist and joined by Byron White, Antonin Scalia, and Clarence Thomas. Rehnquist forthrightly declared that "We believe that *Roe* was wrongly decided, and that it can and should be overruled." He asserted, after citing *Pierce*, *Meyer*, *Loving*, *Skinner*, *Griswold*, and *Eisenstadt*, that those precedents "do not endorse any all-encompassing 'right of privacy,'" and he contended that "the Court in *Roe* read the earlier opinions upon which it based its decision much too broadly." The Court "was mistaken in *Roe* when it classified a woman's decision to terminate her pregnancy as a 'fundamental right,'" and the *Roe* Court "reached too far when it analogized the right to abort a fetus to the rights involved in *Pierce*, *Meyer*, *Loving*, and *Griswold*, and thereby deemed the right to abortion fundamental."

Rehnquist's second emphasis, however, was to insist that the *Casey* trio actually was preserving far less of *Roe* than it imagined. "*Roe* continues to exist," the Chief Justice acknowledged, "but only in the way a storefront on a western movie set exists: a mere facade to give the illusion of reality." The trio's undue burden standard, he argued, is "plucked from nowhere" and "created largely out of whole cloth by the authors of the joint opinion," while their substantial obstacle test "is based even more on a judge's subjective determinations than was the trimester framework." *Roe* v. *Wade*, Rehnquist concluded, "stands as a sort of judicial Potemkin Village, which may be pointed out to passers by as a monument to the importance of adhering to precedent. But behind the facade, an entirely new method of analysis, without any roots in constitutional law, is imported to decide the constitutionality of state laws regulating abortion."[130]

Casey's second dissent, written by Antonin Scalia and joined by Rehnquist, White, and Thomas, unsurprisingly took a far harsher and more sarcastic tone. Scalia mocked Kennedy's comments concerning the "concept of existence, of meaning, of the universe," and complained, after citing the trio's opening statement that "Liberty finds no refuge in a jurisprudence of doubt," that "to come across this phrase in the joint opinion—which calls upon federal district judges to apply an 'undue burden' standard as doubtful in application as it is unprincipled in origin—is really more than one should have to bear." Scalia termed the trio's standard both "inherently manipulable" and "hopelessly unworkable," and decried "the joint opinion's verbal shell game" while lambasting O'Connor for how this present version of "undue burden" admittedly differed from her prior usages. He complained that "It is difficult to maintain the illusion that we are interpreting a Constitution rather than inventing one, when we amend its provisions so breezily," and he taunted the trio by derisively charging that "Reason finds no refuge in this jurisprudence of confusion." Regaining his footing, Scalia remarked that "*Roe* created a vast new class of abortion consumers and abortion proponents by eliminating the moral opprobrium that had attached to the act," but he went on to compare O'Connor, Kennedy, and Souter's stance in *Casey* to that taken by Chief Justice Roger Brooke Taney in *Dred Scott* v. *Sandford* in 1856. "We should get out of this area, where we have no right to be, and where we do neither ourselves nor the country any good by remaining."[131]

Both John Stevens and Harry Blackmun filed individual opinions joining the principal sections of the trio's statement but dissenting from the validation of Pennsylvania's "persuasive" counseling and waiting period provisions. Stevens noted that of the fifteen justices who had sat on the high court since *Roe* was decided, eleven—every one except for *Casey*'s four dissenters—had supported *Roe* at least to the extent of the *Casey* majority. *Roe*, Stevens explained, "was a natural sequel to the protection of individual liberty established in *Griswold*," and "*Roe* is an integral part of a correct understanding of both the concept of liberty and the basic equality of men and women."

Harry Blackmun's opinion was by turns joyful, pensive, and elegiac. Three years earlier, after *Webster*, "All that remained between the promise of *Roe* and the darkness of the plurality was a single, flickering flame. Decisions since *Webster*," such as *Akron Center* and *Rust*,

> gave little reason to hope that this flame would cast much light. But now, just when so many expected the darkness to fall, the flame has grown bright.
>
> I do not underestimate the significance of today's joint opinion. Yet I remain steadfast in my belief that the right to reproductive choice is entitled to the full protection afforded by this Court before *Webster*. And I fear for the darkness as four Justices anxiously await the single vote necessary to extinguish the light.

"Make no mistake," Blackmun went on, "the joint opinion of Justices O'Connor, Kennedy, and Souter is an act of personal courage and constitutional principle." He highlighted all the portions of the trio's holding that spoke for the five-vote majority, and he pointedly observed that "What has happened today should serve as a model for future Justices and a warning to all who have tried to turn this Court into yet another political branch." He emphasized how the Court had voided the spousal notice provision, and he stressed with regard to the other restrictions which the trio had declined to void in this context of a purely facial challenge how he was "pleased that the joint opinion has not ruled out the possibility that these regulations may be shown to impose an unconstitutional burden" once they had been tested by actual practice. "I am confident," Blackmun declared, "that in the future evidence will be produced" showing how they did indeed represent "substantial obstacles" to Pennsylvania women with unwanted pregnancies.

Blackmun restated how "compelled continuation of a pregnancy infringes upon a woman's right to bodily integrity by imposing substantial physical intrusions and significant risks of physical harm" while also depriving "a woman of the right to make her own decision about reproduction and family planning." By "restricting the right to terminate pregnancies," Blackmun added, "the State conscripts women's bodies into its service." He firmly defended both the appropriateness of the trimester framework and the constitutional necessity of upper-level, "strict scrutiny" review of antiabortion regulations. But Blackmun saved his most pointed comments for *Casey*'s dissenters, remarking that "At long last, The Chief Justice and those who have joined him" had finally admitted that they did indeed want to overturn *Roe* v. *Wade*. "The Chief Justice's criticism of *Roe*," Blackmun bluntly maintained, "follows from his stunted conception of individual liberty." Given Rehnquist's "exclusive reliance on tradition, people using contraceptives seem the next likely candidate for his list of outcasts."

Blackmun ended on an apprehensive and deeply personal note. "In one sense," he noted, the approach of the *Casey* majority

> is worlds apart from that of The Chief Justice and Justice Scalia. And yet, in another sense, the distance between the two approaches is short—the distance is but a single vote.
>
> I am 83 years old. I cannot remain on this Court forever, and when I do step down, the confirmation process for my successor well may focus on the issue before us today. That, I regret, may be exactly where the choice between the two worlds will be made.[132]

Public reaction to *Casey*'s stunningly unanticipated result was both voluminous and oddly contradictory. Some pro-choice groups, with their judgment distorted both by organizational agendas and by pessimistic expectations, self-defeatingly tried to insist that "*Roe* v. *Wade* is dead," while right to life activists castigated the O'Connor-Kennedy-Souter trio as "backstabbing" members of a "wimp bloc." Editorialists welcomed the outcome, with the *New York Times* observing that *Roe* had been "a brilliant resolution of seemingly irreconcilable interests" and the *Washington Post* sagely suggesting that "it is possible that those who oppose the 1973 ruling have peaked in terms of their impact on the judicial aspect of this debate." Harvard law professor Laurence H. Tribe correctly noted that the trio opinion "makes sense and puts the right to abortion on a firmer jurisprudential foundation than ever before," and New York University's Ronald Dworkin stated that the coauthors' conclusions "considerably strengthen the case for *Roe*" by giving women's right to choose "an even more secure basis."

Those most upset by *Casey* of course included *Roe*'s two most consistently outspoken critics, former Judge Robert H. Bork and *The New Republic*. Terming the trio opinion constitutionally "radical," Bork proclaimed that "the Constitution contains not one word that can be tortured into the slightest relevance to abortion, one way or the other." Bork again declared that in *Roe* the Court had "offered no legal reasoning for taking the abortion issue from the people," and *The New Republic* announced that "*Casey* is far less defensible than *Roe*" while grousing that "We can imagine any number of plausible ways that *Roe* might have been clearly overturned." Expanding its criticism to cover "the questionable logic" of *Griswold* and even John Harlan's dissent back in *Poe*, *The New Republic* pronounced that "It was *Roe*'s lack of persuasive constitutional support that made the Court look illegitimate to begin with." Abortion, the magazine insisted in a remarkably self-contradictory oxymoron, was simply "a right that should be protected by politics." Unsurprisingly, *The New Republic* failed to describe exactly what role—if any—either the Supreme Court or the Constitution would be left to play if the correct conclusion to be drawn from *Griswold* and *Roe* was that rights ought to be protected only by politics, and not by the judiciary or the law.[133]

Consistent with its resolution of *Casey*, the Supreme Court several months later declined to consider Guam's appeal of the Ninth Circuit decision that had invalidated its hard-line antiabortion statute just a few days before the *Casey* argument. Both Byron White and William Rehnquist—but not Clarence Thomas—joined Antonin Scalia's brief dissent from the Court's refusal to hear the case,[134] and a week later the Court also denied a request to review a Fifth Circuit ruling that had cited *Casey* in upholding Mississippi's imposition of a twenty-four-hour waiting period requirement similar to Pennsylvania's.[135] Early in 1993 the Court also dismissed Louisiana's appeal of the lower court decisions that had voided its all but complete ban on abortions, and not long thereafter the justices additionally refused to stay the enforcement of a new twenty-four-hour waiting period provision in North Dakota.[136]

Early in January 1993, however, in a 6 to 3 decision authored by Antonin Scalia and joined by Byron White, William Rehnquist, Anthony Kennedy, Clarence Thomas, and, in large part, David Souter, the Supreme Court reversed the Fourth Circuit's decision in *Jayne Bray* v. *Alexandria Women's Health Clinic* and vindicated Operation Rescue's claim that the Ku Klux Klan Act of 1871 could not be used by federal judges to combat right to lifers' physical harassment and obstruction of abortion clinics. Writing in dissent, John Stevens observed that "the error that infects the Court's entire opinion is the unstated and mistaken assumption that this is a case about opposition to abortion. It is not. It is a case about the exercise of federal power to control an interstate conspiracy to commit illegal acts." Sandra O'Connor, whose dissent, like Stevens's, was joined by Harry Blackmun, likewise concluded that "This case is not about abortion" but "whether a private conspiracy to deprive members of a protected class of legally protected interests gives rise to a federal cause of action."[137]

On January 22, 1993, the twentieth anniversary of *Roe* v. *Wade* and *Doe* v. *Bolton*, newly inaugurated President Bill Clinton revoked the Reagan-Bush ban on abortion counseling or referral by federally funded clinics that the Supreme Court had upheld two years earlier in *Rust* v. *Sullivan*. Abortion rights supporters celebrated the step as a tangible sign of how the United States had an outspokenly pro-choice president for the first time since *Roe* had been decided, but just six weeks later much of the happiness turned to horror when forty-seven-year-old Dr. David Gunn, who performed abortions at clinics in Florida, Alabama, and Georgia, was shot in the back three times and killed by a thirty-one-year-old right to life activist, Michael F. Griffin, outside a Pensacola clinic. Gunn had long been targeted for harassment by abortion opponents both in Florida and Alabama, and while Operation Rescue founder Randall Terry had repeatedly emphasized that "the doctor is the weak link," Michael Griffin had been participating in a demonstration organized by a different but similar group, Rescue America, just moments before murdering Gunn. One witness told reporters that "It looked like they were just happy," but Rescue America's regional director in Pensacola, former Ku Klux Klansman John Burt, who had himself been convicted of attacking another Pensacola clinic seven years earlier, expressed pro forma regret at Gunn's assassination. Rescue America's national director, Don

Treshman, termed Gunn's killing "unfortunate" but emphasized that as a result, "quite a number of babies' lives will be saved." Treshman characterized Gunn as "a mass murderer in a class with his moral forebears in Nazi Germany and the Soviet Union," and Michael Bray, the spouse of Jayne Bray and himself a convicted felon for a series of Washington-area clinic bombings eight years earlier, made the same point even more explicitly: "From the standpoint of preventing further murders at the hands of Dr. Gunn, the actions of Mr. Griffin could be looked at as a good thing. He should be acquitted of any charges, because his actions were done in defense of people who were scheduled to die."

A spokesman for the National Right to Life Committee sought to dismiss Griffin as "a nutcake," and the U.S. Catholic Conference condemned Gunn's murder, admitting that it "makes a mockery of the pro-life cause." But the most perceptive and astute antiabortion reactions came, quite appropriately, from *Roe* v. *Wade*'s home city of Dallas, where the president of Texans United for Life, Bill Price, frankly confessed that "there has been a philosophical or even moral groundwork laid for assassinating abortionists by certain people in the pro-life movement, and I think they bear some of the blame." Gunn's killing, Price emphasized, "is a defining point in the history of this struggle. Responsible leaders have to speak out against this. If they don't, we will just become a bunch of terrorists."

Many right-to-life activists, however, rejected Price's judgment. Six months later, in August 1993, Rachelle "Shelley" Shannon, a thirty-seven-year-old Oregon woman who had written repeated letters of support to the imprisoned Michael Griffin, telling him that "I know you did the right thing" and "I wish I could trade places with you," shot and wounded Dr. George R. Tiller, the well-known operator of a Wichita clinic. Tiller's wounds were sufficiently minor that he returned to work the very next day—just as Shannon was being apprehended in Oklahoma—but some right-to-life leaders once again openly applauded the shooting. Andrew Burnett of Advocates for Life Ministries volunteered that "I'm supportive of what she did. It was a courageous act." Dawn Stover, an Oregon colleague of Shannon's, stated that "We have been saying abortion is murder, but we have been hypocritical in not treating it that way. Any one of us would use force to protect the lives of our children. We should not view the pre-born any differently." Since 1973, she added, "30 million children have been killed. Now we have one abortionist dead and one wounded. My goodness, who's winning here?"

Rescue America's Don Treshman ominously observed that "We are sure to see more of these incidents," and the very next day Dr. George W. Patterson, the owner of four southeastern abortion clinics, was murdered in Mobile, Alabama, under circumstances that left it unclear as to whether Patterson was an intended or a random victim. The identity of Patterson's killer was not immediately known, but Pensacola right-to-life leader Paul Hill announced that "If indeed a pro-life individual killed Abortionist Patterson, it would be justifiable assault."

Even prior to the shootings of Tiller and Patterson, Dallas's Bill Price had publicly denounced the tactics of Operation Rescue and similar groups and pointedly warned that "there is a tremendous amount of hate and anger in the fringe of this movement." Not long thereafter, Price confirmed that now even *he* was receiving threats of physical harm from more extreme right-to-lifers.[138]

EPILOGUE

Liberty and Sexuality,
1994-1998

Dr. David Gunn's March 10, 1993, murder at the hands of Michael F. Griffin was only the first of five abortion clinic killings that "right-to-life" activists committed during 1993 and 1994. On July 29, 1994, Dr. John Bayard Britton and a volunteer escort, retired Air Force Lt. Col. James H. Barrett, were shot to death outside another Pensacola, Florida, clinic. Five months later, on December 30, 1994, two receptionists at different clinics in Brookline, Massachusetts, Shannon Lowney and Leanne Nichols, were murdered by yet another antiabortion gunman.

During those years, the vulnerability of clinics and abortion providers to deadly terrorist violence seemed to dwarf all the other political and legal dangers that *Roe's* legacy and its defenders had endured in the years since 1973. But the onslaught of terrorism, bloody as it was, proved short-lived: the three subsequent years witnessed both no further shootings and a significant decline in the number of attacks and mass blockades visited upon clinic facilities. This evolution reflected the decline of right-to-life activism as a truly mass movement, but it also reflected the success that both newly muscular federal law enforcement efforts and consistently supportive court rulings had in combatting violent antiabortion protests.[1]

The early months of 1994 witnessed the successful prosecution of Michael Griffin for his killing of Dr. Gunn and the conviction of Rachelle "Shelley" Shannon for her attempted murder of Dr. George R. Tiller in Wichita, Kansas, in August 1993. Those months also witnessed a symbolically important Supreme Court ruling upholding pro-choice groups' ability to use the federal Racketeer-Influenced Corrupt Organizations (RICO) conspiracy statute to pursue civil damage suits against antiabortion activists and an even more significant legislative victory in the overwhelming congressional passage of the new Freedom of Access to Clinic Entrances (FACE) Act of 1994.

The Supreme Court's unanimous RICO decision, in *National Organization for Women* v. *Joseph Scheidler*, mandated that NOW and several Chicago-area clinics could proceed against the well-known Scheidler, and his Pro-Life Action Network, without having to prove that any specifically "economic" motive underlay antiabortion activists' coordinated efforts to close down clinics. Although the case originally was filed in 1986, the January 1994 Supreme Court ruling may mark only a midpoint in its life. In 1997 a U.S. district judge certified it as a nationwide class action suit on behalf of "all women's health centers in the United States at which abortions are performed," and in 1998, after a seven week trial, a Chicago jury found the defendants liable. Further appeals were planned.[2]

When Michael Griffin's murder trial got under way in Pensacola on February 28, 1994, his defense attorneys attempted to shift the blame for the three shots Griffin had fired into the back of the forty-seven-year-old Dr. Gunn on to local Rescue America regional director John Burt, whose antiabortion exhortations had inflamed Griffin's feelings. Griffin and Burt had first met only two months before the killing, and the Florida jurors refused to be diverted. On March 5, after less than three hours' deliberation, they found the defendant guilty of first degree murder. The thirty-two-year-old Griffin was immediately sentenced to life imprisonment, with no release possible for at least twenty-five years.[3]

Three weeks later Shelley Shannon was convicted of attempting to murder Dr. Tiller after confessing to the shooting on the witness stand while insisting that she had intended only to wound, not kill, him. In April, after also confessing to a series of attacks on West Coast clinics, Shannon was sentenced to more than ten years imprisonment. That fall, Shannon was indicted on federal charges for *ten* 1992–1993 arson and/or acid attacks on clinics in Oregon, California, Nevada, and Idaho, and in mid-1995 she pled guilty to six of them and was sentenced to an additional twenty years in prison on top of her penalty for shooting Tiller. Federal investigators had hoped that Shannon might implicate others in her crimes, but in the end she did not.[4]

The FACE legislation, which authorized both criminal charges and civil sanctions against violent abortion opponents, was in part a response to the Supreme Court's January 1993 ruling in *Bray* v. *Alexandria Women's Health Clinic* that federal judges could not use the Ku Klux Klan Act of 1871 against protesters who physically obstructed patients' and providers' access to clinic entrances. The

FACE Act began to make its way through Congress in mid-1993, and both the Senate and the House approved slightly different versions of the measure in November. After agreement was reached on final language, first the House, by a vote of 241 to 174, and then the Senate, by a margin of 69 to 30, gave final approval to the bill, and on May 26, 1994, President Bill Clinton signed it into law. "No person seeking medical care, no physician providing that care should have to endure harassment or threats or obstruction or intimidation or even murder from vigilantes who take the law into their own hands because they think they know what the law ought to be," Clinton declared.[5]

Clinton and his administration also took a resolutely forthright position in insisting that recalcitrant states *had* to abide by newly liberalized federal statutory language providing for Medicaid coverage of abortions occasioned by rape or incest. That slight loosening in the strictures of the annually adopted Hyde Amendment for fiscal year 1994 had represented less than pro-choice lobbyists initially had hoped to win, but the modest expansion was the first time since 1981 that the Hyde limitations had allowed for federally funded abortions other than in cases where a woman's very life was endangered. As many as fourteen states—Arkansas, Colorado, Illinois, Kentucky, Louisiana, Michigan, Missouri, Montana, Nebraska, North Dakota, Oklahoma, Pennsylvania, South Dakota, and Utah—announced their intention to defy the new regulations implementing the rape and incest coverage, but administration officials were unyielding and a series of federal court suits in Colorado, Michigan, Montana, Arkansas, and Louisiana—all decided between mid-May and the end of July—rapidly whipped the laggards into line.[6]

One day after the Senate gave final approval to FACE, President Clinton nominated First Circuit Court of Appeals Chief Judge Stephen G. Breyer as the Supreme Court successor for Justice Harry A. Blackmun, who had announced his end-of-term retirement five weeks earlier. Breyer, who in 1965 as one of Arthur Goldberg's clerks had played a principal role in *Griswold*, had been a close runner-up a year earlier when Clinton had named D.C. federal appellate judge Ruth Bader Ginsburg to the Court to succeed the retiring Byron R. White. Ginsburg's elevation in place of White had represented a one-vote gain for pro-choice voices on the High Court, and Blackmun's replacement with Breyer—who, like Ginsburg, won easy confirmation by the Senate—allowed *Roe*'s author to step down with the comfort that *Casey*, if not all of *Roe* itself, now commanded a six-to-three margin of support on the Court.[7]

Pennsylvania's mandatory counseling and twenty-four-hour waiting period regulations, which the Court in *Casey* had declined to find facially unconstitutional, finally took effect only two weeks prior to Blackmun's announcement amid considerable media attention. Lower court reviews had delayed implementation for almost two full years, with the Third Circuit Court of Appeals refusing Planned Parenthood's request for a reexamination of the challenged provisions while explicitly acknowledging that the Supreme Court's 1992 holding "meant that a future 'as applied' challenge . . . would be possible" after the legislation took effect and that such a post-enforcement challenge "might yield a different result on its constitutionality." Initially the implementation of the twenty-four-hour waiting period restriction meant that women in Pennsylvania had to make two separate clinic visits, the first to hear the state-mandated "counseling" information from a physician and the second for the abortion itself, but within a few months Pennsylvania clinics were able to avert the first trip by having patients listen by telephone to a tape of a doctor reciting the required information. In May 1995, however, state authorities successfully insisted that Pennsylvania providers had to "orally inform" their patients in person, and the two-visit requirement was reinstated. North Dakota and Ohio clinics used telephone messages to comply with their states' waiting period statutes, but in Mississippi, like Pennsylvania, women had to make two separate in-person visits to a doctor.[8]

Potentially far more encouraging for abortion patients and providers was the mid-May news, released just four days after the Senate's passage of FACE, that the European pharmaceutical giant Roussel Uclaf, in response to intense political pressure from the Clinton administration, was turning over its U.S. patent rights and technology for the abortifacient drug RU-486 at no cost to the New York-based nonprofit Population Council. Lawrence Lader's small Abortion Rights Mobilization (ARM) already had manufactured a few doses of mifepristone (the scientific name for the synthetic steroid known more popularly under its Roussel Uclaf designation RU-486) in the United States, but the costs and difficulties involved in producing a large-scale supply of mifepristone for the entire American market would require both significant financing and a major manufacturer. ARM was aiming to launch its own modest American clinical trials of RU-486—no patent infringement would occur if patients received the drug free—but the Population Council envisioned large-scale fall 1994 clinical trials so that the federal Food and Drug Administration (FDA) would be able to complete its review of RU-486 and approve the drug for nation-wide use by sometime in mid-1995. Right-to-life advocates threatened a boycott of other Roussel products, but news reports made it clear that FDA approval and widespread availability of RU-486 would not represent an abortion rights panacea. European experience showed that mifepristone—which impedes a fertilized egg from attaching to the uterine wall—could be used effectively only during the first eight or nine weeks of pregnancy. Indeed, an initial oral dose of mifepristone had to be followed by oral or vaginal application of a second drug, misoprostol, to trigger uterine contractions. This would require at least two medical appointments plus twenty-four-hour-a-day access to emergency medical care should rare but dangerous heavy bleeding ensue. Many women might prefer the "natural" quality of such a "medical" miscarriage to the "surgical" invasiveness of vacuum aspiration, but it required a more time-consuming commitment than a onetime clinic visit.[9]

Abortion proponents emphasized how the availability of mifepristone, which any doctor could administer in a private office, could radically diminish the battleground atmosphere that surrounded many of the well-known specialty clinics where most abortions were performed. The advent of FACE, however, coupled with more and more court rulings restricting and penalizing obstructive or violent protests, signalled that the heyday of right-to-life blockades was quickly fading. That pattern was highlighted on June 30, 1994, when the U.S. Supreme Court, in a case from Melbourne, Florida, *Madsen v. Women's Health Center,* upheld by a six-to-three margin a state trial court injunction that prohibited antiabortion protesters from coming within thirty-six feet of the clinic's doors and driveway. Antonin Scalia penned an angry dissent, which was joined by fellow justices Anthony M. Kennedy and Clarence Thomas, but the majority opinion authored by Chief Justice William H. Rehnquist—no friend of abortion rights—cited the repeated instances of illegal conduct by Operation Rescue activists in upholding both the buffer zone provision and a prohibition on excessive noise.[10]

The first federal arrests for criminal violations of FACE took place in Milwaukee before the new law was hardly twelve days old. A few weeks later, when Operation Rescue, Rescue America, and Joseph Scheidler's Pro-Life Action Network announced plans for a major early July protest in President Clinton's hometown of Little Rock, Arkansas, their press-release assertions turned into empty threats when only about sixty demonstrators showed up to target Little Rock's four clinics. Courtroom challenges to the constitutionality of FACE—which provided both fines and multiyear prison sentences for anyone who "by force or threat of force or by physical obstruction, intentionally injures, intimidates or interferes with or attempts to injure, intimidate, or interfere with any person because that person is or has been, or in order to intimidate such person or any other person or any class of persons from, obtaining or providing reproductive health services"—were quickly and consistently turned aside.[11]

But neither FACE nor any other law could guarantee an end to antiabortion terrorism, and that unavoidable fact was brought home in painfully bloody fashion on the morning of July 29, when Dr. John Bayard Britton, age sixty-nine, and his volunteer driver, retired Air Force Lt. Col. James H. Barrett, seventy-four, were shot to death outside a Pensacola abortion clinic by Paul J. Hill, a well-known right-to-life activist. Armed with a 12-gauge shotgun, Hill had waited for Britton, Barrett, and Barrett's wife, June (who was wounded in the arm), and then methodically gunned them down as they sat in the cab of Barrett's pickup truck in the clinic parking lot. Hill was immediately taken into custody and charged with two counts of capital murder.

Ironically, few observers familiar with Pensacola's history of antiabortion violence were surprised that Hill, age forty, had finally picked up a gun. A onetime minister, Hill had first become a public figure in right-to-life circles soon after the 1993 killing of Dr. David Gunn, when he spoke out in support of Gunn's killer, Michael F. Griffin. Early in 1994, Hill had told the *Dallas Morning News,* "If an abortionist is about to violently take an innocent person's life, you are entirely morally justified in trying to prevent him from taking that life." Hill had insisted to other reporters that he had no intention of acting on his own advice, saying "Violence is not my calling," but in a painfully eerie coincidence, a February 1994 magazine article that profiled John Bayard Britton as "The Abortionist" also pictured Hill as Pensacola's most dangerous protester. "Paul Hill believes in the potentialities of murder," the profile noted; a photo caption added that among regular demonstrators, Paul Hill is "the one who frightens the employees [at the clinic]"—where five months later he would kill Britton and Barrett.

Three months before Hill committed the two shootings, anti-abortion activists met privately at a hotel outside Chicago for an intense debate about the acceptability of murder as a political act. Hill was the most vociferous in support of doctor killing, and Joseph Scheidler later acknowledged that even he was "surprised at how much support there was for Paul Hill." Asked about Hill, newly named Operation Rescue national director Flip Benham of Texas told reporters, "I think what he's saying is heresy, it's sin, it's murder, it's wrong, and it solves nothing, only makes things worse," but Andrew Burnett, an Oregon activist who sided with Hill, said that Benham had lost the debate. "Flip thought he was going to change people's minds. He didn't; he polarized people even farther." Even Benham admitted that Hill's position had prevailed: "I think I was in the minority."[12]

Support for Hill's view had been growing ever since Michael Griffin's killing of David Gunn in March 1993, and Hill was far from the only well-known right-to-life voice who had been advocating the politics of murder. Michael Bray, a Maryland pastor and convicted clinic bomber, had spoken up immediately on Griffin's behalf and subsequently expanded upon his views in both an academic essay and a paperback book memorably entitled *A Time to Kill*. "With the passage of the FACE bill," Bray explained, "the central government has confirmed itself in all three branches as an adversary of Christians." Griffin's killing of Gunn was "justifiable homicide," since the abortions that Gunn had been scheduled to perform that day did not take place and some perhaps never did, "thus firmly establishing the shooting as sensible and salutary." In his book, published by Andrew Burnett's ironically named Advocates for Life, Bray reiterated, "Where baby killing takes place, it is right and good to intervene with force to prevent such a blasphemous deed. The thorny issue of overthrowing our apostate government is another subject."[13]

In the wake of Britton's and Barrett's murders, federal law enforcement authorities stepped up their protection of other clinics and doctors and launched a new investigation into whether any criminal conspiracy linked Hill to other "justifiable homicide" advocates such as Bray, Donald Spitz, the head of Pro-Life Virginia, and David Trosch, a Roman Catholic priest from Alabama. The angry April debate outside Chicago had led to the creation of a new network among those activists who rejected Benham and Operation Rescue's antimurder stance, the inaptly named American Coalition of Life Activists (ACLA). But press attention quickly focused not on the ACLA network but on attorney Michael R. Hirsh, a recent graduate of Pat Robertson's Regent University School of Law in Virginia Beach, Virginia, who had been representing Paul Hill in a preexisting Florida court case and who also had written both a master's thesis and a law review article defending the killing of abortion doctors. The *Regent University Law Review* quickly withdrew and destroyed all copies of the newly printed article, but the thesis—dedicated to Michael Bray—remained available for public review. As with Bray, Hirsh's argument was plausible *if* one agreed with his fundamental premise: "If we believe that an unborn child is in fact a child . . . no consistent basis exists for denying the logical conclusion of our rhetoric: That Michael Griffin's act is justified." Hirsh contended that in killing David Gunn, Griffin had "acted prudently and reasonably," but Hirsh's employer—Robertson's American Center for Law and Justice—fired him when he sought to expand his representation of Paul Hill to include defending the murders of Britton and Barrett.[14]

In addition to facing state capital murder charges, Hill was indicted in federal court under the criminal provisions of FACE. After U.S. District Judge Roger Vinson refused to allow Hill to introduce a "justifiable homicide" defense, Hill dismissed his court-appointed attorneys and, acting as his own attorney, passively refused to cross-examine prosecution witnesses or introduce any of his own during a speedy, three-day trial. On October 5, after just two hours of jury deliberations, Hill was found guilty.[15]

Less than four weeks later Hill's state court trial got under way under similar circumstances. Michael Hirsh was unqualified to represent a Florida defendant facing the death penalty, and again Hill acted on his own behalf. Hill was allowed to introduce a slightly revised version of Hirsh's canceled article as a defense brief, but he again declined to cross-examine prosecution witnesses or to call any of his own. Testimony established that Hill had purchased the 12-gauge pump-action shotgun two days before the murders and had practiced with it twice at a public shooting range. The jury took only twenty minutes to find Hill guilty, and then deliberated for an additional four hours before recommending the death penalty rather than life imprisonment. One month later Judge Frank Bell affirmed the jury's finding and sentenced Hill to death, a sentence endorsed by Operation Rescue national director Flip Benham. Hill told a television interviewer, "I am certainly guilty of no crimes," and went on to say that his shooting of Britton and Barrett was "honorable."

"I'm not saying that what I did was legal, but I'm saying that what I did was moral."

Hill later revealed that he had started thinking about bloodshed after Shelley Shannon had shot George Tiller: "I was encouraged and emboldened by her example." Hill said he had made up his mind eight days in advance and had bought the new shotgun only after one he owned had jammed when he was practicing with it. Asked why he had shot James Barrett as well as Dr. Britton, Hill replied, "Because he was directly between the abortionist and me. I was actually aiming at the abortionist, but he was directly between us." Hill volunteered that he believed in the death penalty—"I couldn't have shot that abortionist if I didn't"—and wanted his own sentence to be carried out, since martyrdom could be politically valuable: "I am hoping it will be upheld and that I will be executed. . . . I think I can save more people dead than alive."[16]

On the medical front, the fall of 1994 brought news that several physicians had successfully begun small-scale tests using another drug, methotrexate, in place of mifepristone (RU-486) to induce early term miscarriages. In addition, the Population Council announced that its initial trials of RU-486 at half a dozen Planned Parenthood clinics across the country were showing that such "medical" abortions were highly popular with most women who underwent the procedure.[17]

In the November elections, Wyoming voters rejected by an overwhelming margin of 69 to 31 percent an antiabortion initiative that right-to-life activists had placed on the statewide ballot. Nationally, however, Republican congressional gains of 39 seats in the House of Representatives and 5 in the Senate meant that the new Congress would be more heavily antichoice—some 218 out of 435 House members and 45 of 100 senators—than at any other time since *Roe v. Wade*.[18]

Deadly right-to-life terrorism reappeared the day before New Year's Eve when a twenty-two-year-old antiabortion protester, John C. Salvi III, gunned down receptionist Shannon Lowney, age twenty-five, at a Planned Parenthood clinic in the Boston suburb of Brookline and then drove a mile and a half down Beacon Street to kill a second receptionist, Leanne Nichols, age thirty-eight, at a Preterm Health Services clinic. Five other people were wounded, including a Preterm security guard who returned fire, forcing Salvi to drop a bag that contained an ammunition purchase receipt, which enabled law enforcement investigators to identify him. As police tried to find him, Salvi drove south and the very next day opened fire outside the Hillcrest Clinic in Norfolk, Virginia. A Norfolk Fire Department arson investigator happened to witness the shooting and immediately summoned police; Salvi was arrested in his pickup truck just a few blocks away.

A student hairdresser whom acquaintances viewed as a withdrawn and deeply religious Roman Catholic, Salvi seemed potentially unbalanced, yet the day before the Brookline killings he had gone to a gun range to practice with his rifle. Questions about Salvi, however, were quickly overshadowed by the defiantly happy reactions of some antiabortion radicals. Asked about Salvi's attack, Donald Spitz told reporters, "It's justified, it's moral, it was a righteous act," for "babies deserve to be defended at any cost." Don Treshman of Rescue America declared, "We're in a war. . . . The only thing is that until recently the casualties have only been on one side. There are 30 million dead babies and only five people on the other side, so it's really nothing to get all excited about."[19]

In a far different response to the killings, Boston's Archbishop Bernard Cardinal Law, an outspoken opponent of abortion, asked for a temporary moratorium on anticlinic protests. Some responded to his request, but Operation Rescue's Flip Benham called it "unconscionable" and the American Coalition of Life Activists (ACLA) distributed a hit list of twelve abortion doctors whom it labeled the "Deadly Dozen." Salvi's parents expressed their regrets over the shootings and apologized for not having gotten psychiatric help for their son after earlier religious delusions. Seven months later, after repeated hearings, a Massachusetts state trial court found Salvi mentally competent to stand trial, and in March 1996 a jury rejected his insanity defense after nine hours of deliberations and found him guilty. Salvi was sentenced to two consecutive terms of life imprisonment without possibility of parole; eight months later he committed suicide in his prison cell using a plastic bag. Only a few news reports highlighted how Michael Bray's Washington-area church sponsored a banquet to honor the actions of Michael F. Griffin, Paul J. Hill, and John C. Salvi III.[20]

While neither shootings nor arson attacks could be prevented by court rulings, in the aftermath of the Brookline killings there were an increasing number of both state and federal judicial decisions aimed at clamping down on dangerous antiabortion protests. Montana's Supreme Court affirmed a ten-year sentence that had been meted out to one protester who had deluged Bozeman clinic owner

Dr. Susan Wicklund with death threat letters that both prosecutors and jurors judged to be the real thing. In Fargo, North Dakota, where antiabortion protests had been a constant fact of life since the Fargo Women's Health Organization, North Dakota's only clinic, first opened in the fall of 1981, U.S. District Judge Rodney S. Webb ordered one particularly menacing demonstrator to remain 100 feet away from both the clinic and its staff members at all times. A Fargo ordinance prohibiting residential picketing was struck down by an appeals court, but when demonstrators brought civil damage actions against the city and its police officers after some protest arrests were dismissed, the federal courts dismissed the protesters' claims.[21]

As intensified law enforcement further reduced abortion opponents' ability to obstruct clinic services by blockading entrances and harassing staff members, right-to-life groups turned to a new method of attacking abortion providers: civil damage suits brought on behalf of women who had had unsatisfactory clinic experiences. Taking the lead in this effort were Louisville, Kentucky, attorney Theodore H. Amshoff, Jr., and Mark Crutcher, founder of Life Dynamics, a well-funded litigation-sponsorship group based in Denton, Texas.

Both men predicted a raft of what one newspaper called "costly settlements and well-publicized jury verdicts against doctors," but their assertions—particularly Crutcher's—of a large and ever-growing caseload of suits on behalf of women who supposedly had been injured by abortion doctors proved impossible to substantiate: comprehensive searches of nationwide judicial and news information databases turned up evidence of only a handful of such cases. Crutcher's professed hope was that aggressive litigation might eventually make insurance coverage unavailable to abortion providers, but he and Amshoff had a further goal as well: to legitimate the notion that women who years later came to regret an earlier abortion could file suit claiming "emotional trauma." That idea had no basis in precedent and generated no courtroom support, but Amshoff was able to litigate successfully at least two cases—one in Pittsburgh, another in Birmingham—in which women had died as the result of improperly performed procedures.[22]

Amshoff's ability to pursue such cases was the result of something that most abortion proponents were loath to discuss in public: "There's a lot of bad medicine being practiced out there in the name of choice," as Dr. Warren Hern, the country's best-known abortion provider, told the *New York Times.* No worse example existed than Dr. Thomas W. Tucker, age fifty, an operator of three clinics in Alabama and Mississippi whose conduct led to the death of Angela Hall, a twenty-one-year-old mother of five who went to Tucker's Birmingham clinic in April 1994 to have a Norplant contraceptive device removed from her arm. Another patient had died in 1991, and Tucker already faced professional charges resulting from that death. Just a few days after Ms. Hall's demise, Tucker's Mississippi medical license was suspended, and two months later he surrendered his Alabama one. In December 1996 a Birmingham jury awarded Hall's family $10 million in damages following a trial that Tucker declined to attend.

But Tucker was not alone. Soon after John Bayard Britton's killing, news reports revealed that the physician who had replaced him, Steven C. Brigham, already had had his medical license suspended in both New York and Georgia and had surrendered it in Pennsylvania. New Jersey hearings on professional charges against Brigham, who had no specialty training in obstetrics and gynecology, showed women had suffered both uterine perforations and cervical lacerations during second-trimester abortions. Early in 1995 Florida suspended Brigham's license and subsequently revoked it; in February 1998 Brigham was convicted of insurance fraud in New York and faced several years of imprisonment.

Early in 1996 Mark Crutcher and Life Dynamics published an impressively footnoted compendium of every recorded complaint lodged against any abortion provider since—and in some instances even before—*Roe* v. *Wade*. The book suffered from both a weird title—*Lime 5: Exploited By Choice*—and a complete use of numbered pseudonyms in place of doctor's real names, but copies of the volume were sent to every member of Congress *and* to every state legislator in all fifty states. Crutcher quoted Warren Hern's criticism that "there's a lot of crummy medicine being practiced out there in providing abortion services," but the book's failure to name names made its recitation of medical horror stories numbingly impersonal. Crutcher, however, like Michael Bray, was no one's fool; his assertion that "the abortion industry needs to acknowledge that they are not being destroyed by any pro-life success but by one of their own failures, . . . [namely that] they have been unable to make abortion socially acceptable," was uncomfortably close to the mark. His further observation that "the abortionist basically exists without a support network, either within or outside the abortion industry," was one few providers would dispute. But Crutcher's pose as primarily a foe of bad medicine was decidedly incomplete; early in 1997 one newspaper, covering a Crutcher speech at the annual dinner of an ostensibly mainstream right-to-life organization, reported that when questioned "Crutcher declined to express an opinion about violence that is directed against abortion clinics."[23]

Even well before the murders committed by Paul Hill and John Salvi, NARAL president Kate Michelman had acknowledged how "provider availability is rapidly becoming the Achilles heel of the pro-choice and reproductive freedom movement." One response to that growing realization was the creation of Medical Students for Choice as a network for incipient pro-choice doctors; another was Planned Parenthood of New York City's initiative to offer abortion-services training in its clinics to young M.D.'s who were in residency training programs at New York hospitals. Research data showed that fewer and fewer hospitals were offering either abortion training or abortions; by the early 1990s only some 7 percent of abortions nationwide took place in hospitals while almost 70 percent were performed at clinics. One chairman of an obstetrics and gynecology program stressed that "the freestanding clinics are much less expensive and much more user-friendly," but an editorial in the *New England Journal of Medicine* rued how the clinics are "isolated and marginalized from the mainstream of our health-care system." A dean at Yale's medical school observed, "If abortion could be more a part of obstetrical practice and not isolated into abortion clinics, we'd be a lot before off," and early in 1995 the American Council for Graduate Medical Education mandated abortion training for all obstetrics and gynecology residents except conscientious objectors.[24]

Many abortion providers acknowledged that right-to-life harassment was less of a problem for them than loneliness and ambivalence. One New England doctor who gave up doing abortions said harassment was not the problem: "I could have put up with some more, but I felt no sense of community support at all. I could have taken a lot more abuse," but the absence of encouragement was enervating. "That demoralized me. It made me pretty bitter." The most comprehensive research—carried out by a onetime clinic owner who also had been president of the National Abortion Federation (NAF), the major providers' group—showed that "the vast majority of abortion workers experience minimal strain despite extensive antiabortion harassment and violence." In a different vein, however, many providers privately admitted to negative feelings concerning "repeaters," women who were returning for a fourth or fifth abortion, and some supportive students of clinic cultures worried about the counseling women received at at least some facilities: "as long as abortion providers share a view of abortion as stigmatized and morally reprehensible, clients will be serviced, but not well-served."[25]

Statistics showed a small, year-by-year decline in the overall number of American abortions during the early 1990s, but researchers were disinclined to attribute the modest decreases to either right-to-life harassment or the concentration of abortion services at freestanding clinics. Difficulty of access involving travel distance appeared to have some effect, but state laws imposing twenty-four-hour "waiting periods," such as those in Pennsylvania and Mississippi, seemed not only to cause some women to travel to less restrictive neighboring states, and others to delay their abortions until later in pregnancy, but also to lead to an approximately 10 percent overall decline in abortions, at least among Mississippi women.[26]

Mississippi was a typical out-of-the-limelight abortion battleground. Up until Susan Hill's National Women's Health Organization, the operator of eight clinics reaching from Florida to Wisconsin, opened the Jackson Women's Health Organization in February 1995, there had been just one provider in the entire state, Dr. Joseph Booker, Jr., who worked in both Jackson and Gulfport. Booker daily had to cope with the efforts of full-time protester Roy McMillan, who was supported by his spouse, Dr. Beverly Smith, a former abortion provider. McMillan had signed a public petition endorsing Paul Hill's killing of Britton and Barrett—"whatever force is legitimate to defend the life of a born child is legitimate to defend the life of an unborn child"—and when the new second clinic opened, McMillan transferred his efforts there. Clinic employees were met with repeated threats of deadly force from McMillan, and within several months federal prosecutors sought and obtained a FACE injunction against McMillan, forcing him to come no closer to the clinic than the far side of the adjoining street. McMillan then shifted his focus back to Booker's clinic, but the legacy of Paul Hill meant that no one took McMillan's ongoing presence lightly.[27]

In Dallas Dr. Norman Tompkins, who had endured perhaps more personal harassment than any other single provider—and who subsequently had left town and stopped performing abortions—successfully pursued a federal civil RICO action against Operation Rescue and thirty-three individual protesters. Tompkins won an $8.4 million judgment from a Dallas jury, but he had no illusions about ever being able to collect more than a small fraction of the award. Several years earlier Portland, Oregon's Lovejoy clinic had won an $8.2

million judgment against Advocates for Life but had been unable to collect more than about $20,000. Likewise, just a year earlier Planned Parenthood of Houston had won more than $200,000 in actual damages and $1 million in punitive damages in a lawsuit against Operation Rescue, but success in collecting the judgment was limited to such a symbolic effort as seizing office furniture that yielded a grand sum of $3,325 when sold at sheriff's auction.[28]

By the spring of 1995 pro-choice forces were winning virtually all of their battles, both in court and on clinic sidewalks, against dangerously obstructionist opponents of abortion, but in June the national abortion debate began to experience its most significant alteration since the Supreme Court's resounding decision in *Planned Parenthood* v. *Casey* three years earlier.

Prior to June 14, 1995, the phrase "partial birth abortion" had hardly appeared in print anywhere in America. The label had no pedigree whatsoever in medical terminology, but that did not stop either the National Right to Life Committee or Florida Republican representative Charles T. Canady from applying it to a late term abortion technique that Ohio provider Dr. Martin Haskell had detailed in a paper delivered at a September 1992 NAF medical seminar in Dallas. For pregnancies of twenty weeks or more, Haskell had found it preferable to remove the fetus from the womb largely intact, after having collapsed the skull so that the fetal head could exit the cervical os, rather than remove it in pieces. As Haskell described it, his technique, which he termed "dilation and extraction," or "D & X," "differs from classic D & E [dilation and evacuation] in that it does not rely upon dismemberment to remove the fetus. Nor are inductions or infusions used to expel the intact fetus," an older, more dangerous method for late term abortions.

Ten months later the *American Medical News,* a professional weekly, published an excellent story on how both Haskell and Dr. James McMahon of Los Angeles had pioneered the technique, which sometimes was called "intact D & E" instead of "D & X." Any such abortion was a three-day procedure, requiring two preparatory days of cervical dilation, and together Haskell and McMahon performed approximately 450 such procedures a year. McMahon, like Warren Hern, who used a different procedure, specialized in postviability third trimester abortions involving fetal defects; Haskell performed *previability* twenty- to twenty-four-week late second trimester abortions, of which he estimated 80 percent were elective rather than medically indicated.

Representative Canady and the National Right to Life Committee, however, of course had no interest in distinguishing between pre- and postviability abortions; their hope was to somehow once again outlaw *all* abortions, and the Partial-Birth Abortion Ban Act that Canady introduced on June 14 was a first step in that direction: any doctor who "partially vaginally delivers a living fetus before killing the fetus and completing the delivery" could be jailed for up to two years and also could be civilly sued by either the fetal parents or its *maternal* grandparents! Following a pro-forma one-day hearing, Canady's own House Judiciary subcommittee approved the bill on a party-line vote of 7 to 5, and six days later the full Judiciary Committee did the same by a margin of 20 to 12. Abortion politics were beginning to reflect just what Republican control of Congress could entail.[29]

Right-to-life activists received an even more publicized boost in mid-August when Norma McCorvey, "Jane Roe" of *Roe* v. *Wade,* suddenly jettisoned her pro-choice stance and signed on with Reverend Flip Benham's Operation Rescue. Both McCorvey and her partner, Connie Gonzales, were working at a Dallas clinic when Benham succeeded in relocating Operation Rescue's office to rental space next door. Initial hostility soon evolved into quasi-friendly, teasing exchanges between McCorvey and the very personable Benham; one magazine commented on "the peculiar warmth" they had developed. Benham understandably appealed to what one journalist termed McCorvey's "insatiable yearning for love and attention," a yearning that pro-choicers had never adequately satisfied. In addition, as McCorvey emphasized in her 1994 autobiography, her retrospective realization that in 1970 Sarah Weddington could have helped her get an abortion, but chose not to, greatly intensified her resentment toward her onetime lawyer. "I was nothing to Sarah and Linda [Coffee], " McCorvey groused, "nothing more than a name on a piece of paper." When Weddington in her own 1992 autobiography revealed for the first time that she had obtained a Mexican abortion well before *Roe,* McCorvey's anger turned to fury. "When I told her then [in 1970] how desperately I needed one, she could have told me where to go for it. But she wouldn't because she [thought she] needed me to be pregnant for her case." A front page *New York Times* news story stressed "the immense symbolic importance" of McCorvey's defection, but her metamorphosis actually had little to do with abortion and far more with how Benham gave her the warmth and respect she rarely had felt from *Roe*'s supporters.[30]

One critic who assigned too much import to McCorvey's conversion was the pseudo-feminist writer Naomi Wolf, who claimed that "McCorvey should be seen as an object lesson for the prochoice movement." In a histrionic essay in the *New Republic,* Wolf called for "a radical shift in the pro-choice movement's rhetoric and consciousness about abortion" and denounced what she called the movement's "abandonment of . . . an ethical core." Hoping to represent what she said were "millions of Americans who want to support abortion as a legal right but still need to condemn it as a moral iniquity," Wolf espoused "a moral framework that admits that the death of a fetus is a real death." Contending that "our current pro-choice rhetoric leads to disaster," Wolf advocated "a new abortion rights language" and "an abortion rights movement willing publicly to mourn the evil . . . that is abortion." Wolf seemed oblivious to the myriad difficulties that would ensue—for a movement, for organizations, for individuals—were they to embrace the notion that what they were championing and defending was in its essence an "evil." Her stance went well beyond that of the Common Ground Network for Life and Choice, a conversation-between-opponents venture that right-to-life lawyer Andrew Puzder and clinic executive B. J. Isaacson-Jones had pioneered in St. Louis. Indeed, even Wolf herself finally questioned the wisdom of her notion that labeling abortion a "necessary evil" strengthened pro-choice defenses: "Let's pray that I'm not wrong about this," she fretted. "God forbid the discourse changes and we lose *Roe.* I'll be the first to fall on my sword."[31]

On November 1, 1995, the full House of Representatives, by an overwhelming vote of 288 to 139, passed the Partial-Birth Abortion Ban Act that Representative Canady and the Judiciary Committee had put forward five months earlier. Seventy-three Democrats joined with all but fifteen Republicans in backing the measure. The bill did allow a physician an "affirmative defense" against criminal charges if a supposed "partial birth" abortion was the only way in which a woman's life could be saved, but the measure contained no reference to fetal age, thereby potentially criminalizing *any* abortion—even previability ones early in the second trimester—in which the method of fetal evacuation might be covered by Canady's ambiguously vague language.

Six days later the U.S. Senate began floor debate on the House-passed bill, but opponents of the act, hoping to win addition of a broader "woman's life" exception, managed to have it sent to the

Senate Judiciary Committee for a one-day hearing. On December 7 the bill returned to the Senate floor with a broader exception, but an effort to expand it to also allow use of the "partial birth" method to preserve women's *health* failed by a 51 to 47 vote. Then the bill itself—now no longer identical to the House-passed measure—won approval on a 54 to 44 tally.[32]

President Clinton promised a veto, but in late February he publicly sent Congress written notification that he would sign such a bill *if* the House and Senate agreed to broaden the "woman's life" exception to also include instances involving "serious adverse health consequences." The House subcommittee held another brief hearing on the measure, and on March 27 the full House adopted the Senate version without alteration by a vote of 286 to 129. Two weeks later the president made good on his earlier promise and vetoed the bill just prior to meeting with five women who had had late term "partial birth" abortions of abnormal fetuses.[33]

Efforts to enact similar bans on "intact" abortions were also under way in a growing number of individual states, but the first such law, in Ohio, was quickly voided in federal court. "Use of the D & X procedure in the late second trimester appears to pose less of a risk to maternal health than does the D & E procedure" or the old-fashioned induction method, U.S. District Judge Walter H. Rice found. But not only did the statute prohibit what potentially was "a safer procedure than all other available abortion procedures," it also—like Canady's bill and even President Clinton's stance—improperly sought to abridge the comprehensive postviability protection of women's health that explicitly was acknowledged in *Doe* v. *Bolton* (and in *U.S.* v. *Vuitch* even earlier) and expressly reaffirmed in *Casey.* A state, Judge Rice noted, "may not constitutionally limit the provision of abortions only to those situations in which a pregnant woman's physical [as distinct from mental] health is threatened. . . . Under *Casey,* such a regulation is clearly unconstitutional."[34]

Another almost equally significant lower court application of *Casey* came in the less-publicized context of ongoing state efforts to impose Pennsylvania-like restrictions on women seeking abortions. In September 1995 Louisiana joined Mississippi and Pennsylvania and became the third state in the nation to require that women make two separate clinic visits in order to receive state-mandated abortion information *in person* from a physician at least twenty-four hours before the procedure rather than merely by telephone. In Indiana, however, a new law imposing such a requirement was blocked by U.S. District Judge David F. Hamilton. Relying heavily on findings that Mississippi's statute had led to a more than 10 percent decline in abortions, Hamilton emphasized how that data represented "evidence that was not available in *Casey* concerning the actual effects of such laws." Fully appreciating *Casey*'s distinction between state laws that *persuaded* women to have fewer abortions and unconstitutional statutes that *obstructed* women's efforts to obtain abortions, Hamilton found that "the 'in the presence' requirement of the Indiana law is likely to have effects in Indiana comparable to the effects of the similar law in Mississippi." Hamilton reiterated that the focus of *Casey*'s "undue burden test is not on added expense or inconvenience. The focus is on practical burdens so great that they would actually prevent a significant number of women from obtaining abortions they would otherwise choose to have." In Indiana, "for a large fraction of women seeking abortions, the law is likely to operate as a substantial obstacle to a woman's choice" and thus was unconstitutional pursuant to *Casey*. Hamilton's opinion was the most astute lower court discussion that *Casey*'s "undue burden test" had yet received, but in September 1996 a fourth state, Utah, also successfully imposed a two-visit requirement.[35]

In late April 1996 the Supreme Court refused to hear South Dakota's appeal of a lower federal court decision voiding a parental-notice statute that failed to include a judicial bypass provision, but the refusal prompted a rare and combative colloquy between three dissenters—Justice Antonin Scalia, joined by Chief Justice William Rehnquist and Justice Clarence Thomas—and Justice John Paul Stevens. The appeals court panel had concluded that *Casey* had implicitly superseded a prior decision, which in no way concerned abortion, with regard to what standard ought to govern facial—as distinct from "as applied"—challenges to statutes. Scalia insisted that the appellate court's reading of *Casey* "cries out for our review," particularly since its interpretation contradicted that of another appeals court which in 1992 had upheld Mississippi's twenty-four-hour waiting period without Supreme Court rebuff. Justice Stevens, in an unusual rebuttal, dismissed Scalia's complaint and volunteered that it "is not at all clear to me" that even that southern appellate court, the Fifth Circuit, would any longer adhere to its 1992 stance.[36]

Two months later the High Court ordered another appeals court to correct the manner in which it had voided a Utah statute that sought to prohibit virtually all post-twenty-week abortions, a voiding that the Supreme Court the following year declined to review,[37] but the most important decision of the Court's 1995–1996 term concerned not abortion but gay rights. In 1992 Colorado voters had approved a state constitutional amendment prohibiting any governmental unit from adopting any policy offering protection against discrimination to gay citizens, as the cities of Aspen, Boulder, and Denver already had. The Colorado Supreme Court had affirmed a trial court's finding that the amendment was unconstitutional, but the state appealed, presenting the U.S. Supreme Court with its most momentous gay rights case since *Bowers* v. *Hardwick* ten years earlier.

On May 20, 1996, the High Court affirmed the unconstitutionality of the antigay amendment in a six-to-three ruling. Remarkably, Justice Anthony M. Kennedy's majority opinion never once referred to the decade-old precedent of *Bowers,* but the dramatic force of the majority's language—especially as underscored by a splenetic dissent from Justice Scalia—left *Bowers* looking mortally wounded if not explicitly abandoned.

Kennedy stated that the Colorado "amendment seems inexplicable by anything but animus toward the class that it affects," and he added that "disqualification of a class of persons from the right to seek specific protection from the law is unprecedented in our jurisprudence." Observing that "it is not within our constitutional tradition to enact laws of this sort," Kennedy and his five colleagues concluded that the amendment "classifies homosexuals not to further a proper legislative end but to make them unequal to everyone else. This Colorado cannot do. A State cannot so deem a class of persons a stranger to its laws."[38]

The importance of the *Romer* majority's opinion was magnified by the angrily sarcastic dissent filed by Justice Scalia and joined by Chief Justice Rehnquist and Justice Thomas. The *Romer* majority, Scalia accurately complained, "places the prestige of this institution behind the proposition that opposition to homosexuality is as reprehensible as racial or religious bias."

As one influential commentator, Thomas C. Grey, noted, "Scalia's dissent made even louder the silence at the heart of the *Romer* majority opinion—its failure so much as to mention *Hardwick*." Grey believed that "not much is left of *Hardwick,*" and another knowledgeable expert, Louis Michael Seidman, fully agreed, saying it was "difficult to see how *Bower's* validation of same-sex sodomy laws survives the Court's analysis. The sound of the Court's silence regarding *Bowers* is deafening."[39]

Seidman accurately termed *Romer* the "first major Supreme Court victory" for gay people in American history, but he also added, "*Romer's* future is indeterminate."[40] Prior to *Romer*, the highest state courts in Texas,[41] Louisiana,[42] and Mississippi[43] in 1994 and in Rhode Island[44] and Oklahoma[45] in 1995 had all declined to void their still-existing criminal sodomy statutes. Some of the holdings deserved more attention than they received, such as the Rhode Island Supreme Court's declaration that "the state may constitutionally prosecute an unmarried consenting heterosexual adult who engages in an act of cunnilingus."[46]

Early in 1996, however, Tennessee's court of appeals, in a ruling left undisturbed by the state supreme court soon after *Romer*, held that the state's Homosexual Practices Act violated the Tennessee Constitution. "Our citizens' fundamental right to privacy," the court announced, "encompasses the right of the plaintiffs to engage in consensual, private, non-commercial sexual conduct."[47] Georgia's supreme court again upheld that state's criminal statute; a five-to-two majority declared that "the proscription against sodomy is a legitimate and valid exercise of state police power in further-ance of the moral welfare of the public." One dissenter criticized that outcome as "pathetic and disgraceful" and cited Tennessee's dissimilar result;[48] a year later the Tennessee opinion was also quoted by the Montana Supreme Court in a unanimous decision voiding that state's same-sex sodomy statute on state constitutional grounds. "The right of consenting adults, regardless of gender, to engage in non-commercial, private, sexual relations free of governmental interference, intrusion and condemnation," wrote Justice James Nelson, lies at "the very core of Montana's constitutional right of individual privacy." "There are certain rights so fundamental that they will not be denied to a minority no matter how despised by society."[49]

The Montana ruling reduced to twenty-one the number of states that still criminalized consensual oral and anal sex, but far more attention was being directed toward another gay rights litigation drive, namely a test case effort to win legalization of same-sex marriages in Hawaii pursuant to the state supreme court's unique reading of the Hawaii constitution. In 1993 the state's high court, in an intermediate ruling, had held that "sex is a 'suspect classification' for purposes of equal protection analysis" and that accordingly the state would have to demonstrate a compelling reason for denying marriage licenses to same-sex couples.

The test case, initially filed in 1991 on behalf of both male and female couples, was then remanded to a lower court for a full-fledged trial under the highly demanding standard of review the state supreme court had mandated. Only three years later did the trial finally commence, and in early December 1996 Circuit Court Judge Kevin S. C. Chang unsurprisingly ruled that the state had failed to meet its burden of proof. Nationally, the Hawaii litigation had inspired congressional passage of the Defense of Marriage Act, ostensibly authorizing other states and the federal government to ignore any same-sex unions that might take place in Hawaii. President Bill Clinton signed the bill into law in September 1996, but the almost universal expectation that Chang's decision eventually would be affirmed by the Hawaii Supreme Court stimulated a strong backlash in Hawaii too. Early in 1997 the Hawaii state legislature proposed amending the state's constitution to explicitly prohibit same-sex marriage while at the same time approving legislation allowing same-sex couples to be recognized as "reciprocal beneficiaries" under state law. Formal adoption of the state constitutional amendment had to await ratification by the state's voters in the November 1998 election, but overwhelming public support for the restriction meant that approval was assured. What if anything the Hawaii Supreme Court might do with Chang's ruling was reduced to a modest curiosity, and the once-bright expectation of a national gay rights breakthrough in Hawaii all but disappeared.[50]

Early in 1996 word spread that the U.S. Department of Justice was ending the investigation it had initiated a year earlier into whether Paul Hill, Shelley Shannon, and other advocates of deadly force were linked to any wider conspiracy to kill doctors and destroy clinics. The Justice Department's failure to establish an actual conspiracy, however, did not represent an end to ongoing law enforcement success in halting and punishing violently obstructive abortion opponents. One young woman who unsuccessfully attempted to burn a Virginia clinic was sentenced to two and a half years in federal prison,[51] and in Oregon one of the two leading lights of Advocates for Life, Paul deParrie, was enjoined from having any contact with one Portland clinic director pursuant to a state antistalking statute. Half a dozen Oregon providers filed a federal class action RICO and FACE suit against the pro-violence American Coalition of Life Activists,[52] and a plethora of federal and state courts continued to affirm both injunctive orders restricting obstructive protests and criminal convictions of offenders.[53]

On the medical front, the Population Council announced in late March 1996 that its large clinical trial of mifepristone, funded largely by wealthy investor Warren Buffett, was now complete and that the final data required for federal approval by the FDA had been submitted. The Council also said that arrangements for full-scale manufacture and distribution of RU-486 were in place, and the president of the private company the Council had set up to oversee those functions declared, "We hope that mifepristone will be available to women in this country by the end of the year." Lawrence Lader's small Abortion Rights Mobilization also had its own trials of mifepristone under way, and the National Abortion Federation disclosed that it was encouraging its members to use methotrexate for medical abortions. In mid-July an FDA advisory committee recommended mifepristone's approval, and in mid-September the FDA announced that it was giving RU-486 conditional approval. Clinical research continued to show widespread patient satisfaction with both mifepristone- and methotrexate-induced medical abortions, and one survey of rural physicians found that while only 4 percent offered surgical abortions to their patients, 26 percent said they would definitely use RU-486 when it was obtainable. Population Council executives stated that they hoped for full-scale national availability of RU-486 by mid-1997.[54]

In mid-September 1996 the Republican congressional leadership scheduled House and Senate override votes for the Partial-Birth Abortion Ban Act that President Clinton had vetoed five months earlier. Abortion opponents received a major boost when first the *Bergen* (N.J.) *Record* and then the *Washington Post* published major stories asserting that the actual number of late second trimester "partial birth" abortions was far greater than the very modest number of postviability third trimester procedures that had drawn the most attention during earlier congressional debates, and on September 19, by a more than two-thirds vote of 285 to 137, the House of Representatives successfully overrode the Clinton veto. Seventy Democrats joined the majority; only fifteen Republicans were in the minority.[55]

One week later the override attempt in the Senate fell eight votes short of the sixty-seven that were needed, but a number of normally pro-choice senators—Republican Arlen Specter and Democrats Sam Nunn and Patrick Leahy—switched sides to support enactment of the ban. Democratic minority leader Tom Daschle said he would attempt to work out a compromise on health-exception language that both the president and right-to-lifers could support, but NAF executive director Vicki Saporta expressed a different view: "I don't think it will ever be over. They [abortion opponents] think they're on to something."[56]

A Mississippi effort to enforce what would have been the nation's most draconian antiabortion regulations was derailed in federal court,[57] but a few weeks later news broke that a major obstacle would indefinitely delay widespread availability of RU-486. A lawsuit filed in Los Angeles Superior Court revealed that the Population Council's carefully chosen overseer of the manufacturing and distribution work, Joseph D. Pike, was a disbarred attorney who had been convicted of forgery in North Carolina earlier in the year and sentenced to eighteen months probation. The Population Council had learned of Pike's record a few months prior and quietly had sought to ease him out of the project, but the Los Angeles suit, filed by former "Gong Show" producer Burt Sugarman, a potential investor in the manufacturing and distribution work who had had a falling out of his own with Pike, propelled everyone's dirty laundry into the newspapers. The Population Council had worked assiduously to keep all its manufacturing and distribution plans as secret as possible so as to shield the project from antiabortion harassment, but now it too filed suit against Pike in New York.

Pike previously had overseen the manufacturing of a Council-sponsored intrauterine device (IUD), but Council president Margaret Catley-Carlson publicly confessed, "We are responsible for not having done due diligence on someone we had had as a partner for ten years." Pike had been given the job of raising the estimated $27 million needed to launch the difficult, large-volume manufacturing work, and by July 1996 he had obtained more than $13 million from interested investors. Some $8 million of that money had gone to the Population Council itself as reimbursement for the approximately $12 million it so far had expended on RU-486, but Pike's investors, such as New York financier Brian M. Freeman, now had their names in the newspapers while also facing a significant delay before there would be any return on their dollars. Finally, in mid-February 1997, the Council announced that a settlement had been reached with Pike and that a new entity, Advances for Choice, would oversee the manufacturing and marketing. RU-486, the Council said, ought to be nationally available by the end of 1997.[58]

Early in 1997 antiabortion bombers struck a clinic in Atlanta, Georgia, and then one in Tulsa, Oklahoma,[59] but one month later, in yet another firm ruling against right-to-life protesters, the U.S.

Supreme Court affirmed in large part an injunction barring demonstrators from coming within fifteen feet of a clinic in Buffalo, New York. The long-running case, *Schenck* v. *Pro-Choice Network of Western New York,* had been in litigation for more than six years and had received en banc consideration from the entire U.S. Second Circuit Court of Appeals soon after the High Court's 1994 ruling in *Madsen.* The six-to-three 1997 ruling, with Justices Scalia, Kennedy, and Thomas again in dissent, reiterated the majority's clear adherence to the principles of *Madsen* while also holding that lower courts could not additionally prohibit protesters from accosting people who were approaching a clinic.[60]

Numerous state and federal courts continued to affirm restrictive injunctions and criminal charges brought under FACE,[61] but in two other, low-visibility abortion cases, one concerning a Montana parental-notice statute and one concerning Montana's insistence that only doctors, not physician assistants, could perform first-trimester abortions, the Supreme Court twice reversed federal appellate court rulings. The parental-notice ruling, *Lambert* v. *Wicklund,* came without dissent,[62] but in the physician assistant case, *Mazurek* v. *Armstrong,* Justices Stevens, Ginsburg, and Breyer gently reprimanded their colleagues for being insufficiently inquisitive about whether Montana had enacted the limitation solely to target one "PA" who did perform abortions under a doctor's supervision, Susan Cahill. Five months later a state court judge blocked the ban pursuant to Montana's *state* constitution.[63]

In late February 1997, just as the new Congress was gearing up for another attempt to pass the Partial-Birth Abortion Ban Act into law over President Clinton's opposition, controversy developed over a claim by one previously little known abortion rights lobbyist, Ron Fitzsimmons, that he had "lied through my teeth" to ABC News more than a year earlier in denying that there were significant numbers of "intact" second trimester abortions. The ABC interview with Fitzsimmons, the executive director of the National Coalition of Abortion Providers, a small competitor of NAF's, actually had never even aired, but Fitzsimmons's strange though self-advertising confession drew considerable attention and generated extensive news media criticism of pro-choice interest groups. One *New York Times* reporter characterized abortion rights supporters as "a movement enveloped by an extremism that prohibits concessions, compromise, maybe even candor," and Fitzsimmons's further claim that abortion "is a form of killing; you're ending a life" gave opponents additional ammunition.[64]

Fitzsimmons soon circulated a somewhat bizarre memo to his members, asserting that "the net effect of this 'confession' has been an appreciable *increase* in credibility and visibility" as NCAP had "emerged as an honest, credible source of information," but hardly anyone else shared his perspective. On March 11 the House and Senate Judiciary Committees held a joint, one-day hearing on the partial birth bill, and National Right to Life Committee legislative director Douglas Johnson testified honestly—though with little news media coverage—that "more than 90 percent of the abortions that would be banned by the Partial-Birth Abortion Ban Act are not third trimester abortions." Johnson also readily acknowledged that "it is true that a subset of the third-trimester partial-birth abortions involve babies who have grave disorders that will result in death of the baby soon after birth." The Right to Life Committee nonetheless supported enactment of a federal criminal statute so as to guarantee that those fetuses' mothers would have no choice but to carry them to term and then experience their deaths.[65]

The National Right to Life Committee was also energetically instigating state legislative consideration of "partial birth" ban laws in more than half the states, but sometimes the proponents were too frank for their own good. Michigan in 1996 had joined Ohio and Utah as the first three states to enact such measures, but antiabortion activist Mark Crutcher conceded to one Michigan newspaper that "there is physically no way to enforce that law" unless doctors somehow were closely surveilled. Republican state senator Jack Horton confessed, "I'm not sure if prosecution was on our mind when we passed this," and added, "Sometimes laws are made to make a statement." Crutcher, however, had a further explanation: "The whole issue is a scam being perpetrated by people on our side of the issue for fund-raising purposes."[66]

On March 20 the House of Representatives passed the federal partial birth bill by a vote of 295 to 136—ten more ayes than it had received six months earlier—after rejecting by an almost equally large margin, 282 to 149, an amendment that would have added a further exception for pregnancies involving "serious adverse long-term physical health consequences" for the woman. Senate minority leader Tom Daschle continued to try to fashion a more tightly worded maternal health amendment that would break the political logjam, and finally settled on an exception for cases that would "risk grievous injury to her physical health," where "grievous injury" was expressly limited to "a severely debilitating disease or impairment specifically caused by the pregnancy." Daschle said he wanted to avoid a congressional ban on one specific procedure that could aid some women, since "politicians cannot anticipate or understand the unique circumstances she and her physician might face," but his eagerness to enact instead a more comprehensive restriction on *all* third trimester procedures ("No post-viability abortions should be allowed—regardless of procedure—unless they are absolutely necessary to protect a mother from death or serious damage to her health") placed him in a position of totally breaching the comprehensive protection of postviability maternal health the Court had established in *U.S.* v. *Vuitch* and *Doe* v. *Bolton.*[67]

That infirmity failed to stop either President Clinton or the otherwise pro-choice American College of Obstetricians and Gynecologists (ACOG) from endorsing Daschle's proposal, but their support did him little good on the Senate floor, where his substitute was defeated by a 64 to 36 margin after a fully pro-choice amendment offered by California Democrat Diane Feinstein lost on a vote of 72 to 28. Some voices, like the editorial page of the *Washington Post,* termed Daschle's effort "a surprisingly good compromise" whose postviability effect "would be broader than" the partial birth ban, but conservative commentator Robert D. Novak correctly called Daschle's offering "a serious retreat by pro-choice forces." Novak highlighted how right-to-lifers' actual goal was to "seek real legislation banning all second- and third-trimester abortions, without loopholes," and one knowledgeable reporter proclaimed that the partial birth initiative represented a "stunning coup for abortion foes" that had brought about "a fundamental shift in the national debate over abortion."[68]

On May 19, 1997, one day before the House-passed partial birth bill was scheduled for debate on the Senate floor, the American Medical Association (AMA) astounded most observers, and some of its own members, by endorsing passage of the measure in exchange for some exceedingly modest changes in the ban agreed to by Senate sponsor Rick Santorum, Republican of Pennsylvania. Observers believed Santorum was now within striking distance of the 67 votes needed to override another presidential veto, but on May 20 Senate passage took place by a margin of only 64 to 36. Among those 64 were three Democrats who previously had opposed the bill, including minority leader Daschle, who tried to explain his flip-flop by saying, "I voted in favor of its passage because I still desire to find common ground with those outside the extremes." More memorably,

Daschle also volunteered that it was "highly likely" that the bill for which he had just voted "will be declared unconstitutional should it be enacted into law."[69]

Antiabortion strategists publicly congratulated themselves on their growing political success. Christian Coalition executive director Ralph Reed told Katharine Q. Seelye of the *New York Times* that the key to their headway lay in an exclusive focus on the fetus: "never get taken off it to talk about the health of the mother or any other rabbit trail." Conservative columnist Fred Barnes noted how on the Senate floor the ostensibly pro-choice Tom Daschle had "sounded like a pro-lifer," and Seelye highlighted the contradictory irony of President Clinton's endorsement of Daschle's measure, which "carried far broader restrictions on abortion than the bill he plans to re-veto." While the right-to-lifers' initiative was "more of a political strategy than a real issue," the debate nonetheless had cost abortion supporters "enormous political capital." Seelye noted, "Rarely has so much energy been expended by so many over something that, in practical terms, would have so little effect," but she emphasized how a comment from conservative activist Gary Bauer illuminated the entire strategy underlying the "partial birth ban" campaign: "When this is over, I want to move on to an up-or-down vote on second- and third-trimester abortions."[70]

In mid-May yet another arsonist struck Portland, Oregon's Love-joy clinic. Several months later federal authorities indicted a fifty-nine-year-old Washington State man, Richard T. Andrews, for three California clinic arsons; Andrews subsequently pled guilty to seven Northwest clinic attacks stretching from California to Montana between 1992 and 1995 and received a seven-year sentence.[71] Even more serious was news that the Population Council's intended man-ufacturer of mifepristone for the American market, the Hungarian drug company Gedeon Richter, had privately told the Council in late February, eighteen months after signing a production con-tract, that it was dropping out of the project. The prospective Ameri-can distributor, Danco Laboratories, had quietly filed a breach-of-contract suit against Gedeon Richter in New York in early May, but the Council admitted that the need to find a new manufacturer probably would result in a multiyear delay in RU-486's availability across the United States.

Lawrence Lader's ARM announced that a grant from the John Merck Fund would allow it to expand its provision of free mifepris-tone beyond the few thousand patients who so far had had medical abortions in ARM-sponsored clinical trials, and discussions began as to whether ARM's small-scale manufacturing process, overseen by young Columbia University chemistry professor David Horne, could to any large degree fill the gap created by Gedeon Richter's withdrawal. ARM's clinical trials, overseen by Rochester medical researcher and physician Eric A. Schaff, had continued to demonstrate mifepristone's popularity and efficacy. Well over 90 percent of women patients with pregnancies of no more than eight weeks now were able to successfully self-administer the second step of the RU-486 procedure, vaginal misoprostol, at home. In sharp contrast to methotrexate, with whose use one-third of women had to wait two to three weeks to expel their pregnancies, mifepristone/misoprostol miscarriages occurred far more quickly. Schaff noted that "some providers may find the 24-hour telephone availability and need for surgical backup for excessive bleeding problematic," and knowledgeable researchers all agreed that "medical abortion will not be a panacea." Given the Population Council's admission that they no longer had any timetable for RU-486's widespread availability, the encouraging clinical findings had only abstract significance for most American women.[72]

Several months later the House of Representatives approved the Senate-amended version of the Partial-Birth Abortion Ban Act by a vote of 296 to 132 and President Clinton once again immediately vetoed the bill. Republican leaders announced they would postpone votes on overriding the veto until sometime in 1998 in the hope that upcoming fall elections might help them gain the three additional votes they would need in the Senate.[73] In the courts, a federal judge in Wisconsin reluctantly declined to strike down a new state statute that, when actually implemented in May 1998, made Wisconsin the fifth state to require in-person provision of state-mandated abortion information at least twenty-four hours before the procedure; Ohio in mid-1998 was poised to become sixth.[74] Many pro-choice lawyers, however, breathed a small sigh of relief when the U.S. Supreme Court, in declining to apply *Casey*'s "liberty" analysis to the issue of physician aid-in-dying for terminally ill patients in two heavily publicized cases, left *Casey*'s abortion-related vitality unaffected.[75]

Potentially of more moment for future abortion politics and litigation, however, was the undeviating track record that began to accumulate throughout the last half of 1997 and the early months of 1998 as more than a dozen newly passed state-level "partial birth ban" statutes were challenged in court: with only one exception, each lawsuit proved successful. The National Right to Life Committee's effort to win enactment of such laws by as many state legislatures as possible was registering impressive success: although several bills were vetoed by governors, in six states—Indiana, Mississippi, South Carolina, South Dakota, Tennessee, and Utah—1997 "partial birth" statutes took effect without judicial review.

But in the first thirteen states where such enactments were challenged in court, however, restraining orders or injunctions soon were issued barring enforcement. The first such measure, in Ohio, had been blocked in December 1995, and in November 1997 the Sixth Circuit Court of Appeals affirmed that ruling in a decision the U.S. Supreme Court declined to review. In Georgia a federal district court judge ruled that the statute could not impinge upon previability abortions; a similar outcome occurred in Alabama after the state attorney general told county prosecutors that the new law applied only to viable fetuses. Rhode Island's law was blocked in mid-July by a U.S. district judge, and Louisiana's—along with a new enactment encouraging suits against doctors—was restrained three days later. Arizona's measure was stopped the following day by a judge who said it clearly was unconstitutional, and Arkansas's was stymied on July 31. Alaska's was curbed by a state judge in early August, and Montana's by a state judge in early October.[76]

But two of the most important rulings came in full dress opinions issued by federal judges in Detroit and Omaha. U.S. District Judge Gerald E. Rosen permanently enjoined enforcement of Michigan's "partial birth" abortion ban act, writing that "the statute leaves physicians at risk of violating its terms virtually every time they perform an abortion after the first trimester." Noting that the Michigan measure was less precise than both the Ohio law that had already been struck down and the federal bill that had been vetoed by President Clinton, Judge Rosen said the Michigan ban was invalid both because it was "hopelessly ambiguous" and because in many instances "it will operate as a substantial obstacle to a woman's choice to undergo an abortion."[77]

Two weeks later U.S. District Judge Richard G. Kopf, acting in a challenge to Nebraska's new law brought by abortion doctor LeRoy Carhart, rendered the strongest and most persuasive judgment to date. Finding that the Nebraska prohibition would have "the effect of subjecting Carhart's patients to an appreciably greater risk of injury or death than would be the case if these women could rely on him to perform his variant of the banned procedure on nonviable fetuses when medically advisable," Judge Kopf ruled that the Nebraska ban was an "undue burden" under *Casey* and thus unconstitutional. "Credible medical evidence establishes that the D & X procedure," Kopf noted, sometimes "is appreciably safer than the D & E procedure" involving fetal dismemberment within the womb. Hence the new law "subordinates maternal life and health to the life and health of a nonviable fetus," and "nonviable fetal life cannot constitutionally be considered superior to maternal life or health."[78]

In December 1997 New Jersey's newly enacted partial birth ban measure became the eleventh such statute to be blocked by a court, and two months later federal district judge Charles P. Kocoras granted a permanent injunction against Illinois's similar new statute. Like previous jurists, Kocoras highlighted the unconstitutionally vague terminology the law featured, but he like Kopf also explicitly underscored the affirmative medical value of the targeted procedure:

> Intact D&E is particularly useful in cases of fetal abnormalities because geneticists often request that the fetus be removed intact to facilitate genetic testing. In addition, the intact D&E reduces the risk of retained tissue and reduces the risk of uterine perforation and cervical laceration because the procedure requires less instrumentation in the uterus. An intact D&E may also result in less blood loss and less trauma for some patients and may take less operating time.

In March 1998 an Idaho federal judge restrained an analogous law there, but in mid-May an exceptionally conservative U.S. district judge in Wisconsin, John C. Shabaz, became the first federal jurist to allow such a state statute actually to take effect before ruling on its constitutionality. Frightened doctors briefly halted *all* abortion services before resuming their practices once local district attorneys agreed that the ban would not be applied expansively.[79]

Judges Kopf's and Kocoras's rulings, however, accurately reflected the two overarching realities of abortion law and politics in 1998: (1) that legislatures rather than demonstrators were the greatest hindrance to the provision of abortion services and (2) that with legislatures as with protesters the courts—state as well as federal—were the foremost guarantors of women's access to abortion.

In the wake of *Casey* and especially in the wake of the 1994 enactment of the federal FACE statute, clinic operators all across the country came to realize that in all honesty antiabortion protesters and even terrorists were *less* of an impediment to the provision of services than were the profusion of regulatory obstacles thrown up by right–to–life dominated legislatures in a growing number of states. No law enforcement authority could prevent the deadly onslaught of someone like Paul Hill or John Salvi, but state and federal prosecutors had brought a virtual halt to the violently obstructive harassment that clinic patients and providers had had to endure in the late 1980s and early 1990s. The complete marginalization of violent protest was sadly underscored by the January 29, 1998, bombing of a Birmingham, Alabama, abortion clinic that killed a thirty-four-year-old city police officer, Robert D. Sanderson, and badly wounded a clinic nurse, Emily Lyons. The accused bomber, Eric Robert Rudolph, eluded capture for months.[80]

While by 1998 abortion opponents had decisively lost the physical battle to obstruct access to clinics or otherwise close them down, right–to–life legislators, in large part through their focus on the supposed "partial birth" procedure, had succeeded in shifting the focus of abortion debates onto the fetus, and away from women, to a greater extent than at any other time since *Roe*. Foes of "intact" abortions often failed to acknowledge that they opposed *all* abortions, not simply one particular procedure, just as state-level proponents of mandatory waiting periods and other restrictive legislation often did a poor job of concealing their desire to deny women a right to choose rather than simply aid them in making better-informed choices. For many right-to-lifers, opposition to all forms of nonprocreative sexuality remained more basic and elemental than protection of either late-term or early-term fetuses; few antiabortion activists supported contraceptive services and hardly any endorsed gay rights. Focus on the fetus might be successful public relations, but it fundamentally obscured the larger, more far-reaching agenda that lay just behind the stalking horse of "partial birth" abortion ban bills.[81]

Casey's explicit tolerance of "persuasive" as distinct from "obstructive" state efforts to delay women's exercise of their right to choose abortion without undue hindrance made judges decidedly more lenient with regard to intrusive statutes than courts had become with intrusive protesters.[82] But *Casey's* prohibitory boundaries were clear if not sharp, and any right–to–life strategist who truly believed that legislation banning the use of one or another abortion technique for previability procedures could survive review in the federal courts was, as Judge Kopf's opinion showed, guilty of grave self-deception.

After 1992 no serious scholar of the Supreme Court could any longer doubt that the constitutional core of *Roe,* as upheld and re-affirmed in *Casey,* was secure for all time. Indeed, not only did such post-*Casey* abortion protest rulings as *Madsen* and *Schenck* reflect a firm majority consensus that the First Amendment rights of demon-strators would not be allowed to infringe on the health care rights of patients and providers, but federal appellate courts' unanimous ratification of the constitutionality of FACE further enshrined the federal judiciary as the most important pro-choice actor in Ameri-can government.

Federal and state trial judges' equally unanimous rulings against the slew of state-level "partial birth" ban laws thus underscored the extent to which the judiciary had become the bulwark of the pro-choice struggle. Federal courts could upend even local zoning prac-tices that obstructed clinic services, and a growing number of state courts, such as Alaska's, held that their *state* constitutions protected access to abortion even more assertively than did *Casey.*[83]

The virtual disappearance of organized medicine from the front ranks of the abortion rights movement was in part the result of the extensive segregation of abortion services into the lonely world of freestanding clinics, but medicine's ambivalence about abortion also reflected a professional distaste for the repetitious routine of suction curettage that might be significantly altered once RU-486 becomes fully available. The advent of new manual syringe techniques for very early "surgical" abortions—even eight to ten days after concep-tion—promises to hasten the shift toward early abortions even with-out universal availability of RU-486.[84]

The Supreme Court's firm commitment to *Casey* accurately re-flected the remarkably imposing stability of American public opin-ion about abortion. Twenty-five years' evidence indicated that while significant numerical variations could be generated by differently worded questions, a clear majority of Americans opposed any gov-ernmental action to overturn the constitutional consensus repre-sented by *Casey.* The best analyses of abortion opinion reflected both Americans' less than impressive levels of political knowledge—"only 30% of Americans can recall unprompted in surveys that *Roe* v. *Wade* is a case dealing with abortion rights"—and the firm distinction that some 10 to 20 percent of respondents drew between the legality of abortion, which they supported, and the morality of abortion, which they opposed. It of course remained true that "a sizeable component of abortion attitudes relates to sexuality itself," but 1997–1998 polling reflected how the legislative debates over "partial birth" ban bills had had less of an impact on Americans' underlying beliefs than many journalists appreciated. Most important, the news media's marked preoccupation with the fetus had reinforced Americans' already well pronounced preference for early rather than late term abortion. One early 1998 *New York Times* polling report simplistically contended that "public opinion has shifted away from general acceptance of legal abortion," but a comprehensive study by the generally conservative American Enterprise Institute concluded that "opinion on abortion remains very much what it was in 1973."[85]

"Partial birth" publicity might generate measurable short-term legislative gains, but the "partial birth" debates offered little long-term encouragement for those who dreamed of a return to the days when most abortions were illegal. Radical activist Matt Trewhella denounced the "partial birth" ban efforts as a "worthless charade" in *Life Advocate* magazine, accurately complaining that "not a single preborn baby will be protected from death by this legislation." In addition, he argued, "the general public now thinks that partial-birth is the *only horrible* abortion procedure." American Life League president Judie Brown made the same point in *USA Today*, saying that abortion opponents had "shot ourselves in the foot" by focusing on "partial birth" abortions. "The implicit message is that all other kinds of abortion aren't as bad," and "that undermines what this movement is trying to do, which is ban all abortions, period." Trewhella's and Brown's consternation appeared to be valid; during Virginia's fall 1997 gubernatorial campaign, successful Republican candidate James S. Gilmore III explicitly soft-peddled his long record of intense opposition to legal abortion by featuring broadcast ads in which he stressed that "the Supreme Court has spoken. No one's going to ban abortions."[86]

During some of the "partial birth" debates, just like after *Casey*, pro-choice activists sometimes used self-defeating rhetoric and unnecessarily surrendered too much ground. Pro-choice groups and litigators erroneously held an overly pessimistic view of *Casey*, and at other times too also manifested an odd desire to treat victories as defeats. In an extreme example, one attorney blasted Judge Rosen's 1997 ruling voiding Michigan's "partial birth" ban as "a disaster"[87] since the jurist went out of his way to detail how unacceptable the measure was, thus potentially giving guidance to legislators who might make another try.

Litigators who believed the sky was falling even when each "partial birth" ban under challenge was blocked were less of a problem, however, than were pro-choice voices who volunteered that abortions were somehow a form of "evil." The contrast to the 1967–1973 era, when virtually all abortion rights activists appreciated how often a safe and legal abortion could represent a significant and life-preserving achievement for a woman suddenly faced with an unwanted pregnancy, could not have been greater. Longtime organizer Frances Kissling, who *did* appreciate the remarkable merits of *Casey,* pointedly complained in *Ms.* magazine, "Sometimes the Supreme Court justices sound more feminist than we do."[88] Among 1998 abortion rights activists, everyone was pro-choice but surprisingly few were explicitly pro-abortion. The wonderfully important title of onetime Wisconsin activist Anne Gaylor's 1975 book, *Abortion Is a Blessing,* seemed like a voice from another age.

And perhaps it was. On the twenty-fifth anniversaries of *Roe* v. *Wade* and *Doe* v. *Bolton,* American women's right to choose no longer was under physical siege by obstructive demonstrators, and American courts had drawn clear lines marking the outer boundaries of both antiabortion protests and restrictive state statutes. A firm Supreme Court majority, and scores of lower court judges, stood behind the guarantees of *Casey* and the protections of FACE; if pro-choice activists had rightful cause for concern, their worries might best focus neither on the judiciary nor even on legislatures. Instead the biggest questions loomed within: could the movement itself offer a more supportive sense of a wider community to those doctors and other staff members who actually provided abortion services in the sometimes isolating environment of freestanding clinics? And could the movement reeducate and remind itself that abortion was *not* an evil and indeed was often a blessing? The legacy of all those who had come before, from Kit Hepburn and Estelle Griswold to Alan Guttmacher, Roy Lucas, and Judy Smith, ought to be a lesson that of course it should.[89]

AFTERWORD

More than six years before Estelle Griswold and Fowler Harper launched *Poe* v. *Ullman*, and more than forty years before the trio of Justices O'Connor, Kennedy, and Souter guaranteed that the legacy of Kit Hepburn, of *Griswold*, and of *Roe* v. *Wade* would be enshrined beside *Brown* for all time in America's constitutional pantheon, Yale's Harold Lasswell stated the basic truth as clearly as anyone ever would: "The presumption in favor of privacy follows from our respect for freedom of choice, for autonomy, for self-direction on the part of everyone."

Constitutionally, the basic principle can be succinctly yet completely stated in just eleven words: "The right to privacy is inherent in the right to liberty."

And, just as basically, as Fowler Harper said a full decade before undertaking *Poe*, the law "is not changed by argument. It is changed by necessity."

"Except for critical periods," Harper stated, "the rule is one of inertia. The old values are encrusted in the law until they are literally forced out by the sheer necessity of events."

More than thirty years after Jean and Marvin Durning volunteered to be the initial "Roes," the "Roes" in *Poe*, Jean explained their willingness to become the first of all the seemingly anonymous plaintiffs who would lead to the other *Roe*, in a phrase that spoke for Kit Hepburn, for Estelle Griswold, for Lee Buxton, and for all those who would come after: "This was something that we thought was right."

And more than thirty years after Ruth and Bob "Oldendorf" became the first "Does" in *Poe*, Bob explained the deeply personal bond that they in their lifelong anonymity had now for two decades felt between *Poe* and *Roe*: "It was a necessary thing for everyone. That's why I went along—for people who didn't have health problems, but for whatever reasons they had. It's up to the person themselves."[1]

ACKNOWLEDGMENTS

The old man was the only other Tuesday morning visitor to the cemetery at Wethersfield's Congregational Church. "Griswold," I answered when he asked who I was looking for. "There are dozens," he replied with a gentle shake of his head. "Estelle Griswold," I added. "Early 1980s." He nodded. "If you start up there, I'll take a look down here."

He had a limp, I realized, but as I began to work my way back and forth along a steep hillock, he slowly walked the rows of gravestones down nearer the road. He was right, there *were* dozens of Griswolds, reaching back many generations, but in less than five minutes, about two thirds of the way up the hillock, I came upon the small flat headstone that was my goal: "Estelle Trebert Griswold—June 8, 1900—August 13, 1981."

I gave him a shout, letting him know that I'd found the one I'd been looking for. A few moments later, as I left, I stopped to say thank you, but I didn't ask his name.

Far more often than we usually remember, books like this do indeed depend upon the kindness of strangers as well as the hospitality of friends. In Waterbury, in New Haven, in Dallas, and in scores of other places, people whose names I likewise didn't catch have many times been just as friendly and eager to help as the old man in Wethersfield.

Bro Adams and Cathy Bruce, and Bill and JoAn Chace, all kindly welcomed me as a house guest on the many trips that took me to Waterbury, Hartford, New Haven, and Middletown. Twenty years ago, as an undergraduate, I spent the better part of four years at Wesleyan, and to go back—especially to Olin Library—for the research on this book supplied a marvelous sense of closure. The happenstance that even in 1974, thanks to the late Clem Vose, all of Roy Lucas's litigation files were in the basement of the same building where I began the thesis that became my first book—*Protest at Selma*—made my 1991 discovery of those long-untouched papers all the more ironic. Clem, Eugene Golob, David Titus, and Richard Buel at Wesleyan, like Peter Fish, David Price, David Paletz, and David Barber at Duke, all long ago taught me some of what scholarship involves, but most of what one learns is the product of time spent alone, not formal instruction. The six years of work on this book, like *Bearing the Cross* before it, have been a deeply satisfying and almost always pleasant endeavor, and the experience of teaching oneself a fundamentally new literature and story—especially one that so far has been much less explored than civil rights history—has been extremely enjoyable.

Six years of work of course accumulates many debts that one does remember. In all of the Connecticut research, I am most deeply indebted to Ann Y. Smith, the director of Waterbury's Mattatuck Museum, whose willingness to help open all sorts of local doors has given the first two chapters of this book a richness they otherwise could not have had. Ann's colleagues Dorothy Cantor and Deborah Grazier were likewise helpful on many occasions, and my Waterbury inquiries also greatly benefitted from many conversations with one of the area's most knowledgeable historians, Jeremy Brecher.

Also in Waterbury, I am deeply thankful to Senator Thomas F. "Tim" Upson for unearthing the fifty-year-old case files of his father, and to Anita Bologna at the *Waterbury Republican* for guiding me through that paper's superb clipping morgue. My other Waterbury debts include John Tobin at the Waterbury Hospital, Brad Ward in the State's Attorney's office, and the staff members at both the Bronson Library and at the Superior Court law library.

At Hartford's superb and pleasant Connecticut State Library and Archives, I was graciously helped by State Archivist Mark H. Jones, Anwar Ahmad, and many other librarians. Wesley W. Horton, Joseph Lynch, Herbert Janick, and Ellsworth S. Grant all gave me kind advice, and the *Hartford Courant* provided me full access to its library. Andrea Haas Hubbell of Connecticut Public Television generously shared with me the transcripts of her interviews, and Randall C. Jimerson at the University of Connecticut was also extremely helpful. Elizabeth A. Swain graciously eased my usage of the Lucas papers at Wesleyan, and James Campbell and his colleagues at the New Haven Colony Historical Society were also repeatedly helpful during my long sojourn there. Ruth C. Emerson and Judge Joseph B. Clark were each instrumental in giving me access to two collections of papers that added tremendous richness to the *Poe* and *Griswold* stories, and Angel Diggs and her colleagues at the *New Haven Register* kindly allowed me to review that paper's clipping morgue. My additional New Haven debts include Nicholas J. Cimmino at Superior Court, Katherine Morton and Judith Schiff at Yale's Sterling Library, Dr. Orvan W. Hess, and Andrew Ullman. Both Elizabeth Phillips and Professor Stephen C. Veltri greatly strengthened my knowledge of Fowler Harper, and the late John McLean Morris and Mrs. Helen Rose enlarged my understanding of Lee Buxton. David Brion Davis, Howard Lamar, Ralph Carlson, and Maud Andrew all provided crucial assistance in helping me locate the *Poe* plaintiffs.

In Northampton, Helen and Dan Horowitz graciously welcomed me into their home, and Susan Grigg and Margery Sly, along with Peter Engelman of the Margaret Sanger Papers Project, made Smith College's Sophia Smith Collection extremely pleasant to work in. George Scialabba kindly hosted me during several visits to Cambridge, and at Radcliffe College's Schlesinger Library, Eva Moseley, Anne Engelhardt, and Susan von Salis were all very helpful, as was Richard Wolfe at Harvard Medical School's Countway Library. Ben Primer, Nanci A. Young, Jean Holliday (and Beverly A. Williams) all made for most pleasant research visits to Princeton's Mudd Library, and Mills and Brenda Thornton graciously hosted me in Ann Arbor.

David Wigdor, Mary Wolfskill, Fred Bauman, Jeff Flannery, and their colleagues in the Manuscript Division at the Library of Congress have for some years now made it a place where I truly look forward to doing research. James Hutson and Jill Brett, as well as Linda Carr and Rosalie Scott, have also gone out of their ways to be extremely helpful during my work in the Library's Madison Building. Trudy H. Peterson, Mary Ronan, and Sue McDonough all helped ease my work at the National Archives, and Judith A. Miller and Peter Buscemi have been my favorite people in Washington for almost a decade now.

In Dallas, Ginny Whitehill time and time again has been exceptionally kind—and crucial—in helping with my work on *Roe*. David Farmer, Kay Bost, and Kristin Jacobsen at SMU's DeGolyer Library were also extremely helpful, and Craig Flournoy and Judy Sall helped arrange my full access to the clipping morgues of both the *Dallas Morning News* and the late *Dallas Times-Herald*. Jim and Carolyn Clark, Doris Middleton, Barbara Richardson, Judy Mohraz, and Karen Denard also extended wonderful courtesies during my visits to Dallas. Margaret Taylor, Julie Lowenberg, Judge Susan Legarde, and Peter Harlan, and Elnore Savage and Carolyn Hames in Fort Worth, were all very helpful as well.

In Austin, Heather Moore at the Ransom Library, Linda Hanson at the Johnson Library, Michael Widener at the Tarlton Law Library, and Katherine J. Adams at the Barker Texas History Center all helped ease my work, as did the staff of the the Texas Legislative Reference Library. Sandra Garrett helped me considerably with stories from *The Rag*, and David McNeely, Marie Maynor, Chris LaPlante, Tony Black, and Pete Cortez all helped me track down important leads in Austin. The clipping files at both the Austin Public Library and the Dallas Public Library also proved useful.

In Atlanta, Margie Pitts Hames, like Ginny Whitehill in Dallas and Ann Smith in Waterbury, was exceptionally helpful and crucial with my work on *Doe*, as was Sidney O. Smith, Jr. Louise Cook (and now Joe Hale) once again made research visits to Atlanta enjoyable and entertaining, and Gary Pomerantz kindly arranged for my access to the library resources of the *Atlanta Constitution* and the late *Atlanta Journal*.

Both the marvelous Archie Motley at the Chicago Historical Society and Stan Oliner at the Colorado Historical Society were extremely helpful, as were Gloria Roberts at PPFA, Caroline Rittenhouse at Bryn Mawr College, and David Klaasen at the University of Minnesota's Social Welfare History Archives. Leigh Ann Wheeler helped review the Minnesota materials for me.

Claudia Dreifus and Barbara Milbauer generously shared with me the fruits of their earlier work, and Marian Faux, Sagar C. Jain, and Harriet Pollack kindly checked to see if they had retained similar materials. Steve Wermeil was especially generous in discussing with me his ongoing work.

I spent a part of 1991 as a fellow at the Virginia Center for the Humanities, where Robert C. Vaughan, Susan Coleman, Ruby Davis, and Carol Hendricks, among others, all made for an exceptionally pleasant stay, and where Mary Carter Bishop, Suzanne W. Morse, and Susan Stein were helpful and interesting colleagues. I also benefitted tremendously from the University of Virginia's superb libraries, and especially from the wonderfully friendly and effective interlibrary loan staff at Alderman Library. This past year I've repeatedly been helped by both Ulla Volk and Carol Salomon at the Cooper Union Library. Thanks to John Jay Iselin, John Harrington, Roxann Clawson, Maria Schiro, and my other entertaining colleagues, teaching at Cooper has been an extremely pleasant experience.

Arthur M. Schlesinger, Jr., kindly introduced and recommended me to the good people at the Twentieth Century Fund, and both Michelle Miller and Richard C. Leone have been most supportive and encouraging of this very large book.

In addition to many of the people whose names are listed among my interviews in the bibliography, Michael Bessie, Dr. David Bingham, Timothy Byrnes, Dan Carter, James H. Cone, Joy Dryfoos, Mary Dudziak, Kim Fellner, Rachel Gorlin, Linda Greenhouse, Dr. Martin Heskell, Nan Hunter, Dennis Hutchinson, John C. Jeffries, Jr., Carol Joffe, Randall Kennedy, Michael Klarman, Uta Landy, Bruce Lee,

Kristin Luker, Matt Mallow, Nick Mills, Teresa Nelson, Richard Newman, James F. O'Brien, Lieutenant General William Odom, Lynn M. Paltrow, Barbara Radford, Evelyn Raiola, Linda Rocawich, Henry Schwarzschild, Joyce Seltzer, Reva Seybolt, Jim Sleeper, Helen A. Stephenson, Tina Welsh, Joanne Whitehead, James W. Williams, Juan Williams, Wendy Williams, and Tinsley Yarbrough all provided thoughtful assistance or advice. In the bibliography itself, those interviews or conversations which took place by telephone, rather than in person, are designated by the symbol (T).

This book shifted from William Morrow & Co. to Macmillan along with my editor, Lisa Drew, and Lisa's assistant, Katherine Boyle, has been exceptionally helpful and astute as this manuscript moved toward publication. Mary Flower handled the huge job of copyediting this book, and David Frost at Macmillan helped ease this forward. At one particular juncture, Macmillan president Barry Lippman was also most considerate. Jane Cushman has been my agent for almost a decade now, and Jeff Gerecke, Karen O'Boyle, Tony Outhwaite, and Tom Cushman at JCA have repeatedly been most helpful. Throughout all of these recent years, Ellen Vercruysse has superbly and economically handled all of my travel arrangements.

Ann Smith kindly reviewed the final draft of chapter one, and Lynn M. Paltrow thoroughly read chapter nine. Ellen Chesler, Pamela S. Karlan, and Susan F. Newcomer all read the entire final manuscript and offered extensive suggestions and corrections. Perhaps moreso than anyone else, Ellen, Pam, and Susan have all talked with me on scores of occasions about one or another part of this story over the last few years, and my cumulative gratitude for all of those conversations and phone calls—above and beyond their comments on the manuscript—is quite considerable.

I began this book—the "privacy book," I then called it—in the fall and winter of 1987–1988, in the immediate wake of the Senate hearings on Robert H. Bork's unsuccessful nomination to the U.S. Supreme Court. Perhaps even more than with *Bearing the Cross*, the researching of this book has introduced me to a large number of wonderful and impressive people. The degree of supportiveness I've received from so many of them has been a tremendous boon, especially when some of those with whom I've spoken—such as Hector Kinloch, Elizabeth "Odegard," and Robert "Oldendorf"—were being asked about the most privately traumatic experiences of their lives. Some people who themselves appear in the book—Jean and Marvin Durning, Ruth Emerson, Margie Hames, Larry Lader, Roy Lucas, and

Ginny Whitehill—have been especially willing to have repeated conversations and send along all sorts of relevant items, but the considerable respect which I feel for all of them does not mean that they will necessarily welcome or agree with every particular aspect of this long but wonderfully important story. Relatively little of this history has ever been brought together, or even brought to light, prior to now, and, much as with *Bearing the Cross*, I hope that this book too will help open the door for others that will follow. Just as Dallas's memorable Judge Irving L. Goldberg once said about judicial opinions, a book too "should have not only a beginning and an end, but a future."

ACKNOWLEDGMENTS TO THE 1998 EDITION

The publication of this expanded paperback edition of *Liberty and Sexuality* and the research involved in preparing the extensive new epilogue covering developments since 1993 have been aided by many friends and colleagues.

My deepest thanks go to Kristin Luker for first suggesting that the University of California Press would be an ideal publisher for a paperback edition. Timothy A. Byrnes, Neal Devins, Davison M. Douglas, Robert F. Drinan, Mary Dudziak, Laura Kalman, Bruce Allen Murphy, David M. O'Brien, Jeffrey Rosen, Gerald N. Rosenberg, Nadine Strossen, and Stephen Wermiel kindly added their voices in support, and Naomi Schneider of the University of California Press rightly encouraged me to prepare a thorough postscript that would update events through May 1998.

I owe deep and extensive debts to the highly skilled librarians and computer support professionals at the Emory University School of Law: Will Haines, Amy Flick, Terry Gordon, Linda Wagner, Gregg Wagner, Dan Nagy and Deborah Mann Keene. I also owe considerable thanks to Gloria Mann, Celeste Katz, and Katie McCormick.

Jodi Michael, Marcy Wilder, and Kate Michelman at NARAL have been exceptionally helpful, as have Stanley Henshaw, Ted Joyce, Eve Gartner, and Carole Joffe. Preparing the new epilogue has been an informative challenge, and this expansion of *Liberty and Sexuality*'s story ought to be helpful for everyone interested in *Roe* v. *Wade*'s wider legacy.

NOTES

CHAPTER ONE

1. Hilda C. Standish, M.D., "Medical Report, Maternal Health Center Annual Meeting," 15 June 1937, PPLC 39-C.
2. "Connecticut," *Birth Control Review*, February-March 1937, p. 4; and "Connecticut," *Birth Control Review*, June 1938, p. 104.
3. *Bridgeport Times-Star*, 18 April 1938, *Bridgeport Post*, 19 April 1938, and *Bridgeport Telegram*, 20 April 1938.
4. Sarah Clement Pease, "President's Report," 8 June 1939, PPLC 10-G.
5. Garrow conversations with Bice Clemow, Katharine H. Hepburn, Robert Hepburn, and Alfred M. Pease, Jr. Sallie Pease's obituary appears in the *Hartford Courant*, 26 May 1983, p. B8.
6. *Hartford Courant*, 9 June 1939, p. 24; *Waterbury Republican*, 9 June 1939, p. 15.
7. The best starting point for an appreciation of Waterbury in the 1930s is Jeremy Brecher et al., *Brass Valley: The Story of Working People's Lives and Struggles in an American Industrial Region* (Philadelphia: Temple University Press, 1982), esp. pp. 105, 215. A very valuable account of the Hayes trial and the political events leading up to it is Barbara A. C. Coyle, "The Waterbury Conspiracy Scandal of 1938: An Aberration in Connecticut State and Local Politics" (unpublished C.A.S. thesis, Wesleyan University, 1982). Also see Carl A. Lundgren et al., "Report of Extraordinary Grand Jury," [19 May 1938], Stevenson Papers; *Newsweek*, 30 May 1938, p. 10; the subsequent Connecticut Supreme Court decision affirming the resulting convictions, *State of Connecticut v. T. Frank Hayes et al.* 127 Conn. 543 (4 March 1941); and Wilbur L. Cross, *Connecticut Yankee: An Autobiography* (New Haven: Yale University Press, 1943), pp. 378-395. Pape's earlier efforts against the Hayes regime are reflected in *Harry C. Post et al. v. Thomas F. Dillane et al.*, 119 Conn. 655 (Conn. Sup. Ct., 3 April 1935), *State ex rel Pape v. John T. Derwin and Peter H. Dunais*, 2 Conn. Supp. 60 (New Haven County Super. Ct., 19 June 1935), and *State ex rel Pape v. Peter H. Dunais & John T. Derwin*, 120 Conn. 562 (Conn. Sup. Ct., 3 December 1935). Other Waterbury histories include an early one by Pape himself, *History of Waterbury and the Naugatuck Valley* (Chicago: S. J. Clarke, 1918), and Cornelius F. Maloney et al., eds., *Waterbury: A Pictorial History, 1674-1974* (Chester, CT: Pequot Press, 1974). On the *Republican* and *American*, an excellent source is Niver W. Beaman, *Fat Man in a Phone Booth: Notes Off a Newspaperman's Cuff* (Chicago: Cloud, 1947); Beaman was a *Republican* reporter and editor from 1928 to 1939. On the *Democrat*, and its subsequent closing, see *Editor & Publisher*, 8 February 1947, pp. 9, 66–67. The Brecher volume can also be supplemented by Cecilia Bucki, *Metal, Minds and Machine: Waterbury at Work* (Waterbury: Mattatuck Historical Society, 1980), and by Deirdre M. Moloney, "Families, Work, and Social Institutions: A Comparative Study of Immigrants and Their Children in Waterbury, Connecticut, 1900–1920" (unpublished M.A. thesis, University of Wisconsin, Madison, 1989), esp. pp. 42–48. Rowland L. Mitchell, Jr., "Social Legislation in Connecticut, 1919–1939" (unpublished Ph.D. dissertation, Yale University, 1954), pp. 16–19, provides an excellent overview of Connecticut immigration; additional sources, often focusing on Italian immigrants in New Haven, include David Rodnick, "Group Frustrations in Connecticut," *American Journal of Sociology* 47 (September 1941): 157–166; Irvin L. Child, *Italian or American? The Second Generation in Conflict* (New Haven: Yale University Press, 1943); Samuel Koenig, "Ethnic Factors in the Economic Life of Urban Connecticut," *American Sociological Review* 8 (April 1943): 193–197; Jerome K. Myers, "Assimilation to the Ecological and Social Systems

of a Community," *American Sociological Review* 15 (June 1950): 367–372; and Myers, "Assimilation in the Political Community," *Sociology and Social Research* 35 (January-February 1951): 175–182.

8. *Waterbury Democrat*, 9 June 1939, p. 1, and 15 May 1939, p. 3. The front-page news story in Saturday's (10 June) *Democrat* repeated Pease's statement and observed that "Her remarks apparently indicated that it was a triumph for the league."

9. *Waterbury Republican*, 10 June 1939, p. 2.

10. *Waterbury American*, 10 June 1939, p. 3. On Jeannie Heppel, who was then fifty-three years old and had been dispensary supervisor since 1919, see a 31 October 1954 *Waterbury Republican* profile marking her retirement, and her obituary in the 21 September 1962 *Republican*, p. 4. The Chase Dispensary building, designed by well-known architect Cass Gilbert, was constructed in 1923–1924.

11. *Waterbury Democrat*, 9 June 1939, p. 1; Parish Annual Reports, 1938, 1939, 1940, for St. Patrick's, Immaculate Conception, Our Lady of Lourdes, Sacred Heart, and others, Archives of the Archdiocese of Hartford; Robert E. Shea, *Saint Patrick's Church, Waterbury, Connecticut* (South Hackensack, NJ: Custombook, 1980); [George F. X. Reilly, ed.], *The Story of 100 Years, 1847–1947* (Waterbury: Immaculate Conception Parish, 1947); *Golden Jubilee, 1899–1949* (Waterbury: Our Lady of Lourdes Church, 1949); *Waterbury Democrat*, 29 April 1939, p. 12, 18 May 1939, pp. 1, 5, and 27 May 1939, p.2; Moloney, "Families, Work, and Social Institutions," pp. 42-48. Cryne obituaries appear in the *Waterbury Republican*, 9 September 1963, and the *Catholic Transcript*, 12 September 1963, p. 10. Cryne and John S. Kennedy were also undeniably well acquainted; see *Waterbury Democrat*, 10 October 1939, p. 5. On Kennedy, a Hartford native (b. 1909) who became associate editor of the *Catholic Transcript* immediately upon his ordination in 1935, and who later served as editor of the *Transcript* throughout the 1950s and 1960s, see the *Hartford Courant*, 13 November 1959, p. 4, and 11 January 1971, and the 26 May 1960 *Transcript*.

   Copies of parish histories for additional Waterbury Catholic churches, including St. Thomas (1948), Sts. Peter and Paul (1970), Sacred Heart (1975), and St. Anne (1987) are also available at the Mattatuck Museum. An exceptionally valuable resource is Thomas S. Duggan (then Vicar-General of the Hartford Diocese), *The Catholic Church in Connecticut* (New York: States History Co., 1930), esp. pp. 375–400. Much less useful is Austin F. Munich's brief pamphlet, *The Beginnings of Roman Catholicism in Connecticut* (New Haven: Yale University Press, 1935).

12. Garrow conversations with Father Robert E. Shea (St. Patrick's) and Father Walter A. Vichis (Blessed Sacrament); *Waterbury Republican*, 12 June 1939, pp. 1, 3; *Waterbury Democrat*, 12 June 1939, p. 1; *Catholic Transcript*, 15 June 1939, p.1.

13. Garrow conversations with Anthony Fitzgerald and William J. Secor, Jr.; *Waterbury Republican*, 12 June 1939, p. 1; *Waterbury Democrat*, 12 June 1939, p. 1.

14. Fitzgerald obituaries, *Waterbury American*, 2 December 1981, pp. 1, 5, and *Waterbury Republican*, 3 December 1981, p. 8; *Waterbury American*, 28 May 1968, p. 1; Lundgren et al., "Report of Extraordinary Grand Jury," pp. 59–60.

15. Garrow conversations with Anthony Fitzgerald, William J. Secor, Jr., and J. Warren Upson; *Hartford Courant*, 3 June 1938, p. 1; *Waterbury Republican*, 8 June 1938; Lewis obituary, *Waterbury Republican*, 19 July 1965; *New York Times*, 3 September 1938.

16. Garrow conversations with J. Warren Upson, William J. Secor, Jr., and Anthony Fitzgerald; J. Warren Upson Interview (Brecher); *Waterbury Democrat*, 11 May 1939, p. 3; *Waterbury Republican*, 19 June 1939, p. 1.

17. *Waterbury Republican*, 12 June 1939, pp. 1, 3. Although unnamed in the story, the Hartford attorney was almost certainly Lucius F. Robinson, Jr.

18. Copies of Fitzgerald's warrant application are in both the J. Warren Upson Papers and in the bound Connecticut Supreme Court Record and Briefs, *State of Connecticut* v. *Certain Contraceptive Materials*, #1780, January Term 1940, A-144, p. 173.

19. *Waterbury Republican*, 12 March 1961; *Waterbury Democrat*, 11 May 1939, p. 3; Garrow conversations with J. Warren Upson and William J. Secor, Jr.; *Waterbury American*, 19 February 1932, p. 7; *Waterbury Republican*, 23 November 1933. On McEvoy's appointment to the

bench, also see George E. Clapp, "The Kaiser of Connecticut," *American Mercury*, June 1933, pp. 229–36, at 233.

20. Connecticut Supreme Court Record and Briefs, *State of Connecticut* v. *Certain Contraceptive Materials*, #1780, January Term 1940, A-144, p. 173ff; *Waterbury Democrat*, 12 June 1939, pp. 1, 4; *Waterbury American*, 12 June 1939, p. 1; *Waterbury Republican*, 13 June 1939, pp. 1, 3; Fitzgerald to J. Warren Upson, 28 June 1939, Upson Papers. Walter Smyth's obituary appears in the *Waterbury Republican*, 5 August 1961, p. 2, and Albert S. Francis's in the *Republican*, 20 November 1963, p. 2, and the *American*, 19 November 1963. On K. G. Alling, see *Waterbury Democrat*, 30 June 1939, p. 22.

21. *Waterbury Democrat*, 12 June 1939, p. 4; Garrow conversations with Katharine H. Hepburn, Robert H. Hepburn, Margaret Hepburn Perry, Ellsworth Grant, Hilda Crosby Standish, and Bice Clemow; *West Hartford News*, 20 September 1979; "Statement of Mrs. Clara McTernan," 12 June 1939, p. 202, Upson Papers.

22. The best presently available source on the early political activities of Kit Hepburn is an early life biography of her daughter, based in part on family interviews: Christopher Andersen, *Young Kate* (New York: Henry Holt & Co., 1988), esp. pp. 44–45, 70, 102–05, 110–15, 163–64. Also valuable is Carole Nichols, "Votes and More for Women: Suffrage and After in Connecticut," *Women & History* 5 (Spring 1983): 1–92, which is a revised version of Nichols's "A New Force in Politics: The Suffragists' Experience in Connecticut" (unpublished M A thesis, Sarah Lawrence College, 1979). A brief (4pp.) untitled autobiographical essay by Kit Hepburn, perhaps a draft of remarks for a speech, and apparently dating from c.14 September 1946, is also significant: Kitchelt Papers, 6–153, as is an impressive Official Program for a 2 May 1914 Votes for Women Pageant and Parade in Hartford, which also includes photos of all the Connecticut activists: Kitchelt Papers, 1–13. In addition to Garrow conversations with Katharine Hepburn, Robert H. Hepburn, and Margaret Hepburn Perry, firsthand family sources include Katharine's autobiographical *Me: Stories of My Life* (New York: Alfred A. Knopf, 1991), esp. pp. 10, 19–21, 27; brief pieces by Katharine in the *Hartford Times Sunday Magazine*, 29 December 1968, pp. 3–6, and in *Family Circle*, 12 January 1982, pp. 64–65; Robert H. Hepburn to Barbara Ryden, 24 May 1983, PPLC 33-J; and two unpublished essays by the late Marion Hepburn Grant: "The Educated Housewife," 29pp., 1977 (Connecticut Historical Society, Hartford), and "Mother Was a Suffragette," 17pp., 21 October 1980, PPLC 24-S. Also useful—although modest conflicts about particular dates and events exist among some of these sources—are Carey E. Gross, "Katharine Houghton Hepburn '00," *Bryn Mawr Alumnae Bulletin*, Fall 1984, pp. 6–7; obituaries of Katharine Hepburn in the *New York Times*, 18 March 1951, p. 90, the *Hartford Courant*, 18 March 1951, pp. 1, 2, and the *Hartford Times*, 19 March 1951, p. 26; Thomas Hepburn's obituary in the *Courant*, 21 November 1962; Lupton A. Wilkinson and J. Bryan III, "The Hepburn Story" *Saturday Evening Post*, 29 November 1941, pp. 9–11, 89–92; Joseph S. Van Why, *Nook Farm* (Hartford: Stowe-Day Foundation, 1975); *Hartford Courant*, 8 November 1984, pp. F1, F2; and William J. Mann, "Hepburn: The Hartford Years," *Hartford Monthly*, February 1990, pp. 26–31, 80. Also see David M. Roth, *Connecticut: A Bicentennial History* (New York: W. W. Norton & Co., 1979), p. 190, and Allan M. Brandt, *No Magic Bullet* (New York: Oxford University Press, 1985), p. 38. Less relevant biographies of Katharine the younger include Anne Edwards, *A Remarkable Woman* (New York: William Morrow & Co., 1985), pp. 27–38; Michael Freedland, *Katharine Hepburn* (London: W. H. Allen, 1984), pp. 1–11; and Gary Carey, *Katharine Hepburn* (New York: St. Martin's Press, 1983). Distinctly unreliable is Charles Higham, *Kate: The Life of Katharine Hepburn* (New York: W. W. Norton & Co., 1975). On Jo Bennett's later life, see *New York Times*, 23 June 1954, p. 26; Nancy Cott, *The Grounding of Modern Feminism* (New Haven: Yale University Press, 1987), pp. 65, 73; and Janice R. and Stephen R. MacKinnon, *Agnes Smedley* (Berkeley: University of California Press, 1988), pp. 129, 256, 323.

23. Senate Judiciary Committee Hearing transcript, 27 February 1917, Connecticut State Library; *Hartford Courant*, 8 March 1917, pp. 8, 16, and 18 October 1917, p. 9; Nichols, "Votes and More," esp. pp. 18–21, 36; Andersen, *Young Kate*, pp. 163–64; and Rosalind Rosenberg, *Divided Lives: American Women in the Twentieth Century* (New York: Hill & Wang,

1992), pp. 69–73. Also see Christine A. Lunardini, *From Equal Suffrage to Equal Rights* (New York: New York University Press, 1986), pp. 6–7, 19, 138, and David Morgan, *Suffragists and Democrats: The Politics of Woman Suffrage in America* (East Lansing: Michigan State University Press, 1972). On Connecticut's ratification, see Edwin M. Dahill, Jr.'s superb "Connecticut's J. Henry Roraback" (unpublished Ed.D. dissertation, Teachers College, Columbia University, 1971), pp. 93–96.

24. Porritt's late daughter, Marjory Nield Blackall, wrote an excellent twenty-one-page biographical essay, "The Story of Annie G. Porritt" (unpublished manuscript, 1976), Porritt Papers, Sophia Smith Collection. Also see Nichols, "Votes and More," p. 8, and Annie Porritt, "Minutes," Executive Committee, Connecticut Society for Social Hygiene, 14 January 1920, Winslow Papers, Box 77. Like her husband, Edward O. Porritt, who authored *The Unreformed House of Commons* (Cambridge University Press, 1909, 2 vols.) (and who died in 1921), Annie Porritt too was a published writer. See for example *The Militant Suffrage Movement in England* (New York: National American Woman Suffrage Association, n.d. [c.1912]), 14pp.; "When I Was Young," *The Independent*, 25 June 1921, pp. 660–661, 677; and "Woman as a Metonymy," *The Independent*, 16 June 1910, pp. 1324–26. About that latter piece an introductory editor's note warned: "The theory propounded by Mrs. Porritt that man is the emotional sex is so novel that we considered it desirable to have it discussed by a competent authority and necessarily by a man," Lester F. Ward.

25. Connecticut *Journal of the House* (23 January 1917), p. 129, notes the introduction of House Bill 221, "An act repealing Section 1327 of the General Statutes," by Mr. Parsons of Enfield. Also see *Journal of the Senate* (24 January 1917), p. 173. A 1918 revision of the Connecticut code changed the section number to 6399, and a 1930 revision altered it to 6246. On Margaret Sanger, by far the best source is Ellen Chesler's impressive *Woman of Valor* (New York: Simon & Schuster, 1992), esp. pp. 85–88, 97–99. On Anthony Comstock and the 1873 federal legislation he championed (17 Stat. 599), the traditional but now very-dated beginning point is Heywood Broun and Margaret Leech, *Anthony Comstock: Roundsman of the Lord* (New York: Albert & Charles Boni, 1927), esp. pp. 128–44; C. Thomas Dienes, *Law, Politics, and Birth Control* (Urbana: University of Illinois Press, 1972), esp. pp. 33–39, 56–73, is better informed. Also see Anna Louise Bates, "Protective Custody: A Feminist Interpretation of Anthony Comstock's Life and Laws" (unpublished Ph.D. dissertation, State University of New York at Binghamton, 1991); Alvah W. Sulloway, *Birth Control and Catholic Doctrine* (Boston: Beacon Press, 1959), p. 3 (noting Comstock's earlier 1869 success in the New York state legislature); Peter Fryer, *The Birth Controllers* (London: Secker & Warburg, 1965), pp. 193–200; Paul S. Boyer, *Purity in Print: The Vice-Society Movement and Book Censorship in America* (New York: Charles Scribner's Sons, 1968); Robert W. Haney, *Comstockery in America* (Boston: Beacon Press, 1960); David J. Pivar, *Purity Crusade: Sexual Morality and Social Control, 1868–1900* (Westport, CT: Greenwood Press, 1973); John T. Noonan, Jr., *Contraception* (Cambridge, MA: Harvard University Press, 1965), pp. 412–13; and particularly John P. Harper, "Be Fruitful and Multiply: Origins of Legal Restrictions on Planned Parenthood in Nineteenth Century America," in Carol R. Berkin and Mary Beth Norton, eds., *Women of America* (Boston: Houghton Mifflin, 1979), pp. 245–65, esp. at 260–64. A sophisticated recent examination of northeastern urban Comstockery is Nicola Beisel, "Class, Culture, and Campaigns Against Vice in Three American Cities, 1872–1892" *American Sociological Review* 55 (February 1990): 44–62. Additional congressional amendments added in 1897 (29 Stat. 512) and 1909 expressly forbid the interstate shipment or importation of contraceptive items. See Henry J. Abraham and Leo A. Hazlewood, "Comstockery at the Bar of Justice: Birth Control Legislation in the Federal, Connecticut, and Massachusetts Courts," *Law in Transition Quarterly* 4 (December 1967): 220–45. The initial convictions under the Comstock statute appear to have been *U.S. v. Bott & Whitehead*, 24 Fed. 1204 (1873), and *U.S. v. Foote*, 25 Fed. 1140 (1876). See Helen I. Clarke, *Social Legislation*, 2nd ed. (New York: Appleton-Century-Crofts, 1957), pp. 173–76, and Norman E. Himes, *Medical History of Contraception* (Baltimore: Williams & Wilkins, 1936), p. 277. Also see *U.S. v. Popper*, 98 Fed. 423 (1899).

26. Chesler, *Woman of Valor*, pp. 97–127; Linda Gordon, *Woman's Body, Woman's Right: A Social*

History of Birth Control in America (New York: Grossman Publishers, 1976), pp. 221–223; and Francis M. Vreeland, "The Process of Reform With Especial Reference to Reform Groups in the Field of Population" (unpublished Ph.D. dissertation, University of Michigan, 1929), p. 60. Despite its odd title, the Vreeland dissertation is a substantial—578pp.—and impressive political history of birth control reform efforts in the years prior to 1927. It is essential reading for any serious student of the subject. Seemingly similar, but actually of very little substantive value, is Henrietta L. Bartleson, "The American Birth Control Movement" (unpublished Ph.D. dissertation, Syracuse University, 1974); also note Rilma Buckman, "Social Engineering: A Study of the Birth Control Movement," *Social Forces* 22 (May 1944): 420–428. Even lengthier—759pp.—than Vreeland is Mary Jane Huth, "The Birth Control Movement in the United States" (unpublished Ph.D. dissertation, St. Louis University, 1955), in whose view "Many of the leaders of the American Birth Control Movement during the late nineteenth and early twentieth centuries were recruited from radical and psychopathic elements in the population—feminists, socialists, freethinkers, and sex reformers" (p. 32).

On the pamphlet, see Joan M. Jensen, "The Evolution of Margaret Sanger's *Family Limitation* Pamphlet," *Signs* 6 (Spring 1981): 548–555, and Lynne Masel-Walters, "For the 'Poor Mute Mothers'?—Margaret Sanger and *The Woman Rebel*," *Journalism History* 11 (Spring/Summer 1984): 3–10, 37. Also see Sanger's own *My Fight For Birth Control* (New York: Farrar & Rinehart, 1931), pp. 91–95, as well as Sanger's *Margaret Sanger: An Autobiography* (New York: W. W. Norton & Co., 1938), pp. 118–122.

27. David M. Kennedy, *Birth Control in America: The Career of Margaret Sanger* (New Haven: Yale University Press, 1970), pp. 72–73, 80; Chesler, *Woman of Valor*, pp. 109, 126–131, 138–140; Gordon, *Woman's Body*, pp. 227–228; James Reed, *The Birth Control Movement and American Society: From Private Vice to Public Virtue*, rev. ed. (Princeton: Princeton University Press, 1983), pp. 90–98; Madeline Gray, *Margaret Sanger* (New York: Richard Marek, 1979), pp. 114–119; Lawrence Lader, *The Margaret Sanger Story* (Garden City, NY: Doubleday & Co., 1955), pp. 83, 94–95; *Survey*, 25 September 1915, p. 567. Also see Sanger's own *My Fight For Birth Control*, pp. 119–126, and Sanger's *Autobiography*, pp. 176–189. Contrary to Sanger's statement in the *Autobiography* (p. 188), and once in Connecticut (*Hartford Courant*, 3 June 1937, p. 8) that Katharine Houghton Hepburn attended the January 1916 dinner (and that she and Hepburn had known each other as children in Corning, New York), the best present evidence indicates that Hepburn and Sanger first met only in Hartford in early 1923. See "Pioneers in Birth Control to Observe 25th Anniversary," *Hartford Times*, 16 October 1941.

In addition to the Chesler, Gordon, Reed, Kennedy, Gray and Lader biographies cited above, the literature on Margaret Sanger is quite extensive, and sometimes combative. Gloria and Ronald Moore, *Margaret Sanger and the Birth Control Movement: A Bibliography, 1911–1984* (Metuchen, NJ: Scarecrow Press, 1986), is comprehensive for its time period. Also see Emily T. Douglas, *Margaret Sanger* (New York: Holt, Rinehart & Winston, 1970); Joan Dash, *A Life of One's Own: Three Gifted Women and the Men They Married* (New York: Harper & Row, 1973), pp. 1–113; Sheila M. Rothman, *Woman's Proper Place* (New York: Basic Books, 1978), pp. 188–209; and, generally, June Sochen, *The New Woman: Feminism in Greenwich Village, 1910–1920* (New York: Quadrangle Books, 1972). An excellent undergraduate thesis on Sanger, by her grandson, is Alexander C. Sanger, "Margaret Sanger: The Early Years, 1910–1917" (unpublished B.A. thesis, Princeton University, 1969). Other useful theses include Robert W. Mack, "Margaret Sanger and the Crusade for Birth Control" (unpublished B.A. thesis, Princeton University, 1962); Susan A. Nicholson, "Margaret Sanger: Rebellion and Respectability" (unpublished M.A. thesis, Smith College, 1973); and Elizabeth S. Wood, "Margaret Sanger: The Making of a Crusader" (unpublished B.A. thesis, Princeton University, 1991).

Essays that express varied, although often critical, opinions concerning the Kennedy, Reed, and/or Gordon books include Constance Lindemann, "Margaret Sanger and the Birth Control Movement," *Women & Health* 3 (1978): 12–21; Nancy F. Cott, "Abortion, Birth Control, and American Public Policy," *Yale Review* 67 (Summer 1978): 600–605; Harriet B.

Presser, "Birth Control and the Control of Motherhood," *Family Planning Perspectives* 10 (November-December 1978): 374–376; David M. Kennedy, "Decrease and Stultify: Contraception and Abortion in American Society," *Reviews in American History* 7 (March 1979): 18–25; Elizabeth Fee and Michael Wallace, "The History and Politics of Birth Control," *Feminist Studies* 5 (Spring 1979): 201–215; Ann J. Lane, "The Politics of Birth Control," *Marxist Perspectives* 2 (Fall 1979): 160–169; Mary P. Ryan, "Reproduction in American History," *Journal of Interdisciplinary History* 10 (Autumn 1979): 319–332; Dorothy Wardell, "Margaret Sanger: Birth Control's Successful Revolutionary," *American Journal of Public Health* 70 (July 1980): 736–742; James Reed, "Public Policy on Human Reproduction and the Historian," *Journal of Social History* 18 (Spring 1985): 383–398; and Esther Katz, "The History of Birth Control in the United States," *Trends in History* 4 (1988): 81–101. Also see Dorothy Green and Mary-Elizabeth Murdock, eds., *The Margaret Sanger Centennial Conference* [1979] (Northampton, MA: Smith College, 1982), esp. p. 46; the *Journal of Social History* 11 (Fall 1978): 269–273, and 12 (Fall 1978): 173–177, and *Signs* 4 (Summer 1979): 804–808. An extensive evaluation of Chesler's *Woman of Valor* is Daniel J. Kevles, "Sex Without Fear," *New York Times Book Review*, 28 June 1992, pp. 1, 34–35.

28. Chesler, *Woman of Valor,* pp. 140–42, 171; Gordon, *Woman's Body*, pp. 228–229; Vreeland, "The Process of Reform," pp. 388–391. The initial organizing of the Allison defense group is documented in multiple 1916 meeting minutes in the PPLM Papers, Box 25. Informative stories include *The Masses*, September 1916, p. 15, and J. Prentice Murphy, "The Allison Case," *Survey,* 9 December 1916, pp. 266–267. An excellent retrospective overview of the early Massachusetts developments is Cerise Carman Jack, "Massachusetts" *Birth Control Review* 2 (April 1918): 7–8; also see Diane McCarrick Gieg's valuable "The Birth Control League of Massachusetts, 1916–1940" (unpublished B.A. thesis, Simmons College, 1973), pp. 14–57. The Massachusetts Supreme Judicial Court's affirmation of Allison's conviction is *Commonwealth* v. *Allison*, 227 Mass. 57, 116 N.E. 265 (25 May 1917).

29. Chesler, *Woman of Valor*, pp. 143–145, 150; and Sanger, "Clinics, Courts and Jails," *Birth Control Review*, April 1918, pp. 8–9. On the Connecticut bill, the minimal surviving state legislative records indicate that there may have been a hearing on the measure on the afternoon of 8 March 1917, but if so, no Connecticut newspapers noted it. Following unfavorable committee reports (which, if actually written, also do not survive), both the House, on March 9, and the Senate, on March 17, rejected the bill. *Journal of the House*, p. 694; *Journal of the Senate*, p. 735. That April 1918 issue of the *Birth Control Review*, in a list of American birth control centers, included Henry F. Fletcher, Room 422, 647 Main Street, Hartford, but no evidence suggests that this was anything more than Fletcher's office.

30. Elizabeth Stuyvesant, "The Brownsville Birth Control Clinic," *Birth Control Review*, March 1917, pp. 6–8; Jonah J. Goldstein, "The Birth Control Clinic Cases," *Birth Control Review*, February 1917, p. 8; and *People of the State of New York* v. *Byrne*, 163 N.Y. Supp. 680, 681 (5 December 1916). Also see Chesler, *Woman of Valor*, pp. 150–152; Lader, *Margaret Sanger*, pp. 107–115, Gray, *Margaret Sanger*, pp. 126–27; Douglas, *Margaret Sanger*, pp. 105–110; and Sanger's *My Fight*, pp. 152–160, and her *Autobiography*, pp. 213–223. On Goldstein, see his obituary, *New York Times*, 23 July 1967, p. 60, and *National Cyclopedia of American Biography*, p. 256; Goldstein's extensive 1965 interview with the Columbia University Oral History Program unfortunately does not discuss this lower court litigation.

31. Goldstein, "The Birth Control Clinic Cases"; *People of the State of New York* v. *Byrne*, 163 N.Y. Supp. 682, 684 (3 February 1917); Chesler, *Woman of Valor*, pp. 152–158; Lader, *Margaret Sanger*, pp. 127–137; and Sanger's *My Fight*, pp. 169–184, and her *Autobiography*, pp. 224–237. A full transcript of Margaret's trial appears at pages 7 through 91 of the case's formal printed record, in the U.S. Supreme Court file, *Sanger* v. *People of the State of New York*, O.T. 1917 #945, National Archives, RG 267, File #26412, Box 7093.

32. Chesler, *Woman of Valor*, pp. 158–60; *People of the State of New York* v. *Sanger*, 179 App. Div. 939 (31 July 1917); *People* v. *Sanger*, 222 N.Y. 192 (8 January 1918); Jack H. Hudson, "Birth Control Legislation," *Cleveland-Marshall Law Review* 9 (May 1960): 245–257, at 246–247; Dienes, *Law, Politics, and Birth Control*, p. 87; *Sanger* v. *People* File, U.S. Supreme Court, n. 31

above; and *Sanger* v. *People*, 251 U.S. 537 (17 November 1919). As Sanger herself later wrote, "The decision in question would have been more thoroly [*sic*] and widely called to the attention of the medical profession had we not hoped that by an appeal to the United States Supreme Court to gain even a greater advantage." "The Legal Right of Physicians to Prescribe Birth Control Measures," *American Medicine* 15 (June 1920): 321–323. Also see Lader, *Margaret Sanger*, pp. 148–149; Sanger's *Autobiography*, pp. 238–250; and Goldstein's recollection of the 1919 Supreme Court oral argument at pp. 81–83 of his 1965 interview with Douglas Scott of the Columbia Oral History Program.

33. Kennedy, *Birth Control in America*, pp. 220–221; Mary Ware Dennett, *Birth Control Laws* (New York: Frederick H. Hitchcock, 1926), pp. 94–95; Sanger, "How Shall We Change the Law," *Birth Control Review*, July 1919, pp. 8–9; Jensen, "The Evolution of Margaret Sanger's *Family Limitation* Pamphlet," pp. 554–555.

34. Chesler, *Woman of Valor*, pp. 200–205; *Hartford Courant*, 15 November 1921, p. 10; *New Republic*, 30 November 1921, p. 9. Also see Vreeland, "The Process of Reform," pp. 132–135; Lader, *Margaret Sanger*, pp. 172–185; Gray, *Margaret Sanger*, pp. 171–174; and Sanger's *My Fight*, pp. 212–237, and *Autobiography*, pp. 301–315. Also see Annie G. Porritt, "Publicity in the Birth Control Movement," in *Report of the 5th International Neo-Malthusian and Birth Control Conference* (London), 14 July 1922, pp. 301–307, at 304, who observed that "the opponents did the maximum of service to the movement. . . . Persecution furnishes perhaps the very best publicity."

35. "Minutes of the First Annual Meeting of the American Birth Control League," 12 January 1922, PPFA Box 1; *Hartford Courant*, 9 October 1922, p. 2, and 10 October 1922, p. 1; Chesler, *Woman of Valor*, p. 236; ABCL "Organization Department Report," n.d.; Annie Porritt, "Minutes," Second Annual Meeting, ABCL, 11 January 1923, PPFA Box 1; and *Laws on Birth Control in the U.S.A.* (New York: ABCL, 1924), pp. 3–4, Porritt Papers, Box 2. Additional 1922 ABCL board of directors meeting minutes—for 12 April, 10 May, 22 May, 5 June, 3 November, and 13 December—all further detail Day and Porritt's participation. Also see Anne Kennedy, "Report of Executive Secretary, American Birth Control League," 1922, p. 5, PPFA Box 1.

36. Chesler, *Woman of Valor*, pp. 226, 232–233, 274; Kennedy, *Birth Control in America*, pp. 182, 222; Connecticut *Journal of the House*, p. 224, and *Journal of the Senate*, p. 285. A copy of House Bill 504 is in the 1923 Connecticut General Assembly Records (RG 2), Box 78.

37. Dienes, *Law, Politics, and Birth Control*, pp. 43–47; Carol F. Brooks, "The Early History of the Anti-Contraceptive Laws in Massachusetts and Connecticut" (unpublished M.A. thesis, Brown University, 1964), pp. 18–27, 49–52; Brooks, "The Early History of the Anti-Contraceptive Laws in Massachusetts and Connecticut," *American Quarterly* 18 (Spring 1966): 3–23; Stephen D. Howard, "The Birth Control Law Conflict in Massachusetts" (unpublished B.A. thesis, Harvard University, 1959), pp. 3–8; Catherine Jackson Tilson to J. Warren Upson, 30 June 1939, Upson Papers; 1879 Connecticut *Journal of the Senate*, pp. 236, 294, 317, 339, 414, 449 and 586; *Journal of the House*, pp. 271, 333, 488, 548, 576 and 594; *Hartford Courant*, 19 March, 20 March, 21 March, and 27 March 1879; and Joseph F. Brodley and Edwin D. Etherington, "Contraception: Human Right or Criminal Deviation?" (unpublished paper, Yale Law School, 25 May 1950) [PPLC 4-M and N], who observe (p. 6): "We know almost nothing about its passage."

The Brooks thesis, pp. 22–27, contains a thorough exegesis and analysis of the legislative language, and correctly raises the clear but unanswerable question of whether the precise wording of the final statute resulted from the possibility that "an extra 'use' was unintentionally included" when the substitute bill was prepared. Neither Neil Harris, *Humbug: The Art of P. T. Barnum* (Boston: Little, Brown, 1973), esp. pp. 186–189 and 196–201, nor A. H. Saxon, *P. T. Barnum: The Legend and the Man* (New York: Columbia University Press, 1989), esp. pp. 247–273, at 270–273, refer to Barnum's involvement in this story. Barnum previously had served in the 1865, 1866, and 1878 legislatures, and in 1875–1876 had been mayor of Bridgeport. Saxon (pp. 270–271) reports that Barnum's principal 1879 legislative focus was opposing capital punishment. Also see the most reliable edition of Barnum's much-amended and reprinted autobiography, George S. Bryan, ed., *Struggles and Triumphs*, 2 vols. (New York: Alfred A. Knopf, 1927), esp. pp. 731–732 and 734, as well as Harvey W. Root, "Barnum as Legislator," *Harper's*, September 1926, pp. 465–475 (which focuses almost exclusively on the 1865 session); Root, *The Unknown Barnum* (New York: Harper & Bros., 1927), esp. pp. 200–202; M. R. Werner, *Barnum* (New York: Harcourt, Brace, 1923); and Irving Wallace, *The Fabulous Showman: The Life and Times of P. T. Barnum* (New York: Alfred A. Knopf, 1959), esp. pp. 260–262.

38. *Hartford Courant*, 12 February 1923, pp. 1, 2; *Hartford Times*, 12 February 1923, p. 6; and Sanger, "Address at Parsons Theatre," 11 February 1923, 31pp., Sanger-LC Box 202, esp. p. 31, which apparently is a transcription from some type of recording, and includes only the formal speech, and not the ensuing question and answer period described in the press coverage. Also see Sanger's *Autobiography*, pp. 293–294, and Joan M. Gaulard, "Woman Rebel: The Rhetorical Strategies of Margaret Sanger and the American Birth Control Movement, 1912 to 1938" (unpublished Ph.D. dissertation, Indiana University, 1978), pp. 98–100.

39. "Pioneers in Birth Control to Observe 25th Anniversary," *Hartford Times*, 16 October 1941; *Hartford Times*, 13 February 1923, p. 25, and 14 February 1923, p. 17; *Hartford Courant*, 14 February 1923, pp. 1, 2; *New Haven Journal-Courier*, 14 February 1923, pp. 1, 4; *New York Times*, 14 February 1923, p. 8; "The Hearing at Hartford," *Birth Control Review*, March 1923, pp. 63–64. The obituary for Butler, later the United States Attorney for Connecticut (1934–1945), appears in the *Courant*, 8 February 1971.

40. Connecticut *Journal of the House*, p. 826 (21 March), and *Journal of the Senate*, p. 832 (23 March); *Hartford Courant*, 21 March 1923, p. 1; *Hartford Times*, 21 March 1923, p. 1. For an overview of the 1923 legislative session, see Dahill's valuable "J. Henry Roraback," which terms it "not particularly noteworthy" (p. 169). Also see Lane W. Lancaster, "Rotten Boroughs and the Connecticut Legislature," *National Municipal Review* 13 (December 1924): 678–683; and Don C. Seitz, "Connecticut: A Nation in Miniature," *The Nation*, 18 April 1923, pp. 461–464.

41. *Birth Control Herald* [Voluntary Parenthood League], 30 January 1924; U.S. Congress, *Cummins-Vaile Bill—Joint Hearings Before the Subcommittee of the Committees on the Judiciary*, 68th Cong., 1st sess., 8 April and 9 May 1924 (U.S. GPO Serial 38, 1924), 79pp.; Dennett, *Birth Control Laws*, pp. 294–298; Chesler, *Woman of Valor*, pp. 232–233; Annie Porritt, "Minutes," ABCL Board of Directors, 27 November 1923, Porritt Box 2; Porritt, "Minutes," ABCL Third Annual Meeting, 10 January 1924, PPFA Box 1; "Birth Control and Federal Legislation," *Birth Control Review*, March 1924, pp. 68–69; and Porritt to Dennett, 18 June 1924, as well as Dennett to Porritt, 19 June 1924, Dennett Papers 16–287.

42. Chesler, *Woman of Valor*, p. 229; Connecticut *Journal of the Senate*, pp. 276 (30 January) and 692 (18 March), and *Journal of the House*, pp. 388 (3 February) and 763 (20 March); Annie Porritt, "Minutes," ABCL Board of Directors, 9 February 1925, Porritt Papers, Box 2; *Hartford Courant*, 12 March 1925, p. 6, 13 March 1925, p. 1, and 19 March 1925, p. 11; *Hartford Times*, 12 March 1925, p. 2, and 13 March 1925, p. 39; *New Haven Journal-Courier*, 13 March 1925, pp. 1, 3; *Meriden Journal*, 18 March 1925; "Report of Anne Kennedy, Executive Secretary, for 1925," ABCL Papers, Houghton Library, Box 11; Louise H. Fisher File, *Hartford Courant* Library. Prior to Hepburn's role at the hearing, the ABCL's top staffer had worried to Mrs. Day that it was "discouraging" that Hepburn "has shown so little response to anything." Kennedy to Day, 1 December 1924, ABCL Papers, Houghton, Box 3. Dahill, "J. Henry Roraback," p. 188, describes 1925 as "a very steady and unexciting legislative session."

43. Day to Kennedy, 3 [January] 1926, Kennedy to Day, 6 January 1926, Fletcher to Kennedy, 19 January 1926, Kennedy to Fletcher, 25 January 1926, Fletcher to Kennedy, 27 January 1926, and Kennedy to Fletcher, 1 February 1926, ABCL Papers, Houghton, Box 7; ABCL schedule documents for January 1926, PPFA Box 33; Chesler, *Woman of Valor*, p. 233; Kennedy, *Birth Control in America*, p. 102.

44. Vreeland, "The Process of Reform," pp. 150–160, 441, 517; Chesler, *Woman of Valor*, pp. 236–238, 278; Porritt to Penelope B. P. Huse, 20 January 1927 and 1 February 1927, and Porritt to Anne Kennedy, 15 April 1926, ABCL Papers, Houghton, Boxes 8 and 6; Connecticut *Journal of the Senate*, pp. 126 and 673 (25 January and 17 March 1927); *Journal of*

the House, pp. 214 and 743–744 (26 January and 22 March 1927); *New Haven Journal-Courier*, 10 March 1927, p. 2; and *Hartford Courant*, 10 March 1927, p. 10, and 20 March 1927, p. 18. Dahill, "J. Henry Roraback," p. 194, characterizes the 1927 legislative session as "orderly and unspectacular." The House that year had 237 Republicans and only 25 Democrats; the Senate thirty-four Republicans and *one* Democrat. Lane W. Lancaster, "The Background of a State 'Boss' System," *American Journal of Sociology* 35 (March 1930): 783–798, at 795.

Another bill that stopped short of the repeal called for by Senate Bill 145, House Bill 105, was introduced by Representative Bridge of Enfield, and was similarly rejected by the Judiciary Committee and by both the House and the Senate. *Journal of the House*, pp. 137 and 713 (20 January and 17 March 1927); *Journal of the Senate*, pp. 135 and 711–712 (25 January and 22 March 1927). Neither the legislative records nor any surviving correspondence, nor any newspaper stories, shed any light on why this second bill also was introduced and what relationship to it the Connecticut women or Henry Fletcher may have had. Almost three years later, however, Katharine Beach Day, in a 19 November 1929 report on the Connecticut League to an ABCL National Birth Control Conference, with apparent reference to the type of doctors-only reform bill that had been put forward in 1925, explained that "We found much opposition to this bill, even in the medical profession, and our doctor friends advised a simple repeal." "Report for Conference, Connecticut Birth Control League," PPFA Box 36.

45. Chesler, *Woman of Valor*, pp. 237–241; Kennedy, *Birth Control in America*, pp. 103–105; Porritt to Jones, 21 September 1928, Porritt, "Minutes," ABCL Board of Directors, 14 February and 16 March 1928, Heck to Porritt, 14 July and 22 July 1928, Grace R. Adkins to Katharine Beach Day, 21 July 1928, Penelope B. P. Huse to S. R. Colladay, 17 May 1928, Huse to Porritt, 6 October 1928, ABCL Connecticut Branch form letter, 15 September 1928, Evelyn Rice to Porritt, 29 October 1928, and Reverend T. F. Rutledge Beale to Porritt, 9 November 1928, all in Porritt Box 2; Penelope B. P. Huse, "Report of Executive Secretary," 13 November 1928, and Katharine Beach Day, Connecticut Birth Control League Annual Report, 16 January 1930, PPFA Box 1. Also see Sanger's *My Fight*, pp. 329–335, and *Autobiography*, pp. 392–397, and, generally, Helena H. Smith, "Birth Control and the Law," *The Outlook*, 29 August 1928, pp. 686–687, 718. The Konikow case events and effects are richly documented by a variety of materials in PPLM Box 25; also see Gieg, "The Birth Control League of Massachusetts," pp. 58–63.

46. Katharine B. Day, Connecticut Birth Control League Annual Report, 16 January 1930, PPFA Box 1; Day to Katherine Seymour Day, 27 December 1928, Day Papers; Hepburn to Sanger, 13 February 1929, and Sanger to Hepburn, 23 February 1929, Sanger-LC Box 135; *Hartford Times*, 28 February 1929, p. 1; *New Haven Journal-Courier*, 1 March 1929, pp. 1, 2, 5; *Hartford Courant*, 1 March 1929, pp. 1, 2.

47. *Hartford Courant*, 6 March 1929, pp. 1, 4, 7 March 1929, p. 11, 9 March 1929, p. 3, 13 March 1929, pp. 1, 14, and 14 March 1929, p. 17; *Journal of the Senate*, pp. 103 and 577 (23 January and 6 March); *Journal of the House*, pp. 152, 634–635, and 663–664 (24 January, 8 March, and 12 March); *Hartford Times*, 12 March 1929, pp. 1, 20; *New Haven Journal-Courier*, 13 March 1929, p. 6; Katharine Beach Day, "Report for Conference; Connecticut Birth Control League," 19 November 1929, and CBCL Annual Report, 16 January 1930, PPFA Boxes 36 and 1; Peck obituaries in *Waterbury Republican*, 30 October 1938, pp. 1, 4, and *Yale University Obituary Record, 1937–1940*, pp. 277–278. Dahill's unpublished "J. Henry Roraback," which is without a doubt the most informative Connecticut political history for this period, says that the 1929 session "set a high mark for efficiency" (p. 207). Another almost equally valuable source, similarly unpublished, is Mitchell's "Social Legislation in Connecticut, 1919–1939," esp. pp. 57–95. The partisan imbalance in the Connecticut legislature in the 1920s is best covered in three articles by Lane W. Lancaster: "The Background of a State 'Boss' System" (n. 44 above), "Rotten Boroughs and the Connecticut Legislature" (n. 40 above), and "The Democratic Party in Connecticut," *National Municipal Review* 17 (August 1928): 451–455. Valuable survey accounts of Connecticut in the 1920s are Albert E. Van Dusen, *Connecticut* (New York: Random House, 1961), pp. 279–290; and Herbert F. Janick, Jr., *A Diverse People: Connecticut 1914 to the Present* (Chester, CT: Pequot Press, 1975), pp. 32–37.

48. Katharine Beach Day, "Report for Conference, Connecticut Birth Control League," 19 November 1929, and CBCL Annual Report, 16 January 1930, PPFA Boxes 36 and 1; *New York Times*, 16 April 1929, p. 31, 19 April 1929, p. 27, 20 April 1929, p. 21, 21 April 1929, p. I-9, 23 April 1929, p. 3, 25 April 1929, p. 31, 26 April 1929, p. 13, 12 May 1929, pp. 1, 15, and 15 May 1929, p. 20; "The Raid," *Birth Control Review*, May 1929, p. 139; Hannah M. Stone, "The Birth Control Raid," *Eugenics* 2 (August 1929): 1–4; Sanger, "The Birth Control Raid," *New Republic*, 1 May 1929, pp. 305–306; Ernst, *A Love Affair with the Law* (New York: Macmillan, 1968), pp. 131–132; Ernst and Gwendolyn Pickett, *Birth Control in the Courts* (New York: Planned Parenthood Federation of America, 1942), pp. 15–17; Dudley Nichols, "Sex and the Law," *The Nation* 128 (8 May 1929): 552–554; Chesler, *Woman of Valor*, pp. 282–283; Kennedy, *Birth Control in America*, p. 224; Lader, *Margaret Sanger*, pp. 254–262. Also see Sanger's *My Fight*, pp. 318–326, and *Autobiography*, pp. 402–408. See as well William J. McWilliams, "Laws of New York and Birth Control," *Birth Control Review* 14 (February 1930): 46–47, 61–63; and Alexander Lindey, "Change the New York Law," *Birth Control Review* 14 (March 1930): 79–80. On Hannah Stone, see the memorial tributes in *Human Fertility* 6 (August 1941): 108–113.

49. "The Raid," *Birth Control Review* 13 (June 1929): 154–155; Patrick J. Ward, "The Catholics and Birth Control," *New Republic*, 29 May 1929, pp. 35–38, at 35; Sanger, "The Next Step," *Birth Control Review* 13 (October 1929): 278–279. Also see *A New Day Dawns for Birth Control* (New York: National Committee on Federal Legislation, 1937), p. 16; Reed, *Birth Control Movement*, p. 120; Ernst, *The Best Is Yet . . .* (New York: Harper & Bros., 1945), pp. 252–253; William M. Morehouse, "The Speaking of Margaret Sanger in the Birth Control Movement from 1916 to 1937" (unpublished Ph.D. dissertation, Purdue University, 1968), p. 148; Helena H. Smith, "They Were Eleven," *New Yorker*, 5 July 1930, pp. 22–25; Chesler, *Woman of Valor*, pp. 233–234, and Dorothy D. Bromley, "The Question of Birth Control," *Harper's*, December 1929, pp. 35–45.

50. Ida H. Timme to Hepburn, 11 October 1929, Hepburn to Timme, 17 October 1929, Sanger to Hepburn, 19 October 1929, Hepburn to Sanger, 21 October 1929, Sanger to Hepburn, 23 October 1929, Timme to Hepburn, 24 October 1929, Sanger to Hepburn, 6 November 1929, Hepburn to Sanger, 9 November 1929, Hepburn to Sanger, 29 November 1929, Sanger to Hepburn, 30 November 1929, all in Sanger-LC Boxes 134 and 135; Gordon, *Woman's Body*, p. 270; Katharine Beach Day, "Report for Conference, Connecticut Birth Control League," 19 November 1929, and CBCL Annual Report, 16 January 1930, PPFA Boxes 36 and 1; Constance Heck to Hepburn, 2 April 1930, Clara Louise [Rowe] McGraw to Day, 2 July 1930, "List of Connecticut Endorsers," 14 February 1930, and Harden Stille to Nancy Rockefeller, 28 July 1930, Sanger-LC Boxes 135 and 134.

51. On Connecticut politics of the period, including Cross's victory and its perceived meaning, see Dahill, "J. Henry Roraback," esp. pp. 2, 19, 55, 229–232, and Mitchell, "Social Legislation," pp. 329–340. Significant contemporaneous stories include Allen B. MacMurphy, "Revolt in Connecticut," *Nation*, 10 September 1930, pp. 263–265, and Bulkley S. Griffin, "Roraback of Connecticut," *New Republic*, 26 November 1930, pp. 41–43. Also see George E. Clapp, "The Kaiser of Connecticut," *American Mercury*, June 1933, pp. 229–236; Roth, *Connecticut*, pp. 196–198; Janick, *A Diverse People*, pp. 43–53; Mary H. Murray, "Wilbur L. Cross: Connecticut Statesman and Humanitarian, 1930–1935" (unpublished Ph.D. dissertation, University of Connecticut, 1972), esp. pp. 50–51; Ernest H. Nelson, Jr., "Years of Transformation: Connecticut in the Time of Wilbur Cross, 1930–1938" (unpublished B.A. thesis, Princeton University, 1961); and Peter J. Lombardo, "Connecticut in the Great Depression, 1929–1933" (unpublished Ph.D. dissertation, University of Notre Dame, 1979). Roraback remained a dominant figure in Connecticut politics until 1936, when he suffered brain damage as a result of an extremely serious fever. Sixteen months later, on 18 May 1937, he committed suicide by shooting himself. See Dahill, "J. Henry Roraback," pp. 270-273, and *Time*, 31 May 1937, p. 20.

52. "Connecticut Birth Control League," *Birth Control Review* 14 (November 1930): 324; Annie Porritt, "Connecticut," *Birth Control Review* 15 (February 1931): 44; Kenyon, "Nullification

or Repeal?," *Birth Control Review* 14 (October 1930): 278–280; "A Symposium on Nullification and Repeal," *Birth Control Review* 14 (November 1930): 309–316. Interestingly, and perhaps in reference to the summer 1930 contact with the Greenwich women, the Connecticut item also said that "As the law is so difficult to change, an effort is being made to get doctors to open clinics and so test it out."

53. *Youngs Rubber Corp.* v. *C. I. Lee & Co.*, 45 F.2d 103 (15 December 1930); "Some Legislative Aspects of Birth Control," *Harvard Law Review* 45 (February 1932): 723–729 at 727; U.S. Congress, Senate, Committee on the Judiciary, *Birth Control—Hearings Before a Subcommittee on S.4582*, 71st Cong., 3rd sess., 13 and 14 February 1931, pp. 2, 28, 30, 50. On *Youngs Rubber*, also see Ernst, "How We Nullify," *The Nation* 134 (27 January 1932): 113–114; Ernst and Lindey, *The Censor Marches On* (New York: Doubleday, Doran & Co., 1940), pp. 157–160; Ernst and Pickett, *Birth Control in the Courts*, pp. 18–20; Kennedy, *Birth Control in America*, pp. 246–248; James S. Murphy, *The Condom Industry in the United States* (Jefferson, NC: McFarland & Co., 1990), pp. 10–11; and Joshua Gamson, "Rubber Wars: Struggles over the Condom in the United States," *Journal of the History of Sexuality* 1 (October 1990): 262–282. On the Senate hearing, also see Chesler, *Woman of Valor*, pp. 328–330; Kennedy, *Birth Control in America*, pp. 228–229; Lader, *Margaret Sanger*, pp. 268–270; Gray, *Margaret Sanger*, pp. 310–311; Morehouse, "The Speaking of Margaret Sanger," pp. 192–195; and Robert E. Riegel and Lawrence Eager, "The Birth Control Controversy," *Current History* 36 (August 1932): 563–568. See as well Sanger's *My Fight*, pp. 346–356, and *Autobiography*, pp. 419–422.

54. See "Birth Control League of Massachusetts," *Birth Control Review* 14 (October 1930): 292; Robert Homans et al., "Legal Opinions Concerning the Right of Doctors to Give Contraceptive Advice," *New England Journal of Medicine* 202 (23 January 1930): 192–197; "The Proposed Amendment . . ." *New England Journal of Medicine* 203 (11 December 1930): 1218–1219; Norman E. Himes, "Does a Minority Rule Massachusetts?" *Birth Control Review* 15 (April 1931): 108–110; John Rock, *The Time Has Come* (New York: Alfred A. Knopf, 1963), pp. 75–77; Gieg, "The Birth Control League of Massachusetts," pp. 74–78; and Antoinette F. Konikow, "The Doctor's Dilemma in Massachusetts," *Birth Control Review* 15 (January 1931): 21–22. Konikow advocated simply opening a facility, arguing "It is likely such a clinic would not be disturbed for years, if at all." Even if raided, she added, "birth control has nothing to fear from a test case and the public's reaction to it."

55. Porritt, "Connecticut," *Birth Control Review*, February 1931, p. 44; *Hartford Courant*, 23 January 1931, p. 17, 30 January 1931, p. 5, 24 February 1931, p. 17, 25 February 1931, p. 2, 21 March 1931, 1 April 1931, pp. 1, 5, 2 April 1931, pp. 1, 18, 3 April 1931, p. 3; *New Haven Journal-Courier*, 24 February 1931, p. 10, 3 April 1931, p. 1; *Hartford Times*, 24 February 1931, p. 1, 1 April 1931, pp. 1, 12, 2 April 1931, pp. 1, 25; *Journal of the House*, pp. 151, 276, 526, 919, 998–1004 (22 January, 29 January, 25 February, 26 March, 1 April); *Journal of the Senate*, pp. 147, 313, 521, 975 (27 January, 30 January, 27 February, 2 April); Porritt to "Dear Friend and Member," 14 February 1931, Day Papers; *Outlook and Independent*, 15 April 1931, p. 518. On Katharine Beach Day, also see Day to Sanger, 17 December 1933, Sanger to Day, 14 February 1934, Day to Ms. Dryden, 4 February 1935, Sanger to Day, 8 February 1935, Day to Bernice Wickham, 15 January 1936, Wickham to Day, 17 January 1936, Day to Sanger, 28 December 1936, and Sanger to Day, 11 January 1937, all in Sanger-LC Box 135. Miller's obituary appears in the *Courant*, 27 October 1971. Initially, two very similar bills, H.B. 156 by Epaphroditus Peck, and H.B. 632 by Marjory Cheney, were both introduced, as the version initially circulated for doctors' approval (#632) was later slightly revised. H.B. 156 became the formal vehicle for the Judiciary Committee's substitute. On the 1931 legislative session in general, see Van Dusen, *Connecticut*, pp. 294–296; and Wilbur L. Cross, *Connecticut Yankee: An Autobiography* (New Haven: Yale University Press, 1943), pp. 250–257.

56. C.-E. A. Winslow to David R. Lyman, 5 May 1931, Winslow Box 96; Charles W. Comfort, Jr., ed., *Proceedings of the Connecticut State Medical Society 1931* (Hartford: CSMS, 1932), pp. 76–80; C.-E. A. Winslow to Elizabeth Reed, 26 May 1931, and Winslow to Clarence Hall, 26 May 1931, Winslow Box 96; "Progress in Connecticut," *Birth Control Review* 15 (July 1931):

219–220; and especially *A Study in Irony: Birth Control in Connecticut* (New Haven: CBCL, February, 1932), 8pp. Winslow's obituary appears in the *New Haven Register*, 9 January 1957. Creadick had been born in Delaware in 1883, had graduated from the University of Pennsylvania (1904) and the University of Pennsylvania Medical School (1908) and had practiced in New Haven since 1917. See *Connecticut State Medical Journal* 15 (May 1951): 414, Orvan W. Hess, M.D., to Garrow, 24 August 1992, and an undated New Haven newspaper obituary clipping reporting Creadick's 23 July 1956 death in North Carolina, kindly supplied by Dr. Hess. One later document, where Creadick decries "the dysgenic effect created by the knowledge of contraception which is at present disseminated amongst the ranks of our people who ought to be having many children, while the dependent groups are proliferating," clearly indicates Creadick's eugenicist perspective. Creadick, "Report of the Medical Advisory Board," CBCL, 26 June 1940, PPLC 10-K.

57. George Packard, "Is Birth Control Legal?" *Birth Control Review* 15 (September 1931): 248–250, 271; Christine E. Nicoll and Robert G. Weisbord, "The Early Years of the Rhode Island Birth Control League," *Rhode Island History* 45 (November 1986): 111–25; Sanger, *My Fight*, p. 356; "Connecticut," *Birth Control Review* 15 (November 1931): 328. Also see p. 320, plus "A Conference of the New England States on Birth Control," Providence, 14 October 1931, PPFA Box 1; as well as *New London Day*, 12 April 1977, p. 12, and Laurel J. Fein, "Waving No Flags: The History of the Planned Parenthood League of Connecticut, 1923–1965" (unpublished Senior History Essay, Yale University, 16 April 1982), pp. 9–10.

58. Creadick to Sanger, 22 February 1932, Sanger-LC Box 134; *New York Times*, 7 March 1932, p. 5, 8 March 1932, p. 3; *New Haven Times*, 7 and 9 March 1932; *New Haven Register*, 9 March 1932; *New Haven Journal-Courier*, 9 March 1932; *Stamford Advocate*, 10 March 1932; Sanger to Creadick, 15 March 1932, Sanger to Hepburn, 16 March 1932, and Sanger to Creadick, 25 March 1932, Sanger-LC Boxes 134 and 135. Katharine Hepburn was at best ambivalent about Sanger's and the CBCL's contacts with Whitney and the Eugenics Society. As she told Sanger, "To my mind the eugenics men are stupid. . . . They're a dumb crowd and a waste of time. Birth Control is more popular than eugenics." Hepburn to Sanger, 8 May 1931, Sanger-LC Box 135. Also early in 1932 the Hartford Federation of Churches endorsed birth control legalization. *Hartford Courant*, 24 February 1932, p. 1; *Hartford Times*, 24 February 1932.

59. U.S. Congress, Senate, Committee on the Judiciary, *Birth Control—Hearings Before a Subcommittee*, 72nd Cong., 1st sess., 12, 19 and 20 May 1932 (concerning S. 4436); U.S. Congress, House of Representatives, Committee on Ways and Means, *Birth Control—Hearings on H.R. 11082*, 72nd Cong., 1st sess., 19 and 20 May 1932, pp. 7, 35; U.S. Congress, House of Representatives, *Amend the Tariff Act of 1930 and the Criminal Code*, Report No. 1435, 72nd Cong., 1st sess., 26 May 1932, p. 2; *New York Times*, 13 May 1932, p. 40, 20 May 1932, p. 3, 25 May 1932, p. 11. Also see Hepburn to Sanger, 9 January 1932, and Sanger to Hepburn, 12 January 1932, Sanger-LC Box 135; U.S. Congress, Senate, Committee on the Judiciary, *Birth Control—Hearings Before a Subcommittee*, 72nd Cong., 1st sess., 24 and 30 June 1932 (concerning S. 4436); Robert S. Allen, "Congress and Birth Control," *The Nation* 134 (27 January 1932): 104–105; Louise S. Bryant, "The Legal Status of Contraception," *Birth Control Review* 16 (November 1932): 263–266; and Sanger's *Autobiography*, pp. 422–424. See as well Francis L. Broderick, *Right Reverend New Dealer: John A. Ryan* (New York: Macmillan, 1963), pp. 148–150; and David J. O'Brien, *American Catholics and Social Reform: The New Deal Years* (New York: Oxford University Press, 1968), pp. 120–149.

60. Creadick, "Report of President," March 1932, and Creadick to Winslow, 27 April 1932, Winslow Box 96; Charles W. Comfort, ed., *Proceedings of the Connecticut State Medical Society 1932* (Hartford: CSMS, 1933), pp. 58–63; *New Haven Journal-Courier*, 27 May 1932, pp. 1, 6.

61. *Report of the Greenwich Committee for Maternal Health*, September 1932 to August 1933, 15pp., Winslow Box 96 and Rockefeller Papers; Harden Stille to Rockefeller, 28 July 1930, Sanger-LC Box 134; Rockefeller in GCMH *Annual Report*, 1 April 1936–31 March 1937, PPLM Box 118; Nancy Rockefeller, Autobiographical Statement, 1 January 1955, PPLC 24-R; Rockefeller Interviews with Esther Smith (pp. 9–11, 39–42) and with Carole Nichols (pp.

12–24); Florence Rose to Rockefeller, 4 August 1932, Sanger-LC Box 134; Cheri Appel Interview with Ellen Chesler, and Appel letter in *New York Times*, 13 February 1990, p. A24. On Florence Darrach, in addition to a Garrow conversation with her daughter-in-law, Mrs. William Darrach IV, see an undated autobiographical resume in PPLC 24-A and her obituary in the *Greenwich Time*, 29 September 1964, p. 2; on William Darrach, see the *New York Herald Tribune*, 6 January 1931, and obituaries in the *New York Times*, 25 May 1948, p. 27, *New York Journal-American*, 24 May 1948, and *New York Herald Tribune*, 25 May 1948, plus a 26 May *Herald* editorial on him. On the Massachusetts clinic, see *Birth Control and the Massachusetts Law* (Boston: PPLM, 1959), and *PPLM Reports* 24 (Spring 1974): 1–4.

62. James W. Cooper, "Change the Connecticut Law," *Birth Control Review* 16 (November 1932): 281–282; *Hartford Courant*, 21 August 1932; Marjory Nield Blackall, "The Story of Annie Porritt" (unpublished manuscript, 1976), pp. 11–14, Porritt Papers; Garrow conversations with Katharine H. Hepburn and Robert H. Hepburn; Henry F. Fletcher to Longshaw K. Porritt, 24 August 1932, and A. Nowell Creadick and Elizabeth Reed to the ABCL, 5 October 1932, Porritt Box 1; Alison Hastings Porritt to Katherine Seymour Day, 16 January 1933, Day Papers; A. H. Palache to Creadick, 20 January 1933, and Creadick to Sanger, 21 January 1933, Sanger-LC Box 134; Mitchell, "Social Legislation," p. 341; *Hartford Courant*, 26 January 1933, p. 3. Also see Sanger to Katherine Seymour Day, 2 February 1933, Day Papers; and *Hartford Courant*, 19 February 1933. On Raymond E. Baldwin, see Baldwin's own *Let's Go Into Politics* (New York: Macmillan, 1952), esp. pp. 53–54; and Baldwin's obituaries in the *New York Times*, 5 October 1986, p. 44, and the *Hartford Courant*, 5 October 1986, pp. A1, A14. Curtiss S. Johnson, *Raymond E. Baldwin: Connecticut Statesman* (Chester, CT: Pequot Press, 1972), has remarkably little to say about Baldwin's years in the legislature.

63. *Journal of the House*, p. 247 (25 January); *Journal of the Senate*, p. 290 (26 January); House Bill 519, 1933 Connecticut General Assembly Records (RG 2), Box 136; *Hartford Courant*, 2 March 1933, pp. 1, 7; *Hartford Times*, 2 March 1933, p. 9; *New Haven Journal-Courier*, 2 March 1933, pp. 1, 5.

64. *New Haven Register*, 28 April 1933; *Hartford Courant*, 2 May 1933, pp. 1, 5, 3 May 1933, pp. 1, 4, 4 May 1933, p. 10, 5 May 1933, p. 8; *Journal of the House*, pp. 1489–1495 (2 May); *Hartford Times*, 2 May 1933, pp. 1, 11, 4 May 1933, p. 1; *New Haven Journal-Courier*, 3 May 1933, pp. 1, 9, 5 May 1933, pp. 1, 3, 6 May 1933; *New York Herald Tribune*, 3 May 1933; *Journal of the Senate*, p. 1586 (4 May); *Waterbury Republican*, 5 May 1933; *Bridgeport Herald*, 7 May 1933; untitled one page CBCL memo, 4 May 1933, PPLC Papers.

65. *Journal of the House*, pp. 1607, 1714, 1775–1782 (9 May, 18 May, 23 May); *Journal of the Senate*, pp. 1636, 1791–1792, 2054 (10 May, 24 May, 6 June); *Hartford Courant*, 10 May 1933, 11 May 1933, p. 3, 19 May 1933, 24 May 1933, pp. 1, 4, 25 May 1933, p. 5, 7 June 1933, pp. 1, 6; *Hartford Times*, 10 May 1933, 23 May 1933, p. 1; 1933 Connecticut General Assembly Records (RG 2), Box 136; *New Haven Journal-Courier*, 24 May 1933, pp. 1, 9; *New York Herald Tribune*, 24 May 1933; Sanger to Creadick, and to Hepburn, 26 May 1933, and Hepburn to Sanger, 27 May 1933, Sanger-LC Boxes 134 and 135; *Springfield Union*, 28 May 1933; *New Haven Register*, 7 June 1933. Two years later Creadick commented to Sanger (10 May 1935, Sanger-LC Box 135) that "Of course, in my opinion, the amendment was wrong in principle but it would have permitted clinics." On the 1933 legislative session in general, see Cross, *Connecticut Yankee*, pp. 277–290; Van Dusen, *Connecticut*, pp. 299–300; and Murray, "Wilbur L. Cross," p. 279. Idiosyncratic at best is Albert Levitt, "Who Owns Connecticut?," *The Nation* 138 (2 May 1934): 505–507.

66. Connecticut Birth Control League program flyer, 23 November 1933, Winslow Box 96; *Report of the Greenwich Committee for Maternal Health*, September 1932 to August 1933, Winslow Box 96, and Rockefeller Papers; *Report of the Greenwich Committee for Maternal Health*, August 1933 to September 1934, Rockefeller Papers and PPLM Box 118; *Greenwich Press*, 21 November 1933, pp. 1, 7, 23 November 1933, 3 May 1934; *Waterbury Republican*, 23 November 1933; *New York Times*, 24 November 1933; *Bridgeport Herald*, 26 November 1933.

67. Sanger to Hepburn, 11 December 1933, Sanger-LC; U.S. Congress, House of Representatives, Committee on the Judiciary, *Birth Control—Hearings on H.R. 5978*, 73rd

Cong., 2nd sess., 18 and 19 January 1934; "Remarks of Mrs. Thomas N. Hepburn," 17 January 1934, 2pp., Sanger-LC Box 135; *New York World-Telegram*, 18 January 1934, pp. 1, 14; Hepburn to Sanger, 23 January 1934, Sanger to Hepburn, 26 January 1934, and Creadick to Sanger, 29 January 1934, Sanger-LC Box 135; Hannah M. Stone, "The Federal Hearing," *Birth Control Review*, March 1934, pp. 2–4; Sanger to Nancy Rockefeller, 27 February 1934, Rockefeller Papers; U.S. Congress, Senate, Committee on the Judiciary, *Birth Control— Hearings Before a Subcommittee on S. 1842*, 73rd Cong., 2nd sess., 1, 20 and 27 March 1934; Kennedy, *Birth Control in America*, pp. 239–240; Guy I. Burch, "Catholics on Birth Control," *New Republic*, 5 September 1934, pp. 98–100; Elizabeth H. Garrett, "Birth Control's Business Baby," *New Republic*, 17 January 1934, pp. 269–272; Sanger, "Birth Control," *State Government* 7 (September 1934): 187–190, at 190 (which no doubt was directly influenced by a 1 February 1933 Ernst to Sanger letter that appears at page four of the 1934 Senate hearings cited above); Grant Sanger Interview with Ellen Chesler, p. 26; U.S. Congress, House of Representatives, Committee on the Post Office and Post Roads, *Offenses Against the Postal Service—Hearings Before Subcommittee No. 8*, 74th Cong., 1st sess., 8 March and 4 and 10 April 1935. Also see Florence Darrach to Sanger, 30 April 1934, and Sanger to Darrach, 4 May 1934, Sanger-LC Box 135; Alison Hastings Porritt to Sanger, 20 June 1934, Clara Louise McGraw to Sanger, 22 June 1934, and Adelaide Pearson to Katharine Beach Day, 28 June 1934, Sanger-LC Box 135; Anthony M. Turano, "Birth Control and the Law," *American Mercury* 34 (April 1935): 466–472; Chesler, *Woman of Valor*, pp. 342–348, 352–354; and Sanger's *Autobiography*, pp. 424–427. The follow-on case to *Youngs* was *Davis* v. *U.S.*, 62 F.2d 473 (6th Cir., 10 January 1933), reversing a wholesaler's conviction for distributing condoms to druggists and doctors. Four years after Garrett's significant *New Republic* piece, an even more detailed and devastating portrait of the commercial contraceptive industry appeared: "The Accident of Birth," *Fortune* 17 (February 1938): 83–86, 108–114. Boldly terming industry profits "extortionate," the article added that "The industry harbors hundreds of scoundrels who make small fortunes out of ignorance." Also see John W. Riley and Matilda White, "The Use of Various Methods of Contraception," *American Sociological Review* 5 (December 1940): 890–903, and Grace Naismith, "The Racket in Contraceptives," *American Mercury* 70 (July 1950): 3–13.

68. *Hartford Courant*, 24 October 1934; Sarah Clement Pease, "Report from Connecticut Birth Control League, 1935," PPFA Box 4; Creadick to Sanger, 29 October 1934, and Hepburn to Sanger, 4 December 1934, Sanger-LC Box 135; Elsa S. Van Zelm, "Minutes," CBCL Board of Directors, 14 November 1934, PPLC 10-B; *Hartford Times*, 29 January 1935, p. 9, 24 March 1935; *Journal of the House*, pp. 320, 547 and 589–590 (31 January, 19 February, 26 February); *Hartford Courant*, 1 February 1935, p. 16, 21 February 1935, p. 10; 27 February 1935, p. 7; *Journal of the Senate*, pp. 391, 516–517 (1 February and 20 February); *Catholic Transcript*, 7 March 1935 and 14 March 1935; *New York News*, 15 March 1935.

69. *Hartford Times*, 5 April 1935, pp. 1, 50, 6 April 1935, 10 April 1935; *Hartford Courant*, 6 April 1935, pp. 1, 18, 5 June 1935; *Stamford Advocate*, 6 April 1935, pp. 1, 8, 21 May 1935; *New Haven Journal-Courier*, 6 April 1935, pp. 1, 5; *Bridgeport Herald*, 7 April 1935; "Brief prepared by Mr. James Wayne Cooper . . . for the Legislative Hearing" [5 April 1935], PPLC 1-H; Sarah Pease to "Dear League Member," 8 April 1935, and "H.C.S." [Hilda Crosby Standish], Letter to Editor, 12 April 1935, PPLC; Elsa Van Zelm to Stella Hanau, 17 April 1935, Sanger-LC Box 134; Van Zelm, "Minutes," CBCL Board of Directors, 8 May 1935 and 4 June 1935, PPLC 10-C; Creadick to Sanger, 10 May 1935 (and attaching Senator John F. Lynch to "Mrs. K," 10 April 1935), and Sanger to Creadick, 19 June 1935, Sanger-LC Box 135. Also see Sanger to Hepburn, 2 April 1935 and 9 April 1935, Sanger-LC Box 84. Cooper was a graduate of Yale College (1926) and Yale Law School (1929); his obituary appears in the *New Haven Register*, 18 January 1989, p. B7. On the 1935 legislative session in general, see Van Dusen, *Connecticut*, pp. 302–303; and Cross, *Connecticut Yankee*, pp. 313–327.

70. Elsa Van Zelm, "Minutes," CBCL Board of Directors, 4 June 1935, PPLC 10-C; *Hartford Courant*, 5 June 1935; *Hartford Times*, 5 June 1935; Sarah Clement Pease, "President's Report," 2 June 1938, PPLC 10-F; Sallie Pease, Round Table Remarks, 19 February 1936,

Boston, p. 7, PPLM Box 81; Pease's 17 June 1936 "President's Report," which also appears in the *Birth Control Review*, October 1936, pp. 4–5; Pease to Clarence J. Gamble, 5 June 1935, Gamble Papers 6–111; Mabel H. Robbins, "Minutes," 26 June 1935, PPLC 39-C. On Lillian Joseloff, who had been born in Ontario in 1894 and was the first female graduate of Columbia University's College of Pharmacy, see her *Hartford Courant* obituary, 15 February 1975, and that of her husband Morris, 20 May 1969, p. 8. On Eleanor Calverly, who died in 1968, see an undated "Autobiographical Sketch" (c.1955) in Calverly Box 137, and her husband Edwin's *Courant* obituary, 23 April 1971. Eleanor Calverly earned her medical degree at the Woman's Medical College of Pennsylvania in 1908 and then with her husband spent two years in Saudi Arabia and eighteen years in what is now Kuwait before moving to Hartford in 1930. She later published a memoir of her years in the Middle East, *My Arabian Days and Nights* (New York: Thomas Y. Crowell, 1958), but it makes no reference to her later birth control involvement. Hilda Crosby Standish often appears as simply Hilda Crosby in the initial 1935 CBCL documents, but her full married name is used here throughout. Background on Dr. Standish comes from her interviews with Carole Nichols, with Garrow, and with Andrea Hubbell, as well as from the *Courant*, 7 July 1970, p. 1; *West Hartford News*, 20 September 1979, and Standish to Jean Stabell, 14 August 1975, PPLC 33-A. Standish graduated from Wellesley in 1924, from Cornell Medical College in 1928, and, after an internship and residency in Philadelphia and St. Louis, spent some eighteen months working in Shanghai, China, before returning to Hartford in 1934. See also the *Courant*, 13 June 1928 and 7 September 1932. Also generally see Mary R. Walsh, *"Doctors Wanted: No Women Need Apply"—Sexual Barriers in the Medical Profession, 1835–1975* (New Haven: Yale University Press, 1977); Regina M. Morantz et al., eds., *In Her Own Words* (Westport, CT: Greenwood Press, 1982), pp. 3–44; and Regina M. Morantz-Sanchez, *Sympathy and Silence: Women Physicians in American Medicine* (New York: Oxford University Press, 1985).

71. Mabel H. Robbins, "Minutes," 26 June 1935, PPLC 39-C; Pease, Round Table Remarks, 19 February 1936, Boston, p. 7, PPLM Box 81; Pease, "Annual Report of the Connecticut Birth Control League," 22–23 January 1936, PPLC 10-D; Robbins, "Minutes," Board of Sponsors, 25 September 1935, PPLC 39-C; Robbins, "Minutes," CBCL Board of Directors, 9 October 1935, PPLC 10-C.

72. *Hartford Courant*, 24 October 1935, 25 October 1935, p. 1; *Hartford Times*, 24 October 1935, pp. 1, 3, 25 October 1935, p. 10; *New Haven Journal-Courier*, 26 October 1935; Pease to Clarence Gamble, 24 October 1935, Gamble 6–111; Henrietta Scott, "Minutes," 29 October 1935, PPLC 39-C. Also see Hepburn to Sanger, 14 October 1935, Sanger-LC Box 84. On Lucius F. Robinson, Jr., who graduated from Yale in 1918 and from Harvard Law School in 1921, see his *Hartford Courant* obituary, 6 February 1987, pp. D1, D8. On Nicholas F. Rago, a 1915 Yale College and a 1917 Yale Law School graduate who served as city prosecuting attorney from 1935 until 1937, see his *Courant* obituary, 6 May 1969.

73. Joy Sweet, "Minutes," CBCL Board, 13 November 1935, PPLC 10-C; Nancy Rockefeller to Mrs. A. F. Howland, 19 January 1936, PPLM Box 15; Luke B. Lockwood to Florence Darrach, 21 October 1935, PPLC 1-I; *Report of the Greenwich Committee for Maternal Health*, September 1934 to March 1936, 12pp., Rockefeller Papers. Perhaps surprisingly, Section 6244 never became an issue in any of Connecticut's subsequent birth control litigation.

74. *Hartford Courant*, 11 December 1935, 13 December 1935, 14 January 1936, 20 January 1936, 21 January 1936, 23 January 1936; *New York Herald Tribune*, 8 January 1936; *Hartford Times*, 13 January 1936, p. 1, 15 January 1936, 20 January 1936, p. 1, 21 January 1936, p. 8, 24 January 1936; Henrietta Scott, "Minutes," Hartford MHC Board, 14 January 1936, PPLC 39-C; Joy Sweet, "Minutes," CBCL Board, 15 January 1936, PPLC 10-D; Pease, "Annual Report of the Connecticut Birth Control League," 22–23 January 1936, PPLC 10-D; Pease, Round Table Remarks, Boston, 19 February 1936, p. 8, PPLM Box 81. The New York decision, by U.S. District Judge Grover M. Moscowitz, was *U.S.* v. *One Package*, 13 F. Supp. 334 (S.D.N.Y., 6 January 1936). Also see the *Journal of Contraception*, November 1935, pp. 11–12, December 1935, pp. 23–24, and January 1936, p. 39. On Andrew Kelly, see Duggan, *The Catholic Church in Connecticut*, pp. 250–251, obituaries in the *Hartford Courant*, 8 June 1948, the

Hartford Times, 8 June 1948, the *New York Herald Tribune*, 9 June 1948, and a much later posthumous profile by Rev. John S. Kennedy in the *Catholic Transcript*, 13 January 1978, all of which also are in Kelly's file in the Archives of the Hartford Archdiocese.

75. Joy Sweet, "Minutes," CBCL Board, 11 March 1936, PPLC 10-D; Elisabeth L. Whittemore to Mary White, 28 April 1936, PPLM Box 118; Sweet, "Minutes," CBCL Board, 13 May 1936, PPLC 10-D; Florence Rose to Hepburn, 29 May 1936, and Adelaide Pearson to Hepburn, 23 November 1936, Sanger-LC Box 135; Henrietta Scott, "Minutes," Hartford MHC, 8 June 1936, PPLC 10-D; *Hartford Courant*, 9 June 1936, p. 24; Ruth Deeds, "Secretary's Report," and Mabel H. Robbins, "Minutes," CBCL Annual Meeting, 17 June 1936, PPLC 10-D; *A Red Letter Year for the Connecticut Birth Control League*, 4pp. pamphlet, July 1936; Robinson to Greenbaum, Wolff & Ernst, 2 September 1936, PPFA Box 99; "News from the States," *Birth Control Review*, October 1936, pp. 4–5; Lillian Joseloff, "Minutes," CBCL Clinical Committee, 29 October 1936, PPLC 10-D; Standish to Clarence Gamble, 11 November 1936, Gamble 6–112; Frances Goodell, "Minutes," CBCL Board, 7 December 1936, PPLC 10-D. Describing a 21 February 1936 Hepburn talk in Bridgeport, the March 1 *Bridgeport Herald* commented that she had "gestures and mannerisms which reminded one of her daughter." Also see Morris Ernst to Mary Ware Dennett, 19 February 1936, Dennett 18–329, characterizing Hepburn as "quite some gal."

76. *U.S.* v. *One Package*, 86 F.2d 737; *New York Times*, 8 December 1936, p. 9; *New York Herald Tribune*, 8 December 1936; *New York Post*, 8 December 1936; Sanger to Hepburn, 2 December 1936, and untitled minutes of 9 and 10 December 1936 meetings, PPFA Box 33; Hannah M. Stone, "Birth Control Wins," *The Nation* 144 (16 January 1937): 70–71; Ernst and Harriet F. Pilpel, "A Medical Bill of Rights," *Journal of Contraception*, February 1937, pp. 35–37; National Committee, *A New Day Dawns for Birth Control*, 47pp., July 1937, pp. 5, 8, 39–41; Ernst, "The Law Catches Up With Science," in *Birth Control: A Symposium* [11 October 1937] (New York: New York Academy of Medicine, 1938), pp. 12–24, at 16–17; Sanger, "The Status of Birth Control," *New Republic*, 20 April 1938, pp. 324-326; Herbert E. Mayer, *Columbia Law Review* 37 (May 1937): 854–856, at 856; and Harry Kalven, Jr., "A Special Corner of Civil Liberties," *New York University Law Review* 31 (November 1956): 1223–1237, at 1226. On *One Package*, also see *Journal of Contraception*, October 1936, p. 176, November 1936, p. 199, and December 1936, pp. 220–222; *Time*, 21 December 1936, p. 24; *Birth Control Review*, January 1937, pp. 3–5; *Virginia Law Review*, April 1937, pp. 709–710; *Harvard Law Review*, May 1937, p. 1312; Benjamin, "Lobbying for Birth Control," pp. 48–49; Ernst and Lindey, *The Censor Marches On*, p. 161; Ernst and Pickett, *Birth Control*, pp. 30–34; Sanger's *Autobiography*, p. 427–428; Lader, *Margaret Sanger*, pp. 301–303; Kennedy, *Birth Control in America*, p. 251, 255, 258, 269–270; Dienes, *Law, Politics, and Birth Control*, pp. 112–115; Reed, *The Birth Control Movement*, pp. 121, 264; Chesler, *Woman of Valor*, pp. 372–375; and the Ernst volume on the case, at the Schlesinger Library.

77. Hadley Cantril, *Public Opinion, 1935–1946* (Princeton: Princeton University Press, 1951), pp. 41–42; Hazel G. Erskine, "The Polls: The Population Explosion, Birth Control, and Sex Education," *Public Opinion Quarterly* 30 (Fall 1966): 490–501, at 491–492. Also see "The Fortune Quarterly Survey," *Fortune* 14 (July 1936): 158; and Henry F. Pringle, "What Do the Women of America Think About Birth Control?," *Ladies' Home Journal*, March 1938, pp. 14–15, 94–97. Cantril's state-by-state breakdown of the May 1936 responses indicates that Connecticut respondents were 78 percent yes, 22 percent no, while Massachusetts was the third lowest (59 yes, 41 no), trailed only by North and South Dakota.

78. James Reed, "Doctors, Birth Control, and Social Values: 1830–1970," in Morris J. Vogel and Charles E. Rosenberg, eds., *The Therapeutic Revolution* (Philadelphia: University of Pennsylvania Press, 1979), pp. 109–133; Kennedy, *Birth Control in America*, pp. 212–217; *New York Times*, 29 January 1937, p. 7, 9 June 1937, pp. 1, 26; National Committee, *A New Day Dawns*, p. 41; *Journal of the American Medical Association* 108 (3 April, 22 May, 26 June 1937): 1179–1180, 1819–1820, 2217–2218; Charles E. Scribner and Ernst, "Interpretation of the Federal Statutes Relating to Contraceptives," 30 April 1937, 7pp., Ernst Box 266; *Time*, 12 July 1937, p. 47; Mabel T. Wood, "Birth Control's Big Year," *Current History* 46 (August

1937): 55–59; Ernst and Pickett, *Birth Control in the Courts*, p. 56; Andrew G. Truxal and Francis E. Merrill, *The Family in American Culture* (New York: Prentice-Hall, 1947), pp. 232–241; Sanger's *Autobiography*, p. 430; and Patricia J. Norton, "Margaret Sanger and the Depression: Birth Control Comes of Age" (unpublished M.A. thesis, Smith College, 1955), p. 94.

79. *Hartford Times*, 5 January 1937, 9 March 1937, p. 6; *Hartford Courant*, 6 January 1937, p. 6, 6 February 1937, p. 9, 3 April 1937; Nancy Rockefeller to Mrs. Cromwell, 12 January 1937, PPFA Box 3; Ruth Deeds, "Minutes," CBCL Board, 21 January 1937, PPLC 10-E; *Waterbury Democrat*, 27 January 1937; Sarah Pease, "Report of the Connecticut Birth Control League," 27–28 January 1937, PPLC 10-E; *Journal of the House*, pp. 366 and 488 (5 February and 2 March); *Waterbury Republican*, 6 February 1937, 23 March 1937, p. 3; Lois Stringfield, "Minutes," CBCL Clinical Committee, 15 February 1937, PPLC 10-E; *Birth Control Review*, February/March 1937, p. 4; *Journal of Contraception*, June/July 1937, p. 140; Hilda C. Standish, "Medical Report," 15 June 1937, and Pease, "Clinic Report," 15 June 1937, PPLC 39-C. On Representative Fitzgerald, also see *Waterbury Democrat*, 11 April 1936.

80. Tilson to Sanger, 5 March 1937, Rose Box 20; *Hartford Times*, 16 March 1937, p. 6; *Hartford Courant*, 16 March 1937, p. 14, 3 June 1937, p. 8. Also see Tilson to Rose, 8 April 1936, Rose to Tilson, 12 April 1936, Tilson to Rose, 1 May 1936, Rose to Tilson, 8 May 1936, Tilson to Tilson, 17 March 1937, Tilson to Sanger, 9 January 1938, and Rose to Tilson, 19 January 1938, Rose Box 20.

81. The most detailed description of the June 3 raid appears in the ninety-page transcript of the 13 July trial, *Commonwealth of Massachusetts* v. *Carolyn T. Gardner, Flora Rand, and Lucille Lord-Heinstein*, PPLM Box 85. Sears's 20 July verdict remarks appear as subsequent pages 91 to 98 in that transcript. Also see Lord-Heinstein, "The Salem Raid and Trial," *Journal of Contraception*, August/September 1937, pp. 156–157 and 167; Minutes, BCLM Executive Board, 4 June 1937, PPLM Box 26; *Journal of Contraception*, June/July 1937, p. 143; two Caroline Carter Davis articles in the *Birth Control Review*, "Progress in Massachusetts," December 1936, p. 6, and "In the 'Cradle of Liberty,'" October 1937, pp. 6–8; *New York Times*, 21 July 1937, p. 22; Loraine Campbell to Linda Hawkridge, 27 July 1937, PPLM Box 5; *New England Journal of Medicine* 217 (12 August 1937): 277–278. On Lord-Heinstein, also see *Boston Globe*, 2 May 1976, pp. 1, 12–13. On the Fitchburg concerns, see Walter A. Barrows to Massachusetts Public Health Commissioner Henry D. Chadwick, 21 April 1937, Chadwick to Barrows, 22 April 1937, Samuel M. Salny to Barrows, 23 April 1937, Barrows to Linda Hawkridge, 23 April 1937, Salny to Barrows, 28 April 1937, and Barrows to Hawkridge, 8 May 1937, PPLM Box 1.

82. See Ilia Galleani, "The Brookline Case," *Journal of Contraception*, October 1937, pp. 178–179, Caroline Carter Davis, "In the 'Cradle of Liberty,'" *Birth Control Review*, October 1937, pp. 6–8; *New York Times*, 4 August 1937, p. 11, 5 August 1937, p. 25, 7 August 1937, p. 5; Linda Hawkridge's "Summary of Police Activities," 5 August 1937, 2pp., and Minutes, BCLM Executive Committee, 4 August 1937, PPLM Box 26; Loraine Campbell's Interview with James Reed, p. 22; "Summary of Conversation with Mr. Dodge by Mrs. Hawkridge," 13 September 1937, PPLM Box 9. Also see Martha G. Waldstein, "A Maternal Health Center Reviews Its Patients," *Journal of Contraception* 4 (November 1939): 203–209.

83. A seventy-nine-page Transcript of Proceedings in *Commonwealth of Massachusetts* v. *Ilia Galleani*, Brookline Municipal Court, No. 1124, 15 September 1937, is in PPLM Box 85. Also see Galleani, "The Brookline Case," *Journal of Contraception*, October 1937, pp. 178–179.

84. "The Massachusetts Hearings," *Birth Control Review*, October 1937, pp. 4–5; Robert G. Dodge to Loraine Campbell, 27 September 1937, PPLM Box 5; Galleani to Campbell, 4 October 1937, PPLM Box 11; Dodge to Hawkridge, 16 October 1937, PPLM Box 9; "Statement Made by Mrs. Mary M. White Regarding the Legal Situation," 20 October 1937, PPLM Box 85; "On the Massachusetts Front," *Birth Control Review*, November 1937, p. 21; Ernst, "The Law Catches Up With Science," in *Birth Control: A Symposium* [11 October 1937] (New York: New York Academy of Medicine, 1938), pp. 12–24, at 16–17.

85. George G. Smith, "The Massachusetts Physicians Protest the Clinic Raids," *Journal of

Contraception, February 1938, pp. 36–37; *Birth Control Review*, December 1937–January 1938, pp. 40–41; Walter A. Barrows to Linda Hawkridge, 8 December 1937, PPLM Box 1; Hepburn to Hawkridge, 27 December 1937, PPLM Box 11.

86. Sarah C. Pease, "1937 Report," 26–27 January 1938, Mabel H. Robbins, "Minutes," CBCL Board, 10 January 1938, and Dorothea H. Scoville to Pease, 28 May 1938, PPLC 10-E; *Stamford Advocate*, 5 April 1938; *Hartford Times*, 28 April 1938; Barbara Molstad, "Report of the New Haven Clinic," 2 June 1938, PPLC 10-F; Pease's "President's Report" for the Hartford clinic, 14 June 1938, PPLC 39-D; *Journal of Contraception*, December 1938, p. 236; Clarence J. Gamble to Pease, 7 June 1937 and 2 October 1937, Pease to Gamble, "Monday" [8 November 1937] and 19 November 1937, Gamble to Pease, 23 November 1937, Pease to Gamble, 26 November 1937, all in Gamble 6–114. On Leah Cadbury, later Leah Cadbury Furtmuller, see her 24 May 1990 obituary in the *Main Line Times*, a 9 November 1937 response to a Bryn Mawr Alumnae Survey, and her extensive 1981–1982 oral history interviews with Carolyn Rittenhouse, which unfortunately do not mention either Gamble or her work in Connecticut. On Gamble, see Reed, *The Birth Control Movement*; also see Doone and Greer Williams, *Every Child a Wanted Child: Clarence James Gamble, M.D. and His Work in the Birth Control Movement* (Boston: Francis A. Countway Library of Medicine, 1978), an unscholarly and family-sponsored biography that is nonetheless informative.

87. Cadbury to Hart, 28 January 1938, PPLC 45-A; Cadbury to Root, 2 February 1938, Cadbury to Mrs. Hetzel, 13 February 1938, Cadbury to Florence Chase, 28 January 1938, Cadbury to Mabel Robbins, 6 February 1938, Cadbury to Rev. John Lewis, 6 February 1938, Cadbury to Dr. Henry Mason, 6 February 1938, and "Coming to Meeting, Monday, February 7," all PPLC 48-A; Cadbury, "Report on First Meeting at Waterbury," 7 February 1938, PPLC 48-B. Edith Chase died on 6 June 1972, and her obituary appears in that day's *Waterbury American*.

88. Cadbury to Chase, 9 February 1938, Chase to Cadbury, 12 February 1938, Cadbury to Ruth Northrop, 13 February 1938, Cadbury to Florence Chase, 13 February 1938, Cadbury to Mildred Ely, 13 February 1938, Cadbury to Mrs. Hetzel, 13 February 1938 (II), Cadbury mimeo letter, 15 February 1938, PPLC 48-A; Cadbury, "Report on Waterbury and Willimantic," 16 February 1938, PPLC 48-B; Ely to Cadbury, 16 February 1938, Hart to Cadbury, 21 February 1938, Cadbury to Millicent Pond, 21 February 1938, Cadbury to Mrs. Heminway, 21 February 1938, PPLC 48-A.

89. Cadbury, "Final Report of Work in Willimantic and Waterbury," 14 March 1938, PPLC 48-B. One of the two doctors, John M. Freiheit, later explained that birth control "can only be used well by intelligent people" and that widespread attempts at use by the poor would only result in more abortions: "I am certain that if you legalize birth control you will sooner or later have to legalize abortions." Instead, "we really should be lecturing the intelligentsia to cut down on contraception and try to catch up with the masses," and if birth control's popularity spread further, "the doctor himself will soon lose control of the matter." Freiheit to Nowell Creadick, 27 August 1940, PPLC 2-M.

90. Cadbury, "Final Report of Work in Willimantic and Waterbury," 14 March 1938, PPLC 48-B. On Clara McTernan, who died 9 April 1982 in Peekskill, New York, the same town where she had been born on 17 March 1899, I have relied principally on a long and valuable conversation with her step-son, John W. McTernan. Charles McTernan died on 26 May 1967, and his obituary appears in the 27 May *Waterbury Republican*.

91. Cadbury to McTernan, 18 March 1938, Gamble 6–115. Also see Millicent Pond to McTernan, 30 March 1938, Gamble 6–115; and Robbins, "Minutes," CBCL Board, 11 April 1938, p. 2, PPLC 10-E.

92. *Bridgeport Post*, 17 April 1938, 18 April 1938, 19 April 1938; *Bridgeport Telegram*, 18 April 1938, 20 April 1938; *Bridgeport Times-Star*, 18 April 1938; *Journal of Contraception*, May 1938, p. 116.

93. Robert G. Dodge and Walter A. Barrows, "Brief for the Defendants," *Commonwealth of Massachusetts* v. *Carolyn T. Gardner et al.*, Massachusetts Supreme Judicial Court, #8689, February 1938, esp. pp. 23–25; Murray F. Hall and Donald J. Hurley, "Brief of Amici

Curiae," *Commonwealth* v. *Gardner*; Hugh A. Cregg and John J. Ryan, Jr., "Brief for the Commonwealth," *Commonwealth* v. *Gardner*, esp. pp. 4–5; and Linda Hawkridge's notes on the oral argument, plus a 2pp. 15 February summary of them, all in PPLM Box 85; *Birth Control Review*, March 1938, pp. 59–60; *Journal of Contraception*, April 1938, pp. 95–96; Hawkridge, "Record of Conversation with Mr. Dodge," 17 February 1938, Dodge to Hawkridge, 9 April 1938, and "Digest of Mr. Robert G. Dodge's Remarks at the Annual Dinner," 12 April 1938, all in PPLM Box 9; Hepburn to Caroline Carter Davis, 25 April 1938, PPLM Box 11.

94. *Commonwealth* v. *Gardner*, 300 Mass 372, 15 N.E.2d 222, 224; *Birth Control Review*, June 1938, p. 104; Hawkridge, "Memo of Conversation with Mr. Dodge and Mr. Barrows," 27 May 1938, Dodge to Hawkridge, 28 May 1938, PPLM Box 9; Hawkridge to Allison Pierce Moore, 15 June 1938, Marguerite Benson to Hawkridge, 16 June 1938, Sanger to Richard N. Pierson, 24 June 1938, PPFA Box 40; Frankfurter to Hawkridge [excerpt], 24 June 1938, PPLM Box 83; Pilpel to Eric Matsner, 28 June 1938, Charles E. Scribner to Pierson, 29 June 1938, PPFA Box 40; "Conference Arranged By American Birth Control League," 29 June 1938, and [Hawkridge], "Minutes of Meeting on the Massachusetts Case," 30 June 1938, PPLM Box 85; Hawkridge, "Report of Conference on Appeal to Supreme Court," 29 June 1938, PPLM Box 26; Dodge to Hazel Moore, 9 July 1938, PPLM Box 9; Edward O. Proctor to Charles E. Cropsey, 26 July 1938, and Cropsey to Proctor, 27 July 1938, *Gardner* Case File (#42,749), National Archives, RG 267, Box 1421; Pearson to Doris L. Rutledge, 28 July 1938, PPLM Box 84; *Birth Control Review*, October 1938, p. 119; Mary M. White, "Minutes," BCLM Board, 4 October 1938, PPLM Box 26 Also see Kennedy, *Birth Control in America*, pp. 252-253; and Dienes, *Law, Politics, and Birth Control*, pp. 117–121. The Jersey City case, which Ernst a year later won in the U.S. Supreme Court, was *Hague* v. *Congress of Industrial Organizations*, 307 U.S. 496 (1939); per the 4 October BCLM minutes, Frankfurter on that date again reiterated to Hawkridge his advice against switching lawyers. Formally speaking there were four distinct appeals, one for each Salem defendant, designated as cases 264–267 in the Supreme Court's October Term 1938.

95. Sarah Pease, "President's Report," 2 June 1938, PPLC-F; Hilda C. Standish, "Medical Report," 14 June 1938, PPLC 39-D; *Bridgeport Telegram*, 3 June 1938; untitled 2pp. memo, n.d., in both Upson Papers and PPLC 2-E; Pease to Clarence Gamble, n.d. [c.September/October 1938], Gamble 6–116. Born 4 October 1909, William A. Goodrich's obituaries appear in the *Hartford Courant*, 12 February 1959, p. 8, and in the 13 February *New Haven Register*. Also see Yale's *History of the Class of 1931*, p. 229, and Garrow conversations with John W. McTernan and with Dr. Goodrich's widow, who later remarried, Elizabeth Dennett [Goodrich] Scafarello, as well as Garrow's interview with Roger B. and Rosalie Nelson. On Charles L. Larkin, Sr., in addition to a Garrow conversation with his son, Charles L. Larkin, Jr., see his obituary in the *Waterbury American*, 9 February 1967, and a memorial notice in *Connecticut Medicine* 31 (June 1967): 457. No reference whatsoever to the birth control clinic appears in the surviving Minute Book for the Waterbury Hospital's Board of Directors for 1938–1939 (pp. 492–503), or in the minutes and annual reports of the Hospital's Medical and Surgical Staff, or in the annual reports that were prepared by Henry Mason, and by Jeannie Heppel for the Chase Dispensary. Heppel's annual reports for the period regularly thank the Junior League for providing clinic volunteers. See Waterbury Hospital's 48th, 49th, 50th, and 51st Annual Reports, for the years ending October 1, 1937, 1938, 1939, and 1940, particularly pp. 51–52, 49–50, 53–54, and 54–55, respectively. It may well be that most substantive business was conducted by the Board's Executive Committee, for which no minutes survive and for which no minutes may ever have been taken.

96. *Gardner* v. *Massachusetts*, 305 U.S. 559 ("appeal dismissed for want of a substantial federal question"); *New York Herald Tribune*, 11 October 1938; Dodge to Hawkridge, 13 October 1938, PPLM Box 9; *Journal of Contraception*, November 1938, pp. 203, 215; *Birth Control Review*, November 1938, p. 129, December 1938, pp. 139–140, and January 1939, p. 156; Minutes, BCLM Executive Committee, 17 October 1938, PPLM Box 26; Ernst and Pickett, *Birth Control In the Courts*, pp. 41–42, 45; Harriet F. Pilpel, "Memorandum Regarding the

United States Supreme Court's Dismissal of the Massachusetts Birth Control Case," 18 October 1938, Upson Papers; "Abstract of Mr. Ernst's Remarks," 19 October 1938, PPLM Box 106; Ernst to Hawkridge, 20 October 1938, PPLM Box 10; Lindey to Ernst, 21 October 1938, Ernst Box 361; Lindey to Hawkridge, 22 October 1938, PPLM Box 13; Ernst to Hawkridge, 22 October 1938, and 27 October 1938, PPLM Box 10; Minutes, BCLM "President's Council," 27 October 1938, PPLM Box 26; Davis to Hepburn, 31 October 1938, PPLM Box 11; Hawkridge, "Legal Conversations," 2 November–25 November 1938, PPLM Box 85; Lindey, "Re: Massachusetts Birth Control," 15 November 1938, Ernst Box 893; Dodge to Ernst, 18 November 1938, PPLM Box 9; Minutes, BCLM Executive Committee, 18 November 1938, PPLM Box 26; Lindey to Hawkridge, 29 November 1938, Lindey to Lydia A. DeVilbiss, 30 November 1938, and Lindey to Mary M. White, 3 December 1938, PPLM Box 13; John Price Jones Corporation, "Survey, Analysis and Plan of Action—Birth Control League of Massachusetts," 10 December 1938, 205pp., Ernst Box 362; Minutes, BCLM Executive Committee, 20 December 1938, PPLM Box 26; Ernst to White, 4 January 1939, PPLM Box 10; White, ". . . 1938 in Review," 11 January 1939, PPLM Box 26; Lindey to Hawkridge, 13 April 1939, PPLM Box 13; Hawkridge to Lindey, 17 April 1939, Ernst Box 893; *Journal of Contraception*, May 1939, pp. 119–120; Loraine Campbell to Ernst, 11 May 1939, PPLM Box 6; Ernst to Campbell, 12 May 1939, PPLM Box 10; Campbell, "Memorandum of Meeting with Mr. Samuel Hoar," 18 May 1939, PPLM Box 6; Ernst to Hoar, 19 May 1939, PPLM Box 10; Campbell to Hoar, and Campbell to Ernst, 23 June 1939, PPLM Box 6.

Dr. Ilia Galleani, the sole defendant in the Brookline case, very reluctantly pled guilty and paid a $100 fine on 19 December 1938. Also see Ernst and Lindey, *The Censor Marches On*, pp. 172–173, and four law review notes critical of the *Gardner* outcome: *New York University Law Quarterly Review* 16 (November 1938): 149–150; *Michigan Law Review* 37 (December 1938): 317–320; *George Washington Law Review* 7 (December 1938): 255–257; and "Contraceptives and the Law," *University of Chicago Law Review* 6 (February 1939): 260–269.

97. *U.S.* v. *Jose S. Belavel et al.*, U.S.D.C. D.P.R., #4589 CR, 19 January 1939. Never officially reported in the Federal Supplement, a copy of Judge Cooper's nine-page opinion does exist in the Upson Papers. Also see *Journal of Contraception*, February 1939, p. 37; Ernst and Pickett, *Birth Control In the Courts*, pp. 34–36; and Doone and Greer Williams, *Every Child A Wanted Child*, pp. 162–163.

98. *New York Times*, 19 January 1939, p. 15; Reed, *The Birth Control Movement*, p. 265; Chesler, *Woman of Valor*, pp. 381–385, 391–393; "Report of Waterbury Maternal Health Center," 11 October 1938 to 1 June 1939, PPLC 10-G and 48-B; Lois W. Stringfield, "Minutes," CBCL Board, 24 October 1938 and 5 December 1938, PPLC 10-F; Sarah Pease, "Annual Report," 18–20 January 1939, PPLC 10-G; *Hartford Courant*, 31 January 1939, p. 3; Barbara Hubbard, Minutes, Hartford MHC Executive Committee, 1 June 1939, PPLC 39-E; Barbara Molstad, "Report of the New Haven Clinic," 8 June 1939, "Hartford County Annual Report," 8 June 1939, PPLC 10-G; Pease, "President's Report," Hartford MHC, 8 June 1939, and Standish, "Clinic Report," 8 June 1939, PPLC 39-E.

99. Garrow conversations with Virginia J. Goss, Deirdre Carmody, and Anthony Fitzgerald; William B. Fitzgerald to J. Warren Upson, 28 June 1939, Upson Papers; [Sallie Pease], untitled 3pp. typescript, "July, 1939," PPFA Box 39; Pease, "President's Report," 8 June 1939, PPLC 10-G; Pease, "Annual Report of the President," 26 June 1940, PPLC 10-K; Woodbridge E. Morris, "Connecticut Situation," 13 June 1939, Gamble 6–117; Morris to A. N. Creadick, 15 June 1939, PPFA Box 38. Born in 1904, Edward T. Carmody, like Bill Fitzgerald, who was two years older, was a fervent Roman Catholic. Warren Upson's obituary appears in the *Waterbury Republican-American*, 15 March 1992, pp. A1, A11; also see a *Waterbury Republican Magazine* profile, 16 September 1984, pp. 4–5.

100. Upson Interviews with Brecher, Garrow, and Hubbell; Coyle, "The Waterbury Conspiracy Scandal," pp. 13–14; *Waterbury Republican*, 4 November 1936, p. 1; *Waterbury Democrat*, 16 June 1939, p. 1; Beaman, *Fat Man in a Phone Booth*, pp. 71–72. The court decisions voiding

the voter registration frauds are cited fully in note seven above. Years later Warren Upson would be the second Waterbury attorney named to the prestigious American College of Trial Lawyers; Bill Fitzgerald had been the first. *Waterbury Republican*, 5 April 1960.

101. *Waterbury American*, 13 June 1939, p. 2, 14 June 1939, p. 2; *Waterbury Democrat*, 13 June 1939, pp. 1, 7, 14 June 1939, p. 1, 15 June 1939, p. 1; Morris to A. N. Creadick, 15 June 1939, PPFA Box 38; Sanger to Creadick, 15 June 1939, Rose Papers Box 41; Upson, untitled sheet of notes headed "6/15/39," [Lewis], untitled, undated 2pp. sheet of notes headed "Upson," and [Upson], "Memorandum for the file," 16 June 1939, 3pp., Upson Papers; Garrow Interviews with Upson and Roger B. Nelson; also Eleanor Searle to Upson, and Pilpel to Upson, 15 June 1939, Upson Papers.

102. *Waterbury Democrat*, 17 June 1939, pp. 1, 2, 19 June 1939, pp. 1, 4, 21 June 1939, p. 1; *Bridgeport Herald*, 18 June 1939; Pease, "Annual Report," 26 June 1940, PPLC 10-K; Upson to Pilpel, 19 June 1939, Upson Papers; *Waterbury American*, 19 June 1939, pp. 1, 10, 20 June 1939, p. 3; *Waterbury Republican*, 20 June 1939, p. 2, 21 June 1939, p. 4, 22 June 1939, p. 3; Record, *State of Connecticut* v. *Certain Contraceptive Materials*, Connecticut Supreme Court, January Term 1940, #1780; "Statement of Mrs. Clara McTernan," 19 June 1939 (and paginated 174 to 203), Upson Papers; Upson to Pease, 19 June 1939, Upson to Roger B. Nelson, 19 June 1939, and Pease to Upson, n.d. [20 June 1939], Upson Papers. In private, Pease was somewhat less enthusiastic, telling the president of the Massachusetts League that "We are particularly sorry that Waterbury was the city selected for a test case because it is predominantly Catholic and the clinic had been opened such a short time." Pease to Linda Hawkridge, 29 June 1939, PPLM Box 14. No transcript of Ginny Goss's interrogation has survived, nor have any copies of the earlier questioning of women patients, but the pagination of McTernan's statement indicates that Fitzgerald already had taken at least 173 pages of statements prior to Mrs. McTernan's appearance. The Waterbury Hospital's Board of Directors held a regular quarterly meeting at 1:30 p.m. on Monday, June 19, but the minimalist minutes make no reference to any discussion of the clinic controversy. Waterbury Hospital Board Minute Book, pp. 498–499. The board's Executive Committee had last met on June 5.

103. Upson to Barker, 20 June 1939, Barker to Upson, 21 June 1939, Upson to Pilpel, 20 June 1939, Creadick to Upson, 21 June 1939, Upson to Pease, 22 June 1939, Transcript of Proceedings, *State* v. *McTernan et al.*, 23 June 1939, 4pp., Upson Papers; Waterbury Superior Court Criminal Docket Book, #6222–6224; Lois Stringfield, Minutes, CBCL Board, 22 June 1939, PPLC 10-G; *Waterbury Democrat*, 23 June 1939, pp. 1, 8, 24 June 1939, p. 3; *Waterbury American*, 23 June 1939, p. 1, 24 June 1939, p. 1; *Hartford Times*, 23 June 1939; *Waterbury Republican*, 24 June 1939, pp. 1, 3; *Hartford Courant*, 24 June 1939, pp. 1, 4; *New York Herald Tribune*, 24 June 1939. Also see Pease to Clarence Gamble, 20 June 1939, Gamble to Pease, 21 June 1939, and Leah Cadbury to Pease, 22 June 1939, Gamble 6–117. On Kenneth Wynne, see a 7 July 1957 *New Haven Register* profile, as well as obituaries in the *Waterbury American*, 20 August 1971, p. 6; *New Haven Register*, 20 August 1971; *Hartford Courant*, 21 August 1971, p. 4; and particularly J. Warren Upson's "Obituary Sketch of Kenneth Wynne," published as an appendix at 161 Conn. 612. Also Garrow conversations with Upson and with William J. Secor, Jr. (Wynne's son-in-law), and G.C. Edgar, "Insurgents in Connecticut," *The Nation* 135 (26 October 1932): 395-396.

104. "Memorandum of Medical Indications of Persons in Case of *State* vs. *McTernan*," n.d., 5pp; [Fitzgerald], "Statement of Facts—State vs. Clara L. McTernan, William A. Goodrich, Roger B. Nelson," n.d., 12pp., Pilpel to Upson, 26 June 1939, Upson to Pilpel, 27 June 1939, Upson to Fitzgerald, 27 June 1939, Fitzgerald to Upson, 28 June 1939, "Report of Mrs. A. L. Wasserman," n.d., 1pp., "Memorandum Re Birth Control Cases," 26 June 1939, 19pp. (two copies, one annotated by Goodrich, the other by Nelson), Upson to Morris, 29 June 1939, Upson to Pease, 29 June 1939, Upson to Creadick, 29 June 1939, Upson to Pilpel, 29 June 1939, Upson to Lucius F. Robinson, Jr., 29 June 1939, Upson to Morris Tyler, 29 June 1939, Upson to Johnson Stoddard, 29 June 1939, Upson to Eleanor Searle, 30 June 1939, Upson Papers. Also see Tyler to Morris, 27 June 1939, PPFA Box 38; Gilbert Colgate, "Minutes,"

BCFA Executive Committee, 27 June 1939, Gamble 134–2339; Upson to Catherine Tilson, 28 June 1939, and Tilson to Upson, 30 June 1939, Upson Papers.

105. Fitzgerald, "Amended Information," 29 June 1939, Upson, "Demurrer to Information," 29 June 1939, Upson Papers; *Waterbury Democrat*, 29 June 1939, pp. 1, 4, 3 July 1939, pp. 1, 4; *Waterbury American*, 29 June 1939, pp. 1, 12, 3 July 1939, pp. 1, 7; *Waterbury Republican*, 30 June 1939, p. 2, 1 July 1939, pp. 1, 12, 2 July 1939, p. 20, 4 July 1939, p. 2; *Hartford Courant*, 30 June 1939, p. 7; Morris to Tyler, 3 July 1939, PPFA Box 38; Upson to Pease, 3 July 1939, PPLC 3-D and Upson Papers.

106. Hereward Wake, "Memo of Discussion . . . July 8th," 11 July 1939, and untitled Johnson Stoddard memo, 26 July 1939, Upson Papers; "Statement on Connecticut Situation," 14 July 1939, Gamble 6–117; Upson to Morris Tyler, 10 July 1939, Upson to Caroline K. Simon, 10 July 1939, Simon to Upson, 11 July 1939, Tyler to Upson, 12 July 1939, Upson to Wake, 14 July 1939, Upson Papers; "Birth Control Probe Bares Racket," *Bridgeport Herald*, 9 July 1939, p. 1; Garrow Interview with Roger and Rosalie Nelson; Upson, "Brief on Demurrer," *State of Connecticut* v. *Roger B. Nelson*, 25 July 1939, Upson Papers and PPLC 2-F; Upson, "Respondent's Brief on Motion to Dismiss," *In re Condemnation of Contraceptive Materials*, 25 July 1939, Upson Papers and PPLC 2-G; *Waterbury Democrat*, 22 July 1939, p. 1, 25 July 1939, p. 2, 26 July 1939, p. 4; *Waterbury American*, 25 July 1939, pp. 1, 16; *Waterbury Republican*, 26 July 1939, p. 4. Also see Sarah Pease, "Birth Control and Sunday Shaving Illegal in State," *Waterbury Republican*, 16 July 1939, p. 8, and Pease, untitled 3pp. memo, 20 July 1939, PPLC 1-B; Pilpel to Upson, 27 July 1939, and Creadick to Upson, 27 July 1939, Upson Papers. The Wisconsin case, *State ex rel Larkin* v. *Ryan*, 70 Wisc. 676, 36 N.W. 823, 825, had held that "there can be no lawful punishment of mere drunkenness, so long as it is concealed in strict privacy, without any exposure to or interference with the public or any individual. In other words, that strictly private and concealed vice of the individual cannot be lawfully made a public offense." Also see *Schloendorff* v. *Society of New York Hospital*, 105 N.E. 92, 93 (1914), where future Supreme Court Justice Benjamin N. Cardozo, writing for the New York Court of Appeals, stated that "Every human being of adult years and sound mind has a right to determine what shall be done with his own body." Upson also cited the liberty language used in two well-known U.S. Supreme Court decisions, *Meyer* v. *Nebraska*, 262 U.S. 390, 399 (1923), and *Pierce* v. *Society of Sisters*, 268 U.S. 510, 535 (1925).

107. Fitzgerald, "State's Brief on Respondent's Motion to Dismiss," *State of Connecticut* v. *Certain Contraceptive Materials*, 29 July 1939, 18pp., and "State's Consolidated Memorandum of Authorities on Demurrers," *State of Connecticut* v. *Roger B. Nelson et al.*, 29 July 1939, 14pp., Upson Papers; *Waterbury Democrat*, 29 July 1939, p. 1; *Waterbury American*, 29 July 1939, pp. 1, 7; *Waterbury Republican*, 30 July 1939, p. 3, 5 August 1939, pp. 1, 4; McEvoy to Fitzgerald and Upson, 31 July 1939, Upson to McEvoy, 31 July 1939, McEvoy to Fitzgerald and Upson (II), 31 July 1939, Upson to Caroline K. Simon, 1 August 1939, Upson to Creadick, 1 August 1939, Upson to Stoddard, 4 August 1939, Upson Papers.

108. *State of Connecticut* v. *Roger B. Nelson et al.*, 7 Conn. Supp. 262, 264; *Waterbury Democrat*, 7 August 1939, pp. 1, 4; *Waterbury American*, 7 August 1939, pp. 1, 7; *Waterbury Republican*, 8 August 1939, pp. 1, 4; *Hartford Courant*, 8 August 1939, pp. 1, 4; *New York Times*, 8 August 1939; *New York Herald Tribune*, 8 August 1939; Upson to Pease, 7 August 1939, Upson to McTernan, 7 August 1939, Upson to Caroline Simon, 11 August 1939, Upson Papers; Upson to Caroline Simon, 14 August 1939, PPFA Box 38. Also see James W. Cooper to Upson, and Morris L. Ernst to Upson, 21 August 1939, Upson Papers; *Hartford Times*, 8 August 1939, p. 14, and 11 August 1939, p. 10; *Journal of Contraception* 4 (August/September 1939): 170–171; and the *Journal of the Connecticut State Medical Society* 3 (September 1939): 513, which praised Wynne for "his realistic opinion" and "fine understanding."

109. McTernan to Upson, 22 August 1939, Upson Papers; *Time*, 28 August 1939, p. 18; Coyle, "The Waterbury Conspiracy Scandal," pp. 44–70; Penelope Huse note about 17 August *New Milford Times*, PPFA Box 39; *State of Connecticut* v. *Certain Contraceptive Materials*, 7 Conn. Supp. 264, 276, 284; *Waterbury American*, 23 August 1939, p. 1, 24 August 1939, p. 3; *Waterbury Republican*, 24 August 1939, pp. 1, 8; *Hartford Courant*, 24 August 1939, p. 1, 26

August 1939, p. 6; *Waterbury Democrat*, 24 August 1939, p. 11; Upson to Ernst, 24 August 1939, Upson Papers; *Hartford Times*, 25 August 1939, p. 14. Also see Edna McKinnon to Clarence Gamble, 4 August, 17 August, 18 August, 19 August and 25 August 1939, Gamble 135–2347; and McKinnon, "Report of Talk with Mr. Morris Ernst," 22 August 1939, PPFA Box 38.

110. Upson to McTernan, 24 August 1939, McTernan to Upson, 29 August 1939, Upson to McTernan, 31 August 1939, Upson to Caroline Simon, 29 August 1939, Simon to Upson, 30 August 1939, Upson to Simon, 31 August 1939, Upson to Pease, 1 September 1939, Upson Papers; "Suggested Plan of Publicity Campaign," 29 August 1939, PPLC 10-G; untitled 2pp. handwritten memo, n.d., Upson Papers; Pease, "Letter to the Board of Waterbury Hospital" [draft], n.d., and "Corrected Statement . . ." 6 September 1939, PPLC 2-E. Also see Lawrence Lewis to Pease, 7 September 1939, PPLC 2-A, and Eleanor Searle to Caroline Simon, 18 September 1939, PPLC 48-B.

111. Transcript of Proceedings, *State v. Nelson et al.*, 21 September 1939, 7pp., Upson Papers; *Waterbury Democrat*, 21 September 1939, p. 5, 22 September 1939, pp. 1, 8, 26 September 1939, p. 3; *Waterbury Republican*, 22 September 1939, p. 15, 23 September 1939, p. 7; *Waterbury American*, 22 September 1939, pp. 1, 10, 26 September 1939, p. 3; Upson to Morris, 22 September 1939, PPLC 2-A; Upson to Mabel Wood, and Maltbie to Fitzgerald and Upson, 26 September 1939, Upson Papers. Also see *Journal of Contraception* 4 (October 1939): 200; Upson to Howard Phillips, 28 September 1939, Phillips to Upson, 2 October and 17 October 1939, and Upson to Phillips, 18 October 1939, Upson Papers. On William M. Maltbie, see his *Hartford Courant* obituary, 16 December 1961, pp. 1, 2, and particularly Justice Howard W. Alcorn's "Obituary Sketch" of Maltbie, published as an appendix at 148 Conn. 740.

112. Morris Tyler to Florence Darrach, 29 September 1939, Upson to Tyler, 30 September 1939, Upson to Pease, 30 September 1939, Upson, "Memorandum," 2 October 1939, Upson to McTernan, 2 October 1939, [Upson], "Memorandum for Mr. Lewis," 6 October 1939, Upson Papers; Lindey to Morris, 6 October 1939, PPFA Box 38; Upson to Lindey, 10 October 1939, [Upson], "Memorandum for the File," 13 October 1939, Lindey to Upson, 23 October 1939, Upson to Lindey, 25 October 1939, Tyler to Upson, 27 October 1939, Upson to Tyler, 28 October 1939, Fitzgerald to Maltbie, 27 October 1939, Maltbie to Wynne, 31 October 1939, Fitzgerald to Wynne, 31 October 1939, Fitzgerald to Upson, 31 October 1939, Upson to Lindey, 1 and 2 November 1939, Upson to McTernan, Goodrich, and Nelson, 1 November 1939, Upson to Tyler, 1 November, Upson Papers; Penelope Huse note on 2 November 1939 *Winsted Citizen*, PPFA Box 39; *Waterbury American*, 3 November 1939, p. 1, 4 November 1939, p. 4; Lindey to Upson, 3 November 1939, Record in *State* v. *Nelson* and in *State* v. *McTernan & Goodrich*, Upson Papers; *Waterbury Republican*, 4 November 1939, pp. 1, 4, 9 November 1939; *New York Herald Tribune*, 4 November 1939; *Waterbury Democrat*, 4 November 1939, p. 1, 9 November 1939; Upson to Pease, 3 November 1939, Upson to Lindey, 4 and 7 November 1939, Lindey to Upson, 6 November 1939, Upson Papers; Tyler to Morris, 8 November 1939, PPFA Box 38.

113. Eleanor Searle, Minutes, CBCL Board, 22 September 1939, PPLC 10-G; McKinnon to Morris, 22 September 1939, McKinnon, "Connecticut Activities Outlined, September 22 to October 12, 1939," 3pp., and McKinnon, "Report of Connecticut Activities, Sept. 22 to Oct. 12, 1939," 10pp., Gamble 6–118; *Hartford Courant*, 23 September 1939, p. 4; McKinnon to Gamble, and to Mary Compton, 25 September 1939, Gamble 135–2347 and 6–118; Tyler to Upson, 29 September 1939, Upson to Tyler, and to Stoddard, 30 September 1939, Upson Papers; McKinnon to Wood, 5 October 1939, Gamble 6–118; *Waterbury Republican*, 11 October 1939, p. 1, 22 October 1939, p. 2; *Waterbury American*, 11 October 1939, p. 20; *Waterbury Democrat*, 11 October 1939, p. 5; Upson to Pease, 19 October 1939, Tyler to Stoddard, 19 October 1939, Stoddard to Pease, 21 and 23 October 1939, PPLC 2-A; Upson to Stoddard, 26 October 1939, Upson Papers; McKinnon, "Connecticut—Work Accomplished," 4 November 1939, Gamble 6–118; Creadick et al., "The Right to Practice is in Jeopardy," *Journal of the Connecticut State Medical Society* 3 (November 1939): 616–617, 635;

Journal of Contraception 4 (November 1939): 224; Upson to Pease, 3 November 1939, Stoddard to Upson, and Pease to Stoddard, 6 November 1939, Tyler to Upson, 6 November 1939, Upson Papers; Pease to Town and County Chairmen, 10 November 1939, and Lois Stringfield, "Minutes," CBCL Board, 20 November 1939, PPLC 10-G; McKinnon to Morris, 15 November 1939, and Lindey to Morris, 17 November 1939, PPFA Box 38. On Edna Rankin McKinnon, who was born in 1893, earned both undergraduate and law degrees at the University of Montana, and died in 1978, the best source is Wilma Dykeman, *Too Many People, Too Little Love—Edna Rankin McKinnon: Pioneer for Birth Control* (New York: Holt, Rinehart & Winston, 1974), a nonscholarly biography which includes no references to McKinnon's many contacts with the Connecticut activists. Also see Hannah Josephson, *Jeanette Rankin* (Indianapolis: Bobbs-Merrill, 1974); and Ted C. Harris, *Jeanette Rankin* (New York: Arno Press, 1982), a reprint of a 1972 dissertation.

114. Upson to Pease, and to McTernan, 21 November 1939, Upson Papers; Tyler to Morris, 22 November 1939, Upson to Greenbaum, Wolff & Ernst, 25 November 1939, Morris to Lindey, 29 November 1939, PPFA Box 38; Stoddard to Upson, 29 November 1939, Upson Papers; Stoddard to CBCL, 29 November 1939, Lindey to Upson, 30 November 1939, Upson to Lindey, 1 December 1939, PPLC 2-A; Upson to Morris, 1 December 1939, Lindey to Upson, 4 December 1939, Upson to Lindey, 5 December 1939, Janney to Creadick, 8 December 1939, Creadick to Upson, 11 December 1939, Upson to Creadick, 12 December 1939, Creadick to Janney, 12 December 1939, Creadick to Upson, 13 December 1939, Janney to Creadick, 14 December 1939, Janney to Upson, 18 December 1939, Upson Papers; Janney, Frederick H. Wiggin and Huntington T. Day, "Petition and Brief of Amici Curiae," *State of Connecticut* v. *Roger B. Nelson et al.*, Connecticut Supreme Court, January Term 1940, #1803–1805, A-144 II 351–374. Also see Janney to Charles E. Scribner, 8 February 1940, PPFA Box 38.

115. Upson and William J. Secor, Jr., "Respondent's Appeal," *State of Connecticut* v. *Certain Contraceptive Materials*, Connecticut Supreme Court, January Term 1940, #1780, 99pp., Upson and Secor, "Brief of Appellee," *State of Connecticut* v. *Roger B. Nelson et al.*, Connecticut Supreme Court, January Term 1940, #1803–1805, 66pp., esp. p. 41, Upson Papers; Fitzgerald, "Brief of Appellant," *State* v. *Roger B. Nelson et al.*, esp. pp. 9, 17–19, and "Brief of Appellant," *State* v. *Certain Contraceptive Materials*, A-144 II 335–350 and A-144 II 256–265. Bill Secor, a Waterbury native and a brand-new graduate of Yale Law School, joined the Bronson firm several weeks after the June 1939 raid and became Upson's principal assistant on the case; see *Waterbury Democrat*, 10 July 1939, p. 2.

116. *Waterbury Republican*, 28 December 1939, p. 2, 5 January 1940, p. 5; *Waterbury American*, 4 January 1940, pp. 1, 6; *Waterbury Democrat*, 4 January 1940, p. 8; *Hartford Courant*, 5 January 1940, p. 6; *Hartford Times*, 5 January 1940, p. 17; Upson to Morris, 4 January 1940, PPFA Box 38; Upson to Greenbaum, Wolff & Ernst, 4 January 1940, Upson to Janney, and to Pease, 4 January 1940, Upson to Lindey, 8 January 1940, Upson to McWilliams, 8 January 1940, Janney to Upson, 8 January 1940, Lindey to Upson, 8 January 1940, Morris to Upson, 15 January 1940, Upson Papers; Pease, "Annual Report," 26 June 1940, PPLC 10-K; Janney to Pease, 11 January 1940, PPLC 2-A; Lois Stringfield, Minutes, CBCL Board, 15 January 1940, PPLC 10-H; Eleanor Searle to Eugene L. Belisle, 22 January 1940, PPLM Box 106; Janney to Gilbert Colgate, 7 February 1940, and Janney to Morris, 9 May 1940, PPFA Boxes 52 and 38.

117. On William Maltbie, see his *Hartford Courant* obituary, 16 December 1961, pp. 1, 2, and the sketch published as an appendix at 148 Conn. 740. On Jennings, see his *Courant* obituary, 28 February 1965, pp. 1, 4, Raymond E. Baldwin's sketch published at 152 Conn. 749, and the *National Cyclopedia of American Biography* 52 (1970): 576. George Hinman's *Courant* obituary is 20 March 1961, p. 4, and a sketch by later Chief Justice John H. King is at 148 Conn. 737. Allyn L. Brown's sketch of Avery appears at 143 Conn. 735, and Avery's *Courant* obituary is 7 May 1956, p. 4. Brown's own *Courant* obituary is 23 October 1973, p. 4; also see 164 Conn. 713. My retrospective understanding of the Connecticut court has benefitted substantially from two September 1991 conversations with Hartford attorney Wesley W. Horton; also see Mary L. Dudziak, "Just Say No: Birth Control in the Connecticut Supreme Court Before

Griswold v. *Connecticut*," *Iowa Law Review* 75 (May 1990): 915–939, at 930–931, and also in Paul Finkelman and Stephen E. Gottlieb, eds., *Toward a Usable Past* (Athens: University of Georgia Press, 1991), pp. 304–338.

118. Pease, "Annual Report," 24 January 1940, PPLC 10-H; Ralph W. Ely to Hartford Birth Control Clinic, 31 January 1940, and Hilda C. Standish to Ely, 2 February 1940, PPLC 40-B; *Hartford Courant*, 12 March 1940, p. 2; *Newsweek*, 5 February 1940, p. 29; Upson to Morris, 26 February 1940, and Morris to Upson, 29 February 1940, Upson Papers; Eleanor Searle, Minutes, CBCL Future Policies Committee, New York, 28 February 1940, PPLC 1-L.

119. *State* v. *Nelson*, 126 Conn. 412, 418, 422, 424, 426, 11 A.2d 856; *State* v. *Certain Contraceptive Materials*, 126 Conn. 428, 11 A.2d 863. Critical notes on the *Nelson* decision include *Human Fertility* 5 (April 1940): 44–45; *University of Detroit Law Journal* 3 (May 1940): 216–218; *Boston University Law Review* 20 (June 1940): 551–554; *Journal of Criminal Law and Criminology* 31 (September-October 1940): 312–314; *Journal of the American Medical Association*, 14 September 1940, p. 962.

120. *Waterbury American*, 20 March 1940, pp. 1, 10; *Waterbury Democrat*, 20 March 1940, pp. 1, 4; *Hartford Times*, 20 March 1940; *Waterbury Republican*, 21 March 1940, pp. 1, 10; *Hartford Courant*, 21 March 1940, pp. 1, 2; *Greenwich Press*, 21 March 1940, pp. 1, 8.

CHAPTER TWO

1. *News and Observer*, 21 March 1940 and *Des Moines Tribune*, 25 March 1940, both quoted in BCFA press release, n.d. [c.1 April 1940], PPFA Box 39; *Waterbury Democrat*, 21 March 1940, pp. 6, 10, 22 March 1940, p. 2, 23 March 1940, pp. 1, 2, 25 March 1940, p. 3; *Waterbury American*, 21 March 1940, pp. 1, 11, 22 March 1940, pp. 1, 10; *New York Times*, 21 March 1940; *New York Herald Tribune*, 21 March 1940; Florence Rose to Sanger, 21 March 1940 (II), Rose Box 41; *Waterbury Republican*, 22 March 1940, p. 17, 23 March 1940, p. 18; 25 March 1940, pp. 1, 4; *Hartford Courant*, 22 March 1940, p. 12, 23 March 1940, p. 10; Upson to Pease, 23 March 1940, Upson to Ernst, 25 March 1940, Morris to Upson, 26 March 1940, Upson Papers; *Bridgeport Herald*, 24 March 1940. Also see Creadick to Upson, 21 March 1940, Fitzgerald to Upson, 23 March 1940, Upson to McTernan, 25 March 1940, Upson Papers; *Hartford Times*, 21 March 1940, p. 14; *Ridgefield Press*, 28 March 1940; *Catholic Transcript*, 28 March 1940, p. 1.

2. Lois Stringfield, Minutes, CBCL Board, 25 March 1940, PPLC 10-H; *Hartford Courant*, 26 March 1940, pp. 1, 10; *Waterbury Republican*, 26 March 1940, pp. 1, 4; *Waterbury Democrat*, 26 March 1940, p. 3; Charles Magill Smith, "Memorandum to Mrs. John Q. Tilson . . ." 25 March 1940, 4pp., PPFA Box 39; [Pease, Hepburn, et al.], untitled memo, n.d. [c.26 March 1940], Gamble 6–117; Darrach, Annotated Copy of Smith's March 25 memo, Winslow Box 96; Gilbert Colgate, "Minutes of Executive Committee," BCFA, 26 March 1940, Winslow Box 95; Rose to Sanger, 27 March 1940, Rose Box 41; [Smith], "Facts About the Connecticut Situation . . ." 29 March 1940, Sanger-LC Box 176. Also see Pease to Tilson, 1 March 1940, PPFA Box 38.

3. *Waterbury American*, 26 March 1940, p. 2, 27 March 1940, p. 1, 29 March 1940, pp. 1, 2; Fitzgerald motion and McEvoy order, 27 March 1940, PPLC 2-J; *Waterbury Democrat*, 27 March 1940, pp. 1, 2; Upson to Pease, and to Creadick, 27 March 1940, Creadick to Upson, 28 March 1940, Upson, "Memorandum for Mr. Secor," 27 March 1940, Upson Papers. Also see *Hartford Courant*, 27 March 1940, p. 10; Luke B. Lockwood to Florence Darrach, 27 March 1940, PPLC 2-B.

4. Upson to Ernst, 29 March 1940, Upson Papers; Upson Interviews with Brecher and Garrow; Garrow interviews with William J. Secor, Jr., Roger and Rosalie Nelson, Elizabeth [Goodrich] Scafarello, John W. McTernan, and Anthony Fitzgerald; *Waterbury Democrat*, 29 March 1940, p. 7, 1 April 1940, pp. 1, 4, 2 April 1940, p. 1, 3 April 1940, p. 5; *Waterbury American*, 2 April 1940, p. 16, 3 April 1940, p. 9; *Waterbury Republican*, 3 April 1940, pp. 1, 4; *Hartford Courant*, 3 April 1940, p. 3; *Human Fertility* 5 (April 1940): 59–62; Upson to Ernst, 3

April 1940, Upson to McTernan, 5 April 1940, Upson Papers. Also see Upson to McTernan, 19 March 1941, Upson Papers.

5. Garrow interviews with Elizabeth [Goodrich] Scafarello, Roger and Rosalie Nelson, John W. McTernan, and Anthony Fitzgerald.

6. Mabel Robbins, Minutes, Hartford MHC Board, 28 March 1940, and Pease to "Dear Patient," n.d., PPLC 39-E; *Hartford Courant*, 29 March 1940, p. 5; Sanger to Pease, 30 March 1940, Sanger-SS; Sanger to Morris, 30 March 1940, PPFA Box 38. Also see Colgate to Executive Committee Members, 29 March 1940, Sanger-LC Box 176; Rose to Morris, 30 March and 1 April 1940, PPFA Box 38; Upson to Morris, 1 April 1940, PPLC 2-A and Upson Papers; Lucy Smith, Minutes, Hartford MHC Board, 3 June 1940, and especially Mabel H. Robbins, "Clinic Report," 18 June 1940, PPLC 39-E, who noted: "The patients promise all kinds of secrecy if we will only furnish it to them. It has been very hard not to weaken, especially while the supplies were still in the closet."

7. Colgate, "Minutes of Special Meeting of Executive Committee," BCFA, 4 April 1940, and Richard Pierson, "Minutes," BCFA Board, 4 April 1940, Winslow Box 95; Ernst to Pease, 5 April 1940, PPLC 2-C.

8. Catherine Tilson, "Minutes of Joint Meeting," and "Preliminary Draft of Minutes of Joint Meeting," 6 April 1940, PPLC 10-H and 2-A; Standish Interviews with Nichols, Garrow, and Hubbell; Standish to Judy Frew, 13 June 1985, PPLC 25-E; *Hartford Courant*, 7 July 1970, p. 1, 29 April 1973; *West Hartford News*, 20 September 1979; Clarence J. Gamble to Hilda Standish, and to Edna McKinnon, 9 April 1940, Gamble 6–119 and 138-2375; *Hartford Courant*, 1 April 1940, p. 4; McKinnon to Gamble, 10 April 1940, Gamble 6–119; Gamble to Sanger, 10 and 12 April 1940, Gamble 195–3090; Sanger to Gamble, n.d. [c.15 April 1940], Gamble 195–3090; Sanger to Stuart Mudd, 15 April 1940, Sanger-SS; Gamble to Sanger, 23 April 1940, Gamble 195–3090; Ernst to Sanger, 30 April 1940, Ernst Box 363. Concerning Sanger, see particularly Harriet F. Pilpel, "Birth Control Federation," 10 May 1940, Ernst Box 363, detailing an 8 May conversation between Sanger, Ernst, Lindey, and Pilpel that included "a full discussion of the Connecticut case. Many of the facts seemed to surprise Mrs. Sanger, who had apparently been misinformed by various members of the Federation. . . . She believes that the National group should have complete say as to local legal problems. We explained to her that actually it was better in the Connecticut situation that [the] Federation did not have any such power since by and large the Connecticut forces were more aggressive and courageous than the Federation."

9. Bronson, Lewis, Bronson, and Upson to CBCL, "Statement," 6 April 1940, [Upson], "Memorandum to Members of the Firm," and [Bronson], "Memorandum to Members of the Firm," 30 April 1940, Hepburn to Upson, 9 May 1940, Upson Papers.

10. Lois Stringfield, Minutes, CBCL Future Policies Committee, 11 April 1940, PPLC 10-H; Winslow to Morris, and to Harriet Janney, 15 April 1940, Winslow Box 95; Pease to Ernst, 22 April 1940, PPLC 2-C; Edward E. Ottenheimer et al., "Report . . . " n.d. [c.22 April 1940], PPLC 2-A and 10-H; Eleanor Searle, Minutes, CBCL Board, 24 April 1940, PPLC 10-H; Stenotypist's Transcript, "Special Meeting of the Board . . ." 24 April 1940, 26pp., PPLC 10-I; Pilpel to Pease, 25 April 1940, PPLC 2-C. A thirty-eight-year-old graduate of Yale who had worked for JPJ for fifteen years, Rose passed away at age sixty-one on 2 August 1963.

11. Eleanor Searle, Minutes, CBCL Steering Committee, 3 May and 21 May 1940, PPLC 10-J; [Franklin], "Notes on Meeting . . ." 13 May 1940, PPLC 1-L; Catherine Tilson to Franklin, 22 May 1940, PPLC 8-J; *Hartford Courant*, 22 May 1940, p. 12, 23 May 1940, pp. 1, 6; Franklin: "Interview with J. Warren Upson," 23 May 1940, PPLC 2-L; "Interview with Mr. Frederick H. Wiggin," 24 May 1940, PPLC 8-H; "Interview with Judge Carroll Hincks," 24 May 1940, PPLC 2-L; "Interview with Judge Albert Bill," 28 May 1940, PPLC 2-L; "Interview with Mr. Moses Berkman," 29 May 1940, PPLC 8-H; "Interview with Lucius Robinson, Jr.," 6 June 1940, PPLC 2-L; "Interview with William Hanna," 8 June 1940, PPLC 2-L; "Interview with Robbins B. Stoeckel," 8 June 1940, PPLC 2-M; "Interview with Mr. Horace D. Taft," 10 June 1940, PPLC 2-L; "Interview with Mr. Raymond J. Dunne," 11 June 1940, PPLC 2-M; Mr. Redfield to Mr. Franklin, 10 June 1940, PPLC 2-M.

12. "Agenda," 10 June 1940, Sanger-LC Box 180; "Minutes," CBCL Steering Committee, 12 June 1940, PPLC 10-J; Pease, "President's Report," 18 June 1940, PPLC 39-E, and "Annual Report of the President," 26 June 1940, PPLC 10-K; "Plan of Publicity," 24 June 1940, PPLC 24-B; "Mrs. Darrach's Report," and CBCL Minutes, 26 June 1940, PPLC 10-J; *Hartford Courant*, 27 June 1940, p. 22; *Hartford Times*, 27 June 1940; *Waterbury Republican*, 28 June 1940, p. 21; Eleanor Searle, Executive Committee Minutes, 9 July 1940, PPLC 10-K; Darrach to Winslow, 14 July 1940, Winslow Box 96. Also see Lucy Smith, "Minutes," and Standish, "Annual Medical Report," Hartford MHC, 18 June 1940, PPLC 39-E; Standish, "Hartford Clinic Annual Report," 26 June 1940, PPLC 10-K; Gilbert Colgate, "Minutes," BCFA Executive Committee, 2 July 1940, Winslow Box 95; Upson to Franklin, 3 and 5 July 1940, PPLC 2-L and 2-C. On Robbins W. Barstow, see his *Hartford Courant* obituary, 19 September 1962, p. 4.

13. Darrach to Campbell, 15 July 1940, PPLM Box 5; [Franklin], "Interview with Governor Baldwin," 16 July 1940, PPLC 2-M. On Baldwin's significance, see Roth, *Connecticut*, p. 194; Johnson, *Raymond E. Baldwin*, pp. 64–71; and especially John W. Jeffries, *Testing the Roosevelt Coalition: Connecticut Society and Politics in the Era of World War II* (Knoxville: University of Tennessee Press, 1979), pp. 23–45, 301.

14. Franklin to A. K. Holding, 25 July 1940, PPLC 2-O; Eleanor Searle, Executive Committee Minutes, 6 August 1940, PPFA Box 38; *Hartford Courant*, 9 August 1940, p. 12; Searle to Rose, 8 August 1940, Morris to Rose, 13 August 1940, Pilpel to Huse, Rose to McWilliams, and Harold J. Seymour to Rose, 19 August 1940, Huse to Rose, 20 August 1940, McWilliams to Rose (II), 24 August 1940, Huse to Rose, 28 August 1940, Rose to Franklin, 12 September 1940, McWilliams to Pilpel, 16 September 1940, Pilpel to McWilliams, 18 September 1940, McWilliams to Rose, 30 September 1940, and Rose to Franklin, 14 October 1940, all PPFA Box 38; Holding, "Interview with Mrs. Sara Crawford," 15 August 1940, PPLC 2-L; "Report of Meeting with Tolland County Leaders," 20 August 1940, PPLC 50-A; Franklin, "Interview with Judge Kenneth Wynne," 29 August 1940, PPLC 8-H; Janney to Franklin, 8 October 1940, PPLC 2-M; *Volunteers Newsletter* Vol. 1, #1, 4 September 1940, and #2, 22 October 1940, PPLC 8-E; Creadick to Dr. Grannis, 13 September 1940, PPLC 2-O; Lucy Smith, Minutes, Hartford MHC, 13 September and 15 October 1940, PPLC 39-F; Eleanor Searle, Executive Committee Minutes, 25 September, 8 October and 28 October 1940, PPLC 8-B; Loraine Campbell to Rose, 10 October 1940, and Pease to Campbell, n.d. [c.17 October 1940], PPLM Box 5; Hartford Board to state Executive Committee, n.d., PPLC 3-F; Lucy Smith to state Executive Committee, 15 October 1940, PPLC 8-B; Morgan Brainard to Darrach, 15 October 1940, Winslow Box 96; Robbins, "Meeting of Committee on Affiliated Organizations," 21 October 1940, PPLC 2-A; Franklin to Mary P. Milmine, 25 October 1940, PPLC 2-E; C.-E. A. Winslow to Brainard, 30 October 1940, Brainard to Winslow, 2 November 1940, Winslow to Brainard, and to Darrach, 4 November 1940, Winslow Box 96.

15. Upson to Franklin, 28 October 1940, PPLC 2-M; *Commonwealth* v. *Corbett*, 307 Mass. 7, 29 N.E.2d 151 (17 September 1940); Pilpel, "The Social and Legal Status of Contraception," *North Carolina Law Review* 22 (February 1944): 212–225, at 223; "Judicial Regulation of Birth Control Under Obscenity Laws," *Yale Law Journal* 50 (February 1941): 682–689, at 686; *Human Fertility* 6 (February 1941): 27–28. Also see *Commonwealth* v. *Werlinsky*, 307 Mass. 608, 29 N.E.2d 150 (18 September 1940); Pilpel to Loraine Campbell, 18 September 1940, PPLM Box 14; Upson to Robert H. Harry, 11 January 1941, Upson Papers; Ernst and Pickett, *Birth Control in the Courts*, pp. 43–45; *Commonwealth* v. *Goldberg*, 316 Mass. 563, 55 N.E.2d 951 (27 June 1944); and the Massachusetts Mothers' Health Council monthly newsletter, *The Family Guardian*, which commenced publication in July/August 1939, as well as Campbell to Hoar, 24 November 1939, and Hoar to Campbell, 27 November 1939, PPLM Boxes 6 and 11. See as well *U.S.* v. *H. L. Blake Co.*, 189 F. Supp. 903 (30 December 1960).

16. *Human Fertility* 5 (October 1940): 158–159, (December 1940): 190–191, 6 (February 1941): 27–28; Eugene L. Belisle, "Church Control versus Birth Control," *The Nation* 155 (28 November 1942): 568–570; Loraine Campbell Interviews with Reed and with Stuart; L.

Foster Wood, "The Free Speech Issue in Holyoke" *Information Service* 20 (22 March 1941): 1–4 [Federal Council of Churches; Ernst Box 894]; and Kenneth W. Underwood, *Protestant and Catholic: Religious and Social Interaction in an Industrial Community* (Boston: Beacon Press, 1957), pp. 3–38, which speaks of Holyoke as "Paper City" and uses pseudonyms for all individual names other than Sanger's. Among the speakers at one Massachusetts birth control conference in Springfield was Roger B. Nelson; see Nelson to Loraine Campbell, 7 November 1940, PPLM Box 81, and *Springfield Evening Union*, 14 November 1940, pp. 1, 2 and *Springfield Union*, 15 November 1940.

17. Paul Franklin to Harold Seymour, "Confidential," 8–13 November 1940, PPLC 2-Q; Eleanor Searle, Executive Committee Minutes, 12 and 26 November and 19 and 27 December 1940, PPLC 8-B and C; A. K. Holding to Franklin, 15 November 1940, Upson, "Memorandum for Mr. Hanna . . ." (II) 20 and 25 November 1940, PPLC 2-Q; Franklin, "Things to Be Done," 21 November 1940, PPLC 2-R; Mabel Robbins to Holding, n.d., Holding to Upson, 25 November 1940, PPLM 2-M; Garrow conversations with Bice Clemow; Franklin to Clemow, 4 December 1940, PPLC 8-J; Barstow to McWilliams, 5 December 1940, and Colgate to Barstow, 13 December 1940, PPFA Box 38; Upson memo, 11 December 1940, PPLC 2-M; Clemow to Darrach, 12 December 1940, PPLC 3-B; Clemow, "Lawyers' Meeting," 14 December 1940, PPLC 8-F; Clemow to Horace Taft, 17 December 1940, PPLC 8-J; [Upson], "Draft of Proposed Sub-Committee Report," n.d. [c.20 December 1940], PPLC 8-E; Mary Lasker, "Minutes," BCFA Executive Committee, 27 December 1940, Winslow Box 95; Clemow to Sub-Committee, "A Doctor for a Test Case," 31 December 1940, PPLC 3-B; "Status of Plans as of January 1, 1941," 8pp., PPLC 8-F; Winslow to Alice Cowgill, 7 January 1941, and to Darrach, 9 January 1941, Winslow Box 96; Robbins, Minutes, Hartford MHC, 8 January 1941, PPLC 39-F; Searle to Clemow, 10 January 1941, PPLC 3-B. On Carroll C. Hincks, who in 1953 ascended to the Second Circuit Court of Appeals (and who, in the 1910s, had practiced law in Waterbury with subsequent Connecticut State Supreme Court Justice Arthur Ells), see *New Haven Register*, 28 March 1948, pp. Magazine 1–2, 15 March 1959, 24 May 1959, p. 22, and his *Register* obituary, 30 September 1964.

18. Eleanor Searle, Board Minutes, 13 and 27 January 1941, PPLC 8-C; *Bridgeport Telegram*, 14 January 1941; *Hartford Courant*, 14 January 1941, p. 4, 15 January 1941, p. 6; Clemow to Darrach, 18 January 1941, PPLC 3-B; Upson to Darrach, 21 January 1941, PPLC 2-M; Darrach to Wiggin, 21 January 1941, Stoddard to Leonard D. Adkins, 21 January 1941, Adkins to Stoddard, 23 January 1941, Wiggin to Darrach, 24 January 1941, PPLC 3-B; Clemow to Darrach, 31 January 1941, PPLC 2-M. Also see Robbins to Upson, 13 January 1943, PPLC 3-I. On F. H. Wiggin, in addition to Garrow conversations with John Q. Tilson, Jr., and Catherine J. Tilson, see Franklin, "Interview with Mr. Frederick H. Wiggin," 24 May 1940, PPLC 8-H, and Wiggin's obituaries in the *New Haven Register* and *New Haven Journal-Courier*, 23 May 1963, p. 1.

19. *Birth Control News* Vol. 1, #1 (February 1941); *Journal of the House*, p. 467 (4 February 1941); *Journal of the Senate*, p. 604 (11 February 1941); "Minutes," Sponsorship Committee, 7 February 1941, PPLC 2-A; Eleanor Searle, Executive Committee Minutes, 17 February 1941, PPLC 8-C; Penelope Huse to Mrs. Damon, 20 February 1941, Rose Box 32; *Hartford Times*, 7 January 1941; *Hartford Courant*, 8 January 1941, p. 20, 7 February 1941, p. 10, 9 February 1941, p. 1, 10 February 1941, 14 February 1941, p. 2, 15 February 1941, p. 4, 18 February 1941, p. 6, 19 February 1941, p. 6, 25 February 1941, p. 6, 26 February 1941, p. 6. Guy E. Shipler, Jr., "Catholics & Birth Control: How the Battle Goes in Connecticut," *Churchman*, 1 May 1941, pp. 14–15, part two of a four-part series, contains some errors. On the Barrett-McTernan exchange, later joined by Horace Taft, see the *Waterbury American*, 19 November 1940, 25 November 1940, p. 8, 29 November 1940, 13 December 1940, 19 December 1940, and 7 January 1941; also see Mrs. Anson Stocking, "Report on Birth Control Activities for Waterbury," n.d. [c.February 1941], PPLC 1-L, who observed that "These letters have done much to interest persons in the subject of birth control" and added that "It is astonishing the number of intelligent people who are under the impression that

Birth Control Clinics mean legalized abortion." See as well *Hartford Courant*, 12 December 1940, p. 1, and 17 December 1940, p. 13.

20. *Hartford Courant*, 28 February 1941, pp. 1, 5, 1 March 1941, p. 12, 3 March 1941, pp. 1, 2, 4 March 1941, pp. 7, 9, 7 March 1941, pp. 6, 15, 10 March 1941, p. 4, 12 March 1941, p. 13, 13 March 1941, p. 8, 23 March 1941, p. 14; *Waterbury Republican*, 21 March 1941, 1 April 1941; *Hartford Times*, 24 March 1941; Clemow to Penelope Huse, 11 March 1941, PPFA Box 38.

21. Clemow to Files, 1 February 1941, Wiggin to Darrach, 3 February 1941, PPLC 3-B; "Statement of Wilder Tileston, M.D." 30 June 1941, *Tileston* Record, Connecticut Supreme Court; Wiggin to Clemow, 19 March 1941, Clemow to Wiggin, 21 March 1941, PPLC 3-B; Wiggin, "Complaint and Subpoena," 20 March 1941, *Tileston* Record and PPLC 3-F. Also see Harriet Pollack, "An Uncommonly Silly Law: The Connecticut Birth Control Cases in the U.S. Supreme Court" (unpublished Ph.D. dissertation, Columbia University, 1967), pp. 88–90. On Dr. Tileston, in addition to a Garrow conversation with his son Peter, see his obituary notices in the *New Haven Register*, 7 May 1969, p. 23, and *Connecticut Medicine* 33 (June 1969): 419–420. On Abraham S. Ullman, see his obituaries in the 21 August 1974 *New Haven Journal-Courier* and the 22 August 1974 *New Haven Register*, and the 27 November 1939 *Register* on his appointment, after eleven years as the assistant state's attorney.

22. *New Haven Register*, 25 March 1941, 6 April 1941, p. 3; *Hartford Times*, 25 March 1941, 1 April 1941, 10 April 1941, p. 2, 11 April 1941, p. 21; *Hartford Courant*, 26 March 1941, p. 22, 11 April 1941, pp. 1, 4, 6; *New York Herald Tribune*, 25 and 26 March 1941; *Greenwich Press*, 27 March 1941; *Birth Control News* Vol. 1, #2 (March 1941) and #3 (April 1941); Transcript of Public Health and Safety Committee Hearing, 10 April 1941, 51pp., Connecticut State Library; [Penelope Huse and Morris Lewis], "Report on Hearing . . . April 10, 1941," 16 April 1941, 7pp., and Morris Lewis to Mrs. Damon, "Massachusetts & Connecticut Hearings," 22 April 1941, PPFA Box 38; *Bridgeport Herald*, 13 April 1941, p. 8.

23. *Catholic Transcript*, 17 April 1941, p. 4; Mabel Robbins, Executive Committee Minutes, 21 April 1941, PPLC 8-C; *Hartford Times*, 25 April 1941, p. 28; *Birth Control News* Vol. 1, #4 (May 1941); Pilpel to Clemow, 8 May 1941, PPLC 3-C; Darrach to Nan Rockefeller, 15 April 1941, Rockefeller Papers.

24. *Hartford Courant*, 14 May 1941, pp. 1, 4, 20 May 1941, pp. 1, 2, 21 May 1941, p. 1, 11, 28 May 1941, p. 2; *Hartford Times*, 14 May 1941, p. 27, 21 May 1941, 22 May 1941, p. 30, 27 May 1941, pp. 1, 2, 28 May 1941; *Journal of the House*, pp. 1498, 1568–1579, 1809 (14 May, 20 May, 28 May 1941); *Journal of the Senate*, pp. 1653, 1748–1750 (21 and 27 May 1941); 1941 Connecticut General Assembly Records (RG 2), Box 201; *Waterbury Republican*, 21 May 1941, pp. 1, 2, 28 May 1941, p. 3; *Waterbury American*, 22 May 1941, p. 1; Bice Clemow, "An Analysis of the Vote in the House," 24 May 1941, and "An Analysis of the Vote in the Senate," 2 June 1941, PPLC 2-Q; *Human Fertility* 6 (June 1941): 95–96. On the 1941 session in general, see Van Dusen, *Connecticut*, pp. 370–371.

25. *Human Fertility* 6 (February 1941): 28, (June 1941): 94–95; John M. Hall to Loraine Campbell, 1 May 1941, PPLM Box 5; *Opinion of the Justices*, 309 Mass. 555 (16 May 1941); Jonathan Daniels, "Birth Control and Democracy," *The Nation* 153 (1 November 1941): 429; Eugene L. Belisle, "Birth Control in Massachusetts," *The New Republic* 105 (8 December 1941): 759–760; Stephen D. Howard, "The Birth Control Law Conflict in Massachusetts" (unpublished B.A. thesis, Harvard University, 1959), pp. 43–55. The votes against the measure were 133 to 77 in the house and 18 to 16 in the state senate.

26. Eleanor Searle, Board Minutes (II), 12 June 1941, PPLC 8-C; Clemow to Executive Committee Members, 12 June 1941, PPLC 10-L; Morris Lewis to Clemow, 6 June 1941, Clemow to Lewis, 9 June 1941, and Lewis to Clemow, 10 June 1941, PPFA Box 38; Darrach to Barstow, 28 June 1941, and Barstow to Darrach, 1 July 1941, PPLC 8-A; Mabel Robbins to Clarence Gamble, 15 July 1941, Gamble 6–119; Robbins, "Minutes," 13 August and 15 September 1941, Peggy Newburger, Executive Committee Minutes, 23 September 1941, PPLC 10-L; Janet S. Williams, "Report of Executive Vice-President," 28 May 1942, PPLC 10-M; *Hartford Times*, 16 October 1941; *Hartford Courant*, 17 October 1941, p. 26, 20 October 1941, p. 2; *Newsweek*, 20 October 1941, pp. 65–66; *Time*, 27 October 1941, p. 74; *The Family*

Guardian #22 (November-December 1941): 3–4; Clemow to Barstow, 22 November 1941, PPLC 3-B.

27. Mabel Robbins, Executive Committee Minutes, 25 November 1941, PPLC 10-L; Wiggin to Barstow, 2 December 1941, PPLC 3-B; *Tileston* Record, pp. 12–17, 24–37, and 40–52; *Hartford Courant*, 4 December 1941, p. 5; *Human Fertility* 6 (December 1941): 191–192; Wiggin to Darrach, 12 December 1941, PPLC 3-C; Janet S. Williams, "Annual Report," 22 December 1941, PPLC 10-L; Peggy Newburger, Board Minutes, 27 January 1941, PPLC 10-M; Wiggin and Tilson, "Brief for the Plaintiff," *Wilder Tileston* v. *Abraham S. Ullman et al.*, Connecticut Supreme Court, February Term 1942, #2164, 29 January 1942; Ullman, Philip R. Pastore, and Fred Trotta, "Brief of the Defendants," *Tileston* v. *Ullman*, #2164, A-172 463–470. Also see Milton C. Winternitz and Henry Bunting, "The Law and Planned Parenthood," *Connecticut State Medical Journal* 6 (February 1942): 102, and *Human Fertility* 7 (December 1942): 175.

28. Wiggin to Janet Williams, 29 January 1942, Williams to Wiggin, 2 and 7 February 1942, Robbins to Wiggin, 4 February 1942, Wiggin to Williams, 6 February 1942, PPLC 3-B; Florence Darrach [by Robbins], "Annual Report," 28 January 1943, PPLC 10-N.

29. Reed, *The Birth Control Movement*, p. 136; *Tileston* v. *Ullman*, 129 Conn. 84, 88, 26 A.2d 582; *Hartford Courant*, 3 June 1942, p. 1, 4 June 1942, p. 13; *Hartford Times*, 3 June 1942, p. 1; *New York Post*, 3 June 1942. On Arthur F. Ells, see Allyn Brown's profile of him at 151 Conn. 747, and his *Courant* obituary, 9 December 1963, p. 27. Commentaries on *Tileston* include *Human Fertility* 7 (June 1942): 89–91; *Ave Maria*, 20 June 1942, pp. 770–771; *Journal of the American Medical Association* 120 (19 December 1942): 1338; and Jerome A. Scoler, *Boston University Law Review* 23 (January 1943): 115–118. In line with the Connecticut Supreme Court's opinion, Superior Court Judge Frank P. McEvoy entered a formal judgment in the case on June 26; *Tileston* Case File, #60475, New Haven County Superior Court. Fritz Wiggin received a total fee of $3,000 for his work on the case; Wiggin and Dana Statement, 5 June 1942, PPLC 3-D.

30. Rose to Janet Williams, 9 June 1942, Peggy Newburger, Executive Committee Minutes, 10 June 1942, PPLC 10-M; Penelope Huse to Rose, 12 June 1942, PPFA Box 38; Darrach to Upson, 13 June 1942, Upson Papers; Robbins to Eugene Belisle, 15 June 1942, PPLM Box 106; "Report on Conference Held in New Haven," 26 June 1942, PPFA Box 38; Robbins, Minutes, 26 June 1942, Darrach to Board Members, 29 June and 27 July 1942, PPLC 10-M; Darrach to Pilpel, 4 July 1942, Darrach to Claude Pierce, 5 August 1942, Ernst Box 363; Pilpel to Upson, 14 August 1942, Pilpel to Wiggin, 17 August 1942, Upson Papers; Ernst and Pilpel, "Statement of Jurisdiction and Opinions," *Wilder Tileston* v. *Abraham S. Ullman et al.*, 25 August 1942, PPLC 3-F; Pilpel to Robbins, 28 August 1942, Ernst to Darrach, 31 August 1942, PPLC 3-D; Ernst to Rose, 31 August 1942, Ernst to Penelope Huse, 1 September 1942, PPFA Box 39; Roger Baldwin to Arthur Hayes, 3 September 1942, Hayes to Baldwin, 9 September 1942, Clifford Forster to Catherine J. Tilson, 18 September 1942, Tilson to Forster, 21 September 1942, ACLU Box 2522; ACLU Board Minutes, 14 September 1942, Box 2356; Pilpel to Robbins, 3 September 1942, Pilpel to Darrach, 11 September 1942, PPLC 3-D; Robbins to Upson, 11 September 1942, Pilpel to Upson, 18 September 1942, Upson Papers; *Hartford Times*, 17 September 1942, 1 October 1942; Ullman, Pastore, and Arthur T. Gorman, "Statement Against Jurisdiction and Motion to Dismiss or Affirm," *Tileston* v. *Ullman*, 20 September 1942, PPLC 3-F; Peggy Newburger, PPLC Executive Committee Minutes, 22 September 1942, Upson Papers; Rose to Ernst et al., 25 September 1942, PPLC 3-D and PPFA Box 38; Pilpel to Upson, and Blake Cabot to Upson, 28 September 1942, Upson Papers; William Darrach et al. to "Dear Doctor," 1 October 1942, and PPLC "1942 Fall Newsletter," PPLC 3-F; *Hartford Courant*, 2 and 3 October 1942; Pilpel to Upson, 1 October 1942, Cabot to Upson, 5 October 1942, and Scribner to Upson, 7 October 1942, Upson Papers; Robbins to Cabot, 5 October 1942, Cabot to Robbins, 7 October 1942, Upson to Cabot, 13 October 1942, PPFA Box 38; Cabot to Upson, 13 October 1942, Scribner to Upson, 14 October 1942, Pilpel to Upson, 14 October 1942, Ullman to Upson, 15 October 1942, Pilpel to Upson, 19 October 1942, Cabot to Upson, 19 October 1942, Upson Papers; Upson to Cabot, 21 October 1942, PPFA Box 39; Ernst to

Upson, 22 October 1942, Upson Papers; Upson to "Dear Doctors," 24 October 1942, PPLC 3-F; Ernst, "Appellant's Brief," *Tileston* v. *Ullman*, U.S. Supreme Court, October Term 1942, #420, 24 October 1942; Lawrence L. Lewis and Upson, "Brief on Behalf of A. Nowell Creadick, M.D. and Others," *Tileston* v. *Ullman*, 24 October 1942, Upson Papers; Scribner, "Brief on Behalf of 166 Physicians," *Tileston* v. *Ullman*, 24 October 1942, PPLC 3-I; *Hartford Courant*, 25 October 1942, pp. 1, 2; Upson to Pilpel, 27 October 1942, Pilpel to Upson, 28 October 1942, Upson Papers.

31. See Eugene L. Belisle, "Church Control versus Birth Control," *The Nation* 155 (28 November 1942): 568–570; Belisle, "The Cardinal Stoops to Conquer," *The New Republic*, 30 November 1942, pp. 710–712; Howard, "The Birth Control Law Conflict in Massachusetts," pp. 56–71; James M. O'Toole, "Prelates and Politicos: Catholics and Politics in Massachusetts, 1900–1970," in Robert E. Sullivan and O'Toole, eds., *Catholic Boston* (Boston: Archdiocese of Boston, 1985), pp. 15–65, at 31–35; and O'Toole, *Militant and Triumphant: William Henry O'Connell and the Catholic Church in Boston, 1859–1944* (Notre Dame: University of Notre Dame Press, 1992), pp. 135–36. Also see *Compton* v. *State Ballot Law Commission*, 311 Mass. 643 (29 May 1942); *Human Fertility* 7 (August 1942): 112–113 and 123, (December 1942): 191; Alvah W. Sulloway, *Birth Control and Catholic Doctrine* (Boston: Beacon Press, 1959), p. 203; and John H. Fenton, *The Catholic Vote* (New Orleans: Hauser Press, 1960), pp. 7–20.

32. Mabel Robbins to Eleanor Sachs, and Florence Darrach to "Dear Friend," 16 November 1942, PPLC 3-D and 10-M; Jeffries, *Testing the Roosevelt Coalition*, pp. 130–131; *Hartford Courant*, 10 November 1942, p. 12; Upson to Pilpel, 13 November 1942, Upson Papers; "VC" [Vern Countryman], "Tileston v. Ullman," n.d., Douglas Papers Box 78.

33. Pilpel to Upson, 16 and 20 November 1942, Upson Papers; Borchard to Pilpel, 24 November 1942, Pilpel to Borchard, 27 November 1942, Borchard to Pilpel, 30 November 1942, Borchard Box 106; Garrow conversation with Peter Tileston; Upson to Darrach, and to Creadick, 27 November 1942, Robbins to Upson, 30 November 1942, Upson Papers; *Human Fertility* 7 (December 1942): 188–190; Eleanor Sachs, Executive Committee Minutes, 1 December 1942, PPLC 10-M; Borchard to Pilpel, 3 December 1942, Pilpel to Borchard, 4 December 1942, Borchard to Pilpel, 5 December 1942, Borchard Box 106; "Report on Connecticut Situation," 4 December 1942, PPFA Box 38; Upson to Darrach, 9 December 1942, Upson to Scribner, 14 December 1942, Scribner to Upson, 16 December 1942, Pilpel to Upson, 18 December 1942, Darrach to Upson, 18 December 1942, Upson Papers; Pilpel to Borchard, 18 December 1942, Borchard to Pilpel, 22 December 1942, Borchard Box 106; Upson to Pilpel, to Scribner, and to Darrach, 28 December 1942, Ernst to Upson, 29 December 1942, Scribner to Upson, 31 December 1942, Upson Papers; Pilpel to Clerk E. C. Cullinan, 31 December 1942, *Tileston* v. *Ullman* Case File, National Archives (RG 267) Box 3166; Upson to Scribner, 2 January 1943, Scribner to Upson, 4 January 1943, Darrach to Upson, n.d. [3 January 1943], Upson to Darrach, 4 January 1943, Upson to Ernst, and to Charles Cropsey, 5 January 1943, Darrach to Upson, 6 January 1943, Upson Papers; Penelope Huse to Rose, 6 January 1943, PPFA Box 39; Pilpel to Borchard, 6 January 1943, Borchard to Pilpel, 7 January 1943, Borchard Box 106; Ernst and Borchard, "Appellant's Reply Brief," *Tileston* v. *Ullman*, 7 January 1943; Lewis and Upson, "Brief on Behalf of A. Nowell Creadick, M.D. and Others," *Tileston* v. *Ullman*, 7 January 1943; Scribner, "Brief on Behalf of 166 Physicians," *Tileston* v. *Ullman*, 7 January 1943; Darrach to Robbins, 11 January 1943, and Robbins to Darrach, 12 January 1943, PPLC 3-D. Also see Pollack, "An Uncommonly Silly Law," pp. 95–97. Somewhat stunningly, Borchard suggested to Ernst (18 December 1942, Borchard Box 106) that in light of their uncertainty as to whether the declaratory judgment form of the case might be troubling the Justices, "Would it be out of the question for me to write Mr. Douglas or the Chief Justice a personal letter and ask which of these points bothered them, saying that if it were the declaratory judgment point I would endeavor to be present in the Court room and argue the question." Douglas and Stone were the two justices he knew best, Borchard said, "but I do not know whether it would be improper practice to make such a personal inquiry." As of the fall of 1942, Borchard had

been teaching at Yale Law School for twenty-five years. See Laura Kalman, *Legal Realism at Yale, 1927–1960* (Chapel Hill: University of North Carolina Press, 1986), pp. 101, 140.

34. Charles E. Scribner, "The Argument of *Tileston* v. *Ullman* in the United States Supreme Court," 15 January 1943, 9pp., PPFA Box 39; Ernst, *The Best Is Yet . . .* (New York: Harper & Brothers, 1945), p. 254; *Hartford Courant*, 14 January 1943, p. 9, 15 January 1943, p. 2, 28 January 1943; *New York Herald Tribune*, 15 January 1943. On William L. Beers, a subsequent Attorney General of Connecticut who had been named a special assistant to Ullman on November 25 for the purpose of assisting with *Tileston*, see the *New Haven Register*, 28 July 1953, and his *Register* obituary, 14 January 1955. Beers received $1,200 for his help, and Ullman was paid $6,000 in addition to his regular annual salary of $6,240 for his work on the case. *New Haven Journal-Courier*, 3 April 1943. Prior to the oral argument Upson was formally admitted to the Bar of the Supreme Court; Ullman and Beer were his official sponsors.

35. Upson to Creadick, and to Darrach, 15 January 1943, Upson to Ullman, and to Beers, 16 January 1943, Upson Papers; Ernst to Loraine Campbell, 21 January 1943, PPLM Box 84; Robbins, "Minutes," 16 January 1943, and Board Minutes, 19 January 1943, PPLC 10-N; Borchard to Ernst, 15 January 1943, Ernst to Stone, 18 January 1943, Borchard Box 106. Borchard's response to the oral argument experience was considerably more peevish than Ernst's and Upson's. If the Justices "had read the record and the briefs and known the case," he complained to a friend, "they would not have asked so many irrelevant and snap judgment questions, questions which diverted the argument from its main course to collateral notions that spontaneously occurred to the Judges from the profundity of their assumed knowledge." Most distressing, Borchard went on, was the Justices' behavior toward Ernst: "Instead of deferring in slight degree to his long experience, they lit into him as if he were a young cub and they magisterial Socrates." Borchard to Henry S. Fraser, 29 January 1943, Borchard Box 106.

36. William O. Douglas Conference Notes, *Tileston* v. *Ullman*, No. 420, 16 January 1943, Douglas Box 78; *Tileston* File, Stone Papers, Box 69; *Tileston* v. *Ullman*, 318 U.S. 44, 46; *New York Times*, 2 February 1943, p. 21; *New York Herald Tribune*, 2 February 1943; *New York Post*, 2 February 1943.

Stone's modest file on *Tileston* includes brief written endorsements of his opinion from six of his seven colleagues: Frank Murphy, Robert H. Jackson, Stanley Reed, Owen Roberts, Felix Frankfurter ("This suits me fine") and Hugo L. Black: "I agree although I preferred deciding the case on its merits. Since my views are in the minority on this point, I do not care to press them." William O. Douglas also concurred; the Court that heard *Tileston* had one vacancy, as Wiley B. Rutledge had not yet been nominated to fill the seat vacated by James F. Byrnes.

Notes on *Tileston* include *Human Fertility* 8 (March 1943): 30–31; Charles E. Carpenter, *Southern California Law Review* 16 (March 1943): 220–228; and H. Peyton Wilmot, *St. John's Law Review* 17 (April 1943): 122–123. Also see Charles E. Scribner, "Memorandum re Proposed Attack . . ." 16 February 1944, PPFA Box 38, Dudley D. Miles, "The Constitutionality of Anti-Birth Control Legislation," *Wyoming Law Journal* 7 (Spring 1953): 138–142, and Borchard, "Challenging 'Penal' Statutes by Declaratory Action," *Yale Law Journal* 52 (June 1943): 445–493, at 454 and 464–465, where he continued to insist that "the injury is done . . . by the *enactment* of the damaging statute or regulation, long before or even quite without any 'threat' of enforcement by an official." Borchard's response to the decision, however, was about as intemperate as his reaction to the oral argument. Stone, he told Ernst, "decided the case for the Court and decided it practically before the argument began, for the opinion follows almost precisely the points he raised at the opening of the case." Borchard was willing to concede that "the complaint was not artistically drawn," but "Only a person entrenched in his prejudice could maintain that it was not a controversy." "It seems to me," Borchard concluded, "that a new suit with perhaps one good woman is the best procedure available." Borchard to Ernst, 4 February 1943, Borchard Box 106.

37. *Hartford Courant*, 2 February 1943, p. 3; Bice Clemow Interview with Garrow; Upson to Ernst, 2 February 1943, and "Memo for Mr. Berkman," 3 February 1943, Upson Papers; Ernst to John Q. Tilson, Jr., 3 February 1943, Ernst to Florence Darrach, 4 February 1943,

PPLC 3-D; Borchard to Ernst, 4 February 1943, Ernst to Borchard, 10 February 1943, Borchard Box 106; *Hartford Times*, 6 February 1943; Ernst to Upson, 10 February 1943, Upson to Ernst, 11 and 12 February and 9 March 1943, Upson Papers.

38. Ernst to Rose, 5 March 1943, PPLC 3-D; *Hartford Courant*, 2 February 1943, 12 February 1943, pp. 1, 6; *Journal of the House*, p. 194 (20 January); *Journal of the Senate*, p. 209 (21 January); Robbins, Legislative Committee Minutes, 17 February 1943, PPLC 10-N; Winslow to Darrach, 19 February 1943, Winslow Box 96; "Report of the Meeting," 15 March 1943, PPLM Box 84; Virginia Wake, Board Minutes, 16 March 1943, PPLC 10-N; Upson to Darrach, "Memorandum," 19 March 1943, [Robbins] to Eleanor Sachs, 19 March 1943, PPLC 3-K.

39. Transcript of Public Health and Safety Committee Hearing, 31 March 1943, 38pp., PPLC 3-L; *Hartford Times*, 31 March 1943, 1 April 1943, 14 April 1943, 21 April 1943; *Hartford Courant*, 1 April 1943, p. 5, 8 April 1943, p. 1, 9 April 1943, p. 1, 15 April 1943, pp. 1, 7, 21 April 1943, 22 April 1943, p. 1; *Waterbury Democrat*, 1 April 1943, p. 4; *Bridgeport Herald*, 4 April 1943; Florence Darrach to "Dear Legislator," 31 March 1943, PPLC 3-L; Robbins to Upson, 2 April 1943, PPLC 3-K; *Journal of the House*, pp. 1299, 1339–1346, 1480 (9, 14, 27 April); *Waterbury Republican*, 10 April 1943; Upson to Joseph R. Neill, 10 and 22 April 1943, Lillian Owen to Mabel Robbins, 13 April 1943, PPLC 3-K and L; *Journal of the Senate*, pp. 1243 and 1313–1315 (15 and 21 April); Upson to Darrach, 22 April 1943, PPLC 3-L; Pilpel to Darrach, 23 April 1943, PPLC 3-D; Janson to Upson, 23 April 1943, Joseph R. Neill to Upson, 28 April 1943, Upson to Neill, 29 April 1943, PPLC 3-K; Virginia Wake, Board Minutes, 27 April 1943, PPLC 10-N. On the 1943 session in general, see Van Dusen, *Connecticut*, pp. 371–372. The number of senate seats had been increased from thirty-five to thirty-six between the 1940 and 1942 elections.

40. Rose to Darrach, 18 May 1943, PPLC 10-O; Upson to Darrach, 27 May 1943, PPLC 3-L; Upson to Rose, 27 May 1943, PPFA Box 38; Virginia Wake, Executive Committee and Board Minutes, 1 June 1943, PPLC 10-O; Alice Klein to Rose, 9 June 1943, Ernst to Upson, 15 June 1943, Upson to Ernst, 16 June 1943, Rose to Upson, 17 June 1943, Upson to Rose, 22 June 1943, Upson to Janney, 24 June 1943, PPFA Box 38; "Minutes of the Meeting," 29 June 1943, PPLM Box 84; Janney to Board Members, 6 July 1943, PPLC 10-O; Alice Klein to Elizabeth Borden, 20 July 1943, PPLM Box 84; Edna McKinnon, "Legal Conferences," 27 August–1 September 1943, PPFA Box 40 and PPLM Box 84. A clear pattern of dramatic summertime slumps in activity occurred in both Connecticut and Massachusetts from the 1920s through the 1940s, and was noted by observers at the time. As Francis Vreeland quoted one leading activist in 1929, "'Reform is a winter pastime for the clubwoman and everything fluctuates with her.'" "The Process of Reform," p. 359.

41. McKinnon, "Report of Exploratory Trip in Massachusetts," 7 September 1943, McKinnon to Elizabeth Borden, 7 September 1943, Rose to Frederick M. Myers and to Joseph T. Bartlett, 10 September 1943, Borden to Rose, 17 September 1943, PPLM Box 84; McKinnon, "Report of Conference with Mr. Laurence Janney . . ." and "Report of Meeting Regarding Test Case," 9 September 1943, McKinnon to Robbins, 9 September 1943, PPFA Box 38; McKinnon, "Report of Exploratory Trip in Connecticut" and "Report of Meeting With a Sub-Committee," 16 September 1943, PPLC 3-N; McKinnon, "Report of Conference with Mrs. Darrach," 22 September 1943, Rose to Borden, 22 September 1943, PPLM Box 84; McKinnon to Buist Anderson, 22 September 1943, Chauncey B. Garver to Rose, 24 September 1943, Morris Hadley to Rose, 27 September 1943, Anderson to McKinnon, 29 September 1943, PPFA Box 38; Ernst to Albert Lasker, 19 October 1943, Sanger-LC Box 180; Borden to Rose, 22 October 1943, PPLM Box 84; Robbins, "Report," and Barbara Davenport, Board and Executive Committee Minutes, 26 October 1943, PPLC 10-O; Janney to Borden, 28 October 1943, PPLM Box 106; Borden to Carolyn Ahern, 28 October and 14 December 1943, Rose to Borden, 15 November 1943, Borden to Rose, 14 December 1943, PPLM Box 84; Clemow, Legal Advisory Committee Minutes, 20 November 1943, PPLC 3-N; Virginia Wake, Executive Committee Minutes, 18 January 1944, Janney, "Annual Narrative Report," January 1944, PPLC 10-P; "The Fortune Survey, *Fortune* 28 (August

1943): 24 and 30; Schmiedler, "Birth Control: A Catholic View," *Reader's Digest*, October 1943, pp. 115–117. Also see *American Mercury* 58 (February 1944): 157–164, (April 1944): 504–506.

Father Schmiedler's analysis of course prefigured by many years a very similar and now-famous thread metaphor. See Transcript of Oral Argument, *Webster* v. *Reproductive Health Services*, U.S. Supreme Court, October Term 1988, #88–605, pp. 11 and 15. Charles Fried, on behalf of the appellants, explained that with regard to *Roe* v. *Wade*, "We are asking the Court to pull this one thread." Frank Susman, attorney for appellees, responded that "It has always been my personal experience that, when I pull a thread, my sleeve falls off."

42. Elizabeth Borden to Rose, 2 February 1944, PPLM Box 84; Rose to Borden and Janney, 9 February 1944, PPLC 10-P; Charles Scribner to Ernst, 15 February 1944, and enclosed memorandum, Ernst Box 267 and PPFA Box 38; Virginia Wake, Board and Executive Committee Minutes, 14 March 1944, PPLC 10-P; McKinnon, "Report of Trip to Connecticut," 15 March 1944, PPFA Box 38; McKinnon, "Report of Conference with Mr. Ernst . . ." 16 March 1944, PPLM Box 84; Pilpel, "Connecticut Birth Control," 16 March 1944, Ernst Box 267; Rose to Borden, 16 March 1944, PPLM Box 84; McKinnon, "Production Schedule . . ." 17 March 1944, PPLM Box 84; McKinnon, "Report of Conference with Dr. Josephine Evarts," 20 March 1944, PPLM Box 106 and PPFA Box 38; McKinnon to Buist Anderson, 20 March 1944, McKinnon to Rose and Mrs. Trent, 24 March 1944, PPFA Box 38; McKinnon to Carolyn Ahern, 24 March 1944, PPLM Box 84; Rose, "Connecticut Legal Case," 30 March 1944, PPFA Box 38; McKinnon, "Connecticut Report No. 2," 3 April 1944, PPLC 10-P; Pilpel, "Re: Planned Parenthood Federation," 5 April 1944, Ernst Box 894; Anderson to Scribner, 6 April 1944, and Janney to McKinnon, [9] April 1944, PPFA Box 38; McKinnon, "Connecticut Report No. 3," 14 April 1944, PPLC 10-P; Hadleigh Howd to Barbara Davenport, 15 April 1944, McKinnon to Rose, 17 April 1944, and McKinnon, "Conference with Mrs. Pilpel," 19 April 1944, PPFA Box 38; Ernst to McKinnon, 11 May 1944, Ernst Box 894. On Dr. Evarts, who died in 1983, see Eunice Trowbridge and April Radbill, *Dr. Josephine Evarts: A Tribute* (n.p.: n.p., 1981)[Smith College Library], and *Hartford Courant*, 3 April 1986, pp. E1, E14.

43. Virginia Wake, Executive Committee and Annual Meeting Minutes, 15 May 1944, PPLC 10-P; Scribner to McKinnon, 12 May 1944, McKinnon to Trent and Rose, 14 May 1944, PPFA Box 38; Stuart Rand to Morris Hadley, 16 May 1944, PPLM Box 84; McKinnon, "Next Steps in Connecticut," 26 May 1944, Cunningham to Janney, 26 May 1944, PPFA Box 38; McKinnon, "Resume of Test Case Situation in Massachusetts," 29 May 1944, Betty Borden, "Report of Meeting . . ." 30 June 1944, PPLM Box 84; Cunningham, "Director's Report," and Leslie Staples, Executive Committee Minutes, 12 September 1944, PPLC 10-P; [Cunningham], "Tentative Plan for Legislative Campaign," 26 September 1944, PPLC 3-N; Rose to Ernst, 31 October 1944, Ernst Box 894; Ernst to Sanger, 12 September 1944, Sanger-LC Box 180. Sanger imperiously and unfairly told Ernst in reply that she thought Ernst himself was largely to blame for the birth control movement's decreased militancy. "Can you take that on the chin? There is a lot more I have pent up for explosion." Reminiscent of Sanger's erratic 1940 assault on Sallie Pease, this attack was equally misdirected. Sanger to Ernst, 19 September 1944, Sanger-LC Box 180.

On Molly Cunningham and her hiring, see the *Stamford Advocate*, 5 April 1938; Edna McKinnon, "Conference with Mrs. Gerald Cunningham," 21 March 1944, PPFA Box 40; *Connecticut Parenthood* No. 1, July 1944; her 21 May 1976 obituaries in the *Hartford Courant* (p. 4) and the *Hartford Times* (p. 5); and especially Charles F. J. Morse's wonderful profile in the *Courant*, 17 February 1963, p. B3.

44. Jeffries, *Testing the Roosevelt Coalition*, p. 195; Wilbert Snow, *Codline's Child: The Autobiography of Wilbert Snow* (Middletown, CT: Wesleyan University Press, 1974), pp. 427–431; Cunningham to Elizabeth Borden, 14 November 1944, PPLM Box 106; Cunningham to McAuliffe, 13 November 1944, McAuliffe to Cunningham, 14 November 1944. McAuliffe died the following month, and early in 1945 was succeeded by Henry J. O'Brien. Also see Cornelius P. Trowbridge, "Catholicism Fights Birth Control," *The New Republic*, 22 January 1945, pp. 106–109.

45. [Cunningham], "Conference in the office of Mr. Morris Ernst," 15 November 1944, PPLC 3-N; Virginia Wake, Board Minutes, 21 November 1944, PPLC 10-R; Ernst to Evarts, 30 November 1944, Ernst Box 894; *Connecticut Parenthood* No. 2, December 1944; Janney to Ernst, 2 December 1944, Ernst to Janney, 8 December 1944, PPLC 3-N and 10-R; McKinnon, "Legal Situation . . ." 9 December 1944, PPLC 3-N and PPLM Box 84; Pilpel, "Connecticut Birth Control, " 13 December 1944, Ernst Box 267; Amelia W. Fisk, "Report of Interview with Mr. Rand," 21 December 1944, "Report on Interview with Drs. DeNormandie and Titus," 28 December 1944, "Report of Telephone Interview with Mr. Rand," 29 December 1944, PPLM Box 84; Cunningham to Ernst, 27 December 1944, Ernst to Cunningham, 3 January 1945, PPLC 3-N; Fisk to Ernst, 28 December 1944, Rand to Fisk, 2 January 1945, PPLM Box 84; McKinnon to Fisk, 4 January 1945, Borden to Ernst, 2 February 1945, PPLM Box 84; Ernst to Evarts, 25 January 1945, Ernst Box 267.

On Ernst, see the superb *Life* profile, by Yale law professor Fred Rodell: "Morris Ernst: New York's Unlawyerlike Liberal Lawyer Is the Censor's Enemy, the President's Friend," *Life*, 21 February 1944, pp. 97–98, 100–107; also see Marquis James, "Morris L. Ernst," *Scribner's Magazine* 104 (July 1938): 7–11, 57–58; "Greenbaum, Wolff & Ernst—A Brief History of the Firm," 1955, and a 1960 Supplement, Ernst Papers Box 846; and Harrison E. Salisbury, "The Strange Correspondence of Morris Ernst and John Edgar Hoover, 1939–1964," *The Nation* 239 (1 December 1984): 575–589. Ernst's is a biography waiting to be written.

46. Virginia Wake, Board Minutes, 15 January and 21 February 1945, PPLC 10-R; Harriet Janney, "PPLC Narrative Report," 23 January 1945, PPLC 11-A; *Hartford Times*, 25 January 1945, p. 4, 1 March 1945, p. 18; *Hartford Courant*, 26 January 1945, p. 5; *Journal of the House*, pp. 263–264 (30 January); *Journal of the Senate*, p. 257 (January 31); Ernst to Cunningham, 28 February 1945, PPLC 3-N and Ernst Box 267; Ernst to Scribner, 7 March 1945, Sanger-LC Box 180; Julie Howson, Board Minutes, 20 March 1945, PPLC 10-R; Ernst to Becket, 10 April 1945, Becket to Ernst, 24 April 1945, Pilpel, "Connecticut Birth Control," 30 April 1945, Becket to Pilpel, 2 May 1945, Ernst Box 267. On the Roper poll, also see *New York Herald Tribune*, 26 June 1947; *Hartford Courant*, 1 July 1947, p. 10; and *Human Fertility*, June 1947, p. 51.

47. Transcript of Hearing, Public Health and Safety Committee, 1 May 1945, 29pp., PPLC 3-O and Connecticut State Library; Harriet Janney, "The Life and Death of House Bill 317," *Connecticut Parenthood* No. 3, July 1945; Mary V. Z. Cunningham, "The Connecticut Hearing," *Human Fertility* 10 (September 1945): 92–94; *Hartford Courant*, 2 May 1945; *Hartford Times*, 2 May 1945, 22 May 1945; Executive Committee Minutes, 15 May 1945, PPLC 10-R; Cunningham, "Annual Report of Director," 29 May 1945, PPLC 11-A. On the 1945 session in general, see Van Dusen, *Connecticut*, pp. 378–379; also see Virginia L. Blood Interview with Joyce Pendery. Fifteen years later, following his election as a United States Senator, Thomas J. Dodd took a decidedly different stance than he had in 1945 (and 1947), telling PPFA's Cass Canfield that "I believe that government should not legislate concerning so private and personal a matter as birth control practices. This is a matter of private conscience and religious conviction which should be approached through persuasion, rather than compulsion." Dodd to Canfield, 12 October 1960, PPFA II-107. On Dodd's subsequent scandal-ridden departure from the U.S. Senate, see James Boyd, *Above the Law* (New York: New American Library, 1968).

48. Leslie Staples, Annual Meeting Minutes, 29 May 1945, PPLC 11-A; Pilpel, "Connecticut Birth Control," 15 June 1945, Becket to Ernst, 16 June 1945, Cunningham to Ernst, 6 July 1945, Ernst to Cunningham, 9 July 1945, Ernst Box 267; Irwin E. Friedman to Ernst, 21 July 1945, [Cunningham], "Record of Conversations with Ernst Office," August to November, 1945, PPLC 3-N; Pilpel, Note to File, 14 August 1945, Pilpel to Becket, 17 August 1945, Cunningham to Pilpel, 4 September 1945, Pilpel to Ernst, 5 and 7 September 1945, Pilpel, "Connecticut Birth Control," 14 September 1945, Ernst Box 267; Mabel Robbins to Warren Upson, 18 September 1945, PPLC 3-M; Ernst to Pilpel, 22 September 1945, Ernst Box 267; Pilpel, "Connecticut Birth Control," 9 October 1945, Becket to Ernst, 10 October 1945, Pilpel, "Connecticut Birth Control," 11 October 1945, Ernst to Becket, 17 October 1945, Pilpel, "Planned Parenthood" (II), 19 October 1945, Pilpel, "Connecticut Birth Control," 22 October 1945, Ernst Box 267; Janet Williams, Board Minutes, 27 November 1945, PPLC 11-

B; [Cunningham], "Report—Conference, Morris Ernst," 30 November 1945, PPLC 3-N; *Connecticut Parenthood* No. 4, December 1945.

49. Cunningham, "Director's Report," 27 November 1945 and 27 March 1946, Virginia Wake, Board Minutes, 27 March 1946, PPLC 11-B and C; Cunningham, "State Director's Report," 28 May 1946, Janney, "President's Report," 28 May 1946, Virginia Wake, Annual Meeting Minutes, 28 May 1946, PPLC 11-D. Julie Howson, a 1907 graduate of Bryn Mawr, was sixty years old when she assumed the presidency. The two-month delay appears to have occurred because Howson was the (unsuccessful) Democratic nominee for a state house seat in Newtown in 1946, and she formally assumed the role in mid-November, soon after the election; Mrs. Barry Morgan served as acting president in the interim.

50. Mary P. Milmine, Medical Advisory Committee Minutes, 10 October 1946, PPLC 15-A; Leslie Staples, Board Minutes, 15 October and 19 November 1946, PPLC 11-D; Jeffries, *Testing the Roosevelt Coalition*, pp. 231, 239; Snow, *Codline's Child*, pp. 442–446; Cunningham to Pilpel, 13 November 1946, PPLC 4-F; Cunningham, "Director's Report," 19 November 1946, PPLC 11-E; Milmine to Jane L. Brown, 22 November 1946, PPLC 4-B; Cunningham to Amelia Fisk, 2 January 1947, PPLM Box 106; Janney, "Annual Report for 1946," 7 January 1947, PPLC 11-E; *Hartford Courant*, 21 January 1947. Regarding the long-pending Josephine Evarts possibility, Ernst told Molly Cunningham that "I am sorry that our client in Connecticut could not be pressed faster to start a suit," and noted that Cam Becket had "found, as we did, a certain amount of reluctance on the part of the client to proceed." Ernst to Cunningham, 18 November 1946, PPLC 4-F; also see Cunningham to Ernst, 20 November 1946, PPLC 4-B, and Becket to Julie Howson, 21 August 1947, PPLC 4-J, who instead explained the delay largely in terms of how overworked J. Howard Roberts had been, plus an eventual Roberts decision that the matter could not be handled by stipulation rather than a public trial. At that stage Roberts was nominated to a Superior Court judgeship.

51. *Journal of the House*, p. 297 (7 February); *Journal of the Senate*, p. 313 (11 February); 1947 Connecticut General Assembly Records (RG 2), Box 250; *Hartford Courant*, 6 February 1947, p. 2, 7 February 1947, p. 6; "Report from Mr. John Alsop," n.d. [7 February 1947], [Cunningham], "Report of Conference with Harry B. Strong," 18 February 1947, PPLC 4-A. On John Alsop, who subsequently remained an insurance executive and never became as well-known as his older brothers Joseph and Stewart, see the *Courant*, 8 September 1980, pp. 1, 32, and 20 May 1984, pp. A1, A14.

52. Lawrence E. Skelly to Joseph L. Hetzel, 6 March 1947, Sister Louise to Allen F. Delevett, 8 March 1947, ACLU 1947 CL-2; Sister Louise to Elwood K. Jones, 8 March 1947, PPLC 4-A; Leslie Staples, Board Minutes, 7 March 1947, PPLC 11-F; *Hartford Courant*, 9 March 1947, 11 March 1947, 12 March 1947; Transcript of Hearing on H.B. #953, Public Health and Safety Committee, 11 March 1947, 66pp., PPLC 4-F and Connecticut State Library; *Waterbury Republican*, 12 March 1947, p. 1; *Hartford Times*, 12 March 1947; *New York Herald Tribune*, 13 March 1947; *Connecticut Parenthood* No. 6, April 1947; *Human Fertility*, March 1947, pp. 28–29.

53. *Hartford Courant*, 19 March 1947, p. 12, 20 March 1947, p. 2, 21 March 1947, pp. 12, 16, 22 March 1947, 30 March 1947, 8 April 1947, pp. 1, 2; Hetzel to Lionel Raymond, 16 March 1947, Meeting Minutes, 17 March 1947, Delevett et al. to O'Brien, 25 March 1947, PPLC 4-A; John J. Hayes to Hetzel, 28 March 1947, Hetzel to Hayes, 29 March 1947, ACLU 1947 CL-2; PPLC, "Where We Stand Right Now," 1 April and 9 April 1947, PPLC 4-C; Skelly to Hetzel, to Delevett, and to Oliver L. Stringfield, 2 April 1947, Delevett et al., "To the Members of the General Assembly," and Stringfield to Skelly, 7 April 1947, ACLU 1947 CL-2; *Waterbury Republican*, 8 April 1947, pp. 1, 2; *New York Times*, 8 April 1947, p. 24; *Hartford Times*, 8 April 1947, p. 12. In early April a sixth doctor, Oliver L. Stringfield of Stamford, was added to the initial list of five.

54. *New York Herald Tribune*, 13 April 1947, p. 56, 17 April 1947, 8 May 1947; *Hartford Times*, 17 April 1947, 25 April 1947, p. 2, 6 May 1947, 8 May 1947, 12 May 1947, 14 May 1947, p. 1; *Time*, 21 April 1947, p. 58; David P. Gaines memos, 17 April 1947, PPLC 4-A and ACLU 1947 CL-2; Clifford L. Forster to Oliver L. Stringfield, 14 April 1947, Stringfield to Forster,

16 April 1947, Hetzel to Forster, 16 and 23 April 1947, Delevett to Forster, 18 April 1947, Forster to Skelly, 21 April 1947, ACLU 1947 CL-2; *Hartford Courant*, 23 April 1947, 25 April 1947, pp. 1, 12, 29 April 1947, 30 April 1947, 2 May 1947, p. 3, 8 May 1947, pp. 1, 2, 13 May 1947, 14 May 1947, p. 1, 15 May 1947, pp. 1, 14; *Waterbury Republican*, 26 April 1947, pp. 1, 3, 9 May 1947, p. 3; Gaines to B. Kenneth Anthony, 28 April 1947, PPLC 4-A; PPLC "Report on Where Things Stand," 25 April 1947, PPLC 4-C; Mabel Robbins, Clergymen's Advisory Committee Minutes, 25 April 1947, PPLC 23-A; *Journal of the House*, pp. 699, 733, 808 (1, 7, 16 May); *New York Times*, 5 May 1947, p. 25, 15 May 1947; *Journal of the Senate*, pp. 719, 752–753 (9 and 14 May 1947); *The New Republic*, 19 May 1947, p. 8; PPLC, "Doctors vs. Politicians: A Connecticut Episode," June 1947, PPLC 3-N; Cunningham to Louis Harris, 5 June 1947, PPLC 24-E; Herbert S. MacDonald, "Some Aspects and Implications of the So-Called 'Connecticut Birth Control Law'" (unpublished paper, October 1953), pp. 14–16, PPLC 5-J.

55. *Hartford Courant*, 15 May 1947, p. 12; *Hartford Times*, 15 May 1947; Field Committee Minutes, 19 May 1947, PPLC 23-D; Hetzel to Forster, 20 May 1947, and Forster to Hetzel, 27 May 1947, ACLU 1947 CL-2; Hetzel to Paul Ashton, 24 May 1947, PPLC 4-A; Pilpel to Cunningham, 28 May 1947, Cunningham to Pilpel, 29 May 1947, PPLC 4-J; Cunningham, "State Director's Report," 28 May 1947, Julie Howson, "President's Report," 28 May 1947, and Barbara Davenport, Annual Meeting Minutes, 28 May 1947, PPLC 11-F; *Waterbury Republican*, 13 May 1947, p. 8; Garrow conversation with Dr. Charles L. Larkin, Jr.; *New York Times*, 18 June 1947, p. 23; [Massachusetts] *Planned Parenthood News*, September 1947; David Loth, "Planned Parenthood and the Modern Inquisition," *The Humanist*, Autumn 1947, pp. 64–68.

56. Pilpel to Cunningham, 2 June 1947, Rose to Janney and Cunningham, 4 June 1947, PPLC 4-J; Forster to Walter Gellhorn, and to Joseph L. Hetzel et al., 5 June 1947, John H. Foster to Forster, 6 June 1947, ACLU 1947 CL-2; Upson to Pilpel, 10 June 1947, "Minutes of Meeting of Six Connecticut Doctors," 11 June 1947, PPLC 4-J; Hetzel to Forster, 12 June 1947, Delevett to Forster, 12 June 1947, Frederick E. Robin to Hetzel, 16 June 1947, Frances Levenson to Hetzel, 19 June and 7 August 1947, ACLU 1947 CL-2; Elizabeth Winslow, Executive Committee Minutes, 17 June 1947, PPLC 11-G; Pilpel to Hetzel, 3 July 1947, PPLC 4-I; Howson to Ernst, 22 July 1947, Pilpel to Upson, 12 August 1947, Cunningham to Upson, 14 August 1947, PPLC 4-J; Upson to Pilpel, 14 August 1947, PPLC 4-K; Hetzel to Levenson, 20 August 1947, Levenson to Pilpel, 22 August 1947, Pilpel to Levenson, 4 September 1947, ACLU 1947 CL-2; Robbins, Executive Committee Minutes, 9 September 1947, PPLC 11-G; Upson to Robbins, 11 September 1947, PPLC 4-J; Howson to Becket, 12 September 1947, Howson to Catherine J. Tilson, 12 September 1947, Tilson to Howson, 15 September 1947, PPLC 4-K; Levenson to Hetzel, 16 September 1947, ACLU 1947 CL-2; Elizabeth Winslow, Planning Committee Minutes, 17 September 1947, Ernst to Howson, 2 October 1947, PPLC 23-K; Winslow, Field Committee Minutes, 2 October 1947, Cunningham, Planning Committee Subcommittee Minutes, 8 October 1947, PPLC 23-E; Forster to Upson, 9 and 15 October 1947, PPLC 4-I; Cunningham, "Director's Report," and "Planning Committee Report," 14 October 1947, PPLC 11-G and 23-K; Winslow, Board Minutes, 14 October 1947, PPLC 11-G; Cunningham, "Director's Report," and Charlotte Moser, Board Minutes, 9 December 1947, PPLC 11-G; Howson, "Annual Report," 26 January 1948, PPLC 11-H; Robbins, Field Committee Minutes, 3 February 1948, PPLC 23-E; *Hartford Courant*, 10 March 1948, p. 1; *Hartford Times*, 10 March 1948; *Connecticut Parenthood*, April 1948; Cunningham, "Director's Report," 6 April 1948, Howson, "President's Report," Cunningham, "Director's Report," and Winslow, Annual Meeting Minutes, 29 April 1948, PPLC 11-H; *Waterbury Republican*, 30 April 1948, p. 3.

57. Eleanor Leiss, Field Committee Report, May 1948, PPLC 23-F; Robbins, Field Committee Minutes, 8 June 1948, PPLC 23-E; Leiss, Planning Committee Minutes, 8 July 1948, PPLC 23-K; *Connecticut Parenthood*, August 1948; John Q. Tilson, Jr. to Cunningham, 31 August 1948, PPLC 4-J; Cunningham, "Director's Report," and Sydney Brucker, Board Minutes, 29 September 1948, PPLC 11-I; *New York Times*, 1 November 1948, p. 15, 2 November 1948, p.

3; *Danbury News-Times*, 1 November 1948; *Manchester Evening Herald*, 1 November 1948; *Hartford Times*, 1 November 1948.

58. Chester Bowles, *Promises to Keep* (New York: Harper & Row, 1971), p. 187. On the 1948 Massachusetts referendum, see John R. Rodman, "Birth Control Politics in Massachusetts" (unpublished M.A. thesis, Harvard University, 1955), pp. 87–108; O'Toole, "Prelates and Politicos," pp. 49–57, and William J. Kenealy, "Contraception—A Violation of God's Law," *Catholic Mind* 46 (September 1948): 552–564, at 558, 560–561, 563. Also see *New York Times*, 13 November 1948, p. 16; *Newsweek*, 15 November 1948, pp. 26–27; [Massachusetts] *Planned Parenthood News*, December 1948 and April 1949; *Churchman*, 1 December 1948, p. 10; *The Nation* 168 (5 March 1949): 262; and Lee N. Robins, "Birth Control in Massachusetts: The Analysis of an Issue Through an Intensive Survey of Opinion" (unpublished Ph.D. dissertation, Harvard University, 1950).

59. Elizabeth Winslow, Planning Committee Minutes, 8 November 1948, PPLC 23-K; Cunningham, "Director's Report," 16 November 1948, PPLC 11-H; William Hamilton to Katharine McKinney, 11 December 1948, Pilpel to Cunningham, 21 December 1948, PPLC 4-L; Cunningham to Pilpel, 5 January 194[9] (and attachment), PPLC 4-J and 4-M; Cunningham, "Director's Report," and Winslow, Board Minutes, 11 January 1949, PPLC 11-I; Pilpel to Cunningham, 28 January 1949, PPLC 4-L; Dorothy Bowles to Nancy Williams, 25 January 1949, PPLC 17-K. Also generally see both Dorothy Bowles and Chester Bowles's 1963 oral history interviews with Neil Gold for the Columbia Oral History Program.

60. *Journal of the House*, p. 307 (4 February); *Journal of the Senate*, p. 368 (8 February); *Hartford Courant*, 5 February 1949, pp. 1, 7, 30 March 1949, 6 April 1949, p. 2, 13 April 1949; Betty Simonds to Sanger, 3 January 1949, McKinney to Mary Compton, 12 January 1949, Cunningham to Sanger, 2 February 1949, Sanger-LC Box 180; Nancy Williams, Clergymen's Advisory Committee Minutes, 7 February 1949, PPLC 23-A; Robbins, Field Committee Minutes, 8 February 1949, PPLC 23-E; Cunningham, "Director's Report," 8 March 1949, PPLC 11-I; Winslow, Executive Committee Minutes, 6 April 1949, PPLC 11-J; *Bridgeport Herald*, 10 April 1949, pp. 13–14; Transcript of Hearing, Public Health and Safety Committee, 12 April 1949, 44pp., Connecticut State Library; *Hartford Times*, 12 and 13 April 1949; *New York Herald Tribune*, 13 April 1949; Samuel C. Harvey to Cunningham, 19 April 1949, PPLC 4-L. On Senator Carl P. Remy's unsuccessful bill "prohibiting future introduction of birth control measures," see *Journal of the Senate*, pp. 272 and 526 (4 February and 31 March), and *Journal of the House*, p. 377 (8 February).

61. *Hartford Courant*, 6 May 1949, pp. 1, 2; Cunningham, "Annual Report," 19 May 1949, PPLC 11-J; Elizabeth Winslow, Annual Meeting Minutes, 19 May 1949, PPLC 11-H; *Connecticut Parenthood*, June 1949 and February 1950; Charlotte Quaile, Executive Committee Minutes, 23 June 1949, Ruth Cain, Executive Committee Minutes, 30 August 1949, Quaile, Board Minutes, 4 October 1949, PPLC 11-J; Fairman C. Cowan to Loraine L. Campbell, 3 November 1949, PPLC 4-M and PPLM Box 106; Pilpel to Cunningham, 29 November 1949, PPLC 4-J; Cunningham, "Director's Report," and Laura Bushby, Board Minutes, 6 December 1949, PPLC 11-H and J; Winslow, Board Minutes, 14 February 1950, PPLC 11-K; Williams, Clergymen's Advisory Committee Minutes, 20 March 1950, PPLC 23-A; Quaile, Executive Committee Minutes, 24 April 1950, PPLC 11-K.

On the 1949 legislative session in general, see particularly Joseph F. Skelley, Jr., "Executive-Legislative Relationship in Connecticut: A Case Study of Legislative Policy-Making" (unpublished B.A. thesis, Wesleyan University, 1950), and Joseph I. Lieberman, *The Power Broker: A Biography of John M. Bailey, Modern Political Boss* (Boston: Houghton Mifflin Co., 1966), pp. 130–132; also see Bowles, *Promises to Keep*, pp. 204–205, and Van Dusen, *Connecticut*, pp. 384-385.

62. Cunningham, "Annual Report," 18 May 1950, PPLC 11-K; *Connecticut Parenthood*, Summer 1950 and Fall 1950; Virginia Dockham, Board Minutes, 19 September 1950, PPLC 11-K. The two Yale Law School students were Joseph F. Brodley and Edwin D. Etherington. Their eighty-page paper, "Contraception: Human Right or Criminal Deviation?" (25 May 1950,

PPLC 4-M and N), reluctantly suggested that another declaratory judgment action was the league's best hope, with there being at least some chance that a favorable three to two majority (composed of *Nelson* and *Tileston* dissenter Newell Jennings and new justices Raymond E. Baldwin and Ernst Inglis, and discounting Allyn Brown and new (Catholic) justice P. B. O'Sullivan) could be achieved. See esp. pp. 67, 70–72, and 80. On October 24, 1950, PPLC sponsored a conference on "Parenthood in a Democracy" at Connecticut College in New London, with Dr. John Rock and Rev. C. Lawson Willard among the speakers; the ten "sponsors" of the conference included retired Justice Christopher Avery, the other *Nelson* and *Tileston* dissenter, and—much more intriguingly—retired Chief Justice William M. Maltbie. One hence might easily infer that Maltbie's votes in *Nelson* and *Tileston* were in no way influenced by any hostility toward or discomfort with birth control.

On the 1950 Connecticut election, see Bowles, *Promises to Keep*, pp. 234, 241; Lieberman, *The Power Broker*, p. 145; Duane Lockard, *New England State Politics* (Princeton: Princeton University Press, 1959), p. 262; Sidney Hyman, *The Lives of William Benton* (Chicago: University of Chicago Press, 1969), pp. 406–413, 441–443; Alden Hatch, *The Lodges of Massachusetts* (New York: Hawthorn Books, 1973), pp. 239–240; John Davis Lodge's 1967 oral history interview (esp. pp. 33–37) with John T. Mason, Jr., for the Columbia Oral History Program; and George Bush's "Foreword" to Phyllis T. Piotrow, *World Population Crisis: The United States Response* (New York: Praeger, 1973), vii. George Bush refers to a Drew Pearson report that alleged his father backed birth control; John Alsop several weeks after the election wrote Molly Milmine that the word in Republican circles was that Bush "was beaten on account of his activities with" Planned Parenthood and that "it will probably have a frightening effect on other Republican politicians." 24 November 1950, PPLC 4-M. No evidence of *any* contact between Prescott Bush and PPLC appears in either the voluminous and seemingly comprehensive PPLC records, or in the Prescott Bush Papers at Yale; also note the similar retrospective denials by both Prescott Bush (and Dorothy Bush) in Prescott Bush's 1966 oral history interview (pp. 62–63) with John T. Mason, Jr., for the Columbia Oral History Program.

63. Ella Embree, Clergymen's Advisory Committee Minutes, 11 December 1950, PPLC 23-A; Milmine to William Vogt, 9 January 1951, PPLC 4-M; Milmine, "Report for the Legislative Committee," 9 January 1951, PPLC 4-O; Virginia Dockham, Board Minutes, 9 January 1951, Williams, Executive Committee Minutes, 19 January 1951, PPLC 11-L; J. Stephen Knight to Milmine, 15 May 1951, PPLC 5-H. Molly Milmine's obituary appears in the 6 March 1984 *Waterbury Republican*.

On Bailey and Cooney in particular, see Lieberman, *The Power Broker*, pp. 46, 52, 56, 131–132, 156; *Hartford Courant*, 26 January 1933, p. 2, 19 April 1965; Cross, *Connecticut Yankee*, pp. 278–280, 314; *Catholic Transcript*, 24 January 1957. Bailey died in 1975; Cooney's obituaries appear in the *Courant*, 16 August 1984, p. D8, and the *New York Times*, 18 August 1984, p. 10. Exceptionally good work on Connecticut state—and especially legislative—politics in the early 1950s was carried out by W. Duane Lockard. See "The Role of Party in the Connecticut General Assembly, 1931–1951" (unpublished Ph.D. dissertation, Yale University, 1952), esp. pp. 76, 111–116, 129–132, 145–146, 181, 215, 239; "Legislative Politics in Connecticut," *American Political Science Review* 48 (March 1954): 166–173, esp. 169–171; and *New England State Politics* (Princeton: Princeton University Press, 1959), pp. 228–304.

64. Williams, "Connecticut Story," n.d. [c.May 1951], PPLC 6-J and 11-L; Milmine to Board Members, "Political Situation," 26 January 1951, PPLC 4-M and 11-L; *Journal of the House*, pp. 273 and 304 (30 and 31 January); *Journal of the Senate*, pp. 192, 266 (30 and 31 January); Mabel Robbins to Lillian Mermin, 16 February 1951, PPLC 38-L; Mermin, "'Uncontrolled' Birth in Connecticut," *The Humanist* 11 (October 1951): 221–226; Virginia Dockham, Board Minutes, 13 March 1951, PPLC 11-L; [Joseph P. Cooney], "Report of Activities and Efforts to Oppose the Planned Parenthood Bill in 1951," n.d., 3pp., Hartford Archdiocese Archives; Transcript of Hearing, Public Health and Safety Committee, 11 April 1951, 26pp., PPLC 4-O and Connecticut State Library; *Hartford Courant*, 12 April 1951, p. 5; *New York Times*, 12

April 1951; *Hartford Times*, 12 April 1951, p. 30; Willard to Public Health and Safety Committee, 21 April 1951, PPLC 4-P. John J. Hayes, chancellor of the Hartford Diocese from 1945 to 1953, was born in 1906, ordained in 1931, and died in 1964.

65. Rev. E. Paul Sylvester to Milmine, 21 April 1951, Milmine to Sylvester, 3 May 1951, PPLC 4-R; Williams, "Director's Annual Report," 16 May 1951, and Williams, "Connecticut Story," n.d. [c.May 1951], Milmine, Annual Report, 16 May 1951, and Virginia Dockham, Annual Meeting Minutes, 16 May 1951, PPLC 11-L. Also see Milmine to Thomas Sugrue, 21 January 1952, PPLC 24-F.

66. *Journal of the House*, pp. 680 and 717–722 (23 and 28 May); *Journal of the Senate*, p. 712 (29 May); Transcript of Proceedings, Connecticut General Assembly, House of Representatives, 28 May 1951, pp. 1453–1467, Connecticut State Library; *Hartford Courant*, 29 May 1951, p. 3; *New York Herald Tribune*, 29 May 1951; PPLC, "Closer and Closer to Victory," n.d., PPLC 11-L; Milmine in *Connecticut Parenthood*, July 1951; Herbert S. MacDonald, "Some Aspects and Implications of the So-Called 'Connecticut Birth Control Law'" (unpublished paper, October 1953), p. 17, PPLC 5-J. Also see Lockard, "The Role of Party," pp. 179, 258-261, who commented that "Bailey virtually runs the Democratic Senate" and that "Bailey is virtually omnipresent in the legislative halls during sessions of the legislature."

67. May-Louise Iszard, Executive Committee Minutes, 20 June 1951, Board Minutes, 18 September 1951, PPLC 11-M; [Milmine], "Opinions of Mr. John Parsons and Mr. Buist Anderson on the Etherington Test Case," 18 September 1951, Wiggin to Williams, 1 October 1951, PPLC 5-H; Charlotte Quaile, Board Minutes, 15 October 1951, PPLC 11-M; Milmine to Riege, 18 October 1951, Milmine to Wiggin, 19 October 1951, Riege to Milmine, 24 October 1951, PPLC 5-H.

68. Riege to Milmine, 5 November 1951, PPLC 5-H; May-Louise Iszard, Board Minutes, 13 November and 14 December 1951, PPLC 11-M; Pilpel to Loraine Campbell, 30 November 1951, PPLM Box 14; [Riege], "Memorandum Re: Recommendations Concerning Possible Legal Actions," n.d. [13 December 1951], 8pp., PPLC 1-B and 5-J; Iszard, Board Minutes, 18 January 1952, PPLC 11-N; Milmine to Riege, 21 January 1952, PPLC 5-K; Milmine to Board Members, 31 January 1952, PPLC 11-N.

69. Mabel Robbins, Executive Committee Minutes, 5 February 1952, PPLC 11-N; Loraine Campbell to Milmine, 29 January 1952, Riege to Campbell, 7 February 1952, PPLM Box 106; Grace Adkins, Executive Committee Minutes, 3 March 1952, PPLC 11-N; Milmine to Seymour, 3 and 11 March 1952, Seymour to Milmine, 5 March 1952, and Milmine to Riege, 11 March 1952, PPLC 5-H; Claudia McGinley, Board Minutes, 18 March 1952, PPLC 11-N; Riege to Milmine, 20 March 1952, Riege to Seymour, 1 May 1952, Seymour to Riege, 5 May 1952, Riege to Milmine, 12 May and 3 June 1952, PPLC 5-H.

70. Laura Bushby, Executive Committee Minutes, 2 May 1952, Nancy Williams, "Director's Annual Report," 15 May 1952, and May-Louise Iszard, Annual Meeting Minutes, 15 May 1952, PPLC 11-N; Ruth Cain, Board Minutes, 14 August 1952, PPLC 11-O; Riege to Seymour, 11 August 1952, Seymour to Riege, 22 August 1952, PPLC 5-H; Riege to Seymour, 9 September 1952, PPLC 5-I; Iszard, Executive Committee Minutes, 9 September 1952, PPLC 11-O; Loraine Campbell to Workum, 11 and 19 September 1952, PPLM Box 106; Riege to Milmine, 22 September 1952, PPLC 5-I.

71. [Riege], "Memorandum Re: Conference with Mr. Whitney North Seymour," 14 October 1952, PPLC 5-I; Ida Abrahams, Board Minutes, 28 October 1952, PPLC 11-O; *Connecticut Parenthood*, Fall 1952; Imogene Monk, Board Minutes, 18 November 1952, PPLC 11-O; Milmine to Buist Anderson, 18 November 1952, PPLC 5-I; Catherine J. Tilson to Jane Daniells, 26 November 1952, PPLC 4-P; Charlotte Quaile, Board Minutes, 9 December 1952, PPLC 11-O; Milmine to John C. Parsons, 15 December 1952, PPLC 4-P; Milmine, "Notes for Legal File," 13 January 1953, PPLC 5-I; Imogene Monk, Board Minutes, 13 January 1953, PPLC 11-P; Seymour to Riege, 15 January 1953, Milmine to Riege, 2 February 1953, PPLC 5-I. On Bruce Manternach, see the *Hartford Courant*, 3 January 1949.

72. *Journal of the House*, p. 269 (3 February); *Journal of the Senate*, p. 279 (4 February); 1953 Connecticut General Assembly Records (RG 2), Box 312; Imogene Monk, Board Minutes,

10 February 1953, PPLC 11-P; Williams to Milmine, 16 February 1953, PPLC 4-R; Milmine to Dr. Charles Seymour, and to Warren Upson, 16 February 1953, PPLC 4-P; Williams to Margaret Bourke-White, 19 February 1953, PPLC 52-I; Jane M. Daniells to Regina Tomlin, 19 February 1953, Lodge Box 548; Milmine to John H. Pinkerman, 20 February 1953, Pinkerman to Milmine, 1 March 1953, PPLC 32-H and 4-R; Florence B. Darrach to Lodge, 4 March 1953, Lodge Box 548; Pinkerman to Williams, 8 March 1953, PPLC 4-R; Imogene Monk, Board Minutes, 10 March 1953, PPLC 11-P.

73. [Penciled Notes], "Maternal Health Bill," Leonard D. Adkins to Lodge, 16 and 25 March 1953, Meade Alcorn to Lodge, 21 March 1953 (and 2pp. 19 March Riege enclosure), Lodge to Adkins, 7 April 1953 (and multiple 27 March drafts of same), Lodge Box 548. Also see *Hartford Courant*, 23 March 1953; *Connecticut Parenthood*, Spring [23 March] 1953; *Bridgeport Herald*, 29 March 1953; Julie B. Howson to Lodge, 6 April 1953, Katherine A. Evarts to Lodge, 13 April 1953, Lodge Box 548; and Lockard, *New England State Politics*, p. 261.

74. Transcript of Hearing, Public Health and Safety Committee, 1 April 1953, 14pp., Connecticut State Library; Arnold Felton, "Report on Hearing . . ." 3 April 1953, PPLM Box 105; *Hartford Courant*, 2 April 1953, 6 April 1953, p. 3; *New Haven Register*, 2 April 1953; *Middletown Press*, 2 April 1953; *Hartford Times*, 2 April 1953, 6 April 1953; [Joseph P. Cooney], untitled, annotated typescript, n.d. [5 April 1953], Birth Control File, Archives of the Hartford Archdiocese.

75. John C. Parsons to Benton H. Grant, 6 April 1953, PPLC 4-R; *Hartford Times*, 7 and 14 April 1953; *Hartford Courant*, 8 and 15 April 1953; Milmine notes, 10 and 11 April 1953, PPLC 4-R; Adkins to Lodge, 13 April 1953, Lodge Box 548; Milmine, "Report on Political Situation," 14 April 1953, Grant to Milmine, and Milmine to Grant, 14 April 1953, Milmine notes, 14 April 1953, PPLC 4-R; Imogene Monk, Board Minutes, 14 April 1953, PPLC 11-P; *New York Times*, 15 April 1953, p. 45; *New York Herald Tribune*, 15 April 1953.

76. *Hartford Times*, 15 and 16 April 1953; *Middletown Press*, 15 April 1953; *Hartford Courant*, 16 April 1953, 17 April 1953, p. 11, 18 April 1953, p. 1; *Waterbury Republican*, 16 April 1953, p. 2; *New York Times*, 16 April 1953, p. 33, 19 April 1953, p. 46; Milmine to Grant, 17 April 1953, PPLC 4-R; Milmine to Lodge, 17 April 1953, PPLC 5-E; Hayes to Lodge, 18 April 1953, and Lodge to Hayes, 6 May 1953, Lodge Box 548. Lodge apparently was already unfavorably disposed toward PPLC as a result of his earlier meeting with Williams and Daniells; a subsequent note reflecting back upon the meeting and its aftermath read: "Apparently their desire is to attack me rather than to obtain action on legislation." "Maternal Health Bill" notes, Lodge Box 548.

77. *Bridgeport Herald*, 19 April 1953, pp. 19, 23; Grant to Milmine, 19 and 21 April 1953, PPLC 4-R; Lodge to Milmine, 21 and 24 April 1953, and Lodge to Adkins, 22 April 1953, Lodge Box 548; John Pinkerman to Milmine, 22 April 1953, PPLC 32-H; Milmine to Grant, 23 April 1953, PPLC 4-S; Grant to "Mrs. Rogers," 28 April 1953, PPLC 5-A and 38-M; Manternach to Fisher, 30 March 1953, PPLC 5-J; Upson to Milmine, 30 April 1953, PPLC 5-E.

78. Imogene Monk, Executive Committee Minutes, 1 May 1953, PPLC 11-P; Milmine to William Vogt, 1 May 1953, PPLC 4-R; Adkins to Lodge, 4 May 1953, Lodge Box 548; *Hartford Times*, 5 and 7 May 1953; *Hartford Courant*, 6 and 10 May 1953, 12 May 1953, p. 2; *New York Times*, 6 May 1953, p. 33; Lodge to Adkins, 12 May 1953, Lodge Box 548; Countryman to Milmine, 8 July 1953, and Milmine to Countryman, 9 July 1953, PPLC 5-F. Also see *State of New Jersey* v. *Tracy*, 102 A.2d 52 (App. Div., N.J. Superior Court, 21 December 1953).

79. *Waterbury Republican*, 13 and 19 May 1953, 21 May 1953, p. 2; Milmine to Regional and Local Chairmen, 14 May 1953, PPLC 11-Q; *Hartford Courant*, 16 May 1953, p. 2, 17 and 21 May 1953; *New York Times*, 16 May 1953; Adkins to Lodge, 17 May 1953, Lodge Box 548; *Journal of the House*, pp. 875–877, 907, 990, 1017 (18, 20, 22 May); *Journal of the Senate*, pp. 809, 883, 895 (20, 22, 24 May); 1953 Connecticut General Assembly Records (RG 2), Box 312, *Hartford Times*, 20 May 1953; Lodge to Adkins, 21 May 1953, Lodge Box 548. Also see *Bridgeport Herald*, 14 June 1953.

PPLC's May 12 annual meeting was relatively uneventful, although one chairperson of a lesser committee reported that "the name of our organization is an increasingly active and powerful force against us," and recommended—apparently without second—that it be changed to "the League for Maternal Health." Mrs. Ralph A. Stevenson, "Report—Public Speaking Committee," and Imogene Monk, Annual Meeting Minutes, 12 May 1953, PPLC 11-Q.

80. *Journal of the House*, pp. 1024–1029 (27 May); Transcript of Proceedings, Connecticut General Assembly, House of Representatives, 27 May 1953, pp. 3214–3240, Connecticut State Library, esp. pp. 3219–3220, 3222, 3229; *Hartford Courant*, 28 May 1953, p. 5, 29 May 1953, p. 3; *Waterbury Republican*, 28 May 1953, pp. 1, 18, 29 May 1953; *Journal of the Senate*, pp. 913 and 941–942 (27 and 28 May); Transcript of Proceedings, Senate, 28 May 1953, pp. 1977–1984; *New York Times*, 29 May 1953, p. 12; *New York Herald Tribune*, 29 May 1953; *Hartford Times*, 29 May 1953; Milmine to Board Members, to Grant, and to Ivor L. Kenway, 29 May 1953, Grant columns, n.d., PPLC 5-A. Also see John H. Pinkerman to Milmine, 24 July 1953, and Milmine to Pinkerman, 30 July 1953, PPLC 32-H.

81. Milmine to Samuel C. Harvey, 29 May 1953, PPLC 4-S; Milmine to Dr. N. William Wawro, 8 June 1953, PPLC 5-J; Imogene Monk, Board Minutes, 9 June 1953, PPLC 11-R; Nancy Williams to Helen I. Clarke, 15 June 1953, PPLC 5-A; Milmine to Rev. Arthur Paterson, 23 June 1953, Milmine to Manternach, 4 August 1953, Manternach to Milmine, 1 October 1953, Milmine to Manternach, 7 October 1953, Milmine to Evarts, and to Fisher, and to Dr. Edward H. Wray, Jr., 15 October 1953, PPLC 5-K; Milmine to Dr. Helen Ferguson, 26 October 1953, PPLC 5-I. Also see Loraine Campbell to Francis Goodale, 4 August 1953, PPLM Box 106.

82. Stanley A. Leavy to Williams, and to Fredrick C. Redlich, 2 July 1953, Milmine to Miriam Harper, 10 November 1953, and Harper to Milmine, 12 November 1953, PPLC 16-H; Imogene Monk, Board Minutes, 13 October and 10 November 1953, PPLC 11-R; Jane Daniells, Program Survey Committee Minutes, 24 October and 6 November 1953, PPLC 23-N; Milmine, "Notes on Talk with Mr. Adkins," 5 November 1953, PPLC 5-F; Roessle McKinney to Milmine, 3 December 1953, Milmine to McKinney, 5 December 1953, PPLC 19-A; Milmine, "President's Report," 18 May 1954, PPLC 11-S. On the early PPLC relationship with the infertility clinic, see *Connecticut Parenthood*, December 1947, and H. M. Feine, "Public Relations Activities," May 1948, PPLC 24-C. On Dr. Thoms, see his obituaries in the *New Haven Register*, 29 October 1972, pp. A1, A6, and the *New Haven Journal-Courier*, 30 October 1972, p. 7. C. Lee Buxton's appointment as Thoms's successor was announced in mid-November; see *Hartford Times*, 21 November 1953.

83. Griswold Interview with Cheek, p. 26; Milmine to Molly Cunningham, 4 December 1953, PPLC 22-K.

CHAPTER THREE

1. Estelle Griswold Interview with Cheek; Yale University "History of the Class of 1919," "Decennial Record of the Class of 1919" (1929), and "A Twenty-Five Year Record of the Class of 1919" (1946), containing biographical entries and updates on both Dick and then also Estelle Griswold, Yale University Archives; Estelle Griswold Resume, 20 November 1953, Schlesinger Library 223-2-13; *New Haven Register*, 10 April 1965, p. 32; New Haven City Directories, 1951–1954; Hilda Crosby Standish Interviews with Nichols and Hubbell; Garrow interviews with Hilda Crosby Standish and Gary R. Trebert. Richard Griswold's obituary appears in the *New Haven Register*, 2 October 1966, p. II-11; Estelle Griswold's obituary appears in the 18 August 1981 *New Haven Register*, and in the 18 August 1981 *New Haven Journal-Courier*, p. 14.

2. Milmine to Cunningham, 4 December 1953, PPLC 22-K; Griswold Interview with Cheek; Standish Interviews with Nichols and Garrow; Imogene Monk, Board Minutes, 8 December 1953, PPLC 11-R; Milmine to Griswold, 8 December 1953, Griswold to Milmine, 11 December 1953, and PPLC press release, 12 January 1954, PPLC 22-H; *New Haven Register*, 14 January 1954. Also see Garrow interviews with Ellen Switzer: "She said she couldn't have

children and she always wanted children," Fran McCoy: "I think there was definite regret," and Cornelia Jahncke: "It was very devastating for her and her husband not to be able to have children." "'I would have liked to have had children but never could,'" Jahncke quoted Estelle as once having said. In one interview, Estelle characterized her initial hesitance about accepting the PPLC post somewhat differently: "I felt I was vulnerable because we have had no children. . . . There were no infertility clinics when we were younger. But then I realized that the work was basic to all the ideas in which I am interested." Gereon Zimmerman, "Contraception and Commotion in Connecticut," *Look*, 30 January 1962, pp. 78–83, at 83.

3. Milmine to Manternach, 20 January 1954, Manternach to Milmine, 21 January 1954, Ann Dingman to Milmine, 2 February 1954, and Milmine to Manternach, 8 February 1954, PPLC 5-K and J.

4. *Connecticut Parenthood*, Winter 1954; Imogene Monk, Board Minutes, 9 February and 9 March 1954, PPLC 11-S. Also see *Greenwich Time*, 17 March 1954, p. 11. Two years earlier, on March 20, 1952, Harper had spoken, along with Herbert Thoms, at another Yale seminar on planned parenthood; in the fall of 1953 someone had suggested him as a possible member of a committee to study PPLC's future. *Connecticut Parenthood*, Spring 1952; Milmine to Molly Cunningham, 23 September 1953, PPLC 22-K. Griswold many years later described her initial sense of the organization much more bluntly than she had put it to the board: "there was little constructive activity" going on. Griswold Interview with Nichols, p. 28.

5. Manternach to Milmine, 10 March 1954, PPLC 5-J; Buxton to Milmine, 12 April and 10 May 1954, PPLC 16-B; Imogene Monk, Board Minutes, 13 April 1954, PPLC 11-S; *Connecticut Parenthood*, Spring 1954; Manternach to Milmine, 11 May 1954, PPLC 5-L; Jane Daniells, "Legislative Committee Annual Report," [18] May 1954, PPLC 22-K; Monk, Annual Meeting Minutes, and Milmine, "President's Report," 18 May 1954, PPLC 11-S. Also see Monk, Board Minutes, 8 June 1954, PPLC 11-S; Milmine to Buxton, 5 and 26 October 1954, PPLC 37-H. As Fran McCoy later commented on Estelle's hiring of her, "She felt that it ought to be integrated." Garrow Interview.

6. Milmine notes, 27 May 1954, PPLC 5-L; Milmine to Oliver L. Stringfield, and to Blaine Anderson, 1 June 1954, Milmine to Stringfield, and to John H. Riege, and to Herbert MacDonald, 17 August 1954, PPLC 37-G; Theodore J. Richard to Simon Frank, 15 September 1954, PPLC 5-F; Norman St. John-Stevas, *Birth Control and Public Policy* (Santa Barbara, CA: Center for the Study of Democratic Institutions, July 1960), p. 25; Milmine to Dr. Francis Sutherland, 8 December 1954, PPLC 5-F.

7. Griswold, "Director's Report, June 9–October 1, 1954," PPLC 11-S; Griswold to Maud Rogers, 24 June 1954, and to Mrs. William Darbee, 14 June 1954, PPLC 37-G. Also see Griswold to Milmine, 26 July 1954, PPLC 37-G; Miriam Garwood to William Vogt, 18 August 1954, PPFA II-185; New London Meeting Minutes, 21 September 1954, PPLC 50-A.

8. Imogene Monk, Board Minutes, 13 October 1954, and Gertrude Carpenter, Board Minutes, 14 December 1954, PPLC 11-S; *New Haven Register*, 21 November 1954; Milmine to Buxton, 6 December 1954, PPLC 37-G; Griswold to Harper, 9 November 1954, PPLC 37-H; *Connecticut Parenthood*, Fall 1954; Lockard, *New England State Politics*, pp. 235–238; Lieberman, *The Power Broker*, p. 188; Manternach to Milmine, 13 January 1955, Milmine to Manternach, 14 January 1955, and Manternach to Milmine, 17 January 1955, PPLC 5-K. Also see Francis Goodale to Loraine Campbell, 1 February 1955, PPLM Box 106.

9. *Journal of the House*, p. 270 (28 January); *Journal of the Senate*, pp. 326–27 (1 February); 1955 Connecticut General Assembly Records (RG 2), Box 334; "Legislative Report," 17 May 1955, PPLC 5-M; *Hartford Courant*, 28 January 1955, 4 February 1955, 21 April 1955, p. 14; *Waterbury Republican*, 28 January 1955, 21 April 1955; *Hartford Times*, 4 February 1955, 16 and 21 April 1955; *Bridgeport Herald*, 13 February 1955; Gertrude Carpenter, Board Minutes, 15 February and 12 April 1955, PPLC 11-T; *Connecticut Parenthood*, Winter 1955; Buxton to Milmine, 18 April 1955, PPLC 5-P; Transcript of Hearing, Public Health and Safety Committee, 20 April 1955, 96pp., PPLC 5-N and Connecticut State Library; Milmine to Albert Levitt, 25 April 1955, PPLC 37-I. Also see *New Haven Journal-Courier*, 24 April 1955, and *New Haven Register*, 25 April 1955.

10. *Hartford Courant*, 4 May 1955, 16 May 1955, 18 May 1955, p. 1, 24 May 1955, p. 3; *Waterbury*

Republican, 4 May 1955, 18 May 1955, p. 5; *New York Herald Tribune*, 8 May 1955; *Journal of the House*, pp. 874, 900, 927, 949–959 (10, 12, 13, 17 May); Transcript of Proceedings, Connecticut General Assembly, House of Representatives, 17 May 1955, pp. 1554–1587, esp. pp. 1570 and 1577, Connecticut State Library; *Journal of the Senate*, pp. 1022 and 1053–1054 (19 and 23 May); Transcript of Proceedings, Senate, 23 May 1955, pp. 1582–1583; *Bridgeport Telegram*, 24 May 1955; *Bridgeport Post*, 24 May 1955.

11. "Legislative Report," 17 May 1955, PPLC 5-M; *Greenwich Time*, 1 June 1955; Lockard, *New England State Politics*, pp. 281–291, at 282; Gertrude Carpenter, Annual Meeting Minutes, 17 May 1955, PPLC 11-S; Griswold, "Director's Report, May 1954–May 1955," PPLC 11-T; *Connecticut Parenthood*, Spring 1955 and Fall 1955; "Memories of Claudia McGinley," 5 May 1983, 2pp., PPLC 33-I; McGinley to Buxton, 2 May 1955, PPLC 17-K; Buxton to McGinley, 4 May 1955, PPLC 38-M. "The whole problem is such a damnably emotional one," Buxton added, "that any crusading within the profession serves no advantageous purpose and produces only intramural bitterness and strife."

12. Griswold to Malin, 9 May 1955, PPLC 5-P; *Bridgeport Herald*, 5 June 1955; Griswold to Malin, 7 June 1955, PPLC 6-K; Lucy Head, Planning Committee Minutes, 8 June 1955, PPLC 23-K; [Griswold], "Legal Action," [13 June 1955], McGinley to William B. Hamilton, 16 June 1955, PPLC 6-E; Harper to Griswold, 16 June 1955, PPLC 16-K; Executive Committee Minutes, 24 June 1955, PPLC 11-T; Griswold to Mrs. Sunde, 11 August 1955, PPLC-37-H1; [Griswold], "Report of Meeting," 18 August 1955, PPLC 6-E and 11-T; Griswold Notes "Re Legal Advisory Committee," 20 August–6 October 1955, Griswold to Roessle McKinney, 20 September 1955, PPLC 6-E; Mrs. Richard Price to Milmine, 20 October 1955, and McGinley to Price, 26 October 1955, PPLC 21-L; "Summary to Date of Plan," PPLC 21-E.

Three years later a peeved Manternach, having learned of the *Poe* v. *Ullman* set of cases only through the newspapers, sent PPLC a bill for $269 for 1953 and 1955 work. Manternach to PPLC, 1 August 1958, and McGinley to Manternach, 11 August 1958, PPLC 7-G.

13. Gertrude Carpenter, Board Minutes, 9 November 1955, PPLC 11-T; Beatrice H. Hessel, "Report of the Planning Committee," 9 November 1955, PPLC 23-K; *Hartford Courant*, 19 November 1955; Griswold to Ralph Brown, 9 December 1955, PPLC 21-F; F.H. Wiggin to Griswold, 13 December 1955, PPLC 6-E; "Summary to Date of Plan," PPLC 21-E; Winfield Best to Mrs. Price, 20 December 1955, Price to Best, 10 January 1956, PPLC 21-F; Carpenter, Executive Committee Minutes, 10 January 1956, and Board Minutes, 24 January 1956, PPLC 12-A; Griswold to Officers and Board, "Proposed Referral Service," [16 January 1956], PPLC 12-A and 21-E; Miriam Garwood to Doris Rutledge, "Conference with Mrs. McGinley . . ." 27 January 1956, PPFA II-185; *Connecticut Parenthood*, Winter 1956; Vogt to Griswold, 30 January 1956, PPLC 21-F; Louis Joughin to Ralph Brown, 2 February 1956, ACLU 1956 Vol. 11; Dorothy Lorenzen, Stamford Minutes, 7 February 1956, PPLC 51-D; Griswold to Herbert S. MacDonald, and to Winfield Best, 14 February 1956, Griswold to William Vogt, 15 February 1956, F. H. Wiggin to Griswold, 16 February 1956, PPLC 21-F; Ralph Brown to Boris Bittker et al., 17 February 1956, ACLU 1956 Vol. 11; Carpenter, Executive Committee Minutes, 23 February 1956, PPLC 12-A.

14. Miriam Lynch, Referral Service Committee Minutes, 12 March 1956, Daisy M. Dennison, "Report on Progress of Referral Service," 27 March 1956, PPLC 21-E; *Newtown Bee*, 2 and 23 March 1956, *Stamford Advocate*, 20 March 1956, *New Haven Register* and *New Haven Journal-Courier*, 22 March 1956, *Middletown Press*, 5 April 1956, and other similar clippings, all in PPLC 19-K; Gertrude Carpenter, Board Minutes, 27 March and 17 April 1956, PPLC 12-A; Milmine, "Report of the Legislative Committee," 27 March 1956, PPLC 22-K; Dennison, "Report of Committee on Referral Service," May 1956, PPLC 21-E; McGinley to Vogt, 18 April 1956, PPLC 21-G.

15. Griswold, "Director's Report, May 1955–[May] 1956," [22 May 1956], PPLC 12-A; Gertrude Carpenter, Annual Meeting Minutes, 22 May 195[6], PPLC 11-T; Hessel, "Annual Report of Planning Committee," 22 May 1956, PPLC 23-K; Milmine, "Report of Legislative Committee," 22 May 1956, PPLC 5-S.

16. Gertrude Carpenter, Board Minutes, 5 June 1956, PPLC 12-A; Griswold, "Meeting . . . Infertility Clinic," 19 June 1956, McGinley to Buxton, 13 July 1956, Buxton to McGinley, 2 August 1956, PPLC 16-C; Griswold to Herbert MacDonald, Fowler Harper, Ralph S. Brown, J. Stephen Knight, and F. H. Wiggin, 31 May 1956, PPLC 21-F; Brown to Griswold, 5 June 1956, Wiggin to Griswold, 6 June 1956, PPLC 21-G; Bruce Manternach to Griswold, 7 June 1956, PPLC 5-L; McGinley to Vogt, 7 June 1956, PPLC 21-G; Winfield Best to Vogt, 8 June 1956, PPFA II-185; Griswold to Milmine, 19 June 1956, PPLC 5-R; Vogt to Sunnen, 19 July 1956, and Alfred L. Severson to Vogt, 25 July 1956, PPFA II-185; Mrs. Price to Griswold and Vogt, 8 August 1956, PPLC 21-O; Milmine to Griswold, 21 June 1956, PPLC 5-S; Dorothy Lorenzen, Executive Committee Minutes, 12 September 1956, PPLC 12-A; Lieberman, *The Power Broker*, p. 201; Lockard, *New England State Politics*, pp. 238–239. Also see Francis Goodale to Loraine Campbell, 8 February 1957, PPLM Box 106.

17. Gertrude Carpenter, Executive Committee Minutes, 12 November 1956, and Board Minutes, 27 November 1956, PPLC 12-A; Lockard, *New England State Politics*, pp. 238–239; Alan Olmstead, *Meriden Record* and *Manchester Evening Herald*, 11 December 1956; Phyllis Rudolph, Executive Committee Minutes, 13 December 1956, PPLC 12-A; Milmine, "Report of Legislative Committee," 10 January 1957, PPLC 5-S; *Journal of the House*, p. 201 (22 January); *Journal of the Senate*, p. 217 (23 January); *Waterbury Republican*, 24 January 1957, p. 35; Cady to Milmine, 25 January 1957, Milmine to Cady, 26 January 1957, and McGinley to Cady, 29 January 1957, PPLC 4-A; Milmine, "Report of Legislative Committee," 28 January 1957, PPLC 5-S; Carpenter, Board Minutes, 28 January 1957, PPLC 12-B; *Connecticut Parenthood*, Winter 1957. Also see Milmine, "Annual Report, Legislative Committee," 28 May 1957, PPLC 5-S.

18. Buxton to Milmine, 6 February 1957, PPLC 4-A and 5-P; Milmine to Buxton, 26 February 1957, PPLC 4-A and 5-R; Milmine to Griswold, 28 February 1957, PPLC 4-A; Buxton to Milmine, 4 March 1957, PPLC 4-A and 5-P; Milmine, "Report of Legislative Committee," 7 March 1957, PPLC 5-S; Gertrude Carpenter, Executive Committee Minutes, 7 March 1957, PPLC 12-B; Miriam Garwood to William Vogt, 7 March 1957, and Best to Vogt, 20 March 1957, PPFA II-185; Milmine to Griswold, 15 March 1957, PPLC 4-A; Norman K. Parsells to Milmine, 18 March 1957, PPLC 5-Q. Theodore Powell's *The School Bus Law: A Case Study in Education, Religion, and Politics* (Middletown, CT: Wesleyan University Press, 1960), esp. p. 170, is an excellent study of the 1957 legislative struggle over the parochial school transportation bill.

19. Transcript of Hearing, Public Health and Safety Committee, 21 March 1957, 77pp., PPLC 6-C and D and Connecticut State Library, esp. pp. 22, 62–63; Buxton to Milmine, 15 March 1957, PPLC 5-P; Buxton Papers Scrapbook; *Hartford Courant*, 22 March 1957, p. 2; *Hartford Times*, 22 March 1957, p. 4; *New Haven Register*, 22 March 1957; *New York Herald Tribune*, 22 March 1957; *New Haven Journal-Courier*, 22 March 1957; *Bridgeport Herald*, 24 March 1957 and 31 March 1957, p. M-7. Eighteen months later Buxton further observed that "an abortion of any kind is the taking of a life and to deny the fetus the right to future life is a decision not to be entered into lightly." Buxton, Book Review, *Eugenics Quarterly* 5 (December 1958): 230–231. Also see Buxton, "Advances in Obstetrics and Gynecology," *The Practitioner* 181 (October 1958): 395–403, at 396-397.

20. Buxton to Griswold, 22 March 1957, PPLC 6-B; *Hartford Courant*, 4 April 1957, p. 1, 18 April 1957, p. 1, 25 April 1957, p. 1; *Waterbury Republican*, 4 April 1957, 18 April 1957, p. 1, 25 April 1957; *Hartford Times*, 4 April 1957, 18 April 1957; *New Haven Journal-Courier*, 4 April 1957, 18 April 1957; *Bridgeport Herald*, 8 April 1957; Gertrude Carpenter, Board Minutes, 9 April 1957, PPLC 12-B; *Journal of the House*, pp. 869 and 944–948 (9 and 17 April); Transcript of Proceedings, Connecticut General Assembly, House of Representatives, 17 April 1957, pp. 1314-1333, Connecticut State Library; *New Haven Register*, 18 April 1957; *New York Herald Tribune*, 18 April 1957; *Journal of the Senate*, pp. 829 and 867 (18 and 24 April); Milmine to Watson, 25 April 1957, and Watson to Milmine, 2 May 1957, PPLC 5-S; Transcript of Proceedings, Senate, 24 April 1957, pp. 1527–1528; *New York Times*, 25 April 1957. Also see Powell, *The School Bus Law*, pp. 197–198, 213–214, 235, and three Milmine retrospectives

regarding her difficulties in projecting an accurate tally within the senate: "Annual Report, Legislative Committee," 28 May 1957, Milmine to William Vogt, 16 July 1957, and "Report of the Legislative Committee," December 1957, PPLC 5-S.

21. Gertrude Carpenter, Executive Committee Minutes, 7 May 1957, PPLC 12-B; McGinley to Vogt, 9 May 1957, PPLC 21-F; Griswold, "Director's Report, May 1956–May [1957]," 28 May 1957, Carpenter, Annual Meeting Minutes, 28 May 1957, PPLC 12-B; *Connecticut Parenthood*, Summer 1957; Winfield Best to Vogt, "Connecticut Situation," 8 July 1957, PPFA II-185.

22. *Connecticut Parenthood*, Summer 1957 and Fall 1957; Anita Ernst, Executive Committee Minutes, 12 September 1957, PPLC 12-B; Griswold to Sanger, 25 June 1958, Sanger-SS Box 119; Ernst, Board Minutes, 26 November 1957 and 25 February 1958, PPLC 12-B and C.

23. See especially Janet Harbison, "The Doctor Tests the Law," *Presbyterian Life*, 1 October 1962, pp. 14–15, 37. Also see William F. Mengert, "Buxton: Birth Control Martyr," *Ob. Gyn. News* 10 ([15] November 1969): 14; John McLean Morris, "Charles Lee Buxton, 1904–1969," *Transactions of the American Gynecological Society* 92 (1969): 165–166; *New Haven Journal-Courier*, 8 July 1969, p. 11; *Princeton Alumni Weekly*, 27 April 1962, p. 16; *New Haven Register*, 7 July 1969, pp. 1, 2; *Connecticut Medicine*, August 1969; Garrow conversations with Helen Rotch [Buxton] Rose and John M. Morris.

24. "Oldendorf" is a pseudonym chosen by this author.

25. "Odegard" is a pseudonym chosen by this author, at the principals' request.

26. Harbison, "The Doctor Tests the Law," pp. 14–15; Steven M. Spencer, "The Birth Control Revolution," *Saturday Evening Post*, 15 January 1966, pp. 21–25, 66–70; Garrow conversations with Helen Rotch [Buxton] Rose, Robert "Oldendorf," Hector Kinloch, and Elizabeth "Odegard." Also see Buxton, "Birth Control Problems in Connecticut," *Connecticut Medicine* 28 (August 1966): 581–584. Medical details and dates appear in the subsequent 22 May 1958 complaints, all in PPLC 6-L.

27. Hector Kinloch to Garrow, 26 April 1992, and Garrow conversation with Kinloch.

28. Garrow conversation with Robert "Oldendorf."

29. Garrow conversation with Elizabeth "Odegard."

30. Garrow conversations with Marvin and Jean Durning; Emerson, "Fowler Vincent Harper," *Yale Law Journal* 74 (March 1965): 601–603.

31. Stephen C. Veltri, "Fowler Vincent Harper," *Writ* [ONU College of Law], Winter 1989–1990, pp. 3–8; Veltri, "Fowler V. Harper and the Right of Privacy: Twenty-Five Years," *Ohio Northern University Law Review* 16 (1989): 359–363; Harper's principal FBI file, HQ 77–32691, kindly supplied by Professor Veltri; and Garrow conversations with Elizabeth Phillips. Also see "Fowler Harper's Close Call," *Ada Record*, 21 June 1922, p. 1; Harper, "The Work of the Federal Security Agency," *Ohio Northern Alumnus*, April 1940, pp. 6–7, 16; *New York Times*, 17 August 1939, p. 4, 11 July 1940, p. 20, 16 November 1941, p. 35, 6 May 1942, p. 15, 19 October 1942, p. 6, 5 December 1942, p. 7, 17 December 1942, p. 36, 19 February 1943, p. 12, 28 February 1943, pp. 1, 38, 11 April 1943, p. 26, 15 April 1943, p. 16, 23 April 1943, p. 11, 28 April 1943, p. 15, 9 May 1943, p. 14, 7 September 1943, p. 17; Laura Kalman, *Abe Fortas* (New Haven: Yale University Press, 1990), p. 110. A comprehensive bibliography of Harper's publications for those years as well as for later ones appears in the *Ohio Northern University Law Review* 16 (1989): 583–589.

32. Veltri, "Fowler V. Harper"; FBI HQ file 77–32691, especially serial 11, an Indianapolis report of 4 December 1946; *Chicago Herald American*, 31 October and 4 December 1946; Harper's 11pp. formal "Statement" to the IU Board of Trustees, 3 December 1946, and a 189pp. Harper deposition, 29 December 1947, Harper Papers, Box 1; "Fowler V. Harper," *National Cyclopedia of American Biography* 52 (1970): 526–527; *New York Times*, 11 March 1947, p. 14, 6 September 1948, p. 4, 10 August 1949, p. 18, 11 August 1949, p. 5; Laura Kalman, *Legal Realism at Yale, 1927–1960* (Chapel Hill: University of North Carolina Press, 1986), pp. 158–159; Harper, "Loyalty and Lawyers," *Lawyers Guild Review* 11 (Fall 1951): 205–209, and Harper, "Decision by Silence," *Atlantic Monthly* 119 (April 1952): 44–48, at 46. Also see Harper, "The Supreme Court Reconsiders," *The Nation*, 10 November 1951, pp. 396–398, "The Record of J. Howard McGrath," *The Nation*, 24 November 1951, pp. 441–443, "Our

Paper Curtain," *The Nation*, 1 March 1952, pp. 198–200, "The Crusade Against Bridges," *The Nation*, 5 April 1952, pp. 323–326, and "Immigrants: Still Fewer Wanted," *The New Republic*, 3 March 1952, pp. 13–15.

33. *National Cyclopedia of American Biography* 52 (1970): 526–527; Garrow conversations with Elizabeth Phillips; Kalman, *Legal Realism at Yale*, p. 282 n.64 (quoting an undated letter from one "Lew Good" in the Provost's Papers, Box 38, Folder 382, Yale University Archives); Harper to Rostow, 10 March 1953, Harper Papers Box 3; *Washington Times Herald*, 27 May 1953, pp. 1, 5, 30 May 1953, p. 6; FBI HQ file 100–389390. Also see Sigmund Diamond, *Compromised Campus* (New York: Oxford University Press, 1992), pp. 164, 165–166, 214, 226–227, 240, 339–340.

34. Harper, *Problems of the Family* (Indianapolis: Bobbs-Merrill, 1952); Kalman, *Legal Realism at Yale*, pp. 191–192; Dudley F. Sicher, Book Review, *Lawyers Guild Review* 13 (Fall 1953): 130–132 (and listing prior reviews in *Psychiatric Quarterly* [October 1952], *Georgetown Law Journal* and *Yale Law Journal* [January 1953], *Marriage and Family Living* [February 1953], *Harvard Law Review* and *Kentucky Law Journal* [March 1953], *Minnesota Law Review* and *American Catholic Sociological Review* [May 1953], and *Sociology and Social Research* [1953] and the *Journal of Legal Education* [1953]); Harper, Book Review, *Yale Law Journal* 63 (April 1954): 895–899; Harper and James, *The Law of Torts* (1956); Veltri, "Fowler V. Harper." Also see Fowler and Miriam Harper, "Lawyers and Marriage Counseling," *Journal of Family Law* 1 (1961): 73–88; and Harper and Jerome H. Skolnick, *Problems of the Family*, rev.ed. (Indianapolis: Bobbs-Merrill, 1962).

35. Garrow conversations with Marvin Durning, David and Louise Trubek, James M. Edwards, Louis H. Pollak, Robert B. Stevens, and Elizabeth Phillips; James, Rostow, and Emerson in "Fowler V. Harper," *Yale Law Journal* 74 (March 1965): 599–605.

36. *New York Times*, 9 January 1965, p. 25; Kalman, *Legal Realism at Yale*, pp. 197–199; *Peters v. Hobby*, 349 U.S. 331 (6 June 1955); *New York Times*, 7 June 1955, p. 18; *Harper v. Adametz*, 142 Conn. 218 (1 March 1955); *New Haven Register*, 16 March 1955; Garrow conversations with Catherine G. Roraback; New Haven Civil Liberties Council file in Emerson Papers, Box 30; *Yale Law Report*, Fall 1956, pp. 3–4, 8.

37. Griswold, "Summary of Action to Date on Five Lawsuits," 15 July 1958, PPLC 6-K; Garrow conversations with Roraback; Roraback, "*Griswold v. Connecticut*: A Brief Case History," *Ohio Northern University Law Review* 16 (1989): 395–401, at 397–398; Dorothy W. Wolfe, "Catherine Roraback: Her Aim is Justice," *Mount Holyoke Alumnae Quarterly*, Summer 1973, pp. 78–81; *Hartford Times*, 1 January 1971, p. B7, 9 June 1975; *New Haven Register*, 22 January 1966; *Hartford Courant*, 9 April 1988, pp. C1, C7; McGinley, "Memories of Claudia McGinley," 5 May 1983, 2pp., Bea Hessel, "PPLC—The 1960s," 11 March 1983, 3pp., PPLC 33-I; Hessel to Loraine Campbell, 22 June 1959, PPLM Box 106.

38. Griswold, "Summary of Action to Date on Five Lawsuits," 15 July 1958, PPLC 6-K; Garrow conversations with Catherine G. Roraback, Jean and Marvin Durning, Robert "Oldendorf," Hector Kinloch, and Elizabeth "Odegard"; Roraback, "*Griswold v. Connecticut*"; Harper to McGinley, 12 May 1958, PPLC 6-E; Roraback, "Complaint" in *Buxton, Doe, Poe, Hoe*, and *Roe v. Ullman*, 22 May 1958, PPLC 6-L; Record and File for all five actions, #87983 through 87987, New Haven County Superior Court Clerk's Office. Neither Hector Kinloch nor Elizabeth "Odegard" in 1992 had any recollection of signing a formal document or of meeting either Harper or Roraback, and no documents signed by the actual plaintiffs, sealed or unsealed, are now part of the official Superior Court case files. Undated and unsigned carbon copies of letters of authorization prepared for "Jane Doe" and the "Poes," but not the Kinlochs or the Durnings, appear in Fowler Harper's files on the cases, now in the Emerson Papers, Boxes 7 and 8. The "Odegards," who arrived in New Haven in September 1957, recall that they were in Connecticut only for seven months before David's employer transferred them elsewhere, and if their recollection is indeed correct, they would have left New Haven—and Connecticut—sometime in early April, well before *Poe v. Ullman* was actually filed. "We were not residents," and "they knew we were leaving town," Elizabeth "Odegard" volunteered in 1992.

39. Roraback, "Complaint," in *Buxton, Poe, Roe, Doe* and *Hoe*, 22 May 1958, PPLC 6-L; Roraback

to Griswold, 5 June 1958, and Griswold to Roraback, 9 June 1958, PPLC 6-K; Griswold, "Executive Director's Report, May 1957–[May] 1958," [27 May 1958], Anita Ernst, Annual Meeting Minutes, 27 May 1958, PPLC 12-C; *Connecticut Parenthood*, Summer 1958. Also see Lucia Jenney Parks, "Referral Report," 25 February 1958 and 27 May 1958, PPLC 21-O, and Helen Kennedy to Griswold, 18 February 1959, PPLC 21-I.

40. Anita Ernst, Executive Committee Minutes, 5 June 1958, PPLC 12-C; *New Haven Register*, 6 June 1958, pp. 1, 3; *New Haven Journal-Courier*, 7 June 1958; *Hartford Courant* 7 June 1958; *New York Times*, 7 June 1958, p. 10; Patrick Malin to Alan Reitman et al., 9 June 1958, Louis Joughin to Ralph Brown, 10 and 18 June 1958, Brown to Reitman, 5 September 1958, ACLU 1961 Vol. 12; Griswold to Herbert Thoms, 30 June 1958, PPLC 17-K.

41. Ernst, Joint Executive/Finance Committee Minutes, 10 July 1958, PPLC 12-C; Griswold, "Summary of Action to Date on Five Lawsuits," 15 July 1958, PPLC 6-K; Planned Parenthood Federation of America, *The Anatomy of a Victory* (New York: PPFA, 1959); Alan F. Guttmacher, *Babies By Choice or By Chance* (Garden City, NY: Doubleday, 1959), pp. 121–129; Murray, "America's Four Conspiracies," in John Cogley, ed., *Religion in America* (Cleveland: Meridian Books, 1958), pp. 12–41, at 33; *U.S. News & World Report*, 22 August 1958, pp. 72–75; James Finn, "Controversy in New York," *Commonweal*, 12 September 1958, pp. 583–586; John Cogley, "Controversy in Connecticut," *Commonweal*, 28 March 1958, p. 657. Also see Murray, *We Hold These Truths* (New York: Sheed & Ward, 1960), pp. 157–159; *Time*, 8 September 1958, pp. 74–75; *Commonweal*, 18 December 1959, and 22 April 1960, pp. 98–99; and William L. Bradley, "Birth Control Laws in Connecticut and Massachusetts," *Social Action* 26 (April 1960): 20–23.

42. Ernst, *Touch Wood: A Year's Diary* (New York: Atheneum, 1960), pp. 25, 32, 35; Garrow conversations with Roraback; Loraine Campbell Notes, 17 October 1958, and Campbell to Harper, 17 October 1958, PPLM Box 106.

43. Alfred Severson to Griswold, 8 October 1958, PPLC 6-K; Ernst, Executive Committee Minutes, 2 October 1958, Board Minutes, 28 October 1958, PPLC 12-C; Dorothy W. Lorenzen, "Legislative Report," 28 October 1958, PPLC 6-E; Loraine Campbell Notes, 21 October 1958, Pilpel to Campbell, 29 October 1958, Campbell to Pilpel, 1 November 1958, PPLM Box 106.

44. *Buxton et al.* v. *Ullman* Case Files, Clerk's Office, New Haven County Superior Court; Cannon, "Demurrer," *Buxton* v. *Ullman* and *Poe* v. *Ullman*, Clerk's Files and PPLC 6-M.

45. Harper to Campbell, 5 November 1958, Pilpel to Campbell and Vogt, 7 November 1958, Campbell Notes, 7 November 1958, Pilpel to Harper, 10 November 1958, PPLM Box 106; Natalie Schwartz, Education Committee Minutes, 13 November 1958, PPLC 20-H; "Outline of Points Discussed at Conference," 14 November 1958, Pilpel to Harper, 14 November 1958, Campbell to Buxton, 17 November 1958, Pilpel to Harper, 1 December 1958, PPLM Box 106.

46. *New Haven Register*, 2 December 1958, 6 December 1958, p. 3; *New Haven Journal-Courier*, 2 December 1958, 6 December 1958; *Hartford Courant*, 2 December 1958, p. 5, 6 December 1958, p. 19; *Hartford Times*, 2 December 1958, 6 December 1958; *New York Post*, 3 December 1958; *Waterbury Republican*, 6 December 1958, p. 1; *New York Times*, 6 December 1958; Cannon, "Brief of Defendant," *Buxton et al.* v. *Ullman*, [1 December 1958], 14pp., Clerk's File, New Haven County Superior Court, esp. pp. 5, 9 and 14; Roraback, "Memorandum of Law in Opposition to Defendant's Demurrers," *Buxton et al.* v. *Ullman*, 5 December 1958, 10pp., Clerk's File, esp. p. 3; Morton David Goldberg to Ernst, "PPFA—Connecticut Birth Control Suit," 9 December 1958, PPLM Box 106; *Connecticut Parenthood*, Fall 1958. Frank Healey, who graduated from Holy Cross in 1921 and from Yale Law School in 1925, had been named to the Superior Court bench only in mid-1957; he died in March of 1963 at age 65. On his earlier affiliation with Father Cryne, see the *Waterbury Democrat*, 11 May 1939, p. 3. On Raymond J. Cannon, who was six years younger than Healey, see his obituary in the *Hartford Courant*, 22 January 1981, p. A20.

47. Campbell, "Memorandum on Luncheon Conference with Morris Ernst," 9 December 1958, 11pp., PPLM Box 106; Campbell Interview with Reed, p. 58; Ernst, *Touch Wood*, p. 150; Campbell Notes, 11 December 1958, PPLM Box 106. On Harriet Pilpel, who had graduated

from Vassar in 1932, from Columbia Law School in 1936, and then immediately joined Greenbaum, Wolff & Ernst, see her obituary in the *New York Times*, 24 April 1991, p. D23, and "Greenbaum, Wolff & Ernst—A Brief History of the Firm," 1955, with a December, 1960, Supplement, Ernst Papers Box 846.

48. Healey, "Memoranda of Decision on Demurrer," *Buxton et al.* v. *Ullman*, 31 December 1958 [Filed 5 January 1959], PPLC 6-M, Clerk's File, New Haven County Superior Court, and *Poe* v. *Ullman* Record, pp. 16–18; *Hartford Courant*, 7 January 1959, 23 February 1959, p. 8; *New York Times*, 7 January 1959; *New York Herald Tribune*, 7 January 1959; *Waterbury Republican*, 7 January and 23 February 1959; *Hartford Times*, 7 January 1959; *Poe* Record, pp. 18–23 (Cannon's 21 January motion, Judge John R. Thim's 30 January order entering judgment, and Roraback's 11 February notice of appeal); Campbell, "Memorandum re Connecticut Test Cases," 24 December 1958, PPLM Box 106; *Bridgeport Herald*, 22 February 1959; [Griswold], "Meeting with Lawyers," 16 January 1959, PPLC 6-K; Garrow conversations with Jean and Marvin Durning.

49. Lotta Moser, Executive Committee Minutes, 4 December 1958, PPLC 12-C; Lieberman, *The Power Broker*, p. 222; Anita Ernst, Executive Committee Minutes, 8 January 1959, and Board Minutes, 27 January 1959, PPLC 12-D; [Griswold], "Meeting with Lawyers," 16 January 1959, PPLC 6-K; *Journal of the House*, p. 276 (22 January); *Journal of the Senate*, p. 292 (22 January); *Waterbury Republican*, 22 January 1959; Harper to Pilpel, 22 January 1959, and Pilpel to Harper, 10 February 1959, PPLM Box 106; "Legislative Committee Report," 27 January 1959, and [Dorothy Lorenzen], "Notes on Meeting," 2[9] January 1959, PPLC 6-E; *Connecticut Parenthood*, Winter 1959. Also see Joseph A. Gianelli, Jr., "An Analysis of the Connecticut Gubernatorial Election of 1958" (unpublished B.A. thesis, Princeton University, 1959).

50. Griswold to John Morris, 18 February 1959, PPLC 6-F; Dorothy Lorenzen, "Legislative Committee Report," 24 March 1959, PPLC 6-E; Morris to Lockard, 26 March 1959, Morris Papers; Transcript of Hearing, Public Health and Safety Committee, 24 April 1959, 65pp., PPLC 6-G and H and Connecticut State Library, esp. pp. 14 and 62; *Hartford Courant*, 25 April 1959, p. 2; *Waterbury Republican*, 25 April 1959; *Hartford Times*, 25 April 1959; *New York Herald Tribune*, 26 April and 3 May 1959; *New York Times*, 2 May 1959; PPLC "Report to Members," [19 May 1959], PPLC 14-D. On the 1959 session in general, see Van Dusen, *Connecticut*, pp. 395–396; Lieberman, *The Power Broker*, pp. 246–247; and James David Barber, *The Lawmakers: Recruitment and Adaptation to Legislative Life* (New Haven: Yale University Press, 1965).

51. Garrow conversations with Marvin and Jean Durning and with David and Louise Grossman Trubek; Louise Trubek Interview with Brecher; Louise Farr to Griswold, 16 February 1959, Harper to Griswold, 13 March 1959, PPLC 6-F; Board Minutes, 24 March 1959, PPLC 12-D; Griswold to Vogt, [9 April 1959], PPFA II-184; Anita Ernst, Executive Committee Minutes, 21 April 1959, PPLC 12-D; *Teague, Livingston, and Willard* v. *Ullman*, #90315 to 90317, New Haven County Superior Court; *Hartford Courant*, 5 May 1959; *Bridgeport Post*, 5 May 1959; *New York Times*, 5 May 1959, p. 24, 27 May 1959, p. 23; *New York Herald Tribune*, 5 May 1959; Roraback, Complaint, *Trubek* v. *Ullman*, #90417, New Haven County Superior Court, 20 May 1959, PPLC 6-L; Roraback to Buxton, and to Mr. and Mrs. David M. Trubek, 20 May 1959, PPLC 7-G; Griswold to Vogt, 22 May 1959, PPLC 6-I; *New Haven Register*, 26 May 1959, 27 May 1959, p. 26; *New Haven Journal-Courier*, 26 May 1959; and New Haven Civil Liberties Council folder in Emerson Papers, Box 30. On C. Lawson Willard, see a *New Haven Register* profile of 29 March 1970, and his *Register* obituary, 10 April 1983, p. B14.

52. *Buxton et al.* v. *Ullman* Case Files #87983 et seq., Clerk's Office, New Haven County Superior Court; Roraback, "Brief of Plaintiffs-Appellants," *Poe* v. *Ullman*, #4796, Connecticut Supreme Court, March Term 1959, pp. 10–11, "Brief of Plaintiff-Appellant," *Buxton* v. *Ullman*, #4794, p. 16; *Connecticut Parenthood*, Summer 1959. Also see Roraback's very similar "Brief of Plaintiffs-Appellants" in *Hoe*, #4797, and *Doe*, #4798, Connecticut Supreme Court, Record and Briefs, March [October] Term 1959, A-380 I 1–96.

53. Pilpel to Harper, 16 April 1959, Pilpel to Fred Jaffe, 5 May 1959, Harper to Pilpel, 7 May

1959, PPLM Box 106; Pilpel to Vogt, 11 May 1959, PPFA II-184; Campbell Notes, 14 May 1959, Pilpel to Roraback, 14 May 1959, Roraback to Pilpel, 18 May 1959, Campbell to Vogt, 19 May 1959, Pilpel to Campbell and Vogt, 4 June 1959, PPLM Box 106; Pilpel to Campbell and Vogt, 10 June 1959, PPFA II-184; Campbell, "Memo on Connecticut Litigation," 10 June 1959, PPLM Box 106. Also see an earlier essay which Harper mentioned in his May 7 letter to Pilpel, an essay he had written with former Yale law student Edwin D. Etherington (who also had coauthored the 1950 litigation strategy paper previously considered by PPLC), "Lobbyists Before the Court," *University of Pennsylvania Law Review* 101 (June 1953): 1172–1179, a critical commentary on the value of amicus briefs which concluded that "for the most part, briefs amici are repetitious at best and emotional explosions at worst."

54. Harper to Pilpel, 18 June 1959, PPLC 6-K and PPFA II-184; Pilpel to Fifield Workum and Francis Goodhue, 18 June 1959, Pilpel to Harper [draft], 19 June 1959, Kay [Mali] to Campbell, 21 June 1959, Hessel to Campbell, 22 June 1959, Margot Baruch to Campbell, 26 June 1959, Campbell to Hessel, 1 July 1959, Griswold to Vogt, [6] July 1959, Vogt to Griswold, 8 July 1959, Pilpel to Harper, 6 July 1959, Francis Goodhue to Vogt, 8 July 1959, Fifield Workum to Vogt, 8 July 1959, Campbell Notes, 11 July 1959, Campbell to Workum, 13 July 1959, Em Workum to Campbell, 15 July 1959, Vogt to Griswold, 17 July 1959, Griswold to Vogt, 20 July 1959, Workum to Vogt, 27 July 1959, PPLM 106.

55. Cannon, "Brief of Defendant-Appellee," *Hoe* v. *Ullman*, #4797, Connecticut Supreme Court, 24 July 1959, 7pp., esp. p. 6, and a 10pp. "Brief" in *Buxton* (#4794) and two 4pp. briefs in *Doe* and *Poe* (#4798 and 4796), referring the Court to the *Hoe* brief, A-380 I; Griswold to Vogt, 31 July, 25 August and 3 September 1959, PPLC 7-A and PPLM Box 106; Roraback to Pilpel, 7 August 1959, Campbell Notes, 11 August 1959, PPLM Box 106; Rebecca Ehrinpries to Winfield Best, 11 August 1959, PPFA II-184; Best to Campbell, 12 August 1959, Pilpel to Roraback, 17 August 1959, PPLM Box 106; *Buxton* v. *Ullman* Case File, New Haven County Superior Court, #87983; Roraback, "Reply Brief of Plaintiffs-Appellants," *Poe* v. *Ullman*, pp. 10 and 12, "Reply Brief of Plaintiff-Appellant," *Buxton* v. *Ullman*, pp. 3–4; and similar reply briefs in *Doe* and *Hoe*, A-380 I.

56. Vogt to Campbell, 5 August 1959, PPLM Box 106; Anita Ernst, Executive Committee Minutes, 10 September 1959, PPLC 12-D; Hessel to Miriam Garwood, 17 September 1959, PPLC 40-J and PPFA II-185; Campbell Notes, 18 September 1959, PPLM Box 106; Griswold to Vogt, 21 September 1959, PPLC 40-J; *New London Day*, 24 September 1959; Johnson, *Raymond E. Baldwin*, pp. 259–260; Campbell Notes, 7 October 1959, PPLM Box 106; Roraback to Rowland Watts, 20 October 1959, ACLU 1961 Vol. 12; Roraback to Pilpel, 20 October 1959, PPLM Box 106; Griswold to Vogt, 2 November 1959, PPFA II-184; Harper to Eugene Gressman, 2 November 1959, Emerson Box 8; Anita Ernst, Board Minutes, 5 November 1959, and Executive Committee Minutes, 10 December 1959, PPLC 12-D.

57. *New York Times*, 26 November 1959, pp. 1, 43, 6 December 1959, pp. 1, 74; Kingsley Davis and Judith Blake, "Birth Control and Public Policy," *Commentary* 29 (February 1960): 115–121; Charles F. Westoff and Norman B. Ryder, "Methods of Fertility Control in the United States: 1955, 1960 and 1965," in William T. Liu, ed., *Family and Fertility* (Notre Dame: University of Notre Dame Press, 1967), pp. 157–169, at 168; Westoff and Larry Bumpass, "The Revolution in Birth Control Practices of U.S. Roman Catholics," *Science* 179 (5 January 1973): 41–44; Phyllis T. Piotrow, *World Population Crisis* (New York: Praeger, 1973), pp. 23, 36–42. On the adoption of the ACLU's policy, see ACLU Office to Due Process Committee, 19 June 1959, Due Process Committee Minutes, 15 July 1959, and ACLU Board of Directors Minutes, 17 August 1959, ACLU 1959 Vol. 1, and *Civil Liberties*, November 1959.

58. *Buxton* v. *Ullman*, 147 Conn. 48, 156 A.2d 508, 513–514; *Hartford Times*, 22 December 1959; *New Haven Register*, 22 December 1959, pp. 1, 2; *New York Post*, 22 December 1959, p. 4; *Hartford Courant*, 23 December 1959, p. 5; *New York Times*, 23 December 1959, pp. 1, 13; *New York Herald Tribune*, 23 December 1959, pp. 1, 4; *Time*, 4 January 1960, pp. 18–19; Baldwin to Mrs. William B. Gandin, 6 September 1960, Baldwin Papers Box 81. Law review

notes on the Connecticut Supreme Court decision in *Buxton* include Erik J. Stapper, *Michigan Law Review* 58 (April 1960): 929–931; Robert E. Slota, *Villanova Law Review* 5 (Summer 1960): 677–680; *Albany Law Review* 25 (January 1961): 143–146; and *New York Law Forum* 7 (February 1961): 73–81. Also see two more substantive essays, Alvah W. Sulloway, "The Legal and Political Aspects of Population Control in the United States," *Law and Contemporary Problems* 25 (Summer 1960): 593–613; and Andrew N. Farley, "Conception, Contraceptives, and the Law: A Connecticut Problem," *University of Pittsburgh Law Review* 22 (October 1960): 91–103.

59. *New York Herald Tribune*, 24 December 1959, p. 12, 27 December 1959; *Washington Post*, 24 December 1959; Griswold to Chasie des Granges, 11 January 1960, PPLM Box 106; Gressman to Harper, 28 December 1959 and 9 January 1960, Harper to Gressman, 14 January 1960, Gressman to Harper, 27 January 1960, Harper to Gressman, 9 February 1960, Emerson Box 8; Garrow conversations with Hector Kinloch and Elizabeth "Odegard."

60. Jerome E. Caplan to Alan Reitman, 7 January 1960, Rowland Watts to Caplan, 13 January 1960, Caplan to ACLU, 19 January 1960, ACLU 1961 Vol. 12; *Hartford Courant*, 19 April 1960; *Hartford Times*, 19 April 1960; Anita Ernst, Board Minutes, 26 January 1960, Executive Committee Minutes, 16 February 1960, Board Minutes, 22 March 1960, PPLC 12-E; Harper to Seymour, 9 February 1960, Emerson Box 8; Vogt to Pilpel, 25 February 1960, and Pilpel to Johanna von Goeckingk, 15 March 1960, PPFA II-184; Gressman to Harper, 12 and 23 March 1960, Emerson Box 8. On *Trubek*, see Judge Elmer W. Ryan, "Memorandum of Decision on Defendant's Demurrer to Plaintiff's Complaint," *Trubek* v. *Ullman*, #90417, New Haven Superior Court, PPLC 6-M; *Trubek* Record, A-391 590; and *New Haven Register*, 27 February 1960; on the ministerial ones, see Roraback to George Teague, 16 February 1960, PPLC 6-I.

61. Harper, "Jurisdictional Statement," *Poe et al.* v. *Ullman*, U.S.S.C., O.T. 1959 #810, 31pp., 23 March 1960, esp. pp. 8–10, 20–22; Harper, "Jurisdictional Statement," *Buxton* v. *Ullman*, U.S.S.C., O.T. 1959 #811, 13pp., 23 March 1960, esp. pp. 5 and 13; *Meyer* v. *Nebraska*, 262 U.S. 390, 399 (1923); *Skinner* v. *Oklahoma*, 316 U.S. 535, 541 (1942); *Public Utilities Commission* v. *Pollak*, 343 U.S. 451 (1952). On the Gallup Poll, see *Hartford Courant*, 17 February 1960 and *New York Herald Tribune*, 18 February 1960. On "the right to be let alone," see Thomas M. Cooley, *Torts*, 2nd ed., p. 29: "The right to one's person may be said to be a right of complete immunity: to be let alone." Also see Samuel D. Warren and Louis D. Brandeis, "The Right to Privacy," *Harvard Law Review* 4 (December 1890): 193–220, at 195; *Union Pacific Railway Co.* v. *Botsford*, 141 U.S. 250, 251 (1891); *Olmstead* v. *U.S.*, 277 U.S. 438, 471 (Brandeis, J., dissenting); *Public Utilities Commission* v. *Pollak*, 343 U.S. 451, 467, 468 (Douglas, J., dissenting); William O. Douglas, *The Right of the People* (Garden City, NY: Doubleday & Co., 1958), pp. 87, 88; Erwin N. Griswold, "The Right to Be Let Alone," *Northwestern University Law Review* 55 (May-June 1960): 216–226, esp. 216–217. Dean Griswold asserted that "'The right to be let alone' is the underlying theme of the Bill of Rights" and "is implicit in many of the provisions of the Constitution and in the philosophic background out of which the Constitution was formulated." See as well Charles B. Nutting, "The Fifth Amendment and Privacy," *University of Pittsburgh Law Review* 18 (Spring 1957): 533–544, at 543 (privacy "is a generalized interest . . . which should receive protection as a 'liberty'" under due process), and Harry Kalven, Jr., "A Special Corner of Civil Liberties," *New York University Law Review* 31 (November 1956): 1223–1237, at 1228 ("the freedom of sex relations within marriage and the freedom to have children when wanted rank high among the basic personal liberties in our society").

62. "SD" [Steven Duke], *Poe et al.* v. *Ullman*, *Buxton* v. *Ullman*, 1959 Term No. 810, 811, 16 May 1960, 1pp., Douglas Papers Box 1247; "TCW" [T. Cecil Wray], *Poe* v. *Ullman*, *Buxton* v. *Ullman*, 16 May 1960, 3pp. and 1pp., Clark Papers Box B178; "MHB" [Murray H. Bring], *Poe* v. *Ullman*, *Buxton* v. *Ullman*, n.d., 7 pp., Warren Papers Box 208; [Howard Lesnick], *Poe* v. *Ullman*, *Buxton* v. *Ullman*, n.d., 2 pp., Harlan Papers Box 117; *Naim* v. *Naim*, 350 U.S. 891 (1955) and 350 U.S. 985 (1956).

63. Docket Sheets recording the *Poe* vote appear in the Warren Papers, Box 374, the Brennan

Papers, Box 407, and the Clark Papers, Box C76; a more informal but identical tally also appears in the Douglas Papers, Box 1247.

64. *Poe et al.* v. *Ullman*, and *Buxton* v. *Ullman*, 362 U.S. 987; *Hartford Times*, 23 May 1960; *New York Times*, 24 May 1960, p. 25; *New York Herald Tribune*, 24 May 1960; *Hartford Courant*, 24 May 1960, p. 2; *New Haven Register*, 24 May 1960; Pilpel to Vogt et al., 25 May 1960, and Pilpel to Harper et al., 27 May 1960, PPFA II-184 and Emerson Box 8; Harper to Gressman, 25 May 1960, and Gressman to Harper, 3 June 1960, Emerson Box 8; Loraine Campbell to McGinley, 27 May 1960, PPLM Box 106; Pilpel to Raymond J. Cannon, 31 May 1960, PPFA II-184; Harper to Connecticut Commissioner for Food and Drugs, 10 June 1960, Attilio R. Frassinelli to Harper, 30 June 1960, and Harper to Frassinelli, 5 July 1960, Emerson Box 7; Mary S. Calderone to Pilpel, 14 June 1960, PPFA II-184; Lee Buxton to various doctors, 10 June 1960, Harper to John Rock, 15 June 1960, Harper to Fifield Workum, 21 June 1960, Emerson Box 8; Pilpel to Harper, 30 June 1960, Pilpel to Vogt et al., 8 July 1960, Cannon to Pilpel, 15 August 1960, Pilpel to Cannon, 25 August 1960, Cannon to Pilpel, 30 August 1960, PPFA II-184. The PPFA brief was actually written by two of Pilpel's junior associates, Julia Perles and Mark J. Kronman; Seymour's brief was largely composed by Richard Hawkins.

Regarding Frankfurter's temporary recusal, the other possible grounds lay in Frankfurter's long friendship with Connecticut League of Women Voters activist Katharine Ludington, who had passed away in 1953 but whose sister, Helen (Mrs. Arthur G.) Rotch, was the mother of Buxton's wife Helen. See Harlan B. Phillips, ed., *Felix Frankfurter Reminisces* (New York: Reynal & Co., 1960), p. 239; on Ludington, see *New York Times*, 9 March 1953, p. 29, and 21 March 1953, p. 16; also see Louise M. Young, *In the Public Interest: The League of Women Voters, 1920–1970* (Westport, CT: Greenwood Press, 1989), pp. 50, 51, 75, 77, 93, 158; Mary Gray Peck, *Carrie Chapman Catt* (New York: H. W. Wilson Co., 1944), pp. 327, 341. Mrs. Rotch herself had once been president of the Massachusetts League of Women Voters, and had been among the leading sponsors of the 1948 birth control referendum. See John R. Rodman, "Birth Control Politics in Massachusetts" (unpublished M.A. thesis, Harvard University, 1955), p. 37.

65. *New York Herald Tribune*, 28 May 1960, p. 10; John Maguire, "Should We Vote for a Birth Control Law?," *Ave Maria*, 11 June 1960, p. 6; *Newsweek*, 27 June 1960, p. 94; Norman St. John-Stevas, *Birth Control and Public Policy* (Santa Barbara, CA: Center for the Study of Democratic Institutions, July, 1960); *Newsweek*, 25 July 1960, p. 70; *Waterbury Republican*, 11 July 1960; *Hartford Times*, 12 July 1960, p. 22; *Bridgeport Telegram*, 12 July 1960; *Bridgeport Herald*, 17 July 1960.

66. Harper to E. P. Cullinan, 11 July 1960, Harper to Gressman, 15 July 1960, Cannon to Harper, 20 July 1960, Gressman to Harper, 21 July 1960, Emerson Box 8; Pilpel to Harper, 10 August 1960, Pilpel to Harper et al., 26 August 1960, Emerson Box 8; Wulf to Ruth Emerson, 22 August 1960, Wulf to Cannon, 24 August 1960, Emerson to Wulf, 25 August 1960, Cannon to Wulf, 26 August 1960, Harper to Wulf, 31 August 1960, ACLU 1961 Vol. 12; Garrow conversations with Ruth Emerson and Mel Wulf; Wulf, "On the Origins of Privacy," *The Nation*, 27 May 1991, pp. 700–704.

67. Roraback, "Brief of Plaintiffs-Appellants," *Trubek et ux.* v. *Ullman*, #4979, Connecticut Supreme Court, 16pp., c.11 July 1960, A-391; Pilpel to Harper, 2 September 1960, Emerson Box 8; Wulf to Roraback, 20 September 1960, and Roraback to Wulf, 26 September 1960, ACLU 1961 Vol. 12; Workum to Vogt, 21 September 1960, and Vogt to Workum, 11 October 1960, PPFA II-184; Anita Ernst, Executive Committee Minutes, 22 September 1960, PPLC 12-E; *New Haven Register*, and *New Haven Journal-Courier*, 26 September 1960; *Civil Liberties*, October 1960; Pilpel to Vogt, 6 October 1960, PPFA II-184; *Hartford Times*, 10 October 1960; [Joseph W. Bartlett] to Earl Warren, *Poe* v. *Ullman*, and Warren notation, n.d., Warren Box 208; undated, unsigned clerk's notes, *Poe* v. *Ullman*, Douglas Box 1247; *Poe* v. *Ullman* Case File, U.S.S.C., RG 267, Box 3551, National Archives; James R. Browning to Rowland Watts, 10 and 17 October 1960, ACLU 1961 Vol. 12; 29 *U.S. Law Week* 3101 (11 October 1960); Cannon, "Brief of Defendant-Appellee," *Trubek et ux.* v. *Ullman*, #4979,

Connecticut Supreme Court, 10pp., c.30 August 1960, A-391 606–610 and Emerson Box 8, esp. p. 9; *Medical World News*, 9 September 1960, pp. 18–19; *New York Herald Tribune*, 22 September 1960, p. 19, and 24 September 1960; "Coming Up in Court," *America*, 15 October 1960, pp. 67–68. Kennedy's well-known 12 September 1960 speech to the Greater Houston Ministerial Association appears in full in Theodore C. Sorensen, ed., *Let the Word Go Forth: The Speeches, Statements, and Writings of John F. Kennedy* (New York: Delacorte Press, 1988), pp. 130–136, at 131.

68. Harper, "Brief for Appellants," *Poe et al.* v. *Ullman* and *Buxton* v. *Ullman*, U.S.S.C., O.T. 1960, #60 and 61, 72pp., PPLC 6-S, esp. pp. 9, 28–29, 72; Seymour, "Motion for Leave to File a Brief and Brief as Amici Curiae for Sixty-Six Doctors," *Buxton* v. *Ullman*, U.S.S.C., O.T. 1960, #61, 15pp., PPLC 6-S; Ernst and Pilpel, "Motion for Leave to File a Brief with Brief and Appendices as Amicus Curiae for the Planned Parenthood Federation of America," *Poe et al.* v. *Ullman* and *Buxton* v. *Ullman*, U.S.S.C., O.T. 1960, #60, 61, 53pp., PPLC 6-S; Osmond K. Fraenkel and Jerome E. Caplan, "Motion for Leave to File Brief for the American Civil Liberties Union and the Connecticut Civil Liberties Union as Amici Curiae," *Poe et al.* v. *Ullman* and *Buxton* v. *Ullman*, U.S.S.C., O.T. 1960, #60, 61, 21pp., PPLC 6-S, esp. pp. 5–10; *Wolf* v. *Colorado*, 338 U.S. 25, 27 (1949); *Palko* v. *Connecticut*, 302 U.S. 319, 325 (1937) ["implicit in the concept of ordered liberty"]; *Olmstead* v. *U.S.*, 277 U.S. 438, 478 (Brandeis, J., dissenting); Wulf Interview with Garrow; *Rochin* v. *California*, 342 U.S. 165 (1952); *Meyer* v. *Nebraska*, 262 U.S. 390, 399 (1923); *Pierce* v. *Society of Sisters*, 268 U.S. 510, 535 (1925); also see *Reynolds* v. *U.S.*, 98 U.S. 145 (1878), and *Jacobson* v. *Massachusetts*, 197 U.S. 11 (1905). See also Wulf, "On the Origins of Privacy," *The Nation*, 27 May 1991, pp. 700–704; see as well *Feldman* v. *U.S.*, 322 U.S. 487, 490 (1944) (acknowledging a "constitutional purpose . . . to maintain inviolate large areas of personal privacy").

69. Campbell to Leo Arffman, 10 October 1960, PPLM Box 106; Pilpel to Griswold, 19 September 1960, Griswold to Pilpel, 20 October 1960, Griswold to Harper, 7 October 1960, Harper to Griswold, 17 October 1960, PPLC 7-A; Cannon, "Brief for Appellee," *Poe et al.* v. *Ullman* and *Buxton* v. *Ullman*, U.S.S.C., O.T. 1960, #60, 61, 17pp., esp. pp. 13, 16.

70. Harper to Griswold, 27 October 1960, PPLC 7-A; Pilpel to Harper, 14 November 1960, PPFA II-184 and Emerson Box 8; *Trubek* v. *Ullman*, 147 Conn. 633, 165 A.2d 158; *New Haven Register*, 15 and 16 November 1960; *New Haven Journal-Courier*, 16 November 1960; *Hartford Courant*, 16 November 1960; *New York Times*, 16 November 1960, p. 28; Louis H. Pollak to Roraback, 18 November 1960, Pilpel to Vogt et al., 28 November 1960, Pilpel to Harper, 23 December 1960, Emerson Box 8; Anita Ernst, Board Minutes, 25 October 1960 and 12 January 1961, PPLC 12-E; Legislative Committee Minutes, 5 December 1960, PPLC 22-K; *Journal of the House*, pp. 281–282 (24 January); *Journal of the Senate*, pp. 353–354 (25 January); *New Haven Journal-Courier*, 29 December 1960, p. 20; *New York Daily News*, 29 December 1960, p. 12; *Hartford Courant* and *Waterbury Republican*, 30 December 1960; *New York Herald Tribune*, 30 December 1960, p. 3; *Hartford Times*, 30 December 1960, p. 19; *Medical World News*, 6 January 1961, pp. 17–18; *New Haven Register*, 29 January 1961; *New England Journal of Medicine*, 9 February 1961, p. 304; *Hartford Times*, 23 February 1961; *New York Times*, 24 February 1961, pp. 1, 16; Clerk's Office to Harper, 24 January 1961, Emerson Box 7. Representative Dorothy Miller of Bolton, PPLC's 1959 sponsor, also introduced a "reform" bill, H.B. 3741.

The *Yale Law Journal* essay, by James O. Freedman, noted both briefs' citations to the various Supreme Court precedents but complained that "these dicta concerning overt forms of intrusion furnish no basis for suggesting the existence of a right to privacy so sweeping in its terms that it would encompass the regulatory intervention of the anticontraceptive statute. Nor do they suggest any guides for defining and limiting so broad a right." Freedman did concede that "It is difficult to imagine any area of human activity which more reasonably ought to be beyond the reach of the state," and he also acknowledged that the Connecticut law "impinges upon a privilege far more basic to the individual's fulfillment and well being and to the protection of the married state than the liberty established in *Meyer* and *Pierce*." He concluded by suggesting that the Court could recognize "either the right to privacy or the more narrow marital right." "Connecticut's Birth Control Law: Reviewing a State Statute Under the Fourteenth Amendment," *Yale Law Journal* 70 (December 1960): 322–334, at 332–333. Also see Richard J. Regan, "The Connecticut Birth Control Ban and Public Morals," *Catholic Lawyer* 7 (Winter 1961): 5–10, 49, at 6, which wisely noted that the Connecticut statute was largely symbolic but that "controversies over symbols very often are fought more bitterly than controversies over realities."

71. [Charles Fried], "Bench Memorandum," *Poe* v. *Ullman*, *Buxton* v. *Ullman*, #60, 61, n.d., 22pp., Harlan Papers Box 117, esp. pp. 1, 10–13, 15–16, 19–21; Garrow conversation with Charles Fried; and Tinsley E. Yarbrough, *John Marshall Harlan* (New York: Oxford University Press, 1992), p. 310.

72. [Richard S. Arnold], "Nos. 60 & 61—The Birth Control Cases," n.d., 14pp., and [Arnold], "Memo on Nos. 60 & 61—The Merits," n.d., 12pp., Brennan Papers Box 55; Garrow conversation with Richard S. Arnold; and Arnold, "A Remembrance: Mr. Justice Brennan, October Term 1960," *Journal of Supreme Court History* 1991, pp. 5–8. On "justiciability," see Justice Frankfurter's subsequent comment on the term in his opinion in *Poe* v. *Ullman*, 367 U.S. 497, 508: "Justiciability is of course not a legal concept with a fixed content or suscepti-ble of scientific verification."

73. Garrow conversations with Catherine Roraback, Elizabeth Phillips, Nancy F. Wechsler, Jerold Israel, and Richard Arnold; Griswold Interview with Cheek, p. 38; Pilpel to Harper, 16 February 1961, Emerson Box 8; *Hartford Courant*, 26 and 28 February 1961; *New York Times*, 28 February 1961; Bea Hessel, "PPLC—The 1960s," 11 March 1983, 3pp., PPLC 3-I.

74. *Poe* v. *Ullman* Oral Argument Tapes, 1 and 2 March 1961, National Archives; "Arguments Before the Court: Birth Control," *U.S. Law Week* 29 (7 March 1961): 3257–3260; [Fred Jaffe], "Supreme Court Hearing on Connecticut Case," 1 and 2 March 1961, 7pp., PPFA II-184; *Medical News*, 24 March 1961, p. 20; *New York Times*, 2 March 1961, p. 14, 3 March 1961, p. 18; *New York Herald Tribune*, 2 March 1961, p. 6, 3 March 1961, p. 17, 5 March 1961; *New York Post*, 2 and 3 March 1961; *Time*, 10 March 1961, pp. 49–50. Also see *Hartford Times*, 1 and 2 March 1961; *Hartford Courant*, 2 March 1961, 3 March 1961, p. 4; *New Haven Register*, 2 and 3 March 1961; *Waterbury Republican*, 3 March 1961, p. 1; *Middletown Press*, 3 March 1961. The five-by-eight file cards which Harper used for his *Poe* oral argument are in the Harper files in the Emerson Papers, Box 7. All quotations from the March 1 portion of the oral argument have been verified with the original audiotape; the recording of the March 2 argument, however, is distorted by variable speed problems, and quotations for that portion have been drawn from press observer accounts.

75. Griswold Interview with Cheek, p. 38; Frances Ferguson to Bea Hessel, 24 March 1961, PPFA II-184 and Emerson Box 8; Anita Ernst, Board Minutes, 28 March 1961, PPLC 12-E; Fred Jaffe to Cass Canfield, 21 April 1961, PPFA II-184; UPI dispatch in *Waterbury Republican*, 3 March 1961, p. 1; *Time*, 10 March 1961, pp. 49–50.

76. Bea Hessel, "PPLC—The 1960s," 11 March 1983, PPLC 33-I. Detailed notes on the March 3 conference were taken by both Justice Brennan and Justice Douglas and appear respectively in Justice Brennan's 1961 Docket Book (Brennan Papers Box 407) and in Justice Douglas's Papers (Box 1247). Far more cryptic notes on the discussion appear on Chief Justice Warren's Docket Sheet for *Poe* (Warren Papers Box 374), and explicit conference vote tallies appear on both the Brennan and Warren Docket Sheets as well as on that of Justice Clark (Clark Papers Box C76). Also see the unattributed discussion in Bernard Schwartz, *Super Chief: Earl Warren and His Supreme Court* (New York: New York University Press, 1983), pp. 378–380, which in fact, although without footnotes, is drawn directly, with some editorial emendations, from Justice Brennan's conference notes. Internal evidence suggests that the Schwartz study does not draw upon the Douglas conference notes, which, perhaps surpris-ingly, are oftentimes distinctly more detailed and extensive than Justice Brennan's.

    As an authoritative and extremely impressive recent study emphasizes in correcting the erroneous but widely repeated descriptions that appear in many political science texts, "a jus-tice's vote is announced at the time he discusses the case" and "there is no formal vote per se" at the overall conclusion of a case's discussion. Hence, as one justice put it, "the vote goes from the most senior to the most junior." See H. W. Perry, *Deciding to Decide: Agenda Setting in the United States Supreme Court* (Cambridge: Harvard University Press, 1991), pp. 44–48.

My discussion of individual justices here draws upon conversations with Jesse Choper, George L. Saunders, Jr., Lawrence Wallace, Daniel K. Mayers, Charles Fried, Richard S. Arnold, Daniel A. Rezneck, James M. Edwards, and Jerold Israel, and upon correspondence from Joseph W. Bartlett and Bernard E. Jacob, as well as upon conversations with additional former clerks from other terms, including G. Edward White. A number of clerks from the 1960 Term have indicated that they have no recollections whatsoever concerning *Poe*. See Murray H. Bring (Warren) to Garrow, 11 June 1992, John D. French (Frankfurter) to Garrow, 19 June 1992, and James E. Knox, Jr. (Clark) to Garrow, 22 June 1992. Also see particularly Richard S. Arnold, "A Remembrance: Mr. Justice Brennan, October Term 1960," *Journal of Supreme Court History* 1991, pp. 5–8. Also note G. Edward White, *Earl Warren: A Public Life* (New York: Oxford University Press, 1982); on Justice Brennan, also see Edward V. Heck, "The Socialization of a Freshman Justice: The Early Years of Justice Brennan," *Pacific Law Journal* 10 (1979): 707–728; and Heck, "Justice Brennan and the Heyday of Warren Court Liberalism," *Santa Clara Law Review* 20 (1980): 841–887. On the now largely forgotten Charles E. Whittaker, who has been omitted from at least one otherwise comprehensive bibliography of all Supreme Court justices, see Henry J. Abraham, *Justices and Presidents* (New York: Oxford University Press, 1974), pp. 247–248, 287. On Potter Stewart, see Tinsley E. Yarbrough, "Justice Potter Stewart," in Lamb and Halpern, eds., *The Burger Court*, pp. 375–406.

77. [Frankfurter], "Re: Poe v. Ullman," 6 March 1961, FF-HLS II-70–376; Dan [Mayers] to "Dear Mr. Justice," n.d., 1pp., FF-HLS II-70–495 and 546. Perhaps quite surprisingly, twenty-nine years later Anthony Amsterdam insists that "my memory relating to *Poe* is a total blank." Amsterdam to Garrow, 28 May 1992.

78. Upson to Harper, 9 and 15 March 1961, Emerson Box 8; *Poe v. Ullman* Case File, U.S.S.C., O.T. 1960, #60, RG 267, Box 3551, National Archives; Frankfurter to Warren, 15 March [1961], Warren Box 354; Dan [Mayers] to "Dear Mr. Justice," n.d., 1pp., FF-HLS-II-70–441; Garrow conversations with Daniel K. Mayers and Anthony Fitzgerald; also see chapter two here, at note four.

79. "Birth Control Statute Brings Local Conviction," *Wallingford Post*, 6 April 1961, pp. 1, 15.

80. Harper, "Jurisdictional Statement," *Trubek v. Ullman*, U.S.S.C., O.T. 1960, #847, 24 March 1961, 14pp., *Trubek* Case File, RG 267, Box 3815, National Archives; Griswold, Executive Committee Minutes, 9 March 1961, Anita Ernst, Board Minutes, 28 March 1961, PPLC 12-E; Transcript of Hearing, Public Health and Safety Committee, 12 April 1961, pp. 12–23, Connecticut State Library, esp. p. 21; *New Haven Register*, 12, 13 and 27 April 1961; *Hartford Courant*, 13 April 1961, p. 28, 27 April 1961; *Waterbury Republican*, 13 April 1961; *New Haven Journal-Courier*, 13 April 1961; *Hartford Times*, 13 April 1961, p. 40, 27 April 1961, 6 and 9 May 1961; *Bridgeport Herald*, 16 April 1961; *Journal of the House*, pp. 881 and 973 (2 and 9 May).

81. Natalie Schwartz, Executive Committee Minutes, 4 May 1961, PPLC 12-E; Griswold, "Director's Report," [24 May 1961], PPLC 14-D; Fred Jaffe to Cass Canfield, 18 May 1961, PPFA II-184; Canfield, Text of Remarks, 24 May 1961, PPLM Box 106; [Griswold], Annual Meeting Minutes, 24 May 1961, PPLC 12-E; *New Haven Journal-Courier*, 25 May 1961; *New Haven Register*, 14 June 1961, p. 48. On Fowler Harper in this period, also see the *Register*, 30 April 1961, 8 May 1961, p. 33, and 21 May 1961. On Lucia Parks's earlier involvement, see *Bridgeport Post*, 17 April 1938; Parks, "1961–1964," n.d. [1983], 4pp., PPLC 33-I; and Garrow conversations with Lucia and Charles Parks. The hilarious essay from which Harper read is [Alan R. Novak], "Man, His Dog and Birth Control: A Study in Comparative Rights," *Yale Law Journal* 70 (June 1961): 1205–1209.

82. Dan [Mayers] to "Dear Mr. Justice," n.d., 1pp., FF-HLS-II-70–511, 512 et. seq., Dan [Mayers] to "Dear Mr. Justice," n.d., 1pp., FF-HLS-II-70–495 et seq., 70–546 et seq., and 70–644 et seq.; Tony [Amsterdam] to "Dear Mr. Justice," n.d., 2pp., FF-HLS-II-70–488; "Tony's draft," n.d., FF-HLS-II-70–622 et seq.; Harlan, "Memorandum to the Conference,"

3 June 1961, Harlan Box 117, Warren Box 476, Brennan Box 55, Clark Box A109; Garrow conversation with Charles Fried; undated, pencil-annotated 60pp. typescript draft, Harlan Papers, Box 117; Yarbrough, *John Marshall Harlan*, pp. 311–313. Also see particularly Charles Fried, *Order and Law* (New York: Simon & Schuster, 1991), pp. 72–73, 76, which mistakenly calls *Poe* "a criminal case" but terms the Harlan dissent "[t]he seminal statement of the constitutional right to privacy." See as well Fried, "The Conservatism of Justice Harlan," *New York Law School Law Review* 36 (1991): 33–52, at 35. Copies of all the printed draft circulations of different opinions appear in both the Warren Papers, Box 476, and the Brennan Papers, Box 55.

83. Garrow conversations with Charles Fried, Richard S. Arnold, Jesse Choper, Jerold Israel, Lawrence Wallace, James M. Edwards, Daniel A. Rezneck, George L. Saunders, Jr., and Daniel K. Mayers. Also see Bernard Jacob to Garrow, 28 May 1992, and especially Richard S. Arnold, "A Remembrance: Mr. Justice Brennan, October Term 1960," *Journal of Supreme Court History* 1991, pp. 5–8, at 6: "the Justice would always sit down with us and go over his notes when he returned from Conference."

84. Typescript draft of Douglas dissent, labeled "OK for printer 3/22/61 WOD," Douglas Papers Box 1247; Garrow conversations with Daniel A. Rezneck and Richard S. Arnold; Whittaker to Frankfurter, 5 June 1961 ("I agree"), FF-HLS-II-70–436; Clark to Frankfurter, 6 June 1961 ("Good riddance! Join me up"), FF-HLS-II-70–437 and Clark Box A109.

85. Garrow conversations with Richard S. Arnold, Jesse Choper, Jerold Israel, and Lawrence Wallace; Frankfurter, "Memorandum for the Conference," 15 June 1961, Harlan Box 117, Warren Box 476, and Brennan Box 55; Warren to Frankfurter, 16 June 1961, FF-HLS-II-70–305 and Warren Box 476. I am most deeply indebted to Judge Arnold, who reviewed his contemporaneous notes in some detail in the course of our discussion.

As Lawrence Wallace later noted, Justice Black's dissent did not speak to the merits, and Black of course certainly did not share John Harlan's view of Fourteenth Amendment due process liberty. And as Charles Fried has emphasized—see *Order and Law*, p.73—Harlan indeed took pleasure in demonstrating how his jurisprudence at times could indeed be more protective of individual rights than that of Black. On *Poe* also see Jesse H. Choper, *Judicial Review and the National Political Process* (Chicago: University of Chicago Press, 1980), p. 407, who describes it as involving a situation "where there was no realistic threat of deprivation of appellants' individual constitutional rights." The dismissal of *Trubek* v. *Ullman* appears at 367 U.S. 907.

86. *Poe et al.* v. *Ullman*, 367 U.S. 497, 501, 502, 504, 508. Also see Frankfurter's opinion in *Joint Anti-Fascist Refugee Committee* v. *McGrath*, 341 U.S. 123, 151 (1951); see as well *Rescue Army* v. *Municipal Court*, 331 U.S. 549, 571 (1947). But see *District of Columbia* v. *John R. Thompson Co.*, 346 U.S. 100, 113–114 (1953), where the Court observed that "The failure of the executive branch to enforce a law does not result in its modification or repeal." A well-known defense of the Frankfurter opinion appears in Alexander M. Bickel, "The Supreme Court, 1960 Term—Foreword: The Passive Virtues," *Harvard Law Review* 75 (November 1961): 40–79, at 59, 64; also see Bickel, *The Least Dangerous Branch* (Indianapolis: Bobbs-Merrill, 1962), pp. 143–156. Bickel in turn was answered by Gerald Gunther, "The Subtle Vices of the 'Passive Virtues'—A Comment on Principle and Expediency in Judicial Review," *Columbia Law Review* 64 (January 1964): 1–25, at 17–21. A superb critical note by Laurence D. Kay appears in the *California Law Review* 50 (March 1962): 137–143; also see *Mississippi Law Journal* 33 (December 1961): 138–139, *Columbia Law Review* 62 (January 1962): 106–132, *Columbia Law Review* 63 (April 1963): 688–707, and Arthur E. Bonfield, "The Abrogation of Penal Statutes," *Iowa Law Review* 49 (Winter 1964): 389–440, at 435–439.

87. *Poe* v. *Ullman*, 367 U.S. 497, 509.

88. *Poe* v. *Ullman*, 367 U.S. 497, 509, 555.

89. *Poe* v. *Ullman*, 367 U.S. 497, 509, 511, 513, 515, 517, 519–520, 521. Also see Norman Redlich, "Are There 'Certain Rights . . . Retained by the People'?," *New York University Law Review* 37 (November 1962): 787–812, at 799; and Note, *Women's Rights Law Reporter* 10 (Winter 1988): 177–208, at 184; but see Robert L. Calhoun, "Democracy and Natural Law," *Natural Law Forum* 5 (1960): 31–69.

90. *Poe v. Ullman*, 367 U.S. 497, 522, 524, 531–534, 539, 543, 548, 550, 552, 553, 554; *Olmstead v. U.S.*, 277 U.S. 438, 478 (1928); *Prince v. Massachusetts*, 321 U.S. 158, 166 (1944). Three months later, in replying to a writer who had offered his comments on the *Poe* dissent, Harlan added that "I cannot see that this statute is far removed from one that sought to punish a marital relationship not resulting in procreation by those possessing such capabilities. . . . The Connecticut statute seems to me to be a very different thing from one that undertakes merely to regulate or prohibit the sale of contraceptives." Harlan to Joseph O'Meara, 19 September 1962, Harlan Box 117. On the Harlan dissent, also see Fowler V. Harper, *Justice Rutledge and the Bright Constellation* (Indianapolis: Bobbs-Merrill, 1965), pp. 104, 339–340; Richard J. Regan, *American Pluralism and the Catholic Conscience* (New York: Macmillan, 1963), pp. 217–231, at 224–226; Sanford Levinson, "Constitutional Rhetoric and the Ninth Amendment," *Chicago-Kent Law Review* 64 (1988): 131–161, at 136 ("Harlan's opinion . . . is one of the greatest achievements in our judicial history"); Laurence H. Tribe and Michael C. Dorf, *On Reading the Constitution* (Cambridge: Harvard University Press, 1991), pp. 76–79; Melvin Wulf, "On the Origins of Privacy," *The Nation*, 27 May 1991, pp. 700–704, at 703; Nadine Strossen, "Justice Harlan and the Bill of Rights," *New York Law School Law Review* 36 (1991): 133–154, at 143; Bruce Ackerman, "The Common Law Constitution of John Marshall Harlan," *New York Law School Law Review* 36 (1991): 5–32, at 21–25; and Norman Dorsen, "Celebrating (?) the Bill of Rights," *Kentucky Law Journal* 80 (1991–92): 843–860, at 856. As noted before, *Mapp v. Ohio* was handed down the same morning as *Poe*, and Justice Clark's majority opinion included several comments about how the Fourth Amendment protected the right to privacy from unreasonable invasion or intrusion by a state. 367 U.S. 643, 654–657.

CHAPTER FOUR

1. *New York Times*, 20 June 1961, pp. 1, 23, 21 June 1961; *Washington Post*, 20 June 1961; *New York Herald Tribune*, 20 June 1961, 21 June 1961, pp. 1, 14; *Hartford Courant*, 20 June 1961, pp. 1, 3, 21 June 1961; *New Haven Register*, 20 June 1961, 21 June 1961, pp. 1, 52; *Hartford Times*, 20 June 1961, 21 June 1961; Griswold Interview with Cheek, pp. 31–32; Press Release, "Planned Parenthood League of Connecticut to Offer Contraceptive Services," 20 June 1961, PPLC 7-Q; *New Haven Journal-Courier*, 21 June 1961; *New Republic*, 3 July 1961, pp. 7–8.

2. *New York Times*, 21 June 1961, p. 36; *Washington Post*, 20 June 1961; *New York Herald Tribune*, 21 June 1961, pp. 1, 14, 24 June 1961; "Ahead: Acid Test of a Law," *Connecticut Life*, 27 July 1961, pp. 8–10; Pilpel to Harper, 20, 23, and 28 June 1961, Emerson Boxes 8 and 7 and PPFA II-184; Clifford R. Kaeser [to Harper], "Memo: What Constitutes the Practice of Medicine in Connecticut?," 26 June 1961, 11pp., Griswold to Harper (and Lucia Parks letter to doctors), 22 June 1961, Emerson Box 7; Griswold Interview with Cheek, p. 32.

3. Calderone to Somers H. Sturgis, 2 June 1961, PPLM Box 106; Buxton to Robert John, 26 June 1961, PPLC 7-J; Fran McCoy, Minutes, Medical Advisory Meeting, 28 June 1961, PPLC 15-E; PPLC press releases, 28 June 1961, PPLC 26-O1; Fred Jaffe to Canfield, "Connecticut Meeting," 29 June 1961, PPFA II-184; *New Haven Register*, 28 and 29 June 1961; *New Haven Journal-Courier*, 28 June 1961; *Hartford Courant*, 28 and 29 June 1961; Calderone to Buxton, 5 July 1961, PPFA II-184; *Hartford Times*, 12 July 1961.

4. Buxton to Ernst, 12 July 1961, PPLC 7-I; "Ahead: Acid Test of a Law," *Connecticut Life*, 27 July 1961, pp. 8–10; Rock, "We Can End the Battle Over Birth Control!," *Good Housekeeping*, July 1961, pp. 44–45, 107–110, and in *Reader's Digest* 79 (September 1961): 103–107; *Catholic Transcript*, 29 June 1961. Also see Rev. John A. O'Brien, "Let's Take Birth Control Out of Politics," *Look*, 10 October 1961, pp. 67–70 (excerpted in the 3 October 1961 *Hartford Times*); William H. Draper, Jr., "Birth Control: The Problem We Fear to Face," *Look*, 5 December 1961, pp. 39–44; and *New York Times*, 2 December 1961, p. 25 (and *Hartford Times*, 2 December, and *Hartford Courant*, 3 December), for an AP dispatch reporting critical comments by Jesuit scholar Rev. Dexter Hanley of Georgetown Law School.

5. Pilpel to Frances Ferguson, 5 July 1961, PPFA II-184; Harper, "Motion for Leave to File and

Petition for Rehearing of Decision," *Poe et al.* v. *Ullman*, 7 July 1961, 7pp., PPLC 6-P and *Poe* Case File, RG 267, Box 3551, National Archives, esp. pp. 2 and 5; Harper to Pilpel, 7 July 1961, and Harper to Gene Gressman, 11 July 1961, Emerson Box 8. Also see Harper's Application for Stay of Issuance of Mandate, granted by Justice Frankfurter on 19 July, and oppositions to both the petition and the application filed by Raymond Cannon in mid-July, *Poe* Case File and Emerson Box 8.

6. William J. Brennan, "Remarks," The Law Society, London, 10 July 1961, 17pp., Harlan Papers Box 587, at pp. 2–3; Fletcher to Canfield, 19 July 1961, Harper to Fletcher, 26 July 1961, Fletcher to Fred Jaffe, 2 August 1961, PPFA II-184. On Joseph F. Fletcher, see his *New York Times* obituary, 30 October 1991, p. D25.

7. Harper to Griswold, 24 July 1961, Griswold to Buxton, 27 July 1961, Buxton to Griswold, 28 July 1961, PPLC 7-A; *New Haven Register*, 2 and 3 August and 7 September 1961; *New Haven Journal-Courier*, 2 August and 7 September 1961; *New York Daily News*, 3 August 1961; *New York Post*, 3 August 1961; Griswold to Harry Cupp, 3 August 1961, PPLC 38-H; Edith M. Gates, "Report on Telephone Conversation . . ." [16 August 1961], Gamble 6–121; Harper to Griswold, and to Buxton, 18 August 1961, PPLC 7-G; Griswold to Clarence Gamble, 23 August 1961, PPLC 42-A1 and Gamble 6–121; *New York Herald Tribune*, 6 September 1961, p. 13.

8. *Stamford Advocate*, 22 September 1961; *Hartford Courant*, 15, 28 and 29 September 1961; *Hartford Times*, 15 and 29 September 1961; *Manchester Herald*, 15 September 1961; *Middletown Press*, 27 September 1961.

9. *Poe* v. *Ullman*, 368 U.S. 869; Griswold to Thomas Fletcher, 10 October 1961, PPLC 38-H; Harper to Pilpel, 12 October 1961, PPFA II-184; Margaret Dinsmore, New Canaan Minutes, 16 October 1961, PPLC 52-M; Frances Winkler, New Haven League Minutes, 17 October 1961, PPLC 41-A; [PPFA] *Planned Parenthood News*, Fall 1961, p. 3; *New York Times*, 27 October 1961; *New York Herald Tribune*, 27 October 1961; *New Haven Register*, 27 October 1961; *Hartford Courant*, 27 October 1961; *Hartford Times*, 27 October 1961. No indications exist that the Court, or any individual justice, gave anything more than habitual considera-tion to the *Poe* petition. An undated clerk's note in the Douglas Papers (Box 1247) observes "nothing new," and a similarly undated one in the Warren Papers (Box 208) by "RGG" [R. Gordon Gooch] also recommends denial.

10. *Connecticut Parenthood*, Winter 1961; Griswold Interview with Cheek, p. 33; *Medical Tribune*, 17 November 1961, 15 and 22 January 1962; PPLC Press Release, 1 November 1961, PPLC 26–O1; *New Haven Register*, 2 November 1961, p. 6, 3 November 1961, pp. 1, 16; *Hartford Times*, 2 November 1961; *New York Times*, 3 November 1961, p. 37; *New Haven Journal-Courier*, 3 November 1961, p. 1; *Hartford Courant*, 3 November 1961, p. 4; *Waterbury Republican*, 3 November 1961; *New York Herald Tribune*, 3 November 1961. On Arthur Gorman and his replacing the retiring Ab Ullman, see the *New Haven Journal-Courier*, 16 May 1961, p. 1; *New Haven Register*, 26 June 1961, pp. 10–11. Gorman was a New Haven native, and a graduate of Catholic University in Washington and Yale Law School, 1927; his obituary appears in the *Register*, 3 February 1967, pp. 1, 2.

11. *New Haven Register*, 3 November 1961, p. 16; Morris to Raymond E. Baldwin, n.d. [15 December 1961], Baldwin Papers Box 81; Morris in "Birth Control and the Law," CBS Reports, 10 May 1962, p. 21; Gereon Zimmerman, "Contraception and Commotion in Connecticut," *Look*, 30 January 1962, pp. 78–83.

12. "Report of Det. John A. Blazi—November 3rd, 1961," I-115-C, 4pp., Clark Papers; *New York Herald Tribune*, 4 November 1961, pp. 1, 10; *Hartford Courant*, 4 November 1961, p. 2; *Hartford Times*, 4 November 1961; *New York Times*, 4 and 5 November 1961; *New York Post*, 4 November 1961; *Waterbury Republican*, 5 November 1961, p. 68; *Bridgeport Herald*, 5 November 1961; *Newsweek*, 13 November 1961, p. 60; *Connecticut Parenthood*, Winter 1961; Gereon Zimmerman, "Contraception and Commotion in Connecticut," *Look*, 30 January 1962, pp. 78–83; *Brookfield Journal* and *New Milford Times*, 1 February 1962; Griswold Interview with Cheek, pp. 33–34; Berg in *New York Times*, 28 May 1989, pp. CN6–7, and in Fred W. Friendly and Martha J. H. Elliott, *The Constitution: That Delicate Balance* (New York:

Random House, 1985), p. 196; Garrow conversations with John A. Blazi, Harold Berg, Frances McCoy and Virginia Stuermer. On Julius Maretz's appointment as circuit prosecutor, see *New Haven Register*, 22 and 27 November 1960; his obituaries appear in the *New Haven Journal-Courier*, 29 November 1979, and the *Register*, 29 November 1979, p. 18. On John Blazi, see an extensive 1 February 1964 *New Haven Register* profile; on Harold Berg, see a 20 February 1976 *Register* item. A superb and justly famous study of New Haven politics and government in that era is Robert A. Dahl, *Who Governs? Democracy and Power in an American City* (New Haven: Yale University Press, 1961). Also see Nelson W. Polsby, *Community Power and Political Theory* (New Haven: Yale University Press, 1963), pp. 69–97; William L. Miller, *The Fifteenth Ward and the Great Society* (Boston: Houghton Mifflin, 1966); Allan R. Talbott, *The Mayor's Game: Richard Lee of New Haven and the Politics of Change* (New York: Harper & Row, 1967); and Fred Powledge, *Model City* (New York: Simon & Schuster, 1970).

13. *Hartford Courant*, 4 November 1961, p. 2; *New York Herald Tribune*, 4 November 1961, pp. 1, 10; *Connecticut Parenthood*, Winter 1961; "Report of Det. John A. Blazi—November 9th, 1961," 1pp., Clark Papers; Forsberg in *Hartford Courant*, 7 June 1985, pp. A1, A8; Forsberg Interview with Hubbell; Garrow conversations with John Blazi, Joan Bates Forsberg, Rosemary Stevens, and Robert B. Stevens; "Statement by Joan B. Forsberg," 2 p.m., 9 November 1961, 3pp., Clark Papers; "Statement by Rosemary Anne Stevens," 3:45 p.m., 9 November 1961, 2pp., Clark Papers. Both of the Stevenses subsequently became prominent scholars and higher education administrators; Robert Stevens's books include *Law School: Legal Education in America from the 1850s to the 1980s* (Chapel Hill: University of North Carolina Press, 1983); Rosemary Stevens's books include *American Medicine and the Public Interest* (New Haven: Yale University Press, 1971), and *In Sickness and in Wealth: American Hospitals in the Twentieth Century* (New York: Basic Books, 1989).

14. "Report of Det. John A. Blazi—November 10th, 1961," 1pp., Clark Papers; Maretz, "Information with Warrant," *State of Connecticut* v. *Estelle T. Griswold*, CR6–5653, and *State* v. *C. Lee Buxton*, CR6–5654, 10 November 1961, *Griswold* Record, Connecticut Supreme Court, A-427; Griswold Interview with Cheek, p. 35; Garrow conversations with Catherine G. Roraback and Lucia Parks; *New York Herald Tribune*, 11 November 1961, pp. 1, 7, 12 November 1961, p. 26; *New Haven Register* and *New Haven Journal-Courier*, 11 November 1961, pp. 1, 2; *New York Times*, 11 November 1961, p. 25; *Hartford Times*, 10 and 11 November 1961; *Hartford Courant*, 11 November 1961, pp. 1, 2, 12 November 1961; *New York Post*, 11 November 1961. Also see Frances Winkler, New Haven League Minutes, 27 November 1961, PPLC 41-A; *Medical Tribune*, 27 November 1961, p. 1; Zimmerman, "Contraception and Commotion," p. 83; Buxton, "Birth Control Problems in Connecticut," *Connecticut Medicine* 28 (August 1964): 581–584; and *New Haven Journal-Courier*, 7 June 1985, pp. 39, 56.

15. Pilpel to Harper, 14 November 1961, PPFA II-184 and Emerson Box 7; Pike to Canfield, 17 November 1961, and Canfield to Pike, 21 November 1961, Emerson Box 7; Rock to Buxton, 14 November 1961, PPLC 7-J; Buxton to Rock, 21 November 1961, PPLC 7-I; Director to SAC, New Haven, 26 May 1961, 100–389390–7, SAC, New Haven to Director, 14 November 1961 (II), 100–389390–11 and 12. Also see Pilpel to Harper, and to Jaffe, 20 November 1961, Emerson Box 7 and PPFA II-184. On the "Reserve Index," see Athan Theoharis, *Spying on Americans* (Philadelphia: Temple University Press, 1978), pp. 43–62.

16. "Report of Det. Harold Berg—Nov. 14th, 1961," and "Report of Det. Harold Berg—Nov. 15th, 1961," 1pp., "Statement by Marie W. Tindall, 2:30 p.m., Nov. 15, 1961," 2pp., "Statement by Rosemary Anne Stevens, 3:30 p.m., Nov. 16, 1961," 1pp., "Statement by Joan B. Forsberg, 9:50 a.m., Nov. 17, 1961," 1pp., Clark Papers; Garrow conversations with Harold Berg, Rosemary Stevens, and Joan Forsberg; Forsberg Interview with Hubbell.

17. Morris to Raymond E. Baldwin, n.d. [15 December 1961], Baldwin Box 81; Zimmerman, "Contraception and Commotion," pp. 80–81; "Statement by James Gibbons Morris, 11:35 a.m., 11–21–61," 2pp., Clark Papers.

18. *New Haven Register*, 24 November 1961, pp. 1, 3; *New Haven Journal Courier*, 24 November

1961, pp. 1, 2; *Hartford Times*, 24 November 1961; *New York Times*, 24 November 1961, 25 November 1961, p. 25; *New Haven Register/Journal-Courier*, 25 November 1961, p. 5; *Hartford Courant*, 25 November 1961; *Waterbury Republican*, 25 November 1961; *Christian Science Monitor*, 25 November 1961; Roraback, "Demurrer," *State of Connecticut* v. *Estelle T. Griswold*, and *State* v. *Buxton*, 24 November 1961, *Griswold* Record A-427, p. 2; Pilpel to Jaffe, "Connecticut Clinic Cases," 27 November 1961, Pilpel to Canfield, 8 December 1961, PPFA II-184; Jack Fox/UPI dispatch in *New York World-Telegram*, 6 December 1961, p. 37, and *Hartford Times*, among other papers.

19. Roraback, "Memorandum of Law in Support of Demurrers," *State of Connecticut* v. *Estelle T. Griswold* and *State* v. *Buxton*, 8 December 1961, 22pp., PPLC 7-B, esp. pp. 4–5, 14; Maretz and Clark, "Brief of State of Connecticut," *State* v. *Buxton*, 8 December 1961, 3pp., Clark Papers; Transcript of Proceedings, *State* v. *Buxton and Griswold*, 8 December 1961, 27pp., Clark Papers, esp. pp. 4–5, 12–13, 17, 19; *New Haven Register*, 9 December 1961, pp. 1, 2, 14 December 1961; *New Haven Journal-Courier*, 9 December 1961, p. 6; *New York Times*, 9 December 1961, p. 12; *Hartford Times*, 9 December 1961; Pilpel to Roraback, 14 December 1961, PPFA II-184.

20. Morris to Baldwin, n.d. [15 December 1961], and Baldwin to Morris, 27 December 1961, Baldwin Box 81.

21. J. Robert Lacey, "Memorandum on Demurrer to Information," *State of Connecticut* v. *C. Lee Buxton*, CR6–5654, and *State* v. *Estelle T. Griswold*, CR6–5653, Sixth Circuit Court, 20 [22] December 1961, 4pp., PPLC 7-C and *Griswold* Record A-427, pp. 1–10; *New Haven Register*, 22 December 1961, pp. 1, 2; *Hartford Times*, 22 and 23 December 1961; *Hartford Courant*, 23 December 1961, p. 2; *New York Times*, 23 December 1961; *Waterbury Republican*, 23 December 1961; Garrow conversations with Joan Forsberg; Griswold to Cordelia May, 26 December 1961, PPLC 42-A1; *Bridgeport Herald*, 31 December 1961.

22. Transcript of Proceedings, *State of Connecticut* v. *C. Lee Buxton and Estelle T. Griswold*, Sixth Circuit Court, 2 January 1961, 135pp., Clark Papers, esp. pp. 63, 84, 96, 100; *New Haven Register*, 2 January 1962, 3 January 1962, pp. 1, 9; *Hartford Times*, 2 January 1962, p. 17, 3 January 1962, p. 13; *New Haven Journal-Courier*, 3 January 1962, pp. 1, 4; *New York Times*, 3 January 1962, p. 16; *New York Herald Tribune*, 3 January 1962; *Hartford Courant*, 3 January 1962, pp. 1, 2; *Waterbury Republican*, 3 January 1962; Griswold Interview with Cheek, p. 36; Garrow conversations with Joan Forsberg, Rosemary Stevens, Robert Stevens, and Catherine G. Roraback.

23. *New York Herald Tribune*, 3 and 6 January 1962; *Newsweek*, 15 January 1962, p. 55; Zimmerman, "Contraception and Commotion in Connecticut," *Look*, 30 January 1962, pp. 78–83; *New Haven Register*, 13, 15 and 16 January 1962; *New Haven Journal-Courier*, 15 January 1962; *Waterbury Republican*, 16 January 1962; *The Reporter*, 8 January 1962, pp. 14–20, and 15 February 1962, p. 12; *Hartford Courant*, 13 and 17 January 1962; *Bridgeport Herald*, 14 January 1962, p. 1; Roraback letter in *Lakeville Journal*, 18 January 1962; *Commonweal*, 26 January 1962, p. 450; Roraback to Griswold, 10 January 1962, and Roraback to Pilpel, 1 February 1962, PPLC 7-F; Roraback, "Request for Finding" and "Draft Finding," *State* v. *Griswold and Buxton*, 31 January 1962, 16pp., Clark Papers; Pilpel, "Connecticut Planned Parenthood," 5 January 1962, Pilpel to Winfield Best, 6 February 1962, and Mary Calderone to Pilpel, 6 March 1962, PPFA II-184; Zelma Moss, Executive Committee Minutes, 8 March 1962, PPLC 12-F; Pilpel to Roraback, 14 March 1962, PPLC 7-F.

24. *Hartford Times*, 16 February 1962, 5 April 1962, p. 17, 26 April 1962, p. 21, 11 May 1962; *New Haven Register*, 21 February 1962, 8 March 1962, 6 and 9 April 1962, 7 May 1962; *Stamford Advocate*, 13 March 1962; Gary G. Barnes to Griswold, 25 March 1962, PPLC 38-H; *Connecticut Daily Campus*, 9 May 1962; Morris to Gorman, 2 February 1962, Clark Papers; *Bridgeport Herald*, 25 February 1962; Transcript of "Birth Control and the Law," CBS Reports, 10 May 1962 (produced and written by Stephen Fleischman), 28pp., esp. pp. 21–25. On the Chicago conflict, see Planned Parenthood Association of the Chicago Area (PPACA), "Chronological History of the Birth Control Controversy in Chicago," n.d. [c.June 1965], 11pp., Schlesinger Library 223–2–18; the files of "Citizens for the Extension of Birth Control

Services" (CEBCS), a very small Planned Parenthood front group, in Box 12 of the PPACA Papers; CEBCS, "A Report," 24 August 1962, 3pp., Myers Papers I-10, and especially John A. Rohr, "Birth Control in Illinois: A Study in Church-State Relations," *Chicago Studies* 4 (Spring 1965): 31–51. Also see *New York Times*, 30 September and 4 December 1962, and Albert Q. Maisel, "The New Battle Over Birth Control," *Reader's Digest* 82 (February 1963): 54–59. On a similar dispute in Phoenix, see a unanimous ruling by the Arizona Supreme Court that a state statute prohibiting the "advertising" of contraceptive information could *not* be applied or construed to forbid the distribution of noncommercial literature from Planned Parenthood announcing the availability of its birth control services to patrons of public health facilities. *Planned Parenthood Committee of Phoenix* v. *Maricopa County*, 375 P.2d 719 (31 October 1962). Also see Kenneth D. McCoy, Jr., *Louisiana Law Review* 23 (June 1963): 773–778.

25. *New Haven Register*, 20 May, 25 and 26 June 1962; *New Haven Journal-Courier*, 26 June 1962.

26. Clark, "Request for Counter Finding," *State* v. *Griswold and Buxton*, 19 February 1962, 8pp., Clark Papers; Griswold to Harry Cupp, 8 June 1962, and to Cass Canfield, 9 July 1962, PPLC 38-H and 7-F; Lacey, "Finding," *State* v. *Griswold and Buxton*, 25 July 1962, 16pp., PPLC 7-C and *Griswold* Record A-427; *New Haven Register*, 26 July 1962, pp. 1, 6; *Hartford Courant*, 27 July 1962; Roraback, "Motion to Correct Finding," *State* v. *Griswold and Buxton*, 31 July 1962, 1pp., PPLC 7-D and *Griswold* Record A-427; Lacey, "Memorandum on Motion to Correct Finding," *State* v. *Griswold and Buxton*, 22 August [13 September] 1962, *Griswold* Record, pp. 32–33; Roraback to Harper, 18 September 1962, PPLC 7-E; Roraback, "Assignment of Errors," *State* v. *Griswold and Buxton*, 26 September 1962, 5pp., *Griswold* Record, pp. 33–40; Juliet Taylor, Executive Committee Minutes, 27 September 1962, PPLC 12-F.

27. Pilpel to Fred Jaffe, 9 October 1962, PPFA II-184; Roraback to Lacey, 8 October 1962, Clark Papers; Roraback, "Appellants' Brief," *State* v. *Griswold and Buxton*, Appellate Division, 15 October 1962, 42pp., PPLC 7-D, esp. pp. 14, 20; Pilpel to Roraback, 15 October 1962, PPFA II-184 and Emerson Box 7; *Hartford Courant*, 20 October 1962, p. 3; *New Haven Register*, 20 October 1962; *Waterbury Republican*, 20 October 1962; *New York Times*, 20 October 1962; *Bridgeport Herald*, 21 October 1962; UPI dispatch in *Waterbury American* and *New Britain Herald*, 15 December 1962; Griswold to Helen Clarke, 18 December 1962, PPLC 7-E. The two other panel members were Erving Pruyn and Searles Dearington.

28. *Hartford Courant*, 28 August 1962, p. 2, 3 October 1962, 11 October 1962, p. 4, 7 January 1963; *New Haven Register*, 14 August 1962, 7 January 1963, p. 28; *Waterbury Republican*, 11 October 1962; *New York Times*, 18 November 1962; Juliet Taylor, Executive Committee Minutes, 27 September and 1 November 1962, PPLC 12-F; Kay Mali to Naomi T. Gray, 17 October 1962, and Gray to Alan Guttmacher, 28 November 1962, PPFA II-185; *Hartford Times*, 5 January 1963, 7 January 1963, p. 15, 9 January 1963, 13 January 1963, 15 January 1963, p. 13. Also see *Bridgeport Herald*, 12 and 26 August 1962.

29. Redlich, "Are There 'Certain Rights . . . Retained by the People'?" *New York University Law Review* 37 (November 1962): 787–812, at 798, 811–812; Wulf to Redlich, 15 January 1963, ACLU 1964 Vol. 16; Roraback, "*Griswold* v. *Connecticut*: A Brief Case History," *Ohio Northern University Law Review* 16 (1989): 395–401, at 401; Garrow conversations with Catherine G. Roraback.

Previous judicial and scholarly commentary on the Ninth Amendment was extremely scanty. See Knowlton L. Kelsey, "The Ninth Amendment of the Federal Constitution," *Indiana Law Journal* 11 (April 1936): 309–323, at 313 ("Natural rights . . . include . . . the right of privacy"); Robert H. Jackson, *The Supreme Court in the American System of Government* (Cambridge: Harvard University Press, 1955), pp. 74–75 ("the Ninth Amendment rights which are not to be disturbed by the Federal Government are still a mystery to me"); Bennett B. Patterson, *The Forgotten Ninth Amendment* (Indianapolis: Bobbs-Merrill, 1955), p. 55 ("the right of privacy may be" a right protected by the Ninth Amendment); Leslie W. Dunbar, "James Madison and the Ninth Amendment," *Virginia Law Review* 42 (June 1956): 627–643; Mitchell Franklin, "The Relation of the Fifth, Ninth and Fourteenth Amendments to the Third Constitution," *Howard Law Journal* 4 (June 1958): 170–192; O. John Rogge, "Unenumerated Rights," *California Law Review* 47 (December 1959): 787–827.

30. *State of Connecticut* v. *Estelle T. Griswold and C. Lee Buxton*, 3 Conn. Cir. 6; *New Haven Register*, 17 January 1963, pp. 1, 2; *Hartford Times*, 17 January 1963, pp. 1, 2; *Middletown Press*, 17 January 1963; *New York Times*, 18 January 1963, p. 2; *Medical Tribune*, 1 February 1963, pp. 1, 17; *Yale Daily News*, 8 February 1963, pp. 1, 4; Roraback, "Petition for Certification By Supreme Court of Errors," *State* v. *Griswold and Buxton*, 31 January 1963, 9pp., PPLC 7-E; Joseph B. Clark, "Respondent's Brief on Petition for Certification," *State* v. *Griswold and Buxton*, 6 February 1963, 4pp., Clark Papers; *State* v. *Griswold and Buxton* Record, A-427, pp. 42–50; Pilpel to Winfield Best, 7 February 1963, Pilpel, "PPFA—Connecticut," 18 February 1963, Pilpel to Roraback, 19 February 1963, PPFA II-184; *New Haven Register*, 21 February 1963, 3 March 1963; Roraback to Raymond E. Baldwin, and to Raymond G. Calnen, 26 February 1963, Clark Papers; Best to Bea Hessel, 26 March 1963, PPFA II-184.

31. *Journal of the House*, p. 327 (29 January); *Journal of the Senate*, p. 392 (30 January); Juliet Taylor, Executive Committee Minutes, 7 March 1963, PPLC 12-F; *Christian Science Monitor*, 16 February 1963; *New Haven Register*, 17 February 1963, 12 April 1963, p. 10, 22 April 1963; Dorothy D. Bromley, *Catholics and Birth Control* (New York: Devin-Adair, 1965), pp. 142–143; Hearing Transcript, Public Health and Safety Committee, 11 April 1963, Connecticut State Library, pp. 11–22; *Hartford Courant*, 12 April 1963, p. 19, 27 April 1963; *Hartford Times*, 12 April 1963; Rock, *The Time Has Come* (New York: Alfred A. Knopf, 1963); Rock, "It Is Time to End the Birth-Control Fight," *Saturday Evening Post*, 20 April 1963, pp. 10, 14; *Life*, 10 May 1963, pp. 37–40. On the Rock-Cushing friendship and Rock's book, see Loretta McLaughlin, *The Pill, John Rock, and the Church: The Biography of a Revolution* (Boston: Little, Brown, 1982), pp. 157–164.

32. Lucia Parks to Louise H. Fleck, 20 February 1963, Fleck to Parks, 27 February 1963, PPLC 18-N; Doris Allen, "Resumé of what I think I said . . ." 11 March 1963, Ruth Zelitch, New Haven League Minutes, 18 March and 8 April 1963, Zelitch to PPLC Board Members, 18 March 1963, Lucia Parks, "Report on Matters Brought Up By Planned Parenthood League of New Haven," 21 March 1963, PPLC 41-A; Bea Hessel to Naomi Gray, 27 March 1963, PPFA II-185; Lucia Jenney Parks, "1961–1964," n.d. [1983], 4pp., PPLC 33-I; Griswold to PPLC Officers and Board Members, 10 April 1963, PPLC 18-N; Griswold to Parks, 17 April 1963, PPLC 22-H; Garrow conversations with Gary Trebert, Frances McCoy, Ellen Switzer, Lucia and Charles Parks, Cornelia Jahncke, Hilda Crosby Standish, Elizabeth Phillips, Joan Forsberg, and Catherine G. Roraback.

33. Howson to Parks, 23 April 1963, Standish to Griswold, and Standish to "Dear Colleagues," 29 April 1963, Schlesinger Library 223–2–14; Parks, "A Suggested Statement," 27 April 1963, PPLC 12-F; "Resolution" to the Executive Committee, n.d. [c.2 May 1963], Juliet Taylor, Executive Committee Minutes, 2 May 1963, PPLC 12-B.

34. Juliet Taylor, Annual Meeting Minutes, 28 May 1963, PPLC 12-F; Griswold, "Director's Report," 1 May 1962—30 April 1963, in PPLC Annual Report, PPLC 14-D; Dorothy Giles, New Haven League Minutes, 3 June 1963, PPLC 41-A; *Hartford Courant*, 21 April 1963, p. 14, 24 April 1963, p. 10, 15 May 1963, pp. 1, 5; *Waterbury Republican*, 21 April 1963, 15 May 1963, pp. 1, 2; *New Haven Register*, 22 April 1963, 15 May 1963; *Bridgeport Herald*, 28 April 1963, p. 7; *Journal of the House*, pp. 1030 and 1132–1135 (8 and 14 May); Transcript of Proceedings, Connecticut General Assembly, House of Representatives, 14 May 1963, pp. 2321–2325; *New Haven Journal-Courier*, 15 May 1963; *New York Times*, 15 May 1963, p. 41, 17 and 19 May 1963; *Journal of the Senate*, p. 1064 (16 May); *Hartford Times*, 31 May 1963; Lee Buxton to Shirley Lapp, 1 August 1963, Buxton Scrapbook.

35. Pemberton to John E. Coons, 31 January 1963, Coons to Pemberton, n.d. [c.11 February 1963], Russell W. Gibbons to Pemberton, 12 February 1963, Pemberton to Coons, and to Gibbons, 14 February 1963, Pemberton to Coons, and to Gibbons, 18 March 1963, Pemberton to Roraback, 15 April 1963, Roraback to Pemberton, 22 April 1963, ACLU 1964 Vol. 16; Pilpel to Fred Jaffe, 24 April and 5 June 1963, PPFA II-184 and 185; George N. Lindsay, Jr., to Roraback, 8 July 1963, Roraback to Lindsay, 29 July 1963, Roraback to Pilpel,

30 July 1963, PPFA II-184; Pemberton to Roraback, 30 July 1963, and Pemberton to Gibbons, 9 August 1963, ACLU 1964 Vol. 16; *Hartford Times*, 6 and 20 August 1963; *Bridgeport Herald*, 11 August 1963; Roraback to Lacey, 13 August 1963, and to Raymond E. Baldwin, 23 August 1963, Clark Papers; *Hartford Courant*, 21 August 1963; Roraback to Pilpel, 23 August 1963, PPFA II-184; Roraback to Griswold, 26 August 1963, PPLC 7-F; Roraback to Pemberton, 29 August 1963, ACLU 1964 Vol. 16; Roraback, "Brief of Defendants-Appellants," *State of Connecticut* v. *Estelle T. Griswold and C. Lee Buxton*, #5485, Connecticut Supreme Court, 62pp., 30 August 1963, A-427 586–616, esp. pp. 16–19; Pilpel to Roraback, 20 August 1963, PPFA II-184.

36. *New York Times*, 5 August 1963, pp. 1, 12, 6 August 1963, pp. 1, 16, 7 August 1963, pp. 1, 18, 8 August 1963, pp. 1, 12; James O'Gara, "Birth Control and Public Policy," *Commonweal*, 23 August 1963, p. 504; John C. Knott, "The Catholic and Contraception," 22 August 1963, 4pp., Archives of the Archdiocese of Hartford; John A. O'Brien, "Let's End the War Over Birth Control," *Christian Century*, 6 November 1963, pp. 1361–1364. Also see Rosemary Ruether, "Why I Believe in Birth Control," *Saturday Evening Post*, 4 April 1964, pp. 12–14; *Bridgeport Herald*, 10 May 1964.

37. Clark, "Brief of State-Appellee," *State of Connecticut* v. *Estelle T. Griswold and C. Lee Buxton*, #5485, Connecticut Supreme Court, 21pp., 1 October 1963, A-427 617–627, esp. p. 15; *Hartford Times*, 19 October 1963, p. 3, 25 October 1963, p. 17, 12 November 1963, pp. 1, 2, 13 November 1963; *New Haven Register*, 10 and 11 November 1963, 12 November 1963, pp. 1, 2, 13 November 1963; *New Haven Journal-Courier*, 13 November 1963; *Hartford Courant*, 13 November 1963; Garrow conversations with Joseph B. Clark and Catherine G. Roraback; Juliet Taylor, Executive Committee Minutes, 21 November 1963, PPLC 12-F.

38. *New Haven Register*, 27 and 29 November 1963, 9 December 1963; *Waterbury Republican*, 10 December 1963, p. 4; *Bridgeport Post* and *Danbury News-Times*, 10 December 1963; Griswold to Thirja Muffatti, 18 December 1963, PPLC 46-O; Griswold to Naomi Gray, 13 March 1964, PPFA II-185; Garrow conversations with Frances McCoy, Hilda Crosby Standish, Gary Trebert, Ellen Switzer, Catherine G. Roraback, Lucia and Charles Parks, Cornelia Jahncke, Helen [Buxton] Rose, and Elizabeth Phillips.

39. Juliet Taylor, Annual Meeting Minutes, 28 April 1964, PPLC 12-G; *Hartford Courant*, 20 April 1964, p. 3, 30 April 1964, 12 May 1964, pp. 1, 5; Griswold, "Executive Director's Report," 1 May 1963–31 March 1964, PPLC 14-D; *State of Connecticut* v. *Griswold et al.*, 151 Conn. 544, 546, 200 A.2d 479; *Hartford Times*, 12 May 1964; *Waterbury Republican*, 12 May 1964; *New Haven Register*, 12 May 1964; *New York Times*, 12 May 1964, p. 39; *New Haven Journal-Courier*, 13 May 1964. On Cornelia Jahncke, a 1939 Vassar graduate and mother of four, see a profile in *Greenwich Time*, 10 May 1982, p. A3.

40. Jim Dull, "Point of View" Editorial, WELI Radio, 12 May 1964, PPLC 24-J; *New Haven Register*, 17 May 1964; Harper to Griswold, 27 May 1964, PPLC 7-H; Stephen Mann to Harper, "Standing of Defendants in Birth Control Case ..." 22 May 1964, Emerson Box 8; Natalie Schwartz, Board Minutes, 19 May 1964, PPLC 12-G; Roraback to John H. King, 18 May 1964, Raymond J. Cannon to Clark, 5 June 1964, Clark Papers; Garrow conversations with Joseph B. Clark; Harper to Pilpel, 13 June 1964, Pilpel to Harper, 16 June 1964, PPFA II-184; Ernst to Pilpel, 12 and 22 May and 1 June 1964, Ernst Box 593; Melvin Wulf to Robert B. Fleming, 14 May 1964, Ernst to Fleming, 15 May 1964, Fleming to Ernst, 21 May and 8 June 1964, Pilpel to Fleming, 16 June 1964, ACLU 1964 Vol. 16; Harper, "Notice of Appeal ..." *State* v. *Griswold and Buxton*, 22 July 1964, 2pp., Clark Papers; Harper to Nancy Wechsler, 28 July 1964, and Pilpel to Harper, 18 August 1964, Emerson Box 7.

41. Harper to Clark, 2 September 1964, Clark Papers; Harper, Jurisdictional Statement, *Griswold and Buxton* v. *State of Connecticut*, U.S.S.C., O.T. 1964, #496, 19pp., 14 September 1964, esp. pp. 3–6, 11–19; *Hartford Times*, 15 September 1964, 21 September 1964, p. 6; *New Haven Register*, 15 and 20 September 1964; *Hartford Courant*, 16 September 1964; *New Haven Journal-Courier*, 16 September 1964; *Waterbury Republican*, 16 September 1964; Pilpel to Harper, 21 September 1964, PPFA II-184. Harper's Jurisdictional Statement is reprinted in full in *Ohio Northern University Law Review* 16 (1989): 373–394.

42. Harper to Griswold, 24 September 1964, Griswold to Harper, 25 September 1964, PPLC 7-H; Natalie Schwartz, Executive Committee Minutes, 10 September 1964, and Board Minutes, 22 September 1964, PPLC 12-G; Dorothy Giles to Cornelia Jahncke, 12 September 1964, "Summary of Reports of President of New Haven Planned Parenthood League," 22 September 1964, Griswold to Fred Jaffe, 8 October 1964, PPFA II-185; Amelia Roe, New Haven Minutes, 13 October 1964, Jahncke to Giles, 17 October 1964, PPLC 41-B; [Griswold], untitled memo on 28 October PPFA meeting, 31 October 1964, Jaffe to Buxton, 2 November 1964, Henrietta Metcalf to [Doris] Allen, n.d., Jaffe to Giles, 5 November 1964, PPLC 44-A.

43. Natalie Schwartz, Executive Committee Minutes, 6 November 1964, PPLC 12-G; Elizabeth Whittall to Giles, 7 November 1964, PPLC 44-A; Schwartz, Board Minutes, 17 November 1964, PPLC 12-G; Mabel Jenkins to PPLC Board, 19 November 1964, PPLC 46-O; Emergency Executive Committee Minutes, 24 November 1964, PPLC 12-G and 41-B; Jahncke to Giles, 1 December 1964, PPLC 44-A; Jahncke to Buxton, 10 December 1964, PPLC 22-H; Giles to Jahncke, 14 December 1964, PPLC 44-A.

44. Clark, "Motion to Dismiss Appeal," *Griswold et al.* v. *State of Connecticut*, U.S.S.C., O.T. 1964, #496, 30 September 1964, 12 pp., esp. p. 9; *New Haven Register*, 4 October 1964, pp. 1, 2; *Hartford Times*, 5 October 1964; *Waterbury Republican*, 6 October 1964; *Yale Daily News*, 6 October 1964; Harper, "Reply to Motion to Dismiss," *Griswold* v. *Connecticut*, 13 October 1964, 6pp.; *Bridgeport Herald*, 25 October 1964, p. 11; Pilpel to Harper, 14 October 1964, Pilpel to Guttmacher and Jaffe, 15 October 1964, Pilpel to Jaffe, 22 October 1964, PPFA II-184.

45. *Hartford Courant*, *New Haven Register* and *New Haven Journal-Courier*, 16 October 1964; Dorsey, "Changing Attitudes Toward the Massachusetts Birth-Control Law," *New England Journal of Medicine* 271 (15 October 1964): 823–827, at 826; Cushing in a 1 August 1964 Foreword for Dorothy D. Bromley, *Catholics and Birth Control* (New York: Devin-Adair, 1965), p. xi; January 1965 Gallup results in *Hartford Courant*, 13 January 1965, and Hazel Erskine, "The Polls: The Population Explosion, Birth Control, and Sex Education," *Public Opinion Quarterly* 30 (Fall 1966): 490–501; Charles F. Westoff and Norman B. Ryder, "Methods of Fertility Control in the United States: 1955, 1960 and 1965," in William T. Liu, ed., *Family and Fertility* (Notre Dame: University of Notre Dame Press, 1967), pp. 157–169, at 168. Also see Ruth and Edward Brecher, "How New Methods and Changing Attitudes are Affecting the Battle Over Birth Control," *Good Housekeeping*, August 1964, pp. 59, 152–158; and a five part series in the *New York Post Daily Magazine*, 12–16 April 1965, p. 1, especially the April 13 installment.

46. Michael M. Maney, "Griswold v. Connecticut," 30 November 1964, 1pp., Harlan Box 235; [Michael W. Maupin], Griswold v. Connecticut, 1 December 1964, 4pp., Clark Box B202; James S. Campbell, Griswold v. Connecticut, 28 November 1964, 1pp., Douglas Box 1346; Ely, Griswold v. Connecticut, 23 November 1964, 4pp., Warren Box 267. Docket sheets recording the unanimous December 3 conference vote appear in both the Warren Papers, Box 379, and the Clark Papers, Box C81.

47. *New Haven Register*, 7 December 1964, pp. 1, 2, 8 and 13 December 1964; *Hartford Times*, 7 December 1964, p. 18; *Waterbury Republican*, 8 December 1964, p. 2; *New York Times*, 8 December 1964, p. 41; *Miami Herald*, 10 December 1964, p. G25. Also see *New Haven Register*, 10 November 1964; *Time*, 18 December 1964.

48. Garrow conversations with Elizabeth Phillips, Ruth Emerson, and Catherine G. Roraback; SAC, New Haven to Director, 30 November 1964, 100–389390–15; Harper, *Justice Rutledge and the Bright Constellation* (Indianapolis: Bobbs-Merrill, 1965); "The Collaborators," *National Review*, 17 July 1962, pp. 8–9; *New York Times*, 30 August 1963, p. 16, 4 November 1965, p. 54, 5 November 1965, p. 26, 13 November 1965, p. 17, 29 April 1966, p. 34. Also see Harper, "Mr. Justice Rutledge and the Fourth Amendment," *University of Miami Law Review* 18 (Fall 1963): 48–67, and a review of the biography by Robert F. Drinan in the *American Journal of Legal History* 9 (1965): 371–375.

49. *Griswold* Case File, U.S.S.C., O.T. 1964, #496, RG 267, Box 5946, National Archives;

Griswold to Emerson, 9 December 1964, PPLC 7-F and Emerson Box 7; Griswold to Harper, 9 December 1964, PPLC 7-H; Pilpel to Jaffe, 11 December 1964, PPFA II-184; Garrow conversations with Ruth Emerson, Catherine G. Roraback, Louis H. Pollak, Robert B. Stevens, Marvin Durning, David and Louise Trubek, and James M. Edwards; Louis H. Pollak, "Thomas I. Emerson, Lawyer and Scholar: Ipse Custodiet Custodes," *Yale Law Journal* 84 (March 1975): 638–655; Pollak, "Thomas I. Emerson: Pillar of the Bill of Rights," *Yale Law Journal* 101 (November 1991): 321–326; Emerson and David Haber, *Political and Civil Rights in the United States* (Boston: Little, Brown, 1952, 2nd ed., 1958). Also see Emerson, "Freedom of Association and Freedom of Expression," *Yale Law Journal* 74 (November 1964): 1–35; Emerson, "Law as a Force for Social Progress," *Connecticut Law Review* 18 (Fall 1985): 1–5; Emerson, *Young Lawyer for the New Deal: An Insider's Memoir of the Roosevelt Years* (Savage, MD: Rowman and Littlefield, 1991); Norman Dorsen, "Thomas Irwin Emerson," *Yale Law Journal* 85 (March 1976): 463–466; *New York Times*, 22 June 1991, p. 21; Guido Calabresi, "Tom Emerson: The Scholar as Hero," *Yale Law Journal* 101 (November 1991): 315–316; Dorsen, "In Memory of Tom Emerson," *Yale Law Journal* 101 (November 1991): 317–320; Sigmund Diamond, *Compromised Campus* (New York: Oxford University Press, 1992), pp. 211, 213–214.

50. Griswold to Emerson, 9 December 1964, PPLC 7-F and Emerson Box 7; Pilpel to Jaffe, 11 December 1964, PPFA II-184; Emerson to E. P. Cullinan, 17 December 1964, *Griswold* Case File, Box 5946 and Emerson Box 7; Emerson to Arthur E. Bonfield, 17 December 1964, Pilpel to Emerson, 22 and 23 December 1964, Emerson to Pilpel, 29 December 1964, Buxton to Pilpel, 7 January 1965, Emerson Box 7; Natalie Schwartz, Executive Committee Minutes, 7 January 1965, PPLC 12-H; Griswold to Miriam Harper, 11 January 1965, PPLC 7-H; *New Haven Register*, 8 January 1965, pp. 1, 2; *New York Times*, 9 January 1965, p. 25; *Yale Daily News*, 11 January 1965; *Yale Law Report*, Winter 1965, p. 32, and Spring 1965, pp. 30–33; Emerson in "Fowler Vincent Harper," *Yale Law Journal* 74 (March 1965): 599–605, at 602.

51. Garrow conversations with Joseph B. Clark; Roger Hunting to Clark, 18 December 1964, Clark to Hunting, 22 December 1964, Melvin Wulf to Clark, 21 December 1964, Clark to Wulf, 29 December 1964, Seymour to Clark, 8 January 1965, Clark to Seymour, 12 January 1965, Fleming to Clark, 7 January 1965, Clark to Fleming, 12 January 1965, Clark to Mancini, 22 January 1965, Mancini to Judge Zarrilli, 25 January 1965, Clark Papers; *New Haven Register*, 22 January 1964, p. 1, 25 January 1965, 15 February 1965.

52. Emerson to E. P. Cullinan, 14 January 1965, *Griswold* Case File, Box 5946; Pilpel to Jaffe, 22 January 1965, Eleanor M. Fox to Jaffe, 22 January 1965, Jaffe to Emerson, and to Fox, 26 January 1965, Pilpel to Jeannie Rosoff and Jaffe, 29 January 1965, Emerson to Jaffe, 2 February 1965, PPFA II-184; Buxton to Emerson, n.d., Emerson Box 7; Buxton to Seymour, 3 February 1965, PPFA II-184; Jahncke to Frances Ferguson, 12 January 1965, PPLC 19-B; *Bridgeport Herald*, 17 January 1965, pp. 1, 16; *Hartford Courant*, 21 January 1965; *Hartford Times*, 21 January and 3 February 1965; Natalie Schwartz, Board Minutes, 26 January 1965, Juliet Taylor, Emergency Executive Committee Minutes, 2 February 1965, Jahncke to Dorothy Giles, 2 February 1961, PPLC 12-H; Giles to Jahncke, [9 February 1965], PPLC 41-B; Lucia Parks, Executive Committee Minutes, 8 March 1965, PPLC 12-H; Amelia Roe, New Haven Minutes, 11 March 1965, PPLC 41-B; Natalie Schwartz, Board Minutes, 16 March 1965, PPLC 12-H; Jahncke to Naomi Gray, 18 March 1965, PPLC 38-C. During an extended late February–early March visit to Tucson, Arizona, Buxton and his wife had the opportunity to meet the ageing Margaret Sanger, whose son Grant had been a medical school classmate of Lee's. Buxton to Emerson, n.d. [February 1965], Emerson Box 7; Garrow conversation with Helen [Buxton] Rose.

53. Emerson, "Brief for Appellants," *Griswold* v. *Connecticut*, U.S.S.C., O.T. 1964, #496, 11 February 1965, esp. pp. 12, 79, 82, 85, 87. Also see a 20 February 1965 letter from Catherine Roraback, explaining the Griswold-Buxton brief's disinclination to advance any desuetude argument, as quoted extensively in Linda and William Rogers, "Desuetude as a Defense," *Iowa Law Review* 52 (August 1966): 1–30, at 8, 15.

54. Ernst, Pilpel and Wechsler, "Motion for Leave to File a Brief with Brief and Appendices as Amicus Curiae for Planned Parenthood Federation of America," *Griswold* v. *Connecticut*, U.S.S.C., O.T. 1964, #496, 15 February 1965, 40pp.; Seymour and Eleanor M. Fox, "Brief as Amici Curiae for Drs. John M. Adams et al.," *Griswold* v. *Connecticut*, 12 February 1965, 19pp.; Fleming, "Motion for Leave to File a Brief with Brief and Appendix as Amicus Curiae for the Catholic Council on Civil Liberties," *Griswold* v. *Connecticut*, 15 February 1965, 15pp., at 7; Rhoda H. Karpatkin and Melvin L. Wulf, "Motion for Leave to File Brief for the American Civil Liberties Union and the Connecticut Civil Liberties Union and Brief Amici Curiae," *Griswold* v. *Connecticut*, 26 February 1965, 18pp., at 11, 16. Also see Emerson to Wulf, 4 March 1965, expressing anger that the CCLU, of which he was the current chairman, had been included in the ACLU brief without any express authorization or consideration of the apparent conflict of interest, and Wulf to Emerson, 9 March 1965, explaining that everything had simply been modeled on the one in *Poe*. ACLU 1964 Vol. 16 and Emerson Box 7.

55. *New Haven Register*, 12 February 1965, pp. 1, 2, 16 February and 10 March 1965; *Hartford Courant*, 13 and 16 February 1965; *Waterbury Republican*, 13 and 16 February 1965; *New York Herald Tribune*, 16 February 1965; *Bridgeport Herald*, 26 February 1965, p. 2; *Hartford Times*, 9 March 1965; *Time*, 26 February 1965, p. 50; *Medical World News*, 12 February 1965, 12 March 1965, p. 78; Information Center on Population Problems, "Birth Control and the Law," 20pp., April 1965; Clark to Peter Smith, 17 February 1965, Clark Papers; Morris Ernst to Emerson, 17 February 1965, Emerson to Ernst, 25 February 1965, Emerson Box 7; Pilpel to John F. Davis, 3 March 1965, Clark Papers; Pilpel to Emerson, 3 March 1965, Emerson to Pilpel, 4 March 1965, Emerson Box 7.

56. Clark, "Brief for Appellee," *Griswold* v. *Connecticut*, U.S.S.C., O.T. 1964, #496, 9 March 1965, 34pp., at 20 and 12; *New Haven Register*, 11 March 1965, pp. 1, 2, 19 March 1965; *Hartford Courant*, 12 March 1965, p. 10; *Waterbury Republican*, 12 March 1965; Earl Warren notations on John Hart Ely memo, 10 March 1965, Warren Box 267; John F. Davis to Pilpel, 15 March 1965, PPFA II-184; E. P. Cullinan to Emerson, 16 March 1965, Emerson Box 7; Roraback to Buxton, 24 March 1965, Buxton Scrapbook. Also see Emerson and Roraback, "Reply Brief for Appellants," *Griswold* v. *Connecticut*, 25 March 1965, 5pp., Emerson Box 7 and PPLC 7-N.

57. *New York Times*, 3 March 1965, p. 31, 4 March 1965, p. 30; Joseph L. Dorsey, "Morals in Massachusetts," *Commonweal*, 30 April 1965, pp. 188–190; Dorsey, "Massachusetts Liberalizes Birth Control Law," *Dartmouth Medical School Quarterly* 3 (Summer 1966): 8–12. Also see Kingsbury Browne, Jr., "Birth Control in Massachusetts," *Boston Bar Journal*, March 1965, pp. 7–10; [PPLM] *Planned Parenthood News*, Spring 1965, and the extensive materials in the PPLM Papers, Boxes 101 and 102.

58. *Journal of the House*, p. 137 (11 February); *Journal of the Senate*, p. 177 (18 February); *Hartford Courant*, 20 and 24 March 1965; Hearing Transcript, Public Health and Safety Committee, 23 March 1965, pp. 1, 3–6, Connecticut State Library; *Hartford Times*, 24 March 1965, p. 35. On Connecticut's long overdue 1964–1965 reapportionment experience, see *Butterworth* v. *Dempsey*, 229 F.Supp. 754 (D. Conn. 1964), affirmed *sub nom. Pinney* v. *Butterworth*, 378 U.S. 564 (22 June 1964); Lieberman, *The Power Broker*, p. 326; and especially I. Ridgway Davis, *The Effects of Reapportionment on the Connecticut Legislature—Decade of the Sixties* (New York: National Municipal League, 1972).

59. Garrow conversations with Michael M. Maney, Michael W. Maupin, James S. Campbell, S. Paul Posner, Lee A. Albert, Stephen Goldstein, and Stephen Breyer; Monroe Price to Garrow, 30 June 1992, Charles R. Nesson to Garrow, 15 June 1992; *Estes* v. *Texas*, 381 U.S. 532 (1965); *Dombrowski* v. *Pfister*, 380 U.S. 479 (1965); *Hanna* v. *Plumer*, 380 U.S. 460 (1965); Ely, "Bench Memorandum," *Griswold* v. *Connecticut*, 26 February 1965, Warren Box 267, esp. pp. 15–23, 28–29; *Yick Wo* v. *Hopkins*, 118 U.S. 356, 375 (1886). Also see "Abstention and Certification in Diversity Suits," *Yale Law Journal* 73 (April 1964): 850–872. Twenty-seven years later Ely explained that "I literally do not remember anything about the Chief's and my interchange concerning *Griswold* that would not have been reflected in the memoranda."

Warren "had a close social relationship with his clerks, but the great bulk of our professional communication was done on paper." Ely to Garrow, 28 May 1992. Also see Dennis M. Flannery to Garrow, 20 June 1992: "I have no information that would be relevant." On Justice White's basketball-playing, also see J. Harvie Wilkinson III, *Serving Justice* (New York: Charterhouse, 1974), p. 40.

60. Garrow conversations with Cornelia Jahncke, Lucia and Charles Parks, Catherine G. Roraback; Transcript of Proceedings, *Griswold* v. *Connecticut*, U.S.S.C., O.T. 1964, #496; Audiotape of *Griswold* Oral Argument, National Archives; *Lochner* v. *New York*, 198 U.S. 45 (1905); *Meyer* v. *Nebraska*, 262 U.S. 390 (1923); *Pierce* v. *Society of Sisters*, 268 U.S. 510 (1925); Griswold Interview with Cheek, p. 38; *New Haven Journal-Courier*, 30 and 31 March 1965; UPI dispatch in *Naugatuck Daily News*, 30 March 1965. A nineteen-page Emerson outline entitled "Griswold v. Connecticut—Oral Argument," is in Emerson Box 7. In later acknowledging that "The lawyer's problem with the case was that the issue did not readily fit into any existing legal pigeonhole," Emerson also conceded that his First Amendment argument "was relatively weak." Emerson, "Nine Justices in Search of a Doctrine," *Michigan Law Review* 64 (December 1965): 219–234, at 219–220, 221.

61. *New Haven Journal-Courier*, 29 March 1965; Garrow conversations with Joseph B. Clark; Transcript of Proceedings, *Griswold* v. *Connecticut*, U.S.S.C., O.T. 1964, #496; Audiotape of *Griswold* Oral Argument, National Archives; *Sanger* v. *People*, 251 U.S. 537 (1919); *Gardner* v. *Massachusetts*, 305 U.S. 559 (1938); *New Haven Journal-Courier*, 31 March 1965; *New York Times*, 30 March 1965, p. 7, 31 March 1965, pp. 41, 46; *Hartford Courant*, 30 March 1965, 31 March 1965, p. 10; *New Haven Register*, 30 and 31 March 1965; *Washington Post*, 30 March 1965; *Hartford Times*, 30 March 1965; UPI dispatch in *Naugatuck Daily News*, 30 March 1965; *New York Daily News*, 31 March 1965, p. 10; *New York Herald Tribune*, 31 March 1965. On Joseph B. Clark, see the *New Haven Register*, 11 May 1961; on his subsequent appointment as a Connecticut Superior Court judge, see the *Register*, 27 January 1984; also see *Hartford Courant*, 9 April 1988, pp. C1, C7.

62. Warren annotations on page one of Ely's "Bench Memorandum," Griswold v. Connecticut, 26 February 1965, Warren Box 267; William O. Douglas, Conference Notes, *Griswold* v. *Connecticut*, 2 April 1965, 3pp., Douglas Box 1346; William J. Brennan, Docket Book Conference Notes, *Griswold* v. *Connecticut*, 2 April 1965, Brennan Box 411; Garrow conversations with Stephen Breyer, Stephen Goldstein, Paul Posner, and Michael Maney; *Schware* v. *Board of Bar Examiners*, 353 U.S. 232 (1957); *Aptheker* v. *Secretary of State*, 378 U.S. 500 (1964). The high degree of congruence and agreement between the Douglas and Brennan notes is extremely striking. On the White and Goldberg nominations, see Henry J. Abraham, *Justices and Presidents* (New York: Oxford University Press, 1974), pp. 253–258; on White also see Daniel C. Kramer, "Justice Byron R. White," in Lamb and Halpern, eds., *The Burger Court*, pp. 407–432; on Goldberg, also see Daniel P. Moynihan, ed., *The Defenses of Freedom: The Public Papers of Arthur J. Goldberg* (New York: Harper & Row, 1966), and David L. Stebenne's forthcoming biography, *Arthur J. Goldberg, New Deal Liberal* (Oxford University Press). Docket Sheets and/or conference lists all clearly showing a 7 to 2 outcome on *Griswold* and the April 5 assignment to Douglas appear in Brennan Box 118, Warren Box 379, and Clark Box C81; both the Warren and Clark docket sheets also each contain a fragmentary note or two on conference discussion comments. Also see the unfootnoted discussion in Bernard Schwartz, *Super Chief: Earl Warren and His Supreme Court* (New York: New York University Press, 1983), pp. 577–580, again based solely on the Brennan notes, as well as Schwartz, *The Unpublished Opinions of the Warren Court* (New York: Oxford University Press, 1985), pp. 227–229, 237; Schwartz, *The Ascent of Pragmatism* (Reading, MA: Addison-Wesley, 1990), pp. 295–296, 409; Schwartz, *The New Right and the Constitution* (Boston: Northeastern University Press, 1990), pp. 55–57.

63. "Byron" to "Bill," n.d., 3pp., and "WOD" to "Tom," n.d., 1pp., Douglas Box 1346; *Escobedo* v. *Illinois*, 378 U.S. 478 (1964); *Robinson* v. *California*, 370 U.S. 660 (1962); *Reynolds* v. *Sims*, 377 U.S. 533 (1964). Also see Howard Ball's reference, based upon a 1986 interview comment made to him by Justice White, to Douglas's taste for ribald jokes in Stephen L. Wasby,

ed., *"He Shall Not Pass This Way Again": The Legacy of Justice William O. Douglas* (Pittsburgh: University of Pittsburgh Press, 1990), p. 26 n.8.

64. Garrow conversations with Joseph B. Clark and Catherine G. Roraback; Emerson to John P. Frank, 2 April 1965, Emerson Box 35; Emerson to Joseph Forer, 5 April 1965, Emerson to Buxton, and to Griswold, 8 April 1965, Griswold to Emerson, 13 April 1965, Emerson Box 7. Also see Emerson comments in *Hartford Courant*, 7 June 1985, pp. A1, A8, and *New York Times*, 28 May 1989, pp. CN6–CN7.

65. Douglas, Handwritten and Typescript Drafts of Opinion for the Court, *Griswold v. Connecticut*, 16 April 1965, Douglas Box 1346; Steven B. Duke in Wasby, ed., *"He Shall Not Pass This Way Again"*, p. 133; Garrow conversation with James S. Campbell.

66. Campbell to Douglas, 22 April 1965, Douglas Box 1346; Douglas 'Print #3,' 23 April 1965, Brennan Box 130; 4pp. draft of Brennan to Douglas letter, Brennan Box 130, and Brennan to Douglas, 24 April 1965, 3pp., Douglas Box 1346 and Brennan Box 130; Brennan Chambers, October Term 1964, pp. ii–xv; Brennan commenting on Douglas in Nat Hentoff, "The Justice Breaks His Silence," *Playboy*, July 1991, pp. 120–122, 154–158, at 122; Garrow conversations with James S. Campbell and S. Paul Posner; *NAACP v. Alabama*, 357 U.S. 449 (1958). Also see Schwartz, *The Unpublished Opinions of the Warren Court*, pp. 231–239; Schwartz, *Super Chief*, pp. 578–580; Schwartz, *Ascent of Pragmatism*, pp. 296–297; Schwartz, *The New Right*, pp. 56–57; David M. O'Brien, *Storm Center: The Supreme Court in American Politics* (New York: W. W. Norton & Co., 1986), pp. 255–256.

67. Posner to Brennan, [27 April 1965], 2pp., and Douglas 'Print #5,' Brennan Box 130; Garrow conversations with S. Paul Posner. Also see Howard Ball in Wasby, ed., *"He Shall Not Pass This Way Again"*, p. 27 n.13.

68. Ely to Warren, "Justice Douglas' Opinion in No. 496, *Griswold v. Connecticut*," 27 April 1965, 5pp., Warren Box 520. Also see again Ely's 1992 comments as quoted in note 59 above.

69. Clark Note on page one of 28 April Douglas opinion, Clark Box A178; Clark to Douglas, 28 April 1965, Goldberg to Douglas, 29 April 1965, Douglas Box 1346; Harlan to Douglas, 29 April 1965, Harlan Box 235 and Douglas Box 1346; Stewart, "Memorandum to the Conference," 29 April 1965, Harlan Box 235, Douglas Box 1346, Clark Box A178, and Warren Box 520; Garrow conversations with James S. Campbell, Stephen Goldstein, and Lee A. Albert.

70. Garrow conversations with James S. Campbell, Stephen Goldstein, and Stephen Breyer; Stewart Draft Opinion, 5 May 1965, Brennan Box 130, Harlan Box 235, Warren Box 520, Clark Box A211; Campbell to Douglas, 7 May 1965, Goldberg to Douglas, 14 May 1965, Douglas Box 1346; and particularly the suggestive but chronologically garbled discussion of Goldberg's recollections in Howard Ball and Phillip J. Cooper, *Of Power and Right: Hugo Black, William O. Douglas, and America's Constitutional Revolution* (New York: Oxford University Press, 1992), p. 288; as well as Dorothy Goldberg, *A Private View of a Public Life* (New York: Charterhouse, 1975), p. 176.

71. Garrow conversations with Stephen Goldstein, Stephen Breyer, and Lee A. Albert; Ely to Warren, "Justice Goldberg's Concurrence in No. 496, *Griswold v. Connecticut*," 17 May 1965, 4pp., Warren Box 520; Goldberg 'Print #4,' 18 May 1965, Brennan Box 130, Harlan Box 235, Clark Box A211, Warren Box 520; White 'Print #1,' 19 May 1965, and 'Print #3,' 20 May 1965, Brennan Box 130, Harlan Box 235, Clark Box A211; Campbell to Douglas, 19 May 1965, Douglas Box 1346; Ely to Warren, "Justice White's Concurrence in No. 496, *Griswold v. Connecticut*," 19 May 1965, 2pp., Warren Box 520; Brennan Chambers, October Term 1964, pp. ii–xv.

72. Natalie Schwartz, Executive Committee Minutes, 27 April 1965, PPLC 12-H; Griswold, "Executive Director's Report," 31 March 1965, 3pp., PPLC 14-D; *Bridgeport Herald*, 9 May 1965; Dorothy Giles, New Haven "Annual Report," and Amelia Roe, New Haven Minutes, 11 May 1965, PPLC 41-B; *Journal of the House*, pp. 971 and 1061–1065 (12 and 18 May 1965); Marion Miller, Executive Committee Minutes, and Natalie Schwartz, Annual Meeting Minutes, 13 May 1965, PPLC 12-H; *Waterbury Republican*, 19 May 1965, p. 13; *Hartford Courant*, *New Haven Register*, and *Hartford Times*, 19 May 1965; *Journal of the Senate*, p. 1008 (20

May 1965). In early May PPLC's two remaining and long-dormant clergy cases that originally had been filed in 1959 on behalf of ministers C. Lawson Willard and Luther Livingston
were dismissed because they had been inactive for more than five years; the third had been
withdrawn in 1961 when Reverend George Teague had left New Haven. After *Poe* none of
them had stood much chance of satisfying a "case or controversy" requirement. See Roraback
to Griswold, 15 September 1961 and 12 May 1965, PPLC 6-I.

73. Black draft opinion, 11pp. handwritten, 8pp. typed, 13 May 1965, Black Box 383; Black 'Print
#1,' 21 May 1965, and 'Print #2,' 22 May 1965, Black Box 383, Harlan Box 235, Warren Box
520, Clark Box A211; Stewart 'Print #2,' 25 May 1965, Harlan Box 235, Warren Box 520,
Clark Box A211; *Lamont* v. *Postmaster General*, 381 U.S. 301, 308 (24 May 1965); Brennan
Chambers, October Term 1964, pp. ii–xv; Campbell to Douglas, 28 May 1965, Harlan to
Douglas, 2 June 1965, Douglas Box 1346; Harlan draft opinion, 8pp. handwritten, and Harlan
'Print #1,' 2 June 1965, Harlan Box 235; White 'Print #5,' 3 June 1965, Goldberg 'Print #9'
(II), 4 June 1965, Brennan Box 130, Harlan Box 235, Warren Box 520 and Clark Box A211;
Garrow conversations with James S. Campbell, Stephen Goldstein, Stephen Breyer, Michael
Maney, Lee A. Albert, and S. Paul Posner; Ball and Cooper, *Of Power and Right*, p. 288;
Goldberg, *A Private View of a Public Life*, p. 176; Schwartz, *Super Chief*, pp. 579–580. Also see
Douglas to Clark, 21 May 1965, Douglas Box 1346 and Clark Box A178.

Douglas *had* cited the Brandeis dissent in *Olmstead* in a concurring opinion two years earlier in which he had spoken of "the need for a pervasive right of privacy against government
intrusion." *Gibson* v. *Florida Legislative Investigation Committee*, 372 U.S. 539, 568–569, 570
(1963). Noting what he called "the right of privacy implicit in the First Amendment,"
Douglas had stated that "Whether the problem involves the right of an individual to be let
alone in the sanctity of his home or his right to associate with others for the attainment of
lawful purposes, the individual's interest in being free from governmental interference is the
same."

74. *Griswold et al.* v. *Connecticut*, 381 U.S. 479, 483, 484, 485–486, 487, 488, 491, 493, 495,
498–499. Also note William M. Beaney, "The Constitutional Right to Privacy in the
Supreme Court," *Supreme Court Review* 1962 (Chicago: University of Chicago Press, 1962),
pp. 212–251, at 214 ("virtually all enumerated rights in the Constitution can be described as
contributing to the right to privacy, if by the term is meant the integrity and freedom of the
individual person and personality"); and Walter B. Hamlin (a member of the Louisiana
Supreme Court), "The Bill of Rights . . ." *Commercial Law Journal* 68 (August 1963): 233–236,
at 236 ("The right 'to be let alone' is one of our inherent rights which has been sustained by
our courts; the right to privacy is inherent"). See as well *York* v. *Story*, 324 F.2d 450 (9th Cir.
1963), cert. denied 376 U.S. 939 (1964).

The statutes as struck down were Connecticut General Statutes 53–32 (the use provision)
and 54–196 (the accessory provision); they had been recodified into those designations in
1958; previously, following a 1949 revision, they had been Sections 8568 and 8875, respectively. Arthur Goldberg, long after his summer 1965 resignation from the Court, revisited his
Griswold opinion in a newspaper op-ed piece. The right to privacy, he wrote in 1987, "is
embraced by the language and concept of liberty protected by the First [Fifth] and
Fourteenth Amendments." Also under the Fourteenth Amendment, "Privacy must be
regarded as a privilege and immunity of citizens, as well as a cherished liberty," and in
Goldberg's 1987 judgment the privacy right undeniably applied to and protected a woman's
right to choose abortion. Arthur J. Goldberg, "Confirming a Supreme Court Nominee,"
Christian Science Monitor, 29 December 1987. Also see Goldberg, *A Private View of a Public Life*,
pp. 145–146. In several 1971 lectures on the Warren Court, Goldberg never once referred
either to *Griswold* or to the Ninth Amendment. Arthur J. Goldberg, *Equal Justice: The Warren
Era of the Supreme Court* (Evanston, IL: Northwestern University Press, 1971).

75. *Griswold et al.* v. *Connecticut*, 381 U.S. 479, 501, 507, 509, 510, 511, 527.

76. Garrow conversations with Catherine G. Roraback, Helen [Buxton] Rose, Frances McCoy,
and Cornelia Jahncke; *New Haven Register*, 7 June 1965, p. 1, 8 June 1965, p. 1, 28 June 1965,
p. 42; *Hartford Times*, 7 June 1965, p. 1; *New Haven Journal-Courier*, 8 June 1965; *Hartford*

Courant, 8 June 1965, pp. 1, 4, 11, 13 June 1965; *New York Herald Tribune*, 8 June 1965, pp. 1, 19; *New York Times*, 8 June 1965, pp. 1, 34–35; *Greenwich Time*, 8 June 1965; *Bridgeport Herald*, 20 June 1965, pp. 2, 13; *Medical Tribune*, 21 June 1965; *Newsweek*, 21 June 1965, p. 60; *Medical World News*, 25 June 1965, pp. 23–25. Also see Joseph B. Clark to James D. St. Clair, 3 August 1967, Clark Papers.

77. *New York Times*, 9 June 1965, p. 46; *Washington Post*, 8 June 1965, p. A18; *Richmond Times-Dispatch*, 10 June 1965, p. 16; *Boston Herald*, 10 June 1965; *Quincy Patriot-Ledger*, 9 June 1965, and *North Adams Transcript*, 14 June 1965; *Worcester Telegram*, 9 June 1965; *Life*, 2 July 1965, p. 4; *America*, 19 June 1965, pp. 875–876; *Commonweal*, 25 June 1965, pp. 427–428. Also see *Hartford Times*, 9 June 1965, p. 34; *New York Times*, 15 June 1965, p. 25; *Business Week*, 19 June 1965, pp. 108–110; *Christian Century*, 23 June 1965, pp. 796–797, and 4 August 1965, pp. 970–973; William B. Ball, "The Court and Birth Control," *Commonweal*, 9 July 1965, pp. 490–493, and letters, 20 August 1965, pp. 578–579, 607; *Christian Science Monitor*, 21 July 1965; William J. Curran, "Privacy, Birth Control and 'An Uncommonly Silly Law,'" *New England Journal of Medicine* 273 (5 August 1965): 322–323; *New York Times*, 26 August 1965, p. 42, 15 November 1966, p. 25; Harriet F. Pilpel, "A Right is Born: Privacy as a Civil Liberty," *Civil Liberties* 231 (November 1965): 1–2; and William B. Ball, "The Constitutional Question Respecting Birth Control and the Right of Privacy," *Lincoln Law Review* 1 (December 1965): 28–38.

   Somewhat oddly, Morris Ernst in the months to come would repeatedly disparage the amicus brief that his longtime partner Harriet Pilpel had filed, and at the same time would lavish undue credit on the amicus brief submitted by the Catholic Council on Civil Liberties. See Ernst to Jack Pemberton, 22 October 1965, ACLU 1965 Vol. 5, Ernst to Milton Eisenhower, 27 January 1966, Sanger-SSC, and Ernst to Grant Sanger, 15 February 1966, Sanger-SSC ("I am happy to say that the court paid little attention to the brief which our office filed, adopting in full the Catholic position").

78. Robbins to Griswold, 21 June 1965, PPLC 38-J; Standish Interviews with Hubbell and Garrow; "Memories of Claudia McGinley," 5 May 1983, 2pp., Lucia Parks, "1961–1964," n.d. [1983], 4pp., PPLC 33-I; Garrow conversations with Lucia and Charles Parks, Cornelia Jahncke, Catherine G. Roraback, Frances McCoy, Helen [Buxton] Rose, Ellen Switzer, Anita Beloff, and Sue Neale.

79. Griswold Interview with Cheek, p. 35; Griswold to Mary Grahame, 11 August 1975, PPLC 33-A.

80. Miriam Harper to Douglas, 9 June 1965, Douglas Box 1346; also see Miriam Harper to Donald B. Straus, 25 June 1965, PPFA II-184. Oddly enough, in his subsequent autobiography of his years on the Court, Douglas made not a single reference to *Griswold*, to privacy, or to any of the subsequent reproductive rights cases. *The Court Years, 1939–1975: The Autobiography of William O. Douglas* (New York: Random House, 1980). Also see Ball and Cooper, *Of Power and Right*, p. 283.

81. Emerson in the *Hartford Courant*, 7 June 1985, pp. A1, A8, in the *New Haven Register*, 30 April 1989, and in Carpenter, "Revisiting *Griswold*," p. 44; Buxton to Emerson, 17 June and 23 July 1965, Emerson Box 7, Buxton to Jaffe, 17 June 1965, PPFA II-184; Helen Buxton to Emerson, 8 June 1965, Emerson Box 7; Garrow conversations with Helen [Buxton] Rose, Ruth Emerson, Catherine G. Roraback, Ellen Switzer, Elizabeth Phillips, Virginia Stuermer, and John M. Morris; *Hartford Times*, 21 July 1966; Buxton to Alan Guttmacher, 2 November 1967, PPFA II-185; John M. Morris, "Charles Lee Buxton, 1904–1969," *Transactions of the American Gynecological Society* 92 (1969): 165–166. Obituaries on Lee Buxton appear in the *New Haven Register* (p. 1), *New Haven Journal-Courier*, *Hartford Courant* (p. 4), and *Hartford Times* of 8 July 1969; Timothy Buxton's obituary appears in the *New Haven Register* of 16 July 1970. On Emerson's recollections, also see *Family Planning Population Reporter* 4 (October 1975): 94–95, and *New Haven Register*, 22 January 1983, pp. 1, 2.

82. Emerson to Jahncke, 15 June 1965, PPLC 7-M; Emerson, "Nine Justices in Search of a Doctrine," *Michigan Law Review* 64 (December 1965): 219–234, at 227, 229, 231, 232. Also see Emerson to Otto Kahn-Freund, 15 June 1965, and to Arthur S. Miller, 21 July 1965, Emerson Box 7.

83. Cooley, *Torts*, 2nd ed., p. 29; E. L. Godkin, "The Rights of the Citizen," *Scribner's Magazine* 8 (July 1890): 58–67, at 67; Warren and Brandeis, "The Right to Privacy," *Harvard Law Review* 4 (December 1890): 193–220, at 193, 206–207, 215–216; "The Right to Privacy," *The Nation*, 25 December 1890, pp. 496–497; Herbert S. Hadley, "The Right to Privacy," *Northwestern Law Review* 3 (October 1894): 1–21, at 20.

Brandeis biographers erroneously have continued to repeat the wholly fictional notion that publication of the Warren and Brandeis *Harvard Law Review* essay was a direct response to unpleasant coverage of a Warren relative's wedding by a Boston newspaper, the *Saturday Evening Gazette*. See Alpheus T. Mason, *Brandeis: A Free Man's Life* (New York: Viking Press, 1946), p. 70, and Philippa Strum, *Louis D. Brandeis* (Cambridge: Harvard University Press, 1984), pp. 37–38; similarly see Morris L. Ernst and Alan U. Schwartz, *Privacy: The Right to Be Let Alone* (New York: Macmillan, 1962), p. 46, and Edward J. Bloustein, "Privacy as an Aspect of Human Dignity," *New York University Law Review* 39 (December 1964): 962–1007. Two very good but little-noted law review articles correct that error and are far more dependable sources for evaluating the Warren and Brandeis essay. See particularly James H. Barron, "Warren and Brandeis, *The Right to Privacy*, 4 Harv. L. Rev. 193 (1890): Demystifying a Landmark Citation," *Suffolk University Law Review* 13 (Summer 1979): 875–922, esp. pp. 892 and 896 ("References to the family were virtually nonexistent, let alone lurid"); see as well Dorothy J. Glancy, "The Invention of the Right to Privacy," *Arizona Law Review* 21 (1979): 1–39. Also note Walter F. Pratt, "The Warren and Brandeis Argument for a Right to Privacy," *Public Law* 1975 (Summer): 161–179; Grant B. Mindle, "Liberalism, Privacy, and Autonomy," *Journal of Politics* 51 (August 1989): 575–598, at 586–592; and Ken Gormley, "One Hundred Years of Privacy," *Wisconsin Law Review* 1992, pp. 1335–1441, at 1343–1357.

Also see Frederick Davis, "What Do We Mean by 'Right to Privacy?'" *South Dakota Law Review* 4 (Spring 1959): 1–24, at 3; William L. Prosser, "Privacy," *California Law Review* 48 (August 1960): 383–423, at 384, 389; Leon Brittan, "The Right of Privacy in England and the United States," *Tulane Law Review* 37 (February 1963): 235–268; Note, "The Right to Privacy in Nineteenth Century America," *Harvard Law Review* 94 (June 1981): 1892–1910, at 1910; Ferdinand Schoeman, "Privacy: Philosophical Dimensions," *American Philosophical Quarterly* 21 (July 1984): 199–213, at 202–203; William S. Gyves, "The Right to Privacy One Hundred Years Later," *St. John's Law Review* 64 (Winter 1990): 315–334; Irwin R. Kramer, "The Birth of Privacy Law: A Century Since Warren and Brandeis," *Catholic University Law Review* 39 (Spring 1990): 703–724; four articles in the *Northern Illinois University Law Review* 10 (1990): Sheldon W. Halpern, "The 'Inviolate Personality'—Warren and Brandeis After One Hundred Years . . ." pp. 387–399, Dorothy Glancy, "Privacy and the Other Miss M," pp. 401–440, Anita L. Allen and Erin Mack, "How Privacy Got Its Gender," pp. 441–478, and Richard C. Turkington, "Legacy of the Warren and Brandeis Article . . ." pp. 479–520; and Sheldon W. Halpern, "Rethinking the Right of Privacy . . ." *Rutgers Law Review* 43 (Spring 1991): 539–563.

84. Augustus N. Hand, "Schuyler Against Curtis and the Right to Privacy," *American Law Register and Review* 45 (December 1897): 745–759, at 759; *Roberson v. Rochester Folding Box Co.*, 171 N.Y. 538 (1902); Wilbur Larremore, "The Law of Privacy," *Columbia Law Review* 12 (December 1912): 693–708, at 694; *Paolo Pavesich v. New England Life Insurance Co.*, 122 Ga. 190, 50 S.E. 68, 69–71 (1905).

With regard to the ongoing influence of the Warren and Brandeis article, see Elbridge L. Adams, "The Right of Privacy, and Its Relation to the Law of Libel," *American Law Review* 39 (January-February 1905): 37–58, at 37; Wilbur Larremore, "The Right of Privacy," *Sewanee Review* 21 (July 1913): 297–310, at 301.

A law review defense of *Roberson* by one of the four members of the New York Court of Appeals who comprised the majority for that decision is Denis O'Brien, "The Right of Privacy," *Columbia Law Review* 2 (November 1902): 437–448, who was particularly upset at a 23 August 1902 *New York Times* editorial that had condemned the holding. An excellent historical discussion appears in Robert E. Mensel, "'Kodakers Lying in Wait': Amateur Photography and the Right of Privacy in New York, 1885–1915," *American Quarterly* 43 (March 1991): 24–45, esp. at 36–40. Also see John G. Speed, "The Right of Privacy," *North*

American Review 173 (July 1896): 64–74; Percy L. Edwards, "Right of Privacy and Equity Relief," *Central Law Review* 55 (15 August 1902): 123–127.

85. Positive responses to *Pavesich* include *Michigan Law Review* 3 (May 1905): 559–563, *Case and Comment* 12 (June 1905): 2–4, and *Virginia Law Register* 12 (June 1906): 91–99. The three pre-Brandeis Supreme Court references are *Boyd v. United States*, 116 U.S. 616, 630 (1886), *Union Pacific Railway Co. v. Botsford*, 141 U.S. 250, 251 (1891) ("No right is held more sacred . . . than the right of every individual to the possession and control of his own person, free from all restraint or interference of others, unless by clear and unquestionable authority of law"), and *Interstate Commerce Commission v. Brimson*, 154 U.S. 447, 479 (1894) ("the principles that embody the essence of constitutional liberty and security forbid all invasions on the part of government and its employees of the sanctity of a man's home, and the privacies of his life"). Also see *Prudential Insurance Co. v. Cheek*, 259 U.S. 530, 542–543 (1922).

Brandeis's previous dissent was in *Gilbert v. Minnesota*, 254 U.S. 325 (1920). On his dissent in *Olmstead*, 277 U.S. 438, 478, also see Mason, *Brandeis*, pp. 567–569, and Strum, *Louis D. Brandeis*, pp. 323–326.

86. *Meyer v. Nebraska*, 262 U.S. 390, 399 (1923); *Pierce v. Society of Sisters*, 268 U.S. 510, 535 (1925); *Prince v. Massachusetts*, 321 U.S. 158, 166–167 (1944); *Skinner v. Oklahoma*, 316 U.S. 535, 541 (1942); *McDonald v. United States*, 335 U.S. 451, 455–456 (1948); *Public Utilities Commission v. Pollak*, 343 U.S. 451, 467, 468 (1952); Douglas, *The Right of the People* (Garden City, NY: Doubleday & Co., 1958), pp. 87–88. Also see *Davis v. United States*, 328 U.S. 582, 587 (1946), *Kovacs v. Cooper*, 336 U.S. 77, 87 (1949), and *Kent v. Dulles*, 357 U.S. 116, 126 (1958) ("outside areas of plainly harmful conduct, every American is left to shape his own life as he thinks best, do what he pleases, go where he pleases"); see as well Richard C. Gossweiler, "The Right of Privacy: Misuse of History" (unpublished Ph.D. dissertation, Ohio State University, 1978), pp. 11–20.

On the application of the privacy right concept in the tort area during that time period, see George Ragland, Jr., "The Right of Privacy," *Kentucky Law Journal* 17 (January 1929): 85–122; Note, "The Right to Privacy Today," *Harvard Law Review* 43 (December 1929): 297–302; Roy Moreland, "The Right of Privacy Today," *Kentucky Law Journal* 19 (January 1931): 101–136; Basil W. Kacedan, "The Right of Privacy," *Boston University Law Review* 12 (June 1932): 353–395 and (November 1932): 600–647; Leon Green, "The Right of Privacy," *Illinois Law Review* 27 (November 1932): 237–260; Gerald Dickler, "The Right of Privacy," *United States Law Review* 70 (August 1936): 435–456; Louis Nizer, "The Right of Privacy," *Michigan Law Review* 39 (February 1941): 526–560; Wilfred Feinberg, "Recent Developments in the Law of Privacy," *Columbia Law Review* 48 (July 1948): 713–731; Jeptha H. Evans, "The Right of Privacy," *Arkansas Law Review* 6 (Fall 1952): 459–472; Samuel H. Hofstadter, *The Development of the Right of Privacy in New York* (New York: Crosby, 1954); and Hofstadter and George Horowitz, *The Right of Privacy* (New York: Central Book Co., 1964).

87. Samuel H. Wilkins, *Mississippi Law Journal* 37 (March 1966): 304–306, at 306; Robert L. Knupp, *Dickinson Law Review* 69 (Summer 1965): 417–424, at 424. Note as well James F. Simon, *Independent Journey: The Life of William O. Douglas* (New York: Harper & Row, 1980), pp. 346–349; [Sheldon S. Adler], "Toward a Constitutional Theory of Individuality: The Privacy Opinions of Justice Douglas," *Yale Law Journal* 87 (July 1978): 1579–1600; Note, "Substantive Due Process Comes Home to Roost," *Women's Rights Law Reporter* 10 (Winter 1988): 177–208, at 184–185; Sanford Levinson, "Constitutional Rhetoric and the Ninth Amendment," *Chicago-Kent Law Review* 64 (1988): 131–161, at 136 (Douglas's opinion "simply does not persuade"); and Kenneth Karst, "The Freedom of Intimate Association," *Yale Law Journal* 89 (March 1980): 624–692, at 652 ("the result in the *Griswold* case seems inescapable; the chief problem before the Supreme Court was not *what* to decide, but *how* to decide"). Also see *American Bar Association Journal* 51 (September 1965): 870–871; Edward V. Long, "The Right to Privacy," *St. Louis University Law Journal* 10 (Fall 1965): 1–29, at 5–6; *Vanderbilt Law Review* 18 (October 1965): 2037–2043; *Harvard Law Review* 79 (November 1965): 162–165; Robert B. McKay, "The Right of Privacy: Emanations and Intimations,"

Michigan Law Review 64 (December 1965): 259–282; Arthur E. Sutherland, "Privacy in Connecticut," *Michigan Law Review* 64 (December 1965): 283–288; W. Thomas Tete, *Louisiana Law Review* 26 (December 1965): 168–175; Richard Bronner, *Western Reserve Law Review* 17 (December 1965): 601–607; *Brooklyn Law Review* 32 (December 1965): 172–175; Virginia Commission on Constitutional Government, *The Supreme Court of the United States: A Review of the 1964 Term* (Richmond, 1965), pp. 52–57; George C. Piper, *Kentucky Law Journal* 54 (1966): 794–799; Michael H. Terry, *Wayne Law Review* 12 (Winter 1966): 479–487; Louis M. Thrasher, *University of Cincinnati Law Review* 35 (Winter 1966): 134–140; *Journal of Family Law* 6 (Winter 1966): 371–375; Helen Garfield, *University of Colorado Law Review* 38 (Winter 1966): 267–270; Mike White, *University of Missouri at Kansas City Law Review* 34 (Winter 1966): 95–120; *Catholic University Law Review* 15 (January 1966): 126–132; [Sherwin S. Zetlin], *Northwestern University Law Review* 60 (January-February 1966): 813–833; Milton R. Konvitz, "Privacy and the Law," *Law and Contemporary Problems* 31 (Spring 1966): 272–280; *Duke Law Journal* 1966 (Spring): 562–577; Jerry K. Levy, *Washburn Law Journal* 5 (Spring 1966): 286–291; Herbert J. Lustig, *Syracuse Law Review* 17 (Spring 1966): 553–556; Stanley J. Mosk, "The Population Explosion and Due Process," *Lincoln Law Review* 1 (June 1966): 149–165; *Notre Dame Lawyer* 41 (June 1966): 681–785, at 751; Frank R. Goldstein, *Maryland Law Review* 26 (Summer 1966): 249–259; Michael R. Perle, "*Griswold* v. *Connecticut*: Peripheral Rights and Rights Retained by the People Under the Ninth Amendment," *Connecticut Bar Journal* 40 (December 1966): 704–717; Ernest Katin, "*Griswold* v. *Connecticut*: The Justices and Connecticut's 'Uncommonly Silly Law,'" *Notre Dame Lawyer* 42 (June 1967): 680–706; Jesse H. Choper, "On the Warren Court and Judicial Review," *Catholic University Law Review* 17 (September 1967): 20–43, at 34 (*Griswold* "might better have been grounded in equal protection").

88. William M. Beaney, "The *Griswold* Case and the Expanding Right to Privacy," *Wisconsin Law Review* 1966 (Fall): 976–995, at 982; Robert G. Dixon, "The *Griswold* Penumbra: Constitutional Charter for an Expanded Right of Privacy?," *Michigan Law Review* 64 (December 1965): 197–218, at 213, 214, 217. See as well Anita L. Allen, "Taking Liberties: Privacy, Private Choice, and Social Contract Theory," *University of Cincinnati Law Review* 56 (1987): 461–491, at 467; and Graham Hughes, *The Conscience of the Courts* (Garden City, NY: Doubleday, 1975), p. 72, emphasizing how it was the ideological heritage of substantive due process that produced "the circuitous reasoning of *Griswold*. Terrified by history to talk openly in terms of substantive liberty rights under the Fourteenth Amendment, the Justices talked instead in fragile and convoluted reasoning of privacy rights swirling around in ectoplasmic emanations." Also note Laurence H. Tribe, *American Constitutional Law*, 2nd ed. (Mineola, NY: Foundation Press, 1988), p. 775 (*Griswold* was "the most important substantive due process decision of the modern period").

89. Paul G. Kauper, "Penumbras, Peripheries, Emanations, Things Fundamental and Things Forgotten: The *Griswold* Case," *Michigan Law Review* 64 (December 1965): 235–258, at 242, 244; Hyman Gross, "The Concept of Privacy," *New York University Law Review* 42 (March 1967): 34–54, at 35; Anthony R. Blackshield, "Constitutionalism and Comstockery," *Kansas Law Review* 14 (March 1966): 403–452, at 404; Edgar Bodenheimer, "Birth Control Legislation and the United States Supreme Court," *Kansas Law Review* 14 (March 1966): 453–460, at 458; Kent Greenawalt, "Criminal Law and Population Control," *Vanderbilt Law Review* 24 (April 1971): 465–494, at 478; Thomas Gerety, "Doing Without Privacy," *Ohio State Law Journal* 42 (1981): 143–165, at 152. Also see G. Edward White, "The Anti-Judge: William O. Douglas and the Ambiguities of Individuality," *Virginia Law Review* 74 (February 1988): 17–86, at 70; David A. J. Richards, *Foundations of American Constitutionalism* (New York: Oxford University Press, 1989), pp. 213, 229, 232–233; Stephen Macedo, *Liberal Virtues* (New York: Oxford University Press, 1990), p. 188; and Richard A. Posner, "Legal Reasoning from the Top Down and from the Bottom Up," *University of Chicago Law Review* 59 (Winter 1992): 433–450, at 445.

90. See Alfred H. Kelly, "Clio and the Court: An Illicit Love Affair," *Supreme Court Review* 1965 (Chicago: University of Chicago Press, 1965), pp. 119–158; and James F. Kelley, "The

Uncertain Renaissance of the Ninth Amendment," *University of Chicago Law Review* 33 (Summer 1966): 814–836. More favorable commentaries on the Ninth Amendment usage include James D. Carroll, "The Forgotten Amendment," *The Nation* 201 (6 September 1965): 121–122; Mitchell Franklin, "The Ninth Amendment as Civil Law Method . . . ," *Tulane Law Review* 40 (April 1966): 487–522; Floyd Abrams, "What Are the Rights Guaranteed by the Ninth Amendment?," *American Bar Association Journal* 53 (November 1967): 1033–1039; and Charles L. Black, Jr., "The Unfinished Business of the Warren Court," *Washington Law Review* 46 (1970): 3–45, esp. at 40–44, Black, *Decision According to Law* (New York: W. W. Norton & Co., 1981), p. 48, and Black, "On Reading and Using the Ninth Amendment," in Myres S. McDougal and W. Michael Reisman, eds., *Power and Policy in Quest of Law* (Dordrecht: Martinus Nijhoff, 1985), pp. 187–197. With regard to Charles Black and the Ninth Amendment, also see William Van Alstyne, "Slouching Toward Bethlehem with the Ninth Amendment," *Yale Law Journal* 91 (November 1981): 207–216, and Russell L. Caplan, "Charles Black's Rediscovery of the Ninth Amendment . . ." *Michigan Law Review* 80 (March 1982): 656–663.

Also see in particular Eugene M. Van Loan III's excellent "Natural Rights and the Ninth Amendment," *Boston University Law Review* 48 (1968): 1–48, at 48 ("None of the opinions adequately explain the origin and nature of the right of privacy or the factors the Court took into consideration in deciding that it was constitutionally protected"), and William O. Bertelsman, "The Ninth Amendment and Due Process of Law," *University of Cincinnati Law Review* 37 (Fall 1968): 777–796, at 784, 787 ("It is the ghost of *Lochner* which inspires the reluctance to recognize unenumerated rights," and, in contrast to any Fourteenth Amendment basis, "the ninth amendment approach seems the better one, in the context of modern times, to minimize the dread of '*Lochner's*' ghost").

Also see generally Thomas R. Vickerman, "The Ninth Amendment," *South Dakota Law Review* 11 (Winter 1966): 173–179; Gary L. Gardner, "The Ninth Amendment," *Albany Law Review* 30 (January 1966): 89–100; Harold H. Boles, *Tulane Law Review* 40 (February 1966): 418–424; David K. Sutelan, "The Ninth Amendment," *William and Mary Law Review* 8 (Fall 1966): 101–120; Luis Kutner, "The Neglected Ninth Amendment," *Marquette Law Review* 51 (Fall 1967): 121–142; Wilfred J. Ritz, "The Original Purpose and Present Utility of the Ninth Amendment," *Washington and Lee Law Review* 25 (Spring 1968): 1–19; *State v. Abellano*, 441 P.2d 333 (Hawaii Sup. Ct.), 23 May 1968; Mark A. Koral, "Ninth Amendment Vindication of Unenumerated Fundamental Rights," *Temple Law Quarterly* 42 (Fall 1968): 46–59; Gerald Kirven, "Under the Ninth Amendment, What Rights Are the 'Others Retained by the People'?" *South Dakota Law Review* 14 (Winter 1969): 80–91; William Eaton, "New Dimensions of Freedom in the Ninth Amendment," in Frederick M. Wirt and Willis D. Hawley, eds., *New Dimensions of Freedom in America* (San Francisco: Chandler Publishing Co., 1969), pp. 266–274; Irvin M. Kent, "Under the Ninth Amendment What Rights Are the 'Others Retained by the People'?" *Federal Bar Journal* 29 (Summer 1970): 219–237; George E. Garvey, "Unenumerated Rights—Substantive Due Process, the Ninth Amendment, and John Stuart Mill," *Wisconsin Law Review* 1971: 922–938; A. F. Ringold, "The History of the Enactment of the Ninth Amendment and Its Recent Development," *Tulsa Law Journal* 8 (Spring 1972): 1–57, esp. at 55–57; Terence J. Moore, "The Ninth Amendment—Its Origin and Meaning," *New England Law Review* 7 (Spring 1972): 215–309; Lyman Rhoades and Rodney R. Patula, "The Ninth Amendment: A Survey of Theory and Practice in the Federal Courts Since *Griswold* v. *Connecticut*," *Denver Law Journal* 50 (1973): 153–176; R. H. Clark, "The Ninth Amendment and Constitutional Privacy," *Toledo Law Review* 5 (Fall 1973): 83–110; John Ely, *Democracy and Distrust* (Cambridge: Harvard University Press, 1980), pp. 34–41; Raoul Berger, "The Ninth Amendment," *Cornell Law Review* 66 (November 1980): 1–26; Bill Gaugush, "The Ninth Amendment in the Federal Courts, 1965–1980: From Desuetude to Fundamentalism?" *Denver Law Journal* 61 (1983): 25–41; Russell L. Caplan, "The History and Meaning of the Ninth Amendment," *Virginia Law Review* 69 (March 1983): 223–268; Simeon C. R. McIntosh, "On Reading the Ninth Amendment," *Howard Law Journal* 28 (1985): 913–941; Gerald G. Watson, "The Ninth Amendment: Source of a

Substantive Right to Privacy," *John Marshall Law Review* 19 (Summer 1986): 959–981; Lawrence E. Mitchell, "The Ninth Amendmennt and the 'Jurisprudence of Original Intention,'" *Georgetown Law Journal* 74 (August 1986): 1719–1742; John P. Kaminski, "Natural Rights and the Ninth Amendment," in Jon Kukla, ed., *The Bill of Rights* (Richmond: Virginia State Library, 1987), pp. 141–150; Calvin R. Massey, "Federalism and Fundamental Rights: The Ninth Amendment," *Hastings Law Journal* 38 (January 1987): 305–344; Charles J. Cooper, "Limited Government and Individual Liberty: The Ninth Amendment's Forgotten Lessons," *Journal of Law and Politics* 4 (Summer 1987): 63–80; Floyd Abrams, "The Ninth Amendment and the Protection of Unenumerated Rights," *Harvard Journal of Law and Public Policy* 11 (Winter 1988): 93–96; Geoffrey G. Slaughter, "The Ninth Amendment's Role in the Evolution of Fundamental Rights Jurisprudence," *Indiana Law Journal* 64 (Winter 1988): 97–110; Andrzej Rapaczynski, "The Ninth Amendment and the Unwritten Constitution: The Problems of Constitutional Interpretation," *Chicago-Kent Law Review* 64 (1988): 177–210; Randy E. Barnett, "Reconceiving the Ninth Amendment," *Cornell Law Review* 74 (November 1988): 1–42; Leonard W. Levy, *Original Intent and the Framers' Constitution* (New York: Macmillan, 1988), chapter 13; and Thomas B. McAffee, "The Original Meaning of the Ninth Amendment," *Columbia Law Review* 90 (June 1990): 1215–1320.

91. Anita L. Allen, "Taking Liberties: Privacy, Private Choice, and Social Contract Theory," *University of Cincinnati Law Review* 56 (1987): 461–491, at 478n. Also see David M. O'Brien, *Privacy, Law, and Public Policy* (New York: Praeger, 1979), p. 180; Christopher Wolfe, *The Rise of Modern Judicial Review* (New York: Basic Books, 1986), p. 290; and Ronald J. Fiscus, "Before the Velvet Curtain: The Connecticut Contraceptive Cases as a Study in Constitutional Law and Supreme Court Behavior" (unpublished Ph.D. dissertation, University of Wisconsin, 1983), pp. 413–414 ("the Penumbra theory never had a chance, whatever its virtues, of becoming an accepted constitutional doctrine because of the reputation of its author. . . . By the time Douglas came to write his *Griswold* opinion, nobody was listening to him on doctrinal matters").

92. Burr Henly, "'Penumbra: The Roots of a Legal Metaphor," *Hastings Constitutional Law Quarterly* 15 (Fall 1987): 81–100; Henry T. Greely, "A Footnote to 'Penumbra' in *Griswold* v. *Connecticut*," *Constitutional Commentary* 6 (Summer 1989): 251–265, esp. at 260; Dorothy J. Glancy, "Douglas's Right of Privacy: A Response to His Critics," in Wasby, ed., *"He Shall Not Pass This Way Again"*, pp. 155–177, esp. at 162; *Olmstead* v. *United States*, 277 U.S. 438, 469; and Glenn H. Reynolds, "Sex, Lies and Jurisprudence: Robert Bork, *Griswold* and the Philosophy of Original Understanding," *Georgia Law Review* 24 (Summer 1990): 1045–1113, at 1064–1065n. Also see R. H. Clark, "Constitutional Sources of the Penumbral Right to Privacy," *Villanova Law Review* 19 (June 1974): 833–884; James B. Stoneking, "Penumbras and Privacy: A Study of the Uses of Fictions in Constitutional Decision-Making," *West Virginia Law Review* 87 (Summer 1985): 859–877; and *New York University Law Review* 48 (October 1973): 670–773, at 672–677.

93. Bork, "The Supreme Court Needs a New Philosophy," *Fortune* 78 (December 1968): 138–141, 170–177, at 170; Bork, "Neutral Principles and Some First Amendment Problems," *Indiana Law Journal* 47 (Fall 1971): 1–17, at 8–11. Also see Bruce Ackerman, "Robert Bork's Grand Inquisition," *Yale Law Journal* 99 (April 1990): 1419–1439, at 1424; Bork Interview with Hubbell; and Garrow conversation with Robert B. Stevens.

94. U.S. Congress, Senate, Committee on the Judiciary, *Hearings on the Nomination of Robert H. Bork to be Associate Justice of the Supreme Court*, 100th Cong., 1st sess., 1987, pp. 114–119, 121, 127–128, 182–183, 241–243, 250, 290, 325, 711–712, 753–754; Text of a 31 March 1982 speech, p. 4, as quoted in *Hearings*, p. 121; Text of a 5 September 1985 interview, as reprinted in full in Patrick B. McGuigan and Dawn M. Weyrich, *Ninth Justice: The Fight for Bork* (Washington, DC: Free Congress Research and Education Foundation, 1990), pp. 285–303, at 293.

95. Bork to Senator Joseph R. Biden, Jr., 1 October 1987, 15pp., in *Hearings*, pp. 3896–3910, at 3903–3904; Bork, *The Tempting of America* (New York: Free Press, 1989), pp. 95–96, 169, 234, 263.

96. Morgan D. S. Prickett, "The Right of Privacy: A Black View of *Griswold* v. *Connecticut*," *Hastings Constitutional Law Quarterly* 7 (Spring 1980): 777–829, at 823, 824, 825–826; Bruce Fein in *Los Angeles Daily Journal*, 10 June 1985, pp. 1, 19; Fein, "*Griswold* v. *Connecticut*: Wayward Decision-Making in the Supreme Court," *Ohio Northern University Law Review* 16 (1989): 551–559, at 554, 555 ("the Court in *Griswold* could have sustained the accessory convictions without ever pronouncing definitively on the right of marital privacy question"); David P. Currie, *The Constitution in the Supreme Court: The Second Century, 1888–1986* (Chicago: University of Chicago Press, 1990), p. 458; Rex Lee quoted in *American Bar Association Journal*, 1 July 1988, p. 70. Also see Hadley Arkes, *First Things* (Princeton: Princeton University Press, 1986), pp. 352, 354–355; Walter Berns, *Taking the Constitution Seriously* (New York: Simon & Schuster, 1987), p. 206; Terry Eastland, "Bork Revisited," *Commentary*, February 1990, pp. 39–43, at 42–43; and Hugh C. Macgill, "Introduction: Observations on Teaching *Griswold*," *Connecticut Law Review* 23 (Summer 1991): 853–860, at 854, 857, who somewhat oddly declares that "I remain enormously respectful of Douglas's achievement in *Griswold*" while nonetheless stating that "the entire Douglas opinion" seems "too ridiculous a piece of work to take seriously."

97. John H. F. Shattuck, *Rights of Privacy* (Skokie, IL: National Textbook Co., 1977), p. 105 (published "in conjunction with" the ACLU).

98. Austin Sarat, "Abortion and the Courts: Uncertain Boundaries of Law and Politics," in Allan P. Sindler, ed., *American Politics and Public Policy* (Washington, DC: Congressional Quarterly Press, 1982), pp. 113–153, at 127.

99. Eva R. Rubin, *Abortion, Politics, and the Courts* (Westport, CT: Greenwood Press, 1982), p. 37. Also see Lee Epstein and Joseph F. Kobylka, *The Supreme Court and Legal Change* (Chapel Hill: University of North Carolina Press, 1992), p. 157.

100. Cannon F. Allen, "Revising Abortion Policy" (unpublished B.A. thesis, Princeton University, 1984), p. 3.

101. Bruce Ackerman, "Constitutional Politics/Constitutional Law," *Yale Law Journal* 99 (December 1989): 453–547, at 537; Ackerman, *We the People: Foundations* (Cambridge: Harvard University Press, 1991), p. 151. Professor Ackerman also (*Foundations*, p. 159) terms the Douglas opinion "nothing less than a brilliant *interpretive* proposal."

102. Louis Lusky, *By What Right?* (Charlottesville, VA: Michie Co., 1975), pp. 339–344, at 342.

103. Wallace Mendelson, "Mr. Justice Douglas and Government by the Judiciary," *Journal of Politics* 38 (November 1976): 918–937, at 924. Mendelson also termed the Douglas opinion "an unnecessary, indeed reckless, judicial exertion." Also see Sheldon Goldman's rejoinder, *Journal of Politics* 39 (February 1977): 148–158, at 153–154.

104. Also see Philip Bobbitt, *Constitutional Fate* (New York: Oxford University Press, 1982), pp. 170–175, at 170; John A. Rohr, "Privacy: Law and Values," *Thought* 49 (December 1974): 353–373, at 366; Robert G. Dixon, Jr., "The 'New' Substantive Due Process and the Democratic Ethic: A Prolegomenon," *Brigham Young University Law Review* 1976: 43–88, at 84; Ken Martyn, "Technological Advances and *Roe* v. *Wade*: The Need to Rethink Abortion Law," *UCLA Law Review* 29 (June-August 1982): 1194–1215, at 1195; W. A. Parent, "A New Definition of Privacy for the Law," *Law and Philosophy* 2 (December 1983): 305–338, at 312; Michael Hedeen, "Constitutional Law—Substantive Due Process . . ." *Southern Illinois University Law Journal* 11 (Summer 1987): 1305–1325, at 1307; Blair R. Haarlow, "The Right to Privacy in Constitutional Law: Toward a New Jurisprudence" (unpublished B.A. thesis, Princeton University, 1991), p. 18; and Darien A. McWhirter and Jon D. Bible, *Privacy as a Constitutional Right* (New York: Quorum Books, 1992), p. 96.

105. Dixon, "The 'New' Substantive Due Process," n. 104 above, at 84; Joel Feinberg, "Autonomy, Sovereignty, and Privacy: Moral Ideals in the Constitution?" *Notre Dame Law Review* 58 (February 1983): 445–492, at 483; Jeffrey S. Koehlinger, "Substantive Due Process Analysis and the Lockean Liberal Tradition: Rethinking the Modern Privacy Cases," *Indiana Law Journal* 65 (Summer 1990): 723–776, at 746.

106. Massachusetts Democrat Edward M. Kennedy in the Bork *Hearings*, n. 94 above, p. 151.

107. Jahncke to Vera Weiner, 11 June and 12 July 1965, PPLC 41-B and 44-A; Marion Miller,

Executive Committee Minutes, 23 June 1965, PPLC 12-H; Louise Fleck, New Haven
Minutes, 24 June and 10 September 1965, PPLC 41-B; *New Haven Register*, 9 July and 25
August 1965; Griswold, Medical Advisory Committee Minutes, 11 August 1965, PPLC 15-
B; *Bridgeport Herald*, 22 August 1965; PPLC Press Release, 25 August 1965, PPLC 24-Q;
Hartford Courant, 26 August 1965, p. 6; *New York Herald Tribune*, 29 August 1965, p. 27;
Cornelia Jahncke, "My Two Terms as President of PPLC," n.d. [c.12 March 1983], 1pp.,
PPLC 33-I; Garrow conversations with Cornelia Jahncke and Frances McCoy. On the New
York state repeal, see *New York Times*, 17 June 1965, p. 1, and 10 July 1965, p. 1. On the
Massachusetts reform, see *New England Journal of Medicine* 273 (29 July 1965): 277–278; *New
York Times*, 3 August 1965, p. 13, 8 August 1965, p. 53; Dienes, *Law, Politics, and Birth Control*,
pp. 200–209, 247; and especially Joseph L. Dorsey, "Massachusetts Liberalizes Birth Control
Law," *Dartmouth Medical School Quarterly* 3 (Summer 1966): 8–12.

108. Marion Miller, Executive Committee Minutes, 8 September 1965, and Board Minutes, 21
September 1965, PPLC 12-H; *Hartford Courant*, 10 November 1965; *Connecticut Parenthood*,
Winter-Spring 1966; *New Haven Register*, 26 January 1966, p. 1, 18 June 1966, p. 34; *National
Observer*, 2 May 1966; *PPLC News*, May 1975. Also see C. Lee Buxton, "Family Planning
Clinics in Connecticut," *Connecticut Medicine* 32 (February 1968): 122–124.

109. Amelia Roe, New Haven Minutes, 7 October 1965, PPLC 41-B; *Hartford Courant*, 13
October 1965; *New Haven Register*, 20 October 1965; Marion Miller, Board Minutes, 26
October 1965, and Executive Committee Minutes, 7 December 1965, PPLC 12-H; Louise
Fleck, New Haven Minutes, 13 December 1965 and 10 January 1966, PPLC 41-C; Mabel
Jenkins to Vera Weiner, 15 January 1966, PPLC 46-O; Garrow conversations with Cornelia
Jahncke and Frances McCoy; Griswold Interview with Cheek, p. 47.

CHAPTER FIVE

1. Guttmacher, *Babies by Choice or by Chance* (Garden City, NY: Doubleday, 1959), p. 11;
Guttmacher, "The Genesis of Liberalized Abortion in New York: A Personal Insight," *Case
Western Reserve Law Review* 23 (Summer 1972): 756–778, at 756–757. Also see Guttmacher,
"A Defense of the Supreme Court's Abortion Decision," *The Humanist* 33 (May-June 1973):
6–7, Guttmacher, "Why I Favor Liberalized Abortion," *Reader's Digest* 103 (November 1973):
143–147, and David Dempsey, "Dr. Guttmacher is the Evangelist of Birth Control," *New
York Times Magazine*, 9 February 1969, pp. 32–33, 79–84. Biographical obituaries of
Guttmacher appear in the *New York Times*, 19 March 1974, p. 38, the *Washington Post*, 20
March 1974, p. B6, and the *New England Journal of Medicine* 290 (9 May 1974): 1085.

2. Guttmacher, "The Genesis of Liberalized Abortion," p. 757–758; Guttmacher, *Babies By
Choice*, pp. 211–213; *New York Times*, 31 January 1942, p. 30.

3. James C. Mohr, *Abortion in America: The Origins and Evolution of National Policy, 1800–1900*
(New York: Oxford University Press, 1978), passim, esp. pp. 202, 230, 237, 242; Mohr,
"Patterns of Abortion and the Response of American Physicians, 1790–1930," in Judith W.
Leavitt, ed., *Women and Health in America* (Madison: University of Wisconsin Press, 1984), pp.
117–123, at 117–118; Kristin Luker, *Abortion and the Politics of Motherhood* (Berkeley:
University of California Press, 1984), pp. 11–62; Marvin Olasky, *Abortion Rites: A Social
History of Abortion in America* (Wheaton, IL: Crossway Books, 1992), passim. Also see Shelley
Gavigan, "The Criminal Sanction as it Relates to Human Reproduction: The Genesis of the
Statutory Prohibition of Abortion," *Journal of Legal History* 5 (May 1984): 20–43; "The
Abortion Movement and the AMA, 1850–1880," in Carroll Smith-Rosenberg, *Disorderly
Conduct* (New York: Alfred A. Knopf, 1985), pp. 217–244; and Philip A. Rafferty, *Roe v.
Wade: The Birth of a Constitutional Right* (Ann Arbor, MI: University Microfilms International,
1992). Only one case involving abortion appears to have reached the U.S. Supreme Court
during this era, but the Court's 6 to 3 decision upholding an 1893 state statute prohibiting a
previously convicted felon from being licensed to practice medicine included no actual discussion of abortion. See *Hawker* v. *New York*, 170 U.S. 1002 (1898).

4. Stella Hanau, "The Birth-Control Conference," *The Nation* 138 (31 January 1934): 129–130 (citing Taussig's remarks); [Thomas E. Harris], "A Functional Study of Existing Abortion Laws," *Columbia Law Review* 35 (January 1935): 87–97, at 93 (citing Taussig); Frederick J. Taussig, *Abortion—Spontaneous and Induced—Medical and Social Aspects* (St. Louis: C. V. Mosby Co., 1936), esp. p. 338; *Time*, 16 March 1936, p. 52; Harrison Reeves, "The Birth Control Industry," *American Mercury* 39 (November 1936): 295–290, at 288; A. J. Rongy, "Abortion: The $100,000,000 Racket," *American Mercury* 40 (February 1937): 145–150; Jack Frost, "Abortion—Need for Legalized Abortion," *Journal of the American Institute of Criminal Law and Criminology* 29 (November-December 1938): 595–598, at 597; James C. Mohr, "The Historical Character of Abortion in the United States Through World War II," in Paul Sachdev, ed., *Perspectives on Abortion* (Metuchen, NJ: Scarecrow Press, 1985), pp. 3–14, at 12. On Taussig, also see Jonathan B. Imber, *Abortion and the Private Practice of Medicine* (New Haven: Yale University Press, 1986), pp. 3–12.

5. F. W. Stella Browne, "The Right to Abortion," in Norman Haire, ed., *Sexual Reform Congress* [World League for Sexual Reform, 3rd Congress, London, 8–14 September 1929] (London: Kegan Paul, 1930), pp. 178–181; Browne, "The Right to Abortion," in Browne et al., *Abortion* (London: George Allen & Unwin, 1935), pp. 11–50, at 29 and 31; Browne, "The Right of Abortion," *Journal of Sex Education* 5 (1952): 29–32, at 30, 32. Also see Sheila Rowbotham, *A New World For Women—Stella Browne: Socialist Feminist* (London: Pluto Press, 1977), pp. 27, 64, 105, 110, 113–114; Colin Francome, *Abortion Freedom* (London: George Allen & Unwin, 1984), pp. 64–65, 68.

6. William J. Robinson, *The Law Against Abortion* (New York: Eugenics Publishing Co., 1933), esp. pp. 6, 13, 115, 117, 119.

7. Abraham J. Rongy, *Abortion: Legal or Illegal?* (New York: Vanguard Press, 1933), esp. pp. 85, 97–98. Also see Rongy, "Abortion: The $100,000,00 Racket," pp. 145–150.

8. [Thomas E. Harris], "A Functional Study of Existing Abortion Laws," *Columbia Law Review* 35 (January 1935): 87–97, at 95; Jack Frost, "Abortion—Need for Legalized Abortion," *Journal of the American Institute of Criminal Law and Criminology* 29 (November-December 1938): 595–598; B. B. Tolnai, "Abortions and the Law," *The Nation*, 15 April 1939, pp. 424–427; *Birth Control Review* for January 1929, as cited in Jonathan B. Imber, "Sociology and Abortion: Legacies and Strategies," *Contemporary Sociology* 8 (November 1979): 826–836; Ernst and Pilpel, "Release From the Comstock Era," *Birth Control Review*, December 1939, pp. 24–25; George A. Glenn to Margaret Sanger, 26 December 1938, BCFA to Glenn, 3 January 1939, Sanger to Glenn, 16 January 1939, and Florence Rose to D. Kenneth Rose, 8 February 1939, Calderone Papers Box 10. My thanks to Ellen Chesler for the latter citations. A painstakingly thorough survey of an abortion-related bill considered by the New York legislature in 1944 appears in Cyril C. Means, Jr., "The Law of New York Concerning Abortion and the Status of the Foetus, 1664–1968," *New York Law Forum* 14 (Fall 1968): 411–515, at 493–498; also see *New York Times*, 7 January 1944, p. 19.

9. Jane Ward, "What Everyone Should Know About Abortion," *American Mercury* 53 (August 1941): 194–200; National Committee on Maternal Health, *The Abortion Problem* (Baltimore: Williams & Wilkins, 1944); [Henry J. Langston?], "Abortion and the Law," *Southern Medicine & Surgery* 104 (July 1942): 408–409. For a suggestive study of actual law enforcement practices, see Leslie J. Reagan, "'About to Meet Her Maker': Women, Doctors, Dying Declarations, and the State's Investigation of Abortion, Chicago, 1867–1940," *Journal of American History* 77 (March 1991): 1240–1264; for a discussion of some similar New York County (Manhattan) data covering 1925 to 1950, see Jerome E. Bates and Edward S. Zawadzki, *Criminal Abortion* (Springfield, IL: Charles C. Thomas, 1964), pp. 61–62.

10. Lloyd A. Bulloch, "Criminal Law—Abortion—Legal or Illegal," *Southern California Law Review* 23 (July 1950): 523–529; Russell S. Fisher, "Criminal Abortion," *Journal of Criminal Law, Criminology and Police Science* 42 (July-August 1951): 242–249; Myer S. Tulkoff, "Legal and Social Control of Abortion," *Kentucky Law Journal* 40 (May 1952): 410–416; Jerome Bates, "The Abortion Mill: An Institutional Analysis," *Journal of Criminal Law, Criminology and Police Science* 45 (July-August 1954): 157–169.

11. Calderone Interview with Reed, pp. 15–16; Schur, "The Abortion Racket," *The Nation*, 5 March 1955, pp. 199–201; Garrow conversation with Edwin M. Schur. Also see Schur, "Abortion and the Social System," *Social Problems* 3 (October 1955): 94–99, and Morton Sontheimer, "Abortion in America Today," *Woman's Home Companion*, October 1955.

12. "One Doctor's Choice," *Time*, 12 March 1956, pp. 46–48. Also see Olasky, *Abortion Rites*, pp. 275–278.

13. Glanville Williams, *The Sanctity of Life and the Criminal Law* (New York: Alfred A. Knopf, 1957), pp. 230–232; Note, "The Law of Criminal Abortion: An Analysis of Proposed Reforms," *Indiana Law Journal* 32 (Winter 1957): 193–205, at 205. Also see Don H. Mills, "A Medicolegal Analysis of Abortion Statutes," *Southern California Law Review* 31 (Winter 1958): 181–199.

14. Calderone, ed., *Abortion in the United States* (New York: Hoeber-Harper, 1958), esp. pp. 181–184; *Time*, 2 June 1958, p. 70.

15. James R. Newman, "A Conference on Abortion as a Disease of Societies," *Scientific American* 200 (January 1959): 149–154; C. Lee Buxton, Book Review, *Eugenics Quarterly* 5 (December 1958): 230–231; Fowler V. Harper, Book Review, *Yale Law Journal* 68 (December 1958): 395–398.

16. Minutes, ACLU Due Process Committee, 19 December 1956 and 15 October 1958, ACLU 1956 Vol. 2 and ACLU 1967 Vol. 19. On Kenyon, see her *New York Times* obituary, 14 February 1972, p. 32, and Susan M. Hartmann, "Dorothy Kenyon," in *Notable American Women*, pp. 395–397.

17. *New York Times* and *New York Herald Tribune*, 9 November 1958; Guttmacher, "The Genesis of Liberalized Abortion in New York," *Case Western Reserve Law Review* 23 (Summer 1972): 756–778, at 760–761; Michael S. Burnhill, "Humane Abortion Services: A Revolution in Human Rights . . ." *Mount Sinai Journal of Medicine* 42 (September-October 1975): 431–438, at 431–432. Guttmacher had also made extensive news with a 1947 survey of doctors' attitudes toward birth control. See *Newsweek*, 24 February 1947, p. 58; Guttmacher, "Conception Control and the Medical Profession," *Human Fertility* 12 (March 1947): 1–20; Guttmacher, "Planned Parenthood's Three Decades," *The Churchman*, 15 March 1947, pp. 15–16; *New York Times*, 21 October 1951, p. 74.

18. David Lowe, *Abortion and the Law* (New York: Pocket Books, 1966), pp. 77–80; Guttmacher, "Changing Attitudes and Practices Concerning Abortion," *Maryland State Medical Journal* 20 (December 1971): 59–63, at 61; Guttmacher, "The Genesis of Liberalized Abortion in New York," p. 762; Guttmacher, "A Defense of the Supreme Court's Abortion Decision," *The Humanist* 33 (May-June 1973): 6–7; *New York Times*, 22 May 1959, p. 15; John T. Noonan, Jr., *A Private Choice: Abortion in America in the Seventies* (New York: Free Press, 1979), p. 35. Also similarly see Joseph W. Dellapenna, "The History of Abortion: Technology, Morality, and Law," *University of Pittsburgh Law Review* 40 (Spring 1979): 359–428, at 409.

19. Herbert L. Packer and Ralph J. Gampell, "Therapeutic Abortion: A Problem in Law and Medicine," *Stanford Law Review* 11 (May 1959): 417–455, esp. at 417, 447, 449, 451. See also Harvey L. Zipf, "Recent Abortion Law Reforms (or Much Ado About Nothing)," *Journal of Criminal Law, Criminology and Police Science* 60 (March 1969): 3–23, at 9 (terming the Packer and Gampell article "Possibly the most significant impetus to legal reform" at that time); Luker, *Abortion and the Politics of Motherhood*, p. 130, and the 16 November 1981 testimony of Herma Hill Kay in U.S. Congress, Senate, Committee on the Judiciary, *Constitutional Amendments Relating to Abortion—Testimony Before the Subcommittee on the Constitution*, 97th Cong., 1st sess., 1981, pp. 770–771.

20. Guttmacher, "The Law That Doctors Often Break," *Redbook*, August 1959, pp. 25, 95–98, at 95, 98; *New York Times*, 28 July 1959, p. 29; Guttmacher, *Babies by Choice or by Chance*, esp. pp. 116, 197–199, 215. Also see Guttmacher, "The Law That Doctors Often Break," *Reader's Digest* 76 (January 1960): 51–54.

21. Tydings to Guttmacher, 1 September 1959, and Guttmacher to Tydings, 17 September 1959, Guttmacher Papers; Garrow conversation with Joseph D. Tydings.

22. Garrow conversations with Zad Leavy; Leavy, "Criminal Abortion: Facing the Facts," *Los*

Angeles Bar Journal 34 (October 1959): 355–360, 373–383, at 360; Kummer, "Don't Shy Away From Therapeutic Abortion!" *Medical Economics* 37 (11 April 1960): 165–171; *New York Times*, 17 June 1960; *New York Post*, 17 June 1960, p. 30; Kummer and Leavy, "Criminal Abortion—A Consideration of Ways to Reduce Incidence," *California Medicine* 95 (September 1961): 170–175, at 171, 174, 175. Also see Leavy and Kummer, "Criminal Abortion: Human Hardship and Unyielding Laws," *Southern California Law Review* 35 (Winter 1962): 123–148.

23. Calderone, "Illegal Abortion as a Public Health Problem," *American Journal of Public Health* 50 (July 1960): 948–954, at 949, 951 (a paper originally presented on 19 October 1959); Ernst to Calderone, 4 April 1960, Ernst Box 592; Calderone to Guttmacher, "Pilot Abortion Service," 8 December 1960, Schlesinger 179–2–8.

24. *New York Herald Tribune*, 16 October 1960; [Marguerite Clark], "The Abortion Racket— What Should Be Done?" *Newsweek*, 15 August 1960, pp. 50–52.

25. Harvey M. Adelstein, "The Abortion Law," *Western Reserve Law Review* 12 (December 1960): 74–89; Leonard Dubin, "The Antiquated Abortion Laws," *Temple Law Quarterly* 34 (Winter 1961): 146–151; Quay, "Justifiable Abortion—Medical and Legal Foundations," *Georgetown Law Journal* 49 (Winter 1960): 173–256 and (Spring 1961): 395–538, at 174, 230, 233–234, 397–399.

26. "Abortion Laws Should Be Revised," *Christian Century*, 11 January 1961, p. 37; *New York Times*, 24 February 1961, pp. 1, 16.

27. Lawrence Lader, *Abortion* (Indianapolis: Bobbs-Merrill, 1966), pp. 111–116; *Manchester Union-Leader*, 8 March 1961, pp. 1, 7; *America*, 25 March 1961, p. 811.

28. Sagar C. Jain and Steven Hughes, *California Abortion Act 1967: A Study in Legislative Process* (Chapel Hill: Carolina Population Center, 1969), p. 17; Luker, *Abortion and the Politics of Motherhood*, pp. 69–71; Bates and Zawadzki, *Criminal Abortion*, p. 137.

29. John Bartlow Martin, "Abortion," *Saturday Evening Post*, 20 May 1961, pp. 19–21, 72–74, 27 May 1961, pp. 20–21, 49–56, and 3 June 1961, pp. 25, 91–92. A year later a legal commentator offered a succinct analysis: "Abortion is in fact illegal because it is dangerous, is dangerous because it is performed by the unskilled, and is performed by the unskilled because it is illegal." Graham Hughes, "Morals and the Criminal Law," *Yale Law Journal* 71 (March 1962): 662–683, at 680.

30. George R. Metcalf to Guttmacher, 18 April 1961, Guttmacher to Metcalf, 13 September 1961, Gerald Blank to Guttmacher, 30 October 1961, Guttmacher to G. L. "Tim" Timanus, 28 March 1962, and Guttmacher to Irene Garrow, 17 April 1963, Guttmacher Papers; Guttmacher, "The Legal and Moral Status of Therapeutic Abortion," *Progress in Gynecology* 4 (1963): 279–300, at 286–287.

31. Maginnis to Guttmacher, 28 March 1962, Guttmacher to Maginnis, 9 April 1962, Guttmacher Papers; Maginnis Interview with Cheek, esp. pp. 72, 79; "Chronological Events of Citizens Committee for Humane Abortion Laws," 2pp., n.d. [c.October 1964]; Louise Butler, "The Society for Humane Abortion" (unpublished paper, 21 May 1965), 41pp., SHA Box 1, Schlesinger; Susan Berman, "The Abortion Crusader," *San Francisco* 12 (July 1970): 16–18, 38.

32. Dr. X as Told to Lucy Freeman, *The Abortionist* (New York: Grove Press, 1962); Margaret W. Moore, *Abortion: Murder or Mercy?* (Greenwich, CT: Fawcett Publications, 1962); *New York Times*, 30 April 1962, p. 55, 25 May 1962, pp. 1, 30; *America*, 5 May 1962, pp. 193–194; "Abortion Laws," WMCA Radio Editorial, 9–10 June 1962, Ernst Box 592; *Time*, 13 July 1962, pp. 52–53; *Newsweek*, 30 July 1962, pp. 22–23. Also see *Henrie v. Griffith*, 395 P.2d 809 (Okla. Sup. Ct. 1964).

33. Ernst in *The Abortionist*, pp. 10–11; Ernst to Calderone, 16 April and 28 August 1962, Ernst Boxes 593 and 528; Ernst to Guttmacher, 23 April 1962, Guttmacher Papers; Ernst letter, *New York Times*, 4 May 1962; Ernst, "There Is Desperate Need of Medical Wisdom to Deal With the Problem of 'Abortion,'" *New Medical Materia* 4 (July 1962): 21–23; Guttmacher to Joseph M. Harris, 17 July 1962, Guttmacher Papers. Also see Ernst, *A Love Affair With the Law* (New York: Macmillan, 1968), pp. 122, 132. Ernst regularly cited *Bours v. United States*, 229 F. 960 (7th Cir. 1915), to support his contentions; also see *Commonwealth v. Wheeler*, 315 Mass. 394 (1944).

34. Sherri Finkbine, "The Baby We Didn't Dare to Have," *Redbook*, January 1963, pp. 50, 99–104; Finkbine, "The Lesser of Two Evils," 9 January 1966, San Francisco, CA, Schlesinger Library 289-1-21 (Transcript paginated as 92 to 105); *Dallas Times-Herald*, 15 February 1981, pp. H1, H9; *Washington Post*, 27 April 1987; *New York Times*, 26 July 1962, p. 25, 27 July 1962, p. 12; *Chicago Tribune*, 27 July 1962, p. 4; *Time*, 3 August 1962, p. 30; *Newsweek*, 6 August 1962, p. 52. An edited version of Finkbine's January 1966 speech appears under its same title in Alan F. Guttmacher, ed., *The Case for Legalized Abortion Now* (Berkeley, CA: Diablo Press, 1967), pp. 15–25. Additional retrospective Finkbine profiles include *New York Journal-American*, 9 July 1964, pp. 1, 2; *Washington Post*, 10 December 1968, pp. D1, D4; *Detroit News*, 8 August 1971, pp. C1, C15; *Newsweek*, 17 March 1975, p. 14; and *New York Times*, 4 June 1975, p. 49. The Detroit one also ran in a variety of other papers, including the *Philadelphia Evening Bulletin* (22 August) and the *Arizona Star* (12 September).

35. Finkbine, "The Baby We Didn't Dare to Have," pp. 99, 102 (with Finkbine characterizing herself as "impulsive, intense and high-strung"); *Chicago Tribune*, 28 July 1962, p. 2, 31 July 1962, pp. 1, 4, 1 August 1962, p. 3; *New York Times*, 30 July 1962, p. 21, 31 July 1962, p. 9, 1 August 1962, p. 19, 2 August 1962, p. 12; Yale McFate, "Memorandum of Opinion," *Good Samaritan Hospital et al.* v. *Attorney General*, Maricopa County Superior Court, #140504, 30 July 1962, 4pp., Lader Box 1; *Los Angeles Times*, 31 July 1962, pp. 1, 13, 1 August 1962, pp. 1, 16, 4 August 1962, pp. 1, 15; *Washington Post*, 31 July 1962, p. 3, 3 August 1962, p. A4; Cheifetz to Lawrence Lader, 12 June 1964, Lader Box 1.

36. *Chicago Tribune*, 4 August 1962, p. 5, 5 August 1962, pp. 1, 2; *Newsweek*, 13 August 1962, p. 54; *New York Times*, 5 August 1962, p. 64, 7 August 1962, p. 15, 8 August 1962, p. 19, 10 August 1962, p. 6, 13 August 1962, p. 16, 19 August 1962, p. 69, 20 August 1962, p. 9. Also see *New York Post*, 20 August 1962; *New York Journal-American*, 4 September 1962, pp. 1, 13.

37. Celeste Condit, *Decoding Abortion Rhetoric* (Urbana: University of Illinois Press, 1990), pp. 28–31, at 29; Charles C. Dahlberg, "Abortion," in Ralph Slovenko, ed., *Sexual Behavior and the Law* (Springfield, IL: Charles C. Thomas, 1965), pp. 379–393, at 380; Luker, *Abortion and the Politics of Motherhood*, pp. 62–65, 79–80; Marvin N. and Susan N. Olasky, "The Crossover in Newspaper Coverage of Abortion from Murder to Liberation," *Journalism Quarterly* 63 (Spring 1986): 31–37, at 31–32. Also see Marvin Olasky, *The Press and Abortion, 1838–1988* (Hillsdale, NJ: Lawrence Erlbaum, 1988), pp. 92–98; Olasky, *Abortion Rites*, pp. 278–282; and Willard D. Lorensen, "Abortion and the Crime-Sin Spectrum," *West Virginia Law Review* 70 (December 1967): 20–39, at 24–25 ("The present-day abortion law reform movement is largely a product of the ripple of national attention that followed in the wake of the Finkbine case").

38. Judith L. Rapoport, "American Abortion Applicants in Sweden," *Archives of General Psychiatry* 13 (July 1965): 24–33, at 24 and 31 ("most women" applicants "expressed the opinion ... that they had the right to achieve or to renounce motherhood"); John L. Moore, Jr., "Therapeutic Abortion," *Journal of the Medical Association of Georgia* 51 (September 1962): 460–461; Philip R. Overton. "Abortion and Texas Law," *Texas State Journal of Medicine* 58 (September 1962): 765; "2 Doctors Debate Legalizing Abortion," *Dallas Morning News*, 21 September 1962; John C. Knott, "Statement on Abortion," 18 September 1962, 1pp., Archives of the Archdiocese of Hartford.

39. Hazel G. Erskine, "The Polls: The Population Explosion, Birth Control, and Sex Education," *Public Opinion Quarterly* 30 (Fall 1966): 490–501, at 498; Gallup Poll, Volume 3, p. 1784.

40. Dorothy Ames to Ernst, 25 October 1962, Ernst to Ames, 29 October 1962, and Ames to Ernst, 1 November 1962, Ernst Box 592. On Ernst's 12 December 1962 talk on "Medicine or Law—At Whose Door Rests the Responsibility for Correcting the Legal Restrictions for Medical Abortion?" to a dinner meeting of two sections of the Westchester Academy of Medicine, see the various news clippings from the *White Plains Reporter Dispatch*, the *Mount Vernon Daily Argus*, and other papers in Ernst Boxes 528 and 592.

41. [California] Assembly Interim Committee on Criminal Procedure, *Abortion Hearing*, 17–18 December 1962, San Diego, 278pp., at pp. 82, 116, and 254; Jain and Hughes, *California Abortion Act*, pp. 17–22; Kummer, ed., *Abortion: Legal and Illegal* [23 November 1963] (Santa

Monica, CA: Santa Monica Printers, 1967), p. 19; Luker, *Abortion and the Politics of Motherhood*, pp. 70–76; Maginnis Interview with Cheek, p. 89; Linda Beck to Guttmacher, 9 January 1963, Maginnis to Guttmacher, 13 February 1963, Guttmacher to Maginnis and to Beck, 6 March 1963, Maginnis, CCHAL *Newsletter* #2, 12 March 1963, and Maginnis to Guttmacher, 27 March 1963, Guttmacher Papers; Beilenson Interviews with Edginton and Garrow.

42. Finkbine, "The Baby We Didn't Dare to Have," p. 104; *Bridgeport Post*, 27 January 1963; James Ridgeway, "One Million Abortions," *The New Republic* 148 (9 February 1963): 14–17; Mary Calderone to J. David Wyles, 13 March 1963, Guttmacher Papers; *Columbia Spectator*, 14 March 1963; Hall, "Thalidomide and Our Abortion Laws," *Columbia Forum* 6 (Winter 1963): 10–13, at 11 and 13; Garrow conversation with Robert E. Hall; Ernst to Erik Wensberg, 21 March 1963, Ernst to Guttmacher, 29 April 1963, Ernst to Hall, 3 May 1963, Guttmacher Papers; Ernst to Hall, 13 May 1963, and Hall to Ernst, 20 May 1963, Ernst Box 729; Ernst to Pilpel, 9 and 19 April 1963, Ernst Box 592; Campbell Interview with Reed, p. 81; Irene Garrow to Guttmacher, 3 April 1963, and Guttmacher to Garrow, 17 April 1963, Guttmacher Papers.

43. *New York Times*, 19 May 1963, p. 81; Edmund W. Overstreet to Anthony C. Beilenson, 6 June 1963, and Overstreet to Lawrence Lader, 27 May 1964, Lader Box 2; Lester Kinsolving, "What About Therapeutic Abortion?," *Christian Century*, 13 May 1964, pp. 632–635; Howard Hammond, "Therapeutic Abortion: Ten Years' Experience With Hospital Committee Control," *American Journal of Obstetrics and Gynecology* 89 (1 June 1964): 349–355 [September 1963 paper followed by comments from Keith P. Russell and Edmund W. Overstreet]; Leavy in Kummer, ed., *Abortion: Legal and Illegal* [23 November 1963], p. 34; William J. Kenealy, "Law and Morals," *Catholic Lawyer* 9 (Summer 1963): 200–210, 264, at 209; Maginnis to Ernst, 15 July 1963, Ernst Box 593. Also see Leavy and Kummer, "Criminal Abortion: A Failure of Law," *American Bar Association Journal* 50 (January 1964): 52–55.

44. Philip D. Merwin to Pilpel, 18 July 1963, Pilpel to Guttmacher, 23 July and 28 October 1963, Guttmacher Papers; Guttmacher, "Induced Abortion," *New York State Journal of Medicine* 63 (15 August 1963): 2334–2335; Guttmacher, "The Legal and Moral Status of Therapeutic Abortion," *Progress in Gynecology* 4 (1963): 279–300, at 298–299.

45. Donald J. Kenney, "Thalidomide—Catalyst to Abortion Reform," *Arizona Law Review* 5 (Fall 1963): 105–111; Marvin M. Moore, "Antiquated Abortion Laws," *Washington and Lee Law Review* 20 (Fall 1963): 250–259; Monroe Trout, "Therapeutic Abortion Laws Need Therapy," *Temple Law Quarterly* 37 (Winter 1964): 172–189; Ralph J. Gampell, "Legal Status of Therapeutic Abortion and Sterilization in the United States," *Clinical Obstetrics and Gynecology* 7 (March 1964): 22–36; Peter S. Raible, "Abortion," 20 October 1963, University Unitarian Church, Seattle, 8pp., YWCA-UW Papers II-12; Kummer, *Abortion: Legal and Illegal* [23 November 1963], pp. 20–22, 26–27. Also see Snell Putney, "Reason and Abortion," *The Campus Voice* #15 (21 October 1963): 2–4; but see Muriel Davidson, "The Deadly Favor," *Ladies' Home Journal*, November 1963, pp. 53–57.

46. Hardin, *Population, Evolution, and Birth Control*, 2nd ed. (San Francisco: W. H. Freeman & Co., 1969), p. 278; Hardin, "The Case for Legalized Abortion" [1 October 1963], in Hardin, *Stalking the Wild Taboo* (Los Altos, CA: William Kaufmann, Inc., 1973), pp. 10–26, at 11 and 22.

47. Guttmacher to Hardin, 30 December 1963, Hardin to Guttmacher, 2 January 1964, Guttmacher Papers.

48. Pilpel, "Abortion," 20 March 1964, 10pp., Lader Box 2, at 3, 5, and 10; "Symposium on 'The Social Problem of Abortion'" [20 March 1964], *Bulletin of the Sloane Hospital for Women* 11 (Fall 1965): 65–79, at 66 and 72; Guttmacher to Jeanne Brown, 10 April 1964, Guttmacher Papers; *White Plains Reporter-Dispatch*, 24 April 1964; Garrow conversation with Robert E. Hall; Daniel H. Bloom letter in *New York Times*, 13 May 1964; Sylvia Bloom to Guttmacher, n.d. [c.15 September 1964], Guttmacher Papers. Also see Mary Calderone, "Abortion: Disease of Society," *Sexology*, April 1964, pp. 604–606; and E. Mike Miller and Donald E. Wintrode, "A New Approach to Old Crimes: The Model Penal Code," *Notre Dame Lawyer* 39 (April 1964): 310–334, at 312 ("abortion is no longer thought of with such animosity as it was in the past").

49. Hardin, "Abortion and Human Dignity," 29 April 1964, 5pp., which also appears in Guttmacher, ed., *The Case for Legalized Abortion Now* (Berkeley, CA: Diablo Press, 1967), pp. 69–86; Hardin, *Stalking the Wild Taboo*, p. 27.

50. Guttmacher, "Voluntary Agencies," in Minoru Muramatsu and Paul A. Harper, eds., *Population Dynamics* (Baltimore: Johns Hopkins University Press, 1965), pp. 119–127 and 171–175, at 175 [May 1964].

51. Lader to Ernst, 14 May 1964, Ernst to Alice Rossi and to Caleb Foote, 12 May 1964, Foote to Ernst, 19 May 1964, Ernst Box 592; Hardin to Lader, 17 April 1964, Lader to Hardin, 11 May 1964, Lader to Raible, 12 May 1964, Raible to Lader, 22 May 1964, Hardin to Lader, 23 May 1964, Lader to Hardin, 27 May 1964, Lader to Jerry Kummer, 13 July 1964, and Kummer to Lader, 15 July 1964, Lader Boxes 1 and 2.

52. Lader to Pilpel, 23 June 1964, Pilpel, untitled paper prepared for presentation at ACLU Conference, Boulder, CO, 21–24 June 1964, p. 2, Lader to Pat Maginnis, 27 May 1964, and Maginnis to Lader, 11 July 1964, Lader Box 2; *San Francisco Chronicle*, 21 July 1964, p. 2; Jain and Hughes, *California Abortion Act*, pp. 22–23; Buxton to Lader, 21 July 1964, Lader Box 1; *Houston Chronicle*, 14–19 June 1964; Bates and Zawadzki, *Criminal Abortion*, pp. 3, 140; Sylvia Bloom to Alan Guttmacher, n.d. [c.15 September 1964], Guttmacher Papers. At the July hearing, Garrett Hardin reiterated his earlier comments, telling the committee that "my personal viewpoint is that abortion should be on demand, that it is simply a part of normal medicine and there should be no restrictions on it whatever. . . . the fact she doesn't want it should be enough of an indication that abortion should be allowed." [California] Assembly Interim Committee on Criminal Procedure, *The Humane Abortion Act*, 20 July 1964, San Francisco, 130pp., at pp. 25–26.

53. Sylvia Bloom to Alan Guttmacher, n.d. [c.15 September 1964] and 8 October 1964, "Committee for a Humane Abortion Law," 7 November 1964, Guttmacher Papers; Garrow conversation with Robert E. Hall; AHA Press Release, 18 February 1965, Ruth Smith Papers Box 1.

54. *New York Post*, 25 November 1964, p. 26; *New York Herald Tribune*, 25 November 1964; "Testimony of Harriet F. Pilpel," 24 November 1964, p. 20; "Therapeutic Abortion," *Bulletin of the New York Academy of Medicine* 41 (April 1965): 406–409 [7 December 1964]; *New York Times*, 14 December 1964, p. 48; *Time*, 25 December 1964, p. 53; Hall to Lader, 1 December 1964, Lader to Hall, 17 and 29 December 1964, Lader Box 2; Smith to Lonny Myers, 2 October 1967, ARAI I-7; Garrow conversation with Robert E. Hall. Also see Pilpel, "Sex vs. the Law: A Study in Hypocrisy," *Harper's* 230 (January 1965): 35–40, which speaks of "a fundamental human right of privacy."

55. "Association for Humane Abortion Organized," *Ethical Culture Today* 1 (February 1965): 1 and 4; AHA Press Release, 18 February 1965, Ruth Smith Papers Box 1; Soll Goodman to Ernst, 28 January and 4 February 1965, Ernst to Goodman, 10 February 1965, Ernst Box 592; *AHA News* Vol. 1, #1, n.d. [c.13 March 1965]; *New York Times*, 31 January 1965, p. 73; *Modern Medicine*, 15 February 1965, pp. 22, 26; *Medical World News*, 5 March 1965, pp. 38–39; Hall, "New York Abortion Law Survey," *American Journal of Obstetrics and Gynecology* 93 (15 December 1965): 1182–1183 ("Education of the laity and even of the legal profession will be time consuming. Meanwhile it devolves upon the obstetricians, who are most familiar with the problem and its need for solution, to define the former and promote the latter"). Also see Hall, "Therapeutic Abortion, Sterilization, and Contraception," *American Journal of Obstetrics and Gynecology* 91 (15 February 1965): 518–532.

56. "A New Abortion Law," *New York Times*, 13 February 1965, p. 26; *New York Times*, 27 February 1965, p. 24 (Byrn), 4 March 1965, p. 30, 16 April 1965, p. 28 (Means), 30 April 1965, p. 34; AHA Press Release, 18 February 1965, Ruth Smith Papers, Box 1; *AHA News* Vol. 1, #1, n.d. [c.13 March 1965]; Lader to Maginnis, 23 February 1965, Lader Box 1; Lee R. Dice, "When Abortion Is Justified," *The Nation* 200 (22 February 1965): 189–191; Sutton to Guttmacher, 4 March 1965, Guttmacher Papers; *New York World-Telegram & Sun*, 19 March 1965, p. 11; Jain and Hughes, *California Abortion Act*, p. 24; Michael S. Sands, "The Therapeutic Abortion Act," *UCLA Law Review* 13 (January 1966): 285–312, esp. 307–312; Alan F. Charles to Lader, 29 January 1965, Lader Box 2. The best-known and most signifi-

cant previous reversal of an M.D.'s conviction was in *People* v. *Ballard*, 335 P.2d 204 (2d Dist. Ct. App. 1959). Also see Edwin M. Schur, *Crimes Without Victims* (Englewood Cliffs, NJ: Prentice-Hall, 1965), pp. 57–58; and Sybil Meloy, "Pre-Implantation Fertility Control and the Abortion Laws," *Chicago-Kent Law Review* 41 (Fall 1964): 183–206; but see John G. Herbert, "Is Legalized Abortion the Solution to Criminal Abortion?," *University of Colorado Law Review* 37 (Winter 1965): 283–292.

57. Duncan Simmons to Guttmacher, 9 March 1965, Guttmacher Papers; *Dallas Morning News*, 20 March 1965; David Lowe, *Abortion and the Law* (New York: Pocket Books, 1966), esp. pp. 37–38, 57–58, 80–88, 90, 114–116; "The Cruel Abortion Law," *New York Times*, 7 April 1965, p. 42, also see 2 June 1965, p. 44. A low-visibility reform bill that was never acted upon (S.B. 349) also was introduced in the Ohio legislature, as was one in Wisconsin. David Lowe produced the CBS documentary, and his paperback book is based directly on it.

58. Lader, "The Scandal of Abortion Laws," *New York Times Magazine*, 25 April 1965, pp. 32ff; William Kopit and Pilpel, "Abortion and the New York Penal Laws," 20 April 1965, ACLU 1966 Vol. 12, pp. 4–5; Means to Ruth P. Smith, 11 April 1965, Lader Box 2; Means to Smith, 18 April 1965, Guttmacher Papers; Means to John Pemberton, 21 April 1965, ACLU 1965 Vol. 7; Means to Lader, 6 May 1965, Means to Jack Star, 21 May 1965, Lader Box 2. On the impact of Lader's article, also see *America*, 15 May 1965, p. 703; and Alan Reitman to ASA, 2 June 1965, ACLU 1965 Vol. 7.

59. *Los Angeles Times*, 13 May 1965, 14 May 1965, p. II-1; *Life*, 4 June 1965, pp. 24–31; Luker, *Abortion and the Politics of Motherhood*, pp. 81–82; *New York Times*, 22 June 1965, p. 42; Allan J. Rosenberg and Emmanuel Silver, "Suicide, Psychiatrists and Therapeutic Abortion," *California Medicine* 102 (June 1965): 407–411, at 410–411. Also see *America*, 19 June 1965, pp. 877–881, and 16 October 1965, pp. 436–438; and both Kenneth R. Niswander, "Medical Abortion Practices in the United States," and Harold Rosen, "Psychiatric Implications of Abortion: A Case Study in Social Hypocrisy," *Western Reserve Law Review* 17 (December 1965): 403–423 and 435–464.

60. Jain and Hughes, *California Abortion Act*, pp. 27–29; *San Francisco Chronicle*, 20 May 1965; Louise Butler, "The Society for Humane Abortion" (unpublished paper, 21 May 1965), SHA Papers Box 1; *SHA Newsletter* Vol. 1, #1 (9 May 1965), #2 (August 1965), #3 (September 1965), #4 (October-November 1965), #5 (December 1965); Maginnis and Lana Clarke Phelan Interviews with Cheek; *San Jose Mercury-News*, 29 August 1965, p. 32.

61. *Washington Post*, 30 August 1965, p. B3; "Mrs. X," "One Woman's Abortion," *The Atlantic* 216 (August 1965): 66–68; *Time*, 17 September 1965, p. 82; Walter Goodman, "Abortion and Sterilization: The Search for Answers," *Redbook*, October 1965, pp. 70–71, 147–150; Jack Star, "The Growing Tragedy of Illegal Abortion," *Look*, 19 October 1965, pp. 149–160; Byrn, "The Abortion Question," *Catholic Lawyer* 11 (Autumn 1965): 316–322, at 322; Drinan, "The Inviolability of the Right to Be Born," *Western Reserve Law Review* 17 (December 1965): 465–479, at 475. Also see "Should Abortion Be Legal?" *Civil Liberties in New York*, October 1965, pp. 1, 6, and *Riverdale Press*, 4 and 11 November 1965; but see A. C. Mietus and Norbert J. Mietus, "Criminal Abortion," *American Bar Association Journal* 51 (October 1965): 924–928.

62. *New York Times*, 26 October 1965, p. 37, 2 December 1965, p. 24, 8 December 1965, p. 46; "Abortion and the Law," *Journal of the American Medical Women's Association* 21 (March 1966): 232; *Atlanta Constitution*, 6 December 1965; Kummer and Leavy, "Therapeutic Abortion Law Confusion," *Journal of the American Medical Association* 195 (10 January 1966): 140–144; B. James George, Jr., "Current Abortion Laws: Proposals and Movements for Reform," and Kenneth J. Ryan, "Humane Abortion Laws and the Health Needs of Society," *Western Reserve Law Review* 17 (December 1965): 371–402 and 424–434; Marvin M. Moore, "Unrealistic Abortion Laws," *Criminal Law Bulletin* 1 (December 1965): 3–13; James S. Bukes and William C. Hewson, "The Legal Status of Therapeutic Abortion," *University of Pittsburgh Law Review* 27 (March 1966): 669–682; Savage to Philip Overton, 6 December 1965, Savage Papers; Charles R. Ross to Guttmacher, 26 October 1965, Guttmacher Papers. Apropos of the *Times*'s figure, a subsequent study estimated that the nationwide 1965 abortion death toll

actually came to 235. Hyman Rodman et al., *The Abortion Question* (New York: Columbia University Press, 1987), p. 46. Early in 1965 the *Times* had reported a 1964 New York *City* illegal abortion death toll totaling seventy-nine, assertedly the lowest on record. 11 January 1965, p. 42. A subsequent review of 223 abortion deaths recorded in one state between August 1957 and December 1965 is Leon P. Fox, "Abortion Deaths in California," *American Journal of Obstetrics and Gynecology* 98 (1 July 1967): 645–653.

63. Erskine, "The Polls," p. 499; *New York Herald Tribune*, 7 March 1966, pp. 17, 19; *New York Times*, 24 April 1966, p. 83; Rossi, "Abortion Laws and Their Victims," *Transaction* 3 (September-October 1966): 7–12; Rossi, "Public Views on Abortion," in Guttmacher, ed., *The Case for Legalized Abortion Now*, pp. 26–53; *America*, 12 February 1966, p. 219. Also note the results of an otherwise undocumented 18 January 1966 CBS News "National Health Quiz" which asked simply "Would you favor relaxation of existing abortion laws?" and reported that 43 percent of whoever the respondents were said yes, and 39 percent no. See Anthony C. Beilenson, "The Therapeutic Abortion Act," *Los Angeles Bar Bulletin* 41 (May 1966): 316–319, 344–346, at 319. On ASA, see Ruth P. Smith, "Executive Director's Report," 27 October 1965, "Headquarters Report," 19 November 1965, and "Report of the Executive Director," 30 March 1966, Smith Papers, Box 1.

64. Russell B. Shaw, *Abortion and Public Policy* (Washington, DC: Family Life Bureau, NCWC, February 1966), esp. p. 9; Buckley, "The Catholic Church and Abortion," *National Review*, 5 April 1966, p. 308; Richard P. Byrne, "A Critical Look at Legalized Abortion," *Los Angeles Bar Bulletin* 41 (May 1966): 320–323, 347–354; *Wall Street Journal*, 15 February 1966, pp. 1, 18; *Atlanta Constitution*, 27 April 1966, pp. 1, 9; *Chicago Tribune Magazine*, 13 February 1966, pp. 18ff; Phelan, "Abortion Laws: The Cruel Fraud," and Transcript, "Twentieth Century Women and Archaic Abortion Laws," 9 January 1966, SHA Papers II-22, esp. pp. 133–134, 139, 149; *SHA Newsletter* Vol. 2 #1 (February-March 1966), #2 (April-May 1966). Three standard volumes survey the development of Roman Catholic doctrine concerning abortion: Roger J. Huser, *The Crime of Abortion in Canon Law* (Washington, DC: Catholic University of America Press, 1942); John Connery, *Abortion: The Development of the Roman Catholic Perspective* (Chicago: Loyola University Press, 1977); Susan Teft Nicholson, *Abortion and the Roman Catholic Church* (Knoxville, TN: Religious Ethics, 1978). Also see John T. Noonan, Jr., "Abortion and the Catholic Church: A Summary History," *Natural Law Forum* 12 (1967): 85–131, Hans Lotstra, *Abortion: The Catholic Debate in America* (New York: Irvington Publishers, 1985), and Patricia B. Jung and Thomas A. Shannon, eds., *Abortion and Catholicism: The American Debate* (New York: Crossroad, 1988).

65. *New York Times*, 3 March 1966, p. 24, 7 March 1966, pp. 26, 28, 8 March 1966, p. 28, 16 March 1965, p. 28, 23 March 1966, p. 46 (Pilpel); "Testimony of Harriet F. Pilpel," 7 March 1966, Lucas Box 28; "Minutes of the Proceedings of a Public Hearing of the Assembly Health Committee on Abortion," 7 March 1966, 141pp., ACLU 1966 Vol. 12, esp. pp. 20 and 100; *New York Post*, 13 March 1966, p. 31; *ASA News*, Spring 1966. Also see Pilpel, "Birth Control, Abortion and Sterilization—The Dynamics of Intervention by Judicial, Administrative, Professional and Lay Action," *American Journal of Orthopsychiatry* 36 (March 1966): 207–208; Pilpel, "The Abortion Crisis—Danger and Opportunity" (unpublished paper, August 1966), 8pp., ARAI 10–6, p. 6 ("The basic theory of the Connecticut birth control decision suggests that if the abortion laws are strictly and literally interpreted, they too, may well be unconstitutional"); Pilpel, "Birth Control and a New Birth of Freedom," *Ohio State Law Journal* 27 (Fall 1966): 679–690; and *Civil Liberties in New York* 18 (April 1970): 2–3. Pilpel's August 1966 paper subsequently appeared as "The Abortion Crisis" in Guttmacher, ed., *The Case for Legalized Abortion Now*, pp. 97–113.

66. ASA Board Minutes, 18 January, 1 March, and 20 April 1966, Lader Box 13; *New York Times*, 31 March 1966, p. 13; Ralph M. Crowley and Robert W. Laidlaw, "Psychiatric Opinion Regarding Abortion," *American Journal of Psychiatry* 124 (October 1967): 559–562; H. Benjamin Munson, "Abortion in Modern Times: Thoughts and Comments," *South Dakota Journal of Medicine* 19 (April 1966): 23–25, 28–30, and Munson, "Let's Legalize Abortions," *United Church Herald*, February 1967, pp. 25–27; *Dallas Morning News*, 16 April 1966; *Houston*

Chronicle, 17 April 1966, 24 April 1966, p. II-4; *Dallas Times Herald*, 18 April 1966; *Houston Post*, 21 April and 22 and 29 May 1966; *Fort Worth Star-Telegram*, 21 June 1966, 22 June 1966, pp. VI-4, 5, 23 June 1966; C. Lincoln Williston to Savage, 10 May 1966, and Joe T. Nelson to Lowell B. Baker, 7 April 1967, Savage Papers. Also see *AMA News*, 23 May 1966, p. 9; *New York Times*, 6 May 1966, p. 31, 20 July 1966, p. 83; Ruth and Edward Brecher, *New York Times Magazine*, 29 May 1966, pp. 6–7ff; and especially Kenneth R. Niswander et al., "Changing Attitudes Toward Therapeutic Abortion," *Journal of the American Medical Association* 196 (27 June 1966): 124–127.

67. Alfred L. Severson to Roemer, to Kinsolving, and to Keith P. Russell, 30 March 1966, Dorothy C. Stolz to Severson, 1 April 1966, Roemer to Kinsolving, 4 April 1966, Stolz to Kinsolving, 5 April 1966, Severson to Kinsolving, 5 April 1966, Kinsolving to Severson, 18 April 1966 (II), Stolz to CCTA Board, 19 May 1966, Kinsolving to Stolz, 23 May 1966, CCTA Board Minutes, 1 June 1966, CCTA Boxes 7 and 1; Jain and Hughes, *California Abortion Act*, p. 36; Roemer to Egeberg and Russell, 18 January 1969, CCTA Box 4; Garrow conversations with Ruth Roemer and Keith P. Russell; Luker, *Abortion and the Politics of Motherhood*, pp. 84–85.

68. Lawrence Sherwin and Edmund W. Overstreet, "Therapeutic Abortion: Attitudes and Practices of California Physicians," *California Medicine* 105 (November 1966): 337–339; Joseph L. Shalant, "Abortion Laws and Why the Court Must Act" (unpublished paper, 25 April 1966), 94pp., ACLU 1966 Vol. 11; *Newsweek*, 6 June 1966, p. 58; *New York Times*, 19 June 1966, p. 88; "The Better Way: The Campaign to Make Legal Abortion Easier," *Good Housekeeping* 164 (March 1967): 191–193; Gerald M. Feigen letter, *Playboy*, May 1967, pp. 149–150; CCTA Board Minutes, 1 June 1966, CCTA Box 7; Ruth P. Smith to Severson, 17 June 1966, Smith Box 1; Kinsolving to CCTA Board, 25 July 1966, CCTA Box 1; *San Francisco Chronicle*, 26 July 1966, 19 August 1966; Roemer to Sunnen, 1 August 1966, CCTA Box 7; *New York Times*, 24 September 1966, p. 19; *San Francisco Examiner*, 26, 27, and 28 September 1966; *SHA Newsletter* Vol. 3 #1 (January-February 1967); Leavy to Joseph L. Carr, 9 September 1966, CCTA Box 1; "Policy Statement on Abortion," ACLU of Southern California, 21 September 1966, ACLU 1967 Vol. 5; Jain and Hughes, *California Abortion Act*, pp. 37–39; Maginnis Interview with Cheek, pp. 105–125; Garrow conversations with Keith P. Russell, Ruth Roemer, and Zad Leavy; Leavy, "The Legalization of Therapeutic Abortion," *Emko Newsletter*, April 1973, pp. 1–3; Luker, *Abortion and the Politics of Motherhood*, pp. 86–87. Also see Lader, *Abortion*, pp. 172–173, 175.

69. Stolz, "Progress Report," 28 September and 26 October 1966, CCTA Box 7; *ASA News*, November-December 1966; Savage, "Report of the Special Committee to Study Abortion Laws in Texas," 1 October 1966, William G. Reid to C. Lincoln Williston, 10 November 1966, Peggy J. Whalley to Savage, 14 December 1966, Williston to Savage, 28 December 1966, Savage Papers; *Houston Post*, 9 November 1966; Blumenthal to Lader, 19 September 1966, John V. P. Lassoe to William Genne, 12 September 1966, Blumenthal and Charles M. Kinsolving, Jr., to Hall, 25 October 1966, Lader to Blumenthal and Kinsolving, 2 November 1966, Lader to Blumenthal, Hall and Kinsolving, 11 November 1966, Lader Box 4; William B. Ober, "We Should Legalize Abortion," *Saturday Evening Post*, 8 October 1966, pp. 14, 20; Ober to John Holloman, 3 November 1966, "Bill" [Ober] to Lader, 8 November 1966, Lader Box 7. On Ober, see his *New York Times* obituary, 1 May 1993, p. 31. Also see CCTA Board Minutes, and Kinsolving, "Progress Report," 28 September 1966, and Roemer to Robert Lamb, 30 September 1966, CCTA Boxes 7 and 1; D. Frank Kaltreider, "Changing Attitudes Toward Abortion, Sterilization, and Contraception," *Texas Medicine* 62 (August 1966): 40–45; and ASA Board Minutes, 19 September 1966, Lader Box 13. Previous New York assembly sponsor Percy Sutton had left the legislature to become Manhattan Borough President.

70. "The Right to Abortion," *The Nation* 203 (17 October 1966): 373–374; *Newsweek*, 14 November 1966, p. 92; *New York Times*, 25 October 1966, p. 29, 4 December 1966, p. 81. Also see *San Francisco Chronicle*, 11 October 1966, pp. 1, 16; Hall, "Abortion in American Hospitals," *American Journal of Public Health* 57 (November 1967): 1933–1936; Hall, "Present

Abortion Practices in Hospitals of New York State," *New York Medicine* 23 (March 1967): 124–126; H. Martin Huddleston, "The Law of Therapeutic Abortion: A Social Commentary on Proposed Reform," *Journal of Public Law* 1966: 386–400; and particularly Thomas S. Szasz, "The Ethics of Abortion," *The Humanist* 26 (September-October 1966): 147–148, who offered a unique argument for repeal and against reform. Calling abortion "no more a medical problem than the use of the electric chair makes capital punishment a problem of electrical engineering," Szasz asserted that if a fetus was a human person, "it is no more reasonable to condone killing the fetus because it threatens the woman's mental health, than it is to condone killing her husband or mother-in-law because they threaten her mental health." "The proper remedy," he concluded, "must be sought not in medically and psychiatrically 'liberal' abortion laws, but in the repeal of all such laws." Also see both Alice S. Rossi, "Public Views on Abortion," and Pat Maginnis, "Elective Abortion as a Woman's Right," in Guttmacher, ed., *The Case for Legalized Abortion Now*, pp. 26–53 and 131–144. Rossi stated (p. 31) that "no woman should bear any child she does not want" and Maginnis (p. 137) criticized reform bills for failing to acknowledge "the individual woman as capable of exercising self determination." Maginnis and her colleague Rowena Gurner were also subsequently arrested in February 1967 in Redwood City for distributing abortion information, and again the charges were eventually dismissed.

On ASA, see ASA Board Minutes, 22 November 1966, Lader Box 13 and Smith Box 1; Hall to Guttmacher, 23 November 1966, Guttmacher Papers; Robert L. Goldberg to Hall, and Louis M. Hellman to Smith, 6 December 1966, Smith to ASA Board, 9 January 1967, Smith Box 1, and Smith to Lonny Myers, 27 March 1967, ARAI 8–7.

71. "A Report," Citizens for the Extension of Birth Control Services, 24 August 1962, Myers 1–10; Myers to Marjorie Pinschmidt, 29 October 1965, ARAI 2–11; Myers to Robert Hartman, 26 October 1966, Myers to Jeanne Spurlock, 22 November 1966, Myers to "Dear Fellow Citizen," February-March 1967, ARAI 2–1 and 1–7 and Lader Box 4; *Chicago Sun-Times*, 9 February 1969, pp. F1, F16; Myers Interview with Chesler; Garrow conversations with Myers and with Shaw; Staggenborg, *The Pro-Choice Movement*, pp. 16–17.

72. Leavy and Kay, "Brief as Amici Curiae for Doctors Gail V. Anderson et al.," *Shively v. Board of Medical Examiners*, Cal. Sup. Ct. #7756, 28 November 1966, 39pp., ACLU 1967 Vol. 19, esp. pp. 17, 23–27; Leavy and Kummer, "Abortion and the Population Crisis: Therapeutic Abortion and the Law; Some New Approaches," *Ohio State Law Journal* 27 (Fall 1966): 647–678, at 672–674; Leavy and Kay, "First Errata Sheet to Brief as Amici Curiae . . ." *Shively and Smith v. Stewart*, #7756, 18pp., 2 December 1966; Leavy to Pilpel, 23 December 1966, CCTA Box 10; Keith Russell to Kinsolving, 18 November 1966, and Kinsolving to Ruth Roemer, 30 December 1966, CCTA Box 1; *CCTA Newsletter*, January 1967.

73. *New York Times*, 13 December 1966, p. 52, 22 December 1966, p. 35, 3 January 1967, p. 36, 7 January 1967, p. 26, 11 January 1967, p. 54, 13 January 1967, p. 22, 18 January 1967, p. 29, 30 January 1967, pp. 1, 40, 31 January 1967, p. 25; Pilpel, "Testimony," 3 February 1967, ACLU 1967 Vol. 5, pp. 8–9; *New York Times*, 4 February 1967, p. 24, 9 February 1967, p. 24, 10 February 1967, p. 39, 11 February 1967, p. 18, 12 February 1967, pp. 61, E5, 13 February 1967, pp. 1, 50, 14 February 1967, pp. 32, 42, 18 February 1967, pp. 1, 28 (Marya Mannes), and 30, 20 February 1967, pp. 1, 24, 21 February 1967, p. 46, 23 February 1967, pp. 1, 41, 25 February 1967, pp. 1, 30; *Medical World News*, 24 February 1967, pp. 58–64; "Abortion and the Law," *JAMA* 199 (16 January 1967): 179–180. Also see Larry P. Pletcher, "New York State Abortion Reform, 1967: A Case Study" (unpublished B.A. thesis, Princeton University, 1968), esp. p. 55; and Mark S. Reingold, "Abortion Law Reform in New York: A Study of Religious, Moral, Medical and Legal Conflict," *Albany Law Review* 31 (June 1967): 290–309, for an explication of the Blumenthal bill's provisions. See as well Marya Mannes, "A Woman Views Abortion," in Guttmacher, ed., *The Case for Legalized Abortion Now*, pp. 54–60, esp. p. 59 ("the right to control what takes place within our own body").

74. *Christian Century*, 1 February 1967, p. 132; Moody, "Man's Vengeance on Woman: Some Reflections on Abortion Laws," *Renewal*, February 1967, pp. 8–9; *Time*, 10 February 1967, p. 47; *Commonweal*, 24 February 1967, pp. 582–583; Byrn, "Abortion in Perspective," *Duquesne*

University Law Review 5 (1966–67): 125–141; Byrn, "Abortion—A Legal View," *Commonweal*, 17 March 1967, pp. 679–681, at 680; Drinan, "Strategy on Abortion," *America*, 4 February 1967, pp. 177–179; Hall, "The Medico-Legal Aspects of Abortion," *Criminologica* 4 (February 1967): 7–10, at 8. See as well John C. Bennett, "The Abortion Debate," *Christianity & Crisis*, 20 March 1967, pp. 47–48; Thomas H. Barnard, Jr., "An Analysis and Criticism of the Model Penal Code Provisions on the Law of Abortion," *Western Reserve Law Review* 18 (January 1967): 540–564; David Granfield, "Law and Morals," *Criminologica* 4 (February 1967): 11–19; Richard J. Neuhaus, "The Dangerous Assumptions," *Commonweal*, 30 June 1967, pp. 408–413; also see Hall to ASA Board, 16 January 1967, Guttmacher Papers.

On the ACLU discussions, see Joel Gora to Alan Reitman, 2 and 19 October 1966, ACLU 1967 Vol. 19, Reitman to Thomas Browning, 5 January 1967, "The Office" to Board Members, "Due Process Committee Recommendation on Abortion," 8 February 1967, ACLU Board Minutes, 14 February 1967, pp. 3–7, Edward J. Ennis to Due Process Committee, 20 February 1967, Kenyon to "Dear Fellow Board Member," 21 February 1967, Ennis to "Dear Fellow Board Member," 24 February 1967, ACLU 1967 Vol. 5; Lois G. Forer to Kenyon, 27 February 1967, Kenyon to Forer, 6 March 1967, Kenyon Boxes 45 and 44; Kenyon, "Women of the U.S.A., Awake!," *N.Y. ADA Bulletin*, March 1967, p. 3; also see George Soll to Ennis, 3 March 1967, Ennis to Soll, 6 March 1967, ACLU Due Process Committee Minutes, 8 March 1967, ACLU 1967 Vols. 19 and 5; Kenyon to Pilpel, 13 and 26 April 1967, Pilpel to Kenyon, 18 April 1967, and Kenyon to Reitman, 19 April 1967, Kenyon Boxes 44 and 45.

75. *Long Island Press*, 5 and 14 May 1965, 8 and 22 September 1965, 6 November 1965; *New York Times*, 10 June 1965, p. 30; *New York Daily News*, 14 May 1965; *New York Herald Tribune*, 16 May and 3 October 1965; *People* v. *Baird*, 262 N.Y.S.2d 947 (Nassau County Dist. Ct. 1965); *New York Post*, 23 September 1965, p. 46; *New York Times*, 13 August 1966, p. 14; *State* v. *Baird*, 50 N.J. 376, 235 A.2d 673 (1967); "Students Picket Planned Parenthood," *Delphian* [Adelphi University], 26 October 1966, pp. 1, 13; *Newsday*, 20 February 1967; *Village Voice*, 18 August 1966, pp. 1, 18–19, 23 February 1967; *National Observer*, 12 December 1966, pp. 1, 12; *Sepia*, July 1967, pp. 31–36; Garrow conversations with Bill Baird and Larry Lader.

76. Connecticut General Assembly, Joint Legislative Hearings Transcript, Judiciary Committees, 21 February 1967, Connecticut State Library, esp. pp. 73, 80; *New York Times*, 22 February 1967, p. 29. On the subsequent measure, H.B. 4767, see Judiciary Committees Hearing Transcript, 21 March 1967, esp. pp. 548–553; Garrow conversation with Donald J. Cantor.

77. Daniel J. O'Neil, *Church Lobbying in a Western State: A Case Study on Abortion Legislation* (Tucson: University of Arizona Press, 1970), esp. pp. 22–26, 35–37, 41–43, 58.

78. Sagar C. Jain and Laurel F. Gooch, *Georgia Abortion Act, 1968: A Study in Legislative Process* (Chapel Hill: University of North Carolina School of Public Health, 1972), pp. 12–17, 27–31; *Atlanta Journal*, 24 January 1967, 8 and 20 February 1967, 2, 14, and 15 March 1967; *Atlanta Constitution*, 6 February 1967, 8 February 1967, p. 1, 14 March 1967, p. 16, 15 March 1967; *New York Times*, 12 February 1967, p. 64; *Georgia Bulletin*, 2 March 1967; Joseph L. Girardeau, "The Abortion Law," *Journal of the Medical Association of Georgia* 56 (August 1967): 340; Garrow interview with W. Newton Long.

79. *New York Times*, 27 February 1967, pp. 1, 21–23, 28, 28 February 1967, p. 26, 6 March 1967, p. 28, 8 March 1967, pp. 1, 37, 44, 9 March 1967, p. 41, 12 March 1967, pp. 81, E2, 13 March 1967, p. 40; *Life*, 3 March 1967, p. 4; Guttmacher to Rockefeller, 15 March 1967, Guttmacher Papers; Lader, *Abortion II*, pp. 11, 24–26, 44; Lassoe to Organizations Interested in Abortion Law Reform, 27 March and 16 May 1967, Lader Box 4; Lader to Cyril Means et al., "Legal Meeting on Test Case," n.d. [c.mid-March 1967], 2pp., Means to Lader, 14 April 1967, Pilpel to Means, 18 April 1967, Lader to Pilpel, 22 April 1967, Means to Pilpel, 26 April 1967, Lader Box 7; Blumenthal to Richard D. Lamm, 5 May 1967, Lamm Papers; Garrow conversations with Lawrence Lader, Milan Vuitch, Robert E. Hall, John V. P. Lassoe, and Jimmye Kimmey. Also see *Newsweek*, 20 March 1967, pp. 71–73; Morris Ernst to Lader, 15 and 31 March 1967, Lader Box 7. Relative to Means, also see the pessimistic comments of B. J. George, Jr., in *Illinois Medical Journal* 131 (May 1967): 666–700, at 699–700 ("liberalization

will not be achieved through new judicial decisions, but only through new legislation that will be passed when the popular pressures for reform become strong enough"). In another indication of ASA's relative moderation, executive director Jimmye Kimmey three months earlier had written to Chicago's Lonny Myers that "The question of abortion on demand is one that I still am not clear about." 21 December 1966, ARAI 10–15.

80. On Indiana, see Robert Force, "Legal Problems of Abortion Law Reform," *Administrative Law Review* 19 (July 1967): 364–382, esp. at 364. On North Dakota, see Faye D. Ginsburg, *Contested Lives* (Berkeley: University of California Press, 1989), pp. 65, 147–150. On Hawaii, see Patricia G. Steinhoff and Milton Diamond, *Abortion Politics: The Hawaii Experience* (Honolulu: University Press of Hawaii, 1977), pp. 8–10. On New Jersey, see *Gleitman* v. *Cosgrove*, 227 A.2d 689, 693 (6 March 1967); *New York Times*, 8 March 1967, p. 37, 14 March 1967, p. 49.

81. "Legalize Abortion Now," and Baird, "Abortions: The Necessity for Legalization," *B.U. News*, 8 March 1967, p. 9; Mungo, *Beyond the Revolution* (Chicago: Contemporary Books, 1990), p. 138; Garrow conversations with William R. Baird.

82. *Boston Herald*, 7 April 1967, pp. 1, 4; *Boston Record American*, 7 April 1967, pp. 1, 2, 32, 6 June 1967, p. 4; *Boston Globe*, 7 April 1967, 8 April 1967, p. 24, 26 April 1967, 7 May 1967, p. 22, 8 May 1967, pp. 1, 16, 10 May 1967, p. 13, 9 November 1969, 4 April 1982, pp. B1, B2; *New York Times*, 7 April 1967, p. 14; *B.U. News*, 12 April 1967, p. 1, 3 May 1967, p. 7, 10 May 1967, p. 1; *Collegiate Cauldron*, 13 April 1967, p. 1; *Boston Traveler*, 8 May 1967, pp. 1, 11; [Massachusetts] *Planned Parenthood News*, May 1967, p. 2; Hazel Sagoff to Katherine Howard, 29 June 1967, Baird Papers; Gene Marine and Art Goldberg, "That'll Be a Big Step Forward, Won't It?," *Ramparts*, July 1967, pp. 45–49, at 48; Art Goldberg, "The Perils of the Pill," *Ramparts*, May 1969, pp. 45–48; Baird and Robert Mamis, "The Rights of Woman," *Boston Magazine*, August 1969; Campbell Interview with Reed, pp. 68–69; Garrow conversations with William R. Baird.

83. Cal Queal, "How Colorado Changed Its Abortion Law," *Denver Post Empire Magazine*, 18 June 1967, pp. 38–45; Robert I. Sanders and Carlton R. Stoiber, "Colorado's New Abortion Law," *University of Colorado Law Review* 40 (Winter 1968): 297–314; Olga Curtis, "The Paradox of Colorado's Abortion Law," *Denver Post Empire Magazine*, 18 January 1970, pp. 30–31; Rose Bacon, "How Liberalized Abortion Became Law in One State," *Ave Maria*, 22 July 1967, pp. 16–18; Douglas G. McConnell, "The Coming of an Idea: Abortion Reform in Colorado" (unpublished paper, Eagleton Institute, 6 May 1968), 67pp., Lader Box 4; Lamm to Paul N. McCloskey, Jr., 28 April 1969, Lamm Papers; Lamm et al., "The Legislative Process in Changing Therapeutic Abortion Laws: The Colorado Experience," *American Journal of Orthopsychiatry* 39 (July 1969): 684–690, esp. at 685; Lamm, "Abortion—A Case Study in Legislative Reform" (unpublished paper, 1970), 21pp., Lader Box 6; Conrad M. Riley to Richard Frank, 22 July 1969, ARAI 1–12; Lamm Interview with Garrow. Also see "Report Submitted by Ruth A. Steel," 15 February 1969, 4pp., ARAI 12–7; Susan Barnes's remarks in "Abortion," *American Journal of Nursing* 70 (September 1970): 1919–1925; and Patricia Donovan's profile of Lamm in *Family Planning/Population Reporter* 3 (December 1974): 120–121.

84. *Denver Post*, 23 February 1967, 1 March 1967, p. 32, 10 March 1967, pp. 1, 3, 17 March 1967, p. 35, 24 March 1967, p. 15; John Bermingham, "Legislative Experience and Tactics," in Warren M. Hern and Bonnie Andrikopoulos, eds., *Abortion in the Seventies* (New York: National Abortion Federation, 1977), pp. 221–222; Lamm et al., "The Legislative Process," pp. 687–689; McConnell, "The Coming of an Idea"; Lamm, "Abortion—A Case Study," p. 9; Jack Star, "Report from Colorado . . ." *Look*, 11 July 1967, pp. 67–69; Sanders and Stoiber, "Colorado's New Abortion Law"; Bacon, "How Liberalized Abortion Became Law"; Lamm Interview with Garrow. Also see Lamm to D. J. Kwitek, 28 February 1967, Lamm to Father John F. Slattery, 1 March 1967, Dorothy E. Walsh to Lamm, 5 March 1967, Daniel Goldbeger to Lamm, Slattery to Lamm, and Lamm to Barbara Rutherford, 7 March 1967, Lamm to Slattery, and Catherine Maloney to Lamm, 10 March 1967, Jack Knudsen to Lamm, and Lamm to Art and Morley Ballantine, 15 March 1967, Lamm Papers; Lamm to

Larry Lader, 17 May 1967 and 28 August 1970, Ruth Steel to Lader, 23 January 1968, Lader Boxes 4 and 6; and Steven Levine, "Report on Survey of Colorado Legislators Regarding the Abortion Law of 1967" (unpublished paper, n.d.), 5pp., Lucas Box 2.

85. *Denver Post*, 29 March 1967, 3 April 1967, p. 15, 4 April 1967, pp. 1, 3, 5 April 1967, 6 April 1967, 7 April 1967, pp. 1, 14, 9 April 1967, 11 April 1967, 12 April 1967, p. B2, 13 April 1967, p. 26, 17 April 1967, p. 14; Bermingham, "Legislative Experience and Tactics," pp. 221–222; *New York Times*, 9 April 1967, p. 34, 26 April 1967, pp. 49, 53, 29 April 1967, p. 34, 30 April 1967, pp. 60, E6; Lamm to Love, "Arguments in Favor of Revision of Abortion Laws," 15 April 1967, 3pp., Lamm Papers; *Saturday Evening Post*, 3 June 1967, p. 96; Sam W. Downing et al., "Abortion Under the New Colorado Law," *Journal of Reproductive Medicine* 2 (May 1969): 256–264, at 258; Olga Curtis, "The Paradox of Colorado's Abortion Law," *Denver Post Empire Magazine*, 18 January 1970, pp. 30–31; Lamm to Lader, 2 May 1967, Lader Box 6; Marks in Jack Star, "Report from Colorado . . ." *Look*, 11 July 1967, pp. 67–69; Lamm Interview with Garrow.

86. *Modern Medicine*, 24 April 1967, pp. 12–16, 22–32, and *New York Times*, 30 April 1967, p. 82; *Dallas Morning News*, 6 January 1967, pp. A1, A11, 8 January 1967, 14 January 1967, p. C8, 22 February 1967, p. A6, 26 February 1967, pp. A28, A31, 21 March 1967, p. D20, 6 May 1967, p. A12; Savage, "Minutes of the Special Committee to Study Abortion Laws in Texas," 20 January 1967, and Savage to Keith P. Russell, 23 January 1967, Savage Papers; 1967 *Texas Senate Journal*, pp. 281 and 485 (21 February and 21 March); *Dallas Times-Herald*, 21 February 1967, p. B26, 25 February 1967, pp. 29, 31, 21 March 1967, p. A4, 6 May 1967, 7 May 1967, pp. 31, 33; Parkhouse Press Release and "Dear Editor" letter, 21 February 1967, Legislative Reference Division, Texas State Library; Texas Committee for the Modernization of Therapeutic Abortion Laws, "The Case for Humane Abortion," undated pamphlet, Whitehill Papers; *Houston Post*, 26 February 1967, p. 5; *Fort Worth Star-Telegram*, 21 March 1967; *Houston Chronicle*, 21 March 1967. On Parkhouse's planned retirement from the legislature, see *Dallas Morning News*, 30 May 1967; for his obituaries see the *Austin American-Statesman*, 25 August 1967, and the *Dallas Times Herald*, 24 August 1967, pp. 1, 18.

87. Sagar C. Jain and Steven W. Sinding, *North Carolina Abortion Law 1967* (Chapel Hill: Carolina Population Center, 1968), passim; "Remarks of Representative Art Jones," [15 July 1967], Chapel Hill, NC, 6pp., Lader Box 4; Jones to Lee Gidding, 20 February 1970, NARAL Box 5; Kuralt to Lader, 24 August 1970, Lader Box 4; [Raleigh] *News & Observer*, 5 May 1967, p. 1, 9 May 1967, p. 6; *New York Times*, 6 May 1967, p. 25, 9 May 1967, p. 36. Also see H. Hugh Stevens, Jr., "Criminal Law—Abortion—The New North Carolina Abortion Statute," *North Carolina Law Review* 46 (April 1968): 585–599.

88. Jain and Hughes, *California Abortion Act 1967*, pp. 41–89; Luker, *Abortion and the Politics of Motherhood*, pp. 89–93, Zad Leavy to Carol Katz et al., 28 March 1967, ACLU 1967 Vol. 19; *New York Times*, 29 April 1967, p. 14, 7 June 1967, p. 35, 14 June 1967, p. 19, 16 June 1967, p. 24; Leavy and Alan F. Charles, "California's New Therapeutic Abortion Act," *UCLA Law Review* 15 (November 1967): 1–31; Brian Pendleton, "The California Therapeutic Abortion Act," *Hastings Law Journal* 19 (November 1967): 242–255, esp. at 246; Beilenson Interviews with Edginton and Garrow. Also see *California Medicine* 106 (April 1967): 318–319; *New York Times*, 13 April 1967, p. 15; and Patricia Donovan's profile of Beilenson in *Family Planning/Population Law Reporter* 2 (April 1973): 34–36; see as well Norbert J. Mietus, *The Therapeutic Abortion Act—A Statement in Opposition* (Sacramento, CA, mimeograph), 104pp., April 1967.

89. Jain and Hughes, *California Abortion Act 1967*, pp. 71, 87; Leavy and Charles, "The Therapeutic Abortion Act of 1967," *Los Angeles Bar Bulletin* 43 (January 1968): 111–114, 133–137, at 112; Garrow conversations with Ruth Roemer, Zad Leavy, and Keith P. Russell.

90. Leland Rayson, "Abortion Law Reform in Illinois?," *Student Lawyer Journal*, December 1968, pp. 18–23; *Chicago Daily News*, 1 March 1967, pp. 29–30; "Medical Implications of the Current Abortion Law in Illinois," *Illinois Medical Journal* 131 (May 1967): 666–700; *Issue* [ICMCA Newsletter] #1 (1 May 1967), #2 (July 1967), #3 (November 1967); Don Shaw to Howard Moody, 4 August 1967, ARAI 1–15; Myers, "Abortion Is a Private Matter,"

Focus/Midwest 5 (#38), n.d. [c.Fall 1967], pp. 38–40; Garrow conversations with Lonny Myers and Don Shaw.

91. On Minnesota, see *St. Paul Pioneer Press*, 14 January 1967, p. C8, and *Minneapolis Tribune*, 7 March 1967, p. 4; also see *Minnesota Medicine* 50 (January 1967): 55–59 and 119–126. On Michigan, where the state Senate Judiciary Committee held a 28 August 1967 hearing on SB 568, see Daniel G. Wylie, "Abortion Reform in Michigan," *Wayne Law Review* 14 (1968): 1006–1029; on Iowa, see James C. Mohr, "Iowa's Abortion Battles of the Late 1960s and Early 1970s," *Annals of Iowa* 50 (Summer 1989): 63–89, at 70–71. On Ohio, see the 1 February and 26 May 1967 issues of the Ohio Committee for Abortion Law Reform's (OCALR) *OCALR Newsletter*, ARAI 4–31, and Sherman Goldberg, "An Analysis of the Proposed Changes to the Ohio Abortion Statute," *University of Cincinnati Law Review* 37 (Spring 1968): 340–360; on Republican state senator Robert L. Prange's Missouri bill, see *St. Louis Post-Dispatch*, 25 May 1967, p. C1. On Alabama, see *Birmingham Post-Herald*, 29 June 1967, p. 5, 25 August 1967, p. 2; and *Birmingham News*, 24 July 1967, p. 17.

92. On Nevada, see James T. Richardson and Sandie W. Fox, "Religious Affiliation as a Predictor of Voting Behavior in Abortion Reform Legislation," *Journal for the Scientific Study of Religion* 11 (December 1972): 347–359; on Maryland, see the remarks of Delegate Allen B. Spector in "Abortion and the Law," *Current Medical Digest*, September 1969, pp. 751–775, at 756. On Oklahoma, see the references in *Modern Hospital*, August 1967, pp. 90–94, and *Medical Economics*, 21 August 1967, pp. 21–35, on Maine, see *New York Times*, 16 June 1967, p. 24. On Florida, see Walter W. Sackett, Jr., to Guttmacher, 18 April 1967, Guttmacher Papers, and *New York Times*, 29 April 1967, p. 14, and 8 June 1967, p. 26.

93. *New York Times*, 21 May 1967, p. 82, 24 June 1967, p. 31; Kenyon and George Soll to ACLU Board, 9 June 1967, 5pp. ("the right to control one's own body is a right so fundamental as to be tantamount to the right to freedom itself"), "Memo on Abortion," 26 May 1967, 12pp., Due Process Committee to ACLU Board, "Further Recommendations," and Legal Department to ACLU Board, "The Constitutionality of Abortion Laws," 12 June 1967, ACLU Board Minutes, 15 June 1967, Algernon Black to Alan Reitman, 19 June 1967, Reitman to Robert E. Hall, 14 July 1967, ACLU 1967 Vol. 5; *New York Times*, 19 June 1967, pp. 23, 34, 22 June 1967, pp. 41, 78; *Wall Street Journal*, 19 June 1967, p. 9; *Time*, 30 June 1967, p. 44; *AMA News*, 3 July 1967, and 11 September 1967, p. 4; "AMA Policy on Therapeutic Abortion," *JAMA* 201 (14 August 1967): 544; Raymond Tatalovich and Byron W. Daynes, *The Politics of Abortion* (New York: Praeger, 1981), p. 53. Also generally see Ronald M. Green, "Abortion and Promise-Keeping," *Christianity & Crisis*, 15 May 1967, pp. 109–113; Robert Coles, "Who's to Be Born?" *New Republic*, 10 June 1967, pp. 10–12; Phil Kerby, "Abortion: Laws and Attitudes," *The Nation*, 12 June 1967, pp. 754–756; Louis B. Schwartz, "Abortion and 19th Century Laws," *Trial*, June/July 1967, pp. 41, 45; Herman Schwartz, "The Parent or the Fetus?—A Survey of Abortion Law Reform," *The Humanist*, July-August 1967, pp. 123–126; J. Robert Willson, "Abortion—A Medical Responsibility?," *Obstetrics and Gynecology* 30 (August 1967): 294–303; and *Georgia Law Review* 1 (Summer 1967): 693–706.

94. *New York Times*, 22 May 1967, pp. 1, 36; *Village Voice*, 25 May 1967, p. 3; Moody and Arlene Carmen, *Abortion Counseling and Social Change* (Valley Forge, PA: Judson Press, 1973), esp. pp. 19–36; Lader, *Abortion II*, pp. 42–47; Carmen Interview with Chesler, esp. p. 6; Celeste M. Condit, *Decoding Abortion Rhetoric* (Urbana: University of Illinois Press, 1990), p. 60; Garrow conversations with Larry Lader and Milan Vuitch. Also see *New York Times*, 8 August 1973; Moody, "Abortion Revisited," *Christianity & Crisis*, 21 July 1975, pp. 166–168; and *Washington Post*, 26 April 1989, pp. D1, D15–D16.

95. Lader to Lassoe, 30 May 1967, [Lassoe], "Ad Hoc Committee on Organization" to Interested Organizations, "Recommendations for Future Operations," 7 June 1967, Lader Box 4; Micki Wolter to Lader, 15 May 1967, Pilpel to Wayne Decker, 31 May 1967, Lader to Pilpel, 27 June 1967, Lader to Pilpel and Ephraim London, "Abortion Test Case," 17 July 1967, Lader Box 7; Bernard Nathanson, *Aborting America* (Garden City, NY: Doubleday & Co., 1979), pp. 29–31; Garrow conversations with Larry Lader and John Lassoe. On Nathanson's initial

introduction to Lader by Ober on June 2, also see Joe Klein, "Born Again," *New York Magazine*, 7 January 1985, pp. 40–45, and *Washington Post*, 24 March 1985, pp. B1, B5–B7.

CHAPTER SIX

1. Garrow conversations with Roy Lucas; Lucas to Clement E. Vose, 2 July 1969, Lucas Box 25; Linda Greenhouse, "Constitutional Question: Is There a Right to Abortion?" *New York Times Magazine*, 25 January 1970, pp. 30–31, 88–91; *The Commentator* [NYU Law School], 25 February 1970, p. 9; Lucas Interview with Vose; [Lucas], "Preludes to *Roe* v. *Wade* and *Doe* v. *Bolton*," n.d., 5pp., Whitehill Papers; Lucas, "Notes on the Efforts in 1965–1973"; *Heart of Atlanta Motel* v. *United States*, 379 U.S. 241 (1964), and *Katzenbach* v. *McClung*, 379 U.S. 294 (1964), both argued 5 October 1964; Garrow conversations with Norman Dorsen; McKay, "The Right of Privacy: Emanations and Intimations," *Michigan Law Review* 64 (December 1965): 259–282; Emerson, "Nine Justices in Search of a Doctrine," *Michigan Law Review* 64 (December 1965): 219–234, at 232; *Loving* v. *Virginia*, 388 U.S. 1 (12 June 1967). See as well [Lucas], "Crowded-Art Doctrine Rejected by District Court," *New York University Law Review* 39 (November 1964): 895–899. Lucas also recalls being influenced by his reading of the abortion section of Edwin M. Schur's *Crimes Without Victims* (Englewood Cliffs, NJ: Prentice-Hall, 1965), pp. 11–66, and by a movie, *The Cardinal*.

   Argued on April 10, the Supreme Court's decision in *Loving* reversed a 1966 ruling by the Virginia Supreme Court (206 Va. 924) and declared, in a unanimous opinion by Chief Justice Warren, that "The freedom to marry has long been recognized as one of the vital personal rights essential to the orderly pursuit of happiness by free men. Marriage is one of the 'basic civil rights of man,' fundamental to our very existence and survival." 388 U.S. 12, quoting *Skinner* v. *Oklahoma*, 316 U.S. 535, 541 (1942). Originally married in June of 1958 in Washington, D.C., Richard P. Loving and Mildred D. Jeter Loving had been arrested six weeks later after returning to their hometown of Central Point in Caroline County, Virginia. After standing trial and then being induced to plead guilty, in January 1959 they were given suspended sentences on the condition that they leave Virginia and not return. Four years later, unhappy with that ongoing state of affairs, they had contacted the U.S. Department of Justice and had been referred to the ACLU, which put them in touch with two Alexandria attorneys, Bernard S. Cohen and Philip J. Hirschkopf. Those lawyers in November 1963 filed a motion in state court to vacate the 1959 sentence, and only in January 1965, under pressure from a newly instituted federal court case, did the state court judge finally deny the motion and allow them to appeal that action to the Virginia Supreme Court, whose 1966 affirmance was then challenged in the U.S. Supreme Court. Also see Walter Wadlington, "The *Loving* Case: Virginia's Anti-Miscegenation Statute in Historical Perspective," *Virginia Law Review* 52 (October 1966): 1189–1223; Simeon Booker, "The Couple That Rocked the Courts," *Ebony*, September 1967, pp. 78–80; Robert F. Drinan, "The *Loving* Decision and the Freedom to Marry," *Ohio State Law Journal* 29 (1968): 358–398; Henry H. Foster, Jr., "Marriage: A 'Basic Civil Right of Man,'" *Fordham Law Review* 37 (October 1968): 51–80; and Robert J. Sickles, *Race, Marriage, and the Law* (Albuquerque: University of New Mexico Press, 1972), pp. 76–91.

2. Garrow conversations with Roy Lucas and Uta Landy; Pilpel to Means, 18 April 1967, Lader Box 7; Lucas, "Preludes to *Roe* v. *Wade*," and "Notes on the Efforts in 1965–73." Unfortunately, no copy of the initial 1967 version of Lucas's paper appears to have survived in either Lucas's, Lader's, or Pilpel's files.

3. *Birmingham Post-Herald*, 29 June 1967, p. 5, 25 August 1967, p. 2; *Birmingham News*, 24 July 1967, p. 17; Lucas to Lader, 10 and 28 August 1967, Lader Box 4; [Lucas], "The Relationship of the Alabama State Abortion Law to Requirements of the United States Constitution," 2pp., n.d., Lader Box 5; Lucas, "Federal Constitutional Limitations on the Enforcement and Administration of State Abortion Statutes," *North Carolina Law Review* 46 (June 1968): 730–778, at 755–756, 761, 777–778; Lader to Alvin J. Conway, 15 August 1967, Lader Box 7;

Dorsen to Lucas, 1 September 1967, Lucas Box 28. Again, no typescript, prepublication copy of the revised paper appears to have survived either in Lader's files or elsewhere. An influential stimulus for his analysis, Lucas emphasizes, was a Note on "Declaratory Relief in the Criminal Law," *Harvard Law Review* 80 (May 1967): 1490–1513, esp. at 1507 ("it is likely that the germinative right to privacy announced in *Griswold* . . . may present situations apt for declaratory resolution").

4. Lader to Alvin J. Conway, 15 August 1967, Lader to John Lassoe, Jr., 28 September 1967, Lader Boxes 7 and 4; Hall in *Medical Economics* 44 (21 August 1967): 21–35; Hardin, "Semantic Aspects of Abortion," *ETC* 24 (September 1967): 263–281, at 270. Also see Hardin, "Abortion—Or Compulsory Pregnancy?," *Journal of Marriage and the Family* 30 (May 1968): 246–251. ICMCA's Don Shaw made the same point as Hardin in a 4 August 1967 letter to Howard Moody: "We feel that the states following the [ALI] model penal code will appear to move forward [but] are actually making future much needed changes more difficult for themselves. . . . Surely the trend is toward a much more enlightened policy than represented in" the ALI provisions. ARAI 1–15.

5. *Washington Post*, 7 September 1967, pp. G1, G2, 9 September 1967, p. E1; *New York Times*, 9 September 1967, p. 30, 10 September 1967, p. E11; *Time*, 15 September 1967, p. 84; Walter W. Sackett, Jr., to Jimmye Kimmey, 1 May 1968, Guttmacher Papers; *Newsweek*, 18 September 1967, pp. 60–61. Subsequently published papers from the conference include Natalie Shainess, "Abortion: Social, Psychiatric, and Psychoanalytic Perspectives," *New York State Journal of Medicine* 63 (1 December 1968): 3070–3073 (proliberalization), and David W. Louisell's tractlike "Abortion, the Practice of Medicine and the Due Process of Law," *UCLA Law Review* 16 (February 1969): 233–254. Selected proceedings of the conference appear in Robert E. Cooke et al., eds., *The Terrible Choice* (New York: Bantam, 1968), which in one chart (p. 57) asserted that the total number of deaths from abortion in the U.S. in 1965 was 235, with 49 of those occurring in New York and 39 in California. Statistician Tietze in his remarks had estimated an annual nationwide total of between five hundred and one thousand. Also see Tietze and Sarah Lewit, "Abortion," *Scientific American* 220 (January 1969): 21–27.

6. *ASA Newsletter* Vol. 2, #3 (Fall 1967): 3. On the initially titled Michigan Abortion Review Council, which by early 1968 had changed its name to the Michigan Council for the Study of Abortion, see the 13 November and 20 December 1967 minutes in the Jack Stack Papers, Box 1. On Lonny Myers's ongoing efforts to build ICMCA, see Myers to Robert E. Hall, 14 September 1967, Ruth Smith Papers, Box 1, Barbara Siegel to Nat Lehrman, 19 September 1967, ARAI 1–7, Jimmye Kimmey to Myers, 28 September 1967, ARAI 10–15, Myers to Lader, 2 October 1967, Smith Box 1, Ruth Smith to Lehrman, 5 October 1967, ARAI 1–7, Lader to Myers, 9 October 1967, and Myers to Hall, 23 October 1967, ARAI 10–15. On Edie Rein's attempts to expand the Wisconsin Committee to Legalize Abortion, see Rein to Lader, 11 August 1967, Lader Box 4; and Anne Nicol Gaylor, *Abortion Is A Blessing* (New York: Psychological Dimensions, 1975), pp. 1–4.

7. Sagar C. Jain and Laurel F. Gooch, *Georgia Abortion Act, 1968: A Study in Legislative Process* (Chapel Hill: University of North Carolina School of Public Health, 1972), pp. 33–34; *Atlanta Journal-Constitution*, 27 August 1967; John L. Moore, Jr., "Abortion Laws," *Journal of the Medical Association of Georgia* 56 (October 1967): 439; *Atlanta Journal*, 6 December 1967; *Atlanta Constitution*, 22 December 1967.

8. Bowers to Estelle Griswold, 24 September 1966, PPLC 38-R; Bowers, "Favoring Reform of Connecticut's Criminal Law on Abortion," 29 May 1967, 2pp., Schlesinger 289–1–13; *New Haven Register*, 21 July 1967; Bowers to Harriet Pilpel, 2 October 1967, PPLC 38-R; Bowers to Cantor, 10 October 1967, and Bowers to Lowell Levin, 30 October 1967, Cantor Papers; Bowers to Lincoln Day, 30 October 1967, PPLC 38-R; Evelyn Warren to ICMCA, 14 November 1967, Warren to Lonny Myers, 18 November 1967, and Bowers to ICMCA, 12 December 1967, ARAI 3–24; Carol Fessenden to Richard D. Lamm, 4 December 1967, Lamm Papers; Bowers to "Dear Director," 21 December 1967, PPLC 38-R; Warren to Lonny Myers, 3 January 1968, ARAI 3–24; Griswold Interview with Cheek, pp. 47–48;

Garrow conversations with Donald J. Cantor and Richard M. Bowers. Also see Buxton, "One Doctor's Opinion of Abortion Laws," *American Journal of Nursing* 68 (May 1968): 1026–1028.

9. *Time*, 13 October 1967, pp. 32–33. Also see "Should Abortion Laws Be Eased?" *Good Housekeeping*, October 1967, pp. 14–22, and "Coping With Abortion," *Mademoiselle*, October 1967, pp. 172–173, 211–216.

10. Abraham Heller and H. G. Whittington, "The Colorado Story: Denver General Hospital Experience with the Change in the Law on Therapeutic Abortion," *American Journal of Psychiatry* 125 (December 1968): 809–816; John T. Foster, "Abortion," *Modern Hospital* 109 (August 1967): 90–94; *Wall Street Journal*, 18 August 1967, p. 1; *Medical World News*, 29 September 1967, pp. 46–52; Lamm to Lader, 18 September 1967, Lader Box 6; *New York Times*, 26 October 1967, p. 1, 20 January 1968, p. 16; Z. Alexander Aarons, "Therapeutic Abortion and the Psychiatrist," *American Journal of Psychiatry* 124 (December 1967): 745–754, at 753. Also see Sam W. Downing, Richard Lamm, and Abraham Heller, "Abortion Under the New Colorado Law," *Journal of Reproductive Medicine* 2 (May 1969): 256–264, at 262, and Arthur Peck, "Therapeutic Abortion: Patients, Doctors, and Society," *American Journal of Psychiatry* 125 (December 1968): 797–804, at 802–803. On North Carolina, see W. Joseph May, "Therapeutic Abortion Experience in North Carolina Under the Liberalized 1967 Law," *North Carolina Medical Journal* 32 (May 1971): 186–187; on the California statute taking effect, see *New York Times*, 17 December 1967, p. 47, *SHA Newsletter* Vol. 3, #2 (December 1967–January 1968), and Hamlet C. Pulley, "Abortions—First Annual Report," *California Medicine* 108 (May 1968): 403. A total of 479 abortions—out of 549 that were applied for—took place in California between November 8 and the end of 1967.

11. "The Abortion Question," *America*, 9 December 1967, p. 706, Drinan, "Abortion," pp. 713–715, Byrn, "Abortion," pp. 710–713; Donald A. Giannella, "The Difficult Quest for a Truly Humane Abortion Law," *Villanova Law Review* 13 (Winter 1968): 257–302, at 302; Drinan, "The Right of the Foetus to be Born," *Dublin Review* 241 (Winter 1967–1968): 365–381, at 374, 381. Also see *New York Times*, 27 March 1968, p. 26, 17 February 1969, p. 32, Drinan, "Catholic Moral Teaching and Abortion Laws in America," *Catholic Theological Society of America Proceedings* 23 (June 1968): 118–130, Drinan, "The Morality of Abortion Laws," *Catholic Lawyer* 14 (Summer 1968): 190–198, 264; Thomas A. Wassmer, "Contemporary Attitudes of the Roman Catholic Church Toward Abortion," *Journal of Religion and Health* 7 (October 1968): 311–323; and Daniel Callahan, *Abortion* (New York: Macmillan, 1970), p. 436. See as well James Voyles, "Changing Abortion Laws in the United States," *Journal of Family Law* 7 (Fall 1967): 496–511; "Abortion Legislation: The Need for Reform," *Vanderbilt Law Review* 20 (November 1967): 1313–1328; Nathan Hershey, *American Journal of Nursing* 67 (November 1967): 2310–2312; [Editorial], *Journal of the Mississippi State Medical Association* 8 (November 1967): 661–665; Paul G. Reiter, "Trends in Abortion Legislation," *St. Louis University Law Journal* 12 (Winter 1967–68): 260–276; Dennis M. Mahoney, "Therapeutic Abortion," *Dickinson Law Review* 72 (Winter 1968): 270–295; Paul Ramsey, "The Morality of Abortion," in Daniel H. Labby, ed., *Life or Death* (Seattle: University of Washington Press, 1968), pp. 60–93; Ralph B. Potter, Jr., "The Abortion Debate," in Donald R. Cutler, ed., *The Religious Situation: 1968* (Boston: Beacon Press, 1968), pp. 112–161; Loren G. Stern, "Abortion: Reform and the Law," *Journal of Criminal Law, Criminology and Police Science* 59 (March 1968): 84–95; Edwin M. Schur, "Abortion," *The Annals* 376 (March 1968): 136–147; "Survey of Abortion Reform Legislation," *Washington Law Review* 43 (March 1968): 644–654; and William Diller, "The Unborn Child," *Suffolk University Law Review* 2 (Spring 1968): 228–243.

12. *Boston Globe*, 13 September 1967, 9 October 1967, p. 13, 18 October 1967; *Boston Record American*, 12 September 1967; *B.U. News*, 13 September 1967, 18 October 1967, p. 3; *New York Times*, 18 October 1967; *Long Island Press*, 18 October 1967; Macaulay, "Report to the Supreme Judicial Court," *Commonwealth* v. *Baird*, #29688 and 29689, 3 November 1967, *Baird* Case File, National Archives; *National Guardian*, 25 November 1967, p. 10, and 2 December 1967, p. 10; *Harvard Graduate Bulletin*, 6 December 1967, pp. 3–4. Also see *Long*

Island Star-Journal, 11 September 1967, p. 4; *Hartford Courant*, 26 October 1967, p. 48.

13. On NOW, see *New York Times*, 22 November 1966, pp. 1, 44; Maren L. Carden, *The New Feminist Movement* (New York: Russell Sage Foundation, 1974), pp. 104–135; Jo Freeman, *The Politics of Women's Liberation* (New York: David McKay, 1975), pp. 71–102; Sheila M. Rothman, *Woman's Proper Place* (New York: Basic Books, 1978), pp. 244–246; Barbara S. Deckard, *The Women's Movement*, 3rd ed. (New York: Harper & Row, 1983), pp. 324–326; Leila J. Rupp and Verta Taylor, *Survival in the Doldrums* (New York: Oxford University Press, 1987), pp. 179–186; Winifred S. Wandersee, *On the Move* (Boston: Twayne, 1988), pp. 36–54; Marcia Cohen, *The Sisterhood* (New York: Simon & Schuster, 1988), p. 141; and especially Flora Davis, *Moving the Mountain* (New York: Simon & Schuster, 1991), pp. 52–59, 66–68.

14. Cusack Interview with Garrow; Cusack to John T. Knox, 16 May 1965, Cusack to Blumenthal, 13 November 1967, Cusack to Duryea, 21 November 1967, Cusack to Gloria [Nelson], 22 November 1967, Duryea to Cusack, 28 November 1967, Cusack et al. to "Fellow Unitarians," December 1967, Cusack to Pat [Maginnis], Rowena [Gurner], and Bob [Bick], 29 December 1967, Cusack, "A Proposal for Elective Abortion," 18 January 1968, Cusack to Anthony J. Travia, and Gloria [Nelson] to Cusack, 22 January 1968, Cusack to New York State legislators, 25 January 1968, Cusack to Blumenthal, and to Duryea, 26 January 1968, Blumenthal to Cusack, 30 January 1968, Duryea to Cusack, 31 January 1968, Maginnis to Cusack, 6 February 1968, Cusack to Duryea, 11 February 1968, Duryea to Cusack, 15 February 1968, Cusack Papers; *Newsday*, 16 January 1970, p. A3 (on Cusack); and Oliver Quayle & Co., "A Survey of Public Opinion on Abortion in New York," January 1968, 33pp., Guttmacher Papers.

15. *New York Times*, 3 January 1968, p. 46, 4 January 1968, pp. 26, 36, 8 January 1968, p. 28, 10 January 1968, pp. 1, 23, 11 January 1968, p. 36, 14 January 1968, p. IV-8, 19 January 1968; McManus, WCBS-TV Editorial Reply, 18 January 1968, Guttmacher Papers. On the ongoing referral work, also see Lader, "The Mother Who Chose Abortion," *Redbook*, February 1968, pp. 76–77, 147–151.

16. *New York Times*, 21 January 1968, pp. 1, 79, 23 January 1968, p. 23, 24 January 1968, p. 26; Myers to Guttmacher, and to Lader, 17 January 1968, Guttmacher Papers and Lader Box 4; Hall to Myers, 22 January 1968, Lader to Myers, 11 February 1968, Fletcher to Myers, 23 January 1968, Ober to Myers, 28 January 1968, ARAI 10–16; Lader, *Abortion II*, p. 62; Guttmacher to Myers, 22 January 1968, and Guttmacher, "Abortion," 2pp., 2 February 1968, Guttmacher Papers.

17. *New York Times*, 7 February 1968, pp. 1, 66, 10 February 1968, p. 32, 25 February 1968, p. 56, 1 March 1968, p. 26, 9 March 1968, p. 1, 17 March 1968, p. 25, 20 March 1968, p. 1, 24 March 1968, p. IV-11; Cusack to Blumenthal, 10 February 1968, Blumenthal to Cusack, 19 February 1968, Cusack to Maginnis, n.d. [c.4 March 1968] and 7 March 1968, Cusack Papers; OALR Press Release, 28 February 1968, ARAI 4–28; Transcript of Hearing, Governor's Select Committee to Review the State's Abortion Law, 29 February 1968, 326pp., Guttmacher Papers; Guttmacher, "The Genesis of Liberalized Abortion in New York," *Case Western Reserve Law Review* 23 (Summer 1972): 756–778; Garrow conversations with Ruth Cusack, John Lassoe, Jimmye Kimmey, and Robert E. Hall. Also see Guttmacher, "When Pregnancy Means Heartbreak," *McCalls*, April 1968, pp. 61, 130–134; Guttmacher's comments in "Law, Morality, and Abortion," *Rutgers Law Review* 22 (Spring 1968): 415–445; and Lader, "The New Abortion Laws," *Parents Magazine*, April 1968.

18. *New York Times*, 31 March 1968, pp. 1, 75, 2 April 1968, p. 10, 4 April 1968, pp. 1, 31, 6 April 1948, p. 38; John V. P. Lassoe, Jr., "This Week's Action on Abortion Law Reform," 10 April 1968, Lader Box 6. Also see Robert M. Byrn, "Demythologizing Abortion Reform," and Wilfred R. Caron, "New York Abortion Reform: A Critique," *Catholic Lawyer* 14 (Summer 1968): 180–189 and 199–213.

19. Jain and Gooch, *Georgia Abortion Act, 1968*, pp. 35–62; *Atlanta Journal*, 2, 16, 17, 19, and 31 January, 26 February and 2 March 1968; *Atlanta Constitution*, 10, 16, 17, 18, 19, and 31 January and 28 February 1968; *New York Times*, 27 February 1968, p. 32. Also see John L. Moore and Trammell E. Vickery, "Therapeutic Abortion Law," *Journal of the Medical*

Association of Georgia 57 (June 1968): 323–328; Cyril Means to Jimmye Kimmey, 12 July 1968, ACLU 1972 Vol. 37; the comments by Smalley and Eugene Griffin in "Abortion and the Law," *Current Medical Digest*, September 1969, pp. 751–775, at 772–775; and James M. Ingram, "Changing Aspects of Abortion Law," *American Journal of Obstetrics and Gynecology* 105 (1 September 1969): 35–45.

20. Jain and Gooch, *Georgia Abortion Act, 1968*, p. 62. On Maryland, where an initial repeal bill was backed by the Maryland Citizens Committee on Abortion Law, see the comments of legislative sponsor Allen B. Spector in "Abortion and the Law," *Current Medical Digest*, September 1969, pp. 751–775, at 756–760; *Newsweek*, 17 March 1969, p. 104; John F. King, "Abortion and the New Maryland Law," *Journal of the American Medical Association* 207 (24 March 1969): 2341–2342; Irvin M. Cushner to Lonny Myers, 6 January 1969, Cushner to Harold S. Goodman, 7 January 1969, ARAI 2–14, and Cushner, "The Aftermath of Abortion Legislation in Maryland," *Advances in Planned Parenthood* 6 (1971): 158–163. Passage of the Maryland law was never noted in the *New York Times*. On Florida see Walter W. Sackett, Jr., to Jimmye Kimmey, 1 May 1968, Guttmacher Papers; on Hawaii see Steinhoff and Diamond, *Abortion Politics*, p. 11; on Connecticut, see *New York Times*, 4 June 1968, p. 22; on New Jersey, see *New York Times*, 2 April 1968, p. 41, 13 May 1968, p. 86, 29 October 1968, p. 40, 14 November 1968, p. 40, 18 March 1969, p. 33, 9 May 1969, p. 15, and a superb six-part series of early June articles by Naomi Rock in the *Perth Amboy Evening News*, reprinted in booklet form, in the Lucas Papers. On Texas see C. Lincoln Williston to Savage, Downs, et al., 28 June 1967, Savage to Downs et al., 12 February 1968, Texas Medical Association, *Transactions of the House of Delegates*, 2–5 May 1968, pp. 76–82, and Ben B. Shaver and Downs to "Dear Doctor," 8 July 1968, Savage Papers; *Houston Post*, 8 October 1967, 31 July 1968; *Dallas Times Herald*, 3 April 1968; *Dallas Morning News*, 2 May 1968, p. A18, 5 May 1968, p. A18; also see *Dallas Morning News*, 17 September 1967, p. 27, 22 September 1967, and 7 November 1967, p. 14; *Dallas Times Herald*, 7 November 1967; John P. Vanderpool and Robert B. White, "Psychiatry and the Abortion Problem," *Texas Medicine* 64 (January 1968): 48–51; *Houston Post*, 17 and 24 March 1968; *Ft. Worth Star-Telegram*, 5 May 1968.

21. On the Santa Barbara conference, see Thomas M. Hart and Thomas P. Lowry, eds., *Abortion Law Reform: A Report on the California Conference on Abortion* (Ross, CA: Association for Repeal of Abortion Laws, 1968), 90pp., esp. p. 39; also see Hart to Lader, 3 September 1967, Lader Box 4, and Leavy to Garrett Hardin, 14 February 1968, CCTA Box 5. On CCTA, see Ruth Roemer to Keith Russell, 10 January 1968, CCTA Box 5, Ellen Studhalter, CCTA Board Minutes, 31 January and 28 May 1968, Roemer to Board Members, 14 June 1968, CCTA Box 4, and *CCTA Newsletter*, August 1968. On the Shively situation, see *New York Times*, 15 February 1968, p. 14, *The Nation*, 26 February 1968, p. 261, and Ned Overstreet to Roemer, 7 June 1968, CCTA Box 5. On the Los Angeles Clergy Consultation Service, see Carmen and Moody, *Abortion Counseling*, pp. 47–48, Luker, *Abortion*, p. 122, and *Los Angeles Times*, 15 May 1968; on the initiative planning, see *SHA Newsletter* Vol. 4, #1 (September 1968).

22. On Nevada, see Bernard Burton to Vanessa Brown, 20 May 1968, and the 28 May CCTA Minutes, CCTA Box 4, Nevada Committee for the Rights of Women, "The Truth About Abortion," n.d., CCTA Box 3, and *CCTA Newsletter*, August 1968, p. 3. On ASA, see Hall to Stephen Enke, 2 February 1968, "Enke Report on Abortion Liberalization," 12 February 1968, Mott to Hall, and Mott to Louis Hellman, 25 April 1968, Hellman to Mott, 2 May 1968, Guttmacher Papers; Mott to Hellman, 27 December 1968, Lader Box 6; *U.S. Medicine*, 1 June 1968, pp. 3, 34; Garrow conversations with Robert E. Hall, Jimmye Kimmey, and John Lassoe. Mott too contributed to the Nevada effort; see Mott to Don Green, 27 December 1968, Lader Box 6.

23. On the ACLU's interminably prolonged internal discussions, see Alan Reitman to Dorothy Kenyon et al., 20 October 1967, Norman Dorsen to Reitman, 26 October 1967, Reitman and Trudy Hayden to ACLU Board, "ACLU Abortion Policy . . ." 31 October 1967, 10pp., Robert E. Hall to Reitman, 1 November 1967 ("I have never before seen a group become so hung up on tangential matters"), Thomas L. Shaffer to Reitman, 6 November 1967, Hayden to Dorsen, 7 November 1967, Pilpel to Reitman, 13 November 1967, Ad Hoc Committee

on Abortion to ACLU Board, 22 November 1967, Minutes, ACLU Plenary Board Meeting, 2–3 December 1967, pp. 19–23, Reitman to Edward Ennis, 7 December 1967, ACLU Board Minutes, 25 January 1968, pp. 3–5, ACLU 1967 Vol. 5; *Civil Liberties*, January 1968, p. 3, and March-April 1968; *New York Times*, 25 March 1968, p. 35; *Current*, May 1968, pp. 26–32; Garrow conversations with Norman Dorsen and Robert E. Hall. Also see Thomas L. Shaffer, "Abortion, the Law and Human Life," *Valparaiso University Law Review* 2 (Fall 1967): 94–106. On ACOG, see *New York Times*, 10 May 1968, p. 21; also see 13 July 1968, p. 28.

24. Myers to Richard Rosenzweig, 14 May 1968, ARAI 8–9, Myers to Bob Hall, 3 June 1968, ARAI 10–15; ICMCA Executive Meeting Minutes, 12 and 26 June 1968, ARAI 7–14, and 9 July 1968, Lader Box 6; Myers to Bob Hall, 10 and 15 July 1968, ARAI 10–15; Lader, *Abortion II*, p. 88; Myers to Lader, and to Garrett Hardin, 2 August 1968, Lader Box 15; Myers to Ruth Smith, 8–9 August 1968, NARAL–NYPL Box 2; Myers to John Lassoe, 22 August 1968, ARAI 1–7; Myers to Joseph Sunnen, 26 August 1968, and Sunnen to Myers, 12 September 1968, ARAI 2–7; Gloria Hunt to John Lassoe, 26 September 1968, Smith Box 1; *ICMCA Journal* #5 (Summer 1968) and #6 (Fall 1968); Garrow conversations with Lonny Myers, Don C. Shaw, Robert E. Hall, and Lawrence Lader.

25. Lader to Myers and Hardin, "Memo No. 1," 3 September 1968, 5pp., Lader Box 15; Lader, *Abortion II*, pp. 1–4, 26, 46; Carmen and Moody, *Abortion Counseling*, p. 102–104. Also see Lader, "Non-Hospital Abortions," *Look*, 21 January 1969, pp. 63–65. Most of the New York CCS expenses were privately covered by Stewart Mott; see Mott to Moody, 27 December 1968, Lader Box 6.

26. *New York Times*, 9 June 1968, p. 33, 19 August 1968, p. 20; *Washington Post*, 16 June 1968, p. G2; David Whieldon, "New Abortion System," *Medical Economics* 45 (28 October 1968): 238–243. The *Times*'s number was erroneous; the actual total for Colorado's first twelve months was 407. William Droegemueller et al., "The First Year Experience in Colorado with the New Abortion Law," *American Journal of Obstetrics and Gynecology* 103 (1 March 1969): 694–702, and John C. Cobb, "Abortion in Colorado 1967–1969: Changing Attitudes and Practices Since the New Law," *Advances in Planned Parenthood* 5 (1970): 186–189.

27. Lucas, "Notes on the Efforts in 1965–1973," pp. 5–7; *Dickey* v. *Troy State University*, 273 F. Supp. 613, *Troy State University* v. *Dickey*, 394 F.2d 490, 402 F.2d 515 (5th Cir. 1968); Morris Dees, *A Season For Justice* (New York: Charles Scribner's Sons, 1991), pp. 89, 94–95, 97–99, 101–103; *Tinker* v. *Des Moines Independent Community School District*, 393 U.S. 503 (1969), 21 L.Ed 975; Linda Greenhouse, "Constitutional Question: Is There a Right to Abortion?," *New York Times Magazine*, 25 January 1970, pp. 30–31, 88–91; *The Commentator* [NYU Law School], 25 February 1970, p. 9; Lucas Interview with Vose; Garrow conversations with Roy Lucas, Morris Dees, Richard G. Singer, Charles Morgan, Cyril Means, Jimmye Kimmey, and Robert E. Hall.

28. Lucas to Wulf, 4 July 1968, ACLU 1972 Vol. 37; Lucas to ASA Board, n.d. [c.12 July 1968], Lucas Papers; Lucas, "Trial Brief for an Abortion Test Case Prepared for the Association for the Study of Abortion, Inc.," n.d., 106pp., ACLU 1972 Vol. 37; Norton to Alan Reitman, "Abortion," 5 December 1967, and Norton to John Fordon, "Abortion Project," 3 July 1968, Fordon to Nat Lehrman, 9 July 1968, ACLU 1967 Vol. 19; Wulf to Lehrman, 16 July 1968, Kimmey to Pilpel et al., "Meeting of July 18," 22 July 1968, ACLU 1972 Vol. 37.

29. James Hennesey, *American Catholics* (New York: Oxford University Press, 1981), pp. 327–329; Jay P. Dolan, *The American Catholic Experience* (Garden City, NY: Doubleday & Co., 1985), pp. 434–436; Mary C. Segers, "The Bishops, Birth Control, and Abortion Policy: 1950–1985," in Segers, ed., *Church Polity and American Politics* (New York: Garland, 1990), pp. 215–231, at 221; Lawrence Lader, *Politics, Power and the Church* (New York: Macmillan, 1987), pp. 41–49; Norman B. Ryder and Charles F. Westoff, *Reproduction in the United States, 1965* (Princeton: Princeton University Press, 1971), pp. 185–221; Westoff and Larry Bumpass, "The Revolution in Birth Control Practices of U.S. Roman Catholics," *Science* 179 (5 January 1973): 41–44. Also see Joseph Roddy, "The Pope's Unsolvable Problem," *Look*, 13 December 1966, pp. 120–128, Ambrogio Valsecchi, *Controversy: The Birth Control Debate, 1958–1968* (London: Geoffrey Chapman, 1968), and Westoff and Ryder, "Experience with

Oral Contraception in the United States, 1960–1965," *Clinical Obstetrics and Gynecology* 11 (September 1968): 734–752.

30. *New York Times*, 3 August 1968, 25 October 1968, p. 93; Andrew J. Eyman, "Findings of Fact and Conclusions of Law," *Shively* v. *Board of Medical Examiners*, #590333, San Francisco County Superior Court, 24 September 1968; *ASA Newsletter* Vol. 3, #3 (Fall 1968); *People* v. *Belous*, Cal. Ct. App., 2d Dist., Div. 3, 13 August 1968; *Los Angeles Times*, 27 September 1968, p. II-6, 25 October 1968, pp. 1, 21; Fred Okrand to Mel Wulf, 9 October 1968, ACLU 1972 Vol. 37; Leavy to Enersen, 3 December 1968, CCTA Box 4; Munger to Lader, 28 February 1972, Lader Box 5; Garrow conversations with Ruth Roemer, Zad Leavy, Keith P. Russell, and Charles T. Munger. A full transcript of Belous's January 1967 trial appears in the U.S. Supreme Court case file on *People* v. *Belous*, O.T. 1970, #971, RG 267, Box 9564. The provider to whom Belous made the referral, Karl Lairtus, testified at the trial that he often sent Belous one hundred dollars for each such referral, but Belous denied ever receiving any money from Lairtus.

31. Cusack to Cook, 19 July 1968, Gloria Nelson to Cusack, 26 and 30 July and 4 August 1968, Cook to Cusack, 19 August 1968, Cusack to Cook, 26 August 1968, Cusack to Arlene Carmen, 31 August 1968, Cook to Cusack, 10 September 1968, Cusack to Blumenthal, and to Manfred Ohrenstein, 13 September 1968, Cusack to Duryea, 14 September 1968, Duryea to Cusack, 19 September 1968, Cusack to Lader, 22 September 1968, Cusack to Robert E. Hall, 1 October 1968, Cusack to Arlene Carmen, 3 October 1968, Cusack to John Lassoe, and to Duryea, 4 October 1968, Duryea to Cusack, 10 October 1968, Hall to Cusack, and Cusack to Franz Leichter, 11 October 1968, Leichter to Cusack, 14 October 1968, Cusack to Duryea, 10 November 1968, Arlene Emery Brown to Lader, 5 December 1971, Cusack to Lader, 19–20 December 1971, Cusack Papers; Cook Interview with Chesler, pp. 32–34; Cusack Interview with Garrow.

32. Pilpel to Wulf, 12 September 1968, ACLU 1972 Vol. 37; Lucas to Ad Hoc Test Case Committee Members, "Consideration of Further Steps," 15 October 1968, Lucas to Ann Israel, 18 October 1968, Pilpel to Lucas, 4 November 1968, Lucas Boxes 16 and 17; Sylvia Bloom, ASA Executive Committee Minutes, 6 November 1968, NARAL Box 6; Means to Ad Hoc Test Committee Members, 30 October 1968, Lucas to Ad Hoc Test Case Committee Members, "*Belous* v. *California* . . ." 12 November 1968, and Hall to Gordon W. Douglas et al., 12 November 1968, ACLU 1972 Vol. 37; Means, "The Law of New York Concerning Abortion," *New York Law Forum* 14 (Fall 1968): 411–515, esp. at 418 and 507; Mel Wulf to Jules Bernfeld, 12 November 1968, ACLU 1968 Vol. 7; Wulf to Aryeh Neier, n.d., and Neier to Wulf, 19 November 1968, ACLU 1972 Vol. 37; Richard H. Schwarz to Lucas, 26 November 1968, Lucas Box 16; Garrow conversations with Roy Lucas and Cyril Means. Also see "Testimony of Cyril C. Means, Jr., Before the Legislative Commission to Review the New Jersey Statutes Relating to Abortion," 28 October 1968, 20pp., Lucas Box 15 and ACLU 1972 Vol. 37; and Pilpel and Kenneth P. Norwick, *When Should Abortion Be Legal?* (New York: Public Affairs Pamphlets, #429, January 1969).

33. Zarky to Paul Halvonik, Wulf, and Lucas, 11 and 21 November 1968, Fred Okrand to Halvonik et al., 19 November 1968, Zarky to Wulf, 11 December 1968, Zarky to Wulf et al., 26 December 1968, ACLU 1972 Vol. 37; Lucas to Ad Hoc Test Case Committee Members, "*Belous* v. *California* . . ." 12 November 1968, ACLU 1972 Vol. 37.

34. *New York Times*, 14 November 1968, p. 50, 15 November 1968, p. 28, 18 November 1968, p. 46, 30 November 1968; *Wall Street Journal*, 15 November 1968, p. 3; *Time*, 15 November 1968, pp. 61–62; Elizabeth Elkind to Richard Lamm, 13 September 1968, Lamm Papers. On Michigan, where the Michigan State Medical Society endorsed *repeal* in September of 1968, see Transcript of Public Hearing, Michigan State Senate Committee on Abortion Law Reform— SR 185, 7 October 1968, Ann Arbor, 152pp., Bursley Papers Box 15; on Minnesota, see *MCLTP Newsletter* #1 (October 1968), and *St. Paul Pioneer Press*, 30 October 1968, p. 8; on the TMA poll, see *Dallas Times-Herald*, 16 September 1968, p. A18, and *Houston Post*, 17 September 1968. On Myers's efforts and NARAL, see Lader to Myers, 22 October 1968, Lader Box 15, ICMCA Board Minutes, 13 November 1968, ARAI 7–14, and Lader to Myers et al., 21 January 1969, NARAL Box 1; on Washington, see *Seattle Times*, 6 August 1968, Peter Raible to Lader,

10 April 1967, Lader Box 4, Byron N. Fujita and Nathaniel N. Wagner, "Referendum 20—Abortion Reform in Washington State," in Howard J. and Joy D. Osofsky, eds., *The Abortion Experience* (Hagerstown, MD: Harper & Row, 1973), pp. 232–260, at 234–235, and Robert G. Morrison, "Choice in Washington: The Politics of Liberalized Abortion" (unpublished M.A. thesis, University of Virginia, 1982), p. 32.

35. The conference proceedings were subsequently published in two volumes: Robert E. Hall, ed., *Abortion In A Changing World* (New York: Columbia University Press, 1970), vol. 1, pp. xix–xx, 141, 173, vol. 2, pp. 144, 156–159, 169; *Epperson v. Arkansas*, 393 U.S. 97 (1968); *New York Times*, 24 November 1968, p. 77; *Newsweek*, 2 December 1968, pp. 82–83; Lader to Myers et al., 21 November 1968, Lader Box 15; Garrow conversations with Hall, Lader, Leavy, Lucas, Ruth Roemer, John Lassoe, and Jimmye Kimmey. Several weeks before the conference, Hall "with great reluctance" turned aside a request from New York NOW that two of its members also be allowed to attend and participate, explaining that "we have tried to limit our invitations to those who are truly expert in abortion in a professional rather than personal sense." Hall emphasized that he was "acutely conscious of the fact that this is basically a woman's issue," but NOW's Jean Faust tartly replied that "we do not see abortion as 'a woman's issue,' but as a *human* issue" and observed that "professionals have for too long been dictating moral, theological and legal decisions to women—without consulting women." Faust to Hall, 28 September 1968, Hall to Faust, 11 October 1968, and Faust to Hall, 16 October 1968, Cusack Papers.

Also see *National Catholic Reporter*, 27 November 1968; *CCTA Newsletter*, January 1969, p. 3; Overstreet to Jack Stack, 21 March 1969, Stack Box 1; Lawrence E. Allan, "Constitutional Aspects of Present Criminal Abortion Laws," *Valparaiso Law Review* 3 (Fall 1968): 102–121, at 116 ("The Courts may well rely on *Griswold* in deciding abortion cases; and it seems clear that the *Griswold* arguments will be advanced with vigor by the advocates of reform"); and *Hospital Practice*, January 1969, pp. 19, 24–25. One week later Rockefeller told a Chicago audience that "Abortion is a medical question. As such, it should be taken out of the law and out of other disciplines and left to the practicing physician." *Chicago Daily News*, 23 November 1968.

36. Hall to Gordon W. Douglas et al., 12 November 1968 and 2 January 1969, Lucas, "Memorandum to Ad Hoc Test Case Committee," 26 December 1968, ACLU 1972 Vol. 37; Hall to Drs. Posner et al., 31 December 1968, Lucas Box 17; Hall, "His Birth Without Permission," *Saturday Review*, 7 December 1968, pp. 78–79, and Hall in *New York Times Magazine*, 29 December 1968, pp. 10–11, 17–20 ("repeal will not come from the legislatures but from the courts"); Beatrice Kornbluh to Leichter, 24 November 1968, Cusack Papers; Cusack to Lader, 19–20 December 1971, Lader Box 5; Lader [press release], "Assemblywoman Constance Cook Announces First Abortion *Repeal* Bill in New York State Legislature," 16 December 1968, NARAL Box 1; Lader, *Abortion II*, p. 92; Garrow conversations with Cusack and Lader; Guttmacher to Mrs. Nelson, 23 December 1968, Guttmacher Papers.

37. Warren to Mrs. Roome, 12 December 1968, ARAI 3–24; *New York Times*, 2 January 1969. On Texas, see *Dallas Morning News*, 19 January 1969, p. A10, 11 February 1969, p. D1, 13 February 1969, 18 February 1969; *Ft. Worth Star-Telegram* [editorial], 25 January 1969; *Dallas Times-Herald*, 12 February 1969; *Texas House Journal*, 13 February 1969, p. 236 (HB 323); C. Lincoln Williston to Clark, 18 February 1969, Clark Papers; Garrow conversations with James H. Clark, Jr. On Clark, a Yale graduate who also had an MBA from Stanford, see *Dallas Times-Herald*, 8 July 1969, pp. 15, 20.

38. Lamm, "Unwanted Child Births Forced by Law," *Denver Post*, 2 February 1969, pp. G1, G5; Lamm Interview with Garrow; Bonser to Lader, 30 January 1969, Lader Box 5 and NARAL Box 2; Keith Monroe, *New York Times Magazine*, 29 December 1968, pp. 10–11, 17–20; *Washington Post*, 10 December 1968, pp. D1, D4. Also see Harvey L. Zipf, "Recent Abortion Law Reforms (or Much Ado About Nothing)," *Journal of Criminal Law, Criminology and Police Science* 60 (March 1969): 3–23, esp. at 23 ("the constitutional right to 'raise a family' must also be a constitutional right to limit family size").

39. Hall to Myers, 13 June 1968, ARAI 10–15; Lassoe to Toba Cohen, 15 November 1968, Nat Lehrman to Cohen, 5 December 1968, Gordon Sherman to Cohen, 13 December 1968 ("the right of a woman to medical abortion is an individual moral choice and should not be subject to legal restrictions by the state"), ARAI 1–7; ICMCA Minutes, 18 December 1968 and 19 February 1969, ARAI 7–14; Cohen to Arnold Maremont, 2 January 1969, ARAI 1–7; Don Shaw to Hall, 24 January 1969, ARAI 13–4, Lassoe to Shaw, 27 January 1969, ARAI 10–5; Hall to Shaw, 27 January 1969, Shaw to Lassoe, 28 January 1969, ARAI 13–4; *New York Times*, 28 March 1969, p. 76; Cohen to Richard Rosenzweig, 21 May 1969, ARAI 1–7.

40. Kimmey to Toba Cohen, 30 December 1968, ARAI 8–10; Myers, untitled 6pp. account of the conference, March 1969, Schlesinger 223–2–19; Friedan, "Abortion: A Woman's Civil Right," 14 February 1969, Lader Box 3 and ARAI 5–5; Breslow, "Abortion: The Case for Repeal," 15 February 1969, Schlesinger 223–2–11; "Report of the Planning Committee, NARAL," 16 February 1969 (transcript of recording, paginated as 62 to 140), ARAI 2–20; *New York Times*, 17 February 1969, p. 32; *Washington Post*, 17 February 1969, p. D1; *Los Angeles Times*, 17 February 1969, pp. IV-1, IV-7, 18 February 1969, pp. 1, 6; Ivan Shapiro to Jack Pemberton, 28 February 1969, ACLU 1969 Vol. 4; Lader to Myers and Shaw, 13 March 1969, Ruth Smith to Gidding, 15 March 1969, NARAL Box 1; Lader, *Abortion II*, p. 95. Also see Nathanson, *Aborting America*, pp. 34, 47–55.

41. Edgar B. Keemer, "Report of First National Conference . . ." 20 February 1969, ACLU 1969 Vol. 4; Keemer, *Confessions of a Pro-Life Abortionist* (Detroit: Vinco Press, 1980), pp. 12, 113, 136, 163–164, 195, 208, 214–215; Keemer, "Looking Back at Luenbach: 296 Non-Hospital Abortions," *Journal of the National Medical Association* 62 (July 1970): 291–293; Ruth Barnett [Bush], *They Weep On My Doorstep* (Beaverton, OR: Halo Publishers, January 1969), pp. 56, 135.

42. *New York Times*, 22 January 1969, p. 47, 27 February 1967, pp. 22, 23; *Village Voice*, 18 August 1966, pp. 1, 18–19; *Time*, 13 October 1967, pp. 32–33; Spencer, "The Performance of Nonhospital Abortions," in Hall, ed., *Abortion in a Changing World*, vol. 1, pp. 218–225, at 218; Brownmiller, "Dr. Spencer, 1889–1969," *Village Voice*, 30 January 1969, pp. 1, 53–54; [Carol Kahn], *Medical World News*, 28 February 1969, pp. 28–29; *Newsweek*, 17 February 1969, p. 92; *Los Angeles Times*, 17 March 1969, pp. 1, 20–21; *Philadelphia Evening Bulletin*, 18 December 1969, pp. 1, 14; Ellen Messer and Kathryn E. May, *Back Rooms: Voices From the Illegal Abortion Era* (New York: St. Martin's Press, 1988), pp. 218–224; Michael T. Kaufman, "Abortion Doctor," *Lear's*, July-August 1989, pp. 84–87; Patricia G. Miller, *The Worst of Times* (New York: HarperCollins, 1993), pp. 122–139; Garrow conversations with John Lassoe, Susan Brownmiller and Michael T. Kaufman.

43. Donald W. Ball, "An Abortion Clinic Ethnography," *Social Problems* 14 (Winter 1967): 293–301, at 298; Nancy Howell Lee, *The Search for An Abortionist* (Chicago: University of Chicago Press, 1969); R. W. Jesse and Frederick J. Spencer, "Abortion—The Hidden Epidemic," *Virginia Medical Monthly* 95 (August 1968): 447–456; Kenneth R. Whittemore, "The Availability of Nonhospital Abortions," in Hall, ed., *Abortion in a Changing World*, vol. 1, pp. 212–217, at 212–214. Along with Lee, also see Peter K. Manning, "Fixing What You Feared: Notes on the Campus Abortion Search," in James M. Henslin, ed., *Studies in the Sociology of Sex* (New York: Appleton-Century-Crofts, 1971), pp. 137–166. For a sympathetic profile of a nonmedical provider, Lorraine Florio, who operated in Lawrence, Mass., between 1958 and 1968, see *Boston Globe*, 16 May 1989, pp. 1, 4–5.

44. Arlene Carmen Interview with Chesler; Carmen and Moody, *Abortion Counseling*, pp. 50–51; Nathanson, *Aborting America*, p. 44; *New York Times*, 3 January 1969, p. 25; *Newsday*, 26 and 27 March 1969, pp. 10–11.

45. Munger to Joseph Sunnen, and to Garrett Hardin, 20 January 1969, Roger O. Egeberg and Keith P. Russell to "Dear Doctor," 28 January 1969, Ruth Roemer to Russell, 28 January 1969, Egeberg to Roemer, 4 February 1969, Munger to Burnham Enersen, 5 February 1969, Munger to Fellow Signers of the Lawyers' Brief, 28 February 1969, CCTA Box 4; Barbara M. Armstrong et al., "Application for Leave to File Brief Amicus Curiae and Brief," *People* v. *Belous*, California Supreme Court, Crim. #12739, January 1969, 32pp., at p. 19; Leavy et al.,

"Amicus Curiae Brief on Behalf of Medical School Deans and Others," *People* v. *Belous*, #12739, 14 January 1969, 48pp., esp. pp. 20–24; Trinkhaus et al., "Amicus Curiae Brief," *People* v. *Belous*, #12739, February 1969, 24pp.; *Los Angeles Times*, 14 February 1969, p. 3, 10 March 1969, pp. 1, 12–13; Lucas, "Memorandum: Report on the Belous v. California Case," 5 March 1969, ACLU 1972 Vol. 37; CCTA Board Minutes, 19 March 1969, CCTA Box 5; *CCTA Newsletter*, April 1969; Lucas in *NARAL News* Vol. 1, #1 (Summer 1969), p. 3; Garrow conversations with Charles T. Munger, Zad Leavy, Ruth Roemer, and Keith P. Russell. One member of the California high court, Stanley Mosk, recused himself from *Belous* because of a family member's prior acquaintance with the doctor, and Chief Justice Traynor placed the case on his court's Sacramento docket, thus assuring that senior Sacramento-area appellate judge Fred R. Pierce, rather than another jurist, would take Mosk's place and become the seventh member of the *Belous* court. 71 Cal.2d 982, and Munger Interview with Garrow. Also see *Open Forum* [Southern California ACLU], February 1969, pp. 4–5, and *SHA Newsletter* Vol. 5, #1 (April 1969). Hostile perspectives also include Luis Kutner, "Due Process of Abortion," *Minnesota Law Review* 53 (November 1968): 1–28; Frank J. Ayd, Jr., "Liberal Abortion Laws," *America*, 1 February 1969, pp. 130–132; and Eugene Quay, "Constitutionality of Abortion Laws: Rights of the Fetus," *Child and Family* 8 (Spring 1969): 169–175.

46. Lucas, "Memorandum: Report on the Belous v. California Case," 5 March 1969, ACLU 1972 Vol. 37; *Morin* v. *Garra*, 54 N.J. 82 (10 December 1968); Lucas and Balk, "Petition for Writ of Certiorari," *Morin* v. *Garra*, U.S.S.C., O.T. 1968, #1289, 25pp., 21 April 1969, at pp. 10, 12 and 17, and Lucas and Balk, "Reply Brief for Petitioner," *Morin* v. *Garra*, #1289, 10pp., Lucas Box 26 and National Archives Box 8961; Leavy to Lucas, 20 March 1969, Pilpel to Lucas, 24 March 1969, Lucas Box 26; *Morin* v. *Garra*, 395 U.S. 935 (2 June 1969); Garrow conversations with Roy Lucas.

Louisiana State Board of Medical Examiners v. *Knight*, 180 So.2d 755 (1965), 195 So.2d 375 (1967), 211 So.2d 433 (1968), *Knight* v. *Louisiana State Board of Medical Examiners*, 252 La. 889, 214 So.2d 716 (25 October 1968), Benjamin E. Smith and Douglas A. Allen, "Petition for Writ of Certiorari," *Knight* v. *Louisiana State Board of Medical Examiners*, U.S.S.C., O.T. 1968, #1075, 32pp., 20 February 1969, esp. pp. 21–23 ("the private right of a woman to determine whether or not to bear a child"); *Knight* v. *Louisiana State Board of Medical Examiners*, 395 U.S. 933 (2 June 1969). Several months earlier the Supreme Court had denied certiorari in another New Jersey case where several defendants' (including one physician) abortion convictions had already been affirmed by the New Jersey Supreme Court. *New Jersey* v. *Moretti*, 235 A.2d 226, 244 A.2d 499 (1968); *Moretti* v. *New Jersey*, 393 U.S. 952 (18 November 1968). Additionally, the very same day that the U.S. Supreme Court rejected *Knight*, the Massachusetts Supreme Judicial Court rejected a vagueness challenge to that state's abortion statute by a doctor whose medical license had been revoked after he had pled guilty to two counts of abortion and been sentenced to three years' probation. *Kudish* v. *Board of Registration in Medicine*, 248 N.E.2d 264 (2 June 1969).

47. Minutes, Citizens for Abortion Law Repeal, 7 January 1969, NARAL Box 4; Cusack to Lader, 19–20 December 1971 ("I was dismayed at the lack of enthusiasm for the abortion issue shown by the chapter as a whole"), Lader Box 5; Cusack Interview with Garrow; *New York Times*, 7 January 1969, p. 40, 15 January 1969, p. 35, 28 January 1969, p. 31, 29 January 1969, p. 40, 30 January 1969, p. 22, 3 February 1969, p. 27, 6 February 1969, p. 38, 7 February 1969, p. 39, 12 February 1969, p. 79, 13 February 1969, p. 28, 14 February 1969, p. 42, 21 February 1969, p. 46, 22 February 1969, p. 35, 23 February 1969, p. E6, 25 February 1969, p. 46, 3 March 1969, p. 40; *Voice of the Women's Liberation Movement* Vol. 1, #1 (March 1968), #2 (June 1968), #3 (August 1968), #4 (October 1968), esp. p. 11, #5 (January 1969), #6 (February 1969); Jo Freeman, *The Politics of Women's Liberation* (New York: David McKay, 1975), esp. pp. 51, 59, 62, 82; *The New Yorker*, 22 February 1969, pp. 28–29; *The Guardian*, 19 April 1969, p. 11; Alice Echols, *Daring to Be Bad: Radical Feminism in America, 1967–1975* (Minneapolis: University of Minnesota Press, 1989), esp. pp. 139–142; Board Minutes, New Yorkers for Abortion Law Repeal, 23 July and 6 and 13 August 1969, Smith Box 1. Also see

Darlene Weide, "The History of New York Abortion Law Repeal: A Case Study" (unpublished B.A. thesis, Barnard College, April 1989), pp. 21–24; Ellen Willis in the *Village Voice*, 3 March 1980, p. 8; and Ninia Baehr, *Abortion Without Apology* (Boston: South End Press, 1990), pp. 38–44.

On Ruth Cusack's point regarding NOW, also see Suzanne Staggenborg, *The Pro-Choice Movement* (New York: Oxford University Press, 1991), p. 20 ("NOW's participation in the abortion movement was . . . limited in the early years. . . . many NOW members and chapters were preoccupied with economic issues"). Even in 1971, one participant-observer emphasized how "the abortion reform effort was already well under way when feminist resurgence began" (Emily C. Moore, "Abortion and Public Policy: What Are the Issues?" *New York Law Forum* 17 [1971]: 411–436, at 420), and California attorney Herma Hill Kay, whose active involvement dated to the early 1960s, subsequently made much the same point: "The abortion law reform movement in California was led, as it was initially in many other states, not by members of the women's movement but by physicians, attorneys, and public health experts." U.S. Congress, Senate, Committee on the Judiciary, *Constitutional Amendments Relating to Abortion—Hearings Before the Subcommittee on the Constitution*, 97th Cong., 1st sess., 16 November 1981, pp. 766–767. Also see Alice S. Rossi and Bhavani Sitaraman, "Abortion in Context: Historical Trends and Future Changes," *Family Planning Perspectives* 20 (November-December 1988): 273–281, 301, at 273 ("American feminists were relative latecomers to the abortion reform movement").

On the early feminist groupings and the various factional shifts that took place among the New York activists, see especially Celestine Ware, *Woman Power: The Movement for Women's Liberation* (New York: Tower Publications, 1970), pp. 16–74, esp. at 29–30 and 38, Roberta Salper, "The Development of the American Women's Liberation Movement, 1967–1971," in Salper, ed., *Female Liberation* (New York: Alfred A. Knopf, 1972), pp. 169–184, Maren L. Carden, *The New Feminist Movement* (New York: Russell Sage Foundation, 1974), esp. pp. 32, 87, 104–132; see as well Lucinda Cisler, "A Campaign to Repeal Legal Restrictions on Non-Prescription Contraceptives: The Case of New York," in Myron H. Redford et al., eds., *The Condom* (San Francisco: San Francisco Press, 1974), pp. 83–108; Leah Fritz, *Dreamers and Dealers* (Boston: Beacon Press, 1979), esp. p. 26; Barbara S. Deckard, *The Women's Movement*, 3rd ed. (New York: Harper & Row, 1983), pp. 327–336; Winifred D. Wandersee, *On the Move* (Boston: Twayne, 1988), pp. 1–15; and Faye D. Ginsburg, *Contested Lives* (Berkeley: University of California Press, 1989), p. 39.

48. Guttmacher to "Dear Friend of Planned Parenthood," 26 February 1969, 4pp.; Guttmacher, "The Genesis of Liberalized Abortion in New York: A Personal Insight," *Case Western Reserve Law Review* 23 (Summer 1972): 756–778, at 775–77; Norman F. Lent, "Report of the Joint Legislative Committee," 10 March 1969, 9pp., Schlesinger 223–1–10; *New York Times*, 28 February 1969, p. 35, 5 March 1969, p. 33, 8 March 1969, p. 28, 11 March 1969, p. 36, 13 March 1969, p. 32, 14 March 1969, p. 40, 17 March 1969, p. 13, 21 March 1969, pp. 46, 50, 22 March 1969, p. 19, 15 April 1969, pp. 44, 46, 17 April 1969, p. 46, 18 April 1969, pp. 1, 48, 19 April 1969, p. 26; Liz Elkind to ARA Board, "Memorandum," n.d. [c.24 March 1969], 3pp., Cusack Papers; Lader, *Abortion II*, pp. 122–123.

49. *Dallas Times-Herald*, 5 March 1969, 7 March 1969, 20 March 1969; *Dallas Morning News*, 6 March 1969, 8 March 1969, p. D1, 20 March 1969, p. A11, 23 March 1969, 24 March 1969, 25 March 1969, pp. C1, C3, 5 April 1969, 9 April 1969, 14 May 1969, p. AA4, 2 August 1969; *Houston Post*, 6 March 1969, 20 March 1969; Charles O. Galvin to Clark, 5 March 1969, James T. Downs III to Clark, 17 March 1969, Clark to Mrs. Fred R. Brown, 31 March 1969, Clark Papers; Garrow conversations with Jim Clark; *Ft. Worth Star-Telegram*, 13 April 1969, p. A8; Savage, "Report of Committee on Abortion Laws in Texas," Texas Medical Association *Program*, May 1969, pp. 96–98, Savage Papers; *Houston Chronicle*, 3 May 1969; *Corpus Christi Caller*, 13 July 1969.

50. On New Mexico, see *New York Times*, 23 February 1969, p. 59, 23 March 1969, p. 44, Jonathan B. Sutin, "New Mexico's 1969 Criminal Abortion Law," *Natural Resources Journal* 10 (July 1970): 591–614, and Robert Shafer, "New Abortion Laws Won't Change Old

Attitudes," *Modern Hospital* 118 (February 1972): 96–98. The one *New York Times* item regarding Arkansas noted simply the bill's passage in the House: 7 February 1969, p. 18. On Kansas, see Lee Derman to Ernest Angell, 5 March 1969, Derman to Alan Reitman, 26 April 1969, ACLU 1969 Vol. 4, *New York Times*, 25 April 1969, p. 26, Derman to Lee Gidding, 30 May 1969, NARAL Box 3. On Oregon, see Alan R. Mitchell, "Abortion, Oregon Style," *Oregon Law Review* 49 (April 1970): 302–321, Marilyn Weaver to Richard Lamm, 9 and 16 August 1968, Lamm Papers, Jimmye Kimmey to Toba Cohen, 27 May 1969, ARAI 1–11, and Gordon B. Fields, *Oregon Law Review* 51 (Spring 1972): 494–514, at 504; on Delaware see *New York Times*, 13 June 1969, p. 14, 22 June 1969, p. 42. Some tallies erroneously counted Mississippi's 1966 addition of rape as a second exception to its standard antiabortion law as a "reform" enactment; given Mississippi's racial politics at that time and the symbolic importance of rape, this book does not.

51. Lassoe to Don Shaw, 27 January 1969, ARAI 10–5; *New York Times*, 26 January 1969, p. 76, 3 June 1969, p. 43; *Hartford Times*, 13 April 1969; Transcript of Judiciary Committee Hearing, 14 April 1969, Connecticut State Library, esp. p. 85; Roraback to Jack Pemberton, 6 May 1969, ACLU 1969 Vol. 4; Transcript of Proceedings, House of Representatives, 9 May 1969, pp. 25–78, Connecticut State Library; Cantor to Emerson, 21 May 1969, and Emerson to Cantor, 15 July 1969, Emerson Box 49; Stephen Fleck to Lee Gidding, 21 April 1969, Gidding to Fleck, 28 May 1969, and Lucas to Gidding, 29 May 1969, NARAL Box 4; Garrow conversations with Donald J. Cantor and Richard Bowers.

52. On Iowa, see James C. Mohr, "Iowa's Abortion Battles of the Late 1960s and Early 1970s," *Annals of Iowa* 50 (Summer 1989): 63–89, at 71, and especially Robert L. Webber to Lee Gidding, 25 August 1969, NARAL Box 3. On Minnesota, see Robert B. Benjamin, "Abortion or Compulsory Pregnancy?," *Minnesota Medicine* 52 (March 1969): 455–457 ("At our own feet must lie some of the responsibility for women who have died following criminal abortions"); *Minnesota Tribune*, 20 March 1969, pp. 1, 7; and Irene Hoebel to Lader, 19 April 1969, NARAL Box 3. On Nevada, see *New York Times*, 10 April 1969, p. 38, and James T. Richardson and Sandie W. Fox, "Religious Affiliation as a Predictor of Voting Behavior in Abortion Reform Legislation," *Journal for the Scientific Study of Religion* 11 (December 1972): 347–359; on Hawaii, see Patricia G. Steinhoff and Milton Diamond, *Abortion Politics: The Hawaii Experience* (Honolulu: University Press of Hawaii, 1977), pp. 13–23. For another unusual medical statement somewhat similar to Dr. Benjamin's, see C. V. Cimmino, "Abortions," *Virginia Medical Monthly* 96 (April 1969): 236–237 ("the parasite growing within her").

53. On Illinois see Richard Lamm to John Henry Kleine, 29 April 1969, ARAI 17–4; Toba Cohen to Cyril Means, 14 May 1969, and Cohen to Jimmye Kimmey, 21 May 1969, ARAI 8–10; Paul Handler to Don Shaw, 3 June 1969, ARAI 8–11; and Shaw to Lassoe, 21 August 1969, ARAI 1–7. Also see Lonny Myers, "Testimony Before the Public Welfare Committee," 18 March 1969, and "Testimony Before Senate Judiciary Committee," 23 April 1969, NARAL Box 3.

On Michigan, see *New York Times*, 5 February 1969, p. 20; Jack Stack to Mary Lou Tanton, 4 March 1969, Michigan Women for Medical Control of Abortion *Newsletter* #6 (April 1969) and #7 (May 1969), Stack Box 1; *New York Times*, 13 June 1969, p. 14; Minutes, Michigan Coordinating Committee for Abortion Law Reform, 28 June 1969, Stack to Stewart Mott, 3 July 1969, Stack Box 1; and Stack, "Abortion Law Reform Progress in Michigan," *Michigan Medicine* 69 (January 1970): 23–27.

On Washington, see William E. Watts, *Northwest Medicine*, March 1969, p. 270; Samuel Goldenberg to Elizabeth Elkind, 10 March 1969, WCAR I-2; Marilyn Ward to Mrs. E. G. Spencer, 5 May 1969, WCAR I-1; Goldenberg to Elizabeth Bannister et al., 6 and 7 May 1969, WCAR II-17; Goldenberg to Jimmye Kimmey, 20 May, 9 July and 6 and 20 August 1969, Goldenberg to Richard Lamm, 24 June 1969, WCAR I-2; Goldenberg to Anne Gaylor, 18 August 1969, WCAR II-2; WCAR Minutes, 19 August and 9 September 1969, WCAR I-4; and especially Robert G. Morrison, "Choice in Washington: The Politics of Liberalized Abortion" (unpublished M.A. thesis, University of Virginia, 1982), pp. 34–47.

54. Lucas to Emerson, 2 April 1969, Emerson to Lucas, 17 April 1969, Lucas to Emerson, 23

April 1969, Emerson to Lucas, 30 April 1969, Emerson Box 13; Lee Gidding to Stephen Fleck, 28 May 1969, NARAL Box 4; Lucas to Clement E. Vose, 2 July and 18 August 1969, Lucas Interview with Vose, 9 July 1969, Lucas Box 25; Brochure, "The James Madison Constitutional Law Institute," n.d. [July 1969], 12pp., Martha Gantt to Emerson, 6 August 1969, Lucas to Emerson, 4 September 1969, and "Cases Presently on Docket," 3 September 1969, Emerson Box 13; Lucas to Mel Wulf, 8 September 1969, and 3 September enclosure, ACLU 1969 Vol. 9; Garrow conversations with Roy Lucas, Morris Dees, Norman Dorsen, Douglas J. Kramer, and Mel Wulf. Also see Lucas, "The Right to Higher Education," *Journal of Higher Education* 41 (January 1970): 55–64.

55. Clark, "Religion, Morality, and Abortion: A Constitutional Appraisal," *Loyola University Law Review* 2 (April 1969): 1–11, at 8 and 9. Also see Gerald N. Rosenberg, *The Hollow Hope* (Chicago: University of Chicago Press, 1991), p. 182 ("Clark's position on when the state's interests become compelling was the standard that the Court adopted" in 1973).

56. *Commonwealth* v. *Baird*, 247 N.E.2d 574, 580, 582; *Boston Globe*, 3 December 1968, 1 May 1969, pp. 1, 13, 19 May 1969, pp. 1, 22, 2 June 1969, pp. 1, 24, 20 June 1969, 9 November 1969; *New York Times*, 3 December 1968, 20 May 1969, p. 49, 3 June 1969, p. 31; James Clapp and Lucinda Cisler, "The Baird Case: Testing Birth Control Laws," June 1969, ARAI Box 2; *NOW–New York Newsletter* Vol. 2, #6 (June 1969): 5; Balliro, "Petition for Writ of Certiorari," *Baird* v. *Massachusetts*, U.S.S.C., O.T. 1969, #707, 31 July 1969, 29pp., and Robert H. Quinn et al., "Brief for the Commonwealth of Massachusetts in Opposition to the Granting of the Petition for Certiorari," *Baird* v. *Massachusetts*, #707, 30 August 1969, p. 6, National Archives RG 267, Box 9840; *New England Journal of Medicine* 281 (4 September 1969): 546–547. Efforts in 1968 and early 1969 to alter the state's birth control statute so as to legalize the distribution of contraceptives to unmarried individuals were twice defeated by very wide margins on the floor of the state House.

57. *New York Times*, 12 May 1969, p. 66; *Los Angeles Times*, 13 May 1969, pp. IV-1, 9, 14 May 1969, pp. IV-1, 2; Carl Reiterman, ed., *Abortion and the Unwanted Child* (New York: Springer Publishing Co., 1971), esp. pp. 9–12, 15, 24. Overstreet also (p. 24) restated a comment he earlier had made at Hot Springs: "Increasingly [women] claim the decision of the U.S. Supreme Court in *Griswold* . . . as a manifesto which gives to the individual woman the right to avoid childbearing."

58. Larry Plagenz, "States Legislate Abortion Reform, But Hospitals Are Reluctant to Comply," *Modern Hospital* 113 (July 1969): 82–85, at 84; "Abortion and the Law," *Current Medical Digest*, September 1969, pp. 751–775, at 751; *Atlanta Journal*, 14 May 1969, p. B21; Roger W. Rochat et al., "An Epidemiological Analysis of Abortion in Georgia," *American Journal of Public Health* 61 (March 1971): 543–552; on North Carolina, see Arthur C. Christakos, "Experience at Duke Medical Center After Modern Legislation for Therapeutic Abortion," *Southern Medical Journal* 63 (June 1970): 655–657, and Eric Pfeiffer, "Psychiatric Indications or Psychiatric Justification of Therapeutic Abortion?," *Archives of General Psychiatry* 23 (November 1970): 402–407; on Maryland, see Irvin M. Cushner, "The Aftermath of Abortion Legislation in Maryland," *Advances in Planned Parenthood* 6 (1971): 158–163, and Theodore Irwin, "The New Abortion Laws: How Are They Working?" *Today's Health* 48 (March 1970): 21–23ff; also see *New York Times*, 2 March 1969, p. 61, 6 June 1969, p. 87.

Also see *New England Journal of Medicine* 280 (29 May 1969): 1240–1241; *JAMA* 209 (14 July 1969): 229–231 and 260–261; Conrad M. Riley to Richard Frank, 22 July 1969, ARAI 1–12; Abraham Heller and H. G. Whittington, "The Colorado Report," in R. Bruce Sloane, ed., *Abortion* (New York: Grune & Stratton, 1971), pp. 151–164; Lamm and Steven Davison, "Abortion and Euthanasia: A Reply," *Rocky Mountain Medical Journal*, February 1971, pp. 40–42; Heller, "Therapeutic Abortion Trends in the United States," *Current Psychiatric Therapies* 12 (1972): 171–184.

59. Leon Marder, "Psychiatric Experience with a Liberalized Therapeutic Abortion Law," *American Journal of Psychiatry* 126 (March 1970): 1230–1236, at 1231; Marder et al., "Psychosocial Aspects of Therapeutic Abortion," *Southern Medical Journal* 63 (June 1970): 657–661; R. Bruce Sloane, "The Unwanted Pregnancy," *New England Journal of Medicine* 280

(29 May 1969): 1206–1213, at 1211; Kummer, "New Trends in Therapeutic Abortion in California," *Obstetrics and Gynecology* 34 (December 1969): 883–887, at 885; Russell and Edwin W. Jackson, "Therapeutic Abortions in California: First Year's Experience Under New Legislation," *American Journal of Obstetrics and Gynecology* 105 (1 November 1969): 757–765, at 760.

60. Hall, "Abortion Laws: A Call For Reform," *DePaul Law Review* 18 (Summer 1969): 584–592, at 586, 590; Albert Q. Maisel, "The Growing Battle Over Abortion Reform," *Reader's Digest*, June 1969, pp. 152–158; *Time*, 6 June 1969, pp. 26–27; Charles F. Westoff et al., "The Structure of Attitudes Toward Abortion," *Milbank Memorial Fund Quarterly* 47 (January 1969): 11–37, at 12; Elise F. Jones and Westoff, "Attitudes Toward Abortion in the United States and the Trend Since 1965," in Westoff and Robert Parke, Jr., eds., *Demographic and Social Aspects of Population Growth* (Washington: U.S. Government Printing Office, 1972), pp. 569–578, at 570; Judith Blake, "Abortion and Public Opinion: the 1960–1970 Decade," *Science* 171 (12 February 1971): 540–549.

Also see Frank W. Peyton et al., "Women's Attitudes Concerning Abortion," *Obstetrics and Gynecology* 34 (August 1969): 182–188; Dennis S. Mileti and Larry D. Barnett, "Nine Demographic Factors and Their Relationship to Attitudes Toward Abortion Legalization," *Social Biology* 19 (March 1972): 43–50; Pilpel, "The Right of Abortion," *Atlantic Monthly* 223 (June 1969): 69–71; Alice S. Rossi, "Abortion and Social Change," *Dissent* 16 (July-August 1969): 338–346; Sidney M. Morris, *Kentucky Law Journal* 57 (Spring 1969): 555–563; Betty Wolf, "Abortion Law Reform at a Crossroad?," *Chicago-Kent Law Review* 46 (Spring-Summer 1969): 102–115; John Montjoy, "Abortion and the Law," *Tulane Law Review* 43 (June 1969): 834–853; Carl E. Wasmuth and Kenet E. Chareau, "Abortion Laws," *Cleveland State Law Review* 18 (September 1969): 503–511; Robert Hoffman, "The Moral Right to Abortion," *Michigan Quarterly Review* 8 (October 1969): 273–277. The rather small number of opposition pieces from mid-1969 include *America*, 3 May 1969, pp. 518–519, and 19 July 1969, pp. 36–39; John T. Noonan, Jr., "Amendment of the Abortion Law: Relevant Data and Judicial Opinion," *Catholic Lawyer* 15 (Spring 1969): 124–135; and Charles P. Kindregan, "Abortion, the Law, and Defective Children," *Suffolk University Law Review* 3 (Spring 1969): 225–276; also see especially *New York Times*, 18 April 1969, p.40.

61. *New York Times*, 25 May 1969, p. 34, 26 May 1969, p. 17, 30 May 1969, p. 26, 17 October 1969, p. 28; Hare in Ellen Messer and Kathryn E. May, *Back Rooms: Voices From the Illegal Abortion Era* (New York: St. Martin's Press, 1988), pp. 203–214; Lader, *Abortion II*, pp. 75–76, 96–102; *Wall Street Journal*, 23 June 1969, pp. 1, 23; Susan Brownmiller, "Abortion Counseling: Service Beyond Sermons," *New York Magazine*, 4 August 1969, pp. 26–31; Lader to Ephraim London, 9 August 1969, Lader Box 4; Jesse Lyons to Burton Roberts, 17 September 1969, and Cyril C. Means, Jr., to Roberts, 18 September 1969, Gerald A. Messerman to Lucas, 6 October 1969, Lucas Box 25; *San Francisco Chronicle*, 4 October 1969, p. 28. Also see *Time*, 28 November 1969, p. 82; *Denver Post Empire Magazine*, 25 January 1970, pp. 26–29; and *Commonwealth* v. *Brunelle*, 171 N.E.2d 850 (1961).

62. *People* v. *Belous*, 458 P.2d 194, 199–200, 202, 206, 71 Cal.2d 954, 80 Cal. Rptr. 354. With regard to Peters's final point, see particularly Edith Barnett, "The Hospital Abortion Committee as an Administrative Body of the State," *Journal of Family Law* 10 (1970): 32–47.

63. *Los Angeles Times*, 6 September 1969, p. 1, 25 September 1969, pp. IV-1, 12; *New York Times*, 14 September 1969, p. 66; *Time*, 19 September 1969, p. 66; Keith P. Russell, "To the Signers of the Physicians' Brief," 28 October 1969, CCTA Box 1; Lucas to W. J. Bryan Henrie, 10 September 1969, Lucas Box 21; *American Medical News*, 22 September 1969, p. 3; Howard Hassard and David E. Willett, "Abortion in California," *California Medicine* 111 (December 1969): 491–492; Leavy, "Current Developments in the Law of Abortion," *Los Angeles Bar Bulletin* 45 (November 1969): 11–15, 36–37. Also see CCTA Board Minutes, 10 September 1969, and CCTA "Open Meeting" Minutes, Santa Monica, 29 October 1969, CCTA Box 4; Jimmye Kimmey to Samuel Goldenberg, 18 September 1969, WCAR I-1; Kimmey, "The Abortion Argument: What It's Not About," *Barnard Alumnae*, Fall 1969; Leavy in *CCTA Newsletter*, October 1969, pp. 1, 2; *The New Republic*, 25 October 1969, p. 12; *Scientific*

American, November 1969, pp. 56–57; *Modern Hospital*, December 1969, pp. 50–52; *Medical Economics*, 22 December 1969, pp. 146–147.

Law journal notes on the case, many of which were quite hostile to the *Belous* majority, include Kathryn L. Powers, "Toward A Judicial Reform of Abortion Laws," *University of Florida Law Review* 22 (Summer 1969): 59–72; Laurens H. Silver, *Clearinghouse Review* 3 (October 1969): 131–133; *Washington University Law Quarterly* 1969 (Fall): 445–451; Richard D. Holper, *Journal of Family Law* 9 (1969): 300–308; *New York Law Forum* 15 (Winter 1969): 941–949; Joseph J. Fabrizio, *Journal of Urban Law* 47 (1969–70): 901–906; Nelson J. Vogel, Jr., *Notre Dame Lawyer* 45 (Winter 1970): 329–339; Edward J. Hund, Jr., *Washburn Law Journal* 9 (Winter 1970): 286–292; R. Eldridge Hicks, *Harvard Civil Rights–Civil Liberties Law Review* 5 (January 1970): 133–150; Jane L. McGrew, *University of Pennsylvania Law Review* 118 (February 1970): 643–659; *Fordham Law Review* 38 (March 1970): 557–568; Kathryn G. Milman, "Abortion Reform: History, Status, and Prognosis," *Case Western Reserve Law Review* 21 (April 1970): 521–548; Stewart M. Weintraub, *Temple Law Quarterly* 43 (Spring 1970): 302–304; *University of Richmond Law Review* 4 (Spring 1970): 351–357; William T. Robinson III, *Kentucky Law Journal* 58 (Spring 1970): 843–850; Hugh Lowe, *Texas Law Review* 48 (May 1970): 937–946; Gary R. Cassavechia, *Duquesne Law Review* 8 (Summer 1970): 439–447; Edward C. Hussie, *Dickinson Law Review* 74 (Summer 1970): 772–781; Patrick L. Baude, "Constitutional Reflections on Abortion Reform," *University of Michigan Journal of Law Reform* 4 (Fall 1970): 1–10; Lyle B. Haskin, "The Abortion Controversy: The Law's Response," *Chicago-Kent Law Review* 48 (Fall-Winter 1971): 191–207. Also see note 69 below.

64. Thomas C. Lynch et al., "Petition for Rehearing," *People* v. *Belous*, 19 September 1969, p. 12 (denied 3 October 1969); Lynch et al., "Petition for Writ of Certiorari," *California* v. *Belous*, U.S.S.C., O.T. 1969, #971, 15 December 1969, 15pp., National Archives RG 267, Box 9564; Russell, "To the Signers of the Physicians' Brief," 28 October 1969, CCTA Box 1; Zarky in *Los Angeles Times*, 25 September 1969, pp. IV-1, 12; Cyril Means to Lucas et al., 29 December 1969, Lucas Box 1; Lucas to W. J. Bryan Henrie, 10 September 1969, Lucas Box 21; Lucas to Zarky, 18 September 1969, Lucas Box 1; Dees to Drs. Nace Cohen and Hugh McGuire, 18 and 19 September 1969, Lucas Box 25; Lucas, "Notes on the Efforts in 1965–1973"; Garrow conversations with Roy Lucas.

65. Garrow conversations with Roy Lucas, Robert E. Hall, and Mel Wulf; ACLU News Release, 30 September 1969, Lucas Box 28; *Washington Post*, 30 September 1969, pp. B1, B2; *New York Times*, 1 October 1969, p. 55; Aryeh Neier to Lucas, and Bart Clausen to Lucas, 1 October 1969, and Lucas draft response, n.d., Lucas Box 25; Pilpel to Hall et al., 30 December 1969, ACLU 1972 Vol. 37.

66. Munger to Lucas, 24 October 1969, CCTA Financial Report, July 1968–June 1969, 11 March 1970, Munger to Anwyl, 27 June 1969, Anwyl to Ruth Roemer, 3 July 1969, Elizabeth Canfield to Joseph Sunnen, 21 December 1969, Munger to Dean Bauer, 30 December 1969, CCTA Box 4; Munger to Lader, 28 February 1972, Lader Box 5; Munger Interview with Garrow.

67. Nancy Stearns and Florynce Kennedy, "Complaint for Declaratory and Injunctive Relief," *Abramowicz* v. *Lefkowitz*, S.D.N.Y. CA#69–4469, 10 October 1969, pp. 11–12; *New York Times*, 8 October 1969, p. 53, 6 November 1969, p. 28, 7 November 1969, p. 14, 10 November 1969, p. 46, 13 December 1969, p. 37; *Hall* v. *Lefkowitz*, 305 F. Supp. 1030 (4 November); *Village Voice*, 4 December 1969, pp. 34, 37; Diane Schulder and Florynce Kennedy, *Abortion Rap* (New York: McGraw-Hill, 1971); Stearns, "Roe v. Wade: Our Struggle Continues," *Berkeley Women's Law Journal* 4 (1988–89): 1–11, at 1–4; Stearns Interview with Garrow. Also see Darlene Weide, "The History of New York Abortion Law Repeal" (unpublished B.A. thesis, Barnard College, 1989), pp. 27–30; and John D. Gregory, "Complaint," *John and Mary Doe et al.* v. *Lefkowitz*, S.D.N.Y. #CA69–4423, 24 October 1969, 13pp., Lucas Box 16.

68. Dees to Charles Flowers, 4 November 1969, Flowers to Dees, 11 November 1969, Dees to Flowers, 17 November 1969, Lucas Box 25; Lucas to Savage, 23 October 1969, Lucas Box 22; Madison Institute "Meeting of the Board of Trustees," 25 October 1969, Emerson Box 13; Jane Lollis to Lucas, "Memorandum," 28 October 1969, 8pp., Lucas Box 23; Lassoe to Don Shaw, 28 October 1969, ARAI 8–11. Also see Patrick E. Treacy to Mel Wulf, 17 October

1969, ACLU 1972 Vol. 37; and Lader to NARAL Executive Committee, "Suggested Projects," 23 October 1969, Lader Box 15. On internal developments within NARAL, also see Conni Finnerty et al. to NARAL Board Members, 30 August 1969, NARAL Executive Committee Minutes, 28 September and 7 November 1969, and Lee Gidding, "Executive Director's Report," 7 November 1969, NARAL Box 1.

69. *United States* v. *Vuitch*, 305 F. Supp. 1032, 1034, 1035; *U.S.* v. *Vuitch* Docket Sheet, #1043-68, Gesell Papers; *Washington Post*, 11 November 1969, pp. A1, A17, B1, B3, 12 November 1969, pp. A1, A16, C1, C10, 18 November 1969, p. A22; *New York Times*, 11 November 1969, p. 30, 12 November 1969, pp. 30, 46, 16 November 1969, p. E9; *National Observer*, 17 November 1969; *Washington Star*, 18 November 1969, p. A12; *Time*, 21 November 1969, pp. 65–66; John F. Dienelt, "Memories of a Year With Judge Gesell (1969–1970)," n.d., 4pp., Gesell Papers; Garrow conversation with John F. Dienelt; Fred Rodell to Gesell, 19 November 1969, and Carol Greitzer to Gesell, 26 November 1969, Gesell Papers. Law journal notes on *Vuitch*—several of which also review *Belous*—include Robert Ross, Jr., *South Texas Law Journal* 11 (1969): 426–434; William E. Sherman, *North Dakota Law Review* 46 (Winter 1970): 249–257; Donald W. Brodie, "Marital Procreation," *Oregon Law Review* 49 (April 1970): 245–259; Jay R. Herman, *Suffolk University Law Review* 4 (Spring 1970): 920–929; *Vanderbilt Law Review* 23 (May 1970): 821–827. On Dr. Vuitch himself, see *Washington Post*, 4 October 1969, p. B1, 19 November 1969; Lader, *Abortion II*, pp. 9–11, 111–113; *Medical World News*, 16 January 1970, pp. 16–17; *Washingtonian*, October 1970, p. 37; *Baltimore News-American*, 24 October 1971, pp. E12–E13; Garrow conversations with Milan Vuitch and Florence Vuitch; and Dr. Vuitch's obituaries in the *Washington Post*, 10 April 1993, p. B6, and the *New York Times*, 11 April 1993, p. 30. On Judge Gesell, a 1935 Yale Law School graduate who had been named to the bench just two years earlier by President Lyndon B. Johnson, see his obituaries in the *New York Times*, 21 February 1993, p. 39, and the *Washington Post*, 21 February 1993, p. B6.

70. Stephen M. Nagler to Richard Samuel, 26 September 1969, Samuel to Abortion Suit Committee, 14 November 1969, Lucas Box 15; *Newark Evening News*, 11 December 1969, pp. 40, 47; [Lucas], "Memorandum Re New Jersey Abortion Case," n.d. [27 December 1969], Lucas Box 15. Also see *State* v. *Raymond*, 257 A.2d 107 (15 September 1969).

71. *Des Moines Register*, 16 November 1969, pp. 1, 2; *ICMCA Journal* #7 (Winter 1969); George S. Daly, Jr., to ACLU, 29 December 1969, ACLU 1972 Vol. 37; Lamm to Lucas, 18 November 1969, Lucas to Lamm, 1 December 1969, Lucas Box 2; *New York Times*, 8 December 1969, pp. 1, 53; Lamm, "The Reproductive Revolution," *American Bar Association Journal* 56 (January 1970): 41–44, at 43; Olga Curtis, "The Paradox of Colorado's Abortion Law," *Denver Post Empire Magazine*, 1 February 1970, pp. 34–35; Lamm Interview with Garrow. To some extent, however, Lucas believed that cases against unreformed statutes should be filed first. "A drive against ALI-type reform laws will follow. If both were considered by the Supreme Court at the same time, there is danger that the resulting decision would represent a compromise." *NARAL News*, Winter 1970, p. 5.

72. Byron N. Fujita and Nathaniel N. Wagner, "Referendum 20—Abortion Reform in Washington State," in Howard J. and Joy D. Osofsky, eds., *The Abortion Experience*, pp. 232–260, at 235–240; David R. Hood to Goldenberg, 24 November 1969, WCAR I-1; WCAR Executive Committee Minutes, 24 November 1969, WCAR I-5; Robert G. Morrison, "Choice in Washington: The Politics of Liberalized Abortion" (unpublished M.A. thesis, University of Virginia, 1982), pp. 61–67; *Seattle Times*, 28 November 1969, 21 December 1969, p. A15; Goldenberg to Lee Gidding, 1 December 1969, NARAL Box 6; Harold H. Green to Ronald Pion, and to Charles S. Fine, 5 December 1969, WCAR I-1; WCAR Executive Committee Minutes, 8 December 1969, WCAR I-3; *New York Times*, 12 December 1969, p. 36; William H. Gates, Jr., to Goldenberg, 18 December 1969, WCAR I-1; Goldenberg to Lee Gidding, 20 December 1969, NARAL Box 5; William E. Watts to WCAR Board, n.d., and Gates to WCAR, 16 January 1970, WCAR I-1. Also see *Northwest Medicine*, November 1969, p. 1068, and Ronald J. Pion et al., "Abortion Request and Post-Operative Response," *Northwest Medicine*, September 1970, pp. 693–698. On Dr. Koome, also see *National Catholic Reporter*, 10 December 1969, and *American Medical News*, 8 June 1970, p. 9.

73. *New York Law Journal*, 10 October 1969, pp. 1, 3; *New York Times*, 12 October 1969, p. 40, 31 October 1969, p. 17, 3 November 1969, p. 37, 18 November 1969, p. 38, 23 November 1969, p. 78, 25 November 1969, p. 51, 30 November 1969, p. 60; *Modern Medicine* 37 (3 November 1969): 18–25; *Washington Post*, 14 November 1969; "The Present Status of Abortion Laws" [1 and 17 December 1969], *Bulletin of the New York Academy of Medicine* 46 (April 1970): 281–286; "Position Statement on Abortion" [12–13 December 1969], *American Journal of Psychiatry* 126 (April 1970): 1554; *Minneapolis Tribune*, 19 November 1969, p. 16; *Minneapolis Star*, 19 November 1969, p. C11; Cook to Lucas, 14 October 1969, Lucas Box 25. Also see Group for the Advancement of Psychiatry, *The Right to Abortion: A Psychiatric View* (New York: Charles Scribner's Sons, 1970); and Richard L. Worsnop, "Abortion Law Reform," *Editorial Research Reports*, 24 July 1970, pp. 545–562.

74. *America*, 29 November 1969, p. 515; Noonan, ed., *The Morality of Abortion* (Cambridge: Harvard University Press, 1970), pp. ix, 234; Noonan, "The Constitutionality of the Regulation of Abortion," *Hastings Law Journal* 21 (November 1969): 51–65, at 62. Also see Rudy J. Gerber, "Abortion: Two Opposing Legal Philosophies," *American Journal of Jurisprudence* 15 (1970): 1–24.

75. Rashbaum, "Proposal for Ambulatory Abortion Service," n.d., 3pp., Hall to Guttmacher, with enclosure, "The New York Abortion Clinic," 2 December 1969, Guttmacher to Solomon Berson et al., 23 December 1969, Guttmacher Papers; Vuitch to Lader, n.d. [c.mid-November 1969], 10pp., Vuitch Papers; Carmen and Moody, *Abortion Counseling*, pp. 67–69; Nathanson, *Aborting America*, pp. 64–66; *New York Times*, 10 December 1969, p. 110, 11 December 1969, pp. 37, 40, 13 December 1969, p. 37; *Washington Post*, 12 December 1969, p. B1; Lee Gidding, "Executive Director's Report," 12 December 1969, NARAL Box 1; Lader, *Abortion II*, p. 114.

76. Lucas to Savage, 1 and 8 December 1969, Lucas Box 22; [Gidding], "Phone Conversation with Roy Lucas," 6 December 1969, NARAL Box 7; Stuart Nelkin to ASA, 1 December 1969, and Jimmye Kimmey to Nelkin, 8 December 1969, Lucas Box 22; Merrill to Mel Wulf, and to ASA, 19 December 1969, Kimmey to Merrill, 22 December 1969, and Wulf to Lucas, 30 December 1969, Lucas Box 22; Merrill to NARAL, 19 December 1969, and Gidding to Merrill, 30 December 1969, NARAL Box 5; Lucas to Merrill, 2 January 1970, Lucas Box 22; Garrow conversations with Roy Merrill, Roy Lucas, and Fred Bruner. Also see Gidding to Samuel Goldenberg, 10 December 1969, NARAL Box 6; *C. W. Thompson* v. *Texas*, U.S.S.C., O.T. 1971, #1200, National Archives RG 267, Box 296; Lucas to John F. Davis, 17 December 1969, and Davis to Lucas, 31 December 1969, regarding the likely timetable for argument should the Supreme Court choose to review *Belous*. National Archives, RG 267, Box 9564. On John R. Brown, see Jack Bass, *Unlikely Heroes* (New York: Simon & Schuster, 1981), pp. 101–108; and Harvey C. Couch, *A History of the Fifth Circuit, 1891–1981* (New Orleans: U.S. Court of Appeals, 1984), pp. 86–194 passim.

CHAPTER SEVEN

1. Garrow conversations with Judy Smith, Jim Wheelis, Victoria Foe, Bea Vogel, and Barbara Hines; Susan Torian Olan, "Blood Debts," Dick J. Reavis, "SDS: From Students to Seniors," Frieda L. Werden, "Adventures of a Texas Feminist," and Danny N. Schweers, "The Community and *The Rag*," in Daryl Janes, ed., *No Apologies: Texas Radicals Celebrate the '60s* (Austin: Eakin Press, 1992), pp. 13–48, 102–107, 191–210, and 213–236; "Abortions," *The Rag*, 29 April 1969, pp. F and G; Susan Torian Olan, "*The Rag*: A Study in Underground Journalism" (unpublished M.A. thesis, University of Texas at Austin, 1981), esp. pp. 86, 104–105, 119. On the SDS National Council meeting in Austin, also see Kirkpatrick Sale, *SDS* (New York: Random House, 1973), pp. 537–538. On Victoria Foe, also see *New York Times*, 15 June 1993, p. B10, 10 August 1993, pp. C1, C12, and *Seattle Times*, 27 July 1993, pp. E1, E7.

2. *Board of Regents* v. *New Left Education Project*, #174,116, Travis County 167th District Court, 8

July 1969; *New Left Education Project* v. *Board of Regents*, U.S.D.C., W.D. Tex., CA# 69–106, 1 August 1969; Garrow conversations with Jim Wheelis, Barbara Hines, Judy Smith, and Ron Weddington. The Austin case was not David Richards's first effort on behalf of an underground newspaper; also see *Stein* v. *Batchelor*, 300 F. Supp. 602 (N.D. Tex.), 9 June 1969, concerning *Dallas Notes*. On David Richards, also see Ann Richards, *Straight From the Heart* (New York: Simon & Schuster, 1989), pp. 69–76, 79–81, and 134–137.

3. Judy [Smith], "Women's Psyches," *The Rag*, 31 July 1969, p. 6; "Why Women's Liberation?," *The Rag*, Vol. 3, #28 [8 September 1969], p. 4; Garrow conversations with Judy Smith, Bea Vogel, Barbara Hines, and Jim Wheelis.

4. "And Their Bodies," *The Rag*, 31 July 1969, p. 6; "Why Women's Liberation?" *The Rag*, Vol. 3, #28 [8 September 1969], p. 4; Barbara Wuensch, "Women's Liberation," *The Rag*, 15 September 1969, p. 3; Bea [Vogel], "On Liberation," *The Rag*, 29 September 1969, pp. 12–13; "Birth Control," *The Rag*, 3 November 1969, p. 17; *Austin American-Statesman*, 15 October 1969; Beatrice R. Vogel to Lee Gidding, 16 February 1970, NARAL Box 5; Garrow conversations with Judy Smith, Bea Vogel, Victoria Foe, and Barbara Hines.

5. Garrow conversations with Judy Smith, Barbara Hines, Bea Vogel, Victoria Foe, and Bob Breihan.

6. Garrow conversations with Judy Smith, Bea Vogel, Sarah Weddington, Jim Wheelis, Ron Weddington, and Barbara Hines; Sarah Weddington, *A Question of Choice* (New York: G. P. Putnam's Sons, 1992), pp. 24–38; Weddington in Vicki Quade, "Our Bodies, Our Law," *The Barrister* 13 (Summer 1986): 14–16ff.; Molly Ivins, "This Right of Privacy," *Texas Observer*, 16 February 1973, pp. 1, 3–5. Sarah Weddington has related her memories of the garage sale query on numerous occasions; at least once, in 1973, she erroneously identified it as occurring "in the spring of 1970." Weddington, "Court Abortion Victory Not Enough," *Daily Texan*, 1 February 1973. Also see *Dallas Times-Herald*, 12 December 1971, p. D10; Weddington Interview with Duke (1973); Weddington in Rachel C. Wahlberg, "Abortion: Landmark Decision," *Dallas Morning News*, 22 and 23 April 1973, pp. E1 and C7; Weddington's 11 April 1975 testimony in U.S. Congress, Senate, Committee on the Judiciary, *Abortion Hearings Before the Subcommittee on Constitutional Amendments*, Part IV, 94th Cong., 1st sess., p. 520; *Dallas Times-Herald*, 14 December 1975, p. D2; Weddington in Warren M. Hern and Bonnie Andrikopoulos, eds., *Abortion in the Seventies* (New York: National Abortion Federation, 1977), p. 278; *Daily Texan*, 8 May 1987, 6 March 1990, 12 November 1991; Weddington, "*Roe* v. *Wade* Began At Garage Sale," *Fulton County Daily Report*, 9 February 1989, pp. 8–9; *Austin American-Statesman*, 29 June 1989; Weddington, "*Roe* v. *Wade*: Past and Future," *Suffolk University Law Review* 24 (Fall 1990): 601–620, at 601–603; and Weddington, "Abortion: The New Focus," in Roy M. Mersky and Gary R. Hartman, eds., *A Documentary History of the Legal Aspects of Abortion in the United States: Webster v. Reproductive Health Services* (Littleton, CO: Fred B. Rothman & Co., 1990), vol. 1, pp. 3–16, at 5–6.

7. Weddington, *A Question of Choice*, pp. 12–14, 18–24. On at least one occasion in later years when Weddington was asked whether she herself had ever had an abortion, she brushed the question aside: "That's irrelevant," she claimed. Quade, "Our Bodies, Our Law," pp. 14–16ff. In an earlier interview, citing her "very strong feeling of self-determination," Weddington noted that upon finishing law school "I was planning to start a practice and a career. There was no question in my mind that I did not want to have a child at that time. I'm sure I would have had no hesitancy . . . to choose an abortion had a choice been necessary." Interview with Cheek, p. 38. On Weddington's background, also see Weddington et al., *Texas Women in Politics* (Austin: Foundation for Women's Resources, 1977), pp. 77–81; and Weddington Interviews with Marcello, Cheek, and Garrow. Worthwhile biographical stories or profiles of Weddington include *Daily Texan*, 2 December 1971; *Austin Sun*, 9 September 1977, p. 11; *Dallas Times-Herald*, 5 September 1978, pp. 1, 6, 22 March 1985, pp. A1, A13; *People Magazine*, 18 September 1978, pp. 36–37; *Towne Hall Notes* [University of Texas Law School], Winter 1979, pp. 6–7; Susan Wood, "The Weddington Way," *Washington Post Magazine*, 11 February 1979, pp. 6–11; *Christian Science Monitor*, 4 May 1979, p. B8; *Austin American-Statesman*, 1 July 1979, pp. E1, E12; *New York Times*, 15 August 1979, p. D14; Mary

Dudley, "The Odyssey of Sarah Weddington," *Texas Woman* 1 (November 1979): 24–31; Linda Stern, "Sarah Weddington," *Working Woman*, February 1980, pp. 35–37, 62; Ann F. Crawford and Crystal S. Ragsdale, *Women in Texas* (Burnet, TX: Eakin Press, 1982), pp. 309–318; *Dallas Morning News*, 25 March 1982, pp. C1, C4, 31 January 1983, 2 October 1983, pp. E1, E4; *Austin Business Journal*, 26 September/2 October 1988, pp. 1, 14; Leslie Bennetts, "A Woman's Choice," *Vanity Fair*, September 1992, pp. 148–158.

8. Garrow conversations with Sarah Weddington, Judy Smith, Jim Wheelis, Barbara Hines, Ron Weddington, and Bea Vogel; Weddington Interview with Duke; Weddington, *A Question of Choice*, pp. 44–47. Somewhat oddly, one newspaper story only two years later quotes Weddington as saying that "Through the women's liberation groups I heard of Linda Coffee and that she was filing a case in Dallas." *Dallas Times-Herald*, 12 December 1971, p. D10.

  After the November 26 hearing, the substantive and procedural history of *New Left Education Project* v. *Board of Regents* became convoluted in the extreme. On December 17 the three-judge panel filed a brief order granting the request that new plaintiffs—including Ron Weddington and Barbara Hines—be allowed to enter the case but declining *The Rag*'s request that they block the Regents' ongoing state court suit against the paper. Two months later attorney Richards requested that Travis County District Judge Tom Blackwell hold the state case in abeyance pending further action in the federal matter, but one day after a February 25 hearing Blackwell *granted* the Regents' request for a temporary injunction against any distribution of *The Rag* on the UT campus. Following a June 26, 1970, hearing on the merits, the federal panel nine weeks later found for *The Rag*, ruling that the Regents' restrictions "are unconstitutionally overbroad." The Regents appealed directly to the U.S. Supreme Court, and after oral argument on December 6, 1971, the high court held by a vote of 6 to 1 (Justice Douglas dissenting) that because of the less than statewide authority of the Regents, the suit originally should have been heard by a single district judge rather than a three-judge panel. Hence UT's appeal was dismissed and referred to the Fifth Circuit Court of Appeals, which in early 1973 affirmed an unreported interim decision by U.S. District Judge Jack Roberts that the Regents' drastic alteration of the antidistribution rules in February of 1972 effectively mooted the case. Eight months later the Supreme Court, acting on a further appeal by the Regents, agreed with the conclusion of mootness but instructed that the earlier judgment against the Regents should also be formally vacated. In addition to the case files now located in the National Archives and in the regional records center in Fort Worth (CA#69–106), see *New Left Education Project* v. *Board of Regents*, 326 F. Supp. 158, 164 (3 September 1970), *Board of Regents* v. *New Left Education Project* (#70–55), 404 U.S. 541 (24 January 1972), *New Left Education Project* v. *Board of Regents*, 472 F.2d 218 (19 January 1973), and *Board of Regents* v. *New Left Education Project* (#72–1485), 414 U.S. 807 (9 October 1973).

9. Garrow conversations with Linda Coffee and Sarah Weddington; Weddington, *A Question of Choice*, pp. 23, 48–49. Biographical items on Linda Coffee appear in the *Dallas Morning News*, 6 February 1960, 2 September 1968, p. C1, and 29 July 1990, p. E4.

10. Hughes Interviews with Frantz, Gantt, and Marcello; Opal H. Allread, "Sarah T. Hughes: A Case Study in Judicial Decision-Making" (unpublished Ph.D. dissertation, University of Oklahoma, 1987), esp. pp. 106–107; *Dallas Morning News*, 13 August 1961, 19 February 1975, p. C1, 5 August 1975, p. D1, 12 November 1975, p. C1, 25 April 1985, pp. A1, A20; *Dallas Morning News Magazine*, 10 May 1981, pp. 8–11; *Dallas Times-Herald*, 16 August 1981, pp. 1, 26, 24 April 1985, pp. 1, 16, 25 April 1985, pp. 1, 12; Garrow conversations with Linda Coffee and Barefoot Sanders. Also see Ann F. Crawford and Crystal S. Ragsdale, *Women in Texas* (Burnet, TX: Eakin Press, 1982), pp. 261–269.

11. Lawrence J. Vilardo and Howard W. Gutman, "With Justice from One: Interview with Hon. Irving L. Goldberg," *Litigation* 17 (Spring 1991): 16–22, 56–57; *Dallas Morning News*, 28 April 1966, 29 June 1966, 26 December 1971, p. A28; Garrow conversations with Linda Coffee, Clarice M. Davis, and Irving L. Goldberg. Also see Frank T. Read and Lucy S. McGough, *Let Them Be Judged* (Metuchen, NJ: Scarecrow Press, 1978), pp. 180–181; Jack Bass, *Unlikely Heroes* (New York: Simon & Schuster, 1981), pp. 304–305 and 327–328; and Harvey C.

Couch, *A History of the Fifth Circuit, 1891–1981* (New Orleans: U.S. Court of Appeals, 1984), p. 134.

12. *Buchanan* v. *Batchelor*, 308 F. Supp. 729 (1970); *Buchanan* v. *Texas*, 471 S.W.2d 401 (Tex. Ct. Crim. App. 1971); *Dallas Morning News*, 17 July 1973, p. A14; Garrow conversations with Linda Coffee. McCluskey filed *Buchanan* one month before both New York's "Stonewall Rebellion" of 27 June 1969 and the widely noted vindication of a gay federal employee's privacy rights by the D.C. Circuit Court of Appeals in *Norton* v. *Macy*, 417 F.2d 1161 (1 July 1969). For earlier discussions of possible legal challenges to police and prosecutorial pursuit of criminal charges against consensual gay sex participants, see *Yale Law Journal* 70 (March 1961): 623–635; *UCLA Law Review* 13 (March 1966): 643–832 and 14 (January 1967): 581–603; *Journal of Public Law* 16 (1967): 159–192; *South Dakota Law Review* 13 (Spring 1968): 384–397; *California Western Law Review* 4 (Spring 1968): 115–131 and 5 (Spring 1969): 232–251; *Natural Resources Journal* 8 (July 1968): 531–541; *Wayne Law Review* 14 (1968): 934–969; and *Kentucky Law Journal* 57 (Spring 1969): 591–598. Particularly valuable commentaries on early gay rights legal efforts include Webster Schott, "A 4-Million Minority Asks for Equal Rights," *New York Times Magazine*, 12 November 1967, pp. 44ff.; Gilbert M. Cantor, "The Need for Homosexual Law Reform," in Ralph W. Weltge, ed., *The Same Sex* (Philadelphia: Pilgrim Press, 1969), pp. 83–94; Kay Tobin and Randy Wicker, *The Gay Crusaders* (New York: Paperback Library, 1972); Laud Humphreys, *Out of the Closets: The Sociology of Homosexual Liberation* (Englewood Cliffs, NJ: Prentice-Hall, 1972); and especially Donn Teal, *The Gay Militants* (New York: Stein and Day, 1971), and John D'Emilio, *Sexual Politics, Sexual Communities* (Chicago: University of Chicago Press, 1983), esp. pp. 211, 231–233, 239. On the definitional history by which sodomy statutes generally came to cover most but not all acts of oral sex, see Lawrence R. Murphy, "Defining the Crime Against Nature: Sodomy in the United States Appeals Courts, 1810–1940," *Journal of Homosexuality* 19 (1990): 49–66; also see *Mercer Law Review* 16 (Fall 1964): 345–347.

13. Coffee to Weddington, 4 December 1969, in Barbara Milbauer, *The Law Giveth* (New York: Atheneum, 1983), pp. 29–30; Garrow conversations with Linda Coffee and Sarah Weddington; *Houston Post*, 23 June 1970, p. II-1; Weddington Interviews with Duke and Cheek; Weddington, *A Question of Choice*, p. 49. Unfortunately neither Weddington, Coffee, nor Milbauer can now locate an actual copy of the December 4 letter.

14. Garrow conversations with Linda Coffee, Sarah Weddington, Judy Smith, Barbara Hines, Bea Vogel, Virginia Whitehill, Patricia [White] Judd, Ellen [Kalina] Lewis, Pat [Cookston] Davidson, Doris Middleton, and Barbara Richardson; Weddington, "*Roe* v. *Wade*: Past and Future," *Suffolk University Law Review* 24 (Fall 1990): 601–620, at 603; Genevieve Scott, Women's Alliance Minutes, 30 September 1969, 7 October 1969, 25 November 1969, and 13 January 1970, First Unitarian Church; "Abortion Law to Be Topic," *Dallas Morning News*, 12 January 1970, p. C4; *Dallas Times-Herald*, 14 January 1970. My deepest thanks go to Doris Middleton for providing me with the extremely valuable Women's Alliance minutes.

15. On Marsha and David King, see their marriage announcements in the 11 July 1968 *Atlanta Constitution* and *Atlanta Journal*, as well as Barbara Richardson's subsequent profile, "Couple Seeks Right Not to Have Child," *Dallas Times-Herald*, 15 March 1970, p. E9, and Marsha King's three-page 5 July 1971 memo to Roy Lucas, "Personal Information on Mary Doe," Lucas Box 22. Also Garrow conversations with Linda Coffee and Virginia Whitehill; *Atlanta Constitution*, 21 December 1983, p. A28.

16. *Buchanan* v. *Batchelor*, 308 F. Supp. 729, 732, 733, 735 (21 January 1970); Allread, "Sarah T. Hughes," pp. 141–143; *Cotner* v. *Henry*, 394 F.2d 873 (17 April 1968), cert. denied 393 U.S. 847 (1968). Also see Charles O. Cotner, "Marital Sodomy Imprisonment," *Playboy*, July 1968, p. 45, R. Thomas Farrar, *University of Miami Law Review* 23 (Fall 1968): 231–236, and especially Jon D. Krahulik, "The Cotner Case: Indiana Witch Hunt," *Indiana Legal Forum* 2 (Spring 1969): 336–350. Married in 1953 and the parents of five children, Charles and Jeane Cotner had an argument in May 1965 that led to Jeane's filing a complaint with local authorities. When she attempted to withdraw it the local judge to their surprise refused, and Charles then and there, without benefit of counsel, decided that the quickest and easiest way to get

rid of the matter would be simply to plead guilty to the sodomy charge. Expecting no punishment, Charles was instead sentenced to two to fourteen years in prison. Only when the Seventh Circuit panel by a vote of 2 to 1 reversed an earlier district court dismissal of his petition for habeas corpus was he released. Also note *Travers* v. *Paton*, 261 F. Supp. 110 (D.Conn., 1966). Law journal notes on the panel decision in *Buchanan* include Ty M. Sparks, *Texas Tech Law Review* 2 (Fall 1970): 115–120; William R. Pakalka, *Texas Law Review* 49 (January 1971): 400–406; and John F. Simmons, *Nebraska Law Review* 50 (Spring 1971): 567–575.

17. Garrow conversations with Norma McCorvey, Linda Coffee, and Sarah Weddington; McCorvey Interview with Dreifus; McCorvey in Angela Bonavoglia, ed., *The Choices We Made* (New York: Random House, 1991), pp. 137–143; Joseph N. Bell, "A Landmark Decision," *Good Housekeeping* 176 (June 1973): 77–79ff; *Parade Magazine*, 8 May 1983; Marian Faux, *Roe v. Wade* (New York: Macmillan, 1988), pp. 6–10; McCorvey in "Search for Justice: The American Stories," WUSA-TV, Washington, D.C., 13 September 1987, 6pp.; *Dallas Morning News*, 9 September 1987, pp. A1, A16, 10 September 1987, pp. A1, A34; *Dallas Times-Herald*, 22 January 1988, pp. A1, A18, 2 July 1991, pp. A1, A6; *Village Voice*, 11 April 1989, p. 44; *People Magazine*, 22 May 1989, pp. 36–41; *Los Angeles Times*, 25 June 1989, pp. 1, 17–18; Marian Faux, "Roe v. Wade," *Memories* 3 (June-July 1990): 94–98. Also see *Dallas Times Herald Magazine*, 18 October 1981, pp. 37–42; *People Magazine*, 5 August 1985, p. 72; *New York Times*, 9 September 1987, p. A23, 9 May 1989, p. A18; *Newsweek*, 17 April 1989, p. 22; *Los Angeles Herald-Examiner*, 1 May 1989, pp. B1, B5. On Dr. Richard Allen Lane, who was subsequently sentenced to two years in prison, see *Dallas Morning News*, 28 June 1968, and 8 December 1970, p. 9. On nonmedical abortion providers in Dallas circa 1970, see *Dallas Morning News*, 14 October 1973, p. A1.

Seventeen months later, in September 1971, Weddington wrote a letter telling a friend that she recently had been in Dallas and that "Meeting Jane Roe was fascinating." While this statement would seem to suggest that perhaps Weddington had not previously met her, Weddington nonetheless firmly believes that she did indeed first meet Norma McCorvey at the Colombo's Pizza Parlor on Mockingbird Lane sometime in January or early February 1970. McCorvey has often recalled how in what she remembers as her first joint meeting with Coffee and Weddington, Sarah spoke about them taking her case to the Supreme Court. In one 1984 interview McCorvey stated that she believed she first met Weddington at Marsha and David King's apartment. That locus, and especially the explicit reference to the Supreme Court, would fit very well into the context of September 1971; such a reference to the Supreme Court would have been extremely unlikely in January or February 1970, for, as Weddington emphasizes, "we weren't thinking of the Supreme Court" at that time. While such factors would seem to buttress the apparent meaning of Weddington's September 1971 letter, she reiterates that the implication that she did not first meet McCorvey until September 1971 could not be correct. "It couldn't. It's just impossible." Such an inference would be "absolutely inaccurate," for it "doesn't make any sense." Weddington also noted, however, that "I can tell you what I remember; I can't tell you what was true or not." Linda Coffee acknowledges graciously that she does "not really" have any specific recollection of the pizza parlor meeting and is "not absolutely positive" that there was a joint meeting before the case was filed. Asked for her interpretation of Weddington's September 1971 statement if indeed an early 1970 initial joint meeting took place, Coffee replied frankly, "That doesn't make any sense." Norma McCorvey candidly confesses that she is uncertain of where she first met the two lawyers together, or even if she did indeed have one or more initial face-to-face meetings with just Coffee. Garrow conversations with Sarah Weddington, Linda Coffee, Norma McCorvey, and Virginia Whitehill; Weddington to Whitehill, 23 September 1971, Whitehill Papers.

18. Garrow conversations with Linda Coffee, Sarah Weddington, Virginia Whitehill, Patricia [White] Judd, Ellen [Kalina] Lewis, Doris Middleton, and Norma McCorvey; Genevieve Scott, Women's Alliance Minutes, 27 January and 3 February 1970; Patricia White, Organizational Meeting Minutes, 11 February 1970, Whitehill Papers; Genevieve Scott,

Women's Alliance Minutes, 24 February and 3 March 1970; Beatrice R. Vogel to Lee Gidding, 16 February 1970, and Gidding to Vogel, 19 February 1970, NARAL Box 5; Allread, "Sarah T. Hughes," pp. 143–146; Doris Middleton, "Alas Roe v. Wade," unpublished essay, 1992; Donna Gordon, "Roe v. Wade Revisited," *The World* [U.U.A.], January-February 1992, p. 56.

19. Garrow conversations with Linda Coffee, Sarah Weddington, and Barbara Richardson; *Roe* v. *Wade*, CA# 3–3690, U.S.D.C. N.D. Tex., *Doe* v. *Wade*, CA#3–3691, U.S.D.C. N.D. Tex., 3 March 1970; *Dallas Times Herald*, 3 March 1970, pp. 1, 8, 5 March 1970, 6 March 1970, p. A28, 8 March 1970, pp. 1, 4, 15 March 1970, p. E9; *Dallas Morning News*, 4 March 1970, p. 1; *The Rag*, 9 March 1970, p. 17. The Texas abortion statute originally dated from 1854, and had been revised and rephrased in 1907. See Amy Johnson, "Abortion, Personhood, and Privacy in Texas," *Texas Law Review* 68 (June 1990): 1521–1544. Also see *Houston Law Review* 18 (May 1981): 819–848.

20. On NARAL and the D.C. situation, see Lader to Executive Committee Members, 13 January and 17 February 1970, NARAL Box 1, Cyril C. Means, Jr., to Donald Harting, 17 January 1970, and Lee Gidding memo, 11 February 1970, NARAL Box 2; also see *New York Times*, 7 February 1970, p. 11; *Washington Post*, 23 February 1970, pp. C1, C2, 24 February 1970, pp. B1, B2, 25 February 1970, pp. C1, C2, 12 March 1970, pp. A1, A14; *Washington Star*, 24 February 1970, pp. B1, B4; and *Medical Annals of the District of Columbia* 39 (March 1970): 133–137, 186 and (May 1970): 275–277. On the New York scene, see *Newsday*, 15 August 1969, p. 7; New Yorkers for Abortion Law Repeal to NARAL Executive Committee, 19 December 1969, NARAL Box 1; Cusack to Cook, 21 December 1969, Cusack to Duryea, 5 January 1970, Citizens for Abortion Law Repeal Minutes, 7 January 1970, Cusack to Clapp, 10 January 1970, and Clapp to Cusack, 19 January 19[70], Cusack Papers; *New Yorkers for Abortion Law Repeal Newsletter* Vol. 2, #2 (February 1970); Ruth P. Smith and Ruth Frey, "Chronicle of the Activities of the Committee for the Cook-Leichter Bill," n.d. [c.30 April 1970], 4pp., NARAL Box 4; *New York Times*, 4 January 1970, p. 48, 26 January 1970, p. 19, 29 January 1970, p. 27, 4 February 1970, p. 42; Lader, *Abortion II*, p. 130; Darlene Weide, "The History of New York Abortion Law Repeal: A Case Study" (unpublished B.A. thesis, Barnard College, 1989).

Also see particularly Lucinda Cisler, "Unfinished Business: Birth Control and Women's Liberation," in Robin Morgan, ed., *Sisterhood Is Powerful* (New York: Random House, 1970), pp. 245–289, at 275–276, and Cisler, "Abortion Law Repeal (Sort of): A Warning to Women" [April 1970], in Anne Koedt, ed., *Radical Feminism* (New York: Quadrangle, 1973), pp. 151–164, at 154. Cisler in her first essay emphasized that "'reform' and repeal are actually fundamentally incompatible ideas," in part because therapeutic reform proponents basically viewed women as "victims—of rape, or of rubella, or of heart disease or mental illness—never as possible shapers of their own destinies." In the second, she insisted that "it *is* the women's movement whose demand for *repeal*—rather than 'reform'—of the abortion laws has spurred the general acceleration in the abortion movement and its influence."

21. Diane Schulder and Florynce Kennedy, *Abortion Rap* (New York: McGraw-Hill, 1971), passim; Claudia Dreifus, "Abortion: This Piece is For Remembrance," in Dreifus, ed., *Seizing Our Bodies* (New York: Vintage, 1978), pp. 131–145; *New York Times*, 27 January 1970, p. 29, 28 January 1970, p. 26; Greenhouse, *New York Times Magazine*, 25 January 1970, pp. 30–31, 88–91. Also see *Science News*, 17 January 1970, pp. 75–76, which quoted ASA's Jimmye Kimmey as saying that "We have stopped pushing for new laws" and instead were looking ahead to a definitive Supreme Court ruling. Subsequent analyses which also highlight the importance of Lucas's article include Betty Sarvis and Hyman Rodman, *The Abortion Controversy* (New York: Columbia University Press, 1973), p. 57 ("a landmark article"); Raymond Tatalovich and Byron W. Daynes, *The Politics of Abortion* (New York: Praeger, 1981), p. 26 ("a landmark article"); Eva R. Rubin, "The Abortion Cases: A Study in Law and Social Change," *North Carolina Central Law Journal* 5 (Spring 1974): 215–253, at 227; Rubin, *Abortion, Politics, and the Courts* (Westport, CT: Greenwood Press, 1982), pp. 41–42, 49 ("The "germinal" article both "supplied the blueprint" and "laid a foundation for much of the later

constitutional argument in lower court challenges and indirectly for Justice Blackmun's opinion in *Roe*." "In many ways, this article supplied a master plan for an extended litigation campaign"); and Elizabeth Mensch and Alan Freeman, *The Politics of Virtue* (Durham, NC: Duke University Press, 1993), pp. 122–123.

22. *Life*, 27 February 1970, pp. 20–29; *St. Louis Post-Dispatch*, 20 February 1970, pp. 1, 4; "Alumni Lead Fight to Remove Abortion Law," *The Commentator* [NYU Law School], 25 February 1970, p. 9; Lucas to Chris Tietze, 22 January 1970, Lucas Box 17; Hall to Lucas, 2 February 1970, Lucas Box 18; Jane Zuckerman to Lucas, 3 February 1970, Lucas Box 25; Pilpel to File, "PP—Abortion Clinic," 4 February 1970, Hall to Pilpel, Guttmacher, and Goldmark, 10 February 1970, Guttmacher Papers; Pilpel to Lucas, 10 February 1970, Lucas Box 25; Pilpel to File, "PP—Abortion Facility," 17 February 1970, Lucas Box 18; Hellman to Guttmacher, 19 February 1970, Guttmacher Papers; *New York Times*, 19 February 1970, p. 51, 4 March 1970, p. 37, 8 March 1970, p. 38; Goldmark and Guttmacher letter, 4 March 1970, ASA Annual Meeting Minutes, 6 March 1970, Guttmacher Papers; Carmen and Moody, *Abortion Counseling*, pp. 68–71; Nathanson, *Aborting America*, pp. 66–69. Also see Jane Ross, "Abortion and the Unwanted Child: An Interview with Alan F. Guttmacher and Harriet F. Pilpel," *Family Planning Perspectives* 2 (March 1970): 16–25, at 16, where Guttmacher forcefully reiterated that "Safe abortion must be available as a rational option for any woman who finds herself pregnant and does not wish to be."

23. Lucas, Norman Dorsen, Harriet F. Pilpel, and Ruth Jane Zuckerman, "Brief of Plaintiffs," *Hall* v. *Hogan*, U.S.D.C. S.D.N.Y., #69-C-4284, 6 March 1970; Marvin J. Diamond to Mel Wulf, 11 February 1970, Lucas Box 4; [Lee Gidding], "Lucas, the Vuitch Case, and NARAL," 19 February 1970, NARAL Box 7; Lucas to Diamond, 20 February 1970, ACLU 1972 Vol. 37; Garrow conversations with Roy Lucas. Also note *Molinaro* v. *New Jersey*, 396 U.S. 365, 19 January 1970, dismissing an appeal of an abortion conviction (254 A.2d 792 [N.J. Sup. Ct.]) by a fugitive nonphysician.

24. *Baird* v. *Massachusetts*, 396 U.S. 1029; *Baird* Case File, O.T. 1969, #707, National Archives, RG 267, Box 9840; *Boston Globe*, 13 January 1970, 20 February 1970, 1 March 1970, p. A3, 14 March 1970, 28 March 1970, pp. 1, 5; *Boston Herald Traveler*, 13 January 1970, p. 3; *Baird* v. *Eisenstadt*, 310 F. Supp. 951; Baird, "The Prison Diary of Bill Baird," *Boston Globe Magazine*, 14 June 1970; *Eisenstadt* v. *Baird*, Appendix to Record, pp. 7–14; Garrow conversations with William R. Baird.

25. *California* v. *Belous*, 397 U.S. 915; William J. Brennan Docket Book (O.T. 1970, #971) and Conference Lists (20 February 1970), Brennan Papers Boxes 417 and 200–201; Judge Paul Mast, *People* v. *Robert C. Robb*, Central Orange County Municipal Court, #149005, 9 January 1970, 9pp.; *Los Angeles Times*, 10 January 1970, p. II-10, 3 March 1970, pp. IV-1, 6, 19 March 1970, pp. 1, 3, 21 March 1970, p. II-10; Joy Connors, "Legalized Abortion—Only a Matter of Time?" *Orange County Illustrated*, May 1970, pp. 25–28, 46–47; Lucas to Salle Soladay, 17 December 1969, Lucas Box 25; Leavy, "Approaches to Attacking the Therapeutic Abortion Act of 1967 by Declaratory Relief Action," n.d., 4pp., Ruth Roemer to Leavy, 18 January 1970, Zarky, "Proposed Plaintiffs—California Federal Case," 20 January 1970, CCTA Box 5; Roemer to Jane and Garrett Hardin, 23 January 1970, Roemer to Philip Corfman, 4 February 1970, CCTA Box 4; Jane Hardin to Thomas Hart, 5 February 1970, Cusack Papers; Zarky to Mel Wulf, 28 February 1970, Lucas Box 25; Jimmye Kimmey to Elizabeth Canfield, 22 January 1970, Roemer to Kimmey, 30 January 1970, Kimmey to Roemer, 5 February 1970, CCTA Board Minutes, 16 March 1970, CCTA Box 4; Moses A. Berman, "Complaint," 15 May 1970, and John Shriver Gwynne, "Declaration," 20 May 1970, in *Gwynne* v. *Hicks*, U.S.D.C. C.D. Cal., CA#70-1088; Judge T. L. Foley in *People* v. *Robert W. Barksdale*, San Leandro-Hayward Municipal Court, 24 March 1970; Thomas G. Moyers, "Abortion Laws: A Study in Social Change," *San Diego Law Review* 7 (May 1970): 237–243, at 241; Garrow conversations with Ruth Roemer, Keith Russell, Zad Leavy, Charles T. Munger, and Anthony C. Beilenson. Also see Cheriel M. Jensen, "A Case Study: The 1970 Abortion Initiative in California," *ZPG National Reporter*, August 1970, pp. 10–11, 38–39.

26. Robert G. Morrison, "Choice in Washington: The Politics of Liberalized Abortion" (unpub-

lished M.A. thesis, University of Virginia, 1982), pp. 87–101; Hall to Marilyn Ward, 20 January 1970, Richard Lamm to Ward, 22 and 30 January 1970, WCAR I-1; *New York Times*, 31 January 1970, p. 20; Lee Gidding to Samuel Goldenberg, 3 February 1970, WCAR I-3; WCAR Executive Committee Minutes, 12 February 1970, WCAR I-5; Goldenberg to David Hood, 13 February 1970, WCAR I-2. Also see Randy L. St. Mary and Patrick B. Cerutti, "Washington Abortion Reform," *Gonzaga Law Review* 5 (Spring 1970): 270–288.

27. On South Carolina, see Gerald E. Berendt, "Abortion Law in South Carolina," *South Carolina Law Review* 24 (1972): 425–438. On Vermont see *New York Times*, 31 January 1970, p. 20, 19 March 1970, p. 36; on Massachusetts, see *New York Times*, 24 March 1970, p. 28. On Iowa, see *Des Moines Register*, 22 February 1970, p. W4; and Robert L. Webber to Lee Gidding, 2 March and 8 April 1970, NARAL Box 3. On Arizona, see William E. Davis, "Therapeutic Abortion," *Arizona Medicine*, December 1969, pp. 1060–1061; *New York Times*, 27 February 1970, p. 72; and [Lee Gidding], "Phone Conversation with Rep. John Roeder," 23 April 1970, and "Arizona Situation," 28 July 1970, NARAL Box 2. On Michigan, see *Detroit Free Press*, 20 January 1970, p. A6 (editorially endorsing repeal), 26 February 1970, p. A6; Transcript of Hearing, Michigan State Senate Committee on Abortion Law Reform, 7 February 1970, Bloomfield Township, 294pp., Beebe Box 2; [Lee Gidding], "Phone Conversation with [Mary Lou] Tanton," 17 February 1970, NARAL Box 3; Transcript of Hearing, Michigan State Senate Committee on Abortion Law Reform, 27 February 1970, Detroit, 461pp., Bursley Box 15; *New York Times*, 16 March 1970, p. 31, 17 May 1970, p. 38.

28. Patricia G. Steinhoff and Milton Diamond, *Abortion Politics: The Hawaii Experience* (Honolulu: University Press of Hawaii, 1977), esp. pp. 22–173; Joan Hayes, "Abortion Law: A Case History—or Helping a 'Hopeless Cause' Become a Political Possibility" (unpublished manuscript, n.d. [c.January 1970]), 14pp., NARAL Box 3; Roy G. Smith et al., "Physicians' Attitudes on the Abortion Law," *Hawaii Medical Journal* 29 (January-February 1970): 209–211; *Honolulu Star-Bulletin*, 31 October 1969, p. A12, 5 November 1969, p. A23, 6 March 1970, p. 2; Joan Hayes to Lee Gidding, 10 January 1970, NARAL Box 3; *New York Times*, 11 February 1970, p. 23, 12 February 1970, p. 74, 25 February 1970, pp. 1, 28; Vincent H. Yano et al. to David C. McClung, Conference Committee Report 3–70, Hawaii Legislature, 19 February 1970, 9pp., WCAR I-1; *Honolulu Advertiser*, 2 March 1970, p. C2; Tom Coffman, *Catch A Wave: A Case Study of Hawaii's New Politics*, 2nd ed. (Honolulu: University Press of Hawaii, 1973), pp. 81, 159; Roy G. Smith, "Changing Hawaii's Abortion Laws," *Pacific Health* 3 (1970): 2–4. On Joan Hayes, also see Mary Finch Hoyt, "How One Woman Changed Her State's Abortion Law," *Ladies' Home Journal*, October 1971. On Vincent Yano, also see *National Catholic Reporter*, 11 December 1970, pp. 14–15.

29. *New York Times*, 3 March 1970, p. 40, 12 March 1970, p. 21, 15 March 1970, p. 69; *Time*, 9 March 1970, p. 34; *Newsweek*, 9 March 1970, p. 46.

30. *Babbitz* v. *McCann*, 306 F. Supp. 400 (E.D. Wis.), 2 December 1969; "Happy Mother Works for Legalized Abortion," *Milwaukee Sentinel*, 31 January 1970, pp. 1, 6, and Rein to Lader, 29 June 1970, Lader Box 4. Also see Anne Nicol Gaylor, *Abortion Is a Blessing* (New York: Psychological Dimensions, 1975), p. 5; and Gaylor to Keith P. Russell, 28 July 1969, CCTA Box 4.

31. Rein to Jimmye Kimmey, 3 January 1970, Lucas Box 24; Rein to Larry Lader, n.d., Lader Box 5; Clifford K. Meldman, "Amicus Curiae Brief of the Wisconsin Committee to Legalize Abortion," *Babbitz* v. *McCann*, U.S.D.C. E.D. Wis., CA#69-C-548, 14 January 1970, 24pp., at pp. 4–5; Pilpel to Lucas and Kimmey, 20 January 1970, Lucas Box 24; Rein to NARAL, 7 February 1970, NARAL Box 6; *Babbitz* v. *McCann*, 310 F. Supp. 293, 298, 299, 301 (E.D. Wis.), 5 March 1970. Law review notes on the panel decision in *Babbitz* include *Georgia Law Review* 4 (Summer 1970): 907–915; James D. Williams, *American University Law Review* 20 (August 1970): 136–151; *Vanderbilt Law Review* 23 (November 1970): 1346–1352; *Wisconsin Law Review* 1970 (#3): 933–943; and Donald P. Doherty, *St. Louis University Law Journal* 15 (Summer 1971): 642–650; also see Robert W. Fox, *American Bar Association Journal* 57 (July 1971): 667–672.

32. Lucas, Samuel, and Richard H. Chused, "Complaint" and "Memorandum of Law in Support

of Motion to Convene a Three-Judge Court," *YWCA of Princeton* v. *Kugler*, U.S.D.C. D.N.J., CA#264–70, 5 March 1970, Lucas Box 15; *Newark Star-Ledger*, 18 January 1970, p. 24, 6 March 1970, p. 1; *New York Times*, 6 March 1970, p. 36, 10 March 1970, p. 27, 13 March 1970, p. 24; *Newark Evening News*, 6 March 1970, p. 1; *Perth Amboy News-Tribune*, 6 March 1970, pp. 1, 4; Lucas et al., "Brief of Plaintiffs," *YWCA of Princeton* v. *Kugler*, 24 April 1970, 135pp., Lucas Box 16, esp. p. 55. Lucas's New Jersey brief closely resembled the one he had filed in *Hall* seven weeks earlier, and the same characterization of *Griswold* had first appeared there. Lucas et al., "Brief of Plaintiffs," *Hall* v. *Hogan*, U.S.D.C. S.D. N.Y., #69-C-4284, 6 March 1970, esp. p. 81.

33. *Doe* v. *Scott*, 310 F. Supp. 688, N.D. Ill. (27 March 1970); *Arnold* v. *Sendak*, U.S.D.C. S.D. Ind., #70-C-217 (29 March 1970); Robert K. McKenzie, Jr., to Lucas, 23 February 1970, Lucas Box 12; Jack M. Stack to Ron Paul, 3 March 1970, Stack Box 1; Paul to Lucas, 9 March 1970, Lucas Box 12; John I. Bain to Stack, 30 March 1970, Stack Box 1; Paul to J. H. Fenwick (Playboy Foundation), 20 April 1970, Lucas Box 12; *State* v. *Jesse Ketchum*, Oakland County District Court, 30 March 1970, 4pp., Lucas Box 12; *New York Times*, 1 April 1970, p. 48; Lader, *Abortion II*, pp. 76–78; *State* v. *Munson*, 7 April 1970, unreported but printed in full in Thomas G. Fritz, "Abortion and the Constitutional Question," *South Dakota Law Review* 15 (Spring 1970): 318–334, at 332–334. On Munson, also see *Rapid City Journal*, 13 August 1969, p. 1; Lucas to Munson, 20 February 1970, Homer Kandaras to Lucas, 4 March 1970, Lucas to Kandaras, 11 March 1970, Kandaras to Lucas, 9 April 1970, Kandaras to Mel Wulf, 13 April 1970, Lucas Box 22.

34. Griswold et al., "Jurisdictional Statement," *U.S.* v. *Milan Vuitch*, U.S.S.C., O.T. 1969, #1155, 8pp., 5 February 1970, pp. 4, 6; Vuitch to Sitnick, 27 February 1970, Lucas Box 4; Sitnick, Nellis, and Lucas, "Motion to Affirm," *U.S.* v. *Vuitch*, #1155, 43pp., 6 March 1970, p. 4; [William T. Lake], *U.S.* v. *Vuitch*, 25 March 1970, 2pp., Harlan Box 427; William O. Douglas notation on [Thomas C. Armitage], *U.S.* v. *Vuitch*, 26 March 1970, Douglas Box 1507; William J. Brennan Docket Book, *United States* v. *Vuitch*, O.T. 1969, #1155, Box 416; Stewart, "Memorandum to the Conference," 27 March 1970, Harlan Box 427, Black Box 437, Brennan Box 200, and Douglas Box 1507; White to Stewart, 28 March 1970, Black to Stewart, 31 March 1970, and Harlan to Stewart, 2 April 1970, Douglas Box 1507; John F. Davis to Griswold and to Sitnick, 31 March 1970, *U.S.* v. *Vuitch* Case File, National Archives, RG 267, Box 10088; Sitnick, Nellis, and Lucas, "Supplemental Memorandum of Appellee," *U.S.* v. *Vuitch*, #1155, 12pp., 14 April 1970; Griswold et al., "Supplemental Memorandum for the United States," *U.S.* v. *Vuitch*, #1155, 9pp., [14] April 1970; [William T. Lake], *U.S.* v. *Vuitch*, 19 April 1970, Harlan Box 427; [Thomas C. Armitage], *U.S.* v. *Vuitch*, 20 April 1970, Douglas Box 1507; *U.S.* v. *Vuitch*, 397 U.S. 1061 (27 April); *New York Times*, 28 April 1970, pp. 1, 31; *Washington Post*, 28 April 1970, pp. A1, A12; Nellis to Vuitch, 29 April 1970, Lucas Box 8; Harlan, "Memorandum to the Conference," 25 June 1970, Harlan Box 427 and Brennan Box 200; E. Robert Seaver to Nellis et al., 29 June 1970, Lucas Box 4; *U.S.* v. *Vuitch*, 399 U.S. 923 (29 June 1970); Lucas, "Developments in Federal Jurisdiction," 3 July 1970, Lucas Box 24; Garrow conversations with Roy Lucas, Larry Lader, Milan Vuitch and Joseph Nellis. On Nellis, a Chicago native and Northwestern Law School graduate who had practiced law in Washington since 1947, also see *Washington Legal Times*, 22 October 1979, p. 5.

35. Cook Interview with Chesler, pp. 28–31, 37–38, 45, 59–63; *New York Times*, 11 March 1970, pp. 1, 73, 16 March 1970, p. 42, 17 March 1970, p. 31, 18 March 1970, p. 32, 19 March 1970, pp. 1, 39, 20 March 1970, pp. 46, 52, 21 March 1970, p. 59, 22 March 1970, p. E8, 24 March 1970, p. 37, 29 March 1970, p. 35, 31 March 1970, pp. 1, 82, 1 April 1970, pp. 1, 44, 48, 5 April 1970, p. E6, 8 April 1970, p. 88, 9 April 1970, pp. 1, 40, 46, 10 April 1970, pp. 1, 42; Dominick Interview with White; *Newsweek*, 20 April 1970, p. 77; *Time*, 20 April 1970, p. 46; Lader to Joseph Sunnen, "Progress Report," 20 April 1970, CCTA Box 1; Lader to Lonny Myers, 15 July 1970, NARAL Box 3; Ben White, "Abortion Law Repeal in New York State, 1970" (unpublished draft manuscript, n.d.), Lader Box 5; Lader, *Abortion II*, pp. 132–144; Frank J. Traina, "Diocesan Mobilization Against Abortion Law Reform" (unpublished Ph.D.

dissertation, Cornell University, 1975); *Washington Post*, 27 April 1989, pp. B1–B3. For a full articulation of Cisler and Clapp's stance, see Clapp, "The New York Abortion Situation," *ZPG National Reporter*, August 1970, pp. 8–9, 39 ("what happened in New York was a *setback* for the cause of abortion law repeal"), which also was reprinted in a slightly expanded pamphlet form under the title "Abortion Legislation in New York State." On George Michaels, also see *New York Times*, 20 April 1970, p. 63, 21 April 1970, p. 35, 23 April 1970, p. 36, 27 April 1970, p. 34, 5 June 1970, p. 40, 24 June 1970, p. 35, 11 August 1970, p. 23; [Lee Gidding], "Phone Conversation with George Michaels," 21 April 1970, NARAL Box 4; Michaels to Lader, 6 December 1971, Lader Box 16; Michaels, "Text of Address to be Delivered at Smith College," 9 December 1971, Lader Box 5, Lader, *Abortion II*, pp. 144–147; and Michaels's *New York Times* obituary, 5 December 1992, p. 27.

36. *New York Times*, 11 April 1970, pp. 1, 17, 30, 12 April 1970, pp. 47, E10, 13 April 1970, pp. 1, 20, 27 April 1970, p. 28, 30 April 1970, p. 1, 3 May 1970, p. E6, 4 May 1970, p. 1; NARAL Emergency Executive Committee Minutes, 17 April 1970, NARAL Box 1; Carmen and Moody, *Abortion Counseling*, pp. 72–73; Lader, *Abortion II*, pp. 149–150.

37. Lucas to Alan Charles, 13 April 1970, Lucas Box 15; "Abortion Laws Workshop," 28 April 1970, Kansas City, NARAL Box 1; Roberts to Lee Gidding, 18 February 1970, NARAL Box 5; *Oregonian*, 15 April 1970; *Oregon Committee for the Legal Termination of Pregnancy Newsletter*, Spring 1970, ARAI Box 1. At least one member of the three-judge New York panel, Circuit Judge Henry J. Friendly, was very happy at *not* having to decide *Hall* v. *Lefkowitz*. See his unpublished 1970 remarks as quoted in Ruth B. Ginsburg, "Some Thoughts on Autonomy and Equality in Relation to *Roe* v. *Wade*," *North Carolina Law Review* 63 (January 1985): 375–386, at 385–386 ("How much better that the issue was settled by the legislature!"); also see Henry J. Friendly, "The Courts and Social Policy: Substance and Procedure," *University of Miami Law Review* 33 (November 1978): 21–42, at 34 (asserting with regard to *Roe* and *Doe* that "there was no real precedential support for the abortion decisions, and it was a bit disingenuous to rest them on a recognized 'right of privacy'"). On the Oregon suit, also see Roberts and Skelton, "Abortion and the Courts," *Environmental Law* 1 (Spring 1971): 225–237.

38. *New York Times*, 24 April 1970, p. 16, 25 April 1970, p. 59, 2 May 1970, p. 26; Drinan, "The State of the Abortion Question," *Commonweal*, 17 April 1970, pp. 108–109; *San Francisco Chronicle*, 30 May 1970, p. 34. Also see Drinan, "The Jurisprudential Options on Abortion," *Theological Studies* 31 (March 1970): 149–169, and Drinan, *The Fractured Dream* (New York: Crossroad, 1991), pp. 34–50. On the bishops' Conference, see Timothy A. Byrnes, *Catholic Bishops in American Politics* (Princeton: Princeton University Press, 1991), pp. 51–55. Contemporaneous repeal voices included Harold Rosen, "Abortion in America," *American Journal of Psychiatry* 126 (March 1970): 1299–1301; Michael J. Halberstam, "Abortion: A Startling Proposal," *Redbook*, April 1970, pp. 78–79, 137–139; William R. Roy, "Abortion: A Physician's View," *Washburn Law Journal* 9 (Spring 1970): 391–411; Patricia E. Kowitz's very unusual "Isolating the Male Bias Against Reform of Abortion Legislation," *Santa Clara Lawyer* 10 (Spring 1970): 301–318; G. Clyde Dodder, "Abortion Laws: An Appeal for Repeal," *Ripon Forum* 6 (May 1970): 20–22; Natalie Shainess, "Abortion Is No Man's Business," *Psychology Today* 3 (May 1970): 18–22, 74–76 ("an unwanted child destroys a woman's mastery of her life"); and Charles Liser, "The Right to Control the Use of One's Body," in Norman Dorsen, ed., *The Rights of Americans* (New York: Random House, 1970), pp. 348–364, at 361–362 ("at least until viability the judgment whether to terminate a pregnancy should belong exclusively to the mother"). Antiabortion contributions included Denis Cavanagh, "Reforming the Abortion Laws," *America*, 18 April 1970, pp. 406–411; Brendan F. Brown, "Recent Statutes and the Crime of Abortion," William J. Kenealy, "Abortion: A Human Problem," and Leon Salzman, "Abortion: A Moral or Medical Problem," all in *Loyola Law Review* 16 (1970): 275–287, 289–293, and 295–298. Intermediate or ambivalent views are expressed in three different essays in the *Christian Century*, 20 May 1970, pp. 624–631.

39. Judith P. Rooks, "Why and How We Legalized Abortion" (unpublished speech, 21 January

1983, Salem, Oregon), 22pp.; Garrow conversations with James L. Waters, W. Newton Long, J. Emmett Herndon, Judith P. [Bourne] Rooks, Peter Bourne, and Robert Hatcher; *Atlanta Journal*, 21, 22, and 25 July 1969. Also see Judith P. Bourne, "Abortion: Influences on Health Professionals' Attitudes," *Hospitals* 46 (16 July 1972): 80–83. On the Virginia action, see *New York Times*, 23 March 1970, p. 20, and 12 April 1970, p. 65. On Emmett Herndon, also see Herndon, "Religious Aspects and Theology in Therapeutic Abortion," *Southern Medical Journal* 63 (June 1970): 651–654; and John Ard, "Newsmaker Interview with Emmett Herndon," *Presbyterian Survey* 60 (6 April 1970): 1–4.

40. *Atlanta Constitution*, 4 December 1969, p. B4, 19 January 1970, 23 January 1970, 28 January 1970, 2 February 1970, 4 February 1970, p. A1, 5 February 1970; Alan Bonser to Lee Gidding, 4 December 1969, NARAL Box 2; Annis Pratt to "Dear Friend," n.d. [December 1969], Herndon Papers; *Atlanta Journal*, 14 January 1970, p. D16, 4 and 5 February 1970; *Atlanta Journal-Constitution*, 1 February 1970; Garrow conversations with Judith [Bourne] Rooks and Peter Bourne. On Grace Towns Hamilton, see her *New York Times* obituary, 20 June 1992, p. 12.

41. *Atlanta Journal*, 6 February 1970, 12 February 1970, 17 February 1970; *Atlanta Constitution*, 7 February 1970, 11 February 1970, p. 1, 12 February 1970, 13 February 1970, 14 February 1970, 15 February 1970, pp. G8, G10, 17 February 1970; *Dallas Morning News*, 8 February 1970, p. A22; Garrow conversations with Judith [Bourne] Rooks and Peter Bourne.

42. Garrow conversations with Judith [Bourne] Rooks, Peter Bourne, Agnes "Ruste" Kitfield, Margie Pitts Hames, Tobiane Schwartz, Elizabeth Roediger Rindskopf, Gale Siegel Messerman, Reber F. Boult, Jr., Charles Morgan, Jr., J. Emmett Herndon, Robert A. Hatcher, James L. Waters and W. Newton Long; Judith Rooks, "Why and How We Legalized Abortion" (unpublished speech, 21 January 1983, Salem, Oregon), 22pp.; [Lee Gidding], "Phone Conversation with Dr. [George] Violin," 19 February 1970, NARAL Box 2; *Atlanta Journal*, 23 February 1970; *Atlanta Constitution*, 24 February 1970; ACLU of Georgia Executive Committee Agenda, 4 March 1970, Georgia ACLU Papers. On Margie Hames, also see *Fulton County Daily Report*, 12 February 1987, pp. 1, 4–5; *Atlanta Constitution*, 22 January 1988, p. B3; and Terry Dunham, "How the Abortion Law Was Killed," *Atlanta Journal-Constitution Magazine*, 11 March 1973, pp. 22–30. On Robert Hatcher, also see a fifteen-part series of front-page articles on population-related issues which he authored for the *Atlanta Constitution* between 5 and 19 April 1970, particularly those of 7 and 16 April, the latter of which includes both an estimate of 20,000 illegal abortions each year in Georgia and a report that the state's cumulative total of reported abortion deaths from 1960 to 1968 was seventy-seven.

43. Kit Young, "Therapeutic Abortion Evaluation Protocol—Sandy Bensing," 12 March 1970; Sandra Bensing Case Card, Atlanta Legal Aid Society, 14 May 1969; Joseph S. Thorpe and John W. Eppes, "Psychological Evaluation—Sandra Bensing," 16 March 1970; Sandra Bensing Affidavits, 16 April and 5 May 1970, Hames Papers; [Bensing], "Answers to Interrogatories," 14 June 1970, *Doe v. Bolton* Record, pp. 63–65; *Atlanta Constitution*, 13 December 1988, pp. A1, A6; Ann Woolner, "'I Am Mary Doe,'" *Fulton County Daily Report*, 9 February 1989, pp. 1, 3–7; *Los Angeles Times*, 25 June 1989, pp. 1, 17–18; Garrow conversations with Judith [Bourne] Rooks, Margie Pitts Hames, Sandra Bensing Cano, Tobi Schwartz, and Peter Bourne. Also see Charles W. Butler, "Psychiatric Indications for Therapeutic Abortion," *Southern Medical Journal* 63 (June 1970): 647–650, in which Butler volunteers that under the operative standard specified by the 1968 reform language—a "serious" threat to a woman's health—"a judgment is virtually impossible." A comprehensive statistical overview of Grady's abortion service from 1968 through 1970 is provided in Lawrence D. Baker and Malcolm G. Freeman, "Statistical Analysis of Applicants and of the Induced Abortion Work-up," *Journal of the Medical Association of Georgia* 60 (December 1971): 392–396, in which they report a total of 6 therapeutic abortions in calendar 1968, 31 in 1969, and 134 in 1970. In that latter year they report a total of 341 applicants, only 202 of whom were formally considered by Grady's Therapeutic Abortion Committee. Forty-three were rejected by the committee, and another fifteen or more withdrew or went elsewhere after or

just before receiving committee approval. Twenty-seven percent of all applicants were already thirteen or more weeks into their pregnancy at the time of applying; *another* 29 percent reached or passed the thirteen-week level while waiting for a committee decision. No month-by-month approval statistics for 1970 are reported.

44. Sandra Bensing, "Affidavit," 16 April 1970, *Doe* v. *Bolton* Case File, Federal Records Center, East Point, GA, 74A-2025, Box 16; Hames and Schwartz, "Complaint for Declaratory and Injunctive Relief," *Doe* v. *Bolton*, U.S.D.C. N.D. Ga., #13676, 16 April 1970, pp. 7 and 12; Hames and Schwartz, "Brief in Support of Motion for Temporary Restraining Order," *Doe* v. *Bolton*, 16 April 1970, p. 6; Garrow conversations with Margie Hames, Tobi Schwartz, Judith [Bourne] Rooks, Sandra Bensing Cano, Peter Bourne, Elizabeth Rindskopf, and Gale Siegel Messerman. Like Judith Bourne, Gale Siegel, a 1969 graduate of Southern Methodist law school, would immediately recall more than twenty years later the first article that voiced the central argument: "Lucas is the one who started the whole thing."

45. *Atlanta Constitution*, 17 April 1970, pp. A1, A19; *Atlanta Journal*, 17 April 1970, p. 1; Stewart R. Perry to Madison Institute, 13 April 1970, Lucas Box 12; Perry to Hodgson, 10 March 1971, Lucas Box 13; Perry, "Complaint for Declaratory Judgment and Injunctive Relief," *Doe* v. *Randall*, U.S.D.C. D. Minn., #3–70 Civ.97, 16 April 1970; Hodgson, "Therapeutic Abortion," 18 November 1969, 5pp., Lader Box 5 and ARAI 12–10, which also subsequently appears as "Therapeutic Abortion in Medical Perspective," *Minnesota Medicine* 53 (July 1970): 755–757; Hodgson in *Ft. Worth Star-Telegram*, 2 February 1971, pp. B1, B3; Hodgson in Peter Irons, *The Courage of Their Convictions* (New York: Free Press, 1988), pp. 253–279, at 269–271; Garrow conversations with Jane E. Hodgson; *Minneapolis Tribune*, 17 and 21 April 1970, 22 May and 30 June 1970; *Minneapolis Star*, 17 April and 1 and 12 May 1970; *Doe* v. *Randall* Record and Case File (including transcripts of the 20 and 27 April 1970 hearings), U.S.S.C., O.T. 1970, #728, National Archives RG 267, Box 10269; *St. Paul Dispatch*, 27 April 1970, 1 and 26 May 1970, 12 June 1970, pp. 17, 20; Pratt to Hodgson, 6 May 1970, Lucas Box 13; *Doe* v. *Randall*, 314 F. Supp. 32 (19 May and 1 July 1970); *St. Paul Pioneer Press*, 22 May and 2 July 1970; Lucas to Perry, 2 June 1970, Lucas Box 12; *New York Times*, 30 June 1970, p. 24; Hodgson in *Minnesota Journal of Education*, October 1970, pp. 30–32. Hachey's formally unreported 29 June opinion appears in the *Social Justice Review* 63 (November 1970): 228–234.

On Jane Hodgson, also see *Minneapolis Tribune*, 7 June 1970, pp. 1, 11; *St. Paul Dispatch*, 24 June 1970, pp. 1, 2, 6; Hodgson, "Abortion: The Law and the Reality, 1970," *Mayo Alumnus* 6 (October 1970): 1–4; *Boston Globe*, 18 October 1970; Edwin Kiester, Jr., "Doctor Hodgson's Choice," *Family Health* 3 (June 1971): 14–17; Hodgson, "Teenage Mothers," *Minnesota Medicine* 55 (January 1972): 49; Hodgson's several contributions in a volume which she edited, *Abortion and Sterilization: Medical and Social Aspects* (New York: Grune & Stratton, 1981); *New York Times*, 25 June 1989, p. 20, 11 July 1989, pp. A1, B4; *Washington Post*, 29 November 1989, pp. B1, B6; *U.S. News & World Report*, 4 December 1989, p. 26; Laura Fraser, "Hodgson's Choice," *Vogue*, July 1990, pp. 206–209, 228. Also see Jule M. Hannaford, "Abortion: Crime or Privilege," *Mayo Clinic Proceedings* 45 (July 1970): 510–516. On MCLTP, see Irene Hoebel to MCLTP Board, 18 February 1970, ARC Box 120–2B, Vincent Yano to [Genevieve] Lane, 2 July 1970, WCAR I-3, and [Lee Gidding], "Minnesota Situation," 28 July 1970, NARAL Box 3; on Robert McCoy, also see *Minneapolis Star*, 21 and 23 January 1970.

46. *Anchorage Daily News*, 27 February 1970, 14 June 1970, pp. 1, 2; *Anchorage Daily Times*, 3 March 1970, 18 April 1970; *New York Times*, 19 April 1970, p. 42, 1 May 1970, p. 10; Helen D. Nienhueser to Mrs. Joseph McLean, 3 June 1970, Lader Box 5; John L. Rader to Lader, 16 December 1971 and 3 January 1972 (20pp.), Lader Box 16; Lader, *Abortion II*, pp. 117–120.

47. *Washington Post*, 25 February 1970, pp. B1, B4, 11 April 1970, p. B1, 14 April 1970, p. C1, 17 April 1970, p. B3, 20 May 1970, p. C1, 27 May 1970, pp. A1, A10; *New York Times*, 19 March 1970, p. 38, 20 March 1970, p. 46, 1 April 1970, pp. 1, 48, 15 April 1970, p. 38, 27 May 1970, p. 43; [Lee Gidding], "Maryland Repeal Bill," 1 April 1970, NARAL Box 3; *Newsweek*, 13 April 1970, pp. 53–61, 8 June 1970, pp. 51–52.

48. George S. Daly, Jr., Michael Katz, and Roy Lucas, "Complaint," *Elizabeth Corkey* v. *Dan Edwards*, U.S.D.C. W.D.N.C., #2665, 12 May 1970; [Raleigh] *News & Observer*, 18 May 1970; Jones to Lee Gidding, 28 May 1970, NARAL Box 5; Daly, "Memorandum in Support of Motion for Summary Judgment," *Corkey* v. *Edwards*, #2665, 2 July 1970, 107pp.

49. See *Southern Patriot*, June 1970, p. 4, and eventually *Crossen* v. *Attorney General*, 344 F.Supp. 587 (E.D. Ky.), 19 May 1972.

50. Thayer, Susman, Irving Achtenberg, and Lucas, "Complaint for Declaratory Judgment and Injunctive Relief," *Rodgers* v. *Danforth*, U.S.D.C. W.D. Mo., #18260–2, 15 May 1970, 15pp., Lucas Box 15. On Susman, also see Patricia Donovan, *Family Planning/Population Reporter* 4 (April 1975): 30–31.

51. Berman, "Complaint," *Gwynne* v. *Cecil Hicks*, U.S.D.C. C.D. Cal., CA#70–1088, 15 May 1970, Gwynne, "Declaration," 20 May 1970, Berman to Lucas, 22 and 29 May and 5 and 26 June 1970, Lucas to Berman, 26 May and 22 June 1970, Zad Leavy to Berman, 1 June 1970, Judge William W. Thomson, *People* v. *Gwynne*, Central Orange Municipal Court, #173309, 16 June 1970, Lucas Box 1.

52. On Connecticut, see Sasha Harmon and Mimi Abramovitz to "Dear Sisters," 20 February 1970, Lader Box 6, and *Hartford Courant*, 15 May 1970; also see Donald J. Cantor, *Escape From Marriage* (New York: William Morrow & Co., 1971), pp. 117–118. On Ohio, see Don Breakstone to Lucas, 22 May 1970, and Leslie L. Knowlton to Lucas, 24 July and 17 August 1970, Lucas Box 21; on New Hampshire, see Marianne Dame to Lucas, 20 May 1970, and Lucas to Dame, 25 May 1970, Lucas Box 25. On South Dakota, see Homer Kandaras to Lucas, 26 May and 9 June 1970 and Lucas to Kandaras, 1 June and 7 August 1970, Lucas Box 22; on Louisiana, see Smith to Lucas, 1 and 15 June 1970, Lucas Box 7. On Arizona, see Seymour Sacks, LeRoy L. Miller, and Stanley G. Feldman, "Complaints," *Planned Parenthood Association of Phoenix et al.* v. *Gary K. Nelson*, U.S.D.C. D. Ariz., Civ. #70–334PHX, 9 June 1970, 7pp., Lucas Box 1; *Arizona Republic*, 11 June 1970; Sacks et al., "Response to Motions to Dismiss," *PPAP* v. *Nelson*, #70–334PHX, 5 August 1970, 44pp., Lucas to Sacks, 13 August 1970, "Judgment," *PPAP* v. *Nelson*, 24 August 1970 (denying defendant's motion to dismiss), Sacks to Lucas, 26 August 1970, Lucas Box 1; Eileen Hulse, *Phoenix*, January 1971, pp. 45–46. Also note two highly unappealing criminal cases, both involving physicians who unsuccessfully attempted to challenge convictions involving women's deaths: *State of Missouri* v. *Richard P. Mucie*, 448 S.W.2d 879 (Mo. Sup. Ct.), 12 January 1970, 398 U.S. 938 (cert. denied), 1 June 1970, and *U.S. ex rel. Jesse Williams II* v. *Follette*, 313 F. Supp. 269 (S.D.N.Y.), 12 May 1970; *U.S. ex rel. Williams* v. *Zelker*, 445 F.2d 451 (2d Cir.), 2 July 1971.

53. Garrow conversations with Roy L. Merrill, Jr., Linda Coffee, Fred Bruner, and William R. Fuller; *Dallas Morning News*, 20 and 28 March 1970; *Dallas Times-Herald*, 20 and 28 March 1970; Bruner and Merrill, "Application for Intervention," and "Intervenor and Plaintiff Hallford's Original Complaint," *Roe* v. *Wade*, #3–3690–B, 19 and 23 March 1970, 10pp., p. 7; *State* v. *Hallford*, #69–2524, 5 May 1969, and #69–5307, 3 October 1969. Jane "Wilhite" is a pseudonym chosen by this author, even though the woman's correct name appears in the public case file. "Francis C. King" is listed as the second witness in addition to Frank Johnson in the October indictment. On Hallford, also see "Affidavit of Plaintiff Hallford in Support of Motion for Summary Judgment," *Roe* v. *Wade*, n.d. [c.20 April 1970], 11pp.; *Dallas Morning News*, 6 December 1964. On Fred Bruner, also see *Dallas Morning News*, 22 April 1956 and 19 March 1964; *Dallas Times-Herald*, 28 January 1973.

54. Garrow conversations with Linda Coffee, Roy Merrill, Fred Bruner, Henry Wade, John B. Tolle, Jay Floyd, and Robert Flowers; Johnston to Crawford C. Martin, 10 March 1970, Alfred Walker to Bob Flowers, 12 March 1970, Texas AG File 70–308; Tolle, "Defendant's Original Answer," *Roe* v. *Wade*, #3–3690–B, 23 March 1970, 2pp.; Johnston, "Motion to Dismiss," 1pp., and "Brief in Support of Defendant's Motion to Dismiss," 1pp., *Doe* v. *Wade*, #3–3691–C, 24 March 1970, Johnston to Floyd, n.d., Texas AG File 70–308; Tolle, "Defendant's Answer to Intervenor Hallford's Original Complaint," *Roe* v. *Wade*, #3–3690–B, 26 March 1970, 4pp. On Henry Wade, also see Richard West, "The Chief," *D Magazine* 13 (May 1986): 108–11, 179–183, and *Dallas Morning News*, 30 December 1986, pp.

A1, A5. On John Tolle, also see *Dallas Morning News*, 31 January 1979. Also see generally *Houston Chronicle*, 19 and 22 March 1970, *Houston Post*, 19 March 1970, and *San Antonio Light*, 1 April 1970.

55. Hughes to Coffee, Bruner, Tolle, and Crawford Martin, 26 March 1970, Floyd notes, n.d., 2pp., Floyd to Alfred Walker, 9 April 1970, Texas AG File 70–308; *Dallas Times-Herald*, 4 April 1970; Garrow conversations with Linda Coffee, Fred Bruner, John Tolle, and Jay Floyd.

56. On Morehouse, see *Dallas Morning News*, 2 April 1970, p. AA1, 10 April 1970, p. A14, 12 May 1970, p. A15; and *The Rag*, 6 April 1970, p. 12. On Austin and Houston developments, also see *Austin American-Statesman*, 29 March 1970, p. F7; Laura Maggi to NARAL, 7 April 1970, Charlene Torrest to NARAL, 9 April 1970, and Lee Gidding to Maggi and to Torrest, 21 April 1970, NARAL Box 5; *Dallas Morning News*, 10 April 1970, p. A5; *The Rag*, 13 April 1970, 27 April 1970, p. 13, 18 May 1970, p. 11; *Houston Post*, 1 May 1970.

57. Ellen Kalina form letters, 6 April and 4 May 1970, Whitehill Papers; *Dallas Times-Herald*, 13 April 1970, pp. 1, 6, 14 April 1970, pp. A15, A17, 16 April 1970, 22 April 1970, p. C5, 24 April 1970, p. 1, 2 May 1970, 6 May 1970, 20 May 1970, pp. 27, 30, 21 May 1970, pp. 21, 36, 10 June 1970; *Dallas Morning News*, 17 April 1970, p. 15, 19 April 1970, p. C37; Kalina and Patricia White to Hugh Savage, 27 April 1970, Savage and Whitehill Papers; Kalina to NARAL, 27 April 1970, Lee Gidding to Kalina, 29 April 1970, NARAL Box 5; Genevieve Scott, Women's Alliance Minutes, 28 April and 5 May 1970, First Unitarian Church; Garrow conversations with Virginia Whitehill, James H. Clark, Jr., and J. Claude Evans. Also see J. Claude Evans, "Defusing the Abortion Debate," *Christian Century*, 31 January 1973, pp. 117–118.

58. Bruner and Merrill, "Brief of Plaintiff James Hubert Hallford," *Roe v. Wade*, #3–3690, 13 April 1970; Weddington and Coffee, "Plaintiff's First Amended Complaint," *Roe v. Wade*, #3–3690, 16 April [filed 22 April] 1970, 4pp.; Coffee and Weddington, "Brief of Plaintiffs Jane Roe, John Doe, and Mary Doe," *Roe et al. v. Wade*, #3–3690, 23 April 1970, 14pp.; Floyd, "Motion to Dismiss" and "State of Texas's Memorandum of Authorities in Support of its Motion to Dismiss," *Roe v. Wade*, #3–3690, 30 April 1970, 2pp. and 16pp.; Tolle, "Defendant's Brief," *Roe et al. v. Wade*, #3–3690, 18 May 1970; Sylvia M. Demarest, "Request for Leave to File Amicus Curiae Brief," *Roe v. Wade*, #3–3690, 18 May 1970; Bruner and Merrill, "Reply Brief of Plaintiff James Hubert Hallford," *Roe v. Wade*, #3–3690, 20 May 1970; Garrow conversations with Roy Merrill, Linda Coffee, Fred Bruner, Sarah Weddington, Jay Floyd, and John Tolle; *Dallas Times-Herald*, 22 May 1970, pp. 1, 10, 27, 29.

59. Garrow conversations with Paul C. Trickett, Bob Breihan, Sarah Weddington, Norma McCorvey, and Linda Coffee; "Affidavit of Dr. Paul C. Trickett," 24 April [filed 21 May] 1970, and "Affidavit of Jane Roe," *Roe v. Wade*, #3–3690, 21 May 1970, *Roe* Record pp. 51 and 56–58. On Trickett's support for repeal, see *Austin American-Statesman*, 21 July 1970. With regard to the continuation of McCorvey's pregnancy, also see Weddington Interview with Cheek, p. 60 ("That's right. We were afraid that if she went ahead and got the abortion, there might be some chance the court would declare the case moot") and Weddington in Warren M. Hern and Bonnie Andrikopoulos, eds., *Abortion in the Seventies* (New York: National Abortion Federation, 1977), p. 279 ("Linda and I explained to her that . . . the case might be declared moot and later thrown out if she had an abortion. She decided to carry the pregnancy to term to save the case"). Years later, Weddington would become highly dismissive of McCorvey's role in the case: "'Her only involvement in this case was that she signed one affidavit,' Weddington said . . . 'It probably took 30 to 40 minutes of her time to become the plaintiff and another 30 to 40 minutes to sign the affidavit.'" *New Haven Register*, 30 April 1989.

60. Lucas to Shreve, 18 May 1970, Lucas Box 22 ("In response to your request for information"); Hughes Interview with Marcello (1979), pp. 17–18; Goldberg Interview with Garrow; *Dallas Morning News*, 26 December 1971, p. A28. On "Mac" Taylor, see *Dallas Morning News*, 29 June 1966, p. D1, 30 December 1967, p. 10, 19 June 1985, pp. A13, A17; *Dallas Times-Herald*, 14 July 1974, p. B3, 27 July 1975, p. A12, 18 June 1985, pp. 1, 5; and *Dallas Times-Herald Magazine*, 10 April 1977, pp. 12–14.

61. Transcript of Oral Argument, *Roe* v. *Wade*, #3–3690, 22 May 1970, *Roe* Record, pp. 75–110; *Stanley* v. *Georgia*, 394 U.S. 557, 564 (1969); Garrow conversations with Irving L. Goldberg, John B. Tolle, Linda Coffee, Sarah Weddington, Fred Bruner, Roy Merrill, Jay Floyd, Clarice Davis, Barbara Richardson, and Virginia Whitehill; *Dallas Morning News*, 23 May 1970, p. D18; *Dallas Times-Herald*, 23 May 1970, p. 1. Also see Richard C. Cortner, *The Supreme Court and Civil Liberties* (Palo Alto, CA: Mayfield Publishing Co., 1975), pp. 33–79, at 41–42. On *Stanley*, also see *State* v. *Robert E. Stanley*, 161 S.E.2d 309, 224 Ga. 259; and Al Katz, "Privacy and Pornography," *Supreme Court Review* 1969 (Chicago: University of Chicago Press, 1969), pp. 203–217; see as well *Henley* v. *Wise*, 303 F. Supp. 62, 67 (N.D. Ind.), 4 June 1969, where a three-judge court including Seventh Circuit Judge Otto Kerner voided Indiana's obscenity statute and observed that "While only the right to *marital* privacy is covered by *Cotner* and *Griswold*, it is clear that this right stems from the greater right to individual privacy. Absent the use of self-destructive force, the state has no interest in prohibiting purely private conduct, i.e. conduct which does not involve another person."

62. Weddington in Hern and Andrikopoulos, eds., *Abortion in the Seventies*, p. 279; Weddington, *A Question of Choice*, pp. 64–67; Coffee in Barbara Milbauer, *The Law Giveth*, p. 37; Garrow conversations with Virginia Whitehill, Barbara Richardson, Sarah Weddington, Linda Coffee, Roy Merrill, Fred Bruner, John Tolle, and Jay Floyd.

63. Garrow conversations with Margie Pitts Hames, Sidney O. Smith, Jr., Judith [Bourne] Rooks, Peter G. Bourne, Sandra [Bensing] Cano, Tobi Schwartz, and Agnes "Ruste" Kitfield; *Atlanta Constitution*, 2 May 1970, p. A6, 8 May 1970, 9 May 1970, 15 May 1970, p. A9, 28 May 1970, p. B14, 10 June 1970, p. A16, 11 June 1970; Smith, "Orders," 25 April and 5 May 1970, *Doe* v. *Bolton* Record, pp. 21 and 39–40; "Mary Doe," "Answers to Interrogatories," 14 June 1970, *Doe* Record, pp. 63–65; Hames to "Dear *Doe* Plaintiffs," 24 February 1989, Hames Papers; Sandra Race Bensing and Joel Lee Bensing Affidavits, 5 May 1970, and Buckley to Hames, 15 May 1970, Hames Papers; ACLU of Georgia Executive Board Minutes, 18 May 1970; *Atlanta Journal*, 18 May 1970, 10 June 1970; Hames, "Brief in Opposition to Motion to Dismiss," *Doe* v. *Bolton*, #13676, 25 May 1970, 6pp.; Affidavits of "Ruth Roe," 12 June 1970, and "Polly Poe," 13 June 1970, Hames Papers. As Hames noted in her 24 February 1989 letter, "It was to our advantage in not mooting our case or her standing as a plaintiff, for her to not have the abortion."

64. Hames, Schwartz, and Rindskopf, "Brief of Plaintiffs," *Doe* v. *Bolton*, #13676, 8 June 1970, 58pp., pp. 9, 30, 35; Charles, "Brief of the National Legal Program on Health Problems of the Poor," *Doe* v. *Bolton*, #13676, 6 June 1970, 30pp.; Buckley, "Brief of Amicus Curiae for the Unborn Child of Mary Doe and Other Unborn Children Similarly Situated," *Doe* v. *Bolton*, #13676, 8 June 1970, 52pp.; Hight, "Brief on the Merits on Behalf of Defendant Lewis R. Slaton," *Doe* v. *Bolton*, #13676, 8 June 1970, 6pp.; Henry L. Bowden and Ralph H. Witt, "Preliminary Brief of Defendant Herbert T. Jenkins," *Doe* v. *Bolton*, #13676, 8 June 1970, 6pp.

65. Garrow conversations with Dorothy T. Beasley and Arthur K. Bolton; Beasley, "Brief of the Attorney General in Support of the Constitutionality of the Georgia Abortion Laws," and "Brief in Support of Motion to Dismiss," *Doe* v. *Bolton*, #13676, 9 and 10 June 1970, 12pp. and 13pp. On Dorothy Beasley, also see *Atlanta Constitution*, 14 January 1972, p. B5, and Margaret Shannon, "Matters of Life and Death," *Atlanta Journal-Constitution Magazine*, 23 April 1972, pp. 7–17.

66. On Lewis R. Morgan, see *Atlanta Journal*, 17 July 1968, pp. A1, A12, 28 July 1968, 7 October 1971; *Atlanta Constitution*, 18 July 1968, pp. 1, 19, 3 August 1968, 7 October 1971; also see Read and McGough, *Let Them Be Judged*, pp. 452–453, and Harvey C. Couch, *A History of the Fifth Circuit, 1891–1981*, p. 144. On Albert J. Henderson, see *Atlanta Constitution*, 26 September 1968, 10 October 1968; *Atlanta Journal*, 3 October 1968 and 27 July 1979. On Sidney Smith, see *Atlanta Journal*, 24 August 1965, pp. 1, 6, 25 August 1965, 8 and 10 September 1965, 28 November 1973, p. A20, 12 June 1974, pp. A1, A10; *Atlanta Journal-Constitution*, 29 August 1965; *Atlanta Journal-Constitution Magazine*, 1 September 1974, pp. 10–12; *Atlanta Constitution*, 28 November 1973, 29 January 1988, p. A16; Garrow conversa-

tions with Sidney O. Smith, Jr., Jeffrey R. Nickerson, Elizabeth Rindskopf, and Margie Hames.

67. Transcript of Hearing, *Doe* v. *Bolton*, #13676, 15 June 1970, 97pp.; *Atlanta Journal*, 15 and 16 June 1970; *Atlanta Constitution*, 16 June 1970; Garrow conversations with Margie Hames, Tobi Schwartz, Elizabeth Rindskopf, Gale Siegel Messerman, Judith [Bourne] Rooks, Sandra [Bensing] Cano, Dorothy T. Beasley, Sidney O. Smith, Jr., Jeffrey R. Nickerson, Agnes "Ruste" Kitfield, Reber Boult, James L. Waters, and W. Newton Long. The hearing transcript which appears in the formal *Doe* Record (pp. 125–160) is edited and is highly incomplete.

68. Garrow conversations with Tobi Schwartz, Margie Hames, Elizabeth Rindskopf, Judith [Bourne] Rooks, and Gale Siegel Messerman; Rindskopf, "Supplemental Brief of Plaintiffs," *Doe* v. *Bolton*, #13676, 24 June 1970, 15pp., p. 2; *Atlanta Constitution*, 25 June 1970; Tony H. Hight, "Supplemental Brief," *Doe* v. *Bolton*, #13676, 30 June 1970, 15pp.; Ferdinand Buckley, "Supplementary Brief," *Doe* v. *Bolton*, #13676, 30 June 1970, 17pp.; Henry Bowden and Ralph Witt, "Supplemental Brief," *Doe* v. *Bolton*, #13676, 2 July 1970, 5pp.; Beasley et al., "Supplemental Brief of Defendant Arthur K. Bolton," *Doe* v. *Bolton*, #13676, 1 July 1970, 19pp., pp. 2–4, 7.

69. Garrow conversations with Irving L. Goldberg, Clarice M. Davis, and Barefoot Sanders; Hughes Interview with Marcello, pp. 18, 20–21; Hughes in undated clipping from the *University Daily* [Texas Tech], April 1973, Hughes Papers; Goldberg in Lawrence J. Vilardo and Howard W. Gutman, "With Justice from One: Interview with Hon. Irving L. Goldberg," *Litigation* 17 (Spring 1991): 16–22, 56–57, at 22; Allread, "Sarah T. Hughes," p. 147 (Hughes too in 1976 termed *Roe* "easy"). No case materials pertaining to *Roe* appear in any of the surviving papers of either Judge Hughes or Judge Taylor. As Judge Goldberg explained in part, "we didn't write each other notes."

70. *Roe* v. *Wade*, 314 F. Supp. 1217, 1221–1224 (17 June 1970); *Dombrowski* v. *Pfister*, 380 U.S. 479, 489–490 (1965). Irving Goldberg would later say that "I am against per curiam opinions." *Litigation* 17 (Spring 1991): 16–22ff., at 22. Law journal notes on the panel decision in *Roe* include Ernest R. Reeves, *Texas Tech Law Review* 2 (Fall 1970): 99–105; Michael J. Appleton, *Texas Law Review* 49 (March 1971): 537–542; and James K. Skillern, *Baylor Law Review* 23 (Fall 1971): 605–615.

71. *Dallas Morning News*, 18 June 1970, p. A1, 19 June 1970, pp. A1, A14, 20 June 1970, p. AA4; *Dallas Times-Herald*, 18 June 1970, pp. A1, A14, C2, 21 June 1970, p. A40; *New York Times*, 18 June 1970, p. 37; Jay Floyd notes, 18 June 1970, and Richard R. Brann to Martin and Wade, 25 June 1970, Texas AG File 70–308; Laura Maggi to NARAL, 18 June 1970, NARAL Box 5; *Fort Worth Star-Telegram*, 19 June 1970, p. A6; *Austin American-Statesman*, 19 June 1970, 3 July 1970, p. 8; *The Rag*, 22 June 1970; *Houston Post*, 23 June 1970, p. II-1; Dallas Committee Minutes, 24 June 1970, Whitehill Papers. On fifty-four-year-old Crawford Martin, a long-time state senator who had first been elected attorney general in November, 1966, see his 1971 LBJ Library interview with David McComb.

72. Price to Paul C. MacDonald, 29 June 1970, and Affidavits of Dr. Paul C. MacDonald (28 July 1971), Dr. Joseph Seitchik (9 August 1971), and Dr. William J. McGanity (13 August 1971), in "Brief for Appellants," *Roe* v. *Wade*, U.S.S.C., O.T. 1971, #70–18, appendices B, C, and D.

73. On the AMA, see *New York Times*, 23 June 1970, p. 16, 26 June 1970, pp. 1, 24, 40, 27 June 1970, p. 1; and *Journal of the American Medical Association* 213 (17 August 1970): 1182–1183. With regard to Callahan, see *Newsweek*, 8 June 1970, pp. 64–65, *New York Times*, 8 June 1970, pp. 1, 29, Harriet Pilpel's review in the *New York Times Book Review*, 14 June 1970, pp. 6, 26, and Callahan, *Abortion: Law, Choice and Morality*, esp. pp. 19, 409, 448, 492–493. Also see Callahan, "Contraception and Abortion: American Catholic Responses," *The Annals* 387 (January 1970): 109–117, and Callahan, "The New Setting of Abortion Decisions," *The Ecumenist* 8 (May-June 1970): 65–68. Also see generally, *Congressional Quarterly Weekly Report*, 24 July 1970, pp. 1913–1916.

74 *New York Times*, 13 May 1970, p. 37, 21 May 1970, p. 34, 22 May 1970, p. 33, 30 May 1970,

pp. 1, 50, 3 June 1970, p. 44, 11 June 1970, p. 18, 19 June 1970, p. 39, 20 June 1970, p. 26, 29 June 1970, pp. 1, 20, 30 June 1970, p. 45, 1 July 1970, p. 36, 2 July 1970, pp. 1, 42–43, 3 July 1970, p. 26, 4 July 1970, p. 18, 5 July 1970, pp. 35, E12, 9 July 1970, p. 75, 11 July 1970, p. 10, 14 July 1970, p. 13, 16 July 1970, p. 24, 17 July 1970, p. 30, 19 July 1970, p. E7, 22 July 1970, p. 38, 26 July 1970, p. 36, 28 July 1970, p. 35, 5 September 1970, p. 19, 17 September 1970, pp. 43, 93, 18 September 1970, pp. 1, 47, 23 September 1970, p. 95; ASA Executive Committee Minutes, 18 May 1970, Pilpel, "Minutes of Ad Hoc Doctors' Committee on New York Abortion Law Implementation," 22 May 1970, Guttmacher Papers; Lael Scott, *New York Magazine*, 25 May 1970, pp. 64–71; "Statement on Implementation" [25 May 1970], *Bulletin of the New York Academy of Medicine* 46 (September 1970): 674–675; *National Observer*, 8 June 1970, pp. 1, 9; Linda Greenhouse, *New York Times Magazine*, 28 June 1970, pp. 7, 26–34; *Wall Street Journal*, 1 July 1970, pp. 1, 23; *Newsweek*, 13 July 1970, p. 60, 5 October 1970, p. 52; *Time*, 7 September 1970, p. 48; Linda Nessel, *New York Magazine*, 28 September 1970, pp. 58–64; *Journal of the American Medical Association* 214 (12 October 1970): 252–256, 362; Howard Eisenberg, *Medical Economics*, 4 January 1971, pp. 35ff.; Susan Edmiston, "A Report on the Abortion Capital of the Country," *New York Times Magazine*, 11 April 1971, pp. 10–11, 36–44.

For further coverage of New York's implementation of repeal, also see *New York Times*, 17 October 1970, p. 60, 18 October 1970, p. 1, 20 October 1970, pp. 1, 29, 25 October 1970, p. E12, 8 November 1970, p. 75, 7 February 1971, p. 70, 21 February 1971, p. 76, 6 April 1971, p. 78; *Buffalo Law Review* 20 (Winter 1971): 524–535; Carol Guercia, "The Effects of the Legalization of Abortion in the State of New York" (unpublished paper, Yale University, 1971), 52pp., Lader Box 3; Anne Barry, *McCall's* 98 (January 1971): 30–33, 105; Jean Pakter et al., "Surveillance of the Abortion Program in New York City," which appears identically in both *Modern Treatment* 8 (February 1971): 169–201 and *Clinical Obstetrics and Gynecology* 14 (March 1971): 267–299; Pakter and Frieda Nelson, "Abortion in New York City: The First Nine Months," *Family Planning Perspectives* 3 (July 1971): 5–12; Anthony J. LaFache, *Albany Law Review* 35 (1971): 644–664; Alan F. Guttmacher, "Abortion U.S.A.," *Resident and Staff Physician*, September 1971, pp. 114–117; Joseph J. Rovinsky, "Abortion in New York City," *Obstetrics and Gynecology* 38 (September 1971): 333–342; Rovinsky, "Abortion in New York City," *Advances in Planned Parenthood* 7 (1972): 169–174; Martin L. Stone et al., "The Impact of a Liberalized Abortion Law on the Medical Schools," *American Journal of Obstetrics and Gynecology* 111 (1 November 1971): 728–735; Abner I. Weisman, *American Journal of Obstetrics and Gynecology* 112 (1 January 1972): 138–143; Pakter and Nelson, "Effects of a Liberalized Abortion Law in New York City," *Mt. Sinai Journal of Medicine* 39 (November-December 1972): 535–543; Sylvia Wassertheil-Smoller et al., "New York State Physicians and the Social Context of Abortion," *American Journal of Public Health* 63 (February 1973): 144–149; David Harris et al., "Legal Abortion 1970–1971—The New York City Experience," *American Journal of Public Health* 63 (May 1973): 409–418; Jean Pakter et al., "Two Years Experience in New York City . . ." *American Journal of Public Health* 63 (June 1973): 524–535; Pakter et al., "A Review of Two Years' Experience in New York City . . ." in Howard J. and Joy D. Osofsky, eds., *The Abortion Experience* (Hagerstown, MD: Harper & Row, 1973), pp. 47–72; Jean Van der Tak, *Abortion, Fertility, and Changing Legislation* (Lexington, MA: D.C. Heath & Co., 1974), pp. 35–39; Timothy A. Deyak and V. Kerry Smith, "The Economic Value of Statute Reform," *Journal of Political Economy* 84 (February 1976): 83–99; and Joanne Miller, "Hospital Response to the Legalization of Abortion in New York State," *Journal of Health and Social Behavior* 20 (December 1979): 363–375.

75. Hall to Lucas, 16 July 1970, Lucas, "Order to Show Cause," *Hall v. Trustees and Officers of the Presbyterian Hospital*, U.S.D.C. S.D.N.Y., #70-3090, 17 July 1970, and Hall notes, n.d., Lucas Box 18; *New York Times*, 18 July 1970, p.10; *New York Post*, 21 July 1970, pp. 1, 2, 22 July 1970, pp. 1, 31; Lucas, "Hall & Poe v. Columbia Presbyterian," 5 April 1973, Lucas Box 18; Garrow conversations with Robert E. Hall and Roy Lucas. Also see Hall, "The Abortion Revolution," *Playboy* 17 (September 1970): 112ff; Hall, "The Truth About Abortion in New York," *Columbia Forum* 13 (Winter 1970): 18–22; Hall, "Abortion: Physician and Hospital Attitudes," *American Journal of Public Health* 61 (March 1971): 517–519; Hall, "The Future of

Therapeutic Abortions in the United States," *Clinical Obstetrics and Gynecology* 14 (December 1971): 1149–1153; *New York Times*, 28 October 1970, p. 55, *Los Angeles Times*, 25 January 1971, pp. IV-1, 8, and *Ob.Gyn. News*, 1 April 1971, pp. 1, 48. *Hall* was dismissed in April 1971 by U.S. District Judge Edward C. McLean on the grounds that both "Sally Poe" and successor plaintiff "Sandy Poe" had indeed already obtained abortions at other hospitals.

76. On Hawaii, see *New York Times*, 23 March 1970, p. 19; *Time*, 6 July 1970, p. 34; Roy G. Smith et al., "Abortion in Hawaii: The First 124 Days," *American Journal of Public Health* 61 (March 1971): 530–542; Smith et al., "Abortion in Hawaii: 1970–1971," *Hawaii Medical Journal*, July-August 1973, pp. 213–220; John F. McDermott and Walter F. Char, "Abortion Repeal in Hawaii," *American Journal of Orthopsychiatry* 41 (July 1971): 620–626; Franklin E. Zimring, *University of Chicago Law Review* 39 (Summer 1972): 699–721; Milton Diamond et al., "Abortion in Hawaii," *Family Planning Perspectives* 5 (Winter 1973): 54–60; and Steinhoff and Diamond, *Abortion Politics: The Hawaii Experience*, pp. 174–191.

On California, see *CCTA Newsletter*, May 1970; *Los Angeles Times*, 26 June 1970, pp. IV-1, 4; *SHA Newsletter*, Summer 1970; Rhonda Levitt and Shirley Radl, "A Day in Sacramento," *ZPG National Reporter*, August 1970, pp. 4–6, 23; *San Francisco Chronicle*, 16 September 1970; Jerome M. Kummer, *Journal of Reproductive Medicine* 5 (October 1970): 67–74; Nancy B. Reardan, *Pacific Law Journal* 2 (January 1971): 186–205; Charles and Bonnie Remsberg, *Good Housekeeping* 172 (February 1971): 86–87, 146–150; E. W. Jackson et al., "Therapeutic Abortions in California," *California Medicine* 115 (July 1971): 28–33; Zad Leavy, "Living with the Therapeutic Abortion Act of 1967," *Clinical Obstetrics and Gynecology* 14 (December 1971): 1154–1164; Kristin Luker, *Abortion and the Politics of Motherhood* (Berkeley: University of California Press, 1984), pp. 94, 134; and especially two very similar but highly informative pieces by Michael S. Goldstein: "Creating and Controlling a Medical Market: Abortion in Los Angeles After Liberalization," *Social Problems* 31 (June 1984): 514–529, and "Abortion as a Medical Career Choice: Entrepreneurs, Community Physicians, and Others," *Journal of Health and Social Behavior* 25 (June 1984): 211–229.

77. On New Mexico, see Robert Shafer, *Modern Hospital* 118 (February 1972): 96–98; on Maryland, see Robert J. Melton et al., "Therapeutic Abortion in Maryland, 1968–1970," *Obstetrics and Gynecology* 39 (June 1972): 923–930; on North Carolina, see W. Joseph May, "Therapeutic Abortion Experience in North Carolina . . ." *North Carolina Medical Journal* 32 (May 1971): 186–187; Takey Crist, "Abortion," *North Carolina Medical Journal* 32 (August 1971): 347–351; and J. F. Hulka, "The Abortion Explosion," *North Carolina Medical Journal* 33 (November 1972): 957–959; also see William B. Walker and Hulka, *Southern Medical Journal* 64 (April 1971): 441–445. With regard to a another reform statute, which took on effect July 1, 1970, also see Robert Bettis and Richard A. Brose, "Physician Attitudes on Abortion and the Kansas Abortion Law," *Journal of the Kansas Medical Society*, August 1971, pp. 344–349.

78. On Lamm's Colorado case, which he had been ready to file for several months, see Lamm to Lucas, 24 February, 28 July and 28 August 1970, Lucas Box 2; *New York Times*, 4 July 1970, p. 18; Lamm Interview with Garrow; and *Doe v. Dunbar*, 320 F. Supp. 1297 (D. Colo.), 22 December 1970 (denying defendants' motion to dismiss). Also see Lamm and Steven G. Davison, "Abortion Reform," *Yale Review of Law and Social Action* 1 (Spring 1971): 55–63. On the Pennsylvania decision, *Commonwealth v. Barry G. Page*, 6 *Centre County Legal Journal* 127 (Centre County Ct. C.P. #353), 23 July 1970 (and supplemental opinions at 6 *CCLJ* 147 and 285), also see Mitchell F. Sikora, Jr., "Abortion: An Environmental Convenience or a Constitutional Right?," *Environmental Affairs* 1 (November 1971): 469–527, at 486, and especially Patricia G. Miller, *The Worst of Times* (New York: HarperCollins, 1993), pp. 268–283. On other less unusual Pennsylvania developments, see *Berman v. Duggan*, 119 *Pittsburgh Legal Journal* 226 and 242 (Allegheny County Ct. C.P.), 6 January 1971; *New York Times*, 7 January 1971, p. 43; Gerald Malick, "Thoughts on the Legalization of Abortion," *Pennsylvania Medicine* 74 (March 1971): 39; Dane S. Wert, "Abortion," *Pennsylvania Medicine* 74 (May 1971): 59–62; *Commonwealth v. Chester S. Beall*, Allegheny County Ct. C.P., #618, 19 October 1971; and Lois G. Forer, "The Case for Abortion on Demand," *Pennsylvania Bar Association Quarterly* 43 (January 1972): 203–211.

Also note two Oklahoma actions. On the pro se declaratory judgment case of *W. J. Bryan*

Henrie v. *G. T. Blankenship*, U.S.D.C. N.D. Okla., #70-C-211, 6 July 1970, see *Tulsa Tribune*, 7 July 1970, pp. A1, A4, and 1 August 1970; Lucas to A. F. Ringold, 12 August 1970, and Henrie to Lucas, 17 August 1970, Lucas Box 21; also see *Osteopathic Physician*, July 1970, pp. 54–57, and *SHA Newsletter* Vol. 6, #4 (Winter 1970–1971). Less than two years later, Dr. Henrie passed away at the age of seventy-six. See *Tulsa Daily World*, 13 May 1972. Regarding efforts to reverse a doctor's criminal abortion conviction in a case involving a woman's death, see O. A. Cargill, Jr., and Stanley Pierce, "Brief of Plaintiff in Error," *Virgil Ray Jobe* v. *State of Oklahoma*, Okla. Ct. Crim. App., #A15732, August 1970, 89pp., and Lucas to Cargill, 12 August 1970, Lucas Box 25; *Oklahoma City Times*, 24 November 1970; *Tulsa Tribune*, 17 December 1970. Also see generally Charles L. Pain, *Oklahoma Law Review* 24 (May 1971): 243–251.

79. *Baird* v. *Eisenstadt*, 429 F.2d 1398, 1401–1402; *New York Times*, 12 July 1970, p. E14. For a critique of the circuit court panel's opinion, see "Due Process of Law—Privacy," *Harvard Law Review* 84 (April 1971): 1525–1535. Also see *Sturgis* v. *Attorney General*, 260 N.E.2d 687, 690, a 5 to 2 29 June 1970 Massachusetts Supreme Judicial Court decision *upholding* the very same statute against a declaratory judgment challenge brought by several physicians. The *Sturgis* majority had asserted that "the *Griswold* case, as the Attorney General argues, affirmed 'beyond doubt' the right of the State of Connecticut to enact statutes regulating the private sexual lives of single persons, stating that the discouraging of extramarital relations is 'admittedly a legitimate subject of state concern.'" 381 U.S. 479, 498 (Goldberg, J., concurring). Also see Scott M. Lewis, *Ohio State Law Journal* 32 (1971): 221–226.

80. *Doe* v. *Bolton*, 319 F. Supp. 1048, 1054–55, 1056 (N.D. Ga.), 31 July 1970; Garrow conversations with Sidney O. Smith, Jr., and Jeffrey R. Nickerson. Notes on the panel decision in *Doe* include John L. Moore, Jr., *Journal of the Medical Association of Georgia* 59 (October 1970): 402–404; and Sylvia G. Haywood, *Mercer Law Review* 22 (Winter 1971): 461–466.

81. *Atlanta Journal*, 31 July 1970, p. 1, 20 and 25 August 1970; *Atlanta Constitution*, 1, 20 and 26 August 1970, p. B2; *Atlanta Journal-Constitution*, 2 August 1970; Judith Bourne to Anne Treseder, 31 August 1970, NARAL Box 2; Roger W. Rochat et al., "An Epidemiological Analysis of Abortion in Georgia," *American Journal of Public Health* 61 (March 1971): 543–552; Malcolm G. Freeman and William L. Graves, "Physician Attitudes Toward Hospital Abortion in Georgia—1970," *Journal of the Medical Association of Georgia* 59 (December 1970): 437–446; *Atlanta Journal*, 6 January 1971, p. B10; John L. Moore, Jr., "The Abortion Survey," *Journal of the Medical Association of Georgia* 59 (December 1970): 459–460; Garrow conversations with Margie Hames, Judith [Bourne] Rooks, Peter Bourne, Robert A. Hatcher, Tobi Schwartz, Dorothy T. Beasley, and Arthur K. Bolton.

82. *Rosen* v. *Louisiana State Board of Medical Examiners*, 318 F. Supp. 1217, 1223, 1231, 1234–35 (E.D. La.), 7 August 1970; *New York Times*, 12 August 1970, p. 42; Lucas, "Memorandum of Telephone Call," 14 August 1970, Lucas Box 7; Lucas to David S. Dolowitz, 2 December 1970, Lucas Box 24 ("For my part, I agree with . . . Cassibry that *Griswold* stands for something more than the right to use a Trojan"). Ainsworth's concluding reference concerning fundamentality is to Justice Cardozo's opinion for the Court in *Snyder* v. *Massachusetts*, 291 U.S. 97, 105 (1934). On Ainsworth, see Read and McGough, *Let Them Be Judged*, pp. 179–180, and Couch, *A History of the Fifth Circuit, 1891–1981*, pp. 134–135. Cassibry's dissent further noted, with regard to the state—and Ainsworth's—contention that the purpose of an antiabortion statute was to protect fetal life, that if that were true, it was thus incongruous that the Louisiana law also penalized attempted abortions upon women who were not actually pregnant, and where hence no fetal "life" was at risk. Cassibry also rhetorically asked, with regard to the state practice of prosecuting abortion providers, but not abortion recipients: "Suppose, for example, that A hires B to kill C; would the State grant A immunity in exchange for his testimony against B? If abortion is truly regarded as the destruction of human life, the mother is the principal criminal; the 'abortionist' is merely her paid executioner. If the State really means to protect the life of the fetus why does it fail to deter the person most directly responsible for taking it?" 318 F. Supp. at 1241–42.

83. On the eventual New Orleans appeal, see Benjamin E. Smith, "Jurisdictional Statement,"

Rosen v. *Louisiana State Board of Medical Examiners,* U.S.S.C., O.T. 1970, #1010, 19 November 1970; *New York Times,* 28 November 1970, p. 56; and Lucas to Smith, 4 February 1971. On the 10 September dismissal of *Rodgers* v. *Danforth,* see Charlotte P. Thayer et al., "Jurisdictional Statement," *Rodgers* v. *Danforth,* U.S.S.C., O.T. 1970, #1402, n.d. [8 February 1971], 23pp., Lucas to Thayer, 23 October 1970, and Frank Susman et al. to "Dear Plaintiff," 25 November 1970, Lucas Box 15.

On the Utah suit, *Doe* v. *Rampton,* filed 8 September 1970 by David S. "Sandy" Dolowitz, see Dolowitz, "Complaint for Three-Judge Court, Declaratory Judgment and Injunctive Relief," *Doe* v. *Rampton,* U.S.D.C. D. Utah, #C-234, 8pp., Chief Judge Willis W. Ritter's 14 September 1970 temporary restraining order concluding that "the plaintiff is likely to prevail on the merits," Dolowitz's amended complaint of 16 September, Alan Charles to Dolowitz, 18 September 1970, Lucas to Dolowitz, 22 October 1970, and Dolowitz to Lucas, 28 October 1970, Lucas Box 24.

On the Pennsylvania case, filed 14 September 1970, see *Phyllis R. Ryan et al.* v. *Arlen Specter,* 321 F. Supp. 1109 (E.D. Pa.), 22 January 1971 (denying defendant's motion to dismiss), and *Ryan* v. *Specter,* 332 F. Supp. 26 (E.D. Pa.), 27 August 1971 (abstaining from any decision until the Pennsylvania Supreme Court ruled upon the appeal of *Commonwealth* v. *Page,* discussed at note 78 above). On the Ohio case of *A. H. Steinberg, M.D., et al.* v. *Paul Brown,* filed by Toledo attorney Gerald B. Lackey on 10 October, see Lackey, "Complaint for Declaratory and Injunctive Relief," *Steinberg* v. *Brown,* U.S.D.C. N.D. Ohio, #C-70-289, Leslie L. Knowlton to Lucas, 14 October 1970, and Lucas to Knowlton, 20 October 1970, Lucas Box 21.

On Massachusetts, see Lucas to Laura Rasmussen, 21 October 1970, Lucas Box 25; also see Melvin L. Taylor, "Abortion Law in Massachusetts," *New England Journal of Medicine* 283 (10 September 1970): 602, and Taylor, "A Medical Case for Abortion Liberalization," *Archives of Surgery* 102 (March 1971): 235.

Also note two nonphysician criminal decisions, *State* v. *Abodeely,* 179 N.W.2d 347 (2 September 1970), [appeal dismissed, 402 U.S. 936, 3 May 1971], in which the Iowa Supreme Court volunteered that a doctor would be entitled to a good faith presumption, and *Spears* v. *State of Mississippi,* 241 So.2d 148 (9 November 1970) and 257 S.2d 876 (Miss. Sup. Ct.), 24 January 1972, cert. denied 409 U.S. 1106; *Spears* v. *State,* 278 So.2d 443 (Miss. Sup. Ct.), 21 May 1973. On *Abodeely,* also see Bruce W. Foudree, *Drake Law Review* 20 (June 1971): 666–673.

84. Alfred Walker to Martin F. McKernan (National Right to Life Committee), 29 June 1970, and McKernan to Walker, 2 July 1970, Texas AG File 70–308; Lee Gidding to Laura Maggi, 30 June 1970, NARAL Box 5; Weddington Interview with Cheek, p. 19; Lucas to Counsel Involved in Federal Litigation Against State Abortion Statutes, "Developments in Federal Jurisdiction," 3 July 1970, 4pp., Lucas Box 24; Tolle, "Notice of Appeal," 9 July 1970, Bruner, "Notice of Appeal," 23 July 1970, Coffee, "Notice of Appeal," 24 July 1970, *Roe* v. *Wade,* #3–3690; *Dallas Times Herald,* 18 July 1970; Robert C. Flowers, "Notice of Appeal to the Supreme Court," 17 August 1970, Coffee and Bruner, "Notice of Appeal," 17 August 1970, *Roe* v. *Wade,* #3–3690; [Lucas], "Memorandum of Telephone Call, August 18, 1970, 4PM, to Linda Coffee," Lucas Box 22; Tolle to Jay Floyd, 17 September 1970, Texas AG File 70–308; Garrow conversations with Roy Lucas, Linda Coffee, Sarah Weddington, Roy Merrill, Fred Bruner, John Tolle, and Jay Floyd. Also see Lucas's comments in "Abortion: Litigative and Legislative Processes," *Human Rights* 1 (July 1971): 23–53, an edited transcript of an August 1970 American Bar Association panel discussion, and Lucas in the *Miami Herald,* 14 July 1970, p. A16. With regard to the 1970 Supreme Court decisions concerning jurisdiction of direct appeals, see *Gunn* v. *University Committee to End the War,* 399 U.S. 383, *Mitchell* v. *Donovan,* 398 U.S. 427, *Rockefeller* v. *Catholic Medical Center,* 397 U.S. 820, and *Goldstein* v. *Cox,* 396 U.S. 471. When she filed the notice of appeal to the Supreme Court, Coffee told reporters "We are appealing to both courts. We are not sure where we belong. Because of recent Supreme Court decisions, it's a little unclear where the jurisdiction is." *Dallas Morning News,* 18 August 1970, p. D1, *Dallas Times-Herald* and *Austin American-Statesman,* 18 August 1970.

In another immediate post-*Roe* development, a black Texas physician in jail because of a criminal abortion charge that led to his parole on a drunken driving conviction being revoked, Dr. W. B. D. Cooper, unsuccessfully filed a habeas corpus petition seeking release on account of the Dallas panel's declaratory ruling. See *Cooper* v. *State*, 447 S.W.2d 179 (Tex. Ct. Crim. App.), 3 December 1969; Cooper, "Application," 29 June [filed 7 July] 1970, and Charles E. and Barbara S. Benson, "Petition for Writ of Certiorari," *Cooper* v. *Beto*, U.S.S.C., O.T. 1970, #893, 23 October 1970, National Archives RG 267, Box 10303; *Dallas Morning News*, 10 July 1970, p. D4; Charles Benson to Lucas, 5 October 1970, and Lucas to Benson, 9 October 1970, Lucas Box 22; *Lubbock Avalanche-Journal*, 22 October 1970, p. E11; *Cooper* v. *Beto*, 400 U.S. 1021 (cert. denied), 25 January 1971.

85. Lucas to Savage, 26 August 1970 ("They now want me to handle the appeal"), Savage to Lucas, 8 September 1970, Lucas Box 22; *Dallas Morning News*, 12 and 19 July 1970; *Fort Worth Star-Telegram*, 19 July 1970, p. A21, 26 July 1970, pp. F1, F9, 27 August 1970; Patricia White to NARAL, 14 August and n.d. [c.10 September] 1970, NARAL Box 5; *Dallas Times-Herald*, 23 August 1970, p. A15; AEC-D Minutes, 26 August 1970, Whitehill Papers; *Houston Chronicle*, 30 August and 16 October 1970; Savage, "Report of Special Committee on Abortion Laws in Texas," 19 September 1970, 2pp., Whitehill Papers; Miriam Kass, *Houston Post*, 27, 28, 29, and 30 September and 1 and 2 October 1970, p. A1; Marjorie Clapp, *San Antonio Light*, 27, 28, 29, and 30 September 1970, p. 1, 1 and 2 October 1970; Pat White to Ginny Whitehill, 2 October 1970, and AEC-D flyer, "Have you ever really *studied* Abortion?" ("A woman has a fundamental right to decide when to bear a child"), n.d., Whitehill Papers; *Dallas Morning News*, 8 October 1970, p. C1; Garrow conversations with Norma McCorvey; Marsha King to Roy Lucas, 5 July 1971 ("My reaction was again one of dread, terror and the helpless feeling that my body and my life had been removed from my control and something terrible was wrong. Again, I felt as if I had discovered I had cancer"), Lucas Box 22. Also note both Roy Merrill's 31 August 1970 "Form for Appearance of Counsel" for the Fifth Circuit (explicitly listing Lucas as lead counsel), and Merrill to Tolle, Flowers, Weddington and Coffee, 1 September 1970 (giving formal notification that Lucas is now an attorney of record for Dr. Hallford), Lucas Box 22.

86. Lucas et al., "Jurisdictional Statement," *Roe et al.* v. *Wade*, U.S.S.C., O.T. 1970, #808, esp. pp. 10, 13–16; 39 *U.S. Law Week* 3151; Lucas to Edward W. Wadsworth (CCA5), 8 September 1970, and Wadsworth to Lucas, 11 September 1970, Lucas Box 22 and Texas AG File 70–308; Roy Merrill to Lucas, 5 October 1970, and Lucas to Hugh Savage, 7 October 1970, Lucas Box 22; Lucas, "Motion to Hold Appeal in Abeyance," *Wade* v. *Roe*, 5th Cir., #30329, 9 October 1970; Tolle, "Appellant's Motion in Opposition to Motion to Hold Appeal in Abeyance," *Wade* v. *Roe*, 5th Cir., #30329, 20 October 1970 [motion granted 28 October 1970]; *Dallas Morning News*, 12 October 1970, p. A10; [Henry Wade to Jim Clark], "Status on Appeal—Jane Roe v. Henry Wade," n.d. [14 October 1970], Clark Papers; Lucas to Tolle, and to Robert C. Flowers, 23 October 1970, Lucas Box 22 and Texas AG File 70–308; *Dallas Times-Herald*, 25 October 1970; Floyd to E. Robert Seaver, 2 November 1970, Floyd, "Reply to Jurisdictional Statement," *Roe* v. *Wade*, U.S.S.C., O.T. 1970, #808, 5 November 1970, National Archives RG 267, Box 9.

87. *Dallas Morning News*, 10 October 1970, p. D5, 15 November 1970, pp. A29, E1, 16 November 1970, p. C8, 17 November 1970, p. C1, 18 November 1970, p. C2, 19 November 1970, p. C3; *Dallas Times-Herald*, 21 October 1970, pp. 21, 24, 1 April 1971, pp. 25, 29; Patricia White to Savage, 23 October 1970, White to Texas Abortion Coalition Members, "Report on November Conference," n.d. [c.15 November 1970], "Minutes of Abortion Coalition Steering Committee," 12 December 1970, Whitehill Papers; *The Rag*, 14 December 1970, p. 4; AEC-D to Morris Harrell, n.d. [c.December 1970], Whitehill and White to Page Keeton, 15 December 1970, AEC-D *Newsletter*, 15 December 1970, Debbie Leonard to Weddington and Whitehill, 18 December 1970, Weddington and Whitehill to TAC Steering Committee Members, 19 December 1970, Evelyn Sell to Whitehill, 19 December 1970, Whitehill to TMA Abortion Committee Members, 23 December 1970, Miriam Kass to Whitehill, 24 December 1970, Whitehill Papers; *Second Coming* Vol. 1, #1 (1 December

1970), pp. 4–5, #2 (11 December 1970), p. 5; *Houston Chronicle*, 6 and 16 December 1970; Garrow conversations with J. Claude Evans, Virginia Whitehill, Judy Smith, Barbara Hines, and Beatrice Vogel. Also see Carol Joffe, "Portraits of Three 'Physicians of Conscience': Abortion Before Legalization in the United States," *Journal of the History of Sexuality* 2 (July 1991): 46–67, regarding the Texas provider whom she calls "David Bennett."

88. Garrow conversations with Margie Hames, Tobi Schwartz, Elizabeth Rindskopf, Gale Siegel Messerman, Reber Boult, Charles Morgan and Roy Lucas; Lucas to Hames, 18 and 28 August 1970, Hames Papers.

89. Garrow conversations with Roy Lucas, Morris Dees, Douglas J. Kramer, Richard G. Singer, Nicholas W. Danforth, Brian L. Sullivan, and Larry Lader; *New York Times*, 22 March 1970, p. 30; Lucas to Lader, 15 April 1970, Lucas Box 25; Lucas to IRS, 8 September 1970, CCTA Box 1; Lucas to Robert L. Loeb, 14 September 1970, Lucas Box 25; NARAL Annual Meeting Minutes, 27–28 September 1970, Boulder, CO, NARAL I-3; Lucas to Richard Lamm, 29 September 1970, Lucas Box 2; Lucas to Carol Crawford, 8 October 1970, Lucas to Lader, 23 October 1970, "James Madison Constitutional Law Institute Income & Expenses, Fifteen Months Ended Oct. 31, 1970," David S. Greenspan to Dees, 1 December 1970, Lucas to Nat Lehrman, and to Bob Hall, 6 December 1970, Lucas to Samuel Landfather, 16 December 1970, Lucas to Greenspan et al., 19 December 1970, Lucas to Hall, 28 December 1970, Lucas to Stewart Mott, 29 December 1970, Lucas Box 25; Lucas Interview with Vose. Also see *New York Times*, 27 May 1970, p. 33.

90. Lucas to Alan Charles, 29 August 1970, Lucas to Allan C. Barnes, 7 September 1970, Lucas Box 25.

91. *Atlanta Journal*, 19, 28, and 29 September 1970, 5 October 1970, pp. A1, A16, 15 October 1970, 16 November 1970; *Atlanta Journal-Constitution*, 4 October 1970, pp. C1, C12, 11 October 1970; Hames, "Petition of Jane Roe to Intervene" and "Motion of Jane Roe for Temporary Restraining Order," *Doe* v. *Bolton*, #13676, 15 September 1970, Hames, "Memorandum in Support of the Petition of Jane Roe to Intervene as Plaintiff and to Clarify and Enforce the Court's Opinion of July 31," *Doe* v. *Bolton*, #13676, 6 October 1970, 13pp., *Doe* Case File 74A–2025, Box 16; Maureen "Filler," "Affidavit," 1 October 1970, *Polly Poe* v. *Fulton-DeKalb Hospital Authority*, U.S.D.C. N.D. Ga., #14223, 7 October 1970, Hames Papers; Supplemental Opinion, *Doe* v. *Bolton*, 319 F. Supp. 1048, 1056, 14 October 1970; *Atlanta Constitution*, 16 October 1970; Trammell Vickery to Judge Sidney O. Smith, 9 October 1970, and Hames to Smith, 20 October 1970, Hames Papers; *Atlanta Constitution*, 22 December 1970, p. A1, 23 December 1970, p. A2, 30 December 1970, p. A4; Ann Woolner, "'I am Mary Doe,'" *Fulton County Daily Report*, 9 February 1989, pp. 1, 3–7; Hames et al., "Jurisdictional Statement," *Doe* v. *Bolton*, U.S.S.C., O.T. 1970, #971, 14 November 1970, 25pp.; Bolton et al., "Motion to Dismiss," *Doe* v. *Bolton*, 28 December 1970, 19pp.; Garrow conversations with Margie Hames, Reber Boult, Elizabeth Rindskopf, Tobi Schwartz, and Sandra [Bensing] Cano.

92. *Babbitz* v. *McCann*, 312 F. Supp. 725 (E.D. Wis.), 11 May 1970; *New York Times*, 23 June 1970, p. 38, 13 October 1970, p. 26, 19 November 1970, p. 58; Lucas to Counsel Involved in Federal Litigation Against State Abortion Statutes, "Developments in Federal Jurisdiction," 3 July 1970, and Lucas annotation of Clifford K. Meldman to Nathaniel D. Rothstein, 10 July 1970, Lucas Box 24; Lucas to Hugh Savage, 26 August 1970, Lucas Box 22; *McCann* v. *Babbitz*, 400 U.S. 1 (12 October 1970); *Milwaukee Journal*, 28 October 1970, pp. 1, 5, 29 October 1970, pp. 1, 4, 18 November 1970, pp. 1, 10; *Babbitz* v. *McCann*, 320 F. Supp. 219 (E.D. Wis.), 18 November 1970; *Milwaukee Sentinel*, 19 November 1970, p. 8, 1 December 1970, 16 January 1971; *McCann* v. *Kerner*, 436 F.2d 1342 (7th Cir.), 14 January 1971; Garrow conversations with Roy Lucas and Joseph L. Nellis. Also see Lee Gidding, "Executive Director's Report," 30 October 1970, NARAL Box 1; *Minneapolis Tribune*, 21 December 1970, pp. 1, 7; and Joseph L. Nellis, "The Lesson of Wisconsin" (unpublished paper, 12 May 1972), 5pp., NARAL I-12.

93. Byron N. Fujita and Nathaniel N. Wagner, "Referendum 20—Abortion Reform in Washington State," in Howard J. and Joy D. Osofsky, eds., *The Abortion Experience*, pp.

232–260; Robert G. Morrison, "Choice in Washington: The Politics of Liberalized Abortion" (unpublished M.A. thesis, University of Virginia, 1982), pp. 101–150, at 130; Archbishop Thomas A. Connolly letters to "Reverend and dear Father," 14 April 1970, 30 April 1970, and 29 September 1970, YWCA/UWash Papers Boxes 2 and 3; *Seattle Post-Intelligencer*, 6 September 1970, p. 8, 4 November 1970, p. 2; *Seattle Times*, 27 September 1970, p. A20; *New York Times*, 25 October 1970, p. 79, 4 November 1970, p. 35; *Daily Olympian*, 27 October 1970. Also see Mike Ferry et al., "Abortion as an Election Issue," *ZPG National Reporter*, January 1971, pp. 12–15; Ricky L. Welborn, *North Carolina Law Review* 49 (June 1971): 487–502, at 502; and Laurie McCutcheon and Nathaniel Wagner, "The People, Religion, and Abortion Reform in Washington State," *ZPG National Reporter*, July 1971, pp. 5–6. For other contemporaneous yet more general Roman Catholic expressions of opposition to abortion liberalization, see *New York Times*, 13 October 1970, p. 2, 14 October 1970, p. 47, 6 December 1970, p. 33, 28 December 1970, p. 63, and 3 January 1971, p. 36.

94. *New York Times*, 29 November 1970, p. 52. Also see *Journal of the American Medical Association* 215 (11 January 1971): 286.

95. Lucas to Fred Graham, 22 July 1970, Lucas Box 12; Lucas to Chris Tietze, 14 September 1970, Lucas Box 25; Lucas et al., "Jurisdictional Statement," *Hodgson* v. *Randall*, U.S.S.C., O.T. 1970, #728, 21 [29] September 1970, 40pp., Lucas et al., "Jurisdictional Statement," *Hodgson* v. *Minnesota*, U.S.S.C., O.T. 1970, #729, 21 September [5 October] 1970, 31pp., Lucas, "Application for Partial Stay," *Hodgson* v. *Randall*, #728, 1 [2] October 1970, 13pp., at p. 6, Lucas to Justice Harry A. Blackmun, 2 November 1970, Lucas, "Application for Stay," *Hodgson* v. *Minnesota*, #729, 3 November 1970, National Archives, RG 267, Boxes 10,269 and 10,270; Hodgson to Lucas, 28 September 1970, Lucas Box 13; E. Robert Seaver to Lucas, 19 October and 6 November 1970, Lucas to William Randall, and to John R. Kenefick, 23 October 1970, Lucas Box 12; Transcript of Hearing, 5 November 1970, Lucas Box 13; *New York Times*, 7 November 1970, p. 14, 15 November 1970, p. 75, 20 November 1970, p. 19, 21 November 1970, p. 15; *St. Paul Dispatch*, 12 November 1970, pp. 1, 14, 13 November 1970, 17 November 1970; *Minneapolis Star*, 12, 13, 14, and 17 November 1970, 18 November 1970, p. A23, 19 and 21 November 1970; *Minneapolis Tribune*, 13, 17, 18, and 20 November 1970; *St. Paul Pioneer Press*, 13, 14, and 18 November 1970; Irvin M. Cushner to Lucas, 1 December 1970, Stewart R. Perry to Hodgson, 10 March 1971, Lucas Box 13; Peter Irons, *The Courage of Their Convictions* (New York: Free Press, 1988), pp. 258–261; Garrow conversations with Jane E. Hodgson and Roy Lucas.

96. Lucas to ASA Executive Committee, "Amicus Brief in *Vuitch* v. *Maryland*," n.d. [c.2 April 1970], Guttmacher Papers and Lucas Box 9; Lucas, "To Whom It May Concern, n.d. [c.10 May 1970], Lucas to Clerk's Office, Maryland Court of Special Appeals, 30 July 1970, Lucas Box 9; Lucas to Bob Hall, 18 August 1980, Lucas Box 8; M. William Adelson et al., "Brief of Appellant," *Vuitch* v. *State*, Md. Ct. Spec. App., September Term 1970, #32, n.d., 25pp.; Lucas et al., "Brief of Amici Curiae Association for the Study of Abortion," *Vuitch* v. *State*, Md. Ct. Spec. App., September Term 1970, #32, 15 August 1970, 44pp.; Lucas to Michael Rodak, 22 July 1970, and Lucas to E. P. Cullinan, 2 September 1970, *U.S.* v. *Vuitch* File, U.S.S.C., O.T. 1970, #84, National Archives, RG 267, Box 10088; *Washington Star*, 9 September 1970; Garrow conversations with Roy Lucas and Milan Vuitch.

97. Sitnick, Nellis, and Lucas, "Brief for Milan M. Vuitch, M.D.," *U.S.* v. *Vuitch*, U.S.S.C., O.T. 1970, #84, 29 September 1970, 70pp., pp. 40–41, 43, 51.

Generally unremarkable amicus briefs in *Vuitch* included a substantive submission by Marilyn Rose and Alan Charles from Los Angeles, and considerably more modest ones (ten to fourteen pages) by the ACLU (Ralph Temple et al., "Brief for Amici Curiae American Civil Liberties Union," 10 September 1970, 10pp.), Sylvia S. Ellison, and Lola Boswell in support of the Gesell ruling. Amicus submissions urging reversal of Gesell were filed by Alfred L. Scanlan et al. ("Brief of Dr. William F. Colliton, Jr., et al. . . ." 14 July 1970, 53pp.), Dennis J. Horan ("Brief of Dr. Bart Heffernan . . ." 14 July 1970, 46pp.), David W. Louisell, and Robert L. Sassone. Also see "DCB" [Dennis C. Brown], *U.S.* v. *Vuitch*, 23 September 1970, Douglas Box 1507.

Per Lucas's *Vuitch* Supreme Court brief at 11, also see *Mindel* v. *U.S. Civil Service Commission*, 312 F. Supp. 485 (N.D. Cal.), 30 March 1970, where the termination of a postal worker for "immoral conduct" because he was living with a woman to whom he was not married was found to violate "his right to privacy as guaranteed by the 9th Amendment" and thus overturned.

98. *Middletown* [Ohio] *Journal*, 11 November 1970; Vuitch, "Motion for Leave to Argue *Pro Hac Vice*," 3 November 1970, *Vuitch* File, Box 10088; [Lucas A. Powe], *U.S.* v. *Vuitch*, #84, 14 November 1970, Douglas Box 1507; Sitnick and Nellis to Lucas, 16 November 1970, 4pp., Hames Papers; Sitnick and Nellis to Seaver, 20 November 1970, Cullinan to Nellis and Sitnick, 20 November 1970, Nellis to Cullinan, 23 November 1970, Sitnick and Nellis, "Response to Appellee's Motion *Pro Hac Vice*," 24 November 1970, 5pp., Vuitch to Clerk, U.S.S.C., 24 November 1970, Nellis to Cullinan, 24 November 1970, *Vuitch* File, Box 10088; Garrow conversations with Roy Lucas, Joseph L. Nellis, Milan Vuitch, and Florence "Lee" Vuitch.

99. Cullinan to Sitnick, Nellis and Lucas, 24 November 1970, *Vuitch* File, Box 10088; Vuitch to Dorsen, 30 November 1970, Dorsen to Vuitch, 7 and 15 December 1970, Dorsen Papers; Dorsen to Cullinan, 22 December 1970, Nellis to Cullinan, 30 December 1970, *Vuitch* File, Box 10088; *Vuitch* v. *State*, 10 Md. App. 389, 271 A.2d 371, 374, 376 (Md. Ct. Spec. App.), 24 November 1970; Garrow conversations with Roy Lucas, Joseph L. Nellis, Milan Vuitch, Florence "Lee" Vuitch, and Norman Dorsen.

100. *Steinberg* v. *Brown*, 321 F. Supp. 741, 746–747, 748, 752, 759 (N.D. Ohio), 18 December 1970; Gerald B. Lackey to Lucas, 31 December 1970, Lucas Box 21.

101. *Newark Star-Ledger*, 15 December 1970, pp. 1, 10; *Woodbridge News Tribune*, 15 December 1970, pp. 1, 9; *Trentonian*, 15 December 1970, p. 3; Stearns Interview with Garrow; Lucas to Hugh Savage, 2 December 1970, Lucas Box 22; Lucas to Sam Landfather, 16 December 1970, Lucas Box 25.

102. C. Thomas Dienes, *Law, Politics, and Birth Control* (Urbana: University of Illinois Press, 1972), pp. 189–191; Bush to Mrs. Jim L. Hunter, 23 October 1970, Whitehill Papers; Elliot Silverstein, "From Comstockery Through Population Control: The Inevitability of Balancing," *North Carolina Central Law Journal* 6 (Fall 1974): 8–47, at 15; P.L. 91-662, 84 Stat. 1973 (8 January 1971). Also see Bush, "Foreword," in Phyllis T. Piotrow, *World Population Crisis: The United States Response* (New York: Praeger, 1973), p. vii.

CHAPTER EIGHT

1. Jane Hodgson to Roy Lucas, 28 September 1970, Lucas Box 13; Garrow conversations with Roy Lucas. The two standard biographies of Lyndon Johnson's ill-fated favorite justice are Bruce A. Murphy, *Fortas* (New York: William Morrow & Co., 1988), and Laura Kalman, *Abe Fortas* (New Haven: Yale University Press, 1990). Also see Robert Shogan, *A Question of Judgment: The Fortas Case and the Struggle for the Supreme Court* (Indianapolis: Bobbs-Merrill, 1972), and Neil D. McFeeley, *Appointment of Judges: The Johnson Presidency* (Austin: University of Texas Press, 1987), pp. 113–120. Perhaps surprisingly, neither Warren E. Burger nor Harry A. Blackmun have yet received any book-length biographical attention. On Burger, see Charles M. Lamb, "Chief Justice Warren E. Burger," in Lamb and Stephen C. Halpern, eds., *The Burger Court* (Urbana: University of Illinois Press, 1991), pp. 129–162, and the special symposium issue of *Oklahoma Law Review* 45 (Spring 1992): 1–168. On Blackmun, see especially Stephen L. Wasby, "Justice Harry A. Blackmun in the Burger Court," *Hamline Law Review* 11 (Summer 1988): 183–245; also see Note, "The Changing Social Vision of Justice Blackmun," *Harvard Law Review* 96 (January 1983): 717–736; Wasby, "Justice Harry A. Blackmun," in Lamb and Halpern, eds., *The Burger Court*, pp. 63–99; John A. Jenkins, "A Candid Talk With Justice Blackmun," *New York Times Magazine*, 20 February 1983, pp. 20–29, 57–66; the special symposium issue of *Hamline Law Review* 8 (January 1985); and David G. Savage, *Turning Right* (New York: John Wiley & Sons, 1992), pp. 234–238. On

Justice Marshall's earlier life, see Marshall's 1977 oral history interviews with Ed Edwin for the Columbia Oral History Program; Michael D. Davis and Hunter R. Clark, *Thurgood Marshall* (New York: Carol Publishing Group, 1992), Carl Rowan, *Dream Makers, Dream Breakers* (Boston: Little, Brown, 1993), and especially Richard Kluger, *Simple Justice* (New York: Alfred A. Knopf, 1976), esp. pp. 173–194 and 214–238. With regard to Marshall on the Supreme Court, see William J. Daniels, "Justice Thurgood Marshall," in Lamb and Halpern, eds., *The Burger Court*, pp. 212–237.

2. Garrow conversations with Roy Lucas, Norman Dorsen, and Joseph L. Nellis.

3. Transcript of Oral Argument, *U.S.* v. *Vuitch*, U.S.S.C., O.T. 1970, #84, 12 January 1971, 64pp., and Tape Recording of *Vuitch* Oral Argument, National Archives; "Arguments Before the Court: Abortion," *U.S. Law Week* 39 (19 January 1971): 3305–3307; *Washington Evening Star*, 12 January 1971; *Chicago Tribune*, 18 January 1971; "Arguments Heard," *Criminal Law Reporter* 8 (20 January 1971): 4120–4122; *Washington Post*, 13 January 1971, p. A5; *New York Times*, 13 January 1971, p. 45; Garrow conversations with Norman Dorsen, Joseph L. Nellis, Roy Lucas, Milan Vuitch and Cyril C. Means. While the transcript itself does not identify which justice asked a particular question, the tape recording of the argument is generally clear enough to allow most—though not all—particular questioners to be identified. The government's attorney, Samuel Huntington, should not be confused with a well-known political science scholar of the same name.

4. Means's comments of 23 January 1971 as cited in both Alan Charles and Susan Alexander, "Abortions for Poor and Nonwhite Women: A Denial of Equal Protection?," *Hastings Law Journal* 23 (November 1971): 147–169, at 159–160, and in Paul Marx's far from friendly reportage in *The Death Peddlers* (Collegeville, MN: Saint John's University Press, 1971), pp. 83–87; Lader in NARAL Executive Committee Minutes, 5 February 1971, NARAL Box 1; Dorsen to Vuitch, and to Lucas, 15 January 1971, Dorsen Papers; Dorsen remarks of early June 1971 in Sarah Lewit, ed., *Abortion Techniques and Services* (Amsterdam: Excerpta Medica, 1972), pp. 89–91; Garrow conversations with Norman Dorsen, Roy Lucas, Cyril C. Means, Joseph L. Nellis, and Larry Lader. Also see Lucas to Irv Cushner, 6 January 1971, Lucas Box 13, Florence Vuitch to Lucas, 14 January 1971, and Milan Vuitch to Lucas, 22 January 1971, Lucas Box 8. Dorsen's second case, argued January 14, was *Tate* v. *Short*, 401 U.S. 395 (2 March 1971), in which Dorsen prevailed unanimously. Also see "U.S. v. Vuitch," *Life*, 5 February 1971, p. 63.

5. Harlan, "Memorandum to the Conference," 14 January 1971, Harlan Box 427, Black Box 437, Brennan Box 236, Douglas Box 1507; Douglas Conference Notes, *U.S.* v. *Vuitch*, 15 January 1971, Douglas Box 1507; Brennan Conference Notes, *U.S.* v. *Vuitch*, O.T. 1970, #84, Box 417; Brennan Conference Lists, Boxes 224 and 226; Assignment List, 28 January 1971, Marshall Box 63; Douglas Notes, "No. 84," [17 February 1971], Douglas Box 1507; "1st Draft, RWS 2–9–71," 18pp., Black Box 437; Garrow conversations with Robert W. Spearman, L. A. Scott Powe, and Thomas Rowe. Also see David M. O'Brien, *Storm Center* (New York: W. W. Norton & Co., 1986), pp. 25–26, and Tinsley E. Yarbrough, *John Marshall Harlan* (New York: Oxford University Press, 1992), p. 314.

6. Brennan Docket Book sheets for *Hodgson* v. *Randall* (#728), *Hodgson* v. *Minnesota* (#729), *Roe* v. *Wade* (#808), *Doe* v. *Bolton* (#971), *Bolton* v. *Doe* (#973), *Rosen* v. *Louisiana State Board of Medical Examiners* (#1010), *Unborn Child of Mary Doe* v. *Mary Doe* (#6172), Brennan Boxes 417 and 419; Brennan Conference Lists, e.g., 8 January 1971, p. 17, Brennan Boxes 224 and 226; [Scott Powe], *Doe* v. *Wade*, 30 December 1970, and [Powe], *Doe* v. *Bolton*, 6 February 1971, Douglas Box 1589; Michael Rodak to Margie Hames, 31 March 1971, Hames Papers. On Jane Hodgson's cases, also see Roy Lucas to Lew Mondy, 23 December 1970 and 5 February 1971, and Mondy to Lucas, 13 January 1971, Lucas Box 13, and *St. Paul Pioneer Dispatch*, 22 January 1971, p. II-1.

7. *Doe* v. *Scott*, 321 F. Supp. 1385, 1388–1391, 1396 (N.D. Ill.), 29 January 1971; *New York Times*, 30 January 1971, p. 25, 2 February 1971, p. 41; *Wall Street Journal*, 1 February 1971, p. 3; *American Medical News*, 8 February 1971, p. 12; *Chicago Tribune*, 11 February 1971, p. 1; *Hanrahan* v. *Doe* Case File, U.S.S.C., O.T. 1970, #1522 and 1523, National Archives, RG 267, Box 34; *Playboy*, September 1971.

8. *Corkey* v. *Edwards*, 322 F. Supp. 1248, 1251–1252 (W.D.N.C.), 1 February 1971; *Rosen* v. *Louisiana State Board of Medical Examiners*, 318 F. Supp. 1217, 1223 (E.D. La.), 7 August 1970, as cited in chapter seven above at note 82. Also note two cases involving criminal abortion prosecutions, *State* v. *Austin L. Jamieson*, 206 Kan. 491, 480 P.2d 87 (Kan. Sup. Ct.), 23 January 1971, where a conviction was reversed because of a faulty information, and *Major* v. *Ferdon*, 325 F. Supp. 1141 (N.D. Cal.), 25 February 1971, where Dr. Robert A. Major unsuccessfully attempted to win federal court injunctive relief against pending state charges. Also see Lucas to Patricia A. Carson, 30 December 1970, Lucas Box 25, and Barbara A. Phillips to E. P. Stephenson, 24 and 25 February 1971, Lucas Box 1.

9. Lamm, "Therapeutic Abortion: The Role of State Government" and Packwood, "The Role of the Federal Government" [22–24 January 1971], *Clinical Obstetrics and Gynecology* 14 (December 1971): 1204–1207, at 1204–05, and 1212–1221, at 1213. Also see *Chicago Daily News*, 11 February 1971, pp. 1, 10, and the additional papers by S. Leon Israel, "The Liberation of Women from Unwanted Pregnancy," and Joseph Fletcher, "The Ethics of Abortion," *Clinical Obstetrics and Gynecology* 14 (December 1971): 1113–1123 and 1124–1129; see as well Marx, *The Death Peddlers*, esp. p. 118, an unfriendly observer at the January symposium who believed that the real problem involved "the *copulation* crisis."

10. Lamm to Whitehill, n.d. [c.6 January 1971], Whitehill Papers; Lamm, "Therapeutic Abortion: The Role of State Government" [22–24 January 1971], *Clinical Obstetrics and Gynecology* 14 (December 1971): 1204–1207, at 1205. On Montana, see Jenny Eichwald to Lee Gidding, 17 March 1971, NARAL Box 4 and Joan Uda to Ginny Whitehill, 30 April 1972, Whitehill Papers; on efforts to start a court case there, see John O'Connor to Lucas, 24 November 1970, William N. Jensen to Lucas, 3 January 1972, Lucas Box 25; and *Great Falls Tribune*, 19 May 1971. On New Mexico, see *Christian Science Monitor*, 3 March 1971. On Iowa, see Barbara Madden, "An Evaluation of the Defeat of the Abortion Issue in the Iowa House," n.d. [c.11 February 1971], [Gidding], "Iowa Vote," 12 February 1971, and Robert L. Webber to Gidding, 28 February 1971, NARAL Box 3; also see James C. Mohr, "Iowa's Abortion Battles of the Late 1960s and Early 1970s," *Annals of Iowa* 50 (Summer 1989): 63–89. On Minnesota, see *St. Paul Pioneer Press*, 23 February 1971, and Bob McCoy to Larry Lader, 14 April 1972, Lader Box 5; on Massachusetts, see *New York Times*, 8 April 1971, p. 50. Also see, with regard to Wyoming, Mai Kirkbride (of the Wyoming Council for the Medical Termination of Pregnancy) to ICMCA, 3 February 1971, ARAI 6–24.

11. On Georgia, see *Atlanta Constitution*, 2 and 23 March 1971; *Atlanta Journal*, 4 and 9 March 1971; Margie Hames to Virgil T. Smith, 2 March 1971, Hames Papers; Margaret A. Downie to Gidding, 29 March 1971, NARAL Box 2. On New York, see *New York Times*, 2 November 1970, pp. 1, 46, 22 November 1970, p. 60, 29 November 1970, p. IV-8, 13 December 1970, p. 66, 30 December 1970, p. 23, 4 January 1971, p. 31, 7 January 1971, p. 27, 22 January 1971, p. 24, 28 January 1971, p. 21, 11 February 1971, p. 38, 30 March 1971, p. 39, 31 March 1971, p. 39, 1 April 1971, pp. 1, 36, 2 April 1971, p. 1, 3 April 1971, pp. 26, 28, 30, 4 April 1971, pp. 1, 28, 33, 5 April 1971, p. 32, 7 April 1971, pp. 43, 54, 16 April 1971, p. 73; Gidding to Betty Friedan, "Threats to the 1970 New York Abortion Law," 9 November 1970, NARAL Box 4; Hall, "Realities of Abortion," *New York Times*, 13 February 1971, p. 27; Arlene Carmen to New York Times, 15 February 1971, NARAL Box 4; R. Bradlee Boal and Rosalyn Udow to "Dear Friend," 5 April 1971, and Udow, "Report of Activities," Committee for Legal Abortion, November 1970–June 1971, 21 June 1971, 6pp., Guttmacher Papers; *Newsweek*, 19 April 1971, pp. 129–131. Also see Hall in "Pregnancy Termination: The Impact of New Laws," *Journal of Reproductive Medicine* 6 (June 1971): 45–72.

12. Gidding to Ruth Steel, 13 November 1970, Lader Box 16; Peter J. Leahy, "The Anti-Abortion Movement" (unpublished Ph.D. dissertation, Syracuse University, 1975), pp. 33–38; Byrnes, *Catholic Bishops in American Politics*, p. 58; National Right to Life Committee, "Special Legal Report," March 1971, Texas AG File 70–308. The late February Supreme Court decisions, four in number, were *Younger* v. *Harris*, 401 U.S. 37, *Samuels* v. *Mackell*, 401 U.S. 66, *Boyle* v. *Landry*, 401 U.S. 77, and *Perez* v. *Ledesma*, 401 U.S. 82, all handed down on 23 February 1971. One antiabortion attorney, Dennis J. Horan, asserted that in the end the

Supreme Court would hold antiabortion statutes constitutional, while Roy Lucas called the outcome "a very close question" and one that might well turn on the concept of viability. "I think it's going to be close, but I'm optimistic." *American Medical News*, 19 April 1971, pp. 10–13. On the *Younger* cases, also see Philip B. Kurland, "1970 Term: Notes on the Emergence of the Burger Court," *Supreme Court Review* 1971 (Chicago: University of Chicago Press, 1971), pp. 265–322, at 293–297.

13. *Atlanta Constitution*, 2 March 1971; *Time*, 29 March 1971, pp. 70, 73; Gidding to Barbara Madden, 30 March 1971, NARAL Box 3. On Michigan, see [Gidding], "Michigan," 12 and 29 March 1971, NARAL Box 3; *Detroit Free Press*, 28 March 1971, pp. A3, A6, 30 March 1971, p. A8; George E. LaCroix to Lader, 20 April 1971, Lader Box 16; also see Ron Paul to Lucas, 19 December 1970, Lucas Box 12; Barbara Serena et al., "Attitudes Toward Michigan's Abortion Law," *Michigan Medicine*, April 1971, pp. 309–316; Clara Raven, "Testimony in Favor of Abortion Reform," *Woman Physician* 26 (November 1971): 584–586; and Era L. Hill and Johan W. Eliot, "Black Physicians' Experience with Abortion Requests and Opinion About Abortion Law Change in Michigan," *Journal of the National Medical Association* 64 (January 1972): 52–58.

14. Evelyn Sell to "Dear Friends," 11 January 1971, Linda Dunson to Whitehill, 15 January 1971, Whitehill Papers; Victoria Foe, "Considerations on Abortion," *Daily Texan*, 13 January 1971, p. 5; *Austin American-Statesman*, 17 and 31 January 1971; *Houston Post*, 17 and 31 January 1971; Weddington to Pat [White] et al., 21 January 1971, Whitehill Papers; Victoria Foe to Alan F. Guttmacher, 24 January 1971, Guttmacher Papers; *Second Coming*, Vol. 1, #3, 25 January 1971, p. 4, #4, 8 February 1971, p. 10; *Dallas Morning News*, 27 January 1971, 3 February 1971; *Dallas Times-Herald*, 27 January 1971; Burnis Cohen to Weddington, 7 February 1971, Whitehill Papers; *The Rag*, 8 February 1971, p. 5; Marian Faux, *Roe v. Wade* (New York: Macmillan, 1988), pp. 208–212; Frieda L. Werden, "Adventures of a Texas Feminist," in Daryl Janes, ed., *No Apologies: Texas Radicals Celebrate the '60s* (Austin: Eakin Press, 1992), pp. 191–210, at 202–203. On Senator Creighton, see his 1975 oral history with Ronald Marcello at North Texas State University.

15. Weddington to Lucas, n.d. [January 1971], Lucas Box 22; *Dallas Times-Herald*, 1 February 1971, p. B2, 18 February 1971, 11 and 12 March 1971; *Ft. Worth Star-Telegram*, 2 February 1971, pp. B1, B3; Doris Hensarling to Hugh Savage, 2 February 1971, Whitehill Papers; *San Antonio Light*, 17 February 1971; *Second Coming*, #5, 22 February 1971, pp. 3, 8, #6, 4 March 1971, p. 11; [Dallas] Abortion Education Committee *Newsletter*, n.d. [c.6 March 1971], Whitehill Papers; *Texas Senate Journal*, 10 March 1971, p. 383 (S.B. 553); *Austin American-Statesman*, 11 March 1971; *Dallas Morning News*, 11 March 1971, p. A5, 14 March 1971, p. A32; *Houston Chronicle*, 11 March 1971.

On the application by "Jean Poe" and attorney Sylvia Demarest to intervene in *Roe*, see *Dallas Times-Herald*, 25 November 1970; *Dallas Morning News*, 26 November 1970, p. B9; *Austin American-Statesman*, 26 November 1970, p. A29; W. M. Taylor, Jr., "Order," and Taylor, Goldberg, and Hughes, "Order Granting Plaintiffs' Motion to Withdraw Their Application for Further Relief," *Roe* v. *Wade*, 19 February 1971, Texas AG File 70–308.

16. *Dallas Times-Herald*, 16 March 1971, 24 March 1971, pp. 31, 34, 1 April 1971, pp. 25, 29, 13 and 14 April 1971; Whitehill et al. to Texas State Legislature, "Abortion Legislation," 18 March 1971, and Patricia White et al., "Dear Legislator," 24 March 1971, Whitehill Papers; *The Rag*, 22 [March] 1971, p. 14, 12 April 1971, p. 4; A. R. Schwartz to Whitehill, 22 March 1971, Whitehill Papers; *Second Coming*, Vol. 1, #7, 22 March 1971, p. 4, #8, 26 April 1971, p. 9; [Dallas] Abortion Education Committee *Newsletter* (2), n.d. [c.24 March and 6 April 1971], and "Abortion Hearing" outline, 29 March 1971, Whitehill Papers; *Amarillo Daily News*, 28 March 1971, pp. C11, C14, 30 March 1971; Lee Gidding to Texas Citizens for Abortion Education, 29 March 1971, NARAL Box 5; *Dallas Morning News*, 30 March 1971, p. D2, 14 April 1971, p. A4; *Houston Post*, 30 March 1971, pp. A1, A10, 14 April 1971; *Houston Chronicle*, 30 March and 14 April 1971; *Austin American-Statesman*, 30 March and 14 April 1971; *Ft. Worth Star-Telegram*, 31 March and 14 April 1971; *Galveston Daily News*, 4–8 April 1971; Whitehill to Lamm, 4 April 1971, and Lamm to "Dear Fellow Legislator," 8 April 1971,

Whitehill Papers; *Texas Senate Journal*, 13 April 1971, p. 642; Evans, "Abortion Law Reform is Inevitable—Even in Texas," *Christian Century*, 5 May 1971, pp. 548–549; Sarah Weddington, *A Question of Choice* (New York: G. P. Putnam's Sons, 1992), pp. 75–78.

17. *Batchelor* v. *Buchanan*, 401 U.S. 989, 29 March 1971; *Dallas Times-Herald*, 2 April 1971, pp. 1, 8; "An Open Letter from the Catholic Bishops of Texas on the Subject of Abortion," n.d. [15 April 1971], Whitehill Papers; *Houston Chronicle*, 16 April 1971; *Austin American-Statesman*, 20 April 1971, pp. 1, 6; *Dallas Morning News*, 20 April 1971; *Texas Catholic*, 24 April 1971, p. 1. Also see Harlan to Black, 15 March 1971, and Brennan to Black, 9 and 16 March 1971, Marshall Box 64. Three months later the Texas Court of Criminal Appeals reversed one of Alvin Buchanan's two trial court sodomy convictions but affirmed the other, and the U.S. Supreme Court subsequently denied McCluskey's petition that it review the remaining conviction. *Buchanan* v. *State*, 471 S.W.2d 401 (14 July 1971), *Buchanan* v. *Texas* [U.S.S.C., O.T. 1971, #5664], 405 U.S. 930 (22 February 1972). Also see *Dallas Morning News*, 6 August 1970, p. D1, 12 July 1971, p. D3; *Pruett* v. *State*, 463 S.W.2d 191 (Tex. Ct. Crim. App.), 25 November 1970, appeal dismissed for want of a substantial federal question, 402 U.S.902 (19 April 1971); and *Dawson* v. *Vance*, 329 F.Supp. 1320 (S.D. Tex.), 29 July 1971.

See as well *In re Labady*, 326 F. Supp. 924, 927 (S.D.N.Y.), 23 March 1971, a naturalization proceeding where a federal district judge cited *Griswold* and *Stanley* in holding that "it is now established that official inquiry into a person's private sexual habits does violence to his constitutionally protected zone of privacy." But see *Hughes* v. *State*, 287 A.2d 299, 305 (Md. Ct. Spec. App.), 16 February 1972, cert. denied 409 U.S. 1025 (20 November 1972); *Connor* v. *State*, 490 S.W.2d 114 (Ark. Sup. Ct.), 29 January 1973, appeal dismissed for want of a substantial federal question, 414 U.S. 991 (5 November 1973), and rehearing denied, 414 U.S. 1138 (7 January 1974), and *Connor* v. *Hutto*, 516 F.2d 853 (8th Cir.), 28 May 1975, as well as the additional cases cited in note 37 of chapter nine.

18. *The Rag*, 19 April 1971, p. 3; *Austin American-Statesman*, 23 May 1971; Garrow conversations with Judy Smith, Barbara Hines, Beatrice Vogel, Bob Breihan, J. Claude Evans and Emmett Herndon. For a study based upon 1971 interviews with 29 ministerial activists in Michigan, see Nanette J. Davis, "Clergy Abortion Brokers: A Transactional Analysis of Social Movement Development," *Sociological Focus* 6 (Fall 1973): 87–109.

19. Melinda Bart Schlesinger and Pauline B. Bart, "Collective Work and Self-Identity: Working in a Feminist Illegal Abortion Collective," in Frank Lindenfeld and Joyce Rothschild-Whitt, eds., *Workplace Democracy and Social Change* (Boston: Porter Sargent, 1982), pp. 139–153; Pauline B. Bart, "Seizing the Means of Reproduction: An Illegal Feminist Abortion Collective—How and Why It Worked," *Qualitative Sociology* 10 (Winter 1987): 339–357; Linnea Johnson, "Something Real: Jane and Me—Memories and Exhortations of a Feminist Ex-Abortionist" (unpublished essay, Chicago Historical Society, 1992), 27pp. On the one raid (May 3, 1972) in which seven "Jane" participants were arrested, see *Illinois Women's Abortion Coalition Newsletter*, n.d. [21 June 1972], CWLU Box 8; the charges were subsequently dropped in March, 1973. Also generally see Pauline Bart in Helen Roberts, ed., *Women, Health and Reproduction* (London: Routledge & Kegan Paul, 1981), pp. 109–128; Kathryn Pyne Parsons, "Moral Revolution," in Julia A. Sherman and Evelyn T. Beck, eds., *The Prism of Sex* (Madison: University of Wisconsin Press, 1979), pp. 189–227, at 204–211; "Just Call Jane," in Marlene G. Fried, ed., *From Abortion to Reproductive Freedom* (Boston: South End Press, 1990), pp. 93–100; Ninia Baehr, *Abortion Without Apology* (Boston: South End Press, 1990), pp. 25–30; Mary Kay Blakely, "Remembering Jane," *New York Times Magazine*, 23 September 1990, pp. 26, 78; Peter Broeman and Jeannette Meier, "Therapeutic Abortion Practices in Chicago Hospitals—Vagueness, Variation, and Violation of the Law," *Law and the Social Order* [Arizona State University] 1971, pp. 757–775; Suzanne Staggenborg, "Stability and Innovation in the Women's Movement: A Comparison of Two Movement Organizations," *Social Problems* 36 (February 1989): 75–92; and Staggenborg, *The Pro-Choice Movement* (New York: Oxford University Press, 1991), pp. 21–22, 39.

20. On the Massachusetts appeal, see Robert H. Quinn et al., "Jurisdictional Statement," *Thomas S. Eisenstadt* v. *William R. Baird*, U.S.S.C., O.T. 1970, #804, 5 October 1970, 10pp.; E. P.

Cullinan to Joseph J. Balliro, 5 January 1971, *Eisenstadt* Case File, #70–804, National Archives, RG 267, Box 8; Balliro, "Motion to Dismiss or Affirm," *Eisenstadt* v. *Baird*, #804, 3 February 1971; 39 *U.S. Law Week* 3367 (1 March 1971); *New York Times*, 2 March 1971, p. 22. Both Justice Brennan's and Justice Douglas's notations indicate that six justices— Marshall, White, Stewart, Harlan, Black, and Burger—voted in favor of hearing the appeal, while Justices Blackmun, Brennan, and Douglas voted simply to affirm the First Circuit's decision. See Brennan Docket Book, O.T. 1970, #804, Brennan Box 417; also see [Scott Powe], *Eisenstadt* v. *Baird*, 30 December 1970 and 13 February 1971, Douglas Box 1543.

21. See [Yale Law Women's Association], *Women vs. Connecticut*, an undated sixteen-page pamphlet [c.October 1970]; Lucas to Ann C. Hill, 26 October 1970, Lucas Box 25; *Hartford Times*, 20 November 1970, pp. B1, B8, 17 January 1971, 13 April 1971, 16 May 1971, pp. A1, A7; *Hartford Courant*, 9 January and 13 April 1971; *Waterbury American*, 26 January 1971; "Dear Doctor" letter, n.d., Emerson Box 10, whose signatories include Tom Emerson, Ann C. Hill, and Hillary Rodham; *Yale Daily News*, 15 February 1971, pp. 1, 6; *New Haven Register*, 29 January and 1 March 1971; *New York Times*, 3 March 1971, p. 40, 8 April 1971, p. 83; Marilyn Seichter Interview with Hubbell; and Nancy Stearns Interview with Garrow. Rodham was among the students in Emerson's spring 1971 Political and Civil Rights course. See *The Nation*, 2 November 1992, p. 492.

22. *Burlington Free Press*, 17 April 1971, p. 3, 18 June 1971, p. 14; Higgins, "The Vermont Abortion Suits," *ZPG National Reporter*, February 1972, pp. 5, 9–10. On ZPG, which initially was begun by Connecticut attorney Richard M. Bowers in the winter of 1968–1969 and expanded from a membership of 3,000 in January 1970 to 34,000 in April 1971, see *ZPG Communicator*, Vol. 1, #1 (March 1969); Larry D. Barnett, "Zero Population Growth, Inc.," *Bioscience* 21 (15 July 1971): 759–765, Barnett, "Zero Population Growth, Inc.: A Second Study," *Journal of Biosocial Science* 6 (January 1974): 1–22; Garrow conversations with Richard Bowers.

23. *McCann* v. *Babbitz*, 402 U.S. 903 (19 April 1971); Brennan Docket Book, Box 417; *McCann* Case File (O.T. 1970, #1353), National Archives, RG 267, Box 10393; *Kennan* v. *Nichol*, 326 F. Supp. 613 (W.D. Wis.), 27 April 1971; *Madison Capital Times*, 22 April 1971, pp. 1, 4, 30 April 1971, pp. 1, 2, 6 May 1971, p. 1, 11 May 1971, pp. 1, 2, 12 May 1971, pp. 1, 8; *New York Times*, 2 May 1971, p. 36; *Kennan* v. *Warren*, 328 F. Supp. 525 (W.D. Wis.), 5 May 1971; *Nichol* v. *Kennan* Case File (U.S.S.C., O.T. 1971, #595), National Archives, RG 267, Box 189; Anne Gaylor, "Abortion in Wisconsin?," *ZPG National Reporter*, July 1971, pp. 1–2; Gaylor, *Abortion Is A Blessing* (New York: Psychological Dimensions, 1975), pp. 6–20. Also see Richard Cates, "Legal Considerations in Wisconsin and Elsewhere" [23 October 1971], in Thomas M. Hart, ed., *Abortion in the Clinic and Office Setting* (San Francisco: Society for Humane Abortion, 1972), pp. 40–41; Paul Halvorsen et al., "Attitudes Toward Abortion" [among Milwaukee ob/gyns], *Wisconsin Medical Journal* 71 (April 1972): 134–139; and two law journal notes on *Babbitz*, *Washington Law Review* 46 (May 1971): 565–575, and Grahame G. Capp, *Journal of Urban Law* 48 (June 1971): 969–982.

24. *U.S.* v. *Vuitch* draft circulations, Harlan, "Memorandum to the Conference," 18 February 1971, Burger to Black, 24 February 1971, Blackmun to Black, 26 February 1971, Blackmun to Harlan, 29 March 1971, Brennan to Harlan, 29 March 1971, Marshall to Harlan, 29 March 1971, Blackmun to Black, 30 March 1971, Blackmun to Black, 13 April 1971, Harlan to Black, 14 April 1971, Douglas to Black, 15 April 1971, Black Box 437, Brennan Box 236, Douglas Box 1507, Harlan Box 427 and Marshall Box 69; Stewart to Black, n.d., and Robert W. Spearman, "Memo on No. 84, the Abortion Case," n.d. [c.14 April 1971], Black Box 438; Garrow conversations with Robert W. Spearman, L. A. Scott Powe and Thomas Rowe; Evan A. Davis to Garrow, 25 June 1992, and Duncan Kennedy to Garrow, 18 September 1992.

25. *U.S.* v. *Vuitch*, 402 U.S. 62, 72–73, 78, 96–97; Harlan to Black, 14 April 1971, Black circulations #5 and #6, 31 March and 14 April 1971, Black Box 437, Brennan Box 236, Douglas Box 1507, Harlan Box 427 and Marshall Box 69. The two substantive sentences deleted by Black at Harlan's request had read: "It is true that this statute touches a subject that tends to arouse the emotions of both jurors and judges. But the lifetime judges of this Court are sim-

ply not empowered to invalidate laws merely because we find them repugnant, ill-conceived or out of step with modern ideas."

Douglas's *Vuitch* dissent was the fifth time since *Griswold* that he had spoken to the right of privacy, always in dissent. See *Schmerber* v. *California*, 384 U.S. 757, 778–779 ("No clearer invasion of this right of privacy can be imagined than forcible blood-letting of the kind involved here"), 20 June 1966; *Lewis* v. *U.S.*, 385 U.S. 206, and *Osborn* v. *U.S.*, 385 U.S. 323, 340, 352 ("various provisions of the Bill of Rights contain this aura of privacy"), 12 December 1966; *Warden* v. *Hayden*, 387 U.S. 294, 312, 322 ("the privacy protected by the Fourth Amendment is much wider than the one protected by the First"), 325 (*Griswold's* "right of privacy . . . is kin to the right of privacy created by the Fourth Amendment"), 29 May 1967; and *Wyman* v. *James*, 400 U.S. 309, 330, 12 January 1971. See as well Douglas's dissent eight weeks later in *Palmer* v. *Thompson*, 403 U.S. 217, 233 ("Rights, not explicitly mentioned in the Constitution, have at times been deemed so elementary to our way of life that they have been labeled as basic rights"), 234, 237, 239, 14 June 1971. Also see Justice Fortas's dissent in *Time, Inc.* v. *Hill*, 385 U.S. 374, 412–414, 415 ("Privacy, then, is a basic right"), 9 January 1967; see as well Laura Kalman, *Abe Fortas* (New Haven: Yale University Press, 1990), pp. 264–266.

Also see *Doe* v. *D.C. General Hospital*, 313 F. Supp. 1170, 434 F.2d 423 (1970), and Philip B. Kurland, "1970 Term: Notes on the Emergence of the Burger Court," *Supreme Court Review* 1971 (Chicago: University of Chicago Press, 1971), pp. 265–322, at 309–311 (*Vuitch* made the D.C. statute "all but unusable against licensed physicians"). Case notes on *Vuitch* include William J. Curran, *New England Journal of Medicine* 285 (1 July 1971): 30–31; Robert G. Tanner, *Wake Forest Law Review* 7 (October 1971): 651–659; and John Wagner, *Nebraska Law Review* 51 (Winter 1971): 340–351. Also see Angela R. Holder, *Journal of the American Medical Association* 216 (3 May 1971): 933–934; Donald T. Kramer, "Validity, Under Federal Constitution, of Abortion Laws," 28 *L.Ed.* 1053–1087 (1971); *Harvard Law Review* 84 (June 1971): 1856–1911, at 1877; *Georgia Law Review* 6 (Fall 1971): 168–193, at 188; Martin F. McKernan, Jr., "Recent Abortion Litigation," *Catholic Lawyer* 17 (Winter 1971): 1–10; Donald W. Brodie, "Privacy: the Family and the State," *University of Illinois Law Forum* 1972, pp. 743–769, at 766; Thomas Polityka, "From *Poe* to *Roe*: A Bickelian View of the Abortion Decision," *Nebraska Law Review* 53 (1974): 31–57, at 49–51; and Richard C. Cortner, *The Supreme Court and Civil Liberties Policy* (Palo Alto, CA: Mayfield Publishing Co., 1975), p. 53.

26. *Washington Evening Star*, 21 April 1971, pp. A1, A5, 22 and 23 April 1971; *Washington Post*, 22 April 1971, pp. A1, A9; *New York Times*, 22 April 1971, pp. 1, 21; *Newsweek*, 3 May 1971, p. 110; *Time*, 3 May 1971, p. 40; *American Medical News*, 3 May 1971, p. 11; *Dallas Morning News*, 12 August 1971, p. C11; Gail Werner and Penelope Lemov, "Abortion," *Washingtonian*, October 1971, pp. 70–73; Lawrence Lader, *Abortion II* (Boston: Beacon Press, 1973), p. 115; Jane E. Hodgson, "Community Abortion Services," *Minnesota Medicine* 56 (March 1973): 239–242 (describing Washington's "Preterm" clinic); Harold L. Hirsh, "Impact of the Supreme Court Decisions on the Performance of Abortions in the United States," *Forensic Science* 3 (June 1974): 209–223, esp. at 214; Pilpel et al., "Memorandum," 29 April 1971, 8pp., ACLU 1972 Vol. 37, p. 6; Garrow conversations with Milan Vuitch and Norman Dorsen. Also see William J. Brennan, "A Tribute to Norman Dorsen," *Harvard Civil Rights—Civil Liberties Law Review* 27 (Summer 1992): 309–314, at 311, noting the *Vuitch* Court's "expansive interpretation of the word 'health'" and how "the Court's holding [in *Vuitch*] prefigures certain themes developed more fully in *Roe*."

On Dr. Vuitch's subsequent career, assorted difficulties, and eventual forced retirement, see *Washington Post*, 7 July 1977, p. MD1, 19 August 1983, p. B2, 11 November 1984, p. B1, 17 November 1984, pp. B1, B7, 28 November 1984, pp. B1, B7, 30 November 1984, p. B4, 15 December 1984, p. B5, 21 December 1984, pp. B1, B6, 23 March 1985, pp. C1, C2.

27. *Daily Texan*, 22 April 1971; *Houston Post*, 23 April 1971; *Houston Chronicle*, 25 and 26 April 1971; *Dallas Times-Herald*, 25 April 1971; Sam Coats to Ginny Whitehill, 30 April 1971, Whitehill Papers.

28. *Hodgson* v. *Randall* and *Hodgson* v. *Minnesota* [U.S.S.C., O.T. 1970, #728 and 729], 402 U.S.

967, 17 May 1971; E. Robert Seaver to Roy Lucas (2), 17 May 1971, Lucas Box 12; Brennan Conference Lists and Docket Book, Brennan Boxes 224, 226 and 417. Justice Brennan's notations indicate that the initial decisions on the *Hodgson* cases were taken on March 24 and reaffirmed on May 13. Also see Black, "Memorandum on Cases Held for *Dombrowski* Group," n.d. [c.8 March 1971], Blackmun to Black, 9 March 1971, Brennan to Black, 9 March 1971, p. 6, Brennan to Black, 16 March 1971, Marshall Box 64. Justice Douglas dissented without comment from the Court's affirmance of *Hodgson* v. *Randall*.

29. In the Louisiana case, *Rosen* v. *State Board of Medical Examiners*, O.T. 1970, #1010, the Court in February (E. Robert Seaver to Sam A. LeBlanc, 10 February 1971) had requested a response on behalf of the state to Ben Smith's November appeal, but following the March 12 filing of a Motion to Affirm or Dismiss, the Court first on April 23 (with Justices Douglas and Harlan voting to take the case) and again on May 13 kept *Rosen* on hold pending action on a nonabortion case involving a Florida obscenity prosecution, *Mitchum* v. *Foster*. Also see White to Black, 10 March 1971, Marshall Box 64. The Missouri case, *Rodgers* v. *Danforth*, #70–89, was also considered at those same two conferences and also put on hold in light of *Mitchum*. On May 21 the Court put both of the appeals stemming from the Illinois three-judge court decision, *Hanrahan* v. *Doe* and *Heffernan* v. *Doe*, #70–105 and 70–106, on hold pending disposition of the Texas and Georgia cases. Conference List, 20 May 1971, Marshall Box 63, and Brennan Docket Book Box 419. On the Illinois cases, also see Mel Wulf to David A. Goldberger, 27 April 1971, and Sybille Fritzsche to Wulf, 11 May 1971, ACLU 1976 Vol. 24.

30. *Roe* v. *Wade*, O.T. 1970, #808, and *Doe* v. *Bolton*, #971, Brennan Docket Books, Boxes 417 and 419; Black, "Memorandum on Cases Held for *Dombrowski* Group," n.d. [c.8 March 1971], Brennan to Black, 9 March 1971, pp. 6–7, White to Black, 10 March 1971, Blackmun to Black, 10 March 1971, Burger to Black, 10 March 1971, Stewart to Black, 12 March 1971, Brennan to Black, 16 March 1971, Brennan, "Memorandum to the Conference," 1 and 21 April 1971, Marshall Box 64; *Roe* v. *Wade* and *Doe* v. *Bolton*, 402 U.S. 941, 3 May 1971. Also see "LAP" [L. A. Scott Powe] to Douglas, *Doe* v. *Wade*, 2 March 1971, and "LAP" [Powe] to Douglas, [*Doe* v. *Bolton*], 13 April 1971, Douglas Box 1589. After initial consideration on April 22, on April 28 the justices unanimously agreed to dismiss both Georgia's cross-appeal, *Bolton* v. *Doe*, #973, and Ferdinand Buckley's similar petition, *Unborn Child of Mary Doe* v. *Mary Doe*, #6172. Conference Lists, Brennan Boxes 224 and 226 and Marshall Box 63, Brennan Docket Book, Box 417; 402 U.S. 936.

31. *New York Times*, 4 May 1971, p. 31; *Washington Post*, 4 May 1971, p. A8; *Dallas Morning News*, 4 May 1971, p. A5; E. Robert Seaver to Lucas, 4 and 18 May 1971, Lucas Box 22; Lucas to Hames, 4 May 1971, Hames Papers; Lucas, "Memorandum to Ad Hoc Group on Amicus Curiae Support for 1970 Supreme Court Cases," and "What the Pro-Abortion Groups Did *NOT* Do in the Court Cases Challenging Abortion Law Restrictions," 4pp., 7 May 1971, ACLU 1972 Vol. 37; Pilpel in "Roundtable: Legal Abortion" [11 May 1971], *Medical Aspects of Human Sexuality* 5 (August 1971): 50–75, at 75, and in ASA Board Minutes, 13 May 1971, Guttmacher Papers; *Houston Chronicle*, 9, 11, and 14 May 1971; *Houston Post*, 9 May 1971; *Dallas Times-Herald*, 9 May 1971, 21 May 1971, p. A40; *Ft. Worth Star-Telegram*, 12 May 1971; Foe to Whitehill, n.d. [c.mid-May 1971], Whitehill Papers.

Also see Heather Sigworth, "Abortion Laws in the Federal Courts—The Supreme Court as Supreme Platonic Guardian," *Indiana Legal Forum* 5 (Fall 1971): 130–142, at 133 and 137, who observed with regard to the Court's May actions that "From the pattern of disposition of these appeals and petitions, it is difficult not to conclude that the Court will give little comfort to those seeking to abolish all abortion laws" and "is unlikely to be sympathetic to the 'privacy' argument." *Vuitch* in particular, this commentator contended, "must indicate that the Court is of no mind to strike down all substantive limitations on abortion." Also note *Lashley* v. *Maryland*, 402 U.S. 991, 24 May 1971, dismissing an appeal of a nonphysician's abortion conviction (268 A.2d 502) with only Justice Douglas in dissent.

32. Hames to Michael Rodak, 11 May 1971, *Doe* Case File, National Archives, RG 267, Box 16; Lucas to E. Robert Seaver, 8 June 1971, and Seaver to Lucas, 14 June 1971, *Roe* Case File,

National Archives, RG 267, Box 9; Lucas to Roy Merrill, 13 April 1971, Lucas Box 22; [Lucas], "Texas Abortion Law Test Case: Appeal Pending Before the Supreme Court," n.d. [c.late May 1971], 4pp., Whitehill Papers; *Houston Chronicle*, 28 May 1971; *Galveston Daily News*, 28 May 1971, pp. A1, A4; Coffee to Robert L. Sassone, 4 June 1971, and Coffee to Ephraim London, 29 July 1971 (also referring to Lucas as "lead counsel"), Lucas Box 22; "Contributions as of 3/15/71," Whitehill Papers; Jay Floyd notes, 24 May 1971, and Floyd to Lucas, 7 June 1971, Texas AG File 70–308; Barbara Milbauer, *The Law Giveth* (New York: Atheneum, 1983), p. 52; Sarah Weddington, *A Question of Choice* (New York: G. P. Putnam's Sons, 1992), pp. 75–76, 84; Garrow conversations with Roy Lucas, Sarah Weddington, Ron Weddington, Linda Coffee, and Virginia Whitehill.

33. Pilpel to Dorsen et al., 19 and 25 May 1971, Kimmey to Allan Barnes et al., 27 May and 8 June 1971, Hames Papers; Sarah Lewit, ed., *Abortion Techniques and Services* (Amsterdam: Excerpta Medica, 1972), esp. pp. 91 and 111–113; [Hames], "Memo—Re: Roy Lucas— Abortion Cases," 2pp., n.d. [c.6 June 1971], [Hames], "Memo—Re: Roy Lucas," 1pp., n.d. [c.6 June 1971], Zarky to Hames, 8 June 1971, and Hames to Zarky, 16 June 1971, Hames Papers; Lucas to Timothy Bloomfield, 22 June 1971, Lucas Box 8; Kimmey to Barnes et al., "Amicus Briefs Report," 23 June 1971, Whitehill Papers; Pilpel to Hames, 25 June 1971, Hames Papers; Garrow conversations with Nancy Wechsler, Jane Zuckerman, Roy Lucas, Norman Dorsen, Cyril Means, Jimmye Kimmey, Mel Wulf, Margie Hames, Judith [Bourne] Rooks, Larry Lader, and Joseph Nellis. Also see Nathanson, *Aborting America*, pp. 152–154. Cyril Means's obituary appears in the *New York Times*, 6 October 1992, p. D23; also see Means, "The Constitutional Aspects of a National Population Policy," *Villanova Law Review* 15 (Summer 1970): 854–862, and Means's additional symposium comments at pp. 876–877.

34. *New York Times*, 9 April 1971, p. 28, 12 April 1971, p. 34, 13 April 1971, p. 43, 15 April 1971, pp. 31, 42, 22 April 1971, pp. 30, 46, 25 April 1971, p. 32, 27 April 1971, p. 47, 28 April 1971, p. 51, 29 April 1971, p. 1, 2 May 1971, pp. 58, V-22, 4 May 1971, p. 38, 7 May 1971, pp. 1, 24, 37, 9 May 1971, pp. 8, VI-80, 11 May 1971, pp. 27, 43, 12 May 1971, p. 1, 13 May 1971, p. 1, 14 May 1971, pp. 1, 66, 15 May 1971, p. 34, 16 May 1971, p. IV-6, 17 May 1971, p. 35, 20 May 1971, p. 57, 27 May 1971, p. 30, 3 June 1971, pp. 29, 43, 4 June 1971, pp. 15, 38, 6 June 1971, p. 64, 8 June 1971, p. 21, 19 June 1971, p. 28, 21 June 1971, p. 15, 24 June 1971, p. 34, 29 June 1971, pp. 22, 35, 30 June 1971, pp. 43, 72, 1 July 1971, p. 42, 2 July 1971, p. 8; *American Medical News*, 17 May 1971, p. 3; *City of New York v. Wyman*, 321 N.Y.S.2d 695, 707, 709–710 (N.Y. County Sup. Ct.), 18 May 1971, 322 N.Y.S.2d 957 (Sup. Ct. App. Div., 1st Dept.), 1 July 1971; Lader, "A Guide to Abortion Laws in the United States," *Redbook*, June 1971, pp. 51–58; *Wall Street Journal*, 1 June 1971, pp. 1, 29; *Newsday*, 30 June 1971, pp. A4, A5; *S.P.S. Consultants, Inc. v. Lefkowitz*, 333 F. Supp. 1370, 1373 (S.D.N.Y.), 8 July and 5 October 1971; *Newsweek*, 19 July 1971, pp. 50–52.

On for-profit abortion brokers, also see *New York Times*, 19 December 1970, p. 21, 10 February 1971, pp. 45, 47, 12 February 1971, p. 38, 27 February 1971, p. 34, 28 February 1971, p. E5, 5 April 1971, p. 26, 8 January 1972, p. 33; *Time*, 15 March 1971, p. 64. Also see a subsequent and suggestively different Michigan federal court ruling, *Mitchell Family Planning, Inc. v. City of Royal Oak*, 335 F. Supp. 738 (E.D. Mich.), 5 January 1972.

Subsequent *New York Times* stories concerning New York implementation also include 26 July 1971, p. 10, 21 August 1971, p. 26, 27 September 1971, p. 27, 13 October 1971, p. 15, 15 October 1971, p. 38, 4 January 1972, p. 22, and 20 February 1972, p. 61. Also see Art Spikol, "Across the Border and Into the Mill: The Boston-New York Abortion Run," *Boston Magazine*, July 1971, pp. 34–39, 58–59, John Pennington, "Abortion," *Atlanta Journal-Constitution Magazine*, 30 January 1972, pp. 10–18, and Ardis H. Danon, "Organizing an Abortion Service," *Nursing Outlook* 21 (July 1973): 460–64.

35. *New York Times*, 5 July 1971, p. 17; *National Clergy Consultation Service on Abortion Newsletter* Vol. 2, #1 (July 1971). Also see *Christian Century*, 21 July 1971, p. 871, which characterized Medeiros's remarks as an "indiscriminate harangue." For a vastly different and strikingly liberal Catholic analysis, see John F. Dedek, "Abortion: A Theological Judgment," *Chicago*

Studies 10 (Fall 1971): 313–333, at 332 ("perhaps even grave socio-economic reasons could justify an abortion before the beginning of the third week," or possibly even later).

On Illinois, see *Chicago Sun-Times*, 18 May 1971; on Maine, see *New York Times*, 20 May 1971, p. 25, and *Christian Science Monitor*, 22 May 1971, p. 4; on Ohio, see *Columbus Dispatch*, 6 June 1971, p. A45, and 9 June 1971, p. B15. On North Dakota, see Faye D. Ginsburg, *Contested Lives* (Berkeley: University of California Press, 1989), pp. 65–67.

On Michigan, see [Lee Gidding], "Michigan," 29 March 1971, NARAL Box 3; George E. LaCroix to Lader, 20 April 1971, Lader Box 16; *Detroit News*, 6 June 1971, p. B11; *New York Times*, 14 July 1971, p. 71; also see Doreen Bierbrier, "The 1972 Abortion Referendum in Michigan" (unpublished paper, University of Michigan, December, 1973), Bentley Historical Library. Led by Detroit attorney Barbara G. Robb, in late August several *hundred* female plaintiffs filed a constitutional challenge against the existing Michigan abortion law in state court. See Linda Nordquist, "Michigan Women's Abortion Suit," 6 August 1971, MARC Box 2; *Detroit News*, 27 August 1971, pp. D1, D3; and Robb et al., "Amended Complaint," *Lorraine B. Beebe et al. v. William Cahalan*, Wayne County Cir. Ct., #CA188-670-R, 23 September 1971, Lucas Box 12.

36. On Connecticut, see the subsequent Second Circuit ruling, *Abele v. Markle*, 452 F.2d 1121, 13 December 1971; on Kentucky, see *Crossen v. Breckenridge*, 446 F.2d 833, 23 June 1971. On the Arizona case, see *Arizona Republic*, 18 May 1971, p. 21, and 19 June 1971, p. 35; *Planned Parenthood Association v. Nelson*, 327 F. Supp. 1290 (D. Ariz.), 11 June 1971; and Seymour Sacks to Harriet Pilpel, 10 December 1971, Pilpel-SSC.

On New Jersey, see Lucas to Felix H. Vann, 14 September 1971, Lucas Box 25; on Colorado, see *Denver Post*, 22 May 1971, p. 19; on Oklahoma, see *Tulsa Tribune*, 1 March 1971, pp. B1, B6, 2 March 1971, pp. B1, B5, and 3 and 4 March 1971. On the South Dakota *Munson* case, see Lucas to Homer Kandaras, 4 November 1970, Kandaras to Lucas, 14 December 1970, Munson to Lucas, 19 January 1971, Lucas to Kandaras, 15 April 1971, Mel Wulf to Kandaras, 20 April 1971, Lucas to Kandaras, 13 May 1971, C. J. Kelly to Kandaras, 1 June 1971, Kandaras to Lucas, 2 June 1971, Lucas to Kandaras, 7 June 1971, Kandaras to Lucas, 13 July 1971, Lucas to Kandaras, 16 July 1971, Kelly to Kandaras, 27 July 1971, Kandaras to Lucas, 28 July 1971, Lucas to Kandaras, 31 July 1971, Kandaras to Lucas, 12 August 1971, and Kandaras and Lucas, "Respondent's Brief," *State v. Munson*, S.D. Sup. Ct. [1 September 1971], 58pp., Lucas Box 22.

37. On Missouri, see *Rodgers et al. v. Danforth*, St. Louis County Cir. Ct., #315512, 7 June 1971, 3pp., Lucas Box 15, *St. Louis Post-Dispatch*, 8 June 1971, p. A8, *St. Louis Globe-Democrat*, 8 June 1971, p. 1. On Florida, see *Landreth v. Hopkins*, 331 F. Supp. 920 (N.D. Fla.), 22 September 1971, and *Walsingham v. State*, 250 So.2d 857 (Fla. Sup. Ct.), 12 July 1971.

On California, see *Ballard v. Anderson*, 4 Cal.3d 873 (19 May 1971); *San Francisco Chronicle*, 20 May 1971; *New York Times*, 20 May 1971, p. 25, and 18 July 1971, p. 29; *State v. Pettegrew*, 96 Cal. Rptr. 189 (Cal. Ct. App., 2d Dist.), 12 July 1971; *State v. Barksdale*, 96 Cal. Rptr. 265, 272 (Cal. Ct. App., 1st Dist.), 22 July 1971; also see Ruth Roemer to Joseph Sunnen, 18 and 25 August 1971, CCTA Box 1; *Los Angeles Times*, 21 November 1971, pp. E1, E20, 22 November 1971, pp. II-1, II-13, II-15, 23 November 1971, pp. II-1, II-6, 24 November 1971, pp. IV-2, IV-4; and Daniel M. Schneider, *University of Cincinnati Law Review* 41 (1972): 235–244.

38. Garrow conversations with Margie Hames, Reber Boult, Pamela D. Walker, Tobiane Schwartz, Elizabeth Rindskopf, Gale Siegel Messerman, Charles Morgan, Jr., and Sandra [Bensing] Cano; *Atlanta Constitution*, 22 December 1970, p. A1, 23 December 1970, p. A2, 30 December 1970, p. A4, 26 January 1971, p. A6; [Sandra Bensing] Affidavit, 9 March 1971, Hames Papers; Ann Woolner, "'I Am Mary Doe,'" *Fulton County Daily Report*, 9 February 1989, pp. 1, 3–7.

39. Marsha King to Lucas, 5 July 1971, Lucas Box 22; Garrow conversations with Roy Lucas, Linda Coffee, Norma McCorvey, Sarah Weddington, and Virginia Whitehill; Patricia Thomas, "Abortion: Is It a Constitutional Right?," *ZPG National Reporter*, July 1971, pp. 6–7; *Second Coming*, Vol. 1, #9, 15 July 1971, p. 2; *Houston Post*, 18 July 1971.

On the SWP and WONAAC, see especially "More Trots," *The Rag*, 13 March 1972, pp. 12–13, plus Garrow conversations with Judy Smith and Barbara Hines; also see "Dear Sister" letter, 4 June 1971, Barbara Roberts, "Abortion Laws Murder Women," 12 June 1971, Debbie Notkin to "Dear Sister," 18 June 1971, and "Dear Sister" letter, 17 July 1971, Chicago Women's Liberation Union Papers, Box 8; *New York Times*, 20 July 1971, p. 30, and 15 October 1971, p. 53; *WONAAC National Newsletter* [#1], 16 September 1971; Judith Papachristou, *Women Together* (New York: Alfred A. Knopf, 1976), pp. 248–249; Suzanne Staggenborg, "Coalition Work in the Pro-Choice Movement: Organizational and Environmental Opportunities and Obstacles," *Social Problems* 33 (June 1986): 374–390, at 378; Staggenborg, *The Pro-Choice Movement* (New York: Oxford University Press, 1991), p. 26; and especially Flora Davis, *Moving the Mountain* (New York: Simon & Schuster, 1991), pp. 138–141.

40. Weddington, *A Question of Choice* (New York: G. P. Putnam's Sons, 1992), pp. 80, 84–98; Lucas to Michael Rodak, 7 July 1971, Lucas Box 22; Lucas to Weddington, "Re: Hodgson Brief," n.d. [c.7 July 1971], Lucas Box 12; Brian Sullivan to Margie Hames, 8 July 1971, Hames Papers; Weddington in Texas Citizens for Abortion Education [*Newsletter*], July–August [1971], p. 3, and Weddington to Whitehill, n.d. [11 July 1971], Whitehill Papers; Lucas to Hames, 17 July 1971, Hames Papers; Lucas, "Memorandum to Trustees— Monthly Report: July, 1971" [c.19 July 1971], Emerson Box 13 and Lucas Box 25; Weddington to John Tolle, 19 July 1971, and Tolle to Weddington, 22 July 1971, Lucas Box 22; Lucas to Rodak, 20 July 1971, and E. Robert Seaver to Lucas, 3 August 1971, *Roe* Case File, National Archives, RG 267, Box 9; Hames to Seaver, 7 July 1971, and to Rodak, 28 July 1971, *Doe* Case File, National Archives, RG 267, Box 16; Marian Faux, *Roe v. Wade* (New York: Macmillan, 1988), pp. 204, 219–223; Garrow conversations with Sarah Weddington, Ron Weddington, Roy Lucas, Nicholas W. Danforth, Brian L. Sullivan, David M. Tundermann, Daniel M. Schneider, Richard G. Singer, Jane E. Hodgson, and Virginia B. Whitehill.

The three affidavits from the Texas physicians—Paul C. MacDonald, chairman of ob/gyn at the University of Texas Southwestern Medical School in Dallas (28 July 1971), Joseph Seitchik, chairman of ob/gyn at the University of Texas Medical School at San Antonio (9 August 1971), and William J. McGanity, chairman of ob/gyn at the University of Texas Medical Branch at Galveston (13 August 1971), appear as appendices B-1, C-1, and D-1 in the *Roe* brief.

On the North Carolina appeal, see Lucas and George S. Daly, Jr., "Jurisdictional Statement," *Corkey* v. *Edwards*, U.S.S.C., O.T. 1971, #92, 27pp., 19 July 1971, National Archives, RG 267, Box 97; Daly to Richard L. Burt et al., 20 July 1971, Lucas Box 20; and *Washington Post*, 21 July 1971, p. B2. On 5 November 1971 the justices privately decided to hold *Corkey* in abeyance until *Roe* and *Doe* were resolved. Brennan Docket Book, Box 419.

On the *Hodgson* case, also see Brian Sullivan to Lucas, "Supreme Court of Minnesota," 21 May 1971, 4pp., Lucas Box 13; Steering Committee Minutes, Hodgson Defense Fund, 24 June 1971, St. Paul, MARC Papers, Box 120-2B; Lucas et al., "Appellant's Brief," *Hodgson* v. *State*, Minnesota Sup. Ct., #42966, 77pp., 6 August 1971, and Lucas and Weddington, "First Hospital Abortion Case Appealed in Minnesota," 6 August 1971, Lucas Box 14.

41. Weddington, *A Question of Choice*, pp. 89–98; Glen M. Wilkerson to Sarah and Ron Weddington, "Memorandum: In Re Texas Abortion Case," 22 August 1971, 12pp., Lucas Box 23; Garrow conversations with Roy Lucas, Sarah Weddington, Ron Weddington, Nicholas W. Danforth, Brian L. Sullivan, David M. Tundermann, Daniel M. Schneider, Beatrice Vogel, Barbara Hines, and Margie Hames. Also see Ron Weddington's comments in Leslie Bennetts, "A Woman's Choice," *Vanity Fair*, September 1992, pp. 148, 152–158.

With regard to Means's well-known article, "The Law of New York Concerning Abortion and the Status of the Foetus, 1664–1968: A Case of Cessation of Constitutionality," *New York Law Forum* 14 (Fall 1968): 411–515, Tundermann reported that Means's "own conclusions sometime strain credibility: in the presence of manifest public outcry over fetal deaths just prior to the passage of New York's 1872 abortion law, Means disclaims any impact upon the legislature of this popular pressure (even though the statute itself copies the language of a pro-fetal group)." He added that "Where the important thing is to win the case no matter how, however, I suppose I agree with Means's technique: begin with a scholarly attempt at historical research; if it doesn't work, fudge it as necessary; write a piece so long that others will read only your introduction and conclusion; then keep citing it until courts begin picking it up. This preserves the guise of impartial scholarship while advancing the proper ideological goals." David [Tundermann] to Roy [Lucas], "Legislative Purpose et al.," 5 August 1971, Lucas Box 13.

42. Roy [Lucas], "Memorandum to Sarah Re: Doe v. Bolton," 10 August 1971, Lucas Box 5; Garrow conversations with Roy Lucas, Nicholas W. Danforth, David W. Tundermann, Brian L. Sullivan, and Daniel M. Schneider.

43. Lucas, "Brief as Amici Curiae for the American College of Obstetricians and Gynecologists et al.," Doe v. Bolton, U.S.S.C., O.T. 1971, #70–40, 96pp., 14 August 1971; Lucas et al., "Brief for Appellants," Roe v. Wade, U.S.S.C., O.T. 1971, #70–18, 145pp., 18 August 1971, esp. pp. 91–95, 101–102, 123; Jacobson v. Massachusetts, 197 U.S. 11, 29–30; Hames et al., "Brief of the Appellants," Doe et al. v. Bolton, U.S.S.C., O.T. 1971, #70–40, 57pp., 17 August 1971; Pilpel, Wechsler, and Zuckerman, "Brief for Planned Parenthood Federation of America," Roe v. Wade and Doe v. Bolton, 45pp., 11 August 1971, esp. pp. 10–11, 30, 32, 34; Stearns, "Brief Amicus Curiae on Behalf of New Women Lawyers, Women's Health and Abortion Project, Inc., and Women's National Abortion Action Coalition," Roe v. Wade and Doe v. Bolton, 60pp., 2 August 1971, p. 7; Ryan, "Brief of the American College of Obstetricians and Gynecologists et al.," Roe v. Wade, 18pp., 17 August 1971, p. 16; Garrow conversations with Roy Lucas, Ron Weddington, and Sarah Weddington.

The additional August amicus briefs were Norma G. Zarky, "Brief Amicus Curiae" for the AAUW, YWCA, and NOW, Roe v. Wade and Doe v. Bolton, 37pp., 10 August 1971; Marttie L. Thompson and Marcia Lowry, "Brief Amicus Curiae for State Communities Aid Association," Roe v. Wade and Doe v. Bolton, 16pp., 14 August 1971; Helen L. Buttenwieser, "Brief Amicus Curiae for the American Ethical Union, the American Friends Service Committee, the American Jewish Congress, the Episcopal Diocese of New York et al.," Roe v. Wade and Doe v. Bolton, 35pp., 16 August 1971; and Alan F. Charles and Susan G. Alexander, "Brief Amicus Curiae for the National Legal Program on Health Problems of the Poor, the National Welfare Rights Organization, and the American Public Health Association," Roe v. Wade, 42pp., 17 August 1971. Also see Jimmye Kimmey to All Attorneys, "Amicus Briefs in Roe v. Wade and Doe v. Bolton," 25 August 1971, Guttmacher Papers. One other supportive amicus brief was submitted two months later: Charles and Alexander, "Brief Amicus Curiae," Doe v. Bolton, 53pp., 12 October 1971 (for the same three groups as their earlier brief in Roe).

On the Doe amicus brief, also see Warren E. Magee to Lucas, 5 August 1971, Lucas Box 5; Lucas to Milan Vuitch, 12 August 1971, Lucas Box 8; New York Times, 15 August 1971, p. 56; and American Medical News, 23 August 1971, p. 10. On the Roe brief, also see Dallas Morning News, 5 September 1971, p. A14, and Norman Dorsen to Lucas, 8 September 1971, Lucas Box 22. With regard to Georgia, also see ACLU of Georgia Executive Committee Minutes, 21 July 1971, Georgia ACLU Papers, and Atlanta Constitution, 3 August 1971.

44. Lucas to Means, 12 August 1971, Lucas Box 25; Means to Hames, 17 August 1971, Hames Papers; Means to Larry Lader, 29 August 1971, Lader Box 16; Weddington, A Question of Choice, p. 99; Garrow conversations with Sarah Weddington, Ron Weddington, Cyril Means, Margie Hames, and Roy Lucas.

45. Weddington to Michael Rodak, 30 August and 8 September 1971, Lucas Box 22; Lucas to Nathan H. Rappaport, 14 September 1971, Lucas Box 25; Lucas to Homer Kandaras, 14 September 1971, Lucas Box 22; Lucas Interview with Vose; Garrow conversations with Roy Lucas and Sarah Weddington.

On the Kansas case, Poe v. Menghini, filed 24 September 1971, see Frank D. Menghini to Roosevelt Butler, 29 July 1971, and a 23 September 1971 agreement between Lucas, Dr. Lynn D. Weller, Jr., and the Douglass Hospital of Kansas City, Kansas, Lucas Box 7; as well as Lucas to A. F. "Tony" Ringold, 27 September 1971, Lucas Box 21; *Kansas City Star*, 24 September 1971, and *Kansas City Times*, 21 October 1971; also see Lader, *Abortion II*, pp. 181–182. U.S. District Judge Wesley Brown on 28 September denied Lucas's 24 September request for a temporary restraining order against the Kansas statute, but a full hearing before a three-judge federal panel took place in Kansas City on October 20.

46. Lucas to Hames, 19 September 1971, and Hames to Lucas, 28 September 1971, Hames Papers; Garrow conversations with Roy Lucas and Margie Hames.

47. "Statement from the Nominating Committee," 13 September 1971, Lucas Box 27; John Cowles to Frank M. Rarig, Jr., 21 September 1971, and Rarig, Hodgson Legal Defense Fund Steering Committee Minutes, 30 September 1971, MARC Box 120-2B; Lucas, "Statement on Medical Referral Agencies," 27 September 1971, and "Memorandum to NARAL Board Members and Others," 1 October 1971, Lucas Box 25. Also see Lucas to Rarig, 7 October 1971, MARC 120-2B.

48. Gidding to Lamm, 12 August 1971, and Biddy Hurlbut to Gidding, 16 September 1971, NARAL Boxes 2 and 3; *New York Times*, 20 August 1971, p. 9, 18 September 1971, p. 1, 24 September 1971, p. 1, 4 October 1971, p. 27, 5 October 1971, p. 28; NARAL Annual Meeting Minutes, 3–4 October 1971, "Statement by Lawrence Lader," 3 October 1971, NARAL I-5; Lucas to Frank Rarig, 7 October 1971, MARC 120-2B; *American Medical News*, 18 October 1971, p. 7; Lucas, "Memorandum to NARAL Membership," 8 November 1971, and "The Threat of the Lucas Case," n.d. [c.18 November 1971], NARAL I-25; Robert L. Webber to Lader, 16 November 1971, PPFA II-120; Jones to Gidding, 22 November 1971, NARAL Box 5; Lader, *Abortion II*, pp. 180–181. Also see Hurlbut to Gidding, 21 October and 6 November 1971, NARAL Box 3; *Time*, 27 September 1971, pp. 67–70; Nathanson, *Aborting America*, pp. 154–155; and especially Nellis to Means, 1 November 1971, Lader Box 16, which indicates that the anti-Lucas rebuttal ("The Threat of the Lucas Case," above) was prepared for Means and Lader at least in part by Joe Nellis.

On Black and Harlan's retirements, see *New York Times*, 18 September 1971, pp. 1, 12, and 24 September 1971, pp. 1, 20; on Black's and then Harlan's deaths, see *New York Times*, 25 September 1971, p. 1, and 30 December 1971, pp. 1, 29. On the two justices' final years on the Court, see Howard Ball, "Justice Hugo L. Black," and Wallace Mendelson, "Justice John M. Harlan," in Lamb and Halpern, eds., *The Burger Court*, pp. 35–62 and 193–211.

49. Weddington, *A Question of Choice*, p. 100; Weddington to Virginia Whitehill, 23 September 1971, "Thursday" [14] October 1971, and 28 October 1971, Whitehill Papers; Weddington to Margie Hames, "Friday" [15] October 1971, Hames Papers; *Dallas Morning News*, 16 September 1971, p. D1, 22 September 1971, p. A14. The official sponsor of Weddington's September 15 admission to the Supreme Court bar was U.S. District Judge Sarah T. Hughes. With regard to Weddington's statement in the 23 September letter that "Meeting Jane Roe was fascinating," also see the discussion in note 17 of chapter seven.

50. On the Utah case, *Doe* v. *Rampton*, U.S.D.C. D.Utah, #C-234-70, which had been argued in late January, see the unreported, eight-page 8 September 1971 "Opinion and Judgment" which the panel's 2 to 1 majority, Circuit Judge J. Oliver Seth and Senior District Judge A. Sherman Christensen, filed on 29 September, and Chief District Judge Willis W. Ritter's energetic ten-page dissent; also see *Ogden Standard-Examiner*, 27 January 1971. Plaintiffs' attorney David "Sandy" Dolowitz filed his jurisdictional statement of appeal with the Supreme Court on 4 November 1971. *Doe* v. *Rampton*, U.S.S.C., O.T. 1971, #5666, National Archives, RG 267, Box 194.

51. *Vuitch* v. *Maryland*, 404 U.S. 868; E. Robert Seaver to E. Barrett Prettyman, Jr., 12 October 1971, Lucas Box 9; *Washington Post*, 13 October 1971; Nellis to Lader, 13 October 1971, NARAL Box 7; *Vuitch* v. *Hardy*, C.A.#71–1129 (D. Md.), 13 October 1971; Garrow conversations with Roy Lucas and Milan Vuitch. Also see Lucas et al., "Petition for a Writ of Certiorari," *Vuitch* v. *Maryland*, U.S.S.C., O.T. 1970, #1533, 20pp., March 1971, Lucas Box 8, and Justice Brennan's 4 October 1971 conference tally, showing the 5 to 2 vote, in Brennan Docket Book, Box 417.

52. 404 U.S. 813, 12 October 1971; E. Robert Seaver to Lucas, 12 October 1971. The Court also

granted permission for the filing of the various amicus briefs that had been submitted in the case, and rejected the request appended to Nancy Stearns's amicus submission that she be allowed to participate in the oral argument. Justice Douglas's notes indicate that while both of the actions with regard to oral argument were unanimously agreed upon, four justices— Douglas, Brennan, Stewart, and White—approved the filing of all the amicus briefs, while two—Burger and Blackmun—voted against accepting those submissions, except with regard to the ACOG one, which Justice Blackmun took no part in considering. Douglas's notations do not indicate whether Justice Marshall was absent or simply did not participate. See Douglas's notations on "KRR" [Kenneth R. Reed], *Roe v. Wade*, *Doe v. Bolton*, 2 October 1971, Douglas Box 1589.

53. Beasley to E. Robert Seaver, 18 August 1971 (requesting extension until 15 November) and Seaver to Beasley, 24 August 1971 (granted only until 15 October), *Doe* Case File, National Archives, RG 267, Box 16; Floyd to Michael Rodak, 10 September 1971, and Seaver to Floyd, 14 September 1971 (requesting and receiving extension until 15 October), *Roe* Case File, National Archives, RG 267, Box 9; Arthur K. Bolton et al., "Brief for Appellees," *Doe v. Bolton*, U.S.S.C., O.T. 1971, #70–40, 79pp., 15 October 1971; Margaret Shannon, "Matters of Life and Death," *Atlanta Journal-Constitution Magazine*, 23 April 1972, pp. 7–17; Garrow conversations with Dorothy Beasley, Elizabeth Rindskopf, Arthur K. Bolton, and Jay Floyd. Also see Ferdinand Buckley et al., "Brief of Ferdinand Buckley as Amicus Curiae," *Doe v. Bolton*, 17 pp., 14 October 1971. Beasley's earlier Supreme Court argument against Rindskopf came on 23 March 1971 in *Bell v. Burson*, 402 U.S. 535, decided by a unanimous Court on 24 May 1971.

54. Crawford C. Martin et al., "Brief for Appellee," *Roe v. Wade*, U.S.S.C., O.T. 1971, #70–18, 58pp., 19 October 1971; McKernan to Alfred Walker, 2 July 1970, Alfred L. Scanlan to William R. "Bud" Considine, 26 August 1971, Jerome A. Frazel, Jr., to Floyd, 9 September 1971, Dennis J. Horan to Floyd, 16, 21, and 24 September 1971, Texas AG File 70–308; Floyd in *Dallas Morning News*, 15 May 1989, pp. C1, C3, *Boston Globe*, 15 May 1989, pp. 8, 11, and *Dallas Times-Herald*, 4 July 1989, p. A13; Garrow conversations with Jay Floyd, John Tolle, Henry Wade, and Robert C. Flowers. The book to which Horan referred Floyd was Germain Grisez, *Abortion* (New York: Corpus Books), at pages 382–389.

Four of the six other antiabortion amicus briefs were largely unremarkable. See Charles E. Rice, "Brief Amicus Curiae of Americans United for Life," *Roe v. Wade*, 11pp., 30 August 1971; Eugene J. McMahon, "Brief of Women for the Unborn et al.," *Roe v. Wade*, 18pp., 17 September 1971; Robert E. Dunne, "Brief of Amicus Curiae Robert L. Sassone [president of "LIFE," the "League for Infants, Fetuses, and the Elderly"]," *Doe v. Bolton*, 55pp., 12 October 1971; and Joseph P. Witherspoon, "Brief Amicus Curiae," *Roe v. Wade*, October 1971. Also see note 53 above and note 55 below. See as well Witherspoon to E. Robert Seaver, 20 November 1971, *Roe* Case File, National Archives, RG 267, Box 9; and William K. Kimble, *Texas Southern Law Review* 1 (1971): 173–180.

55. Martin et al., "Brief for Appellee," *Roe v. Wade*, 19 October 1971, pp. ii, iii, 9, 10, 12, 16, 20, and 26; Horan, Frazel, et al., "Motion and Brief Amicus Curiae of Certain Physicians . . . " *Roe v. Wade* and *Doe v. Bolton*, 79pp., 15 October 1971; Scanlan et al., "Brief Amicus Curiae of the National Right to Life Committee," *Roe v. Wade* and *Doe v. Bolton*, 61pp., 8 October 1971, p. 7. Also see McKernan to "Gentlemen," 27 October 1971, Texas AG File 70–308 (telling Floyd "I am very pleased that you found it possible to insert some of the medical evidence which I had suggested to you" and congratulating him for "what I feel is a fine piece of legal writing both in organization and content"). The duplication between the two briefs can be traced by comparing pages 30 to 54 of Texas's "Brief for Appellee" with pages 7 to 26 of Horan and Frazel's "Brief Amicus Curiae." Also compare the "Brief for Appellee" at p. 27 with the Scanlan amicus brief at p. 24; also see Cyril C. Means, "The Phoenix of Abortional Freedom," *New York Law Forum* 17 (1971): 335–410, at 406.

56. *New York Times*, 22 October 1971, pp. 1, 24 and 25, 24 October 1971, p. IV-1, 26 October 1971, p. 1, 28 October 1971, p. 26; Nellis to Means, 15 November 1971, Lader Box 16. On Justice Powell, see J. Harvie Wilkinson III, *Serving Justice: A Supreme Court Clerk's View* (New York: Charterhouse, 1974), Wilkinson, "Honorable Lewis F. Powell, Jr.: Five Years on the

Supreme Court," *University of Richmond Law Review* 11 (Winter 1977): 259–267; Jacob W. Landynski, "Justice Lewis F. Powell, Jr.," in Lamb and Halpern, eds., *The Burger Court*, pp. 276–314; and John C. Jeffries, Jr.'s forthcoming *Justice Lewis F. Powell, Jr.: A Biography* (New York: Macmillan, 1994). On now Chief Justice Rehnquist, see Sue Davis, *Justice Rehnquist and the Constitution* (Princeton: Princeton University Press, 1989), and Davis, "Justice William H. Rehnquist," in Lamb and Halpern, eds., *The Burger Court*, pp. 315–342; also see Donald E. Boles, *Mr. Justice Rehnquist, Judicial Activist: The Early Years* (Ames: Iowa State University Press, 1987).

57. *New York Times*, 28 October 1971, pp. 1, 22; Gerald Lipson and Dianne Wolman, "Polling Americans on Birth Control and Population," *Family Planning Perspectives* 4 (January 1972): 39–42.

58. Lucas to Weddington, 2 November 1971, Lucas Box 22; *Thompson v. State*, 493 S.W.2d 913; *Dallas Times Herald*, 2 November 1971, pp. 19, 21, 21 November 1971, p. A34; *New York Times*, 3 November 1971, p. 17; *Washington Post, Dallas Morning News, Houston Chronicle, Houston Post* and *Austin American-Statesman*, all for 3 November 1971; Scanlan to Floyd, 5 November 1971, Texas AG File 70–308. A full transcript of Dr. C. W. Thompson III's May 1969 trial—at which the young woman who had undergone an incomplete abortion testified against him—is located in the subsequent U.S. Supreme Court case file, *Thompson v. Texas*, O.T. 1971, #1200, National Archives, RG 267, Box 296.

59. Weddington to Means, 3 November 1971, Pilpel-SSC; Lucas to Stuart Kinard, 5 November 1971, Lucas Box 22; Weddington to Whitehill, 14 and 28 October 1971, Whitehill Papers; Lucas to Weddington, 7 November 1971, Lucas Box 7; Garrow conversations with Sarah Weddington, L. A. Scott Powe, Roy Lucas, Linda Coffee, and Ron Weddington.

60. E. Robert Seaver to Lucas, 15 November 1971, and Lucas to Seaver, 18 November 1971, Lucas Box 22; *Houston Post*, 18 November 1971; Weddington to Whitehill, 23 November 1971, Whitehill Papers; Coffee to Seaver, 24 November 1971, Seaver notes, 29 November 1971, and Weddington to Seaver, 29 November 1971, *Roe* Case File, National Archives, RG 267, Box 9; Weddington to Lucas, 29 November 1971, Whitehill Papers; Seaver to Weddington, 30 November 1971, Lucas Box 22; Lucas to Weddington, 23 July 1972, Whitehill Papers; Weddington, *A Question of Choice*, p. 102; Garrow conversations with Sarah Weddington, Ron Weddington, Roy Lucas, Linda Coffee, and Roy Merrill. No copy of Marsha King's November 22 telegram appears to have survived. Two decades later, Lucas would assert that "Cyril, et al. found in Sarah an opportunistic, very inexperienced, malleable individual who technically had to do no more than persuade" the three clients to support her claim and "who risked the results of an important social movement to gratify her own ego and ambition." Lucas, "Notes on the Efforts in 1965–1973," pp. 27, 94.

61. Robert H. Quinn et al., "Brief for the Appellant," *Eisenstadt v. Baird*, U.S.S.C., O.T. 1970, #70–17, 14 May 1971; Pilpel, Wechsler and Zuckerman, "Brief of the Planned Parenthood Federation of America," *Eisenstadt v. Baird*, #70–17, 14 June 1971; Roger P. Stokey and Stephen M. Weiner, "Brief for Amicus Curiae Planned Parenthood League of Massachusetts," *Eisenstadt v. Baird*, #70–17, 14 June 1971; Sylvia S. Ellison, "Brief for Human Rights for Women, Inc.," *Eisenstadt v. Baird*, #70–17, 15 July 1971; Balliro, "Brief for the Appellee," *Eisenstadt v. Baird*, #70–17, 15 July 1971; Matthew H. Feinberg to Mel Wulf, 16 April 1971, Wulf to John A. Robertson, 1 July 1971, Robertson to Wulf, 7 July 1971, and Tydings to Wulf, 15 November 1971, ACLU 1975 Vol. 19; Gruening to Baird, 14 September 1971, Baird Papers; Tydings to E. Robert Seaver, 28 September 1971, Balliro to Seaver, 27 October and 1 November 1971, and Baird to Seaver, 1 November 1971, *Eisenstadt* Case File, National Archives, RG 267, Box 8; Wulf, Lawrence G. Sager, and Robertson, "Brief of the American Civil Liberties Union and the Civil Liberties Union of Massachusetts," *Eisenstadt v. Baird*, #70–17, 26pp., 26 October 1971, pp. 9, 11, 14; Tydings and David W. Rutstein, "Supplemental Brief of Appellee," *Eisenstadt v. Baird*, #70–17, 1 November 1971; Garrow conversations with William R. Baird, Joseph D. Tydings and Jane Zuckerman. Also see *New York Times*, 21 September 1971, p. 30, and *Manfredonia v. Barry*, 401 F. Supp. 762 (E.D.N.Y.), 25 September 1975.

62. Transcript of Oral Argument, *Eisenstadt v. Baird*, U.S.S.C., O.T. 1971, #70–17, 17 November 1971, 41pp., esp. pp. 11–14, 16, 21, 28, 39–40.

63. Douglas Conference Notes, *Eisenstadt* v. *Baird*, 19 November 1971, Douglas Box 1543. Brennan in resisting any First Amendment holding had cited *U.S.* v. *O'Brien* (391 U.S. 367, 1968); White in saying that the law ought to be affirmed cited *Ferguson* v. *Skrupa* (372 U.S. 726, 1963). Justice Brennan's docket book sheets on *Eisenstadt* contain no notes on the conference discussion aside from a vote tally showing a 5 to 2 majority in favor of affirmance, with Chief Justice Burger and Justice White marked as dissenters. Brennan Docket Books, Boxes 418 and 419.

64. "RLJ" [Richard L. Jacobson] to "Dear Mr. Justice," 23 November 1971, Douglas Box 1543; Burger to Douglas, and Douglas to Burger, 23 November 1971, Douglas Box 1543 and Brennan Box 255; Brennan assignment sheet, 23 November 1971, Brennan Box 249; Brennan circulations of 13, 23, and 29 December 1971, Marshall to Brennan, 13 December 1971, Stewart to Brennan, 22 December 1971, Brennan Box 255 and Marshall Box 81; Burger to Douglas, 28 December 1971, Brennan Box 255, Douglas Box 1543 and Marshall Box 81; Garrow conversations with Paul R. Hoeber, Gerald Goldman, Paul Gewirtz, Richard L. Jacobson, William H. Alsup, Benjamin W. Heineman, Jr., and Richard D. Parker. No written materials reflecting or documenting the preparation or composition of the Brennan opinion in advance of the initial December 13 typeset circulation appear in any of Justice Brennan's files.

65. Hames to Cyril Means, 15 November 1971, Hames to Graham, 18 November 1971, Hames to Paul Shimek, Jr., 18 November 1971, Hames Papers; *Atlanta Constitution*, 24 November 1971, p. B3; Graham to Hames, 29 November 1971, Hames Papers; Garrow conversations with Margie Hames. *Reed* v. *Reed*, 404 U.S. 71 (22 November 1971), was argued on October 19; the Florida case was *Mitchum* v. *Foster*, 407 U.S. 225 (1972).

66. Floyd, "Motion to Postpone Argument and Submission," *Roe* v. *Wade*, 30 November 1971, *Roe* Case File, National Archives, RG 267, Box 9; Weddington, *A Question of Choice*, p. 102; *American Medical News*, 6 December 1971, pp. 12–13 and 20 December 1971, p. 4; "WHA" [William H. Alsup] note, 2 December 1971, Douglas Box 1589; *New York Times*, 7 December 1971, p. 1, 11 December 1971, p. 1, 14 December 1971, p. 21; *Roe* v. *Wade*, 404 U.S. 981 (7 December 1971); Garrow conversations with Paul Gewirtz, Richard L. Jacobson, Benjamin W. Heineman, Jr., Richard D. Parker, William H. Alsup, and Gerald Goldman. Powell and Rehnquist officially joined the Court on 7 January 1972.

67. *New York Times*, 4 December 1971, pp. 29, 37, 10 December 1971, p. 32, 17 December 1971, p. 48, 23 December 1971, p. 24; Lucas to James Nespole, 17 December 1971, Lucas Box 19; *Minneapolis Tribune* and *St. Paul Dispatch*, 10 December 1971; Lucas to Irene Hoebel, 21 December 1971, MARC 120-2B; Lucas, "Annual Report to [Madison Institute] Trustees," 28 December 1971, Emerson Box 13; *San Francisco Chronicle*, 9 December 1971, p. 25; *San Francisco Examiner*, 9 December 1971, p. 44; Zad Leavy, Norma G. Zarky, and Alan F. Charles, "Amicus Curiae Brief on Behalf of Medical School Deans, Professors and Others," *People* v. *Pettegrew* and *People* v. *Barksdale*, Cal. Sup. Ct., Crim. #15841 and 15866, 47pp., 18 November 1971; Ruth Roemer to Lucas, 19 January 1972, Lucas Box 25; Garrow conversations with Ruth Roemer and Zad Leavy.

On WONAAC and the Wheeler case, also see Means to Hames, 20 October 1971, Hames Papers; *Austin American-Statesman*, 17 October 1971, p. 2, and 23 October 1971; Nellis to Means, 1 November 1971, Lader Box 16; *New York Times*, 21 November 1971, p. 95; Ellen Frankfort, *Vaginal Politics* (New York: Quadrangle Books, 1972), pp. 97–100; and Lader, *Abortion II*, pp. 188–189. On Byrn, also see Byrn, "Abortion on Demand: Whose Morality?," *Notre Dame Lawyer* 46 (Fall 1970): 5–40; *Science News*, 29 January 1972, p. 75; and Frankfort, *Vaginal Politics*, pp. 94–97.

68. *Daily Texan*, 2 December 1971; *Dallas Times Herald*, 12 December 1971, p. D10; Weddington Interview with Cheek, pp. 20–21, 36; Weddington in Vicki Quade, "Our Bodies, Our Law," *The Barrister* 13 (Summer 1986): 14ff., at 16; Milbauer, *The Law Giveth*, pp. 53–54; Weddington, *A Question of Choice*, pp. 101, 106–108; Garrow conversations with Margie Hames, Sarah Weddington, Ron Weddington, Joseph Nellis, Cyril Means, Nancy Wechsler, and Jane Zuckerman.

69. Texas Citizens for Abortion Education [*Newsletter*], March 1972, p. 2; Weddington, *A Question of Choice*, p. 109; Floyd note sheet, n.d., Texas AG File 70–308; Garrow conversations with Sarah Weddington, Ron Weddington, Linda Coffee, Virginia Whitehill, Roy Merrill, Fred Bruner, Margie Hames, Tobi Schwartz, Ruste Kitfield, Judith [Bourne] Rooks, Peter Bourne, Gale Siegel Messerman, Reber F. Boult, Jr., Pamela Walker, Roy Lucas, Bob Hall, Jimmye Kimmey, Brian Sullivan, Nicholas W. Danforth, Daniel M. Schneider, and David W. Tundermann.

70. Transcripts and Tape Recordings of *Roe* v. *Wade* and *Doe* v. *Bolton* Oral Arguments, 13 December 1971, National Archives; [Floyd], "Introduction [Outline of Oral Argument Presentation]," n.d. [c.13 December 1971], 11pp., and "1st Contention [earlier draft of the same]," n.d., 10pp., Texas AG File 70–308; *Washington Post*, 14 December 1971, p. A3; *Dallas Morning News*, 14 December 1971, p. A9; *Houston Chronicle*, 14 December 1971; *American Medical News*, 20 December 1971, pp. 4, 9; Weddington in *Dallas Morning News*, 22 April 1973, p. E1; Weddington Interview with Duke, pp. 4–5; Weddington Interview with Cheek, pp. 23–24; Weddington in *Fulton County Daily Report*, 9 February 1989, pp. 8–9; Weddington, *A Question of Choice*, pp. 115–119; Hames in *Atlanta Journal-Constitution Magazine*, 11 March 1973, pp. 22ff.; Woodward and Armstrong, *The Brethren*, pp. 165–167; Milbauer, *The Law Giveth*, pp. 52, 55; O'Brien, *Storm Center*, pp. 26–28; Garrow conversations with Sarah Weddington, Jay Floyd, Margie Hames, Dorothy Beasley, Linda Coffee, Ron Weddington, Peter Bourne, and Jimmye Kimmey. The article which Weddington cited is Cyril C. Means, "The Phoenix of Abortional Freedom," *New York Law Forum* 17 (1971): 335–410, esp. at 336 and 402–403.

Also see *Ft. Worth Star-Telegram*, 13 December 1971; *Atlanta Journal*, 13 December 1971; *Atlanta Constitution*, 14 December 1971; *Dallas Times-Herald*, 14 December 1971; and 10 *Criminal Law Reporter* 4117–4119. Published versions of the *Roe* transcript contain a modest number of errors that can be detected only when a listener carefully compares the transcript to the actual audio recording of the argument. The identity of most but not all questioners can also be determined from the tapes.

71. Garrow conversations with Sarah Weddington, Margie Hames, Jay Floyd, Dorothy Beasley, Linda Coffee, Tobi Schwartz, Ron Weddington, Jimmye Kimmey, Peter Bourne, Brian Sullivan, Gale Siegel Messerman, Virginia Whitehill and Pamela Walker; Weddington to Jay Floyd, 20 December 1971, Texas AG File 70–308; Lucas to Morton Goldstein and to Barbara Phillips, 3 January 1972, Lucas Box 25; Nancy Stearns to Hames, 5 January 197[2], Hames Papers; *Science News*, 29 January 1972, p. 75; Weddington, *A Question of Choice*, p. 121. Also see Lynne N. Henderson, "Legality and Empathy," *Michigan Law Review* 85 (June 1987): 1574–1653, at 1621–22, who asserts that "*Roe* v. *Wade* was not well argued—counsel for both sides . . . seemed unprepared to answer questions, did not respond to questions, did not have facts at their disposal," and Lee Epstein and Joseph F. Kobylka, *The Supreme Court and Legal Change* (Chapel Hill: University of North Carolina Press, 1992), pp. 179–182, who characterize Floyd's performance as "downright awful" and Weddington's as "less than stellar," since "she sounded more like a lobbyist staking out a policy question than an attorney making a legal claim." Also note H. W. Perry, Jr., *Deciding to Decide* (Cambridge: Harvard University Press, 1991), p. 127, who observes that in interviews with five sitting justices and some sixty-four clerks, most of whom served in the late 1970s, "Time and again, I was told that most state attorneys general are terrible litigators."

72. Douglas Conference Notes on *Roe* and *Doe*, 16 December 1971, Douglas Box 1588; Brennan Docket Book Conference Notes, 16 December 1971, Brennan Boxes 418 and 419. Also see Woodward and Armstrong, *The Brethren*, pp. 169–170; James F. Simon, *Independent Journey* (New York: Harper & Row, 1980), pp. 438–442; O'Brien, *Storm Center*, pp. 28–29, and especially Bernard Schwartz, *The Unpublished Opinions of the Burger Court* (New York: Oxford University Press, 1988), pp. 84–86, and Schwartz, *The Ascent of Pragmatism* (New York: Addison-Wesley, 1990), pp. 47, 298–299.

73. Brennan Conference List for 16 December 1971, Brennan Box 249; 17 and 20 December 1971 Assignment Lists, Brennan Box 249 and Marshall Box 75; Douglas Conference Notes,

16 December 1971, Douglas Box 1588; Douglas to Burger, 18 December 1971, Burger to Douglas, 20 December 1971, Brennan Box 281 and Douglas Box 1589; Garrow conversations with William H. Alsup, Richard L. Jacobson, Paul R. Hoeber, Paul Gewirtz, Benjamin W. Heineman, Jr., Richard D. Parker, Larry A. Hammond, and G. Edward White. Brennan's docket book sheets contain no vote tallies for the 1971 *Roe* and *Doe* discussions, and no conference notes or docket book pages for the 1971 Term appear among Justice Marshall's otherwise voluminous Supreme Court papers. Also see Woodward and Armstrong, *The Brethren*, pp. 170–172; Melvin I. Urofsky, ed., *The Douglas Letters* (Bethesda, MD: Adler & Adler, 1987), pp. 181–182; Schwartz, *The Unpublished Opinions of the Burger Court*, pp. 86–87; *Port of Portland* v. *United States*, 408 U.S. 811 (29 June 1972).

On Douglas's widespread reputation for unfriendly moodiness, see Schwartz, *The Ascent of Pragmatism*, pp. 19–20 ("the quintessential loner—a lover of humanity who did not like people") and Howard Ball and Melvin Urofsky's contributions in Stephen L. Wasby, ed., *"He Shall Not Pass This Way Again": The Legacy of William O. Douglas* (Pittsburgh: University of Pittsburgh Press, 1990), pp. 32 and 36–37. Urofsky quotes Justice Marshall, in a 17 May 1988 interview, as characterizing Douglas as "about as independent a cuss as I knew."

74. Blackmun in Bill Moyers's 1987 PBS "In Search of the Constitution," and in *Washington Post*, 20 April 1992, pp. A1, A4; Douglas to Brennan, 22 December 1971, with attachment, and Brennan to Douglas, 30 December 1971, Brennan Box 281 and Douglas Box 1589. Douglas's December 22 draft also appears in Schwartz, *The Unpublished Opinions of the Burger Court*, pp. 87–102, at 93–102. Also see Schwartz, *The New Right and the Constitution* (Boston: Northeastern University Press, 1990), pp. 59–60. In mid-January Douglas also mentioned *Griswold* and the Ninth Amendment in a short public dissent from the Court's denial of certiorari in a case where a California high school had suspended a male student who had refused to shorten the length of his hair. Under *Griswold*, Douglas said, "liberty" "includes at least the fundamental rights 'retained by the people' under the Ninth Amendment," and a decision about the length of one's hair was "a purely private choice." *Olff* v. *East Side Union High School District*, 404 U.S. 1042, 1043–44 (17 January 1972), denying cert. to 445 F.2d 932 (9th Cir., 1971), which in turn had reversed 305 F. Supp. 557 (N.D. Cal., 1969). Also see Dale J. Galvin, *Willamette Law Journal* 8 (June 1972): 277–283. A profusion of additional "hair length" cases, many involving discussions of either the Ninth Amendment and/or *Griswold*, percolated in a significant number of federal district and circuit courts between 1966 and 1972, but in no instance did the Supreme Court accord any of them substantive review. See *Ferrell* v. *Dallas Independent School District*, 261 F. Supp. 545 (N.D. Tex., 1966), affirmed 392 F.2d 697 (5th Cir., 1968), cert. denied 393 U.S. 856 (15 October 1968); *Anderson* v. *Laird*, 437 F.2d 912, 916 (7th Cir., 1971), cert. denied 404 U.S. 865 (12 October 1971); and *Freeman* v. *Flake*, 448 F.2d 258, 261 (10th Cir., 1971), cert. denied 405 U.S. 1032 (Douglas dissenting), 27 March 1972. Also see *Breen* v. *Kahl*, 296 F. Supp. 702 (W.D. Wis.), 20 February 1969; *Richards* v. *Thurston*, 424 F.2d 1281, 1284–85 (1st Cir.), 28 April 1970; *Watson* v. *Thompson*, 321 F. Supp. 394, 401–02 (E.D. Tex.), 6 January 1971; *Berryman* v. *Hein*, 329 F. Supp. 616, 620 (D. Idaho), 17 February 1971; *Bishop* v. *Colaw*, 450 F.2d 1069, 1075 (8th Cir., 1971); *Stull* v. *School Board*, 450 F.2d 339, 347 (3d Cir., 1972); and especially *Karr* v. *Schmidt*, 460 F.2d 609, 614, 619, 624 (5th Cir., 1972). Also note 401 U.S. 1201, and *Murphy* v. *Pocatello School District*, 94 Idaho 32, 480 P.2d 878, 883 (Idaho Sup. Ct. 1971).

75. Blackmun to Burger, 18 January 1972, Brennan Box 249 and Marshall Box 99; "WHA" [William H. Alsup] to Douglas, 25 January 1972, Douglas Box 1589; *Hanrahan* v. *Doe*, 404 U.S. 1012 (10 January 1972); *Nichol* v. *Kennan*, 404 U.S. 1055 (24 January 1972); *Chicago Tribune*, 25 January 1972, p. 2. Also see Woodward and Armstrong, *The Brethren*, p. 176. On *Kennan* and the highly complex procedural developments in the Wisconsin litigation, also see Joseph L. Nellis, "Memorandum re *Babbitz* v. *McCann*," 14 June 1971, and Nellis to Otto J. Kerner, 18 June 1971, NARAL Box 6; *Nichol* v. *Kennan*, 404 U.S. 879 (19 October 1971), and 404 U.S. 1036 (17 January 1972); "KRR" [Kenneth R. Reed] to Douglas, 14 October 1971, Douglas Box 1539; Robert A. Warren et al., "Jurisdictional Statement," *Nichol* v. *Kennan*, 29 October 1971, *Nichol* Case File #71–595, National Archives, RG 267, Box 189; Nellis to

Nathaniel Rothstein and Milton Bordow, 1 November 1971, Lader Box 5; *Babbitz* v. *McCann*, 404 U.S. 988 (14 December 1971); Nellis et al., "Brief and Appendix for Appellant," *Babbitz* v. *McCann*, 7th Cir., #71–1763, 34pp., January 1972; Nellis to Cyril Means et al., 3 February 1972, NARAL Box 6 and Lader Box 16; Nellis to Margie Hames, 22 February 1972, Hames Papers; Nellis to Means, 16 and 20 March 1972, NARAL Boxes 6 and 7, Nellis to Jimmye Kimmey, 25 September 1972, NARAL Box 6; and especially "WHA" [William H. Alsup] to Douglas, 5 January 1972, 3pp., Douglas Box 1539, which provides a comprehensive chronological summary of the earlier developments while also observing how "Given that the Court is indicating it will invalidate the Texas and Ga. abortion laws, it would not make much sense to deprive these Wisconsin women of the operation in the meantime. The equities of irreparable harm are clearly in favor of the lower court's action."

76. *Abele* v. *Markle*, 452 F.2d 1121, 13 December 1971; *New York Times*, 6 January 1972, p. 24, 7 January 1972, p. 26, 12 January 1972, p. 45, 1 February 1972, p. 34, 11 February 1972, p. 35, 13 February 1972, p. 59, 18 February 1972, p. 34, 26 February 1972, pp. 1, 9, 24 March 1972, p. 45; *Byrn* v. *New York City Health and Hospitals Corp*, 329 N.Y.S.2d 722 (App. Div. Sup. Ct.), 24 February 1972, and 333 N.Y.S.2d 63; *City of New York* v. *Wyman*, 330 N.Y.S.2d 385 (N.Y. Ct. App.), 10 February 1972. On the Connecticut case, also see *Hartford Courant*, 18 December 1971; and Elizabeth Gilbertson Wilhelm to Marjorie Fine, and to Stewart Mott, 27 March 1971, Emerson Box 49 and NARAL Box 2. For another unsuccessful effort similar to Professor Byrn's, see *McGarvey* v. *Magee-Womens Hospital*, 340 F. Supp. 751 (W.D. Pa.), 17 March 1972, affirmed without opinion, 474 F.2d 1339 (3d Cir., 1973).

77. *Beecham* v. *Leahy*, 287 A.2d 836, 840, 14 January 1972; *State* v. *Barquet*, 262 So.2d 431, 437–38, 14 February 1972; *Miami Herald*, 15 February 1972, pp. A1, A8, 8 April 1972, p. A22; *New York Times*, 15 February 1972, p. 18; Lawrence Justiz to Lee Gidding, 27 April 1972, NARAL Box 2. On the Vermont case, see particularly Willis E. Higgins, "The Vermont Abortion Suits," *ZPG National Reporter*, February 1972, pp. 5, 9–10; also see Lee Gidding to Larry Lader, 22 December 1971, NARAL Box 5; Lucas to Frederick Cross, 9 February 1972, Lucas Box 7; Higgins, "The Phoenix Stirs: Common Law Abortion in Vermont" (unpublished paper, 12 May 1972), 6pp., NARAL I-12; and Lader, *Abortion II*, p. 190. On the Florida decisions, also see C. Ken Bishop, *University of Florida Law Review* 24 (Winter 1972): 346–352; and Joseph M. Ellis, *Florida Bar Journal* 47 (January 1973): 18–22; for legislative background, see Cliff Reuter to Lader, 23 September 1970, Lee Gidding, "Florida Situation," 27 October 1970, [Gidding], "Florida Situation," 17 December 1971, and [Gidding], "Florida," 16 and 24 February 1972, NARAL Box 2.

78. On North Dakota, see Dick Schlorf (North Dakota Citizens for the Legal Termination of Pregnancy) to the Michigan Coordinating Committee for Abortion Law Reform, [10 February 1972], MARC Box 3 ("so far we are operating in sort of an underground manner"), and Faye D. Ginsburg, *Contested Lives* (Berkeley: University of California Press, 1989), pp. 67–70; on Michigan, see Durlin Hickok and Colin Campbell, "Attitudes Toward Abortion Law Reform . . . " *Michigan Medicine*, April 1972, pp. 327–329; and *Poe* v. *Scodeller*, U.S.D.C. W.D. Mich., CA# G53–72 [6 March 1972], Lucas Box 12. Also note *Tennessee Woman* v. *David Pack*, U.S.D.C. M.D. Tenn., #CA 6538, a challenge to Tennessee's antiabortion statute in which a federal three-judge panel in an unreported four page opinion on 21 March 1972 declined to order injunctive relief. Texas AG File 70–308.

79. On Oklahoma, see *New York Times*, 2 March 1972, p. 33; on Georgia, see *Atlanta Constitution*, 26 and 27 January, 25 and 26 February and 4 March 1972; Sarah Stewart to Lee Gidding, 29 January and 3 March 1972, NARAL Box 2; *Atlanta Journal*, 23 February 1972, p. B5, 4 March 1972; *Atlanta Journal-Constitution*, 23 April 1972. Also see Lee Gidding, "Iowa," 16 February 1972, NARAL Box 3.

80. *Austin American-Statesman*, 26 January 1972, 7 February 1972, p. 21, 11 February 1972, 30 April 1972, p. D9; *Dallas Morning News*, 6 February 1972, p. A30, 30 May 1972, p. B7; Ginny Whitehill to Lee Gidding, 9 February, 25 March and 22 April 1972, NARAL Box 5; *Houston Chronicle*, 23 February 1972; *Houston Post*, 23 February 1972 and 2 April 1972, p. B8; *Abilene Reporter-News*, 18 March 1972, p. B3; Whitehill to Ruth [Bowers], 1 April 1972, and

Whitehill to Bowers and Weddington, 22 April 1972, Whitehill Papers; *New York Times*, 17 April 1972, p. 28; *Dallas Times-Herald*, 28 April 1972; Garrow conversations with Sarah Weddington and Virginia Whitehill. On Weddington's legislative campaign, also see Ann Richards, *Straight From the Heart* (New York: Simon & Schuster, 1989), pp. 138–144, and Weddington, *A Question of Choice*, p. 125.

81. On the ABA, see *New York Times*, 8 February 1972, p. 37, and James A. Knecht, *University of Illinois Law Forum* 1972, pp. 177–197; on the Commission on Population Growth and the American Future, see *New York Times*, 12 March 1972, p. 1, and 17 March 1972, pp. 1, 18. For the January Gallup numbers, see Gerald Lipson and Dianne Wolman, "Polling Americans on Birth Control and Population," *Family Planning Perspectives* 4 (January 1972): 39–42. With regard to the "stall," see Lader to David Huber, 2 February 1972, Lader Box 21; Hall, "Induced Abortion in the United States, 1971," *Journal of Reproductive Medicine* 8 (June 1972): 345–347, and Hall's "Foreword" in David F. Walbert and J. Douglas Butler, eds., *Abortion, Society and the Law* (Cleveland: Case Western Reserve University Press, 1973), p. ix. On the Massachusetts case, see *Commonwealth* v. *Hare*, 280 N.E. 138, 28 February 1972, Gerald A. Messerman in Walbert and Butler, *Abortion, Society and the Law*, pp. 251–253, and Ellen Messer and Kathryn E. May, *Back Rooms* (New York: St. Martin's Press, 1988), p. 211; on earlier developments, see *Burlington Free Press*, 12 December 1969; *Boston Globe*, 26 February 1970, pp. 1, 14; *Boston Herald-Traveler*, 27 February 1970; and Lader, *Abortion II*, pp. 75–76. Also see generally *Time*, 20 March 1972, pp. 89–90; *National Clergy Consultation Service on Abortion Newsletter*, Vol. 3, #1 (May 1972); and compare "A Statement on Abortion by One Hundred Professors of Obstetrics," *American Journal of Obstetrics and Gynecology* 112 (1 April 1972): 992–998, with Harvey Karman, "The Paramedic Abortionist," *Clinical Obstetrics and Gynecology* 15 (June 1972): 379–387.

82. NARAL memo, 13 January 1972, NARAL I-25; Lucas to Irene Hoebel, 21 December 1971, MARC Box 120-2B; Lucas, "Annual Report to Trustees," 28 December 1971, Emerson Box 13; Lucas to Pilpel, 3 January 1972, and Pilpel to Lucas, 17 January 1972, Lucas Box 19; Lucas to Ralph Brown, 13 January 1972, Lucas Box 25; Lucas to Richard L. Cates, 18 January 1972, Lucas Box 24; Lucas to James K. Foley, 2 August 1972, Lucas Box 11; Robert E. Hall to Lucas, 22 March 1972, Charles L. Black, Jr., to Lucas, 3 April 1972, and Norman Dorsen to Lucas, 27 April 1972, Emerson Box 13; Garrow conversations with Roy Lucas, Joseph Nellis, Milan Vuitch, Florence "Lee" Vuitch, Larry Lader, and Cyril Means.

83. Stearns to George H. Barlow et al., 26 January 1972, and Forman to Stearns, 31 January 1972, Brennan Box 281; *YWCA* v. *Kugler*, 342 F. Supp. 1048, 1069, 1071, 1072, 1082, 29 February 1972. Supreme Court Justice William J. Brennan, as the "circuit" or supervisory justice assigned to the Third Circuit, which encompassed New Jersey, received a copy of both Stearns's letter and Forman's reply. Law journal notes on *YWCA* v. *Kugler* include Lawrence E. Allison, Jr., *Mississippi Law Journal* 43 (November 1972): 728–732, and A. G. J. McIntyre, *Journal of Urban Law* 50 (February 1973): 505–513. Also see "New Jersey's Abortion Law: An Establishment of Religion?," *Rutgers Law Review* 25 (Spring 1971): 452–475, which, despite its face date, actually *postdates* the *Kugler* decision, and similarly note Joseph S. Oteri et al., "Abortion and the Religious Liberty Clauses," *Harvard Civil Rights-Civil Liberties Law Review* 7 (May 1972): 559–599. Some two years later, in 1974, the *Kugler* decision was affirmed without opinion by the Third Circuit Court of Appeals (493 F.2d 1402), and certiorari was denied by the U.S. Supreme Court (415 U.S. 989).

84. *New York Times*, 2 March 1972, p. 31, 5 March 1972, p. 77, 8 March 1972, p. 46, 31 March 1972, p. 36, 9 May 1972, p. 26, 14 May 1972, p. 106, 25 June 1972, p. 69; *Trentonian*, 2 March 1972, p. 33; *Philadelphia Inquirer*, 5 March 1972, p. A18; *Newark Star-Ledger*, 5 March 1972, p. 26; *YWCA Magazine*, June 1972, pp. 12, 32; Lader to NARAL Executive Committee Members, 2 March 1972, and Lader to Biddy Hurlbut, 8 March 1972, NARAL Box 1; Lader, *Abortion II*, pp. 191–192. Also see Marianne Dame to Lucas, 6 [March] 1972, and Lucas to Dame, 16 March 1972, Lucas Box 25.

85. Frederick K. Cross to Delmas C. Hill et al., 15 February 1972, Lucas Box 7; *Poe* v. *Menghini*, 339 F. Supp. 986, 992–993, 13 March 1972; Means to Lucas, 15 March 1972, Lader Box 5 and Hames Papers; Lucas to Allan Barnes, 8 May 1972, Lucas Box 10.

86. Brennan Circulations (particularly 13 December 1971, p. 15, as well as 16 and 21 March 1972), White Circulations (7 February and 2 March 1972), Blackmun to White, 29 February 1972, Douglas Circulations (13 December 1971, 5 January 1972, and 17, 20, and 21 March 1972), Burger Circulations (10 and 21 March 1972), Brennan Box 255, Douglas Box 1543, and Marshall Box 81; "RLJ" [Richard L. Jacobson] to Douglas (2), 17 March 1972, Douglas Box 1543; Brennan Notes, 5pp., n.d. [22 March 1972], Brennan Box 255; *Eisenstadt* v. *Baird*, 405 U.S. 438, 443, 447, 448, 453, 455, 460, 463–64, 465, 472; Garrow conversations with Gerald Goldman, Paul Gewirtz, and Richard L. Jacobson. Also see *Stanley* v. *Illinois*, 405 U.S. 645, 651, where Justice White on behalf of a Court majority stated, with a reference to Arthur Goldberg's concurrence in *Griswold*, that "The integrity of the family unit has found protection" under the due process and equal protection clauses and the Ninth Amendment.

87. *Boston Evening Globe*, 22 March 1972, pp. 1, 51; *Boston Globe* and *Boston Herald Traveler*, 23 March 1972; *Worcester Telegram*, 23 March 1972, p. 16; *Washington Post*, 23 March 1972, pp. A1, A14; *New York Times*, 23 March 1972, p. 22, 25 March 1972, p. 30; Lucas to Henry Cowie, Jr., 23 March 1972, Lucas Box 13; Hames in *Macon Telegraph*, 13 April 1972; Richard A. Posner, "The Uncertain Protection of Privacy by the Supreme Court," *Supreme Court Review* 1979 (Chicago: University of Chicago Press, 1980), pp. 173–216, at 198; John F. Kippley, *Birth Control and Christian Discipleship* (Cincinnati: Couple to Couple League, 1985), p. 9; John T. Noonan, Jr., *A Private Choice* (New York: Free Press, 1979), p. 21; Mary Ann Glendon, *Rights Talk* (New York: Free Press, 1991), p. 57, William Van Alstyne, "Closing the Circle of Constitutional Review . . . " *Duke Law Journal* 1989 (December): 1677–1688, at 1678. Also see Posner, *Sex and Reason* (Cambridge: Harvard University Press, 1992), pp. 329–331; Van Alstyne, "The Enduring Example of John Marshall Harlan," *New York Law School Law Review* 36 (1991): 109–126, at 122; Graham Hughes, *The Conscience of the Courts* (Garden City, NY: Doubleday, 1975), pp. 33, 55, and 71; Michael J. Sandel, "Moral Argument and Liberal Toleration," *California Law Review* 77 (May 1989): 521–538, at 527–528; and Peter S. Wenz, *Abortion Rights as Religious Freedom* (Philadelphia: Temple University Press, 1992), pp. 28–30.

Note also Harriet F. Pilpel, Nancy F. Wechsler, and Ruth Jane Zuckerman, "U.S. Supreme Court Decision in the Massachusetts Birth Control Case," 14 April 1972, 12pp.; Pilpel and Wechsler, "Implications of the Baird Decision," *Family Planning/Population Reporter* 1 (December 1972): 6–7; William J. Curran, *New England Journal of Medicine* 286 (1 June 1972): 1198–1199; Morgan S. Bragg, *University of Florida Law Review* 25 (Fall 1972): 139–159, at 157 (*Eisenstadt* is "a startling expansion of *Griswold*"); Gerald Gunther, *Harvard Law Review* 86 (November 1972): 1–42, at 29–36; *Harvard Law Review* 86 (November 1972): 116–122; *Yale Law Journal* 82 (November 1972): 123–154, at 126–128; and Philip B. Kurland, "1971 Term: The Year of the Stewart-White Court," *Supreme Court Review* 1972 (University of Chicago Press, 1972), pp. 181–329, at 247–249. Additional law journal notes on *Eisenstadt* include Christel E. Marquardt, *Washburn Law Journal* 12 (Fall 1972): 97–101, and Katherine R. Jones, *New York University Review of Law and Social Change* 3 (Winter 1973): 56–69.

88. *Abele* v. *Markle*, 342 F. Supp. 800, 802, 805, 18 April 1972; *New York Times*, 19 April 1972, pp. 1, 94, 20 April 1972, p. 91, 22 April 1972, p. 34, 23 April 1972, p. IV-3, 10 May 1972, p. 51, 13 May 1972, pp. 1, 38, 15 May 1972, p. 24, 16 May 1972, p. 51, 17 May 1972, p. 53, 19 May 1972, p. 44, 20 May 1972, p. 13, 23 May 1972, pp. 1, 32, 24 May 1972, pp. 1, 51, 25 May 1972, p. 38, 27 May 1972, p. 12, 28 May 1972, p. IV-5, 10 June 1972, p. 35, 18 June 1972, p. 35, 1 July 1972, p. 8; Hearing Transcript, Public Health and Safety Committee, 19 May 1972, 239pp., Transcript of Proceedings, Connecticut House, 22 May 1972, pp. 2–107, and 23 May 1972, pp. 1–14, Transcript of Proceedings, Connecticut Senate, 22 May 1972, pp. 1–145, and 23 May 1972, pp. 1–15, Connecticut State Library; *Abele* Case File, National Archives, RG 267, Box 386; *New Haven Journal-Courier*, 1 July 1972 and 5 July 1972, p. 1. Meskill's attitude toward a rape exception was not unique; twelve years later a prominent antiabortion legal scholar, Basile J. Uddo, would assert that "allowing abortion for rape invites a flood of bogus rape abortions." Uddo, "Pregnancy Due to Rape and Incest," in James Bopp, Jr., ed., *Restoring the Right to Life* (Provo, UT: Brigham Young University Press, 1984), pp. 175–191, at 185.

89. Means to Pilpel, 25 May 1972, Lader Box 3 and PPFA II-184; *New York Times*, 9 April 1972,

p. 70, 14 April 1972, p. 42, 17 April 1972, p. 27, 18 April 1972, p. 43, 19 April 1972, p. 94, 20 April 1972, p. 44, 23 April 1972, p. IV-3, 24 April 1972, p. 24, 25 April 1972, pp. 40, 42, 26 April 1972, p. 31, 27 April 1972, pp. 16, 35, 28 April 1972, pp. 26, 45, 29 April 1972, pp. 30, 35, 1 May 1972, pp. 29, 32, 2 May 1972, p. 32, 3 May 1972, pp. 18, 33, 46, 5 May 1972, pp. 40, 46, 6 May 1972, pp. 1, 12; Lader to NARAL Executive Committee Members, 18 April 1982, NARAL Box 1. Also see "We Have Had Abortions," *Ms.*, Spring 1972, pp. 34–35, Paul Hoffman, "The Politics of Abortion," *The Nation*, 5 June 1972, pp. 712–713, and Fred C. Shapiro, "'Right to Life' Has a Message for New York State Legislators," *New York Times Magazine*, 20 August 1972, pp. 10, 34–44. When the Illinois plaintiffs' attorneys, citing Marshall's refusal to stay the Connecticut order, petitioned to have the stay he *had* issued in their case vacated, the request was denied first by Justice Rehnquist and then by the entire Court, with only Justice Douglas dissenting. *Doe v. Hanrahan*, 407 U.S. 902, 12 June 1972.

90. *New York Times*, 6 May 1972, p. 1, 7 May 1972, pp. 1, 29, 8 May 1972, pp. 1, 36, 43, 9 May 1972, pp. 1, 26, 10 May 1972, pp. 1, 51, 11 May 1972, pp. 1, 37, 40, 41, and 44, 12 May 1972, p. 46, 14 May 1972, pp. 1, 53, 62 and IV-4, 15 May 1972, p. 34, 16 May 1972, p. 1, 21 May 1972, p. IV-7, 25 May 1972, p. 11, 26 May 1972, pp. 34, 40, 27 May 1972, p. 16, 31 May 1972, p. 26; Larry Lader to NARAL Executive Committee Members, 16 May 1972, NARAL Box 1; *Wall Street Journal*, 17 May 1972; *Time*, 22 May 1972, p. 23; *Newsweek*, 22 May 1972, p. 32; Lader in *NARAL News*, Summer 1972, p. 3; [Alfred F. Moran], "Proposal," 20 June 1972, Schlesinger 223–1–3; Joan Cassell, *A Group Called Women* (New York: David McKay, 1977), p. 117. Also see *New York Times*, 1 June 1972, p. 47, 2 June 1972, p. 41, 8 June 1972, p. 53, 14 June 1972, p. 37, and 17 June 1972, p. 14; Lader, *Abortion II*, pp. 196–207. See as well Natalie Shainess, "Abortion: Inalienable Right," *New York State Journal of Medicine* 72 (1 July 1972): 1772–1775, at 1773 ("a nonsentient, nonindependently viable, noncognitive cell mass is not a human life"); and Suzannah Lessard, *Washington Monthly*, August 1972, pp. 29–37.

91. *New York Times*, 25 May 1972, p. 49, 8 June 1972, p. 53, 5 June 1972, p. 28, 21 June 1972, p. 56, 23 June 1972, p. 38; Lee Gidding to Sam Landfather, 22 May 1972, Lader Box 21; *Crossen v. Attorney General*, 344 F. Supp. 587 (E.D. Ky.), 19 May 1972.

92. Blackmun, "Memorandum to the Conference," 18 May 1972, and attachment, esp. p. 15, Brennan to Blackmun, 18 May 1972, Douglas to Blackmun, 19 May 1972, Brennan Box 282, Douglas Box 1588 and Marshall Box 99; Brennan Chambers, October Term 1971; Blackmun to Douglas, 22 May 1972, Douglas Box 1589; Garrow conversations with Benjamin W. Heineman, Jr., Paul Gewirtz, and Richard L. Jacobson. Douglas on Monday the 22nd gave updated copies of his *Doe* draft to both Marshall and Brennan, and wrote but did not send a memo to them, to Stewart and (surprisingly) to White saying that in light of Blackmun's "apparent problems with the case, I thought it best to circulate" his own *Doe* draft "to the group of five, thinking we might have a talk about it this week" and volunteering that suggestions would be welcome. "Time is getting late and the case was argued seven [*sic*] months ago and assigned by the Chief who represented a minority view." Douglas memo, ("not sent"), 22 May 1972, Douglas Box 1589; Douglas Circulation, 22 May 1972, Marshall Box 99 ("For Justice Marshall—not circulated") and Brennan Box 281.

Also see Woodward and Armstrong, *The Brethren*, pp. 183–184; O'Brien, *Storm Center*, p. 29; Melvin U. Urofsky, ed., *The Douglas Letters* (Bethesda, MD: Adler & Adler, 1987), pp. 182–185; Schwartz, *The Ascent of Pragmatism*, pp. 300–305; Phillip J. Cooper, "Justice William O. Douglas," in Lamb and Halpern, eds., *The Burger Court*, pp. 163–192, at 185; and especially Schwartz, *The Unpublished Opinions of the Burger Court*, pp. 103–119 and 144–151.

93. Blackmun, "Memorandum to the Conference," with attachment, 25 May 1972, Brennan Box 282, Douglas Box 1589 and Marshall Box 99; "WHA" [William H. Alsup] to Douglas, "Mary Doe," 25 and 26 May 1972, Douglas Box 1589; Douglas to Blackmun, 25 May 1972 (2), Brennan to Blackmun, 25 May 1972, Marshall to Blackmun, 25 May 1972, Blackmun, "Memorandum to the Conference," 26 May 1972, Brennan Box 282, Douglas Box 1589 and Marshall Box 99; Garrow conversations with Richard L. Jacobson, William H. Alsup, and Paul Gewirtz. Also see Schwartz, *The Unpublished Opinions of the Burger Court*, pp. 120–140.

Douglas's papers contain apparently the only surviving copy of a four-page typescript draft of a letter to Blackmun which the Brennan Chambers prepared on May 25 but which Brennan then decided not to send. Addressed "Dear Harry," the draft states that "I am particularly delighted that there appears to be a Court to confront the central issue in the abortion field and to dispose of it in the way your opinion has so artfully done." While Brennan's recommended changes would not "require significant rewriting or delay decision in the case," should not the Georgia statute, which lacked any fetal time ceiling, be "held invalid in full," "particularly in view of our recognition that there may be a compelling state interest in protecting such life at some point in pregnancy?" Additionally, "Should we make explicit what appears to be implicit . . . namely that (1) the fundamental right of choice to have an abortion belongs to the individual pregnant woman, whether married or single, and (2) any state subordinating interest may be asserted only by requirements not merely rationally related, but necessary to its achievement?" Also, "do you think it would be desirable to add an express statement that a physician cannot be subjected to criminal punishment so long as he exercises sound medical judgment, along the lines of Potter's *Vuitch* opinion?" Lastly, the opinion ought to make clear that abortions could be performed in licensed clinics as well as in hospitals. No similar copy appears in Justice Brennan's Papers, but Brennan reportedly conveyed the contents of the letter to a seemingly receptive Blackmun face-to-face. "No. 70–40," n.d. [25 May 1972], Douglas Box 1589; Brennan Chambers, October Term 1971.

94. Blackmun, "Memorandum to the Conference," 26 May 1972, Stewart to Blackmun, 30 May 1972, White Circulation in *Roe*, 3pp., 29 May 1972, Brennan Box 282, Douglas Box 1589, Marshall Box 99. Also see Schwartz, *The Unpublished Opinions of the Burger Court*, pp. 141–143. At a conference on May 29, the justices also agreed to hold the appeal in *Thompson* v. *Texas* until they had decided *Roe*. See Stuart M. Nelkin and Stuart Kinard, "Jurisdictional Statement," *C. W. Thompson* v. *Texas*, U.S.S.C., O.T. 1971, #1200, 20 March 1972, and Michael Rodak to Carol Vance, 3 May 1972, *Thompson* Case File, National Archives, RG 267, Box 296; "PG" [Paul Gewirtz] to Marshall, 1 May 1972, Marshall Box 75; and Brennan Docket Book, Box 419.

95. Blackmun, "Memorandum to the Conference," 31 May 1972, Douglas to Blackmun, 31 May 1972, Brennan to Blackmun, 31 May 1972, Marshall to Blackmun, 31 May 1972, Burger, "Memorandum to the Conference," 31 May 1972, Brennan Box 282, Douglas Box 1589, and Marshall Box 99; Brennan Chambers, October Term 1971. Also see Schwartz, *The Unpublished Opinions of the Burger Court*, pp. 143–146. Blackmun's reference to a "licensed medical facility" appears to mesh with one of the latter suggestions contained in the unsent Brennan letter discussed in note 93 above. Privately Blackmun also felt that the Court should not strike down both abortion statutes and the death penalty (see note 98 below) at the same time.

96. "WHA" [William H. Alsup] to Douglas, "Mary Doe," 1 June 1972, Douglas Box 1589; Douglas to Burger, 1 June 1972, Powell, "Memorandum to the Conference," 1 June 1972, Brennan Box 281, Douglas Box 1589, and Marshall Box 99; Garrow conversations with William H. Alsup, Richard L. Jacobson, Paul Gewirtz, and Benjamin W. Heineman, Jr.; Brennan Chambers, October Term 1971. Also see Schwartz, *The Unpublished Opinions of the Burger Court*, pp. 146–147.

97. Rehnquist, "Memorandum to the Conference," 1 June 1972, Brennan Box 281, Douglas Box 1589, and Marshall Box 99; "Memorandum from Mr. Justice Douglas," 4pp. typescript ["OK for printer WOD 6/1/72"] and typeset copy, 2 June 1972, "Mr. Justice Douglas" ["6th draft" (annotation of #5)], 8 June 1972, Douglas Box 1588; "Bill" ["from Justice Brennan"], 2pp., n.d., and "Bill" to "Bill," ["70–40"], n.d., Douglas Box 1589; White, "Memorandum to the Conference," 5 June 1972, Brennan Box 281, Douglas Box 1589, and Marshall Box 99; Douglas memorandum, print #6, 13 June 1972, Marshall Box 99; Douglas to Michael Rodak, 26 June 1972, Brennan Box 281 and Douglas Box 1589; Brennan Chambers, October Term 1971; 40 *U.S. Law Week* 3617 and 404 U.S. 919 (26 June 1972); Garrow conversations with William H. Alsup, Richard L. Jacobson, Benjamin W. Heineman, Jr., Richard D. Parker, and Paul Gewirtz. Brennan's references were to *U.S.* v. *Wade*, 388 U.S. 218 (1967), and *Miranda* v. *Arizona*, 384 U.S. 436 (1966). Also see Woodward and Armstrong, *The*

Brethren, pp. 187–189; Simon, *Independent Journey,* p. 440; Howard Ball in Wasby, ed., *"He Shall Not Pass This Way Again,"* pp. 7–8, Ball and Cooper, *Of Power and Right,* pp. 308–309, and Nat Hentoff, "The Justice Breaks His Silence," *Playboy,* July 1991, pp. 120–122, 154–158, at 122.

98. Michael Rodak, Jr., to Lucas, and Lucas to "Dear Al," 26 June 1972, Lucas Box 22; *New York Times,* 27 June 1972, p. 24; *Dallas Morning News,* 27 June 1972, p. A6; *Medical World News,* 14 July 1972; Means in *NARAL News,* Summer 1972, p. 2; Garrow conversations with Roy Lucas, Sarah Weddington, Ron Weddington, Linda Coffee, Jay Floyd, Margie Hames, and Dorothy Beasley. On Weddington's legislative campaign, see *Austin American-Statesman,* 7 May 1972, p. A1, 4 June 1972, p. A1; and Weddington, *A Question of Choice,* pp. 125 and 134. Beasley's two death penalty cases, *Furman* v. *Georgia* and *Jackson* v. *Georgia,* 408 U.S. 238, had been argued on January 17 and were announced on June 29. *Peters* v. *Kiff,* 407 U.S. 493, a habeas corpus challenge to the exclusion of black jurors from the trial of a white criminal defendant, was argued on February 22 and decided on June 22. Also see *Atlanta Constitution,* 14 January 1972, p. B5, and *Atlanta Journal-Constitution Magazine,* 23 April 1972, pp. 7–17.

99. *Washington Post,* 4 July 1972, pp. A1, A10; *Austin American-Statesman,* 4 July 1972, pp. 1, 6; *New York Times,* 5 July 1972, p. 27; Douglas to Burger, 4 July 1972, Burger to Douglas, 27 July 1972, and Douglas to Burger, 7 August 1972, Brennan Box 281, Douglas Box 1588, and Marshall Box 78; Woodward and Armstrong, *The Brethren,* p. 229; Blackmun as quoted in Note, "The Changing Social Vision of Justice Blackmun," *Harvard Law Review* 96 (January 1983): 717–736, at 723 (characterizing in a 1979 speech in France his "two full weeks" of summer 1972 research as "personally and very privately performed"); *Washington Post,* 20 April 1992, pp. A1, A4; Garrow conversations with three firsthand observers or participants. Also see *The Rag,* 31 July 1972, p. 5, and Urofsky, ed., *The Douglas Letters,* pp. 185–186. Although Burger told Douglas in the July 27 letter that he was writing so as "to allow any future scholar who may peruse the current press accounts or papers of Justices to have the 'due process' benefit of all the facts in context," twenty years later, even when presented with his own 1972 statement, the retired Chief Justice declined to make his *Roe* and *Doe* notes and other materials available for review. "I have made it a firm practice not to open my files to third parties for any reason, and I do not believe that it is appropriate for other Justices to do so." Garrow to Burger, 16 June 1992, and Burger to Garrow, 19 June 1992, author's files.

100. Weddington to Lee Gidding, 31 August 1972, NARAL Box 5; *New York Times,* 8 June 1972, p. 38, 19 June 1972, p. 68, 21 June 1972, p. 48, 27 June 1972, p. 30, 28 June 1972, pp. 21, 34, 13 July 1972, pp. 1, 34, 15 July 1972, p. 1, 6 August 1972, pp. 28, 40, 9 August 1972, p. 12, 11 August 1972, p. 8, 17 August 1972, p. 35, 18 August 1972, p. 36, 5 September 1972, p. 1, 25 September 1972, p. 42, 4 October 1972, p. 32; Martin F. McKernan, Jr., "Constitutional Amendments on the Rights of the Unborn," June 1972, 2pp., Texas AG File 70–308; Garrow conversations with Sarah Weddington, Ron Weddington, and Margie Hames. On Powell's August 13 speech, also see *U.S. News & World Report,* 28 August 1972, and Wilkinson, *Serving Justice,* pp. 102–107, at 105.

101. *Vuitch* v. *Hardy,* CA#71–1129 (D. Md.), unreported opinion of Judge Joseph H. Young, 22 June 1972, p. 12; *Washington Post,* 23 June 1972, pp. C1, C7; *Baltimore Sun,* 23 June 1972, p. C22; *Washington Evening Star,* 23 June 1972, 25 June 1972, pp. D1, D3. On subsequent appellate developments, see Lucas et al., "Brief of Respondent in Opposition," *Hardy* v. *Vuitch,* U.S.S.C., O.T. 1971, #1686, 4pp., n.d. [c.July 1972]; 409 U.S. 851 (denying cert.), 10 October 1972; and Lucas et al., "Brief of Appellee," *Hardy* v. *Vuitch,* 4th Cir., #72–1890, 51pp., n.d. [c.November 1972]. See also Lucas, "Verified Complaint in Class Action," *WONAAC et al.* v. *District of Columbia City Council et al.,* CA#72–1991 (D.D.C.), 37pp., 4 October 1972, Lucas Box 2.

102. *Byrn* v. *New York City Health and Hospitals Corporation,* 335 N.Y.S.2d 390, 392, 31 N.Y.2d 194, 286 N.E.2d 887, 7 July 1972; *New York Times,* 8 July 1972, pp. 1, 23, 21 July 1972, p. 31, 22 July 1972, p. 31, 27 July 1972, p. 63, 2 August 1972, p. 39, 4 August 1972, p. 35; Thomas J. Ford, "Jurisdictional Statement," *Byrn* v. *New York City Health and Hospitals Corporation,* U.S.S.C., O.T. 1972, #434, 17pp., 14 September 1972, National Archives, RG 267, Box 441; *Klein* v. *Nassau County Medical Center,* 347 F. Supp. 496 (E.D.N.Y.), 24 August 1972; *New York Times,* 25 August 1972, pp. 1, 67, 26 August 1972, p. 16, 29 August 1972, p. 37, 30 August

1972, p. 34, 31 August 1972, p. 37, 1 September 1972, p. 23, 4 September 1972, p. 14, 15 September 1972, p. 41, 20 September 1972, p. 17, 27 September 1972, p. 27. On the New York Court of Appeals decision in Byrn, also see Virginia N. Duin, "New York's Abortion Reform Law: Unanswered Questions," *Albany Law Review* 37 (1972): 22–60; *Fordham Law Review* 41 (December 1972): 439–449; and James A. Kearns, *Notre Dame Lawyer* 48 (February 1973): 715–727; on *Klein,* also see Alan F. Charles, *Clearinghouse Review* 6 (November 1972): 422–424, and 412 U.S. 925 (1973).

103. *New York Times*, 11 August 1972, p. 26, 13 August 1972, p. 73, 25 August 1972, p. 67, 16 September 1972, p. 64, 3 October 1972, p. 94, 2 November 1972, p. 91; *Cheaney v. State*, 285 N.E.2d 265 (Ind. Sup. Ct.), 24 July 1972, cert. denied, 410 U.S. 991 (1973) [nonphysician appellant]; *American Medical News*, 14 August 1972; *People v. Nixon*, 201 N.W.2d 635, 640–641 (Mich. Ct. App.), 23 August 1972. On Dr. Robert M. Livingston's unsuccessful effort to have the New Jersey prosecution blocked by one or another federal court, also see "Opinion of Mr. Justice Douglas," *Livingston v. Kugler*, 9 September 1972, Brennan Papers Box 279.

104. *New York Times*, 25 August 1972, pp. 1, 67, 26 August 1972, p. 37, 1 September 1972, p. 56; *Dallas Morning News*, 3 September 1972, p. E1; William C. McCready and Andrew M. Greeley, "The End of American Catholicism?," *America*, 28 October 1972, pp. 334–338, at 336. On the Gallup data, see especially Richard Pomeroy and Lynn C. Landman, "Public Opinion Trends," *Family Planning Perspectives* 4 (October 1972): 44–55, and both Pomeroy and Landman, "American Public Opinion and Abortion in the Early Seventies," and Judith Blake, "Elective Abortion and Our Reluctant Citizenry," in Howard J. and Joy D. Osofsky, eds., *The Abortion Experience* (Hagerstown, MD: Harper & Row, 1973), pp. 447–467 and 482–495; also see Shana Alexander, *Newsweek*, 2 October 1972, p. 29; Patricia Donovan, "Support for Abortion Reform Increases," *Family Planning/Population Reporter* 1 (December 1972): 13–14; John C. Bennett, *Christianity & Crisis*, 8 January 1973, pp. 287–288; and the 1972 Harris poll numbers cited in Connie deBoer, "The Polls: Abortion," *Public Opinion Quarterly* 41 (Winter 1977–1978): 553–564.

105. Larry Lader to NARAL Board Members, 7 July 1972, NARAL Box 1; *NARAL News*, Summer 1972, pp. 1, 3–4; Michigan Abortion Referendum Committee Minutes, 2 August 1972, MARC Box 2; *New York Times*, 10 September 1972, p. 71, 11 September 1972, p. 14; *Detroit News*, 14 September 1972, pp. A1, A20, 5 October 1972, pp. A1, A17.

106. Lucas to Weddington, 23 July 1972, Whitehill Papers; Garrow conversations with Roy Lucas and Sarah Weddington. Also see William F. Buckley's "Firing Line" (with Lucas and John Noonan), taped 25 July 1972 (and broadcast 5 November 1972); *San Antonio Light*, 2 August 1972; Lucas to Ermo Ingel, 3 August 1972, Lucas Box 11.

107. Weddington to Lee Gidding, 31 August 1972, and Gidding to Weddington, 8 September 1972, NARAL Box 5; Weddington, *A Question of Choice*, p. 134, and Garrow conversations with Sarah Weddington; Weddington et al., "Supplemental Brief for Appellants," *Roe v. Wade*, U.S.S.C., O.T. 1972, 17pp., 16 September 1972, esp. pp. 8 and 10; Hames et al., "Supplemental Brief of the Appellants," *Doe v. Bolton*, U.S.S.C., O.T. 1972, 9pp., 25 September 1972, esp. pp. 2–3; *Atlanta Constitution*, 28 August 1972; Pilpel et al., "Supplemental Brief for Amici Curiae Planned Parenthood Federation of America," *Roe v. Wade* and *Doe v. Bolton*, 31pp., 15 September 1972, esp. p. 30; Joan K. Bradford, "Brief Amici Curiae on Behalf of the California Committee to Legalize Abortion, et al.," *Roe v. Wade* and *Doe v. Bolton*, 31pp., 20 September 1972; Gary K. Nelson et al., "Brief Amicus Curiae of the Attorneys General of Arizona, Connecticut, Kentucky, Nebraska and Utah," *Roe v. Wade*, 10pp., 20 September 1972; McKernan to Floyd, 20 July 1972, Floyd to McKernan, 24 July 1972, McKernan to Floyd, 9 August 1972, Floyd to John Danforth, George Kugler, Robert K. Killian, Gary K. Nelson et al., 25 August 1972, Texas AG File 70–308. Also see *Atlanta Cooperative News Project v. United States Postal Service*, 350 F. Supp. 234 (N.D. Ga.), 29 September 1972, and *Atlanta Constitution*, 30 September 1972, regarding a successful suit brought by *The Great Speckled Bird*, Atlanta's "underground" newspaper, against an attempt by the post office to deny mailing privileges to the paper because it printed abortion referral advertising.

108. *Abele* v. *Markle*, 351 F. Supp. 224, 227, 228–229, 230 (D. Conn.), 20 September 1972; *New York Times*, 21 September 1972, pp. 1, 42, 22 September 1972, p. 85, 4 October 1972, pp. 51, 100.

109. *State* v. *Munson*, 201 N.W.2d 123 (S.D. Sup. Ct.), 26 September 1972; *Rodgers* v. *Danforth*, 486 S.W.2d 258 (Mo. Sup. Ct.), 3 October 1972; *Kansas City Times*, 4 October 1972; *New York Times*, 27 September 1972, p. 27, 28 September 1972, p. 34, 3 October 1972, p. 22, 4 October 1972, p. 100, 6 October 1972, p. 47. On *Munson*, also see Roy Lucas and Homer Kandaras, "Jurisdictional Statement," *Munson* v. *South Dakota*, U.S.S.C., O.T. 1972, #631, 11pp., 24 October 1972, and Michael Rodak to Gordon Mydland, 20 December 1972, *Munson* Case File, National Archives, RG 267, Box 476.

110. NARAL Annual Meeting Minutes, 6–8 October 1972, and Greitzer, "Annual Message," 7 October 1972, NARAL I-6; *New York Times*, 8 October 1972, pp. 1, 20, 9 October 1972, p. 9, 12 October 1972, p. 36; Michigan Abortion Referendum Committee Minutes, 27 September and 4 and 11 October 1972, MARC Box 2; MARC *Newsletter #3*, 10 October 1972; *National Observer*, 21 October 1972.

111. Pilpel to John Robbins, 19 September 1972, PPFA II-49; *San Antonio Light*, 15 September 1972; *Austin American-Statesman*, 8 October 1972, p. F7; *Ft. Worth Star-Telegram*, 10 October 1972; Weddington Interviews with Duke and Cheek; Weddington, *A Question of Choice*, p. 136; Garrow conversations with Sarah Weddington, Ron Weddington, Linda Coffee, Roy Lucas, Margie Hames, Cyril Means, and Joseph Nellis.

112. Transcripts and Tape Recordings of Oral Arguments, *Roe* v. *Wade* and *Doe* v. *Bolton*, 11 October 1972, National Archives; [Roy Lucas], Notes on *Roe* and *Doe* Oral Arguments, 11 October 1972, 9pp., Lucas Box 24; [Tobiane Schwartz], Notes on *Roe* Oral Argument, n.d. [11 October 1972], Hames Papers; *Dallas Times Herald*, 11 October 1972, 12 October 1972, p. B3; *Atlanta Journal*, 11 October 1972; *Houston Post*, 12 October 1972; *Washington Post*, 12 October 1972, p. A2; *Dallas Morning News*, 12 October 1972, p. A4; Weddington to Ginny Whitehill, "Sunday" [15 October 1972], Whitehill Papers; Weddington in *Dallas Morning News*, 23 April 1973, p. C7, and in Joseph Bell, "A Landmark Decision," *Good Housekeeping*, June 1973, pp. 77–79ff.; O'Brien, *Storm Center*, pp. 31–34; Marian Faux, *Roe v. Wade*, pp. 280–287; Weddington, *A Question of Choice*, p. 137; Flowers to Michael Rodak, 8 September 1972, Texas AG File 70–308; Garrow conversations with Sarah Weddington, Robert C. Flowers, Margie Hames, and Dorothy T. Beasley. On Flowers, also see *Dallas Morning News*, 21 September 1973, p. A11.

113. Weddington to Ginny Whitehill, "Sunday" [15 October 1972], Whitehill Papers; *Houston Chronicle*, 9 March 1973; Weddington in Joseph Bell, "A Landmark Decision," *Good Housekeeping*, June 1973, pp. 77–79ff.; Weddington Interviews with Cheek and Marcello; Weddington, *A Question of Choice*, p. 137; Hames in *Atlanta Journal-Constitution Magazine*, 11 March 1973, pp. 7–17; Lucas to Cyril Means, 25 October 1972, and Weddington to Whitehill, 9 November 1972, Whitehill Papers; Garrow conversations with Sarah Weddington, Ron Weddington, Linda Coffee, Margie Hames, Tobi Schwartz, and Roy Lucas. Also see Epstein and Kobylka, *The Supreme Court and Legal Change*, pp. 190–192, who assert that Weddington's performance was "worse the second time around" and fault her "strategic naiveté." Robert Flowers, however, "was worse," for he "was unprepared and faltered at almost every turn," such that "he practically gave away his case."

114. William O. Douglas Conference Notes, *Roe* and *Doe*, 13 October 1972, Douglas Box 1588; Brennan Conference Notes and Vote Tallies on *Roe* and *Doe*, Brennan Docket Books, Boxes 418 and 419; Garrow conversations with Larry A. Hammond; Douglas to "Janet" [Meek] and "Carol" [Bruch], n.d. [c.13 October 1972], Douglas Box 1589. While Justice Douglas's conference notes are explicitly labeled October 13, Justice Brennan's conference lists suggest that *Roe* and *Doe* actually may have been discussed only on October 24, rather than at either the regular Friday conference on October 13 or the following one on October 20. Justice Marshall's papers indicate that the Court had 3:30 p.m. conferences on both Wednesday the 11th and Tuesday the 17th, and that the regular conference of October 20 was reconvened on October 24. Conference Lists, Brennan Boxes 277 and 278, Marshall Box 95.

A copy of Jon Newman's opinion in the Connecticut case, *Abele* v. *Markle,* appears in Justice Brennan's *Roe* and *Doe* file (Brennan Box 281), and the Court's October 13 conference agreed to hold both of Connecticut's two appeals in abeyance until *Roe* and *Doe* were decided. See Burger, "Memorandum for the Conference: *Markle* v. *Abele,*" 11 October 1972, 6pp., Brennan Box 279; October 13 Conference List, Brennan Box 278; 409 U.S. 908 (16 October 1972); *New York Times,* 17 October 1972, p. 45; 409 U.S. 1021 (20 November 1972); and *Markle* Case Files (#72–56 and 72–530), National Archives, RG 267, Boxes 386 and 491. On November 3 the justices also agreed to continue holding both Roy Lucas's appeal in the North Carolina case, *Corkey* v. *Edwards,* and Professor Byrn's appeal of *Byrn.* Brennan Conference List, 3 November 1972, Brennan Box 278; also see Lucas and George S. Daly, Jr., "Motion to Set Questions . . . for Briefing and Argument," *Corkey* v. *Edwards,* #71–92, 17 October 1972, and Michael Rodak, Jr., to Lucas, 6 November 1972, *Corkey* Case File, National Archives, RG 267, Box 97; 409 U.S. 975; on *Byrn,* see *New York Times,* 12 January 1973, p. 30.

On *Roe* and *Doe,* also see Woodward and Armstrong, *The Brethren,* pp. 230–231; Schwartz, *The Unpublished Opinions of the Burger Court,* pp. 148–149, and Schwartz, *The Ascent of Pragmatism,* p. 305, the latter two of which, based only upon the Brennan conference notes, erroneously (but understandably) both render Stewart's reference to "Jon Newman" as "John Harlan."

115. Harry M. Clor, "Constitutional Interpretation: An Interview with Justice Lewis Powell," *Kenyon College Alumni Bulletin,* Summer 1979, pp. 14–18, at 17.

116. Paul Hendrickson, "The Admen Who Beat Abortion," *Detroit Free Press Magazine,* 4 March 1973, pp. 10–15; *Detroit News,* 19 October 1972, pp. A1, A19, 3 November 1972, pp. A1, A8; MARC Board Minutes, 1 November 1972, MARC Box 2; *Wall Street Journal,* 3 November 1972, p. 30; *New York Times,* 8 November 1972, p. 15; Whitehill to Stack, 6 December 1972, Whitehill Papers; Lader to Barbara Madden, 16 November 1972, NARAL Box 3; *American Medical News,* 20 November 1972, pp. 1, 6; Kimmey to Ruth Roemer, 30 November 1972, CCTA Box 6. Also see *Detroit News,* 9 June 1972, pp. A1, A8; Edgar B. Keemer, "Update on Abortion in Michigan," *Journal of the National Medical Association* 64 (November 1972): 518–519; *National Review,* 22 December 1972, p. 1407; *Christianity Today,* 22 December 1972, pp. 24–25; and Doreen Bierbrier, "The 1972 Abortion Referendum in Michigan" (unpublished paper, December 1973), 19pp., Bentley Historical Library. On North Dakota, also see *Minneapolis Tribune,* 5 November 1972, pp. B1, B21; and Faye Ginsburg, *Contested Lives,* pp. 67–70. In general, see Warren M. Hern, "The Politics of Abortion," *The Progressive* 36 (November 1972): 26–29, and *Newsweek,* 13 November 1972, p. 70.

117. *Austin American-Statesman,* 9 November 1972, p. 1, 19 November 1972, p. H4; Weddington, *A Question of Choice,* p. 142; Cathy Bonner to Ginny Whitehill, 23 and 30 November 1972, Whitehill to Jack Stack, 6 December 1972, Whitehill to James Roderick, 3 January 1973, Whitehill Papers.

118. Bea Blair to Al Moran and John Robbins, 12 October 1972, John Robbins to Fred Jaffe et al., 23 October 1972, Shirley Gordon to John Robbins, 14 November 1972, Betty Dietz to John Robbins, 20 November 1972, Bea Blair to Pam Veerhusen and Robbins, 27 November 1972, Gordon to Robbins, 30 November 1972, and Guttmacher, "Memorandum on [December 13] Conference with Governor Rockefeller," 20 December 1972, Schlesinger 223–1–3; *New York Times,* 18 October 1972, p. 38, 22 October 1972, p. 1, 11 November 1972, p. 32, 16 November 1972, p. 51, 19 November 1972, p. 66, 20 November 1972, p. 43, 22 November 1972, p. 35, 23 November 1972, p. 17, 25 November 1972, p. 13, 28 November 1972, p. 90, 12 December 1972, p. 49, 19 December 1972, p. 25, 23 December 1972, p. 17, 31 December 1972, p. 32, 2 January 1973, p. 1, 7 January 1973, p. IV-2, 10 January 1973, p. 48, 11 January 1973, p. 25, 12 January 1973, p. 30, 15 January 1973, p. 63; *Commonweal,* 24 November 1972, pp. 175–178; *Washington Post,* 8 January 1973; *Newsday,* 8 January 1973, pp. A4, A5; Beatrice Blair Interview with Chesler, p. 41. Also see Delpfine Welch, "Defending the Right to Abortion in New York," *International Socialist Review,* January 1973, pp. 10–13.

119. *New York Times,* 16 November 1972, p. 53, 21 November 1972, p. 20, 1 December 1972, p.

17, 13 December 1972, p. 53; *Time,* 11 December 1972, p. 32; *American Medical News,* 11 December 1972; Lader to NARAL Board Members, "The Damage to the Abortion Movement," 5 December 1972, NARAL Box 7; Lader to NARAL Board Members, n.d. [c.7 January 1973], Guttmacher Papers; Kimmey in *Kansas City Times,* 26 December 1972, p. E6. Also see NARAL Executive Committee Minutes, 27 November 1972, NARAL Box 1; Kimmey to Lee Gidding et al., "Education Campaign re Abortion Rights," 12 December 1972, NARAL Box 6; and, with regard to the power of fetal photos, Celeste Condit, *Decoding Abortion Rhetoric,* pp. 79–94.

120. *People v. Barksdale,* 503 P.2d 257, 263–264, and *People v. Pettegrew,* 503 P.2d 276, 22 November 1972; *New York Times,* 23 November 1972, p. 17; Zad Leavy, Memo on *People v. Barksdale,* 1 December 1972, Leavy Papers; Garrow conversations with Zad Leavy. On Dr. Koome, see *Seattle Times,* 23 November 1972, p. A17; *Seattle Post-Intelligencer,* 23 November 1972, p. A13, 3 December 1972, p. G5; *In re Koome,* 82 Wash.2d 816, 514 P.2d 520 (1973), and *State v. Koome,* 84 Wash.2d 901, 530 P.2d 260 (7 January 1975), finally dismissing the 1972 conviction. On Minnesota, see Minnesota Supreme Court Administrator to Members of the Press, 28 December 1972, Lucas Box 14.

On other pending matters, see *Nelson v. Planned Parenthood Center of Tucson,* 505 P.2d 580 (Ariz. Ct. App.), 3 January 1973, and *New York Times,* 7 January 1973, p. 22; also see a preliminary holding, *Planned Parenthood Center of Tucson v. Marks,* 497 P.2d 534 (Ariz. Ct. App.), 30 May 1972. In late December of 1972, a new federal court suit was filed challenging Maine's abortion law. *New York Times,* 24 December 1972, p. 47.

121. Blackmun, "Memorandum to the Conference," 21 November 1972, Blackmun *Roe* and *Doe* Circulations (each designated as print #2), 22 November 1972, esp. Roe pp. 38, 47–48, Brennan Box 281, Douglas Box 1589, Marshall Box 99; Blackmun to Brennan, 21 November 1972, Brennan Box 282. Also see Woodward and Armstrong, *The Brethren,* pp. 230–232; and Schwartz, *The Unpublished Opinions of the Burger Court,* pp. 148–149.

122. Douglas to Blackmun, 24 November 1972, Douglas Circulation #1, 25 November 1972, Stewart to Blackmun, 27 November 1972, White to Blackmun, 1 December 1972, Rehnquist to Blackmun, 4 December 1972, Powell to Blackmun, 5 December 1972, Brennan Box 282, Douglas Box 1589, Marshall Box 99; William J. Maledon, "The Law and the Unborn Child: The Legal and Logical Inconsistencies," *Notre Dame Lawyer* 46 (Winter 1971): 349–372, at 372; "MVT" [Mark V. Tushnet] to "Dear Judge," n.d. [c.22 November 1972], 2pp., Marshall Box 99; Garrow conversations with William J. Maledon, James W. Ziglar, Geoffrey R. Stone, Mark V. Tushnet, L. Michael Seidman, Peter M. Kreindler, Larry A. Hammond, Frederick W. Lambert, and John G. Koeltl; Gerald M. Rosberg to Garrow, 23 June 1992. Also see Woodward and Armstrong, *The Brethren,* pp. 232–235; O'Brien, *Storm Center,* pp. 34–35; Urofsky, *The Douglas Letters,* pp. 186–187; and Schwartz, *The Ascent of Pragmatism,* pp. 306–307. Several O.T. 1972 clerks have indicated that they have no recollections concerning *Roe* and *Doe.* Richard J. Urowsky to Garrow, 16 June 1972, David M. Schulte to Garrow, 17 June 1992, and Stuart C. Stock to Garrow, 23 June 1992.

Ten years later, Mark Tushnet's evaluation of the Blackmun opinion had changed dramatically. "It seems to be generally agreed that, as a matter of simple craft, Justice Blackmun's opinion for the Court was dreadful," while William O. Douglas's concurrence was "brilliant." See Tushnet, "Following the Rules Laid Down: A Critique of Interpretivism and Neutral Principles," *Harvard Law Review* 96 (February 1983): 781–827, at 820–821; also see Tushnet, "The Supreme Court on Abortion," in J. Douglas Butler and David F. Walbert, eds., *Abortion, Medicine, and the Law,* 3rd ed. (New York: Facts on File, 1986), pp. 161–176.

123. Blackmun, "Memorandum to the Conference, Re: *Abortion Cases,*" 11 December 1972, Douglas to Blackmun, 11 December 1972, Brennan Box 282, Douglas Box 1589, Marshall Box 99; [Mark Tushnet], one-page typescript draft of Marshall letter to Blackmun, n.d. [c.12 December 1972], Marshall Box 99; Marshall to Blackmun, "Re: *Abortion Cases,*" 12 December 1972, Brennan Box 282, Douglas Box 1589, Marshall Box 99; Garrow conversations with William J. Maledon, Geoffrey R. Stone, Mark V. Tushnet, L. Michael Seidman, and James W. Ziglar. The sole word that Marshall added was "here" in the letter's final sen-

tence. It should be emphasized that Professor Tushnet neither suggested nor fully subscribes to this appraisal of the December 12 Marshall to Blackmun letter. Also see Schwartz, *The Unpublished Opinions of the Burger Court*, pp. 149–150. Many years later, Tushnet would mount a brief but unpersuasive attack on the usefulness of the viability concept. See "Two Notes on the Jurisprudence of Privacy," *Constitutional Commentary* 8 (Winter 1991): 75–85, at 80–85.

124. Brennan to Blackmun, 13 December 1972, Brennan Box 282; Brennan Chambers, October Term 1972, pp. 58–70. Also see Schwartz, *The Unpublished Opinions of the Burger Court*, pp. 150–151.

125. Burger to Blackmun, 13 December 1972, Stewart to Blackmun, 14 December 1972, Blackmun, "Memorandum to the Conference: Re: *Abortion Cases*," 15 December 1972, Brennan Box 282, Douglas Box 1589, Marshall Box 99; Brennan Chambers, October Term 1972, pp. 58–70. Also see Schwartz, *The Unpublished Opinions of the Burger Court*, pp. 150–151; *Washington Post*, 22 January 1989, pp. D1, D2.

126. Blackmun, "Memorandum to the Conference," 21 December 1972, and Blackmun *Roe* (51pp.) and *Doe* (28pp.) Circulations #3, 21 December 1972, Douglas to Blackmun, 22 December 1972, Marshall to Blackmun, 26 December 1972, Brennan to Blackmun, 27 December 1972, Stewart to Blackmun, 27 December 1972, Stewart Circulation #2, 28 December 1972, Douglas Circulation #2, 29 December 1972, Powell to Blackmun, 4 January 1973, Brennan Box 282, Douglas Box 1589, Marshall Box 99; Carol [Bruch] to Douglas, 23 December 1972, 4pp., and 1 January 1973, Douglas Box 1589; Brennan Chambers, October Term 1972, pp. 58–70; Garrow conversations with Geoffrey R. Stone, L. Michael Seidman, William J. Maledon, Larry A. Hammond, and Mark V. Tushnet. Also see O'Brien, *Storm Center*, p. 35.

127. White Circulation #1, Rehnquist Circulations #1 in both *Roe* and *Doe*, 11 January 1973, Rehnquist to White, 11 January 1973, Burger to Blackmun, 16 January 1973, Blackmun, "Memorandum to the Conference," 16 January 1973, Blackmun *Doe* Circulation #4, 16 January 1973, Blackmun *Roe* Circulation #4, 17 January 1973, Powell to Blackmun, 16 January 1973, Brennan to Blackmun, 17 January 1973, Burger Circulation #1, 18 January 1973, Brennan Box 282, Douglas Box 1589, and Marshall Box 99; Assignment Sheet, Brennan Box 277; Woodward and Armstrong, *The Brethren*, p. 236; Garrow conversations with Geoffrey R. Stone, L. Michael Seidman, and Mark V. Tushnet. Ten years later, Justice Blackmun would frankly recall that Warren Burger "was never very enthusiastic about joining the majority." John A. Jenkins, "A Candid Talk with Justice Blackmun," *New York Times Magazine*, 20 February 1983, pp. 20ff., at 28.

128. *Houston Post*, 31 December 1972, p. AA2; *Dallas Morning News*, 7 January 1973; Whitehill to Lee Gidding, 10 January 1973, NARAL Box 5; Weddington, *A Question of Choice*, p. 145; "Abortion on Demand," *Time*, 29 January 1973, pp. 46–47; Woodward and Armstrong, *The Brethren*, pp. 237–238; Garrow conversations with Larry A. Hammond.

129. *New York Times*, 23 January 1973, pp. 1, 20; *Roe v. Wade*, 410 U.S. 113, 116–117, 129, 140–141, 149, 150, 152–153, 154, 156–159, 160, 162–164, 165, 166. The *Roe* majority opinion also included one citation to former Justice Clark's article (at 140) and two references (154 and 158) to the second Connecticut decision by Judge Newman. Nancy Stearns would later observe, with reference to 410 U.S. 153, that "Blackmun's description of the physical and emotional harm to women of an unwanted pregnancy, the stigma of an out-of-wedlock pregnancy, and the problems associated with bearing an unwanted child bears a striking resemblance to the language used by the Connecticut court." "*Roe v. Wade:* Our Struggle Continues," *Berkeley Women's Law Journal* 4 (1988–89): 1–11, at 5. Also see John A. Jenkins, "A Candid Talk with Justice Blackmun," *New York Times Magazine*, 20 February 1983, pp. 20ff., at 26: "I believe everything I said in the second paragraph of that opinion, where I agonized, initially not only for myself, but for the Court."

130. *Doe v. Bolton*, 410 U.S. 179, 195, 197, 199.

131. Douglas concurring in both *Roe* and *Doe*, 410 U.S. 209, 211, 212, 213, 214, 215, 217, 218, 220.

132. Stewart concurring in *Roe* v. *Wade*, 410 U.S. 167, 168, 169–170. Also see Benjamin W. Heineman, Jr., "A Balance Wheel on the Court," *Yale Law Journal* 95 (June 1986): 1325–1327.

133. Burger concurring in *Roe* and *Doe*, 410 U.S. 207, 208. As two subsequent commentators observed, "The majority opinion in *Roe* seemed irreconcilable with Chief Justice Burger's concurrence." Daniel A. Farber and John E. Nowak, "Beyond the *Roe* Debate: Judicial Experience with the 1980's 'Reasonableness' Test," *Virginia Law Review* 76 (April 1990): 519–538, at 522.

134. White dissenting in *Roe* and *Doe*, 410 U.S. 221, 222.

135. Rehnquist dissenting in *Roe*, 410 U.S. 171, 172, 174; Rehnquist dissenting in *Doe*, 410 U.S. 223. Also see Rehnquist, "Is an Expanded Right of Privacy Consistent with Fair and Effective Law Enforcement?," *Kansas Law Review* 23 (Fall 1974): 1–22, at 5 and 21 ("widely divergent claims, which upon analysis have very little in common with one another, are lumped under the umbrella of 'privacy'").

136. Blackmun with Bill Moyers, "In Search of the Constitution: Mr. Justice Blackmun," 26 April 1987, PBS. Also see *New York Times*, 8 March 1986, p. 7.

CHAPTER NINE

1. *Dallas Times-Herald*, 23 January 1973, 28 January 1973, 30 January 1973, p. B1, 15 May 1989, pp. B1, B3; *Dallas Morning News*, 23 January 1973, pp. A5, A16, D1 and D4, 27 January 1973, p. A30, 22 January 1982, p. A6; *Austin American-Statesman*, 23 January 1973, pp. 1, 2, 7; *Daily Texan*, 23 January 1973; Robert O'Brien, *Baptist Standard*, 31 January 1973, p. 4; *Jackson Clarion-Ledger*, 3 February 1973; Joseph N. Bell, "A Landmark Decision," *Good Housekeeping* 176 (June 1973): 77–79ff.; McCorvey Interview with Dreifus; *New Haven Register*, 29 September 1985; *Village Voice*, 11 April 1989, p. 44; *Life*, May 1989, pp. 111–118; *People*, 22 May 1989, pp. 36–41; *Los Angeles Times*, 25 June 1989, pp. 1, 17, 18; Weddington Interviews with Duke and Cheek; Weddington, *A Question of Choice*, pp. 146–148; Garrow conversations with Norma McCorvey, Sarah Weddington, and Linda Coffee. With regard to Linda Coffee and a significant case that she filed in December of 1973, see *Johnson* v. *Republic National Bank of Dallas*, 78 F.R.D. 352 (N.D. Tex.), 15 March 1978, 505 F. Supp. 224 (N.D. Tex.), 22 October 1980, and *Dallas Morning News*, 26 October 1980, pp. E1, E8.

2. Marsha King to Ginny Whitehill, 12 February 1973, Whitehill Papers; *Dallas Times-Herald*, 23 January 1973; Evans, "The Abortion Decision: A Balancing of Rights," *Christian Century*, 14 February 1973, pp. 195–197. In September 1973 Marsha entered law school at Emory University, and in 1976 she received her law degree. Also see Woodward and Armstrong, *The Brethren*, p. 240. On Henry McCluskey's murder and his convicted killer, William David Hovila, whose death sentence was subsequently commuted to life imprisonment by Texas authorities in 1982, see *Dallas Morning News*, 29 June 1973, p. D1, 30 June 1973, p. E1, 3 July 1973, 10 July 1973, 11 July 1973, 17 July 1973, p. A14, 13 August 1973, p. A22, 23 November 1976, p. A10, 24 November 1976, p. C8, 11 May 1978, 23 January 1979; *Dallas Times-Herald*, 8, 10, and 17 July 1973, 12 August 1973, p. B4, 13 August 1973; *State* v. *Hovila*, 562 S.W.2d 243 (Tex. Ct. Crim. App. 1978); and *Hovila* v. *Texas*, 439 U.S. 1135 (22 January 1979).

3. *Dallas Times-Herald Magazine*, 18 October 1981, pp. 37–42; *Dallas Times-Herald*, 22 January 1988, pp. A1, A18; *New Haven Register*, 30 April 1989; *Dallas Morning News*, 15 May 1989, pp. C1, C3; Garrow conversations with Jay Floyd, Henry Wade, and John B. Tolle.

4. *Atlanta Constitution*, 23 January 1973, pp. A1, A14, 13 December 1988, pp. A1, A6; Western Union to Michael Rodak, 23 January 1973, and Hames to Rodak, 13 February 1973, *Doe* Case File, National Archives, RG 267, Box 16; *Atlanta Journal*, 23 January 1973, p. B4; Sandra Race Cano, "Motion to Unseal," 9 December 1988, and Judge J. Owen Forrester, "Order," 2 May 1989, *Doe* v. *Bolton* Case File, 74A-2025, Box 16; Ann Woolner, "'I Am Mary Doe,'" *Fulton County Daily Report*, 9 February 1989, pp. 1, 3–7; *Atlanta Journal-Constitution*, 23 April 1992, p. A12; Garrow conversations with Arthur K. Bolton, Dorothy Toth Beasley, Sandra

Bensing Cano, Margie Hames, and Tobi Schwartz. Additional coverage of Sandra Bensing Cano's 1988–89 effort to reopen *Doe* includes *Atlanta Constitution*, 5 January 1989, pp. D1, D5, 23 February 1989, p. C4, 3 May 1989, p. C4; *Fulton County Daily Report*, 22 and 27 February 1989; *Atlanta Journal-Constitution*, 7 April 1989, pp. C1, C4; Mark Curriden, *ABA Journal*, July 1989, p. 26; and *Los Angeles Times*, 11 November 1989, pp. B1, B4.

5. Gidding to Whitehill, 7 February 1973, Whitehill Papers; Lader, "The Abortion Revolution," *The Humanist*, May/June 1973, pp. 4–7; Lader, *Abortion II* (inside cover); Stearns in Janice Goodman et al., "*Doe* and *Roe*: Where Do We Go From Here?," *Women's Rights Law Reporter* 1 (Spring 1973): 20–38, at 23 and 37; Beatrice Blair Interview with Chesler, p. 63; Garrow conversations with Cyril Means. Also see Gidding, "Translating the Supreme Court Decision into Practice," 7 February 1973, NARAL Box 1, and Lucinda Cisler, "Abortion: A Major Battle Is Over—But the War is Not," *Feminist Studies* 1 (1973): 121–131.

6. *Dallas Morning News*, 28 January 1973, p. A2; Lucas to Hames, 6 March 1973, Hames Papers; Garrow conversations with Roy Lucas.

7. *New York Times*, 23 January 1973, pp. 1, 20, 24 January 1973, pp. 13, 14, and 89, 27 January 1973, p. 8, 28 January 1973, pp. 45, IV-3; *Washington Post*, 23 January 1973, p. A1; *Newsweek*, 5 February 1973, pp. 27–28, 66, 69; *Time*, 5 February 1973, pp. 50–51; *U.S. News & World Report*, 5 February 1973, p. 36. An informative analysis of the abortion-related coverage of the *New York Times*, *Washington Post*, *Los Angeles Times*, *Boston Globe*, and *Chicago Tribune* between January 22 and February 22, 1973, is John C. Pollock et al., "Media Agendas and Human Rights: The Supreme Court Decision on Abortion," *Journalism Quarterly* 55 (Autumn 1978): 544–548, 561. On the Catholic hierarchy, see Byrnes, *Catholic Bishops in American Politics*, p. 57.

8. *New York Times*, 24 January 1973, p. 40; *Washington Post*, 31 January 1973, p. A18; *Los Angeles Times*, 23 January 1973, p. II-6; *Boston Globe*, 23 January 1973; *Wall Street Journal*, 26 January 1973, p. 12; *Philadelphia Inquirer*, 24 January 1973; *Pittsburgh Post-Gazette*, 24 January 1973; *Atlanta Constitution*, 24 January 1973; *News and Observer*, 24 January 1973; *Arkansas Democrat*, 27 January 1973; *St. Louis Post-Dispatch*, 28 January 1973; *Houston Chronicle*, 26 January 1973; *San Angelo Standard-Times*, 27 January 1973, p. A6; *San Antonio Light*, 26 January 1973. Also see Joseph Kraft, *Washington Post*, 25 January 1973, p. A15, and Anthony Lewis, *New York Times*, 3 February 1973, p. 29.

9. Drinan, "The Abortion Decision," *Commonweal*, 16 February 1973, pp. 438–440; Buckley in the *Dallas Morning News*, 1 February 1973, p. A23; *Christianity Today*, 16 February 1973, pp. 32–33; Callahan in *Hastings Center Report* 3 (April 1973): 4–7, at 7; Lincoln, "Why I Reversed My Stand on Laissez-Faire Abortion," *Christian Century*, 25 April 1973, pp. 477–479, at 479; Noonan, "Raw Judicial Power," *National Review*, 2 March 1973, pp. 260–264, at 261; "Abortion," *The New Republic*, 10 February 1973, p. 9. Also see William Murchison, *Dallas Morning News*, 7 February 1973, David Hawkins, *Dallas Morning News*, 8 March 1973, p. D2; and, far more moderately, Daniel A. Degnan, *New York Times*, 10 March 1973, p. 31. Also note Charles E. Curran, "Abortion: Law and Morality in Contemporary Catholic Theology," *The Jurist* 33 (Spring 1973): 162–183.

10. Robert E. Hall, "The Supreme Court Decision on Abortion," *American Journal of Obstetrics and Gynecology* 116 (1 May 1973): 1–8; Hall letter in *New York Times*, 19 February 1984, p. IV-18; Alan A. Stone, "Abortion and the Supreme Court: What Now?," *Modern Medicine*, 30 April 1973, pp. 32–37; "33,000 Doctors Speak Out on Abortion," *Modern Medicine*, 14 May 1973, pp. 31–35; *New York Times*, 13 May 1973, p. 40; *ASA Newsletter* Vol. 8, #3–4. Also see Paul T. Murray and Herman Jew, "Mississippi Physicians' Attitudes Toward the Supreme Court Abortion Decision," *Journal of the Mississippi State Medical Association* 15 (July 1974): 291–294; Gail L. Pratt et al., "Connecticut Physicians' Attitudes Toward Abortion," *American Journal of Public Health* 66 (March 1976): 288–290; and Charles H. Franklin and Liane C. Kosaki, "Republican Schoolmaster: The U.S. Supreme Court, Public Opinion, and Abortion," *American Political Science Review* 83 (September 1989): 751–771.

11. Blackmun, "Memorandum to the Conference—Abortion Holds," 23 January 1973, Brennan Box 282; *Cedar Rapids Gazette*, 25 January 1973, pp. 1, 7; *Washington Post*, 26 January 1973, p. A2.

12. David M. Kendall to John Hill, *"Roe* v. *Wade,"* 24 January 1973, 10pp., John H. Hagler to Henry Wade, *"Roe* v. *Wade,"* 30 January 1973, 5pp., Joseph P. Witherspoon to Hill, 6 February 1973, Mary Jane Bode to Larry York, *"Roe* vs. *Wade,"* 12 February 1973, Texas AG File 70–308; *Dallas Morning News,* 1 February 1973, 7 February 1973, p. D3, 16 February 1973, p. A20, 17 February 1973, pp. A4, D2; John Hill et al., "Petition for Rehearing," *Roe* v. *Wade,* 15 February 1973; Arthur K. Bolton et al., "Petition for Rehearing," *Doe* v. *Bolton,* 16 February 1973; George D. Stoughton and Daniel R. Schaefer, "Brief of State of Connecticut, Amicus Curiae, in Support of Petitions for Rehearing Filed by the States of Georgia and Texas," *Doe* v. *Bolton* and *Roe* v. *Wade,* 16 February 1973; Dennis J. Horan et al., "Motion to Intervene . . . of Dr. Bart T. Heffernan," *Roe* v. *Wade* and *Doe* v. *Bolton,* 16 February 1973; *Abilene Reporter-News,* 17 February 1973, p. B3; Brennan Docket Book, Brennan Box 419; *Roe* v. *Wade,* 410 U.S. 959; *Doe* v. *Bolton,* 410 U.S. 959; *Rodgers* v. *Danforth,* 410 U.S. 949, *Corkey* v. *Edwards,* 410 U.S. 950, *Doe* v. *Rampton,* 410 U.S. 950, *Crossen* v. *Attorney General,* 410 U.S. 950, *Munson* v. *South Dakota,* 410 U.S. 950, *Thompson* v. *Texas,* 410 U.S. 950, *Kruze* v. *Ohio,* 410 U.S. 951, *Sasaki* v. *Kentucky,* 410 U.S. 951, *Markle* v. *Abele I* and *II,* 410 U.S. 951, *Hanrahan* v. *Doe,* 410 U.S. 950, *Heffernan* v. *Doe,* 410 U.S. 950; *Byrn* v. *New York City Health and Hospitals Corporation,* 410 U.S. 949 (appeal dismissed for want of a substantial federal question); *New York Times,* 27 February 1973, p. 22; *Dallas Morning News,* 27 February 1973, p. A5; *Austin American-Statesman,* 27 February 1973; *Markle* v. *Abele,* 411 U.S. 940, and *Byrn* v. *New York City Health and Hospitals Corporation,* 411 U.S. 940, 16 April 1973; *New York Times,* 5 April 1973, p. 32, 17 April 1973, p. 28; *Rosen* v. *Louisiana,* 412 U.S. 902, 21 May 1973. *Sasaki,* which had not been listed in Blackmun's memorandum, vacated *Sasaki* v. *Commonwealth,* 485 S.W.2d 897, 6 October 1972, in which the Kentucky Supreme Court, relying almost wholly on the May 1972 federal court upholding of Kentucky's abortion statute in *Crossen* v. *Attorney General,* 344 F. Supp. 587 (E.D. Ky.), had affirmed a physician's conviction. On the subsequent dispositions of several of these cases, also see *Danforth* v. *Rodgers,* 414 U.S. 1035, 19 November 1973; *Doe* v. *Rampton,* 366 F. Supp. 189 (D. Utah), 7 September 1973; *State* v. *Munson,* 206 N.W.2d 434 (S.D. Sup. Ct.), 5 April 1973; *State* v. *Thompson,* 493 S.W.2d 793 (Tex. Ct. Crim. App.), 1 May 1973; *State* v. *Kruze,* 295 N.E.2d 916 (Ohio Sup. Ct.), 2 May 1973; and *Abele* v. *Markle,* 369 F. Supp. 807 (D. Conn.), 26 April 1973. On South Dakota's Dr. Munson, also see *Minneapolis Tribune,* 21 August 1977.

13. *State* v. *Hodgson,* 204 N.W.2d 199, 2 February 1973; *Vuitch* v. *Hardy,* 473 F.2d 1370, 20 February 1973; *Jobe* v. *State,* 509 P.2d 481 (Okla. Ct. Crim. App.), 31 January 1973; *People* v. *Frey* and *People* v. *Mermelli,* 294 N.E.2d 257 (Ill. Sup. Ct.), 20 March 1973; *People* v. *Norton,* 507 P.2d 862 (Colo. Sup. Ct.), 5 March 1973, *New York Times,* 6 March 1973, p. 83; *State* v. *Page* and *State* v. *King,* 303 A.2d 215 (Pa. Sup. Ct.), 29 March 1973, *New York Times,* 30 March 1973, p. 8; *State* v. *Wahlrab,* 509 P.2d 245 (Ariz. Ct. App.), 24 April 1973; *Larkin* v. *Cahalan,* 208 N.W.2d 176 (Mich. Sup. Ct.), 18 June 1973; *State* v. *Lawrence,* 198 S.E.2d 253 (S.C. Sup. Ct.), 16 July 1973; *Doe* v. *Burk,* 513 P.2d 643 (Wyo. Sup. Ct.), 28 August 1973; *Doe* v. *Woodahl,* 360 F. Supp. 20 (D. Mont.), 29 May 1973; *Doe* v. *Turner,* 361 F. Supp. 1288 (S.D. Iowa), 3 August 1973.

The unreported February 1 decision in *Tennessee Woman* v. *Pack* is noted in both Mark B. Anderson et al., *Vanderbilt Law Review* 26 (May 1973): 823–836, at 823, and in *Memphis State Law Review* 3 (Spring 1973): 359–364, at 363; the unreported February 7 decision in *Women of Rhode Island* v. *Israel* is noted in *New York Times,* 9 February 1973, p. 15. On Illinois, also see *New York Times,* 8 February 1973, p. 33, and 2 March 1973, p. 11; on New Mexico, see *New York Times,* 10 February 1973, p. 38; and on Indiana, see *New York Times,* 6 March 1973, p. 83. Also note *State* v. *Hultgren,* 204 N.W.2d 197 (Minn. Sup. Ct.), 2 February 1973; *Henrie* v. *Derryberry,* 358 F. Supp. 719 (N.D. Okla.), 2 April 1973; *May* v. *State,* 492 S.W.2d 888 (Ark. Sup. Ct.), 9 April 1973, *New York Times,* 10 April 1973, p. 28; *People* v. *Bricker,* 208 N.W.2d 172 (Mich. Sup. Ct.), 18 June 1973; *State* v. *New Times, Inc.,* 511 P.2d 196 (Ariz. Ct. App., Div. 1), 3 July 1973; *State* v. *Ingel,* 308 A.2d 223 (Md. Ct. Spec. App.), 6 August 1973; and *State* v. *Nixon,* 212 N.W.2d 797 (Mich. Ct. App., Div. 3), 27 September 1973. On Texas, see Mary Ann Beaty, *American Journal of Criminal Law* 2 (Summer 1973): 231–243; on Georgia, see J. Winston Huff, "The New Georgia Abortion Law," *Journal of the Medical Association of*

Georgia 62 (June 1973): 241–243, and Elizabeth J. Appley, "Two Decades of Reproductive Freedom Litigation and Activism in Georgia: From *Doe* v. *Bolton* to *Atlanta* v. *Operation Rescue,*" *Georgia State Bar Journal* 28 (August 1991): 34–41.

14. *Dallas Morning News*, 1 February 1973; *New York Times*, 16 February 1973, pp. 1, 46, 17 February 1973, p. 62, 21 February 1973, p. 31, 2 March 1973, p. 75, 19 March 1973, p. 32, 20 May 1973, p. 35; Frederick S. Jaffe et al., *Abortion Politics* (New York: McGraw Hill, 1981), pp. 31–41. Two studies that examine hospital responses to *Roe* in Harris County (Houston), Texas, are David W. Brady and Kathleen Kemp, "The Supreme Court's Abortion Rulings and Social Change," *Social Science Quarterly* 57 (December 1976): 535–546, and Kemp et al., "The Supreme Court and Social Change: The Case of Abortion," *Western Political Quarterly* 31 (March 1978): 19–31. Also see Jon R. Bond and Charles A. Johnson, "Implementing a Permissive Policy: Hospital Abortion Services After *Roe* v. *Wade,*" *American Journal of Political Science* 26 (February 1982): 1–24, Johnson and Bond, "Policy Implementation and Responsiveness in Nongovernmental Institutions: Hospital Abortion Services After *Roe* v. *Wade,*" *Western Political Quarterly* 35 (September 1982): 385–405; as well as Johnson and Bond, "Coercive and Noncoercive Abortion Deterrence Policies: A Comparative State Analysis," *Law & Policy Quarterly* 2 (January 1980): 106–128, and Susan B. Hansen, "State Implementation of Supreme Court Decisions: Abortion Rates Since *Roe* v. *Wade,*" *Journal of Politics* 42 (May 1980): 372–395. More generally, also note John H. Knowles, "The Health System and the Supreme Court Decision: An Affirmative Response," *Family Planning Perspectives* 5 (Spring 1973): 113–116; Helen Dudar, "Abortion for the Asking," *Saturday Review*, April 1973, pp. 30–35; Christopher Tietze, "The Public Health Effects of Legal Abortion in the United States," *Family Planning Perspectives* 16 (January-February 1984): 26–28; and Patricia B. Richard, "Alternative Abortion Policies: What Are the Health Consequences?," *Social Science Quarterly* 70 (December 1989): 941–955.

15. *New York Times*, 1 February 1973, pp. 22, 73, 2 February 1973, p. 35, 4 February 1973, pp. 39, 66, 68, 10 February 1973, p. 35, 15 February 1973, p. 20, 18 February 1973, p. IV-10, 26 February 1973, p. 62, 28 February 1973, p. 47, 2 March 1973, p. 11, 10 March 1973, pp. 15, 31, 16 March 1973, p. 86, 15 April 1973, p. 73; Bea Blair, "Abortion: Can We Lose Our Right to Choose?," *Ms.*, October 1973, pp. 92–95. The full text of the Bishops' February 13 "Pastoral Message" appears in U.S. Congress, Senate, Committee on the Judiciary, *Abortion Hearings Before the Subcommittee on Constitutional Amendments*, 93rd Cong., 2nd sess., 1974, pp. 237–240. Also see *Commonweal*, 23 March 1973, pp. 51–52; *America*, 2 June 1973, pp. 506–507; Mary T. Hanna, *Catholics and American Politics* (Cambridge: Harvard University Press, 1979), pp. 175–197; and William Lasser, *The Limits of Judicial Power* (Chapel Hill: University of North Carolina Press, 1988), p. 215.

16. Robert M. Byrn, "An American Tragedy: The Supreme Court on Abortion," *Fordham Law Review* 41 (May 1973): 807–862 (reprinted in part as *"Wade* and *Bolton:* Fundamental Legal Errors and Dangerous Implications," *Catholic Lawyer* 19 [Autumn 1973]: 243–250); Byrn, "Good-bye to the Judeo-Christian Era in Law," *America*, 2 June 1973, pp. 511–514; Byrn, "The Abortion Amendments: Policy in the Light of Precedent," *St. Louis University Law Journal* 18 (Spring 1974): 380–406; Joseph O'Meara, "Abortion: The Court Decides a Non-Case," *Supreme Court Review* 1974 (Chicago: University of Chicago Press, 1975), pp. 337–360, at 358; Charles E. Rice, "The Dred Scott Case of the Twentieth Century," *Houston Law Review* 10 (Winter 1972–73): 1059–1086; Rice, "Overruling *Roe* v. *Wade*: An Analysis of the Proposed Constitutional Amendments," *Boston College Industrial and Commercial Law Review* 15 (December 1973): 307–341; Albert Broderick, "A Constitutional Lawyer Looks at the *Roe-Doe* Decisions," *The Jurist* 33 (Spring 1973): 123–133; Patrick T. Conley and Robert J. McKenna, "The Supreme Court on Abortion—A Dissenting Opinion," *Catholic Lawyer* 19 (Winter 1973): 19–28.

Also see Arnold H. Loewy, *North Carolina Law Review* 52 (December 1973): 223–243, at 224; David Goldenberg, *Catholic Lawyer* 19 (Winter 1973): 36–57; William R. Hopkin, Jr., *Temple Law Quarterly* 47 (Summer 1974): 715–738; Jacqueline N. Haley, *Suffolk University Law Review* 9 (Fall 1974): 145–184; Stanley M. Harrison, *New York Law Forum* 19 (Winter 1974): 685–701; and Baruch Brody, *Abortion and the Sanctity of Human Life* (Cambridge, MA:

MIT Press, 1975), pp. 123–131. Subsequent but generally similar writings also include John J. Coleman III, *"Roe v. Wade:* A Retrospective Look at a Judicial Oxymoron," *St. Louis University Law Journal* 29 (1984): 7–44; George P. Grant, *English-speaking Justice* (Notre Dame, IN: University of Notre Dame Press, 1985), pp. 69–73; William Mathie, "Reason, Revelation and Liberal Justice: Reflections on George Grant's Analysis of *Roe v. Wade," Canadian Journal of Political Science* 19 (September 1986): 443–466; and Stephen Schwarz, *The Moral Question of Abortion* (Chicago: Loyola University Press, 1990).

More significant hostile critiques include Joseph W. Dellapenna, "Neither Piety nor Wit: The Supreme Court on Abortion," *Columbia Human Rights Law Review* 6 (Fall-Winter 1974–75): 379–413, at 384 (*Roe* is "an exceptional example of poor craftsmanship"); Dellapenna, "The History of Abortion: Technology, Morality, and Law," *University of Pittsburgh Law Review* 40 (Spring 1979): 359–428, at 424 ("The Court's discussion of history is inaccurate and inconclusive, and, in any event, unrelated to its later conclusions"); Lynn D. Wardle, "The Gap Between Law and Moral Order: An Examination of the Legitimacy of the Supreme Court Abortion Decisions," *Brigham Young University Law Review* 1980: 811–835, at 832 ("As examples of judicial craftsmanship, the *Roe* and *Doe* opinions are an embarrassment to the profession"); and James S. Witherspoon, "Reexamining *Roe:* Nineteenth-Century Abortion Statutes and the Fourteenth Amendment," *St. Mary's Law Journal* 17 (1985): 29–71, at 70 ("the Supreme Court's analysis in *Roe v. Wade* of the development, purposes, and the understandings underlying the nineteenth-century antiabortion statutes, was fundamentally erroneous").

17. Unremarkable notes on *Roe* and *Doe* include H. Cam Zachry, *Journal of Family Law* 12 (1972–73): 459–475; David Granfield, *The Jurist* 33 (Spring 1973): 113–122; Edward McG. Gaffney, *The Jurist* 33 (Spring 1973): 134–152; Robert C. Timmons, *University of Miami Law Review* 27 (Spring/Summer 1973): 481–487; William J. Curran, *New England Journal of Medicine* 288 (3 May 1973): 950–951; Lauren P. Braunstein, *Tulane Law Review* 47 (June 1973): 1159–1167; Tom Riggs, *San Diego Law Review* 10 (June 1973): 844–856; Harley Riedel, *University of Florida Law Review* 25 (Summer 1973): 779–794; A. J. Alexis Gelinas, *Washington and Lee Law Review* 30 (Summer 1973): 628–646; *Georgetown Law Journal* 61 (July 1973): 1559–1575; Arthur G. Scotland, *Pacific Law Journal* 4 (July 1973): 821–860; Edwin J. Holman, *Journal of the American Medical Association* 225 (9, 16, and 23 July 1973): 215–216, 343–344, and 447–448; L. Wayne Gilleland, *Georgia State Bar Journal* 10 (August 1973): 153–162; Dorothy E. Patton, *Columbia Human Rights Law Review* 5 (Fall 1973): 497–521; William D. Bayliss, *University of Richmond Law Review* 8 (Fall 1973): 75–87; Robert L. Watt III, *North Carolina Law Review* 51 (October 1973): 1573–1584; *Harvard Law Review* 87 (November 1973): 75–85; Peter D. Coddington, *Albany Law Review* 37 (1973): 776–797; Marilyn B. Cane, *Family Law Quarterly* 7 (1973): 413–432; Carolyn V. Minter, *Ohio Northern University Law Review* 1 (1973): 119–129; Michael J. Satris, *University of California Davis Law Review* 7 (1974): 432–456; Linda Goodnight and Judy Rutledge, *Baylor Law Review* 27 (Winter 1975): 122–138. Subsequent articles that merit less attention than their titles might suggest include Michael R. Hagan, *"Roe v. Wade:* The Rhetoric of Fetal Life," *Central States Speech Journal* 27 (Fall 1976): 192–199; David Fuqua, "Justice Harry A. Blackmun: The Abortion Decisions," *Arkansas Law Review* 34 (1980): 276–296; and Janet LaRue, "Abortion: Justice Harry A. Blackmun and the *Roe v. Wade* Decision," *Simon Greenleaf Law Review* 2 (1982): 122–145.

18. Ely, "The Wages of Crying Wolf: A Comment on *Roe v. Wade," Yale Law Journal* 82 (April 1973): 920–949, at 920n3, 924, 926, 927, 928, 929, 943, 947; Francis J. Flaherty, "Abortion, the Constitution, and the Human Life Statute," *Commonweal,* 23 October 1981, pp. 586–593, at 588; *Los Angeles Daily Journal,* 21 January 1983, pp. 1, 15, at 15; Ely in U.S. Congress, Senate, Committee on the Judiciary, *Abortion Hearing Before the Subcommittee on Constitutional Amendments,* Part III, 93rd Cong., 2nd sess. (8 October 1974), pp. 251–252.

19. Heymann and Barzelay, "The Forest and the Trees: *Roe v. Wade* and Its Critics," *Boston University Law Review* 53 (May 1973): 765–784, at 765, 766, 775, 779, 784.

20. Noonan, *A Private Choice* (New York: Free Press, 1979), p. 21; Louise A. Wheeler and Shirley L. Kovar, *"Roe v. Wade:* The Right of Privacy Revisited," *Kansas Law Review* 21 (Summer

1973): 527–548, at 527 and 529; Cox, *The Role of the Supreme Court in American Government* (New York: Oxford University Press, 1976), pp. 53–54, 113.

Also see Richard Epstein, "Substantive Due Process by Any Other Name," *Supreme Court Review* 1973 (Chicago: University of Chicago Press, 1974), pp. 159–185; Norman Vieira, *"Roe* and *Doe*: Substantive Due Process and the Right of Abortion," *Hastings Law Journal* 25 (March 1974): 867–879, at 877; Louis Lusky, *By What Right?* (Charlottesville, VA: Michie Co., 1975), p. 15; Michael J. Perry, "Abortion, the Public Morals, and the Police Power: The Ethical Function of Substantive Due Process," *UCLA Law Review* 23 (April 1976): 689–736, at 690–691, Perry, *The Constitution, the Courts, and Human Rights* (New Haven: Yale University Press, 1982), p. 144 ("the Court failed to articulate anything like a rigorous argument"), and Perry, *Morality, Politics, and the Law* (New York: Oxford University Press, 1988), p. 175.

21. Friendly, "The Courts and Social Policy: Substance and Procedure," *University of Miami Law Review* 33 (November 1978): 21–42, at 35; Gunther, "Some Reflections on the Judicial Role: Distinctions, Roots, and Prospects," *Washington University Law Quarterly* 1979 (Summer): 817–828, at 820, 819; Richard G. Morgan, *"Roe v. Wade* and the Lesson of the Pre-*Roe* Case Law," *Michigan Law Review* 77 (August 1979): 1724–1748, at 1731 and 1725–1726. Also see Note, "Fornication, Cohabitation, and the Constitution," *Michigan Law Review* 77 (December 1978): 252–306, at 293.

22. Van Alstyne, "The Fate of Constitutional *Ipse Dixits," Journal of Legal Education* 33 (December 1983): 712–721, at 720; Van Alstyne, "Closing the Circle of Constitutional Review from *Griswold v. Connecticut* to *Roe v. Wade*: An Outline of a Decision Merely Overruling *Roe," Duke Law Journal* 1989 (December): 1677–1688, at 1680–81, 1683–84, and 1688. Also see Philip Bobbitt, *Constitutional Fate* (New York: Oxford University Press, 1982), pp. 157 and 159 (*Roe* an "unpersuasive opinion" and "a doctrinal fiasco").

23. Ginsburg, "Some Thoughts on Autonomy and Equality in Relation to *Roe v. Wade," North Carolina Law Review* 63 (January 1985): 375–386, at 376, 381 and 385–86; Ginsburg, "A Moderate View on *Roe," Constitution,* Spring-Summer 1992, p. 17. Also see Ginsburg, "Speaking in a Judicial Voice," 9 March 1993, New York University Law School, esp. pp. 22–37, at 32 and 36 (reprinted in part in *Legal Times,* 5 April 1993, pp. 10–11), and Garrow, *Washington Post,* 20 June 1993, p. C3.

See as well Carl E. Schneider, "Moral Discourse and the Transformation of American Family Law," *Michigan Law Review* 83 (August 1985): 1803–1879, esp. 1864–1870, at 1869 (*Roe* is "uncommonly unpersuasive"), and Schneider, "State-Interest Analysis in Fourteenth Amendment 'Privacy' Law," *Law and Constitutional Problems* 51 (Winter 1988): 79–122, at 93–94; Kent Greenawalt, "Religious Convictions and Lawmaking," *Michigan Law Review* 84 (December 1985): 352–404, at 371 (*Roe* "was wrongly decided"); Helen Garfield, "Privacy, Abortion, and Judicial Review: Haunted by the Ghost of *Lochner," Washington Law Review* 61 (April 1986): 293–365, at 313 and 316; Hal Miller, *The Abandoned Middle: The Ethics and Politics of Abortion in America* (Salem, MA: Penumbra Press, 1988), pp. 72–73; Linda R. Hirshman, "Bronte, Bloom, and Bork: An Essay on the Moral Education of Judges," *University of Pennsylvania Law Review* 137 (November 1988): 177–231, at 202 (*Roe*'s "opinion lacks a certain high rhetorical tone we have come to expect from path-breaking developments in the Supreme Court"); Note, "Substantive Due Process Comes Home to Roost," *Women's Rights Law Reporter* 10 (Winter 1988): 177–208, at 188; Harry F. Tepker, Jr., "Abortion, Privacy and State Constitutional Law: A Speculation If (or When) *Roe v. Wade* Is Overturned," *Emerging Issues in State Constitutional Law* 2 (1989): 173–187, at 176 (Blackmun "pastes together several precedents and principles that have little to do with the abortion issue").

24. Calabresi, *Ideals, Beliefs, Attitudes, and the Law* (Syracuse, NY: Syracuse University Press, 1985), pp. 92, 97, 101–102, 106, 110; Law, "Rethinking Sex and the Constitution," *University of Pennsylvania Law Review* 132 (June 1984): 955–1040, at 1020.

With regard to equal protection, also see Kathryn H. Snedaker, "Reconsidering *Roe v. Wade*: Equal Protection Analysis as an Alternative Approach," *New Mexico Law Review* 17 (Winter 1987): 115–137; Rhonda Copelon, "Unpacking Patriarchy: Reproduction, Sexuality, Originalism, and Constitutional Change," in Jules Lobel, ed., *A Less Than Perfect Union* (New

York: Monthly Review Press, 1988), pp. 303–334, at 326; Cass R. Sunstein, "Sexual Orientation and the Constitution: A Note on the Relationship Between Due Process and Equal Protection," *University of Chicago Law Review* 55 (Fall 1988): 1161–1179, at 1175; Sunstein, "Six Theses on Interpretation," *Constitutional Commentary* 6 (Winter 1989): 91–96; Sunstein, "Why the Unconstitutional Conditions Doctrine Is an Anachronism . . ." *Boston University Law Review* 70 (July 1990): 593–621, at 617–620; Sunstein, "Neutrality in Constitutional Law," *Columbia Law Review* 92 (January 1992): 1–52, at 31n; Sunstein, *The Partial Constitution* (Cambridge, MA: Harvard University Press, 1993), pp. 270–285; Catharine A. MacKinnon, "Reflections on Sex Equality Under Law," *Yale Law Journal* 100 (March 1991): 1281–1328, at 1319; Ruth Colker, *Abortion & Dialogue* (Bloomington: Indiana University Press, 1992), p. 100; Reva Siegel, "Reasoning from the Body: A Historical Perspective on Abortion Regulation and Questions of Equal Protection," *Stanford Law Review* 44 (January 1992): 261–381; and Andrew Koppelman, "Forced Labor: A Thirteenth Amendment Defense of Abortion," *Northwestern University Law Review* 84 (Winter 1990): 480–535, at 483–84, who also makes the additional argument that "When women are compelled to carry and bear children, they are subjected to 'involuntary servitude' in violation of the Thirteenth Amendment." Also note Laura W. Stein, "Living with the Risk of Backfire: A Response to the Feminist Critiques of Privacy and Equality," *Minnesota Law Review* 77 (May 1993): 1153–1191, at 1171–1182; and Ronald Dworkin, "Feminism and Abortion," *New York Review of Books*, 10 June 1993, pp. 27–29.

25. On autonomy, see Note, "On Privacy: Constitutional Protection for Personal Liberty," *New York University Law Review* 48 (October 1973): 670–773, at 701; Tyler Baker, "*Roe* and *Paris*: Does Privacy Have a Principle?," *Stanford Law Review* 26 (May 1974): 1161–1189; Louis Henkin, "Privacy and Autonomy," *Columbia Law Review* 74 (December 1974): 1410–1433, at 1424; Graham Hughes, *The Conscience of the Courts* (Garden City, NY: Doubleday, 1975), pp. 34, 71; June A. Eichbaum, "Towards an Autonomy-Based Theory of Constitutional Privacy," *Harvard Civil Rights–Civil Liberties Law Review* 14 (Summer 1979): 361–384; Thomas Huff, "Thinking Clearly About Privacy," *Washington Law Review* 55 (1980): 777–794, at 789; Rogers M. Smith, "The Constitution and Autonomy," *Texas Law Review* 60 (February 1982): 175–205; Edward T. Mulligan, "*Griswold* Revisited in Light of *Uplinger*," *New York University Review of Law and Social Change* 13 (1984–85): 51–82, at 75, 78, and 81; David A. J. Richards, *Toleration and the Constitution* (New York: Oxford University Press, 1986), p. 237; Joseph Kupfer, "Privacy, Autonomy, and Self-Concept," *American Philosophical Quarterly* 24 (January 1987): 81–89; Rhonda Copelon, "Beyond the Liberal Idea of Privacy: Toward a Positive Right of Autonomy," in Michael W. McCann and Gerald L. Houseman, eds., *Judging the Constitution* (Glenview, IL: Scott, Foresman & Co., 1989), pp. 287–314; and Daniel R. Ortiz, "Privacy, Autonomy, and Consent," *Harvard Journal of Law & Public Policy* 12 (Winter 1989): 91–97.

On "liberty," see Paul Bender, "Privacies of Life," *Harper's* 248 (April 1974): 36–45; Judith J. Thomson, "The Right to Privacy," *Philosophy and Public Affairs* 4 (Summer 1975): 295–314; W. A. Parent, "Recent Work on the Concept of Privacy," *American Philosophical Quarterly* 20 (October 1983): 341–355; Helen Garfield, "Privacy, Abortion, and Judicial Review," *Washington Law Review* 61 (April 1986): 293–365, at 318 and 322; and Robert B. Hallborg, Jr., "Principles of Liberty and the Right to Privacy," *Law and Philosophy* 5 (August 1986): 175–218, at 175.

Also note J. Braxton Craven, Jr., "Personhood: The Right to Be Let Alone," *Duke Law Journal* 1976 (September): 699–720; Tom Gerety, "Redefining Privacy," *Harvard Civil Rights–Civil Liberties Law Review* 12 (Spring 1977): 233–296, and Gerety, "Doing Without Privacy," *Ohio State Law Journal* 42 (1981): 143–165; Ruth Gavison, "Privacy and the Limits of Law," *Yale Law Journal* 89 (January 1980): 421–471; H. J. McCloskey, "Privacy and the Right to Privacy," *Philosophy* 55 (January 1980): 17–38; Raymond Wacks, "The Poverty of 'Privacy,'" *Law Quarterly Review* 96 (January 1980): 73–89; Rosalind Petchesky, "Giving Women a Real Choice," *The Nation*, 28 May 1990, pp. 732–735; Julie C. Inness, *Privacy, Intimacy, and Isolation* (New York: Oxford University Press, 1992), p. 120 ("the common denominator of constitutional privacy is intimacy"); and Mark A. Racanelli, "Reversals:

Privacy and the Rehnquist Court," *Georgetown Law Journal* 81 (December 1992): 443–479. But see Thomas I. Emerson, "The Right of Privacy and Freedom of the Press," *Harvard Civil Rights–Civil Liberties Law Review* 14 (Summer 1979): 329–360, at 340–41 ("We will not make much progress if we frame the problem in terms of a broader quest for 'liberty.' The recent tendency of the Supreme Court to look upon privacy as merely an undifferentiated aspect of an amorphous right to 'liberty' is a regressive step").

26. Wellington, "Common Law Rules and Constitutional Double Standards: Some Notes on Adjudication," *Yale Law Journal* 83 (December 1973): 221–311, at 301; Susan F. Appleton, "Doctors, Patients and the Constitution: A Theoretical Analysis of the Physician's Role in 'Private' Reproductive Decisions," *Washington University Law Quarterly* 63 (1985): 183–236, at 187–88 and 197. Also see especially Andrea Asaro, "The Judicial Portrayal of the Physician in Abortion and Sterilization Decisions: The Use and Abuse of Medical Discretion," *Harvard Women's Law Journal* 6 (Spring 1983): 51–102, at 51, 59, and 93; see as well Julie Conger, "Abortion: The Five-Year Revolution and Its Impact," *Ecology Law Quarterly* 3 (Spring 1973): 311–347, at 329–330; Laurence H. Tribe, "The Supreme Court, 1972 Term—Foreword: Toward a Model of Roles in the Due Process of Life and Law," *Harvard Law Review* 87 (November 1973): 1–53, at 38n ("the Court's decision to cast *Roe* and *Doe* in medico-technocratic terms"), and Tribe, "Seven Deadly Sins of Straining the Constitution Through a Pseudo-Scientific Sieve," *Hastings Law Journal* 36 (November 1984): 155–172, at 168 and 170; Nancy S. Erickson, "Women and the Supreme Court: Anatomy is Destiny," *Brooklyn Law Review* 41 (Fall 1974): 209–282, at 242–55; and Tina C. Oh, "An Exercise in Anachronism: Blackmun's Analysis of 19th Century Anti-Abortion Legislation" (unpublished B.A. thesis, Princeton University, 1990), pp. 67 and 70. But note George J. Annas et al., "The Right of Privacy Protects the Doctor-Patient Relationship," *Journal of the American Medical Association* 263 (9 February 1990): 858–861, at 861 ("*Roe* is also a physicians' rights case" and "Those who seek to overrule *Roe* are fundamentally arguing for state control of what can and cannot be done and said by physicians").

27. Robertson, "Gestational Burdens and Fetal Status: Justifying *Roe* v. *Wade*," *American Journal of Law & Medicine* 13 (Summer-Fall 1987): 189–212, at 193 and 203–204; Rhoden, "Trimesters and Technology: Revamping *Roe* v. *Wade*," *Yale Law Journal* 95 (March 1986): 639–697, at 640n, 648, and 656; H. Tristram Engelhardt, Jr., "Viability, Abortion, and the Difference Between a Fetus and an Infant," *American Journal of Obstetrics and Gynecology* 116 (1 June 1973): 429–434. Also see Rhoden, "The New Neonatal Dilemma: Live Births from Late Abortions," *Georgetown Law Journal* 72 (June 1984): 1451–1509; and Roger Wertheimer, "Understanding Blackmun's Argument: The Reasoning of *Roe* v. *Wade*," in Jay L. Garfield and Patricia Hennessey, eds., *Abortion: Moral and Legal Perspectives* (Amherst: University of Massachusetts Press, 1984), pp. 105–122.

On the appropriateness of viability, also see Engelhardt, "The Ontology of Abortion," *Ethics* 84 (April 1974): 217–234, at 232; L. W. Sumner, "Toward A Credible View of Abortion," *Canadian Journal of Philosophy* 4 (September 1974): 163–181, and Sumner, *Abortion and Moral Theory* (Princeton: Princeton University Press, 1981), esp. pp. 150, 157; Chris Macaluso, "Viability and Abortion," *Kentucky Law Journal* 64 (1975): 146–164; Jane English, "Abortion and the Concept of a Person," *Canadian Journal of Philosophy* 5 (October 1975): 233–243; Patricia A. King, "The Juridical Status of the Fetus: A Proposal for Legal Protection of the Unborn," *Michigan Law Review* 77 (August 1979): 1647–1687, at 1687; Alan Zaitchik, "Viability and the Morality of Abortion," *Philosophy and Public Affairs* 10 (Winter 1981): 18–26; Gerald Dworkin, "Morality, Legality, and Abortion," *Society* 19 (May-June 1982): 51–53; Deborah L. Rhode, *Justice and Gender* (Cambridge: Harvard University Press, 1989), pp. 211–212; Rhoden, "A Compromise on Abortion?," *Hastings Center Report*, July-August 1989, pp. 32–37; Jed Rubenfeld, "On the Legal Status of the Proposition that 'Life Begins at Conception,'" *Stanford Law Review* 43 (February 1991): 599–635, at 635; and Ronald Dworkin, "Unenumerated Rights: Whether and How *Roe* Should be Overruled," *University of Chicago Law Review* 59 (Winter 1992): 381–432, at 430 ("the arguments for choosing viability as the key date remain impressive").

28. Richard A. Posner, *Sex and Reason* (Cambridge: Harvard University Press, 1992), p. 337; Fried, *Order and Law* (New York: Simon & Schuster, 1991), pp. 75, 72, and 79.

29. Tribe, "The Supreme Court, 1972 Term—Foreword: Toward a Model of Roles in the Due Process of Life and Law," *Harvard Law Review* 87 (November 1973): 1–53, at 7 and 4n; Tribe in U.S. Congress, Senate, Committee on the Judiciary, *Constitutional Amendments Relating to Abortion—Hearings Before the Subcommittee on the Constitution*, 97th Cong., 1st sess., 5 October 1981, pp. 101 and 77; Tribe, *Abortion: The Clash of Absolutes* (New York: W. W. Norton & Co., 1990), p. 110; Tribe, *American Constitutional Law*, 2nd ed. (Mineola, NY: Foundation Press, 1988), p. 1349. Also see Tribe and Michael C. Dorf, *On Reading the Constitution* (Cambridge: Harvard University Press, 1991), p. 60 (the constitutional question of abortion is "profound-ly difficult" and *Roe* is "the hardest case of all").

30. "The Unborn and the Born Again," *The New Republic*, 2 July 1977, pp. 5–6; *Newsweek*, 5 June 1978, pp. 37–47; "Good News on Abortion," *The New Republic*, 31 July 1989, pp. 5–6; Glendon, *Rights Talk* (New York: Free Press, 1991), p. 58; Ginsburg, "A Moderate View on *Roe*," *Constitution*, Spring-Summer 1992, p. 17; Ehrenreich, "Mothers Unite," *The New Republic*, 10 July 1989, pp. 30–33. Also see Ginsburg, "Some Thoughts on Autonomy and Equality," p. 381; Ginsburg, "Speaking in a Judicial Voice," 9 March 1993, New York University Law School, esp. pp. 32–36 (reprinted in part in *Legal Times*, 5 April 1993, pp. 10–11); Eva R. Rubin, *Abortion, Politics, and the Courts* (Westport, CT: Greenwood Press, 1982), p. 166 ("the cause of elective abortion might have fared better if its supporters had continued the state-by-state legislative battle instead of moving into the courts"); Larry R. Churchill and Jose J. Siman, "Abortion and the Rhetoric of Individual Rights," *Hastings Center Report* 12 (February 1982): 9–12; Roger M. Williams, "The Power of Fetal Politics," *Saturday Review*, 9 June 1979, pp. 12–15, at 12 ("Success . . . came too easily"); and Charles Krauthammer, New York *Daily News*, 5 July 1992, p. 31 (1973 as "a time when state after state, reflecting changes in national mores, was liberalizing abortion laws"). Also note Garrow, *Washington Post*, 20 June 1993, p. C3.

31. On the 1973 congressional scene, see particularly *Congressional Quarterly Weekly Report*, 10 November 1973, pp. 2973–76; also see Arlie Schardt, "Saving Abortion," *Civil Liberties*, September 1973, pp. 1–2; Bea Blair, "Abortion: Can We Lose Our Right to Choose?," *Ms.*, October 1973, pp. 92–95; and Karen Mulhauser, "Congressional Activities," in Warren M. Hern and Bonnie Andrikopoulos, eds., *Abortion in the Seventies* (New York: National Abortion Federation, 1977), pp. 225–228. On Rhode Island, see *Doe* v. *Israel*, 358 F. Supp. 1193, 1201 (D.R.I.), 16 May 1973, *Doe* v. *Israel*, 482 F.2d 156 (1st Cir.), 6 June 1973, and *Israel* v. *Doe*, 416 U.S. 993 (cert. denied), 13 May 1974; on Minnesota, see *Hodgson* v. *Anderson*, 378 F. Supp. 1008 (D. Minn.), 28 June 1974; appeal dismissed *sub nom. Spannaus* v. *Hodgson*, 420 U.S. 903, 27 January 1975.

On the hospital access litigation, see *New York Times*, 2 July 1973, p. 11; *Nyberg* v. *City of Virginia*, 361 F. Supp. 932 (D. Minn.), 10 August 1973, *Nyberg* v. *City of Virginia*, 495 F.2d 1342 (8th Cir.), 19 February 1974, *City of Virginia* v. *Nyberg*, 419 U.S. 891 (appeal dismissed), 21 October 1974; *Doe* v. *Hale Hospital*, 369 F. Supp. 970 (D. Mass.), 30 January 1974, *Doe* v. *Hale Hospital*, 500 F.2d 144 (1st Cir.), 12 July 1974, *Hale Hospital* v. *Doe*, 420 U.S. 907 (cert. denied), 27 January 1975; and *Doe* v. *Mundy*, 378 F.Supp. 731 (E.D. Wis.), 24 July 1974, *Doe* v. *Mundy*, 419 U.S. 813 (stay denied), 15 October 1974, *Doe* v. *Mundy*, 514 F.2d 1179 (7th Cir.), 30 January 1975. Also note *City of Virginia* v. *Nyberg*, 462 U.S. 1125 (dismissing an appeal of 667 F.2d 754, with White and Rehnquist, JJ., dissenting), 20 June 1983; *New York Times*, 21 June 1983, p. A21.

On the Florida litigation, see *Coe* v. *Gerstein*, 376 F. Supp. 695 (S.D. Fla.), 14 August 1973, *Gerstein* v. *Coe*, 417 U.S. 279 (appeal dismissed for want of jurisdiction), and *Poe* v. *Gerstein*, 417 U.S. 281, 3 June 1974, *Poe* v. *Gerstein*, 517 F.2d 787 (5th Cir.), 18 August 1975. In general, see Richard Wasserman, "Implications of the Abortion Decisions: Post *Roe* and *Doe* Litigation and Legislation," *Columbia Law Review* 74 (March 1974): 237–268; and "A Review of State Abortion Laws Enacted Since January 1973," *Family Planning/Population Reporter* 4 (December 1975): 108–113.

32. *Wall Street Journal*, 2 August 1973, pp. 1, 27; John Deedy, "The Church in the World: Catholics, Abortion, and the Supreme Court," *Theology Today* 30 (October 1973): 279–286, at 281; *Time*, 4 February 1974, pp. 60–61; *Newsweek*, 4 February 1974, p. 57; U.S. Congress,

Senate, Committee on the Judiciary, *Abortion Hearings Before the Subcommittee on Constitutional Amendments*, 93rd Cong., 2nd sess. (parts I–IV), 6–7 March 1974. The National Conference of Catholic Bishops' 18 September and 13 November 1973 resolutions appear in the *Senate Hearings* at pp. 227–230. Also see Nick Thimmesch, *Newsweek*, 9 July 1973, p. 7; *Hospital Practice*, October 1973, pp. 199–201; *Dallas Times-Herald*, 20 January 1974, p. D5; Marion K. Sanders, "Enemies of Abortion," *Harper's* 248 (March 1974): 26–30; *U.S. News & World Report*, 4 March 1974, pp. 43–44; Robert Edelstein et al., "Moral Consistency and the Abortion Issue," *Commonweal*, 22 March 1974, pp. 59–61; Jim Castelli, "The Catholic Church and Abortion," *The Progressive* 38 (April 1974): 9; *The New Republic*, 18 May 1974, pp. 6–7; Daniel A. Degnan, "Law, Morals and Abortion," *Commonweal*, 31 May 1974, pp. 305–308; and Richard A. McCormick, "Notes on Moral Theology: The Abortion Dossier," *Theological Studies* 35 (June 1974): 312–359.

33. *New York Times*, 13 April 1974, pp. 1, 10, 17 February 1975, p. 41, 19 February 1975, p. 34, 29 April 1975, p. 31, 2 November 1975, p. 39, 6 April 1976, p. 25, 18 December 1976, p. 1; *Time*, 27 May 1974, p. 84, 24 February 1975, p. 67, 3 March 1975, pp. 54–55; *Newsweek*, 27 January 1975, p. 55, 24 February 1975, p. 20, 3 March 1975, pp. 18–30; *Commonwealth* v. *Edelin*, 359 N.E.2d 4, 17 December 1976; Nathan Lewin, "Abortion and Dr. Edelin," *The New Republic*, 1 March 1975, pp. 16–19; Connie Paige, *The Right to Lifers* (New York: Summit Books, 1983), esp. pp. 26 and 119–20. Also see *New England Journal of Medicine* 290 (6 June 1974): 1301–02; and William A. Nolen, *The Baby in the Bottle* (New York: Coward, McCann & Geoghegan), 1978.

34. Jeannie I. Rosoff, "Is Support of Abortion Political Suicide?" *Family Planning Perspectives* 7 (January-February 1975): 13–22; Elizabeth B. Stengel, "Abortion: The Battle's Not Over," *Ms.*, February 1975, pp. 98–99; *New York Times*, 3 February 1975, pp. 1, 42; *Newsweek*, 17 February 1975, p. 97; James J. Diamond, "The Troubled Anti-Abortion Camp," *America*, 10 August 1974, pp. 52–54; Raymond G. Decker, "The Abortion Decision: Two Years Later—More Christian Than Its Critics," *Commonweal*, 14 February 1975, pp. 384–392, at 385–86; *Congressional Quarterly Weekly Report*, 3 May 1975, pp. 917–922. Also see Richard J. Orloski, "Abortion: Legal Questions and Legislative Alternatives," *America*, 10 August 1974, pp. 50–51; *Time*, 2 September 1974, p. 56, 28 April 1975, pp. 75–76; Charles E. Curran, "Civil Law and Christian Morality: Abortion and the Churches," in Curran, ed., *Ongoing Revisions in Moral Theology* (Notre Dame, IN: Fides, 1975), pp. 107–143; U.S. Commission on Civil Rights, *Constitutional Aspects of the Right to Limit Childbearing* (Washington: USCCR), April 1975; Harriet F. Pilpel, "Abortion: U.S.A. Style," *Journal of Sex Research* 11 (May 1975): 113–118; Joseph F. Donceel, "Why Is Abortion Wrong?," *America*, 16 August 1975, pp. 65–67; Denise Spalding, "Abortions: Legal but How Available?," *Ms.*, September 1975, pp. 103–105; Robert A. Destro, "Abortion and the Constitution: The Need for a Life-Protective Amendment," *California Law Review* 63 (September 1975): 1250–1351; and Joseph P. Witherspoon, "The New Pro-Life Legislation: Patterns and Recommendations," *St. Mary's Law Journal* 7 (1976): 637–697.

35. *Congressional Quarterly Weekly Report*, 19 April 1975, pp. 814–816; *New York Times*, 18 September 1975, p. 34, 21 November 1975, p. 19, 29 April 1976, p. 35; *Time*, 1 December 1975, p. 59; *America*, 27 December 1975, pp. 454–455; Robert N. Lynch, "'Abortion' and 1976 Politics," *America*, 6 March 1976, pp. 177–178; U.S. Congress, House of Representatives, Committee on the Judiciary, *Proposed Constitutional Amendments on Abortion—Hearings Before the Subcommittee on Civil and Constitutional Rights*, 94th Cong., 2nd sess., 4–5 February and 22–26 March 1976; Jim Castelli, "Anti-Abortion, the Bishops and the Crusaders," *America*, 22 May 1976, pp. 442–444; Byrnes, *Catholic Bishops in American Politics*, pp. 58–60. Also see Lucy Komisar, *Newsweek*, 9 June 1975, p. 11; Mary C. Segers, "Abortion: The Last Resort," *America*, 27 December 1975, pp. 456–458; Meg Greenfield, *Newsweek*, 16 February 1976, p. 92; James Armstrong, "The Politics of Abortion," *Christian Century*, 10 March 1976, pp. 215–216; Paul J. Weber, "Bishops in Politics: The Big Plunge," *America*, 20 March 1976, pp. 220–223; Harriet F. Pilpel, "The Collateral Legal Consequences of Adopting a Constitutional Amendment on Abortion," *Family Planning/Population Law Reporter* 5 (June 1976): 44–48; Robert M. Byrn, "Confronting Objections to an Anti-Abortion

Amendment," *America,* 19 June 1976, pp. 529–534; and John D. Rockefeller III, *Newsweek,* 21 June 1976, p. 11.

36. William R. Arney and William H. Trescher, "Trends in Attitudes Toward Abortion, 1972–1975," *Family Planning Perspectives* 8 (May-June 1976): 117–124; Judith Blake, "The Abortion Decisions: Judicial Review and Public Opinion," in Edward Manier et al., eds., *Abortion* (Notre Dame, IN: University of Notre Dame Press, 1977), pp. 51–82; Blake, "The Supreme Court's Abortion Decisions and Public Opinion in the United States," *Population and Development Review* 3 (March-June 1977): 45–62; Theodore C. Wagenaar and Ingeborg W. Knol, "Attitudes Toward Abortion: A Comparative Analysis of Correlates for 1973 and 1975," *Journal of Sociology and Social Welfare* 4 (July 1977): 927–944; Elise F. Jones and Charles F. Westoff, "How Attitudes Toward Abortion Are Changing," *Journal of Population* 1 (Spring 1978): 5–21; Eric M. Uslaner and Ronald E. Weber, "Public Support for Pro-Choice Abortion Policies in the Nation and States: Changes and Stability After the *Roe* and *Doe* Decisions," *Michigan Law Review* 77 (August 1979): 1772–1789; Lucky R. Tedrow and E. R. Mahoney, "Trends in Attitudes Toward Abortion: 1972–1976," *Public Opinion Quarterly* 43 (Summer 1979): 181–189; Mark Evers and Jeanne McGee, "The Trend and Pattern in Attitudes Toward Abortion in the United States, 1965–1977," *Social Indicators Research* 7 (January 1980): 251–267; Stephen J. Cutler et al., "Aging and Conservatism: Cohort Changes in Attitudes About Legalized Abortion," *Journal of Gerontology* 35 (January 1980): 115–123; Helen R. F. Ebaugh and C. Allen Haney, "Shifts in Abortion Attitudes: 1972–1978," *Journal of Marriage and the Family* 42 (August 1980): 491–499; and Donald Granberg and Beth W. Granberg, "Abortion Attitudes, 1965–1980: Trends and Determinants," *Family Planning Perspectives* 12 (September-October 1980): 250–261.

37. Webster Schott, "A 4-Million Minority Asks for Equal Rights," *New York Times Magazine,* 12 November 1967, pp. 44–72, at 59; *Delaney* v. *Florida,* 387 U.S. 426, 29 May 1967 (dismissing appeal of *State* v. *Delaney,* 190 So.2d 578 [Fla. Sup. Ct.], for want of a substantial federal question, with only Justice Douglas voting to note probable jurisdiction); *Baker* v. *Nelson,* 409 U.S. 810, 10 October 1972 (dismissing an appeal from Minn. Sup. Ct., 191 N.W.2d 185); *Canfield* v. *Oklahoma,* 414 U.S. 991, 5 November 1973 (dismissing appeal of 506 P.2d 987 [Okla. Ct. Crim. App.], for want of a substantial federal question); *Carter* v. *Arkansas,* 416 U.S. 905, 1 April 1974 (denying certiorari to *State* v. *Carter,* 500 S.W.2d 368 [Ark. Sup. Ct.]); *Brewer* v. *United States,* 416 U.S. 990, 13 May 1974 (denying certiorari to *United States* v. *Brewer,* 363 F. Supp. 606 [M.D. Pa.], aff'd memo, 491 F.2d 751 [3d Cir.].

Also note *Acanfora* v. *Board of Education of Montgomery County,* 419 U.S. 836, 15 October 1974 (denying certiorari to 359 F. Supp. 843 [D. Md.], affirmed 491 F.2d 498 [4th Cir.]). Also see Arthur J. Silverstein, "Constitutional Aspects of the Homosexual's Right to a Marriage License," *Journal of Family Law* 12 (1972–73): 607–634; Silverstein, "The Legality of Homosexual Marriage," *Yale Law Journal* 82 (January 1973): 573–589; Walter Barnett, *Sexual Freedom and the Constitution* (Albuquerque: University of New Mexico Press), 1973, esp. pp. 15–16 and 97 (*Griswold* "can be read to mean that sexual fulfillment is a fundamental human right"); Ellen Chaitin and V. Roy Lefcourt, "Is Gay Suspect?" *Lincoln Law Review* 8 (1973): 24–54; Note, "The Constitutionality of Laws Forbidding Private Homosexual Conduct," *Michigan Law Review* 72 (August 1974): 1613–1637; Kent Greenawalt, "Privacy and Its Legal Protections," *Hastings Center Studies* 2 (September 1974): 45–68, at 53; Lawrence M. Goldyn, "Legal Ideology and the Regulation of Homosexual Behavior" (unpublished Ph.D. dissertation, Stanford University, 1979); Vern L. Bullough, "Lesbianism, Homosexuality, and the American Civil Liberties Union," *Journal of Homosexuality* 13 (Fall 1986): 23–33; and Richard D. Mohr, "Mr. Justice Douglas at Sodom: Gays and Privacy," *Columbia Human Rights Law Review* 18 (Fall-Winter 1986–87): 43–110.

38. *California* v. *LaRue,* 409 U.S. 109, 132n (Marshall, J., dissenting), 5 December 1972; *Fisher* v. *Snyder,* 346 F. Supp. 396 (D. Neb.), 10 August 1972, affirmed, 476 F.2d 375 (8th Cir.), 16 April 1973; *Drake* v. *Covington County Board of Education,* 371 F. Supp. 974 (M.D. Ala.), 23 January 1974. But see *Wishart* v. *McDonald,* 500 F.2d 1110, 1114 (1st Cir.), 10 July 1974 (affirming 367 F. Supp. 530) (upholding dismissal of teacher who each Thursday evening played on his lawn with a life-sized mannequin: "The right to be left alone in the home

extends only to the home and not to conduct displayed under the street lamp on the front lawn"); and especially *Sullivan* v. *Meade County Independent School District*, 387 F. Supp. 1237 (D.S.D.), 21 February 1975, affirmed, 530 F.2d 799 (8th Cir.), 26 February 1976.

Also see *Dixon* v. *State*, 268 N.E.2d 84, 90 (Ind. Sup. Ct., DeBruler, J., dissenting), 6 April 1971 ("I see no valid reason to limit the right of sexual privacy to married persons. . . . Sexual acts between consenting adults in private do not harm anyone else and should be free from state regulation"); *Davis* v. *Meek*, 344 F. Supp. 298 (N.D. Ohio), 5 May 1972; *Commonwealth* v. *Balthazar*, 318 N.E.2d 478, 481 (Mass. Sup. Jud. Ct.), 1 November 1974; and *Major* v. *Hampton*, 413 F. Supp. 66 (E.D. La.), 23 February 1976. But see *Pettit* v. *State Board of Education*, 513 P.2d 889 (Cal. Sup. Ct.), 7 September 1973; and note Robert E. Willett, *California Law Review* 61 (December 1973): 1442–1462.

39. *Wainwright* v. *Stone*, 414 U.S. 21, 5 November 1973, reversing *Stone* v. *Wainwright*, 478 F.2d. 390 (5th Cir.), 19 April 1973 (also see *Stone* v. *State*, 264 So.2d 81, 267 So.2d 329 [Fla. Sup. Ct.], and *Franklin* v. *State*, 257 So.2d 21 [Fla. Sup. Ct.], 17 December 1971); *Rose* v. *Locke*, 423 U.S. 48, 51, 55, 17 November 1975, reversing *Locke* v. *Rose*, 514 F.2d 570 (6th Cir.), 4 April 1975 (also see *Locke* v. *State*, 501 S.W.2d 826 [Tenn. Ct. Crim. App.], 2 October 1973); Thomas C. Grey, "Eros, Civilization and the Burger Court," *Law and Contemporary Problems* 43 (Summer 1980): 83–100, at 86n. Also note *State* v. *Crawford*, 478 S.W.2d 314 (Mo. Sup. Ct.), appeal dismissed for want of a substantial federal question, *Crawford* v. *Missouri*, 409 U.S. 811, 10 October 1972; and *Jellum* v. *Culp*, 475 F.2d 829 (9th Cir.), 6 March 1973, 476 P.2d 205 (Or. Ct. App.), 1970.

Also see *Paris Adult Theater* v. *Slaton*, 413 U.S. 49, 65–67, *United States* v. *12 200-Ft. Reels of Super 8mm. Film*, 413 U.S. 123, 126–127, and *United States* v. *Orito*, 413 U.S. 139, 142, 21 June 1973; *Cleveland Board of Education* v. *LaFleur*, 414 U.S. 632, 639–640, 21 January 1974; *Village of Belle Terre* v. *Boraas*, 416 U.S. 1, 1 April 1974; *Lehman* v. *City of Shaker Heights*, 418 U.S. 298, 307 (Douglas, J., dissenting), 25 June 1974; and *Kelley* v. *Johnson*, 425 U.S. 238, 244, 251, 5 April 1976.

40. *Doe* v. *Commonwealth's Attorney*, 403 F. Supp. 1199, 1203, 1205 (E.D. Va.), 24 October 1975; Edward T. Mulligan, "*Griswold* Revisited in Light of *Uplinger*," *New York University Review of Law and Social Change* 13 (1984–1985): 51–82, at 55; Philip J. Hirschkop and John D. Grad, "Jurisdictional Statement," *Doe* v. *Commonwealth's Attorney*, U.S.S.C., O.T. 1975, #896, 19 November 1975, 12pp., pp. 7, 9–10; *Doe* v. *Commonwealth's Attorney*, 425 U.S. 901, 29 March 1976; *New York Times*, 30 March 1976, pp. 1, 17, 31 March 1976, p. 40, 8 April 1976, p. 37; *Los Angeles Times*, 30 March 1976, pp. 1, 8, 1 April 1976, p. II-6; *Wall Street Journal*, 5 April 1976, p. 12; *Time*, 12 April 1976, p. 50. Also see Toby Marotta, *The Politics of Homosexuality* (Boston: Houghton Mifflin, 1981), pp. 22–23, 322–324, and 330, identifying research chemist Tony Segura, a founding member of the New York Mattachine Society chapter, as a leading Richmond activist at the time of *Doe*'s filing; Ronald J. Bacigal, *May It Please the Court: A Biography of Judge Robert R. Merhige, Jr.* (Lanham, MD: University Press of America, 1992); H. W. Perry, Jr., *Deciding to Decide* (Cambridge, MA: Harvard University Press, 1991), pp. 49, 257, concerning clerks' impressions of the Court's reluctance to decide gay rights cases; Woodward and Armstrong, *The Brethren*, p. 425; and *Enslin* v. *North Carolina*, 425 U.S. 903, 29 March 1976, denying certiorari to *State* v. *Enslin*, 214 So.2d 318.

On John Paul Stevens, see Robert J. Sickels, *Justice John Paul Stevens and the Constitution* (University Park: Pennsylvania State University Press, 1989); Bradley C. Canon, "Justice John Paul Stevens," in Charles M. Lamb and Stephen C. Halpern, eds., *The Burger Court* (Urbana: University of Illinois Press, 1991), pp. 343–374; and Woodward and Armstrong, *The Brethren*, pp. 400–402. For Stevens' prior stance toward the right to privacy, see his opinion in *Fitzgerald* v. *Porter Memorial Hospital*, 523 F.2d 716, 719, 720 (7th Cir.), 26 September 1975 (noting "our tradition of respect for the dignity of individual choice in matters of conscience" and observing that "neither the conception that produced *Griswold*, nor its progeny, is narrowly limited to marital rights").

41. E. Carrington Bogan to Mel Wulf, 6 April 1976, and Wulf to Harriet Pilpel, 22 April 1976, ACLU 1978 Vol. 30; Wulf et al., "Consolidated Petition for Rehearing," *Doe* v. *Commonwealth's Attorney* and *Enslin* v. *North Carolina*, U.S.S.C., O.T. 1975, #896 and 897, 22

April 1976, 6pp., pp. 4–5; William Thom and Marilyn G. Haft, "Brief Amicus Curiae of the National Gay Task Force in Support of Petition for Rehearing," *Doe* v. *Commonwealth's Attorney,* #896, 26 April 1976; E. Carrington Bogan, "Brief Amicus Curiae of Lambda Legal Defense and Educational Fund, Inc., in Support of Petitions for Rehearing," *Doe* v. *Commonwealth's Attorney* and *Enslin* v. *North Carolina,* #896 and 897, 26 April 1976; *New York Times,* 9 May 1976, p. 26, 20 May 1976, p. 31; *Doe* v. *Commonwealth's Attorney,* 425 U.S. 985, 19 May 1976.

Comments on the Court's action in *Doe* include Kent Greenawalt, "The Burger Court and Claims of Privacy," *Hastings Center Report* 6 (August 1976): 19–20; W. Cecil Jones, "*Doe* v. *Commonwealth's Attorney*: Closing the Door to a Fundamental Right of Sexual Privacy," *Denver Law Journal* 53 (1976): 553–576, esp. at 574; Nathan Lewin, "Avoiding the Supreme Court," *New York Times Magazine,* 17 October 1976, pp. 31, 90–100, at 98; Leslie L. Cooney, *Duquesne Law Review* 15 (Fall 1976): 123–132; James J. Rizzo, "The Constitutionality of Sodomy Statutes," *Fordham Law Review* 45 (December 1976): 553–595, at 570, 574, and 592; *Iowa Law Review* 62 (December 1976): 568–590; *Brigham Young University Law Review* 1977: 170–188; Tim O'Neill, "*Doe* v. *Commonwealth's Attorney*: A Set-Back for the Right of Privacy," *Kentucky Law Journal* 65 (Spring 1977): 748–763; Martin R. Levy and C. Thomas Hectus, "Privacy Revisited: The Downfall of *Griswold,*" *University of Richmond Law Review* 12 (Summer 1978): 627–646, at 627; David L. Bazelon, "Probing Privacy," *Gonzaga Law Review* 12 (Summer 1977): 587–619, at 616–617; and Yale L. Rosenberg, "Notes from the Underground: A Substantive Analysis of Summary Adjudication by the Burger Court, Part II," *Houston Law Review* 19 (July 1982): 831–897, at 848 (*Doe* is "One of the most criticized decisions rendered by the Court in recent years").

On public opinion statistics, see especially Eugene E. Levitt and Albert D. Klassen, Jr., "Public Attitudes Toward Homosexuality," *Journal of Homosexuality* 1 (Fall 1974): 29–43, at 30, 35, and 40; also see Jon P. Alston, "Attitudes Toward Extramarital and Homosexual Relations," *Journal for the Scientific Study of Religion* 13 (December 1974): 479–481; Kenneth L. Nyberg and Alston, "Analysis of Public Attitudes Toward Homosexual Behavior," *Journal of Homosexuality* 2 (Winter 1976–77): 99–107; Norval D. Glenn and Charles N. Weaver, "Attitudes Toward Premarital, Extramarital, and Homosexual Relations in the U.S. in the 1970s," *Journal of Sex Research* 15 (May 1979): 108–118; and Tom W. Smith, "The Polls—The Sexual Revolution?," *Public Opinion Quarterly* 54 (Fall 1990): 415–435. Also note Gilbert Geis et al., "Reported Consequences of Decriminalization of Consensual Adult Homosexuality in Seven American States," *Journal of Homosexuality* 1 (Summer 1976): 419–426.

42. Richard E. Crouch to Mel Wulf, 27 May 1976, and Wulf to General Counsel, 2 June 1976, ACLU 1978 Vol. 38; *Lovisi* v. *Virginia,* 405 U.S. 936, 22 February 1972, 405 U.S. 998, 20 March 1972 (with Douglas, J., dissenting), 405 U.S. 1048, 3 April 1972 (with Douglas, J., dissenting); *Lovisi* v. *Virginia,* 212 Va. 848, 188 S.E.2d 206, 207, 24 April 1972, cert. denied, 407 U.S. 922, 19 June 1972; *Lovisi* v. *Slayton,* 363 F. Supp. 620, 624, 625, 626, 627, (E.D. Va.), 31 August 1973; *Lovisi* v. *Slayton,* 539 F.2d 349, 351, 355 (4th Cir.), 12 May 1976, cert. denied, *Lovisi* v. *Zahradnick,* 429 U.S. 977, 29 November 1976.

Also see *State* v. *Bateman,* 547 P.2d 6 (Ariz. Sup. Ct.), 10 March 1976 (stay denied, 429 U.S. 1302, 16 August 1976 [Rehnquist, Crct. J.], cert. denied, *Bateman* v. *Arizona,* 429 U.S. 864, 4 October 1976), reversing both *State* v. *Bateman,* 540 P.2d 732 (Ariz. Ct. App., Div. 1), 30 September 1975, and *State* v. *Callaway,* 542 P.2d 1147 (Ariz. Ct. App., Div. 2), 26 November 1975. Also note Judith E. Sirkis, *Arizona State Law Journal* 1976: 499–524.

But see *State* v. *Pilcher,* 242 N.W.2d 348, 359 (Iowa Sup. Ct.), 19 May 1976, a 5 to 4 holding that "the rationale expressed in *Eisenstadt* extends to protect the manner of sexual relations performed in private between consenting adults of the opposite sex not married to each other." Also note *State* v. *Pilcher,* 242 N.W.2d 367 (Iowa Sup. Ct.), 19 May 1976; *Washington University Law Quarterly* 1977 (Spring): 337–348, and *Iowa Law Review* 63 (October 1977): 248–265.

Law journal notes on *Lovisi* include Keith M. Wiener, *Emory Law Journal* 25 (Fall 1976): 959–981; E. Clifton Knowles, *Tennessee Law Review* 44 (Fall 1976): 179–188; *Journal of*

Criminal Law and Criminology 68 (March 1977): 77–82; Joseph L. Koplin, *George Washington Law Review* 45 (May 1977): 839–861; Carleton H. A. Taber, *Hastings Constitutional Law Quarterly* 4 (Summer 1977): 637–664; Stephen A. Yeagy, *Rutgers Camden Law Journal* 8 (Summer 1977): 707–713; and June A. Eichbaum, "*Lovisi* v. *Slayton*: Constitutional Privacy and Sexual Expression," *Columbia Human Rights Law Review* 10 (Fall-Winter 1978–79): 525–540.

Also see *Warner* v. *State*, 489 P.2d 526 (Okla. Ct. Crim. App.), 1 September 1971; and *Chesebrough* v. *State*, 255 So.2d 675 (Fla. Sup. Ct.), 8 December 1971, cert. denied, 406 U.S. 976, 7 June 1972.

43. *Planned Parenthood of Central Missouri* v. *Danforth*, 392 F. Supp. 1362 (E.D. Mo.), 31 January 1975; 420 U.S. 918 (enforcement stayed pending appeal), 18 February 1975; Blackmun, "Memorandum to the Conference" (and attachment), 17 June 1975, Stewart to Blackmun, 17 June 1975, Brennan to Blackmun, 17 June 1975, and Marshall to Blackmun, 18 June 1975, Marshall Box 166; Woodward and Armstrong, *The Brethren*, pp. 414–416; 423 U.S. 819 (probable jurisdiction noted), 6 October 1975; *New York Times*, 7 October 1975, p. 1, 12 October 1975, p. IV-4; *Wulff* v. *Singleton*, 508 F.2d 1211 (8th Cir.), 1975 (reversing 380 F. Supp. 1137 [E.D. Mo.], 1974); *Baird* v. *Bellotti*, 393 F. Supp. 847 (D. Mass.), 28 April 1975. On the Massachusetts statute, see Virginia G. Cartoof, "Massachusetts' Parental Consent Law: Origins, Implementation and Impact" (unpublished Ph.D. dissertation, Brandeis University, 1985).

Also see especially *Connecticut* v. *Menillo*, 423 U.S. 9, 11 November 1975 (vacating and remanding 362 A.2d 962); and *Word* v. *Poelker*, 495 F.2d 1349 (8th Cir.), 20 February 1974. Also note *Wolfe* v. *Schroering*, 388 F. Supp. 631 (W.D. Ky.), 19 November 1974; *Doe* v. *Zimmerman*, 405 F. Supp. 534 (M.D. Pa.), 3 December 1975; *Roe* v. *Arizona Board of Regents*, 549 P.2d 150 (Ariz. Sup. Ct.), 11 May 1976 (reversing 534 P.2d 285 [Ariz. Ct. App.]); and M. David Bryant, Jr., "State Legislation on Abortion After *Roe* v. *Wade*," *American Journal of Law and Medicine* 2 (Summer 1976): 101–132.

44. Blackmun, *Danforth* Circulation #2, 26 May 1976, Brennan to Blackmun, 28 May 1976, Stevens to Blackmun, 28 May 1976, Stewart to Blackmun, 1 June 1976, Stevens *Danforth* Prints #2 and 3, 1 and 4 June 1976, Marshall to Blackmun, 2 June 1976, White to Blackmun, 4 June 1976, Marshall Box 166; Blackmun Bellotti typescript circulation, 7 June 1976, Stevens to Blackmun, 8 June 1976, Brennan to Blackmun, 9 June 1976, Stewart to Blackmun, 9 June 1976, Powell to Blackmun, 9 June 1976, Blackmun Bellotti Prints #1 and 2, 10 and 15 June 1976, Marshall to Blackmun, 10 June 1976, Rehnquist to Blackmun, 11 June 1976, White to Blackmun, 14 June 1976, and Burger to Blackmun, 16 June 1976, Marshall Box 170; White *Danforth* typescript circulation, 16 June 1976, Rehnquist to White, 17 June 1976, Stewart Danforth typescript circulation, 17 June 1976, Stevens to Blackmun, 17 June 1976, Powell to Stewart, 18 June 1976, Stewart Print #1, 21 June 1976, Blackmun, "Memorandum to the Conference" (*Danforth*), 21 June 1976, Marshall Box 166; Blackmun, "Memorandum to the Conference" (*Bellotti*), 21 June 1976, Marshall Box 170; Blackmun *Danforth* Print #3, 26 June 1976, Blackmun, "Memorandum to the Conference," 28 June 1976, Stewart to Blackmun, 28 June 1976, Blackmun, "Memorandum to the Conference," 28 June 1976, Powell to Blackmun, 28 June 1976, White Print #2, 28 and 30 June 1976, Burger to White, 30 June 1976, Stewart Print #2, 29 June 1976, Blackmun, "Memorandum to the Conference," 29 June 1976, White, "Memorandum to the Conference," 29 June 1976, Marshall Box 166.

45. *Planned Parenthood of Central Missouri* v. *Danforth*, 438 U.S. 52, 64, 71, 74, 78–79, 89, 92; *Singleton* v. *Wulff*, 428 U.S. 106, *Bellotti* v. *Baird*, 428 U.S. 132, 1 July 1976; *New York Times*, 2 July 1976, pp. A1, A8. Also see Epstein and Kobylka, *The Supreme Court and Legal Change*, pp. 216–220. Relevant law journal notes include Merrill S. Schell, "Third Party Consent to Abortions Before and After *Danforth*," and George W. Moss III, "Abortion Statutes After *Danforth*," *Journal of Family Law* 15 (1976–77): 508–536 and 537–567.

46. *New York Times*, 26 August 1976, p. 15, 16 September 1976, pp. 1, 30, 17 September 1976, p. 22, 18 September 1976, pp. 1, 9, 30 September 1976, p. 1, 1 October 1976, p. 1, 2 October

1976, p. 1, 23 October 1976, p. 1, 9 November 1976, p. 1, 14 November 1976, p. IV-8, 15 February 1977, p. 49; *McRae* v. *Mathews*, 421 F. Supp. 533, 22 October 1976; *Buckley* v. *McRae*, 429 U.S. 935, 8 November 1976 (stay denied), *Buckley* v. *McRae*, 429 U.S. 1085, 22 February 1977 (stay again denied); Maris A. Vinovskis, "The Politics of Abortion in the House of Representatives in 1976," *Michigan Law Review* 77 (August 1979): 1790–1827, at 1793–1799. Also see Joyce Gelb and Marian L. Palley, "Women and Interest Group Politics: A Comparative Analysis of Federal Decision Making," *Journal of Politics* 41 (May 1979): 362–392, at 375–377; Gelb and Palley, *Women and Public Policies*, rev. ed. (Princeton: Princeton University Press, 1987), pp. 129–161; Charles Fimian, "The Effects of Religion on Abortion Policy-Making: A Study of Voting Behavior in the U.S. Congress, 1976–1980" (unpublished Ph.D. dissertation, Arizona State University, 1983); and Raymond Tatalovich and David Schier, "The Persistence of Ideological Cleavage in Voting on Abortion Legislation in the House of Representatives, 1973–1988," *American Politics Quarterly* 21 (January 1993): 125–139.

47. *Sendak* v. *Arnold*, 429 U.S. 968, 29 November 1976 (affirming 416 F. Supp. 22). On abortion's role in the 1976 presidential campaign, see especially Byrnes, *Catholic Bishops in American Politics*, pp. 68–81; also see Byrnes, "The Bishops and Electoral Politics: A Case Study," in Segers, ed., *Church Polity and American Politics*, pp. 121–141; Sandra Stencel, "Abortion Politics," *Editorial Research Reports* 15 (22 October 1976): 767–784; and Byron W. Daynes and Raymond Tatalovich, "Presidential Politics and Abortion, 1972–1976," *Presidential Studies Quarterly* 22 (Summer 1992): 545–561, at 546–49.

See as well *Whalen* v. *Roe*, 429 U.S. 589, 22 February 1977, at 605n: "The constitutional right vindicated in *Doe* was the right of a pregnant woman to decide whether or not to bear a child," Justice Stevens observed on behalf of all nine justices. "The statutory restrictions on the abortion procedures were invalid because they encumbered the woman's exercise of that constitutionally protected right by placing obstacles in the path of the doctor. . . . If those obstacles had not impacted upon the woman's freedom to make a constitutionally protected decision, if they had merely made the physician's work more laborious or less independent without any impact on the patient, they would not have violated the Constitution." Also see 429 U.S. 609, Stewart, J., concurring: "Whatever the *ratio decidendi* of *Griswold*, it does not recognize a general interest in freedom from disclosure of private information."

Also note *Garger* v. *New Jersey*, 429 U.S. 922, 1 November 1976, denying cert. to *In re Quinlan*, 355 A.2d 647, 663–64 (N.J. Sup. Ct.), 31 March 1976; *Superintendent of Belchertown State School* v. *Saikewicz*, 370 N.E.2d 417, 424, 426 (Mass. Sup. Jud. Ct.), 28 November 1977; *In re Eichner*, 423 N.Y.S.2d 580, 593 (Nassau County Sup. Ct.), 6 December 1979; *Eichner* v. *Dillon*, 426 N.Y.S.2d 517, 537–541 (App. Div. Sup. Ct., 2d Dept.), 27 March 1980; *Satz* v. *Perlmutter*, 379 So.2d 359 (Fla. Sup. Ct.), 17 January 1980 (affirming 362 So.2d 160); and *Rasmussen* v. *Fleming*, 741 P.2d 674, 682 (Ariz. Sup. Ct.), 23 July 1987 ("The right to refuse medical treatment is a personal right sufficiently 'fundamental' or 'implicit in the concept of ordered liberty' to fall within the constitutionally protected zone of privacy contemplated by the Supreme Court"). See too Edward M. Kay, "The Right to Die," *University of Florida Law Review* 18 (Spring 1966): 591–605, at 604 ("The right to die complements and falls within the right to be let alone concept"); Richard Delgado, "Euthanasia Reconsidered—The Choice of Death as an Aspect of the Right of Privacy," *Arizona Law Review* 17 (1975): 474–494, at 478 ("the decision to die is even more intimate than the decision to abort since no potentially independent entity is destroyed"); William F. Smith, "*In re Quinlan*: Defining the Basis for Terminating Life Support Under the Right of Privacy," *Tulsa Law Journal* 12 (1976): 150–167; Norman L. Cantor, "*Quinlan*, Privacy, and the Handling of Incompetent Dying Patients," *Rutgers Law Review* 30 (Winter 1977): 243–266; Patricia Archbold, "*Roe* v. *Wade* and *In re Quinlan*: Individual Decision and the Scope of Privacy's Constitutional Guarantee," *University of San Francisco Law Review* 12 (Fall 1977): 111–153, at 130 ("preserving individual decision is the essence of privacy's constitutional role"); David A. J. Richards, "Constitutional Privacy, the Right to Die and the Meaning of Life," *William and Mary Law Review* 22 (Spring 1981): 327–419; and Joyce A. Howell, "Guaranteeing the Right to Privacy: A Proposal," *Rutgers Law Journal* 17 (Spring-Summer 1986): 615–657.

48. *Carey* v. *Population Services International*, 431 U.S. 678, 687, 688–689, 693, 703, 9 June 1977 (affirming 398 F. Supp. 321). Also see Brian DeBoice, "Due Process Privacy and the Path of Progress," *University of Illinois Law Forum* 1979: 469–546, at 505.

See also *Moore* v. *City of East Cleveland*, 431 U.S. 494, 499, 503, 31 May 1977 (Powell, J., writing for only a four-justice plurality); and *Smith* v. *Organization of Foster Families for Equality and Reform*, 431 U.S. 816, 844, 13 June 1977; note as well *Harvard Law Review* 91 (November 1977): 128–152, at 136 and 150; and Robert A. Burt, "The Constitution of the Family," *Supreme Court Review* 1979 (Chicago: University of Chicago Press, 1980), pp. 329–395, at 388–391.

49. *Maher* v. *Roe*, 432 U.S. 464, 473–474, 475, 484, (reversing 408 F. Supp. 660); *Beal* v. *Doe*, 432 U.S. 438, 450, 462 (reversing 523 F.2d 611); *Poelker* v. *Doe*, 432 U.S. 519 (reversing 515 F.2d 541), 20 June 1977.

Also see Powell, "Memorandum to the Conference" (and *Maher* Print #1), 15 April 1977, Stevens to Powell, 18 April 1977, Powell Print #2, 28 April 1977, Stewart to Powell, 28 April 1977, Rehnquist to Powell, 28 April 1977, Marshall Box 186; Powell Circulation #1 in *Beal*, 28 April 1977, Stevens to Powell, 29 April 1977, Brennan to Powell, 2 May 1977, Powell Print #2, 2 May 1977, Rehnquist to Powell, 3 May 1977, Stewart to Powell, 3 May 1977, Marshall Box 182; Powell Per Curiam Circulation #1 in *Poelker*, 2 May 1977, Brennan to Powell, 2 May 1977, Stevens to Powell, Stewart to Powell, and Rehnquist to Powell, all 3 May 1977, Marshall Box 181; Powell *Maher* Print #3, 6 May 1977, Burger Concurrence Print #1, 11 May 1977, Brennan Dissent Print #2, 31 May 1977, Marshall to Brennan, 31 May 1977, Blackmun to Brennan, 1 June 1977, White to Powell, 1 June 1977, Powell Print #4, 2 June 1977, Marshall Box 186; Brennan *Beal* Dissent Print #1, 31 May 1977, Marshall to Brennan, 31 May 1977, Blackmun to Brennan, 1 June 1977, Blackmun Dissent Print #1, 1 and 2 June 1977, White to Powell, 1 June 1977, Burger to Powell, 1 June 1977, Marshall Box 182; Brennan *Poelker* Dissent Print #1, 31 May 1977, Marshall to Brennan, 31 May 1977, Blackmun to Brennan, 1 June 1977, Burger to Powell, 1 June 1977, White to Powell, 1 June 1977, Brennan to Blackmun, 14 June 1977, Marshall to Blackmun, 14 June 1977, Marshall Box 181; Powell to Brennan, 13 June 1977, Marshall Box 186. Marshall apparently first circulated his seven-page typescript dissent in all three cases on 10 January 1977, the day before they were argued. *Maher* File, Marshall Box 186.

50. *New York Times*, 18 June 1977, p. 1, 21 June 1977, pp. 1, 13, 22 June 1977, pp. 17, 22, 26 June 1977, p. IV-1, 27 June 1977, 30 June 1977, pp. 1, 20, 1 July 1977, p. 24, 3 July 1977, p. 32, 5 July 1977, p. 28, 6 July 1977, p. 12, 10 July 1977, p. 23, 13 July 1977, pp. 1, 10, 14 July 1977, p. 38, 17 July 1977, p. IV-10, 29 July 1977, p. 1, 31 July 1977, p. IV-2, 3 August 1977, p. 11, 5 August 1977, pp. 1, 9, 6 August 1977, p. 16; *Califano* v. *McRae*, 433 U.S. 916, 29 June 1977; Jeanne B. Nicholson and Debra W. Stewart, "The Supreme Court, Abortion Policy, and State Response: A Preliminary Analysis," *Publius* 8 (Winter 1978): 159–178. On Judge Dooling himself, see *New York Times*, 1 August 1977, p. 42. Also see *Ms.*, July 1977, pp. 54–55; Richard N. Ostling, "The Changing Abortion Debate," *Theology Today* 34 (July 1977): 161–166; *The New Republic*, 2 July 1977, pp. 5–6; Eugene J. McMahon, *America*, 9 July 1977, pp. 12–14; Peter Steinfels, "The Politics of Abortion," *Commonweal*, 22 July 1977, p. 456; Lance Morrow, *Time*, 11 August 1977, p. 49; Howard A. Palley, "Abortion Policy: Ideology, Political Cleavage and the Policy Process," *Policy Studies Journal* 7 (Winter 1978): 224–233; Peter Skerry, "The Class Conflict Over Abortion," *The Public Interest* 52 (Summer 1978): 69–84; and Marc I. Steinberg, *St. Louis University Law Journal* 22 (1979): 596–600.

51. Kristen B. Glen, "Abortion in the Courts: A Laywoman's Historical Guide to the New Disaster Area," *Feminist Studies* 4 (February 1978): 1–26, at 1; Moody in *Christianity & Crisis*, 19 September 1977, pp. 202–207, at 203; Susman, "*Roe* v. *Wade* and *Doe* v. *Bolton* Revisited in 1976 and 1977—Reviewed?; Revived?; Revested?; Reversed? or Revoked?" *St. Louis University Law Journal* 22 (1979): 581–595, at 584; Law in Patricia Donovan, *Family Planning/Population Reporter* 6 (October 1977): 66–67; *New York Times,* 17 August 1977, p. 1, 13 September 1977, p. 14, 27 September 1977, p. 24, 28 September 1977, p. 1, 30 September 1977, pp. 20, 26, 1 October 1977, p. 8, 2 October 1977, p. IV-4, 6 October 1977, p. A21, 14 October 1977, p. 14, 23 October 1977, pp. 1, 24, 1 November 1977, p. 29, 2 November 1977,

p. 19, 4 November 1977, p. 1, 5 November 1977, p. 9, 27 November 1977, p. IV-4, 28 November 1977, p. 19, 30 November 1977, p. 20, 7 December 1977, p. 19, 8 December 1977, pp. 1, 14, 9 December 1977, p. 16, 25 December 1977, p. 20.

Also see Mary C. Segers, "Abortion and the Supreme Court: Some Are More Equal Than Others," *Hastings Center Report* 7 (August 1977): 5–6; Janet Benshoof, "Mobilizing for Abortion Rights," *Civil Liberties Review* 4 (September-October 1977): 76–79; Michael Kinsley, *The New Republic*, 19 November 1977, pp. 13–15; David T. Hardy, "Privacy and Public Funding: *Maher* v. *Roe* as the Interaction of *Roe* v. *Wade* and *Dandridge* v. *Williams*," *Arizona Law Review* 18 (1977): 903–938; Alan J. Shefler, "Indigent Women and Abortion: Limitation of the Right of Privacy in *Maher* v. *Roe*," *Tulsa Law Journal* 13 (1977): 287–303; Barnett M. Sneideman, "Abortion: A Public Health and Social Policy Perspective," *New York University Review of Law and Social Change* 7 (Spring 1978): 187–213; Michael J. Perry, "The Abortion Funding Cases," *Georgetown Law Journal* 66 (June 1978): 1191–1245; Dennis J. Horan and Thomas J. Marzen, "The Moral Interest of the State in Abortion Funding: A Comment on *Beal, Maher*, and *Poelker*," *St. Louis University Law Journal* 22 (1979): 566–579; Debra W. Stewart and Jeanne B. Nicholson, "Abortion Policy in 1978: A Follow-Up Analysis," *Publius 9* (Winter 1979): 161–167; Susan J. Tolchin, "The Impact of the Hyde Amendment on Congress: Effects of Single Issue Politics on Legislative Disfunction, June 1977–June 1978," *Women and Politics* 5 (Spring 1985): 91–106; and Kathleen R. Scharf, "Abortion and the Body Politic: An Anthropological Analysis of Legislative Activity in Massachusetts" (unpublished Ph.D. dissertation, Boston University, 1981).

52. *Time,* 19 December 1977, pp. 12–13; "A Call to Concern," *Christianity & Crisis*, 3 October 1977, pp. 222–224, and *Christian Century,* 12 October 1977, pp. 912–14. Also see Gloria Steinem, "Abortion Alert," *Ms.*, November 1977, p. 118.

In later years, some writers would blame the supposed passivity of abortion rights advocates for antiabortionists' increasing success. See, e.g., Samuel Walker, *In Defense of American Liberties* (New York: Oxford University Press, 1990), p. 303 (after *Roe*, "the abortion rights legislative movement evaporated"), Marlene Gerber Fried, in Fried, ed., *From Abortion to Reproductive Rights* (Boston: South End Press, 1990), p. 5 ("The abortion rights movement essentially folded after abortion became legal"), and Susan G. Mezey, *In Pursuit of Equality* (New York: St. Martin's Press, 1991), p. 210 (until 1989, pro-choice proponents had been "largely quiescent since 1973"). Also see Pamela J. Conover and Virginia Gray, *Feminism and the New Right* (New York: Praeger, 1983), p. 67. However, as Suzanne Staggenborg has correctly noted, "Contrary to some accounts . . . the pro-choice movement did not demobilize in response to the victory." Staggenborg, "Organizational and Environmental Influences on the Development of the Pro-Choice Movement," *Social Forces* 68 (September 1989): 204–240, at 221; also see Staggenborg, *The Pro-Choice Movement* (New York: Oxford University Press, 1991), pp. 10, 57.

53. James T. Burtchaell, *Christianity & Crisis*, 14 November 1977, pp. 270–271; Frederick S. Jaffe et al., *Abortion Politics* (New York: McGraw-Hill, 1981), pp. 10, 32 (reporting 1977 statistics); *New York Times*, 20 February 1978, p. 12, 2 March 1978, 3 March 1978, p. 8, 4 March 1978, p. 24, 10 March 1978, p. 16; *Congressional Quarterly Weekly Report*, 1 July 1978, pp. 1677–1679; Patricia Donovan, *Family Planning/Population Reporter* 7 (August 1978): 62–64; *Newsweek*, 5 June 1978, pp. 37–47. On Burtchaell, also see *New York Times*, 3 December 1991, p. A20.

See also *Christianity & Crisis,* 31 October 1977, pp. 253–255, 14 November 1977, pp. 264–266, and 26 December 1977, pp. 311–318; Lawrence Lader, *New York Times*, 11 January 1978, p. A19; *New York Times*, 22 January 1978, p. D19, 23 January 1978, pp. A18, B2, 24 January 1978, p. A12, 4 May 1978, p. A17, 20 May 1978, p. 24; *Time*, 10 April 1978, p. 26, 22 May 1978, p. 24; and Judy Barton, "Abortion Clinics Under Siege," *The Progressive*, March 1979, pp. 27–29.

54. *New York Times,* 14 March 1978, p. 37, 14 June 1978, p. 1, 20 June 1978, p. 16, 20 June 1978, pp. 1, 16, 16 August 1978, p. 128, 4 October 1978, p. 75, 13 October 1978, p. 3, 16 October 1978, p. 5, 5 December 1978, p. 18, 26 December 1978, p. B14; Margaret Steinfels et al., "Is Abortion a Religious Issue?," *Hastings Center Report* 8 (August 1978): 12–17; *Commonweal*, 8

December 1978, pp. 771–773, 2 February 1979, pp. 35–38; Aryeh Neier, "Theology and the Constitution," *The Nation*, 30 December 1978, pp. 723, 726–727; "Does the First Amendment Bar the Hyde Amendment?," *Christianity & Crisis*, 5 March 1979, pp. 34–43; *Beal* v. *Franklin*, 435 U.S. 913 (probable jurisdiction noted), 6 March 1978 (argued 3 October 1978); *New York Times*, 7 March 1978, p. 12, 17 October 1978, p. 29, 31 October 1978, p. 20; *Bellotti* v. *Baird*, 439 U.S. 925 (probable jurisdiction noted), 30 October 1978; *New York Times*, 13 November 1978, p. 18, 16 November 1978, p. 27, 22 November 1978, p. 1; *Time*, 29 January 1979, pp. 62–63. Also see Richard A. McCormick, *America*, 22 July 1978, pp. 26–30; *Wall Street Journal*, 15 August 1978.

55. *Colautti* v. *Franklin*, 439 U.S. 379, 386, 387, 388, 393, 394, 409, 9 January 1979; *New York Times*, 10 January 1979, p. D18, 14 January 1979, p. IV-22, 23 January 1979, p. C10. Also see especially *Anders* v. *Floyd*, 440 U.S. 445, 5 March 1979 (vacating and remanding 440 F.Supp. 535), and *New York Times*, 6 March 1979, p. B7, as well as *Planned Parenthood Association* v. *Fitzpatrick*, 401 F. Supp. 554 (E.D. Pa.), *Franklin* v. *Fitzpatrick* and *Beal* v. *Franklin*, 428 U.S. 901, 6 July 1976; Leslie Ann Cohen, "Fetal Viability and Individual Autonomy: Resolving Medical and Legal Standards for Abortion," *UCLA Law Review* 27 (August 1980): 1340–1364, at 1354–55; Eugene Griffin, "Viability and Fetal Life in State Criminal Abortion Laws," *Journal of Criminal Law & Criminology* 72 (Spring 1981): 324–344; and Ken Martyn, "Technological Advances and *Roe* v. *Wade*: The Need to Rethink Abortion Law," *UCLA Law Review* 29 (June-August 1982): 1194–1215. Blackmun first circulated an initial print of his *Colautti* opinion on 22 November 1978, and it was joined by Justices Marshall (22 November), Brennan, Stewart, Stevens (all 27 November) and Powell (7 December). Also see White to Blackmun, 24 November 1978, White Print #1, 29 December 1978 (joined 2 January 1979 by both Rehnquist and Burger), and White to Blackmun, 4 January 1979, all in Marshall Box 226. On "right to life" efforts in Pennsylvania, see especially Michael Margolis and Kevin Neary, "Pressure Politics Revisited: The Anti-Abortion Campaign," *Policy Studies Journal* 8 (Spring 1980): 698–716.

Also note *Zablocki* v. *Redhail*, 434 U.S. 374, 384, 18 January 1978 ("the right to marry is part of the fundamental 'right of privacy' implicit in the Fourteenth Amendment's Due Process Clause"). See as well "The Constitution and the Family," *Harvard Law Review* 93 (April 1980): 1156–1383, at 1250.

56. *New York Times*, 1 March 1979, p. B20, 12 March 1979, p. 16, 22 April 1979, p. 49, 1 May 1979, p. C22, 15 May 1979, p. B6, 20 May 1979, p. 52, 28 June 1979, p. B14, 29 June 1979, p. 15, 3 July 1979, p. 9; *Bellotti* v. *Baird*, 443 U.S. 622, 649, 651, 655, 2 July 1979 (affirming 450 F. Supp. 997); Stevens to Powell, 5 June 1979, Marshall Box 235. Also see *Baird* v. *Attorney General*, 360 N.E.2d 288 (Mass. Sup. Jud. Ct.), and *Baird* v. *Bellotti*, 428 F. Supp. 854.

Powell first circulated his opinion on June 1, and in a cover note highlighted how in part he was working from *Bellotti I*'s specification of whether or not a statutory requirement posed an "undue burden" (428 U.S. 145) on a pregnant minor's right to an abortion. Powell, "Memorandum to the Conference," 1 June 1979 (with attachment). Prior to subsequently joining Powell's opinion, Potter Stewart initially contended "that a pregnant minor should not have even the rather light burden that you would require of satisfying the Superior Court that her parents would probably deny consent and seek to obstruct her efforts to seek judicial relief. In my opinion, her burden should be only to convince the Court that she is sufficiently mature to decide the matter for herself or that an abortion would be in her best interest." Their disagreement, Stewart added, "probably depends ultimately upon a differing assessment of what is an 'undue burden'" per *Bellotti I*. Stewart to Powell, 4, 5, and 25 June 1979. Also see Rehnquist to Powell (2), 5 June 1979, Stevens typescript circulation, 6 June 1979, and Print #1, 8 June 1979, White to Powell, 7 June 1979, Rehnquist to Powell, 8 June 1979, Burger to Powell, 8 June 1979, Brennan to Stevens, 8 June 1979, Blackmun to Powell, 18 June 1979 ("I have been through these woods before and I know how sticky and difficult the going is in this general area"), Blackmun to Stevens, 18 June 1979, Marshall to Stevens, 19 June 1979, Rehnquist to Powell, 25 June 1979, Burger to Powell, 25 June 1979, all in Marshall Box 235.

Also note Juli Loesch, "Abortion and an Attempt at Dialogue," *America*, 24 March 1979, pp. 234–236; Rhonda Copelon, *Ms.*, May 1979, pp. 91–92; Elizabeth R. Dobell, *Redbook*, June 1979, pp. 42, 86–97; and especially Roger M. Williams, "The Power of Fetal Politics," *Saturday Review*, 9 June 1979, pp. 12–15; as well as Robert B. Keiter, "Privacy, Children, and Their Parents: Reflections On and Beyond the Supreme Court's Approach," *Minnesota Law Review* 66 (March 1982): 459–518, at 472–477.

57. *New York Times*, 20 July 1979, p. A14, 18 September 1979, p. B8, 29 September 1979, pp. 1, 24, 2 October 1979, p. B13, 4 October 1979, p. 30, 10 October 1979, p. 1, 13 October 1979, p. 1, 11 November 1979, p. 43, 14 November 1979, p. 22, 16 November 1979, p. 9, 17 November 1979, p. 10, 26 November 1979, p. 18, 27 November 1979, p. B18; *Williams* v. *Zbaraz*, 444 U.S. 962 (26 November 1979).

On public opinion, see Judith Blake and Jorge H. Del Pinal, "Predicting Polar Attitudes Toward Abortion in the United States," in James T. Burtchaell, ed., *Abortion Parley* (Kansas City: Andrews & McMeel, 1980), pp. 29–56, and "Negativism, Equivocation, and Wobbly Assent: Public 'Support' for the Pro-Choice Platform on Abortion," *Demography* 18 (August 1981): 309–320; Donald and Beth W. Granberg, "Pro-Life Versus Pro-Choice: Another Look at the Abortion Controversy in the U.S.," *Sociology and Social Research* 65 (July 1981): 424–434; Michael W. Coombs and Susan Welch, "Blacks, Whites, and Attitudes Toward Abortion," *Public Opinion Quarterly* 46 (Winter 1982): 510–520, at 514; Herbert McClosky and Alida Brill, *Dimensions of Tolerance* (New York: Russell Sage Foundation, 1983), pp. 218–231; Cynthia H. Deitch, "Ideology and Opposition to Abortion: Trends in Public Opinion, 1972–1980," *Alternative Lifestyles* 6 (Fall 1983): 6–26; Helen R. F. Ebaugh and C. Allen Haney, "Abortion Attitudes in the United States: Continuities and Discontinuities," and Donald and Beth W. Granberg, "Social Bases of Support and Opposition to Legalized Abortion," both in Paul Sachdev, ed., *Perspectives on Abortion* (Metuchen, NJ: Scarecrow Press, 1985), pp. 163–77 and 191–204; Allen L. McCutcheon, "Sexual Morality, Pro-Life Values, and Attitudes Toward Abortion: A Simultaneous Latent Structure Analysis for 1978–1983," *Sociological Methods and Research* 16 (November 1987): 256–275; Ted G. Jelen, "Changes in the Attitudinal Correlations of Opposition to Abortion, 1977–1985," *Journal for the Scientific Study of Religion* 27 (June 1988): 211–228; Robert F. Szafran and Arthur F. Clagett, "Variable Predictors of Attitudes Toward the Legalization of Abortion," *Social Indicators Research* 20 (June 1988): 271–290; and Michael W. Gillespie et al., "Secular Trends in Abortion Attitudes: 1975–1980–1985," *Journal of Psychology* 122 (July 1988): 323–341. Also note Ross K. Baker et al., "Matters of Life and Death: Social, Political, and Religious Correlates of Attitudes on Abortion," *American Politics Quarterly* 9 (January 1981): 89–102; Howard Schuman et al., "Context Effects on Survey Responses to Questions About Abortion," *Public Opinion Quarterly* 45 (Summer 1981): 216–223; Gregory Casey, "Intensive Analysis of a 'Single' Issue: Attitudes on Abortion," *Political Methodology* 10 (1984): 97–124; and George F. Bishop et al., "The Importance of Replicating a Failure to Replicate: Order Effects on Abortion Items," *Public Opinion Quarterly* 49 (Spring 1985): 105–114.

Also see generally Andrew Hacker, "Of Two Minds About Abortion," *Harper's* 259 (September 1979): 16–22, at 18 ("Support for abortion comes primarily from men and women who admit to enjoying sexual activity.... They compose a new class of Americans, for whom intercourse is an important leisure pursuit"); Edward A. Langerak, "Abortion: Listening to the Middle," *Hastings Center Report 9* (October 1979): 24–28; and *ABA Journal*, November 1979, pp. 1634–35.

58. Kristin Luker, *Abortion and the Politics of Motherhood* (Berkeley: University of California Press, 1984), pp. 137–138, 193, 224, 241; Stephen L. Markson, "Normative Boundaries and Abortion Policy: The Politics of Morality," *Research in Social Problems and Public Policy* 2 (1982): 21–33, at 32; Linda Gordon and Allen Hunter, "Sex, Family & the New Right," *Radical America* 11/12 (December 1977–February 1978): 9–25, at 11; Patrick J. Sheeran, *Women, Society, the State, and Abortion* (New York: Praeger, 1987), at pp. 125 and 127–28; Rosalind P. Petchesky, "Antiabortion, Antifeminism, and the Rise of the New Right," *Feminist Studies* 7 (Summer 1981): 206–246, at 207 and 210. Also note Petchesky,

"Reproductive Freedom: Beyond 'A Woman's Right to Choose,'" *Signs* 5 (Summer 1980): 661–685; Faye Ginsburg, "Procreation Stories: Reproduction, Nurturance, and Procreation in Life Narratives of Abortion Activists," *American Ethnologist* 14 (November 1987): 623–636; Suzanne Staggenborg, "Life-Style Preferences and Social Movement Recruitment: Illustrations from the Abortion Conflict," *Social Science Quarterly* 68 (December 1987): 779–797; and Elizabeth A. Cook et al., *Between Two Absolutes: Public Opinion and the Politics of Abortion* (Boulder, CO: Westview Press, 1992), pp. 5, 86–87 and 108.

Also see Donald Granberg, "Pro-Life or Reflection of Conservative Ideology?—An Analysis of Opposition to Legalized Abortion," *Sociology and Social Research* 62 (April 1978): 414–429; William A. McIntosh et al., "The Differential Impact of Religious Preference and Church Attendance on Attitudes Toward Abortion," *Review of Religious Research* 20 (Spring 1979): 195–213; Granberg, "The Abortion Activists," *Family Planning Perspectives* 13 (July-August 1981): 157–163; Mary Jo Neitz, "Family, State, and God: Ideologies of the Right-to-Life Movement," *Sociological Analysis* 42 (Fall 1981): 265–276; Granberg, "Comparison of Members of Pro- and Anti-Abortion Organizations in Missouri," *Social Biology* 28 (Fall-Winter 1981): 239–252; Granberg, "Family Size Preferences and Sexual Permissiveness as Factors Differentiating Abortion Activists," *Social Psychology Quarterly* 45 (March 1982): 15–23; Granberg, "What Does It Mean to Be 'Pro-Life'?" *Christian Century*, 12 May 1982, pp. 562–566; Granberg, "Comparison of Pro-Choice and Pro-Life Activists: Their Values, Attitudes, and Beliefs," *Population and Environment* 5 (Summer 1982): 75–94; Peter J. Leahy et al., "The Anti-Abortion Movement and Symbolic Crusades: Reappraisal of a Popular Theory," *Alternative Lifestyles* 6 (Fall 1983): 27–47; Ted G. Jelen, "Respect for Life, Sexual Morality, and Opposition to Abortion," *Review of Religious Research* 25 (March 1984): 220–231; Mary H. Benin, "Determinants of Opposition to Abortion," *Sociological Perspectives* 28 (April 1985): 199–216; Robert J. Spitzer, *The Right to Life Movement and Third Party Politics* (Westport, CT: Greenwood Press, 1987), p. 85; John D. McCarthy, "Pro-Life and Pro-Choice Mobilization: Infrastructure Deficits and New Technologies," in Mayer N. Zald and McCarthy, eds., Social Movements in an Organizational Society (New Brunswick, NJ: Transaction Books, 1987), pp. 49–66; Amy Fried, "Abortion Politics as Symbolic Politics: An Investigation Into Belief Systems," *Social Science Quarterly* 69 (March 1988): 137–154; and James L. Guth et al., "The Sources of Antiabortion Attitudes," *American Politics Quarterly* 21 (January 1993): 65–80.

59. *New York Times*, 13 January 1980, p. 22, 16 January 1980, pp. A1, B2, 17 January 1980, p. B3, 20 January 1980, p. IV-18, 23 January 1980, p. 12, 13 February 1980, p. B7, 15 February 1980, p. 30, 20 February 1980, p. 1, 21 February 1980, p. B11, 22 February 1980, p. 14, 24 February 1980, p. 29; *McRae v. Harris*, 491 F. Supp. 630 (E.D.N.Y.), 15 January 1980; *Harris v. McRae*, 444 U.S. 1069, 19 February 1980; *Congressional Quarterly Weekly Report*, 19 April 1980, pp. 1037–1041.

Also see Mary Meehan, *Commonweal*, 18 January 1980, pp. 13–16; Mary C. Segers, *Christianity & Crisis*, 18 February 1980, pp. 21–27; and especially Eve W. Paul and Paula Schaap, "Abortion and the Law in 1980," *New York Law School Law Review* 25 (1980): 497–525.

60. "CRS" [Cass R. Sunstein], Bench Memo, *Williams v. Zbaraz*, n.d. [c.March 1980], p. 8, Marshall Box 239; "JMC" [Janet M. Cooper], Bench Memo, *Harris v. McRae*, n.d. [c.early April 1980], 7pp., Marshall Box 240; *New York Times*, 20 April 1980, p. IV-8, 22 April 1980, p. B12; Brennan to Marshall, Blackmun and Stevens, 28 April 1980, Stewart, "Memorandum to the Conference" (with attached 54pp. typescript for *Harris*), 6 June 1980, Stevens to Stewart, Marshall to Stewart, and Powell to Stewart, 9 June 1980, Rehnquist to Stewart, and White to Stewart, 10 June 1980, Stewart Print #1, 11 June 1980, Stevens typescript, 13 June 1980, Brennan to Stevens, and Brennan typescript, 20 June 1980, Blackmun to Brennan, 23 June 1980, Blackmun typescript, Marshall typescript, White typescript, and Stevens Print #1, 23 June 1980, Burger to Stewart, 23 June 1980, Marshall to Brennan, 24 June 1980, Marshall Print #1, Blackmun Print #1, and White Print #1, 25 June 1980, Brennan Print #1, 26 June 1980, Marshall Box 258; Stewart *Zbaraz* typescript, 11 June 1980, Powell to Stewart,

Rehnquist to Stewart, and White to Stewart, 16 June 1980, Stewart *Zbaraz* Print #1, 17 June 1980, Marshall Box 253.

61. *Harris* v. *McRae,* 448 U.S. 297, 316, 317, 318, 325, 326, 330, 331n, 352 (reversing 491 F. Supp. 630); *Williams* v. *Zbaraz,* 448 U.S. 358, 369 (vacating 469 F. Supp. 1212), 30 June 1980. Also see *Zbaraz* v. *Quern,* 572 F.2d 582 and 596 F.2d 196 (7th Cir.); also note *Pre-term, Inc.* v. *Dukakis,* 591 F.2d 121 (1st Cir.).

62. *New York Times,* 30 June 1980, p. B15, 1 July 1980, pp. A1, A18, B8, B9, 4 July 1980, p. 10, 6 July 1980, pp. IV-4, IV-16, 7 July 1980, p. B2, 26 July 1980, p. 6; *Congressional Quarterly Weekly Report,* 5 July 1980, pp. 1860–63; *Time,* 14 July 1980, pp. 10–13; Michael J. Perry, "Why the Supreme Court Was Plainly Wrong in the Hyde Amendment Case: A Brief Comment on *Harris* v. *McRae,*" *Stanford Law Review* 32 (July 1980): 1113–1128, at 1120; Mary C. Segers, "Governing Abortion Policy," in Richard A. Gambitta et al., eds., *Governing Through Courts* (Beverly Hills, CA: Sage Publications, 1981), pp. 283–300, at 289; Dennis J. Horan, "The Supreme Court on Abortion Funding: The Second Time Around," *St. Louis University Law Journal* 25 (1981): 411–427, at 426.

On *Harris,* also see Leslie F. Goldstein, "A Critique of the Abortion Funding Decisions: On Private Rights in the Public Sector," *Hastings Constitutional Law Quarterly* 8 (Fall 1980): 313–342; John T. Noonan, Jr., and David Mechanic, in *Hastings Center Report* 10 (December 1980): 14–16 and 17–19; Robert W. Bennett, "Abortions and Judicial Review," *Northwestern University Law Review* 75 (February 1981): 978–1017; Tinsley E. Yarbrough, "The Abortion-Funding Issue: A Study in Mixed Constitutional Cues," *North Carolina Law Review* 59 (March 1981): 611–627; David T. Hardy, "*Harris* v. *McRae*: Clash of a Nonenumerated Right with Legislative Control of the Purse," *Case Western Reserve Law Review* 31 (Spring 1981): 465–508; Susan F. Appleton, "Beyond the Limits of Reproductive Choice: The Contributions of the Abortion-Funding Cases to Fundamental Rights Analysis and to the Welfare Rights Thesis," *Columbia Law Review* 81 (May 1981): 721–758; Paul M. Sommers and Laura S. Thomas, "Restricting Federal Funds for Abortion: Another Look," *Social Science Quarterly* 64 (June 1983): 340–346; and Kenneth J. Meier and Deborah R. McFarlane, "The Politics of Funding Abortion," *American Politics Quarterly* 21 (January 1993): 81–101. Also note Jean G. Platt et al., "Special Project—Survey of Abortion Law," *Arizona State Law Journal* 1980: 67–216; and Epstein and Kobylka, *The Supreme Court and Legal Change,* pp. 221–231.

63. *New York Times,* 18 August 1980, p. A15, 30 September 1980, p. 16, 1 October 1980, p. 16, 2 October 1980, pp. 18, 19, 6 November 1980, p. B9, 7 November 1980, pp. 14, 16, 9 November 1980, p. IV-8, 10 November 1980, p. 21, 13 December 1980, p. 1, 14 December 1980, pp. 1, 31; Patricia Donovan, "The Defeat of the Toledo Abortion Ordinance: An Anatomy of a Crucial Victory," *Family Planning/Population Reporter* 9 (August 1980): 64–67; George G. Higgins, "The Pro-life Movement and the New Right," *America,* 13 September 1980, pp. 107–110; Donald Granberg and James Burlison, "The Abortion Issue in the 1980 Elections," *Family Planning Perspectives* 15 (September-October 1983): 231–238; and Byrnes, *Catholic Bishops in American Politics,* pp. 82–91.

Also see *Life,* November 1981, pp. 45–54; *Commonweal,* 12 February 1982, pp. 75–84, at 78; Stanley K. Henshaw and Greg Martire, "Abortion and the Public Opinion Polls: Morality and Legality," *Family Planning Perspectives* 14 (March-April 1982): 53–60; Jerome S. Legge, Jr., "The Determinants of Attitudes Toward Abortion in the American Electorate," *Western Political Quarterly* 36 (September 1983): 479–490; and Granberg, "An Anomaly in Political Perception," *Public Opinion Quarterly* 49 (Winter 1985): 504–516.

64. *H. L.* v. *Matheson,* 445 U.S. 903, 25 February 1980; *New York Times,* 26 February 1980, p. D19, 12 October 1980, pp. 35, IV-8; "MM" [Martha Minow], Bench Memo, *H. L.* v. *Matheson,* n.d. [c.late October 1980], 5pp., Marshall Box 261; Marshall Print #1, 7 November 1980, Stewart to Marshall, 10 November 1980, Powell to Marshall, 12 November 1980, Blackmun to Marshall, 12 November 1980, Marshall Box 279. Blackmun's "out there" reference echoed a phrase—"another world 'out there'"—he had used three years earlier in *Beal* v. *Doe,* 432 U.S. at 463. Also note Nanette Dembitz, "The Supreme Court and a Minor's Abortion Decision," *Columbia Law Review* 80 (October 1980): 1251–1263.

65. *Moe* v. *Secretary of Administration and Finance*, 382 Mass. 629, 651, 18 February 1981; *New York Times*, 19 February 1981, p. A20; *Committee to Defend Reproductive Rights* v. *Myers*, 29 Cal.3d 252, 282, 284–85, 20 March 1981. Also generally see Gerald B. Cope, Jr., "Toward a Right of Privacy as a Matter of State Constitutional Law," *Florida State University Law Review* 5 (Fall 1977): 631–745; and Mark Silverstein, "Privacy Rights in State Constitutions: Models for Illinois?" *University of Illinois Law Review* 1989: 215–296.

On Massachusetts, also note William L. Pardee, "The Massachusetts Right of Privacy Statute," *Suffolk University Law Review* 9 (Summer 1975): 1254–85; on California, also note Lewis A. Kornhauser, "Privacy: The New Constitutional Language and the Old Right," *California Law Review* 64 (March 1976): 347–369; Peter H. Behr, "Privacy: To Be or Not to Be, That Is the Question," *Pacific Law Journal* 10 (July 1979): 663–671; *City of Santa Barbara* v. *Adamson*, 610 P.2d 436, 440n (Cal. Sup. Ct.), 15 May 1980 ("the federal right of privacy in general appears to be narrower than what the voters approved in 1972 when they added 'privacy' to the California Constitution"); and Robert S. Gerstein, "California's Constitutional Right to Privacy," *Hastings Constitutional Law Quarterly* 9 (Winter 1982): 385–427.

Regarding other states, also note Joan Uda, "*Roe* v. *Wade* and the Montana Dilemma," *Montana Law Review* 35 (Winter 1974): 103–118, and Larry M. Elison and Dennis NettikSimmons, "Right of Privacy," *Montana Law Review* 48 (Winter 1987): 1–52; James C. Harrington, "Privacy and the Texas Constitution," *Vermont Law Review* 13 (Spring 1988): 155–177; and John Devlin, "Privacy and Abortion Rights Under the Louisiana State Constitution," *Louisiana Law Review* 51 (March 1991): 685–732.

No doubt the most unusual state constitutional privacy holding of the 1970s and 1980s was the Alaska Supreme Court's unanimous 1975 ruling that the privacy language added to that state's Constitution in 1972 ("The right of the people to privacy is recognized and shall not be infringed") effectively decriminalized the use and possession of small amounts of marijuana within the home. *Ravin* v. *State*, 537 P.2d 494, 27 May 1975. Also note *New York Times*, 28 May 1975, p. 8, as well as *State* v. *Kanter*, 493 P.2d 306, 313–14 (Hawaii Sup. Ct., Levinson, J., dissenting), 20 January 1972 (cert. denied, *Kantner* v. *Hawaii*, 409 U.S. 948, 24 October 1972). Law journal notes on *Ravin* include Lynda Mae Wong, *UCLA–Alaska Law Review* 5 (Fall 1975): 178–229; Janet K. Breece, *North Carolina Central Law Journal* 7 (Fall 1975): 163–174; Gerald Solk, *Texas Southern University Law Review* 4 (1976): 50–65; David E. Rohrer, *Wisconsin Law Review* 1976: 305–330; Bruce Brashear, *Tulsa Law Journal* 11 (1976): 563–586; and Bruce M. Botelho, *Willamette Law Journal* 12 (Spring 1976): 394–400. Also note Mark Soler, *Connecticut Law Review* 6 (Summer 1974): 601–723; and Michael A. Lamson, *Arizona Law Review* 18 (1976): 207–231.

66. *H. L.* v. *Matheson*, 450 U.S. 398, 420 (affirming 604 P.2d 907), 23 March 1981; *New York Times*, 24 March 1981, p. 1, 29 March 1981, p. IV-7. Also see especially *Gary-Northwest Indiana Women's Services, Inc.* v. *Orr*, 451 U.S. 934, 27 April 1981 (affirming 496 F. Supp. 894), with Justices Brennan, Marshall, and Blackmun indicating that they would note probable jurisdiction; *New York Times*, 28 April 1981, p. D23. Note also Elizabeth Buchanan, "The Constitution and the Anomaly of the Pregnant Teenager," *Arizona Law Review* 24 (1982): 553–610; and Janet Benshoof, "Reproductive Freedom," in Kenneth P. Norwick, ed., *Lobbying For Freedom in the 1980s* (New York: Wideview/Perigee), 1983, pp. 71–111, at 83 (*H. L.* "a very narrow" decision).

On *H. L.*, also see Blackmun to Marshall, and Brennan to Marshall, 13 November 1980, Marshall Print #2, 17 November 1980, Burger to Marshall, and White to Burger, 24 November 1980, Burger Print #1, 16 December 1980, Stevens Print #1, 17 December 1980, Powell to Burger and Marshall (and attachment), 8 January 1981, Stewart to Powell, 9 January 1981, Burger, "Memorandum to the Conference" (and Print #2), 10 January 1981, Burger to Powell, 15 January 1981, Powell to Burger, 16 January 1981, Stewart to Powell, Stewart to Burger, and Rehnquist to Burger, 22 January 1981, Marshall Dissent Print #1, 25 February 1981, Blackmun to Marshall, 26 February 1981, Brennan to Marshall, 27 February 1981, White to Burger, 4 March 1981, Marshall Box 279.

67. Stephen H. Galebach, "A Human Life Statute," *Human Life Review* 7 (Winter 1981): 3–31;

New York Times, 23 January 1981, p. 14, 15 February 1981, p. 38, 16 February 1981, p. B6, 7 March 1981, p. 11, 13 March 1981, p. A18, 21 March 1981, p. 22, 27 March 1981, p. 1, 28 March 1981, p. 9, 19 April 1981, p. IV-16, 22 April 1981, p. 25, 23 April 1981, p. B9, 24 April 1981, p. 16, 25 April 1981, p. 7, 26 April 1981, pp. IV-1, 9, and 24, 3 May 1981, p. 31, 4 May 1981, p. B12, 18 May 1981, p. 18, 21 May 1981, p. B12, 22 May 1981, p. 16, 24 May 1981, p. IV-19, 2 June 1981, p. B9, 11 June 1981, p. 18, 13 June 1981, p. 10, 14 June 1981, p. IV-8, 19 June 1981, p. A16, 20 June 1981, p. 10; *Congressional Quarterly Weekly Report*, 28 February 1981, pp. 383–384; Timothy Noah, "The Right-to-Life Split," *The New Republic*, 21 March 1981, pp. 7–9; *Time*, 6 April 1981, pp. 20–28; U.S. Congress, Senate, Committee on the Judiciary, *The Human Life Bill—Hearings Before the Subcommittee on Separation of Powers*, 97th Cong., 1st sess., 23–24 April, 20–21 May, and 1, 10, 12, and 18 June 1981, pp. 195–97, 310, 328, and 426. Also see Bernard N. Nathanson, *The Abortion Papers* (New York: Frederick Fell, 1983), pp. 7–11, 17–18; Edward Keynes, *The Court vs. Congress* (Durham, NC: Duke University Press, 1989), pp. 245–300, at 285–91; Susan R. Burgess, *Contest for Constitutional Authority* (Lawrence: University Press of Kansas, 1992), pp. 28–48; and especially Charlotte Low, "The Pro-Life Movement in Disarray," *American Spectator*, October 1987, pp. 23–26.

Also note Charles Hartshorne, *Christian Century*, 21 January 1981, pp. 42–45; Gloria Steinem, *Ms.*, February 1981, pp. 43–44; Lisa C. Wohl, *Ms.*, February 1981, pp. 48, 81–82; Deirdre English, *Mother Jones*, February-March 1981, pp. 16–26; John Hart Ely and Laurence H. Tribe, *New York Times*, 17 March 1981, p. A17 (as well as 12 April 1981, p. IV-22, and 20 April 1981, p. 18); and Stacey Oliker, *Socialist Review* 11 (March-April 1981): 71–95.

On Galebach's proposal, also see Rhonda Copelon, *Ms.*, February 1981, pp. 46, 72–74; Charles E. M. Kolb, "The Proposed Human Life Statute: Abortion as Murder?," *ABA Journal* 67 (September 1981): 1123–26; Francis J. Flaherty, "Abortion, the Constitution, and the Human Life Statute," *Commonweal*, 23 October 1981, pp. 586–593; Basile J. Uddo, "The Human Life Bill: Protecting the Unborn Through Congressional Enforcement of the Fourteenth Amendment," *Loyola Law Review* 27 (Fall 1981): 1079–97; Samuel Estreicher, "Congressional Power and Constitutional Rights: Reflections on Proposed 'Human Life' Legislation," *Virginia Law Review* 68 (February 1982): 333–458; Thomas I. Emerson, "The Power of Congress to Change Constitutional Decisions of the Supreme Court: The Human Life Bill," *Northwestern University Law Review* 77 (April 1982): 129–142; David Westfall, "Beyond Abortion: The Potential Reach of a Human Life Amendment," *American Journal of Law & Medicine* 8 (Summer 1982): 97–135; John G. Ferreira, "The Human Life Bill: Personhood Revisited, or Congress Takes Aim at *Roe* v. *Wade*," *Hofstra Law Review* 10 (Summer 1982): 1269–1290; Henry J. Hyde, "The Human Life Bill: Some Issues and Answers," and Harriet F. Pilpel, "Hyde and Go Seek: A Response to Representative Hyde," both in *New York Law School Law Review* 27 (1982): 1077–1100 and 1101–1123.

68. *New York Times*, 10 July 1981, p. 12, 12 July 1981, p. IV-2, 22 September 1981, p. B5, 31 October 1981, p. 11, 6 November 1981, p. 1, 17 November 1981, p. 20, 18 November 1981, pp. A1, B4, 19 November 1981, p. 19, 26 November 1981, p. B8, 13 December 1981, p. 39, 17 December 1981, p. B15, 22 January 1982, pp. A12, A20, 23 January 1982, p. 1, 25 January 1982, p. 31, 23 February 1982, p. 18, 3 March 1982, p. 22, 10 March 1982, p. 26, 11 March 1982, p. 1, 7 August 1982, p. 44, 17 August 1982, p. 18, 18 August 1982, p. 9, 19 August 1982, p. 23, 20 August 1982, pp. A26, D16, 21 August 1982, p. 9, 25 August 1982, p. 22, 7 September 1982, pp. A18, A22, 9 September 1982, p. 18, 10 September 1982, p. D17, 11 September 1982, p. 7, 14 September 1982, p. 19, 16 September 1982, p. 1, 17 September 1982, p. 19, 20 September 1982, p. B10, 25 September 1982, p. 9, 1 November 1982, p. D13; *Congressional Quarterly Weekly Report*, 11 July 1981, p. 1253; U.S. Congress, Senate, Committee on the Judiciary, *Constitutional Amendments Relating to Abortion—Hearings Before the Subcommittee on the Constitution*, 97th Cong., 1st sess., 5, 14, and 19 October, 4, 5, 12, and 16 November, and 7 and 16 December 1981; Tim Miller, *National Journal*, 20 March 1982, pp. 511–513; Mary C. Segers, "Can Congress Settle the Abortion Issue?," *Hastings Center Report* 12 (June 1982): 20–28; Roger H. Davidson, "Procedures and Politics in Congress," in Gilbert Y. Steiner, ed., *The Abortion Dispute and the American System* (Washington, DC: Brookings Institution, 1983), pp. 30–46. Also note Nathanson, *The Abortion Papers*, pp. 37–42.

Also see Donald Granberg, "The Abortion Controversy: An Overview," *The Humanist*, July-August 1981, pp. 28–38, 66; Carol Joffe, "The Abortion Struggle in American Politics," *Dissent* 28 (Summer 1981): 268–271; William J. Voegeli, Jr., "A Critique of the Pro-Choice Argument," *Review of Politics* 43 (October 1981): 560–571; Peter Steinfels, *Commonweal*, 20 November 1981, pp. 660–664, at 664 ("The goal ... should be the prohibition of abortion after eight weeks of development"); Richard Polenberg, "The Second Victory of Anthony Comstock," *Society* 19 (May-June 1982): 32–38; and Granberg and Donald Denney, "The Coathanger and the Rose," *Society* 19 (May-June 1982): 39–46.

69. *Right to Choose* v. *Byrne*, 91 N.J. 287, 306 (also acknowledging "the fundamental right of a woman to control her body and destiny"), 18 August 1982; *New York Times*, 19 August 1982, p. B4.

70. Joe Caldwell, "Memorandum to the Conference—Pending Abortion Cases," 29 April 1982, Marshall Box 304; *Simopoulos* v. *Virginia* (probable jurisdiction noted), *City of Akron* v. *Akron Center for Reproductive Health* and *Planned Parenthood Association of Kansas City* v. *Ashcroft* (cert. granted), 456 U.S. 988, 24 May 1982; *New York Times*, 25 May 1982, p. B7, 29 July 1982, p. 17, 30 July 1982, p. D16, 4 August 1982, p. 22, 31 August 1982, pp. 1, 12, 1 December 1982, p. B4, 5 December 1982, p. 49, 19 December 1982, p. IV-18; Blackmun to O'Connor, and Brennan to O'Connor, 13 August 1982, O'Connor to Blackmun, O'Connor to Alexander L. Stevas, and Blackmun to O'Connor, 3 September 1982, Marshall Box 304; "LT" [Lawrence Tu], "Bench Memo," *Simopoulos* v. *Virginia*, 29 November 1982, 7pp., "PM" [Paul Mogin], "Bench Memo," *City of Akron* v. *Akron Center*, n.d. [c.29 November 1982], 8pp., "Bench Memo," *Planned Parenthood Association of Kansas City* v. *Ashcroft*, n.d. [c.29 November 1982], 8pp., Marshall Box 305; Transcript of Oral Argument, *City of Akron* v. *Akron Center*, 30 November 1982, pp. 12 and 14.

On Justice Stewart's retirement and Justice O'Connor's nomination and confirmation, see *New York Times*, 19 June 1981, pp. 1, 14, 20 June 1981, p. 9, 8 July 1981, p. 1, 9 July 1981, p. 17, 10 July 1981, p. 11, 12 July 1981, p. IV-20, 16 July 1981, p. 14, 19 July 1981, p. IV-4, 10 September 1981, p. B14, 22 September 1981, p. 1, 26 September 1981, p. 8; Epstein and Kobylka, *The Supreme Court and Legal Change*, pp. 235–236. Also see Richard A. Cordray and James T. Vradlis, "The Emerging Jurisprudence of Justice O'Connor," *University of Chicago Law Review* 52 (Spring 1985): 389–459; Beverly B. Cook, "Justice Sandra Day O'Connor," in Charles M. Lamb and Stephen C. Halpern, eds., *The Burger Court* (Urbana: University of Illinois Press, 1991), pp. 238–275; and Howard Kohn, *Los Angeles Times Magazine*, 18 April 1993, pp. 14ff. Just a few months prior to O'Connor's nomination, one prominent liberal had emphasized that progressives' concern over possible Reagan Supreme Court nominees was "a misplaced worry." Michael Walzer, "The Courts, the Elections, and the People," *Dissent* 28 (Spring 1981): 153–155.

71. "Abortion Cases," n.d. [c.16 December 1982], 4pp., Burger, "Memorandum to the Conference," 10 and 13 December 1982, Brennan, "Memorandum to the Conference—Abortion Cases," 16 December 1982, Marshall Vote Tally Sheet, 16 December 1982, Powell, "Memorandum to the Conference," 17 December 1982, Marshall Box 304; Powell Print #1, *Simopoulos* v. *Virginia*, 3 March 1983, Stevens to Powell, O'Connor to Powell,, and Rehnquist to Powell, 7 March 1983, Blackmun to Powell, 8 March 1983, Burger to Powell, 11 March 1983, Powell, "Memorandum to the Conference" (and Print #3), 28 April 1983, O'Connor Concurrence, Print #1, 5 May 1983, Rehnquist to O'Connor, 5 May 1983, White to O'Connor, 6 May 1983, Burger to Powell, 16 May 1983, Powell Print #4, 23 May 1983, Marshall to Powell, Blackmun to Powell, and Brennan to Powell, 23 May 1983, Marshall Box 312; Powell Print #1, *Akron*, 3 March 1983, Stevens to Powell, 4 March 1983, O'Connor to Powell, and Rehnquist to Powell, 7 March 1983, Brennan to Powell, 8 March 1983, Powell to Brennan, 9 March 198[3], Brennan to Powell, 9 March 1983, Blackmun to Powell, 8 March 1983, Powell to Blackmun, 9 March 198[3], Blackmun to Powell, 10 March 1983, Marshall to Powell, 14 March 1983, O'Connor Dissent, Print #1, 5 May 1983, Rehnquist to O'Connor, 5 May 1983, White to O'Connor, 6 May 1983, Burger to Powell, 9 June 1983, Marshall Boxes 314 and 315; Powell Print #1, *Ashcroft*, 4 March 1983, Blackmun to Powell, 4 March 1983, O'Connor to Powell, Rehnquist to Powell, and Stevens to Powell,

7 March 1983, O'Connor Print #1, 5 May 1983, Rehnquist to O'Connor, 5 May 1983, White to O'Connor, 6 May 1983, Blackmun Circulation #1, 17 May 1983, Brennan to Blackmun, 23 May 1983, Marshall to Blackmun, 25 May 1983, Stevens to Blackmun, 1 June 1983, Burger to Powell, 1 June 1983, Marshall Box 318. Warren Burger apparently cast no votes whatsoever at the December 16 conference.

72. *City of Akron* v. *Akron Center for Reproductive Health*, 462 U.S. 416, 419–20, 421n, 427, 429n, 433–34, 453, 454, 457, 458, 459, *Planned Parenthood Association of Kansas City* v. *Ashcroft*, 462 U.S. 476, 485–86, 490, *Simopoulos* v. *Virginia*, 462 U.S. 506, 15 June 1983. Also see *Bellotti* v. *Baird*, 428 U.S. 132, 145, *Maher* v. *Roe*, 432 U.S. 464, 474; and Epstein and Kobylka, *The Supreme Court and Legal Change*, pp. 238–47. On *Akron*, also see 651 F.2d 1198 (6th Cir.); on *Ashcroft*, also see 483 F. Supp. 679 (E.D. Mo.), 655 F.2d 848 (8th Cir.), and 664 F.2d 687 (8th Cir.); *Simopoulos* affirmed 277 S.E.2d 194 (Va. Sup. Ct.). On Dr. Simopoulos, also see *New York Times*, 28 July 1984, p. 9; on the rarity of third-trimester abortions—only some two hundred a year—see Nancy K. Rhoden et al., "Late Abortion and Technological Advances in Fetal Viability," *Family Planning Perspectives* 17 (July-August 1985): 160–164.

73. *New York Times*, 16 June 1983, pp. A1, B10, B11, 17 June 1983, pp. A16, A26, 19 June 1983, p. IV-7, 14 July 1983, p. A20; *Time*, 27 June 1983, pp. 14–15; *Newsweek*, 27 June 1983, pp. 62–63; Laura Fox, "The 1983 Abortion Decisions," *University of Richmond Law Review* 18 (Fall 1983): 137–159, at 157; Nancy Ford, "The Evolution of a Constitutional Right to an Abortion," *Journal of Legal Medicine* 4 (September 1983): 271–322, at 272. Also see John A. Robertson, "Procreative Liberty and the Control of Conception, Pregnancy, and Childbirth," *Virginia Law Review* 69 (April 1983): 405–464; Curt S. Rush, "Genetic Screening, Eugenic Abortion, and *Roe* v. *Wade*: How Viable is *Roe*'s Viability Standard?," *Brooklyn Law Review* 50 (Fall 1983): 113–142; and Leonard H. Glantz, "Limiting State Regulation of Reproductive Decisions," *American Journal of Public Health* 74 (February 1984): 168–169.

74. *New York Times*, 14 January 1983, p. A27, 15 January 1983, pp. 4, 17, 22 January 1983, p. 33, 23 January 1983, pp. 18, IV-20, 20 April 1983, p. 12, 12 June 1983, p. 27, 28 June 1983, p. A14, 29 June 1983, pp. A1, A16, 1 July 1983, p. A22; U.S. Congress, Senate, Committee on the Judiciary, *Legal Ramifications of the Human Life Amendment—Hearings Before the Subcommittee on the Constitution*, 98th Cong., 1st sess., 28 February and 7 March 1983; Donald Granberg, "The U.S. Senate Votes to Uphold *Roe* Versus *Wade*," *Population Research and Policy Review* 4 (June 1985): 115–131. Also see William Lasser, *The Limits of Judicial Power* (Chapel Hill: University of North Carolina Press, 1988), pp. 221–222; Marshall H. Medoff, "Constituencies, Ideology, and the Demand for Abortion Legislation," *Public Choice* 60 (February 1989): 185–191; and George A. Chressanthis, "Ideology, Constituent Interests, and Senatorial Voting: The Case of Abortion," *Social Science Quarterly* 72 (September 1991): 588–600.

75. *New York* v. *Uplinger*, 464 U.S. 812, 3 October 1983; *New York Times*, 4 October 1983, p. A24; "TF" [William "Terry" Fisher], "Bench Memorandum," *New York* v. *Uplinger*, 16 January 1984, 7pp., Marshall Box 329; *People* v. *Uplinger* and *People* v. *Butler*, 447 N.E.2d 62, 460 N.Y.S.2d 514 (N.Y. Ct. App.), 23 February 1983 (reversing 449 N.Y.S.2d 916); *People* v. *Onofre*, 415 N.E.2d 936, 434 N.Y.S.2d 947, 949, 951, 954–55, 956–57, 960 (N.Y. Ct. App.), 18 December 1980 (affirming 424 N.Y.S.2d 566, 568, 24 January 1980), cert. denied., *New York* v. *Onofre*, 451 U.S. 987, 18 May 1981; *State* v. *Saunders*, 381 A.2d 333, 339, 340, 342 (N.J. Sup. Ct.), 13 December 1977; *Commonwealth* v. *Bonadio*, 415 A.2d 47, 50, 51, 52 (Pa. Sup. Ct.), 30 May 1980. On *Uplinger*, also see 444 N.Y.S.2d 373, 443 N.Y.S.2d 40, and 442 N.Y.S.2d 46; on *Saunders*, also see 361 A.2d 111 and 326 A.2d 84.

Also note *State* v. *Santos*, 413 A.2d 58, 68 (R.I. Sup. Ct.), 20 March 1980 ("we do not believe that the decision of an unmarried adult to engage in private consensual sexual activity is of such a fundamental nature or is so 'implicit in the concept of ordered liberty' to warrant its inclusion in the guarantee of personal privacy"); and *Commonwealth* v. *Stowell*, 449 N.E.2d 357, 360 (Mass. Sup. Jud. Ct.), 13 May 1983 ("Whatever the precise definition of the right of privacy and the scope of its protection of private sexual conduct, there is no fundamental personal privacy right implicit in the concept of ordered liberty barring the prosecution of consenting adults committing adultery in private"); see as well Anne W. Hulecki, *Suffolk University Law Review* 18 (1984): 83–90.

Law journal notes on the New York Court of Appeals decision in *Onofre* include Bennett Wolff, "Expanding the Right of Sexual Privacy," *Loyola Law Review* 27 (Fall 1981): 1279–1300; Katheryn D. Katz, "Sexual Morality and the Constitution: *People* v. *Onofre*," *Albany Law Review* 46 (Winter 1982): 311–362, at 312n ("*Onofre* is the first decision in which the right of the individual to engage in homosexual sexual acts was explicitly protected"); and Douglas E. Schwartz, *Western New England Law Review* 5 (Summer 1982): 75–102. Also note David A. J. Richards, "Homosexuality and the Constitutional Right to Privacy," *New York University Review of Law and Social Change* 8 (1979): 311–316, at 314 ("There is no principled way to defend the earlier right to privacy cases and not extend the right to homosexuality, other than the circular and question-begging assumption that homosexuality, as such, is intrinsically immoral and unnatural"); and *ABA Journal* 66 (July 1980): 836.

Notes on *Saunders* include Lawrence M. Ross, *Buffalo Law Review* 27 (Spring 1978): 395–409; Roger B. Coven, *Suffolk University Law Review* 12 (Fall 1978): 1312–1328; and Kathryn J. Humphrey, *Wayne Law Review* 25 (July 1979): 1067–1084; on *Bonadio*, see Debra Barnhart, *University of Pittsburgh Law Review* 43 (Fall 1981): 253–284.

76. *Gaylord* v. *Tacoma School District*, 434 U.S. 879, 3 October 1977 (denying certiorari to 559 P.2d 1340 [Wash. Sup. Ct.]); *Hollenbaugh* v. *Carnegie Free Library*, 439 U.S. 1052, 1055, 1058, 11 December 1978 (denying certiorari to 578 F.2d 1374 [3d Cir.], 6 June 1978, which had summarily affirmed 436 F. Supp. 1328 [W.D. Pa.], 15 September 1977); *Poe* v. *North Carolina*, 445 U.S. 947, 31 March 1980 (dismissing the appeal of *State* v. *Poe*, 259 S.E.2d 304 [N.C. Sup. Ct.], 252 S.E.2d 843 [N.C. Ct. App.], for want of a substantial federal question); *Whisenhunt* v. *Spradlin*, 464 U.S. 965, 970–971, 7 November 1983 (denying certiorari to *Shawgo* v. *Spradlin*, 701 F.2d 470 [5th Cir.], 28 March 1983).

Also note *Ratchford* v. *Gay Lib*, 434 U.S. 1080, 21 February 1978 (Rehnquist, Blackmun, and Burger dissenting from denial of certiorari to 558 F.2d 848); on *Hollenbaugh*, also see 545 F.2d 382 (3d Cir.), 405 F. Supp. 629 (W.D. Pa.), and Susan M. Slaff, *Western New England Law Review* 4 (Summer 1981): 171–197.

77. *Berg* v. *Claytor*, 436 F. Supp. 76, 79 (D.D.C.), 27 May 1977; Thomas F. Coleman, "Procedure and Strategy in Gay Rights Litigation," *New York University Review of Law and Social Change* 8 (1979): 317–323, at 319 and 323; *Hicks* v. *Miranda*, 422 U.S. 332; Dominick Veltri, "The Legal Arena: Progress for Gay Civil Rights," *Journal of Homosexuality* 5 (Fall-Winter 1979–80): 25–34, at 30; Thomas C. Grey, "Eros, Civilization and the Burger Court," *Law and Contemporary Problems* 43 (Summer 1980): 83–100, at 87 and 98. Also see *Washington Post*, 11 December 1979, p. A3; and Bruce C. Hafen, "The Constitutional Status of Marriage, Kinship, and Sexual Privacy," *Michigan Law Review* 81 (January 1983): 463–574, at 538 ("a right of sexual freedom cannot reasonably be inferred from the procreative rights recognized by the Court"). But see *Miller* v. *Rumsfeld*, 647 F.2d 80, 84–85 (9th Cir.), 15 May 1981 (Norris, J., dissenting). On Vernon Berg, also see Mary Ann Humphrey, *My Country, My Right to Serve* (New York: HarperCollins, 1990), pp. 72–79.

78. *Baker* v. *Wade*, 553 F. Supp. 1121, 1133, 1134n, 1138, 1140, 1141, 1144 (N.D. Tex.), 17 August 1982. Also see Michael Ennis, "What Do These Rugged Texas He-Men Have in Common?," *Texas Monthly*, June 1980, pp. 107–113, 209–226; and especially Thomas J. Coleman, Jr., "Disordered Liberty: Judicial Restraint on the Rights to Privacy and Equality in *Bowers* v. *Hardwick* and *Baker* v. *Wade*," *Thurgood Marshall Law Review* 12 (Fall 1986): 81–108, at 84–88.

79. Brennan Print #1, 1 March 1984, Blackmun to Brennan, Rehnquist to Brennan, and O'Connor to Brennan, 1 March 1984, Brennan Print #2, 6 March 1984, Powell to Brennan, 6 March 1984, Marshall to Brennan, 7 March 1984, Rehnquist Circulation, 5pp., 8 March 1984 (withdrawn 15 March), White Print #1, 9 March 1984, O'Connor to White, 13 March 1984, Burger to White, and Rehnquist to White, 15 March 1984, White Print #2, 17 March 1984, Brennan Prints #s 3 and 4, 14 and 19 March 1984, Stevens to Brennan, and Stevens circulation, 21 May 1984; *New York* v. *Uplinger*, 467 U.S. 246, 247n, 249, 30 May 1984. Also

see Edward T. Mulligan, "*Griswold* Revisited in Light of *Uplinger*," *New York University Review of Law & Social Change* 13 (1984–85): 51–82, at 56–57, who inferred that "one or more of the majority who voted to dismiss *Uplinger* would likely have sided with their conservative brethren had they not been able to avoid the issue."

Also note *Roberts* v. *U.S. Jaycees*, 468 U.S. 609, 617, 618, 619, 3 July 1984 ("certain intimate human relationships" implicate "a fundamental element of personal liberty" and "freedom of intimate association" such that the Court "must afford the formation and preservation of certain kinds of highly personal relationships a substantial measure of sanctuary from unjustified interference by the State." The "ability independently to define one's identity that is central to any concept of liberty" includes "the creation and sustenance of a family—marriage . . . childbirth . . . the raising and education of children . . . and cohabitation with one's relatives").

80. *Dronenburg* v. *Zech*, 741 F.2d 1388, 1391, 1392, 1395, 1396, 1397 (D.C. Cir.), 17 August 1984; *New York Times*, 18 August 1984, pp. 1, 10, 23 August 1984, p. B8. On James L. Dronenburg, also see Humphrey, *My Country, My Right to Serve*, pp. 89–92.

Law journal notes on the Bork opinion include Katherine M. Allen, *North Carolina Law Review* 63 (April 1985): 749–766; Jeffrey M. Winn, *Pace Law Review* 5 (Summer 1985): 847–878; Richard C. McQuown, *Capital University Law Review* 14 (1985): 313–326; and Kelly Carbetta-Scandy, *University of Cincinnati Law Review* 54 (1986): 1055–1067. Also see Steven O. Ludd, "The Aftermath of *Doe* v. *Commonwealth's Attorney*," *University of Dayton Law Review* 10 (Spring 1985): 705–743, at 739–742; and Richard B. Saphire, "Gay Rights and the Constitution," *University of Dayton Law Review* 10 (Spring 1985): 767–813. But note Arthur E. Brooks, *William and Mary Law Review* 26 (Summer 1985): 645–682, at 646 ("all sodomy should be subject to criminalization"), and Charles Rice, *Legalizing Homosexual Conduct: The Role of the Supreme Court in the Gay Rights Movement* (Cumberland, VA: Center for Judicial Studies, 1984), p. 21 ("The AIDS epidemic shows the wisdom of the common law position which was derived from the religious condemnation of homosexuality").

81. *Dronenburg* v. *Zech*, 749 F.2d 1579, 1580, 1582, 1583 (D.C. Cir.), 15 November 1984. Also see Andrew B. Jones, "*Dronenburg* v. *Zech*: Judicial Restraint or Judicial Prejudice?," *Yale Law & Policy Review* 3 (Fall 1984): 245–262; and Howard L. Pearlman, "*Dronenburg* v. *Zech*: Strict Construction or Abdication of Judicial Responsibility?," *Hastings Constitutional Law Quarterly* 12 (Summer 1985): 669–697.

82. *New York Times*, 20 January 1984, p. A23, 24 January 1984, p. A8, 18 February 1984, p. 10, 25 June 1984, p. D13, 8 July 1984, p. 14, 8 September 1984, p. 8, 12 September 1984, p. B9, 13 September 1984, p. B16, 14 September 1984, pp. A1, A22, 15 September 1984, p. 29, 17 September 1984, p. B12, 20 September 1984, p. A31, 23 September 1984, p. 34, 24 September 1984, p. B3, 28 September 1984, p. A22, 6 October 1984, pp. 10, 26, 10 October 1984, p. A12, 14 October 1984, pp. 1, 30 and IV-3, 16 October 1984, pp. A1, B2, 17 October 1984, p. A24, 5 November 1984, p. B15, 20 November 1984, p. A14, 22 November 1984, p. A16, 25 November 1984, p. IV-2, 5 December 1984, p. A23, 6 December 1984, p. B20, 21 December 1984, p. A35, 26 December 1984, p. A20, 27 December 1984, p. A14, 29 December 1984, p. 5, 31 December 1984, p. A8, 1 January 1985, p. 6, 2 January 1985, p. A15, 3 January 1985, p. A17, 4 January 1985, p. A1, 7 January 1985, p. A12, 11 January 1985, p. A1, 17 January 1985, p. B5, 18 January 1985, p. A12, 19 January 1985, p. 22, 20 January 1985, p. 24, 21 January 1985, p. A10, 22 January 1985, p. A10. Also see Sidney and Daniel Callahan, *Commonweal*, 5 October 1984, pp. 520–523; *Newsweek*, 3 December 1984, p. 31, and 14 January 1985, pp. 20–29; *Public Opinion*, April-May 1985, pp. 25–28; Byrnes, *Catholic Bishops in American Politics*, pp. 114–126; George Gallup, Jr., and Jim Castelli, *The People's Religion* (New York: Macmillan, 1989), pp. 167–179; and, on Pensacola, Dallas A. Blanchard and Terry J. Prewitt, *Religious Violence and Abortion* (Gainesville: University Press of Florida, 1993).

83. *New York Times*, 23 January 1985, pp. A1, A15 and A22, 25 January 1985, p. B8, 6 February 1985, p. A14, 16 February 1985, p. 46, 25 February 1985, p. A10, 5 March 1985, p. A1, 11 March 1985, p. A18, 13 March 1985, p. A18, 24 March 1985, p. 29, 16 April 1985, p. D27, 17 April 1985, p. A16, 21 April 1985, p. 32, 24 April 1985, p. A16, 25 April 1985, p. A23, 22 May 1985, p. A18, 26 May 1985, p. IV-5, 18 June 1985, p. A14, 3 July 1985, p. A19, 13 July 1985,

p. 42; U.S. Congress, House of Representatives, Committee on the Judiciary, *Abortion Clinic Violence—Oversight Hearings Before the Subcommittee on Civil and Constitutional Rights*, 99th Cong., 1st sess., 6 and 12 March and 3 April 1985, pp. 52–53; Joseph M. Scheidler, *Closed: 99 Ways to Stop Abortion* (San Francisco: Ignatius Press, 1985); *Wall Street Journal*, 16 April 1985, pp. 1, 21; Blanchard and Prewitt, *Religious Violence and Abortion*, pp. 150–151, 165–172.

Also see Patricia Donovan, *Family Planning Perspectives* 17 (January-February 1985): 5–9; *New Republic*, 25 February 1985; *Newsweek*, 25 March 1985, p. 16; U.S. Congress, Senate, Committee on the Judiciary, *Abortion Funding Restriction Act—Hearings Before the Subcommittee on the Constitution*, 99th Cong., 1st sess., 2 April and 22 July 1985; Amanda Spake, Ms., July 1985, pp. 88–92, 112–14; and Marjorie R. Hershey, "Direct Action and the Abortion Issue," in Allan J. Cigler and Burdett A. Loomis, eds., *Interest Group Politics*, 2nd ed. (Washington: CQ Press, 1986), pp. 27–45.

Also note Randall A. Lake, "The Metaethical Framework of Anti-Abortion Rhetoric," *Signs* 11 (Spring 1986): 478–499; Rosalind P. Petchesky, "Fetal Images: The Power of Visual Culture in the Politics of Reproduction," *Feminist Studies* 13 (Summer 1987): 263–292; James W. Prescott, "The Abortion of *The Silent Scream*," *The Humanist*, September-October 1986, pp. 10–17, 28; Michael P. Thompson, "The Facts of Life: Rhetorical Dimensions of the Pro-Life Movement in America" (unpublished Ph.D. dissertation, Rensselaer Polytechnic Institute, 1985); and especially Celeste M. Condit, *Decoding Abortion Rhetoric* (Urbana: University of Illinois Press, 1990), p. 87 ("if *The Silent Scream* had really been silent, it would have had no rhetorical impact").

On clinic violence, also see David C. Nice, "Abortion Clinic Bombings as Political Violence," *American Journal of Political Science* 32 (February 1988): 178–195; Michele Wilson and John Lynxwiler, "Abortion Clinic Violence as Terrorism," *Terrorism* 11 (1988): 263–273; and David A. Grimes et al., "An Epidemic of Antiabortion Violence in the United States," *American Journal of Obstetrics and Gynecology* 165 (November 1991): 1263–1268, reporting a total of 110 building attacks from 1977 to 1988, with an annual peak of 29 in 1984.

84. *Board of Education of Oklahoma City* v. *National Gay Task Force*, 470 U.S. 903, 26 March 1985 (affirming 729 F.2d 1270 [10th Cir.]); *Rowland* v. *Mad River Local School District*, 470 U.S. 1009, 1016, 25 February 1985 (denying certiorari to 730 F.2d 444 [6th Cir.]); Stevens per curiam circulation (dismissing the appeal and denying certiorari), 10 January 1985, *Thornburgh* v. *ACOG*, #84–495, Rehnquist to Stevens, 10 January 1985, Blackmun to Stevens, and Brennan to Stevens, 14 February 1985, Marshall to Stevens, 19 February 1985, Rehnquist dissent circulation, 10 April 1985, Burger to Rehnquist, and O'Connor to Rehnquist, 10 April 1985, Marshall Box 382; *Thornburgh* v. *ACOG*, 471 U.S. 1014, 15 April 1985; *New York Times*, 16 April 1985, p. A23; *Diamond* v. *Charles*, 471 U.S. 1115, 20 May 1985; *New York Times*, 21 May 1985, p. A25, 15 July 1985, p. A1, 16 July 1985, p. A8, 18 July 1985, pp. A18, A22, 25 July 1985, p. A23. Also see *City of North Muskegon* v. *Briggs*, 473 U.S. 909, 1 July 1985 (White, Burger, and Rehnquist dissenting from denial of certiorari to 746 F.2d 1475 [6th Cir.], 2 October 1984, a summary affirmance of 563 F. Supp. 585 [W.D. Mich.], 5 May 1983).

On Justice Powell's prostate surgery and subsequent hospitalization, see *New York Times*, 5 January 1985, p. 6, 16 March 1985, p. 28, 18 March 1985, p. A15, and 26 March 1985, p. A17. The Oklahoma City case, with Laurence H. Tribe representing the National Gay Task Force, was argued on 14 January, during Powell's absence.

85. *Dallas Morning News*, 13 March 1983, p. A40; *Baker* v. *Wade*, 743 F.2d 236 (5th Cir.), 21 September 1984; *Baker* v. *Wade*, 106 F.R.D. 526 (N.D. Tex.), 1 July 1985; *Doe* v. *Duling*, 603 F. Supp. 960, 966, 967, 968 (E.D. Va.), 27 February 1985. On *Baker* v. *Wade*, also see Thomas J. Coleman, Jr., *Thurgood Marshall Law Review* 12 (Fall 1986): 81–108, at 97–98.

86. *Hardwick* v. *Bowers*, 760 F.2d 1202, 21 May 1985; Louis Levenson et al., "Complaint," *Hardwick et al.* v. *Bowers et al.*, U.S.D.C. N.D. Ga., #C83–273, 14 February 1983; Art Harris, "The Unintended Battle of Michael Hardwick," *Washington Post*, 21 August 1986, pp. C1, C4; Richard Laermer, "Michael Hardwick: The Man Behind the Georgia Sodomy Case," *The Advocate*, 2 September 1986, pp. 38–41, 110; Hardwick in Bill Moyers's "In Search of the Constitution—For the People," PBS, 1987; Hardwick in Peter Irons, *The Courage of Their*

Convictions (New York: Free Press, 1988), pp. 379–403; Stephen J. Schnably, "Beyond *Griswold*: Foucauldian and Republican Approaches to Privacy," *Connecticut Law Review* 23 (Summer 1991): 861–954, at 865n; and Anne B. Goldstein, "History, Homosexuality, and Political Values: Searching for the Hidden Determinants of *Bowers* v. *Hardwick*," *Yale Law Journal* 97 (May 1988): 1073–1103. Also see Yao Apasu-Gbotsu et al., "Survey on the Constitutional Right to Privacy in the Context of Homosexual Activity," *University of Miami Law Review* 40 (January 1986): 521–657, at 523 ("the facts of *Hardwick* present the 'purest' right to privacy case the Supreme Court could hear"). On Frank M. Johnson, Jr., see Jack Bass, *Taming the Storm* (New York: Doubleday, 1993), esp. pp. 423–427.

87. Robert H. Hall, "Order," *Hardwick* v. *Bowers*, #C83–273, 15 April 1983; *Hardwick* v. *Bowers*, 760 F.2d 1202, 1211, 1212 (11th Cir.), 21 May 1985, 765 F.2d 1123, 13 June 1985 (rehearing en banc denied without opinion); *National Law Journal*, 17 June 1985, p. 10; Michael E. Hobbs, "Petition for Writ of Certiorari," *Bowers* v. *Hardwick*, U.S.S.C., O.T. 1985, #140, 25 July 1985; Wilde, "Brief of Respondents in Opposition," *Bowers* v. *Hardwick*, 18pp., 12 September 1985, pp. 9 and 11. Law journal notes on the appellate decision include Elisa L. Fuller, *University of Miami Law Review* 39 (September 1985): 973–995; *Journal of Family Law* 24 (1985–86): 348–352; Leslie Denny, *Oklahoma Law Review* 39 (Summer 1986): 233–256; and especially Robert Glazier, "*Bowers* v. *Hardwick*: The Extension of the Right to Privacy to Private Consensual Homosexual Conduct," *Nova Law Journal* 10 (Fall 1985): 175–215.

88. Michael E. Hobbs, "Brief of Petitioner in Reply," *Bowers* v. *Hardwick*, U.S.S.C., O.T. 1985, #140, 8 October 1985, p. 1; *Baker* v. *Wade*, 769 F.2d 289, 292 (5th Cir.), 26 August 1985; *Baker* v. *Wade*, 774 F.2d 1285, 1286–87, 23 October 1985. Also see generally Kenneth R. Wing, *American Journal of Public Health* 76 (February 1986): 201–204; and Karen A. Corti, "Beyond *Dronenburg*: Rethinking the Right to Privacy," *Vermont Law Review* 11 (Spring 1986): 299–342.

89. Marshall Docket Book, Marshall Box 543; White Circulation, 17 October 1985, Rehnquist to White, 17 October 1985, Brennan to White, 17 October 1985, Brennan, "Memorandum to the Conference," 23 October 1985, Burger, "Memorandum to the Conference," 24 October 1985, Marshall Box 393; *Bowers* v. *Hardwick*, 474 U.S. 943, 4 November 1985; *New York Times*, 5 November 1985, p. A25.

90. *New York Times*, 11 August 1985, p. 22, 18 August 1985, p. 35, 22 August 1985, p. A12, 26 August 1985, p. B6, 1 September 1985, p. 29, 4 September 1985, p. A20, 19 September 1985, p. A32, 3 October 1985, p. B7, 18 October 1985, p. B2, 20 October 1985, p. 48, 22 October 1985, p. A21, 6 November 1985, pp. A22, B4, 7 November 1985, p. B11; "DR" [Daniel Richman], "Bench Memorandum," *Thornburgh* v. *ACOG*, October 1985, 13pp., Marshall Box 375; Brennan to Burger, 12 November 1985 (*Thornburgh*), Marshall Box 382; Brennan to Burger, 20 November 1985 (*Diamond*), Marshall Box 387; Mark E. Rust, "The Abortion Cases," *ABA Journal*, February 1986, pp. 50–53; Patricia Donovan, "Letting the People Decide: How the Antiabortion Referenda Fared," *Family Planning Perspectives* 18 (May-June 1986): 127–128, 144.

Also see George Scialabba, "The Trouble with *Roe* v. *Wade*," *Village Voice*, 16 July 1985, pp. 25–26; Stephen L. Carter, *Wall Street Journal*, 21 August 1985; Jan Jarvis, "The Question of Abortion," *Dallas Morning News Magazine*, 6 October 1985, pp. 8–12; *ABA Journal*, January 1986, p. 42; Dawn E. Johnsen, "The Creation of Fetal Rights: Conflicts with Women's Constitutional Rights to Liberty, Privacy, and Equal Protection," *Yale Law Journal* 95 (January 1986): 599–625; and Daniel Callahan, "How Technology Is Reframing the Abortion Debate," *Hastings Center Report* 16 (February 1986): 33–42.

91. *New York Times*, 5 December 1985, p. A18, 9 December 1985, p. B9, 11 December 1985, p. B8, 12 December 1985, p. B10, 31 December 1985, p. 6, 1 January 1986, p. 6, 17 January 1986, p. A12, 23 January 1986, p. D25, 24 January 1986, p. D19, 25 January 1986, p. 7, 23 February 1986, p. IV-22, 10 March 1986, p. B4, 27 March 1986, p. A18; Warren M. Hern, "The Politics of Choice: Abortion as Insurrection," in W. Penn Handwerker, ed., *Births and Power* (Boulder, CO: Westview Press, 1990), pp. 127–145; Blanchard and Prewitt, *Religious Violence and Abortion*, p. 283.

92. *Doe* v. *Duling*, 782 F.2d 1202 (4th Cir.), 7 February 1986; Tribe et al., "Brief for Respondent," *Bowers* v. *Hardwick*, U.S.S.C., O.T. 1985, #140, 36pp., 31 January 1986, pp. 9, 11–12; "DR" [Daniel Richman], "Bench Memorandum," *Bowers* v. *Hardwick*, March 1986, p. 3, Marshall Box 376; Transcript of Oral Argument, *Bowers* v. *Hardwick*, 31 March 1986; *New York Times*, 1 April 1986, p. A24, 25 May 1993, pp. A1, A16. Also see *Newsweek*, 7 April 1986, p. 74; David Robinson, Jr., "Sodomy and the Supreme Court," *Commentary* 82 (October 1986): 57–61; Christopher J. Cherry, "The Hard Road to *Hardwick*: The Constitutional Challenge to Sodomy Statutes" (unpublished M.A. thesis, University of Virginia, 1989), pp. 17–24; Andrea Sachs, "Laurence Tribe," *Constitution* 3 (Spring-Summer 1991): 24–32; Lynne N. Henderson, "Legality and Empathy," *Michigan Law Review* 85 (June 1987): 1574–1653, at 1639–45 ("Hardwick never appeared in the briefs or arguments as a human being"); and Stephen J. Schnably, "Beyond *Griswold*: Foucauldian and Republican Approaches to Privacy," *Connecticut Law Review* 23 (Summer 1991): 861–954, 869n, who notes that "It is striking . . . that the Brief for Respondent filed in *Bowers* . . . never refers to Hardwick as gay, and refers only obliquely . . . to the fact that his sexual partner was another man. . . . The brief's reticence presumably reflects a tactical decision to do everything possible to present the case as one involving sexual privacy rather than gay rights."

93. Marshall Docket Book, Marshall Box 543; *Robinson* v. *California*, 370 U.S. 660; Brennan to Burger, 4 April 1986, Marshall Box 378; Powell, "Memorandum to the Conference," 8 April 1986, Stevens to Powell, 8 April 1986, Burger to White, 9 April 1986, White Print #1, 21 April 1986, Blackmun to White, 21 April 1986, Marshall to White, 22 April 1986, Powell to White, 22 April 1986, Rehnquist to White, 23 April 1986, White Prints #2 and 3, 28 April and 20 May 1986, Marshall Box 393. Also see Schwartz, *The Ascent of Pragmatism*, pp. 314–319; and additional notes.

94. *Diamond* v. *Charles*, 476 U.S. 54, 30 April 1986 (dismissing the appeal of *Charles* v. *Daley*, 749 F.2d 452 [7th Cir.], for want of jurisdiction); *New York Times*, 22 April 1986, p. A20, 1 May 1986, p. B8; *Thornburgh* v. *ACOG*, 476 U.S. 747, 759, 764, 772, 778, 782, 785, 790, 792, 814, 11 June 1986 (affirming 737 F.2d 283 [3d Cir.]); *New York Times*, 12 June 1986, pp. A1, A10, A11, 16 June 1986, p. B8, 17 June 1986, p. A26. Also see Epstein and Kobylka, *The Supreme Court and Legal Change*, pp. 252–60.

On *Diamond*, also see *Charles* v. *Carey*, 627 F.2d 772 (7th Cir.), 1980; *Charles* v. *Carey*, 579 F. Supp. 377 and 579 F. Supp. 464 (N.D. Ill.), 1983; Blackmun Print #1, 14 February 1986, Marshall to Blackmun, 14 February 1986, Brennan to Blackmun, and Stevens to Blackmun, 18 February 1986, Powell to Blackmun, and O'Connor to Blackmun, 25 February 1986, O'Connor Concurrence #1, 10 April 1986, White to Blackmun, 15 April 1986, Rehnquist to O'Connor, 16 April 1986, Burger to O'Connor, 24 April 1986, Marshall Box 387.

On *Thornburgh*, also see *New York Times*, 12 June 1982, p. 9, 10 December 1982, p. 16; 552 F. Supp. 791 (E.D. Pa.); Blackmun to Marshall, 7 February 1986, Blackmun to Brennan, Marshall and Powell, 10 February 1986, Brennan to Blackmun, 10 and 11 February 1986, Blackmun Print #1, 11 February 1986, Marshall to Blackmun, Powell to Blackmun, and Stevens to Blackmun, 12 February 1986, White to Blackmun, and O'Connor to Blackmun, 18 February 1986, White Print #1, 12 March 1986, Rehnquist to White, 12 March and 14 April 1986, O'Connor to Blackmun, 14 March 1986, Stevens Print #1, 30 April 1986, O'Connor Print #1, 6 May 1986, Rehnquist to O'Connor, 7 May 1986, Burger Print #1, 29 May 1986, Marshall Box 382; *Harvard Law Review* 100 (November 1986): 200–210; Leonard H. Glantz, "Abortion and the Supreme Court: Why Legislative Motive Matters," *American Journal of Public Health* 76 (December 1986): 1452–1455; Harold H. Koh, "Rebalancing the Medical Triad: Justice Blackmun's Contributions to Law and Medicine," *American Journal of Law & Medicine* 13 (Summer-Fall 1987): 315–334, at 328–329 (noting that Blackmun's more recent abortion opinions "no longer champion a physician's discretion for its own sake" and that Blackmun's "*Thornburgh* opinion reflects a considered determination to shift *Roe*'s emphasis toward the autonomy of the individual, and not the doctor"); and Rhonda Copelon, "Losing the Negative Right of Privacy," *New York University Review of Law and Social Change* 18 (1990–91): 15–50, at 42–43.

Law review notes on *Thornburgh* include Jason H. Brown, *Suffolk University Law Review* 21 (Fall 1987): 877–889; Mary E. Quinn, *Creighton Law Review* 20 (1987): 917–948; and Ann E. Fulks, *Journal of Family Law* 26 (1988): 771–792; see as well Dennis J. Horan et al., "Two Ships Passing in the Night: An Interpretivist Review of the White-Stevens Colloquy on *Roe* v. *Wade*," *St. Louis University Public Law Review* 6 (1987): 229–311. Also note John A. Robertson, "Embryos, Families, and Procreative Liberty: The Legal Structure of the New Reproduction," *Southern California Law Review* 59 (July 1986): 939–1041; Norma J. Wikler, "Society's Response to the New Reproductive Technologies," *Southern California Law Review* 59 (July 1986): 1043–1057; Gary B. Gertler, "Brain Birth: A Proposal for Defining When a Fetus Is Entitled to Human Life Status," *Southern California Law Review* 59 (July 1986): 1061–1078; and A. S. Cohan, "No Legal Impediment: Access to Abortion in the United States," *Journal of American Studies* 20 (August 1986): 189–205.

95. *New York Times*, 18 June 1986, pp. 1, 30, 31; O'Connor to White, 19 June 1986, Powell Prints #1 and #2, 19 and 23 June 1986, Burger Print #1, 22 June 1986, Blackmun Print #1, 23 June 1986, Stevens to Blackmun, 23 June 1986, Stevens Print #1, 24 June 1986, Marshall to Blackmun, Marshall to Stevens, Brennan to Blackmun, Burger to White, and Blackmun to Burger, 24 June 1986, Powell Print #3, 25 June 1986, White Print #4, 25 June 1986, Brennan to Stevens, 28 June 1986, Marshall Box 393.

96. *Bowers* v. *Hardwick*, 478 U.S. 186, 190–91, 194, 196, 197, 198, 199, 200, 203n, 208, 214, 216, 218, 219, 30 June 1986. White's internal quotations are from *Moore* v. *City of East Cleveland*, 431 U.S. 494, 503 (1977), and *Palko* v. *Connecticut*, 302 U.S. 319, 325 (1937); Blackmun's reference is to *Katz* v. *United States*, 389 U.S. 347 (1967). Also note *O'Connor* v. *Donaldson*, 422 U.S. 563, 575, 26 June 1975 ("Mere public intolerance or animosity cannot constitutionally justify the deprivation of a person's physical liberty").

97. *New York Times*, 1 July 1986, pp. A1, A19, 2 July 1986, p. A30, 10 July 1986, p. A23; *Washington Post*, 2 July 1986, pp. A1, A8, 3 July 1986, p. A23; Brest, *Los Angeles Times*, 13 July 1986, p. V-2; Gewirtz, *New York Times*, 8 July 1986, p. A21; Thomas J. Maroney, "*Bowers* v. *Hardwick*: A Case Study in Federalism, Legal Procedure and Constitutional Interpretation," *Syracuse Law Review* 38 (1987): 1223–1250, at 1244; Thomas B. Stoddard, "*Bowers* v. *Hardwick*: Precedent by Personal Predilection," *University of Chicago Law Review* 54 (Spring 1987): 648–656, at 649; *The New Republic*, 28 July 1986, p. 4; *Newsweek*, 14 July 1986, pp. 36–38; Daniel O. Conkle, "The Second Death of Substantive Due Process," *Indiana Law Journal* 62 (Spring 1987): 215–242, at 235; Charles Colson, *Christianity Today*, 19 September 1986, p. 72; Abby R. Rubenfeld, "Lessons Learned: A Reflection Upon *Bowers* v. *Hardwick*," *Nova Law Review* 11 (Fall 1986): 59–70, at 65.

Also see *Time*, 14 July 1986, pp. 23–24, 21 July 1986, pp. 12–22; *U.S. News & World Report*, 14 July 1986, p. 18; Gerald Gillerman, *Boston Bar Journal* 30 (September-October 1986): 4–10, at 4 ("whether or not you are a criminal depends not on what you do, but who you are"); also note *Legal Times*, 21 July 1986, pp. 5, 12; *America*, 9 August 1986, p. 41; Richard J. Neuhaus, *National Review*, 15 August 1986, p. 40; David R. Carlin, Jr., *Commonweal*, 12 September 1986, pp. 456–457; Robert J. Bresler, *USA Today* 115 (November 1986): 6–7; and Alida Brill, *Nobody's Business: Paradoxes of Privacy* (Reading, MA: Addison-Wesley, 1990), p. 125. On poll results, also see Tom W. Smith, "The Polls—The Sexual Revolution?," *Public Opinion Quarterly* 54 (Fall 1990): 415–435, at 424.

Law journal notes critical of the *Bowers* majority include Ali Khan, *San Diego Law Review* 23 (September-October 1986): 957–977; *Harvard Law Review* 100 (November 1986): 210–220; Mark F. Kohler, *Connecticut Law Review* 19 (Fall 1986): 129–142; Gary S. Caplan, *Journal of Criminal Law & Criminology* 77 (Fall 1986): 894–930; Jo Marie Escobar, *Western State University Law Review* 14 (Fall 1986): 309–323; Loren George, *Southern University Law Review* 12 (1986): 307–317; James J. Bromberek, *John Marshall Law Review* 20 (Winter 1986–87): 325–342; Jim Gibb, *Capital University Law Review* 16 (Winter 1986–87): 301–323; Shaun A. Roberts, *University of Dayton Law Review* 12 (Winter 1986–87): 429–440; Angelina M. Massari, *Washington University Journal of Urban and Contemporary Law* 31 (Winter 1987): 403–417; Rahel E. Kent, *Whittier Law Review* 9 (1987): 115–149; Bruce A. Wilson, *Creighton Law Review* 20 (1987): 833–866; Margaret J. Siderides, *University of Bridgeport Law Review* 8

(1987): 229–253; Shelley R. Wieck, *South Dakota Law Review* 32 (1987): 323–343; Randi Maurer, *Loyola of Los Angeles Law Review* 20 (April 1987): 1013–1054; Roger D. Strode, Jr., *Marquette Law Review* 70 (Spring 1987): 599–611; Donna L. Smith, *Tulsa Law Journal* 22 (Spring 1987): 373–397; John A. Gordon, *Boston College Law Review* 28 (July 1987): 691–721; Daniel J. Langin, *Iowa Law Review* 72 (July 1987): 1443–1460; Michael Hedeen, *Southern Illinois University Law Journal* 11 (Summer 1987): 1305–1325; Richard G. Duplantier, *Loyola Law Review* 33 (Summer 1987): 483–498; Orene Bryant, *Toledo Law Review* 18 (Summer 1987): 835–870; Shari A. Levitan, *Suffolk University Law Review* 21 (Fall 1987): 853–876; Paul L. Alpert, *New York Law School Journal of Human Rights* 5 (Fall 1987): 129–162; John R. Hamilton, *Kentucky Law Journal* 76 (Fall 1987): 301–324; Joseph R. Thornton, *North Carolina Law Review* 65 (October 1987): 1100–1123; Robin S. Foreman, *Wake Forest Law Review* 22 (1987): 629–647; Yvonne L. Tharpes, *Howard Law Journal* 30 (1987): 537–549, at 547 ("Erotophobia permeates the *Bowers* opinions and effectively ignores the reality that anal and oral sexual practices are nearly universal modes of sexual expression in America"); Serena L. Nowell, *Howard Law Journal* 30 (1987): 551–565; Michael R. Engelman, *Journal of Family Law* 26 (1987–88): 373–393; Nancy S. Cameron, *Gonzaga Law Review* 22 (1987–88): 577–603; Mark J. Kappelhoff, *American University Law Review* 37 (Winter 1988): 487–512; Joan B. Dressler, *North Carolina Central Law Journal* 17 (1988): 100–118; George W. M. Thomas, *Syracuse Law Review* 39 (1988): 875–896; Caroline W. Ferree, *Denver University Law Review* 64 (1988): 599–612; and Mitchell L. Pearl, *New York University Law Review* 63 (April 1988): 154–190. Note as well Christopher W. Weller, *Cumberland Law Review* 16 (1986): 555–592; Paul L. Alpern, *Harvard Journal of Law & Public Policy* 10 (Winter 1987): 213–227; Julia K. Sullens, *Tulane Law Review* 61 (March 1987): 907–929; *Missouri Law Review* 52 (Spring 1987): 467–484; Daniel L. Pulter, *Oklahoma City University Law Review* 12 (Fall 1987): 865–905; and Richard J. Wittbrodt, *Pepperdine Law Review* 14 (1987): 313–335.

Also see especially Jeffrey W. Soderberg, "*Bowers v. Hardwick*: The Supreme Court Redefines Fundamental Rights Analysis," *Villanova Law Review* 32 (February 1987): 221–258; also note Annamay T. Sheppard, "Private Passion, Public Outrage: Thoughts on *Bowers v. Hardwick*," *Rutgers Law Review* 40 (Winter 1988): 521–559; Sylvia A. Law, "Homosexuality and the Social Meaning of Gender," *Wisconsin Law Review* 1988: 187–235, at 187 ("the disapprobation of homosexual behavior is a reaction to the violation of gender norms, rather than simply scorn for the violation of norms of sexual behavior"); Janet Self, "*Bowers v. Hardwick*: A Study of Aggression," *Human Rights Quarterly* 10 (August 1988): 395–432; Norman Vieira, "*Hardwick* and the Right of Privacy," *University of Chicago Law Review* 55 (Fall 1988): 1181–1191; Claude Millman, "Sodomy Statutes and the Eighth Amendment," *Columbia Journal of Law and Social Problems* 21 (1988): 267–307; Andrew Koppelman, "The Miscegenation Analogy: Sodomy Law as Sex Discrimination," *Yale Law Journal* 98 (November 1988): 145–164, at 147 ("sodomy laws discriminate on the basis of sex—for example, permitting men, but not women, to have sex with women—in order to impose traditional sex roles"); J. Drew Page, "Cruel and Unusual Punishment and Sodomy Statutes," *University of Chicago Law Review* 56 (Winter 1989): 367–396; A. S. Cohan, "The State in the Bedroom: What Some Adults May Not Do Privately After *Hardwick v. Bowers*," *Journal of American Studies* 23 (April 1989): 41–62; "Sexual Orientation and the Law," *Harvard Law Review* 102 (May 1989): 1508–1671; Judith W. DeCew, "Constitutional Privacy, Judicial Interpretation, and *Bowers v. Hardwick*," *Social Theory and Practice* 15 (Fall 1989): 285–303; Stephen Macedo, *The New Right v. The Constitution*, 2nd ed. (Washington, DC: Cato Institute, 1988), pp. 69–74; Macedo, *Liberal Virtues* (New York: Oxford University Press, 1990), pp. 192–197; Sheldon Leader, "The Right to Privacy, the Enforcement of Morals, and the Judicial Function: An Argument," *Current Legal Problems* 43 (1990): 115–134; and "Constitutional Barriers to Civil and Criminal Restrictions on Pre- and Extramarital Sex," *Harvard Law Review* 104 (May 1991): 1660–1680, at 1660 ("Sex is undoubtedly the world's oldest recreational activity").

98. David Robinson, Jr., "Sodomy and the Supreme Court," *Commentary* 82 (October 1986): 57–61, at 60; James J. Knicely, "The *Thornburgh* and *Bowers* Cases," *Mississippi Law Journal* 56 (August 1986): 267–323, at 270–271; Fried, *Order and Law* (New York: Simon & Schuster,

1991), pp. 82–83; Fein, "*Griswold* v. *Connecticut:* Wayward Decision-Making in the Supreme Court," *Ohio Northern University Law Review* 16 (1989): 551–559, at 559. Also see Alan J. Wertjes, *Washington University Law Quarterly* 64 (1986): 1233–1250; Walter Berns, *Taking the Constitution Seriously* (New York: Simon & Schuster, 1987), p. 226; Mary Jane Morrison, "Constitutional Reasoning for Rights," *Missouri Law Review* 54 (Winter 1989): 29–73, at 69 ("The proper question in *Bowers* is whether Georgia constitutionally may criminalize all sodomy; and the proper answer is that Georgia may"); Earl M. Maltz, *Brigham Young University Law Review* 1989: 59–93; and Gerard V. Bradley, *Wake Forest Law Review* 25 (1990): 501–546.

99. *Washington Post*, 13 July 1986, pp. A1, A8; White, "Memorandum to the Conference-Holds for *Bowers*," 25 June 1986, Marshall Box 378; *Baker* v. *Wade*, 478 U.S. 1022, 7 July 1986; *State* v. *Walsh*, 713 S.W.2d 508, 510, 511, 512–13 (Mo. Sup. Ct.), 15 July 1986; Tribe et al., "Petition for Rehearing," *Bowers* v. *Hardwick*, U.S.S.C., O.T. 1985, #140, 24 July 1986, pp. 2, 7, 9–10; *Bowers* v. *Hardwick*, 478 U.S. 1039, 11 September 1986; *Oklahoma* v. *Post*, 479 U.S. 890, 14 October 1986 (denying certiorari to *Post* v. *State*, 717 P.2d. 1151, 14 April 1986, and 715 P.2d 1105, 26 February 1986 [Okla. Ct. Crim. App.]); *Lambeth* v. *State*, 354 S.E.2d 144 (Ga. Sup. Ct.), 9 April 1987; *Gordon* v. *State*, 360 S.E. 2d 253 (Ga. Sup. Ct.), 24 September 1987; *Washington Post*, 26 October 1990, p. A3; *New York Law Journal*, 26 October 1990, p. 1, 20 November 1990, p. 2; *National Law Journal*, 5 November 1990, p. 3. Also see Tribe and Michael C. Dorf, *On Reading the Constitution*, p. 117 (*Bowers* was "egregiously wrong"); and Tribe, "Contrasting Constitutional Visions," *Harvard Civil Rights–Civil Liberties Law Review* 22 (Winter 1987): 95–109, at 104–106.

Regarding Oklahoma, also see *Hinkle* v. *State*, 771 P.2d 232 (Okla. Ct. Crim. App.), 20 March 1989, reaffirming *Post* despite the intervening ruling in *Bowers*. On Georgia, also see *Atlanta Constitution*, 28 August 1989, p. A8, 1 September 1989, p. C3; *Wall Street Journal*, 6 September 1989, p. B7; and *Playboy*, February 1990, p. 44, concerning the incarceration and release of one James D. Moseley, who had served nineteen months of a two-and-a-half-year prison sentence after being convicted of performing oral sex on his wife. Concerning Michael Hardwick, also see *Atlanta Constitution*, 8 September 1986, p. A7; and *Miami Herald*, 17 December 1990, pp. C1, C2. On other post-*Bowers* legal prospects, see Nan Feyler, "The Use of the State Constitutional Right to Privacy to Defeat State Sodomy Statutes," *New York University Review of Law and Social Change* 14 (1986): 973–994; *Washington Post*, 4 February 1987, p. A16; David C. Nice, "State Deregulation of Intimate Behavior," *Social Science Quarterly* 69 (March 1988): 203–211; Regina O. Matthews, "The Louisiana Constitution's Declaration of Rights: Post-*Hardwick* Protection for Sexual Privacy?," *Tulane Law Review* 62 (March 1988): 767–812; and Juli A. Morris, "Challenging Sodomy Statutes: State Constitutional Protections for Sexual Privacy," *Indiana Law Journal* 66 (Spring 1991): 609–624.

100. Bill Moyers, "In Search of the Constitution: Mr. Justice Blackmun," PBS, 26 April 1987; *New York Times*, 18 September 1986, pp. 1, 26, 11 June 1986, p. A21, 14 June 1986, p. 27, 15 June 1986, p. 21, 13 July 1986, p. 33, 15 October 1986, p. B36, 30 October 1986, pp. A30, B7, 12 November 1986, p. B3, 13 November 1986, p. B10, 4 December 1986, p. A32, 5 December 1986, p. A16, 15 December 1986, p. B3, 16 December 1986, p. B4, 19 December 1986, p. B3, 21 January 1987, p. A24, 22 January 1987, p. A27, 23 January 1987, p. A10, 26 January 1987, p. A22, 19 February 1987, p. B4, 20 February 1987, p. B3, 23 February 1987, p. A1, 25 February 1987, p. B1, 8 April 1987, p. D31, 7 May 1987, p. B1, 19 May 1987, p. B8, 13 June 1987, p. 31, 5 August 1987, p. B2, 3 September 1987, p. B1; Blackmun, "Memorandum to the Conference," 24 June 1986, Marshall Box 378; Scalia, "Memorandum to the Conference," 26 March 1987, and Stevens to Scalia, 26 March 1987, Marshall Box 407; *Hartigan* v. *Zbaraz*, 479 U.S. 881, 14 October 1986, 480 U.S. 944, 30 March 1987, 481 U.S. 1008, 7 April 1987. Also see *SHARE* v. *Bering*, 479 U.S. 1050 (dismissing a petition seeking review of *Bering* v. *SHARE*, 721 P.2d 918 [Wash. Sup. Ct.] for want of jurisdiction), Powell to Rehnquist, 9 January 1987, Marshall Box 407, and Bonny E. Sweeney, *Case Western Reserve Law Review* 38 (1988): 698–728; also note *Turner* v. *Safley*, 482 U.S. 78, 95–97, 1 June 1987.

Also see generally Elizabeth Fee and Ruth Finkelstein, "Abortion: The Politics of

Necessity and Choice," *Feminist Studies* 12 (Summer 1986): 361–373, at 372 ("we must stop framing the abortion argument in terms of an individual right to privacy"); *Harper's*, July 1986, pp. 35–43; *Christianity & Crisis*, 14 July 1986, pp. 232–250; Carol Joffe, "Abortion and Antifeminism," *Politics and Society* 15 (1986–87): 207–212; Sharon E. Rush, *University of Florida Law Review* 39 (Winter 1987): 55–111; Janice Steinschneider, *Harvard Women's Law Journal* 10 (Spring 1987): 284–294; and Marvin N. Olasky, "Abortion Rights: Anatomy of a Negative Campaign," *Public Relations Review* 13 (Fall 1987): 12–23.

101. *New York Times*, 27 June 1987, p. 1, 8 July 1987, pp. A1, A20, 13 July 1987, p. A12, 14 July 1987, p. A22, 9 August 1987, p. 25, 13 September 1987, p. IV-7, 14 September 1987, p. B9, 15 September 1987, p. A21, 19 September 1987, p. 10, 22 September 1987, p. A1; *Washington Post*, 19 July 1987, pp. C6, C7, 5 August 1987, p. A20; Michael Pertschuk and Wendy Schaetzel, *The People Rising: The Campaign Against the Bork Nomination* (New York: Thunder's Mouth Press, 1989), pp. 135–137, 144, 257–258; Ethan Bronner, *Battle for Justice* (New York: W. W. Norton & Co., 1989), pp. 152, 159, 221–22, 266–70; U.S. Congress, Senate, Committee on the Judiciary, *Hearings on the Nomination of Robert H. Bork*, 100th Cong., 1st sess., 15–30 September 1987, pp. 184–85, 265, 1176, 3547–49, 3789, 3896–3910, 4455; Mark Gitenstein, *Matters of Principle* (New York: Simon & Schuster, 1992), pp. 105 and 112–117; Bork, *The Tempting of America* (New York: Free Press, 1989), pp. 120, 250. Also see *Time*, 21 September 1987, pp. 14–15.

On public opinion polls concerning the right to privacy, also see Louis Harris et al., *The Dimensions of Privacy: A National Opinion Research Survey of Attitudes Toward Privacy* (Stevens Point, WI: Sentry Insurance, April 1979), p. 15 (When more than 1,500 respondents were asked: "The United States was founded on the belief that the rights to life, liberty, and the pursuit of happiness were fundamental for both the individual and a just society. Do you think we should or should not add today the right of privacy to this list?" in December 1978, 76 percent chose "should," 17 percent said "should not," and 7 percent had no opinion); and *National Law Journal*, 26 February 1990, pp. 1, 36–37 (73 percent of 805 respondents to a January 1990 survey believe that the Constitution guarantees a right of privacy; 51 percent believe it is written in the Constitution, and only 41 percent can name even one member of the Supreme Court).

102. U.S. Congress, Senate, *Congressional Record*, 9 October 1987, pp. 14011–12; Gitenstein, *Matters of Principle*, p. 322; Frank Michelman, "Law's Republic," *Yale Law Journal* 97 (July 1988): 1493–1537, at 1533–34; Sanford Levinson, "Constitutional Rhetoric and the Ninth Amendment," *Chicago-Kent Law Review* 64 (1988): 131–161, at 135; Lackland H. Bloom, Jr., "The Legacy of *Griswold*," *Ohio Northern University Law Review* 16 (1989): 511–544, at 543; Gary McDowell, "Congress and the Courts," *The Public Interest*, Summer 1990, pp. 89–101, at 100. The internal quotation is from *West Virginia State Board of Education* v. *Barnette*, 319 U.S. 624, 642 (1943).

Also see Lilian R. BeVier, "What Privacy Is Not," *Harvard Journal of Law & Public Policy* 12 (Winter 1989): 99–103, at 102 ("by calling the abortion right a right of privacy, the Court has appropriated, or rather misappropriated, much of the good will that the word 'privacy' itself has quite legitimately accumulated"); Glenn H. Reynolds, "Sex, Lies and Jurisprudence: Robert Bork, *Griswold* and the Philosophy of Original Understanding," *Georgia Law Review* 24 (Summer 1990): 1045–1113, at 1105 (*Griswold* "is in fact a rather popular opinion—so popular that when word went out that Robert Bork was against it, his fate was largely sealed"); and Harry H. Wellington, *Interpreting the Constitution* (New Haven: Yale University Press, 1990), p. 121 ("the hearings suggest strong political approval of the principle advanced in *Griswold*").

On *Griswold*'s influence overseas, see *Mary McGee* v. *Attorney General*, 1974 Irish Reports 284, 326–28, 335–36 (Supreme Court of Ireland), 19 December 1974; also see Robert A. Burt, "Privacy and Contraception in the American and Irish Constitutions," *St. Louis University Public Law Review* 7 (1988): 287–296. Non-American legal decisions that have favorably cited *Roe* include *Paton* v. *United Kingdom*, 3 E.H.R.R. 408, 415 (European Commission of Human Rights), 1980; *The Queen* v. *Bayliss and Culleon*, 9 Qld Lawyer Reps. 8, 10, 49, 54–56 (Queensland, Australia), 1986; and *Morgenthaler* v. *Her Majesty, The Queen*, 1

S.C.R. 30, 40 D.L.R. 4th 385 (Supreme Court of Canada), 28 January 1988. Also see *New York Times*, 29 January 1988, p. A3.

103. Bork, *The Tempting of America*, pp. 112, 116, 158–59. Also see *Dallas Morning News*, 10 July 1989, p. A13; David A. Kaplan, "Is *Roe* Good Law?," *Newsweek*, 27 April 1992, pp. 49–51 (criticizing Blackmun's "sloppy use of legal doctrine" and concluding that *"Roe* is a lousy opinion," "almost devoid of the things we expect from our judges"); and Elizabeth Mensch and Alan Freeman, *The Politics of Virtue* (Durham, NC: Duke University Press, 1993), p. 126 (*Roe* "may be fairly characterized as a mistake for three combined reasons: it was legally problematic at best, sociologically inaccurate, and politically disastrous").

104. New York Times, 30 October 1987, p. A1, 1 November 1987, p. IV-7, 4 November 1987, p. B32, 8 November 1987, p. A1, 12 November 1987, p. A1, 15 December 1987, p. B16, 21 January 1988, p. A18, 23 January 1988, p. 50; Legal Times, 23 November 1987, p. 1; Blackmun, "Memorandum to the Conference," 7 December 1987, and Rehnquist, "Memorandum to the Conference," 8 December 1987, Marshall Box 439; *Hartigan* v. *Zbaraz*, 484 U.S. 171, 14 December 1987; U.S. Congress, Senate, Committee on the Judiciary, *Hearings on the Nomination of Anthony M. Kennedy*, 100th Cong., 1st sess., 14–16 December 1987, pp. 88, 121, 164–65, 166, 233; Ethan Bronner, *Battle For Justice* (New York: W. W. Norton & Co., 1989), pp. 328–338. Also see Sallie Tisdale, *Harper's*, October 1987, pp. 66–70.

105. *New York Times*, 4 February 1988, pp. A1, A18, 19 February 1988, p. A10, 3 May 1988, p. B1, 4 May 1988, p. B2, 5 May 1988, p. B3, 8 May 1988, p. 28, 10 May 1988, p. A20, 20 July 1988, p. A19, 30 July 1988, 7 August 1988, p. 20, 13 August 1988, p. 6, 26 August 1988, p. A12, 29 August 1988, p. A15, 31 August 1988, p. A14, 10 September 1988, p. 6, 14 September 1988, p. A24; U.S. Congress, Senate, Committee on the Judiciary, *Report—Nomination of Anthony M. Kennedy to Be an Associate Justice of the United States Supreme Court*, 100th Cong., 2nd sess., #100–13, 1 February 1988, pp. 18–19, 51, 58–59; Charles Fager, "Fetal Distraction," *The New Republic*, 30 May 1988, pp. 21–22; *Washington Post*, 14 September 1988; *U.S. News & World Report*, 3 October 1988, pp. 23–31. Also see Stephen F. Rohde, *Los Angeles Lawyer*, March 1988, pp. 45–53; Ernest A. Braun, *Los Angeles Lawyer*, June 1988, pp. 27–28; Paul Reidinger, *ABA Journal*, July 1988, pp. 66–70; and Julie Hairston and Molly McGuire's articles on "Operation Rescue" in *Southern Exposure*, Summer 1990, pp. 15–18.

Also note Justice Kennedy's opinion for the Court in *United States Catholic Conference* v. *Abortion Rights Mobilization*, 487 U.S. 72, 20 June 1988 (reversing and remanding 824 F.2d 156), with only Marshall, J., dissenting, plus *Abortion Rights Mobilization* v. *United States Catholic Conference*, 495 U.S. 918, 30 April 1990 (denying certiorari to 885 F.2d 1020, 6 September 1989). See as well 544 F. Supp. 471 (1982) and 603 F. Supp. 970 (1985); *New York Times*, 27 September 1987, p. 52, 8 December 1987, p. A21, 19 April 1988, p. A23, 21 June 1988, p. A17, 29 July 1988, p. A27, 7 September 1989, p. B3, 1 May 1990, p. A18.

106. *New York Times*, 5 October 1988, p. A22, 27 October 1988, p. A27, 30 October 1988, p. 26, 11 November 1988, p. A20, 14 November 1988, p. B10, 24 December 1988, p. 8, 26 December 1988, p. 12, 10 January 1989, p. B5; Patricia Donovan, "The 1988 Abortion Referenda," *Family Planning Perspectives* 21 (September-October 1989): 218–223; *Washington Post*, 11 November 1988, pp. A1, A4, 10 January 1989, pp. A1, A5; "PE" [Paul Englemayer], *Webster* v. *Reproductive Health Services*, 29 December 1988, 2pp., Marshall Box 454; *Webster* Docket Sheet, Marshall Box 554; *Webster* v. *Reproductive Health Services*, 488 U.S. 1003, 9 January 1989. Marshall's docket sheet does not indicate any votes for Justices Scalia and Kennedy regarding *Webster* at the January 6 conference.

107. *New York Times*, 15 January 1989, pp. 25, IV-28, 21 January 1989, p. A26, 22 January 1989, p. 21, 24 January 1989, p. A1, 31 January 1989, p. A22, 21 March 1989, p. A19, 26 March 1989, p. 19, 5 April 1989, p. A23, 6 April 1989, p. B10, 9 April 1989, pp. 28, IV-24, 10 April 1989, pp. A1, A17, B6, 11 April 1989, p. A20, 16 April 1989, p. 28, 18 April 1989, p. C1, 19 April 1989, p. A23, 21 April 1989, p. B5, 26 April 1989, pp. A1, A25, 2 July 1989, p. 14; William C. Bryson et al., "Brief for the United States as Amicus Curiae Supporting Appellants," *Webster* v. *Reproductive Health Services*, #88–605, 23 February 1989, pp. 1, 5–6, 12; William L. Webster

et al., "Brief for Appellants," *Webster* v. *Reproductive Health Services*, #88–605, 23 February 1989, pp. 9, 14, 17; Roger K. Evans et al., "Brief for Appellees," *Webster* v. *Reproductive Health Services*, #88–605, 30 March 1989, p. 2; *Time*, 1 May 1989, pp. 20–28; Sylvia A. Law et al., "Brief of 281 American Historians as Amicus Curiae Supporting Appellees," *Webster* v. *Reproductive Health Services*, #88–605, 31pp., 30 March 1989; Law, "Conversations Between Historians and the Constitution," *The Public Historian* 12 (Summer 1990): 11–17; Stevens to Rehnquist, 17 April 1989, Marshall Box 480; Webster et al., "Appellants' Reply Brief," *Webster* v. *Reproductive Health Services*, #88–605, 20 April 1989, p. 5. On the origins of the Missouri statute, see Cynthia Gorney, "Taking Aim at *Roe* v. *Wade*," *Washington Post Magazine*, 9 April 1989, pp. 18–26, 42–44; on the amicus briefs, see Kathryn Kolbert, *Women's Rights Law Reporter* 11 (1989): 153–162; *Family Planning Perspectives* 21 (May-June 1989): 134–136; and especially Susan Behuniak-Long, "Friendly Fire: Amici Curiae and *Webster* v. *Reproductive Health Services*," *Judicature* 74 (February-March 1991): 261–270. Also note Ruth Colker, "Feminist Litigation: An Oxymoron?—A Study of the Briefs Filed in *William L. Webster* v. *Reproductive Health Services*," and Sarah E. Burns, "Notes from the Field: A Reply to Professor Colker," *Harvard Women's Law Journal* 13 (Spring 1990): 137–188 and 189–206. On the historians' brief in particular, also see the articles by James C. Mohr (pp. 19–26), Estelle B. Freedman (pp. 27–32), and others in *The Public Historian* 12 (Summer 1990); as well as Gerard V. Bradley, "Academic Integrity Betrayed," *First Things*, August-September 1990, pp. 10–11. Also note Roy M. Mersky and Gary R. Hartman, *A Documentary History of the Legal Aspects of Abortion in the United States: Webster v. Reproductive Health Services (Littleton, CO: Fred B. Rothman and Co.,* 1990), 8 vols.

Also see Mary Ann Glendon, *The New Republic*, 20 February 1989, pp. 19–20; *Ms.*, April 1989, pp. 87–95; Dawn Johnsen and Marcy Wilder, "Will *Roe* v. *Wade* Survive the Rehnquist Court?" *Nova Law Review* 13 (Spring 1989): 457–469; James Bopp, Jr. and Richard E. Coleson, "The Right to Abortion: Anomalous, Absolute, and Ripe for Reversal," *B.Y.U. Journal of Public Law* 3 (1989): 181–355; Bopp, "Will There Be a Constitutional Right to Abortion After the Reconsideration of *Roe* v. *Wade*?," *Journal of Contemporary Law* 15 (1989): 131–173; *Commonweal*, 5 May 1989, pp. 259–60, 267–69; Henry Reske, *ABA Journal*, May 1989, pp. 60–64; and Walter Dellinger, *The New Republic*, 8 May 1989, pp. 11–12.

On public opinion in the late 1980s, also see Jacqueline Scott, "Conflicting Beliefs About Abortion: Legal Approval and Moral Doubts," *Social Psychology Quarterly* 52 (December 1989): 319–326; and Elizabeth A. Cook et al., "Generational Differences in Attitudes Toward Abortion," *American Politics Quarterly* 21 (January 1993): 31–53; also note Jacqueline Scott and Howard Schuman, "Attitude Strength and Social Action in the Abortion Dispute," *American Sociological Review* 53 (October 1988): 785–793; and Robert Lerner et al., "Abortion and Social Change in America," *Society*, January-February 1990, pp. 8–15.

108. Transcript of Oral Argument, *Webster* v. *Reproductive Health Services*, 26 April 1989, pp. 11–12, 15–17; *New York Times*, 26 April 1989, pp. A24, A25, 27 April 1989, pp. A1, B14, 28 April 1989, pp. A38, B12, 30 April 1989, p. IV-25, 16 May 1989, p. A20; *Washington Post*, 27 April 1989, pp. A1, A14; Ronald Dworkin, "The Great Abortion Case," *New York Review of Books*, 29 June 1989, pp. 49–53; Rhonda Copelon and Kathryn Kolbert, *Ms.*, July-August 1989, pp. 42–44; Marian Faux, *Crusaders* (New York: Carol Publishing Group, 1990), esp. pp. 52–61. Also see *Newsweek*, 1 May 1989, pp. 28–37.

109. Marshall Docket Sheet, Marshall Box 554; Rehnquist Print #1, 25 May 1989, 23pp., p. 23, Blackmun to Rehnquist, 26 May 1989, Brennan to Rehnquist, Marshall to Rehnquist, White to Rehnquist, Kennedy to Rehnquist, and Stevens to Rehnquist, 30 May 1989, Rehnquist Print #2, 6 June 1989, Blackmun Print #1, 21 June 1989, pp. 1–2, 26, Brennan to Blackmun, and Marshall to Blackmun, 21 June 1989, O'Connor typescript circulation, 22 June 1989, Stevens to O'Connor, 22 and 23 June 1989, O'Connor Print #1, 23 June 1989, Marshall to O'Connor, and Blackmun to O'Connor, 26 June 1989, Stevens Circulation #1, and Scalia Print #1, 26 June 1989, Rehnquist, "Memorandum to the Conference," and Rehnquist Print #4, 27 June 1989, Stevens to Rehnquist, 27 June 1989, Blackmun Print #2, 28 June 1989 (with earlier references to "majority" now changed to "plurality"), Marshall Box 480. Also

see *Los Angeles Times*, 13 December 1992, p. A1; *Washington Post*, 23 May 1993, pp. A1, A21, and *New York Times*, 24 May 1993, p. A10.

110. *Webster* v. *Reproductive Health Services*, 492 U.S. 490, 509, 511, 517, 518, 519, 520, 525–26, 530, 531, 532, 535, 536n, 538, 547n, 556, 557n, 560 (reversing 851 F.2d 1071 [8th Cir.]), 3 July 1989. Also see 662 F. Supp. 407 and 655 F. Supp. 1300 (W.D. Mo.), 1987, as well as Epstein and Kobylka, *The Supreme Court and Legal Change*, pp. 265–292, and Savage, *Turning Right*, pp. 227–228, 260–272, and 288–298.

111. *New York Times*, 30 June 1989, p. A8, 3 July 1989, pp. A8, A10, 4 July 1989, pp. 1, 10, 11, and 28, 5 July 1989, p. A1, A17, A18, and A21, 6 July 1989, p. A21, 9 July 1989, p. IV-1; *Washington Post*, 4 July 1989, pp. A1, A6, A7; *Time*, 17 July 1989, p. 96; Bopp and Richard E. Coleson, "What Does *Webster* Mean?," *University of Pennsylvania Law Review* 138 (November 1989): 157–177, at 157–58; Susan R. Estrich and Kathleen M. Sullivan, "Abortion Politics: Writing for an Audience of One," *University of Pennsylvania Law Review* 138 (November 1989): 119–155, at 119–20 and 123; Daniel A. Farber, "Abortion After *Webster*," *Constitutional Commentary* 6 (Summer 1989): 225–230, at 225–27; Walter Dellinger and Gene B. Sperling, "Abortion and the Supreme Court: The Retreat from *Roe* v. *Wade*," *University of Pennsylvania Law Review* 138 (November 1989): 83–118, at 83 and 98n.

Also see especially Kathryn Kolbert, "The *Webster* Amicus Curiae Briefs: Did the Amici Effort Make a Difference?" *American Journal of Law and Medicine* 15 (1989): 153–168; Susan Behuniak-Long, "Friendly Fire: Amici Curiae and *Webster* v. *Reproductive Health Services*," *Judicature* 74 (February-March 1991): 261–270, at 270; Ronald Dworkin, "The Future of Abortion," *New York Review of Books*, 28 September 1989, pp. 47–51; Paul D. Simmons, "Religious Liberty and the Abortion Debate," *Journal of Church and State* 32 (Summer 1990): 567–584; and a four-part *Los Angeles Times* series, 1–4 July 1990, pp. A1ff.; note as well James R. Kelly, *America*, 19 August 1989, pp. 79–83; William Saletan, T*he New Republic*, 18–25 September 1989, pp. 18–20; John Robertson, "The Future of Early Abortion," *ABA Journal*, October 1989, pp. 72–75; Mary Anne Warren, "The Abortion Struggle in America," *Bioethics* 3 (October 1989): 320–332; George J. Annas, *New England Journal of Medicine* 321 (26 October 1989): 1200–1203; Frances Olsen, "Unraveling Compromise," *Harvard Law Review* 103 (November 1989): 105–135; Leonard A. Cole, "The End of the Abortion Debate," *University of Pennsylvania Law Review* 138 (November 1989): 217–223; Christopher A. Crain, "Judicial Restraint and the Non-Decision in *Webster* v. *Reproductive Health Services*," *Harvard Journal of Law & Public Policy* 13 (Winter 1990): 263–318; Kevin W. Saunders, "Privacy and Social Contract: A Defense of Judicial Activism in Privacy Cases," *Arizona Law Review* 33 (1991): 811–857; Karen L. Bell, "Toward a New Analysis of the Abortion Debate," *Arizona Law Review* 33 (1991): 907–935; and Donald P. Judges, *Hard Choices, Lost Voices* (Chicago: Ivan R. Dee, 1993), pp. 190–199.

112. Rehnquist, "Memorandum to the Conference," 28 June 1989, Marshall Box 463; *Hodgson* v. *Minnesota*, 492 U.S. 917, *Ohio* v. *Akron Center for Reproductive Health*, 492 U.S. 916, and *Turnock* v. *Ragsdale*, 492 U.S. 916, 3 July 1989; *New York Times*, 25 June 1989, p. 20, 6 July 1989, p. A16, 8 July 1989, p. 7, 9 July 1989, p. 19, 16 July 1989, p. A1, 21 July 1989, p. A6, 26 July 1989, p. A12, 31 July 1989, p. A8, 3 August 1989, p. A18, 12 August 1989, p. 6, 13 August 1989, p. 23, 25 August 1989, p. A1, 29 September 1989, pp. A1, A13, 6 October 1989, p. A15, 7 October 1989, p. 9, 11 October 1989, p. A1, 12 October 1989, pp. A1, A22, A23, 13 October 1989, p. A1, 14 October 1989, p. 1, 15 October 1989, pp. 24, 29, IV-1, 16 October 1989, p. A18, 22 October 1989, p. 32, 26 October 1989, p. A20, 29 October 1989, p. A1, 7 November 1989, p. A16, 8 November 1989, p. A18, 9 November 1989, p. B14, 10 November 1989, p. A1, 13 November 1989, p. A14; *In re T.W.*, 551 So.2d 1186 (Fla. Sup. Ct.), 5 October 1989 (affirming 543 So.2d 837); *Washington Post*, 6 October 1989, pp. A1, A9, 7 October 1989, p. A6.

On the 1980 Florida privacy amendment and *In re T.W.*, also see Gerald B. Cope, Jr., "To Be Let Alone: Florida's Proposed Right of Privacy," *Florida State University Law Review* 6 (Summer 1978): 671–773; John M. Devlin, "State Constitutional Autonomy Rights in an Age of Federal Retrenchment," *Emerging Issues in State Constitutional Law* 3 (1990): 195–246, at 224–26; Martha M. Ezzard, *Denver University Law Review* 67 (1990): 401–419; Daniel R.

Gordon, "One Privacy Provision, Two Privacy Protections: The Right to Privacy in Florida After *Roe* v. *Wade*," *Wisconsin Women's Law Journal 5 (1990): 81–122;* and Rebecca M. Salokar, "The First Test of Webster's Effect: The Florida Church," in Timothy A. Byrnes and Mary C. Segers, eds., *The Catholic Church and the Politics of Abortion* (Boulder, CO: Westview Press, 1992), pp. 48–70. On Congress, also see James L. Regens and Brad Lockerbie, "Making Choices About Choice: House Support for Abortion Funding," *Social Science Research* 22 (March 1993): 24–32; on New Jersey, also see Mary C. Segers, *Commonweal*, 12 January 1990, pp. 10–13; and Segers, "Abortion Politics Post-Webster: The New Jersey Bishops," in Byrnes and Segers, eds., *The Catholic Church and the Politics of Abortion*, pp. 27–47.

Also generally see Jack Fowler, *National Review*, 4 August 1989, pp. 35–36; *Commonweal*, 11 August 1989, pp. 425–428; Morton Kondracke, *The New Republic*, 28 August 1989, pp. 17–19; Barbara Barnett, *Southern Exposure*, Summer 1990, pp. 20–23; and especially Glen Halva-Neubauer, "Abortion Policy in the Post-Webster Age," *Publius* 20 (Summer 1990): 27–44; Alissa Rubin, "Interest Groups and Abortion Politics in the Post-*Webster* Era," in Allan J. Cigler and Burdett A. Loomis, eds., *Interest Group Politics*, 3rd ed. (Washington, DC: CQ Press, 1991), pp. 239–255; and Glen Halva-Neubauer, "Legislative Agenda-Setting in the States: The Case of Abortion Policy" (unpublished Ph.D. dissertation, University of Minnesota, 1992). Also note Ruth Ann Strickland and Marcia L. Whicker, "Political and Socioeconomic Indicators of State Restrictiveness Toward Abortion," *Policy Studies Journal* 20 (Winter 1992): 598–617; Carolyn L. Cooke, "Holding the Line: A View of Evolving Abortion Policy" (unpublished Ph.D. dissertation, Indiana University, 1992); Marilyn A. Yale, "Abortion in State Level Electoral Politics: A Content Analysis of Press Coverage During Four Gubernatorial Campaigns" (unpublished Ph.D. dissertation, University of Houston, 1992); and Malcolm L. Goggin, "Understanding the New Politics of Abortion," and Michael B. Berkman and Robert E. O'Connor, "Do Women Legislators Matter? Female Legislators and State Abortion Policy," *American Politics Quarterly* 21 (January 1993): 4–30 and 102–124.

113. *New York Times*, 20 September 1989, p. A16, 3 October 1989, p. A19, 4 October 1989, p. B24, 17 October 1989, p. A17, 25 October 1989, p. A1, 8 November 1989, p. A18, 15 November 1989, p. A19, 19 November 1989, p. 38, 23 November 1989, p. A1, 24 November 1989, p. A1, 30 November 1989, pp. A1, B16, 3 December 1989, p. IV-4, 7 December 1989, p. A34; Stevens to Rehnquist, 28 August 1989, Marshall Box 463; *Turnock* v. *Ragsdale*, 493 U.S. 802, 2 October 1989 (Stevens not participating), *Turnock* v. *Ragsdale*, 493 U.S. 987, 1 December 1989 (granting motion to defer any further proceedings); "GP" [Gregory Priest], "Bench Memorandum," *Ohio* v. *Akron Center*, 27 November 1989, 6pp., Marshall Box 483; Alexander Wohl, "The Abortion Cases," *ABA Journal*, February 1990, pp. 68–71; O'Connor, "Memorandum to the Conference," 4 December 1989, Marshall Box 492; Stevens to Rehnquist (2), 7 December 1989, Marshall Boxes 498 and 500; O'Connor to Rehnquist (2), 8 December 1989, Marshall Boxes 498 and 500; Rehnquist, "Memorandum to the Conference," 8 December 1989, and Rehnquist to O'Connor, 8 December 1989, Marshall Box 492; Brennan to Marshall, Blackmun, and Stevens, 11 December 1989, and Blackmun to Brennan, 11 December 1989, Marshall Box 498. Also see *Washington Post*, 23 May 1993, p. A21.

On the 1989 passage of the Pennsylvania statute, also see Thomas J. O'Hara, "The Abortion Control Act of 1989: The Pennsylvania Catholics," in Byrnes and Segers, eds., *The Catholic Church and the Politics of Abortion*, pp. 87–104. On Illinois, see the earlier Eighth Circuit decision in *Ragsdale* v. *Turnock*, 841 F.2d 1358, as well as MaryAnne Borrelli, "The Consistent Life Ethic in State Politics: Joseph Cardinal Bernardin and the Abortion Issue in Illinois," in Byrnes and Segers, eds., *The Catholic Church and the Politics of Abortion*, pp. 71–86.

On earlier action in the Minnesota case, see 648 F. Supp. 756, 479 U.S. 1102 (denying certiorari), 827 F.2d 1191, 835 F.2d 1546, and 853 F.2d 1452; Rachel N. Pine, "Speculation and Reality: The Role of Facts in Judicial Protection of Fundamental Rights," *University of Pennsylvania Law Review* 136 (January 1988): 655–727; and *New York Times*, 28 August 1987, p. A1, 9 August 1988, p. A1; on earlier action in the Ohio case, see 633 F. Supp. 1123, 854 F.2d 852, and *New York Times*, 13 August 1988, p. 6.

On lower federal court abortion behavior, see Steve Alumbaugh and C. K. Rowland, "The Links Between Platform-Based Appointment Criteria and Trial Judges' Abortion

Judgments," *Judicature* 74 (October-November 1990): 153–162, at 162 ("the Reagan appointees were much more resistant to abortion rights than were the appointees of his predecessors" while "Carter's appointees were much more supportive of abortion claims than were the appointees of other presidents").

114. *New York Times*, 12 January 1990, p. A18, 23 January 1990, p. A18, 29 January 1990, p. A17, 7 February 1990, p. A25, 10 March 1990, p. 8, 16 March 1990, p. A1, 20 March 1990, p. A14, 21 March 1990, p. A24, 22 March 1990, p. A1, 23 March 1990, p. A12, 25 March 1990, p. 29, 26 March 1990, p. B8, 27 March 1990, p. A24, 30 March 1990, p. A12, 31 March 1990, p. 1, 1 April 1990, p. IV-5, 2 April 1990, p. A14, 3 April 1990, p. A18, 6 April 1990, p. A1, 18 April 1990, p. A14, 19 April 1990, p. A25, 22 April 1990, p. 30, 27 April 1990, p. A10, 28 April 1990, pp. 1, 28, 29 April 1990, pp. 1, 26, 31 July 1990, p. A12, 5 August 1990, p. 24, 24 August 1990, p. A12, 25 August 1990, p. 8, 22 September 1990, p. 8; *Guam Society of Obstetricians and Gynecologists* v. *Ada*, 776 F. Supp. 1422, 23 August 1990; *Planned Parenthood of Southeastern Pennsylvania* v. *Casey*, 744 F. Supp. 1323, 24 August 1990; *New Haven Register*, 18 April 1990, 28 April 1990, and 1 May 1990; Connecticut General Statute 19A-602 (1991).

On the Connecticut events, also see Paul Baumann, *Commonweal*, 15 June 1990, pp. 373–375; Spencer M. Clapp, "Leading the Nation After Webster: Connecticut's Abortion Law," in Byrnes and Segers, eds., *The Catholic Church and the Politics of Abortion*, pp. 118–136; Barbara Hinkson Craig and David M. O'Brien, *Abortion and American Politics* (Chatham, NJ: Chatham House, 1993), pp. 284–292; and Eugene P. Falco, "Connecticut as a Model in an Era Without *Roe*" (unpublished paper, University of Connecticut Law School, Spring 1992); as well as *New York Times*, 4 April 1991, p. B3 (identifying Senator Upson as the only vocal opponent of Connecticut's repeal of its criminal adultery law) and *New York Times*, 18 April 1991, p. B6, and 23 April 1991, pp. B1, B4 (concerning Connecticut's adoption of a "gay rights" bill [as distinct from sodomy law repeal] due to what the measure's chief sponsor said was "the tacit support of the state's Roman Catholic church").

Also generally see Frances Kissling, "Ending the Abortion War," and James R. Kelly, "Beyond Slogans," *Christian Century*, 21 February 1990, pp. 180–84 and 184–86; U.S. Congress, Senate, Committee on Labor and Human Resources, *Hearings—Freedom of Choice Act of 1989*, 101st Cong., 2nd sess., 27 March and 23 May 1990; and especially Sue Hertz, *Caught in the Crossfire: A Year on Abortion's Front Line* (New York: Prentice Hall, 1991).

115. Jonathan B. Imber, "Abortion Policy and Medical Practice," *Society*, July-August 1990, pp. 27–34, at 33; *New York Times*, 8 January 1990, pp. A1, B8, 8 September 1991, p. 18, 15 March 1992, pp. 1, 18, 12 May 1993, p. A18, 19 June 1993, pp. 23–24; *Washington Post*, 1 May 1991, p. A16, 20 April 1993, p. H7; *Time*, 4 May 1992, pp. 26–32; *Chronicle of Higher Education*, 6 May 1992, pp. A39, A40; *Wall Street Journal*, 12 March 1993, pp. B1, B6; Warren Hern, *New York Times*, 13 March 1993, p. 21; Harold J. Morowitz and James S. Trefil, *The Facts of Life: Science and the Abortion Controversy* (New York: Oxford University Press, 1992), pp. 19, 116, 119, 133, 146. Also see Rivers Singleton, Jr., "Paradigms of Science/Society Interaction: The Abortion Controversy," *Perspectives in Biology and Medicine* 32 (Winter 1989): 174–193; *New York Times*, 18 February 1989, p. 29, 25 November 1992, p. A21; Lawrence Lader, *RU 486* (Reading, MA: Addison-Wesley, 1991); and Kim M. Blankenship et al., "Reproductive Technologies and the U.S. Courts," *Gender & Society* 7 (March 1993): 8–31.

116. Kennedy *Akron Center* Print #1, 11 January 1990, Marshall to Kennedy, 12 January 1990, Brennan to Kennedy, Blackmun to Kennedy, White to Kennedy, and Stevens to Kennedy, 16 January 1990, Rehnquist to Kennedy, 18 January 1990, Scalia to Kennedy, 23 January 1990, Stevens Concurrence #1, 7 February 1990, O'Connor to Kennedy, 19 March 1990, Marshall Box 498; Stevens *Hodgson* Print #1, 7 February 1990, Marshall to Stevens, 12 February 1990, Kennedy to Stevens, 28 February 1990, Marshall Print #1, 13 March 1990, Kennedy Print #1, 6 June 1990, Rehnquist to Kennedy, and White to Kennedy, 6 June 1990, O'Connor, "Memorandum to the Conference," and O'Connor Print #1, 11 June 1990, Stevens, "Memorandum to the Conference," and Stevens Print #4, 11 June 1990, Brennan to Stevens, 13 June 1990, Kennedy, "Memorandum to the Conference," and Stevens to Kennedy, 13 June 1990, Brennan to Marshall, 13 June 1990, Brennan to Stevens, 14 June 1990, Stevens,

"Memorandum to the Conference," and Stevens Print #5, 15 June 1990, Marshall to Stevens, 15 June 1990, Stevens to Marshall, 18 June 1990, Stevens to Blackmun, 18 June 1990, Marshall to Stevens, 18 June 1990, Blackmun to Stevens, 18 June 1990, Blackmun to Brennan, Marshall (and Stevens), 18 June 1990 ("the three of us should be together as much as possible"), Brennan to Blackmun, 18 June 1990 ("I am in wholehearted agreement . . . especially now that Sandra has agreed to invalidate at least part of an abortion law"), Stevens to Marshall and Blackmun, 19 June 1990, Kennedy Print #2, and Scalia Print #1, 20 June 1990, Scalia to Kennedy, Brennan to Marshall, and Blackmun to Marshall, 20 June 1990, Marshall Boxes 499 and 500; Kennedy *Akron Center* Print #3, Scalia Print #1, and Blackmun Print #1, 19 June 1990, Stevens to Kennedy, 19 June 1990, Brennan to Blackmun, 19 June 1990, Marshall to Blackmun, 20 June 1990, Marshall Box 498.

117. *Hodgson* v. *Minnesota*, 497 U.S. 417, 110 Sup. Ct. 2926, 111 L.Ed. 2d 344, 370, 379, 25 June 1990; *Ohio* v. *Akron Center for Reproductive Health*, 497 U.S. 502, 110 Sup. Ct. 2972, 111 L.Ed.2d 405, 424, 25 June 1990; *New York Times*, 26 June 1990, pp. A1, A20, 27 June 1990, p. A14; *Time*, 9 July 1990, pp. 22–27. Also see Anita L. Allen, *National Law Journal*, 13 August 1990, pp. S8, S14; David J. Zampa, *Notre Dame Law Review* 65 (1990): 731–780; Savage, *Turning Right*, pp. 307–313, 342–345; and Judges, *Hard Choices*, pp. 200–206.

118. *New York Times*, 10 June 1990, p. 29, 15 June 1990, p. A13, 18 June 1990, p. A18, 24 June 1990, p. 23, 25 June 1990, p. A1, 27 June 1990, p. A14, 28 June 1990, p. A18, 7 July 1990, p. 10, 8 July 1990, p. 10, 9 July 1990, p. A1, 10 July 1990, p. A17, 13 July 1990, p. A9, 21 July 1990, p. A1, 24 July 1990, p. A1, 25 July 1990, p. A1, 28 July 1990, p. A1, 1 August 1990, p. A12, 14 September 1990, p. A1, 19 September 1990, p. A24, 3 October 1990, p. A1, 9 October 1990, pp. A1, A22, 21 October 1990, p. 24, 8 November 1990, p. B10; U.S. Congress, Senate, Committee on the Judiciary, *Hearings on the Nomination of David H. Souter*, 101st Cong., 2nd sess., 13–19 September 1990, pp. 54, 268–69, 277, and 910–11.

On Louisiana, also see Christine Day, "Abortion and Religious Coalitions: The Case of Louisiana," in Byrnes and Segers, eds., *The Catholic Church and the Politics of Abortion*, pp. 105–117. On David Souter, also see Jeff Rosen, *The New Republic*, 24 September 1990, pp. 20–24; and U.S. Congress, Senate, Committee on the Judiciary, *Report—Nomination of David H. Souter to Be an Associate Justice of the United States Supreme Court*, 101st Cong., 2nd sess., #101–32, 1 October 1990. More generally, also note Fred Siegel, "Nothing in Moderation," *Atlantic*, May 1990, pp. 108, 110; Walter Dellinger, "Should We Compromise on Abortion?" *The American Prospect*, Summer 1990, pp. 30–37; and Margaret L. McConnell, "Living with *Roe* v. *Wade*," *Commentary*, November 1990, pp. 34–38, at 36 ("casting abortion as a right takes the weight of morality out of the balance. For, by definition, a right is something one need not feel guilty exercising").

119. *New York Times*, 30 January 1988, p. 1, 2 February 1988, p. A12, 7 February 1988, p. IV-7, 14 August 1988, p. 24, 3 November 1989, p. B1, 30 May 1990, p. B6, 9 September 1990, p. 29, 31 October 1990, p. A1; *Rust* v. *Sullivan*, 495 U.S. 956, 29 May 1990; "SB" [Scott Brewer], "Bench Memorandum," *Rust* v. *Sullivan*, 24 October 1990, 10pp., Marshall Box 513; Marshall Docket Sheet, Marshall Box 558; Marshall, "Memorandum to the Conference," 7 November 1990, Rehnquist Print #1, 13 December 1990, Marshall to Rehnquist, 13 December 1990, White to Rehnquist, and Blackmun to Rehnquist, 14 December 1990, Stevens to Rehnquist, 18 December 1990, O'Connor to Rehnquist, 17 January 1991, Scalia to Rehnquist, 7 February 1991, Blackmun Print #1, 7 February 1991, Stevens to Blackmun, 8 February 1991, Marshall to Blackmun, 11 February 1991, White to Rehnquist, 13 February 1991, O'Connor Print #1, 13 February 1991, Kennedy to Rehnquist, 19 February 1991, Rehnquist Print #4, 20 February 1991, White to Rehnquist, 20 February 1991, Scalia to Rehnquist, 22 February 1991, Rehnquist to Souter, 29 April 1991, Stevens Print #1, 3 May 1991, Stevens to Blackmun, 8 May 1991, Souter to Rehnquist, 9 May 1991, Marshall Box 530.

For the lower court decisions in *Rust*, see 690 F. Supp. 1261 and 889 F.2d. 401 (2d Cir.); for the different holdings in the two other circuits, see *Massachusetts* v. *Secretary of Health and Human Services*, 899 F.2d 53 (1st Cir.), and *Planned Parenthood Federation of America* v. *Sullivan*, 913 F.2d 1492 (10th Cir.).

120. *Rust* v. *Sullivan*, 111 Sup. Ct. 1759, 114 L.Ed.2d 233, 255, 260, 261, 270, 23 May 1991; *Washington Post*, 24 May 1991, pp. A1, A18; *New York Times*, 24 May 1991, pp. A1, A18, 25 May 1991, p. A23, 26 May 1991, p. IV-1, 31 May 1991, p. A31, 25 June 1991, p. A23, 26 June 1991, p. A1. Also see Savage, *Turning Right*, pp. 383–388, 409–412; and Judges, *Hard Choices*, pp. 207–211.

121. *U.S. Army* v. *Watkins*, 111 Sup. Ct. 384, 5 November 1990; *Watkins* v. *U.S. Army*, 541 F. Supp. 249 (W.D. Wash.), 18 May 1982; *Watkins* v. *U.S. Army*, 551 F. Supp. 212 (W.D. Wash.), 5 October 1982; *Watkins* v. *U.S. Army*, 721 F.2d 687 (9th Cir.), 9 December 1983; *Watkins* v. *U.S. Army*, 837 F.2d 1428, 1453, 1457 (9th Cir.), 10 February 1988; *Watkins* v. *U.S. Army*, 847 F.2d 1329 and 847 F.2d 1362 (9th Cir.), 8 June 1988; *Watkins* v. *U.S. Army*, 875 F.2d 699 (9th Cir.), 3 May 1989.

   Ben-Shalom v. *Stone*, 494 U.S. 1004 (cert. denied), 26 February 1990; *Ben-Shalom* v. *Alexander*, 489 F. Supp. 964 (E.D. Wis.), 20 May 1980; *Ben-Shalom* v. *Secretary of the Army*, 826 F.2d 722 (7th Cir.), 18 August 1987; *Ben-Shalom* v. *Marsh*, 690 F. Supp. 774 (E.D. Wis.), 3 August 1988; *Ben-Shalom* v. *Marsh*, 703 F. Supp. 1372 (E.D. Wis.), 10 January 1989; *Ben-Shalom* v. *Marsh*, 881 F.2d 454 (7th Cir.), 7 August 1989.

   Concurring in the en banc ruling in *Watkins* on expressly constitutional grounds, Circuit Judge William A. Norris, acknowledging the influence of a recent article by University of Chicago law professor Cass Sunstein ("Sexual Orientation and the Constitution: A Note on the Relationship Between Due Process and Equal Protection," *University of Chicago Law Review* 55 [Fall 1988]: 1161–1179), commented with regard to *Bowers* that "It is perfectly consistent to say that homosexual sodomy is not a practice so deeply-rooted in our traditions as to merit due process protection, and at the same time to say, for example, that because homosexuals have historically been subject to invidious discrimination, laws which burden homosexuals as a class should be subjected to heightened scrutiny under the equal protection clause. Indeed, the two propositions may be complementary: In all probability, homosexuality is not considered a deeply-rooted part of our traditions *precisely because* homosexuals have historically been subjected to invidious discrimination." 875 F.2d at 719. Circuit Judge Harlington Wood, however, writing on behalf of the *Ben-Shalom* panel, cited *Bowers* in explicitly rejecting Norris's contention: "If homosexual conduct may constitutionally be criminalized, then homosexuals do not constitute a suspect or quasi-suspect class entitled to greater than rational basis scrutiny for equal protection purposes." 881 F.2d at 464.

   On Perry Watkins, also see *Army Times*, 1 December 1971, p. 58; *Newsweek*, 22 February 1988, p. 55; *The New Republic*, 7 March 1988, p. 9; *New York Times*, 4 May 1989, pp. A1, A22, 6 November 1990, p. A16, 31 January 1991, p. C19; and Humphrey, *My Country, My Right to Serve*, pp. 248–257.

   On Miriam Ben-Shalom, also see 807 F.2d 982 (Fed. Cir.), 1986; *New York Times*, 10 August 1989, p. A14, 27 February 1990, pp. A1, A18; and Humphrey, *My Country*, pp. 187–193.

   Also see generally Rodrick W. Lewis, *Nebraska Law Review* 68 (1989): 851–866; *New York Times*, 25 October 1989, p. A24, 21 December 1990, p. B6; John C. Hayes, "The Tradition of Prejudice Versus the Principle of Equality: Homosexuals and Heightened Equal Protection Scrutiny After *Bowers* v. *Hardwick*," *Boston College Law Review* 31 (March 1990): 375–475; Arthur Leonard, The Nation, 2 July 1990, pp. 12–15; *Steffan* v. *Cheney*, 780 F. Supp. 1 (D.D.C.), 9 December 1991; and Thomas B. Stoddard, "Lesbian and Gay Rights Litigation Before A Hostile Federal Judiciary: Extracting Benefit From Peril," *Harvard Civil Rights–Civil Liberties Law Review* 27 (Summer 1992): 555–573.

122. *Parrillo* v. *Parrillo*, 554 A.2d 1043 (R.I. Sup. Ct.), 7 March 1989; *New York Times*, 12 March 1989, p. 27; *Boston Globe*, 10 May 1989, pp. 49, 53; *Parrillo* v. *Parrillo*, 493 U.S. 954 (cert. denied), 6 November 1989; *Schochet* v. *State*, 541 A.2d 183, 188–89, 194–95, 197 (Md. Ct. Spec. App.), 19 May 1988; Mark Cohen, *Baltimore* Magazine, September 1989, pp. 9–10; *Washington Post*, 28 April 1990, pp. B1, B3; *Schochet* v. *State*, 580 A.2d 176, 183 (Md. Ct. App.), 9 October 1990.

123. *State* v. *Morales*, 826 S.W.2d 201, 204 (Tex. Ct. App.), 11 March 1992; 35 Tex. Sup. Ct. J. 1117; *Commonwealth* v. *Wasson*, 842 S.W.2d 487, 491, 502, 512, 514, 518 (Ky. Sup. Ct.), 24

September 1992; *New York Times*, 25 September 1992, p. A13. See also *Commonwealth* v. *Wasson*, 785 S.W.2d 67 (Ky. Ct. App.), 1990; *Harvard Law Review* 106 (April 1993): 1370–1375; Shirley A. Wiegand and Sara Farr, "Part of the Moving Stream: State Constitutional Law, Sodomy, and Beyond," *Kentucky Law Journal* 81 (1993): 449–482; note as well Thomas P. Lewis, "*Commonwealth* v. *Wasson*: Invalidating Kentucky's Sodomy Statute," and John C. Roach, "Rule of Men," *Kentucky Law Journal* 81 (1993): 423–448 and 483–510.

124. *New York Times*, 21 January 1991, p. A18, 23 January 1991, p. A16, 17 February 1991, p. 28, 26 February 1991, p. A21,15 May 1991, p. A22, 5 June 1991, p. A18, 6 June 1991, p. A21, 15 June 1991, p. 9, 19 June 1991, p. A1, 20 June 1991, pp. A1, A18, 21 June 1991, p. A11, 30 July 1991, p. A16, 3 August 1991, p. 8, 4 August 1991, p. 20, 6 August 1991, p. A14, 7 August 1991, p. A10, 8 August 1991, p. A16, 9 August 1991, p. A1, 10 August 1991, p. 6, 11 August 1991, p. 16, 12 August 1991, p. A1, 13 August 1991, p. A13, 14 August 1991, p. A16, 18 August 1991, p. 23, 20 August 1991, p. A20, 21 August 1991, p. A20, 22 August 1991, p. A22, 25 August 1991, p. 26, 26 August 1991, p. A14, 27 August 1991, p. A17, 28 August 1991, p. A14, 30 August 1991, p. A19, 31 August 1991, p. 10, 8 September 1991, p. 18; Marshall Docket Sheet (#90–985), Marshall Box 562; Kennedy, "Memorandum to the Conference," 19 February 1991, Marshall Box 524; *Bray* v. *Alexandria Women's Health Clinic*, 111 Sup. Ct. 1070, 25 February 1991.

For the lower court decisions in *Bray*, see *National Organization for Women* v. *Operation Rescue*, 726 F. Supp. 1483 (E.D. Va.), 1989, and *National Organization of Women* v. *Operation Rescue*, 914 F.2d 582 (4th Cir.), 1990. On Louisiana, also see Ruth Colker, "Reflections on Abortion: A Roll of the Dice in Louisiana," *SMU Law Review* 46 (Summer 1992): 47–55.

Also generally see Jeff Rosen, *The New Republic*, 1 July 1991, pp. 19–20; Ronald Dworkin, *New York Review of Books*, 18 July 1991, pp. 23–28; *The New Republic*, 7 October 1991, pp. 7–8; and Susan Faludi, *Backlash* (New York: Crown Publishers, 1991), pp. 400–402.

125. *New York Times*, 28 June 1991, p. A1, 2 July 1991, p. A1, 3 July 1991, p. A1, 11 September 1991, p. A1, 12 September 1991, p. A1, 14 September 1991, p. 7, 20 September 1991, p. A17, 16 October 1991, p. A1; *Washington Post*, 4 July 1991, p. A12. The object of Thomas's praise was Lewis E. Lehrman. See Lehrman, "The Right to Life and the Restoration of the American Republic," *National Review*, 29 August 1986, pp. 25–28, and Lehrman, "Natural Right and the Right to Life," *American Spectator*, April 1987, pp. 21–23.

126. *New York Times*, 17 October 1991, pp. A1, A20, 22 October 1991, p. A1, 8 November 1991, p. A1, 22 November 1991, p. A16, 10 December 1991, p. A29, 13 December 1991, p. B12, 18 December 1991, p. A28, 29 December 1991, p. 17, 22 January 1992, pp. A1, A17, 23 January 1992, pp. A1, A18, 24 January 1992, p. A12, 5 March 1992, p. A16, 6 April 1992, pp. A1, B8, 7 April 1992, p. A25, 17 April 1992, p. A13; *Planned Parenthood* v. *Casey*, 947 F.2d 682 (3d Cir.), 21 October 1991; *Washington Post*, 15 December 1991, p. A14, 22 January 1992, pp. A1, A4, 26 January 1992, pp. A8, A9, 31 March 1992, p. A15, 6 April 1992, pp. A1, A20, 7 April 1992, p. A22, 17 April 1992, pp. A1, A10; *Planned Parenthood* v. *Casey*, 112 Sup. Ct. 931, 21 January 1992, 112 Sup. Ct. 1554, 30 March 1992; *Wall Street Journal*, 22 January 1992, p. A16, 15 April 1992, p. A22; *Guam Society of Obstetricians and Gynecologists* v. *Ada*, 962 F.2d 1366 (9th Cir.), 16 April 1992.

127. Transcript of Oral Argument, *Planned Parenthood of Southeastern Pennsylvania* v. *Casey*, 22 April 1992, pp. 1, 2, 3, 8, 14, 18; *New York Times*, 20 April 1992, pp. A1, B11, 23 April 1992, pp. A1, B10, B11, 24 April 1992, pp. A1, A17, B7, 27 April 1992, p. A14; *Washington Post*, 22 April 1992, pp. A1, A7, A19, 23 April 1992, pp. A1, A12, A13; *Newsweek*, 27 April 1992, pp. 44–47. Also see Leon Friedman, ed., *The Supreme Court Confronts Abortion* (New York: Farrar, Straus & Giroux, 1993), pp. 311–338.

128. *The New Republic*, 18 May 1992, p. 7; *Bray* v. *Alexandria Women's Health Clinic*, 112 Sup. Ct. 2935, 8 June 1992; *New York Times*, 9 June 1992, pp. A1, A21; *Washington Post*, 9 June 1992, pp. A1, A6.

Also see generally Mark Clements, "Should Abortion Remain Legal?," *Parade Magazine*, 17 May 1992, pp. 4–5; Katha Pollitt, *The Nation*, 25 May 1992, pp. 718–726; and *New York Times*, 19 June 1992, p. A16.

129. *Planned Parenthood of Southeastern Pennsylvania* v. *Casey*, 112 Sup. Ct. 2791, 120 L.Ed.2d 674,

693, 694, 695, 697, 698, 699, 701–02, 703, 704, 708–09, 710, 711–12, 714–15, 719–20, 721, 29 June 1992. Regarding the composition of the trio opinion in *Casey*, see especially David G. Savage, *Los Angeles Times*, 13 December 1992, p. A1, and Paul M. Barrett, *Wall Street Journal*, 2 February 1993, pp. A1, A6. Also note *Legal Times*, 6 July 1992, p. 21; Richard C. Reuben, *Los Angeles Daily Journal*, 21 August 1992, p. 1; Rowland Evans and Robert Novak, *New York Post*, 4 September 1992, p. 25; Linda Greenhouse, *New York Times*, 25 October 1992, pp. 1, 31; Richard C. Reuben, "Man in the Middle," and Terry Carter, "Crossing the Rubicon," *California Lawyer* 12 (October 1992): 35–40 and 103–104; and Terry Eastland, "The Tempting of Justice Kennedy," *American Spectator*, February 1993, pp. 32–37. The best present indications are that Justice Kennedy, after indicating at the April 24 *Casey* conference that he would join a Rehnquist majority to uphold the Pennsylvania regulations but not to void *Roe*, subsequently decided, following the circulation of a first draft of Rehnquist's ostensible majority opinion, that he would instead join with Souter and O'Connor in their separate statement. When the joint opinion was first distributed, Savage reports "Rehnquist and Scalia were stunned. So, too, was Blackmun." Carter, visiting with Kennedy the morning of *Casey*'s announcement, quotes the justice as wistfully observing that "Sometimes you don't know whether you're Caesar about to cross the Rubicon, or Captain Queeg cutting your own tow line," just a few moments before the decision was announced.

130. *Planned Parenthood of Southeastern Pennsylvania* v. *Casey*, 112 Sup. Ct. 2791, 120 L.Ed.2d 674, 758, 763, 764, 765, 772, 773, 29 June 1992.

131. *Planned Parenthood of Southeastern Pennsylvania* v. *Casey*, 112 Sup. Ct. 2791, 120 L.Ed.2d 674, 782, 785, 786, 787, 788–89, 790, 792, 797, 29 June 1992.

132. *Planned Parenthood of Southeastern Pennsylvania* v. *Casey*, 112 Sup. Ct. 2791, 120 L.Ed.2d 674, 738, 744, 746, 747, 748, 756, 758, 29 June 1992.

133. *New York Times*, 30 June 1992, pp. A1, A15–A18, A22, 1 July 1992, pp. A1, A12, A17, 3 July 1992, pp. A1, A16; *Washington Post*, 30 June 1992, pp. A1, A9–A10, A18; *Wall Street Journal*, 30 June 1992, pp. A1, A4; Dworkin, "The Center Holds!," *New York Review of Books*, 13 August 1992, pp. 29–33; Bork, *New York Times*, 8 July 1992, p. A19; *The New Republic*, 27 July 1992, p. 7.

Also see Garrow, "A Landmark Decision," *Dissent* 39 (Fall 1992): 427–429; Anita L. Allen, "Autonomy's Magic Wand: Abortion and Constitutional Interpretation," *Boston University Law Review* 72 (September 1992): 683–698; Center for Reproductive Law and Policy, *An Analysis of Planned Parenthood* v. *Casey*, November 1992, 12pp.; Wendy K. Mariner, "The Supreme Court, Abortion, and the Jurisprudence of Class," *American Journal of Public Health* 82 (November 1992): 1556–62; Kathleen M. Sullivan, "Foreword: The Justices of Rules and Standards," *Harvard Law Review* 106 (November 1992): 24–123, at 27–34; *Harvard Law Review* 106 (November 1992): 201–210; Charles Krauthammer, *Washington Post*, 4 December 1992, p. A31; Sylvia A. Law, "Abortion Compromise: Inevitable and Impossible," *University of Illinois Law Review* 1992: 921–941, at 926–932; Earl M. Maltz, "Abortion, Precedent, and the Constitution," *Notre Dame Law Review* 68 (1992): 11–32; Teresa L. Scott, "Burying the Dead: The Case Against Reviving Pre-*Roe* and Pre-*Casey* Abortion Statutes in a Post-*Casey* World," *New York University Review of Law and Social Change* 19 (1992): 355–389; David Capper, "Judging the United States Supreme Court: An Outsider's View of the Right of Privacy," *University of Detroit Mercy Law Review* 69 (1992): 545–579, at 562–565; Michael J. Gerhardt, "The Pressure of Precedent: A Critique of the Conservative Approaches to *Stare Decisis* in Abortion Cases," *Constitutional Commentary* 10 (Winter 1993): 67–86; Martha A. Field, "Abortion Law Today," *Journal of Legal Medicine* 14 (March 1993): 3–24; Janet Benshoof, "Planned Parenthood v. Casey," *Journal of the American Medical Association* 269 (5 May 1993): 2249–2257; Ronald Dworkin, *Life's Dominion* (New York: Alfred A. Knopf, 1993), p. 169; and Judges, *Hard Choices*, pp. 224–252.

134. *Ada* v. *Guam Society of Obstetricians and Gynecologists*, 113 Sup. Ct. 633, 30 November 1992; *New York Times*, 1 December 1992, pp. A1, A22; *Washington Post*, 1 December 1992, pp. A1, A9; *Wall Street Journal*, 1 December 1992, p. A2. Also note *Jane L.* v. *Bangerter*, 809 F. Supp. 865 (D. Utah), 17 December 1992.

135. *Barnes* v. *Moore*, 113 Sup. Ct. 656, 7 December 1992, denying certiorari to 970 F.2d 12 (5th Cir.), 17 August 1992; *New York Times*, 13 October 1992, p. A14, 8 December 1992, p. A22; *Washington Post*, 8 December 1992, pp. A1, A15. Also see *Barnes* v. *Mississippi*, 992 F.2d 1335 (5th Cir.), 26 May 1993 (upholding a parental consent law), cert. denied, 510 U.S. 976, 15 November 1993, and *New York Times*, 30 May 1993, p. 28.

136. *Edwards* v. *Sojourner T.*, 113 Sup. Ct. 1414, 8 March 1993, denying certiorari to *Sojourner T.* v. *Edwards*, 974 F.2d 27 (5th Cir.), 22 September 1992; *New York Times*, 23 September 1992, p. A25, 23 December 1992, p. B6, 9 March 1993, p. A13; *Washington Post*, 9 March 1993, p. A8; *Fargo Women's Health Organization* v. *Sinner*, 819 F. Supp. 862 (D.N.D.), 19 February 1993; *Fargo Women's Health Organization* v. *Schafer*, 819 F. Supp. 865 (D.N.D.), 9 March 1993; *Fargo Women's Health Organization* v. *Schafer*, 113 Sup. Ct. 1668, 2 April 1993; *New York Times*, 3 April 1993, p. 8. Justice O'Connor, in a brief comment in the *Fargo* case joined only by Justice Souter, reiterated that "a law restricting abortions constitutes an undue burden, and hence is invalid, if, 'in a large fraction of the cases in which [the law] is relevant, it will operate as a substantial obstacle to a woman's choice to undergo an abortion.'"

137. *Bray* v. *Alexandria Women's Health Clinic*, 113 Sup. Ct. 753, 122 L.Ed. 34, 94, 101, 13 January 1993; *New York Times*, 7 October 1992, p. A14, 13 January 1993, p. A21, 14 January 1993, pp. A1, D24–D25; *Washington Post*, 7 October 1992, p. A14, 14 January 1993, pp. A1, A10. Also see *NOW* v. *Scheidler*, 968 F.2d 612 (7th Cir.), 29 June 1992, cert. granted, 113 Sup. Ct. 2958, 14 June 1993; see as well *New York Times*, 20 January 1993, p. A16, 15 June 1993, p. A22; and *Washington University Law Quarterly* 71 (Spring 1993): 175–187.

138. *New York Times*, 23 January 1993, pp. 1, 10, 6 March 1993, p. 6, 11 March 1993, pp. A1, B10, 12 March 1993, pp. A1, A17, A28–A29, 13 March 1993, p. 6, 14 March 1993, p. 24, 19 March 1993, p. A12, 30 March 1993, p. A21, 20 August 1993, p. A12, 21 August 1993, p. 5, 22 August 1993, p. 29, 24 August 1993, p. A10, 28 August 1993, pp., 1, 8, 29 August 1993, p. 24, 5 September 1993, p. 31; *Washington Post*, 23 January 1993, pp. A1, A9, 11 March 1993, pp. A1, A4, 12 March 1993, pp. A1, A4, 13 March 1993, pp. A20, A21, B1, B5, 15 March 1993, p. A11, 8 April 1993, pp. A1, A16, A17; 24 August 1993, p. A4, 5 September 1993, p. A31, *Dallas Morning News*, 13 March 1993, pp. A29, A32, A33, 19 March 1993, pp. A29, A33, 20 March 1993, pp. A33, A34, 25 March 1993, pp. A31, A36, 7 July 1993, pp. A1, A25; *Newsday*, 25 March 1993, p. 95; Karen Houppert, "John Burt's Holy War," *Village Voice*, 6 April 1993, pp. 27–31. With some understatement, Price added that "I have never been treated this way by supporters of abortion." On the earlier Pensacola terrorism, see Blanchard and Prewitt, *Religious Violence and Abortion*, passim.

EPILOGUE

1. This author first voiced this interpretation in the immediate aftermath of the Lowney and Nichols murders. See Garrow, "A Deadly, Dying Fringe," *New York Times,* 6 January 1995, p. A27. Also see *New York Times,* 12 September 1993, p. 31, and 30 September 1993, p. A16.

General 1993 and later treatments of the abortion issue whose particular contributions are not otherwise specifically noted below include Jane B. Wishner, ed., *Abortion and the States: Political Change and Future Regulation* (Chicago: American Bar Association, 1993) [a volume whose contributions were already well dated by the time of its publication]; Malcolm L. Goggin, ed., *Understanding the New Politics of Abortion* (Newbury Park, CA: Sage Publications, 1993); Ruth Colker, *Pregnant Men: Practice, Theory, and the Law* (Bloomington: Indiana University Press, 1994); Neal Devins, ed., *Federal Abortion Politics: A Documentary History,* 3 vols. (New York: Garland Publishing, 1995); Ian Shapiro, ed., *Abortion: The Supreme Court Decisions* (Indianapolis: Hackett Publishing Co., 1995); Barbara M. Yarnold, *Abortion Politics in the Federal Courts* (Westport, CT: Praeger, 1995) [a slim volume whose content actually predates the 1992 *Casey* decision]; Jenni Parrish, ed., *Abortion Law in the*

United States, 3 vols. (New York: Garland Publishing, 1995) [an unremarkable collection of reprints]; Karen O'Connor, *No Neutral Ground? Abortion Politics in an Age of Absolutes* (Boulder, CO: Westview Press, 1996); Marianne Githens and Dorothy M. Stetson, eds., *Abortion Politics* (New York: Routledge, 1996) [a mostly comparative volume]; Neal Devins, *Shaping Constitutional Values: Elected Government, the Supreme Court, and the Abortion Debate* (Baltimore: Johns Hopkins University Press, 1996); Mark A. Graber, *Rethinking Abortion: Equal Choice, the Constitution, and Reproductive Politics* (Princeton: Princeton University Press, 1996); Janet Hadley, *Abortion: Between Freedom and Necessity* (Philadelphia: Temple University Press, 1996); Eileen L. McDonagh, *Breaking the Abortion Deadlock: From Choice to Consent* (New York: Oxford University Press, 1996) [an original and highly provocative perspective that received much less attention than it might have]; Raymond Tatalovich, *The Politics of Abortion in the United States and Canada* (Armonk, NY: M. E. Sharpe, 1997); and Alison M. Jaggar, "Regendering the U.S. Abortion Debate," *Journal of Social Philosophy* 28 (Spring 1997): 127–140.

A small relatively modest number of post-1993 books and articles make substantive contributions to one or more chapters of the earlier history. With regard to the pre-*Griswold* era, Janet Farrell Brodie's *Contraception and Abortion in Nineteenth-Century America* (Ithaca: Cornell University Press, 1994) is an important work; valuable too, and previously uncited, is Simone M. Caron, "Race, Class, and Reproduction: The Evolution of Reproductive Policy in the United States, 1800–1989" (unpublished Ph.D. dissertation, Clark University, 1989). Also note Carole R. McCann, *Birth Control Politics in the United States, 1916–1945* (Ithaca: Cornell University Press, 1994) [neither Morris Ernst nor Dorothy Kenyon merit even a mention]; James W. Reed, "The Birth Control Movement Before *Roe v. Wade,*" *Journal of Policy History* 7 (1995): 22–52; and, autobiographically, Bill Baird, "The Politics of God, Government, and Sex: A Thirty-one-Year Crusade," *Saint Louis University Public Law Review* 13 (1993): 139–182. Also see Beth Bailey's excellent study of Lawrence, Kansas: "Prescribing the Pill: Politics, Culture, and the Sexual Revolution in America's Heartland," *Journal of Social History* 30 (Summer 1997): 827–856. Doctrinal treatments of *Griswold*-related privacy and liberty themes are Sheldon Gelman, "'Life' and 'Liberty': Their Original Meaning, Historical Antecedents, and Current Significance in the Debate Over Abortion Rights," *Minnesota Law Review* 78 (February 1994): 585–698; Jeffrey L. Johnson, "Constitutional Privacy," *Law and Philosophy* 13 (May 1994): 161–193; David Helscher, "*Griswold v. Connecticut* and the Unenumerated Right of Privacy," *Northern Illinois University Law Review* 15 (Fall 1994): 33–61; and William C. Heffernan, "Privacy Rights," *Suffolk University Law Review* 29 (Fall 1995): 737–808. Less valuable are Patricia Boling, "Privacy as Autonomy vs. Privacy as Familial Attachment," *Policy Studies Review* 13 (Spring-Summer 1994): 91–100; and Judith Wagner DeCew, *In Pursuit of Privacy* (Ithaca: Cornell University Press, 1997); also note the previously uncited William E. Coyle, "The Ninth Amendment and The Right to Privacy: The *Griswold* Case" (unpublished Ph.D. dissertation, Florida State University, 1966).

Regarding the early abortion era, *Wolf v. Colorado,* 338 U.S. 25 (1949) is a well-known citation for its holding "incorporating" the Fourth Amendment's prohibition of unreasonable searches or seizures against state governments; previously uncited is the fact that the two defendants, Julius A. Wolf and A. H. Montgomery, had been sentenced to twelve to eighteen months imprisonment for conspiracy to commit abortion: *Wolf v. People,* 187 P.2d 926 and 928 (Col.S.Ct.), 3 and 24 November 1947. Also to be noted, concerning *Liberty and Sexuality*'s discussion of the American Law Institute's 1959 consideration of abortion law reform (pp. 277 and 829 n.18 above), are the *Proceedings of the 36th Annual Meeting* (Philadelphia: American Law Institute, 1960), pp. 252–282.

The most notable post-1993 book concerning the pre-*Roe* era is Leslie J. Reagan's excellent *When Abortion Was a Crime: Women, Medicine, and the Law in the United States, 1867–1973* (Berkeley: University of California Press, 1997) [reviewed by this author in the *Journal of American History,* December 1997, pp. 1091–1092]. Also see Reagan's "Linking Midwives and Abortion in the Progressive Era," *Bulletin of the History of Medicine* 69 (Winter 1995): 569–598, and Rickie Solinger, "Extreme Danger: Women Abortionists and

Their Clients Before *Roe* v. *Wade,*" in Joanne Meyerowitz, ed., *Not June Cleaver: Women and Gender in Postwar America, 1945–1960* (Philadelphia: Temple University Press, 1994), pp. 335–357. Highly disappointing is Solinger's *The Abortionist: A Woman Against the Law* (New York: Free Press, 1994), concerning Portland's Ruth Barnett Bush; see Regina Morantz Sanchez's evaluation in the *New York Times Book Review,* 6 November 1994, p. 29. Leslie Reagan's work underscores how many mainstream physicians quietly provided illegal abortions to needy women; it also conclusively disproves the claim voiced by antiabortion activist Clarke D. Forsythe that "abortion laws can be successfully enforced, and abortion can be contained." See Forsythe, "The Effective Enforcement of Abortion Law Before *Roe* v. *Wade,*" in Brad Stetson, ed., *The Silent Subject: Reflections on the Unborn in American Culture* (Westport, CT: Praeger, 1996), pp. 179–227, at 206. Also simply note Kathryn Ann Farr, "Shaping Policy Through Litigation: Abortion Law in the United States," *Crime & Delinquency* 39 (April 1993): 167–183, and Mark A. Graber, "The Ghost of Abortion Past: Pre-*Roe* Abortion Law in Action," *Virginia Journal of Social Policy and the Law* 1 (Spring 1994): 309–381. Rosemary A. Nossiff, "Abortion Policy in New York and Pennsylvania, 1965–1972" (unpublished Ph.D. dissertation, Cornell University, 1994), is enriched by interviews with a number of New York political participants. Poorly informed in the extreme is Christopher Z. Mooney and Mei-Hsien Lee, "Legislating Morality in the American States: The Case of Pre-*Roe* Abortion Regulation Reform," *American Journal of Political Science* 38 (August 1995): 599–627. Forthcoming work by Gene Burns promises to be of vastly superior quality and will also address Mississippi's 1966 addition of a rape exception, noted above here at p. 852 n.50; see also *Jackson Clarion-Ledger,* 10 March 1966, pp. A1, A16, and 19 May 1966, p. A18.

Two previously uncited films, Dorothy Fadiman, *When Abortion Was Illegal: Untold Stories* (Santa Monica: Direct Cinema, 1992), and Daniel Friedman and Sharon Grimberg, *Back Alley Detroit: Abortion Before Roe v. Wade* (New York: Filmakers Library, 1992), offer brief portraits of the earlier era. Also note Fadiman's two subsequent sequels, *From Danger to Dignity: The Fight for Safe Abortion* (Menlo Park: Concentric Media, 1995) and *The Fragile Promise of Choice: Abortion in the United States Today* (Menlo Park: Concentric Media, 1996). Carole Joffe's invaluable *Doctors of Conscience: The Struggle to Provide Abortion Before and After Roe v. Wade* (Boston: Beacon Press, 1995) would be even more valuable were not most of the physician's identities—excepting Jane Hodgson—masked by pseudonyms. Knowledgeable readers will recognize "David Bennett" (pp. 86–95) as Curtis Boyd; see Curtis Boyd, "The Morality of Abortion: The Making of a Feminist Physician," *Saint Louis University Public Law Review* 13 (1993): 303–314. Also see Joffe, "The Unending Struggle for Legal Abortion: Conversations With Jane Hodgson," *Journal of the American Medical Women's Association* 49 (September-October 1994): 160–163, and Hodgson's own wonderfully autobiographical "The Twentieth-Century Gender Battle," in Rickie Solinger, ed., *Abortion Wars* (Berkeley: University of California Press, 1998), pp. 290–306. Chicago's unique abortion organization is detailed in Charles R. King, "Calling Jane: The Life and Death of a Women's Illegal Abortion Service," *Women & Health* 20 (1993): 75–93, and in Laura Kaplan, *The Story of Jane: The Legendary Underground Feminist Abortion Service* (New York: Pantheon Books, 1996), which unfortunately suffers badly both from the use of pseudonyms and the absence of any footnotes.

Lawrence Lader adds some further autobiographical reflections in *A Private Matter: RU486 and the Abortion Crisis* (Amherst, NY: Prometheus Books, 1995), as does Bernard Nathanson in *The Hand of God* (Washington, D.C.: Regnery Publishing, 1996). When the hardback edition of this book appeared, Roy Lucas told me, "I'm horrified at myself when I relive and rethink some of my abusive behavior toward Sarah [Weddington] and Margie [Hames]. I think I got really, really carried away over the fear of losing that hospitalization requirement issue [in *Doe* v. *Bolton*] that they were so totally disinterested in and seemingly unprepared on and I guess in retrospect looking back on it I sure should have had an awful lot more tact back in those days." Lucas to Garrow, 8 January 1994. Also see Rhett Lucas, "New Painting Surfaces for a New Age," *American Artist,* February 1995, pp. 52–55. Useful commentary on the female attorneys who litigated *Abele* v. *Markle* appears in Amy Kesselman's essay, "Women versus Connecticut," in Rickie Solinger, ed., *Abortion Wars* (Berkeley: University of California Press, 1998), pp. 42–67.

Regarding events inside the Supreme Court, note John C. Jeffries, Jr.'s *Justice Lewis F. Powell, Jr.* (New York: Charles Scribner's Sons, 1994) [stating at p. 341 that Powell "later said privately that the abortion opinions were 'the worst opinions I ever joined'"], but not all particulars can be relied upon, e.g., the claim (p. 356) that the abortion issue "barely surfaced" during the 1972 presidential campaign. Jeffries's book contains a significant discussion of *Bowers* v. *Hardwick* (pp. 511–530), but likewise errs (pp. 520 and 527) in failing to note Hardwick's jailing, claiming, "He had not been punished at all."

Thurgood Marshall clerk Mark Tushnet, in a modest volume entitled *Abortion* (New York: Facts on File, 1996), addresses his authorship of Marshall's 12 December 1972 letter by saying (p. viii) that "Marshall, after learning that Justices William Brennan and Potter Stewart had been expressing some concern about Justice Harry Blackmun's proposed opinion, decided to send Blackmun a letter saying that he agreed with what he understood to be their concerns." Tushnet adds (p. 71) that the letter "had been discussed with Justice Brennan's law clerks"; Tushnet also was questioned about the Marshall letter by Representative Henry Hyde in U.S. Congress, House of Representatives, Committee on the Judiciary, *Origins and Scope of Roe v. Wade—Hearings Before the Subcommittee on the Constitution,* 104th Cong., 2nd sess., 22 April 1996, pp. 119–120.

Byron White clerk Richard Hoffman, in an unprecedented interview with CNN for "*Roe* Versus *Wade* Plus 25," a 22 January 1998 broadcast, described a heated personal exchange between himself and the justice: "We were standing by his fireplace and standing right next to each other . . . and we went at it. I just felt . . . that it was a question of personal liberty of the woman . . . and he felt there was no constitutional warrant to do what the court was doing. . . . We were kind of screaming at each other."

Harry Blackmun OT 1971 clerk George Frampton, in an interview on that same CNN broadcast, attributed Warren Burger's vote in *Roe* to Blackmun's influence: "In the end, Justice Blackmun, who really worked on the chief justice to do this, ended up swaying the chief justice rather than vice versa, and it may be simply that the chief justice did not want to be on the wrong side of history."

Harry Blackmun clerk Randall P. Bezanson discusses his OT 1972 experience in "Self-Reliance," *North Dakota Law Review* 71 (1995): 29–40; also note Bezanson's "Emancipation as Freedom in *Roe* v. *Wade,*" *Dickinson Law Review* 97 (Spring 1993): 485–512, at 511 ("Freedom is what Justice Blackmun had in mind in *Roe*"). Last, with particular reference to William J. Brennan's role, see my own essay, "Reproductive Rights and Liberties: The Long Road to *Roe,*" in E. Joshua Rosenkranz and Bernard Schwartz, eds., *Reason and Passion: Justice Brennan's Enduring Influence* (New York: W. W. Norton & Co., 1997), pp. 105–116.

Two impressive books for younger readers make much of *Liberty and Sexuality*'s story available to secondary school students: Leonard A. Stevens, *The Case of Roe v. Wade* (New York: G. P. Putnam's Sons, 1996), and Nancy Tompkins, *Roe v. Wade* (Danbury, CT: Franklin Watts, 1996). Anyone tempted to make use of Peter Irons's *May It Please the Court: Arguments on Abortion* (New York: New Press, 1995) had best beware; see Edward Lazarus, "Electronic Hash," *Atlantic Monthly,* October 1994, pp. 36–41, and Lazarus, *Los Angeles Times Book Review,* 10 August 1997, p. 12.

Regarding post-*Roe* events, Jack E. Rossotti et al., "Nonlegal Advice: The Amicus Briefs and *Webster* v. *Reproductive Health Services,*" *Judicature* 81 (November–December 1997): 118–121, is helpful; Edward Lazarus's *Closed Chambers* (New York: Times Books, 1998), pp. 459–486, presents the most comprehensively suggestive history of *Casey.*

Concerning *Liberty and Sexuality* itself, out of some sixty-odd book reviews a number are worth noting because of the reviewers' own expertise: Kristin Luker, *New York Times Book Review,* 20 February 1994, pp. 7–8; Linda Gordon, *Los Angeles Times Book Review,* 27 February 1994, pp. 3, 13; Marian Faux, *Newsday,* 23 January 1994, pp. 35, 40; Suzanna

Sherry, *Washington Post Book World,* 13 February 1994, p. 4; Sheila Kuehl, *California Lawyer* (January 1994): 64–65; Anita L. Allen, *Christian Science Monitor,* 4 April 1994, p. 15; Jeffrey Rosen, *Atlantic Monthly,* May 1994, pp. 121–127; Kathleen M. Sullivan, *New Republic,* 23 May 1994, pp. 42–46; Simon Heller, *The Lancet,* 18 June 1994, pp. 1555–1556; Leslie F. Goldstein, *Constitution* (Spring 1994): 95–96; R. Alta Charo, *Family Planning Perspectives* (July-August 1994): 181–182; Gerald N. Rosenberg, *Contemporary Sociology* (September 1994): 656–658; Laura Kalman, *Reviews in American History* (December 1994): 725–731; Donald T. Critchlow, *Journal of American History* (March 1995): 1662–1663, Neal Devins, *Michigan Law Review* (May 1995): 1433–1459; Robin West, *Law and History Review* (Fall 1995): 433–437; Mark Tushnet, *Journal of Interdisciplinary History* (Autumn 1995): 356–357; and James C. Mohr, *Journal of Women's History* (Spring 1996): 172–184.

Reviews that fundamentally disagree with *Liberty and Sexuality'*s evaluation of *Griswold* and *Roe* range from the professional (James R. Kelly, *America,* 31 December 1994, pp. 26–27) to the hostile (Alan Freeman and Elizabeth Mensch, *Commonweal,* 21 October 1994, pp. 19–23) to the hilarious (Robert A. Destro, *Human Life Review* [Summer 1994]: 28–48). Also see Michael M. Uhlmann, *First Things* (August-September 1994): 52–55; Brennan Nierman, *Perspectives in Political Science* (Winter 1995): 43–44; and Robert J. McKeever, *Society* (September-October 1996): 81–83.

2. *National Organization for Women, Inc. v. Scheidler,* 510 U.S. 249, 262 (24 January 1994). Also see *NOW, Inc. v. Scheidler,* 25 F.3d 1053 (7th Cir.), 16 May 1994, cert. denied *sub nom. Scheidler v. Delaware Women's Health Organization,* 513 U.S. 1058, 12 December 1994; *NOW, Inc. v. Scheidler,* 897 F.Supp. 1047 (N.D. Ill.), 25 July 1995; *NOW, Inc. v. Scheidler,* 172 F.R.D. 351, 363 (N.D. Ill.), 31 March 1997; *New York Times,* 9 December 1993, p. A18, 25 January 1994, pp. A1, A17, 30 January 1994, p. IV-4, 13 December 1994, p. B11, 21 April 1998, pp. A1, A15; *Chicago Daily Law Bulletin,* 17 April 1997, p. 3; and *Chicago Tribune,* 21 April 1998, p. 1. Similarly note *Libertad v. Welch,* 53 F.3d 428 (1st Cir.), 28 April 1995, and Susan L. Ronn, "'FACE'-ing RICO: A Remedy for Antiabortion Violence?" *Seattle University Law Review* 18 (Winter 1995): 357–387.

3. *New York Times,* 21 February 1994, p. A10, 22 February 1994, p. A17, 28 February 1994, p. A13, 1 March 1994, p. A20, 2 March 1994, p. A13, 3 March 1994, p. A14, 4 March 1994, p. A20, 5 March 1994, p. 6, 6 March 1994, p. 20, and 7 March 1994, p. A15. Also see Craig Vetter, "Death at the Clinic Door," *Playboy,* July 1994, pp. 108ff.

4. *New York Times,* 26 March 1994, p. 7, 27 April 1994, p. A12, 18 June 1995, pp. 1, 18, 9 September 1995, p. 7; *Washington Post,* 26 April 1994, p. A6, 25 October 1994, p. A15, 1 April 1997, p. A4. Also see Peter Korn, "The Mysterious Violence of Shelley Shannon," *Self,* March 1997, pp. 98, 103–104, and James Risen and Judy Thomas, *Wrath of Angels: The American Abortion War* (New York: HarperCollins, 1998), chap. 14; note as well Barbara Radford and Gina Shaw, "Antiabortion Violence: Causes and Effects," *Women's Health Issues* 3 (Fall 1993): 144–151; and Susan G. Mezey et al., "Keeping Abortion Clinics Open," *Policy Studies Review* 13 (Spring-Summer 1994): 111–126.

5. *New York Times,* 16 September 1993, p. A18, 17 November 1993, p. A16, 19 November 1993, p. A16, 6 May 1994, p. A20, 13 May 1994, pp. A1, A22, 25 May 1994, p. B8, 26 May 1994, p. A20, 27 May 1994, p. A18, and 11 June 1994, pp. 1, 9. Also see Deborah R. McFarlane, "U.S. Abortion Policy Since *Roe v. Wade,*" *American Journal of Gynecologic Health* 7 (July-August 1993): 17–25. With regard to the interpretation of the 1871 statute at issue in *Bray,* also see *National Abortion Federation v. Operation Rescue,* 8 F.3d 680 (9th Cir.), 29 October 1993, and *New York Times,* 30 October 1993, p. 8.

6. *New York Times,* 29 September 1993, p. A19, 9 November 1993, p. A15, 25 December 1993, pp. 1, 10, 26 December 1993, p. 23, 28 December 1993, p. D18, 5 January 1994, pp. A1, A12, 7 January 1994, p. A16, 10 January 1994, p. A13, 19 January 1994, p. A12, 26 March 1994, p. 7, 1 April 1994, p. A20, 3 April 1994, p. 15, 7 May 1994, pp. 1, 10, 19 August 1994, p. A18, and 16 September 1994, p. A12; *Washington Post,* 19 October 1993, p. A4, and 25 December 1993, pp. A1, A7.

On the federal court litigation, see *Hern v. Beye,* 1994 WL 192366 (D. Col.), 12 May

1994, affirmed 57 F.3d 906 (10th Cir.), 8 June 1995, cert. denied *sub nom. Weil* v. *Hern,* 516
U.S. 1011, 4 December 1995; *Planned Parenthood Affiliates of Michigan* v. *Engler,* 860 F.Supp.
406 (W.D. Mich.), 18 July 1994, affirmed 73 F.3d 634 (6th Cir.), 16 January 1996; *Planned
Parenthood of Missoula* v. *Blouke,* 858 F.Supp. 137 (D. Mont.), 19 July 1994; *Little Rock Family
Planning Services* v. *Dalton,* 860 F.Supp. 609 (E.D. Ark.), 25 July 1994, affirmed 60 F.3d 497
(8th Cir.), 25 July 1995, judgment reversed in part, *Dalton* v. *Little Rock Family Planning Services,* 516 U.S. 474, 18 March 1996; *Orr* v. *Nelson,* 902 F.Supp. 1019 and 874 F.Supp. 998,
(D. Neb.), 4 November 1994 and 25 January 1995, affirmed 60 F.3d 497 (8th Cir.), 25 July
1995, cert. denied, 516 U.S. 1074, 16 January 1996; and *Hope Medical Group for Women* v.
Edwards, 860 F.Supp. 1149 (E.D. La.), 28 July 1994, application for stay denied, 512 U.S.
1301 (Scalia, Circuit Justice), 17 August 1994, affirmed 63 F.3d 418 (5th Cir.), 11 September 1995, cert. denied *sub nom. Foster* v. *Hope Medical Group for Women,* 517 U.S. 1104, 25
March 1996. Also see the subsequent similar rulings in *Elizabeth Blackwell Health Center for
Women* v. *Knoll,* 1994 WL 512365 (E.D. Pa.), 15 September 1994, affirmed, 61 F.3d 170
(3rd Cir.), 25 July 1995, cert. denied, 516 U.S. 1093, 22 January 1996, *Planned Parenthood* v.
Wright, 1994 WL 750638 (N.D. Ill.), 6 December 1994, *Stangler* v. *Shalala,* 1994 WL
764104 (W.D. Mo.), 28 December 1994, *Fargo Women's Health Organization* v. *Wessman,*
1995 WL 465830 (D. N.D.), 15 March 1995, and *Utah Women's Clinic* v. *Graham,* 892
F.Supp. 1379 (D. Ut.), 20 June 1995. Per *Dalton,* also note *Unborn Child Amendment Committee* v. *Ward,* 943 S.W.2d 591 (Ark.S.Ct.), 5 May 1997, *Knowlton* v. *Ward,* 889 S.W.2d 721
(Ark.S.Ct.), 5 December 1994, and *Unborn Child Amendment Committee* v. *Ward,* 883
S.W.2d 817 (Ark.S.Ct.), 3 October 1994.

Also see, for two state constitutionally based holdings prohibiting state authorities in
West Virginia and Minnesota from refusing to provide Medicaid funds for medically necessary abortions, *Women's Health Center of West Virginia* v. *Panepinto,* 446 S.E.2d 658
(W.Va.S.Ct.), 17 December 1993 [noted in *Washington Post,* 18 December 1993, p. A11],
and the even broader *Women of the State of Minnesota* v. *Gomez,* 542 N.W.2d 17, 31
(Minn.S.Ct.), 15 December 1995 ("the right of privacy under our constitution protects
not simply the right to an abortion, but rather it protects the woman's *decision* to abort; any
legislation infringing on the decision-making process, then, violates this fundamental
right"). Also note the Idaho outcome reported in *Roe* v. *Harris,* 917 P.2d 403 (Id.S.Ct.), 21
May 1996. For a contrary Michigan state constitutional holding, reversing an affirmative
trial court ruling, see *Mahaffey* v. *Attorney General,* 564 N.W.2d 104 (Mich.Ct.Apps.), 14
March 1997; for a contrary North Carolina holding, see *Rosie J.* v. *North Carolina Department of Human Resources,* 491 S.E.2d 535 (N.C.S.Ct.), 3 October 1997. Also see Linda M.
Vanzi, "Freedom at Home: State Constitutions and Medicaid Funding for Abortions," *New
Mexico Law Review* 26 (Summer 1996): 433–454.

7. On Blackmun's April 6 announcement, Breyer's May 13 nomination, and Breyer's
87–9 Senate approval on July 29, see *New York Times,* 7 April 1994, p. A1, 10 April 1994,
p. IV-3, 14 May 1994, p. 1, and 30 July 1994, p. 1. Also see Garrow, "Blackmun's Journey
Toward Feminism," *Boston Globe,* 10 April 1994, pp. 69, 72; Susie Blackmun, "*Roe* v. *Wade:*
Its Impact Upon the Author and His Family," *Conscience* 18 (Winter 1997–1998): 17–18;
and Tony Mauro's excellent profile, *USA Today,* 20 January 1998, p. A3. Breyer in his Senate
confirmation hearing testimony, U.S. Congress, Senate, Committee on the Judiciary, *Nomination of Stephen G. Breyer to be an Associate Justice of the Supreme Court of the United States
—Hearings,* 103rd Cong., 2nd sess., 12–15 July 1994, twice addressed *Roe* and *Casey*
(pp. 138 and 268–269); he also briefly commented on his involvement with *Griswold*
(pp. 200–201). On the *Casey* decision, also see my 1994 profile of David H. Souter, "Justice
Souter: A Surprising Kind of Conservative," *New York Times Magazine,* 25 September 1994,
pp. 36–43ff., and my essay "From *Brown* to *Casey:* The U.S. Supreme Court and the Burdens of History," in Austin Sarat, ed., *Race, Law, and Culture* (New York: Oxford University
Press, 1997), pp. 74–88, which also appears in Neal Devins and Davison M. Douglas, eds.,
Redefining Equality (New York: Oxford University Press, 1997), pp. 205–217.

On White's 1993 retirement and Ginsburg's nomination and 96-to-3 confirmation by the Senate, see *New York Times*, 20 March 1993, p. 1, 15 June 1993, p. A1, and 4 August 1993, p. A1. Ginsburg addressed *Roe* and/or *Casey* at five different junctures during her three days of Senate confirmation hearing testimony; see U.S. Congress, Senate, Committee on the Judiciary, *Nomination of Ruth Bader Ginsburg to be Associate Justice of the Supreme Court of the United States—Hearings*, 103rd Cong., 1st sess., 20–23 July 1993, pp. 148–150, 207–208, 242–244, 270–274, and 302. Concerning her earlier criticisms of Blackmun's opinions in *Roe* and *Doe*, also see Garrow, "History Lesson for the Judge: What Clinton's Supreme Court Nominee Doesn't Know About *Roe*," *Washington Post*, 20 June 1993, p. C3, and Rosemary Nossiff, "Why Justice Ginsburg Is Wrong About States Expanding Abortion Rights," *PS* 27 (June 1994): 227–231.

Also passing more permanently from the scene that summer was another major figure in *Roe* and *Doe*, Margie Pitts Hames, who died unexpectedly in Atlanta at age sixty. See *Atlanta Journal-Constitution*, 20 July 1994, p. A1, 21 July 1994, p. C6, 22 July 1994, p. A14, and *New York Times*, 22 July 1994, p. B18.

Worthwhile commentaries on the *Casey* decision that postdate the immediate surge of 1992–1993 responses include James Boyd White, *Acts of Hope* (Chicago: University of Chicago Press, 1994), pp. 153–183 ["this opinion enhances the dignity of the Court and the nation alike," p. 179]; Tom R. Tyler and Gregory Mitchell, "Legitimacy and the Empowerment of Discretionary Legal Authority: The United States Supreme Court and Abortion Rights," *Duke Law Journal* 43 (February 1994). 703–815; Alan Brownstein, "How Rights Are Infringed: The Role of Undue Burden Analysis in Constitutional Doctrine," *Hastings Law Journal* 45 (April 1994): 867–959; Patricia A. Sullivan and Steven R. Goldzwig, "A Relational Approach to Moral Decision-making: The Majority Opinion in *Planned Parenthood* v. *Casey*," *Quarterly Journal of Speech* 81 (May 1995): 167–190; Christina E. Wells, "Abortion Counseling as Vice Activity: The Free Speech Implications of *Rust* v. *Sullivan* and *Planned Parenthood* v. *Casey*," *Columbia Law Review* 95 (November 1995): 1724–1764; Sarah Stroud, "Dworkin and *Casey* on Abortion," *Philosophy & Public Affairs* 25 (Spring 1996): 140–170 (especially at pp. 166–169 concerning *Casey's* all-but-forgotten invocation of "purpose" as well as "effect" in establishing its undue burden/substantial obstacle test); and Robert D. Goldstein, "Reading *Casey*: Structuring the Woman's Decision-making Process," *William and Mary Bill of Rights Journal* 4 (Summer 1996): 787–880.

Also note Kathryn Kolbert and David H. Gans, "Responding to *Planned Parenthood* v. *Casey*: Establishing Neutrality Principles in State Constitutional Law," *Temple Law Review* 66 (Winter 1993): 1151–1170; Robin L. West, "The Nature of the Right to an Abortion," *Hastings Law Journal* 45 (April 1994): 961–967; Anita L. Allen, "The Proposed Equal Protection Fix for Abortion Law," *Harvard Journal of Law & Public Policy* 18 (Spring 1995): 419–455; and, from the other side of the street, Basile J. Uddo, "The Public Law of Abortion: A Constitutional and Statutory Review of the Present and Future Legal Landscape," in R. Randall Rainey and Gerard Magill, eds., *Abortion and Public Policy* (Omaha: Creighton University Press, 1996), pp. 163–182 (especially at p. 179: "we may have seen all that *Casey* will allow in those provisions of the Pennsylvania law upheld.")

Less notable are Gillian E. Metzger, "Unburdening the Undue Burden Standard: Orienting *Casey* in Constitutional Jurisprudence," *Columbia Law Review* 94 (October 1994): 2025–2089; Valerie J. Pacer, "Salvaging the Undue Burden Standard—Is It a Lost Cause?" *Washington University Law Quarterly* 73 (Spring 1995): 295–332; Erin Daly, "Reconsidering Abortion Law: Liberty, Equality, and the New Rhetoric of *Planned Parenthood* v. *Casey*," *American University Law Review* 45 (October 1995): 77–150; and John C. Ford, "The *Casey* Standard for Evaluating Facial Attacks on Abortion Statutes," *Michigan Law Review* 95 (March 1997): 1443–1471.

Of little if any utility are Sullivan and Goldzwig, "Abortion and Undue Burdens: Justice Sandra Day O'Connor and Judicial Decision-making," *Women & Politics* 16 (1996): 27–54, and Katherine E. Sheehan, "Toward a Jurisprudence of Doubt," *UCLA Women's Law Journal* 7 (Spring-Summer 1997): 201–262.

8. For the post–Supreme Court litigation, see *Planned Parenthood of Southeastern Pennsylvania* v. *Casey,* 978 F.2d 74 (3rd Cir.), 30 October 1992, on remand, 822 F.Supp. 227 (E.D. Pa.), 12 May 1993, reversed 14 F.3d 848, 861–62, 863 (3rd Cir.), 14 January 1994, application for stay denied, 510 U.S. 1309 (Souter, Circuit Justice), 7 February 1994. Also see *New York Times,* 15 January 1994, p. 22, 30 January 1994, p. 23, 8 February 1994, p. A10, 9 February 1994, p. A8, 17 February 1994, p. A18, 19 March 1994, p. 9, 22 March 1994, p. A12, 26 September 1994, p. A14; *Pittsburgh Post-Gazette,* 23 November 1994, p.A1, 24 May 1995 p. A1; and Secretary of the Commonwealth Yvette Kane's letter in the *Harrisburg Patriot,* 2 June 1995, p. A10; the in-person requirement was mandated on 23 May 1995. Also note Susan B. Hansen, "What Didn't Happen: The Implementation of the *Casey* Abortion Decision in Pennsylvania," *Comparative State Politics* 14 (1993): 9–18, and Kathryn Kolbert and Andrea Miller, "Government in the Examining Room: Restrictions on the Provision of Abortion," *Journal of the American Medical Women's Association* 49 (September–October 1994): 153–155. On the North Dakota statute, see *Fargo Women's Health Organization* v. *Schafer,* 18 F.3d 526 (8th Cir.), 10 February 1994, and *New York Times,* 11 February 1994, p. A11, and 15 March 1997, p. A21.

9. *New York Times,* 13 October 1993, p. A17, 18 February 1994, pp. A1, A18, 17 March 1994, p. A23, 23 March 1994, p. C12, 17 May 1994, pp. A1, A16, A18, 22 May 1994, p. IV-16, 23 May 1994, p. B6, and 2 June 1994, p. A21; *Washington Post,* 17 May 1994, p. A1. Also see more generally R. Alta Charo, "A Political History of RU-486," in Kathi E. Hanna, ed., *Biomedical Politics* (Washington, D.C.: National Academy Press, 1991), pp. 43–93; Mary Ann Castle and Francine M. Coeytaux, "RU 486 Beyond the Controversy: Implications for Health Care Practice," *Journal of the American Medical Women's Association* 49 (September–October 1994): 156–159, 164; and Beverly Winikoff, "Acceptability of First-Trimester Medical Abortion," in David T. Baird et al., eds., *Modern Methods of Inducing Abortion* (Oxford, U.K.: Blackwell Science, 1995), pp. 145–169. See as well John A. Robertson, *Children of Choice: Freedom and the New Reproductive Technologies* (Princeton: Princeton University Press, 1994), and Janet L. Dolgin, *Defining the Family: Law, Technology, and Reproduction in an Uneasy Age* (New York: New York University Press, 1997).

10. *Madsen* v. *Women's Health Center,* 512 U.S. 753, 776. The prior lower court rulings are *Operation Rescue* v. *Women's Health Center,* 626 So.2d 664 (Fla.S.Ct.), 28 October 1993, and the conflicting *Cheffer* v. *McGregor,* 6 F.3d 705 (11th Cir.), 20 October 1993. The subsequent rulings on remand are 644 So.2d 86 (Fla.S.Ct.), 20 October 1994, and 41 F.3d 1421, 1422 (11th Cir.), 14 December 1994. Also see *New York Times,* 22 January 1994, p. 6, 28 April 1994, pp. A1, A8, 29 April 1994, p. A7, and 1 July 1994, pp. A1, A17.

Other state court rulings from late 1993 and early 1994, prior to *Madsen,* that upheld similar antiobstruction injunctions and were also appealed to the High Court were *Kaplan* v. *Prolife Action League of Greensboro,* 431 S.E.2d 828 (N.C. Ct.Apps.), 20 July 1993, affirmed 436 S.E.2d 379 (N.C.S.Ct.), 7 October 1993, cert. denied *sub nom. Winfield* v. *Kaplan,* 512 U.S. 1253, 30 June 1994 (with Justices Scalia, Kennedy, and Thomas again dissenting); *Feminist Women's Health Center* v. *Blythe,* 22 Cal.Rptr.2d 184 (Cal.App. 3 Dist.), 19 August 1993, vacated and remanded (for further consideration in light of *Madsen*) *sub nom. Reali* v. *Feminist Women's Health Center,* 512 U.S. 1249, 30 June 1994, on remand, 39 Cal.Rptr.2d 189 (Cal.App. 3 Dist.), 8 March 1995, cert. denied, 516 U.S. 987, 27 November 1995; *Murray* v. *Lawson,* 642 A.2d 338 (N.J.S.Ct.), 6 April 1994, vacated and remanded (for further consideration in light of *Madsen*), 513 U.S. 802, 3 October 1994, modified on remand, 649 A.2d 1253 (N.J.S.Ct.), 1 December 1994, cert. denied, 515 U.S. 1110, 30 May 1995 (with Scalia concurring) [note also *New York Times,* 7 April 1994, p. B6, and 31 May 1995, p. B7]; *Planned Parenthood Shasta-Diablo* v. *Williams,* 851 P.2d 774 and 873 P.2d 1224 (Cal.S.Ct.), 13 May 1993 and 26 May 1994, vacated and remanded (for further consideration in light of *Madsen*), 513 U.S. 956, 31 October 1994, on remand, 898 P.2d 402 (Cal.S.Ct.), 31 July 1995, cert. denied, 117 S.Ct. 1285, 17 March 1997; and *Planned Parenthood League of Massachusetts* v. *Blake,* 631 N.E.2d 985 (Mass.S.J.Ct.), 11 April 1994, cert. denied, 513 U.S. 868, 3 October 1994. Also note the subsequent *Commonwealth*

v. *Blake,* 654 N.E.2d 64 (Mass.Apps.Ct.), 23 August 1995. See as well *State* v. *Loce,* 630 A.2d 792 (N.J.Super.Ct. App.Div.), 30 June 1993, review denied, 636 A.2d 520 (N.J.S.Ct.), 21 October 1993, cert. denied *sub nom. Love* v. *New Jersey,* 510 U.S. 1165, 28 February 1994, and *U.S.* v. *Terry,* 17 F.3d 575 (2nd Cir.), 25 February 1994 (affirming 815 F.Supp. 728, 10 March 1993), cert. denied, 513 U.S. 946, 17 October 1994 [note also *New York Times,* 27 February 1994, p. 39, and 18 October 1994, p. A23]. Subsequent U.S. Supreme Court denials of review involving *Madsen*-like questions are *Vittitow* v. *City of Upper Arlington,* 43 F.3d 1100 (6th Cir.), 12 January 1995 [reversing 830 F.Supp. 1077 (S.D. Ohio), 19 August 1993], cert. denied, 515 U.S. 1121, 5 June 1995 [noted in *New York Times,* 6 June 1995, p. A16], and *City of San Jose* v. *Superior Court,* 38 Cal.Rptr.2d 205 (Cal.App. 6 Dist.), 15 February 1995, cert. denied *sub nom. Thompson* v. *San Jose,* 516 U.S. 932, 16 October 1995.

Also see *Horizon Health Center* v. *Felicissimo,* 638 A.2d 1260 (N.J.S.Ct.), 6 April 1994, on remand, 659 A.2d 1387 (N.J.Super. Ct.App.Div.), 5 July 1995, cert. denied, 667 A.2d 191 (N.J.S.Ct.), 18 October 1995, *Robbinsdale Clinic* v. *Pro-Life Action Ministries,* 515 N.W.2d 88 (Minn.Ct.Apps.), 19 April 1994, *City of Missoula* v. *Asbury,* 873 P.2d 936 (Mon.S.Ct.), 27 April 1994, and *State* v. *Trewhella,* 520 N.W.2d 291 (Wis.Ct.Apps.), 7 June 1994, review denied, 524 N.W.2d 141 (Wis.S.Ct.), 26 August 1994. Also note *Women's Health Care Services* v. *Operation Rescue,* 24 F.3d 107 and 25 F.3d 1059 (10th Cir.), 11 May 1994, reversing and remanding U.S. District Judge Patrick F. Kelly's 1991 orders regarding protests in Wichita, Kansas, in light of the January 1993 Supreme Court ruling in *Bray.* See as well *U.S.* v. *Turner,* 44 F.3d 900 (10th Cir.), 24 January 1995, cert. denied, 515 U.S. 1104, 30 May 1995, rehearing denied, 515 U.S. 1178, 11 August 1995.

11. *New York Times,* 7 June 1994, p. A14, 17 June 1994, p. A20, 26 June 1994, p. 19, 4 July 1994, p. 9, 8 July 1994, p. A18, 9 July 1994, p. 10, 23 September 1994, p. A16. On the Milwaukee protests, also see Verlyn Klinkenborg, "Violent Certainties," *Harper's,* January 1995, pp. 37–52, *Hoover* v. *Wagner,* 47 F.3d 845 (7th Cir.), 2 February 1995, *State* v. *Baumann,* 532 N.W.2d 144 (Wis.Ct.Apps.), 28 February 1995, and *State* v. *Lescher,* 1995 Wis.App. Lexis 960, 8 August 1995. FACE's criminal provisions are codified at 18 U.S.C. 248(a) and (b).

Early cases affirming the constitutionality of FACE were *American Life League* v. *Reno,* 855 F.Supp. 137 (E.D.Va.), 16 June 1994, affirmed, 47 F.3d 642 (4th Cir.), cert. denied, 516 U.S. 809, 2 October 1995; *Council for Life Coalition* v. *Reno,* 856 F.Supp. 1422 (S.D.Cal.), 6 July 1994; *Cheffer* v. *Reno,* 1994 WL 644873 (M.D. Fla.), 26 July 1994, affirmed, 55 F.3d 1517 (11th Cir.); *Cook* v. *Reno,* 859 F.Supp. 1008 (W.D. La.), 5 August 1994, vacated and remanded, 74 F.3d 97 (5th Cir.), 6 February 1996; *Riely* v. *Reno,* 860 F.Supp. 693 (D. Ariz.), 12 August 1994; and *U.S.* v. *Brock,* 863 F.Supp. 851 (E.D. Wis.), 23 September 1994, affirmed *sub nom. U.S.* v. *Soderna,* 82 F.3d 1370 (7th Cir.), 30 April 1996, cert. denied *sub nom. Hatch* v. *U.S.,* 117 S.Ct. 507, 2 December 1996. Also see *Woodall* v. *Reno,* 47 F.3d 656 (4th Cir.), 13 February 1995, cert. denied, 515 U.S. 1141, 19 June 1995 [noted in *New York Times,* 20 June 1995, p. B7]; *U.S.* v. *Dinwiddie,* 885 F.Supp. 1286 (W.D.Mo.), 21 March 1995, 885 F.Supp. 1299 (W.D.Mo.), 12 April 1995, affirmed, 76 F.3d 913 (8th Cir.), 16 February 1996, cert. denied, 117 S.Ct. 613, 16 December 1996; *U.S.* v. *Lucero,* 895 F.Supp. 1419 and 141 (D. Kan.), 25 May 1995; *U.S.* v. *White,* 893 F.Supp. 1423 (C.D. Cal.), 23 June 1995; *U.S.* v. *Wilson,* 1994 WL 777319 (E.D.Wis.), 30 November 1994, 880 F.Supp. 621 (E.D.Wis.), 16 March 1995, reversed, 73 F.3d 675 (7th Cir.), 29 December 1995, cert. denied (also *sub nom. Skott, Ketchum, Balint,* and *Stambaugh* v. *U.S.*), 117 S.Ct. 46, 47, 7 October 1996.

An excellent law journal review of the cases is Kristine L. Sendek, "'FACE'-ing the Constitution: The Battle Over the Freedom of Access to Clinic Entrances Shifts from Reproductive Health Facilities to the Federal Courts," *Catholic University Law Review* 46 (Fall 1996): 165–241; also see Alan E. Brownstein, "Rules of Engagement for Cultural Wars: Regulating Conduct, Unprotected Speech, and Protected Expression in Anti-Abortion Protests," *U.C. Davis Law Review* 29 (Spring 1996): 553–638, and "Section II," 29 (Summer 1996): 1163–1216, Amy H. Nemko, "Saving FACE: Clinic Access Under A New Commerce Clause," *Yale Law Journal* 106 (November 1996): 525–530; and Arianne K. Tepper, "In Your F.A.C.E.: Federal Enforcement of the Freedom of Access to Clinic Entrances Act of 1994," *Pace Law Review* 17 (Spring 1997): 489–551.

12. *New York Times,* 30 July 1994, pp. 1, 26, 31 July 1994, p. 26, 1 August 1994, p. A10, 5 August 1994, p. A10, 6 August 1994, pp. 1, 6, 10 August 1994, p. A12, 18 August 1994, p. B11, 19 August 1994, p. A18; *St. Louis Post-Dispatch,* 31 July 1994, p. A1; Paul J. Hill, "Who Killed the Innocent—Michael Griffin or Dr. David Gunn," *Life Advocate,* August 1993, pp. 40–43; *Dallas Morning News,* 30 January 1994, p. A18, 9 February 1994, pp. A1, A14; *Washington Post,* 26 April 1994, p. A6; Tom Junod, "The Abortionist," *GQ,* February 1994, pp. 150–57, 190–92; Tom Bates, *Rocky Mountain News,* 28 November 1994, p. A28. On Hill, also see Craig Vetter, "The Christian Soldier," *Playboy,* December 1994, pp. 54ff.

13. Michael Bray, "Abortion and the Disarmed Church," unpublished paper, Evangelical Theological Society, 1993, pp. 1, 3; Bray, *A Time to Kill* (Portland, OR: Advocates for Life Publications, 1994), p. 172. Also note Cathy Ramey, *In Defense of Others: A Biblical Analysis and Apologetic on the Use of Force to Save Lives* (Portland, OR: Advocates for Life Publications, 1995) [32pp.]. On Bray, also see James Risen and Judy Thomas, *Wrath of Angels: The American Abortion War* (New York: HarperCollins, 1998), chap. 4, and James Moore, *Very Special Agents* (New York: Pocket Books, 1997), pp. 244–277; more generally also note Faye Ginsburg's two related essays, "Saving America's Souls: Operation Rescue's Crusade Against Abortion," in Martin E. Marty and R. Scott Appleby, eds., *Fundamentalisms and the State* (Chicago: University of Chicago Press, 1993), pp. 557–588, which reappears in updated form as "Rescuing the Nation" in Rickie Solinger, ed., *Abortion Wars* (Berkeley: University of California Press, 1998), pp. 227–250.

14. *New York Times,* 2 August 1994, p. A14, 4 August 1994, pp. A1, A14, 24 August 1994, p. 12, 26 August 1994, p. A22, 31 August 1994, p. B7; *Washington Post,* 13 August 1994, pp. A1, A10, 23 August 1994, p. B2; *Norfolk Virginian-Pilot,* 19 August 1994, p. A18; *National Law Journal,* 26 September 1994, p. A17; *ABA Journal* (December 1994): 26; Michael R. Hirsh, "Use of Force in Defense of Another: An Argument for Michael Griffin" (unpublished J.D./M.A. thesis, Regent University, 1993), pp. 7, 53. Also see Frederick Clarkson, *Eternal Hostility* (Monroe, ME: Common Courage Press, 1997), pp. 139–157.

15. *New York Times,* 13 August 1994, p. 6, 16 August 1994, p. A11, 18 September 1994, p. 44, 2 October 1994, p. 22, 3 October 1994, p. B11, 4 October 1994, p. A19, 5 October 1994, p. A18, 6 October 1994, p. A18, 7 October 1994, p. A24. *U.S. v. Hill,* 893 F.Supp. 1034, 1039, 1044, and 1048 (N.D. Fla.), 15, 16, and 28 September, and 7 October 1994, are four separate court rulings on preliminary matters relating to Hill's federal criminal trial.

16. *New York Times,* 25 October 1994, p. A19, 26 October 1994, p. A18, 1 November 1994, p. A24, 3 November 1994, pp. A1, A27, 4 November 1994, p. A20, 14 November 1994, p. A12, 7 December 1994, p. A16, 22 December 1994, p. B11, 10 March 1995, p. A14, 24 September 1995, p. IV-7; *Washington Post,* 2 November 1994, p. A7, 7 December 1994, pp. A1, A20, 21 December 1994, p. A2; "In Defense of Another: The Paul Hill Brief," *Regent University Law Review* 5 (Spring 1995): 31–82; Roger Parloff, *American Lawyer* (June 1995): 76ff.; *Washington Times,* 6 July 1995, p. A3, 2 June 1996, p. A1; *Ft. Lauderdale Sun-Sentinel,* 21 October 1995, p. A27; *Orlando Sentinel,* 1 June 1996, p. D1; *Hill v. State,* 656 So.2d 1271 and 688 So.2d 901 (Fla. S.Ct.), 22 June 1995 and 27 November 1996, cert. denied, 118 S. Ct. 265, 6 October 1997. Also see Charles E. Rice and John P. Tuskey, "The Legality and Morality of Using Deadly Force to Protect Unborn Children from Abortionists," *Regent University Law Review* 5 (Spring 1995): 83–151.

17. *New York Times,* 10 October 1994, pp. A1, B12, 20 October 1994, p. A21, 28 October 1994, p. A28, 20 November 1994, p. 43, 30 January 1995, pp. A1, A11, 1 March 1995, p. B7, 31 August 1995, pp. A1, B12; *Washington Post,* 19 October 1994, pp. A1, A9.

18. *Wyoming NARAL v. Karpan,* 881 P.2d 281 (Wy.S.Ct.), 7 September 1994; *Washington Post,* 31 October 1994, p. A13, 5 December 1994, pp. A1, A14, 7 May 1995, p. C3; *New York Times,* 10 November 1994, p. B7; *New Republic,* 5 December 1994, pp. 10–11. On

abortion's role in national partisan politics, see Alan I. Abramowitz, "It's Abortion, Stupid: Policy Voting in the 1992 Presidential Election," *Journal of Politics* 57 (February 1995): 176–186; Mary C. Segers, "The Pro-Choice Movement Post-*Casey*," in Segers and Timothy A. Byrnes, eds., *Abortion Politics in American States* (Armonk, NY: M. E. Sharpe, 1995), pp. 225–245; and Greg D. Adams, "Abortion: Evidence of an Issue Evolution," *American Journal of Political Science* 41 (July 1997): 718–737.

19. *New York Times,* 31 December 1994, pp. 1, 8, 9, 1 January 1995, pp. 1, 17, 26, 2 January 1995, pp. 1, 10, 3 January 1995, p. A12, 4 January 1995, p. A16, 5 January 1995, p. A16, 6 January 1995, p. A12, 7 January 1995, p. 7.

20. *New York Times,* 9 January 1995, pp. A1, A16, 10 January 1995, p. A12, 14 January 1995, p. 12, 15 January 1995, p. 16, 17 January 1995, p. A10, 21 January 1995, p. 7, 22 January 1995, p. 14, 23 January 1995, pp. B1, B4, 24 January 1995, p. A12, 28 January 1995, pp. 9, 18, 4 February 1995, p. 18, 11 May 1995, p. A18, 25 July 1995, p. A9, 24 August 1995, p. B14, 15 February 1996, p. A14, 4 March 1996, p. A10, 16 March 1996, p. 6, 19 March 1996, p. A12, 30 November 1996, p. 9, 4 December 1996, p. A17; *Washington Post,* 17 January 1995, pp. A1, A8, 3 May 1995, p. D3, 26 July 1995, p. A2, 27 July 1995, p. A3, 29 July 1995, p. A14, 6 February 1996, p. A8, 17 March 1996, p. A18, 19 March 1996, pp. A1, A8, 30 November 1996, p. A3; *Los Angeles Times,* 24 January 1996, p. A7; Washington Times, 2 June 1996, p. A1.

21. *State v. Russ,* 889 P.2d 161 (Mon.S.Ct.), 24 January 1995; *Washington Post,* 19 January 1995, p. A12; *New York Times,* 1 March 1995, p. B7, 3 March 1995, p. A16; *U.S.* v. *Lindgren,* 883 F.Supp. 1321 (D. N.D.), 1 May 1995; *Kirkeby* v. *Furness,* 52 F.3d 772 (8th Cir.), 20 April 1995, following remand, 92 F.3d 655 (8th Cir.), 8 August 1996; *Habiger* v. *City of Fargo,* 905 F.Supp. 709 (D. N.D.), 23 January 1995, affirmed, 80 F.3d 289 (8th Cir.), 4 April 1996, cert. denied, 117 S.Ct. 518, 2 December 1996; *Veneklase* v. *City of Fargo,* 904 F.Supp. 1038 (D. N.D.), 17 February 1995, reversed and remanded, 78 F.3d 1264 (8th Cir.), 6 March 1996, cert. denied, 117 S.Ct. 178, 7 October 1996. Also similarly see *Fischer* v. *City of St. Paul,* 894 F.Supp. 1318 (D. Minn.), 9 August 1995. For a brief but excellent treatment of Fargo's response to the protests, see Jon G. Lindgren [mayor of Fargo 1978–1994] and H. Elaine Lindgren [a FWHO clinic defense volunteer], "Social Change Within the 'Establishment': A City's Response to National Antiabortion Protesters," *Journal of Applied Behavioral Science* 31 (December 1995): 475–489.

Also see *National Organization for Women* v. *Operation Rescue,* 37 F.3d 646 (D.C. Cir.), 18 October 1994, on remand, 929 F.Supp. 461 (D. D.C.), 30 May 1996; *New York State NOW* v. *Terry,* 996 F.2d 1351 (2nd Cir.), 2 July 1993, vacated and remanded *sub nom. Pearson* v. *Planned Parenthood Margaret Sanger Clinic,* 512 U.S. 1249, 30 June 1994, 41 F.3d 794 (2nd Cir.), 2 December 1994, on remand, 952 F.Supp. 1033 (S.D. N.Y.), 17 January 1997; *Roe* v. *Operation Rescue,* 54 F.3d 133 (3rd Cir.), 18 April 1995, on remand, 1995 WL 464269 (E.D. Pa.), 31 July 1995; and *Commonwealth* v. *Filos,* 649 N.E.2d 1085 (Mass.S.J.Ct.), 16 May 1995.

22. *Legal Times,* 14 February 1994, p. 1; *Wall Street Journal,* 28 October 1994, p. B12; *U.S. News & World Report,* 14 November 1994, p. 67; *Washington Post,* 21 December 1994, p. B4; *Trial,* February 1995, pp. 12–13; *Front Lines Research* [PPFA], February 1995, pp. 10–11; Diane M. Gianelli, *American Medical News,* 6 February 1995, pp. 3, 22; *Time,* 13 March 1995, p. 65; *New York Times,* 9 April 1995, pp. 1, 30, 4 April 1996, p. B14, 24 September 1996, p. A18; *Louisville Courier-Journal,* 15 April 1995, p. A1, 11 December 1996, p. B5; *Texas Lawyer,* 22 April 1996, p. 1; *Pittsburgh Post-Gazette,* 14 January 1997, p. C4; *Memphis Commercial-Appeal,* 8 December 1996, p. B1. Also see Thomas R. Eller, "Informed Consent Civil Actions for Post-Abortion Psychological Trauma," *Notre Dame Law Review* 71 (1996): 639–670, and Thomas W. Strahan, "Negligent Physical or Emotional Injury Related to Induced Abortion," *Regent University Law Review* 9 (Fall 1997): 149–217.

More general post-1993 surveys of antiabortion activism are Dallas A. Blanchard, *The Anti-Abortion Movement and the Rise of the Religious Right* (New York: Twayne, 1994); James R. Kelly, "Seeking a Sociologically Correct Name for Abortion Opponents," in Ted G. Jelen and Marthe A. Chandler, eds., *Abortion Politics in the United States and Canada* (Westport, CT: Praeger, 1994), pp. 15–40; Carol J. C. Maxwell, "Meaning and Motivation in Pro-Life Direct Action" (unpublished Ph.D. dissertation, Washington University, 1994); Keith Cassidy, "The Right to Life Movement: Sources, Development, and Strategies," *Journal of Policy History* 7 (1995): 128–159; both Carol J. C. Maxwell's and Mary C. Segers's contributions to Ted G. Jelen, ed., *Perspectives on the Politics of Abortion* (Westport, CT: Praeger, 1995), pp. 1–20 and 87–130; J. Bryan Hehir, "The Church and Abortion in the 1990s: The Role of Institutional Leadership," in R. Randall Rainey and Gerard Magill, eds., *Abortion and Public Policy* (Omaha: Creighton University Press, 1996), pp. 203–228; and Dallas A. Blanchard, *The Anti-Abortion Movement: References and Resources* (New York: G. K. Hall & Co., 1996). On the important but little-noted role of the Arthur S. DeMoss Foundation, see Mark Johnson, *Richmond Times Dispatch*, 13 June 1994, p. A1.

23. *Memphis Commercial Appeal*, 12 April 1994, p. A11, 16 April 1994, p. A16, 30 June 1994, p. B2; 8 December 1996, p. B1; *New York Times*, 23 April 1994, p. 7, 24 April 1994, p. 25, 30 September 1994, p. A19, 23 November 1994, p. B6, 6 February 1995, p. A15, 9 April 1995, pp. 1, 30; *St. Petersburg Times*, 8 June 1996, pp. B1, B3; *Albany Times Union*, 29 September 1996, p. D1, 11 February 1998, p. B1; Crutcher, *Lime 5: Exploited By Choice* (Denton, TX: Life Dynamics, 1996), pp. 114–115, 192, 280; *Washington Times*, 19 April 1996, p. A2; *Omaha World Herald*, 26 January 1997, p. B3.

On Warren Hern, see especially Hern, "Life on the Front Lines," *Women's Health Issues* 4 (Spring 1994): 48–54, and Steve Jackson's lengthy and impressive profile in the weekly Denver newspaper *Westword*, 13 February 1997, as well as updates of 3 April 1997 and 15 May 1997. Also see Hern et al., "Outpatient Abortion for Fetal Anomaly and Fetal Death from 15–34 Menstrual Weeks' Gestation," *Obstetrics & Gynecology* 81 (February 1993): 301–306.

Also note the 1997 *murder* indictment of Dr. Bruce S. Steir, a California provider with a checkered career, following the death of abortion patient Sharon Hamptlon. *Riverside Press-Enterprise*, 19 December 1996, p. A1, 20 December 1996, p. A1, 23 October 1997, p. A1, 1 February 1998, p. A1, 4 February 1998, p. B1, 19 February 1998, p. B1.

24. *New York Times*, 12 September 1993, p. 31, 11 January 1995, p. C11, 15 February 1995, pp. A1, A14, 20 February 1995, pp. A1, B2, 14 October 1997, p. A17; Barbara R. Gottlieb, *New England Journal of Medicine* 332 (23 February 1995): 532–533; Diane Gianelli, *American Medical News*, 6 March 1995, p. 3; Dana Swartzberg, *JAMA* 274 (11 October 1995): 1107–1108; Mary Ann Castle et al., "Abortion Education for Residents," *Obstetrics & Gynecology* 87 (April 1996): 626–629; Delia M. Rios, *Oregonian*, 4 May 1997, p. A1; and Ellen S. Lazarus's very impressive "Politicizing Abortion: Personal Morality and Professional Responsibility of Residents Training in the United States," *Social Science and Medicine* 44 (May 1997): 1417–1425.

Also see Carolyn Westhoff et al., "Residency Training in Contraception, Sterilization, and Abortion," *Obstetrics & Gynecology* 81 (February 1993): 311–314; H. Trent McKay and Andrea P. McKay, "Abortion Training in Obstetrics and Gynecology Residency Programs," *Family Planning Perspectives* 27 (May-June 1995): 112–115; *New York Times Magazine*, 18 January 1998, pp. 20–27ff.; and *USA Today*, 22 January 1998, pp. D1, D2. On Medical Students for Choice, see Carole Joffe et al., "The Crisis in Abortion Provision and Pro-Choice Medical Activism in the 1990s," in Rickie Solinger, ed., *Abortion Wars* (Berkeley: University of California Press, 1998), pp. 320–333; on NARAL, also see *National Journal*, 5 March 1994, pp. 521–525.

25. *Boston Globe*, 1 November 1994, p. 1; Glenna Halvorson Boyd, "Surviving a Holy War: How Health Care Workers in U.S. Abortion Facilities Are Coping with Antiabortion Harassment" (unpublished Ph.D. dissertation, The Fielding Institute, 1990), p. 151; Diane Gianelli, *American Medical News*, 12 July 1993, pp. 3, 23, 25; Wendy Simonds, "At an Impasse: Inside an Abortion Clinic," *Current Research on Occupations and Professions* 6 (1991): 99–115, at 114.

Also see Simonds's equally excellent "Feminism on the Job: Confronting Opposition in

Abortion Work," in Myra Marx Ferree and Patricia Yancey Martin, eds., *Feminist Organizations* (Philadelphia: Temple University Press, 1995), pp. 248–260; and Simonds, *Abortion at Work: Ideology and Practice in a Feminist Clinic* (New Brunswick: Rutgers University Press, 1996). See as well Kathleen M. Roe, "Private Troubles and Public Issues: Providing Abortion Amid Competing Definitions," *Social Science and Medicine* 29 (1989): 1191–1198; Warren M. Hern, "Proxemics: The Application of Theory to Conflict Arising from Antiabortion Demonstrations," *Population and Environment* 12 (Summer 1991): 379–388; Patricia Lunneborg, *Abortion: A Positive Decision* (New York: Bergin & Garvey, 1992), pp. 177–194; Catherine Cozzarelli and Brenda Major's commendably frank "The Effects of Anti-Abortion Demonstrators and Pro-Choice Escorts on Women's Psychological Responses to Abortion," *Journal of Social and Clinical Psychology* 13 (1994): 404–427; and Mark Donald's profile of retiring clinic operator Charlotte Taft, *Dallas Observer,* 18–24 May 1995, pp. 21–30. Also simply note Suzanne T. Poppema, *Why I Am an Abortion Doctor* (Amherst, NY: Prometheus Books, 1996); Abigail Stewart and Sharon Gold-Steinberg, "Women's Abortion Experiences as Sources of Political Mobilization," in M. Brinton Lykes et al., eds., *Myths About the Powerless* (Philadelphia: Temple University Press, 1996), pp. 275–295; and Sumi Hoshiko, *Our Choices: Women's Personal Decisions About Abortion* (New York: Haworth Press, 1993).

26. *New York Times,* 16 June 1994, pp. A1, D23, 24 December 1994, p. 7, 18 December 1995, p. B6, 22 March 1996, p. A14, 5 December 1997, p. A10; *Washington Post,* 3 October 1995, p. H6; *Chicago Tribune,* 16 January 1996, p. 1; *Harrisburg Patriot,* 30 June 1997, p. 1; Robert W. Brown and R. Todd Jewell, "The Impact of Provider Availability on Abortion Demand," *Contemporary Economic Policy* 14 (April 1996): 95–106; Frances A. Althaus and Stanley K. Henshaw, "The Effects of Mandatory Delay Laws on Abortion Patients and Providers," *Family Planning Perspectives* 26 (September-October 1994): 228–233; and Theodore Joyce et al., "The Impact of Mississippi's Mandatory Delay Law on Abortions and Births," *JAMA* 278 (27 August 1997): 653–658.

Also see Deborah Haas-Wilson, "The Economic Impact of State Restrictions on Abortion," *Journal of Policy Analysis and Management* 12 (Summer 1993): 498–511; Stephan F. Gohmann and Robert L. Ohsfeldt, "Effects of Price and Availability on Abortion Demand," *Contemporary Policy Issues* 11 (October 1993): 42–55; Rebecca M. Blank et al., *State Abortion Rates: The Impact of Policies, Providers, Politics, Demographics and Economic Environment* (Cambridge, MA: National Bureau of Economic Research, Working Paper #4853, September 1994); Jon F. Merz et al., "A Review of Abortion Policy: Legality, Medicaid Funding, and Parental Involvement," *Women's Rights Law Reporter* 17 (Winter 1995): 1–61; Phillip B. Levine et al., *Roe v. Wade and American Fertility* (Cambridge, MA: National Bureau of Economic Research, Working Paper #5615, June 1996); Henshaw and Kathryn Kost, "Abortion Patients in 1994–1995: Characteristics and Contraceptive Use," *Family Planning Perspectives* 28 (July-August 1996): 140–147, 158; Kenneth J. Meier et al., "The Impact of State-Level Restrictions on Abortion," *Demography* 33 (August 1996): 307–312; and Patricia Gober, "The Role of Access in Explaining State Abortion Rates," *Social Science and Medicine* 44 (April 1997): 1003–1016.

27. Lisa Belkin, *New York Times Magazine,* 30 October 1994, pp. 47–51ff.; *U.S. v. McMillan,* 946 F.Supp. 1254 (S.D. Miss.), 22 November 1995; Tina Rosenberg, *Rolling Stone,* 27 June 1996, pp. 46–50, 67–68.

In his 1997 "vanity press" autobiography, *Preparing for Secession . . .* (New York: Vantage Press), McMillan voices an explicitly defeatist attitude, especially in light of FACE: "The faithful who have been arrested so many times have grown weary and have run out of the ability or willingness to be 'hammered' by jail time and fines (I have) . . . [W]e realize that the political change, which was one goal of the rescue movement, will not come" (p. 122). McMillan adds (p. 132), "The abortion debate is all but over in the United States. . . . [T]here will be a few abortion abolitionists willing to make greater sacrifices and to take great risks through the use of force and violence, but I believe it will not appreciably affect the abortion holocaust."

28. *Dallas Morning News,* 6 September 1993, pp. A27, A32, 8 April 1994, pp. A21, A26, 20 April 1995, pp. A33, A35, 2 May 1995, p. A20, 11 October 1995, pp. A23, A27, 26 October 1995, pp. A1, A11, 5 February 1998, p. A27; *New York Times,* 7 May 1994, p. 10, 10 May 1994, pp. A1, A16, 11 June 1994, pp. 1, 9, 21 April 1995, p. A18, 26 October 1995, p. A16; *American Lawyer,* December 1995, p. 33; *Austin American-Statesman,* 17 January 1997, p. B2. Also see *Cyr v. Tompkins,* 1994 WL 110719 (Tex.Ct.Apps.), 30 March 1994, and *Tompkins v. Cyr,* 878 F.Supp. 911 (N.D.Tex.), 17 February 1995. On Lovejoy, see *Lovejoy Specialty Hospital* v. *Advocates for Life,* 855 P.2d 159 (Or.Ct.Apps.), 16 June 1993, review denied, 863 P.2d 1267 (Or.S.Ct.), cert. denied, 511 U.S. 1070, 2 May 1994, and *Portland Oregonian,* 3 May 1994, p. A1. Also see Peter Korn's superbly done *Lovejoy: A Year in the Life of an Abortion Clinic* (New York: Atlantic Monthly Press, 1996). On the Houston case, also see *Operation Rescue-National* v. *Planned Parenthood of Houston and Southeast Texas,* 937 S.W.2d 60 (Tex.App.-Houston-14th), 19 December 1996.

29. Martin Haskell, "Dilation and Extraction for Late Second Trimester Abortion," 13 September 1992, in *Second Trimester Abortion: From Every Angle* [Fall Risk Management Seminar, 9/13–14/92, Dallas, TX] (Washington: National Abortion Federation, 1992), pp. 27–33; *American Medical News,* 5 July 1993, pp. 3, 21, 22; *Washington Post,* 14 June 1995, p. A4, 22 June 1995, p. A10, 16 July 1995, p. C7; U.S. Congress, House of Representatives, Committee on the Judiciary, *Partial-Birth Abortion: Hearing Before the Subcommittee on the Constitution,* 104th Cong., 1st sess., 15 June 1995; *New York Times,* 16 June 1995, p. A19, 19 June 1995, pp. A1, A9, 2 July 1995, p. 22, 5 July 1995, p. A10; U.S. Congress, House of Representatives, *Partial-Birth Abortion Ban Act of 1995—Report #104–267,* 104th Cong., 1st sess., 27 September 1995.

30. *Dallas Morning News,* 31 March 1995, pp. A27, A32; *New York Times,* 28 July 1994, p. C9, 1 April 1995, p. 6, 11 August 1995, p. A12, 12 August 1995, pp. 1, 9; *Washington Post,* 16 April 1995, p. A3, 11 August 1995, pp. F1, F5; Helen Thorpe, *Texas Monthly,* July 1995, pp. 34–39; Debbie Nathan, *Texas Observer,* 29 September 1995, pp. 9–11, Debbie Nathan, "The Death of Jane Roe," *Village Voice,* 30 April 1996, pp. 31–39; McCorvey with Andy Meisler, *I Am Roe* (New York: HarperCollins, 1994), p. 127. Neither *I Am Roe* nor McCorvey's second as-told-to autobiography (McCorvey with Gary Thomas, *Won By Love: Norma McCorvey Speaks Out Against Abortion* [Nashville: Thomas Nelson, 1998]) ought to be relied upon for factual specifics. By far the best McCorvey profile is Meghan O'Hara and Ilene Findler's 1998 television documentary, "Roe vs. Roe: Baptism by Fire"; also see *New York Times,* 28 January 1998, p. B5.

31. Naomi Wolf, "Our Bodies, Our Souls," *New Republic,* 16 October 1995, pp. 26–35; *New York Times,* 18 August 1995, p. A17, 5 June 1996, p. A10, 18 June 1996, p. A23, 3 April 1997, p. A17; *Los Angeles Times,* 24 May 1996, p. E1; *Washington Post,* 28 July 1996, pp. C1, C4, 27 October 1996, p. A20; *Bergen Record,* 18 May 1997, p. R1. Regarding Wolf's stance, also see James Q. Wilson, "On Abortion," *Commentary,* January 1994, pp. 21ff.; George McKenna, "On Abortion: A Lincolnian Position," *Atlantic Monthly,* September 1995, pp. 51ff.; and Noemie Emery, "Abortion and the Republican Party," *Weekly Standard,* 25 December 1995, pp. 26–31. Concerning "common grounds'" origins in St. Louis, see James R. Kelly's contribution in Mary C. Segers and Timothy A. Byrnes, eds., *Abortion Politics in American States* (Armonk, NY: M. E. Sharpe, 1995), pp. 205–224; *St. Louis Post-Dispatch,* 22 May 1997, p. A1; Cynthia Gorney, *Articles of Faith* (New York: Simon & Schuster, 1998); and *Chicago Tribune,* 25 January 1998, p. W1.

32. *New York Times,* 2 November 1995, pp. A1, B13, 6 November 1995, p. B7, 8 November 1995, p. D25, 9 November 1995, pp. A1, B15, 29 November 1995, p. A23; *Washington Post,* 2 November 1995, pp. A1, A12, 8 November 1995, p. A4, 9 November 1995, p. A5, 8 December 1995, pp. A1, A4; U.S. Congress, Senate, Committee on the Judiciary, *The Partial-Birth Abortion Ban Act of 1995—Hearing,* 104th Cong., 1st sess., 17 November 1995.

33. *New York Times,* 9 December 1995, p. 10, 28 February 1996, p. A13, 28 March 1996, pp. A1, B8, 11 April 1996, pp. A1, B10, 15 April 1996, p. B2, 21 April 1996, p. 35, 22 April 1996, pp. B3, B7; Alissa Rubin, *New Republic,* 4 March 1996, pp. 27ff.; U.S. Congress, House of

Representatives, Committee on the Judiciary, *Effects of Anesthesia During a Partial-Birth Abortion—Hearing Before the Subcommittee on the Constitution,* 104th Cong., 2nd sess., 21 March 1996, esp. pp. 123–124; *Washington Post,* 28 March 1996, pp. A1, A11, 11 April 1996, pp. A1, A14, 12 April 1996, p. A6, 17 April 1996, p. A14.

34. *Women's Medical Professional Corp.* v. *Voinovich,* 911 F. Supp. 1051, 1070, 1080–81 (S.D. Ohio), 13 December 1995; *Dayton Daily News,* 9 December 1995, p. B2.

35. *Baton Rouge Advocate.* 27 September 1995, p. A13, regarding Louisiana R.S.40.1299.35.6 (B)(1), which took effect on 25 September 1995; *A Woman's Choice–East Side Women's Clinic* v. *Newman,* 904 F.Supp. 1434, 1442, 1445–46, 1462 (S.D. Ind.), 9 November 1995; *Salt Lake Tribune,* 11 August 1996, p. B1, 20 October 1996, p. C1, regarding Utah Code 76–7–305(1)(a) ["in a face-to-face consultation"], which took effect 1 September 1996. On Indiana, also see *A Woman's Choice-East Side Women's Clinic* v. *Newman,* 671 N.E.2d 104 (Ind.S.Ct.), 7 August 1996; and 980 F.Supp. 972 (S.D.Ind.), 14 October 1997, where Judge Hamilton reluctantly allowed Indiana's eighteen-hour waiting period requirement to take effect while continuing to enjoin the "in the presence" provision.

On May 24, 1997, Florida enacted the Woman's Right to Know Act providing that a physician must "orally, in person" provide a woman with abortion information, but with no twenty-four-hour advance requirement. Enforcement was temporarily enjoined by Palm Beach County Circuit Judge Kathleen Kroll on July 2 and Kroll's order was subsequently affirmed. *St. Petersburg Times,* 10 July 1997, p. B1, 19 February 1998, p. A1; *Ft. Lauderdale Sun-Sentinel,* 16 August 1997, p. B1; *State* v. *Presidential Women's Center,* 1998 WL 64072 (Fla.App. 4 Dist.), 18 February 1998.

36. *Janklow* v. *Planned Parenthood, Sioux Falls Clinic,* 517 U.S. 1174, 29 April 1996, denying cert. to *Planned Parenthood, Sioux Falls Clinic* v. *Miller,* 63 F.3d 1452 (8th Cir.), 31 August 1995, which affirmed 860 F.Supp. 1409 (D. S.D.), 22 August 1994; *New York Times,* 1 September 1995, p. A20; *Washington Post,* 30 April 1996, p. A4, 2 May 1996, p. A28. See also *Causeway Medical Suite* v. *Ieyoub,* 109 F.3d 1096 (5th Cir.), 14 April 1997 (petition for rehearing en banc denied [with seven judges dissenting], 123 F.3d 849, 23 September 1997), cert. denied, 118 S.Ct. 357, 20 October 1997. The panel ruling, affirming 905 F.Supp. 360 (E.D. La.), 24 October 1995, expressly declined Justice Stevens's invitation in light of the fact that the Louisiana parental notice provision at issue would be unconstitutional under either approach.

Also note *Planned Parenthood of Southern Arizona* v. *Neely,* 942 F.Supp. 1578, 1583 (D. Ariz.), 8 October 1996 [voiding a new Arizona parental consent statute because it "places an undue burden on a pregnant minor's freedom to terminate her pregnancy"], 130 F.3d 400 (9th Cir.), 21 November 1997, *Dallas Morning News,* 13 December 1997, p. A42, 21 January 1998, p. D12; *Planned Parenthood League of Massachusetts* v. *Attorney General,* 677 N.E.2d 101 (Mass.S.J.Ct.), 18 March 1997 [a state constitutional holding voiding a statute requiring unmarried minors to seek consent from both parents], and the important California Supreme Court ruling in *American Academy of Pediatrics* v. *Lungren,* 940 P.2d 797 (Cal.S.Ct.), 5 August 1997, *New York Times,* 6 August 1997, p. A9. Also note *Manning* v. *Hunt,* 119 F.3d 254 and 86 F.3d 1151 (4th Cir.), 11 July 1997 and 22 May 1996; *Planned Parenthood of the Blue Ridge* v. *Camblos,* 116 F.3d 707 (4th Cir.), 30 June 1997, 125 F.3d 884 (4th Cir.), 20 October 1997; *Washington Post,* 25 June 1997, p. B1, 1 July 1997, pp. A1, A7, 3 March 1998, p. A1, 4 March 1998, p. B4; *Washington Times,* 2 July 1997, p. C3, 4 July 1997, p. C6; and *Memphis Planned Parenthood* v. *Sundquist,* 121 F.3d 708 (6th Cir.), 1 August 1997.

Concerning the debate about *U.S.* v. *Salerno,* 481 U.S. 739, 26 May 1987, see especially Michael C. Dorf, "Facial Challenges to State and Federal Statutes," *Stanford Law Review* 46 (January 1994): 235–305, at 236–238 and 271–276; also see Sandra Lynne Tholen and Lisa Baird, "Con Law Is as Con Law Does: A Survey of *Planned Parenthood* v. *Casey* in the State and Federal Courts," *Loyola of Los Angeles Law Review* 28 (April 1995): 971–1046, at 1005; and Ruth Burdick, "The *Casey* Undue Burden Standard: Problems Predicted and Encountered, and the Split Over the *Salerno* Test," *Hastings Constitutional Law Quarterly* 23 (Spring 1996): 825–876.

Concerning parental-notice statutes and judicial bypass mechanisms, see Robert L. Ohsfeldt and Stephan F. Gohmann, "Do Parental Involvement Laws Reduce Adolescent Abortion Rates?" *Contemporary Economic Policy* 12 (April 1994): 65–76 [yes, by approximately 18 percent]; Suellyn Scarnecchia and Julie Kunce Field, "Judging Girls: Decision Making in Parental Consent to Abortion Cases," *Michigan Journal of Gender & Law* 3 (1995): 75–113; Deborah Haas-Wilson, "The Impact of State Abortion Restrictions on Minors' Demand for Abortions," *Journal of Human Resources* 31 (Winter 1996): 140–158 [a 20 percent decrease]; Christine C. Sensibaugh and Elizabeth R. Allgeier, "Abortion and Judicial Bypass: Factors Considered by Ohio Juvenile Court Judges in Judicial Bypass Judgments: A Policy Capturing Approach," *Politics and the Life Sciences* 15 (March 1996): 35–47; and Maggie O'Shaughnessy, "The Worst of Both Worlds? Parental Involvement Requirements and the Privacy Rights of Mature Minors," *Ohio State Law Journal* 57 (1996): 1731–1765.

More practically, also see K Kaufmann's impressively informative *The Abortion Resource Handbook* (New York: Simon & Schuster, 1997), pp. 38–78, which notes (p. 42), "The only states with parental involvement laws that do not have judicial or other bypass provisions are Idaho and Utah." See, per *H.L.* v. *Matheson* (discussed above at pp. 637–638), Utah Code Annotated 76–7–304(2) [a doctor shall "notify, if possible, the parents or guardian of the woman upon whom the abortion is to be performed, if she is a minor"], and Idaho Code 18–609(6) ["if the pregnant patient is unmarried and under eighteen (18) years of age or unemancipated, the physician shall provide notice, if possible, of the pending abortion to the parents or legal guardian of the pregnant patient at least twenty-four (24) hours prior to the performance of the abortion"].

37. *Leavitt* v. *Jane L.,* 518 U.S. 137, 17 June 1996, reversing and remanding *Jane L.* v. *Bangerter,* 61 F.3d 1493 (10th Cir.), 2 August 1995 (which had reviewed 809 F.Supp. 865, 17 December 1992). On remand, 102 F.3d 1112 (10th Cir.), 23 December 1996, the appellate panel explicitly relied upon the 8th Circuit application of *Casey* that Justice Scalia unsuccessfully had attacked in his exchange with Justice Stevens in the South Dakota case; the High Court's subsequent 1997 declining of review was without comment: *Leavitt* v. *Jane L.,* 117 S.Ct. 2453, 16 June 1997. Also see *New York Times,* 5 August 1996, p. 9, 17 June 1997, p. A18; *Washington Post,* 18 June 1996, pp. A1, A5, 20 June 1996, p. A26, 19 June 1997, p. A20; *Salt Lake Tribune,* 17 June 1997, p. A1. Note as well *Utah Women's Clinic* v. *Leavitt,* 844 F.Supp. 1482 (D. Utah), 1 February 1994, affirmed, 75 F.3d 564 (10th Cir.), 22 November 1995, cert. denied, 116 S.Ct. 2551, 24 June 1996; *Salt Lake Tribune,* 25 June 1996, p. A6.

38. *Romer* v. *Evans,* 517 U.S. 620, 20 May 1996, affirming 882 P.2d 1335 Col.S.Ct.), 11 October 1994. Also see *Evans* v. *Romer,* 854 P.2d 1270 (Col.S.Ct.), 19 July 1993, cert. denied, 510 U.S. 959, 1 November 1993. See as well *New York Times,* 15 December 1993, p. A22, 12 October 1994, pp. A1, A13, 9 June 1995, p. A22, 21 May 1996, p. A1, 26 May 1996, p. IV-4; *Washington Post,* 19 December 1993, pp. A1, A28; and James W. Button et al., *Private Lives, Public Conflicts: Battles Over Gay Rights in American Communities* (Washington, D.C.: CQ Press, 1997). Also note *Equality Foundation of Greater Cincinnati* v. *City of Cincinnati,* 838 F.Supp. 1235 (S.D. Ohio), 19 November 1993, 860 F.Supp. 417 (S.D. Ohio), 9 August 1994, reversed, 54 F.3d 261 (6th Cir.), 12 May 1995, vacated and remanded for further consideration in light of *Romer,* 518 U.S. 1001, 17 June 1996, on remand, 128 F.3d 289 (6th Cir.), 23 October 1997, where the appellate panel unpersuasively sought to limit *Romer,* and 1998 WL 101701 (6th Cir.), 5 February 1998. See *Washington Post,* 24 October 1997, p. A3; also see *New York Times,* 12 February 1998, p. A1, concerning Maine.

39. 116 S.Ct. at 1629; Thomas C. Grey, "*Bowers* v. *Hardwick* Diminished," *University of Colorado Law Review* 68 (Spring 1997): 373–386 at 373, 374; Louis Michael Seidman, "*Romer's* Radicalism: The Unexpected Revival of Warren Court Activism," 1996 *Supreme Court Review* (Chicago: University of Chicago Press, 1997), pp. 67–121, at 82. Also see this author's discussion of *Romer* in a larger context: Garrow, "The Rehnquist Years," *New York Times Magazine,* 6 October 1996, pp. 64–71, 82, 85, at 82.

Other commentaries on *Romer* include Andrew M. Jacobs, "*Romer* Wasn't Built in a Day: The Subtle Transformation in Judicial Argument Over Gay Rights," 1996 *Wisconsin Law Review* 893–969; Akhil R. Amar, "Attainder and Amendment 2: *Romer's* Rightness," *Michigan Law Review* 95 (October 1996): 203–235; Courtney G. Joslin, "Equal Protection and Anti-Gay Legislation: Dismantling the Legacy of *Bowers* v. *Hardwick*," *Harvard Civil Rights–Civil Liberties Law Review* 32 (Winter 1997): 225–247; and Janet E. Halley, "*Romer* v. *Hardwick*," *University of Colorado Law Review* 68 (Spring 1997): 429–452.

Pre-*Romer* commentaries now seem inescapably dated. See Andrew M. Jacobs, "The Rhetorical Construction of Rights: The Case of the Gay Rights Movement, 1969–1991," *Nebraska Law Review* 72 (1993): 723–759; Patricia A. Cain, "Litigating for Lesbian and Gay Rights: A Legal History," *Virginia Law Review* 79 (October 1993): 1551–1641; Janet E. Halley, "Reasoning About Sodomy: Act and Identity in and After *Bowers* v. *Hardwick*," *Virginia Law Review* 79 (October 1993): 1721–1780; and Mary C. Dunlap, "Gay Men and Lesbians Down by Law in the 1990s USA: The Continuing Toll of *Bowers* v. *Hardwick*," *Golden Gate University Law Review* 24 (Spring 1994): 1–39. An interestingly original critique of the Supreme Court's handling of *Bowers* is Donald A. Dripps, "*Bowers* v. *Hardwick* and the Law of Standing: Noncases Make Bad Law," *Emory Law Journal* 44 (Fall 1995): 1417–1449.

40. Seidman, "*Romer's* Radicalism," at 67–68 and 98.

41. *State* v. *Morales*, 869 S.W.2d 941 (Tex.S.Ct.), 12 January 1994. Also see *City of Sherman* v. *Henry*, 928 S.W.2d 464 (Tex.S.Ct.), 8 July 1996, cert. denied, 117 S.Ct. 1098, 24 February 1997, concerning a negative personnel action against an adulterous police officer; similarly note *Oliverson* v. *West Valley City*, 875 F.Supp. 1465 (D. Utah), 10 January 1995.

42. *State* v. *Baxley*, 633 So.2d 142 and 656 So.2d 973 (La.S.Ct.), 28 February 1994 and 22 May 1995. Also see Evan Wolfson and Robert S. Mower, "When the Police Are in Our Bedrooms, Shouldn't the Courts Go After Them? An Update on the Fight Against 'Sodomy' Laws," *Fordham Urban Law Journal* 21 (Summer 1994): 997–1055.

43. *Miller* v. *State*, 636 So.2d 391 (Miss.S.Ct.), 14 April 1994.

44. *State* v. *Lopes*, 660 A.2d 707 (R.I. S.Ct.), 22 June 1995, cert. denied, 516 U.S. 1123, 20 February 1996; *State* v. *Chiaradio*, 660 A.2d 276 (R.I. S.Ct.), 30 June 1995. In June 1998 the Rhode Island legislature voted to repeal the state sodomy statute; see *New York Times*, 10 May 1998, p. 14; *Providence Journal Bulletin*, 3 June 1998, p. B1.

45. *Sawatzky* v. *City of Oklahoma City*, 906 P.2d 785 (Ok.Ct.Crim.Apps.), 21 November 1995, cert. denied, 517 U.S. 1156, 22 April 1996.

46. *State* v. *Chiaradio*, 660 A.2d 276, 277, 30 June 1995.

47. *Campbell* v. *Sundquist*, 926 S.W.2d 250, 266 (Tenn.Ct.Apps.), 26 January 1996 ["Application for Permission to Appeal Denied by Supreme Court, June 10, 1996"]. Also see *Lesbian/Gay Law Notes* (Summer 1996): 91–92.

48. *Christensen* v. *State*, 468 S.E.2d 188, 190, 192 (Ga.S.Ct.), 11 March 1996. Also see *Fulton County Daily Report*, 19 August 1997, pp. 1, 2, 16 October 1997, pp. 1, 4, 20 May 1998, p. 1, *National Law Journal*, 1 June 1998, p. A11, concerning the Georgia Supreme Court's 1998 review of *State* v. *Powell*, a criminal case involving a five-year prison sentence for ostensibly consensual heterosexual cunnilingus.

49. *Gryczan* v. *State*, 942 P.2d 112, 125, 126 (Mon.S.Ct.), 2 July 1997; *New York Times*, 4 July 1997, p. A11. As of early 1998, cases challenging state sodomy laws were under way in Arkansas and Maryland, but a Kansas court refused to void that state's same-sex-only sodomy law. *Arkansas Democrat-Gazette*, 30 May 1998, p. B6; *Washington Post*, 6 February 1998, p. D5; *City of Topeka* v. *Movsovitz*, #77,372 (Kans.Ct.Apps.), 24 April 1998.

50. *Baehr* v. *Lewin*, 852 P.2d 44, 67 (Haw.S.Ct.), 5 May 1993, 875 P.2d 225, 27 May 1993; *New York Times*, 25 April 1994, pp. A1, B8, 6 March 1996, p. A13, 28 July 1996, p. 12, 4 December 1996, pp. A1, A26, 5 December 1996, p. B16, 25 January 1997, p. 8, 18 April 1997, p. A10, 1 May 1997, p. A14, 10 July 1997, p. A15; *Baehr* v. *Miike*, 910 P.2d 112 (Haw.S.Ct.), 23 January 1996; Paul M. Barrett's superb *Wall Street Journal* story, 17 June 1996, p. A1; *Washington Post*, 10 September 1996, pp. A1, A4, 22 September 1996, p. A21, 4 December

1996, pp. A1, A22, 5 December 1996, p. A3; *Baehr* v. *Miike,* 23 Family Law Reporter 2001 (Haw.Cir.Ct.), 3 December 1996; *Los Angeles Times,* 7 July 1997, p. A3.

Also see Evan Wolfson, "Crossing the Threshold: Equal Marriage Rights for Lesbians and Gay Men and the Intra-Community Critique," *New York University Review of Law and Social Change* 21 (1994–1995): 567–615; "In Sickness and in Health, In Hawaii and Where Else? Conflict of Laws and the Recognition of Same-Sex Marriages," *Harvard Law Review* 109 (June 1996): 2038–2055; William N. Eskridge, Jr., *The Case for Same-Sex Marriage* (New York: Free Press, 1996); Mark Strasser, *Legally Wed: Same-Sex Marriage and the Constitution* (Ithaca: Cornell University Press, 1997); Evan Wolfson and Michael F. Melcher, "DOMA's House Divided: An Argument Against the Defense of Marriage Act," *Federal Lawyer* 44 (September 1997): 30–36; *Anchorage Daily News,* 28 February 1998, p. A1.

51. *Washington Post,* 28 November 1995, pp. B1, B3, 27 December 1995, pp. C1, C2, 25 January 1996, pp. A1, A15, 26 January 1996, pp. B1, B6, 24 February 1996, p. B3, 29 February 1996, p. B6, 27 March 1996, p. A22; *New York Times,* 26 January 1996, p. A12; *Kansas City Star,* 29 April 1996, p. B1; *Norfolk Virginian-Pilot,* 17 May 1996, p. B3, 5 November 1996, p. B3, 13 February 1997, p. B1, 22 February 1997, p. B7; *Los Angeles Times,* 26 January 1997, p. A20.

52. *Oregonian,* 17 May 1996, p. A1, 10 June 1996, p. B1, 26 January 1997, p. B1; *New York Times,* 27 October 1995, p. A21, 21 May 1996, p. A16; *Planned Parenthood of the Columbia/ Willamette* v. *American Coalition of Life Activists,* 945 F.Supp. 1355 (D. Or.), 18 September 1996. The de Parrie ruling later was reversed. *Hanzo* v. *de Parrie,* 326 Ore. 525 (Or.Ct.Apps.), 18 February 1998. Also note *Feminist Women's Health Center* v. *Codispoti,* 63 F.3d 863 (9th Cir.), 17 August 1995, and 69 F.3d 399 (9th Cir.), 7 November 1995. Also see Amy M. Sneirson, "No Place to Hide: Why State and Federal Enforcement of Stalking Laws May Be the Best Way to Protect Abortion Providers," *Washington University Law Quarterly* 73 (Summer 1995): 635–664; and Christina Couch, "Wanted: Privacy Protection for Doctors Who Perform Abortions," *American University Journal of Gender and the Law* 4 (Spring 1996): 361–414.

53. See *People* v. *Terry,* 45 F.3d 17 (2nd Cir.), 5 January 1995, and *People* v. *Operation Rescue National,* 80 F.3d 64 (2nd Cir.), 29 March 1996, cert. denied *sub nom. Broderick* v. *U.S.,* 117 S.Ct. 85, 7 October 1996; *Roe* v. *Operation Rescue,* 54 F.3d 133 (3rd Cir.), 18 April 1995; *U.S.* v. *Arena,* 894 F. Supp. 580 and 918 F.Supp. 561 (N.D. N.Y.), 25 July 1995 and 19 March 1996; *Douglas* v. *Brownell,* 88 F.3d 1511 (8th Cir.), 9 July 1996; *McKusick* v. *City of Melbourne,* 96 F.3d 478 (11th Cir.), 27 September 1996; *U.S.* v. *Unterburger,* 97 F.3d 1413 (11th Cir.), 23 October 1996; cert. denied, 117 S.Ct. 2517, 27 June 1997; *U.S.* v. *Roach,* 947 F.Supp. 872 (E.D. Pa.), 29 November 1996; *Planned Parenthood Association of Southeastern Pennsylvania* v. *Walton,* 949 F.Supp. 290 (E.D. Pa.), 3 December 1996; and *Terry* v. *Reno,* 101 F.3d 1412 (D.C. Cir.), 10 December 1996, cert. denied, 117 S.Ct. 2431, 9 June 1997. Also see *Washington Post,* 18 March 1998, p. D1.

In state courts, see *Planned Parenthood Association of San Mateo County* v. *Operation Rescue of California,* 57 Cal.Rptr.2d 736 (Cal.App. 1 Dist.), 28 October 1996, cert. denied *sub nom. Cochran* v. *Planned Parenthood Association of San Mateo County,* 118 S.Ct. 54, 6 October 1997; and *Commonwealth* v. *Manning,* 673 N.E.2d 73 (Mass.Apps.Ct.), 22 November 1996, review denied, 676 N.E.2d 55 (Mass.S.J.Ct.), 27 January 1997. Also note *Options* v. *Lawson,* 670 A.2d 1081 (N.J.Super.Ct.App.Div.), 2 February 1996, and *Kaplan* v. *Prolife Action League of Greensboro,* 474 S.E.2d 408 and 475 S.E.2d 247 (N.C.Ct.Apps.), 3 and 17 September 1996, review denied, 485 S.E.2d 54 (N.C.S.Ct.), 10 April 1997.

54. *New York Times,* 14 March 1996, p. A17, 30 March 1996, pp. 1, 7, 1 April 1996, p. A12, 19 July 1996, p. A10, 20 July 1996, pp. 1, 7, 28 July 1996, p. IV-14, 12 September 1996, p. A17, 19 September 1996, pp. A1, B12; *San Francisco Chronicle,* 14 March 1996, p. A3; *New York Magazine,* 1 April 1996, pp. 37–41; *Omaha World-Herald,* 21 April 1996, p. A1; *Washington Post,* 19 July 1996, p. A2, 20 July 1996, pp. A1, A10, 19 September 1996, pp. A1, A9, 21 September 1996, pp. D1, D2.

In the medical literature, see Mitchell D. Creinin et al., "Acceptability of Medical Abortion with Methotrexate and Misoprostol," *Contraception* 52 (July 1995): 41–44; Beverly

Winikoff, "Acceptability of Medical Abortion in Early Pregnancy," *Family Planning Perspectives* 27 (July-August 1995): 142–148, 185; Eric A. Schaff et al., "Combined Methotrexate and Misoprostol for Early Induced Abortion," *Archives of Family Medicine* 4 (September 1995): 774–779; Mary Ann Castle et al., "Listening and Learning from Women About Mifepristone," *Women's Health Issues* 5 (Fall 1995): 130–138; Eric A. Schaff et al., "Methotrexate and Misoprostol for Early Abortion," *Family Medicine* 28 (March 1996): 198–203; Schaff et al., "Methotrexate and Misoprostol When Surgical Abortion Fails," *Obstetrics & Gynecology* 87 (March 1996): 450–452; Mitchell D. Creinin et al., "Methotrexate and Misoprostol for Early Abortion: A Multicenter Trial. I. Safety and Efficacy," *Contraception* 53 (June 1996): 321–327; Creinin, "Oral Methotrexate and Vaginal Misoprostol for Early Abortion," *Contraception* 54 (July 1996): 15–18; and Creinin and Anne E. Burke, "Methotrexate and Misoprostol for Early Abortion: A Multicenter Trial. Acceptability," *Contraception* 54 (July 1996): 19–22. Creinin and Burke report in the latter piece that at one of their trial sites, George Tiller's clinic in Kansas, recruits were difficult to come by: "when women were offered this alternative free of charge in Wichita, they still overwhelmingly chose to pay for a surgical procedure which requires fewer visits, has a higher success rate, and has less vaginal bleeding."

On doctors' interest in RU-486, see Roger A. Rosenblatt et al., "Abortions in Rural Idaho: Physicians' Attitudes and Practices," *American Journal of Public Health* 85 (October 1995): 1423–1425.

55. *Washington Post,* 13 September 1996, p. A3, 17 September 1996, pp. A1, A8 and H12–H14, H17, H19, 20 September 1996, pp. A1, A18, Warren Hern, 17 October 1996, p. A22; Ruth Padawer, *Bergen Record,* 15 September 1996, p. R1; *New York Times,* 19 September 1996, p. B12, 20 September 1996, pp. A1, A22. Also see Wendy Chavkin, *American Journal of Public Health* 86 (September 1996): 1204–1206.

56. *New York Times,* 27 September 1996, p. A20, 14 December 1996, pp. 1, 8, 10; *Washington Post,* 27 September 1996, pp. A4, D1, D2. Also see Garrow, "The Perils of Congress Imposing Its Medical Ideas," *Philadelphia Inquirer,* 25 September 1996, p. A23. The official Senate vote was 57–41, but majority leader Trent Lott switched his vote from "yes" to "no" for purely procedural purposes, and one absentee also supported override, thus making for a "real" total of 59, 8 less than the 67 necessary.

57. *New York Times,* 14 August 1996, p. B6, 29 September 1996, p. 30, 6 November 1996, p. A16; *Washington Post,* 29 September 1996, p. A4.

58. *New York Times,* 1 November 1996, p. A20, 6 November 1996, p. A16, 25 January 1997, p. 6, 13 February 1997, p. A14; *Los Angeles Times,* 6 November 1996, p. D2; *Washington Post,* 12 January 1997, pp. A1, A18, A19, 13 February 1997, pp. A1, A15; Gayle Kirshenbaum, "The Stealth Operation to Market RU-486," *George,* April 1997, pp. 112–115, 124–125.

59. *New York Times,* 17 January 1997, pp. A1, A9, 18 January 1997, p. 6, 20 January 1997, p. A9, 21 January 1997, p. A6, 23 January 1997, p. A8, 7 February 1997, p. A9. After anonymous letters claimed credit for the Atlanta bombing and for a second one at a gay Atlanta nightclub on behalf of the "Army of God," reporter Judy Thomas asked Michael Bray whether any such organization existed. "Who would know? And who would tell you if he did?" Bray answered. "I would say it's reasonable to suppose there's an association of people out there." *Kansas City Star,* 26 February 1997, p. A1.

60. *Schenck v. Pro-Choice Network of Western New York,* 117 S.Ct. 855, 19 February 1997, affirming in part and reversing in part 67 F.3d 377 (2nd Cir. en banc), 28 September 1995, which had reversed a two to one panel ruling, 67 F.3d 359 (2nd Cir.), 6 September 1994, which had in turn in large part reversed U.S. District Judge Richard J. Arcara's rulings, 828 F.Supp. 1018 and 799 F.Supp. 1417 (N.D. N.Y.), 30 July 1993 and 14 February 1992; *New York Times,* 8 September 1994, p. B5, 20 February 1997, pp. A1, A16. Also note *Pro-Choice Network v. Walker,* 994 F.2d 989 (2nd Cir.), 26 May 1993, and Deborah A. Ellis and Yolanda S. Wu, "Of Buffer Zones and Broken Bones: Balancing Access to Abortion and Anti-Abortion Protestors' First Amendment Rights in *Schenck v. Pro-Choice Network,*" *Brooklyn Law Review* 62 (Summer 1996): 547–583.

Also compare *Hill* v. *Colorado,* 117 S.Ct. 1077, 24 February 1997, vacating and remanding *Hill* v. *City of Lakewood,* 911 P.2d 670 (Col.Ct.Apps.), 13 July 1995, for further consideration in light of *Schenck,* on remand, *Hill* v. *City of Lakewood,* 949 P.2d 107 (Col.Ct. Apps.), 26 June 1997 [*upholding* an *eight-* as opposed to fifteen-foot personal distance statute], with *Sabelko* v. *Phoenix,* 117 S.Ct. 1077, 24 February 1997, vacating and remanding 68 F.3d 1169 (9th Cir.), 19 October 1995 [which had reversed 846 F.Supp. 810 (D. Ariz.), 11 February 1994], for further consideration in light of *Schenck,* on remand, 120 F.3d 161 (9th Cir.), 14 July 1997 [*voiding* an *eight-*foot personal distance ordinance]; *New York Times,* 25 February 1997, p. A12, 15 July 1997, p. A11. Also see *Williams* v. *Planned Parenthood Shasta-Diablo,* 117 S.Ct. 1285, 17 March 1997 (more fully detailed in note 10 above); *New York Times,* 18 March 1997, p. A14; *People* v. *Conrad,* 64 Cal.Rptr. 848 (Cal.Ct.App.-1st), 15 May 1997; and, per *Sabelko, Edwards* v. *City of Santa Barbara,* 70 F.3d 1277 (9th Cir.), 22 November 1995, vacating and remanding 883 F.Supp. 1379 (C.D. Cal.), 14 March 1995.

61. See *Planned Parenthood League of Massachusetts* v. *Bell,* 677 N.E.2d 204 (Mass.S.J.Ct.), 18 March 1997 [affirming an injunction prohibiting Bell from coming within fifty feet of Planned Parenthood's Brookline clinic]; *U.S.* v. *Scott,* 958 F.Supp. 761, 775 and 919 F.Supp. 76 (D. Conn.), 2 April 1997 and 18 March 1996 [enjoining Scott's protests outside a Bridgeport clinic and noting Scott's declaration to women patients, "You've had your dirty sex and now you have to pay for it"], *U.S.* v. *Vazquez,* 1998 WL 234725 (2nd Cir.), 12 May 1998; *U.S.* v. *Weslin,* 964 F.Supp. 83 (W.D. N.Y.), 6 May 1997; *State* v. *Stambaugh,* 570 N.W. 2d 63 (Wis.Ct.Apps.), 29 July 1997, review denied, 215 Wis. 2d 425 (Wis.S.Ct.) 20 November 1997; *Lucero* v. *Trosch,* 121 F.3d 591 (11th Cir.), 8 September 1997 [also see 928 F.Supp. 1124 and 904 F.Supp. 1336 (D. Ala.), 28 May 1996 and 1 November 1995]; *Hoffman* v. *Hunt,* 126 F. 3d 575 (4th Cir.), 19 September 1997 (cert. denied, 66 *USLW* 3755, 26 May 1998), reversing 923 F.Supp. 791 (W.D. N.C.), 1 April 1996 [also see (Raleigh) *News and Observer,* 8 June 1996, p. A3, and 845 F. Supp. 340 (W.D. N.C.), 22 February 1994]; and *U.S.* v. *Bird,* 124 F.3d 667 (5th Cir.), 24 September 1997, cert. denied 118 S.Ct. 1189, 9 March 1998.

Note too *U.S.* v. *Lynch,* 952 F.Supp. 167 (S.D. N.Y.), 10 January 1997 (review now pending in the Second Circuit Court of Appeals), 104 F.3d 357 (2nd Cir.), 11 December 1996, cert. denied, 117 S.Ct. 1436, 14 April 1997; *New York Times,* 31 October 1995, p. B4, 20 January 1997, p. A13, 22 January 1997, p. A18, 23 April 1997, p. B2; *Washington Post,* 8 February 1997, p. A20; *New York Law Journal,* 16 July 1997, p. 1, 10 September 1997, p. 1; also note *Palmetto State Medical Center* v. *Operation Lifeline,* 117 F.3d 142 (4th Cir.), 2 July 1997.

Also see *Raney* v. *Aware Women Center,* #97-1197-CV (M.D. Fla.), 3 December 1997; and *Florida Today,* 2 March 1997, p. A1, 7 October 1997, p. B1, 19 November 1997, p. B1.

62. *Lambert* v. *Wicklund,* 117 S.Ct. 1169, 31 March 1997, reversing and remanding *Wicklund* v. *Salvagni,* 93 F.3d 567, 16 August 1996, on remand, 112 F.3d 1040 (9th Cir.), 2 May 1997, and 979 F.Supp. 1285 (D. Mont.), 9 October 1997; *New York Times,* 23 December 1993, p. A12, 1 April 1997, p. A13, 17 June 1997, p. A11. State trial court judge Dorothy McCarter subsequently blocked the law on *state* constitutional grounds.

63. *Mazurek* v. *Armstrong,* 117 S.Ct. 1865, 1866, 1867, 16 June 1997 (the appellate ruling "is inconsistent with our treatment of the physician-only requirement at issue in *Casey*" notwithstanding "the fact that an anti-abortion group drafted the Montana law. But that says nothing about the legislature's purpose in passing it."), reversing and remanding 94 F.3d 566 (9th Cir.), 27 August 1996, which had vacated and remanded 906 F.Supp. 561 (D. Mont.), 29 September 1995; *Los Angeles Times,* 17 June 1997, p. A10.

64. *New York Times,* 26 February 1997, p. A10, 27 February 1997, p. A11, 3 March 1997, pp. A1, A12, 9 March 1997, pp. IV-3, IV-15, 10 March 1997, p. A12; *Bergen Record,* 27 February 1997, p. A1; *Washington Post,* 27 February 1997, p. A4; *American Medical News,* 3 March 1997, p. 54; *U.S. News and World Report,* 10 March 1997, p. 19; *USA Today,* 11 March 1997, p. D1; *New Republic,* 24 March 1997, pp. 19ff.

65. Fitzsimmons memo, 4 April 1997, author's files; U.S. Congress, Senate, Committee on the Judiciary, *Partial-Birth Abortion: The Truth—Joint Hearing,* 105th Cong., 1st sess., 11 March

1997, pp. 38, 49; *New York Times,* 12 March 1997, p. A12; *Washington Post,* 12 March 1997, p. A4; U.S. Congress, House of Representatives, *Partial-Birth Abortion Ban Act of 1997—Report #105–24,* 105th Cong., 1st sess., 14 March 1997.

66. Raja Mishra, *Detroit Free Press,* 15 April 1997, p. A1; *New York Times,* 5 May 1997, pp. A1, A11. Also see *American Medical News,* 5 May 1997, p. 5, and also note three Frank Rich columns, *New York Times,* 11 May 1997, p. IV-15, 25 May 1997, p. IV-11, 29 May 1997, p. A19.

67. *New York Times,* 21 March 1997, pp. A1, A14, 23 March 1997, p. 15, 9 May 1997, p. A14, 13 May 1997, p. A9, 17 May 1997, p. 7; *Washington Post,* 21 March 1997, p. A12, Tom Daschle, 2 May 1997, p. A19; *Los Angeles Times,* 2 April 1997, p. E1, 3 April 1997, p. E1.

68. *New York Times,* 14 May 1997, p. A14, 15 May 1997, p. A16, 16 May 1997, pp. A1, A13, William Safire, 18 May 1997, p. IV-17; *Washington Post,* 14 May 1997, pp. A1, A6, 15 May 1997, p. A11, 16 May 1997, pp. A1, A6, A7, 17 May 1997, p. A24, Robert D. Novak, 19 May 1997, p. A21; Albert R. Hunt, *Wall Street Journal,* 22 May 1997, p. A15; Ruth Padawer, *Bergen Record,* 18 May 1997, p. R1. On ACOG, see *American Medical News,* 3 March 1997, p. 3.

69. *New York Times,* 20 May 1997, pp. A1, A12, 21 May 1997, pp. A1, A12, A18, 25 June 1997, p. A11; *Washington Post,* 20 May 1997, pp. A1, A8, 21 May 1997, pp. A1, A4, 30 May 1997, p. A7, 30 June 1997, p. A19; *Los Angeles Times,* 20 May 1997, p. A1; 143 *Congressional Record* S4715; *Modern Healthcare,* 26 May 1997, p. 3; *American Medical News,* 26 May 1997, pp 1, 25, 2 June 1997, p. 3, 7 July 1997, p. 3. On Santorum, see Joe Klein, "The Senator's Dilemma," *New Yorker,* 5 January 1998, pp. 30–35.

70. Katharine Q. Seelye, *New York Times,* 22 May 1997, p. A9, Seelye, *New York Times,* 25 May 1997, p. IV-5; *New York Times,* 24 May 1997, p. 19; Fred Barnes, *Weekly Standard,* 26 May 1997, p. 12; *New Republic,* 2 June 1997, p. 6; Garrow, "When 'Compromise' Means Caving In," *Washington Post,* 1 June 1997, p. C3.

71. *Oregonian,* 23 May 1997, p. A1, 24 May 1997, p. C1; *New York Times,* 24 May 1997, p. 9, 11 February 1998, p. A20, 29 April 1998, p. A18; *Seattle Times,* 13 October 1997, p. B3; *Spokane Spokesman-Review,* 24 October 1997, p. B1; *Rocky Mountain News,* 15 November 1997, p. A48.

72. *Washington Post,* 11 June 1997, pp. A1, A20, 12 June 1997, p. A3; *New York Times,* 13 June 1997, p. A14, 2 July 1997, p. A12, 13 November 1997, p. A11, 30 April 1998, p. A20; *Drug Topics,* 7 July 1997, p. 8; *Boston Globe Magazine,* 23 November 1997, pp. 18ff.; Eric A. Schaff et al., "Vaginal Misoprostol Administered at Home After Mifepristone (RU486) for Abortion," *Journal of Family Practice* 44 (April 1997): 353–360, at 358; David A. Grimes, "Medical Abortion in Early Pregnancy: A Review of the Evidence," *Obstetrics & Gynecology* 89 (May 1997): 790–796, at 795.

Also especially see Mitchell D. Creinin et al., "Early Abortion: Surgical and Medical Options," *Current Problems in Obstetrics, Gynecology and Fertility* 20 (January-February 1997): 6–32; F. Cadepond et al., "RU 486 (Mifepristone): Mechanisms of Action and Clinical Use," *Annual Review of Medicine* 48 (1997): 129–156; Schaff et al., "Methotrexate: A Single Agent for Early Abortion," *Journal of Reproductive Medicine* 42 (January 1997): 56–60; and Irving M. Spitz et al., "Early Pregnancy Termination with Mifepristone and Misoprostol in the United States," *New England Journal of Medicine* 338 (30 April 1998): 1241–1247. Note also Susan J. Mackensie and Seonae Yeo, "Pregnancy Interruption Using Mifepristone (RU-486)," *Journal of Nurse-Midwifery* 42 (March-April 1997): 86–90, and Creinin et al., "Misoprostol for Medical Evacuation of Early Pregnancy Failure," *Obstetrics & Gynecology* 89 (May 1997): 768–772; dated and of little utility is Gwendolyn Prothro, "RU 486 Examined: Impact of a New Technology on an Old Controversy," *University of Michigan Journal of Law Reform* 30 (Summer 1997): 715–741.

73. *New York Times,* 9 October 1997, pp. A1, A13, 10 October 1997, p. A11, 11 October 1997, p. A9; *Washington Post,* 9 October 1997, p. A8; *Los Angeles Times,* 9 October 1997, p. A22, 11 October 1997, p. A22. One representative, New York Democrat Charles Rangel, mistakenly voted yes rather than no, thus making the "true" tally 295 to 133—virtually identical to the earlier March vote. Also lurking on 1998's congressional horizon was S.1645, the

Child Custody Protection Act, a bill introduced by Michigan Republican senator Spencer Abraham which would provide up to one year's imprisonment for anyone who knowingly transported a woman under the age of eighteen across a state line so as to obtain an abortion in avoidance of a home-state parental involvement law. See *Washington Times*, 14 May 1998, p. A8; *New York Times*, 21 May 1998, p. A14, 29 May 1998, p. A18; *Legal Times*, 25 May 1998, pp. 1, 18–19; *Los Angeles Times*, 30 May 1998, p. A4.

74. *Karlin* v. *Foust*, 975 F.Supp. 1177 (W.D. Wis.), 20 June and 2 October 1997, concerning W.S.A. 253.10(3)(b) [a physician must "in person, orally inform"]; *Wisconsin State Journal*, 6 October 1996, p. A1, 20 June 1997, p. A1, 4 October 1997, p. A1, 6 February 1998, p. A1, 15 April 1998, p. B1; *Milwaukee Journal Sentinel*, 20 June 1997, p. 1, 4 October 1997, p. 5, 7 February 1998, p. 5, 24 April 1998, p. 2, 22 May 1998, p. 3, 31 May 1998, p. 1; *Madison Capital Times*, 6 February 1998, p. A2, 22 May 1998, p. A2; *New York Times*, 31 May 1998, p. 18. On Ohio, see *Cincinnati Post*, 15 September 1997, p. A10, 23 September 1997, p. A10, 18 April 1998, p. A1; *Cleveland Plain Dealer*, 15 January 1998, p. A1; *Columbus Dispatch*, 18 January 1998, p. C5, 5 February 1998, p. C9; *Cincinnati Enquirer*, 24 April 1998, p. D2.

Commenting on *Casey*, Judge Crabb noted (p. 1210) that "after the Supreme Court's recent decision in *Armstrong* [the Montana physician assistant case] the impermissible purpose prong of the undue burden test appears almost impossible to prove in the absence of a confession like that in *Bangerter*," where the 10th Circuit Court of Appeals' voiding of a restrictive Utah statute had just been left undisturbed by the High Court. See note 37 above. Concluding (p. 1229), "I am bound by the holding in *Casey* to find that most of the obstacles" created by Wisconsin "do not constitute undue burdens," Judge Crabb observed that "so long as the state stops short of preventing women from obtaining abortions and clothes its laws with the veneer of 'persuasion,' *Casey* permits almost any effort by the state to influence what *Roe* protected and kept private." For another decidedly pessimistic commentary on *Casey's* "weak and confusing" undue burden standard, see Janet Benshoof, "Abortion Rights and Wrongs," *Nation*, 14 October 1996, pp. 19–20; also see Kathryn Kolbert, *National Law Journal*, 26 January 1998, p. A21 (calling *Casey* a "Pyrrhic victory"). On restrictive state statutes more generally also see Kathryn Kolbert and Andrea Miller's essay in Rickie Solinger, ed., *Abortion Wars* (Berkeley: University of California Press, 1998), pp. 95–110.

A Kansas twenty-four-hour waiting period statute took effect July 1, 1997, but did not mandate two in-person visits. *Kansas City Star*, 10 August 1997, p. B1; a similar Kentucky law was scheduled to take effect July 15, 1998. *Louisville Courier-Journal*, 16 April 1998, p. A1.

75. *Washington* v. *Glucksberg*, 117 S.Ct. 2258, and *Vacco* v. *Quill*, 117 S.Ct. 2293, 26 June 1997. *Glucksberg* reversed *Compassion in Dying* v. *State of Washington*, 79 F.3d 790 (9th Cir. en banc), 6 March 1996, which in turn had reversed 49 F.3d 586 (9th Cir.), 9 March 1995, which had reversed 850 F.Supp. 1454 (W.D. Wash.), 3 May 1994. Both the district judge, Barbara Rothstein, and U.S. Circuit Judge Stephen Reinhardt, writing for the en banc majority, had relied very heavily on *Casey* in striking down the Washington state antiassistance statute. *Vacco* reversed 80 F.3d 716 (2nd Cir.), 2 April 1996, which in turn had reversed *Quill* v. *Koppell*, 870 F.Supp. 78 (S.D. N.Y.), 15 December 1994.

Also see, regarding Oregon, *Lee* v. *Harcleroad*, 118 S.Ct. 328, 14 October 1997, denying cert. to *Lee* v. *State of Oregon*, 107 F.3d 1382 (9th Cir.), 27 February 1997, which had reversed 891 F.Supp. 1421 and 869 F.Supp. 1491 (D. Or.), 3 August 1995 and 27 December 1994.

My own commentaries on these cases include "The Justices' Life or Death Choices," *New York Times*, 7 April 1996, p. IV-6; "Nine Justices and a Funeral," *George*, June 1997, pp. 56–63; "Letting the Public Decide About Assisted Suicide," *New York Times*, 29 June 1997, p. IV-4; "The Oregon Trail," *New York Times*, 6 November 1997, p. A27; and "A New View of Death," *Oregonian*, 6 November 1997, p. D11.

76. See in general *National Law Journal*, 22 September 1997, p. A10; *Time*, 20 October 1997, p. 50; and Garrow, "The Reach of *Roe*," *Washington Post*, 18 January 1998, pp. C1, C6.

On Ohio, see *Women's Medical Professional Corp.* v. *Voinovich*, 130 F.3d 187 (6th Cir.), 18 November 1997, cert. denied, 118 S.Ct. 1347, 23 March 1998; *New York Times*, 19 November 1997, p. A16, 24 March 1998, p. A13; *Cincinnati Enquirer,* 6 December 1997, p. A1; *Columbus Dispatch,* 24 March 1998, p. A1.

On Georgia, see *Midtown Hospital* v. *Miller,* #97–1786 (N.D. Ga.), 27 June and 24 July 1997; *Atlanta Constitution,* 21 June 1997, p. D1, 1 July 1997, p. B1, 2 July 1997, p. B5; *Fulton County Daily Report,* 30 June 1997, pp. 1,2, 28 July 1997, pp. 1, 5.

On Alabama, see *Montgomery Advertiser,* 8 August 1997, p. B1, 6 September 1997, p. B5, 3 December 1997, p. A11, 27 January 1998, p. A1; *Summit Medical Associates* v. *James,* 984 F. Supp. 1404 (M.D. Ala.), 26 January 1988, #1970713 (Ala.S.Ct.), 11 February 1998, 1998 WL 125776 (M.D. Ala.), 19 March 1998.

On Rhode Island, see *Rhode Island Medical Society* v. *Pine,* #97–416 (D. R.I.), 11 July 1997; *Providence Journal-Bulletin,* 12 July 1997, p. A1, 1 August 1997, p. B1, 3 April 1998, p. B1, 10 April 1998, p. B1.

On Louisiana, see *Causeway Medical Suite* v. *Foster,* #97–2211 (E.D. La.), 14 July 1997; *New York Times,* 30 June 1997, p. A12; *New Orleans Times-Picayune,* 16 July 1997, p. A4, 15 August 1997, p. A17; *Baton Rouge Advocate,* 22 August 1997, 18 September 1997, p. B9, 14 October 1997, p. B4; *Baton Rouge Capital City Press,* 18 October 1997, p. A13. In the second case, *Okpalobi* v. *Foster,* 981 F.Supp. 977 (E.D. La.), 7 January 1998, a temporary restraining order issued on August 14 was converted into a preliminary injunction early in 1998.

On Arizona, see *Planned Parenthood of Southern Arizona* v. *Woods,* 982 F. Supp. 1369 (D. Ariz.), 27 October 1997; *USA Today,* 22 September 1997, p. A10.

On Arkansas, see *Little Rock Family Planning Services* v. *Jegley,* #97–581 (E.D. Ark.), 31 July 1997; *Arkansas Democrat-Gazette,* 29 July 1997, p. B1, 13 September 1997, p. B7, 10 October 1997, p. B1, 5 November 1997, p. B2; *Memphis Commercial Appeal,* 1 August 1997, p. A12.

On Alaska, see *Planned Parenthood of Alaska* v. *State,* #97-06019 Civil (Super.Ct., 3rd Jud Dist.), 31 July 1997; and *Anchorage Daily News,* 13 August 1997, p. B2, 27 February 1998, p. A1, 14 March 1998, p. A1.

On Montana, see *Intermountain Planned Parenthood* v. *State,* #BDV 97-477, Mon. 1st Jud. Dist. Ct., 1 October 1997.

77. *Evans* v. *Kelley,* 977 F.Supp. 1283, 1311, 1318 (E.D. Mich.), 31 July 1997; *New York Times,* 1 August 1997, p. A20, 4 August 1997, p. A10.

78. *Carhart* v. *Stenberg,* 972 F.Supp. 507, 509, 525, 523, 531 (D. Neb.), 14 August 1997; *Omaha World-Herald,* 14 August 1997, p. 1, 15 August 1997, p. 1, 24 March 1998, p. 11, 25 March 1998, p. 19, 26 March 1998, p. 20.

79. On New Jersey, see *Planned Parenthood of Central New Jersey* v. *Verniero,* Civ. #97-6170 (D. N.J.), 24 December 1997; *New York Times,* 15 December 1997, p. A15, 16 December 1997, p. A17, 17 December 1997, pp. A18, A20, 23 February 1998, p. A10; *New Jersey Law Journal,* 22 December 1997, p. 6; *Bergen Record,* 25 December 1997, p. A1.

On Illinois, see *Hope Clinic* v. *Ryan,* 1998 WL 95222 (N.D. Ill.), 12 February 1998; *Peoria Journal Star,* 13 November 1997, p. A9; *Chicago Tribune,* 17 December 1997, p. 3, 13 February 1998, p. 1; *Chicago Daily Law Bulletin,* 16 April 1998, p. 5.

On Idaho, see *Weyhrich* v. *Lance,* #98–117 (D.Id.), 27 March 1998; *Idaho Statesman,* 14 March 1998, p. A1, 17 March 1998, p. A1.

On Wisconsin, see *Wisconsin State Journal,* 1 May 1998, p. C1, 6 May 1998, p. B3, 14 May 1998, p. A1, 15 May 1998, p. A1, 16 May 1998, p. A1, 19 May 1998, p. A1, 20 May 1998, p. A1, 27 May 1998, p. B1, 3 June 1998, p. C1, 5 June 1998, p. C1; *Milwaukee Journal Sentinel,* 14 May 1998, p. 3, 16 May 1998, p. 1, 21 May 1998, p. 1, 28 May 1998, p. 3, 5 June 1998, p. 5; *Madison Capital Times,* 14 May 1998, p. A1, 15 May 1998, p. A1, 18 May 1998, p. A1, 19 May 1998, p. A2, 20 May 1998, p. A2, 21 May 1998, p. A1, 22 May 1998, p. A12, 4 June 1998, p. A1; *New York Times,* 15 May 1998, p. A14, 16 May 1998, p. A26, 20 May 1998, p. A13; *Washington Post,* 15 May 1998, p. A1, 20 May 1998, p. D16; *National Law Journal,* 1 June 1998, p. A7.

Seven other states—Florida, Iowa, Kansas, Kentucky, Oklahoma, Virginia, and West Virginia, for a cumulative total of 28—also adopted partial birth ban laws during the first five months of 1998. Oklahoma's took effect without judicial challenge, but cases attacking the

Florida, Iowa, Kansas, Virginia, and West Virginia ones were quickly filed, and reproductive rights lawyers predicted that Kentucky's would be challenged, too.

On Florida, see *St. Petersburg Times,* 4 April 1998, p. B5, and *Orlando Sentinel,* 2 June 1998, p. D1. On Iowa, see *Des Moines Register,* 5 March 1998, p. 4. On Kansas, see *Kansas City Star,* 28 April 1998, p. A1, 3 May 1998, p. A1, 4 May 1998, p. A2, 4 June 1998, p. A1. On Kentucky, see *Louisville Courier-Journal,* 16 April 1998, p. A1. On Oklahoma, see *Daily Oklahoman,* 9 April 1998, p. 1, 16 April 1998, p. 8. On Virginia, see *Washington Post,* 14 April 1998, pp. B1, B7, *Richmond Times Dispatch,* 22 May 1998, p. B1. On West Virginia, see *Charleston Gazette,* 9 April 1998, p. A1, 9 June 1998, p. A1.

80. *New York Times,* 30 January 1998, p. A1, 31 January 1998, p. A7, 3 February 1998, p. A10, 7 February 1998, p. A9, 15 February 1998, p. 14, 27 February 1998, p. A15, 28 February 1998, pp. A1, A8, 3 March 1998, p. A16, 11 March 1998, p. A10, 30 April 1998, p. A24, 6 May 1998, p. A16, 17 May 1998, p. 14; *Washington Post,* 30 January 1998, p. A1, 15 February 1998, p. A3. Dallas Blanchard observed that "as the movement weakens, it tends to get more and more violent." *Atlanta Journal Constitution,* 30 January 1998, p. A11. Also see Christopher Swope, "Abortion," *Governing,* May 1998, pp. 44–49.

81. For a stark example of the renewed focus on the fetus, see Sheryl Stolberg, *New York Times,* 11 January 1998, p. IV-3; with regard to sexuality, see Garrow, "Abortion and the Future," *Chicago Tribune,* 21 January 1998, p. I-13. Also see Garrow, "All Over But the Legislating," *New York Times Book Review,* 25 January 1998, pp. 14–16; *Washington Post,* 1 May 1998, p. E3.

82. As Janet Benshoof has correctly observed, in *Casey* "the Court codified into constitutional law the view that women seeking abortions are morally shallow and incapable of making decisions in their own best interests." "Revisiting the Fundamentals," *Conscience* 18 (Winter 1997–1998): 16–17.

83. With regard to zoning, see *Planned Parenthood of Greater Iowa* v. *Atchison,* 126 F.3d 1042 (8th Cir.), 25 September 1997, and *New York Times,* 15 February 1998, p. 15.

For the Alaska Supreme Court's holding that the state constitution protects abortion as a fundamental right, see *Valley Hospital Association* v. *Mat-Su Coalition for Choice,* 948 P.2d 963 (Alas.S.Ct.), 21 November 1997, and *New York Times,* 15 February 1998, p. 15. Also see *Anchorage Daily News,* 27 February 1998, p. A1.

Far differently, in late 1997 the South Carolina Supreme Court, in reinstating a woman's criminal child neglect conviction—and *eight-year* prison sentence—following the birth of a "crack"-affected baby, held by a three-to-two vote that the word "child" includes viable fetuses. *Whitner* v. *State,* 492 S.E.2d 777 (S.C.S.Ct.), 27 October 1997, cert. denied, 66 USLW 3754, 26 May 1998; *New York Times,* 30 October 1997, p. A17, 13 January 1998, pp. A1, A8, 27 May 1998, p. A18.

Also see *Davis* v. *Fieker,* 952 P. 2d 505 (Okla.S.Ct.), 23 December 1997, where Oklahoma's highest court overlooked a glaring problem of standing and ordered the state board of health to begin enforcing several statutes, including one requiring that all post–first trimester abortions be performed in hospitals, that the state attorney general in 1984 had said were constitutionally unenforceable. *Tulsa World,* 26 December 1997, p. A1.

84. *New York Times,* 21 December 1997, pp. 1, 18; *New York Times Magazine,* 18 January 1998, pp. 20–27ff.

85. Robert J. Blendon et al., "The Public and the Controversy over Abortion," *Journal of the American Medical Association* 270 (15 December 1993): 2871–2875, at 2872; Michael R. Welch et al., "Attitudes Toward Abortion Among U.S. Catholics: Another Case of Symbolic Politics?" *Social Science Quarterly* 76 (March 1995): 142–157, at 152; *New York Times,* 16 January 1998, pp. A1, A16; Everett C. Ladd and Karlyn H. Bowman, *Public Opinion about Abortion: Twenty-five Years after Roe v. Wade* (Washington, D.C.: AEI Press, 1997), p. 17. Also note Neil Nevitte et al., "The American Abortion Controversy: Lessons from Cross-National Evidence," *Politics and the Life Sciences* 12 (February 1993): 19–30, at 25 ("support for legalizing abortion appears to be approximately 10 to 20 percept higher than support for abortion per se"); Matthew E. Wetstein, *Abortion Rates in the United States: The Influence of Opinion and Policy* (Albany: State University of New York Press, 1996), p. 73 ("Americans

have come to hold stable views on abortion"); *New York Times,* 21 October 1997, pp. A1, A14, 17 January 1998, pp. A1, A7, 24 January 1998, p. A13; Garrow, "Abortion and the Future," *Chicago Tribune,* 21 January 1998, p. I-13; *Bergen Record,* 6 March 1998, p. A3; Lydia K. Saad, *Public Perspective,* February/March 1998, pp. 7–11, and *Orlando Sentinel,* 15 March 1998, p. G1; *Louisville Courier-Journal,* 17 March 1998, p. A1; and a multi-part discussion in *The Hotline,* 17–20 March 1998.

Also see especially Christopher B. Wlezien and Malcolm L. Goggin, "The Courts, Interest Groups, and Public Opinion about Abortion," *Political Behavior* 15 (December 1993): 381–405; Raymond J. Adamek, "Public Opinion and *Roe v. Wade:* Measurement Difficulties," *Public Opinion Quarterly* 58 (Fall 1994): 409–418; Matthew E. Wetstein and Robert B. Albritton, "Effects of Public Opinion on Abortion Policies and Use in the American States," *Publius* 25 (Fall 1995): 91–105; R. Michael Alvarez and John Brehm, "American Ambivalence Towards Abortion Policy . . . ," *American Journal of Political Science* 39 (November 1995): 1055–1082; and William Saletan, "Electoral Politics and Abortion," in Rickie Solinger, ed., *Abortion Wars* (Berkeley: University of California Press, 1998), pp. 111–123.

Note also Bhavani Sitaraman, *The Middleground: The American Public and the Abortion Debate* (New York: Garland Publishing, 1994); Kimberly J. Cook, *Divided Passions: Public Opinions on Abortion and the Death Penalty* (Boston: Northeastern University Press, 1998); Robert E. O'Connor and Michael B. Berkman, "Religious Determinants of State Abortion Policy," *Social Science Quarterly* 76 (June 1995): 447–459; and Matthew E. Wetstein, "The Abortion Rate Paradox: The Impact of National Policy Change on Abortion Rates," *Social Science Quarterly* 76 (September 1995): 607–618.

86. Matt Trewhella, "Coming Home to Roost," *Life Advocate* 12 (January-February 1998); *USA Today,* 17 November 1997, p. A17; *New York Times,* 21 October 1997, pp. A1, A14; *Los Angeles Times,* 17 November 1997, p. A5; *Washington Post,* 18 January 1998, p. A4.

87. Janet Benshoof, as quoted in the *National Law Journal,* 22 September 1997, p. A10. Frances Kissling rightly complains that "we no longer talk about rights. . . . We try to co-opt conservatives by stressing their buzz words." *Conscience* 18 (Winter 1997–1998): 3.

88. *Ms.,* January-February 1998, p. 77. Kissling also noted, "Now there is a lot more ambivalence and a lot more need for justification. When it is legal, then you can start to think about 'Is it right?'" *Washington Post,* 22 January 1998, pp. A1, A8.

89. An impressively powerful articulation of just what *is* needed is given by Madison provider Elizabeth Karlin in Rickie Solinger, ed., *Abortion Wars* (Berkeley: University of California Press, 1998), pp. 273–289. Also see Patricia Lunneborg, *Abortion: A Positive Decision* (New York: Bergin & Garvey, 1992), p. x: "Abortion is *not* the lesser of two evils. Abortion is pro-family, prolife, moral, and good."

On the *Roe* and *Doe* anniversary, see in general *New York Times,* 15 January 1998, p. A14, 23 January 1998, p. A11; *U.S. News and World Report,* 19 January 1998, pp. 20–32; and *Wall Street Journal,* 22 January 1998, p. A18.

AFTERWORD

1. Harold D. Lasswell, "The Threat to Privacy," in R. M. MacIver, ed., *Conflict of Loyalties* (New York: Harper & Bros., 1952), pp. 121–140, at 134; John B. Young, "A Look at Privacy," in Young, ed., *Privacy* (New York: John Wiley, 1978), pp. 1–10, at 1; Harper, "The Law and Sex Behavior," *Survey,* April 1948, p. 117; Garrow conversations with Jean and Marvin Durning and Robert "Oldendorf." Also note Oliver Wendell Holmes's often-quoted observation that "The life of the law has not been logic; it has been experience. The felt necessities of the time, the prevalent moral and political theories, intuitions of public policy, avowed or unconscious, even the prejudices which judges share with their fellow-men, have had a good deal more to do that the syllogism in determining the rules by which men should be governed." *The Common Law* (Boston: Little, Brown & Co., 1881), p. 1.

BIBLIOGRAPHY

SELECTED BOOKS

Ackerman, Bruce. *We the People: Foundations*. Cambridge, MA: Harvard University Press, 1991.

Allen, Anita L. *Uneasy Access: Privacy for Women in a Free Society*. Totowa, NJ: Rowman & Littlefield, 1988.

Andersen, Christopher. *Young Kate*. New York: Henry Holt & Co., 1988.

Baehr, Ninia. *Abortion Without Apology*. Boston: South End Press, 1990.

Ball, Howard, and Phillip J. Cooper. *Of Power and Right: Hugo Black, William O. Douglas, and America's Constitutional Revolution*. New York: Oxford University Press, 1992.

Barnett, Randy E., ed. *The Rights Retained by the People: The History and Meaning of the Ninth Amendment*. Fairfax, VA: George Mason University Press, 1989.

Barnett, Ruth. *They Weep on My Doorstep*. Beaverton, OR: Halo Publishers, 1969.

Barnett, Walter. *Sexual Freedom and the Constitution*. Albuquerque: University of New Mexico Press, 1973.

Bates, Jerome E., and Edward S. Zawadzki. *Criminal Abortion: A Study in Medical Sociology*. Springfield, IL.: Charles C. Thomas, 1964.

Beaman, Niver W. *Fat Man in a Phone Booth: Notes Off a Newspaperman's Cuff*. Chicago: Cloud, 1947.

Berger, Margaret A. *Litigation on Behalf of Women*. New York: Ford Foundation, 1980.

Blanchard, Dallas A., and Terry J. Prewitt. *Religious Violence and Abortion*. Gainesville: University Press of Florida, 1993.

Blasi, Vincent, ed. *The Burger Court: The Counter-Revolution That Wasn't*. New Haven: Yale University Press, 1983.

Bonavoglia, Angela, ed. *The Choices We Made*. New York: Random House, 1991.

Bopp, James, Jr. *Restoring the Right to Life: The Human Life Amendment*. Provo, UT: Brigham Young University Press, 1984.

Bork, Robert H. *The Tempting of America*. New York: Free Press, 1989.

Bowles, Chester. *Promises to Keep: My Years in Public Life, 1941–1969*. New York: Harper & Row, 1971.

Boyer, Paul S. *Purity in Print: The Vice Society Movement and Book Censorship in America*. New York: Charles Scribner's Sons, 1968.

Brecher, Jeremy, et al. *Brass Valley: The Story of Working People's Lives and Struggles in an American Industrial Region*. Philadelphia: Temple University Press, 1982.

Bromley, Dorothy D. *Catholics and Birth Control*. New York: Devin-Adair, 1965.

Broun, Heywood, and Margaret Leech. *Anthony Comstock*. New York: Albert & Charles Boni, 1927.

Browne, F. W. Stella, et al. *Abortion*. London: George Allen & Unwin, 1935.

Burtchaell, James T., ed. *Abortion Parley*. Kansas City: Andrews & McMeel, 1980.

Burtchaell, James T. *Rachel Weeping: The Case Against Abortion*. San Francisco: Harper & Row, 1982.

Butler, J. Douglas, and David F. Walbert. *Abortion, Medicine, and the Law*, 3rd ed. New York: Facts on File, 1986.

Byrnes, Timothy A. *Catholic Bishops and American Politics*. Princeton: Princeton University Press, 1991.

Byrnes, Timothy A., and Mary C. Segers, eds. *The Catholic Church and the Politics of Abortion*. Boulder, CO: Westview Press, 1992.

Calabresi, Guido. *Ideals, Beliefs, Attitudes, and the Law*. Syracuse, NY: Syracuse University Press, 1985.

Calderone, Mary S., ed. *Abortion in the United States*. New York: Hoeber-Harper, 1958.

Callahan, Daniel. *Abortion: Law, Choice and Morality*. New York: Macmillan, 1970.

Callahan, Sidney, and Daniel Callahan, eds. *Abortion: Understanding Differences*. New York: Plenum Press, 1984.

Carden, Maren L. *The New Feminist Movement*. New York: Russell Sage Foundation, 1974.

Carmen, Arlene, and Howard Moody. *Abortion Counseling and Social Change*. Valley Forge, PA: Judson Press, 1973.

Cassell, Joan. *A Group Called Women: Sisterhood and Symbolism in the Feminist Movement*. New York: David McKay, 1977.

Chesler, Ellen. *Woman of Valor: Margaret Sanger and the Birth Control Movement in America*. New York: Simon & Schuster, 1992.

Coffman, Tom. *Catch a Wave: A Case Study of Hawaii's New Politics*, 2nd ed. Honolulu: University Press of Hawaii, 1973.

Cohen, Sherrill, and Nadine Taub, eds. *Reproductive Laws for the 1990s*. Clifton, NJ: Humana Press, 1989.

Colker, Ruth. *Abortion and Dialogue*. Bloomington: Indiana University Press, 1992.

Condit, Celeste M. *Decoding Abortion Rhetoric*. Urbana: University of Illinois Press, 1990.

Connery, John. *Abortion: The Development of the Roman Catholic Perspective*. Chicago: Loyola University Press, 1977.

Cook, Elizabeth A., et al. *Between Two Absolutes: Public Opinion and the Politics of Abortion*. Boulder, CO: Westview Press, 1992.

Cooke, Robert E., et al. *The Terrible Choice: The Abortion Dilemma*. New York: Bantam, 1968.

Cornish, Mary Jean, et al. *Doctors and Family Planning*. New York: National Committee on Maternal Health, 1963.

Cortner, Richard C. *The Supreme Court and Civil Liberties Policy*. Palo Alto, CA: Mayfield Publishing Co., 1975.

Costain, Anne N. *Inviting Women's Rebellion*. Baltimore: Johns Hopkins University Press, 1992.

Cott, Nancy. *The Grounding of Modern Feminism*. New Haven: Yale University Press, 1987.

Craig, Barbara Hinkson, and David M. O'Brien. *Abortion and American Politics*. Chatham, NJ: Chatham House, 1993.

Coughlan, Michael J. *The Vatican, the Law and the Human Embryo*. Iowa City: University of Iowa Press, 1990.

Crawford, Ann F., and Crystal S. Ragsdale. *Women in Texas*. Burnet, TX: Eakin Press, 1982.

Cross, Wilbur L. *Connecticut Yankee: An Autobiography*. New Haven: Yale University Press, 1943.

Davis, Flora. *Moving the Mountain: The Women's Movement in America Since 1960*. New York: Simon & Schuster, 1991.

Davis, Nanette J. *From Crime to Choice: The Transformation of Abortion in America*. Westport, CT: Greenwood Press, 1985.

D'Emilio, John, and Estelle B. Freedman. *Intimate Matters: A History of Sexuality in America*. New York: Harper & Row, 1988.

Dennett, Mary Ware. *Birth Control Laws*. New York: Frederick H. Hitchcock, 1926.

Dienes, C. Thomas. *Law, Politics, and Birth Control*. Urbana: University of Illinois Press, 1972.

Dionisopoulos, P. Allan, and Craig R. Ducat. *The Right to Privacy*. St. Paul, MN: West Publishing Co., 1976.

Dolan, Jay P. *The American Catholic Experience*. Garden City, NY: Doubleday, 1985.

Dollen, Charles. *Abortion in Context: A Select Bibliography*. Metuchen, NJ: Scarecrow Press, 1970.

Douglas, William O. *The Court Years, 1939–1975: The Autobiography of William O. Douglas*. New York: Random House, 1980.

Douglas, William O. *The Right of the People*. Garden City, NY: Doubleday, 1958.

Duggan, Thomas S. *The Catholic Church in Connecticut*. New York: States History Co., 1930.

Dworkin, Ronald. *Life's Dominion*. New York: Alfred A. Knopf, 1993.

Echols, Alice. *Daring to Be Bad: Radical Feminism in America, 1967–1975*. Minneapolis: University of Minnesota Press, 1989.

Eisler, Kim I. *A Justice for All*, New York: Simon & Schuster, 1993.

Ely, John H. *Democracy and Distrust*. Cambridge, MA: Harvard University Press, 1980.

Emerson, Thomas I. *Young Lawyer for the New Deal: An Insider's Memoir of the Roosevelt Years*. Savage, MD: Rowman & Littlefield, 1991.

Epstein, Lee, and Joseph F. Kobylka. *The Supreme Court and Legal Change*. Chapel Hill: University of North Carolina Press, 1992.

Ernst, Morris L. *A Love Affair with the Law*. New York: Macmillan, 1968.

Ernst, Morris L. *Touch Wood: A Year's Diary*. New York: Atheneum, 1960.

Ernst, Morris L., and Alexander Lindey. *The Censor Marches On*. New York: Doubleday, Doran & Co., 1940.

Ernst, Morris L., and Gwendolyn Pickett. *Birth Control in the Courts*. New York: Planned Parenthood Federation of America, 1942.

Ernst, Morris L., and Alan U. Schwartz. *Privacy: The Right to Be Let Alone*. New York: Macmillan, 1962.

Evans, Sara M. *Born for Liberty: A History of Women in America*. New York: Free Press, 1989.

Falik, Marilyn. *Ideology and Abortion Policy Politics*. New York: Praeger, 1983.

Faux, Marian. *Crusaders: Voices from the Abortion Front*. New York: Carol Publishing Group, 1990.

Faux, Marian. *Roe v. Wade*. New York: Macmillan, 1988.

Floyd, Mary K. *Abortion Bibliography for 1970*. Troy, NY: Whitson Publishing Co., 1972.

Floyd, Mary K. *Abortion Bibliography for 1971*. Troy, NY: Whitson Publishing Co., 1973.

Floyd, Mary K. *Abortion Bibliography for 1972*. Troy, NY: Whitson Publishing Co., 1973.

Floyd, Mary K. *Abortion Bibliography for 1973*. Troy, NY: Whitson Publishing Co., 1974.

Floyd, Mary K. *Abortion Bibliography for 1974*. Troy, NY: Whitson Publishing Co., 1975.

Floyd, Mary K. *Abortion Bibliography for 1975*. Troy, NY: Whitson Publishing Co., 1976.

Francome, Colin. *Abortion Freedom: A Worldwide Movement*. London: George Allen & Unwin, 1984.

Freeman, Jo. *The Politics of Women's Liberation*. New York: David McKay, 1975.

Freeman, Lucy. *The Abortionist*. New York: Grove Press, 1962.

Fried, Charles. *Order and Law*. New York: Simon & Schuster, 1991.

Fried, Marlene G., ed. *From Abortion to Reproductive Freedom*. Boston: South End Press, 1990.

Friedman, Leon, ed. *The Supreme Court Confronts Abortion: The Briefs, Argument and Decision in Planned Parenthood v. Casey*. New York: Farrar, Straus & Giroux, 1993.

Friendly, Fred W., and Martha J. H. Elliott. *The Constitution: That Delicate Balance*. New York: Random House, 1985.

Fritz, Leah. *Dreamers and Dealers: An Intimate Appraisal of the Women's Movement*. Boston: Beacon Press, 1979.

Frohock, Fred M. *Abortion: A Case Study in Law and Morals*. Westport, CT: Greenwood Press, 1983.

Garfield, Jay L., and Patricia Hennessey, eds. *Abortion: Moral and Legal Perspectives*. Amherst: University of Massachusetts Press, 1984.

Gaylor, Anne N. *Abortion Is a Blessing*. New York: Psychological Dimensions, 1975.

Geis, Gilbert. *Not the Law's Business*. Rockville, MD: National Institute of Mental Health, 1972.

Ginsburg, Faye D. *Contested Lives: The Abortion Debate in an American Community*. Berkeley: University of California Press, 1989.

Glendon, Mary Ann. *Abortion and Divorce in Western Law*. Cambridge, MA: Harvard University Press, 1987.

Glendon, Mary Ann. *Rights Talk*. New York: Free Press, 1991.

Gordon, Linda. *Woman's Body, Woman's Right*, rev. ed. New York: Penguin Books, 1990.

Grant, Nicole J. *The Selling of Contraception*. Columbus: Ohio State University Press, 1992.

Grisez, Germain G. *Abortion*. New York: Corpus Books, 1970.

Guttmacher, Alan F. *Babies by Choice or by Chance*. Garden City, NY: Doubleday, 1959.

Guttmacher, Alan F., ed. *The Case for Legalized Abortion Now*. Berkeley, CA: Diablo Press, 1967.

Hall, Robert E., ed. *Abortion in a Changing World*, 2 vols. New York: Columbia University Press, 1970.

Hall, Robert E. *A Doctor's Guide to Having an Abortion*. New York: New American Library, 1971.

Hanna, Mary T. *Catholics and American Politics*. Cambridge, MA: Harvard University Press, 1979.

Hardin, Garrett. *Mandatory Motherhood: The True Meaning of 'Right to Life.'* Boston: Beacon Press, 1974.

Hardin, Garrett. *Stalking the Wild Taboo*. Los Altos, CA: William Kaufmann, 1973.

Harper, Fowler V. *Justice Rutledge and the Bright Constellation*. Indianapolis: Bobbs-Merrill, 1965.

Harris, Louis, and Alan F. Westin. *The Dimensions of Privacy*. Stevens Point, WI: Sentry Insurance Co., 1979.

Harrison, Beverly W. *Our Right to Choose*. Boston: Beacon Press, 1983.

Hartmann, Susan M. *From Margin to Mainstream: American Women and Politics Since 1960*. New York: Alfred A. Knopf, 1989.

Hennesey, James. *American Catholics*. New York: Oxford University Press, 1981.

Hepburn, Katharine. *Me: Stories of My Life*. New York: Alfred A. Knopf, 1991.

Hern, Warren M., and Bonnie Andrikopoulos, eds. *Abortion in the Seventies*. New York: National Abortion Federation, 1977.

Hertz, Sue. *Caught in the Crossfire: A Year on Abortion's Front Line*. New York: Prentice-Hall, 1991.

Hilgers, Thomas W., and Dennis J. Horan, eds. *Abortion and Social Justice*. New York: Sheed & Ward, 1972.

Hilgers, Thomas W., et al., eds. *New Perspectives on Human Abortion*. Frederick, MD: University Publications of America, 1981.

Himes, Norman E. *Medical History of Contraception*. Baltimore: Williams & Wilkins, 1936.

Hodgson, Jane E., ed. *Abortion and Sterilization*. New York: Grune & Stratton, 1981.

Horan, Dennis J., et al. *Abortion and the Constitution: Reversing Roe v. Wade Through the Courts*. Washington, DC: Georgetown University Press, 1987.

Huser, Roger J. *The Crime of Abortion in Canon Law*. Washington, DC: Catholic University of America Press, 1942.

Imber, Jonathan B. *Abortion and the Private Practice of Medicine*. New Haven: Yale University Press, 1986.

Irons, Peter. *The Courage of Their Convictions*. New York: Free Press, 1988.

Irons, Peter, and Stephanie Guitton, eds. *May It Please the Court*. New York: The New Press, 1993.

Jaffe, Frederick S., et al. *Abortion Politics*. New York: McGraw-Hill, 1981.

Jain, Sagar C., and Laurel F. Gooch. *Georgia Abortion Act, 1968: A Study in Legislative Process*. Chapel Hill: University of North Carolina School of Public Health, 1972.

Jain, Sagar C., and Steven Hughes. *California Abortion Act 1967: A Study in Legislative Process*. Chapel Hill: Carolina Population Center, 1969.

Jain, Sagar C., and Steven W. Sinding. *North Carolina Abortion Law 1967*. Chapel Hill: Carolina Population Center, 1968.

Janes, Daryl, ed. *No Apologies: Texas Radicals Celebrate the '60s*. Austin, TX: Eakin Press, 1992.

Janick, Herbert F., Jr. *A Diverse People: Connecticut 1914 to the Present*. Chester, CT: Pequot Press, 1975.

Jeffries, John W. *Testing the Roosevelt Coalition: Connecticut Society and Politics in the Era of World War II*. Knoxville: University of Tennessee Press, 1979.

Judges, Donald P. *Hard Choices, Lost Voices*. Chicago: Ivan R. Dee, 1993.

Kalman, Laura. *Legal Realism at Yale, 1927–1960*. Chapel Hill: University of North Carolina Press, 1986.

Kamm, F. M. *Creation and Abortion*. New York: Oxford University Press, 1992.

Keemer, Ed. *Confessions of a Pro-Life Abortionist*. Detroit: Vinco Press, 1980.

Kelley, J. Ralph. *Catholics in Eastern Connecticut: The Diocese of Norwich*. Norwich: Diocese of Norwich, 1985.

Kennedy, David M. *Birth Control in America: The Career of Margaret Sanger*. New Haven: Yale University Press, 1970.

Krason, Stephen M. *Abortion*. Lanham, MD: University Press of America, 1984.

Kummer, Jerome M., ed. *Abortion: Legal and Illegal*. Santa Monica, CA: Santa Monica Printers, 1967.

Lader, Lawrence. *Abortion*. Indianapolis: Bobbs-Merrill, 1966.

Lader, Lawrence. *Abortion II: Making the Revolution*. Boston: Beacon Press, 1973.

Lader, Lawrence. *The Margaret Sanger Story*. Garden City, NY: Doubleday, 1955.

Lamb, Charles M., and Stephen C. Halpern, eds. *The Burger Court: Political and Judicial Profiles*. Urbana: University of Illinois Press, 1991.

Lamoreux, Stephen. *The Right of Privacy—A Bibliography: 71 Years, 1890–1961*. Spokane: Washington State University, 1961.

Lee, Nancy H. *The Search for an Abortionist*. Chicago: University of Chicago Press, 1969.

Lieberman, Joseph I. *The Legacy: Connecticut Politics 1930–1980*. Hartford: Spoonwood Press, 1981.

Lieberman, Joseph I. *The Power Broker: A Biography of John M. Bailey, Modern Political Boss*. Boston: Houghton Mifflin, 1966.

Linden-Ward, Blanche, and Carol Hurd Green. *Changing the Future: American Women in the 1960s*. New York: Twayne, 1993.

Liptak, Delores Ann. *European Immigrants and the Catholic Church in Connecticut, 1870–1920*. New York: Center for Migration Studies, 1987.

Littlewood, Thomas B. *The Politics of Population Control*. Notre Dame, IN: University of Notre Dame Press, 1977.

Lockard, Duane. *New England State Politics*. Princeton: Princeton University Press, 1959.

Lowe, David. *Abortion and the Law*. New York: Pocket Books, 1966.

Luker, Kristin. *Abortion and the Politics of Motherhood*. Berkeley: University of California Press, 1984.

Lunardini, Christine. *From Equal Suffrage to Equal Rights*. New York: New York University Press, 1986.

McDonnell, Kathleen. *Not an Easy Choice: A Feminist Re-examines Abortion*. Boston: South End Press, 1984.

McGuigan, Patrick B., and Dawn M. Weyrich. *Ninth Justice: The Fight for Bork*. Washington, DC: Free Congress Research and Education Foundation, 1990.

McKeegan, Michele. *Abortion Politics*. New York: Free Press, 1992.

McLaughlin, Loretta. *The Pill, John Rock, and the Church: The Biography of a Revolution*. Boston: Little Brown, 1982.

McWhirter, Darien A., and Jon D. Bible. *Privacy as a Constitutional Right*. New York: Quorum Books, 1992.

Manier, Edward, et al., eds. *Abortion: New Directions for Policy Studies*. Notre Dame, IN: University of Notre Dame Press, 1977.

Marx, Paul. *The Death Peddlers: War on the Unborn*. Collegeville, MN: Saint John's University Press, 1971.

Mason, Mary Paul. *Church-State Relationships in Education in Connecticut, 1633–1953*. Washington, DC: Catholic University of America Press, 1953.

Mensch, Elizabeth, and Alan Freeman. *The Politics of Virtue: Is Abortion Debatable?* Durham, NC: Duke University Press, 1993.

Mersky, Roy M., and Gary R. Hartman, eds. *A Documentary History of the Legal Aspects of Abortion in the United States: Webster v. Reproductive Health Services*. 8 vols. Littleton, CO: Fred B. Rothman & Co., 1990.

Merton, Andrew. *Enemies of Choice*. Boston: Beacon Press, 1981.

Messer, Ellen, and Kathryn E. May. *Back Rooms: Voices from the Illegal Abortion Era*. New York: St. Martin's Press, 1988.

Milbauer, Barbara. *The Law Giveth: Legal Aspects of the Abortion Controversy*. New York: Atheneum, 1983.

Miller, Patricia G. *The Worst of Times*. New York: HarperCollins, 1993.

Mohr, James C. *Abortion in America: The Origins and Evolution of National Policy, 1800–1900*. New York: Oxford University Press, 1978.

Moore, Gloria, and Ronald Moore. *Margaret Sanger and the Birth Control Movement: A Bibliography, 1911–1984*. Metuchen, NJ: Scarecrow Press, 1986.

Moore, Maurice J. *Death of a Dogma? The American Catholic Clergy's Views of Contraception*. Chicago: Community and Family Study Center, University of Chicago, 1973.

Morowitz, Harold J., and James S. Trefil. *The Facts of Life: Science and the Abortion Controversy*. New York: Oxford University Press, 1992.

Muldoon, Maureen. *Abortion: An Annotated Indexed Bibliography*. New York: Edwin Mellen Press, 1980.

Muldoon, Maureen. *The Abortion Debate in the United States and Canada: A Source Book*. New York: Garland Publishing, 1991.

Nathanson, Bernard. *Aborting America*. Garden City, NY: Doubleday, 1979.

National Committee on Maternal Health. *The Abortion Problem*. Baltimore: Williams & Wilkins, 1944.

Neier, Aryeh. *Only Judgment: The Limits of Litigation in Social Change*. Middletown, CT: Wesleyan University Press, 1982.

Nicholson, Susan Teft. *Abortion and the Roman Catholic Church*. Knoxville, TN: Religious Ethics, 1978.

Noonan, John T., Jr. *Contraception: A History of Its Treatment by the Catholic Theologians and Canonists*. Cambridge, MA: Harvard University Press, 1965.

Noonan, John T., Jr. *A Private Choice: Abortion in America in the Seventies*. New York: Free Press, 1979.

Noonan, John T., Jr., ed. *The Morality of Abortion*. Cambridge, MA: Harvard University Press, 1970.

O'Brien, David M. *The Right of Privacy—Its Constitutional and Social Dimensions*. Austin: Tarlton Law Library, University of Texas Law School, 1980.

O'Brien, David M. *Storm Center: The Supreme Court in American Politics*. New York: W. W. Norton & Co., 1986.

Olasky, Marvin. *Abortion Rites: A Social History of Abortion in America*. Wheaton, IL: Crossway Books, 1992.

Olasky, Marvin. *The Press and Abortion, 1838–1988*. Hillsdale, NJ: Lawrence Erlbaum, 1988.

O'Neil, Daniel J. *Church Lobbying in a Western State: A Case Study on Abortion Legislation*. Tucson: University of Arizona Press, 1970.

Osofsky, Howard J., and Joy D. Osofsky, eds. *The Abortion Experience*. Hagerstown, MD: Harper & Row, 1973.

O'Toole, James M. *Militant and Triumphant: William Henry O'Connell and the Catholic Church in Boston, 1859–1944*. Notre Dame, IN: University of Notre Dame Press, 1992.

Paige, Connie. *The Right to Lifers*. New York: Summit Books, 1983.

Patterson, Bennett B. *The Forgotten Ninth Amendment*. Indianapolis: Bobbs-Merrill, 1955.

Perry, H. W., Jr. *Deciding to Decide: Agenda Setting in the United States Supreme Court*. Cambridge, MA: Harvard University Press, 1991.

Petchesky, Rosalind P. *Abortion and Woman's Choice*, rev. ed. Boston: Northeastern University Press, 1990.

Piotrow, Phyllis T. *World Population Crisis: The United States Response*. New York: Praeger, 1973.

Posner, Richard A. *Sex and Reason*. Cambridge, MA: Harvard University Press, 1992.

Rafferty, Philip A. *Roe v. Wade: The Birth of a Constitutional Right*. Ann Arbor, MI: University Microfilms International, 1992.

Reed, James. *The Birth Control Movement and American Society: From Private Vice to Public Virtue*, rev. ed. Princeton: Princeton University Press, 1983.

Reese, Thomas J. *Archbishop: Inside the Power Structure of the American Catholic Church*. San Francisco: Harper & Row, 1989.

Reese, Thomas J. *A Flock of Shepherds: The National Conference of Catholic Bishops*. Kansas City: Sheed & Ward, 1992.

Reiterman, Carl, ed. *Abortion and the Unwanted Child*. New York: Springer Publishing Co., 1971.

Robinson, Victor. *Pioneers of Birth Control in England and America*. New York: Voluntary Parenthood League, 1919.

Robinson, William J. *The Law Against Abortion*. New York: Eugenics Publishing Co., 1933.

Rock, John. *The Time Has Come*. New York: Alfred A. Knopf, 1963.

Rodman, Hyman, et al. *The Abortion Question*. New York: Columbia University Press, 1987.

Rongy, Abraham J. *Abortion: Legal or Illegal?* New York: Vanguard Press, 1933.

Rosen, Harold. *Abortion in America*, rev. ed. Boston: Beacon Press, 1967.

Rosenberg, Gerald N. *The Hollow Hope*. Chicago: University of Chicago Press, 1991.

Rosenberg, Rosalind. *Divided Lives: American Women in the Twentieth Century*. New York: Hill and Wang, 1992.

Rosenblatt, Roger. *Life Itself*. New York: Random House, 1992.

Roth, David M. *Connecticut: A Bicentennial History*. New York: W. W. Norton & Co., 1979.

Rothman, Sheila M. *Woman's Proper Place*. New York: Basic Books, 1978.

Rowbotham, Sheila. *A New World for Women—Stella Browne: Socialist Feminist*. London: Pluto Press, 1977.

Rubin, Eva R. *Abortion, Politics, and the Courts: Roe v. Wade and Its Aftermath*, rev. ed. Westport, CT: Greenwood Press, 1987.

Rupp, Leila J., and Verta Taylor. *Survival in the Doldrums: The American Women's Rights Movement, 1945 to the 1960s*. New York: Oxford University Press, 1987.

Ruzek, Sheryl B. *The Women's Health Movement: Feminist Alternatives to Medical Control*. New York: Praeger, 1978.

Ryan, Barbara. *Feminism and the Women's Movement*. New York: Routledge, 1992.

Ryder, Norman B., and Charles F. Westoff. *Reproduction in the United States, 1965*. Princeton: Princeton University Press, 1971.

Sachdev, Paul, ed. *Perspectives on Abortion*. Metuchen, NJ: Scarecrow Press, 1985.

St. John-Stevas, Norman. *The Agonizing Choice: Birth Control, Religion and the Law*. Bloomington: Indiana University Press, 1971.

St. John-Stevas, Norman. *Birth Control and Public Policy*. Santa Barbara, CA: Center for the Study of Democratic Institutions, 1960.

Samar, Vincent J. *The Right to Privacy: Gays, Lesbians, and the Constitution*. Philadelphia: Temple University Press, 1991.

Sanger, Margaret. *Margaret Sanger: An Autobiography*. New York: W. W. Norton & Co., 1938.

Sanger, Margaret. *My Fight for Birth Control*. New York: Farrar & Rinehart, 1931.

Sarvis, Betty, and Hyman Rodman. *The Abortion Controversy*. New York: Columbia University Press, 1973.

Savage, David G. *Turning Right: The Making of the Rehnquist Supreme Court*. New York: John Wiley & Sons, 1992.

Schulder, Diane, and Florynce Kennedy. *Abortion Rap*. New York: McGraw-Hill, 1971.

Schur, Edwin M. *Crimes Without Victims*. Englewood Cliffs, NJ: Prentice-Hall, 1965.

Schwartz, Bernard. *The Ascent of Pragmatism*. Reading, MA: Addison-Wesley, 1990.

Schwartz, Bernard. *A History of the Supreme Court*. New York: Oxford University Press, 1993.

Schwartz, Bernard. *Super Chief: Earl Warren and His Supreme Court*. New York: New York University Press, 1983.

Schwartz, Bernard. *The Unpublished Opinions of the Burger Court*. New York: Oxford University Press, 1988.

Schwartz, Bernard. *The Unpublished Opinions of the Warren Court*. New York: Oxford University Press, 1985.

Segers, Mary C., ed. *Church Polity and American Politics*. New York: Garland Publishing, 1990.

Shaw, Russell B. *Abortion and Public Policy*. Washington, DC: Family Life Bureau, National Catholic Welfare Conference, 1966.

Shaw, Russell. *Abortion on Trial*. Dayton, OH: Pflaum Press, 1968.

Sheeran, Patrick J. *Women, Society, the State, and Abortion*. New York: Praeger, 1987.

Silverman, Milton, and Philip R. Lee. *Pills, Profits, and Politics*. Berkeley: University of California Press, 1974.

Simon, James F. *Independent Journey: The Life of William O. Douglas*. New York: Harper & Row, 1980.

Smith, David T., ed. *Abortion and the Law*. Cleveland: Case Western Reserve University Press, 1967.

Smith-Rosenberg, Carroll. *Disorderly Conduct*. New York: Alfred A. Knopf, 1985.

Snow, Wilbert. *Codline's Child: The Autobiography of Wilbert Snow*. Middletown, CT: Wesleyan University Press, 1974.

Sochen, June. *Movers and Shakers: American Women Thinkers and Activists, 1900–1970*. New York: Quadrangle Books, 1973.

Staggenborg, Suzanne. *The Pro-Choice Movement*. New York: Oxford University Press, 1991.

Steiner, Gilbert Y., ed. *The Abortion Dispute and the American System*. Washington, DC: Brookings Institution, 1983.

Steinhoff, Patricia G., and Milton Diamond. *Abortion Politics: The Hawaii Experience*. Honolulu: University Press of Hawaii, 1977.

Sulloway, Alvah W. *Birth Control and Catholic Doctrine*. Boston: Beacon Press, 1959.

Sumner, L. W. *Abortion and Moral Theory*. Princeton: Princeton University Press, 1981.

Tatalovich, Raymond, and Byron W. Daynes. *The Politics of Abortion*. New York: Praeger, 1981.

Taussig, Frederick J. *Abortion*. St. Louis: C. V. Mosby Co., 1936.

Tooley, Michael. *Abortion and Infanticide*. Oxford: Clarendon Press, 1983.

Tribe, Laurence H. *Abortion: The Clash of Absolutes*. New York: W. W. Norton & Co., 1990.

Tribe, Laurence H. *American Constitutional Law*, 2nd ed. Mineola, NY: Foundation Press, 1988.

Tribe, Laurence H., and Michael C. Dorf. *On Reading the Constitution*. Cambridge, MA: Harvard University Press, 1991.

U.S. Congress, House of Representatives, Committee on the Judiciary. *Abortion Clinic Violence—Oversight Hearings Before the Subcommittee on Civil and Constitutional Rights*, 99th Cong., 1st and 2nd sess., 6 March 1985–17 December 1986.

U.S. Congress, House of Representatives, Committee on the Judiciary. *Proposed Constitutional Amendments on Abortion—Hearings Before the Subcommittee on Civil and Constitutional Rights*, 94th Cong., 2nd sess., 4 February–26 March 1976.

U.S. Congress, Senate, Committee on the Judiciary. *Abortion Hearings Before the Subcommittee on Constitutional Amendments*, 93rd Cong., 2nd sess., and 94th Cong., 1st sess., 6 March 1974–8 July 1975, 4 parts.

U.S. Congress, Senate, Committee on the Judiciary. *Constitutional Amendments Relating to Abortion—Hearings Before the Subcommittee on the Constitution*, 97th Cong., 1st sess., 5 October–16 December 1981.

U.S. Congress, Senate, Committee on the Judiciary. *Hearings on the Nomination of Robert H. Bork to Be Associate Justice of the Supreme Court of the United States*, 100th Cong., 1st sess., 15–30 September 1987.

U.S. Congress, Senate, Committee on the Judiciary. *Hearings on the Nomination of Anthony M. Kennedy to Be Associate Justice of the Supreme Court of the United States*, 100th Cong., 1st sess., 14–16 December 1987.

U.S. Congress, Senate, Committee on the Judiciary. *Hearings on the Nomination of David H. Souter to Be Associate Justice of the Supreme Court of the United States*, 101st Cong., 2nd sess., 13–19 September 1990.

U.S. Congress, Senate, Committee on the Judiciary. *The Human Life Bill—Hearings Before the Subcommittee on Separation of Powers*, 97th Cong., 1st sess., 23 April–18 June 1981.

Van Dusen, Albert E. *Connecticut*. New York: Random House, 1961.

Walbert, David F., and J. Douglas Butler, eds. *Abortion, Society and the Law*. Cleveland: Case Western Reserve University Press, 1973.

Walker, Samuel. *In Defense of American Liberties*. New York: Oxford University Press, 1990.

Wandersee, Winifred. *On the Move: American Women in the 1970s*. Boston: Twayne, 1988.

Wardle, Lynn D. *The Abortion Privacy Doctrine*. Buffalo, NY: William S. Hein & Co., 1980.

Wardle, Lynn D., and Mary Anne Q. Wood. *A Lawyer Looks at Abortion*. Provo, UT: Brigham Young University Press, 1982.

Ware, Cellestine. *Woman Power: The Movement for Women's Liberation*. New York: Tower Publications, 1970.

Ware, Susan. *Holding Their Own: American Women in the 1930s*. Boston: Twayne, 1982.

Wasby, Stephen L., ed. *"He Shall Not Pass This Way Again": The Legacy of Justice William O. Douglas*. Pittsburgh: University of Pittsburgh Press, 1990.

Weddington, Sarah. *A Question of Choice*. New York: G. P. Putnam's Sons, 1992.

Weddington, Sarah, et al. *Texas Women in Politics*. Austin, TX: Foundation for Women's Resources, 1977.

Wenz, Peter S. *Abortion Rights as Religious Freedom*. Philadelphia: Temple University Press, 1992.

Westin, Alan F. *Privacy and Freedom*. New York: Atheneum, 1967.

Wilkinson, J. Harvie III. *Serving Justice: A Supreme Court Clerk's View*. New York: Charterhouse, 1974.

Williams, Glanville. *The Sanctity of Life and the Criminal Law*. New York: Alfred A. Knopf, 1957.

Woodward, Bob, and Scott Armstrong. *The Brethren: Inside the Supreme Court*. New York: Simon & Schuster, 1979.

Yarbrough, Tinsley E. *John Marshall Harlan*. New York: Oxford University Press, 1992.

Yates, Gayle G. *What Women Want: The Ideas of the Movement*. Cambridge, MA: Harvard University Press, 1975.

SELECTED ARTICLES

Abraham, Henry J., and Leo A. Hazlewood. "Comstockery at the Bar of Justice: Birth Control Legislation in the Federal, Connecticut, and Massachusetts Courts." *Law in Transition Quarterly* 4 (December 1967): 220–245.

Arnold, Richard S. "A Remembrance: Mr. Justice Brennan, October Term 1960." *Journal of Supreme Court History* 1991, pp. 5–8.

Asaro, Andrea. "The Judicial Portrayal of the Physician in Abortion and Sterilization Decisions: The Use and Abuse of Medical Discretion." *Harvard Women's Law Journal* 6 (Spring 1983): 51–102.

Ball, Donald W. "An Abortion Clinic Ethnography." *Social Problems* 14 (Winter 1967): 293–301.

Barron, James H. "Warren and Brandeis, *The Right to Privacy*, 4 Harv. L. Rev. 193 (1890): Demystifying a Landmark Citation." *Suffolk University Law Review* 13 (Summer 1979): 875–922.

Bart, Pauline B. "Seizing the Means of Reproduction: An Illegal Feminist Abortion Collective— How and Why It Worked," in Helen Roberts, ed., *Women, Health and Reproduction* (London: Routledge & Kegan Paul, 1981), pp. 109–128, and in *Qualitative Sociology* 10 (Winter 1987): 339–357.

Beaney, William M. "The Constitutional Right to Privacy in the Supreme Court." *Supreme Court Review* 1962, pp. 212–251.

Beilenson, Anthony C. "The Therapeutic Abortion Act: A Small Measure of Humanity." *Los Angeles Bar Bulletin* 41 (May 1966): 316–319, 344–346.

Bell, Joseph N. "A Landmark Decision." *Good Housekeeping*, June 1973, pp. 77–79ff.

Benshoff, Janet. "Reproductive Freedom," in Kenneth P. Norwick, ed., *Lobbying for Freedom in the 1980s* (New York: Wideview/Perigee, 1983), pp. 71–111.

Blake, Judith. "Abortion and Public Opinion: The 1960–1970 Decade." *Science* 171 (12 February 1971): 540–549.

Bloom, Lackland H., Jr. "The Legacy of *Griswold*." *Ohio Northern University Law Review* 16 (1989): 511–544.

Bork, Robert H. "Neutral Principles and Some First Amendment Problems." *Indiana Law Journal* 47 (Fall 1971): 1–17.

Bork, Robert H. "The Supreme Court Needs a New Philosophy." *Fortune* 78 (December 1968): 138–141, 170–177.

Brooks, Carol F. "The Early History of the Anti-Contraception Laws in Massachusetts and Connecticut." *American Quarterly* 18 (Spring 1966): 3–23.

Browne, F. W. Stella. "The Right of Abortion," in Norman Haire, ed., *Sexual Reform Congress* (London: Kegan Paul, 1930), pp. 178–181.

Brownmiller, Susan. "Abortion Counseling: Service Beyond Sermons." *New York Magazine*, 4 August 1969, pp. 26–31.

Buxton, C. Lee. "Advances in Obstetrics and Gynecology." *The Practitioner* 181 (October 1958): 395–403.

Buxton, C. Lee. "Birth Control Problems in Connecticut: Medical Necessity, Political Cowardice and Legal Procrastination." *Connecticut Medicine* 28 (August 1964): 581–584.

Buxton, C. Lee. "Family Planning Clinics in Connecticut." *Connecticut Medicine* 32 (February 1968): 122–124.

Buxton, C. Lee. "One Doctor's Opinion of Abortion Laws." *American Journal of Nursing* 68 (May 1968): 1026–1028.

Byrn, Robert M. "The Abortion Amendments: Policy in the Light of Precedent." *St. Louis University Law Journal* 18 (Spring 1974): 380–406.

Byrn, Robert M. "Abortion in Perspective." *Duquesne University Law Review* 5 (1966–67): 125–141.

Byrn, Robert M. "Abortion-on-Demand: Whose Morality?" *Notre Dame Lawyer* 46 (Fall 1970): 5–40.

Byrn, Robert M. "The Abortion Question: A Nonsectarian Approach." *Catholic Lawyer* 11 (Autumn 1965): 316–322.

Byrn, Robert M. "An American Tragedy: The Supreme Court on Abortion." *Fordham Law Review* 41 (May 1973): 807–862.

Byrn, Robert M. "Demythologizing Abortion Reform." *Catholic Lawyer* 14 (Summer 1968): 180–189.

Calderone, Mary S. "Illegal Abortion as a Public Health Problem." *American Journal of Public Health* 50 (July 1960): 948–954.

Callahan, Daniel. "Contraception and Abortion: American Catholic Responses." *The Annals* 387 (January 1970): 109–117.

Cisler, Lucinda. "Abortion: A Major Battle Is Over—But the War Is Not." *Feminist Studies* 1 (1973): 121–131.

Cisler, Lucinda. "Abortion Law Repeal (Sort Of): A Warning to Women," in Anne Koedt et al., eds., *Radical Feminism* (New York: Quadrangle, 1973), pp. 151–164.

Cisler, Lucinda. "A Campaign to Repeal Legal Restrictions on Non-Prescription Contraceptives: The Case of New York," in Myron H. Redford et al., eds., *The Condom* (San Francisco: San Francisco Press, 1974), pp. 83–108.

Cisler, Lucinda. "Unfinished Business: Birth Control and Women's Liberation," in Robin Morgan, ed., *Sisterhood Is Powerful* (New York: Random House, 1970), pp. 245–289.

Clark, Tom C. "Religion, Morality, and Abortion: A Constitutional Appraisal." *Loyola University Law Review* 2 (April 1969): 1–11.

Copelon, Rhonda. "Beyond the Liberal Idea of Privacy: Toward a Positive Right of Autonomy," in Michael W. McCann and Gerald L. Houseman, eds., *Judging the Constitution* (Glenview, IL: Scott, Foresman & Co., 1989), pp. 287–314.

Copelon, Rhonda. "Unpacking Patriarchy: Reproduction, Sexuality, Originalism, and Constitutional Change," in Jules Lobel, ed., *A Less Than Perfect Union* (New York: Monthly Review Press, 1988), pp. 303–334.

Cowan, Ruth B. "Women's Rights Through Litigation: An Examination of the American Civil Liberties Union Women's Rights Project, 1971–1976." *Columbia Human Rights Law Review* 8 (Spring-Summer 1976): 373–412.

Craven, J. Braxton, Jr. "Personhood: The Right to Be Let Alone." *Duke Law Journal* 1976 (September): 699–720.

Curran, Charles E. "Abortion: Law and Morality in Contemporary Catholic Theology." *The Jurist* 33 (Spring 1973): 162–83.

Davis, Nanette J. "Clergy Abortion Brokers: A Transactional Analysis of Social Movement Development." *Sociological Focus* 6 (Fall 1973): 87–109.

DeBoice, Brian. "Due Process Privacy and the Path of Progress." *University of Illinois Law Forum* 1979, pp. 469–546.

Dellapenna, Joseph W. "The History of Abortion: Technology, Morality, and Law." *University of Pittsburgh Law Review* 40 (Spring 1979): 359–428.

Dellapenna, Joseph W. "Nor Piety nor Wit: The Supreme Court on Abortion." *Columbia Human Rights Law Review* 6 (Fall-Winter 1974–75): 379–413.

Dellinger, Walter, and Gene B. Sperling. "Abortion and the Supreme Court: The Retreat from *Roe* v. *Wade*." *University of Pennsylvania Law Review* 138 (November 1989): 83–118.

Dixon, Robert G. "The *Griswold* Penumbra: Constitutional Charter for an Expanded Law of Privacy?" *Michigan Law Review* 64 (December 1965): 197–218.

Drinan, Robert F. "Catholic Moral Teaching and Abortion Laws in America." *Catholic Theological Society of America Proceedings* 23 (June 1968): 118–130.

Drinan, Robert F. "The Inviolability of the Right to Be Born." *Western Reserve Law Review* 17 (December 1965): 465–479.

Drinan, Robert F. "The Jurisprudential Options on Abortion." *Theological Studies* 31 (March 1970): 149–169.

Drinan, Robert F. "The Morality of Abortion Laws." *Catholic Lawyer* 14 (Summer 1968): 190–198, 264.

Drinan, Robert F. "The Right of the Foetus to Be Born." *Dublin Review* 241 (Winter 1967–1968): 365–381.

Dudziak, Mary L. "Just Say No: Birth Control in the Connecticut Supreme Court Before *Griswold* v. *Connecticut*," *Iowa Law Review* 75 (May 1990): 915–939, and in Paul Finkelman and Stephen E. Gottlieb, eds., *Toward a Usable Past* (Athens: University of Georgia Press, 1991), pp. 304–338.

Dworkin, Ronald. "Unenumerated Rights: Whether and How *Roe* Should Be Overruled." *University of Chicago Law Review* 59 (Winter 1992): 381–432.

Ely, John H. "The Wages of Crying Wolf: A Comment on *Roe* v. *Wade*." *Yale Law Journal* 82 (April 1973): 920–949.

Emerson, Thomas I. "Nine Justices in Search of a Doctrine." *Michigan Law Review* 64 (December 1965): 219–234.

Emerson, Thomas I. "The Power of Congress to Change Constitutional Decisions of the Supreme Court: The Human Life Bill." *Northwestern University Law Review* 77 (April 1982): 129–142.

Emerson, Thomas I. "The Right of Privacy and Freedom of the Press." *Harvard Civil Rights–Civil Liberties Law Review* 14 (Summer 1979): 329–360.

Ernst, Morris L. "There Is Desperate Need of Medical Wisdom to Deal with the Problem of 'Abortion.'" *New Medical Materia* 4 (July 1962): 21–23.

Estrich, Susan R., and Kathleen M. Sullivan. "Abortion Politics: Writing for an Audience of One." *University of Pennsylvania Law Review* 138 (November 1989): 119–155.

Evans, J. Claude, "The Abortion Decision: A Balancing of Rights," *Christian Century*, 14 February 1973, pp. 195–197.

Evans, J. Claude. "Abortion-Law Reform Is Inevitable—Even in Texas." *Christian Century*, 5 May 1971, pp. 548–549.

Evans, J. Claude. "Defusing the Abortion Debate." *Christian Century*, 31 January 1973, pp. 117–118.

Farber, Daniel A., and John E. Nowak. "Beyond the *Roe* Debate: Judicial Experience with the 1980's 'Reasonableness' Test." *Virginia Law Review* 76 (April 1990): 519–538.

Farrell, Margaret G. "Revisiting *Roe* v. *Wade*: Substance and Process in the Abortion Debate." *Indiana Law Journal* 68 (Spring 1993): 269–362.

Faulkner, William. "On Privacy—The American Dream: What Happened to It." *Harper's* 211 (July 1955): 33–38.

Faux, Marian. "*Roe* v. *Wade*." *Memories* 3 (June-July 1990): 94–98.

Fein, Bruce. "*Griswold* v. *Connecticut*: Wayward Decision-Making in the Supreme Court." *Ohio Northern University Law Review* 16 (1989): 551–559.

Finkbine, Sherri. "The Baby We Didn't Dare to Have." *Redbook*, January 1963, pp. 50, 99–104.

Fried, Charles. "The Conservatism of Justice Harlan." *New York Law School Law Review* 36 (1991): 33–52.

Fried, Charles. "Privacy." *Yale Law Journal* 77 (January 1968): 475–493.

Gamson, Joshua. "Rubber Wars: Struggles Over the Condom in the United States." *Journal of the History of Sexuality* 1 (October 1990): 262–282.

Garfield, Helen. "Privacy, Abortion, and Judicial Review: Haunted by the Ghost of *Lochner*." *Washington Law Review* 61 (April 1986): 293–365.

Gavigan, Shelley. "The Criminal Sanction as It Relates to Human Reproduction: The Genesis of the Statutory Prohibition of Abortion." *Journal of Legal History* 5 (May 1984): 20–43.

George, B. James, Jr. "Current Abortion Laws: Proposals and Movements for Reform." *Western Reserve Law Review* 17 (December 1965): 371–402.

Ginsburg, Ruth B. "Some Thoughts on Autonomy and Equality in Relation to *Roe* v. *Wade*." *North Carolina Law Review* 63 (January 1985): 375–386.

Glancy, Dorothy J. "The Invention of the Right to Privacy." *Arizona Law Review* 21 (1979): 1–39.

Glen, Kristin B. "Abortion in the Courts: A Laywoman's Historical Guide to the New Disaster Area." *Feminist Studies* 4 (February 1978): 1–26.

Godkin, E. L. "The Right of the Citizen." *Scribner's Magazine* 8 (July 1890): 58–67.

Goldstein, Michael S. "Creating and Controlling a Medical Market: Abortion in Los Angeles After Liberalization." *Social Problems* 31 (June 1984): 514–529.

Goodman, Janice, et al. "*Doe* and *Roe*: Where Do We Go From Here?" *Women's Rights Law Reporter* 1 (Spring 1973): 20–38.

Gordon, Linda, and Hunter, Allen. "Sex, Family and the New Right: Anti-Feminism as a Political Force." *Radical America* 11–12 (December 1977–February 1978): 9–25.

Greely, Henry T. "A Footnote to 'Penumbra' in *Griswold* v. *Connecticut*." *Constitutional Commentary* 6 (Summer 1989): 251–265.

Greenhouse, Linda J. "Constitutional Question: Is There a Right to Abortion?" *New York Times Magazine*, 25 January 1970, pp. 30–31, 88–91.

Grey, Thomas C. "Eros, Civilization and the Burger Court." *Law and Contemporary Problems* 43 (Summer 1980): 83–100.

Guttmacher, Alan F. "Changing Attitudes and Practices Concerning Abortion: A Sociomedical Revolution." *Maryland State Medical Journal* 20 (December 1971): 59–63.

Guttmacher, Alan F. "A Defense of the Supreme Court's Abortion Decision." *The Humanist* 33 (May-June 1973): 6–7.

Guttmacher, Alan F. "The Genesis of Liberalized Abortion in New York: A Personal Insight." *Case Western Reserve Law Review* 23 (Summer 1972): 756–778.

Guttmacher, Alan F. "The Legal and Moral Status of Therapeutic Abortion." *Progress in Gynecology* 4 (1963): 279–300.

Hall, Robert E. "Abortion in American Hospitals." *American Journal of Public Health* 57 (November 1967): 1933–1936.

Hall, Robert E. "Abortion Laws: A Call for Reform." *DePaul Law Review* 18 (Summer 1969): 584–592.

Hall, Robert E. "Abortion: Physician and Hospital Attitudes." *American Journal of Public Health* 61 (March 1971): 517–519.

Hall, Robert E. "The Abortion Revolution." *Playboy* 17 (September 1970): 112ff.

Hall, Robert E. "The Future of Therapeutic Abortions in the United States." *Clinical Obstetrics & Gynecology* 14 (December 1971): 1149–1153.

Hall, Robert E. "The Medico-Legal Aspects of Abortion." *Criminologica* 4 (February 1967): 7–10.

Hall, Robert E. "The Medicolegal Aspects of Abortion." *Obstetrics & Gynecology Annual* 1972, pp. 339–350.

Hall, Robert E. "New York Abortion Law Survey." *American Journal of Obstetrics and Gynecology* 93 (15 December 1965): 1182–1183.

Hall, Robert E. "Thalidomide and Our Abortion Laws." *Columbia University Forum* 6 (Winter 1963): 10–13.

Hall, Robert E. "The Truth About Abortion in New York." *Columbia Forum* 13 (Winter 1970): 18–22.

Halva-Neubauer, Glen. "Abortion Policy in the Post-*Webster* Age." *Publius* 20 (Summer 1990): 27–44.

Hand, Augustus N. "*Schuyler* Against *Curtis* and the Right to Privacy." *American Law Register and Review* 45 (December 1897): 745–759.

Hardin, Garrett. "Abortion—Or Compulsory Pregnancy?" *Journal of Marriage and the Family* 30 (May 1968): 246–251.

Hardin, Garrett. "The History and Future of Birth Control." *Perspectives in Biology and Medicine* 10 (Autumn 1966): 1–18.

Hardin, Garrett. "Semantic Aspects of Abortion." *ETC* 24 (September 1967): 263–281.

Harper, John P. "Be Fruitful and Multiply: Origins of Legal Restrictions on Planned Parenthood in Nineteenth-Century America," in Carol R. Berkin and Mary Beth Norton, eds., *Women of America* (Boston: Houghton Mifflin, 1979), pp. 245–265.

Harrison, Irwin P. "Connecticut's Contraceptive Statute: A Recurring Problem in Constitutional Law." *Connecticut Bar Journal* 35 (September 1960): 310–319.

Henly, Burr. "'Penumbra': The Roots of a Legal Metaphor." *Hastings Constitutional Law Quarterly* 15 (Fall 1987): 81–100.

Hepburn, Katharine. "Let's Face the Facts About Abortion." *Family Circle*, 12 January 1982, pp. 64–65.

Hern, Warren M. "The Politics of Choice: Abortion as Insurrection," in W. Penn Handwerker, ed., *Births and Power* (Boulder, CO: Westview Press, 1990), pp. 127–145.

Herndon, J. Emmett. "Religious Aspects and Theology in Therapeutic Abortion." *Southern Medical Journal* 63 (June 1970): 651–654.

Heymann, Philip B., and Douglas E. Barzelay. "The Forest and the Trees: *Roe* v. *Wade* and Its Critics." *Boston University Law Review* 53 (May 1973): 765–784.

Hirsch, Harold L. "Impact of the Supreme Court Decisions on the Performance of Abortions in the United States." *Forensic Science* 3 (June 1974): 209–223.

Hodgson, Jane E. "Abortion: The Law and the Reality." *Mayo Alumnus* 6 (October 1970): 1–4.

Hodgson, Jane E. "Community Abortion Services." *Minnesota Medicine* 56 (March 1973): 239–242.

Hodgson, Jane E. "Therapeutic Abortion in Medical Perspective." *Minnesota Medicine* 53 (July 1970): 755–757.

Humphries, Drew. "The Movement to Legalize Abortion: A Historical Account," in David F. Greenberg, ed., *Corrections and Punishment* (Beverly Hills, CA: Sage Publications, 1977), pp. 205–224.

Hunter, Nan D. "Life After *Hardwick*." *Harvard Civil Rights–Civil Liberties Law Review* 27 (Summer 1992): 531–554.

Jaffe, Frederick S. "Knowledge, Perception, and Change: Notes on a Fragment of Social History." *Mount Sinai Journal of Medicine* 42 (July-August 1975): 286–299.

Janick, Herbert F., Jr. "The New Social History in Twentieth-Century Connecticut." *Connecticut History* 23 (April 1982): 153–167.

Jenkins, John A. "A Candid Talk with Justice Blackmun." *New York Times Magazine*, 20 February 1983, pp. 20–29, 57–66.

Jesse, R. W., and Frederick J. Spencer. "Abortion—The Hidden Epidemic." *Virginia Medical Monthly* 95 (August 1968): 447–456.

Joffe, Carol. "Portraits of Three 'Physicians of Conscience': Abortion Before Legalization in the United States." *Journal of the History of Sexuality* 2 (July 1991): 46–67.

Johnson, Amy. "Abortion, Personhood, and Privacy in Texas." *Texas Law Review* 68 (June 1990): 1521–1544.

Johnson, R. Christian. "Feminism, Philanthropy and Science in the Development of the Oral Contraceptive Pill." *Pharmacy in History* 19 (1977): 63–78.

Karst, Kenneth. "The Freedom of Intimate Association." *Yale Law Journal* 89 (March 1980): 624–692.

Katz, Esther. "The History of Birth Control in the United States." *Trends in History* 4 (1988): 81–101.

Kauper, Paul G. "Penumbras, Peripheries, Emanations, Things Fundamental and Things Forgotten: The *Griswold* Case." *Michigan Law Review* 64 (December 1965): 235–258.

Kenealy, William J. "Contraception—A Violation of God's Law." *Catholic Mind* 46 (September 1948): 552–564.

Koh, Harold H. "Rebalancing the Medical Triad: Justice Blackmun's Contributions to Law and Medicine." *American Journal of Law & Medicine* 13 (Summer-Fall 1987): 315–334.

Koppelman, Andrew. "Forced Labor: A Thirteenth Amendment Defense of Abortion." *Northwestern University Law Review* 84 (Winter 1990): 480–535.

Kummer, Jerome M. "Don't Shy Away from Therapeutic Abortion!" *Medical Economics* 37 (11 April 1960): 165–171.

Kummer, Jerome M. "New Trends in Therapeutic Abortion in California." *Obstetrics and Gynecology* 34 (December 1969): 883–887.

Kummer, Jerome M., and Zad Leavy. "Criminal Abortion—A Consideration of Ways to Reduce Incidence." *California Medicine* 95 (September 1961): 170–175.

Lader, Lawrence. "The Scandal of Abortion Laws." *New York Times Magazine*, 25 April 1965, pp. 32ff.

Lamm, Richard D. "The Reproductive Revolution." *American Bar Association Journal* 56 (January 1970): 41–44.

Lamm, Richard D. "Therapeutic Abortion: The Role of State Government." *Clinical Obstetrics & Gynecology* 14 (December 1971): 1204–1207.

Lamm, Richard D., et al. "The Legislative Process in Changing Therapeutic Abortion Laws: The Colorado Experience." *American Journal of Orthopsychiatry* 39 (July 1969): 684–690.

Lamm, Richard D., and Steven G. Davison. "Abortion Reform." *Yale Review of Law and Social Action* 1 (Spring 1971): 55–63.

Law, Sylvia. "Rethinking Sex and the Constitution." *University of Pennsylvania Law Review* 132 (June 1984): 955–1040.

Leavy, Zad. "Criminal Abortion: Facing the Facts." *Los Angeles Bar Journal* 34 (October 1959): 355–360, 373–383.

Leavy, Zad. "Current Developments in the Law of Abortion: 1969—A Landmark Year." *Los Angeles Bar Bulletin* 45 (November 1969): 11–15, 36–37.

Leavy, Zad. "Living with the Therapeutic Abortion Act of 1967." *Clinical Obstetrics & Gynecology* 14 (December 1971): 1154–1164.

Leavy, Zad, and Jerome M. Kummer. "Abortion and the Population Crisis: Therapeutic Abortion and the Law; Some New Approaches." *Ohio State Law Journal* 27 (Fall 1966): 647–678.

Leavy, Zad, and Jerome M. Kummer. "Criminal Abortion: Human Hardship and Unyielding Laws." *Southern California Law Review* 35 (Winter 1962): 123–148.

Linton, Paul. "Enforcement of State Abortion Statutes After *Roe*: A State by State Analysis." *University of Detroit Law Review* 67 (Winter 1990): 157–259.

Lucas, Roy. "Federal Constitutional Limitations on the Enforcement and Administration of State Abortion Statutes." *North Carolina Law Review* 46 (June 1968): 730–778.

Lucas, Roy. "The Right to Higher Education." *Journal of Higher Education* 41 (January 1970): 55–64.

MacKinnon, Catharine. "The Male Ideology of Privacy: A Feminist Perspective on the Right to Abortion." *Radical America* 17 (July-August 1983): 23–35.

Maledon, William J. "Justice William Brennan: A Personal Tribute." *Arizona State Law Journal* 22 (Winter 1990): 820–827.

Maledon, William J. "The Law and the Unborn Child: The Legal and Logical Inconsistencies." *Notre Dame Lawyer* 46 (Winter 1971): 349–372.

Manning, Peter K. "Fixing What You Feared: Notes on the Campus Abortion Search," in James M. Henslin, ed., *Studies in the Sociology of Sex* (New York: Appleton-Century-Crofts, 1971), pp. 137–166.

Martin, John Bartlow. "Abortion." *Saturday Evening Post*, 20 May 1961, pp. 19–21, 72–74, 27 May 1961, pp. 20–21, 49–56, and 3 June 1961, pp. 25, 91–92.

Means, Cyril C., Jr. "The Constitutional Aspects of a National Population Policy." *Villanova Law Review* 15 (Summer 1970): 854–862.

Means, Cyril C., Jr. "The Law of New York Concerning Abortion and the Status of the Foetus, 1664–1968: A Case of Cessation of Constitutionality." *New York Law Forum* 14 (Fall 1968): 411–515.

Means, Cyril C., Jr. "The Phoenix of Abortional Freedom: Is A Penumbral or Ninth Amendment Right About to Arise From the Nineteenth Century Legislative Ashes of a Fourteenth Century Common Law Liberty?" *New York Law Forum* 17 (1971): 335–410.

Mensel, Robert E. "'Kodakers Lying in Wait': Amateur Photography and the Right of Privacy in New York, 1885–1915." *American Quarterly* 43 (March 1991): 24–45.

Mohr, James C. "Iowa's Abortion Battles of the Late 1960s and Early 1970s: Long-Term Perspectives and Short-Term Analyses." *Annals of Iowa* 50 (Summer 1989): 63–89.

Mohr, James C. "Patterns of Abortion and the Response of American Physicians, 1790–1930," in Judith W. Leavitt, ed., *Women and Health in America* (Madison: University of Wisconsin Press, 1984), pp. 117–123.

Moody, Howard. "Man's Vengeance on Woman: Some Reflections on Abortion Laws." *Renewal*, February 1967, pp. 6–8.

Morgan, Richard G. "*Roe* v. *Wade* and the Lesson of the Pre-*Roe* Case Law." *Michigan Law Review* 77 (August 1979): 1724–1748.

Moynihan, Ruth B. "Coming of Age: Four Centuries of Connecticut Women and Their Choices." *Connecticut Historical Society Bulletin* 53 (Winter-Spring 1988): 9–112.

Mulligan, Edward T. "*Griswold* Revisited in Light of *Uplinger*: An Historical and Philosophical Exposition of Implied Autonomy Rights in the Constitution." *New York University Review of Law & Social Change* 13 (1984–85): 51–82.

Munson, H. Benjamin. "Abortion in Modern Times." *South Dakota Journal of Medicine* 19 (April 1966): 23–25, 28–30.

Nichols, Carole. "Votes and More for Women: Suffrage and After in Connecticut." *Women & History* 5 (Spring 1983): 1–92.

Nicholson, Jeanne B., and Debra W. Stewart. "The Supreme Court, Abortion Policy, and State Response: A Preliminary Analysis." *Publius* 8 (Winter 1978): 159–178.

Nicoll, Christine E., and Robert G. Weisbord. "The Early Years of the Rhode Island Birth Control League." *Rhode Island History* 45 (November 1986): 111–125.

Noonan, John T., Jr. "Abortion and the Catholic Church: A Summary History." *Natural Law Forum* 12 (1967): 85–131.

Noonan, John T., Jr. "Amendment of the Abortion Law: Relevant Data and Judicial Opinion." *Catholic Lawyer* 15 (Spring 1969): 124–135.

Noonan, John T., Jr. "The Constitutionality of the Regulation of Abortion." *Hastings Law Journal* 21 (November 1969): 51–65.

Noonan, John T., Jr. "The Root and Branch of *Roe* v. *Wade*." *Nebraska Law Review* 63 (1984): 668–679.

Ober, William B. "We Should Legalize Abortion." *Saturday Evening Post*, 8 October 1966, pp. 14, 20.

O'Connor, Karen, and Lee Epstein. "Beyond Legislative Lobbying: Women's Rights Groups and the Supreme Court." *Judicature* 67 (September 1983): 134–143.

Olasky, Marvin. "Abortion News in the Late 1920s: A New York City Case Study." *Journalism Quarterly* 66 (Autumn 1989): 724–726.

Olasky, Marvin. "Engineering Social Change: Triumphs of Abortion Public Relations from the Thirties Through the Sixties." *Public Relations Quarterly* 33 (Winter 1988–89): 17–21.

Olasky, Marvin. "Victorian Secret: Pro-Life Victories in 19th-Century America." *Policy Review* 60 (Spring 1992): 30–37.

Olasky, Marvin, and Susan N. Olasky. "The Crossover in Newspaper Coverage of Abortion from Murder to Liberation." *Journalism Quarterly* 63 (Spring 1986): 31–37.

O'Toole, James M. "Prelates and Politicos: Catholics and Politics in Massachusetts, 1900–1970," in Robert E. Sullivan and O'Toole, eds., *Catholic Boston* (Boston: Archdiocese of Boston, 1985), pp. 15–65.

Packer, Herbert L., and Ralph J. Gampell. "Therapeutic Abortion: A Problem in Law and Medicine." *Stanford Law Review* 11 (May 1959): 417–455.

Pearson, Albert M., and Paul M. Kurtz. "The Abortion Controversy: A Study in Law and Politics." *Harvard Journal of Law and Public Policy* 8 (Spring 1985): 427–464.

Petchesky, Rosalind P. "Antiabortion, Antifeminism, and the Rise of the New Right." *Feminist Studies* 7 (Summer 1981): 206–246.

Petchesky, Rosalind P. "Fetal Images: The Power of Visual Culture in the Politics of Reproduction." *Feminist Studies* 13 (Summer 1987): 263–292.

Petchesky, Rosalind P. "Reproductive Freedom: Beyond 'A Woman's Right to Choose.'" *Signs* 5 (Summer 1980): 661–685.

Pilpel, Harriet F. "Birth Control and a New Birth of Freedom." *Ohio State Law Journal* 27 (Fall 1966): 679–690.

Pilpel, Harriet F. "The Right of Abortion." *Atlantic* 223 (June 1969): 69–71.

Pilpel, Harriet F. "Sex vs. the Law: A Study in Hypocrisy." *Harper's* 230 (January 1965): 35–40.

Pine, Rachael N., and Sylvia A. Law. "Envisioning a Future for Reproductive Liberty: Strategies for Making the Rights Real." *Harvard Civil Rights–Civil Liberties Law Review* 27 (Summer 1992): 407–463.

Posner, Richard A. "Legal Reasoning from the Top Down and from the Bottom Up: The Question of Unenumerated Constitutional Rights." *University of Chicago Law Review* 59 (Winter 1992): 433–450.

Posner, Richard A. "The Uncertain Protection of Privacy By the Supreme Court." *Supreme Court Review* 1979, pp. 173–216.

Prickett, Morgan D. S. "The Right of Privacy: A Black View of *Griswold* v. *Connecticut*." *Hastings Constitutional Law Quarterly* 7 (Spring 1980): 777–829.

Prosser, William L. "Privacy." *California Law Review* 48 (August 1960): 383–423.

Quay, Eugene. "Justifiable Abortion—Medical and Legal Foundations." *Georgetown Law Journal* 49 (Winter 1960): 173–256 and (Spring 1961): 395–538.

Ray, Joyce M., and F. G. Gosling. "American Physicians and Birth Control, 1936–1947." *Journal of Social History* 18 (Spring 1985): 399–411.

Reagan, Leslie J. "'About to Meet Her Maker': Women, Doctors, Dying Declarations, and the State's Investigation of Abortion, Chicago, 1867–1940." *Journal of American History* 77 (March 1991): 1240–1264.

Redlich, Norman. "Are There 'Certain Rights . . . Retained by the People'?" *New York University Law Review* 37 (November 1962): 787–812.

Reed, James. "Doctors, Birth Control, and Social Values: 1830–1970," in Morris J. Vogel and Charles E. Rosenberg, eds., *The Therapeutic Revolution* (Philadelphia: University of Pennsylvania Press, 1979), pp. 109–133.

Regan, Richard J. "The Connecticut Birth Control Ban and Public Morals." *Catholic Lawyer* 7 (Winter 1961): 5–10, 49.

Rehnquist, William H. "Is an Expanded Right of Privacy Consistent with Fair and Effective Law Enforcement?" *Kansas Law Review* 23 (Fall 1974): 1–22.

Reynolds, Glenn H. "Sex, Lies and Jurisprudence: Robert Bork, *Griswold* and the Philosophy of Original Understanding." *Georgia Law Review* 24 (Summer 1990): 1045–1113.

Rhoden, Nancy K. "Trimesters and Technology: Revamping *Roe* v. *Wade*." *Yale Law Journal* 95 (March 1986): 639–697.

Richards, David A. J. "Constitutional Legitimacy and Constitutional Privacy." *New York University Law Review* 61 (November 1986): 800–862.

Robertson, John A. "Gestational Burdens and Fetal Status: Justifying *Roe* v. *Wade*." *American Journal of Law & Medicine* 13 (Summer-Fall 1987): 189–212.

Rodell, Fred. "Morris Ernst: New York's Unlawyerlike Liberal Lawyer Is the Censor's Enemy, the President's Friend." *Life*, 21 February 1944, pp. 97–98, 100–107.

Roemer, Ruth. "Abortion Law Reform and Repeal: Legislative and Judicial Developments." *American Journal of Public Health* 61 (March 1971): 500–509.

Roraback, Catherine G. "*Griswold* v. *Connecticut*: A Brief Case History." *Ohio Northern University Law Review* 16 (1989): 395–401.

Rossi, Alice S. "Abortion Laws and Their Victims." *Transaction* 3 (September-October 1966): 7–12.

Rossi, Alice S. "Abortion and Social Change." *Dissent* 16 (July-August 1969): 338–346.

Rossi, Alice S., and Bhavani Sitaraman. "Abortion in Context: Historical Trends and Future Changes." *Family Planning Perspectives* 20 (November-December 1988): 273–281, 301.

Rubenfeld, Jed. "On the Legal Status of the Proposition That 'Life Begins at Conception.'" *Stanford Law Review* 43 (February 1991): 599–635.

Rubenfeld, Jed. "The Right of Privacy." *Harvard Law Review* 102 (February 1989): 737–807.

Rubin, Alissa. "Interest Groups and Abortion Politics in the Post-*Webster* Era," in Allan J. Cigler and Burdett A. Loomis, eds., *Interest Group Politics*, 3rd ed. (Washington, DC: CQ Press, 1991), pp. 239–255.

Salper, Roberta. "The Development of the American Women's Liberation Movement,

1967–1971," in Salper, ed., *Female Liberation* (New York: Alfred A. Knopf, 1972), pp. 169–184.

Sandel, Michael J. "Moral Argument and Liberal Toleration: Abortion and Homosexuality." *California Law Review* 77 (May 1989): 521–538.

Sauer, R. "Attitudes to Abortion in America, 1800–1973." *Population Studies* 28 (March 1974): 53–67.

Schatz, Ronald W. "Connecticut's Working Class in the 1950s: A Catholic Perspective." *Labor History* 25 (Winter 1984): 83–101.

Schlesinger, Melinda Bart, and Pauline B. Bart. "Collective Work and Self-Identity: Working in a Feminist Illegal Abortion Collective," in Frank Lindenfeld and Joyce Rothschild-Whitt, eds., *Workplace Democracy and Social Change* (Boston: Porter Sargent, 1982), pp. 139–153.

Schneider, Carl E. "State-Interest Analysis in Fourteenth Amendment 'Privacy' Law: An Essay on the Constitutionalization of Social Issues." *Law and Contemporary Problems* 51 (Winter 1988): 79–122.

Segers, Mary C. "Governing Abortion Policy," in Richard A. L. Gambitta et al., eds., *Governing Through Courts* (Beverly Hills, CA: Sage Publications, 1981), pp. 283–300.

Siegel, Reva. "Reasoning from the Body: A Historical Perspective on Abortion Regulation and Questions of Equal Protection." *Stanford Law Review* 44 (January 1992): 261–381.

Sigworth, Heather. "Abortion Laws in the Federal Courts—The Supreme Court as Supreme Platonic Guardian." *Indiana Legal Forum* 5 (Fall 1971): 130–142.

Smith, Peter. "The History and Future of the Legal Battle over Birth Control." *Cornell Law Quarterly* 49 (Winter 1964): 275–303.

Thomson, Judith J. "A Defense of Abortion." *Philosophy and Public Affairs* 1 (Fall 1971): 47–66.

Thomson, Judith J. "The Right to Privacy." *Philosophy and Public Affairs* 4 (Summer 1975): 295–314.

Tribe, Laurence H. "Contrasting Constitutional Visions: Of Real and Unreal Differences." *Harvard Civil Rights–Civil Liberties Law Review* 22 (Winter 1987): 95–109.

Tribe, Laurence H. "The Supreme Court, 1972 Term—Foreword: Toward a Model of Roles in the Due Process of Life and Law." *Harvard Law Review* 87 (November 1973): 1–53.

Tushnet, Mark V. "Following the Rules Laid Down: A Critique of Interpretivism and Neutral Principles." *Harvard Law Review* 96 (February 1983): 781–827.

Tushnet, Mark V. "Two Notes on the Jurisprudence of Privacy." *Constitutional Commentary* 8 (Winter 1991): 75–85.

Uslaner, Eric M., and Ronald E. Weber. "Public Support for Pro-Choice Abortion Policies in the Nation and States: Changes and Stability After the *Roe* and *Doe* Decisions." *Michigan Law Review* 77 (August 1979): 1772–1789.

Van Alstyne, William. "Closing the Circle of Constitutional Review from *Griswold* v. *Connecticut* to *Roe* v. *Wade*: An Outline of a Decision Merely Overruling *Roe*." *Duke Law Journal* 1989 (December): 1677–88.

Van Alstyne, William. "The Enduring Example of John Marshall Harlan: 'Virtue as Practice' in the Supreme Court." *New York Law School Law Review* 36 (1991): 109–126.

Vanderford, Marsha L. "Vilification and Social Movements: A Case Study of Pro-Life and Pro-Choice Rhetoric." *Quarterly Journal of Speech* 75 (May 1989): 166–182.

Veltri, Stephen C. "Fowler V. Harper and the Right of Privacy: Twenty-five Years." *Ohio Northern University Law Review* 16 (1989): 359–363.

Wardle, Lynn D. "Rethinking *Roe* v. *Wade*." *Brigham Young University Law Review* 1985, pp. 231–264.

Warren, Mary Anne. "On the Moral and Legal Status of Abortion." *The Monist* 57 (January 1973): 43–61.

Warren, Samuel D., and Louis D. Brandeis. "The Right to Privacy." *Harvard Law Review* 4 (December 1890): 193–220.

Weddington, Sarah. "The Right to Decide." *Engage/Social Action* 2 (February 1974): 6–14.

Weddington, Sarah. "*Roe* v. *Wade* Began at Garage Sale," *Fulton County Daily Report*, 9 February 1989, pp. 8–9.

Weddington, Sarah. "*Roe* v. *Wade*: Past and Future." *Suffolk University Law Review* 24 (Fall 1990): 601–620.

Weddington, Sarah. "The Woman's Right of Privacy." *Perkins Journal* 27 (Fall 1973): 35–41.

Wellington, Harry H. "Common Law Rules and Constitutional Double Standards: Some Notes on Adjudication." *Yale Law Journal* 83 (December 1973): 221–311.

Westoff, Charles F., et al. "The Structure of Attitudes Toward Abortion." *Milbank Memorial Fund Quarterly* 47 (January 1969): 11–37.

White, G. Edward. "The Anti-Judge: William O. Douglas and the Ambiguities of Individuality." *Virginia Law Review* 74 (February 1988): 17–86.

Wilkinson, J. Harvie III, and G. Edward White. "Constitutional Protection for Personal Lifestyles." *Cornell Law Review* 62 (March 1977): 563–625.

Witherspoon, James S. "Reexamining *Roe*: Nineteenth-Century Abortion Statutes and the Fourteenth Amendment." *St. Mary's Law Journal* 17 (1985): 29–71.

Wulf, Melvin L. "On the Origins of Privacy." *The Nation*, 27 May 1991, pp. 700–704.

Zimmerman, Gereon. "Contraception and Commotion in Connecticut." *Look*, 30 January 1962, pp. 78–83.

Zipf, Harvey L. "Recent Abortion Law Reforms (or Much Ado About Nothing)." *Journal of Criminal Law, Criminology and Police Science* 60 (March 1969): 3–23.

UNPUBLISHED DISSERTATIONS, THESES, AND ESSAYS

Allen, Cannon F. "Revising Abortion Policy." B.A. thesis, Princeton University, 1984.

Allread, Opal H. "Sarah T. Hughes: A Case Study in Judicial Decision-Making." Ph.D. dissertation, University of Oklahoma, 1987.

Baker, James W. "A Study of the Historical Development and Contemporary Use of Arguments in the Birth Control Controversy Within the Roman Catholic Church." Ed.D. dissertation, Columbia University, 1974.

Bartleson, Henrietta L. "The American Birth Control Movement." Ph.D. dissertation, Syracuse University, 1974.

Bates, Anna Louise. "Protective Custody: A Feminist Interpretation of Anthony Comstock's Life and Laws." Ph.D. dissertation, State University of New York at Binghamton, 1991.

Becker, Barrie. "Connecticut's Legislative Battle over Birth Control: 1945–1965." Senior History Essay, Yale University, 1987.

Bierbrier, Doreen. "The 1972 Abortion Referendum in Michigan." Bentley Historical Library, University of Michigan, December 1973.

Blackall, Marjory N. "The Story of Annie G. Porritt." Sophia Smith Collection, Smith College, 1976.

Brodley, Joseph F., and Edwin D. Etherington. "Contraception: Human Right or Criminal Deviation?" Yale Law School, 25 May 1950.

Brooks, Carol F. "The Early History of the Anti-Contraception Laws in Massachusetts and Connecticut." M.A. thesis, Brown University, 1964.

Burke, Tracy. "The American Medical Profession and Reproductive Rights: A Case Study of Connecticut." Senior History Essay, Yale University, 1987.

Butler, Louise. "The Society for Humane Abortion." Schlesinger Library, SHA Papers, 21 May 1965.

Buutap, Nguyenphuc. "Legislation, Public Opinion, and the Press: An Interrelationship Reflected in the *New York Times*' Reporting of the Abortion Issue." Ph.D. dissertation, University of Chicago, 1979.

Carpenter, Dale A. II. "Revisiting *Griswold*: An Exploration of Its Political, Social, and Legal Origins." Senior History Essay, Yale University, 1989.

Cartoof, Virgina G. "Massachusetts' Parental Consent Law: Origins, Implementation and Impact." Ph.D. dissertation, Brandeis University, 1985.

Cherry, Christopher J. "The Hard Road to *Hardwick*: The Constitutional Challenge to Sodomy Statutes." M.A. thesis, University of Virginia, 1989.

Cooke, Carolyn L. "Holding the Line: A View of Evolving Abortion Policy." Ph.D. dissertation, Indiana University, 1992.

Coyle, Barbara A. C. "The Waterbury Conspiracy Scandal of 1938: An Aberration in Connecticut State and Local Politics." C.A.S. thesis, Wesleyan University, 1982.

Dahill, Edwin M., Jr. "Connecticut's J. Henry Roraback." Ed.D. dissertation, Teachers College, Columbia University, 1971.

Dillberger, Cigi B. "From Woman Rebel to Birth Control Advocate: Margaret Sanger's Transformation, 1914–1915." M.A. thesis, Florida Atlantic University, 1987.

Doggett, Cynthia V. "The Abortion Controversy and Public Opinion." B.A. thesis, Princeton University, 1983.

Epstein, Lee J. "Interest Groups, Controversy and the Court: An Analysis of Abortion Litigation." M.A. thesis, Emory University, 1982.

Erhart, Joseph F. "The Birth Control Debate in the Roman Catholic Church." Ph.D. dissertation, University of Pittsburgh, 1973.

Fein, Laurel J. "Waving No Flags: The History of the Planned Parenthood League of Connecticut, 1923–1965." Senior History Essay, Yale University, 1982.

Fimian, Charles. "The Effects of Religion on Abortion Policy-Making: A Study of Voting Behavior in the U.S. Congress, 1976–1980." Ph.D. dissertation, Arizona State University, 1983.

Fiscus, Ronald J. "Before the Velvet Curtain: The Connecticut Contraceptive Cases as a Study in Constitutional Law and Supreme Court Behavior." Ph.D. dissertation, University of Wisconsin, Madison, 1983.

Gaulard, Joan M. "Woman Rebel: The Rhetorical Strategies of Margaret Sanger and the American Birth Control Movement, 1912 to 1938." Ph.D. dissertation, Indiana University, 1978.

Gianelli, Joseph A., Jr. "An Analysis of the Connecticut Gubernatorial Election of 1958." B.A. thesis, Princeton University, 1959.

Gieg, Diane McCarrick. "The Birth Control League of Massachusetts, 1916–1940." B.A. thesis, Simmons College, 1973.

Glauberman, Steven L. "Abortion: An Issue of Public Policy." B.A. thesis, Princeton University, 1973.

Goldstein, Cynthia. "The Press and the Beginning of the Birth Control Movement in the United States." Ph.D. dissertation, Pennsylvania State University, 1985.

Goldyn, Lawrence M. "Legal Ideology and the Regulation of Homosexual Behavior." Ph.D. dissertation, Stanford University, 1979.

Gossweiler, Richard C. "The Right of Privacy: Misuse of History." Ph.D. dissertation, Ohio State University, 1978.

Grant, Marion Hepburn. "The Educated Housewife." Connecticut Historical Society, 1977.

Grant, Marion Hepburn. "Mother Was a Suffragette." Women's Association Lecture, PPLC Box 24, 21 October 1980.

Guercia, Carol. "The Effects of the Legalization of Abortion in the State of New York." Senior Essay, Yale University, Lader Box 3, 1971.

Haarlow, Blair R. "The Right to Privacy in Constitutional Law: Toward a New Jurisprudence." B.A. thesis, Princeton University, 1991.

Halva-Neubauer, Glen A. "Legislative Agenda-Setting in the States: The Case of Abortion Policy." Ph.D. dissertation, University of Minnesota, 1992.

Hartouni, Valerie A. "Abortion Politics and the Negotiation of Public Meanings." Ph.D. dissertation, University of California at Santa Cruz, 1987.

Hayes, Joan. "Abortion Law: A Case History—Or Helping a 'Hopeless Cause' Become a Political Possibility." NARAL Box 3, January 1970.

Howard, Stephen D. "The Birth Control Law Conflict in Massachusetts." B.A. thesis, Harvard University, 1959.

Huth, Mary Josephine. "The Birth Control Movement in the United States." Ph.D. dissertation, St. Louis University, 1955.

Johnson, Linnea. "Something Real: Jane and Me—Memories and Exhortations of a Feminist Ex-Abortionist." Chicago Historical Society, 1992.

Joosten, Richard L., Jr. "The Abortion Revolution." B.A. thesis, Princeton University, 1979.

Kramer, Karen W. "The Press and Symbols: The *New York Times* and Abortion from *Roe* to *Webster*." B.A. thesis, Princeton University, 1990.

Krason, Stephen M. "The Supreme Court's Abortion Decisions: A Critical Study of the Shaping of a Major American Public Policy and a Basis for Change." Ph.D. dissertation, State University of New York at Buffalo, 1983.

Lamm, Richard D. "Abortion—A Case Study in Legislative Reform." Lader Box 6, 1970.

Leahy, Peter J. "The Anti-Abortion Movement: Testing a Theory of the Rise and Fall of Social Movements." Ph.D. dissertation, Syracuse University, 1975.

Liptak, Delores Ann. "European Immigrants and the Catholic Church in Connecticut, 1870–1920." Ph.D. dissertation, University of Connecticut, 1978.

Livingston, Barbara F. "Dreams and Inspirations: A Footnote to Biography of Margaret Sanger." B.A. thesis, Wesleyan University, 1974.

Lockard, Walter Duane. "The Role of Party in the Connecticut General Assembly, 1931–1951." Ph.D. dissertation, Yale University, 1952.

Lombardo, Peter J. "Connecticut in the Great Depression, 1929–1933." Ph.D. dissertation, University of Notre Dame, 1979.

Lucas, Roy. "Notes on the Efforts in 1965-73 Leading Up to *Roe* v. *Wade* and *Doe* v. *Bolton*." 114pp., September 1992.

Lynch, Patricia T. C. "Abortion Politics and Family Life." Ph.D. dissertation, University of Massachusetts, 1981.

McCann, Carole R. "Race, Class and Gender in U.S. Birth Control Politics, 1920–1945." Ph.D. dissertation, University of California at Santa Cruz, 1987.

McConnell, Douglas G. "The Coming of an Idea: Abortion Reform in Colorado." Eagleton Institute Paper, Lader Box 4, 6 May 1968.

MacDonald, Herbert S. "Some Aspects and Implications of the So-Called 'Connecticut Birth-Control Law.'" PPLC Box 5, October, 1953.

Mack, Robert W. "Margaret Sanger and the Crusade for Birth Control." B.A. thesis, Princeton University, 1962.

Mandarino, Helena Ann. "Constitutional Privacy: The Evolution of A Doctrine." M.A. thesis, University of Nevada, Las Vegas, 1990.

Marcus, Erin N. "Everybody's Issue: Connecticut's Organized Movement for the Legalization of Contraceptives, 1922–1965." Senior History Essay, Yale University, 1985.

Markson, Stephan L. "Citizens United for Life: Status Politics, Symbolic Reform and the Anti-Abortion Movement." Ph.D. dissertation, University of Massachusetts, 1979.

Middleton, Doris. "Alas *Roe* v. *Wade* . . . We Knew Thee Well." 1992.

Mitchell, Rowland L., Jr. "Social Legislation in Connecticut, 1919–1939." Ph.D. dissertation, Yale University, 1954.

Moloney, Deirdre M. "Families, Work, and Social Institutions: A Comparative Study of Immigrants and Their Children in Waterbury, Connecticut, 1900–1920." M.A. thesis, University of Wisconsin, Madison, 1989.

Morain, Thomas J. "The Emergence of the Women's Movement, 1960–1970." Ph.D. dissertation, University of Iowa, 1974.

Morehouse, William M. "The Speaking of Margaret Sanger in the Birth Control Movement From 1916 to 1937." Ph.D. dissertation, Purdue University, 1968.

Morrison, Robert G. "Choice in Washington: The Politics of Liberalized Abortion." M.A. thesis, University of Virginia, 1982.

Murray, Mary Hickson. "Wilbur L. Cross: Connecticut Statesman and Humanitarian, 1930–1935." Ph.D. dissertation, University of Connecticut, 1972.

Neef, Marian H. "Policy Formation and Implementation in the Abortion Field." Ph.D. dissertation, University of Illinois, 1979.

Nelson, Ernest H., Jr. "Years of Transformation: Connecticut in the Time of Wilbur Cross, 1930–1938." B.A. thesis, Princeton University, 1961.

Nicholson, Susan A. "Margaret Sanger: Rebellion and Respectability." M.A. thesis, Smith College, 1973.

Norton, Patricia J. "Margaret Sanger and the Depression: Birth Control Comes of Age." M.A. thesis, Smith College, 1955.

Oh, Tina C. "An Exercise in Anachronism: Blackmun's Analysis of 19th Century Anti-Abortion Legislation." B.A. thesis, Princeton University, 1990.

Olan, Susan Torian. "The *Rag*: A Study in Underground Journalism." M.A. thesis, University of Texas at Austin, 1981.

Pilpel, Harriet F. "The Abortion Crisis—Danger and Opportunity." Abortion Reform Association of Illinois Papers Box 10, August 1966.

Pletcher, Larry B. "New York State Abortion Reform, 1967: A Case Study." B.A. thesis, Princeton University, 1968.

Plutzer, Eric. "Attitudes Toward Abortion: A Study of the Social and Ideological Bases of Public Opinion." Ph.D. dissertation, Washington University, 1986.

Pollack, Harriet. "'An Uncommonly Silly Law': The Connecticut Birth Control Cases in the U.S. Supreme Court." Ph.D. dissertation, Columbia University, 1967.

Putka, John S. "The Supreme Court and Abortion: The Socio-Political Impact of Judicial Activism." Ph.D. dissertation, University of Cincinnati, 1979.

Railsback, Celeste C. "The Contemporary American Abortion Controversy: A Case Study of Public Argumentation." Ph.D. dissertation, University of Iowa, 1982.

Reedy, Cheryl D. "The Supreme Court and Congress on Abortion: An Analysis of Comparative Institutional Capacity." Ph.D. dissertation, University of Minnesota, 1982.

Robins, Lee N. "Birth Control in Massachusetts: The Analysis of an Issue Through an Intensive Study of Opinion." Ph.D. dissertation, Harvard University, 1950.

Rodman, John R. "Birth Control Politics in Massachusetts." M.A. thesis, Harvard University, 1955.

Roe, Kathleen M. "Abortion Work: A Study of the Relationship Between Private Troubles and Public Issues." Ph.D. dissertation, University of California at Berkeley, 1985.

Rooks, Judith P. "Why and How We Legalized Abortion, and What Difference It Has Made: *Doe* v. *Bolton*—The 'Other' Supreme Court Case." Address at annual meeting of Oregon NARAL, Salem, 21 January 1983.

Rosengren, Arne. "Connecticut Government and Politics." M.A. thesis, Wesleyan University, 1949.

Sadler, Paul L. "The Abortion Issue Within the Southern Baptist Convention, 1969–1988." Ph.D. dissertation, Baylor University, 1991.

Sanger, Alexander C. "Margaret Sanger: The Early Years, 1910–1917." B.A. thesis, Princeton University, 1969.

Scharf, Kathleen R. "Abortion and the Body Politic: An Anthropological Analysis of Legislative Activity in Massachusetts." Ph.D. dissertation, Boston University, 1981.

Schreiner, Elizabeth. "Public Law and Private Rights: The Path to *Griswold* v. *Connecticut*." B.A. thesis, Wesleyan University, 1981.

Scribner, F. Jay. "Modern Catholics and Birth Control." B.A. thesis, Princeton University, 1967.

Shalant, Joseph L. "Abortion Laws and Why the Court Must Act." UCLA Law School paper, ACLU Papers 1966 Vol. 11, 25 April 1966.

Singer, Toby. "Abortion as a Constitutional Right: The Path of Litigation." B.A. thesis, Wesleyan University, 1974.

Skelley, Joseph F., Jr. "Executive-Legislative Relationship in Connecticut: A Case Study of Legislative Policy-Making." B.A. thesis, Wesleyan University, 1950.

Smith, Alphonsus P. "The '*Roe* v. *Wade*' and '*Doe* v. *Bolton*' Decisions on Abortion: An Analysis, Critique, and Examination of Related Issues." Ph.D. dissertation, Drew University, 1981.

Snyder, Robin V. "The Two Worlds of Public Opinion: Media Opinion and Polled Opinion on the Abortion Issue." Ph.D. dissertation, Rutgers University, 1985.

Stillson, Marion. "The Confluence of Choice and Chance in the Construction of a Successful Legal Strategy: A Case Study of *Griswold* v. *Connecticut*." Georgetown Law School paper, Spring 1986.

Strumph, Paul. "Contraception in Connecticut: The Decade of Change, 1960–1969." American Studies paper, Yale University, 1981.

Thompson, Michael P. "The Facts of Life: Rhetorical Dimensions of the Pro-Life Movement in America." Ph.D. dissertation, Rensselaer Polytechnic Institute, 1985.

Traina, Frank J. "Diocesan Mobilization Against Abortion Law Reform." Ph.D. dissertation, Cornell University, 1975.

Vreeland, Francis M. "The Process of Reform with Especial Reference to Reform Groups in the Field of Population." Ph.D. dissertation, University of Michigan, 1929.

Weide, Darlene. "The History of New York Abortion Law Repeal: A Case Study." B.A. thesis, Barnard College, 1989.

Wood, Elizabeth S. "Margaret Sanger: The Making of a Crusader." B.A. thesis, Princeton University, 1991.

Yale, Marilyn A. "Abortion in State Level Electoral Politics: A Content Analysis of Press Coverage During Four Gubernatorial Campaigns." Ph.D. dissertation, University of Houston, 1992.

Yates, Herschel W., Jr. "American Protestantism and Birth Control: An Examination of Shifts Within a Major Religious Value Orientation." Ph.D. dissertation, Harvard University, 1968.

Yeh, I-Tien. "The Opening of the Griswold-Buxton Clinic: Legislative and Judicial History of the Connecticut Birth Control Statutes." Undergraduate paper, Yale University, 1977.

INTERVIEWS, CONVERSATIONS, AND ORAL HISTORIES

Albert, Lee A. Garrow, 13 May 1993, Buffalo, NY (T).

Alsup, William H. Garrow, 6 August 1992, San Francisco, CA (T).

Appel, Cheri. Ellen Chesler, 1 February 1989, New York, NY. Sophia Smith Collection.

Arnold, Richard S. Garrow, 22 May 1992, Little Rock, AR (T).

Baird, Bill. Garrow, 26 May 1992, Hempstead, NY.

Beasley, Dorothy Toth. Garrow, 31 July 1992, Atlanta, GA.

Beilenson, Anthony C. Steven Edginton, 27 March 1982, Los Angeles, CA. UCLA.

Beilenson, Anthony C. Garrow, 24 May 1993, Washington, DC.

Beloff, Anita. Garrow, 6 September 1991, Hamden, CT (T).

Berg, Harold. Garrow, 21 July 1992, Hamden, CT (T).

Blair, Beatrice. Ellen Chesler, 13 April 1976, New York, NY. Schlesinger Library.

Blazi, John A. Garrow, 21 July 1992, Hamden, CT (T).

Blood, Virginia L. Joyce Pendery, 7 August 1980, Darien, CT. UConn.

Bolton, Arthur K. Garrow, 4 August 1992, Griffin, GA (T).

Bork, Robert H. Andrea Haas Hubbell, 21 April 1992, Washington, DC.

Boult, Reber F., Jr. Garrow, 5 August 1992, Albuquerque, NM (T).

Bourne, Peter. Garrow, 3 March 1992, Washington, DC.

Bowers, Richard M. Garrow, 7 July 1992, Delancey, NY (T).

Bowles, Chester. Neil N. Gold, 29 March and 19 April 1963, Washington, DC. Columbia Oral History Program.

Bowles, Dorothy S. Neil N. Gold, 23 May and 8 June 1963, Washington, DC. Columbia Oral History Program.

Breihan, Robert E. Garrow, 8 July 1992, Austin, TX (T).

Breyer, Stephen. Garrow, 19 June 1992, Boston, MA (T).

Bruner, Fred. Garrow, 6 February 1992, Dallas, TX.

Bush, Prescott. John T. Mason, Jr., 1 July 1966, Greenwich, CT. Columbia Oral History Program.

Cadbury, Leah T. Caroline Rittenhouse, 11 August 1981–26 May 1982, Bryn Mawr, PA. Bryn Mawr College Archives.

Calderone, Mary S. James W. Reed, 7 August 1974, New York, NY. Schlesinger Library.

Campbell, James S. Garrow, 23 June 1992, Washington, DC (T).

Campbell, Loraine L. Martha Stuart, 14 July 1967, Boston, MA. Schlesinger Library.

Campbell, Loraine L. James W. Reed, 3 December 1973–22 March 1974, Cambridge, MA. Schlesinger Library.

Cano, Sandra Bensing. Garrow, 30 July 1992, Atlanta, GA (T).

Cantor, Donald J. Garrow, 1 June 1992, Hartford, CT.

Carmen, Arlene. Ellen Chesler, January 1976, New York, NY. Schlesinger Library.

Carmody, Deirdre. Garrow, 17 July 1992, New York, NY (T).

Choper, Jesse. Garrow, 22 June 1992, Berkeley, CA (T).

Clark, Joseph B. Garrow, 10 September 1991, New Haven, CT.

Clark, Tom C. Joe B. Frantz, 7 October 1969, Austin, TX. LBJ Library.

Clemow, Bice. Garrow, 7 November 1991, West Hartford, CT.

Coffee, Linda N. Garrow, 5 February and 8 August 1992, Dallas, TX.

Cook, Constance E. Ellen Chesler, 13 January 1976, Ithaca, NY. Schlesinger Library.

Creighton, Tom. Ronald E. Marcello, 15 July 1975, Austin, TX. University of North Texas Library, Denton.

Cusack, Ruth P. Garrow, 25 June 1993, Miller Place, NY.

Danforth, Nicholas W. Garrow, 14 August 1992, Washington, DC (T).

Darrach, Mrs. William IV. Garrow, 5 August 1992, Sargentville, ME (T).

Davis, Clarice M. Garrow, 14 February 1992, Dallas, TX.

Dees, Morris. Garrow, 31 May 1992, Middletown, CT.

Dienelt, John F. Garrow, 3 June 1993, Washington, DC (T).

Dominick, D. Clinton III. Ben White, August 1970, Albany, NY. Lader Box 5.

Dorsen, Norman. Garrow, 17 March 1992, New York, NY.

Durning, Jean and Marvin. Garrow, 9 June and 24 September 1992, Seattle, WA (T) and New York, NY.

Durning, Jean and Marvin. Andrea Haas Hubbell, 25 September 1992, Hartford, CT.

Edwards, James M. Garrow, 18 June 1992, New York, NY (T).

Emerson, Ruth C. Garrow, 6 November 1991, New Haven, CT.

Evans, J. Claude. Garrow, 14 August 1992, Waynesville, NC (T).

Ferguson, Frances Hand. James W. Reed, 3 June 1974, New York, NY. Schlesinger Library.

Fitzgerald, Anthony. Garrow, 10 September 1991, New Haven, CT.

Flowers, Robert C. Garrow, 10 February 1992, Austin, TX (T).

Floyd, Jay. Garrow, 11 February 1992, Llano, TX.

Foe, Victoria E. Garrow, 25 July 1993, Seattle, WA (T).

Forsberg, Joan Bates. Garrow, 1 June 1992, New Haven, CT.

Forsberg, Joan Bates. Andrea Haas Hubbell, 16 March 1992, New Haven, CT.

Fried, Charles. Garrow, 27 May 1992, Cambridge, MA (T).

Fuller, William R. Garrow, 25 August 1992, Carrollton, TX (T).

Gewirtz, Paul. Garrow, 3 July 1992, New Haven, CT (T).

Goldberg, Irving L. Garrow, 6 February 1992, Dallas, TX.

Goldman, Gerald. Garrow, 20 July 1992, Washington, DC (T).

Goldstein, Jonah J. Douglas Scott, 28 October 1965, New York, NY. Columbia Oral History Program.

Goldstein, Stephen. Garrow, 7 July 1992, Jerusalem, Israel (T).

Goss, Virginia J. Garrow, 5 November 1991, Sanibel, FL (T).

Griswold, Estelle T. Jeannette B. Cheek, 17 March 1976, Fort Myers, FL. Schlesinger Library.

Hall, Robert E. Garrow, 14 April 1992, Riverdale, NY.

Hames, Margie Pitts. Garrow, 10 June (T), 28 July and 1 August 1992, Atlanta, GA.

Hammond, Larry A. Garrow, 22 May 1993, Phoeniz, AZ (T).

Hatcher, Robert A. Garrow, 29 July 1992, Atlanta, GA (T).

Heineman, Benjamin W., Jr. Garrow, 18 August 1992, Fairfield, CT (T).

Hepburn, Katharine H. Garrow, 15 April 1992, New York, NY.

Hepburn, Robert H. Garrow, 13 January 1992, West Hartford, CT.

Herndon, J. Emmett. Garrow, 31 July 1992, Atlanta, GA.

Hines, Barbara. Garrow, 24 August 1992, Austin, TX (T).

Hodgson, Jane E. Garrow, 22 July 1992, St. Paul, MN (T).

Hoeber, Paul R. Garrow, 26 June 1992, San Francisco, CA (T).

Hughes, Sarah T. Joe B. Frantz, 7 October 1968, Washington, DC. LBJ Library.

Hughes, Sarah T. Fred Gantt, January–May 1969, Dallas, TX. University of North Texas Library, Denton.

Hughes, Sarah T. Ronald E. Marcello, 23 August 1979, Dallas, TX. University of North Texas Library, Denton.

Israel, Jerold. Garrow, 2 June 1992, Ann Arbor, MI (T).

Jacobson, Richard L. Garrow, 29 June 1992, Washington, DC (T).

Jahncke, Cornelia. Garrow, 9 November 1991, Greenwich, CT.

Judd, Patricia [White]. Garrow, 25 July 1993, Santa Fe, NM (T).

Kennedy, Duncan. Garrow, 18 September 1992, Cambridge, MA (T).

Kimmey, Jimmye. Garrow, 13 April 1992, New York, NY.

Kinloch, Hector. Garrow, 19 May 1992, Ainslie, Australia (T).

Kitfield, Agnes "Ruste." Garrow, 31 July 1992, Woodstock, GA (T).

Koeltl, John G. Garrow, 17 June 1992, New York, NY (T).

Kramer, Douglas J. Garrow, 20 March 1992, New York, NY (T).

Kreindler, Peter M. Garrow, 29 June 1992, Morristown, NJ (T).

Lader, Lawrence. Garrow, 29 March 1992, New York, NY.

Lambert, Frederick W. Garrow, 5 May 1993, Durham, NC (T).

Lamm, Richard D. Garrow, 30 April 1993, Denver, CO (T).

Larkin, Charles L., Jr. Garrow, 15 September 1991, Waterbury, CT (T).

Lassoe, John V. P. Garrow, 21 April 1992, New York, NY.

Leavy, Zad. Garrow, 8 May 1992, Carmel, CA.

Lewis, Ellen [Kalina]. Garrow, 25 July 1993, Hayden Lake, ID (T).

Lodge, John Davis. John T. Mason, Jr., 5 and 9 October 1967, New York, NY. Columbia Oral History Program.

Long, W. Newton. Garrow, 30 July 1992, Atlanta, GA.

Lucas, Roy. Clement E. Vose, 9 July 1969, New York, NY. Lucas Box 25.

Lucas, Roy. Clement E. Vose, 4 February 1973, Middletown, CT.

Lucas, Roy. Garrow, 27 August and 11–13 September 1992, Whitefish, MT.

McCorvey, Norma. Claudia Dreifus, 6–8 July 1984, Dallas, TX.

McCorvey, Norma. Garrow, 22 July 1992, Dallas, TX (T).

McCoy, Frances. Garrow, 12 September 1991, Hamden, CT.

McTernan, John W. Garrow, 7 September 1991, East Arlington, VT (T).

Maginnis, Patricia T. Jeannette B. Cheek, 16–18 November 1975, San Francisco, CA. Schlesinger Library.

Maledon, William J. Garrow, 8 June 1993, Phoenix, AZ (T).

Maney, Michael M. Garrow, 5 June 1992, New York, NY.

Marshall, Thurgood. Ed Edwin, February–June 1977, Washington, DC. Columbia Oral History Program.

Martin, Crawford C. David McComb, 4 May 1971, Austin, TX. LBJ Library.

Maupin, Michael W. Garrow, 24 June 1992, Richmond, VA (T).

Mayers, Daniel K. Garrow, 2 June 1992, Washington, DC (T).

Means, Cyril C., Jr. Garrow, 25 March 1992, Great Neck, NY.

Merrill, Roy L., Jr. Garrow, 5 February 1992, Dallas, TX.

Messerman, Gale Siegel. Garrow, 17 August 1992, Cleveland, OH (T).

Morgan, Charles, Jr. Garrow, 13 March 1992, Washington, DC (T).

Morris, John M. Garrow, 1 October 1991, New Haven, CT.

Munger, Charles T. Garrow, 6 May 1993, Los Angeles, CA (T).

Myers, Lonny. Ellen Chesler, 24 September 1976, Chicago, IL. Schlesinger Library.

Myers, Lonny. Garrow, 10 August 1992, Chicago, IL.

Neale, Sue. Garrow, 7 July 1992, Killingworth, CT (T).

Nellis, Joseph L. Garrow, 3 March 1992, Washington, DC.

Nelson, Roger B. and Rosalie. Garrow, 13 May 1992, Ann Arbor, MI.

Nickerson, Jeffrey R. Garrow, 29 and 31 July 1992, Atlanta, GA (T).

"Odegard," Elizabeth. Garrow, 8 July 1992, "Moab, UT" (T).

"Oldendorf," Robert S. Garrow, 26 April 1992, New Haven, CT (T).

Parker, Richard D. Garrow, 6 August 1992, Cambridge, MA (T).

Parks, Lucia J. and Charles H. Garrow, 14 July 1992, Southport, CT.

Pease, Alfred M., Jr. Garrow, 5 November 1991, West Hartford, CT (T).

Perry, Margaret Hepburn. Garrow, 24 June 1992, Canton, CT (T).

Phelan, Lana C. Jeannette B. Cheek, 21 November 1975, Long Beach, CA. Schlesinger Library.

Phillips, Elizabeth. Garrow, 24 June 1992, New Haven, CT (T).

Pollak, Louis H. Garrow, 1 July 1992, Philadelphia, PA (T).

Posner, S. Paul. Garrow, 19 June 1992, New York, NY.

Powe, Lucas A. "Scott." Garrow, 17 June 1992, Austin, TX (T).

Rezneck, Daniel A. Garrow, 22 June 1992, Washington, DC (T).

Richardson, Barbara. Garrow, 7 July 1992, Stephenville, TX (T).

Rindskopf, Elizabeth R. Garrow, 16 August 1992, Washington, DC (T).

Rockefeller, Nancy Carnegie. Esther H. Smith, 3 October 1975, Greenwich, CT. Greenwich Public Library.

Rockefeller, Nancy Carnegie. Carole Nichols, 1 February 1981, Greenwich, CT. UConn.

Roemer, Ruth. Garrow, 5 May 1992, Los Angeles, CA.

Rooks, Judith [Bourne]. Garrow, 29 April and 20 July 1992, Portland, OR (T).

Roraback, Catherine G. Garrow, 17 September 1991, Canaan, CT.

Rose, Helen [Buxton]. Garrow, 23 March 1992, Lakeville, MA.

Rowe, Thomas. Garrow, 17 June 1992, Durham, NC (T).

Russell, Keith P. Garrow, 7 May 1992, Los Angeles, CA.

Sanders, Barefoot. Garrow, 6 February 1992, Dallas, TX.

Sanger, Grant. Ellen Chesler, 4–5 August 1976, New York, NY. Schlesinger Library.

Saunders, George L., Jr. Garrow, 18 June 1992, Chicago, IL (T).

Scafarello, Elizabeth [Goodrich]. Garrow, 2 June 1992, Fort Myers, FL (T).

Schneider, Daniel M. Garrow, 4 August 1992, DeKalb, IL (T).

Schur, Edwin. Garrow, 14 April 1992, New York, NY (T).

Schwartz, Tobiane. Garrow, 19 June and 6 August (T) 1992, New York, NY.

Secor, William J., Jr. Garrow, 19 August 1991, Waterbury, CT.

Secor, William J., Jr. Andrea Haas Hubbell, 16 April 1992, Waterbury, CT.

Seichter, Marilyn. Andrea Haas Hubbell, 5 May 1992, Hartford, CT.

Seidman, L. Michael. Garrow, 17 June 1992, Washington, DC (T).

Shaw, Don C. Garrow, 11 August 1992, Chicago, IL.

Shea, Robert E. Garrow, 14 September 1991, Waterbury, CT (T).

Singer, Richard G. Garrow, 26 August 1992, Camden, NJ (T).

Smith, Judy. Garrow, 26 July (T) and 14 September 1992, Missoula, MT.

Smith, Sidney O., Jr. Garrow, 29 July 1992, Atlanta, GA.

Spearman, Robert W. Garrow, 15 and 24 July 1992, Raleigh, NC (T).

Standish, Hilda Crosby. Carole Nichols, 28 July 1980, Hartford, CT. UConn.

Standish, Hilda Crosby. Garrow, 11 September 1991, West Hartford, CT.

Standish, Hilda Crosby. Andrea Haas Hubbell, 20 November 1991, West Hartford, CT.

Stearns, Nancy. Garrow, 13 May 1993, New York, NY.

Stevens, Robert B. Garrow, 17 August 1992, London, UK (T).

Stevens, Rosemary A. Garrow, 14 August 1992, Philadelphia, PA (T).

Stone, Geoffrey R. Garrow, 29 June 1992, Chicago, IL (T).

Stuermer, Virginia M. Garrow, 1 June 1992, New Haven, CT.

Stuermer, Virginia M. Andrea Haas Hubbell, 5 May 1992, New Haven, CT.

Sullivan, Brian L. Garrow, 13 August 1992, New York, NY.

Switzer, Ellen. Garrow, 15 April 1992, New York, NY.

Tileston, Peter. Garrow, 12 July 1992, Vineyard Haven, MA.

Tilson, Catherine J. Garrow, 9 September 1991, Hamden, CT.

Tilson, John Q. Garrow, 10 September 1991, New Haven, CT.

Tolle, John B. Garrow, 6 February 1992, Dallas, TX.

Trebert, Gary R. Garrow, 8 August 1992, Dallas, TX.

Trickett, Paul C. Garrow, 24 June 1992, Austin, TX (T).

Trubek, David M. and Louise G. Garrow, 30 May 1992, Philadelphia, PA.

Trubek, Louise G. Jeremy Brecher, 6 April 1992, Madison, WI.

Tundermann, David W. Garrow, 19 August 1992, Salt Lake City, UT (T).

Tushnet, Mark V. Garrow, 8 June 1992, Washington, DC.

Tydings, Joseph D. Garrow, 2 March 1992, Washington, DC.

Upson, J. Warren. Jeremy Brecher, 9 and 18 April 1986, Woodbury, CT.

Upson, J. Warren. Garrow, 15 August 1991, Southbury, CT.

Upson, J. Warren. Andrea Haas Hubbell, 21 November 1991, Southbury, CT.

Vichis, Walter A. Garrow, 14 September 1991, Waterbury, CT (T).

Vogel, Beatrice. Garrow, 15 July 1992, Helena, MT (T).

Vuitch, Florence R. "Lee." Garrow, 29 May 1993, Silver Spring, MD.

Vuitch, Milan. Garrow, 17 January 1993, Silver Spring, MD.

Wade, Henry. Garrow, 17 February 1992, Dallas, TX (T).

Wallace, Lawrence. Garrow, 7 July 1992, Washington, DC (T).

Walker, Pamela D. Garrow, 19 August 1992, Little Rock, AR (T).

Waters, James L. Garrow, 30 July 1992, Atlanta, GA.

Wechsler, Nancy F. Garrow, 19 March 1992, New York, NY.

Weddington, Ron. Garrow, 10 February 1992, Austin, TX.

Weddington, Sarah R. Patricia Duke, 30 March 1973, Austin, TX. Texas Collection, Carroll Library, Baylor University, Waco.

Weddington, Sarah R. Ronald E. Marcello, 8 July 1975, Austin, TX. University of North Texas Library, Denton.

Weddington, Sarah R. Jeannette B. Cheek, 12 March 1976, Philadelphia, PA. Schlesinger Library.

Weddington, Sarah R. Andrea Haas Hubbell, 12 March 1992, Hartford, CT.

Weddington, Sarah R. Garrow, 5 June 1992, New York, NY.

Wheelis, Jim. Garrow, 6 August (T) and 13 September 1992, Missoula and Whitefish, MT.

White, G. Edward. Garrow, 30 June 1992, Charlottesville, VA (T).

Whitehill, Virginia B. Garrow, 16 February 1992, Dallas, TX.

Wulf, Melvin. Garrow, 19 March 1992, New York, NY.

Ziglar, James W. Garrow, 2 July 1993, Washington, DC (T).

Zuckerman, Ruth Jane. Garrow, 26 August 1992, New York, NY.

TELEVISION TRANSCRIPTS AND VIDEO INTERVIEWS

"Birth Control and the Law." *CBS Reports*, with Eric Sevareid; written and produced by Stephen Fleischman; 10 May 1962.

"Glimpses of Our Past." Produced for PPLC by Cecily Slade and Faith Middleton, 13 May 1983; New Haven Colony Historical Society.

"In Search of the Constitution"—"Mr. Justice Blackmun," "Strictly Speaking," and "For the People," with Bill Moyers, April-June 1987, PBS Video.

"Search for Justice: American Stories," with Carl Rowan; WUSA-TV, Washington, DC, 13 September 1987.

NEWSPAPERS

Atlanta Constitution
Atlanta Journal
Austin American-Statesman
Boston Globe

Bridgeport Herald
Catholic Transcript (Hartford, CT)
Dallas Morning News
Dallas Times-Herald
Hartford Courant
Hartford Times
Los Angeles Times
New Haven Journal-Courier
New Haven Register
New York Herald Tribune
New York Times
Wall Street Journal
Washington Post
Waterbury American
Waterbury Democrat
Waterbury Republican

NEWSLETTERS AND PERIODICALS

America
American Journal of Obstetrics and Gynecology
American Journal of Public Health
American Medical News
American Mercury
ASA (Association for the Study of Abortion) *News*
Birth Control Herald
Birth Control News (Hartford)
Birth Control Review
CCTA (California Committee for Therapeutic Abortion) *Newsletter*
California Medicine
Christian Century
Christianity & Crisis
[National] Clergy Consultation Service on Abortion Newsletter
Commonweal
Connecticut Parenthood
Eugenics
Family Planning Perspectives
Family Planning/Population Reporter
Hastings Center Report
Human Fertility
Issue/ICMCA (Illinois Citizens for the Medical Control of Abortion) *Journal*
Journal of Contraception
Journal of Social Hygiene
Journal of the American Medical Association
Journal of the Medical Association of Georgia
Medical World News
Michigan Medicine
Minnesota Medicine
Modern Medicine
Ms.
NARAL News
The Nation
National Review

New England Journal of Medicine
The New Republic
News Exchange (PPFA)
Newsweek
New Yorkers for Abortion Law Repeal Newsletter
Northwest Medicine
PPFA Newsletter
[Massachusetts] *Planned Parenthood News*
Planned Parenthood News/Newsletter (PPFA)
The Rag (Austin, TX)
Second Coming (Austin, TX)
SHA (Society for Humane Abortion) *Newsletter*
Texas Medicine
Time
Voice of the Women's Liberation Movement
WONAAC (Women's National Abortion Action Coalition) *Newsletter*
ZPG National Reporter

PAPERS AND ARCHIVAL COLLECTIONS

Abortion Rights Association of Illinois Papers, Special Collections Department, University of Illinois Library, Chicago.

Abortion Rights Council Papers, Social Welfare History Archives, University of Minnesota, Minneapolis.

American Birth Control League (ABCL) Papers, Houghton Library, Harvard University, Cambridge, MA.

American Civil Liberties Union of Georgia Papers, Atlanta, GA.

American Civil Liberties Union Papers, Mudd Manuscript Library, Princeton University, Princeton, NJ.

Archives of the Archdiocese of Hartford, Hartford, CT.

Library Files of the *Atlanta Constitution* and the *Atlanta Journal*, Atlanta, GA.

Bill Baird Papers, Hempstead, NY.

Raymond E. Baldwin Papers, Connecticut State Archives, Hartford.

Lorraine Beebe Papers, Bentley Historical Library, University of Michigan, Ann Arbor.

Birth Control League of Massachusetts Papers, Schlesinger Library, Radcliffe College, Cambridge, MA.

Hugo L. Black Papers, Manuscript Division, Library of Congress, Washington, DC.

Edwin Borchard Papers, Manuscripts Division, Sterling Library, Yale University, New Haven, CT.

William J. Brennan Papers, Manuscript Division, Library of Congress, Washington, DC.

Gilbert E. Bursley Papers, Bentley Historical Library, University of Michigan, Ann Arbor.

C. Lee Buxton Scrapbook, Lakeville, MA.

Mary S. Calderone Papers, Schlesinger Library, Radcliffe College, Cambridge, MA.

California Committee for Therapeutic Abortion Papers, Special Collections Department, Research Library, University of California, Los Angeles.

Eleanor T. Calverly Papers, Hartford Seminary Foundation Library, Hartford, CT.

Donald J. Cantor Papers, Hartford, CT.

Chicago Women's Liberation Union Papers, Chicago Historical Society, Chicago, IL.

James H. Clark, Jr., Papers, Special Collections, DeGolyer Library, Southern Methodist University, Dallas, TX.

Joseph B. Clark Papers, New Haven, CT.

Tom C. Clark Papers, Tarlton Law Library, University of Texas Law School, Austin.

Connecticut General Assembly Records (RG 2), Connecticut State Archives, Hartford.

Case Records and Briefs, Connecticut Supreme Court, Hartford.

Ruth P. Cusack Papers, Miller Place, NY.

Library Files of the *Dallas Morning News* and the *Dallas Times-Herald*, Dallas, TX.

Katherine Seymour Day Papers, Stowe-Day Foundation, Hartford, CT.

Mary Ware Dennett Papers, Schlesinger Library, Radcliffe College, Cambridge, MA.

Norman Dorsen Papers, New York, NY.

William O. Douglas Papers, Manuscript Division, Library of Congress, Washington, DC.

Thomas I. Emerson Papers, Manuscripts Division, Sterling Library, Yale University, New Haven, CT.

Morris Ernst Papers, Ransom Humanities Research Center, University of Texas, Austin.

Morris Ernst Volume, Schlesinger Library, Radcliffe College, Cambridge, MA.

Felix Frankfurter Papers, Harvard Law School Library, Cambridge, MA.

Clarence J. Gamble Papers, Countway Library, Harvard Medical School, Boston, MA.

Gerhard A. Gesell Papers, Manuscript Division, Library of Congress, Washington, DC.

Alan F. Guttmacher Papers, Countway Library, Harvard Medical School, Boston, MA.

Robert E. Hall Papers, New York, NY.

Margie Pitts Hames Papers, Atlanta, GA.

John M. Harlan Papers, Mudd Manuscript Library, Princeton University, Princeton, NJ.

Fowler V. Harper Collection, Ohio Northern University College of Law, Ada.

Fowler V. Harper Papers, Manuscripts Division, Sterling Library, Yale University, New Haven, CT.

Library Files of the *Hartford Courant*, Hartford, CT.

Hartford Times Clipping Morgue, Southern Connecticut State University, New Haven.

J. Emmett Herndon Papers, Atlanta, GA.

Sarah T. Hughes Papers, University of North Texas Library, Denton.

Dorothy Kenyon Papers, Sophia Smith Collection, Smith College, Northampton, MA.

Florence L. C. Kitchelt Papers, Schlesinger Library, Radcliffe College, Cambridge, MA.

Lawrence Lader Papers, New York Public Library, New York, NY.

Richard D. Lamm Papers, Colorado Historical Society, Denver.

Zad Leavy Papers, Carmel, CA.

John Davis Lodge Papers, Connecticut State Archives, Hartford.

Lucille Lord-Heinstein Papers, Schlesinger Library, Radcliffe College, Cambridge, MA.

Roy Lucas Papers, Olin Library, Wesleyan University, Middletown, CT.

Edna Rankin McKinnon Papers, Schlesinger Library, Radcliffe College, Cambridge, MA.

Thurgood Marshall Papers, Manuscript Division, Library of Congress, Washington, DC.

Michigan Abortion Referendum Committee Papers, Bentley Historical Library, University of Michigan, Ann Arbor.

John M. Morris Papers, New Haven, CT.

Lonny Myers Papers, Special Collections Department, University of Illinois Library, Chicago.

National Abortion Rights Action League Papers, New York Public Library, New York, NY.

National Abortion Rights Action League Papers, Schlesinger Library, Radcliffe College, Cambridge, MA.

Case Records and Files, New Haven County Superior Court, New Haven, CT.

Criminal Docket Book, New Haven County Superior Court at Waterbury, Waterbury, CT.

Library Files of the *New Haven Register*, New Haven, CT.

Harriet F. Pilpel Papers, Sophia Smith Collection, Smith College, Northampton, MA.

Harriet F. Pilpel Files, Schlesinger Library, Radcliffe College, Cambridge, MA.

Planned Parenthood Federation of America (PPFA) Papers, Sophia Smith Collection, Smith College, Northampton, MA.

Planned Parenthood League of Connecticut (PPLC) Papers, New Haven Colony Historical Society, New Haven, CT.

Planned Parenthood League of Massachusetts (PPLM) Papers, Sophia Smith Collection, Smith College, Northampton, MA.

Annie G. Porritt Papers, Sophia Smith Collection, Smith College, Northampton, MA.

Nancy Carnegie Rockefeller Papers, Manuscripts Division, University of Connecticut Library, Storrs.

Florence Rose Papers, Sophia Smith Collection, Smith College, Northampton, MA.

Margaret Sanger Papers, Manuscript Division, Library of Congress, Washington, DC.

Margaret Sanger Papers, Sophia Smith Collection, Smith College, Northampton, MA.

Hugh W. Savage Papers, Special Collections, DeGolyer Library, Southern Methodist University, Dallas, TX.

Ruth Proskauer Smith Papers, Schlesinger Library, Radcliffe College, Cambridge, MA.

Society for Humane Abortion Papers, Schlesinger Library, Radcliffe College, Cambridge, MA.

Jack Stack Papers, Bentley Historical Library, University of Michigan, Ann Arbor.

E. Robert Stevenson Papers, Mattatuck Museum, Waterbury, CT.

Harlan Fiske Stone Papers, Manuscript Division, Library of Congress, Washington, DC.

Case Files, Office of the Attorney General of Texas, Texas State Archives, Austin.

Legislative Reference Files, Texas State Library, Austin.

U.S. District Court Case Files, National Archives Regional Archives, East Point, GA, and Fort Worth, TX.

U.S. Supreme Court Case Files (RG 267), National Archives, Washington, DC.

U.S. Supreme Court, Tape Recordings of Oral Arguments, National Archives, Washington, DC.

J. Warren Upson Papers, Mattatuck Museum, Waterbury, CT.

Milan Vuitch Papers, Silver Spring, MD.

Earl Warren Papers, Manuscript Division, Library of Congress, Washington, DC.

Washington Citizens for Abortion Reform (WCAR) Papers, Manuscripts Division, University of Washington Library, Seattle.

Records and Reports of the Waterbury Hospital, Waterbury, CT.

Library Files of the *Waterbury Republican-American*, Waterbury, CT.

Virginia B. Whitehill Papers, Special Collections, DeGolyer Library, Southern Methodist University, Dallas, TX.

Charles-Edward A. Winslow Papers, Manuscripts Division, Sterling Library, Yale University, New Haven, CT.

Women's Alliance Papers, First Unitarian Church, Dallas, TX.

YWCA–University of Washington Papers, Manuscripts Division, University of Washington Library, Seattle.

INDEX

ABC News, 729
Abele v. Markle, 544, 566, 568, 574, 583, 588, 956*n*1
Able, Melissa, 603
Abortion (Lader), 318
Abortion Education Committee of Dallas, 461, 462
Abortion Reform Association (ARA), 360, 370, 381–384 *passim*
Abortion Rights Mobilization (ARM), 708, 727, 732–733
Abortionist, The (Rappaport), 284, 285, 504
Abraham, Spencer, 973*n*73
Abramowicz v. Lefkowitz, 380–381, 408, 502
Abrams, Robert, 649
Ad Hoc Committee for Abortion Law Reform, 317
Adametz, Jere, 151
Adkins, Leonard D., 126, 129
Advances for Choice, 728
Advocates for Life Ministries, 703, 711, 719, 726
Ainsworth, Robert A., 459–460, 482
Ajello, Carl, Jr., 545
Akron. See *City of Akron v. Akron Center for Reproductive Health*
Akron Center. See *Ohio v. Akron Center for Reproductive Health*
Alabama, 1967 legislature, 332, 338
Alaska, passes 1970 repeal bill, 431–432, 457
Alcorn, Meade, 126
Alliance for Humane Abortions, 431
Alling, Koland G., 8, 65
Allison, Van Kleeck, 12, 46

Alsop, John deK., 113–115, 117, 118
Alsup, William H., 532, 551
America, 256, 282, 303, 313, 342, 385, 562, 619
American Association of University Women (AAUW), 412, 495
American Baptist Convention, 333
American Bar Association (ABA), 539, 561, 589
American Birth Control League, 14–20 *passim,* 25, 29, 49, 56, 60, 274
American Center for Law and Justice, 712
American Civil Liberties Union (ACLU), 115–116, 139, 200, 267, 351, 613; and *Poe* cases, 154, 164, 166, 170, 171, 173, 231; and *Griswold,* 216, 221, 225, 232, 234, 297; and abortion, 276, 296, 313–314, 333, 349, 352, 370, 371; and Bill Baird, 321–322, 517; and abortion litigation, 379–380, 383, 388, 424, 463, 492, 494, 497, 505; and post-*Roe* abortion issues, 616, 690; and post-*Roe* sexual privacy cases, 621–624 *passim,* 653, 654, 665
American Coalition of Life Activists (ACLA), 711–712, 714, 726
American College of Obstetricians and Gynecologists (ACOG), 278, 350, 491, 501, 504, 505, 731
American Council for Graduate Medical Education, 717
American Enterprise Institute, 738
American Eugenics Society, 21, 30
American Humanist Association, 291

American Law Institute (ALI), 277
American Life League, 738
American Medical Association (AMA), 614; and birth control, 43–44, 48; and abortion, 302, 312, 333, 455, 456, 491, 589, 669; and partial-birth abortions, 731
American Medical News, 378, 719
American Medical Women's Association, 501
American Psychiatric Association, 501
American Public Health Association (APHA), 357, 361, 589
American Social Hygiene Association, 9
Americans for Democratic Action (ADA), 312
Amshoff, Theodore H., Jr., 715
Amsterdam, Anthony, 186, 190, 191, 371
Anderson, Buist, 123
Anderson, Kenneth, 340
Andrews, Richard T., 732
Andrus, Cecil, 682
Anwyl, J. Hugh, 380
Appel, Cheri, 31, 34
Aptheker v. *Secretary of State,* 243
Arizona, 1967 legislature, 316, 317, 319, 327, 332; 1970 legislature, 412
Arizona Republic, 285, 286
Arkansas, passes 1969 reform bill, 369
Arkansas Democrat, 606
"Army of God," 971n59
Army Times, 686
Arnold, Anne, 92
Arnold, Richard S., 175–176, 184–185, 190–191, 192–193
Arnold, Thurman, 151
Ashcroft. See *Planned Parenthood Association of Kansas City* v. *Ashcroft*
Association for Humane Abortion (AHA), 297–298, 300. *See also*

Association for the Study of Abortion (ASA).
Association for the Study of Abortion (ASA), 300, 302–303, 305, 308, 340, 345, 388, 507, 577, 579; and Robert Hall, 313, 317, 318, 339, 356, 360, 371, 376, 456, 483, 607; relative conservatism of, 344, 346, 349, 374; funds Means and Lucas, 352, 353; holds crucial conference, 357–359, 363, 364; and *Hall* case, 379, 409; and amicus briefs, 468, 492, 494
Atlanta Constitution, 303, 422, 423, 606
Atlanta Journal, 422
Atlantic Monthly, The, 149, 301
Austin American-Statesman, 392
Avery, Christopher L., 76, 78, 100

Babbitz, Sidney G., 414–415, 465, 469, 487
Babbitz v. *McCann,* 414–415, 416; influence of, 417, 428, 442, 446, 448, 453, 459–460, 481, 482, 495, 496; appeals of, 465, 468, 469, 487, 488
Babies by Choice or by Chance (Guttmacher), 278
Bailey, John M., 121, 122, 123, 138
Baird, William R., early activism of, 314–315, 317; 1967 Boston arrest, conviction, and jailing of, 320–323, 325, 343, 372–374, 376, 410; appellate victory of, 457; and U.S. Supreme Court, 487, 517–520, 541–543; and *Bellotti I,* 625, 626; and *Bellotti II,* 631, 632
Baird v. *Massachusetts,* 373–374, 410. See also *Eisenstadt* v. *Baird*
Baker, Donald F., 647–648, 656
Baker v. *Wade,* 647–648, 652, 656, 666
Bakke. See *Regents of the University of California* v. *Bakke*

Baldwin, Raymond E., 28, 32, 33, 151; as Governor of Connecticut, 89, 91, 96, 102, 109, 119; as Connecticut Chief Justice, 163–165, 211–212, 222
Baldwin, Simeon, 67
Balk, Jacob, 366
Balliro, Joseph J., 322, 343, 373, 410, 517
Barber, James C., 647
Barker, Creighton, 67
Barlotta, Rose, 45
Barlow, George H., 540
Barnes, Fred, 732
Barnes, James T., 328
Barnes, Susan Graham, 323, 324
Barnum, Phineas T., 16, 78, 116, 193, 195, 472, 757–758n37
Barrett, Francis J., 93
Barrett, James H., 705, 710–713, 718
Barrett, June, 710
Barrows v. Jackson, 512
Barstow, Robbins, 88, 93, 95
Barzelay, Douglas E., 611–612
Bauer, Gary, 732
Beal v. Doe, 627, 628
Beale, T. F. Rutledge, 21
Beasley, Dorothy Toth, 446–447, 449, 450, 458; appeals Doe to Supreme Court, 459, 465, 509–510; and first Doe argument, 523, 527–528; and second Doe argument, 557, 565, 571–572, 599; and Doe aftermath, 602
Becket, G. Campbell, 111, 112
Beckwith, David, 588
Beddingfield, Edgar T., Jr., 328, 329
Beebe, Lorraine, 567
Beers, William L., 104, 105–106
Beilenson, Anthony C., 446, 634; sponsors California reform bill, 290, 292, 296, 298–300, 301, 304, 305, 307, 344; helps pass 1967 reform bill, 330–332, 349,

355; sponsors 1970 repeal bill, 457
Bell, Alden, 330
Bell, Frank, 712
Bellotti, Francis, 625
Bellotti v. Baird I, 625–626, 643, 697
Bellotti v. Baird II, 631, 632, 637, 638
Beloff, Anita, 137
Belous, Leon P., 354–356, 364–366, 377–379. See also People v. Belous, California v. Belous
Ben-Shalom, Miriam, 687
Benham, Flip, 520, 711, 712, 714
Bennett, John C., 630
Bennett, Josephine Day, 9, 10, 14, 16, 21
Benshoof, Janet, 975n82, 976n87
Bensing, Joel Lee, 426–427, 444, 445, 465, 497
Bensing, Sandra, 426–427, 444–445, 447, 450, 465, 497, 523, 598; and Doe aftermath, 602–603
Benton, William, 120
Berg, Harold, 202–204, 206, 208, 209–210, 212
Bergen (N.J.) Record, 727
Berman, Moses, 433
Bermingham, John, 324
Bernardin, Joseph L., 620
Berniere, Walter, 188
Bezanson, Randall P., 581, 607, 956n1
Bick, Robert N., 301
Biddle, Craig, 330, 331
Biden, Joseph R., Jr., 669, 670, 672
Bingham, Alfred M., 92, 93, 95, 97
Birth Control Clinical Research Bureau, 15, 19, 20, 23–24, 31, 58, 60, 81
Birth Control Federation of America (BCFA), 274; 1939 creation of, 2, 60; and 1939 Waterbury arrests, 63, 64, 71, 73–74; and aftermath of Nelson, 79–81,

Birth Control Federation of
     America (BCFA), (cont.)
     83–88, 92, 94, 96; becomes
     PPFA, 100, 271. See also Planned
     Parenthood Federation of
     America (PPFA)
Birth Control League of Massachu-
     setts (BCLM), 12, 20, 27, 31; and
     1937 raids, 45–48, 54–56; and
     Gardner decision, 58–60. See also
     Massachusetts Mothers' Health
     Council
Birth Control Review, 14, 18, 19, 20,
     24, 274
Black, Charles, 371
Black, Hugo L., 513; and Poe v.
     Ullman, 169, 179, 181–186
     passim, 191, 193, 194; and
     Griswold, 237–244 passim, 251,
     254–255, 256, 263, 266; and
     Vuitch, 475–480 passim, 488–490;
     and Roe v. Wade, 491; retirement
     of, 507, 509, 511, 512
Blackmun, Harry A., 473–474, 624,
     707; and Vuitch, 475–478, 480,
     489; and Roe v. Wade, 491, 501,
     521; and Eisenstadt, 519–520,
     536, 541, 542; and first Roe/Doe
     conference, 530–534; and initial
     opinion drafting, 535, 537–538;
     first circulates Roe/Doe draft
     opinions, 547–552; advocates
     reargument of Roe and Doe,
     552–556, 557; and summer work
     on Roe/Doe opinions, 558–559,
     560, 561; and second Roe/Doe
     oral argument, 568–573; and
     second Roe/Doe conference,
     573–576; and final drafting of
     Roe/Doe opinions, 580–587;
     formally announces Roe and
     Doe decisions, 588–595, 596,
     598–599; and initial reactions to
     Roe and Doe, 601, 605–608 pas-
     sim, 617; academic criticisms of,

     609–614; and later citations of
     Roe/Doe opinions, 623; and
     Planned Parenthood v. Danforth,
     625–626; and Maher, 628; and
     Colautti, 631–632; and Bellotti II,
     632; and Harris v. McRae, 635;
     and H. L., 637–638; and Akron,
     641–643; and sexual privacy
     cases, 646; and Uplinger, 648; and
     Bowers, 656–657, 659–667
     passim, 670; and Thornburgh, 661,
     667–668, 673; and Webster,
     675–679; and Akron Center, 682,
     684; and Rust, 685–686; and
     Bray, 689, 702; and Casey,
     691–692, 693, 697, 698–700
Blackstone, William, 569
Blazi, John A., 202–204, 205, 206,
     212
Block, Donald L., 444, 447
Bloom, Daniel, 295, 296
Bloom, Sylvia, 295, 296
Blumenthal, Albert H.: sponsors
     New York reform bill, 308, 311,
     312, 315, 317, 318, 344–347
     passim; and 1969 legislature, 356,
     367–369; backs 1970 repeal
     effort, 408
Bolton, Arthur K., 428, 446, 459,
     465, 571, 599, 602
Bonser, Alan, 340, 360, 422, 423
Booker, Joseph, Jr., 718
Bopp, James, Jr., 679–680
Borchard, Edwin, 103, 104,
     781–782n33, 782nn35, 36
Bork, Robert H.: and Griswold,
     264–267, 268; and Roe, 639; and
     Dronenburg, 649–650, 656, 662,
     666; Supreme Court nomination
     of, 668–672; and Casey, 701
Boston Globe, 410, 606
Boston Herald, 256
Boult, Reber F., Jr., 463, 464, 497,
     523, 527
Bourne, Judith, 422–428, 438,

444–445, 450, 459, 483, 492, 523, 598–599

Bourne, Peter, 422–427 *passim,* 444–445, 523

Bowden, Henry, 446

Bowers, Michael, 654, 655, 656

Bowers, Richard M., 340

Bowers, Ruth McLean, 500, 509, 523, 528, 572

Bowers v. *Hardwick,* ix, 654–657, 658–661, 663–667, 670, 674, 686–687, 724, 956n1

Bowles, Chester, 118–119, 120

Bowles, Dorothy, 118–119

Boyd, Curtis, 955n1

Bozell, L. Brent, 151

Bradford, Dorothy, 45

Bradley, Frank J., 403

Bradley, Kenneth J., 37

Brandeis, Louis D., 172, 195, 252, 254, 260–262, 536, 596, 664, 821n83

Brandlin, Joseph J., 365

Bray, Jayne, 702, 703

Bray, Michael, 651, 652, 703, 711, 714, 971n59

Bray v. *Alexandria Women's Health Clinic,* 688, 689, 692, 702, 706

Breihan, Bob, 392–393, 439, 486

Brennan, William J., Jr., 474; and *Poe* v. *Ullman,* 175–186 *passim,* 190–194, 198–199, 225, 269; and *Griswold,* 237, 242–243, 246–253; and *Vuitch,* 417, 479, 489, 490, 509; and *Roe* v. *Wade,* 491, 521; and *Eisenstadt,* 518–520, 541–544, 566, 571, 596, 597, 599, 621; and first *Roe/Doe* conference, 529–533; and initial opinion drafting, 534–537; and first Blackmun draft opinions, 548–549, 551; opposes reargument of *Roe/Doe,* 553, 555–556, 560; and second *Roe/Doe* conference, 573, 574,

576; and final drafting of *Roe/Doe* opinions, 580–587; and sexual privacy cases, 621, 622, 646, 652; and *Planned Parenthood* v. *Danforth,* 625; and *Carey,* 627–628; and *Maher,* 628; and *Bellotti II,* 632; and *Harris* v. *McRae,* 635; and *H. L.,* 637–638; and *Akron,* 641–642; and *Uplinger,* 646, 648, 649; and *Bowers,* 656–657, 659–660, 664; and *Akron Center,* 682, 684; retires from Court, 684

Breslow, Lester, 361

Brest, Paul, 665

Breyer, Stephen G., 250, 707, 729

Bridgeport Herald, 69

Bridgeport Maternal Health Center, 1, 49, 54

Brigham, Steven C., 716

Bring, Murray H., 168

Britton, John Bayard, 705, 710–713, 716, 718

Bronson, Richardson, 86

Brown, Allyn, 76, 77, 100

Brown, Charles, 58, 65

Brown, John R., 387, 388, 398, 436, 444

Brown, Judie, 738

Brown, Ralph E., 309

Brown, Ralph S., 139

Brown v. *Board of Education,* x, 136, 473, 690, 692, 695, 741

Browne, F. W. Stella, 272–273, 274, 293

Brownmiller, Susan, 363, 408

Brunelle, Pierre V., 376–377

Bruner, Fred, 388, 434–439, 441–443, 454, 461, 501, 516, 523

Bruno, Leopoldo, 392–393

Bryan, Albert V., 621–622

Brydges, Earl W., 311, 409, 418–419, 421, 545

B.U. News, 320, 322

Buchanan, Alvin L., 398

Buchanan, Patrick J., 546

Buchanan v. *Batchelor,* 398, 401–402, 403, 436, 448, 485, 487, 620, 621, 647

Buchmeyer, Jerry, 647–648, 652, 656

Buckley, Ferdinand, 348, 444, 446, 448, 449, 450

Buckley, James, 609

Buckley, William F., Jr., 149, 151, 230; and abortion, 303, 606

Buffett, Susan, 355

Buffett, Warren, 355, 380, 727

Bulkeley, Morgan G., 109

Burger, Warren E., 473–474; and *Vuitch,* 418, 476–480, 489; and *Roe* v. *Wade,* 491, 501, 521, 524, 526; and *Eisenstadt,* 518–520, 541, 543; and first *Roe/Doe* conference, 528–530, 532–534, 537, 548, 549; supports reargument of *Roe/Doe,* 553–560, 564; and second *Roe/Doe* argument, 568–573; and second *Roe/Doe* conference, 573–574, 576; and final drafting of *Roe/Doe* opinions, 581, 585, 586–588; final *Roe/Doe* concurrence by, 597, 600; and *Planned Parenthood* v. *Danforth,* 626; and *Sendak,* 627; and *Carey,* 628; and *Bellotti II,* 632; and *Colautti,* 632; and *Harris* v. *McRae,* 634; and *H. L.,* 637, 638; and *Akron,* 642; and *Uplinger,* 644, 646, 649; and *Thornburgh,* 652, 657, 662; and *Bowers,* 657, 659, 661, 663; retires from Court, 662–663, 668

Burnett, Andrew, 703, 711

Burns, John A., 412–414

Burrall, Lucy, 66

Burrall, Mary, 66

Burt, John, 658, 702, 706

Bush, George, 472, 673, 684, 689

Bush, Prescott, 120, 124, 788–789n62

Bush, Ruth Barnett, 362, 955n1

Bushby, Laura, 124

Bushby, Wilkie, 124

Butler, Charles W., 427

Butler, Robert P., 17

Buxton, C. Lee, initial involvement with PPLC, 135–142 *passim;* and abortion, 142, 259, 260, 276, 296, 302, 309, 340, 364, 370, 795n19; organizes *Poe* v. *Ullman,* 143–147, 152–157 *passim,* 161, 163, 165–169 *passim,* 173–179 *passim,* 182, 187, 195; and 1961 clinic opening, 196–198, 200–201, 203–210; trial and conviction of, 212–217, 221, 222; and *Griswold* appeal, 224–233 *passim,* 237, 239, 244, 251, 252; and *Griswold* aftermath, 255, 257–259, 260, 267, 268, 269, 315, 599, 741

Buxton, Helen, 130, 143–144, 224, 257, 258–259, 260

Buxton v. *Ullman,* 154, 164–169 *passim,* 175, 177, 186, 193, 211, 212. See also *Poe* v. *Ullman.*

Byrn, Robert M., 298, 301, 313, 342, 346, 522, 538, 561, 608, 609

Byrn v. *New York City Health and Hospitals Corp.,* 522, 568, 574

Byrne, Ethel, 12, 13

Byrne, Richard P., 330

Cabot, Thomas, 500

Cadbury, Leah Tapper, 49–54, 72, 599, 768n86

Cady, Francis C., 141

Cahill, Susan, 729

Calabresi, Guido, 613–614

Calderone, Mary S., 197, 275–276, 280–281, 285, 293, 302

Calhoun, Frank E., 123, 128

California, 1961 legislature, 282–283; 1963 legislature, 290, 292, 296; 1965 legislature, 298–299, 301; 1967 legislature passes reform bill, 330–332;

limited impact of 1967 law, 360, 375; impact of *Belous* decision in, 380, 411, 457

California v. *Belous,* 410. See also *People* v. *Belous*

California Committee for Therapeutic Abortion (CCTA), 305–308, 309, 323, 354, 374; and 1967 reform bill, 330, 332, 349, 375–376; and *Belous,* 355, 364, 365, 366, 378, 411

California Medical Association, 306, 330, 378

California Medicine, 280

Callahan, Daniel, 455–456, 606

Calverly, Eleanor Taylor, 37, 41, 50, 57, 76, 92

Campbell, James S., 245, 246, 249, 250, 252

Campbell, Loraine, 47, 88, 89, 285, 291; and *Poe* cases, 155–159 *passim,* 162–163, 164, 169, 172; on Bill Baird, 322–323

Campbell, R. Paul, 457

Campbell, William, 481, 513

Canady, Charles T., 719, 720, 721

Canfield, Cass, 196, 199, 208

Cannon, Raymond J., 156–164 *passim,* 170–171, 173, 176, 178–180, 232

Cano, Sandra Bensing. *See* Bensing, Sandra

Cantor, Donald, 340, 370

Cardozo, Benjamin, 264

Carey v. *Population Services International,* 627–628, 645, 648, 655, 658, 664, 694

Cargo, David F., 369

Carhart, LeRoy, 734

Carmen, Arlene, 350–351

Carmody, Dorothy Chase, 61

Carmody, Edward T., 61–62

Carraba, Salvatore, 142

Carswell, G. Harrold, 474

Carter, Jimmy, 636, 637

Carter, Robert, 337

Casey. See Planned Parenthood of Southeastern Pennsylvania v. *Casey*

Casey, Robert P., 681

Cassibry, Fred J., 460

Catholic Council on Civil Liberties (CCCL), 221, 225, 228, 232, 234

Catholic Transcript, 35, 96, 198

Catley-Carlson, Margaret, 728

Catt, Carrie Chapman, 10

CBS Reports, 214–215

Cedar Rapids Gazette, 607

Chamberlain, Jerome, 438

Chang, Kevin S. C., 726

Charles, Alan F., 299, 330, 332, 446, 464

Chase, Edith, 49, 50, 51, 66

Chase, Florence, 49

Chase, Nancy, 328

Cheifetz, Walter, 286–287

Cheney, Marjory, 23, 28

Chicago Herald American, 148

Chicago Tribune, 303

Chicago Women's Liberation Union, 486–487

Child Custody Protection Act, 973n73

Choper, Jesse, 371

Christ, Ernest W., 22

Christian Century, The, 281, 312

Christian Coalition, 732

Christianity Today, 606, 609

Cisler, Lucinda "Cindy," 374, 408, 420, 863n20

Citizens' Abortion Discussion Group, 358, 371

Citizens' Committee for Humane Abortion Laws, 284, 290. *See also* Society for Humane Abortion (SHA)

Citizens for Abortion Law Repeal, 367

Citizens for the Extension of Birth Control Services, 309, 810–811n24

City of Akron v. *Akron Center for Reproductive Health,* 640–643, 657, 661, 679, 690, 691, 696
Clapp, James, 374, 408, 420
Clarie, T. Emmet, 496, 544, 566
Clark, Beatrice V., 45
Clark, James H., Jr., 359, 369, 438
Clark, Joseph B., 210, 215, 222–223, 224; and *Griswold,* 228, 229, 232, 234, 236, 239–240, 244
Clark, Ramsey, 372
Clark, Tom C., 149, 473; and *Poe* v. *Ullman,* 168, 169, 183, 185, 186, 191; and *Griswold,* 241–242, 244, 248, 249; influential abortion essay by, 372, 416, 441, 453, 468, 471, 478, 481, 500, 501, 502, 536, 541, 550, 564, 596, 909*n*129
Clemow, Bice, 92, 94, 97, 98, 109
Clergy Consultation Service on Abortion (CCS), 333–334, 347, 349, 350, 362, 364, 376–377, 386, 392, 409, 438, 486, 495, 539
Clinton, Bill, 702, 707, 722, 726, 727, 731, 732, 733
Closed: 99 Ways to Stop Abortion (Scheidler), 651
Coats, Sam, 491
Coccomo, Thomas, 188
Coffee, Linda N., first approached by Weddington, 396, 398–400; seeks plaintiffs for case, 400–401, 403–405; files *Roe* v. *Wade,* 406–407, 433–434, 436, 437–439; and three-judge hearing of *Roe,* 440–444, 447; and three-judge decision, 453, 454; and Supreme Court appeal of *Roe,* 460–461, 492, 497, 501, 563, 877–878*n*84; and first oral argument of *Roe,* 516–517, 523; and *Roe* reargument, 557, 568, 572, 599; and *Roe* aftermath, 600–601, 602; treatment of

Norma McCorvey, 720
Colautti v. *Franklin,* 631–632
Coleman v. *Miller,* 661
Colgate, Gilbert, 81
Colorado, passes 1967 reform bill, 323–325, 327, 329, 332; limited impact of 1967 law, 341–342, 351, 360, 375; 1971 legislature, 483
Colson, Charles, 665–666
Columbia Law Review, 42
Columbia Spectator, 291
Comfort, Charles W., 32, 36
Comley, John M., 224
Committee for the Cook-Leichter Bill, 408
Common Ground Network for Life and Choice, 721
Commonweal, 155, 222, 257, 312, 313
Commonwealth v. *Bonadio,* 645
Commonwealth v. *Corbett,* 90, 99, 100, 128
Commonwealth v. *Gardner,* 56, 58–60, 80, 88, 322; and *State* v. *Nelson,* 64, 69–71, 75, 77, 90; and *Tileston,* 99, 100, 102, 124; and *Poe* v. *Ullman,* 161; and *Griswold,* 228, 239, 240
Complete Book of Birth Control, The (Guttmacher), 200
Comstock, Anthony, 10, 15, 42, 285, 472, 754*n*25
Cone, James H., 630
Connecticut Birth Control League (CBCL), and initial public clinics, 1–3, 7, 37–41, 44, 48–54, 56–58, 60–61; early legislative efforts of, 16–37 *passim;* and Waterbury arrests, 61–77; and *Nelson* aftermath, 78–81, 83–90, 91–94; and *Tileston,* 94–100; becomes PPLC, 100. *See also* Planned Parenthood League of Connecticut (PPLC).

Connecticut Civil Liberties Union (CCLU), 166, 170, 171, 173, 189, 370

Connecticut Council of Catholic Women, 19, 32

Connecticut Council of Churches, 159

Connecticut General Assembly, 1917 session, 10; 1923 session, 15–17; 1925 session, 18–19; 1927 session, 19–20; 1929 session, 20–23; 1931 session, 25, 27–28; 1933 session, 31–34; 1935 session, 35–37; 1937 session, 44; 1941 session, 86–90, 91–94, 95–97; 1943 session, 102, 106–107; 1945 session, 109–111; 1947 session, 113–116; 1949 session, 118–119; 1951 session, 120–123; 1953 session, 125–128; 1955 session, 137–138; 1957 session, 141–142; 1959 session, 159–160; 1961 session, 173, 189; 1963 session, 217, 221; 1965 session, 235, 251; 1967 session, 316; 1969 session, 348, 370; 1972 special session, 544–545; codifies *Roe* v. *Wade* in 1990, 682

Connecticut League for Abortion Law Reform, 340, 370; becomes Connecticut League for Abortion Law *Repeal,* 433

Connecticut League of Women Voters, 8, 10, 15, 34

Connecticut Social Hygiene Association, 9, 10, 29

Connecticut State Medical Society, 28, 32, 36, 67, 87; endorses birth control, 29, 31, 43, 115, 119; and abortion, 487

Connecticut Women's Suffrage Association, 9

Connolly, Thomas A., 466

Converse, Frank C., 35, 36

Conway, Alvin, 319

Cook, Constance E., 356, 359, 367, 368, 385, 408, 418–420

Cooke, Lawrence, 645

Cooke, Terence, 546, 605, 619, 620

Cookston, Pat, 400, 405

Cooley, Thomas M., 168, 172, 260

Cooney, Joseph P., as state senator, 34, 97; as diocesan lobbyist, 114, 119, 121–122, 126–127, 137, 141–142, 160, 189, 217, 235; and abortion, 316

Cooper, Clarence P., 417

Cooper, James F., 18

Cooper, James Wayne, 36

Cooper, Robert A., 60

Cooper, Robert O., 438

Cooper Union, 109

Cooper v. *Aaron,* 692

Corbett, Lewis, 90

Corkey v. *Edwards,* 432, 482, 498, 499, 508, 526

Cornell, John A., 72–73, 74

Cotner v. *Henry,* 402, 861–862n16

Countryman, Vern, 102, 128–129, 151

Cowles, John, 506

Cox, Archibald, 335, 612, 639

Craig, Glenn, 278

Craven, Braxton, 482

Creadick, A. Nowell, 29–35 *passim,* 87, 92, 104, 125, 200, 761–762n56; and Waterbury arrests, 63, 67, 70, 74

Creighton, Tom, 484, 485, 490

Cross, Wilbur L., 25, 32, 67, 89

Crouch, Richard E., 623

Crutcher, Mark, 715, 716–717, 730

Cryne, Eugene P., 4–5, 6, 50, 157, 599

Cullinan, E. P., 469

Cummings, Homer, 43

Cunningham, Gerald, 108

Cunningham, Mary Van Zile, 108–114 *passim,* 116–119, 128, 133

Curtis, Philip, 110, 111
Cusack, Ruth P., 344–345, 347,
    356, 361, 367, 368
Cushing, Richard J., 117, 118, 217,
    218, 228–229, 234–235, 256

Daily Worker, The, 151
Dallas Committee for the Study of
    Abortion (DCSA), 405, 406, 438.
    See also Abortion Education
    Committee of Dallas.
Dallas Gay Alliance, 647
Dallas Legal Services Project, 439,
    485
Dallas Morning News, 406, 423, 454,
    509, 601, 608
Dallas Times-Herald, 400, 405,
    406–407, 454, 485
Daly, George S., Jr., 432
Daly, John, 188
Danaher, Cornelius J., 96, 106–107
Danco Laboratories, 732
Danforth. See *Planned Parenthood of
    Central Missouri* v. *Danforth.*
Danforth, Nicholas W., 498, 500,
    523, 564
Daniells, Jane, 126
Darrach, Florence Borden, 31, 39;
    and *Nelson* aftermath, 78, 79,
    86–90, 96, 102; and *Tileston,* 92,
    97
Daschle, Tom, 727, 730–732
Davenport, Barbara, 112
Davids, Georgina, 23
Davis, Caroline Carter, 46, 47, 59
Davis, Clarice, 452–453
Davis, Edith, 66
Davis, Edward H., 53, 66
Davis, Ruth A., 51
Day, George H., 9
Day, Katharine Beach, 9–10, 16, 22,
    25, 27, 29, 32; and American
    Birth Control League, 14–15,
    19
Decker, Raymond G., 618

Decker, Wayne, 318, 334
DeConcini, Dennis, 669
Dees, Morris, 351, 352, 371, 372,
    379, 381, 463, 504
Defense of Marriage Act, 726
Delaware, passes 1969 reform bill,
    370
Delevett, Allen F., 114
Dennett, Mary Ware, 10, 12, 14, 15,
    17–18, 19, 26
Dennis v. *United States,* 149
Dennison, Daisy M., 95
Denver Post, 324, 360
deParrie, Paul, 726
Des Moines Tribune, 79
Detroit Free Press, 412
Detroit News, 563, 576–577
Devitt, Edward J., 430
Devlin, Raymond J., 33
DeVries, Julian, 286
DeWolf, L. Harold, 630
Diamond v. *Charles,* 657, 661
Dickinson, Robert L., 43
Dixon, Robert G., 263
Dodd, Thomas J., 111, 114, 785n47
Dodge, Robert G., 45, 54–56,
    58–59
Doe v. *Bolton,* ix; filing of, 423–428,
    431, 444–446; three-judge hear-
    ing of, 447–450, 451; three-judge
    decision in, 457–459, 481, 482,
    518, 541, 561; three-judge deci-
    sion appealed to Supreme Court,
    459, 460, 462–463, 464–465,
    468, 471, 480; initial Supreme
    Court consideration of, 491–492,
    493, 494, 497–510 *passim,* 513,
    514–515, 517, 520–522; first oral
    argument of, 523, 526–528, 541;
    first Supreme Court conference
    on, 528, 530–534; initial opinion
    drafting in, 534–538; and *Eisen-
    stadt,* 542–544; first Blackmun
    draft opinion in, 547–552; tussle
    over rearguing of, 552–560;

second oral argument of, 563,
565, 567–568, 571–573; second
conference on, 573–576; final
opinion drafting in, 580–587;
Supreme Court decision formally announced, 588, 594–597,
598; immediate aftermath of,
600, 602–609, 618, 620, 621,
633; academic criticisms of,
609–616, 618; and *Danforth,* 626;
and *Maher,* 628, 629, 630; and
Colautti, 631; and *H. L.,* 637; and
Akron, 641; anniversary of, 702,
739; postviability protection
of women's health in, 722, 731;
Lucas's retrospective on, 955n1
Doe v. *Commonwealth's Attorney,*
621–622, 623, 624, 646–650
passim, 655, 656
Doe v. *Randall,* 428–430
Doe v. *Scott,* 480–481, 513
Doe v. *Ullman,* 154, 156, 157, 164,
166, 193. See also *Poe* v. *Ullman*
Doe v. *Wade,* 406, 407, 415, 433,
436, 437. See also *Roe* v. *Wade*
Dombrowski v. *Pfister,* 235
Dominick, D. Clinton, 419
Dooling, John F., Jr., 627, 629, 631,
633, 634, 635
Dorsen, Norman, 336, 371, 379;
and *Vuitch,* 470, 474, 477–478,
479, 490; and *Roe* v. *Wade,*
492–493, 494, 501
Dorsey, Joseph L., 228–229
Douglas, Cathy, 557–558, 560
Douglas, William O., 357, 474; and
Tileston, 102, 103, 105; and *Poe* v.
Ullman, 168, 169, 182, 183, 186,
191–194 *passim,* 221, 225; and
Griswold, 235, 240, 241–254,
372; *Griswold* opinion assessed,
256, 258, 262–267, 566, 590,
649, 650, 654; and *Baird,* 410;
and *Hodgson* cases, 467; and
Vuitch, 479–480, 488–489, 509;

and *Babbitz,* 487; and *Roe* v.
Wade, 491, 512, 521, 528; and
Eisenstadt, 519–520, 536, 541,
542; and *Doe* v. *Bolton,* 527; and
first *Roe/Doe* conference,
529–534; and initial opinion
drafting, 534–538; and first
Blackmun draft opinions,
548–551; opposes reargument of
Roe and *Doe,* 553–560, 561; and
second *Roe/Doe* conference, 573,
574, 576; and final drafting of
Roe/Doe opinions, 581, 583, 586;
final *Roe/Doe* concurrence by,
595–597; retires from Court, 622
Downs, James T., III, 326
Doyle, James E., 488
Draper, William, 517
Dred Scott v. *Sandford,* 699
Drinan, Robert F., 228, 299, 301,
313, 341, 342–343, 412, 413,
421; and *Roe,* 606
Dronenburg, James L., 649–650
Dronenburg v. *Zech,* 649–650, 656,
662, 666
Duffee, Charles, 45
Dukakis, Michael S., 234–235, 673
Duke, Steven, 168
Dunn, Earl, 623–624
Durning, Jean Cressy, 146–147, 153,
156, 159, 161, 205, 266, 267, 741
Durning, Marvin, 146–147, 152,
153, 156, 159, 160, 161, 205,
266, 267, 741
Duryea, Perry B., Jr., 344–345, 356,
368, 419, 420
Dusenbury, Fred, 297
Dworkin, Ronald, 701

East, John P., 639
Edelin, Kenneth C., 617–618
Egeberg, Roger O., 306, 365
Ehrenreich, Barbara, 616
Ehrlichman, John D., 546
Eisenhower, Arthur, 185

Eisenhower, Dwight D., 140–141, 164
Eisenstadt, Thomas, 410
Eisenstadt v. *Baird*, 457, 517–520, 536, 541–544, 545, 625; subsequent influence of, 544, 561, 566, 611, 620–624 *passim*, 627, 644, 647, 649; and *Doe*, 550, 565; and *Roe*, 564, 571, 591, 592, 596, 597, 599; and *Bowers*, 655, 658, 663, 664–665, 687; and *Casey*, 694, 698. See also *Baird* v. *Massachusetts*
Ells, Arthur F., 85, 88, 100, 106
Elton, Deborah, 66
Ely, John Hart, 229, 236–237, 240, 241, 248–252 *passim*, 255; and *Roe* v. *Wade*, 609–611, 612, 615
Ely, Mildred Chase, 49, 50, 51
Emerson, Ruth Calvin, 170, 171–172, 231, 237
Emerson, Thomas I., 153, 170, 370; and Fowler Harper, 147–151 *passim*, 198; inherits *Griswold* appeal, 231–234, 236–237; argues *Griswold*, 237–238, 240–241, 244, 250; and *Griswold* decision, 255, 258–260, 264, 310, 337, 446; and Roy Lucas, 371
Enersen, Burnham, 355, 365–366
Ernst, Morris L., 24, 26, 73, 785*n*45; and *One Package* decision, 42, 43–44; and *Gardner*, 47–48, 55–56, 59; and *Nelson*, 79, 81, 84–85, 86, 92; and *Tileston*, 101, 102–106; and post-*Tileston* strategizing, 107–113 *passim*, 124; and *Poe* cases, 153, 155–159 *passim*, 162, 171, 197; and *Griswold*, 225, 234; and abortion, 274, 280, 284–285, 288–296 *passim*, 386
Escobedo v. *Illinois*, 244
Estes, Joe, 397
Estes v. *Texas*, 235

Evans, J. Claude, 438, 462, 485, 486, 601
Evans, Orinda, 425
Evarts, Josephine, 108–112 *passim*, 119, 129, 135
Evarts, Katherine, 173, 235
Expressen, 287, 288
Eyman, Andrew J., 354

Family Limitation (Sanger), 11–12
Fargo (North Dakota) Women's Health Organization, 715
Farr, Louise Evans, 160
Fein, Bruce, 666
Feinstein, Diane, 731
Ferguson, Frances Hand, 163
Ferraro, Geraldine, 651
Ferris, Pamelia, 47
Fielding, Virginia, 405
Finkbine, Robert, 286–289
Finkbine, Sherri Chessen, 285–289, 291, 293, 300, 302, 360
First Unitarian Church of Dallas, 289, 400, 405, 438
Fisher, Evelyn, 173
Fisher, Louise H., 19, 22, 32–33, 36, 106, 111, 114, 119, 122
Fisher, Robert L., 128, 129, 141, 142
Fitzgerald, Anthony, 83
Fitzgerald, John G., 44
Fitzgerald, William B., 5–7, 157; and Waterbury arrests, 7–8, 61–71, 72–73, 599; and *Nelson* case, 74–78, 79, 81–83, 85, 186–188, 194
Fitzpatrick, James W., 36
Fitzsimmons, Ron, 729–730
Flanagan, John P., 54
Flast v. *Cohen*, 512
Fleming, Robert B., 225, 232, 234
Fletcher, Henry F., 10, 12, 14, 15, 16, 19, 20, 21
Fletcher, Joseph F., 199, 298, 346
Flood, Thomas W., 200

Florida, 1967 legislature, 332; 1968 legislature, 348; passes 1972 reform statute, 538; 1997 legislation, 967n35

Florio, Jim, 681

Flowers, Robert C., 437, 569–570, 592

Floyd, Jay, 437, 438, 439, 441–443; and *Roe* appeal to Supreme Court, 462, 509–512, 513–514, 521, 608, 636; and first *Roe* oral argument, 523, 525–526, 527; and second *Roe* argument, 557, 565, 569, 599; and *Roe* aftermath, 602

Foe, Victoria, 389–392, 484, 492

Ford, Gerald, 622

Forman, Philip, 540

Forrester, Owen, 446

Forsberg, Joan Bates, 204–205, 206, 208, 209, 212

Forsythe, Clarke D., 955n1

Fortas, Abe, 473

Fortune, 42

Foster, Carl, 82

Foster, John G., 58, 65

Fowler, Henry, 237

Fox, David A., 28

Frampton, George, 548, 551, 559, 956n1

Francis, Albert S., 8, 65

Frankfurter, Felix, 55–56, 264; and *Poe* v. *Ullman,* 169, 170, 172, 176–194 *passim,* 224, 242, 243, 266, 802n64

Franklin, Paul, 87–90, 92

Frazel, Jerome A., Jr., 510–511

Freedom of Access to Clinic Entrances (FACE) Act, x, 705, 706–710, 712, 718, 726, 729, 735, 736, 739

Freeman, Brian M., 728

Freeman, Jo, 367

French, John D., 186

Freund, Paul, 175, 182, 186

Fried, Charles, 174–175, 190–191, 611, 615, 666, 783–784n41; and *Webster,* 673, 674–675

Friedan, Betty, 343, 356, 361, 561

Friedman, Irwin E., 112

Friendly, Henry J., 381, 612, 867n37

Frothingham, Channing, 54

Fuller, Jack, 558

Fuller, Lon L., 155–156

Fuller, William R., 434–435

Furman v. *Georgia,* 509

Gabrielli, Domenick, 645

Galleani, Ilia, 46–47

Gamble, Clarence J., 49, 85

Gampell, Ralph J., 278–281 *passim,* 283, 290

Gardner. See *Commonwealth* v. *Gardner*

Gardner, Carolyn T., 45, 47

Garrity, B. L., 21

Garth, Leonard, 540

Garth, Thomas H., 19

Gaylor, Anne, 739

Geddes, Minna, 117–118

Gedeon Richter, 732

George, B. James, Jr., 358

Georgetown Law Journal, 281

Georgia, 1967 legislature, 316–317, 319, 332; passes 1968 reform bill, 347–348; limited impact of 1968 law, 360, 375; 1970 legislature, 422–423; 1971 legislature, 483, 484; 1972 legislature, 538

Georgia Citizens for Hospital Abortions, 340, 360, 422–428 *passim,* 445

Gesell, Gerhard A., 646–647; rules for Vuitch, 382, 383, 386, 407, 409, 415, 424, 441, 599; Supreme Court reviews ruling by, 417, 468, 471, 475, 477, 479–480, 488–490, 599

Gewirtz, Paul, 665

Gidding, Lee, 361, 387–388, 483, 484, 506–508, 539, 561, 567, 588; and *Roe* aftermath, 603

Giles, Dorothy, 226, 227

Gilhuly, Mae, 206

Gillett, Frederick H., 26

Gilman, Lawrence M., 119

Gilmore, James S., III, 738

Ginsberg, Martin, 369, 408

Ginsburg, Douglas, 672

Ginsburg, Ruth Bader, 613, 614, 616, 707, 729

Gitenstein, Mark, 671

Glendon, Mary Ann, 616

Glenn, George A., 274

Godkin, E. L., 260, 261

Goldberg, Arthur J., 224, 236, 473; and *Griswold,* 238, 239, 242–243, 249–255, 264, 453, 566, 590, 707

Goldberg, Irving L., 397–398, 621, 656; and *Buchanan,* 398, 401–402, 485; and *Roe v. Wade,* 436, 440–444, 447, 451–454, 599

Goldberg, Samuel J., 98

Goldenberg, Samuel, 371, 384

Goldman, Emma, 10

Goldmark, Carl, Jr., 298, 302, 409

Goldstein, Jonah J., 12–13

Goldstein, Stephen, 250

Gonzales, Connie, 600, 720

Goodrich, Elizabeth D., 83

Goodrich, William A., and opening of Waterbury clinic, 4, 7, 57–58, 61, 65; and Waterbury arrests, 66–68, 70, 72–73, 81–83

Gordon, Felix, 287

Gordon, James H., Jr., 667

Gordon, Marion O., 446

Gordon, Myron L., 414, 465

Gorman, Arthur T., 201, 214

Goss, Virginia J., 8, 57, 61–62, 63, 65, 66

Graham, Callan, 461

Graham, Fred, 382, 425, 520, 602

Grant, Benton H., 127, 129

Grant, Marion Hepburn, 10

Grassley, Charles, 669

Gray, Wilford D., 47

Green, Ben C., 471

Greenhouse, Linda, 408, 493

Greenwich Maternal Health Center, 1, 31, 34, 37, 39–40

Greitzer, Carol, 567

Gressman, Eugene, 166, 170, 198

Grey, Thomas C., 647, 724

Griffin, Michael F., 702, 703, 705, 706, 710, 711, 712, 714

Griggs, Harriet, 57, 65

Griswold, Erwin, 417, 418

Griswold, Estelle Trebert, 739; joins PPLC, 130–135; as PPLC executive director in 1950s, 135–142, 159; and *Poe v. Ullman,* 143, 152–155, 161–163, 165, 172–173, 176–177; opens clinic in 1961, 189, 195–210 *passim;* trial and conviction of, 212–217, 221, 223, 224; and internal PPLC tensions, 218–220; and Supreme Court appeal, 225–233, 237, 239, 244, 251; and aftermath of *Griswold,* 252, 255–259, 267–269, 315, 334, 599, 741; and abortion, 269, 340, 370

Griswold, Frank, 131

Griswold, Richard W., 131, 132–133, 218, 223–224

Griswold v. Connecticut, ix; initial Supreme Court appeal of, 225–226, 228–237, 297; oral argument of, 237–240; justices' deliberations over, 240–244; drafting of opinions in, 245–252, 609; final opinions announced, 252–255; initial reactions to, 255–260, 320; scholarly criticisms of, 263–268, 385; legacy of, 269, 372; influences abortion activists, 302, 304, 306, 307, 309–310, 312, 334, 358, 384; influences

Roy Lucas, 337, 338–339, 353, 356, 371, 408, 416; and *Belous,* 355, 365, 366, 377, 378, 379; and *Eisenstadt* v. *Baird,* 373, 374, 518–519, 541–543; and *Vuitch,* 382, 468, 473, 474, 478, 489, 490; and *Buchanan,* 398, 401–402; and *Roe* v. *Wade,* 405, 453, 461–462, 493, 501, 502, 507, 512; and *Babbitz,* 415–416; and *Doe* v. *Bolton,* 428, 446, 448, 449, 450; and Pennsylvania case, 457; and Louisiana case, 460; and *Hodgson* cases, 467; and Ohio case, 471; and Illinois case, 481; and *Wyman* case, 495; and *Roe* and *Doe* in Supreme Court, 524, 527, 532, 534, 536, 550, 568, 569, 571, 574, 576, 588, 590, 592, 596, 597, 599; and New Jersey case, 540; and Kansas case, 541; and Connecticut cases, 544, 566; and Maryland case, 561; post-*Roe* commentary on, 611, 613, 614, 615, 620, 621, 622; post-*Roe* judicial citations of, 623, 624, 635, 645, 647–650 *passim,* 688; and *Carey,* 627; and *Bowers,* 654, 655, 658, 659, 663–667 *passim,* 687; and Bork nomination, 668–671; and Kennedy nomination, 672; and *Webster,* 675, 678; and Souter nomination, 684; and *Casey,* 690, 694–695, 698, 699, 701, 741

Gruening, Ernest, 517

Grunsky, Donald, 330

Gunn, David, 702–703, 705, 706, 710, 711, 712

Gunther, Gerald, 612

Gurner, Rowena, 301

Gustafson, Carl H., 323–324

Guttmacher, Alan F., 197, 200, 227, 228, 358, 364, 739; and early abortion reform, 270 272,

275–285 *passim,* 288–299 *passim,* 305, 309, 362; and Rockefeller commission, 317, 346, 347; and Roy Lucas, 336; moves toward endorsing repeal, 359, 361, 368, 384, 484; as *Hall* case plaintiff, 379, 385; and initial clinic idea, 386, 407, 409; and New York repeal law, 421, 456, 578; and *Roe* v. *Wade,* 501, 599, 605

Guttmacher, Manfred, 270, 277

Gwynne, John Shriver, 411, 433

H. L. v. *Matheson,* 637–638, 640

Hachey, Ronald E., 430

Hadley, Morris, 108

Hague, Frank, 55

Hall, Angela, 716

Hall, Robert E., 291, 294–295, 318, 363, 371, 411; and creation of AHA/ASA, 296, 297–298, 305; advocates reform, 308, 313, 317; backs amicus briefs, 309, 364; and initial test case idea, 339, 352, 353, 356, 359; eventually endorses repeal, 346, 349, 376, 384; and ARA, 360, 370; and *Hall* v. *Lefkowitz,* 379–380; and initial clinic idea, 386, 409; and 1970 New York implementation, 456–457, 483; and *Roe* v. *Wade,* 501, 523, 599, 607; and 1972 events, 539

Hall, Robert H., 654–655

Hall v. *Lefkowitz,* 379–381, 382, 385, 386, 387, 408–409, 410, 416, 418, 420, 439; mooted by New York repeal statute, 421, 612

Hallford, James Hubert, 388, 392; joins in *Roe* v. *Wade,* 433–436, 438, 441, 453, 454; and *Roe* appeal to Supreme Court, 461, 462, 492, 500, 523, 528, 529, 581, 589; and *Roe* aftermath, 601–602

Hames, Margie Pitts, files *Doe* v. *Bolton*, 424–428, 444–446; and three-judge hearing of *Doe*, 447–450; and three-judge decision, 459; and *Doe* appeal to Supreme Court, 462–463, 464–465; and initial Supreme Court consideration of *Doe*, 492–497 *passim*, 499–501, 503, 504–506, 509, 515, 516, 520–521; and first oral argument of *Doe*, 523, 525–528 *passim*; and *Eisenstadt*, 543; and second *Doe* argument, 557, 561, 565, 567–568, 571–572, 573, 599; and *Roe* aftermath, 602–603, 604–605; death of, 958–959*n*7

Hames, William, 425

Hamilton, David F., 723

Hamilton, Grace Towns, 422

Hamilton, James, 321

Hammond, Larry, 575

Hamptlon, Sharon, 964*n*23

Hancock, Frank, 30

Hand, Augustus N., 261

Hand, Learned, 163, 264, 277

Hanes, Myles, 327

Hanna, William, 92

Hanna v. *Plumer*, 236

Hanrahan, Edward V., 481

Hardin, Garrett, 293–298 *passim*, 301, 308, 340, 344, 349, 360, 368; helps create NARAL, 350

Hardwick, Michael, 653–655, 658–660, 663–667, 687

Hardwick v. *Bowers*. See *Bowers* v. *Hardwick*

Hare, Robert W., 377, 539

Harlan, John Marshall, 124, 357, 611; and *Poe* v. *Ullman*, 169, 174, 178, 180, 182–186 *passim*, 190–195 *passim*, 197; *Poe* dissent utilized in *Griswold*, 210, 215, 216, 221, 225, 237, 267; and *Griswold*, 229, 235, 238, 240, 242, 243, 249, 252, 254, 255, 263, 372, 566, 574, 623, 684; and *Vuitch*, 417–418, 479–480, 488–490; and *Kennan*, 488; and *Roe* v. *Wade*, 491; retirement of, 507, 509, 511, 512; post-1965 influence of *Poe* dissent, 518–519, 597, 599, 615, 642, 649, 658, 675, 693, 701

Harmer, John L., 330

Harper, Fowler V., 135, 137, 139, 183, 264, 275, 276, 371; and filing of *Poe* v. *Ullman*, 145, 147–164; appeals *Poe* to U.S. Supreme Court, 165–181, 186–189, 195–200, 237; and 1961 clinic opening, 201, 205–208, 210, 214, 215; and early stages of *Griswold*, 216–217, 220, 221; appeals *Griswold* to Supreme Court, 224–226, 228, 230–232, 250, 297; legacy of, 258–260, 269, 599, 741

Harper, Grace G., 147

Harper, Miriam Cohen, 130, 135, 139, 149, 151, 152, 170, 176, 226, 230–231, 237, 258

Harper v. *Jere Adametz*, 151

Harris v. *McRae*, 634–636, 638, 677, 685

Harrison, Beverly W., 630

Harrison, Irwin P., 232, 239

Hart, Anne Chase, 49, 51

Hartford Courant, 2, 16, 17, 23, 28, 33–34, 39, 40, 41, 93–94, 106, 114, 115, 116, 142

Hartford Maternal Health Center, 1, 7, 37–41, 48, 52–53, 57; 1940 closing of, 83

Hartford Times, 18, 39, 116, 122

Hartigan, Neil, 681

Harvard Law Review, 260

Haskell, Martin, 719

Hastie, William H., 232

Hatch, Orrin, 639–640, 643, 669

Hatcher, Robert A., 348, 425, 428, 459
Hatfield, Henry D., 30
Hawaii, 1967 legislature, 319; 1968 legislature, 348; 1969 legislature, 371; passes 1970 repeal bill, 412–414, 421, 431, 457; same-sex marriages in, 725–726
Hawaii Medical Association, 412
Hawkridge, Linda M., 46, 47, 48, 54–56, 58–59
Hayes, Joan Eames, 412, 414
Hayes, John J., 121–122, 127
Hayes, Patrick, 14
Hayes, T. Frank, 3, 6, 62, 71
Haynsworth, Clement F., Jr., 473, 624
Healey, Frank T., 157, 158, 159
Heck, Constance, 20
Heflin, Howell, 669
Hefner, Hugh, 352, 360
Heidepriem, Nikki, 669
Heiser, Jennie, 130, 135, 136
Hellman, Louis M., 298, 379, 409
Helms, Jesse, 620, 639, 640
Henderson, Albert J., Jr., 444, 447, 458
Henderson, Keith, 200
Henrie, William Jennings Bryan, 284
Hepburn, Katharine, 9
Hepburn, Katharine Houghton, 98, 122, 134, 257, 269, 472, 599, 739, 741; early birth control work of, 1–2, 16–22 passim, 25–30 passim, 32, 34–42 passim, 758n42, 762n58; early Connecticut activism of, 9–10, 753n22; and Massachusetts raids, 48, 55, 59; and Waterbury arrests, 62, 64, 66–67, 71; and Nelson aftermath, 80–81, 83–87, 109; 1941 Wesleyan speech by, 93–94, 113
Hepburn, Robert H., 122
Hepburn, Thomas N., 9, 132

Heppel, Jeannie, 3, 4, 8, 25, 63, 66
Hern, Warren, 715, 716, 719
Herndon, J. Emmett, 422, 425, 426, 428, 459, 486
Hessel, Beatrice, 140, 152, 153, 220; as PPLC president, 162, 163, 176, 177, 180, 189
Hetzel, Joseph L., 49, 114, 116
Hewitt, Norman, 160
Heymann, Philip B., 190, 611–612
Hickey, William F., 189
Hicks v. Miranda, 647
Higgins, George G., 636–637
Higgins, Willis E., 487
Hight, Tony, 446, 449
Hill, Anita F., 689
Hill, John, 602
Hill, Paul J., 704, 710–713, 714, 718, 726, 736
Hill, Susan, 718
Himes, Norman, 26
Hincks, Carroll, 92
Hines, Barbara, 389–390, 395, 500
Hinman, George E., 76, 77–78, 85, 88
Hinman, John J., 111
Hirsh, Michael R., 712
Hoar, Samuel, 59, 60
Hobbs, Michael, 659
Hodgson, Jane E., 1970 prosecution of, 428–430, 466–468, 471, 474, 476, 479; appeals conviction, 480, 484, 491, 498, 506, 522, 580; and Roe v. Wade, 501, 515, 523, 608; and 1990 case, 681; portrayal in Doctors of Conscience, 955n1
Hodgson v. Minnesota (1973), 469, 499, 580
Hodgson v. Minnesota (1990), 681–682, 683–684
Hoe v. Ullman, 154, 164. See also Poe v. Ullman
Hoffman, Richard, 956n1
Hogan, Frank, 409
Hogan, Lawrence J., 609

Holmes, Oliver Wendell, 264, 537, 977*n*1
Holohan, William, 202
Honolulu Star-Bulletin, 413
Hood, David, 384
Hooper, William T., 34, 36
Horan, Dennis J., 510–511, 521, 524, 608, 636, 657, 661
Horne, David, 733
Horton, Jack, 730
House, Charles S., 115, 126
Houston Chronicle, 296, 606
Howard, T. R. M., 361
Howson, Julie, 112, 117, 120, 124, 219
Huber, Sallie Craig, 426
Hughes, Charles Evans, 191
Hughes, George, 397
Hughes, Richard J., 320
Hughes, Sarah T., 387, 388, 396–398, 399, 484; and *Buchanan,* 398, 401–402, 485; and *Roe* v. *Wade,* 436–444 *passim,* 447, 451–454, 599
Humphrey, Hubert H., 357
Hunter, Nan, 665
Huntington, Samuel, 475–476, 478
Hurlbut, Biddy, 507
Hurley, Robert A., 91
Hyde, Henry J., 626, 639
Hyde Amendment, 626–627, 629–630, 631, 632–633, 634–635, 707

Ickes, Harold, 147
Idaho, Medicaid funds for abortions in, 957–958*n*6
Illinois, 1967 legislature, 332; 1969 legislature, 371; 1971 legislature, 496
Illinois Citizens for the Medical Control of Abortion (ICMCA), 308–309, 332, 350, 360, 382, 383
Indiana, 1967 legislature, 319; 1997 legislation, 734

Iowa, 1967 legislature, 332; 1969 legislature, 370; 1970 legislature, 412; 1971 legislature, 483
Isaacson-Jones, B. J., 721
Israel, Jerold, 177

Jackson, Arthur H., 114
Jackson, Jesse, 579
Jackson, Robert H., 103, 512
Jackson v. *Georgia,* 510
Jackson (Mississippi) Women's Health Organization, 718
Jacobson, Richard L., 532
Jacobson v. *Massachusetts,* 502, 536
Jaffe, Fred, 196, 199, 227, 228, 232, 258
Jahncke, Cornelia, 221, 224, 226, 227, 231, 237, 259, 268
James, Fleming, 150
James Madison Constitutional Law Institute (JMCLI), 371–372, 379, 381, 461, 463, 492, 494, 498–501, 504, 508, 509, 516, 528, 539, 540, 557, 564
"Jane," 486–487, 955*n*1
Janney, Harriet Crawford, 107–112 *passim*
Janney, Laurence A., 74, 89, 92
Janson, C. William, 106, 107
Javits, Jacob, 311
Jenkins, Herbert T., 428, 446, 449
Jennings, Kathryn, 57, 66
Jennings, Newell, 76, 78, 100
John Merck Fund, 732
John Price Jones Corp., 86–90, 91
Johnson, Douglas, 730
Johnson, Frank, 434–435
Johnson, Frank M., Jr., 351, 653, 655, 656, 659, 660
Johnson, Lyndon B., 235, 315, 387, 397, 440, 447, 473, 600
Johnston, Wilson, 436, 437, 455
Joint Commission on Accreditation of Hospitals (JCAH), 348

Jones, Arthur H., 327–329, 375, 432, 508
Jones, Eleanor Dwight, 20
Jones, Elwood K., 114
Jones, Francis E., 17, 27–28
Jones, Perry, 392
Jordan, Joseph M., 321, 343
Joseloff, Lillian Leiterman, 37, 49, 50
Journal of Homosexuality, 647
Journal of the American Medical Association (JAMA), 43, 312
Julian, Anthony J., 410

Kahn, Cindy, 323
Kahn, Ed, 323
Kandaras, Homer, 433
Kansas, passes 1969 reform bill, 369–370
Kaplan, Benjamin, 155
Karlin, Elizabeth, 976n89
Katz v. *United States,* 664
Kay, Herma Hill, 309, 330, 338, 364
Keemer, Ed, 361–362, 364, 508
Keeton, Page, 326
Kehrer, Betty, 425
Kelly, Andrew J., 41, 93, 94, 98, 113, 114
Kelly, Patrick F., 688
Kelsey, George, 630
Kenealy, William J., 118, 292
Kennan, Alfred Lee, 487–488, 508, 538
Kennard, Don, 454, 484–485, 491
Kennedy, Anne, 19
Kennedy, Anthony M., 672–673; and *Webster,* 675–678; and *Akron Center,* 682, 683–684; and *Rust,* 685; and *Bray,* 688, 702; and *Casey,* 691–700 *passim,* 741; and *Madsen* v. *Women's Health Center,* 709; and *Romer,* 724; and *Schenck,* 729
Kennedy, Edward M., 669
Kennedy, Ethel, 237
Kennedy, John F., 171, 235, 236, 447

Kennedy, John J., 118
Kennedy, John S., 3
Kennedy, Robert F., 311–312
Kenyon, Dorothy, 26, 276, 296, 308, 313–314, 333, 386
Kepler, Johannes, 264
Kerner, Otto, 332, 414, 465
Killian, Robert K., 607
Kimmey, Jimmye, 308, 353, 360, 374, 375, 376, 388; and *Roe* v. *Wade,* 492, 494, 523, 577, 579
King, David Garth, 401, 405–407, 437, 440, 454, 497–498; and oral argument of *Roe,* 515–516, 523, 528; and *Roe* aftermath, 601
King, John Hamilton, 164, 222–223
King, Marsha, 400–401, 404–407, 437, 440, 454, 461, 497–498, 509; and oral argument of *Roe,* 515–517, 522, 523, 528, 563, 572; and *Roe* aftermath, 601
Kinloch, Anne, 144, 145, 152, 154, 166, 175
Kinloch, Hector, 144, 145, 152, 154, 166, 175
Kinsey, Alfred, 150
Kinsolving, Lester, 306
Kissling, Frances, 739
Kitchell, Helen, 33
Kitfield, Agnes "Ruste," 424–425, 523
Kleine, John Henry, 332
Knight, Sidney C., 367
Knott, John C., 215, 222, 256, 289
Knox, John T., 282–283, 284, 290, 344
Kocoras, Charles P., 735
Kolbert, Kathryn, 690–691, 692, 693
Konikow, Antoinette F., 20
Koome, A. Frans, 384, 579
Kopf, Richard G., 734–735, 736
Kosicki, Bernard, 215, 217
Kramer, Douglas J., 372
Krause, Marshall, 304

Kravitch, Phyllis A., 655
Kroll, Kathleen, 967n35
Ku Klux Klan Act, 706
Kummer, Jerome M., 280, 281, 283,
    290, 292, 310, 375, 501
Kuralt, Wallace, 327–328

LaBelle, John D., 200
Lacey, J. Robert, 207, 210–213, 215
Lader, Lawrence, 295–296, 299,
    300, 305, 325, 341, 359, 360,
    599; and ASA, 298, 346; begins
    test case discussions, 308, 318–
    319, 335, 338–339, 350–351; and
    creation of CCS, 318, 333–334,
    345, 376; publishes *Abortion,* 318,
    337; and creation of NARAL,
    350, 360–361, 364; and initial
    clinic idea, 386, 407; and Roy
    Lucas, 417, 464, 493, 506, 507,
    513, 539–540; and *Vuitch,* 478;
    and 1972 developments, 508,
    540, 545, 546, 567, 577, 579;
    cited by Supreme Court, 589;
    and *Roe* aftermath, 603, 604; and
    RU-486, 708, 727, 732
Ladies Home Journal, 43
Laidlaw, Robert, 299
Lamb, Robert, 309
Lambert v. *Wicklund,* 729
Lambeth, James A., 667
Lamm, Richard D., 411, 507; and
    1967 Colorado reform bill,
    323–325, 327, 329; criticizes new
    reform law, 341, 351, 360, 374,
    375; organizes court challenge
    to reform law, 383–384, 457;
    advocates repeal, 482, 485
Lamont v. *Postmaster General,* 251
Landy, Uta Henkel, 336, 499, 503
Lane, Richard Allen, 402, 403
Larkin, Charles L., 4, 7, 57, 58, 63,
    65, 116
Lassoe, John V. P., Jr., 317, 318, 319,
    334, 339, 360, 363, 370, 382

Lasswell, Harold, 741
Law, Cardinal Bernard, 714
Law, Sylvia, 614, 629
Law Against Abortion, The
    (Robinson), 273
Law of Torts, The (Harper and James),
    150
Leahy, Patrick, 727
Leavy, Zad, 446; and early abortion
    reform, 279–281, 283, 290;
    authors *Shively* brief, 307,
    309–310, 338; and 1967 Califor-
    nia bill, 330, 332; considers possi-
    ble test case, 349, 358, 410; and
    Belous, 354–355, 364–366, 377,
    378
Lee, Rex E., 641
Lee, Richard, 202
Lefcourt, Gerald, 381
Leichter, Franz, 356, 359, 367, 385,
    386, 408
Lent, Norman, 368
Lesnick, Howard, 169, 174
Leventhal, David, 189
Lewis, Ann, 669
Lewis, Helen, 23
Lewis, Lawrence L., 6, 62, 63–64,
    65, 66, 67, 72
Lewis, Oren R., 621
Lewittes, Joel, 408
Life, 110, 256, 300, 317, 408
Life Advocate magazine, 738
Life Dynamics, 715, 716
Lime 5: Exploited By Choice
    (Crutcher), 716
Lincoln, C. Eric, 606
Lindey, Alexander, 26, 73, 75
Livingston, Luther, 160
Lochner v. *New York,* 238, 245, 246,
    252
Lockard, Frank P., 160
Lockwood, Luke B., 39–40
Lodge, John Davis, 120, 125–127, 129
Long, W. Newton, 348, 422, 426,
    428, 447

Look, 208, 213, 301
Lord-Heinstein, Lucille, 45, 47
Los Angeles Bar Journal, 279
Los Angeles Times, 300, 363, 374, 378, 606, 622, 665
Lott, Trent, 971*n*56
Louisell, David, 619
Love, John, 325
Lovejoy Specialty Hospital, 718–719, 732
Loving v. *Virginia,* 337, 377, 382, 534, 536, 591, 592, 596, 659, 663, 664, 842*n*1; and *Casey,* 690, 698
Lovisi, Aldo, 623–624
Lovisi, Margaret, 623–624
Lovisi v. *Slayton,* 623–624, 647
Lowney, Shannon, 705, 713
Loyola University Law Review, 372, 537
Lucas, Roy, 334, 739; background of, 335–337; envisions test case, 338–339; publishes landmark article, 351–352, 424, 863–864*n*21; prepares model brief, 352–354, 356–357, 358–359; and *Belous,* 356, 366, 378, 379; creates Madison Institute, 371–372; and *Baird,* 374; files *Hall* case, 379–381, 408–409, 421, 439; envisions Texas case, 381, 384, 386–388, 433; and *Vuitch,* 382, 409, 417, 464, 468–470, 474, 478; and New Jersey case, 383, 416, 471; and North Carolina case, 432; and South Dakota case, 433; and *Roe* v. *Wade,* 440, 461–462, 484–485, 491–495, 497, 498–502, 503, 513, 556–557, 599; and *Doe* v. *Bolton,* 446, 462–463, 504–506, 520; and Louisiana case, 459, 460; and NARAL, 464, 506–508, 539–540; and *Babbitz,* 465; and *Hodgson* cases, 467; and first *Roe*

oral argument, 503–504, 509, 514–517, 522, 523, 528; and *Vuitch* v. *Hardy,* 509, 561; and *Poe* v. *Menghini,* 540–541; and *Eisenstadt,* 543; and second *Roe* oral argument, 563–564, 568, 573; and *Roe* aftermath, 604–605, 617, 640
Lucey, Robert E., 369
Lumbard, J. Edward, 566
Lynch, Robert, 619–620
Lynch, Thomas C., 365, 378
Lyons, Emily, 736
Lyons, William J., 33

Macaulay, Donald B., 343, 373
MacDonald, Herbert S., 115–116, 123
Maddox, Lester, 348
Madison, James, 254
Madsen v. *Women's Health Center,* 709, 729, 737
Maginn, Edward J., 311
Maginnis, Patricia T., 284, 290, 292, 298, 301, 303–304, 307, 308, 333, 340, 344, 349
Maher v. *Roe,* 627–629, 634–635, 638, 643, 677, 685
Maine, 1967 legislature, 332; 1971 legislature, 496
Maledon, William J., 581–582, 583, 593
Malin, Patrick, 139
Maltbie, William M., 72–73, 76, 77, 88, 99–100, 106, 124, 788–789*n*62
Mancini, Philip F., Jr., 232
Mandel, Marvin, 432
Maney, Michael M., 229
Manternach, Bruce W., 125, 128, 129, 135, 139
Mapp v. *Ohio,* 192
Marbury v. *Madison,* 641
Maretz, Julius, 201–202, 204, 206–215 *passim,* 222–223, 232, 239

Marks, Floyd, 325

Marshall, Thurgood, 473–474; and *Vuitch,* 478, 480, 489, 490; and Illinois case, 481; and *Kennan,* 488; and *Roe* v. *Wade,* 491, 521, 526; and *Eisenstadt,* 519–520, 536, 541; and first *Roe/Doe* conference, 529–533; and Connecticut cases, 544, 545, 566; and initial Blackmun *Roe/Doe* opinions, 548–549, 550; opposes reargument of *Roe/Doe,* 553, 555, 560; and second *Roe/Doe* argument, 570, 571–572, 573; and second *Roe/Doe* conference, 574, 576; and final drafting of *Roe/Doe* opinions, 581–584, 586; and sexual privacy cases, 621, 622, 646, 652; and *Planned Parenthood* v. *Danforth,* 625; and *Maher,* 628; and *Bellotti II,* 632; and *Harris* v. *McRae,* 635; and *H. L.,* 637–638; and *Akron,* 641–642; and *Uplinger,* 646, 648; and *Bowers,* 656–657, 658, 659–660, 664; and *Webster,* 675, 677, 679; and *Akron Center,* 682, 684; and *Rust,* 686; retires from Court, 689

Martin, Crawford, 455, 460

Martin, John Bartlow, 283

Martinez, Bob, 680

Maryland, 1967 legislature, 332; passes 1968 reform bill, 348; limited impact of 1968 law, 375, 457; 1970 legislature, 432; 1971 legislature, 483

Mason, B. Henry, 4, 7, 8, 49, 53–54, 58, 63, 65

Massachusetts, 1942 birth control referendum in, 90–91, 97, 101–102; 1948 birth control referendum in, 116, 118; 1966 revision of birth control statute, 269, 320, 826–827n107; 1970 legislature, 412; 1971 legislature, 483; 1972 legislature, 547

Massachusetts Civil Liberties Union, 321

Massachusetts Medical Society, 48

Massachusetts Mothers' Health Council, 60

Matthies, Bernard, 96

Mattox, Jim, 652

May, Cordelia Scaife, 349

Mayers, Daniel K., 186, 190

Mazurek v. *Armstrong,* 729

McAuliffe, Maurice F., 4, 36, 110

McCann, E. Michael, 414, 465

McCarter, Dorothy, 972n62

McCluskey, Henry J., Jr., 398–404 *passim* 436, 437, 448, 485, 487, 600, 602, 620, 647

McConaughy, James L., 94, 113, 119

McCormack, John W., 27

McCorvey, Elwood, 402

McCorvey, Norma Nelson, 402–406, 439–440, 461, 497–498, 509, 516, 523, 598; and *Roe* aftermath, 600–602; reversal of pro-choice stance, 720–721

McCoy, Frances, 136, 137, 207

McCoy, Robert, 345, 429

McDonald v. *United States,* 262

McEvoy, Frank P., 6, 7–8, 65, 69–73 *passim* 75, 78, 81

McFate, Yale, 287

McGinley, Claudia, 220, 257; as PPLC president, 138, 139, 140, 142; and *Poe* cases, 152, 153, 154, 155, 158, 162

McGovern, George, 561

McGrath, John J., 45

McGuire, James P., 618

McHale, Edward, 321

McHugh, James, 484, 524, 562

McIntyre, James, 331, 365

McKay, Robert B., 337, 338, 371, 494

McKernan, Martin F., Jr., 510, 565
McKinney, Katharine B., 119–120
McKinnon, Edna Rankin, 74, 85, 107, 108
McLain, George, 290
McLean, George P., 19
McMahon, James, 719
McManus, William F., 345–346
McMillan, Roy, 718
McNamara, Ann K., 23, 24
McNulty, James V., 306, 365
McNutt, Paul V., 147
McTernan, Charles C., 52, 57, 83
McTernan, Clara, 187, 599; and Waterbury arrests, 8–9, 62–73 *passim;* and opening of Waterbury clinic, 52 54, 57–58, 60–61; and *Nelson* decision, 77, 79, 81–83, 93
McTernan, John, 83
McWilliams, William J., 64, 75
Mead, Margaret, 291
Means, Cyril C., Jr., 300, 346; opposes test case idea, 318–319, 334, 338, 356–357; historical work of, 352, 353, 408, 511, 544, 891–892n41; and *Vuitch,* 478; and *Roe* v. *Wade,* 492–494, 500–501, 503, 504, 512–516 *passim,* 523, 524, 525, 527, 563, 567, 573, 599; and NARAL, 506, 507, 539–540; and Wheeler case, 522; and Connecticut case, 545; cited by Supreme Court, 589; and *Roe* aftermath, 603, 605
Mecklenburg, Marjory, 579
Medeiros, Humberto S., 495
Medical Association of Georgia, 316, 348
Medical Students for Choice, 717
Medical World News, 363
Meldman, Clifford K., 415
Mencken, H. L., 270
Merhige, Robert R., Jr., 621, 623–624, 652, 658

Merrill, Roy L., Jr., 388, 433–439, 441, 443, 501, 516, 517, 523
Merriman, H. Heminway, Jr., 61–62
Meskill, Thomas J., 544–545
Metcalf, George R., 283
Meyer v. *Nebraska,* 166, 172, 234, 238, 242, 243, 245, 253, 262, 377, 468, 478, 501, 550, 663, 667, 698; cited in *Roe* v. *Wade,* 590, 591, 592
Michaels, George M., 420
Michelman, Kate, 717
Michigan, 1967 legislature, 332; 1969 legislature, 371; 1970 legislature, 412; 1971 legislature, 484, 496; and 1972 abortion referendum, 496, 538, 547, 562–563, 566–567, 576–577, 578, 616; Medicaid funds for abortions in, 957–958n6
Michigan Abortion Referendum Committee, 563
Michigan Law Review, 337
Militant, The, 361
Mill, John Stuart, 645
Miller, Dorothy, 159
Miller, James Raglan, 21, 27, 32, 36, 98
Miller, Keith, 431
Milmine, Mary Parker, 120, 122–125, 127–131, 133–138, 140–141, 142
Minneapolis Star, 506
Minneapolis Tribune, 506
Minnesota, 1967 legislature, 332; 1969 legislature, 370, 385; 1971 legislature, 483; Medicaid funds for abortions in, 957–958n6
Minnesota Citizens Concerned for Life, 430
Minnesota Council for the Legal Termination of Pregnancy, 370, 385, 429
Miranda v. *Arizona,* 556
Mirikitani, Percy, 412

Mississippi, 1966 legislature, 852–853*n*50, 955*n*1; 1997 legislation, 734
Missouri, 1967 legislature, 332
Modern Hospital, 375
Modern Medicine, 607
Moffett, Jim, 348
Monchun, Frank J., 123
Mondale, Walter, 651
Montana, 1971 legislature, 482–483
Montgomery, A. H., 954*n*1
Moody, Howard, 629; advocates repeal, 312, 350–351; helps create CCS, 318, 333, 345–351 *passim,* 392, 409, 438, 486, 495–496
Moore, Herman, 327, 328
Moore, John L., 348
Morehouse, Wray, 438
Morgan, Charles, Jr., 351
Morgan, Lewis R., 444, 447–450, 458
Morin v. *Garra,* 366
Morris, James G., 202, 204, 209–215 *passim,* 223
Morris, Steven, 286
Morris, Woodbridge E., 2, 60; and Waterbury case, 63, 67–68, 71, 73, 75–76, 79, 84
Mott, Stewart R., 317, 349, 361, 364
Moynihan, Daniel Patrick, 671
Ms. magazine, 739
Munger, Charles T., 355, 364, 365, 378, 380, 411
Mungo, Raymond, 320
Munson, H. Benjamin, 417, 433, 522. See also *State* v. *Munson*
Murphy, James D., 305
Murphy, Lawrence P., 311
Murray, J. Edward, 286
Murray, John Courtney, 155
Murray, John G., 17
Musselman, Luther, 135
Myers, Caroline R. "Lonny," 309, 332, 346, 359, 368; and creation of NARAL, 350, 358, 360

NAACP v. *Alabama,* 246, 253
Nagler, Stephen M., 383
Naim v. *Naim,* 169
Nathanson, Bernard, 334, 361, 364, 376, 409, 456, 651
Nation, The, 149, 261, 298
National Abortion Federation (NAF), 717, 727
National American Woman Suffrage Association (NAWSA), 10
National Association for the Repeal of Abortion Laws (NARAL), 545, 579, 651, 668, 717; creation of, 350, 358, 360–361, 362, 364; and 1969-1970 developments, 386, 388, 407–408; and Lee Gidding, 387, 483, 484, 561, 588; and Roy Lucas, 464, 506–508, 539; and 1972 Michigan vote, 562–563, 566–567, 577; and *Roe* aftermath, 603
National Birth Control League (NBCL), 11, 12, 13, 14
National Catholic Welfare Conference, 27, 107, 164, 215, 222, 256; and abortion, 289, 303
National Coalition of Abortion Providers (NCAP), 729, 730
National Committee for a Human Life Amendment, 619
National Committee on Federal Legislation for Birth Control, 24–25, 34, 43–44
National Committee on Maternal Health, 274
National Conference of Catholic Bishops, 421–422, 609, 617, 619, 636, 682
National Council of Churches, 173, 282
National Gay Task Force, 621, 622
National Organization for Women (NOW), 343–344, 356, 367, 373–374, 495, 546, 849*n*35, 851–52*n*47

National Organization for Women v. *Joseph Scheidler,* 706

National Review, 230, 303

National Right to Life Committee (NRLC), 484, 510, 512, 524, 561, 565, 680, 682, 703, 719, 720, 730, 734

National Woman's Party (NWP), 10

National Women's Health Organization, 718

Nebraska, 1967 legislature, 319

Nellis, Joseph L., 417, 465, 468–470, 474, 476–477, 504, 505, 539; and *Roe* v. *Wade,* 493–494, 503, 507, 512–513, 514, 521, 523, 563, 567

Nelson. See *State* v. *Nelson*

Nelson, James, 725

Nelson, Roger B., and opening of Waterbury clinic, 4, 57–58, 61; and Waterbury arrests, 66–73 *passim,* 81–83

Nelson, Rosalie, 69

Nerreau, Thomas, 188

Nevada, 1967 legislature, 332; 1969 legislature, 370

Nevada Committee for the Rights of Women, 349

New England Journal of Medicine, 27, 228, 375, 717

New Hampshire, 1961 legislature, 282

New Haven Journal-Courier, 18, 21, 33, 39

New Haven Register, 154, 214

New Jersey, 1997 legislation, 735

New Mexico, 1965 legislature, 299; 1967 legislature, 319; passes 1969 reform bill, 369, 457; 1971 legislature, 483

New Republic, The, 14, 35, 606–607, 609, 616, 665, 692, 701, 721

New York, 1965 legislature, 298; 1966 legislature, 304–305; 1967 legislature, 308, 310–312, 317–318, 319, 332; 1968 legislature, 344–345, 346–347; 1969 legislature, 356, 359, 367–369; passes 1970 repeal bill, 385, 407–408, 431; impact and implementation of repeal law in, 456–457; 1971 legislature, 483, 495; 1972 legislature, 545–547; 1973 legislature, 566–567, 578, 616

New York v. *Uplinger,* 644, 646–649 *passim*

New York Civil Liberties Union, 300, 305

New York Herald Tribune, 165, 170

New York Radical Women, 367

New York Times, and birth control, 6, 24, 43, 256, 259; pre-1970 abortion coverage of, 271, 277, 278, 284, 297, 308, 318, 326, 333, 337, 351, 359, 360, 363, 368, 380, 382; endorses abortion reform, 298, 300, 302, 305, 310–312, 317, 345, 347, 357–358; 1970-1973 abortion coverage of, 408, 414, 418, 419, 420, 455–456, 466, 483, 493, 501, 507, 513, 520, 522, 543, 546, 557, 566; welcomes *Roe/Doe* decisions, 605–606, 701; post-*Roe* coverage by, 620, 622, 629, 633, 635, 636, 649, 683, 737; and *Bowers,* 665; and Bork nomination, 668, 669; on McCorvey's defection, 720; characterization of abortion rights supporters, 729; on partial-birth abortions, 732

New York World, 109

New Yorkers for Abortion Law Repeal, 367, 374, 408, 420

Newman, Jon O., 544, 566, 568, 574, 583, 588, 597, 599, 909*n*129

News and Observer (Raleigh, NC), 79, 606

Newsweek, 170, 281, 284, 308, 340,
    341, 359, 363, 414, 455, 605,
    616, 631, 665
Nichol, Gerald C., 487–488
Nichols, Leanne, 705, 713
Nichols, Louis B., 149
Nickerson, Jeffrey, 458
Nienhueser, Helen, 431
Ninth Amendment, 216, 225–226,
    811–812*n*29; and *Griswold,* 233,
    236, 238, 242, 248, 250, 253–
    254, 255; post-*Griswold* com-
    mentary on, 260, 264; post-
    Griswold judicial usage of, 415,
    540, 544; and *Roe* v. *Wade,* 441–
    442, 443, 451, 453, 454, 502, 524,
    525, 529, 530, 547, 548, 568, 574,
    575, 590–591, 595–596; and *Doe*
    v. *Bolton,* 448, 531, 535, 551, 572;
    and post-*Roe* commentary, 610
Nixon, Richard M., 357, 471,
    473–474, 483, 507, 509, 510,
    512, 546, 561, 578, 639
Nolan, Joseph R., 343, 373, 410,
    518–519
Noonan, John T., Jr., 277, 330, 385,
    606, 612, 619
Norris, George W., 19
North Carolina, passes 1967 reform
    bill, 327–329, 332; limited impact
    of 1967 law, 341, 375, 457; Med-
    icaid funds for abortions in,
    957–958*n*6
North Carolina Law Review, 351,
    366, 379, 408
North Carolina Medical Society,
    328, 329
North Dakota, 1967 legislature,
    319; 1972 abortion referendum,
    496, 538, 567, 577; 1971 legisla-
    ture, 496
Northrop, Ruth, 49, 50, 66, 72
Northwestern Law Review, 261
Norton, Eleanor Holmes, 352, 371
Novak, Robert D., 731

Nunn, Sam, 727
NYU Law Review, 336

Ober, William B., 308, 318, 319,
    334, 346, 350
O'Brien, Henry J., 114, 141, 256
O'Brien, Robert, 601
O'Brien, Timothy E., 290
O'Connor, John, 651
O'Connor, Sandra Day, 640; *Akron*
    dissent by, 642, 643; and *Uplinger,*
    644, 646, 649; and *Bowers,* 660,
    663; and *Webster,* 673, 675,
    677–680; and *Akron Center,*
    681–682, 683–684; and *Rust,*
    685–686; and *Casey,* 690–693,
    696–697, 698–699, 700, 741; and
    Bray, 702
"Odegard," David, 146, 152, 154,
    166
"Odegard," Elizabeth, 144, 146, 152,
    154, 166
Ohio, 1965 legislature, 756*n*57;
    1967 legislature, 332; 1971 legis-
    lature, 496
Ohio v. *Akron Center for Reproductive*
    Health, 681–682, 683–684,
    699
Ohrenstein, Manfred, 298
Oklahoma, 1967 legislature, 332;
    1972 legislature, 538
Okrand, Fred, 355, 364–365
"Oldendorf," Robert, 145, 152, 266,
    267, 741
"Oldendorf," Ruth, 141, 144, 145,
    152, 154, 201, 210, 266, 267, 741
Olmstead v. *United States,* 252, 254,
    261–262, 264, 536, 596, 664
On Liberty (Mill), 645
O'Neill, William, 682
Onofre, Ronald, 644. See also *People*
    v. *Onofre*
Operation Rescue, 603, 673, 683,
    688, 689, 692, 702, 704, 709,
    711, 718, 719, 720

Oregon, passes 1969 reform bill, 370

Oregon Committee for the Legal Termination of Pregnancy, 370

Organizations for Abortion Law Reform, 347

Our Bodies, Our Selves, 390

Overstreet, Edmund W., 292, 307, 330, 358, 374, 501

Packer, Herbert L., 278–281 *passim,* 283, 290

Packwood, Robert, 482, 494

Palko v. Connecticut, 675

Pankhurst, Emmeline, 9

Pape, William J., 3, 62

Pappas, David, 487–488

Parker, Philip S., 46–47

Parkhouse, George, 326–327

Parks, Charles, 237

Parks, Lucia, 189, 196, 197, 201, 218–220, 224, 237, 257

Parsells, Norman K., 125, 126

Partial-Birth Abortion Ban Act, 720, 721–722, 727, 729–732, 733

Paterson, Basil A., 311

Patterson, George W., 704

Paul, Alice, 10

Pavesich, Paolo, 261

Pavesich v. New England Life Insurance Co., 261

Pearson, Mabel H., 56–57

Pease, Sarah Clement, 29, 134, 599; as president of Connecticut Birth Control League, 1, 2–3, 35, 36, 48–52 *passim,* 57, 60–61; and initial Hartford clinic, 37–39, 40, 41; and Waterbury arrests, 62, 64, 66–67, 70, 71, 72, 74; and *Nelson* decision, 75–76, 78; and *Nelson* aftermath, 79–81, 83–90, 92, 98, 109, 269

Peck, Epaphroditus, 22, 23, 28, 33, 34

Peck, Gregory, 668

Pemberton, John, 221

Pennsylvania, 1967 legislature, 332; 1972 legislature, 547, 578

People for the American Way, 668, 669

People v. Barksdale, 496–497, 522–523, 579

People v. Belous, 355, 356, 357, 364–366, 371, 372, 377–379, 850–851*n*45; California impact of, 380, 411; national influence of, 381–385 *passim,* 388, 409, 415, 416, 417, 428, 429, 459, 468, 477, 481, 495, 496; and *Roe v. Wade,* 399, 400, 442, 453, 599

People v. Onofre, 644, 645, 648, 649

People v. Pettigrew, 496–497, 522–523, 579

People v. Sanger, 13, 239, 240

People v. Uplinger, 644. See also *New York v. Uplinger.*

Perry, Stewart R., 429–430, 467

Peters, John P., 150, 151

Peters, Raymond E., 366, 377–378, 379, 380, 415

Phelan, Lana Clarke, 304

Philadelphia Inquirer, 606

Phillips, Charles, 328

Phillips, Elizabeth, 151, 176

Pickrell, Robert, 286

Pierce v. Society of Sisters, 172, 234, 238, 241, 242, 243, 245, 253, 262, 377, 468, 534, 550, 635, 663, 667, 698; cited in *Roe v. Wade,* 591, 592, 596

Pierson, Richard N., 60

Pike, James A., 208, 306

Pike, Joseph D., 728

Pilpel, Harriet F., 139, 285; and *Gardner,* 56, 59; and *State v. Nelson,* 64, 67, 68, 79; and post-*Nelson strategizing,* 88, 92; and *Corbett,* 90; and *Tileston,* 96, 101, 102; and post-*Tileston* strategizing, 107–113 *passim,* 118; and

Pilpel, Harriet F. (*cont.*)
  Poe cases, 155–164 *passim,* 166,
    169–173 *passim,* 176–179 *passim,*
    197; and *Griswold,* 207–208, 210,
    213, 215, 221, 225, 228, 231,
    232, 234; and early abortion
    reform, 274, 291–300 *passim,*
    313–314; advocates repeal over
    reform, 304–305, 311, 347;
    and early test case discussions,
    318–319, 334, 335, 353, 357,
    409; and Roy Lucas, 337–338,
    379, 464, 539–540; and *Vuitch,*
    490; and *Roe* v. *Wade,* 491–493,
    495, 502, 503, 523, 545; and
    Eisenstadt, 517; and second *Roe/
    Doe* oral argument, 565, 567,
    568, 572; and *Roe* aftermath, 603
Pittsburgh Post-Gazette, 606
*Planned Parenthood Association of
  Kansas City* v. *Ashcroft,* 640–643,
  657
Planned Parenthood Federation
  of America (PPFA), 1940s Connecticut involvement of, 100,
  101, 106–108 *passim;* 1950s
  Connecticut involvement of,
  137, 139, 140; and *Poe* v. *Ullman,*
  153, 155–159, 162–163, 166,
  169–170, 171, 180, 181; and
  1961 Connecticut clinic opening, 196–201 *passim,* 208; and
  Griswold, 221, 225–228 *passim,*
  232, 233, 234, 258, 269; and
  abortion, 275, 280, 285, 291, 294,
  295, 297, 357, 368, 464, 578; and
  Bill Baird, 315, 322, 517; and *Roe*
  v. *Wade,* 495, 502, 565, 605
Planned Parenthood League of
  Connecticut (PPLC), succeeds
  CBCL, 100; and *Tileston,* 100–
  106; and post-*Tileston* strategies,
  107–120; in early 1950s, 120–
  129, 184; hires Estelle Griswold,
  130–142; sponsors *Poe* v. *Ullman,*

143, 152–164, 169, 173, 177,
  180, 189, 193; and 1961 clinic
  opening, 196–212; suffers internal tensions, 218–221, 226–228;
  and *Griswold* convictions,
  223–224; and *Griswold* appeal,
  229–233, 237, 251; and *Griswold*
  victory, 255–260, 268–269
Planned Parenthood League of
  Massachusetts (PPLM), 169,
  322, 343. *See also* Birth Control
  League of Massachusetts,
  Massachusetts Mothers' Health
  Council
Planned Parenthood of Atlanta, 428
*Planned Parenthood of Central
  Missouri* v. *Danforth,* 624–626,
  629, 631, 632, 638, 662
Planned Parenthood of Houston,
  719
Planned Parenthood of New York
  City, 578, 668, 717
Planned Parenthood of Phoenix,
  433
*Planned Parenthood of Southeastern
  Pennsylvania* v. *Casey,* ix,
  689–701, 708, 719, 722–723,
  733, 735, 736–739,
  951–952*n*129, 973–974*n*74
Platt, Caroline T., 22–23
Playboy Foundation, 352, 360
Plessy v. *Ferguson,* 686
Plunkett, J. Jerome, 467
Poe v. *Ullman,* 154, 164, 359, 532,
  611, 741; considered by U.S.
  Supreme Court, 168–169 *passim;*
  decided by Supreme Court,
  190–200; and *Griswold,* 210, 211,
  212, 224–226, 229–230, 232,
  237, 241, 242, 246, 249, 253,
  254, 262, 263, 267; post-1965 influence of Harlan dissent in, 372,
  519, 597, 599, 615, 642, 649,
  658, 675, 693, 701
Poelker v. *Doe,* 627, 628, 629

Poland, Kay, 431
Political and Civil Rights in the United States (Emerson and Haber), 231
Pollak, Louis H., 151
Pond, Millicent, 52, 53
Population Council, 708, 709, 713, 727, 728, 732–733
Porritt, Alison Hastings, 29
Porritt, Annie Webb, 9, 10, 16–21 *passim*, 27, 29, 32, 754n24; and American Birth Control League, 14–15
Port of Portland v. *United States*, 532
Porter, Paul, 151
Posner, S. Paul, 246–247, 248
Powe, L. A. "Scott," 513
Powell, Lewis F., Jr., 561, 652; appointed to Supreme Court, 512, 513, 521–522, 534, 537, 557; supports reargument of *Roe* and *Doe*, 548, 552, 554–556; and second *Roe/Doe* argument, 571, 572, 573; and second *Roe/Doe* conference, 575–576; and final drafting of *Roe/Doe* opinions, 581, 586, 587, 588; and *Planned Parenthood* v. *Danforth*, 625–626; and *Carey*, 628; and *Maher*, 628; and *Bellotti II*, 632; and *Harris* v. *McRae*, 634–635; and *H. L.* v. *Matheson*, 637–638; and *Akron*, 641–643; and *New York* v. *Uplinger*, 648; and *Bowers*, 658–667 *passim*; retires from Court, 668, 672, 673
Powell, Wesley, 282
Pratt, Annis, 422
Pratt, Joseph H., 429, 430, 467, 474, 501
Preate, Ernest D., Jr., 689, 691
Price, Bill, 703, 704
Price, C. J. "Jack," 455
Prince v. *Massachusetts*, 262, 591, 663, 694
Pritchard, Joel, 358, 384, 411

Pro-Life Action League, 651, 706, 709
Pro-Life Virginia, 711
Problems of the Family (Harper), 150, 156
Public opinion, on birth control, 42–43, 107, 167, 216, 229; on abortion, 289, 302–303, 376, 385, 513, 539, 562; on *Roe* v. *Wade*, 605, 607; on abortion since *Roe* v. *Wade*, 620, 629, 633, 636, 639–640, 657–658, 680; on partial-birth abortions, 732, 737–738
Public Utilities Commission v. *Pollak*, 167, 262
Puzder, Andrew, 721

Quattlebaum, Frank, 428
Quay, Eugene, 281
Quinn, Robert H., 374

Racketeer-Influenced Corrupt Organizations (RICO) conspiracy statute, 705–706, 718, 726
Rader, John L., 431–432
Rag, The, 389–391, 393, 395, 438, 439, 454
Rago, Nicholas F., 38, 39
Raible, Peter S., 292, 296
Rand, Flora, 45, 47
Randall, William, 429–430, 467
Rangel, Charles, 973n73
Rankin, Jeanette, 10, 74
Rappaport, Nathan G., 315, 361, 363, 504
Rashbaum, William, 386
Raymond, John M., 46
Raymond, Sherwin H., 383
Rayson, Leland, 332
Reader's Digest, 107, 278, 376
Reagan, Ronald, 331, 615, 634, 636, 637, 640, 649, 651, 662, 668, 672
Redbook, 278, 291, 301

Redlich, Norman, 216–217, 221, 226
Redstockings, 367–368
Reed, Elizabeth, 29
Reed, Kenneth R., 532
Reed, Ralph, 732
Reed v. Reed, 521
Regent University Law Review, 712
Regents of the University of California v. Bakke, 674
Rehnquist, William H., appointed to Supreme Court, 512, 513, 521–522, 534, 537, 557, 560; supports reargument of Roe and Doe, 548, 552, 554–555, 556; and second Roe/Doe argument, 570, 571, 572; and second Roe/Doe conference, 576; and final drafting of Roe/Doe opinions, 581, 586; final dissent in Roe and Doe, 597, 598, 606, 609; and Planned Parenthood v. Danforth, 626; and Sendak, 627; and Carey, 628; and Bellotti II, 632; and Colautti, 632; and Harris v. McRae, 634; and Akron, 642; and Uplinger, 644, 646, 649; and Thornburgh, 652, 657, 662; and Bowers, 656, 659, 661, 663; becomes Chief Justice, 662, 667; and Webster, 673, 675–680; and Akron Center, 681–682, 683; and Rust, 685; and Bray, 688, 702; and Casey, 691–692, 698, 700, 701, 723; and Madsen v. Women's Health Center, 709; and Romer, 724
Reid, Clarence A., 416–417
Rein, Edith, 414–415, 465
Reinhardt, Stephen, 686, 974n75
Reinhardt, Wilton, 122
Reising, Simon P., 202
Rescue America, 702, 703, 709
Reuther, Rosemary R., 630
Reynolds, John W., 414
Reynolds v. Sims, 244

Rezneck, Daniel A., 184
Rhode Island Birth Control League, 30
Rhoden, Nancy K., 614–615
Ribicoff, Abraham, 141
Rice, Walter H., 722
Richards, David R., 390
Richardson, Barbara, 400, 405, 407, 454
Richman, Daniel, 658
Richmond Times-Dispatch, 256
Riege, John H., 123–126, 139
Rindskopf, Elizabeth Roediger, 425, 428, 446, 447, 450, 509
Rindskopf, Peter, 425
Robbins, Mabel, 50, 52, 99–100, 101, 125, 257
Roberson, Abigail, 261
Roberson v. Rochester Folding Box Co., 261
Roberts, Betty, 421
Roberts, Burton, 376
Roberts, J. Howard, 111, 112
Roberts, Marion, 23
Robertson, John A., 517–518, 614
Robinson, David, 128
Robinson, Lucius F., Jr., 38, 39, 41
Robinson, William J., 273
Robinson v. California, 244, 659, 660
Robson, Edwin A., 480–481
Rock, John, 43, 48, 54, 198, 208, 218, 222
Rockefeller, John D., III, 358, 463
Rockefeller, Nancy Carnegie, 31
Rockefeller, Nelson, 310, 317, 345–347, 421, 483, 495, 545–547, 578, 605
Rockefeller Foundation, 464
Rodell, Fred, 149
Rodham, Hillary, 886n21
Roe v. Ullman, 154, 159, 160. See also Poe v. Ullman
Roe v. Wade, ix, 737; initial filing of, 405–407, 415, 431, 433, 436, 437–439; three-judge hearing of,

440–444, 446; three-judge decision in, 451–455, 456; influence of three-judge decision, 459–460, 481, 482, 496; three-judge decision appealed to Supreme Court, 460–462, 465, 468, 469, 471, 480, 485; initial Supreme Court consideration of, 491–504 *passim,* 507–517 *passim;* first oral argument of, 520–527 *passim,* 541; first Supreme Court conference on, 528–530, 531–535; initial opinion drafting in, 535, 537–538; and *Eisenstadt,* 542–544, 545; first Blackmun draft opinion in, 547–552; tussle over rearguing of, 552–560; second oral argument of, 563–565, 567–571, 572–573; second conference on, 573–576; final opinion drafting in, 580–587; Supreme Court decision formally announced, 588–589; immediate aftermath of, 600–602, 603–609, 617, 620, 621, 625, 633; academic criticisms of, 609–616, 618, 639; subsequent citations of, 622, 623, 645, 647, 649–650; and *Danforth,* 626; and *Carey,* 627; and *Maher,* 628, 629, 630; and *Colautti,* 631–632; and *Harris* v. *McRae,* 635–636; and *H. L.,* 638; and O'Connor nomination, 640; and *Akron,* 641–643; later congressional opposition to, 644; and *Thornburgh,* 652, 657, 661, 662, 667–668; and *Bowers,* 656, 658, 663, 665–666, 667; and Bork nomination, 668–671; and Kennedy nomination, 672–673; and *Webster,* 673–680; codified by 1990 Connecticut law, 682; and *Akron Center,* 684; and Souter nomination, 684; and *Rust,* 686; and Thomas nomination, 689; and *Casey,* 689–701,

702, 703, 741; violence as legacy of, 705, 706, 710–715, 717, 718–719, 726, 728–729, 732, 735–736; complaints against abortion providers since, 716; anniversary of, 739

Roemer, Buddy, 684

Roemer, Ruth, 306, 332

Romer v. *Evans,* x, 724–725

Romney, Seymour L., 379

Ronan, Charles N., 286, 287

Rongy, Abraham J., 273

Root, J. Harold, 49

Roper, Elmo, 110

Roraback, Catherine G., 151, 173; and *Poe* v. *Ullman,* 152–157, 159, 161–166, 170, 176–177; and *Griswold,* 207–213 *passim,* 215, 217, 219, 221–224, 228, 231, 237, 255, 258, 260; and abortion, 370, 487, 496

Roraback, J. Henry, 25, 32, 89, 121, 152

Rose, D. Kenneth, 86–87, 88, 100, 107, 108

Rose, Florence, 81

Rosen, Gerald E., 734, 738

Rosen, Isadore I., 433, 459–460, 484, 608

Rosen v. *Louisiana State Board of Medical Examiners,* 459–460, 482

Rossi, Alice S., 302–303

Rostow, Eugene V., 150–151, 232

Rothstein, Barbara J., 686, 974n75

Roussel Uclaf, 708–709

Rowe, Clara Louise, 15

Rowland, Alice V., 117–118, 119

RU-486, 708–709, 713, 727, 728, 732–733, 737

Ruby, Jack, 235

Rudolph, Eric Robert, 736

Russell, Keith P., 290, 306, 330, 365, 375, 378, 501

Rust v. *Sullivan,* 684–686, 692, 699, 702

Rutledge, Neal, 232
Rutledge, Wiley B., 230, 232, 262
Ryan, Carol, 494, 502
Ryan, Elmer S., 127
Ryan, John J., Jr., 54, 55

Sagoff, Hazel, 322
St. Louis Post-Dispatch, 409, 606
Salvi, John C., III, 713–714, 736
Samovar, Phillip G., 365–366
Samuel, Richard, 383, 416
San Angelo Standard-Times, 606
San Antonio Light, 606
San Francisco Chronicle, 331
Sanderson, Robert D., 736
Sanger, Margaret, 21, 25, 32, 49, 94,
    96, 109, 119, 143, 158, 327, 344,
    599, 784n43; 1923-25 Connecti-
    cut visits, 1, 16–17, 18–19; early
    birth control career, 2, 9, 10–15,
    269; and Birth Control Clinical
    Research Bureau, 20, 37; and
    1929 New York raid, 23–24;
    at 1931-1934 congressional hear-
    ings, 26–27, 30–31, 34–35; and
    U.S. v. One Package, 42, 43, 44;
    and *Gardner* decision, 56; and
    creation of BCFA, 60; and
    Waterbury crisis, 63, 64, 81,
    83–84, 85, 88, 776n8; 1940
    Holyoke visit of, 91; and
    abortion, 274
Sanger, William, 10, 11
Santorum, Rick, 731
Saporta, Vicki, 728
Saturday Evening Post, 215, 283, 308
Savage, Hugh W., and early Texas
    reform efforts, 302, 305, 308,
    326–327, 348; and 1969 reform
    drive, 360, 369; and Roy Lucas,
    381, 384, 386–388; and *Roe,* 454,
    471, 501; endorses repeal, 461, 462
Scalia, Antonin, 649–650, 662,
    667–668; and *Webster,* 675,
    677–679; and *Akron Center,*

683–684; and *Rust,* 685; and
    Bray, 688, 702; and *Casey,*
    690–692, 698–701, 723, 968n37;
    and *Madsen v. Women's Health
    Center,* 709; and *Romer,* 724; and
    Schenck, 729
Scanlan, Alfred L., 512, 513, 524
Scanlan, John, 413
Schaff, Eric A., 733
Scheidler, Joseph, 651–652, 706,
    709, 711
*Schenck v. Pro-Choice Network of
    Western New York,* 729, 737
Schmiedler, Edgar, 107–108
Schneider, Daniel M., 498, 499, 523
Schochet, Steven, 687
Schur, Edwin M., 275, 371
Schware v. Board of Bar Examiners,
    243, 253
Schwartz, Tobiane, 425, 427, 428,
    444–450, 497, 523, 527; and *Doe*
    aftermath, 602–603
Scientific American, 276, 293
Scoville, Dorothea H., 48
Scribner, Charles E., 56, 101, 103,
    108
Scribner's Magazine, 260
Sears, George B., 45–46, 47
Seaver, E. Robert, 516–517
Seelye, Katharine Q., 732
Seidman, Louis Michael, 724–725
Selvin, Herman F., 365–366
Sevareid, Eric, 214
Severson, Al, 306
Sexual Behavior in the Human Female
    (Kinsey), 150
Seymour, Whitney North, Sr., 124,
    125, 162, 166, 170, 171, 232
Seymour, Whitney North, Jr., 124,
    125
Shabaz, John C., 735
Shaffer, John, 431
Shannon, James, 157
Shannon, Rachelle "Shelley," 703,
    705, 706, 713, 726

Shapp, Milton, 578
Shaw, Don C., 309, 360
Shea, Daniel E., 28
Sherman, Gordon, 360
Sherman, Lewis, 330
Shively, J. Paul, 307, 309–310, 312, 338, 349, 354, 355, 365
Short, Alan, 330
Shreve, Randy, 440
Siegel, Gale, 428
Silent Scream, The, 651
Simopoulos, Chris, 640, 641
Simopoulos v. Virginia, 640–641
Simpson, Alan, 669, 670
Simpson, Earnest C., 98
Singleton v. Wulff, 625–626
Sisisky, Samuel, 15, 16, 17
Sitnick, Joseph, 417, 468, 469
Skelly, Lawrence E., 114–115
Skelton, Keith, 421
Skinner v. Oklahoma, 167, 468, 478, 534, 550, 591, 592, 596, 663, 698
Slaton, Lewis R., 428, 446, 654
Smalley, Robert H., Jr., 316, 347–348
Smith, Benjamin E., 433, 459, 460
Smith, Beverly, 718
Smith, Carlos, 15
Smith, Charles Magill, 80, 81, 83
Smith, J. Joseph, 62
Smith, Judy, 389–393, 395–396, 400, 407, 598, 739
Smith, Kenneth L., 630
Smith, Linda, 390
Smith, Philip T., 30
Smith, Regina, 682
Smith, Roy G., 412–413
Smith, Ruth Proskauer, 297, 308, 507
Smith, Seymour P., 307
Smith, Sidney O., Jr., 444, 447–450, 457–459, 464, 599
Smith, Virgil, 423
Smyth, Walter, 8, 63, 65
Sobeloff, Simon E., 335

Socialist Workers Party (SWP), 498, 522, 539
Society for Humane Abortion (SHA), 301, 303–304, 307, 308, 344
Souter, David H., 684; and Rust, 685; and Casey, 691–697, 699, 700, 741; and Bray, 702
South Carolina, passes 1970 reform bill, 412; 1997 legislation, 734
South Dakota, 1966 legislature, 305; 1997 legislation, 734
Southern California ACLU, 307, 355, 364
Spearman, Robert W., 480
Specter, Arlen, 669, 670, 727
Spector, Allen B., 432
Spencer, Robert D., 318, 362–363, 364
Spiegel, Samuel A., 495
Spitz, Donald, 711, 714
Stack, Jack, 563, 567, 577
Standish, Hilda Crosby, 36–41 passim, 57, 76, 78, 85, 95, 119, 164, 764–765n70; and Estelle Griswold, 132, 134, 137, 219–220, 224, 257
Stanford Law Review, 277
Stanley v. Georgia, 441, 468, 536, 550, 590, 592, 621–622, 644, 645, 657, 658, 659, 664
Starnes, Richard L., Jr., 316–317, 340, 347
Starr, Kenneth W., 685, 691–692
State v. Griswold and Buxton, 212, 216, 221. See also Griswold v. Connecticut
State v. Munson, 417, 453
State v. Nelson, 77–82, 84, 88, 90, 92, 107; and Tileston, 98, 99, 100, 103, 104, 124; and Poe v. Ullman, 156, 157, 159, 161, 163, 165, 178, 186–188, 193–194, 198; and Griswold, 211, 212, 217, 224, 266, 269

State v. *Saunders,* 644–645

Stearns, Nancy, 471, 502, 522, 540,
603–604

Steel, Ruth, 324

Steinberg v. *Brown,* 470–471, 481

Steinem, Gloria, 561

Steingut, Stanley, 385

Steir, Bruce S., 964*n*23

Stevens, John Paul, and sexual
privacy cases, 622, 646; and
Planned Parenthood v. *Danforth,*
625–626; and *Carey,* 627;
and *Bellotti II,* 632; and *Harris*
v. *McRae,* 635; and *Akron,*
641–642; and *Uplinger,* 648–649;
and *Bowers,* 659–661, 663,
664–665; and *Thornburgh,* 662;
and *Webster,* 673, 675–679; and
Akron Center, 681–682, 683–684;
and *Rust,* 685–686; and *Casey,*
691–692, 693, 697, 699, 723,
968*n*37; and *Bray,* 702; and
Mazurek v. *Armstrong,* 729

Stevens, Robert, 205–206

Stevens, Rosemary, 205–206,
208–209, 212

Stewart, Potter, 340; and *Poe* v. *Ullman,* 169, 177–180 *passim,* 184,
185–186, 193, 194; and *Griswold,*
238–239, 242, 243, 249–251
passim, 254–256 *passim,* 266;
and *Vuitch,* 417–418, 475–480,
489–490; and *Roe* v. *Wade,* 491,
512, 521, 524–526, 564; and
Eisenstadt, 518–520, 536, 541;
and first *Roe/Doe* conference,
528–529, 531–533; and initial
Blackmun opinions, 548–549,
551–552; opposes reargument
of *Roe/Doe,* 553, 555–556, 558,
560; and second *Roe/Doe* oral
argument, 568–570, 573; and
second *Roe/Doe* conference,
574, 576; and final drafting of
Roe/Doe opinions, 581, 585, 586;

final concurrence in *Roe* and
Doe, 597, 598; and sexual privacy
cases, 621; and *Planned Parenthood*
v. *Danforth,* 625–626; and *Bellotti
II,* 632; and *Harris* v. *McRae,*
634–635; and *H. L.,* 637, 638;
retires from Court, 640

Stockton, Ruth, 324

Stoddard, Johnson, 64, 67, 80, 85, 86

Stoddard, Thomas B., 665

Stolz, Dorothy, 306, 308

Stone, Hannah M., 19, 20, 23, 31,
40, 42, 44

Stone, Harlan Fiske, 103–105, 262

Story, Jopseh, 254

Stover, Dawn, 703

Strauss, Robert, 397

Stringfield, Oliver L., 116

Stroffolino, Stanley, 117, 118

Strong, Harry B., 113

Students for a Democratic Society
(SDS), 389–390

Stuermer, Virginia, 203, 268

Sugarman, Burt, 728

Sugrue, Francis J., 94

Sullivan, Brian L., 498, 523

Sunnen, Joseph, 204, 314, 361;
supports PPLC, 139, 140, 156;
creates CCTA, 305–306, 307,
354; sponsors Nevada repeal
effort, 349, 370; and Roy Lucas,
463, 504

Susman, Frank, 433, 567, 629, 675,
783–784*n*41

Sutton, John, 394–395

Sutton, Percy E., 298, 304–305,
361

Swingers Life, 623

Switzer, Ellen, 137

Swygert, Luther M., 480–481

Talmadge, Herman, 447

Taney, Roger B., 699

Taussig, Frederick J., 272

Taylor, William M., Jr., 397, 398,

401, 485; and *Roe v. Wade,* 436, 440, 451–452

Teague, George, 160

Tennessee, 1997 legislation, 734

Tennessee Homosexual Practices Act, 725

Terry, Randall, 673, 702

Texans United for Life, 703

Texas, 1967 legislature, 326–327, 332; 1969 legislature, 359–360, 369; 1971 legislature, 484–486, 490–491

Texas Abortion Coalition, 462, 484

Texas Catholic Conference, 326, 369, 461, 485

Texas Citizens for Abortion Education, 484

Texas Committee for the Modernization of Therapeutic Abortion Laws, 326

Texas Medical Association (TMA), 289; and early reform efforts, 302, 305, 308, 326–327, 348, 358, 360, 369; endorses repeal, 461, 462

Thaler, Seymour, 367, 419

Thayer, Charlotte, 433

Thomas, Clarence, 689; and *Casey,* 692, 698, 701, 723; and *Bray,* 702; and *Madsen v. Women's Health Center,* 709; and *Romer,* 724; and *Schenck,* 729

Thomas, Judy, 971n59

Thompson, C. W., 388

Thompson v. Texas, 513, 524, 525

Thoms, Herbert, 29, 130

Thornburgh v. American College of Obstetricians and Gynecologists (ACOG), 652, 657, 661–662, 667, 668; and *Casey,* 690, 691, 696

Tiers, Montgomery C., 33

Tietze, Christopher, 340, 346, 501

Tileston, Wilder, 94–95, 98, 101–105

Tileston v. Ullman, 94–101, 102–106, 123–124, 128, 143; and *Poe v. Ullman,* 156, 157, 159, 161, 163, 165; and *Griswold,* 211, 212, 224

Tiller, George R., 703, 704, 705, 706, 713, 970–971n54

Tilson, Catherine J., 44, 79

Tilson, John Q., Jr., 98, 99, 105

Timanus, G. Lotrell, 271, 275, 283–284, 291, 299, 315, 362

Time, 180, 275, 284, 301, 312, 341, 342, 358, 363, 376, 378, 414, 484, 588, 605, 618, 622, 630

Time Has Come, The (Rock), 218

Time to Kill, A (Bray), 711

Tindall, Marie Wilson, 208, 212

Tinker v. Des Moines Independent Community School District, 351

Todd, Malcolm, 330

Tolle, John B., 436–437, 439, 440–443, 461, 499, 523

Tompkins, Norman, 718

Torrick, Keith, 653

Townsend, Killian, 422, 483

Tracy, Spencer, 599

Travia, Anthony J., 311

Traynor, Roger, 366

Trebert, Jennie Church, 131

Trebert, Raymond, 131

Treshman, Don, 702–703, 714

Trewhella, Matt, 738

Tribe, Laurence H., 615, 616, 658, 659, 664, 666–667, 701

Trickett, Paul C., 439

Trinkaus, Walter, 299

Trosch, David, 711

Trubek, David, 160–161, 171, 205

Trubek, Louise Grossman, 160–161, 171, 205

Trubek v. Ullman, 161, 164, 166, 170, 173, 189, 193, 211, 212, 224

Truman, Harry, 183

Tucker, Thomas W., 715–716

Tundermann, David, 498–499, 500
Turner, B. L., 392
Turner, Jack, 160
Tushnet, Mark V., 582, 583, 908*n*122, 956*n*1
Tuttle, Elbert P., 653, 655
Twentieth Century Fund, 352, 356, 372, 498
Tydings, Joseph D., 279, 517, 518–519
Tyler, Harold R., Jr., 381
Tyler, Margaret, 94
Tyler, Morris, 64, 73, 85

Ullman, Abraham S., and *Tileston* case, 94, 98–102, 104, 105–106; and *Poe* cases, 143, 154, 155, 156, 201
Union Pacific Railway Co. v. *Botsford,* 590
Unitarian Universalist Association, 291–292
United States Catholic Conference, 484, 524, 562, 703
United States v. *Belaval,* 60, 69
United States v. *One Package,* 42, 43, 44, 46, 48, 54, 60, 64, 69, 261, 285, 309
United States v. *Salerno,* 967–968*n*36
United States v. *Vuitch,* Gesell decision in, 382–385 *passim;* government appeal of, 387, 407, 409, 417, 449, 459; national impact of Gesell's ruling, 388, 400, 415, 416, 424, 428, 429, 441, 442, 446, 453, 481; Supreme Court consideration of, 417–418, 468–470, 471, 473, 474–480, 493–494, 495, 504, 505, 507, 510, 516, 521, 539; Supreme Court decision in, 488–491; and *Roe* v. *Wade,* 524, 529, 534, 552, 555, 564, 571, 575, 580, 597; and *Doe* v. *Bolton,* 550, 574;

definition of women's health in, 722, 731
United States v. *Wade,* 556
Uplinger. See *New York* v. *Uplinger*
Upson, J. Warren, 599; and *Nelson* case, 62–79, 81, 86, 99; and post-*Nelson* strategizing, 85, 87–88, 90, 92, 106, 107, 128; and *Tileston,* 101, 103–105; and *Poe* v. *Ullman,* 187, 194
Upson, Thomas F., 682
USA Today, 738
Utah, 1997 legislation, 734

Valdambrini, Joseph, 4, 50
Van Alstyne, William, 371, 613
Van Buren, Edgar T., 340
Verba, Berta, 8, 63
Vermont, 1970 legislature, 412
Village Voice, 363
Vinson, Fred M., 242
Vinson, Roger, 712
Virginia, passes 1970 reform bill, 422
Voeller, Bruce, 622
Vogel, Beatrice, 389–391, 393, 395, 500
Vogt, William, 157
Voice of the Women's Liberation Movement, 367
Voluntary Parenthood League, 14
Vuitch, Florence R., 469, 478, 604
Vuitch, Milan M., 318, 333, 350, 494, 504; and Gesell decision, 382–383, 386, 539, 646; and Supreme Court, 417–418, 464, 465, 468–470, 474–480, 490; and *Hardy* case, 509, 561, 608. See also *United States* v. *Vuitch; Vuitch* v. *Hardy*
Vuitch v. *Hardy,* 509, 561

Waddell, Myron C., 351
Wade, Henry, 396; and filing of *Roe,* 406, 436–437, 439; and three-

judge court, 442, 443, 452, 455; and Supreme Court appeal, 460–461, 499, 510, 523, 599; and *Roe* aftermath, 602; and *Baker* case, 647–648, 652

Walker, Alfred, 437, 438

Walker, Pamela D., 497, 523

Wall, William X., 321

Wall Street Journal, 303, 606

Wallace, Henry, 231

Wallingford Post, 188

Ward, Bernard, 396

Ward, Marilyn, 411

Warren, Earl, 473; and *Poe v. Ullman,* 168–169, 177, 179–187 *passim,* 191–193, 198; and *Griswold,* 229, 236–237, 240–244, 248–253, 255, 609

Warren, Evelyn, 359

Warren, Robert, 488

Warren, Samuel D., 260–261

Washington, 1969 legislature, 358, 371; 1970 statewide referendum, 384, 411, 412, 431, 466, 483, 496, 538; 1992 referendum codifies *Roe,* 689

Washington Citizens for Abortion Reform (WCAR), 371, 384

Washington Post, 256, 360, 380, 418, 543, 557–558, 559, 561, 606, 666, 668, 701, 727, 731

Washington Times Herald, 150

Waterbury American, 3, 4, 93

Waterbury Democrat, 3, 4, 8, 63, 79

Waterbury Maternal Health Center, initial creation of, 2–5, 49–54, 57–58, 60–61; 1939 raid against, 7–8, 61–78

Waterbury Republican, 2–3, 4, 5, 7, 8, 62

Waters, James L., 422, 426, 428

Waters, Vincent, 329

Watkins, Perry J., 686–687

Watkins v. U.S. Army, 686–687

Watson, Elmer S., 142

Webb, Rodney S., 715

Webster, William H., 625

Webster, William L., 673, 674

Webster v. Reproductive Health Services, 673–681, 683, 691–692, 699

Wechsler, Herbert, 277

Wechsler, Nancy F., 176, 177, 232, 234, 492, 502

Weddington, Ron, 393–394, 396, 492, 499, 503, 509, 561, 564; and *Roe v. Wade,* 500–502, 523, 568, 572

Weddington, Sarah R., first asked about abortion case, 393–396; approaches Linda Coffee, 396, 398–400; and filing of *Roe v. Wade,* 404–406, 437–439, 862n17, 871n59; and three-judge hearing of *Roe,* 440–444; and three-judge decision, 453; and Supreme Court appeal of *Roe,* 461, 462, 492, 494; and *Roe* brief, 499–501; and first Supreme Court argument of *Roe,* 503–504, 507–510 *passim,* 513–517, 521–528 *passim;* wages successful 1972 legislative race, 538, 557, 577, 587–588; and second *Roe* argument, 561, 563–565, 567–573, 599; and *Roe* aftermath, 600–601; treatment of Norma McCorvey, 720

Weinfeld, Edward, 381

Weller, Lynn, 504, 508

Wellington, Harry H., 614

Wesleyan University, 32, 93

West Virginia, Medicaid funds for abortions in, 957–958n6

Wheeler, Shirley, 522

Wheelis, Jim, 389, 393, 395–396

White, Byron R., 224, 236, 707; and *Griswold,* 240, 242–244, 249–252 *passim,* 254–255, 566; and *Vuitch,* 476–477, 480, 489; and *Roe v.*

White, Byron R. (*cont.*),
  Wade, 491, 521, 525; and
  Eisenstadt, 519–520, 541–543;
  and first *Roe/Doe* conference,
  529, 531–533; initial dissent by,
  552; supports reargument of
  Roe/Doe, 554, 555, 556, 557,
  560; and second *Roe/Doe* oral
  argument, 568–571, 572; and
  second *Roe/Doe* conference, 574,
  576; and final drafting of *Roe/
  Doe* opinions, 581, 586; final dissent in *Roe* and *Doe,* 597–598,
  609; and *Planned Parenthood* v.
  Danforth, 626; and *Carey,* 627;
  and *Sendak,* 627; and *Bellotti II,*
  632; and *Colautti,* 632; and *Harris*
  v. *McRae,* 634; and *Akron,* 642;
  and *Uplinger,* 644, 646, 649; and
  Thornburgh, 652, 657, 662; and
  Bowers, 656, 659, 661, 663–666,
  674; and *Webster,* 673, 675–678;
  and *Akron Center,* 683; and *Rust,*
  685; and *Bray,* 688, 702; and
  Casey, 692, 698, 701
White, Jack, 328
Whitehill, Virginia B., 400–401,
  405, 438, 462, 482, 485, 492,
  577; and *Roe* v. *Wade,* 443, 500,
  509, 513, 514, 515, 523, 539,
  573, 588; and *Roe* aftermath, 601,
  603
Whitney, Leon F., 21, 30
Whittaker, Charles E., 169, 178,
  185, 186, 191, 224, 242
Whittemore, Elisabeth L., 29, 94
Wicklund, Susan, 715
Widmyer, Nancy K., 428–430,
  466–467
Widmyer, Ronald R., 428
Wiggin, Frederick H., 92, 94–95,
  98–105, 123, 157
Wilde, Kathleen, 655
Wilder, L. Douglas, 681
"Wilhite," Jane, 435

Wilkerson, Glen, 500
Wilkinson, J. Harvie III, 658
Willard, C. Lawson, III, 122, 137,
  157, 160
Williams, Glanville, 275
Williams, J. Whitridge, 270
Williams, Nancy Doggett, 117, 118,
  120, 122–124, 126, 130
Williams v. *Zbaraz,* 633, 634–635
Willis, Ellen, 368
Willkie, Wendell, 89
Wilson, Malcolm, 578
Winslow, Charles-Edward A., 29, 106
Wintersheimer, Donald C., 688
Wirin, A. L., 355, 364–366
Wisconsin, 1965 legislature, 834n57
Wisconsin Committee to Legalize
  Abortion, 414–415, 465
Wisdom, John Minor, 452
Witt, Ralph, 446, 449
Wolf, Julius A., 953–957n1
Wolf, Naomi, 721
Wolf v. *Colorado,* 171–172,
  953–957n1
Wolf v. *People,* 953–957n1
Woman Rebel, The, 10
Women's Equity Action League
  (WEAL), 343, 498, 509
Women's National Abortion Action
  Coalition (WONAAC), 498,
  502, 522
Woodward, Bob, 558
Woodward, W. C., 43
Worcester Telegram, 256
Workum, Fifield, 124
Wray, T. Cecil, 168
Wright, Charles Alan, 513, 639
Wuensch, Barbara, 390
Wulf, Melvin L., 371, 517, 624;
  and *Poe* v. *Ullman,* 170, 171–172;
  and *Griswold,* 216, 217; and
  first abortion test case, 352–353,
  357, 379; and *Roe* and *Doe,* 492,
  505
Wynne, Kenneth, 67–76 *passim,* 90